FAMILY LAW

ASPEN CASEBOOK SERIES

FAMILY LAW

Fifth Edition

LESLIE JOAN HARRIS
Dorothy Kliks Fones Professor
University of Oregon School of Law

JUNE CARBONE
Robina Chair in Law, Science and Technology
University of Minnesota Law School

LEE E. TEITELBAUM
the late Hugh B. Brown Professor of Law
University of Utah

Wolters Kluwer
Law & Business

Wolters Kluwer Law & Business serves customers worldwide with CCH, Aspen
Publishers, and Kluwer Law International products. (www.wolterskluwerlb.com)

To contact Customer Service, e-mail customer.service@wolterskluwer.com, call
1-800-234-1660, fax 1-800-901-9075, or mail correspondence to:

Wolters Kluwer Law & Business
Attn: Order Department
PO Box 990
Frederick, MD 21705

Printed in the United States of America.

1 2 3 4 5 6 7 8 9 0

ISBN 978-1-4548-2512-8

Library of Congress Cataloging-in-Publication Data

Harris, Leslie J., 1952- author.
    Family law / Leslie Joan Harris, Dorothy Kliks Fones Professor of Law, University
of Oregon; June Carbone, Edward A. Smith/Missouri Chair of Law, the Constitution
and Society, University of Missouri-Kansas City; Lee E. Teitelbaum, the late Hugh
B. Brown Professor of Law, University of Utah. — Fourth edition.
       pages cm. — (Aspen casebook series)
    Includes bibliographical references and index.
    ISBN 978-1-4548-2512-8 (alk. paper)
    1. Domestic relations — United States. I. Carbone, June, author. II. Teitelbaum,
Lee E., author. III. Title.
    KF504.H33 2014
    346.7301′5 — dc23
                                                                            2014023577

Certified Sourcing
www.sfiprogram.org
SFI-01042

SFI label applies to the text stock

About Wolters Kluwer Law & Business

Wolters Kluwer Law & Business is a leading global provider of intelligent information and digital solutions for legal and business professionals in key specialty areas, and respected educational resources for professors and law students. Wolters Kluwer Law & Business connects legal and business professionals as well as those in the education market with timely, specialized authoritative content and information-enabled solutions to support success through productivity, accuracy and mobility.

Serving customers worldwide, Wolters Kluwer Law & Business products include those under the Aspen Publishers, CCH, Kluwer Law International, Loislaw, ftwilliam.com and MediRegs family of products.

CCH products have been a trusted resource since 1913, and are highly regarded resources for legal, securities, antitrust and trade regulation, government contracting, banking, pension, payroll, employment and labor, and healthcare reimbursement and compliance professionals.

Aspen Publishers products provide essential information to attorneys, business professionals and law students. Written by preeminent authorities, the product line offers analytical and practical information in a range of specialty practice areas from securities law and intellectual property to mergers and acquisitions and pension/benefits. Aspen's trusted legal education resources provide professors and students with high-quality, up-to-date and effective resources for successful instruction and study in all areas of the law.

Kluwer Law International products provide the global business community with reliable international legal information in English. Legal practitioners, corporate counsel and business executives around the world rely on Kluwer Law journals, looseleafs, books, and electronic products for comprehensive information in many areas of international legal practice.

Loislaw is a comprehensive online legal research product providing legal content to law firm practitioners of various specializations. Loislaw provides attorneys with the ability to quickly and efficiently find the necessary legal information they need, when and where they need it, by facilitating access to primary law as well as state-specific law, records, forms and treatises.

ftwilliam.com offers employee benefits professionals the highest quality plan documents (retirement, welfare and non-qualified) and government forms (5500/PBGC, 1099 and IRS) software at highly competitive prices.

MediRegs products provide integrated health care compliance content and software solutions for professionals in healthcare, higher education and life sciences, including professionals in accounting, law and consulting.

Wolters Kluwer Law & Business, a division of Wolters Kluwer, is headquartered in New York. Wolters Kluwer is a market-leading global information services company focused on professionals.

To My Family
June Carbone

To Charlie and Danny
Leslie Harris

Summary of Contents

Contents

II FAMILY DISSOLUTION

III   CHILDREN, PARENTS, AND THE STATE

Preface

This casebook is intended for a basic course in family law. In the preface to every edition since the first we have commented on how rapidly the law concerning families, parents and children, spouses, and domestic partners is changing. This seems more true today than ever. Long-settled principles and practices regarding marriage, divorce, marital property, spousal support, and custody, to mention only a few areas, have been abandoned or substantially modified over the last few decades. Same-sex couples, unmarried cohabitants, and single-parent families are increasingly important.

This book compares innovative developments in some states with the reaffirmation of traditional principles in others, and does so in the context of a wider focus on family and the state, the role of mediating institutions, and the efficacy of law and particular methods of enforcing the law. In assessing these developments, we present many different voices and accounts without, we hope, privileging any particular account as representing that of the book as a whole. Perspectives in this book shift regularly, through the notes and questions.

Understanding family law requires appreciation not just for the difficult social and theoretical issues underlying changes in legal doctrine, but the settings in which family practice occurs. Many students will practice domestic relations shortly after graduation, and a family law course must introduce them to the doctrine, procedures, and techniques they will encounter in law offices and courts.

In other areas, introduction to a body of statutory and judicial doctrine in the field will serve that purpose. Family law, however, draws on doctrines in a number of other areas, such as property, contracts, torts, criminal law, conflict of laws, and constitutional law, whose principles must be introduced or reviewed. Moreover, as families have become more complex, so has the law that serves them. Family law issues routinely intersect with eligibility for public assistance, social security, bankruptcy and other forms of assistance.

The practice of family law is — even more than most other areas — cross-disciplinary. The foundation of family wealth has changed from land, cars and bank accounts to employment and benefits — and therefore pensions, businesses, and degrees. Some notion of financial principles (such as the time value of money) is essential to valuation of property at divorce. As paternity has become more contested, knowledge of genetics and statistics has become more important to the determination of parenthood, and some understanding of clinical psychology is regularly necessary in custody disputes. Social history is important to understanding the context in which the law has developed and to the interpretation of current bodies of doctrine. And discussions of legal and policy responses to domestic violence must draw on social scientific evidence regarding the incidence, distribution, and causes of such violence.

Moreover, family law cannot be effectively taught without some attention to process. The text incorporates materials that address counseling, negotiation, alternative dispute resolution and ethics.

The casebook deals with the complexity of family law both in the organization of the chapters — separate units on family contracts, jurisdiction, and practice, for example, can be shortened, skipped, or taught in almost any order — and the diversity of material within each chapter. Each unit combines primary cases with comprehensive notes, supplemented with academic and policy analyses that provide a foundation for evaluation. Detailed problems extend the coverage or apply the commentary to real world examples.

Finally, the casebook tries to convey our continued excitement about the study of family law, and our conviction that family practice requires appreciation of the complex interaction between human relations and legal process.

Leslie J. Harris
June Carbone

August 2014

Editors' note: Throughout the book, footnotes to the text and to opinions and other quoted materials are numbered consecutively from the beginning of each chapter. Some footnotes in opinions and secondary authorities are omitted. Editor's footnotes added to quoted materials are indicated by the abbreviation: — Ed.

Acknowledgments

We thank John Devins and others at Aspen for their assistance in many ways over many years, as well as members of The Froebe Group for editorial assistance.

June Carbone thanks her research assistant Jessica Qian.

The late Lee Teitelbaum, former professor and dean of the University of Utah, was a principal author of the first two editions of this book, and his contributions to the book continue to be important. Professor Carol A. Weisbrod was a coauthor of the first edition of this book, and we gratefully acknowledge her contributions.

Altman, Irwin. "Husbands and Wives in Contemporary Polygamy." *JL & Fam. Stud.* 8 (2006): 389.

American Academy of Matrimonial Lawyers, Bounds of Advocacy, Standard 1.2, 1.3, 1.4, 1.5, 6.1, 6.2, Comments to Standard 1.5 (2012). Reprinted by permission of the American Academy of Matrimonial Lawyers.

American Law Institute, Principles of the Law of Family Dissolution, Sections 2.05, 2.08, 5.02, 5.03, 7.04, 7.05, and 7.09 (2002). Copyright 2002 by the American Law Institute. Reproduced with permission. All rights reserved. The complete publication, *Principles of the Law of Family Dissolution: Analysis and Recommendations*, is available in hardcover or softcover through the American Law Institute at www.ALI.org or 1-800-253-6397.

Bartholet, Elizabeth, International Adoption: Propriety, Prospects and Pragmatics, 13 J. Am. Acad. Matrimonial L. 181 (1996). Reprinted by permission.

Beld, Jo Michelle & Len Biernet, Federal Intent for State Child Support Guidelines: Income Shares, Cost Shares, and the Realities of Shared Parenting, 37 Fam. L. Q. 165 (2003). Reprinted by permission.

Bennett, Jessica. Only You. And You. And You.: Polyamory — Relationships with Multiple, Mutually Consenting Partners — Has a Coming-out Party, Newsweek July 28, 2009.

Bix, Brian, Bargaining in the Shadow of Love: The Enforcement of Premarital Agreements and How We Think About Marriage, 40 Wm. & Mary L. Rev. 145 (1998). Reprinted by permission.

Bowman, Cynthia Grant, Social Science and Legal Policy: The Case of Heterosexual Cohabitation, 9 J. L. & Fam. Stud. 1 (2007). Reprinted by permission of Professor Bowman and the Journal of Law & Family Studies.

Braver, Sanford L., and Ira Mark Ellman. "Citizens' Views About Fault in Property Division." 47 Fam. L.Q. 419 (2013) at 419, 423, 431, 433-35.

Carbone, June, The Futility of Coherence: The ALI's Principles of the Law of Family Dissolution, Compensatory Spousal Payments, 4 J.L. & Fam. Stud. 43 (2002). Reprinted by permission.

Carbone, June & Naomi Cahn, The Triple System of Family Law, 2013 Mich. St. L. Rev. 113.

Case, Mary Anne. "Enforcing Bargains in an Ongoing Marriage." *Wash. UJL & Pol'y* 35 (2011): 225.

Carnevale, Anthony P., Stephen J. Rose, and Ban Cheah. "The college payoff: Education, occupations, lifetime earnings." (2013). Georgetown University Center on Education and the Workforce.

Chambers, David, Stepparents, Biologic Parents, and the Law's Perceptions of "Family" After Divorce. Reprinted from Divorce Reform at the Crossroads 102. Copyright © 1990 by Yale University Press. Reprinted by permission.

Cherlin, Andrew J., American Marriage in the Early Twenty-first Century, 15(2) The Future of Children: Marriage and Child Well-Being 33 (2005). A publication of the Center for the Future of Children. Copyright © The Center for the Future of Children, The David and Lucile Packard Foundation.

Eisenberg, Melvin, The Bargaining Principle and Its Limits, 95 Harv. L. Rev. 741 (1982). Copyright © 1982 by the Harvard Law Review Association. Reprinted by permission of Professor Eisenberg and the Harvard Law Review Association.

Ellman, Ira Mark, The Misguided Movement to Revive Fault Divorce, and Why Reformers Should Look Instead to the American Law Institute, 11 Int'l J.L. Pol'y & Fam. 216 (1997). Reprinted by permission.

England, Paula & George Farkas, Householders, Employment and Gender: A Social, Economic and Demographic View 55-56. Copyright © 1986 Aldine de Gruyter, A Division of Walter de Gruyter, Inc. Reprinted with permission.

Estin, Anne Laquer, Maintenance, Alimony and the Rehabilitation of Family Care, 71 N.C. L. Rev. 721 (1993). Copyright © the North Carolina Law Review Association. Reprinted by permission. The publisher bears responsibility for any errors which have occurred in reprinting or editing.

Fabricius, William V., Sandford L. Braver & Kindra Deneau, Divorced Parents' Financial Support of their Children's College Expenses, 41 Fam. Ct. Rev. 224 (2003). Reprinted by permission.

Fineman, Martha A., Why Marriage?, 9 Va. J. Soc. Pol'y & L. 239 (2001). Reprinted by permission of Professor Fineman and Virgina Journal of Social Policy and the Law.

Freud, Anna, Painter v. Bannister, 7 The Writings of Anna Freud 247-255 (1966-1970). Reprinted by permission of International Universities Press.

Friedman, Lawrence, Rights of Passage: Divorce in Historical Perspective, 63 Or. L. Rev. 649. Copyright © 1984 by University of Oregon. Reprinted by permission of the Oregon Law Review and of Professor Friedman.

Galbraith, John Kenneth, Economics and the Public Purpose 31-37. Copyright © 1973 by John Kenneth Galbraith. Reprinted by permission of Houghton Mifflin Company. All rights reserved.

Garrison, Marsha, The Economic Consequences of Divorce, 32 Fam. & Conciliation Cts. Rev. 10 (1994). Copyright © 1994 by Sage Publications, Inc. Reprinted by permission of Sage Publications, Inc.

Garrison, Marsha. "The decline of formal marriage: Inevitable or reversible?" *Family Law Quarterly* (2007): 491-520.

Ginzburg, Rebecca, Note, Altering "Family": Another Look at the Supreme Court's Narrow Protection of Families in Belle Terre, 83 B.U. L. Rev. 875 (2003). Reprinted by permission.

Glendon, Mary Ann, Marriage and the State: The Withering Away of Marriage, 62 Va. L. Rev. 663 (1976). Copyright © the Virginia Law Review Association. Reprinted by permission of the Virginia Law Review Association and Fred B. Rothman & Co.

Grossberg, Michael, Governing the Hearth. Reprinted from Governing the Hearth: Law and the Family in Nineteenth-Century America, by Michael Grossberg. Copyright © 1988 by the University of North Carolina Press. Used by permission of the publisher and Professor Grossberg.

Harris, Leslie Joan, The New ALI Child Support Proposal, 35 Willamette L. Rev. 473 (1999). Reprinted by permission.

Harris, Leslie Joan. Reforming Paternity Law to Eliminate Gender, Status and Class Inequality 2013 Mich. St. L. Rev. 1295, 1299-1302.

Harris, Leslie, Dennis Waldrop & Lori Waldrop, Making and Breaking Connections Between Parents' Duty to Support and Right to Control Their Children, 69 Or. L. Rev. 689 (1990). Copyright © 1990 University of Oregon. Reprinted by permission.

Hedeen, Timothy & Peter Salem, What Should Family Lawyers Know? Results of a Survey of Practitioners and Students, 44 Fam. Ct. Rev. 601, 605-606, 608-611 (2006). Reprinted by permission.

Kay, Herma Hill, Equality and Difference: A Perspective on No-Fault Divorce and Its Aftermath, 56 U. Cin. L. Rev. 1 (1987). Copyright © University of Cincinnati. Reprinted by permission.

Mechoulan, Stéphane, Divorce Laws and the Structure of the American Family, 35 J. Legal Stud. 143, 144-147, 165-166 (2006). Reprinted with permission of Professor Mechoulan and the publisher.

Melli, Marygold S., Constructing a Social Problem, Am. B. Found. Res. J. 759 (1986). Copyright © 1986 The University of Chicago Press. Published by the University of Chicago Press. Reprinted by permission of Professor Melli and the publisher.

Melli, Marygold S., Howard S. Erlanger & Elizabeth Chambliss, The Process of Negotiation: An Exploratory Investigation in the Context of No-Fault Divorce, 40 Rutgers L. Rev. 1133 (1988). Copyright © 1988 by Rutgers University. Reprinted by permission of Professors Melli, Erlanger, and Chambliss.

Menolascino, Frank J. & Michael L. Egger, Medical Dimensions of Mental Retardation xx-xxii (1978), published by the University of Nebraska Press. Reprinted by permission.

Mnookin, Robert H. & Lewis Kornhauser, Bargaining in the Shadow of the Law: The Case of Divorce, 88 Yale L.J. 950 (1979). Copyright © The Yale Law Journal Company. Reprinted by permission of The Yale Law Journal Company and Fred B. Rothman & Company from the Yale Law Journal and by permission of Professor Mnookin.

Murphy, Jane C. "Legal Images of Fatherhood: Welfare Reform, Child Support Enforcement, and Fatherless Children." 81 Notre Dame L. Rev. 325, 350-352 (2005).

Oldham, J. Thomas, Management of the Community Estate During an Intact Marriage, 56 L. & Contemp. Probs. (No. 2) 99 (1993). Copyright © 1993 Journal of Law and Contemporary Problems. Reprinted by permission of the publisher and Professor Oldham.

Paul, Diane B. & Hamish G. Spencer, "It's Ok, We're Not Cousins by Blood": The Cousin Marriage Controversy in Historical Perspective, 6(12) PLoS Biol e320. doi:10.1371/journal.pbio.0060320 (2008), open-access license.

Peele, Catherine J., Social and Psychological Effects of the Availability and the Granting of Alimony on the Spouses, 6 Law & Contemp. Probs. 283 (1939). Copyright © 1939 Journal of Law and Contemporary Problems. Reprinted by permission.

Perry, Twila, Alimony: Race, Privilege, and Dependency in the Search of Theory, 82 Geo. L.J. 2481 (1994). Copyright © Georgetown Law Journal & Georgetown University. Reprinted with the permission of the publisher.

_____, Transracial and International Adoption: Mothers, Hierarchy, Race and Feminist Legal Theory, 10 Yale J.L. & Feminism 102 (1998). Reprinted by permission of the Yale Journal of Law & Feminism, Inc.

Pleck, Elizabeth, Domestic Tyranny: The Making of Social Policy Against Family Violence from Colonial Times to the Present 7-9. Copyright © 1987 Oxford University Press. Reprinted by permission.

Polikoff, Nancy D., Ending Marriage as We Know It, 32 Hofstra L. Rev. 201 (2003). Reprinted with the permission of Hofstra Law Review Association.

Prager, Susan W., Sharing Principles and the Future of Marital Property Law, 25 UCLA L. Rev. 1 (1981). Copyright © by the Regents of the University of California, University of California, Los Angeles and Fred B. Rothman and Company. Reprinted by permission.

Resnik, Judith, Naturally Without Gender: Women, Jurisdiction, and the Federal Courts, 66 N.Y.U. L. Rev. 1682 (1991). Copyright © Judith Resnik. Reprinted by permission of Professor Resnik.

Reynolds, Suzanne, Catherine T. Harris & Ralph A. Peeples, Back to the Future: An Empirical Study of Child Custody Outcomes, 85 N.C. L. Rev. 1629, 1631 (2007). Reprinted by permission.

Salmon, Marylynn. *Women and the law of property in early America*. Chapel Hill: University of North Carolina Press, 1986.

Sanger, Carol, A Case for Civil Marriage, 27 Cardozo L. Rev. 1311 (2006). Reprinted by permission of Professor Sanger and the Cardozo Law Review.

Schneider, Andrea Kupfer & Nancy Mills, What Family Lawyers Are Really Doing When They Negotiate, 44 Fam. Ct. Rev. 612 (2006). Reprinted by permission.

Schneider, Carl E., Rethinking Alimony: Marital Decisions and Moral Discourse, B.Y.U. L. Rev. 197 (1991). Copyright © J. Reuben Clark Law School. Reprinted by permission.

Jana B. Singer, Dispute Resolution and the Postdivorce Family: Implications of a Paradigm Shift, 47 Fam. Ct. Rev. 363 (2009). Reprinted with permission.

Smith, Livingston, Susan, Ruth McRoy, Madelyn Freundlich, and Joe Kroll. "Finding families for African American children: The role of race and law in adoption from foster care." Retrieved February 15 (2008): 2010. Donaldson Adoption Institute. All Rights Reserved.

Sokoloff, Burton Z., Antecedents of American Adoption, 3(1) The Future of Children: Adoption 17 (1993). A publication of the Center for the Future of Children. Copyright © The Center for the Future of Children, The David and Lucile Packard Foundation.

Spaht, Katherine Shaw, Covenant Marriage Seven Years Later: Its as Yet Unfulfilled Promise, 65 La. L. Rev. 605 (2005). Reprinted by permission.

Starnes, Cynthia Lee. "Lovers, Parents, and Partners: Disentangling Spousal and Co-Parenting Commitments." *Arizona Law Review* 54.1 (2012).

Teitelbaum, Lee E., Family History and Family Law, 1985 Wis. L. Rev. 1135. Copyright © 1985 by The Board of Regents of the University of Wisconsin System; Reprinted by permission of the Wisconsin Law Review.

Turley, Ruth N. López, and Matthew Desmond. "Contributions to college costs by married, divorced, and remarried parents." *Journal of Family Issues* 32.6 (2011): 767-790.

Uniform State Laws: The following have been reproduced in whole or in part: Uniform Adoption Act, Uniform Child Custody Jurisdiction and Enforcement Act, Uniform Interstate Family Support Act, Uniform Marriage and Divorce Act, Uniform Probate Code, Uniform Parentage Act, Uniform Premarital Agreements Act, Copyright © The National Conference of Commissioners on Uniform State Laws. Reprinted by permission of the National Conference of Commissioners on Uniform State Laws.

Venohr, Jane C. "Child Support Guidelines and Guidelines Reviews: State Differences and Common Issues." *Family Law Quarterly* 47.3 (2013): 327-352.

Vernier, Chester G. & John B. Hurlbut, The Historical Background of Alimony Law and Its Present Structure, 6 Law & Contemp. Probs. 197 (1939). Copyright © 1939 Journal of Law and Contemporary Problems. Reprinted by permission.

Wardle, Lynn E., Deconstructing Family: A Critique of the ALI's "Domestic Partners" Proposal, 2001 BYU L. Rev. 1190 (2001). Reprinted by permission.

Wax, Amy L., Engines Of Inequality: Class, Race, And Family Structure, 41 Fam. L.Q. 567, 568-573, 581-582 (2007). Reprinted by permission.

Wilkinson-Ryan, Tess & Deborah Small Winter, Negotiating Divorce: Gender and the Behavioral Economics of Divorce Bargaining, 26 Law & Ineq. 109 (2008). Reprinted by permission.

Williams, Joan, Is Coverture Dead: Beyond a New Theory of Alimony, 82 Geo. L.J. 2227 (1994). Copyright © by Joan Williams. Reprinted by permission of Professor Williams.

Williams, Robert G., Guidelines for Setting Levels of Child Support Orders, 21 Fam. L.Q. 281 (1987). Copyright © Robert G. Williams. Reprinted by permission of Robert G. Williams, President, Policy Studies, Inc.

Wizner, Stephen & Miriam Berkman, Being a Lawyer for a Child Too Young to Be a Client: A Clinical Study. 68 Neb. L. Rev. 330. Copyright © 1989 Nebraska Law Review. Reprinted by permission.

Younger, Judith T. Lovers' Contracts in the Courts: Forsaking the Minimum
    Decencies, 13 Wm. & Mary J. Women & L. 349, 419-420 (2007).
    Reprinted by permission.

____, A Minnesota Comparative Family Law Symposium: Antenuptial Agree-
    ments, 28 Wm. Mitchell L. Review L. Rev. 697 (2001). Reprinted by
    permission.

FAMILY LAW

MARRIAGE AND ITS ALTERNATIVES

I

When Are Adult Partners a Family?

1

A generation or two ago, *family* had a fairly clear connotation, although many people even then did not live in families that fit the standard image. Today, however, the meaning of *family* is contested in many realms of life, including the law. This chapter introduces some of the recurring themes in the legal debates:

- Should the law make distinctions among people based on their family status at all?
- When family membership matters, how should it be determined? On the basis of formal markers such as blood relationship or legal ceremony, or on the basis of function?
- If family is defined by function, what kinds of behavior indicate that people belong to a family?
- What are the roles of legislatures and judges in making these decisions?

These issues will continue to arise throughout the following three chapters in this part. Chapter 2 explores in some detail the myriad ways in which the law does treat adults differently if they are considered "married" or the equivalent thereof. Chapter 3 examines the law of formal marriage, and Chapter 4 deals with informal domestic arrangements among adults. Chapter 13 returns to some of these issues in the context of the parent-child relationship.

In 2013 the Centers for Disease Control reported that between 2006 and 2010, almost half of all women lived with a partner rather than marrying as their first family-like union, compared to about a third of women in 1995. Cohabitation was especially common among less educated women; 70 percent of them cohabited as a first union, compared to 47 percent of women with a bachelor's degree. Casey E. Copen et al., First Premarital Cohabitation in the United States: 2006-2010 National Survey of Family Growth (National Health Statistics Reports No. 64, Apr. 4, 2013). In 2010, for the first time, less than 50 percent of all American households consisted of married couples; 20 percent of all households consisted of married couples with children, down from 44 percent in 1960, and

28 percent consisted of married couples without children, compared to 31 percent in 1960. Linda A. Jacobson et al., Household Change in the United States, 67(1) Population Bulletin 3 (Sept. 2012). This study also found that marriage was much more common among the well-educated. Commenting on this trend six years earlier, a demographic trends analyst said, "We seem to be reverting to a much older pattern, when elites marry and a great many others live together and have kids." Blaine Harden, Numbers Drop for the Married with Children: Institution Becoming the Choice of the Educated, Affluent, Washington Post, Mar. 4, 2007. The following materials begin to explore whether, in light of this social development, the law should make a distinction between marriage and cohabitation and, if so, under what circumstances.

MARTHA ALBERTSON FINEMAN, *WHY MARRIAGE?*

9 Va. J. Soc. Pol'y & L. 239, 245-246 (2001)

. . . I argue that for all relevant and appropriate societal purposes we do not need marriage, per se, at all. To state that we do not need marriage to accomplish many societal objectives is not the same thing as saying that we do not need a family to do so for some. However, family as a social category should not be dependent on having marriage as its core relationship. Nor is family synonymous with marriage. Although both of these things might historically have been true, things have changed substantially in the past several decades. Marriage does not have the same relevance as a societal institution as it did even fifty years ago, when it was the primary means of protecting and providing for the legal and structurally devised dependency of wives.

The pressing problems today do not revolve around the marriage connection, but the caretaker-dependent relationship. In a world in which wives are equal partners and participants in the market sphere, and in which the consensus is that bad marriages should end, women do not need the special protection of legal marriage. Rather than marriage, we should view the parent-child relationship as the quintessential or core family connection, and focus on how policy can strengthen this tie. Thus, in a responsive society, one could have a marriage [or other long-term sexual affiliation] without necessarily constituting a "family" entitled to special protection and benefits under law. Correspondingly, one might have dependents, thereby creating a family and gaining protection and benefits, without having a marriage.

If this suggestion seems extreme and radical, it only serves to demonstrate the extent to which marriage continues to be uncritically central to our thinking about the family. What is bizarre is that it remains central in spite of the fact that the traditional marital family has become a statistical minority of family units in our society. The tenacity of marriage as a concept explains the relatively unsophisticated and uninformed policy debates. Marriage, as the preferred societal solution, has become the problem. The very existence of this institution eclipses discussion and debate about the problems of dependency and allows us to avoid confronting the difficulty of making the transformations necessary to address these problems.

Carol Sanger, *A Case for Civil Marriage*

27 Cardozo L. Rev. 1311, 1311-1322 (2006)

... Professor Edward Stein has posed a straightforward question: Should civil marriage simply be abolished? In this mini-symposium, Professors Edward Zelinsky and Daniel Crane have provided two answers to his question: yes and yes.

Let me explain the double positive. Both authors agree that marriage should not, in Professor Zelinsky's words, be "recognized, defined, or regulated by the state."[1] Both are content to use contract to create enforceable marriage-like obligations. Yet their reasons for abolition differ in ways that distinguish their yeses. Both agree that civil marriage should be abolished, but as we see from their paper titles, Professor Zelinsky wants to deregulate marriage and Professor Crane wants to privatize it. ...

Zelinsky offers several practical reasons why the state should get out of the marriage business. He explains that marriage is no longer necessary for issues of parentage, custody, or adoption; it is not necessary for significant areas of wealth transmission, such as pensions or inheritance. Moreover, the benefits that are often associated with marriage—medical decision-making, evidentiary privilege, hospital visitation—are not as robust as most people think. In short, Zelinsky argues that, if civil marriage is abolished, the world will not look so very different than it does now. It will certainly not look worse and, from a marital perspective, it may well look much better. Active competition among firms will strengthen the institution. People will feel more committed to domestic arrangements that they have affirmatively chosen. The polity itself will be better off because there will be less squabbling over the meaning of marriage. We can each be "married" in our own way.

As a Contracts professor, I am honored that my subject has been chosen for this important assignment. At the same time, I am wary about just how well it is going to perform. ...

... I agree with Professor Zelinsky that many couples, even those who are represented by lawyers, will contract incompletely and then turn to gap fillers provided by the state. It is interesting to think for a moment about why parties to a marriage contract may be especially unlikely to provide for the range of likely disputes. As Lynn Baker and Robert Emery discovered in their study of newlyweds, there is an enormous optimism about marriage by those standing on its cusp. Although the study's subjects were well aware of the general dismal statistics on divorce, not one of them thought that their own marriage would bust up. In addition to the optimism bias, all the standard reasons that contracting parties leave things out apply: fear of introducing the deal breaker and a reluctance of parties in on-going relationships to spell out every expectation, demand, or obligation. For all these reasons, there is likely to be substantial recourse to gap fillers.

I wonder, however, whether the default rules will begin to operate as a shadow regime, establishing baselines for marital obligation and support so that the law of marriage contract will over time not differ much from the law of civil

---

1. Edward A. Zelinsky, Deregulating Marriage: The Pro-Marriage Case for Abolishing Civil Marriage, 27 Cardozo L. Rev. 1161, 1164 (2006).

marriage. If, as Professor Zelinsky acknowledges, marriage contracts are a unique kind of contract and therefore "require . . . unique rules," I would prefer to have the rules straight up rather than through indirect resort to contract.

My greater concern, however, is not about the terms parties leave out but about the enforcement of terms they explicitly include. What is a court to do with provisions that limit the number of children to the marriage or that forbid the use of contraception by either spouse? What about a contract that provides only fault-based grounds for dissolution or no grounds for divorce at all? The immediate answer is that the complaining parties consented to the agreement and are stuck with their bargain. But how will courts handle breach in cases where the wife has used a diaphragm or the husband has had an affair in violation of contract terms? Should judges enforce liquidated damage clauses that deny the breaching spouse property? Can a plaintiff sue for specific performance so that the defendant spouse might be enjoined from marrying again, just as defecting sports players cannot sign with other teams?

There is also a deeper question about the contract-based marital regime. Professor Zelinsky envisions an array of standard form contracts from which couples may choose. I am sure this will be so should his proposal prevail; we are energetic capitalists and just as umbrellas appear for sale on every Manhattan corner within two minutes of a thundershower, marriage entrepreneurs will be out there faster than you can say "Party of the First Part." There will be contract options to cater to every relationship taste and preference. But how customized can a marriage contract be before it falls outside the marital regime altogether? Is there a list of topics or terms that must be included before the arrangement is not marriage but something else, something perhaps closer to an employment contract or a property transfer or a friendship pact? Must the contracting parties reside together or be economically interdependent? Must there be provision for mutual support? . . .

It may be that this question — what have we got here? — is no longer the state's business. If states get out of the marriage business, they would seem to have little room to object to whatever arrangements substitute in. That, I think, is part of Professor Zelinsky's goal. Marriage law has produced virulent debate over the meaning of the institution. If marriage is deregulated, gay and lesbian couples can marry just like any other persons with contractual capacity. Getting rid of civil marriage takes a contentious issue off the political table: there is no more state interest in private domestic arrangements other than policing the contracts by which the relationships are established. . . .

I fear that the preference for deregulation reflects something of an insider's perspective. Marriage may seem like very little when it can be declined, but it is much more significant when it is withheld. . . .

Professor Crane has presented a theological case for the privatization of marriage. . . .

. . . Each religious tradition can offer and can "realize its own vision with respect to . . . marital obligation, divorce, and remarriage," limited only by respect for "the minimal norms of a liberal democratic society." When disputes arise, the parties turn, for arbitrated resolution, to "tribunals specialized in the religious traditions of the relevant family." . . .

. . . [Professor Crane] assures us that nothing too bad can happen under this form of privatization because the religious regime cannot fall below the "minimal norms of liberal democratic society." That sounds good and upon first reading the phrase, all my liberal, feminist, upper west side fears were allayed. Let the churches take back marriage; the minimum norms of a liberal democratic society will protect anything I might be worried about. But the matter is not quite so simple.

To begin, what are the minimum norms of a liberal democratic society? The phrase is not a determinate one and has no technical meaning. Because we are all law-trained, we can probably fill in a likely set of minimum norms without much trouble. I suspect our list would include concerns about equality, participation, the rule of law, and perhaps respect for autonomy.

But these are exactly the areas where religion lets us down. In few religions do women and men participate equally with one another, whether as celebrants, members, and certainly as founders. As political theorist Susan Okin has stressed, Christianity, Judaism, and Islam, certainly in their more orthodox forms, are organized around the authority of husbands and the subservience of women. Husbands control such things as the punishment of children and wives, the availability of divorce, and the distribution of property. This is not a feminist claim; it is a descriptive statement. I am sure that most of us can uncontroversially come up with examples from within our own traditions.

Participatory norms are also challenged by religious marriage. Not all religions permit marriage outside the faith so that marriage to one's chosen partner may not be permitted at all. To demonstrate the value of civil law in such circumstances, political theorist Jeremy Waldron directs us to Romeo and Juliet, that most unhappily married couple. Prevented from marrying by the "traditions of the relevant family," the star-crossed lovers had to leave their respective communities and decamp to Verona. Waldron uses the case to illustrate the importance of an external "structure of rights that people can count on for organizing their lives, a structure which stands somewhat apart from communal or affective attachments and which can be relied on to survive as a basis for action no matter what happens to those attachments." Civil marriage performs exactly this function: it provides a "basis on which individuals . . . can reconstitute their relations and take new initiatives in social life without having to count on the affective support of the communities to which they have hitherto belonged."

Just as some religious traditions restrict entrance to marriage, not all faiths permit exit from the institution. Restrictions on divorce implicate issues of autonomy and of equal participation, particularly for women. As Okin has explained, women's vulnerability within a marriage is intensified by their inability to leave it. The distribution of power at home impacts significantly on participation and influence in the public realm: "the more a culture requires or expects of women in the domestic sphere, the less opportunity they have of achieving equality with men in either sphere." . . .

Without using the vocabulary of multi-culturalism, Professor Crane's privatization endorses a multi-cultural regime for marriage. Each couple (or each plurality in the case of polygamous religions) chooses and then is bound by the religious traditions to which they feel most closely tied. From the perspective of cultural accommodation, this is good. The authority of the group is recognized; its autonomy strengthened. But such accommodation is also likely to work against less powerful members within the group, those whom Les Green has called minorities within minorities. As Green observes, "without respect for internal minorities, a liberal society risks becoming a mosaic of tyrannies." This may be particularly true in the area of family law where as Shachar has noted, "the violation of rights are systemic rather than accidental." . . .

For all these reasons, it is therefore not enough simply to invoke minimum norms to satisfy concerns about unjust practices in religious marriage. Religions are markedly undemocratic, concerned not with rights or equality or principles of non-discrimination but with the demands of faith. Moreover, I suspect few religions would accept the importation of democratic norms, minimal or not, as a condition of governance. It means nothing to cede authority to religious tradition if the religion must first sign on to an incompatible set of civic values and practices. . . .

. . . However, I think it is worth letting all committed couples ask this of one another: to commit to the full extent that is possible at law. And it is marriage law—not contract law—that ought to do the heavy lifting here, not as a functional matter—we can probably kick contract law into sufficient shape to do the job if necessary—but as a matter of the legitimacy of state authority over marriage. Just as the state has interests in marriage, citizens have an interest in the state articulating and defending its interests, as it was eventually unable to do with miscegenation, prohibitions on contraception, or as an absolute requirement for parenting. The nature of the state's interest in marriage is often contested, as it should be. As historian Nancy Cott has pointed out, "the public benefit of governmental involvement in marriage no longer goes without saying." But the explication of the state's interest is less likely to be produced by adjusting the definition of consideration or narrowing the application of injunctive relief.

MARSHA GARRISON, <i>THE DECLINE OF FORMAL MARRIAGE:</i>
INEVITABLE OR REVERSIBLE?

49 Fam. L.Q. 491, 493-499, 501-503, 516-519 (2007)

Formal marriage signals intention. It signals each partner who enters into a new marital union, their friends, and their families. It also signals strangers; those who meet or do business with the married couple understand that each spouse has entered into a binding commitment that entails expectations of fidelity, sharing, and lifetime partnership. Formal marriage also signals intention to the state; government officials can and do assume that the married couple has undertaken obligations to each other that both justify treating them as an economic unit and assuming that a deceased spouse would want his or her marital partner to obtain the lion's share of the decedent spouse's assets.

Formal marriage accomplishes all of these signaling functions prospectively, efficiently, and unequivocally. After a couple marries, there is no question about what sort of relationship they intend. No litigation will be necessary to determine their relational status. No decisionmaker will be required to sift through heaps of self-serving testimony about individual promises made and understandings reached. One partner cannot surprise the other by bringing a fraudulent claim, nor can one partner surprise the other by trying to evade a just claim.

Informal marriage lacks all of these merits. It must be proven and thus offers only a retrospective status. Gaining that status will almost invariably necessitate costly and time-consuming litigation.

These basic disadvantages of informal marriage are compounded by the evidentiary problems inherent in fact-based determination of marital status. Marital intent is subjective; when not publicly expressed, it is extraordinarily hard to prove. This basic problem is exacerbated by the range of meanings associated with cohabitation and the fact that cohabitants often do not agree about the nature of their relationship. . . .

Given the lack of uniformity in cohabitants' understandings and behaviors, the mere fact of living together provides little evidence of what understandings a particular relationship has produced. One partner may deeply believe that the relationship is committed; the other may deeply believe the reverse. A breakup can only enhance such disagreement, setting the stage for disappointed expectations and resulting litigation. These difficulties are bad enough when both cohabitants are able to testify at a hearing; they are even worse when the issue of marital understanding is tested in a proceeding brought after one partner dies. . . .

Formal marriage is also associated with a range of benefits to adult partners and their children. Cross-national surveys show that marriage is associated with higher levels of subjective well-being throughout the industrialized and nonindustrialized world. Researcher after researcher has reported that married individuals typically live longer and healthier lives than the unmarried; husbands and wives get more sleep, eat more regularly, and visit the doctor more often; they abuse addictive substances and engage in risky behaviors less frequently. Married men and women also do better economically than their unmarried counterparts. Married men earn more than either single men or cohabitants. Married couples also have a higher savings rate and thus accrue greater wealth than the unmarried.

The marital advantage also provides benefits to a couple's children. Because of the greater stability that marriage provides, marital children are exposed to many fewer financial, physical, and educational risks; these lower risks are associated with higher levels of well-being. There is also evidence that the advantages conferred by marital childbearing and rearing transcend the specific benefits associated with residential and economic stability. For example, married fathers appear to be more involved and spend more time with their children than unmarried fathers; if parental separation occurs, they see their children more often and pay child support more regularly. . . .

For both adults and children, the marital advantage is concentrated in low-conflict relationships. Researchers have found that the continuation of a high-conflict marriage is *negatively* associated with the health and happiness; indeed, longitudinal surveys show that "parents' marital unhappiness and discord have a broad negative impact on virtually every dimension of offspring well-being." . . .

Selection effects also explain away a significant portion of the marital advantage. To the extent that those who marry are wealthier — or happier, or healthier — before marriage, they should maintain these advantages after marriage. Although the jury is still out on the extent to which the marriage "premium" derives from preexisting characteristics or the married state, we know that both marriage and marital parenting are strongly associated with higher socioeconomic status. . . .

However, despite these caveats, the evidence strongly suggests that the marital advantage is real, and that it persists across national, cultural, and socioeconomic boundaries. . . .

Despite the advantages associated with formal marriage, all across the industrialized world young adults are marrying later and increasing numbers may not marry at all. With the notable exceptions of Asia and southern Europe, the proportion of children born outside of marriage has also skyrocketed.

The decline of marriage and marital childbearing is not evenly distributed across the population, however. College-educated women were once less likely to marry than others; this is no longer the case and, at least in the United States, these well-educated women are equally or more likely to stay married than they were several decades ago. In the United States and, to a lesser extent, some European nations, nonmarital fertility is also concentrated among the poorly educated. Because of these divergent trends, in the mid-1990s, only 10% of the children of U.S. college-educated women lived in single-parent households — a percentage that has not increased since 1980 — as compared with more than 40% of children whose mothers lacked a high-school diploma.

Marital and reproductive behavior also diverges sharply by race and ethnicity. In the United States, the decline of marriage has been much more pronounced among black than white Americans. Blacks have long had a high rate of marital disruption, but they are now much less likely to marry, too. Slightly more than two-thirds of black women born between 1960 and 1964 married by age forty, compared to eighty-seven percent of those born two decades earlier and eighty-nine percent of non-Hispanic white women. Conversely, sixty-eight percent of black children are now born outside of marriage, compared to twenty-eight percent of non-Hispanic white children. Black cohabitants are also much less likely than white cohabitants to marry after their child's birth or even to remain a couple. . . .

Because the decline of marriage results from a number of different factors, policymakers face large difficulties in reversing the trend. These policy-making difficulties are magnified because the personal benefits of marriage are concentrated in long-term, harmonious marital relationships. Initiatives that encourage couples with weak, highly conflicted relationships to enter into formal marriage along with those who have strong, unconflicted relationships may foster the signaling function of marriage but cannot produce significant gains in adult or child well-being. Ideally, then, public policy would encourage couples to defer marriage — formal or informal — and childbearing until they have determined that their relationship has good prospects for long-term success. It would also encourage them to enter into formal, ceremonial marriage when and if they make a positive determination about their long-term prospects. Achieving a result this nuanced is obviously very difficult given the range of variables that appear to affect marital decision-making and our limited understanding of how those variables work together. . . .

Given these concerns, shifts in the law that assimilate some cohabitational relationships to marriage would appear to be particularly undesirable. These shifts seem to be motivated, in large part, by the sense that women in long-term cohabitational relationships are disadvantaged at relationship dissolution as compared to their married peers and aim at reducing that disadvantage. Some such schemes rely on individualized fact-finding; others, more numerous, rely on the duration of cohabitation or the birth of a common child. The individualized schemes [create] fact-finding problems . . . ; the durational and common-child approaches resolve some of the fact-finding difficulties of the individualized schemes but reduce individual autonomy and risk the imposition of obligations on individuals who lack marital understandings or — worse — who have affirmatively chosen to avoid marital obligations by remaining single. Although these reasons alone should deter policymakers from initiating such "conscriptive" regulatory schemes, policy-makers inclined toward this type of initiative should additionally consider the fact that conscriptive schemes not so subtly signal that the decision to marry is unimportant. Such a signal has the potential to contribute to the perception that public support for formal marriage is declining and thus to trigger exactly that. . . .

On the other hand, policies that neutrally, but sharply, distinguish marriage from cohabitation appear to be warranted and appropriate. These policies reinforce the perception that marriage is not just a piece of paper and thus encourage both thoughtful marital decisions and decisions that segregate those with marital intentions from those without such intentions. These policies may also reinforce public opinion in favor of formal marriage for those with marital intentions and childbearing within such relationships.

Cynthia Grant Bowman, *Social Science and Legal Policy: The Case of Heterosexual Cohabitation*

9 J.L. & Fam. Stud. 1, 36-42 (2007)

The social science findings about cohabitation support the extension of legal protections to cohabitants. Cohabitation is likely, though not always, a less stable relationship than marriage, one that is more likely to involve domestic violence; and it involves substantial economic interdependence. A large number of individuals involved are likely to be poor, to come from disadvantaged racial or ethnic minorities, and to have children. All of these are powerful reasons to recognize their unions for purposes of government benefits, to extend a variety of legal remedies upon the ending of their relationships, and to grant them rights against third parties. The very instability of cohabiting unions is a strong reason to provide rights to property and support upon dissolution, so long as the relationship has lasted a certain period of time or has produced a child.

If, as recent studies indicate, cohabitants are more likely to merge their finances than to keep them separate, and the presence of a cohabitant in the household adds substantially to the ability of an otherwise single mother to support her child, then we need to worry about vulnerability of the parties if the relationship ends. Legal remedies for the custodial parent (usually the mother) — remedies beyond the child support she can presumably command from the child's biological father — may be very important for the welfare of the children involved. . . .

A number of legal scholars argue that we should not give legal protection to cohabitation because to do so will harm the institution of marriage, which is, or should be, the societal ideal. Given the statistics on the increase in cohabitation, this could be a case of sacrificing the good in a futile search for the best. . . .

The argument that to give legal status to cohabitants will harm the ideal embodied in marriage assumes that refusal to recognize cohabitation will lead people to marry instead, and that marriage by many of the people currently cohabiting would not be characterized by the bad effects that accompany their cohabitation. Arguments to this effect are seriously flawed in a number of respects.

First, legal incentives do not seem to affect people's private behavior in this way. Indeed, most people are unlikely even to know what their legal rights and obligations are, at least until they get divorced. . . . Many people in the United States mistakenly believe that the law in fact does protect them after a certain period of cohabitation, although common law marriage is recognized only in a handful of states. . . .

We now have a number of studies, primarily in the context of welfare reform, about the impact of legal incentives upon the rate of marriage. Without exception they show that welfare programs designed to encourage marriage have had no statistically significant effect on the marriage rate. Indeed, one study suggests that entry into marriage is *negatively* associated with the incentives offered by the new federal welfare initiatives which drastically limit payment of benefits to unmarried mothers. These results are consistent with evidence that variations in welfare benefits do not affect the non-marital birth rate either. Human beings apparently do not regulate behavior as private as union formation and childbirth in response to incentives from the state.

If people did think and act in this way, however, the incentive structure provided by the current legal treatment of cohabitation in this country is perverse. By not imposing any legal obligations on cohabitants, the stronger partner economically is given an incentive *not* to marry, because to do so would mean being required to share his or her property upon dissolution of the relationship and possibly to support the former partner in the short or long run. . . .

The comparisons of most immediate interest are those with Western European countries that have in fact extended legal protections to cohabiting couples, such as the Netherlands, Sweden, and France. In the Netherlands, heterosexual couples may choose between marriage and registration as domestic partners, which is virtually identical to marriage in legal status. Yet the rate of cohabitation to marriage in the Netherlands (25% of unions are cohabitations) is identical to that in the U.K., where legal protections are denied to heterosexual cohabitants. In Sweden, heterosexual cohabitation has been accepted for the longest period of time and is given very favorable treatment by the government, and cohabitants' property is distributed equally between them at the end of their relationships. Yet Eurobarometer surveys show that 90% of Swedish young people are in favor of marriage, and 61.2% of cohabiting women aged 15 to 44 in Sweden eventually marry their partners, compared with 48% in the United States. In short, giving positive legal treatment to cohabitation does not seem to discourage the transition to marriage and may in fact encourage it.

In France, where the Pacte Civil de Solidarité allows cohabitants who register to receive some of the benefits of marital status, about 83.5% of adult women will cohabit between ages 15 and 45, compared to about 50% in the U.S. Approximately equal proportions of cohabitants will end their cohabitation by marrying or by separating: 46.3% will marry in France and 48% in the U.S.; 53.7% will separate in France and 52% in the U.S. . . .

In sum, offering legal recognition and support to cohabitants and making their lives easier does not appear to discourage marriage, and in fact the opposite may be true. . . .

HEWITT V. HEWITT

394 N.E.2d 1204 (Ill. 1979)

UNDERWOOD, J. The issue in this case is whether plaintiff Victoria Hewitt, whose complaint alleges she lived with defendant Robert Hewitt from 1960 to 1975 in an unmarried, family-like relationship to which three children have been born, may recover from him "an equal share of the profits and properties accumulated by the parties" during that period.

Plaintiff initially filed a complaint for divorce, but at a hearing on defendant's motion to dismiss, admitted that no marriage ceremony had taken place and that the parties have never obtained a marriage license. . . .

Plaintiff thereafter filed an amended complaint alleging the following bases for her claim: (1) that because defendant promised he would "share his life, his future, his earnings and his property" with her and all of defendant's property resulted from the parties' joint endeavors, plaintiff is entitled in equity to a one-half share; (2) that the conduct of the parties evinced an implied contract entitling plaintiff to one-half the property accumulated during their "family relationship"; (3) that because defendant fraudulently assured plaintiff she was his wife in order to secure her services, although he knew they were not legally married, defendant's property should be impressed with a trust for plaintiff's benefit; (4) that because plaintiff has relied to her detriment on defendant's promises and devoted her entire life to him, defendant has been unjustly enriched.

The factual background alleged or testified to is that in June 1960, when she and defendant were students at Grinnell College in Iowa, plaintiff became pregnant; that defendant thereafter told her that they were husband and wife and would live as such, no formal ceremony being necessary, and that he would "share his life, his future, his earnings and his property" with her; that the parties immediately announced to their respective parents that they were married and thereafter held themselves out as husband and wife; that in reliance on defendant's promises she devoted her efforts to his professional education and his establishment in the practice of pedodontia, obtaining financial assistance from her parents for this purpose; that she assisted defendant in his career with her own special skills and although she was given payroll checks for these services she placed them in a common fund; that defendant, who was without funds at the time of the marriage, as a result of her efforts now earns over $80,000 a year and has accumulated large amounts of property, owned either jointly with her or separately; that she has given him every assistance a wife and mother could give, including social activities designed to enhance his social and professional reputation.

The amended complaint was also dismissed, the trial court finding that Illinois law and public policy require such claims to be based on a valid marriage. The appellate court reversed, stating that because the parties had outwardly lived a conventional married life, plaintiff's conduct had not "so affronted public policy that she should be denied any and all relief," and that plaintiff's complaint stated a cause of action on an express oral contract. We granted leave to appeal. Defendant apparently does not contest his obligation to support the children, and that question is not before us. . . .

. . . The issue of unmarried cohabitants' mutual property rights, however, as we earlier noted, cannot appropriately be characterized solely in terms of contract law, nor is it limited to considerations of equity or fairness as between the parties to such relationships. There are major public policy questions involved in determining whether, under what circumstances, and to what extent it is desirable to accord some type of legal status to claims arising from such relationships. Of substantially greater importance than the rights of the immediate parties is the impact of such recognition upon our society and the institution of marriage. Will the fact that legal rights closely resembling those arising from conventional marriages can be acquired by those who deliberately choose to enter into what have heretofore been commonly referred to as "illicit" or "meretricious" relationships encourage formation of such relationships and weaken marriage as the foundation of our family-based society? In the event of death shall the survivor have the status of a surviving spouse for purposes of inheritance, wrongful death actions, workmen's compensation, etc.? And still more importantly: what of the children born of such relationships? What are their support and inheritance rights and by what standards are custody questions resolved? What of the sociological and psychological effects upon them of that type of environment? Does not the recognition of legally enforceable property and custody rights emanating from nonmarital cohabitation in practical effect equate with the legalization of common law marriage at least in the circumstances of this case? And, in summary, have the increasing numbers of unmarried cohabitants and changing mores of our society reached the point at which the general welfare of the citizens of this State is best served by a return to something resembling the judicially created common law marriage our legislature outlawed in 1905? . . .

. . . We cannot confidently say that judicial recognition of property rights between unmarried cohabitants will not make that alternative to marriage more attractive by allowing the parties to engage in such relationships with greater security. As one commentator has noted, it may make this alternative especially attractive to persons who seek a property arrangement that the law does not permit to marital partners. This court, for example, has held void agreements releasing husbands from their obligation to support their wives. In thus potentially enhancing the attractiveness of a private arrangement over marriage, we believe that the appellate court decision in this case contravenes the [Illinois Marriage and Dissolution of Marriage] Act's policy of strengthening and preserving the integrity of marriage. . . .

We accordingly hold that plaintiff's claims are unenforceable for the reason that they contravene the public policy, implicit in the statutory scheme of the Illinois Marriage and Dissolution of Marriage Act, disfavoring the grant of mutually enforceable property rights to knowingly unmarried cohabitants. The judgment of the appellate court is reversed and the judgment of the circuit court of Champaign County is affirmed.

Appellate court reversed; circuit court affirmed.

NOTES AND QUESTIONS

1. In 1960 marriage was widely accepted as necessary to provide support for children and their caregiving mothers. A man who impregnated a woman was expected to marry her, and she needed to be married if she were to raise the child and remain "respectable." Marriages prompted by an unplanned pregnancy increased during the 1950s, and at the time that the Hewitts had their first child, 30 percent of brides gave birth within eight and a half months of the nuptials. The Hewitts, in almost every respect except their failure to formalize their relationship, were very much like many other couples of their era.

Had the Hewitts been married, when they broke up Victoria could have asserted claims against Robert for a share of the property acquired during the marriage, for spousal support, or both. Since they were not married, their relationship was essentially that of long-term roommates. Each owned the property in his or her name, and she had no basis on which to claim support. Why would Victoria have agreed to live in a relationship that left her so economically vulnerable? Does the reason that she agreed matter now that she is seeking legal relief?

Why do many women today make the same decision Victoria made — to live with a man and raise a child with him with little or no protection in the event of family dissolution?

2. The *Hewitt* court was concerned that allowing Victoria to make a claim against Robert would undermine marriage. Professor Garrison makes the same argument. Why does Professor Bowman disagree? In what ways would allowing her to make a claim make living together more desirable than marriage? Are there ways in which marriage would still be more desirable to the individuals involved?

3. Professor Garrison argues against treating cohabitation and marriage similarly based on objective factors in part because it may result in some people having obligations imposed on them that they did not intend. Perhaps Mr. Hewitt would think himself to be in that category. What did Ms. Hewitt intend? If their intentions differ, whose should the law protect and why?

4. Professor Sanger contrasts marriage, which involves traditions, expectations, and default terms imposed from without, with contract as a legal arrangement that couples negotiate for themselves. If the Hewitts had negotiated a contract at the time they began to live together, what terms do you think it would have included? Would those terms differ if they were to enter into a contract in similar circumstances today? Is such a contract likely to address the realistic needs of a full-time homemaker adequately? Is the negotiation process likely to bring them closer together or drive them further apart?

5. Professor Fineman favors the deregulation of adult relationships, effectively replacing marriage with contract, but continuing state recognition of the parent-child tie and support to alleviate the dependency that accompanies the assumption of caretaking responsibilities. As a practical matter, what would this have meant for Victoria Hewitt? Would Fineman grant a remedy to Victoria if she and Robert had not had children but still lived a role-divided life in which Victoria maintained the home and Robert worked as a children's dentist?

6. As we will see in Chapter 4, in most states today Victoria would be able to state a claim against Robert for common law marriage or, where common law marriage is not permitted, based upon the contract or equity theories that the

Illinois court in *Hewitt* rejected. However, the Illinois courts still refuse to allow cohabitants to make claims against each other at the end of their relationships, affirming *Hewitt. See, e.g.,* Costa v. Oliven, 849 N.E.2d 122 (Ill. App. 2006).

BRASCHI V. STAHL ASSOCIATES COMPANY

543 N.E.2d 49 (N.Y. 1989)

TITONE, J. Appellant, Miguel Braschi, was living with Leslie Blanchard in a rent-controlled apartment located at 405 East 54th Street from the summer of 1975 until Blanchard's death in September of 1986. In November of 1986, respondent, Stahl Associates Company, the owner of the apartment building, served a notice to cure on appellant contending that he was a mere licensee with no right to occupy the apartment since only Blanchard was the tenant of record. In December of 1986 respondent served appellant with a notice to terminate informing appellant that he had one month to vacate the apartment and that, if the apartment was not vacated, respondent would commence summary proceedings to evict him.

Appellant then initiated an action seeking a permanent injunction and a declaration of entitlement to occupy the apartment. By order to show cause appellant then moved for a preliminary injunction, pendente lite, enjoining respondent from evicting him until a court could determine whether he was a member of Blanchard's family within the meaning of 9 NYCRR 2204.6(d). After examining the nature of the relationship between the two men, Supreme Court concluded that appellant was a "family member" within the meaning of the regulation and, accordingly, that a preliminary injunction should be issued. . . .

The Appellate Division reversed, concluding that section 2204.6(d) provides noneviction protection only to "family members within traditional, legally recognized familial relationships." . . . We now reverse.

The present dispute arises because the term "family" is not defined in the rent-control code and the legislative history is devoid of any specific reference to the noneviction provision. All that is known is the legislative purpose underlying the enactment of the rent-control laws as a whole. Rent control was enacted to address a "serious public emergency" created by "an acute shortage in dwellings," which resulted in "speculative, unwarranted and abnormal increases in rents." These measures were designed to regulate and control the housing market so as to "prevent exactions of unjust, unreasonable and oppressive rents and rental agreements and to forestall profiteering, speculation and other disruptive practices tending to produce threats to the public health . . . [and] to prevent uncertainty, hardship and dislocation." . . .

To accomplish its goals, the Legislature recognized that not only would rents have to be controlled, but that evictions would have to be regulated and controlled as well. Hence, section 2204.6 of the New York City Rent and Eviction Regulations (9 NYCRR 2204.6), which authorizes the issuance of a certificate for the eviction of persons occupying a rent-controlled apartment after the death of the named tenant, provides, in subdivision (d), noneviction protection to those occupants who are either the "surviving spouse of the deceased tenant or some other member of the deceased tenant's family who has been living with the tenant [of record]." The manifest intent of this section is to restrict the landowners' ability to evict a narrow class of occupants other than the tenant of record. The question presented here concerns the scope of the protections provided. Juxtaposed against this intent favoring the protection of tenants is the over-all objective of a gradual "transition from regulation to a normal market of free bargaining between land-lord and tenant." One way in which this goal is to be achieved is "vacancy decontrol," which automatically makes rent-control units subject to the less rigorous provisions of rent stabilization upon the termination of the rent-control tenancy.

Emphasizing the latter objective, respondent argues that the term "family member" as used in 9 NYCRR 2204.6(d) should be construed, consistent with this State's intestacy laws, to mean relationships of blood, consanguinity and adoption in order to effectuate the over-all goal of orderly succession to real property. Under this interpretation, only those entitled to inherit under the laws of intestacy would be afforded noneviction protection. . . .

Contrary to all of these arguments, we conclude that the term "family," as used in 9 NYCRR 2204.6(d), should not be rigidly restricted to those people who have formalized their relationship by obtaining, for instance, a marriage certificate or an adoption order. The intended protection against sudden eviction should not rest on fictitious legal distinctions or genetic history, but instead should find its foundation in the reality of family life. In the context of eviction, a more realistic, and certainly equally valid, view of a family includes two adult lifetime partners whose relationship is long term and characterized by an emotional and financial commitment and interdependence. This view comports both with our society's traditional concept of "family" and with the expectations of individuals who live in such nuclear units. In fact, Webster's Dictionary defines "family" first as "a group of people united by certain convictions or common affiliation." Hence, it is reasonable to conclude that, in using the term "family," the Legislature intended to extend protection to those who reside in households having all of the normal familial characteristics. Appellant Braschi should therefore be afforded the opportunity to prove that he and Blanchard had such a household.

This definition of "family" is consistent with both of the competing purposes of the rent-control laws: the protection of individuals from sudden dislocation and the gradual transition to a free market system. Family members, whether or not related by blood or law, who have always treated the apartment as their family home will be protected against the hardship of eviction following the death of the named tenant, thereby furthering the Legislature's goals of preventing dislocation and preserving family units which might otherwise be broken apart upon eviction. This approach will foster the transition from rent control to rent stabilization by drawing a distinction between those individuals who are, in fact, genuine family members, and those who are mere roommates or newly discovered relatives hoping to inherit the rent-controlled apartment after the existing tenant's death.

The determination as to whether an individual is entitled to noneviction protection should be based upon an objective examination of the relationship of the parties. In making this assessment, the lower courts of this State have looked to a number of factors, including the exclusivity and longevity of the relationship, the level of emotional and financial commitment, the manner in which the parties have conducted their everyday lives and held themselves out to society, and the reliance placed upon one another for daily family services. These factors are most helpful, although it should be emphasized that the presence or absence of one or more of them is not dispositive since it is the totality of the relationship as evidenced by the dedication, caring and self-sacrifice of the parties which should, in the final analysis, control. Appellant's situation provides an example of how the rule should be applied.

Appellant and Blanchard lived together as permanent life partners for more than 10 years. They regarded one another, and were regarded by friends and family, as spouses. The two men's families were aware of the nature of the relationship, and they regularly visited each other's families and attended family functions together, as a couple. Even today, appellant continues to maintain a relationship with Blanchard's niece, who considers him an uncle. In addition to their interwoven social lives, appellant clearly considered the apartment his home. He lists the apartment as his address on his driver's license and passport, and receives all his mail at the apartment address. Moreover, appellant's tenancy was known to the building's superintendent and doormen, who viewed the two men as a couple. Financially, the two men shared all obligations including a household budget. The two were authorized signatories of three safe-deposit boxes, they maintained joint checking and savings accounts, and joint credit cards. In fact, rent was often paid with a check from their joint checking account. Additionally, Blanchard executed a power of attorney in appellant's favor so that appellant could make necessary decisions — financial, medical and personal — for him during his illness. Finally, appellant was the named beneficiary of Blanchard's life insurance policy, as well as the primary legatee and coexecutor of Blanchard's estate. Hence, a court examining these facts could reasonably conclude that these men were much more than mere roommates.

. . . Accordingly, the order of the Appellate Division should be reversed and the case remitted to that court for a consideration of undetermined questions. The certified question should be answered in the negative.

SIMONS, J. (dissenting). I would affirm. The plurality has adopted a definition of family which extends the language of the regulation well beyond the implication of the words used in it. In doing so, it has expanded the class indefinitely to include anyone who can satisfy an administrator that he or she had an emotional and financial "commitment" to the statutory tenant. Its interpretation is inconsistent with the legislative scheme underlying rent regulation, goes well beyond the intended purposes of 9 NYCRR 2204.6(d), and produces an unworkable test that is subject to abuse. . . .

. . . [T]here are serious practical problems in adopting the plurality's interpretation of the statute. Any determination of rights under it would require first a determination of whether protection should be accorded the relationship (i.e., unmarrieds, nonadopted occupants, etc.) and then a subjective determination in each case of whether the relationship was genuine, and entitled to the protection of the law, or expedient, and an attempt to take advantage of the law. Plaintiff maintains that the machinery for such decisions is in place and that appropriate guidelines can be constructed. He refers particularly to a formulation outlined by the court in 2-4 Realty Assocs. v. Pittman, 137 Misc. 2d 898, 902, 523 N.Y.S.2d 7, which sets forth six different factors to be weighed. The plurality has essentially adopted his formulation. The enumeration of such factors, and the determination that they are controlling, is a matter best left to Legislatures because it involves the type of policy making the courts should avoid, but even if these considerations are appropriate and exclusive, the application of them cannot be made objectively and creates serious difficulties in determining who is entitled to the statutory benefit. Anyone is potentially eligible to succeed to the tenant's premises and thus, in each case, the agency will be required to make a determination of eligibility based solely on subjective factors such as the "level of emotional and financial commitment" and "the manner in which the parties have conducted their everyday lives and held themselves out to society."

[The concurring opinion of Bellacosa, J., is omitted.]

NOTES AND QUESTIONS

1. The governing statute in this case provides protections to members of a decedent's "family." Upon what theory does the majority find that Miguel Braschi and Leslie Blanchard were a family?

2. How does the majority determine whether a relationship constitutes a family? How would the dissent determine this question? What role do stereotypes and cultural norms play in these definitions? If Miguel and Leslie had been a married heterosexual couple who lived apart for half the year, maintained separate finances, and kept their marriage secret from family and friends, would Miguel have been a surviving family member for purposes of the statute as interpreted by the majority? The dissent?

3. Today, Miguel Braschi and Leslie Blanchard could marry in New York. If they had exactly the same relationship described in the case, but *chose* not to marry, would that change the outcome of the case?

4. What values are promoted by the majority's test for "family"-ness? By the dissent's? The dissent says that this value choice should be made by the legislature, not the court. Do you agree? Why or why not? On facts such as this, is it possible for a court not to make a value choice?

5. *Braschi* has not been broadly applied by the New York courts. For example, the Court of Appeals refused to apply *Braschi*'s analytical approach to a custody dispute between a biological mother and her former mate, even though the two women had agreed to have the child and had functioned as parents together for the first two years of the child's life. Alison D. v. Virginia M., 572 N.E.2d 27 (N.Y. 1991). Four years later, the court affirmed *Alison D.* and held that the lesbian partner of a biological mother may adopt and so become a legal parent under the statute. Matter of Jacob, 660 N.E.2d 397 (N.Y. 1995). The court explained, "*Alison D.*, in conjunction with second-parent adoption, creates a bright-line rule that promotes certainty in the wake of domestic breakups otherwise fraught with the risk of "disruptive . . . battle[s]." 660 N.E.2d at 397. In 2010 the court again confirmed that parentage should be based on legal forms, not function, in Debra H. v. Janice R., 930 N.E.2d 184 (N.Y. 2010), which held that a child born during a Vermont civil union was the legal child of both women, not just the biological mother, because Vermont law regards both partners in a civil union as a child's parents, and New York would grant comity to that rule.

6. Whether cohabitants are entitled to public benefits dependent on family relationships has arisen in a number of other situations, with mixed results. *See, e.g.,* MacGregor v. Unemployment Insurance Appeals Board, 689 P.2d 453 (Cal. 1984) (allowing unemployment compensation benefits to a woman who quit work to follow fiance); Norman v. Unemployment Insurance Appeals Board, 663 P.2d 904 (Cal. 1983) (denying unemployment benefits to a woman who quit work to follow cohabitant because this was not "good cause"). Some jurisdictions have statutes that provide relief in specific instances. *See, e.g.,* Or. Rev. Stat. § 656.226:

> In case an unmarried man and an unmarried woman have cohabited in this state as husband and wife for over one year prior to the date of an accidental injury received by one or the other as a subject worker, and children are living as a result of that relation, the surviving cohabitant and the children are entitled to compensation under this chapter [workers' compensation] the same as if the man and woman had been legally married.

7. Several courts have held that granting benefits to spouses while denying them to domestic partners (of the same or opposite sex) does not violate state antidiscrimination law, the state constitution, or both. *See, e.g.,* Monson v. Rochester Athletic Club, 759 N.W.2d 60 (Minn. App. 2009) (club's refusal to grant family rates to same-sex couple does not violate state human rights act or state constitution); National Pride at Work, Inc. v. Governor, 732 N.W.2d 139 (Mich. 2007); Rutgers Council of AAUP Chapters v. Rutgers University, 689 A.2d 828 (N.J. Super. App. Div. 1997) (granting benefits to employees' spouses does not violate New Jersey Law Against Discrimination or New Jersey Constitution).

Other state courts have reached a contrary conclusion. For example, University of Alaska v. Tumeo, 933 P.2d 1147 (Alaska 1997), held that denial of health benefits to university employees' same-sex partners violates the Alaska Human Rights Act barring discrimination in employment on the basis of marital status. As the *Tumeo* court noted, however, while the case was pending the Human Rights Act was amended to allow employers to offer coverage only to spouses of employees. Thereafter, the Alaska Supreme Court held under the state constitution that offering benefits only to spouses of public employees violates the equal protection rights of employees with same-sex domestic partners. Alaska Civil Liberties Union v. State, 122 P.3d 781 (Alaska 2005). Similarly, the Oregon Court of Appeals held in Oregon Health Sciences University v. Tanner, 971 P.2d 435 (Or. App. 1998), that state statutes that allowed public employers to offer benefits to employees' spouses and to deny them to same-sex domestic partners constituted sex-based discrimination in violation of the state constitution.

CITY OF LADUE v. HORN

720 S.W.2d 745 (Mo. App. E.D. 1986)

CRANDALL, Judge. Defendants, Joan Horn and E. Terrence Jones, appeal from the judgment of the trial court in favor of plaintiff, City of Ladue (Ladue), which enjoined defendants from occupying their home in violation of Ladue's zoning ordinance and which dismissed defendants' counterclaim. We affirm.

The case was submitted to the trial court on stipulated facts. Ladue's Zoning Ordinance No. 1175 was in effect at all times pertinent to the present action. Certain zones were designated as one-family residential. The zoning ordinance defined family as: "One or more persons related by blood, marriage or adoption, occupying a dwelling unit as an individual housekeeping organization." The only authorized accessory use in residential districts was for "[a]ccommodations for domestic persons employed and living on the premises and home occupations." The purpose of Ladue's zoning ordinance was broadly stated as to promote "the health, safety, morals and general welfare" of Ladue.

In July, 1981, defendants purchased a seven-bedroom, four-bathroom house which was located in a single-family residential zone in Ladue. Residing in defendants' home were Horn's two children (aged 16 and 19) and Jones's one child (age 18). The two older children attended out-of-state universities and lived in the house only on a part-time basis. Although defendants were not married, they shared a common bedroom, maintained a joint checking account for the household expenses, ate their meals together, entertained together, and disciplined each other's children. Ladue made demands upon defendants to vacate their home because their household did not comprise a family, as defined by Ladue's zoning ordinance, and therefore they could not live in an area zoned for single-family dwellings. When defendants refused to vacate, Ladue sought to enjoin defendants' continued violation of the zoning ordinance. Defendants counterclaimed, seeking a declaration that the zoning ordinance was constitutionally void. They also sought attorneys' fees and costs. The trial court entered a permanent injunction in favor of Ladue and dismissed defendants' counterclaim. Enforcement of the injunction was stayed pending this appeal. . . .

. . . Defendants allege that the United States and Missouri Constitutions grant each of them the right to share his or her residence with whomever he or she chooses. They assert that Ladue has not demonstrated a compelling, much less rational, justification for the overly proscriptive blood or legal relationship requirement in its zoning ordinance.

Defendants posit that the term "family" is susceptible to several meanings. They contend that, since their household is the "functional and factual equivalent of a natural family," the ordinance may not preclude them from living in a single-family residential Ladue neighborhood. Defendants argue in their brief as follows:

> The record amply demonstrates that the private, intimate interests of Horn and Jones are substantial. Horn, Jones, and their respective children have historically lived together as a single family unit. They use and occupy their home for the identical purposes and in the identical manners as families which are biologically or maritally related.

To bolster this contention, defendants elaborate on their shared duties, as set forth earlier in this opinion. Defendants acknowledge the importance of viewing themselves as a family unit, albeit a "conceptual family" as opposed to a "true nonfamily," in order to prevent the application of the ordinance.

The fallacy in defendants' syllogism is that the stipulated facts do not compel the conclusion that defendants are living as a family. A man and woman living together, sharing pleasures and certain responsibilities, does not *per se* constitute a family in even the conceptual sense. To approximate a family relationship, there must exist a commitment to a permanent relationship and a perceived reciprocal obligation to support and to care for each other. Only when these characteristics are present can the conceptual family, perhaps, equate with the traditional family. In a traditional family, certain of its inherent attributes arise from the legal relationship of the family members. In a non-traditional family, those same qualities arise in fact, either by explicit agreement or by tacit understanding among the parties.

While the stipulated facts could arguably support an inference by the trial court that defendants and their children comprised a non-traditional family, they do not compel that inference. Absent findings of fact and conclusions of law, we cannot assume that the trial court's perception of defendants' familial status comported with defendants' characterization of themselves as a conceptual family. In fact, if a finding by the trial court that defendants' living arrangement constituted a conceptual family is critical to a determination in defendants' favor, we can assume that the court's finding was adverse to defendants' position. Ordinarily, given our deference to the decision of the trial court, that would dispose of this appeal. We decline, however, to restrict our ruling to such a narrow basis. We therefore consider the broader issues presented by the parties. We assume, *arguendo*, that the sole basis for the judgment entered by the trial court was that defendants were not related by blood, marriage or adoption, as required by Ladue's ordinance.

We first consider whether the ordinance violates any federally protected rights of the defendants. Generally, federal court decisions hold that a zoning classification based upon a biological or a legal relationship among household members is justifiable under constitutional police powers to protect the public health, safety, morals or welfare of the community.

More specifically, the United States Supreme Court has developed a two-tiered approach by which to examine legislation challenged as violative of the equal protection clause. If the personal interest affected by the ordinance is fundamental, "strict scrutiny" is applied and the ordinance is sustained only upon a showing that the burden imposed is necessary to protect a compelling governmental interest. If the ordinance does not contain a suspect class or impinge upon a fundamental interest, the more relaxed "rational basis" test is applied and the classification imposed by the ordinance is upheld if any facts can reasonably justify it. Defendants urge this court to recognize that their interest in choosing their own living arrangement inexorably involves their fundamental rights of freedom of association and of privacy. . . .

In the Village of Belle Terre v. Boraas, 416 U.S. 1 (1974), the court addressed a zoning regulation of the type at issue in this case. The court held that the Village of Belle Terre ordinance involved no fundamental right, but was typical of economic and social legislation which is upheld if it is reasonably related to a permissible governmental objective. The challenged zoning ordinance of the Village of Belle Terre defined family as:

> One or more persons related by blood, adoption or marriage, living and cooking together as a single housekeeping unit [or] a number of persons but not exceeding two (2) living and cooking together as a single housekeeping unit though not related by blood, adoption, or marriage. . . .

The court upheld the ordinance, reasoning that the ordinance constituted valid land use legislation reasonably designed to maintain traditional family values and patterns.

The importance of the family was reaffirmed in Moore v. City of East Cleveland, 431 U.S. 494 (1977), wherein the United States Supreme Court was confronted with a housing ordinance which defined a "family" as only certain closely related individuals. Consequently, a grandmother who lived with her son and two grandsons was convicted of violating the ordinance because her two grandsons were first cousins rather than brothers. The United States Supreme Court struck down the East Cleveland ordinance for violating the freedom of personal choice in matters of marriage and family life. The court distinguished Belle Terre by stating that the ordinance in that case allowed all individuals related by blood, marriage or adoption to live together; whereas East Cleveland, by restricting the number of related persons who could live together, sought "to regulate the occupancy of its housing by slicing deeply into the family itself." The court pointed out that the institution of the family is protected by the Constitution precisely because it is so deeply rooted in the American tradition and that "[o]urs is by no means a tradition limited to respect for the bonds uniting the members of the nuclear family."

Here, because we are dealing with economic and social legislation and not with a fundamental interest or a suspect classification, the test of constitutionality is whether the ordinance is reasonable and not arbitrary and bears a rational relationship to a permissible state objective.

Ladue has a legitimate concern with laying out guidelines for land use addressed to family needs. "It is ample to lay out zones where family values, youth values, and the blessings of quiet seclusion and clean air make the area a sanctuary for people." The question of whether Ladue could have chosen more precise means to effectuate its legislative goals is immaterial. Ladue's zoning ordinance is rationally related to its expressed purposes and violates no provisions of the Constitution of the United States. Further, defendants' assertion that they have a constitutional right to share their residence with whomever they please amounts to the same argument that was made and found unpersuasive by the court in Belle Terre. . . .

For purposes of its zoning code, Ladue has in precise language defined the term "family." It chose the definition which comports with the historical and traditional notions of family; namely, those people related by blood, marriage or adoption. That definition of family has been upheld in numerous Missouri decisions. See, e.g., London v. Handicapped Facilities Board of St. Charles County, 637 S.W.2d 212 (Mo. App. 1982) (group home not a "family" as used in restrictive covenant); Feely v. Birenbaum, 554 S.W.2d 432 (Mo. App. 1977) (two unrelated males not a "family" as used in restrictive covenant); Cash v. Catholic Diocese, 414 S.W.2d 346 (Mo. App. 1967) (nuns not a "family" as used in a restrictive covenant).

Decisions from other state jurisdictions have addressed identical constitutional challenges to zoning ordinances similar to the ordinance in the instant case. The reviewing courts have upheld their respective ordinances on the ground that maintenance of a traditional family environment constitutes a reasonable basis for excluding uses that may impair the stability of that environment and erode the values associated with traditional family life.[2]

The essence of zoning is selection; and, if it is not invidious or discriminatory against those not selected, it is proper. There is no doubt that there is a governmental interest in marriage and in preserving the integrity of the biological or legal family. There is no concomitant governmental interest in keeping together a group of unrelated persons, no matter how closely they simulate a family. Further, there is no state policy which commands that groups of people may live under the same roof in any section of a municipality they choose.

The stated purpose of Ladue's zoning ordinance is the promotion of the health, safety, morals and general welfare in the city. Whether Ladue could have adopted less restrictive means to achieve these same goals is not a controlling factor in considering the constitutionality of the zoning ordinance. Rather, our focus is on whether there exists some reasonable basis for the means actually employed. In making such a determination, if any state of facts either known or which could reasonably be assumed is presented in support of the ordinance, we must defer to the legislative judgment. We find that Ladue has not acted arbitrarily in enacting its zoning ordinance which defines family as those related by blood, marriage or adoption. Given the fact that Ladue has so defined family, we defer to its legislative judgment.

The judgment of the trial court is affirmed.

NOTES AND QUESTIONS

1. Why did the City of Ladue limit buildings in this part of town to "single family dwellings"? How does the Ladue zoning ordinance define "single family"? What assumptions about the meaning of "family" does this definition make? Is this definition of "family" consistent with the goal of the ordinance? If Horn and Jones had lived together without their children, would they be able to meet the requirements of the single family ordinance? If they had married, but not adopted each other's children, would this have changed the result? Which arrangement — two

2. *See, e.g.*, City of White Plains v. Ferraioli, 34 N.Y.2d 300, 357 N.Y.S.2d 449, 313 N.E.2d 756 (1974) (married couple, their two children and 10 foster children not a family under city's ordinance); Rademan v. City and County of Denver, 186 Colo. 250, 526 P.2d 1325 (1974) (two married couples living as a "communal family" not a family); Town of Durham v. White Enterprises, Inc., 115 N.H. 645, 348 A.2d 706 (1975) (student renters not a family); Prospect Gardens Convalescent Home, Inc. v. City of Norwalk, 32 Conn. Supp. 214, 347 A.2d 637 (1975) (nursing home employees living together not a family). *See generally* Annot., 12 A.L.R.4th 238 (1985). A number of jurisdictions have found restrictive zoning ordinances invalid. *See, e.g.*, City of Des Plaines v. Trottner, 34 Ill. 2d 432, 216 N.E.2d 116 (1970) (ordinance with restrictive definition of family violates authority delegated by state legislature in the enabling statute); City of Santa Barbara v. Adamson, 27 Cal. 3d 123, 164 Cal. Rptr. 539, 610 P.2d 436 (1982) (zoning ordinance limiting the number of unrelated persons who could live together, but not related persons, did not further legislative goals); Charter Township of Delta v. Dinolfo, 419 Mich. 253, 351 N.W.2d 831 (1984) (restrictive definition of family not rationally related to achieving township's goals).

unmarried adults or a married couple with adult children from different, prior relationships — better fits the idea of family in the Ladue ordinance and in the readings above? How does marriage without children or the presence of children from different relationships affect Horn and Jones's suitability as residents of this neighborhood? Could the court have interpreted the ordinance in a manner similar to that in *Braschi*, or did the statutory language prevent this? Consider the following comment.

Zoning urban, suburban, and rural areas has proven a useful tool for local and state governments to control population, traffic, pollution, and other social problems. Unfortunately, zoning has also been used to control the identity of the population, and with some success. The ordinance at issue in *Belle Terre* was a common instance of this kind of control; it limited the number of unrelated people that could live in a home, but put no such limit on the number of related people that may live together. Using this type of zoning ordinance, many municipalities have successfully kept out or forced out unrelated people living communally and other non-traditional families. This sort of discrimination, although purportedly for the lawful purpose of protecting traditional family values, effectively imposes the municipality's social preferences on the individuals in the community. Not only does this seem contrary to the most basic and often quoted American themes of plurality and individuality, it summarily dismisses the value of the voluntary family. . . .

The 1960s and 1970s were a period of great social and political upheaval. Along with the era's more familiar symbols of protest and civil unrest — anti-war demonstrations, civil rights demonstrations, and the "hippie" movement — many Americans expressed their discontent with mainstream culture by moving into cooperative-living communities, such as communes.

Communes, however, were nothing new to the United States in the 1960s and 1970s. That period of communal development was the fourth such period in the nineteenth and twentieth centuries; the previous periods took place between 1842 and 1848, between 1894 and 1900, and during the 1930s. Like the movement of the 1960s and 1970s, the others "coincided with [periods] of millennial anticipation" and with fifty to fifty-five year waves, known as Kondratiev cycles, that corresponded to economic fluctuations. Motivation for the movement of the 1960s and 1970s differed from the others, however. Communes in existence through 1845 often formed as a result of religious issues; economic and political issues were the impetus behind many developed between 1820 and 1930; and psychosocial issues provoked the establishment of communes between the Second World War and the 1970s. Interestingly, a study of some of the 1960s communards demonstrated that they came predominantly from nuclear families that they described as "loving and intimate," and from homes in which their parents had nurtured and loved them unconditionally. The study seems to suggest, then, that the communards of the 1960s and 1970s were not seeking a better family, as they left perfectly good ones behind. Instead, they were moved by a sense of alienation, by ideological, relational, and personal reasons, and for convenience. Many hoped to find utopia or experiment with a new way of life. . . .

. . . By contrast, many of today's communards are seeking a place to settle down with some measure of efficiency and community. New communards "tend not to reject the values of society, but select what they like from mainstream society and supplement their lives with those aspects of communal living which enhance and strengthen their sense of self." If trends continue as some sociologists expect, communal arrangements of the twenty-first century "will focus more and more on issues related to health, the environment, stress reduction, personal morality, and building community," rather than a vision of utopia.

Communards today also represent a wider cross-section of Americans. Many communards of the past were individuals who either became ideologically disillusioned by the socio-political state of affairs in the "outside world" or decided to venture out on a spiritual journey; more importantly, they were people who had the time and resources to take this step. Today, communal living draws people wishing to share resources and community, including a large number of single parents and elderly people struggling to live independently on inadequate social security payments.

Co-housing groups are comprised of a group of households "looking for a way to share some of the responsibilities of day-to-day living—preparing and sharing meals, providing child care, maintaining a garden and even sharing cars." Co-housing communities attempt to strike a balance between privacy and cooperation, while also coming together as a community. Within a typical co-housing development, some space is shared by the whole group, but there are also self-sufficient residences. Individuals, couples, or related groups might have their own "apartment" and share a common play area, a common dining area, or a common work space. In this way, members can enjoy peace and quiet or company as they wish, an arguably less all-encompassing and intrusive arrangement than in a traditional family's home.

No doubt the law-abiding citizens of Belle Terre believed that the Supreme Court had saved their neighborhood. After all, if those students were allowed to live there, others could follow, until the streets were lined with traffic and empty beer bottles. Once the "weirdos" got in, they might never be able to get rid of them, and the quiet of their waterfront enclave would be forever lost.

Those students were not the weirdos the villagers thought, however. In fact, they were probably making better use of the six-bedroom house than anyone else had ever made of it. They shared responsibilities and intellectual conversations, and lived as efficiently as they could on their limited means. During the summer, they, like everyone else in town, looked forward to relaxing on the beach with their family. This family was simply a little bit different in character than the others: there were no noisy children and no wedding rings. Instead there was friendship, camaraderie, and a well-run household.

Rebecca Ginzburg, Note, Altering "Family": Another Look at The Supreme Court's Narrow Protection of Families in *Belle Terre*, 83 B.U. L. Rev. 875, 877, 878-879, 888-890 (2003).

2. Horn and Jones argued that the zoning ordinance should be subject to strict scrutiny under the equal protection clause because it adversely affects their fundamental rights of freedom of association and of privacy. To succeed, they would have had to distinguish their situation from that in Belle Terre v. Boraas and analogize it to the situation in Moore v. City of East Cleveland. If you had represented them, how would you have made this argument? If you represented the City of Ladue, how would you have responded?

3. The federal Fair Housing Act of 1968, 42 U.S.C. §§ 3601-3619 and 3631, prohibits discrimination on the basis of familial status, but this provision protects families with children and does not mention marital status. However, 21 states and the District of Columbia have enacted statutes forbidding housing discrimination on the basis of marital status. Andrew Kravis, Is the Inability to Marry a Marital Status? Levin v. Yeshiva University and the Intersection of Sexual Orientation and

Marital Status in Housing Discrimination, 24 Colum. J. Gender & L. 1, 23 Tbl. 1 (2012). Not all these statutes have been interpreted as requiring landlords to rent to unmarried cohabitants, though. *Id.* at 3-4.

4. Until 2008, the city of Black Jack, Missouri, prohibited unmarried couples and the children of either party from living within its borders. The city changed its housing ordinance after it settled a lawsuit brought by the ACLU on behalf of an unmarried couple denied an occupancy permit by the town. Brian Flinchpaugh, Black Jack Expands Definition of "Family," St. Louis Post Dispatch, July 23, 2008.

BOROUGH OF GLASSBORO V. VALLOROSI

568 A.2d 888 (N.J. 1990)

PER CURIAM. . . . In July 1986, the Borough [of Glassboro] amended its zoning ordinance, apparently in response to a rowdy weekend celebration by Glassboro State College students. The amendment applied to the Borough's residential districts and limited the use and occupancy of "detached dwellings" and structures with "two dwelling units" to "families" only. The ordinance defined a "family" as

> one or more persons occupying a dwelling unit as a single non-profit housekeeping unit, who are living together as a stable and permanent living unit, being a traditional family unit or the functional equivalency [sic] thereof.

The amendment included a statement of purpose that plainly reflected the Borough's intention to confine college students either to the dormitories provided by Glassboro State College or to the other zoning districts that permit apartments and townhouses:

> The preservation of "family style living" and the preservation of the character of residential neighborhoods as such are legitimate zoning goals. The Borough of Glassboro is concerned with maintaining the stability and permanence generally associated with single family occupancy throughout its residential neighborhoods. A municipality may endeavor, by legitimate means, to secure and maintain the blessings of quiet seclusion and to make available to its inhabitants the refreshment of repose and the tranquility of solitude. The Borough of Glassboro possesses these goals and, by the regulation herein contained, implements them in a manner which bears a reasonable relationship to the problem sought to be ameliorated. That problem is the use and occupancy of single family and two family dwellings, interspersed among the residential neighborhoods of the community, by groups of individuals whose living arrangements, although temporarily in the same dwelling unit, are transient in nature and do not possess the elements of stability and permanency which have long been associated with single family occupancy. Such living arrangements are not compatible with the family style living sought to be preserved. Such occupancies are in the nature of rooming houses, boarding homes, hotels, motels, and the like. Such uses do not meet the definition of family as contained in this ordinance and are prohibited in detached dwellings and structures with two dwelling units in all residential zones. This ordinance provides zoning classifications which allow for ample apartment and townhouse uses, and there are presently many such uses in existence throughout the Borough. Likewise, Glassboro State College maintains

substantial dormitory and apartment facilities for students and faculty members. Therefore, ample housing exists within the Borough for college students and others who choose to live under arrangements which do not meet the definition of family as provided in this ordinance.

In June 1986, defendants purchased a home located in the restricted residential zone. The purchase was intended to provide a college home for Peter Vallorosi, the brother of defendant Diane Vallorosi and the son of two partners in S & V Associates, a real-estate investment partnership. (Under the partnership agreement, S & V Associates acquired equitable title to the premises when defendants purchased the home.) It was contemplated that nine of Peter's friends would share the house with him while the group attended Glassboro State College. Seven of the ten students renting the house were sophomores at the time their lease took effect. They were all between the ages of eighteen and twenty. All ten students entered into separate, renewable leases for a semester-long period of four months. At the end of each semester, a student could renew the lease for another term "if the house is found to be in order at [the] end of [the preceding] term."

The students moved into their new home in early September 1986. The house had one large kitchen, which was shared by all ten students. The students often ate meals together in small groups, cooked for each other, and generally shared the household chores, grocery shopping, and yard work. A common checking account paid for food and other bills. They shared the use of a telephone. Although uncertain of living arrangements after graduation, the students intended to remain tenants as long as they were enrolled at Glassboro State College.

The Borough commenced this action in September 1986, seeking an injunction against the use and occupancy of the house by the students. The complaint alleged that the occupants did not constitute a "family" as defined in the Borough's ordinance. . . . [D]efendants argued that the communal nature of the students' occupancy, coupled with their intention to live there together throughout their college careers, satisfied the ordinance's requirement that any occupancy be functionally equivalent to "a traditional family unit."

The Chancery Division . . . focused on whether the specific circumstances of the students' occupancy satisfied the ordinance's requirements:

> The testimony that was most helpful to the Court in determining if a group of young men living together exhibited the "generic character" of a family was that of the students themselves. They stated that they do not just rent a room, but that they rent the whole house. The common areas are shared by all with free access; there is one kitchen that is used by the students and meals are either eaten together or in small groups. There is a common checkbook from which the bills of running the house are paid. Although their leases are for a short period of time, they intend to stay in Glassboro so long as they attend the college.

Based on this testimony, the court concluded that the relationship among the students "shows stability, permanancy and can be described as the functional equivalent of a family." The Appellate Division affirmed on the basis of the trial court's analysis.

We granted the Borough's petition for certification. . . .

During the pendency of this appeal, the Court was notified that Peter Vallorosi withdrew from Glassboro State College and that the use of the home by the students ended effective September 1, 1988. Nevertheless, we render a decision on the merits because of the important issues presented.

II.

The legal principles determinative of this appeal are clear and well-settled. The courts of this state have consistently invalidated zoning ordinances intended "to cure or prevent . . . anti-social conduct in dwelling situations." Kirsch Holding Co. v. Borough of Manasquan, 59 N.J. 241, 253-54, 281 A.2d 513 (1971). We have insisted that the municipal power to adopt zoning regulations

> be reasonably exercised; they may be neither unreasonable, arbitrary nor capricious. The means chosen must have a real and substantial relation to the end sought to be achieved. Moreover, the regulation must be reasonably designed to resolve the problem without imposing unnecessary and excessive restrictions on the use of private property.

In Kirsch Holding Co. v. Borough of Manasquan, *supra*, 59 N.J. 241, 281 A.2d 513, we invalidated ordinances in two shore communities that restrictively defined "family" and prohibited seasonal rentals by unrelated persons. We held that the challenged ordinances "preclude so many harmless dwelling uses . . . that they must be held to be so sweepingly excessive, and therefore legally unreasonable, that they must fall in their entirety." . . .

In Berger v. State, *supra*, 71 N.J. 206, 364 A.2d 993, we expressed our agreement with the principle that "[t]he concept of a one family dwelling is based upon its character as a single housekeeping unit." A significant issue in *Berger* was the validity of a restrictive zoning ordinance limiting the definition of family to "persons related by blood, marriage or adoption." . . . The challenged use was a group home for eight to twelve multi-handicapped, pre-school children who would reside in a twelve-room ocean-front house with a married couple experienced as foster parents. Staff hired by the New Jersey Department of Institutions and Agencies would provide support services but would not reside on the premises. We concluded that the State's proposed use of the premises was reasonable and thus immune from regulation by the local zoning ordinance. . . . Finally, we held that an ordinance limiting the term "family" to persons related by blood, marriage, or adoption cannot "satisfy the demands of due process." Such an ordinance

> so narrowly delimits the persons who may occupy a single family dwelling as to prohibit numerous potential occupants who pose no threat to the style of family living sought to be preserved.

Accordingly, we expressed our clear preference for zoning provisions that equated the term "single family" with a "single housekeeping unit."

In State v. Baker, 81 N.J. 99, 405 A.2d 368 (1979), we invalidated the City of Plainfield's zoning ordinance that defined "family" in terms of a "single non-profit housekeeping unit" but limited to four the number of persons unrelated by blood, marriage, or adoption that would constitute a "family." Defendant was convicted of violating the ordinance when he and his wife, their three children, and Mrs. Conata and her three children lived in his home. Defendant, an ordained Presbyterian minister, testified that the Bakers and Conatas had common religious beliefs and lived together as an extended family, sharing common areas and household expenses. Recognizing that the municipality's goal of preserving stable, single-family residential areas was entirely proper, we nevertheless held that the ordinance was violative of our state constitution because "the means chosen [did] not bear a substantial relationship to the effectuation of that goal." . . .

We noted that municipalities could appropriately deal with overcrowding or congestion by ordinance provisions that limit occupancy "*in reasonable relation to available sleeping and bathroom facilities or requiring a minimum amount of habitable floor area per occupant.*" Declining to follow the United States Supreme Court's decision in Village of Belle Terre v. Boraas, 416 U.S. 1 (1974), which upheld a comparable ordinance, we concluded that "[r]estrictions based upon legal or biological relationships such as Plainfield's impact only remotely upon [over-crowding and congestion] and hence cannot withstand judicial scrutiny."

Several of our reported cases involve municipalities whose zoning ordinances defined "family" in terms of a "single housekeeping unit" as suggested by Berger v. State, *supra*. In Township of Washington v. Central Bergen Community Mental Health Center, Inc., 383 A.2d 1194 (Law Div. 1978), the municipality challenged the occupancy of a residential dwelling used as a transitional residence for five former mental patients who shared rent, expenses, and housekeeping chores under the supervision of a community mental-health center. . . . The Law Division held that the challenged occupancy qualified as a single housekeeping unit, observing that "the residents present a picture very much akin to that of a traditional family and their lifestyle is not of a transient or temporary nature. . . ."

In Township of Pemberton v. State, 429 A.2d 360 (App. Div. 1981), the township challenged the use of residential property as a group home for six to eight boys, ages eight to thirteen, who had been committed to the State Training School for Boys but were considered suitable for diversion from that institution to a residential setting that approximated a normal family environment. The boys would be supervised by a married couple with appropriate professional training. They would attend local schools, be encouraged to participate in scouting and Little League, and otherwise be expected to integrate with the community. The arrangement contemplated a residency period of approximately six months. . . . Reversing a Law Division decision enjoining the proposed use, the Appellate Division concluded that the use was permitted by the ordinance, noting that our case law afforded "protection for groups of unrelated persons which have been formed for the purpose of permitting traditionally institutional functions to be performed in the more salutary and constructive context of a 'reproduced' single-family setting." *Accord* Holy Name Hosp. v. Montroy, 153 N.J. Super. 181, 188-89, 379 A.2d 299 (Law Div. 1977) (invalidating local zoning ordinance limiting occupancy by more than three unrelated persons, upholding ordinance only as limiting occupancy by single housekeeping unit, and holding that three residences occupied by groups of nuns constituted single housekeeping units).

By contrast, in Open Door Alcoholism Program, Inc. v. Board of Adjustment of New Brunswick, 200 N.J. Super. 191, 491 A.2d 17 (App. Div. 1985), the court held that a halfway house for ten recovering alcoholics did not constitute a single-family dwelling, on the basis that the occupants lacked the "generic characteristics of a single family." The residents of the halfway house were referred there after having satisfactorily completed treatment for alcoholism. The average occupancy was for six months, although an occupant was free to leave at any time. The residents shared cooking and household chores and took meals together. A resident manager administered the facility. . . . The court concluded that the halfway house occupants did not constitute a single housekeeping unit:

> It is thus evident that in order for a group of unrelated persons living together as a single housekeeping unit to constitute a single family in terms of a zoning regulation, they must exhibit a kind of stability, permanency and functional lifestyle which is equivalent to that of the traditional family unit. In our view, the residents of plaintiff's proposed halfway house, although comprising a single housekeeping unit, would not bear these generic characteristics of a single family. While the residents would share in the household responsibilities and dine together, their affiliation with one another would be no different than if they were fellow residents of a boarding house. Clearly, their living arrangements would not be the functional equivalent of a family unit. The individual lifestyles of the residents and the transient nature of their residencies would not permit the group to possess the elements of stability and permanency which have long been associated with single-family occupancy.

Thus, our cases preclude municipalities from adopting zoning regulations that unreasonably distinguish between residential occupancy by unrelated persons in comparison with occupancy by individuals related by blood, marriage, or adoption. Our decisions permit zoning regulations to restrict uses in certain residential zones to single housekeeping units. But the standard for determining whether a use qualifies as a single housekeeping unit must be functional, and hence capable of being met by either related or unrelated persons.

III.

The Glassboro ordinance at issue here defines "family" by a standard consistent with our decisional law. . . . It provides a functional description of a single housekeeping unit, in terms of "persons . . . living together as a stable and permanent living unit, being a traditional family unit or the functional equivalency [sic] thereof." The ordinance's statement of purpose clearly reflects Glassboro's assumption that the occupancy of residential dwellings by college students would not satisfy the ordinance's standard, but the ordinance makes no impermissible distinction between college students and any other group of unrelated individuals.

. . . The narrow issue before us is whether there is sufficient credible evidence in this record to sustain the trial court's factual finding that the occupancy of defendants' dwelling by these ten college students constituted a single housekeeping unit as defined by the Glassboro ordinance.

Kids can drop out of college ⇒ Does that instill a sense of "stability?"

In view of the unusual circumstances of this case, we find adequate evidence to uphold the Law Division's ruling. The uncontradicted testimony reflects a plan by ten sophomore college students to live together for three years under conditions that correspond substantially to the ordinance's requirement of a "stable and permanent living unit." To facilitate the plan, the house had been purchased by relatives of one of the students. The students ate together, shared household chores, and paid expenses from a common fund. Although the students signed four-month leases, the leases were renewable if the house was "in order" at the end of the term. Moreover, the students testified to their intention to remain in the house throughout college, and there was no significant evidence of defections up to the time of trial. As noted above, the students' occupancy ended in September 1988 because of Peter Vallorosi's post-trial withdrawal from college.

It is a matter of common experience that the costs of college and the variables characteristic of college life and student relationships do not readily lead to the formation of a household as stable and potentially durable as the one described in this record. On these facts, however, we cannot quarrel with the Law Division's conclusion that the occupancy at issue here "shows stability, permanency and can be described as the functional equivalent of a family."

It also bears repetition that noise and other socially disruptive behavior are best regulated outside the framework of municipal zoning. . . .

NOTES AND QUESTIONS

1. The Borough of Glassboro enacted its "single family" zoning ordinance after the New Jersey Supreme Court, parting ways with the U.S. Supreme Court in *Belle Terre*, held that zoning ordinances based on traditional definitions of "family" violated the state constitution. How does the analysis of the two courts differ?

2. Consider the definition of family in the Glassboro ordinance. What is the "functional equivalent" of a "traditional family unit"? What is a "single non-profit housekeeping unit"? Do the cases discussed in *Vallorosi* make the meaning clear? Under these definitions, what is the role of the court in defining "family"?

3. Does the "single housekeeping unit" test suggested by the New Jersey court adequately protect a community's interests in restricting some areas to "single family dwellings"? What does the breakup of the group of college students in *Vallorosi* suggest about the utility of this definition? On the other hand, would there be any question that a married couple who divorced after a few months were still, while they were married, a "single family"?

4. Most lower courts have upheld restrictive applications of single-family zoning laws, applying *Belle Terre*. State court decisions interpreting state constitutions as providing greater protection to nontraditional families, in addition to those in New Jersey, include Baer v. Town of Brookhaven, 537 N.E.2d 619 (N.Y. 1989) (four former mental patients who lived with a family were the functional equivalent of a family for purposes of zoning laws; zoning laws violated state constitution because they limited cohabitation of unrelated persons while not limiting the number of related people who could live together); City of Santa Barbara v. Adamson, 610 P.2d 436 (Cal. 1980); and Charter Township of Delta v. Dinolfo, 351 N.W.2d 831 (Mich. 1984).

The Importance of Being a Family

2

A. INTRODUCTION

In United States v. Windsor, 133 S. Ct. 2675, 2690 (2013), the Supreme Court observed that more than 1,000 federal statutes factor marital status into determining individual rights and responsibilities, such as immigration preferences and Social Security benefits. A 2004 General Accounting Office report listed 1,138 such statutes. GAO, Defense of Marriage Act: Update to Prior Report (Jan. 23, 2004). As we saw in Chapter 1, state law also uses marital status or its equivalent or sometimes familial status as a basis for granting benefits to and imposing responsibilities on people in dozens of ways. Invoking the doctrine of family privacy or the family unit, courts also routinely treat people differently because they are in a marital relationship or its equivalent or a family. The image of the family unit is ubiquitous in modern legal discourse; it is not practicable to collect even the relatively recent references by judges and lawyers to the "family unit."

The metaphor of the family unit is related to the "marital unit," which has ancient roots. The Book of Genesis (Genesis 2:24) declares that a husband must leave the home of his parents to be joined to his wife, "and they shall become one flesh," a declaration Paul repeats in his Epistle to the Ephesians (Ephesians 5:31). Bracton, writing in the thirteenth century, said that husband and wife "are *quasi* one person, for they are one flesh and one blood." 4 Bracton on the Laws and Customs of England 335 (Samuel E. Thorne trans., 1977). Blackstone explained, "[b]y marriage, the husband and wife are one person in law: that is, the very being or legal existence of the woman is suspended during the marriage, or at least incorporated and consolidated into that of the husband." William Blackstone, Commentaries on the Laws of England *442 (W. Lewis ed., 1897). The first American treatise on Husband and Wife explained the common law identity of spouses as a fiction designed to protect wives from coercion. Tapping Reeve, The Law of Baron and Femme: of Parent and Child, of Guardian and Ward, of Master and Servant, and of the Powers of Courts of Chancery 98 (1816).

However, as many careful legal commentators have pointed out, the myth of marital unity was never employed to the maximum extent that its logic would imply, and it does not provide a satisfactory analytical basis for family law doctrine. Pollock and Maitland, for example, observed:

> If we look for any one thought which governs the whole of this province, we shall hardly find it. In particular we must be on our guard against the common belief that the ruling principle is that which sees an "unity of person" between husband and wife. This is a principle which suggests itself from time to time; it has the warrant of holy writ; it will serve to round a paragraph; and may now and again lead us out of or into a difficulty; but a consistently operative principle it can not be. We do not treat the wife as a thing or as somewhat that is neither thing nor person; we treat her as a person. Thus Bracton tells us that if either the husband without the wife, or the wife without the husband, brings an action for the wife's land, the defendant can take exception to this "for they are *quasi* one person, for they are one flesh and one blood." But this impracticable proposition is followed by a real working principle: — "for the thing is the wife's own and the husband is guardian as being the head of the wife." The husband is the wife's guardian: — that we believe to be the fundamental principle; and it explains a great deal, when we remember that guardianship is a profitable right.

2 Frederick Pollock & Frederic W. Maitland, The History of English Law 405-406 (2d ed. 1968).

Still, the myth of marital unity has substantially influenced how family law has developed. The idea of the "family unit" is often invoked to explain doctrines once justified by reference to the doctrine of marital unity. In many settings "the family" seems to be conceived as an entity having claims separate from those of the state and the individual members of the family. This usage suggests that the family stands independent of the state and even that it is a vehicle for governance with claims to "sovereignty." At the least, regard for the family unit suggests that governmental agencies — whether courts, legislatures, or others — should carefully consider the extent to which and the ways in which their rules affect relations within the family.

However, the idea of the family as a "unit" or "entity" is itself subject to question, since these terms tend to make legal treatment of the family seem inevitable or "natural" and to obscure the effects of that treatment on family members. *See* Lee E. Teitelbaum, Family History and Family Law, 1985 Wis. L. Rev. 1135. The materials in this chapter provide an opportunity to consider the meaning of a couple being legally regarded as a family and the tension between a traditional view of the family as a unit and a more recent tendency to view the family as an association of independent actors. Most of the cases involve couples who are formally married, but the same issues may arise for other couples who are regarded as being a family. Section B, dealing with family property, introduces the common law and community property systems. The section explores the doctrines that allocate ownership and management of wealth between adult partners. Notions of family privacy and family protection will compete with the interests of individual family members in making decisions about how wealth is used.

Section C, which addresses the legal treatment of violence between adult family members, presents the same tension as courts and legislatures consider whether notions of family privacy or other concerns should prevent criminal or civil prosecution of one intimate partner for assault of another, and the recognition of tort liability between spouses.

Section D considers reproductive rights and interests, and the last part, Section E, examines medical decision making for incompetent adults. Both sections concern authority for decision making between partners themselves as well as claims that society as a whole has an interest in affecting or controlling these decisions.

B.   MARITAL PROPERTY

This section provides an overview of the significance of marriage or its equivalent for ownership, management, control, and distribution of property or, more generally, wealth. More particularly, the first part deals with doctrines relating to the ownership of real and personal property, including what is often called "new property"—public and private entitlements related to employment. The next part concerns the power of spouses to manage and control family wealth with respect to each other and with respect to creditors.

The concepts and doctrines discussed here are, of course, relevant when the parties' relationship is dissolved, and, accordingly, this section provides a background for the extensive treatments of property distribution upon dissolution of a marriage or cohabiting relationship that appear later in this book. However, the subject of family property is important not only at dissolution. Management and control of wealth during the relationship may be highly significant for the partners themselves. While we expect and hope that family members arrange their financial affairs by mutual agreement, whether articulated or not, questions of right and power may nonetheless arise overtly for couples who do not intend to separate. Moreover, for each case where questions arise overtly, there are many more relationships where the fact or appearance of lawful control defines how each person understands the allocation of decisional authority within the family. If, for example, husbands possess the legal authority to manage available family wealth (as was once true in common law and community property jurisdictions alike), wives may accept—perhaps without even conscious thought about it—their husbands' ultimate responsibility for determining where and how they will live, who will work at what and how much, and the myriad other matters that involve decisions about the acquisition and expenditure of wealth.

The location and character of property ownership may also substantially affect the position of third parties who deal with a married person. Creditors, for example, may find themselves situated differently with respect to property owned by a single person or the "nonmarital" wealth of a spouse than they are with respect to property characterized as "marital."

Finally, consideration of family property, broadly understood, includes kinds of wealth that are not distributable at dissolution and may or may not be available to a surviving spouse upon the other's death. This aspect of marital property incorporates public, and some private, benefit schemes that are as important to the economic condition of beneficiary families as are farms and bonds to the middle and upper socioeconomic groups.

1. Ownership and Control of Wealth

Generally speaking, the marital property systems of Western nations today are divided into two types: "those in which husband and wife own all property separately except those items that they have expressly agreed to hold jointly (in a nontechnical sense) and those in which husband and wife own a substantial portion or even all of their property jointly unless they have expressly agreed to hold it separately." Charles Donahue, Jr., What Causes Fundamental Legal Ideas? Marital Property in England and France in the Thirteenth Century, 78 Mich. L. Rev. 59 (1979). The scheme of separate property ownership is the common law system, which operates or has operated in some fashion in most Anglo-American jurisdictions. The system of joint property is found, in some fashion, in many countries of Western Europe and in nine American states.[1]

These labels — "common law property" and "community property" — capture certain substantial differences in the ways the two systems treat wealth acquired during the marriage. However, there are important aspects in which both regimes in their traditional forms treat the property of married persons alike, particularly with respect to the management of wealth generated during the marriage.

a. The Common Law Tradition[2]

In a common law property state, each spouse owns the property that he or she buys or is given. Spouses can own property jointly as tenants in common, joint tenants, or, in some states, tenants by the entirety. These forms of joint ownership must be expressly created, either at the time the property is originally conveyed to the spouses or later, when one spouse "adds the other to the title" of property that had been separately owned.

---

1. The nine states are Arizona, California, Idaho, Louisiana, Nevada, New Mexico, Texas, Washington, and (by legislation enacted in the 1980s) Wisconsin. Puerto Rico has also adopted community property. Almost a third of the U.S. population lives in these jurisdictions. J. Thomas Oldham, Everything Is Bigger in Texas, Except the Community Property Estate: Must Texas Remain a Divorce Haven for the Rich?, 44 Fam. L.Q. 293 (2010).

2. To talk of the "common law tradition," however conventional, risks two kinds of errors. One is to suggest that the common law treatment of marital property was static, that is, that marital property was treated alike over a lengthy period and that this treatment was the province of courts rather than legislation. The other is to suggest that the common law at a single point in time treated all forms of property alike. Both of these are untrue. English law developed significantly in this as in other respects over time, and by statute as well as by judicial decision. *See, e.g.*, Charles Donahue, Jr., What Causes Fundamental Legal Ideas? Marital Property in England and France in the Thirteenth Century, 78 Mich. L. Rev. 59 (1979), on early developments of marital property doctrine.

Under the common law principles that prevailed before the middle of the nineteenth century, a single woman could manage the property that she owned, and she could enter into contracts and sue and be sued. However, a woman lost these rights when she married. For the duration of the marriage, her husband was entitled to manage her real property and to use any revenue it produced as he saw fit.

The situation changed, however, when one of the spouses died. A wife who survived her husband recaptured her rights with respect to the real property she brought into the marriage. Equally important, her husband could not, during his life, alienate that property without her active participation. Moreover, a married woman had an inchoate life interest in some part of the land that her husband had owned and possessed (of which he was "seised") during the time of their marriage. If the couple had children, the wife had this dower right in one-third of the husband's property and in one-half if they had no children. A wife's dower interest was a life estate (or in some places a life estate unless she remarried) in the dower lands, including the right to rents and profits generated by those lands. A wife's dower was jealously protected against alienation by her husband, who could not sell his land free of that interest unless his wife consented. Moreover, her consent was valid only if given in a judicial proceeding (a "fine"), during which she would be examined privately to ensure that her consent was voluntary.[3] If a husband survived his wife and the couple had no children, her real property passed to her heirs. If they had children, however, the husband had the right to possession and enjoyment of her real property for the rest of his life. Only at death did it pass to her heirs.

The husband's rights in the wife's personal property were even more extensive. Except for certain personal items (such as clothing, jewelry, and the like), he owned and could do as he wished with her personal wealth. Concomitantly, a married man assumed responsibility for his wife's debts and civil wrongs.

By about 1840, American legislatures began to enact statutes that had the effect of reducing or eliminating the more obvious disabilities associated with marriage. The thrust of these laws, generally called Married Women's Property Acts, was to give married women the same legal capacity to deal with their property that single women had. The 1861 Illinois Married Women's Act, for example, provided as follows:

> Section 1. *Be it enacted* . . . That all property, both real and personal, belonging to any married woman, as her sole and separate property, or which any woman hereafter married owns at the time of her marriage, or which any married woman, during coverture, acquires, in good faith, from any person, other than her husband, by descent, devise or otherwise, together with all the rents, issues, increase and profits thereof, shall, notwithstanding her marriage, be and remain, during coverture, her sole and separate property, under her sole control, and be held, owned, possessed and enjoyed by her the same as though she was sole and unmarried; and shall be exempt from execution or attachment for the debts of her husband.

---

3. Although the procedure of the fine was not followed in the American colonies generally, the requirement of a private examination concerning the wife's volition in joining a conveyance of land in which she held an interest was often recognized, although with varying degrees of strength. *See* Marylynn Salmon, Women and the Law of Property in Early America 17-37 (1986).

1861 Ill. Laws 1433. It is important to recognize that these acts, which are still in effect generally, address only a married woman's *separate* property—that is, property she acquired before marriage or by her efforts or gift during marriage. They do not create any interest in the wife in her husband's separate property. Accordingly, this legislation did not affect the wife's position in the common situation where she did not bring wealth into the marriage, inherit wealth, or work in the paid economy during marriage.

PROBLEM

George and Martha were married in 1990. At that time, Martha owned a small portfolio of stocks (worth approximately $25,000) given her by her parents; George owned nothing. During their marriage, Martha was a homemaker, and George was first an employee and then a partner in a real estate group. Fifteen years after their marriage, George and Martha decided to evaluate their financial arrangements because George is concerned about a potential liability as a result of some recent unsuccessful investments on his part. Assuming that the stocks remain titled in Martha's name, that the current value of the real estate partnership is approximately $100,000, and that George has over the years purchased a house and made investments in his own name that amount to approximately $250,000, advise them on the following questions. Under a Married Women's Property Act like the Illinois statute quoted above, who owns what property? Under the statute, which of their assets can George's creditors reach to collect what he owes them?

Married Women's Property Acts address only property given to or earned by women; they generally have no effect on property titled in one spouse's name to which both spouses have in some way contributed. In this situation, spouses sometimes seek relief through generally applicable equitable remedies,[4] particularly resulting and constructive trusts.

---

4. The terms *equity* and *equitable* appear in a number of property contexts. Their meanings within each are specific, and the meaning within one context cannot safely be employed in another. Sometimes these terms refer to remedies created by courts of equity, such as the wife's separate estate in equity (based on an express trust), or the resulting and constructive trust remedies described immediately below, which are extensions, with some modification, of generally applicable doctrines recognizing ownership interests that are not reflected in the legal title. Such equitable interests in specific items of wealth may be recognized at any time.

These uses should be distinguished from "equitable distribution," which is *not* intended to reflect ownership interests in particular items of property but deals only with the distribution of all family property at divorce. Equitable distribution is discussed in detail in Chapter 6.

Adams v. Jankouskas

452 A.2d 148 (Del. 1982)

Moore, Justice. . . . On December 23, 1944 John married Stella in Elkton, Maryland. Both had been married before, and each had children by their prior marriages. . . .

At the time of the marriage, Stella was the owner and operator of a small beauty shop which she had purchased a few months earlier. She apparently saved parsimoniously to buy the shop (even putting her 2 young sons by her previous marriage in an orphanage), but when she married John it was not a particularly profitable enterprise. Before the marriage John had held a string of jobs with various companies and, at the time of the marriage, he was earning approximately $150 a week. In 1948, he secured employment with the duPont Company where he worked until his retirement in 1978.

With the assistance of counsel Stella set up a corporation in July 1947 named "Jan's Apartments," and all 100 shares of the common stock of the corporation were issued in her name. In addition to accumulating other assets, the initial investment of "Jan's Apartments" was in an apartment building at 829 Washington Street which John renovated. About five years later Stella moved her beauty parlor to this building. The corporation also acquired a house at 2409 Franklin Street, which became John and Stella's family residence. John paid monthly rent to the Corporation for their joint use of the house.

Stella was clearly the dominant partner in the marriage and she mainly controlled the family finances. From the beginning of the marriage John surrendered his paycheck to Stella, who then deposited it either in their joint account or the corporate account of Jan's Apartments. John in turn received a nominal sum from Stella for spending money. Early in the marriage the funds in the joint account were used primarily for basic living expenses, but later some of these funds were invested by Stella in stocks, bonds, certificates of deposit and other assets.

The trial testimony indicates that John and Stella voluntarily pooled John's earnings from duPont, and the earnings of the beauty parlor and the corporation. Several witnesses testified that John and Stella were saving "so that they could enjoy their retirement together." In effect they were "planning for the future" and setting aside a "nest egg" for their old age. John testified that the pooling was based upon their agreement that, "what's mine is yours and what's yours is mine." According to John, the understanding was "if [he] died she had everything and if she died [he] had everything."

Stella died in October 1977 leaving an estate valued at over $350,000, approximately $40,000 of which consisted of personal property held in their joint names. Except for this property, a diamond ring, an automobile and $10,000 in cash, all bequeathed to John, Stella's will purported to make her niece, Dolores Adams, the daughter of Stella's sister and executrix, her sole ultimate beneficiary. Virtually all the assets acquired by either party during the marriage were considered by the executrix to be assets of Stella's estate.

. . . John brought this action on September 27, 1979, almost two years after Stella's death. Following trial, the former Chancellor awarded John 50% of the estate left by Stella on the theory that the transactions between Stella and John created a constructive or resulting trust on Stella's part for the benefit of John. . . .

The Chancellor imposed a constructive or resulting trust over the assets of the estate held by Stella's executrix. These two trust theories are similar in that they are both "implied" trusts, that is, their existence is not based upon a valid written trust agreement. Although a constructive trust and a resulting trust are similar in effect, they are based upon entirely different theories.

A resulting trust arises from the presumed intentions of the parties and upon the circumstances surrounding the particular transaction. In imposing a resulting trust, the court presumes, absent contrary evidence, that the person supplying the purchase money for property intends that its purchase will inure to his benefit, and the fact that title is in the name of another is for some incidental reason. Conversely, a constructive trust does not arise from the presumed intent of the parties, but is imposed when a defendant's fraudulent, unfair or unconscionable conduct causes him to be unjustly enriched at the expense of another to whom he owed some duty.[5]

Although most resulting trust cases involve the purchase of real property, the theory upon which they are based equally applies to acquisitions of personality. It has also been applied to situations in which the purchase price for property has been paid out of partnership or community assets. In a case involving purchases made with partnership or community funds, the trust "results" in favor of the partnership or the community. This rule is applicable when, as here, the property was bought with joint funds.

In reviewing the evidence, the Chancellor found:

Here, it is established by the evidence adduced at trial that at the inception of their marriage both parties contributed their earnings to a species of joint account,

---

5. A good discussion of the differences between these two trusts is as follows:

Resulting trusts arise where the legal estate is disposed of or acquired, not fraudulently or in the violation of any fiduciary duty, but the intent in theory of equity appears or is inferred or assumed from the terms of the disposition, or from the accompanying facts and circumstances, that the beneficial interest is not to go with the legal title. In such a case a trust "results" in favor of the person from whom the equitable interest is thus assumed to have been intended, and whom equity deems to be the real owner (see §§ 1031 et seq.).

Constructive trusts are by equity for the purpose of working out right and justice, where there was no intention of the party to create such a relation, and often directly contrary to the intention of the one holding the legal title. All instances of constructive trust may be referred to what equity denominates fraud, either actual or constructive, including acts or omissions in violation of fiduciary obligations. If one party obtains the legal title to property, not only by fraud or by violation of confidence or of fiduciary relations, but in any other unconscientious manner, so that he cannot equitably retain the property which really belongs to another, equity carries out its theory of a double ownership, equitable and legal, by impressing a constructive trust upon the property in favor of the one who is in good conscience entitled to it, and who is considered in equity as the beneficial owner (see §§ 1044 et seq.). Courts of equity, by thus extending the fundamental principle of trusts — that is, the principle of a division between the legal estate in one and the equitable estate in another — to cases of actual or constructive fraud and breaches of good faith, are enabled to wield a remedial power of tremendous efficacy in protecting the rights of property.

1 Pomeroy's Equity Jurisprudence § 166, at 210-211 (5th ed. 1941) (emphasis in original).

petitioner's contributions initially constituting a large percentage of such funding. The evidence also establishes that title to such acquisitions was placed in the name of the decedent. I am satisfied after trial that the source of funds used by the decedent to acquire her initial holdings was from the parties' pooled funds since there is no other credible source of money for such acquisitions.

[In addition,] Stella's ultimate beneficiary, Dolores Adams, an apparently hostile witness, conceded the occurrence of three transactions during the later years of the marriage in which Stella withdrew funds from the joint account and deposited them in a savings account in her name only. Presumably, other such transactions could have been proven, but many of the records pertaining to Stella's affairs were destroyed by the executrix, or someone purportedly acting on advice of her counsel.[6]

Thus, the Court of Chancery properly imposed either a resulting or constructive trust on the assets accumulated from joint contributions. It is important to note that this is not a case where a party was disappointed with what he received under a will. Rather, it is one in which joint funds were committed in obvious trust to one partner and then pooled to purchase property and make investments for the mutual benefit of both. Under these circumstances Chancery may impose this trust upon the accumulated assets in whatever form they now take. . . .

Affirmed. . . .

NOTES AND QUESTIONS

1. The court indicates that the evidence showed that Stella lied to John about her intentions regarding the investment assets and that she never planned to leave them to him. If, instead, Stella originally intended to leave the assets to John but just changed her mind, would that justify imposing a constructive trust in his favor?

2. The chancellor found that the money used to purchase the assets that were in Stella's name came from the parties' pooled funds and that, therefore, Stella held part of the assets on resulting trust for the benefit of John. Why didn't the court

---

6. There also was sufficient competent evidence that Stella never intended to keep her word to John about the ultimate use of the assets accumulated from their joint funds, thus supporting the Chancellor's conclusion that grounds existed for the imposition of a constructive trust. One of Stella's former employees testified:

A.   . . . The only thing she talked about all the time was her will, and she changed her mind about that so many times.

Q.   What did she say about her will?

A.   Well she told me on several occasions that when she died Mr. Jann was going to be in for a real surprise; that he wasn't going to get half of what he thought he was going to get (T-38).

Stella's son also testified:

Basically one of the things that I always felt irritable about is the fact that I knew that she was trying to cut Mr. Jann out from the will.

simply find that John had made a gift to Stella of the money that he put into the account in her name?

Any time one person hands over property to another, the question can always arise as to whether the transaction was intended as a gift or whether the person who received the property was intended to hold the beneficial interest in the property on resulting trust for the original owner. In theory, the answer depends on the intent of the parties, but often the evidence regarding intent is unclear. Therefore, the outcome will be decided on the basis of whether or not the transaction was presumed to be a gift.

If two unrelated persons purchase property and title it in the name of only one, the presumption will be that the person whose name is not on the title did not intend to make a gift; in other words, the presumption will be in favor of a resulting trust.

At common law, a distinct body of law developed in connection with gifts between spouses. Transfers from husband to wife, such as when the husband purchased property from wealth he controlled and placed title in the wife's name alone or in joint ownership, were generally presumed to be gifts to her or to the marital estate. *See* Maxwell v. Maxwell, 109 Ill. 588 (1884) (gift presumed although both parties treated property as husband's); Brown v. Brown, 507 A.2d 1223 (Pa. Super. Ct. 1986) (titling property jointly is strong evidence of intent of donor to make gift to marital estate). Where, however, the wife transferred wealth to her husband, courts often treated the transfer as a loan or as a bailment for safekeeping and would impose a constructive trust for her benefit on that property. *See* Comment, Transfers from Wife to Husband: A Reexamination of Presumptions in Illinois, 53 Nw. U. L. Rev. 781 (1959). Modern equal protection doctrine and, where applicable, equal rights amendments have cast doubt on inconsistent treatment of transfers by spouses. *See* Butler v. Butler, 347 A.2d 477 (Pa. 1975).

In what direction should the presumption concerning gifts run, assuming that a common presumption will apply to transfers by husbands and wives?

3. Assume that John had not contributed money to the bank account from which the assets were purchased, but he had done a great deal of work on the real property that Stella purchased and titled in her name. While John's work added significant value, he did not contribute cash or its equivalent to the property and so would not be entitled to claim a share of the beneficial interest on a resulting trust theory. *See* the opinion of the Canadian Supreme Court in Murdoch v. Murdoch, [1975] 1 S.C.R. 423 (S.C.C.).

4. As we will see in Chapter 6, in most states divorce courts have authority to distribute property acquired during the marriage through labor of either spouse "equitably," which would allow a court to award some of the property to John. However, states do not allow equitable distribution when a marriage ends because of the death of one of the parties. The estate of the decedent consists of property he or she owned during life, and the only way that the surviving spouse can lay claim to any of the decedent's property (which is not willed to him or her) is by establishing the basis for a resulting or constructive trust or by claiming the surviving spouse's elective share.

PROBLEMS

1. For many years, Mr. and Ms. Wirth worked and pooled their earnings. After some time, however, the husband started a "crash" savings program for, as he told his wife, "our latter days." From then on, the wife's earnings were used for family expenses and the husband's earnings were invested, entirely in his name. The family house was also in the husband's name, having been purchased with a down payment of $6500 supplied by his mother. Does the wife have any interest in these properties? What arguments would be made for her position?

2. William and Mary were married in 1957. Shortly afterward, William, together with a partner, established a business. William's initial investment came from savings the couple had accumulated over the first few years of their marriage. During the early years of the business, the wife helped out as a business advisor and bookkeeper. After the birth of their children, she still assisted with the bookkeeping. She has been paid a salary by the company for these services. In conversations with his wife, William often referred to the business as "our company" and its profits as "our security blanket." However, Mary never owned any of the stock in this closely held corporation, nor did she hold any management office in it. The business is now worth approximately one-half million dollars. Assuming that all of the stock in the company is held in the husband's name, does the wife have any legal or equitable interest in the company?

3. Stephanie inherited $170,000 from her aunt before her marriage, which she used to purchase a home for herself and her boyfriend, Daniel. The home was titled solely in the name of Daniel, who later became her husband. Stephanie said that she put sole title in Daniel because she feared that if her name were on the title, her former husband's creditors would try to attach the home. Daniel has recently died, and his estate claims the house. Stephanie seeks an order imposing a constructive trust on the house for her benefit. Daniel's best friend would testify that Daniel had told him shortly before his death that Stephanie claimed she never meant to give the house to him, but that earlier, when they were first married, she had said something different, that she wanted to make a gift to him and for him to be head of the household. What arguments should the parties make?

b.   Community Property

The law of community property, which is often traced to Visigothic Spain, generally recognizes that both spouses own wealth acquired by the labor of either of them during the marriage. As with common law property, the notion of community property has been understood and applied differently at different times and in different places. Community property jurisdictions differ in their treatment of debts and of property owned prior to or inherited during marriage. In one scheme (the Roman-Dutch), all property becomes community property upon marriage; in the Spanish form commonly followed in U.S. community property states and in South America, premarital wealth is regarded as separate property, and its ownership is not affected by marriage. And there are, as one would expect, intermediate schemes as well as differences with respect to the treatment of the income produced by premarital (separate) assets.

Despite these variations, community property interests seem very different from those in a separate property system, where, even under Married Women's Property Acts, each spouse *owns* only what he or she has been given or earns during the marriage.[7] Moreover, community and common law property schemes differ substantially in their treatment of wealth *not* earned during the marriage but brought into the marriage as separate property. Whereas a married woman lost her right to manage her real and personal property during marriage at common law, that was never the case under community property principles. Except for her dowry, a wife has always enjoyed the exclusive rights to control, manage, and dispose of her separate property and can, without her husband's consent, convey her separate property.[8] Similarly, she has had the right to deal with the rents and profits of her separate property in jurisdictions where such rents and profits are separate rather than community property.

Lest one believe, however, that the wife under community property principles stood entirely equal to her husband, it should be added that she occupied much the same position as her sisters in common law jurisdictions before Married Women's Property Acts with respect to management of wealth generated *during* the marriage. While she held an ownership interest in that wealth that wives in common law states did not possess, her interest was passive as long as her husband was alive; the husband possessed full power to manage all of the community property, absent an agreement to the contrary. This state of the law resulted, according to the leading commentators on community property principles, "from the consideration of the husband as head of the family,[9] as the one who due to economic and biological factors has been the member of the marital partnership more

---

7. *See* Dana V. Kaplan, Note: Women of the West: The Evolution of Marital Property Laws in the Southwestern United States and Their Effect on Mexican-American Women, 26 Women's Rts. L. Rep. 139 (2005), describing the development of community property systems in the Southwest and analyzing how rights of married women in those jurisdictions compared to rights in the common law states during the nineteenth century.

8. The Spanish law recognized three kinds of property at the time of marriage: dowry, paraphernalia, and other separate property. The dowry was, of course, the consideration, or part of the consideration, paid the husband for marrying his wife. Accordingly, the right of management and control was placed in his hands. However, as with the wife's realty at common law, neither the husband nor his heirs (assuming they were not also hers) had any interest in dower property after dissolution of the marriage.

Paraphernalia included personal property brought by the wife into the marriage, but for her separate use. She retained all rights of control in this property unless she placed the management in her husband's hands by an express writing. *Other separate property* included wealth owned by the wife but not brought by her into the marriage for common use. Here again, the husband had no right of management.

If the wife received property by gift or inheritance, this was treated as other separate property, and the donee wife retained the power of management and distribution. *See* William Q. de Funiak & Michael J. Vaughan, Principles of Community Property 270-273 (2d ed. 1971).

9. Without reference to a doctrine of marital unity, Spanish law — quite as clearly as English law — declared that "the husband was head of the family, with the duty to provide for its wants and the right to choose its place of residence." de Funiak & Vaughan, *supra* at 270.

practiced and experienced in the acquisition and management of property." W. de Funiak & M. Vaughan at 276.

Sole management power in the husband disappeared during the 1970s as legislatures, either on principle or in anticipation of equal protection challenges, revised their statutes to provide that each spouse or both spouses could manage community wealth. In Kirchberg v. Feenstra, 450 U.S. 455 (1981), the U.S. Supreme Court upheld a Fifth Circuit decision holding the Louisiana "head-and-master" rule unconstitutional.

> By granting the husband exclusive control over the disposition of property, Art. 2404 clearly embodies the type of express gender-based discrimination that we have found unconstitutional absent a showing that the classification is tailored to further an important governmental interest. . . . [Appellant's claim that wives may choose to avoid the impact of Art. 2404] overlooks the critical question: Whether Art. 2404 substantially furthers an important government interest. As we have previously noted, the "absence of an insurmountable barrier" will not redeem an otherwise unconstitutionally discriminatory law. Instead the burden remains on the party seeking to uphold the statute that expressly discriminates on the basis of sex to advance an "exceedingly persuasive justification" for the challenged classification. Because appellant has failed to offer such a justification . . . we affirm the judgment of the Court of Appeals invalidating Art. 2404.

Id. at 459-461.

Statutory formulations now commonly allow either spouse to manage and control community property. *E.g.*, Ariz. Rev. Stat. §25-214 (2014); Cal. Fam. Code §1100 (2014); N.M. Stat. Ann. §40-3-14 (2014). However, equalization of authority over community wealth has not been easy to accomplish in practice. After the demise of sole male authority, three different systems have been used to allocate management authority. A "joint management" system requires spouses to make joint decisions regarding community wealth. "Sole management" allocates to one spouse the sole power to manage particular community assets; for example, a spouse may have sole authority to manage his or her earnings. An "equal management" approach authorizes *either* spouse, acting alone, to manage the community property. Professor Thomas Oldham provides the following review of these schemes.

J. THOMAS OLDHAM, *MANAGEMENT OF THE COMMUNITY ESTATE DURING AN INTACT MARRIAGE*

56 Law & Contemp. Probs. 99, 106-107 (1993)

Each system has its drawbacks. Joint management ensures that both owners will have the opportunity to participate in management of the community, but this requirement could place a substantial burden upon commerce, particularly if it were applied to all transactions involving any amount of community property. Furthermore, some spouses might not want to manage; the joint management system would burden them, unless some way of opting out were created. Also, what should occur under such a system if only one spouse purports to transfer community property? . . .

The sole management system clearly specifies who will have management power over each item of community property. However, if each spouse does not accumulate (or in some states have record ownership of) the same amount of property during marriage, this system would grant one spouse power over more than half of the community estate, even though both spouses possess a present, vested fifty percent interest. If one spouse works outside the home and the other does not, in many instances the spouse working in the home would manage little or no community property.

The equal management system, like the joint management system, reflects a general norm of equality; it does present a problem, however, if the spouses disagree, and especially if they give contradictory instructions to a third party. In addition, even though either spouse in theory may exercise management power, one might argue that the system facilitates the usurpation of management of the community by the dominant spouse. Also, equal and sole management both permit one spouse to affect the property interests of the other without giving that spouse notice.

No state has accepted one of these management systems for all transactions involving community property. Each has adopted a combination of management rules, in which some transactions are governed by one set of rules, and others by another set.

Similar problems arise with regard to the authority of married persons in community property states to make gifts of community assets. Community property states differ greatly in their responses. California law requires the written consent of the other spouse to make a gift of community personal property, and both spouses generally must join in gifts of real property. Cal. Fam. Code §§ 1100(b) (personal property), 1102(a) (real property). Texas, by contrast, allows the managing spouse to make "moderate gifts for just causes outside the community," but the managing spouse bears the burden of proving fairness to the other spouse. *See* Mazique v. Mazique, 742 S.W.2d 805 (Tex. App. 1987). Wisconsin, on the third hand, allows unilateral gifts to third persons up to an amount of $1,000 per donee. Wis. Stat. Ann. § 766.53. For an extensive analysis of these and the many other problems of management, *see* Oldham, above.

NOTES AND QUESTIONS

1. A good starting point for understanding community property is that any property acquired by the productive efforts of either spouse during the marriage is community property, while property owned before marriage or given to only one spouse during marriage is separate property. Because life is more complicated than this simple formula, classification of property as community or separate is also more complicated. We will look at the major points of difficulty in Chapter 6.

On the level of principle, community property seems more consistent with the idea of "marital unity." However, efforts to convince common law property states to change to a community property system have been spectacularly unsuccessful. The Uniform Marital Property Act, promulgated in 1984, would create a community property system during marriage. Only one state, Wisconsin, has enacted the Uniform Act. What might explain the persistence of the common law system in most states?

A recent discussion of these issues is Alicia Brokars Kelly, Money Matters in Marriage: Unmasking Interdependence in Ongoing Spousal Economic Relations, 47 Louisville L. Rev. 113 (2008).

2. Assume that you were a married woman living in the era before Kirchberg v. Feenstra was decided. Would you be better off living in Louisiana or Alabama, a state with common law property, from the perspective of being able to manage your financial affairs independently of your husband? How much control would you have in a modern community property state using a joint management system? An equal management system?

3. Professor Andrea Carroll criticizes some community property rules, particularly those affecting creditors' rights and the spouses' inability to terminate the community during marriage, as creating incentives to divorce. Andrea B. Carroll, Incentivizing Divorce, 30 Cardozo L. Rev. 1925 (2009).

PROBLEMS

1. If George and Martha, the couple in the problem on page 38 above, lived at all times in a community property state, which assets would be community property, and which would be the separate property of George or Martha? Who would have the ability to sell the assets under a joint management system? An equal management system?

2. How would problems 1, 2, and 3 on page 43 above be analyzed in a community property state?

2. "New" Property

To this point, we have largely been concerned with traditional forms of property: houses, ranches, bank accounts, and the like. A great deal of wealth, however, takes a different form: what is sometimes called "the new property." That phrase is most strongly associated with a series of writings by Charles Reich, including The New Property, 73 Yale L.J. 733 (1964); Individual Rights and Social Welfare: The Emerging Legal Issues, 74 Yale L.J. 1245 (1965); and The Greening of America (1970). He observed in the first of these that "today more and more of our wealth takes the form of rights or status rather than of tangible goods. An individual's profession or occupation is a prime example. To many others, a job with a particular employer is the principal form of wealth." 73 Yale L.J. at 738. The importance of this new form of wealth was suggested 25 years ago by Peter Drucker, who characterized the modern American economy as "pension socialism":

If "socialism" is defined as "ownership of the means of production by the workers" — and this is the most orthodox definition — then the United States is the most "socialist" country in the world. . . .

[T]he largest employee pension funds . . . own a controlling interest in practically every single one of the "command positions" in the economy. . . . Indeed, a larger sector of the American economy (outside of farming) today is owned by the American worker — through his investment agent, the pension fund — than Allende in Chile proposed to bring under government ownership to make Chile a "socialist country. . . ."

Peter Drucker, Pension Fund "Socialism," *in* The Public Interest 3-6 (Winter 1976). Whether this is indeed socialism or rather a way for capitalism to assert control over labor's financial resources even after workers cease their labor is an interesting question. *See* William Graebner, A History of Retirement: The Meaning and Function of an American Institution: 1885-1978, 220-221 (1980).

The importance of this form of property for its holders as well as for the economy has grown enormously. Professor Glendon observed:

[F]or the majority in modern welfare states, old property (in the sense of traditional assets of real and personal property) is less important than individual earning power and public and private benefits based on such labor. To the extent that there are savings apart from home equity in a middle-aged middle-income family, they tend less to be represented by bank accounts or tangible assets than by employment-related pension plans, profit-sharing plans, insurance or other benefits. . . .

Mary Ann Glendon, The New Family and the New Property 93-94 (1981).

An enormous amount of personal wealth rests in pension funds, which held $6.35 trillion in assets in 2011. Employee Benefits Security Administration, Private Pension Plan Bulletin: Abstract of 2011 Form 5500 Annual Reports 1 (2013). However, between 2010 and 2011, the total number of pension plans decreased by 2.5 percent, and the number of people actively participating in plans declined by 3.9 percent. *Id.* In 2012, 61 percent of all workers over age 16 worked for an employer that sponsored a pension or retirement plan, up from 59 percent in 2009, but only 46 percent of all workers actually participated in such a plan, a decline from a high of 48 percent in 2003. Employee Benefit Research Institute, Retirement Plan Participation: Survey of Income and Program Participation (SIPP) Data, 2012 at 1 (Aug. 2013). Of nonagricultural workers, 49.1 percent participated in an employer's retirement plan. Pension coverage is more common for higher-earning workers than for lower-earning workers and for older rather than younger workers. Only 34 percent of workers who were 21 to 30 years old participated in a retirement plan, while 62 percent of those age 51 to 60 did. Fourteen percent of workers earning less than $5,000 a year had a pension plan, while 79 percent of those earning $50,000 or more did. These trends have been stable for many years. *Id.* at 4.

In addition, government programs directed to employment security, social insurance benefits, and a variety of other aspects of income maintenance and protection of health and welfare constitute significant forms of wealth in a modern

welfare society. These benefits substantially increased during the 1970s from earlier levels, as did the level of wages subject to Social Security tax.

Statutory and judicial decisions have increasingly come to accept Reich's
understanding of the importance of "new property." The Employee Retirement
Income Security Act of 1974 (ERISA), 29 U.S.C. §§ 1001 et seq., sets forth a
comprehensive scheme for the regulation of private pension plans to protect
their participants and beneficiaries. Government pension plans are not covered,
although they may include provisions similar to those found in the federal statute.

The relationship between ERISA, as modified by the Retirement Equity Act
of 1984, and state laws generally governing the ownership of wealth by family
members is of great importance. In general, state laws define the treatment of
wealth earned or held by one or more members of a family and the extent to
which family members may dispose of that wealth. ERISA, however, incorporates
a critical principle that affects the power of pension plan participants to deal with
their pension funds and, concomitantly, the power of others — particularly spouses
and creditors — to reach or use those funds. ERISA § 206(d)(1) requires that
"[e]ach pension plan shall provide that benefits provided under the plan may
not be assigned or alienated." The relationship between that principle and other
aspects of ERISA to state laws governing marital property (and especially community property) is explored in the following case.

Boggs v. Boggs

520 U.S. 833 (1997)

KENNEDY, J., delivered the opinion of the Court, in which STEVENS, SCALIA,
SOUTER and THOMAS, JJ., joined, and in which REHNQUIST, C.J., and GINSBURG, J.,
joined as to Part III. BREYER, J., filed a dissenting opinion, in which O'CONNOR, J.,
joined, and in which REHNQUIST, C.J., and GINSBURG, J., joined except as to
Part II-B-3. . . .

Isaac Boggs worked for South Central Bell from 1949 until his retirement in
1985. Isaac and Dorothy, his first wife, were married when he began working for
the company, and they remained husband and wife until Dorothy's death in 1979.
They had three sons. Within a year of Dorothy's death, Isaac married Sandra, and
they remained married until his death in 1989.

Upon retirement, Isaac received various benefits from his employer's
retirement plans. One was a lump-sum distribution from the Bell System Savings
Plan for Salaried Employees (Savings Plan) of $151,628.94, which he rolled over
into an Individual Retirement Account (IRA). He made no withdrawals and the
account was worth $180,778.05 when he died. He also received 96 shares of AT&T
stock from the Bell South Employee Stock Ownership Plan (ESOP). In addition,
Isaac enjoyed a monthly annuity payment during his retirement of $1,777.67 from
the Bell South Service Retirement Program.

The instant dispute over ownership of the benefits is between Sandra (the
surviving wife) and the sons of the first marriage. The sons' claim to a portion of
the benefits is based on Dorothy's will. Dorothy bequeathed to Isaac one-third of
her estate, and a lifetime usufruct in the remaining two-thirds. A lifetime usufruct

is the rough equivalent of a common-law life estate. She bequeathed to her sons the naked ownership in the remaining two-thirds, subject to Isaac's usufruct. All agree that, absent pre-emption, Louisiana law controls and that under it Dorothy's will would dispose of her community property interest in Isaac's undistributed pension plan benefits. A Louisiana state court, in a 1980 order entitled "Judgment of Possession," ascribed to Dorothy's estate a community property interest in Isaac's Savings Plan account valued at the time at $21,194.29.

Sandra contests the validity of Dorothy's 1980 testamentary transfer, basing her claim to those benefits on her interest under Isaac's will and 29 U.S.C. § 1055. Isaac bequeathed to Sandra outright certain real property including the family home. His will also gave Sandra a lifetime usufruct in the remainder of his estate, with the naked ownership interest being held by the sons. Sandra argues that the sons' competing claim, since it is based on Dorothy's 1980 purported testamentary transfer of her community property interest in undistributed pension plan benefits, is pre-empted by ERISA. The Bell South Service Retirement Program monthly annuity is now paid to Sandra as the surviving spouse.

After Isaac's death, two of the sons filed an action in state court requesting the appointment of an expert to compute the percentage of the retirement benefits they would be entitled to as a result of Dorothy's attempted testamentary transfer. They further sought a judgment awarding them a portion of: the IRA; the ESOP shares of AT&T stock; the monthly annuity payments received by Isaac during his retirement; and Sandra's survivor annuity payments, both received and payable.

In response, Sandra Boggs filed a complaint in the United States District Court for the Eastern District of Louisiana, seeking a declaratory judgment that ERISA pre-empts the application of Louisiana's community property and succession laws to the extent they recognize the sons' claim to an interest in the disputed retirement benefits. The District Court granted summary judgment against Sandra Boggs. It found that, under Louisiana community property law, Dorothy had an ownership interest in her husband's pension plan benefits built up during their marriage. The creation of this interest, the court explained, does not violate 29 U.S.C. § 1056(d)(1), which prohibits pension plan benefits from being "assigned" or "alienated," since Congress did not intend to alter traditional familial and support obligations. In the court's view, there was no assignment or alienation because Dorothy's rights in the benefits were acquired by operation of community property law and not by transfer from Isaac. Turning to Dorothy's testamentary transfer, the court found it effective because "[ERISA] does not display any particular interest in preserving maximum benefits to any particular beneficiary."

A divided panel of the Fifth Circuit affirmed. . . .

. . . In large part the number of ERISA pre-emption cases reflects the comprehensive nature of the statute, the centrality of pension and welfare plans in the national economy, and their importance to the financial security of the Nation's workforce. ERISA is designed to ensure the proper administration of pension and welfare plans, both during the years of the employee's active service and in his or her retirement years.

This case lies at the intersection of ERISA pension law and state community property law. None can dispute the central role community property laws play in the nine community property States. It is more than a property regime. It is a commitment to the equality of husband and wife and reflects the real partnership inherent in the marital relationship. State community property laws, many of ancient lineage, "must have continued to exist through such lengths of time because of their manifold excellences and are not lightly to be abrogated or tossed aside." 1 W. de Funiak, Principles of Community Property 11 (1943). . . .

The nine community property States have some 80 million residents, with perhaps $1 trillion in retirement plans. This case involves a community property claim, but our ruling will affect as well the right to make claims or assert interests based on the law of any State, whether or not it recognizes community property. Our ruling must be consistent with the congressional scheme to assure the security of plan participants and their families in every State. In enacting ERISA, Congress noted the importance of pension plans in its findings and declaration of policy, explaining:

> [T]he growth in size, scope, and numbers of employee benefit plans in recent years has been rapid and substantial; . . . the continued well-being and security of millions of employees and their dependents are directly affected by these plans; . . . they are affected with a national public interest [and] they have become an important factor affecting the stability of employment and the successful development of industrial relations. . . . 29 U.S.C. § 1001(a).

ERISA is an intricate, comprehensive statute. Its federal regulatory scheme governs employee benefit plans, which include both pension and welfare plans. All employee benefit plans must conform to various reporting, disclosure and fiduciary requirements, while pension plans must also comply with participation, vesting, and funding requirements. The surviving spouse annuity and QDRO provisions, central to the dispute here, are part of the statute's mandatory participation and vesting requirements. These provisions provide detailed protections to spouses of plan participants which, in some cases, exceed what their rights would be were community property law the sole measure.

ERISA's express pre-emption clause states that the Act "shall supersede any and all State laws insofar as they may now or hereafter relate to any employee benefit plan. . . ." § 1144(a). We can begin, and in this case end, the analysis by simply asking if state law conflicts with the provisions of ERISA or operates to frustrate its objects. We hold that there is a conflict, which suffices to resolve the case. . . .

III

Sandra Boggs, as we have observed, asserts that federal law pre-empts and supersedes state law and requires the surviving spouse annuity to be paid to her as the sole beneficiary. We agree.

The annuity at issue is a qualified joint and survivor annuity mandated by ERISA. . . . ERISA requires that every qualified joint and survivor annuity include an annuity payable to a nonparticipant surviving spouse. The survivor's annuity may not be less than 50% of the amount of the annuity which is payable during the joint lives of the participant and spouse. Provision of the survivor's annuity may not be waived by the participant, absent certain limited circumstances, unless the spouse consents in writing to the designation of another beneficiary, which designation also cannot be changed without further spousal consent, witnessed by a plan representative or notary public. Sandra Boggs, as the surviving spouse, is entitled to a survivor's annuity under these provisions. She has not waived her right to the survivor's annuity, let alone consented to having the sons designated as the beneficiaries.

Respondents say their state-law claims are consistent with these provisions. Their claims, they argue, affect only the disposition of plan proceeds after they have been disbursed by the Bell South Service Retirement Program, and thus nothing is required of the plan. . . .

We disagree. The statutory object of the qualified joint and survivor annuity provisions . . . is to ensure a stream of income to surviving spouses. . . .

ERISA's solicitude for the economic security of surviving spouses would be undermined by allowing a predeceasing spouse's heirs and legatees to have a community property interest in the survivor's annuity. Even a plan participant cannot defeat a nonparticipant surviving spouse's statutory entitlement to an annuity. It would be odd, to say the least, if Congress permitted a predeceasing nonparticipant spouse to do so. Nothing in the language of ERISA supports concluding that Congress made such an inexplicable decision. . . .

Louisiana law, to the extent it provides the sons with a right to a portion of Sandra Boggs' § 1055 survivor's annuity, is pre-empted.

IV

Beyond seeking a portion of the survivor's annuity, respondents claim a percentage of: the monthly annuity payments made to Isaac Boggs during his retirement; the IRA; and the ESOP shares of AT&T stock. As before, the claim is based on Dorothy Boggs' attempted testamentary transfer to the sons of her community interest in Isaac's undistributed pension plan benefits. Respondents argue further — and somewhat inconsistently — that their claim again concerns only what a plan participant or beneficiary may do once plan funds are distributed, without imposing any obligations on the plan itself. Both parties agree that the ERISA benefits at issue here were paid after Dorothy's death, and thus this case does not present the question whether ERISA would permit a nonparticipant spouse to obtain a devisable community property interest in benefits paid out during the existence of the community between the participant and that spouse.

The principal object of the statute is to protect plan participants and beneficiaries. . . .

ERISA confers beneficiary status on a nonparticipant spouse or dependent in only narrow circumstances delineated by its provisions. For example, as we have discussed, § 1055(a) requires provision of a surviving spouse annuity in covered pension plans, and, as a consequence the spouse is a beneficiary to this extent. Section 1056's QDRO provisions likewise recognize certain pension plan community property interests of nonparticipant spouses and dependents. A QDRO is a type of domestic relations order which creates or recognizes an alternate payee's right to, or assigns to an alternate payee the right to, a portion of the benefits payable with respect to a participant under a plan. . . . A domestic relations order must meet certain requirements to qualify as a QDRO. QDRO's, unlike domestic relations orders in general, are exempt from both the pension plan anti-alienation provision, and ERISA's general pre-emption clause. . . . These provisions are essential to one of REA's central purposes, which is to give enhanced protection to the spouse and dependent children in the event of divorce or separation, and in the event of death the surviving spouse. Apart from these detailed provisions, ERISA does not confer beneficiary status on nonparticipants by reason of their marital or dependent status. . . .

The surviving spouse annuity and QDRO provisions, which acknowledge and protect specific pension plan community property interests, give rise to the strong implication that other community property claims are not consistent with the statutory scheme. ERISA's silence with respect to the right of a nonparticipant spouse to control pension plan benefits by testamentary transfer provides powerful support for the conclusion that the right does not exist. . . .

We conclude the sons have no claim under ERISA to a share of the retirement benefits. To begin with, the sons are neither participants nor beneficiaries. A "participant" is defined as an "employee or former employee of an employer, or any member or former member of an employee organization, who is or may become eligible to receive a benefit." A "beneficiary" is a "person designated by a participant, or by the terms of an employee benefit plan, who is or may become entitled to a benefit thereunder." § 1002(8). Respondents' claims are based on Dorothy Boggs' attempted testamentary transfer, not on a designation by Isaac Boggs or under the terms of the retirement plans. . . .

The conclusion that Congress intended to pre-empt respondents' nonbeneficiary, nonparticipant interests in the retirement plans is given specific and powerful reinforcement by the pension plan anti-alienation provision. Section 1056(d)(1) provides that "[e]ach pension plan shall provide that benefits provided under the plan may not be assigned or alienated." Statutory anti-alienation provisions are potent mechanisms to prevent the dissipation of funds. . . . The anti-alienation provision can "be seen to bespeak a pension law protective policy of special intensity: Retirement funds shall remain inviolate until retirement."

Dorothy's 1980 testamentary transfer, which is the source of respondents' claimed ownership interest, is a prohibited "assignment or alienation." An "assignment or alienation" has been defined by regulation, with certain exceptions not at issue here, as "[a]ny direct or indirect arrangement whereby a party acquires from a participant or beneficiary" an interest enforceable against a plan to "all or any part of a plan benefit payment which is, or may become, payable to the participant or beneficiary." Those requirements are met. Under Louisiana law community property interests are enforceable against a plan. If respondents' claims were allowed to succeed they would have acquired, as of 1980, an interest in Isaac's pension plan at the expense of plan participants and beneficiaries.

As was true with survivors' annuities, it would be inimical to ERISA's purposes to permit testamentary recipients to acquire a competing interest in undistributed pension benefits, which are intended to provide a stream of income to participants and their beneficiaries. Pension benefits support participants and beneficiaries in their retirement years, and ERISA's pension plan safeguards are designed to further this end. . . . Under respondents' approach, retirees could find their retirement benefits reduced by substantial sums because they have been diverted to testamentary recipients. Retirement benefits and the income stream provided for by ERISA-regulated plans would be disrupted in the name of protecting a nonparticipant spouse's successors over plan participants and beneficiaries. Respondents' logic would even permit a spouse to transfer an interest in a pension plan to creditors, a result incompatible with a spendthrift provision such as § 1056(d)(1). . . .

The axis around which ERISA's protections revolve is the concepts of participant and beneficiary. When Congress has chosen to depart from this framework, it has done so in a careful and limited manner. Respondents' claims, if allowed to succeed, would depart from this framework, upsetting the deliberate balance central to ERISA. It does not matter that respondents have sought to enforce their rights only after the retirement benefits have been distributed since their asserted rights are based on the theory that they had an interest in the undistributed pension plan benefits. Their state-law claims are pre-empted. The judgment of the Fifth Circuit is

Reversed.

Justice BREYER, with whom Justice O'CONNOR joins, and with whom THE CHIEF JUSTICE and Justice GINSBURG join except as to Part II-B-3, dissenting. The question in this case is whether the Employee Retirement Income Security Act of 1974 (ERISA), 29 U.S.C. § 1001, et seq., "pre-empts," and thereby nullifies, state community property law. The state law in question would permit a wife to leave to her children her share of the pension assets that her husband has earned (or, to put the matter in "community property" terms, that she and her husband together have earned) during their marriage. From the perspective of property law, the issue is unusually important, for, we are told, the answer potentially affects nine community property States, with more than 80 million residents, and over $1 trillion in ERISA-qualified pension plans — plans that are often a couple's most important lifetime assets. In my view, Congress did not intend ERISA to pre-empt this testamentary aspect of community property law — at least not in the circumstances present here, where a first wife's bequest need not prevent a second wife from obtaining precisely those benefits that ERISA specifically sets aside for her. See § 1055(a). The Fifth Circuit's determination is consistent with this view. I would therefore affirm its judgment. . . .

The state law in question concerns the ownership of benefits. I concede that a primary concern of ERISA is the proper financial management of pension and welfare benefit funds themselves, and that payment of benefits (which amounts to the writing of checks from those funds) is closely "connected with" that management. . . . But, even so, I cannot say that the state law at issue here concerns a subject that Congress wished to place outside the State's legal reach.

My reason in part lies in the fact that the state law in question involves family, property, and probate — all areas of traditional, and important, state concern. When this Court considers pre-emption, it works "on the 'assumption that the historic police powers of the States were not to be superseded by the Federal Act unless that was the clear and manifest purpose of Congress.'"

I can find no reasonably defined relevant category of state law that Congress would have intended to displace. Obviously, Congress did not intend to pre-empt all state laws that govern property ownership. After all, someone must own an interest in ERISA plan benefits. Nor, for similar reasons, can one believe that Congress intended to pre-empt state laws concerning testamentary bequests. . . . The question, "who owns the property?" needs an answer. Ordinarily, where federal law does not provide a specific answer, state law will have to do so.

Nor can I find some appropriately defined forbidden category by looking to the congressional purpose of establishing uniform laws to regulate the administration of pension funds. This case does not involve a lawsuit against a fund. I agree with the majority that ERISA would likely pre-empt state law that permitted such a suit. But this is not such a case; nor is there reason to believe Louisiana law would produce such a case. . . .

NOTES AND QUESTIONS

1. The Supreme Court in *Boggs* concludes that recognizing Dorothy's community property interests in the pensions at Isaac's death would undermine Congress's purposes in requiring that pensions be inalienable. What are these purposes, according to the Court? Do you agree with the Court's conclusion as to each of the three kinds of rights — the lump sum distribution that Isaac took at retirement and rolled into an IRA, the shares of stock purchased through the employee stock ownership plan, and the surviving spouse's annuity?

If Dorothy and Isaac had divorced, the divorce court would have been able to award Dorothy her community property interests in the pensions that Isaac earned during marriage, as we will see in Chapter 6. For this reason, Professor Andrea Carroll criticizes ERISA as interpreted by *Boggs* as giving spouses in Dorothy's position an incentive to divorce. Andrea B. Carroll, Incentivizing Divorce, 30 Cardozo L. Rev. 1925 (2009).

2. The supremacy clause of the United States Constitution states that the "laws of the United States . . . shall be the supreme law of the Land." Accordingly, state laws inconsistent with federal law are void. Federal legislation may preempt state law in two ways. It may undertake to provide the sole body of law in a field, either by express statutory provision or by implication. Even if Congress has not expressly or implicitly undertaken to occupy the entire field, state law is preempted to the extent of any conflict with a federal statute. Such a "conflict" preemption arises when a private party cannot comply with both federal and state law or when compliance with the challenged state law will frustrate accomplishment of important federal purposes embodied in congressional legislation.

The preemption issue in *Boggs* arose because ERISA regulates pension plans for the benefit of individual beneficiaries and specified others, while community property law treats pension plan wealth as property owned by both the employee and his or her then-current spouse at the time the pension is earned. For an analysis of subsequent Supreme Court decisions in related cases, *see* Albert Feuer, How the Supreme Court and the Department of Labor May Dispel Myths About ERISA's Family Law Provisions and Protect the Benefit Entitlements That Arise Thereunder, 45 J. Marshall L. Rev. 635 (2012).

3. A similar issue can arise when any federal law addresses what a state may regard as community property. In Rodrigue v. Rodrigue, 218 F.3d 432 (5th Cir.

2000), *cert. denied*, 532 U.S. 905 (2001), the question was whether the wife of a highly successful Louisiana artist was entitled to rights in the husband's copyrighted works. The husband argued that the Copyright Act of 1976 provided that ownership of a copyright "vests initially in the author" at the time of the creation of the work. From this, the husband contended, it follows that the community property principle that property acquired during marriage is owned equally by the spouses had been preempted by federal law assigning full ownership solely in the author, and thus his copyrighted works were separate property not subject to division at divorce.

While Section 301 of the Copyright Act provides that the Act governs "all legal or equitable rights that are equivalent to any of the exclusive rights with the general scope of copyright," the Fifth Circuit concluded that this language did not amount to a preemption of the entire field of marital property. Rather, it held that the Act protects five exclusive rights: reproduction, adaptation, publication, performance, and display of protected works. The Act does not treat enjoyment of the economic benefits of copyrighted materials as an exclusive right of the author, and the Act does not preempt the entire field of copyright ownership.

Accordingly, the question was whether the operation of Louisiana community property law conflicted with the purposes of particular provisions of the Act. The strongest argument for finding a conflict — an argument adopted by the district court — was that Louisiana state law would give the nonauthor spouse equal management rights to copyrighted works, which was functionally inconsistent with Copyright Act's grant to authors of exclusive rights related to management. The Fifth Circuit agreed that dividing these management rights, as opposed to the right to enjoy income or other economic benefits from copyrighted works, would conflict with the federal scheme. However, the court held that the conflict was not ineluctable and that Louisiana community property law was not preempted to the extent that it allowed a nonauthor spouse the right to share in the economic benefits created by copyrighted works during the existence of the marriage. For more information, *see* Llewellyn Joseph Gibbons, Love's Labor's Lost: Marry for Love, Copyright Work Made-for-Hire, and Alienate at Your Leisure, 101 Ky. L.J. 113 (2012-2013); Ann Bartow, Intellectual Property and Domestic Relations: Issues to Consider When There Is an Artist, Author, Inventor, or Celebrity in the Family, 35 Fam. L.Q. 383 (2001).

4. In addition to preemption, the opinion in *Boggs* discusses the anti-alienation provision of ERISA, which precludes any person, including the plan participant, from using pension benefit funds prior to retirement. In that respect, it resembles a spendthrift trust, where the corpus and expected future income cannot be transferred by the beneficiary or attached by the beneficiary's creditors. This result reflects deference to the interests of the grantor and a recognition that the creditor has no special right to rely on the availability of those assets.

The purpose of the spendthrift trust is to protect the beneficiary from his or her own improvidence. As John Langbein and Bruce Wolk point out, however, ERISA's alienation rule is an even more dramatic protective strategy than its private trust analog. For one thing, in most states the spendthrift trust is exceptional, usually employed only when the settlor has some special reason to mistrust the beneficiary's judgment. ERISA makes the protective feature universal. For another, spendthrift clauses do not prevent creditors who have supplied necessaries to the beneficiary from collecting from the trust; creditors are not exempt from the ban on alienation imposed by ERISA. John H. Langbein & Bruce A. Wolk, Pension and Employee Benefit Law 546 (2d ed. 1995).

5. ERISA covers only benefit plans established by (1) employers who are engaged in or affect interstate commerce or (2) employee organizations representing employees engaged in or affecting commerce, or both. While many of its provisions apply to all benefit plans, including welfare benefit plans such as health insurance or vacation plans, the anti-alienation provision applies only to pension benefit plans. Mackey v. Lanier Collection Agency & Service, Inc., 486 U.S. 825 (1988). As the Court notes in *Boggs*, however, benefits other than annuity payments — there, employee stock option benefits and profit sharing plans — may qualify as "pension benefits" and therefore come under the anti-alienation provisions of ERISA.

6. Government benefit programs directed to employment security, social insurance benefits, and a variety of other aspects of income now constitute significant forms of wealth. Federal legislation extends immunity from execution for debt to a considerable array of benefits associated with retirement or disability. Exemptions have been enacted for Social Security payments (42 U.S.C. § 407 (1988)), Civil Service retirement benefits (5 U.S.C. § 8346(a) (1988)), Railroad Retirement Act benefits (45 U.S.C. § 231(m)(a) (1988)), and veterans' benefits (38 U.S.C. § 3101(a) (1988)), among others. These exemptions are typically based on policy judgments about the importance of preserving these benefits to avoid impoverishment (and the need for public support) of debtors.

State legislatures have created exemptions for analogous entitlements. Public assistance and unemployment benefits typically are immunized from forcible collection, *e.g.*, Cal. Civ. Proc. Code § 704.120 (unemployment) (2014). Workers' compensation benefits are also largely exempted from execution by state law. To varying extents, the same treatment is given to accident and disability insurance proceeds, but less often to tort judgments for personal injuries. Theodore Eisenberg, Debtor-Creditor Law 37-03[B].

3. Family Support Duties

McGuire v. McGuire

59 N.W.2d 336 (Neb. 1953)

Messmore, J. The plaintiff, Lydia McGuire, brought this action in equity in the district court for Wayne County against Charles W. McGuire, her husband, as defendant, to recover suitable maintenance and support money, and for costs and attorney's fees. Trial was had to the court and a decree was rendered in favor of the plaintiff.

The district court decreed that the plaintiff was legally entitled to use the credit of the defendant and obligate him to pay for certain items in the nature of improvements and repairs, furniture, and appliances for the household in the amount of several thousand dollars; required the defendant to purchase a new automobile with an effective heater within 30 days; ordered him to pay travel expenses of the plaintiff for a visit to each of her daughters at least once a year; that the plaintiff be entitled in the future to pledge the credit of the defendant for what may constitute necessaries of life; awarded a personal allowance to the plaintiff in the sum of $50 a month; awarded $800 for services for the plaintiff's attorney; and as an alternative to part of the award so made, defendant was permitted, in agreement with plaintiff, to purchase a modern home elsewhere. . . .

The record shows that the plaintiff and defendant were married in Wayne, Nebraska, on August 11, 1919. At the time of the marriage the defendant was a bachelor 46 or 47 years of age and had a reputation for more than ordinary frugality, of which the plaintiff was aware. She had visited in his home and had known him for about 3 years prior to the marriage. After the marriage the couple went to live on a farm of 160 acres located in Leslie precinct, Wayne County, owned by the defendant and upon which he had lived and farmed since 1905. The parties have lived on this place ever since. The plaintiff had been previously married. Her first husband died in October 1914, leaving surviving him the plaintiff and two daughters. . . .

At the time of trial plaintiff was 66 years of age and the defendant nearly 80 years of age. No children were born to these parties. The defendant had no dependents except the plaintiff.

The plaintiff testified that she was a dutiful and obedient wife, worked and saved, and cohabited with the defendant until the last 2 or 3 years. She worked in the fields, did outside chores, cooked, and attended to her household duties such as cleaning the house and doing the washing. For a number of years she raised as high as 300 chickens, sold poultry and eggs, and used the money to buy clothing, things she wanted, and for groceries. She further testified that the defendant was the boss of the house and his word was law; that he would not tolerate any charge accounts and would not inform her as to his finances or business; and that he was a poor companion. The defendant did not complain of her work, but left the impression to her that she had not done enough. On several occasions the plaintiff asked the defendant for money. He would give her very small amounts, and for the last 3 or 4 years he had not given her any money nor provided her with clothing, except a coat about 4 years previous. The defendant had purchased the groceries the last 3 or 4 years, and permitted her to buy groceries, but he paid for them by check. There is apparently no complaint about the groceries the defendant furnished. The defendant had not taken her to a motion picture show during the past 12 years. They did not belong to any organizations or charitable institutions, nor did he give her money to make contributions to any charitable institutions. The defendant belongs to the Pleasant Valley Church, which occupies about 2 acres of his farm land. At the time of trial there was no minister for this church, so there were no services. For the past 4 years or more, the defendant had not given the plaintiff money to purchase furniture or other household necessities. Three years ago he did purchase an electric, wood-and-cob combination stove which was installed in the kitchen, also linoleum floor covering for the kitchen. The plaintiff further testified that the house is not equipped with a bathroom, bathing facilities, or inside toilet. The kitchen is not modern. She does not have a kitchen sink. Hard and soft water is obtained from a well and cistern. She has a mechanical Servel refrigerator, and the house is equipped with electricity. There is a pipeless furnace, which she testified had not been in good working order for 5 or 6 years, and she testified she was tired of scooping coal and ashes. She had requested a new furnace, but the defendant believed the one they had to be satisfactory. She related that the furniture was old and she would like to replenish it, at least to be comparable with some of her neighbors; that her silverware and dishes were old and were primarily gifts, outside of what she purchased; that one of her daughters was good about furnishing her clothing, at least a dress a year, or sometimes two; that the defendant owns a 1929 Ford coupe equipped with a heater which is not efficient, and on the average of every 2 weeks he drives the plaintiff to Wayne to visit her mother; and that he also owns a 1927 Chevrolet pickup which is used for different purposes on the farm. The plaintiff was privileged to use all of the rent money she wanted to from the 80-acre farm, and when she goes to see her daughters, which is not frequent, she uses part of the rent money for that purpose, the defendant providing no funds for such use. . . . At the present time the plaintiff is not able to raise chickens and sell eggs. She has about 25 chickens. The plaintiff has had three abdominal operations for which the defendant has paid. She selected her own doctor, and there were no restrictions placed in that respect. When she has requested various things for the home or personal effects, defendant has informed her on many occasions that he did not have the money to pay for the same. She would like to have a new car. She visited one daughter in Spokane, Washington, in March 1951 for 3 or 4 weeks, and visited the other daughter living in Fort Worth, Texas, on three occasions for 2 to 4 weeks at a time. She had visited one of her daughters when she was living in Sioux City some weekends. The plaintiff further testified that she had very little funds, possibly $1,500 in the bank, which was chicken money and money which her father furnished her, he having departed this life a few years ago; and that use of the telephone was restricted, indicating that defendant did not desire that she make long distance calls; otherwise she had free access to the telephone.

It appears that the defendant owns 398 acres of land with 2 acres deeded to a church, the land being of the value of $83,960; that he has bank deposits in the sum of $12,786.81 and government bonds in the amount of $104,500; and that his income, including interest on the bonds and rental for his real estate, is $8,000 or $9,000 a year. There are apparently some Series E United States Savings Bonds listed and registered in the names of Charles W. McGuire or Lydia M. McGuire purchased in 1943, 1944, and 1945, in the amount of $2,500. Other bonds seem to be in the name of Charles W. McGuire, without a beneficiary or co-owner designated. The plaintiff has a bank account of $5,960.22. This account includes deposits of some $200 and $100, which the court required the defendant to pay his wife as temporary allowance during the pendency of these proceedings. One hundred dollars was withdrawn on the date of each deposit. . . .

The defendant assigns as error that the decree is not supported by sufficient evidence; that the decree is contrary to law; [and] that the decree is an unwarranted usurpation and invasion of defendant's fundamental and constitutional rights. . . .

The plaintiff relies upon the following cases from this jurisdiction, which are clearly distinguishable from the facts in the instant case, as will become apparent.

In the case of Earle v. Earle, the plaintiff's petition alleged . . . that the defendant sent his wife away from him, did not permit her to return, contributed to her support and maintenance separate and apart from him, and later refused and ceased to provide for her support and the support of his child. The wife instituted a suit in equity against her husband for maintenance and support without a prayer for divorce or from bed and board. The question presented was whether or not the wife should be compelled to resort to a proceeding for a divorce, which she did not desire to do, or from bed and board. On this question, in this state the statutes are substantially silent and at the present time there is no statute governing this matter. The court stated that it was a well-established rule of law that it is the duty of the husband to provide his family with support and means of living—the style of support, requisite lodging, food, clothing, etc., to be such as fit his means, position, and station in life—and for this purpose the wife has generally the right to use his credit for the purchase of necessaries. The court held that if a wife is abandoned by her husband, without means of support, a bill in equity will lie to compel the husband to support the wife without asking for a decree of divorce. . . .

In the instant case the marital relation has continued for more than 33 years, and the wife has been supported in the same manner during this time without complaint on her part. The parties have not been separated or living apart from each other at any time. In the light of the cited cases it is clear, especially so in this jurisdiction, that to maintain an action such as the one at bar, the parties must be separated or living apart from each other.

The living standards of a family are a matter of concern to the household, and not for the courts to determine, even though the husband's attitude toward his wife, according to his wealth and circumstances, leaves little to be said in his behalf. As long as the home is maintained and the parties are living as husband and wife it may be said that the husband is legally supporting his wife and the purpose of the marriage relation is being carried out. Public policy requires such a holding. It appears that the plaintiff is not devoid of money in her own right. She has a fair-sized bank account and is entitled to use the rent from the 80 acres of land left by her first husband, if she so chooses. . . .

For the reasons given in this opinion, the judgment rendered by the district court is reversed and the cause remanded with directions to dismiss the cause.

Reversed and remanded with directions to dismiss.

YEAGER, J. (dissenting). I respectfully dissent. . . . From the beginning of the married life of the parties the defendant supplied only the barest necessities and there was no change thereafter. He did not even buy groceries until the last 3 or 4 years before the trial, and neither did he buy clothes for the plaintiff. . . .

There is and can be no doubt that, independent of statutes relating to divorce, alimony, and separate maintenance, if this plaintiff were living apart from the defendant she could in equity and on the facts as outlined in the record be awarded appropriate relief.

The principle supporting the right of a wife to maintain an action in equity, independent of statute, for maintenance was first announced in this jurisdiction in Earle v. Earle, 27 Neb. 277, 43 N.W. 118, 119, 20 Am. St. Rep. 667. In the opinion it was said: "While the statute books of this and other states amply provide for the granting of divorces in meritorious cases, yet we do not apprehend that it is the purpose of the law to compel a wife, when the aggrieved party, to resort to this proceeding, and thus liberate her husband from all obligations to her, in order that the rights which the law gives her, by reason of her marital relations with her husband, may be enforced. Such a conclusion would not generally strike the conscience of a court of equity as being entirely equitable." . . .

If relief is to be denied to plaintiff under this principle it must be denied because of the fact that she is not living separate and apart from the defendant and is not seeking separation.

In the light of what the decisions declare to be the basis of the right to maintain an action for support, is there any less reason for extending the right to a wife who is denied the right to maintenance in a home occupied with her husband than to one who has chosen to occupy a separate abode?

The *McGuire* case raises central questions about the relationship of government, particularly courts, to family governance. These questions, and the case itself, have been the subjects of wide comment and some disagreement. The following materials explore some aspects of that debate, including the importance, utility, and implications of treating the family as an economic and social unit.

MARY ANNE CASE, *ENFORCING BARGAINS IN AN ONGOING MARRIAGE*

35 Wash. U. J.L. & Pol'y 225, 239-242 (2011)

The inability to obtain enforcement in an ongoing marriage is far from a universal feature of the law of marriage in all legal systems at all times. For example, Montesquieu declared at the beginning of the eighteenth century that, in France, "husbands have only a vestige of authority over wives," because "the law intervenes in every dispute between them." Indeed, historians of late medieval and early modern France and Italy provide evidence of a pattern of judicial enforcement of women's rights within an ongoing marriage that seems to resemble the U.S. corporate law norm:

> For women, property separations emerged as a more viable option than separations of person and property. The relative ease with which property separations were granted provided married women with the leverage to counter, whether by threat or by actual petition, the legal privileges their husbands had over marital property and to check other kinds of behavior than the narrow management of property.
>
> . . . [In litigated cases, h]usbands' competence was questioned rather than assumed; indeed, some women in these cases . . . were able to use separation petitions to reshape the political economies of their households to protect their own interests if their husbands came up short. . . .
>
> . . .
>
> . . . For the state as represented by its judges, for the local community, and for kin anxious to protect their lineage property, separations were a means of disciplining and regulating households. But all three parties sought to limit the disruption by trying to reconcile husbands and wives and by favoring property separations as checks on the internal problems of households over the disintegration of households that separations of person and property entailed.

Perhaps one reason why continental judges were more willing than their English contemporaries to follow what became the modern rule for corporations is that continental marriages, particularly among the urban bourgeoisie, resembled closely held corporations more than did those of the English landed gentry. Women in intact marriages in early modern France, for example, had their own capital in the form of lineage property, and the level of detailed judicial decision making required to vest control of such property in a wife was far less than the micromanagement inevitably involved in determining, for example, the appropriate living standards of the McGuire household. "In England, by contrast, where there was no lineage property, there was also no common-law right to separate property and no separate property agreement until the nineteenth century, and separate domicile was easier for women to obtain than separate property."

The historians' evidence suggests that bargaining in the shadow of possible judicial enforcement—as the modern law and economics literature would predict—strengthened the hand of women in continental Europe negotiating with recalcitrant husbands, not only over property issues such as household expenditures and investments, but also when it came to matters such as domestic violence. For example, in her study of separated couples in fourteenth-century Venice, historian Linda Guzzetti describes cases settled before judicial proceedings were brought, in which:

> it was a question of the husband undertaking, for the future, neither to beat his wife, nor to abuse her, but to treat her well. The promises were made with the aim that the wives accept living again with the husbands from whom they had fled. These reconciliation agreements contained formulas similar to those in all other notarial contracts: for non-fulfilment of promise a financial penalty was envisaged, and each party could take the other to court.

Whereas differences in marital property regimes between England and the continent may help account for the comparative willingness of courts in early modern continental Europe to enforce bargains in an ongoing marriage, the fact that their approach to marriage is more thoroughgoingly contractual and juridical may help explain why Jewish and Islamic legal systems have also long been more willing to enforce bargains in an ongoing marriage than the Anglo-American legal system, whose approach to civil marriage evolved from Christian canonical notions of marriage as a sacrament of union.

According to Elimelech Westreich, the McGuire case would have been decided very differently under Jewish law: "The living standards are definitely a matter for the courts to determine. [This] is accepted without reservations by the Misnah, Talmud, Mishneh Torah, Sefer Ha-Turim, Shulchan Aruch, and in other Jewish law sources including the verdicts of the rabbinical courts of Israel."

LEE E. TEITELBAUM, *FAMILY HISTORY AND FAMILY LAW*

1985 Wis. L. Rev. 1135, 1144-1145, 1174-1178

[The social history of the nineteenth- and twentieth-century American family] is developmental, moving from an hierarchically ordered household closely integrated with the community towards an egalitarian, companionate family sharply separated from the public world. The trend is not so much toward a nuclear as an enucleated family. . . .

. . . "[P]rivacy" for the household is often given an objective meaning. . . . The meaning given to privacy . . . is the familiar one of autonomy or freedom from governmental control. A clear statement of this association has been provided by Judith Stiehm:

> In this country, intrafamily relations are a private rather than a governmental concern. The state does establish a legal basis for the family's existence, but this defining function is exercised principally when families are either being founded, as in marriage or adoption, or dissolved, as in divorce or death. Even then, the state's role is minimal unless property is involved. The government is only too happy to avoid having either to forbid or to require particular interpersonal behavior.

Judith Stiehm, Government and the Family: Justice and Acceptance, in Changing Images of the Family 361, 362 (V. Tufte & B. Myerhoff eds., 1979).

Both the notion of family privacy and its meaning of autonomy or freedom from governmental concern are used in legal discussions as well. . . . Generally, the notion of family privacy includes two situations: those in which courts decline to intervene to resolve intra-familial disputes for prudential reasons and those in which they say that law may not properly regulate certain aspects of family relationships. The most familiar illustration of the first situation is the reluctance of courts to order the financial and personal arrangements of spouses. Where the marriage is "intact," meaning that proceedings for separation or divorce have not been instituted, courts traditionally have refused to enter support decrees unless gross and dangerous neglect is proved. . . .

. . . When courts refuse to resolve intra-spousal financial disputes, that decision is founded on the principle of family autonomy. . . . However, the practical consequence of many, if not all, of these decisions is to confer or ratify the power of one family member over others. . . . Certainly Mrs. McGuire was not "free to work out her own role" in the marriage if Mr. McGuire had all the money. She could not get the new cloth coat she wanted, or new linoleum for the kitchen, or a warm heater for their old car. Her only choice lay without the marriage, in seeking a judicial separation or divorce. When the majority in McGuire say that "the living standards of the family are a matter of concern to the household," they mean only that they propose to leave the parties where they are. The "household" does not make decisions about living standards, unless that is informally agreed. Otherwise, the husband will make those decisions. . . .

[Analysis that assumes that the state does not intervene in the family unit] depends on a particular conceptualization of law. We mean by intervention public activity through proscriptive and prescriptive rules: "Thou shalt not steal" or "Thou shalt support thy wife." Commands of these kinds are sharply distinguished from facilitative rules and from silence or abstention, which are considered instances of nonregulation. A rule that says "Fathers must leave at least one-third of their wealth to their children at death" is considered different in kind from one that says "Any testamentary provision made in a certain form will be enforced." Similarly, a rule reciting that "Husbands shall adequately support their wives" is different, not only in its content but in its nature, from one that says,

"The state will not resolve financial disputes between spouses." The first of these pairs of rules would be considered an instance of intervention because each manifestly limits individual choice; the second of these pairs would ordinarily be regarded as facilitating or conveying autonomy. . . .

The entity approach . . . hides decisions about family relationships that are worth examining. Although only prescriptive and proscriptive rules are taken as cases of intervention, it is surely true that all forms of societal behavior — including facilitative rules and silence — involve policy choices. Moreover, the choice of strategies is not simply between domination (intervention) and freedom (nonintervention), but between two kinds of authority. When government acts by commands, it thereby authorizes an exercise of public authority. . . .

Facilitative rules and silence, by contrast, leave people to their own strengths and thereby authorize personal authority. If bargains will always be enforced, the making of that bargain reflects only the power, skill, and knowledge of the parties. When the parties are in fact unequal in these characteristics, the weaker party is subject to the domination of the stronger. That domination is personal rather than public; law only ratifies the naturally existing or socially created inequalities which have led to the victory of one over the other.

By regarding the family as an entity which is left free by governmental silence, the effects of a policy permitting personal domination are obscured. When . . . Mrs. McGuire is left to her own resources in dealing with her husband, she is subject to his personal authority in seeking a car or a coat. No rules require that he treat her as other husbands treat their wives, or as he treated a former wife, had he married previously. It does not in principle matter that her neighbors have bought cars, coats, or an electric range for their wives. . . . Because we focus on "the family" rather than on Mrs. McGuire, however, her condition becomes invisible.

BRUCE C. HAFEN, *THE FAMILY AS AN ENTITY*

22 U.C. Davis L. Rev. 865, 909, 912 (1989)

We might help to restore a more familistic perspective on family relationships by regarding the family as a structurally significant and legally meaningful entity that affects both individual and social interests. . . .

This notion of entity is nothing more mysterious than what most Americans still assume (even if partly as myth) is "the dominant American ideal" — namely, relationships based upon marriage and kinship in which legal, biological, and social expectations convey long-term, normative, familistic assumptions. Those who accept membership in such an entity implicitly accept in a general — even if, in many ways, unenforceable — sense the familistic model's characteristics. . . .

Emphasizing the family's "internal" institutional autonomy may leave some deserving individuals without legal recourse for unequal treatment or other wrongs (short of actual abuse) that they may suffer within the sphere of family privacy. However, unless we to some degree assume that risk, constant legal intervention (or the threat of it) will destroy the continuity that is critically necessary for meaningful, ongoing relationships and developmental nurturing. Even the "direct, prolonged conflict" that may characterize some family continuity may play a significant role in "forging communal bonds." . . .

Moreover, when we increase state intervention in an ongoing family to protect the autonomy of some family members against others, we may be simply exchanging one threat to autonomy for another. We must then ask which threat is worse — the state or other family members? In cases of serious spousal or child abuse, the threat from within the family is obviously worse. Over the long run, however, liberal thought has usually, and accurately, perceived the state as a more frightening enemy of personal liberty.

NOTES AND QUESTIONS

1. During the 34 years of the marriage before Mrs. McGuire brought suit, she and her children paid for the things that she needed that Mr. McGuire did not provide. Was she not entitled to support from him then? A number of cases say that a married woman was entitled to support even when she had earnings or property of her own or when her children provided her with funds. *See* Pezas v. Pezas, 201 A.2d 192 (Conn. 1964); Ewell v. State, 114 A.2d 66 (Md. 1955); Ulrich v. State, 59 A.2d 460 (Del. 1948).

2. Mrs. McGuire relied on the earlier decision in Earle v. Earle to support her claim. How did the court distinguish that case? Why did the difference matter?

3. If you had represented Mrs. McGuire after this decision, what would you have advised her to do if she still wanted to get Mr. McGuire to loosen his purse strings? Remember that in Nebraska in the 1950s, divorce was granted only upon proof of fault.

4. Courts in North Carolina and South Carolina have recently held that courts should not entertain suits in which a wife who is living with her husband seeks spousal support because the separate maintenance statutes assume that the parties are in fact living separately. Bauman-Chacon v. Baumann, 710 S.E.2d 431 (N.C. App. 2011); Theisen v. Theisen, 716 S.E.2d 271 (S.C. 2011). In addition, the *Theisen* court explained that it was concerned about

> the relative ease with which parties might otherwise bring their minor disputes into the spotlight of the family court, thereby working irreparable damage to the family unit. The potential for unnecessary litigation will work more harm to a marriage than the requirement that a spouse's discontent with the marriage ordinarily must be sufficient for him or her to leave the marital home prior to receiving separate maintenance.

716 S.E.2d at 279. The dissent responded:

> In my opinion, public policy does not require parties live in separate residences in order to bring a separate maintenance and support suit. Instead, I would allow such a suit where the parties no longer have a "romantic" relationship. We allow a divorce action to be brought where the parties share a residence, *Watson, supra,* and have allowed a separate maintenance and support suit under the same circumstances. *Murray, supra.* Both *Watson* and *Murray* recognize the hardship placed on a parent

in a custody situation if the parent must leave the home in order to commence marital litigation. In a similar vein, public policy should recognize that financial impossibility may prevent a spouse from establishing a separate residence prior to receiving court-ordered support. We should not deny access to the family court to a party who must, of financial necessity, remain in the marital abode.

716 S.E.2d at 278. How would a court determine whether the parties no longer have a "romantic relationship"?

SHARPE FURNITURE, INC. V. BUCKSTAFF

299 N.W.2d 219 (Wis. 1980)

BEILFUSS, C.J. This controversy centers around the purchase of a sofa from Sharpe Furniture, Inc. (Sharpe). The purchase was made by Karen Buckstaff on August 15, 1973. On that date, Mrs. Buckstaff signed in her own name a special order for a "Henredon 6800 Sofa." Under the terms of the order she was to pay $621.50 within 60 days after the item was received from the factory. Interest at a rate of 1.5 percent per month was charged on the unpaid balance after that 60-day period. No representations were made to Sharpe at the time of the purchase that Mrs. Buckstaff was acting on behalf of her husband in purchasing the furniture. Indeed, John Buckstaff had previously written to the local credit bureau service to advise that office that he would not be responsible for any credit extended to his wife.

The Henredon sofa was received from the factory and delivered to the residence of the defendants on February 8, 1974. This piece of furniture has been a part of the Buckstaff home ever since its delivery. Despite this fact, neither John Buckstaff nor his wife have tendered payment for the sofa.

On November 20, 1975, Sharpe commenced this action against both Buckstaffs. The parties agreed to allow the trial court to decide the dispute on the basis of the undisputed facts as they appeared in the trial memoranda submitted by counsel. In addition to the facts already stated above, the informal stipulation of the parties reveals that John Buckstaff, Jr., is the president of Buckstaff Company of Oshkosh, Wisconsin. Mrs. Buckstaff is a housewife. Mr. Buckstaff earns a substantial income and the Buckstaff family is one of social and economic prominence in the Oshkosh area. It was further set forth that Mr. Buckstaff has always provided his wife with the necessaries of life and has never failed or refused to provide his wife with items which could be considered necessaries.

On the basis of these facts, the trial court found that Karen Buckstaff was liable on her contract and that John Buckstaff was also liable for the amount due on the sofa under the common law doctrine of necessaries. . . .

There are two issues which we must consider in reviewing the decision of the court of appeals:

1. Whether, under the common law doctrine of necessaries and in the absence of any contractual obligation on his part, a husband may be held liable for sums due as payment for necessary items purchased on credit by his wife.

2. Whether, in an action for recovery of the value of necessaries supplied on credit to a wife, it is essential for the plaintiff-creditor to prove either that the

husband has failed, refused or neglected to provide the items which have been supplied by the plaintiff-creditor or that the items supplied were reasonably needed by the wife or the family.

Before proceeding to a discussion of the merits of this case, we examine the substance of the doctrine of necessaries.

The Wisconsin Supreme Court restated the common law rule of necessaries early on in the history of the jurisprudence of this state. In 1871, in the case of Warner and Ryan v. Heiden, 28 Wis. 517, 519 (1871), the court wrote:

> The husband is under legal obligations to support his wife, and nothing but wrongful conduct on her part can free him from such obligation. If he fails to provide her with suitable and proper necessaries, any third person who does provide her therewith, may maintain an action against him for the same. 1 Bishop on Mar. and Div., sec. 553. The same learned author, in the next section (sec. 554), thus defines what are necessaries which the husband is bound to furnish to his wife: "And, in general, we may say, that necessaries are such articles of food, or apparel, or medicine, or such medical attendance and nursing, or such provided means of locomotion, or provided habitation and furniture, *or such provision for her protection in society*, and the like, as the husband, considering his ability and standing, ought to furnish to his wife for her sustenance, and the preservation of her health and comfort."

This doctrine traditionally required the creditor to show that he supplied to the wife an item that was, in fact, a necessary and that the defendant had previously failed or refused to provide his wife with this item. . . . When such a showing was made, the creditor was entitled to recovery as against the husband despite the fact that the husband had not contractually bound himself by his own act or by the act of an agent. The doctrine of necessaries is not imposed by the law of agency. This duty is placed upon a husband by virtue of the legal relationship of marriage. It arises as an obligation placed on him as a matter of public policy.

The appellant challenges the continued vitality of this common law rule. Mr. Buckstaff charges that the necessaries doctrine conflicts with contemporary trends toward equality of the sexes and a sex neutral society. . . .

It is true that the necessaries rule has been justified in the past on the basis of a social view of the married woman as a person without legal capacity. However, the nature of the woman's obligations under the necessary rule in relation to the obligation of her husband is not at issue here. That question has been treated in our decision in Estate of Stromsted, ____ Wis. 2d ____, 299 N.W.2d 226 (1980), wherein we concluded the husband was primarily liable for necessities and the wife secondarily liable. The question presented in this case involves a consideration of the nature of the husband's obligation. We must decide whether such a liability imposed upon the husband furthers a proper purpose in contemporary society.

We are of the opinion that the doctrine of necessaries serves a legitimate and proper purpose in our system of common law. The heart of this common law rule is a concern for the support and the sustenance of the family and the individual members thereof. The sustenance of the family unit is accorded a high order of importance in the scheme of Wisconsin law. . . . The necessaries rule encourages the extension of credit to those who in an individual capacity may not have the ability to make these basic purchases. In this manner it facilitates the support of the family unit and its function is in harmony with the purposes behind the support laws of this state. The rule retains a viable role in modern society. . . .

We conclude that when an item or service is obtained for the benefit of the family which is necessary and no payment for that item or service has been made, the elements of an action for an implied-in-law contract exist and the husband is primarily liable. . . .

Mr. Buckstaff's second argument is that, as a matter of law, he is not liable for the necessaries purchased by his wife because Sharpe did not plead or prove that he as a husband failed, refused or neglected to provide a sofa for his wife. It is also argued that liability cannot be found in the face of the parties' stipulation which states that Mr. Buckstaff has always provided his wife with the necessaries of life and has never failed or refused to provide her with items which would constitute necessaries. . . .

In the case of Eder v. Grifka, 149 Wis. 606, 136 N.W. 154 (1912), it was held that, besides demonstrating that necessaries were furnished by the creditor to the defendant's spouse, a plaintiff-creditor must also plead and prove that the defendant wilfully refused to provide the necessaries for his wife. . . .

The merchant's burden of proof was modified by the decision in Simpson Garment Co. v. Schultz, 182 Wis. 506, 196 N.W. 783 (1924). . . .

The *Simpson Garment Company* rule required only that the creditor show that the item was "reasonably needed" by the wife or family, and not that the husband wilfully refused to provide his wife with the necessary item as suggested by Eder v. Grifka, supra. . . .

Buckstaff's first argument, that the court's judgment of liability is invalid in the absence of a finding of refusal or neglect by a husband, must be rejected. Under *Simpson Garment Company*, the refusal or neglect of the husband is not an element essential to recovery by the creditor. Mr. Buckstaff's second contention is that the sofa should not be considered a necessary in view of the stipulation that he as a husband provided his wife with all necessaries. Whether or not, as a general matter, a man provides his wife with necessaries is irrelevant to a determination of whether a particular item is reasonably needed under the *Simpson Garment Company* rule. . . .

We have reviewed the stipulation of the parties in this matter and we are satisfied that ample evidence supported the trial court's conclusion that the Henredon sofa was a legally necessary item. The Buckstaffs are a prominent family and their socio-economic standing justifies a finding that the sofa at issue here was a suitable and proper item for their household. With reference to the element of reasonable need, we note that the sofa has been in use in the Buckstaff home since its delivery. Such continued use gives rise to an inference of reasonable need. This inference is not rebutted by the stipulation stating that Mr. Buckstaff provided his wife with "all necessaries." . . .

The decision of the court of appeals is affirmed.

ABRAHAMSON, J. (concurring). I join the court in retaining the doctrine of necessaries and imposing liability on Mr. Buckstaff for the cost of the sofa. I do not agree, however, with that portion of the opinion in which the court adopts a rule placing primary liability on the husband to the creditor for necessaries supplied to the family. . . .

. . . [I]f the common law doctrine of necessaries is to survive as a rule of law it must be modified in accordance with the developing laws recognizing equal rights and responsibilities of both marital partners and the changes in the economic and social conditions of society. The common law doctrine of necessaries was premised on the legal disability of the married woman and on the husband's duty to support. Today, the married woman is free to contract, and the duty of support rests not on the husband alone but on both the husband and wife. While these changes in the law will require an alteration of the doctrine of necessaries, I would leave that alteration to a case in which the application of the common law doctrine conflicts with the married women statutes and the support statutes. This is not the case.

I believe the court has erred in adopting a flat, general rule which places primary liability on the husband to the creditor who supplies necessaries to the family. In my opinion, the rule suffers from two infirmities: First, the rule is not in harmony with the legislatively established public policy of this state, which is to impose the obligation to support on both the husband and wife on the basis of their respective economic resources and not on one spouse or the other on the basis of gender. Second, the rule discriminates against men and thus contravenes the state and federal constitutional guarantees of equal protection of law. . . .

I am persuaded that the majority rule which effects an unequal distribution of economic benefits and burdens on the basis of gender cannot pass muster under the federal and Wisconsin constitutions. Craig v. Boren, 429 U.S. 190 (1977); Weinberger v. Wiesenfeld, 420 U.S. 636 (1975).

The New Jersey Supreme Court similarly concluded that a rule imposing liability for necessaries solely on the husband was unconstitutional under the federal and state constitutions, reasoning as follows:

> Under the [common law] rule, even a husband who is economically dependent on his wife would be liable for the necessary expenses of both spouses, while the wife would not be liable for either. In perpetuating additional benefits for a wife when the benefits may not be needed, the rule runs afoul of the equal protection clause. *Orr*, supra, 440 U.S. at 282-283.
>
> We recognize that in many instances the present rule correctly operates to favor a needy wife. Even wives who have entered the work force generally earn substantially less than their husbands. . . . However, that is an insufficient reason to retain a gender based classification that denigrates the efforts of women who contribute to the finances of their families and denies equal protection to husbands. Weinberger v. Weisenfeld, supra, 420 U.S. at 645.

JOHN KENNETH GALBRAITH, *ECONOMICS AND THE PUBLIC PURPOSE*

31-37 (1973)

In preindustrial societies women were accorded virtue, their procreative capacities apart, for their efficiency in agricultural labor or cottage manufacture or, in the higher strata of society, for their intellectual, decorative, sexual or other entertainment value. Industrialization eliminated the need for women in such cottage employments as spinning, weaving or the manufacture of apparel. . . . Meanwhile rising standards of popular consumption, combined with the disappearance of the menial personal servant, created an urgent need for labor to administer and otherwise manage consumption. In consequence a new social virtue came to attach to household management — the intelligent shopping for goods, their preparation, use and maintenance and the care and maintenance of the dwelling and other possessions. The virtuous woman became the good housekeeper or, more comprehensively, the good homemaker. . . .

The conversion of women into a crypto-servant class was an economic accomplishment of the first importance. . . . The value of services of housewives has been calculated, somewhat impressionistically, at roughly one fourth of total Gross National Product. . . . If it were not for this service, all forms of household consumption would be limited by the time required to manage such consumption — to select, transport, prepare, repair, maintain, clean, service, store, protect and otherwise perform the tasks that are associated with the consumption of goods. . . .

As just noted, the labor of women to facilitate consumption is not valued in national income or product. This is of some importance for its disguise; what is not counted is often not noticed. The neoclassical model has, however, a much more sophisticated disguise for the role of women. That is the household. . . .

. . . Though a household includes several individuals — husband, wife, offspring, sometimes relatives or parents — with differing needs, tastes and preferences, all neoclassical theory holds it to be the same as an individual. Individual and household choices are, for all practical purposes, interchangeable.

The household having been made identical with the individual, it then distributes its income to various uses so that satisfactions are roughly equal at the margin. This, as observed, is the optimal state of enjoyment, the neoclassical consumer equilibrium. An obvious problem arises as to whose satisfactions are equated at the margin — those of the husband, the wife, the children with some allowance for age or the resident relatives, if any. But on this all accepted theory is silent. Between husband and wife there is evidently a compromise which accords with the more idyllic conception of the sound marriage. . . .

In fact, the modern household does not allow expression of individual personality and preference. It requires extensive subordination of preference by one member or another. The notion that economic society requires something approaching half of its adult members to accept subordinate status is not easily . . . reconciled with a system of social thought which not only esteems the individual but acclaims his or her power. So neoclassical economics resolves the problem by burying the subordination of the individual within the household, the inner relationships of which it ignores. Then it recreates the household as an individual consumer. There the matter remains. The economist does not invade the privacy of the household.

The common reality is that the modern household involves a simple but highly important division of labor. With the receipt of the income, in the usual case, goes the *basic* authority over its use. This usually lies with the male. Some of this authority is taken for granted. The place where the family lives depends overwhelmingly on the convenience or necessity of the member who makes the income. And both the level and nature or style of expenditure are also extensively influenced by its source — by whether the recipient is a business executive, lawyer, artist, accountant, civil servant, artisan, assembly-line worker or professor. More important, in a society which sets store by pecuniary achievement, a natural authority resides with the person who earns the money. This entitles him to be called the *head* of the family.

The administration of the consumption resides with the woman. This involves much choice as to purchases. . . . The conventional wisdom celebrates this power; it is women who hold the purse strings. In fact this is normally the power to implement decisions, not to make them. Action, within the larger strategic framework, is established by the man. . . .

Thomas Oldham, *Management of the Community Estate During an Intact Marriage*

56 Law & Contemp. Probs. 99, 101-104 (Spring 1993)

Factors other than legal rules affect how spouses make decisions about the expenditure of marital funds. For example, a study of management decisions conducted two decades ago in England (a common law jurisdiction where, at least according to the law, a spouse has no vested property right in the other's accumulations during marriage) found that more than fifty percent of all couples took title to their houses jointly. About forty percent of the couples had joint bank accounts.

A 1983 English study by Jan Pahl of management decisions by spouses found that fifty-six percent of the couples studied pooled their funds. [J. Pahl, Money and Marriage (1989).] Additionally, in fourteen percent of the marriages, the wife had by spousal agreement sole management over marital funds, while in none of the marriages did the spouses agree that the husband alone should make all management decisions regarding marital funds. So, although the husbands in the sample generally made much more money than their spouses, and were therefore the legal owners and managers of that money, by private agreement the wife could manage funds earned by the husband in seventy percent of the marriages.

These two studies suggest that factors other than legal rules have a significant effect upon how spouses manage their money. . . .

Even if one accepts that a number of factors other than legal rules affect how spouses manage marital funds, this does not render legal rules irrelevant. . . . Pahl attempted to learn more about how the couples made management decisions. She discovered that the manner in which the spouses said they managed their money did not accurately depict who really controlled important decisions. She found that in all marriages studied, even in those where the spouses pooled resources, one spouse controlled financial decisions. She therefore categorized the spouses into four types: marital resources controlled by the wife alone; marital resources controlled by the husband alone; pooled resources controlled by the wife; and pooled resources controlled by the husband.

. . . [W]hen a wife earned less than thirty percent of what her husband earned, she controlled the household's finances thirty-one percent of the time. When she earned over thirty percent of what her husband earned, however, she had financial control sixty-four percent of the time. This strongly suggests that if the wife works and contributes a significant amount to the household budget, it is much more likely that she will have financial control.

The study does not establish what causes this increased level of control by the working wives. It could be attributed to Britain's legal rule that each wife "owns" those wages that she contributes to the household. Alternatively, the employment could raise her self-esteem so that she feels more able or entitled to participate in management of household funds. Also, women who make a substantial wage might be members of a group who are generally more assertive than others. It is reasonable to conclude from Pahl's study that, although legal rules may have some effect upon the manner in which spouses manage marital funds, it is likely that management patterns selected by spouses for their marriages can be substantially affected by considerations unrelated to legal rules.

NOTES AND QUESTIONS

1. Discussions of McGuire v. McGuire frequently observe that Mrs. McGuire could have pledged her husband's credit to purchase necessaries, *e.g.*, Bruce C. Hafen, The Family as an Entity, 22 U.C. Davis L. Rev. 865 (1989). How useful is the power to pledge a husband's credit for the wife who does not possess independent means? Consider the situation from the creditor's point of view. If the husband did not pay, what would the creditor have to prove to recover from him? Consider also that it was traditionally a defense to an action for necessaries that the wife had forfeited her right to support by adultery or abandonment of her husband. *See* Homer H. Clark, Jr., The Law of Domestic Relations in the United States 252-257 (2d ed. 1988).

2. The obligation to supply necessaries is sometimes said to rest on a theory that the wife acts as the husband's agent for the purchase of such items. That theory has the appeal of preserving a notion of family unity. Is *Buckstaff* consistent with such a theory? If the Buckstaffs had discussed the purchase of the sofa, had disagreed, and Mr. Buckstaff had then told Sharpe Furniture not to sell the sofa to his wife, would he be liable if the store nonetheless sold the sofa to Mrs. Buckstaff?

The court describes the furniture as a "suitable and proper item for their household." Did the Buckstaff "household" make this purchase? Is the "household" sued for the price in this case? Does the "household" now own the sofa? Is a "household" a legal entity for any purpose?

3. The Henredon sofa cost Mr. Buckstaff $621.50 (in 1973 dollars). On what basis does the court decide that this, rather than a less expensive piece of furniture, is a suitable and proper item for their household? Could a fur coat be a "necessary"? *See* Gimbel Bros., Inc. v. Pinto, 145 A.2d 865 (Pa. Super. 1958). On the other hand, would Mr. McGuire likely be required to pay for a $621.50 sofa if Mrs. McGuire charged it?

After reading *McGuire*, how would one describe the level of support to which a married woman who works only in the home is entitled? What level does *Buckstaff* suppose? How does one explain the difference?

4. The husband's responsibility for necessaries is explained in *Buckstaff* and most other cases as a device for enforcing his duty of support. Why is the wife privileged to undertake piecemeal steps to ensure her level of support but not to bring a support action to secure that right through a single, overall remedy? Is one or the other strategy more respectful of "family autonomy"?

5. There are at least four schemes of ordering the liability of spouses for "necessaries" purchased by one of them. At common law, of course, the husband was liable for both his own debts and those incurred by his wife: a perhaps inevitable result having regard to his virtually plenary control over the wife's wealth during the marriage. A second approach is that developed in Estate of Stromsted, 299 N.W.2d 226 (Wis. 1980), and employed in *Buckstaff*: The husband is primarily liable for necessaries and the wife only secondarily responsible. Accordingly, a creditor must first seek satisfaction from the husband and can go against the wife only if the husband's assets are inadequate. A third possibility is to impose joint and several liability, allowing the creditor to choose either or both spouses as the target(s) for collection. *See* Cooke v. Adams, 183 So. 2d 925 (Miss. 1966). The fourth is to hold that the creditor should seek to recover first against the spouse incurring the obligation, making the other secondarily liable. This is the result reached in Jersey Shore Medical Center v. Baum, 417 A.2d 1003 (N.J. 1980), discussed by Justice Abrahamson.

6. For further discussion, *see* Marie T. Reilly, In Good Times and in Debt: The Evolution of Marital Agency and the Meaning of Marriage, 87 Neb. L. Rev. 373 (2008).

"NECESSARIES" AND NEW PROPERTY

The obligation to provide necessaries is not always invoked only in the comfortable middle-class setting of *Buckstaff* or even in the less comfortable setting of *McGuire*. It can also arise in connection with the "new property."

Consider, for example, the situation of a person needing nursing home care. Medicare, a federal program available to everyone 65 or older who is eligible for Social Security benefits (and to certain others on Social Security disability), is regarded as an insurance program on which one may draw as a matter of right. Medicare coverage does not, however, cover the costs of custodial care for a disabled person.

A person without enough money to pay for needed nursing home care may turn to Medicaid, a joint federal and state program that provides medical assistance to the poor. Because Medicaid is a welfare program for the poor, persons with property or income above certain levels do not qualify. For those who do qualify, most of their income must be used to pay for care, and Medicaid picks up the remaining cost. Determining the income of a married applicant brings into play spousal support issues.

If the institutionalized spouse is the primary income producer, federal law provides that the community spouse is entitled to a portion of that income for his or her living expenses. The amount of the community spouse's living allowance is determined by a standardized formula that is updated annually, and all the rest of the institutionalized spouse's income goes toward his or her care. The amount of the community spouse's allowance is low enough that the spouse's standard of living may decline significantly when his or her mate goes into the nursing home. Generally, however, states exempt from the eligibility calculation portions of the institutionalized spouse's income that must be paid to support dependents pursuant to a court order. This rule clearly applies to court orders that preexist the application for Medicaid. What is not so clear is whether the community spouse can circumvent the income rules discussed above by getting a court order for a higher level of support than the rules allow.

The New York Court of Appeals held in In the Matter of Gomprecht, 652 N.E.2d 936 (N.Y. 1995), that if the community spouse initiates an action in state court for support after the institutionalized spouse has applied for Medicaid, the court must apply the Medicaid rule that support above the formula amount is ordered only if the community spouse proves exceptional circumstances resulting in financial duress. In *Gomprecht*, an institutionalized husband had income of $5721.31 per month. His wife, who had two residences assessed at more than $430,000, was entitled to a standard community spouse allowance of only $306.71 from her husband's income. She sought an increase in order to maintain her standard of living before her husband was institutionalized. The trial and intermediate appellate courts held that Family Court was not limited by the Medicaid rules and awarded her an increased allowance of $3339.26. The Court of Appeals reversed, saying that the purpose of the federal provisions for the community spouse is to "end the pauperization of the community spouse by assuring that the community spouse has a sufficient — but not excessive — amount of income and resources available." On the facts of the case, the court concluded that allowing the wife such a large portion of her husband's income was inconsistent with the purposes of the federal act.

In contrast, the New Jersey intermediate appellate court has held that state courts have more discretion under domestic relations law to enter an order providing for the community spouse. M.E.F. v. A.B.F., 925 A.2d 12 (N.J. Super. 2007).

Now consider the situation in which the community spouse has most of the income. To what extent is he or she obligated to contribute that income to pay for nursing home care of the institutionalized spouse? Since 1988, federal law has said that the community spouse has no obligation; only the institutionalized spouse's income is considered in determining Medicaid eligibility. However, this is a special rule applicable only to nursing home cases. In other situations, if one spouse applies for Medicaid, the income of the other is deemed to be available to the applicant, and eligibility is determined on the basis of the combined income of the spouses. In Schweiker v. Gray Panthers, 453 U.S. 34 (1981), the Supreme Court upheld spousal income deeming rules as consistent with the statutory language and with legislative history indicating a congressional intent to hold spouses responsible for each other's support.

NOTES AND QUESTIONS

1. In what ways do the Medicaid rules regarding spousal support obligations differ from those in *McGuire* and *Buckstaff*? What might explain the difference in approaches?

2. What is the theory behind "deeming" the income of one spouse to be available to the other? Is it simply an application of the general rule that a creditor

may recover against one spouse for the necessaries supplied to the other? Are the positions of the creditor and the state Medicaid administrator alike?

3. Federal and state statutes also allow for setting aside a portion of an institutionalized person's income to support the person's or the person's spouse's minor child, dependent child, dependent parent, or dependent sibling if more than half of the needs of the child, parent, or sibling have been provided by the institutionalized person or the person's spouse. 42 U.S.C. § 1396r-5(d)(1)(C). In another New York case, In the Matter of Schachner, 648 N.E.2d 1321 (N.Y. 1995), a community spouse claimed an increase in his allowance from his institutionalized wife's income to pay for their daughter's education in a private high school and in college. The Court of Appeals concluded that under the governing statutes a community spouse is entitled to an increased allowance only for true financial hardships caused by circumstances over which the spouse has no control, and that voluntary support of a child in private school does not fall into this category.

4. For a further explanation and critique of Medicaid rules affecting spousal property and support rights and estate planning techniques, *see* Julia Belian, Medicaid, Elective Shares, and the Ghosts of Tenures Past, 38 Creighton L. Rev. 1111 (2005).

4.   *Constitutional Limits on Gender-Based Classifications*

PROBLEM

Your office represents Dr. Willa Sanchez, an oral surgeon. She has recently treated Ms. Alicia Duran, whom she has also known socially for some time. Dr. Sanchez has billed Ms. Duran $2300 for this surgery but would prefer to collect from Ms. Duran's husband, Roberto, both because she would like to accommodate Ms. Duran's desire that she do so and because she thinks Mr. Duran ought to pay the bill.

Interviews with Dr. Sanchez and Ms. Duran, who is cooperative, reveal the following facts. Ms. Duran has been married to Roberto for five years. Before and during her marriage, Ms. Duran has been employed as a caseworker in the state Department of Human Services, an occupation she enjoys and thinks worthwhile, and in which she has had considerable success. She is well on her way to achieving a Master's of Social Work degree, which is the standard professional credential for personnel occupying supervisory positions in the department. Reviews of her performance to this point suggest that she will achieve a promotion when or soon after she receives this degree.

Mr. Duran is a contractor and a native of Florida. The construction business has been in decline in your state for the last several years, and no substantial improvement is in sight. Mr. Duran has essentially given up — in his own words, "no more" — and decided to return to Florida, where construction continues to boom. Ms. Duran has repeatedly urged him to remain here and equally often declares that she had no desire to leave her job and go to Florida.

Three months ago, Mr. Duran took the car and most of their liquid assets with him to Fort Lauderdale. His departure followed an argument during which he insisted that Alicia go with him and her refusal to do so. Ms. Duran has, since her husband's departure, been able to manage on her salary except for the expenses associated with oral surgery.

She notified Mr. Duran of this bill, and he has refused to pay it while repeating his insistence that she join him in Florida. He has also consulted a lawyer in Florida — not for purposes of divorce, which is for religious reasons unacceptable to both him and Ms. Duran — but in order to cut off any financial obligations he may have as long as she remains away from him.

Your research has disclosed the statutory provisions set out immediately below. Please prepare a memorandum analyzing the legal possibility of collecting the debt from Mr. Duran, assuming that he will (as seems likely) return to the state at least temporarily. Your analysis should incorporate the materials considered to this point, as well as the following materials.

a. Relevant Statutes

Section 1. Both wives and husbands have the duty to support each other during marriage. However, when either party to a marriage incurs a debt for purchase of an item or service that is reasonably necessary to maintenance of the household, the husband shall be primarily liable for that debt and the wife shall be secondarily liable for that debt.

Section 2. Notwithstanding the provisions of Section 1, there shall be no liability for debts incurred by a spouse if the spouse incurring the debt has been given adequate resources to purchase the item or service, nor shall a husband be liable for the debts incurred by his wife if she has abandoned the marital home.

Section 3. If the parties cannot agree upon the location of the marital home, the spouse earning the most money shall determine its location.

b. Additional Materials Concerning Liability for Necessaries

MARSHFIELD CLINIC V. DISCHER, 314 N.W.2d 326, 329-331 (Wis. 1982): While the necessaries doctrine remains important in modern society, it is clear from *Stromsted* that the old common law rule, whereby the husband was solely responsible for his family's necessaries, is out of touch with the changing role of women. Thus, *Stromsted* held that wives share with their husbands the legal duty of support of the family. But it is also inappropriate to impose this obligation in the form of joint and several liability on the husband and the wife. Although many more married women are now working than were in the past, they still contribute less to the typical family income than do their husbands.

We do not view [the *Stromsted*] rule as one which "denigrates the efforts of women who contribute to the finances of their families." Nor do we feel that it is paternalistic or based on an "archaic and overbroad generalization." Schlesinger v. Ballard, 419 U.S. 498, 508 (1975). Rather, we feel that this rule accurately reflects the position of married women in contemporary society. . . . [D]espite great progress, married women still lag far behind their husbands in earning power. This may be due to any number of reasons, such as: discrimination that still exists in the job market; a socialized tendency for women to choose lower paying jobs; the fact that many married women still do not work outside the home, or at least work only part time. For the purposes of this case, these reasons are irrelevant. What is relevant is the verifiable fact that wives are still far from equal with their husbands in economic resources.

The United States Supreme Court has not upheld classifications based on gender when the classifications ". . . command dissimilar treatment for men and women who are . . . similarly situated." Schlesinger v. Ballard. But when the classification reflects a demonstrable fact that men and women are not similarly situated in a certain respect, then the classification has been upheld.

NORTH OTTAWA COMMUNITY HOSPITAL V. KIEFT, 578 N.W.2d 267 (Mich. 1998): The Michigan Supreme Court struck down the common law necessaries doctrine on equal protection grounds in *Kieft*. The suit was brought by plaintiff hospital against Ms. Kieft for medical services rendered to Mr. Kieft prior to his death. The state Married Women's Property Act (MWPA) found in both statutory and state constitutional provisions declared that a married woman's property was not liable for debts of any other person, including those of her husband. The court concluded that these provisions made it impossible for Michigan courts to extend the common law necessaries doctrine, which imposed liability only on husbands, to make wives liable as well. And if a wife could not be liable for her husband's debts, the common law obligation on husbands was a gender-based classification that could not be justified in modern times and thus offended the equal protection clause:

> [T]he common-law necessaries doctrine imposing the support burden only on a husband could be justified in the past because it was substantially related to the important governmental objective of providing necessary support to dependent wives. However, the contemporary reality of women owning property, working outside the home, and otherwise contributing to their own economic support calls for abrogation of this sex-discriminatory doctrine from early common law.

The court also noted that the legislature might choose to modify the statutory and constitutional provisions of the Michigan MWPA so as to permit enforcement of obligations for necessaries supplied to husbands against the property of wives and to extend the necessaries doctrine to both spouses.

c.   Empirical Data

The median *weekly* earnings of full-time women workers in 2011 were 82 percent of that of men working full-time. Bureau of Labor Statistics, Current Population Survey, Table 39: Median Weekly Earnings of Full-time Wage and Salary Workers by Detailed Occupation and Sex, 2012 (2013). However, the median *annual* income of all full-time women workers was 77 percent that of full-time men workers. Carmen DeNavas-Walt, Bernadette D. Proctor & Jessica

C. Smith, U.S. Census Bureau, Income, Poverty, and Health Insurance Coverage in the United States: 2012 at 7, Tbl. 1 (Current Population Reports, P60-245, 2013). The wage gap increased with age. Women aged 16 to 24 and 25 to 34 earned 92 percent and 93 percent as much as men of the same age. For 45- to 54-year-olds, women earned only 76 percent as much as men. Bureau of Labor Statistics, Highlights of Women's Earnings in 2011 at 1 (Oct. 2012). Proportionately more women work part time than men, 26 percent of all workers compared to 13 percent. Men and women who worked part time earned similar amounts on average. *Id.* at 2 (Oct. 2012). The narrowing of the wage gap is mainly caused by women's rising earnings while men's remained relatively static. Women's wages have risen because they are getting more education, are participating in the labor force more, and are working in better-paying jobs. However, as people move into parenthood, women's earnings continue to fall behind men's, as their careers are much more likely to be interrupted or limited for family-related reasons. Pew Research Social and Demographic Trends, On Pay Gap, Millennial Women Near Parity—For Now (Dec. 11, 2013), available at http://www.pewsocial trends.org/2013/12/11/on-pay-gap-millennial-women-near-parity-for-now/#fn-17876-5.

d.   Constitutional Decisions

CRAIG V. BOREN, 429 U.S. 190, 197-200 (1976): [Oklahoma law prohibited the sale of 3.2 percent beer to males under the age of 21 and to females under the age of 18.] To withstand constitutional challenge, previous cases establish that classifications by gender must serve important governmental objectives and must be substantially related to achievement of those objectives. Thus, in [Reed v. Reed, 404 U.S. 71 (1971),] the objectives of "reducing the workload on probate courts" and "avoiding intrafamily controversy" were deemed of insufficient importance to sustain use of an overt gender criterion in the appointment of administrators of intestate decedents' estates. Decisions following *Reed* similarly have rejected administrative ease and convenience as sufficiently important objectives to justify gender-based classifications. . . . And only two terms ago, Stanton v. Stanton expressly stating that Reed v. Reed was "controlling," held that *Reed* required invalidation of a Utah differential age-of-majority statute, notwithstanding the statute's coincidence with and furtherance of the State's purpose of fostering "old notions" of role typing and preparing boys for their expected performance in the economic and political worlds.

Reed v. Reed has also provided the underpinning for decisions that have invalidated statutes employing gender as an inaccurate proxy for other, more germane bases of classification. Hence, "archaic and overbroad" generalizations concerning the financial position of servicewomen and working women could not justify use of a gender line in determining eligibility for certain governmental entitlements. Similarly, increasingly outdated misconceptions concerning the role of females in the home rather than in the "marketplace and world of ideas" were rejected as loose-fitting characterizations incapable of supporting state statutory schemes that were premised upon their accuracy. . . .

We accept for purposes of discussion the District Court's identification of the objective underlying [the statute] as the enhancement of traffic safety. Clearly, the protection of public health and safety represents an important function of state and local governments. However, appellees' statistics in our view cannot support the conclusion that the gender-based distinction closely serves to achieve that objective and therefore the distinction cannot under *Reed* withstand equal protection challenge. . . .

The most focused and relevant of the statistical surveys, arrests of 18-20-year-olds for alcohol-related driving offenses, exemplifies the ultimate unpersuasiveness of this evidentiary record. Viewed in terms of the correlation between sex and the actual activity that Oklahoma seeks to regulate . . . the statistics establish that .18% of females and 2% of males in that age group were arrested for that offense. While such a disparity is not trivial in a statistical sense, it hardly can form the basis for employment of a gender line as a classifying device. Certainly if maleness is to serve as a proxy for drinking and driving, a correlation of 2% must be considered an unduly tenuous "fit." Indeed, prior cases have consistently rejected the use of sex as a decision making factor even though the statutes in question certainly rested on far more predictive empirical relationships than this.

ORR v. ORR, 440 U.S. 268 (1979): Brennan, J. The question presented is the constitutionality of Alabama alimony statutes which provide that husbands, but not wives, may be required to pay alimony upon divorce. . . .

In authorizing the imposition of alimony obligations on husbands, but not on wives, the Alabama statutory scheme "provides that different treatment be accorded . . . on the basis of . . . sex. The fact that the classification expressly discriminates against men rather than women does not protect it from scrutiny. Craig v. Boren, 429 U.S. 190 (1976). To withstand scrutiny under the Equal Protection Clause, "classifications by gender must serve important governmental objectives and must be substantially related to achievement of those objectives." We shall, therefore, examine the three governmental objectives that might arguably be served by Alabama's statutory scheme.

Appellant views the Alabama alimony statutes as effectively announcing the State's preference for an allocation of family responsibilities under which the wife plays a dependent role, and as seeking for their objective the reinforcement of that model among the State's citizens. . . . We agree, as he urges, that prior cases settle that this purpose cannot sustain the statutes. Stanton v. Stanton, 421 U.S. 7, 10 (1975), held that the "old notion" that "generally it is the man's primary responsibility to provide a home and its essentials," can no longer justify a statute that discriminates on the basis of gender. "No longer is the female destined solely for the home and the rearing of the family, and only the male for the marketplace and the world of ideas. . . ."

The opinion of the Alabama Court of Civil Appeals suggests other purposes that the statute may serve. . . . One is a legislative purpose to provide help for needy spouses, using sex as a proxy for need. The other is a goal of compensating women for past discrimination during marriage, which assertedly has left them unprepared to fend for themselves in the working world following divorce. We concede, of course, that assisting needy spouses is a legitimate and important governmental objective. We have also recognized "[r]eduction of the disparity in economic condition between men and women caused by the long history of discrimination against women . . . as . . . an important governmental objective," Califano v. Webster, 430 U.S., at 317. It only remains, therefore, to determine whether the classification at issue here is "substantially related to achievement of those objectives."

Ordinarily, we would begin the analysis of the "needy spouse" objective by considering whether sex is a sufficiently "accurate proxy," Craig v. Boren, 429 U.S. at 204, for dependency to establish that the gender classification rests "upon some ground of difference having a fair and substantial relation to the object of the legislation. . . . Similarly, we would initially approach the 'compensation' rationale by asking whether women had in fact been significantly discriminated against in the sphere to which the statute applied a sex-based classification, leaving the sexes *not* similarly situated with respect to opportunities in that sphere."

But in this case, even if sex were a reliable proxy for need, and even if the institution of marriage did discriminate against women, these factors still would "not adequately justify the salient features of" Alabama's statutory scheme. Under the statute, individualized hearings at which the parties' relative financial circumstances are considered *already* occur. There is no reason, therefor, to use sex as a proxy for need. . . . In such circumstances, not even an administrative convenience rationale exists to justify operating by generalization or by proxy. Similarly, since individualized hearings can determine which were in fact discriminated against vis-à-vis their husbands, as well as which family units defied the stereotype and left the husband dependent on the wife, Alabama's alleged compensatory purpose may be effectuated without placing burdens solely on husbands. . . . "Thus, the gender-based distinction is gratuitous. . . ."

Legislative classifications which distribute benefits and burdens on the basis of gender carry the inherent risk of reinforcing stereotypes about the "proper place" of women and their need for special protection. Thus, even statutes purportedly designed to compensate for and ameliorate the effects of past discrimination must be carefully tailored. Where, as here, the State's compensatory and ameliorative purposes are as well served by a gender-neutral classification as one that gender classifies and therefore carries with it the baggage of sexual stereotypes, the State cannot be permitted to classify on the basis of sex.

KIRCHBERG V. FEENSTRA, 450 U.S. 455 (1981): See above, page 45.

UNITED STATES V. VIRGINIA, 518 U.S. 515 (1996): The United States sued Virginia Military Academy (VMI) and the state of Virginia, claiming that VMI's exclusively male admissions policy violated the Equal Protection Clause. After the Fourth Circuit reversed a trial court decision in VMI's favor, the state proposed establishment of a parallel program for women. The district court found that this proposal satisfied the equal protection requirement and the Fourth Circuit affirmed, although it recognized that the new school would lack the historical benefit and prestige of VMI.

The United States Supreme Court reversed, holding that any gender-based government action must rest on an "exceedingly persuasive justification." To meet this burden, a state must demonstrate "at least that the classification serves 'important governmental objectives' and that the discriminatory means employed are 'substantially related to the achievement of those objectives.'" The justification must be genuine and not merely pretextual or post hoc, and must not rely on overbroad generalizations about the different talents, abilities, or preferences of men and women. The majority also observed that, under its decisions, sex classifications may be used to compensate women for particular economic disabilities they have suffered, to promote equality of employment opportunity, but not to create or perpetuate the legal, social, and economic inferiority of women.

The categorical exclusion of women from VMI did not meet this test. The state's claim that VMI's "adversative" method of training to instill physical and mental discipline could neither be made available to women nor modified sufficiently without great compromise to VMI's program was not proved and thus rested on overbroad notions concerning the roles and abilities of males and females. The Supreme Court also held that the creation of a separate program for women did not cure the constitutional violation. The violation was the categorical exclusion of women, without regard for their individual capacities, from an educational opportunity provided to men. The proposed alternative institution was different in kind and unequal in tangible and intangible resources, and thus did not provide substantial equality in educational opportunities.

NGUYEN V. IMMIGRATION AND NATURALIZATION SERVICE, 533 U.S. 53 (2001): Under 8 U.S.C. §1409, the right of a child born outside the United States to unmarried parents, only one of whom is an American citizen, to claim American citizenship varies with the gender of the parents. If the citizen parent is the mother, the child is automatically entitled to claim American citizenship, but if the citizen parent is the father, the child may claim American citizenship only if, while the child was younger than 18, the father legitimated the child, the father acknowledged paternity in writing under oath, or the father's paternity was adjudicated by a court. Tuan Anh Nguyen was born in Saigon to an American father and a Vietnamese mother, who were not married. Nguyen came to the United States with his father when he was five years old, became a lawful permanent resident, and was raised by his father. When Nguyen was 22, the INS instituted deportation proceedings against him after he had been convicted of two felonies, and while the immigration proceedings were pending, his father obtained a court order of parentage from a state court, based on DNA testing. Nguyen's claim to citizenship was denied by the INS, based on the statute. In the courts he argued that the statute violated equal protection. The Supreme Court rejected his claim by a 5-4 vote. The majority explained: "The first governmental interest to be served [by the statutory distinction] is the importance of assuring that a biological parent-child relationship exists. . . . Fathers and mothers are not similarly situated with regard to proof of biological parenthood. The imposition of a different set of rules for making that legal determination with respect to fathers and mothers is neither surprising nor troublesome from a constitutional perspective. Section 11409(a)(4)'s provision of three options for a father seeking to establish paternity . . . is designed to ensure an acceptable documentation of paternity. . . .

The second important government interest . . . is the determination to ensure that the child and the citizen parent have some demonstrated opportunity or potential to develop not just a relationship that is recognized, as a formal matter, by the law, but one that consists of the real, everyday ties that provide a connection between child and citizen parent and, in turn, the United States. In the case of a citizen mother and a child born overseas, the opportunity for a meaningful relationship between citizen parent and child inheres in the very event of birth. . . . The same opportunity does not result from the event of birth, as a matter of biological inevitability, in the case of the unwed father. . . .

WASHINGTON V. DAVIS, 426 U.S. 229 (1976): [Respondents, unsuccessful black applicants for positions on the District of Columbia police force, claimed that a test measuring verbal ability, reading comprehension, and vocabulary resulted in a higher percentage of blacks failing the test and therefore unconstitutionally discriminated against them. There was no claim that use of the test was an intentional or purposeful act of discrimination.]

The central purpose of the Equal Protection Clause of the Fourteenth Amendment is the prevention of official misconduct discriminating on the basis of race. [However,] our cases have not embraced the proposition that a law or other official act, without regard to whether it reflects a racially discriminatory purpose, is unconstitutional *solely* because it has a racially disproportionate impact. . . .

This is not to say that the necessary discriminatory racial purpose must be express or appear on the face of the statute, or that a law's disproportionate impact is irrelevant in cases involving Constitution-based claims of racial discrimination. A statute, otherwise neutral on its face, must not be applied so as invidiously to discriminate on the basis of race. . . .

Necessarily, an invidious discriminatory purpose may often be inferred from the totality of the relevant facts, including the fact, if it is true, that the law bears more heavily on one race than another. Nevertheless, we have not held that a law, neutral on its face and serving ends otherwise within the power of government to pursue, is invalid under the Equal Protection Clause simply because it may affect a greater proportion of one race than of another. Disproportionate impact is not irrelevant, but it is not the sole touchstone of an invidious racial discrimination forbidden by the Constitution. Standing alone, it does not trigger the rule, that racial classifications are to be subjected to the strictest scrutiny and are justifiable only by the weightiest of considerations. . . .

VILLAGE OF ARLINGTON HEIGHTS V. METROPOLITAN HOUSING DEVELOPMENT CORP., 429 U.S. 252 (1977): [Respondent sought rezoning of a parcel in Arlington Heights in order to build low- and moderate-income housing. Denial of the request was challenged as racially discriminatory.] Determining whether invidious discriminatory purpose was a motivating factor demands a sensitive inquiry into such circumstantial and direct evidence of intent as may be available. The impact of the official action [may] provide an important starting point. Sometimes a clear pattern, unexplainable on grounds other than race, emerges from the effect of the state action even when the governing legislation appears neutral on its face. The evidentiary inquiry is then relatively easy. But such cases are rare. . . . [I]mpact alone is not determinative, and the Court must look to other evidence.

The historical background of the decision is one evidentiary source, particularly if it reveals a series of official actions taken for invidious purposes.

The specific sequence of events leading up to the challenged decision also may shed some light on the decisionmaker's purposes. [Deviations] from the normal procedural sequence also might afford evidence that improper purposes are playing a role. . . .

[In this case, respondents] simply failed to carry their burden of proving that discriminatory purpose was a motivating factor in the Village's decision.

PERSONNEL ADMINISTRATOR v. FEENEY, 442 U.S. 256 (1979): Stewart, J. This case presents a challenge to the constitutionality of the Massachusetts veterans' preference statute on the ground that it discriminates against women in violation of the Equal Protection Clause of the Fourteenth Amendment. Under [the statute], all veterans who qualify for state civil service positions must be considered for appointment ahead of any qualifying nonveterans. The preference operates overwhelmingly to the advantage of males. . . .

If the impact of this statute could not be plausibly explained on a neutral ground, impact itself would signal that the real classification made by the law was in fact not neutral. But there can be but one answer to the question whether this veteran preference excludes significant numbers of women from preferred state jobs because they are women or because they are nonveterans. Apart from the facts that the definition of "veterans" in the statute has always been neutral as to gender and that Massachusetts has consistently defined veteran status in a way that has been inclusive of women who have served in the military, this is not a law that can plausibly be explained only as a gender-based classification. Indeed, it is not a law that can rationally be explained on that ground. Veteran status is not uniquely male. Although few women benefit from the preference, the nonveteran statute is not substantially all female. . . .

. . . [It] cannot seriously be argued that the Legislature of Massachusetts could have been unaware that most veterans are men. . . . It would thus be disingenuous to say that the adverse consequences of this legislation for women were unintended, in the sense that they were not volitional or in the sense that they were not foreseeable.

"Discriminatory purpose," however, implies more than intent as volition or intent as awareness of consequences. It implies that the decisionmaker [chose] or reaffirmed a particular course of action at least in part "because of," not merely "in spite of," its adverse effects upon an identifiable group. Yet nothing in the record demonstrates that this preference for veterans was originally devised or subsequently reenacted because it would accomplish the collateral goal of keeping women in a stereotypic and predefined place in the Massachusetts Civil Service.

C. DOMESTIC VIOLENCE

Domestic violence presents hard questions of law, history, and social science. Two leading scholars of family violence observe that "[n]o doubt, acts of violence and willful neglect within families have been occurring as long as there have been human families." Lloyd Ohlin & Michael Tonry, Family Violence in Perspective, *in* Family Violence 1 (Lloyd Ohlin & Michael Tonry eds., 1989). Does that mean, however, that there are kinds of conduct that everyone has always regarded as "violence" and "neglect" (and therefore wrongful), or does it mean that the kinds of conduct we now regard as violent and neglectful have always occurred but previously were largely tolerated?

The original view of domestic violence — that men are almost always the perpetrators and women almost always the victims — has been challenged by family violence researchers since the 1970s. Feminist advocates define the core problem as some men's illegitimate assertion of power and control over women, while the family violence group understands the problem as a manifestation of interpersonal conflict. *Compare, e.g.*, Russell P. Dobash et al., The Myth of Sexual Symmetry in Marital Violence, 39 Soc. Probs. 71 (1992), *with* Linda D. Kelly, Disabusing the Definition of Domestic Abuse: How Women Batter Men and the Role of the Feminist State, 30 Fla. St. U. L. Rev. 791 (2003); Richard J. Gelles, The Politics of Research: The Use, Abuse and Misuse of Social Science Data — The Cases of Intimate Partner Violence, 45 Fam. Ct. Rev. 42 (2007). *See also* Richard J. Gelles & Murray A. Straus, Intimate Violence (1988); Jeffrey Fagan & Angela Browne, Violence Between Spouses and Intimates: Physical Aggression Between Women and Men in Intimate Relationships, *in* 3 Understanding and Preventing Violence 115-211 (Albert J. Reiss, Jr. & Jeffrey A. Roth eds., 1994).

Closer examinations of the conflicting data upon which these views are based show that the researchers are studying different populations; those who find a great gender disparity are surveying victims who have become involved with agencies that deal with domestic violence, including shelters, hospitals, the police, and courts, while those who find gender equality are studying the general population. Michael P. Johnson, Conflict and Control: Gender Symmetry and Asymmetry in Domestic Violence, 12 Violence Against Women 1003 (2006). Johnson, a leading proponent of this interpretation, divides domestic violence into four categories: intimate terrorism, where the perpetrator is violent and controlling and in heterosexual couples is almost always a man; violent resistance, where the perpetrator is violent but not controlling and in heterosexual couples is almost always a woman; situational couple violence, in which neither is violent and controlling; and mutual violence, where both are violent and controlling. Situational couple violence is the dominant form reported in general surveys, while intimate terrorism and violent resistance are dominant in surveys done by courts, police, hospitals, and shelters. *See also* Nancy Ver Steegh & Clare Dalton, Report from the Wingspread Conference on Domestic Violence and Family Courts, 46 Fam. Ct. Rev. 454 (2008) (different types of family violence call for different responses, with important variables being the impact on the victim and the intent of the perpetrator; categories include violence used by a perpetrator in the exercise of coercive control over the victim, violent resistance or self-defense, violence driven by conflict, separation-instigated violence, and violence stemming from severe mental illness).

What counts as a "legal response" to violence within families is also unclear. The historian Elizabeth Pleck reports that the "first law against wife abuse anywhere in the Western World was written into a new criminal code of the Massachusetts Bay Colony [during the middle of the seventeenth century]."

Elizabeth Pleck, Criminal Approaches to Family Violence: 1640-1980, *in* Family Violence, above, at 19, 22. However, ecclesiastical courts had long recognized serious physical abuse as a ground for legal separation, allowing the victim to live apart from the abuser while requiring the abuser to continue providing support for her.

Furthermore, an event occurring in real life must first be discovered, and the observer or victim must decide to bring the matter to official attention before the law can respond to it. For domestic violence, which rarely occurs on the street, official notice depends heavily on whether the victims so identify themselves, how seriously they regard the conduct, and whether they wish to become involved in the formal processing of a complaint. Thus, the definition of domestic violence is largely in the control of family members.

Police officers, lawyers, social workers, and judges all have some role in the response to complaints of domestic violence. How they respond will be influenced by both institutional and personal views of the gravity of the behavior, the perceived utility of various kinds of response, and interpretations of the outcomes that will likely be associated with judicial processing of the complaint.

In considering the following materials, it may be useful to consider not only the doctrinal issues that arise in connection with family violence but the associated problems of defining and responding to conduct between spouses and domestic partners at various levels of practical responsibility.

ELIZABETH PLECK, *DOMESTIC TYRANNY: THE MAKING OF SOCIAL POLICY AGAINST FAMILY VIOLENCE FROM COLONIAL TIMES TO THE PRESENT*

7-9 (1987)

The history of reform against family violence . . . , although similar in some respects to many [other social movements in the United States], has had one aspect that necessarily limited it and made it more controversial.

The single most consistent barrier to reform against domestic violence has been the Family Ideal — that is, [related] but nonetheless distinct ideas about family privacy, conjugal and parental rights, and family instability. In this ideal with origins possibly extending into antiquity, the "family" consists of a two-parent household with minor children. Other constellations, such as a mother and her two children, were seen not as a family but as a deviation from it.

One crucial element of the Family Ideal was belief in domestic privacy. . . .

By the 1830s the private sphere came to acquire a deeply emotional texture; it became a refuge from the hard, calculating dealings of the business world. . . . Even more than before, intervention in the family was viewed as problematic, a violation of family intimacy. Although there have been many periods of American history since the 1830s when family privacy has declined in importance, belief in it has persisted to the present day. Modern defenders are likely to argue that the family has a constitutional right to privacy or insist that the home is the only setting where intimacy can flourish, providing meaning, coherence, and stability in personal life.

A second element of the Family Ideal is a belief in conjugal and parental rights. In ancient times, the head of the household had the power to compel obedience from his wife, children, and servants and maintain domestic harmony. . . .

The Romans had the most extensive legal definition of these traditional rights. A Roman wife remained under the guardianship of her husband, who possessed *patria potestas*, including the power to sell his wife and children into slavery or put them to death. Since Roman times, the husband's power has been gradually restricted, and the rights of women and children have correspondingly increased. Yet in many areas of law a stranger is entitled to more legal protection than a family member. In most states, a wife does not have the right to charge her husband with rape, nor in many can a family member sue a relative for damages arising from assault. . . .

A third element of the Family Ideal is belief in the preservation of the family. Marriage was supposed to be life long, for religious reasons and for the responsibility of raising children. Conservatives of the nineteenth century argued that women were dependent on the family for their happiness. They were tethered to it because of their children and in order to make the home a place of affection. . . .

. . . [R]eform against family violence is an implicit critique of each element of the Family Ideal. It inevitably asserts that family violence is a public matter, not a private issue. Public policy against domestic violence offers state intervention in the family as a major remedy for abuse, challenges the view that marriage and family should be preserved at all costs, and asserts that children and women are individuals whose liberties must be protected.

1. Police Response to Domestic Violence Calls

Well into the 1970s, police forces commonly treated domestic violence calls differently from other reports of crimes. Officers were taught to try to defuse the situation by getting the alleged aggressor to take a walk and cool off and to use arrest only as a last resort. Laurie S. Kohn, The Justice System and Domestic Violence: Engaging the Case but Divorcing the Victim, 32 N.Y.U. Rev. L. & Soc. Change 191, 212 (2008), quoting International Association of Chiefs of Police, Training Key 16: Handling Disturbance Calls (1967), and American Bar Assn., Standards Relating to the Urban Police Function 107 (1973). In addition to the family privacy rationale, many police and prosecutors believed that domestic violence complainants were unreliable, prone to return to their attackers, and likely to refuse to cooperate as witnesses. Even if the aggressor was arrested and prosecuted, if the alleged victim asked to have the case dismissed, the charges would be dropped.

Battered women's advocates severely criticized these practices, arguing that sometimes victims' requests to drop charges were coerced; that leaving the decision about whether to prosecute in their hands placed them at greater risk of harm from their assailants; and that domestic violence victims are often ambivalent for good reasons, including lack of independent financial resources and social support, desire to preserve their families, love for the attacker, and depression and post-traumatic stress disorder. The efforts of these advocates, as well as data from an influential empirical study, led to mandatory arrest and no-drop policies. These policies were also supported by the argument that the public has an interest independent of the victim's in seeing a person who has committed a crime brought to justice. *See generally* Deborah Epstein, Effective Intervention in Domestic Violence Cases: Rethinking the Roles of Prosecutors, Judges, and the Court System, 11 Yale J.L. & Feminism 3 (1999); Cheryl Hanna, No Right to Choose: Mandated Victim Participation in Domestic Violence Prosecutions, 109 Harv. L. Rev. 1849 (1996).

WILLIAMS V. STATE

151 P.3d 460 (Alaska App. 2006)

COATS, Chief Judge. . . . Thomas A. Williams was charged almost two and one-half years ago with assaulting his wife of twenty-three years. He is apparently still awaiting trial. As required by AS 12.30.027(b), one of the conditions of his pre-trial release forbids him from returning to the residence he shared with his wife and daughter. . . .

On April 21, 2004, the police responded to a report by a passerby that a man was strangling a woman in a house on Henderson Loop in Anchorage. When the police arrived at the house, they contacted Terese Williams. Williams said her husband, Thomas Williams, had grabbed her around the neck during an argument and pushed her to the ground. She said he kept a firm grip on her throat and squeezed for several minutes and that she was very scared. Then he let go and she got up. She was shaken and went to smoke a cigarette; her husband grabbed his bags and left. . . . The investigating officer noted that Terese Williams was "visibly shaken" and had a scratch on her chin, a finger impression under her right ear, and a small red mark on the left of her neck.

Based on these allegations, Thomas Williams was charged with fourth-degree assault. The conditions of his pre-trial release barred him from contacting his wife or returning to the residence they had shared.

Several weeks after his release, Williams asked the court to modify his release conditions so he could have contact with his wife. His attorney said Williams and his wife had been together for more than twenty years and that both parties wished to renew contact. The State did not oppose the request. The prosecutor told the court that "in looking at Mr. Williams's record and the facts in this case, the State [is] confident or at least hopeful that it was an isolated incident." The court modified the bail conditions to allow contact, but emphasized that, by statute, Williams was still barred from the residence.

Several months later, Williams asked the court for permission to stay in the residence to care for the house and dog while his wife and daughter were in London. Williams's wife supported the request, and the State did not oppose. The court also granted that request.

On December 23, 2004 — eight months after the incident — Williams, again with his wife's support, asked the court for permission to return to the residence for Christmas. He also filed a motion challenging the constitutionality of AS

12.30.027(b). Williams argued that the statute infringed his fundamental right to maintain his marital relationship and violated his rights to both due process and equal protection of the laws. . . .

Relying on AS 12.30.027(b), District Court Judge Sigurd E. Murphy denied Williams's request to return to the residence. The court then scheduled a hearing on Williams's motion challenging the constitutionality of the statute.

That hearing was held in January 2005. At the hearing, Terese Williams reiterated that she had been in regular contact with her husband and that she did not feel he was a threat. She said Williams was in counseling and that it was her wish that he return to the residence. She also asserted that the police and witnesses had exaggerated the seriousness of the incident. The State opposed the motion but did not present any evidence. The prosecutor simply observed that the domestic violence in the home had escalated, noting that Williams had threatened his wife with a fire poker in 2002 (he was convicted of disorderly conduct for that offense), and was now charged with assault for strangling his wife.

On February 2, 2005, Judge Murphy denied the motion. . . .

We have previously subjected restrictions on marital association to heightened scrutiny. In Dawson v. State, we observed that "[a] condition of probation restricting marital association plainly implicates the constitutional rights of privacy, liberty, and freedom of association and . . . must be subjected to special scrutiny."

The State nevertheless argues that no fundamental right is at stake in this case because Williams's conditions of release permit him to see his wife — just not in their home. Hence, the State argues, the residence restriction has "at most a modest, incidental, and temporary effect" on the marital relationship. This argument understates the integral relationship between cohabitation and marriage. Moreover, apart from any burden imposed on Williams's relationship with his wife and family, Williams has a liberty interest in choosing his family living arrangements.

In Moore v. City of East Cleveland, the United States Supreme Court addressed a city ordinance that limited the occupancy of a dwelling to members of a single family. While that limitation in itself is unremarkable, this ordinance defined "family" so narrowly that it forbade Inez Moore from living in her home with her son and two young grandsons because the grandsons were cousins, not brothers. When Moore refused to remove the offending grandson from her home, she was convicted of a crime. The Supreme Court rejected the city's claim that it was required to uphold the ordinance if it bore a rational relationship to permissible government objectives:

> When a city undertakes such intrusive regulation of the family . . . the usual deference to the legislature is inappropriate. "This Court has long recognized that freedom of personal choice in matters of marriage and family life is one of the liberties protected by the Due Process Clause of the Fourteenth Amendment." . . . Of course, the family is not beyond regulation. But when the government intrudes on choices concerning family living arrangements, this Court must examine carefully the importance of the governmental interests advanced and the extent to which they are served by the challenged regulation.

This liberty interest does not disappear because a person has been charged with a crime. We hold based on this authority that Williams has an important, if not fundamental, right to live in his home with his wife and family while on pre-trial release, and that any state infringement of that right must be carefully scrutinized.

There is no legislative history to illuminate the legislature's purpose in enacting the residence restriction in AS 12.30.027(b). But the State undoubtedly has a legitimate and compelling interest in preventing domestic violence — and in preventing a person accused of domestic violence from tampering with the alleged victim's testimony. On the other hand, the government has no legitimate interest in barring a person who poses no appreciable risk of harming or intimidating the victim from returning to a shared residence. Given the importance of the right to live with a member of one's family, we will invalidate the classification if we find an insufficiently tight fit between the purposes of the statute and the means used to accomplish those purposes and if less restrictive alternatives are available.

The State argues that a blanket prohibition on returning to the alleged victim's residence is necessary because of the peculiar dynamics of domestic violence — in particular, the well-documented tendency of victims to remain with their abusers. The State argues that the victims of domestic violence are influenced by psychological and emotional forces that "too often make impossible an accurate assessment of whether the victim's safety can be assured if the defendant is allowed to return to [the] residence." The State concludes that a court's evaluation of whether a defendant poses a risk to the alleged victim is therefore likely to be "little more than an educated guess." We agree that it can be difficult for judges to accurately predict whether a particular defendant will be dangerous in the future. But judges confront this task "countless times each day throughout the American system of criminal justice." . . .

As the State points out, courts are not obliged to credit a victim's assertion that her abuser is no threat — even if that testimony is undisputed. And in this case, in urging us to affirm the district court, the State lists ample circumstantial evidence Judge Murphy could have relied on to discredit Terese Williams's statements: the couple's lengthy marriage; Terese Williams's testimony about the financial strain of maintaining separate residences; Williams's prior conviction for threatening his wife with a fire poker; the fact that Terese Williams had resumed living with Williams after that prior incident; the eyewitness reports that Williams had strangled his wife; and the investigating officer's observations of Terese Williams's injuries. . . .

Of course, the residence restriction in AS 12.30.027(b) generally will only burden the liberty interest of a person who was living with the alleged victim at the time of the offense. But even within this narrower context, it is easy to imagine situations in which the condition would serve no legitimate governmental purpose. . . .

Judge Murphy provided another example of how the residence restriction might create a significant hardship without advancing the State's interest in reducing domestic violence:

> *Court*:   Let's say you have a case where a couple have been married for a long period of time. There's no criminal activity. They get along pretty

well. As married couples often do, they have little fights and disagreements. Well, one night they both have been drinking and the
husband calls the wife a fat pig or some other obnoxious statement,
and the wife slaps him. He then goes ahead and calls the police.
The police arrive.

> Now . . . I assume the prosecutor acknowledges that the [Anchor-
age Police Department] has a policy in domestic violence cases that if
they go there on a call, they're going to arrest somebody, right?

Prosecutor: Yes, Your Honor.

Court: So let's say they arrest a woman for slapping her husband. They take
her to jail and she's prohibited from returning to the home that she
lived in for maybe a quarter of a century, and she has school-aged
children to raise, and she is a home provider, and she prepares all the
meals for the kids. . . . And the husband, who works full-time on
the North Slope, or maybe [like Williams] he works in the valley
in the Department of Corrections, isn't there to do that. There's
been a total disruption to the home.

As the above examples illustrate, under Alaska's far-reaching definition of
domestic violence, probable cause to believe a person has committed a domestic
violence offense cannot necessarily be equated with probable cause to believe that
the person poses an ongoing risk to the alleged victim's safety. . . .

Moreover, it appears that other jurisdictions have found less restrictive alternatives adequate to protect the victims of domestic violence. The Model Code on
Domestic and Family Violence, which served as a blueprint for Alaska's 1996
Domestic Violence Prevention and Victim Protection Act (the law that authorized
the residence restriction at issue in this case), contains no blanket prohibition on a
person charged with domestic violence returning to the residence of the alleged
victim. Rather, the Model Code gives courts discretion to remove the accused from
the home if the court finds that doing so is necessary to protect the alleged victim.
Apparently no other state follows Alaska's rule. At least two states restrict a
person charged with domestic violence from returning to the alleged victim's
residence for one to three days after the incident — but the victim can waive
that requirement. . . .

In *Dawson*, we recognized that restrictions on marital association might be
justified in domestic violence cases. But we also recognized that those restrictions
should be carefully considered:

> In certain types of cases, such as cases involving domestic violence, limiting marital
> association would plainly be defensible. In any type of case, it is conceivable that such
> a limitation might be justified by case-specific circumstances demonstrating actual
> necessity and the lack of less restrictive alternatives. In such a case, however, to avoid
> unnecessary intrusion on marital privacy, it would seem appropriate to tailor a close
> fit between the scope of the order restricting marital association and the specific
> needs of the case at hand.

We struck down the probation condition in *Dawson* — which forbade the
defendant from any contact with his wife unless the contact was approved by his

probation officer — after concluding that the court had made no apparent effort to tailor the scope of the condition to the specific circumstances of Dawson's case. Similarly here, the State has failed to show that the less restrictive alternatives adopted by the Model Code and other jurisdictions — for instance, conditioning the residence restriction on a judicial finding, following a hearing, that the person charged with domestic violence poses an ongoing risk to the alleged victim — would fail to accomplish the government's interests. The legislation is thus impermissibly overinclusive: it prohibits all persons charged with crimes that meet the broad definition of domestic violence from returning to the victim's residence, even persons who pose no appreciable risk of assaulting the victim or tampering with the victim's testimony. . . .

We therefore hold that AS 12.30.027(b), as applied to individuals on pre-trial release, violates article I, section 1 of the Alaska Constitution. (We express no opinion as to whether this statute is constitutional as applied to individuals on post-conviction release.) . . .

NOTES AND QUESTIONS

1. Does the court in *Williams* use the doctrine of family privacy in the same way that the court in *McGuire* did? Would the *Williams* court have held that Thomas's constitutional rights were violated if Terese had not supported his request that he be allowed to return home?

Professor Jeannie Suk argues that an unintended consequence of efforts to change police policies in domestic violence cases has been to criminalize conduct that is ordinarily not criminal — being in one's home — and that prosecutions for violations of restraining orders have become a surrogate for punishing domestic violence itself. When orders are issued incidental to arrests and prosecutions, they deny women autonomy and effectively reallocate property in the home, impose de facto divorce (if the couple was married), and criminalize decisions to live as intimate partners. Jeannie Suk, Criminal Law Comes Home, 116 Yale L.J. 2 (2006).

2. *Williams* indicates that a statute would be constitutional if it gave a court discretion to decide whether to exclude a defendant charged with a crime of domestic violence from the home he shared with the victim. What is the constitutional significance of the difference between a blanket rule and a discretionary rule? Could it have been argued in support of the statute that the legislature had determined that a person charged with a crime of domestic violence always posed a risk to the victim?

If the statute in *Williams* had granted the judge discretion about whether to exclude the husband from the home, and the prosecution had asked for an order, should it have been granted? How much weight should the court give to the wife's expressed wish that her husband be allowed to return home? To the fact that Mr. Williams had battered his wife before? That this time he had injured her fairly severely?

3. One of the most obvious expressions of the family privacy doctrine with regard to domestic violence is the common law rule that a man could not legally rape his wife. 1 Matthew Hale, History of Pleas of the Crown 629 (1736). By 1995 almost all states had abandoned this rule in its absolute form. Lalenya Weintraub

Siegel, Note, The Marital Rape Exemption: Evolution to Extinction, 43 Clev. St. L. Rev. 351, 367-369 (1995). However, many states criminalize a narrower range of offenses if committed within marriage, subject marital rape to less serious sanctions than nonmarital rape, and/or create special procedural requirements for prosecutions of marital rape. Jill Elaine Hasday, A Legal History of Marital Rape, 88 Cal. L. Rev. 1373, 1375, 1484-1485 (2000).

4. Other provisions of the Constitution besides due process limit the state's authority to define conduct as domestic violence that can be sanctioned. The First Amendment and state constitutional protections for free speech prevent the state from entering certain orders that prohibit communication. For example, in In re Marriage of Suggs, 93 P.3d 161 (2004), a court restrained a woman from "knowingly and willfully making invalid and unsubstantiated allegations or complaints to third parties which are designed for the purpose of annoying, harassing, vexing, or otherwise harming" her former husband. The court observed that the order was a prior restraint on speech, which is especially hard to justify against a constitutional challenge. While a court could restrain her from slandering her former husband, the language in the order was so broad and vague that it could be interpreted as covering protected speech. *See also* In re Marriage of Meredith, 201 P.3d 1056 (Wash. App. 2009).

PROBLEM

Scott and Janet had a stormy marriage, marked by frequent heated arguments, many of which ended with Scott threatening Janet. Last year she filed for a restraining order against him but dropped it within a few days. In May they fought again, and she became frightened that he was going to hurt her badly. She left their home and went to stay with her parents in Canada, taking their son and some belongings. Two months later, she returned at Scott's request and after he promised that he had changed and would not hit her any more. On the third day after she came home, Janet and Scott began fighting again, and Scott took the baby and left the house. Janet called the police, reporting the fight and her fear for her child's safety. When the police arrived, she opened the door a crack and told the officers that her call had been a misunderstanding, that nothing was wrong. She refused to answer the officer's questions, kept glancing furtively over her shoulder, and finally said, "Go! Just please go!"

The Fourth Amendment limits the ability of police officers to enter a dwelling without a warrant, but one exception to the requirement allows them to enter if they have probable cause to believe that an immediate response is necessary to protect someone's life or safety. On these facts, would the exception apply so that the police can enter, despite what Janet said?

NOTE: THE IMPACT OF MANDATORY ARREST AND NO-DROP POLICIES

The first study of the impact of arrest on domestic violence showed that arrest significantly reduced the violence, compared to more traditional "cooling-off" strategies." However, replications of the study produced a more complicated picture. Effectiveness of arrest varied from city to city, and arrest was much more effective in stopping violence committed by men who were employed, married, high school graduates, and white than with other populations. The validity of these replication studies has, in turn, been challenged. *See* sources cited in Kimberly D. Bailey, The Aftermath of *Crawford* and *Davis*: Deconstructing the Sound of Silence, 2009 BYU L. Rev. 1, 9-10.

Some women's advocates have challenged mandatory arrest and prosecutorial no-drop policies for ignoring victims without necessarily making them safer. Laurie S. Kohn, The Justice System and Domestic Violence: Engaging the Case but Divorcing the Victim, 32 N.Y.U. Rev. L. & Soc. Change 191 (2008); *see also* Bailey, above; G. Kristian Miccio, A House Divided: Mandatory Arrest, Domestic Violence, and the Conservatization of the Battered Women's Movement, 42 Hous. L. Rev. 237 (2005); Aya Gruber, A "Neo-Feminist" Assessment of Rape and Domestic Violence Law Reform, 15 J. Gender Race & Just. 583 (2012). Some critics also argue that the common view that the only solution to battering is for the victim to leave oversimplifies domestic violence and illegitimately disregards the wishes of women who want to end the violence but preserve the relationship. *See, e.g.*, Sally F. Goldfarb, Reconceiving Civil Protection Orders for Domestic Violence: Can Law Help End the Abuse Without Ending the Relationship?, 29 Cardozo L. Rev. 1487 (2008).

If a victim of domestic violence is unwilling to testify against the defendant, a prosecutor may try to proceed without the victim's testimony, relying on physical evidence and the victim's hearsay statements at or near the time of the violence. However, this option is severely limited by a line of Supreme Court decisions beginning with Crawford v. Washington, 541 U.S. 36 (2004), where the Supreme Court held that "testimonial" hearsay cannot be admitted against a criminal defendant unless the declarant is presently available for cross-examination, or is presently unavailable but was once available for cross-examination by the defendant. Davis v. Washington, 547 U.S. 813 (2006), held that statements made to police officers when "the primary purpose of interrogation is to enable police assistance to meet an ongoing emergency" are not testimonial and are not inadmissible under *Crawford*. *Davis* concerned the admissibility of a 911 call in which a woman said that her boyfriend was hitting her. The Court said that these excited utterances to a police officer about "an ongoing emergency" were non-testimonial and could be admitted in the criminal prosecution of the boyfriend. However, in a companion case, the Court held that a woman's written statement given to police officers who were investigating her call for help after her husband hit and shoved her were testimonial and could not be admitted in a criminal prosecution. For more information, *see* Tom Lininger, The Sound of Silence: Holding Batterers Accountable for Silencing Their Victims, 87 Tex. L. Rev. 857 (2009).

2.   *Protective Orders*

The most widely used judicial response to domestic violence is the protective order. Protective orders are civil orders restraining the offender from conduct that endangers the person seeking the order. Such orders are available in every state for threats to the safety of a domestic partner. The statutes typically authorize courts to grant temporary protective orders after a hearing or ex parte; if the latter is authorized, a respondent is entitled to a full due process hearing within a few days. In some states, these hearings are automatic, as in the next case; in other states, the respondent must ask for a hearing. *See, e.g.*, Or. Rev. Stat. § 107.716 (2014). At the full hearing, the petitioner has the burden of proof. The next case considers the type of notice that a petition for a restraining order must provide, as well as what kind of conduct can provide the basis for an order.

J.D. v. M.D.F.

25 A.3d 1045 (N.J. 2011)

Justice HOENS delivered the opinion of the Court. . . . From 1993 until 2006, plaintiff, J.D., and defendant, M.D.F., were engaged in a long-term relationship. Although they never married, they resided together and two children were born to them. After they ended their relationship, they sought the assistance of the courts in a variety of disputed proceedings, including a litigated palimony suit, the details of which are not apparent from the record on appeal in this matter. What is clear from the record is that following their separation, their relationship continued to deteriorate and they were on the verge of becoming embroiled in a custody dispute when the events that gave rise to this appeal occurred.

Throughout the proceedings relating to the domestic violence allegations in the trial court, the parties appeared without attorneys. As a result, the record has presented challenges to courts at every level. Relevant to this dispute, it appears that at all times since the end of the relationship, plaintiff continued to reside in the home that she and defendant had purchased together. The couple's two children resided with her, as did an older child of hers that she had from a relationship prior to the one with defendant. By the time of the events in issue, plaintiff had begun a relationship with a new person, R.T., who she referred to as her boyfriend, and who was present during the events in question.

. . . Plaintiff's domestic violence complaint, which was filed on September 19, 2008, was apparently compiled with the assistance of court personnel based on information plaintiff supplied and was transcribed on a court-approved form. According to the complaint, plaintiff and her boyfriend, R.T., observed defendant outside of plaintiff's residence at 1:42 A.M. taking flash photographs. In the complaint, plaintiff alleged that as soon as her boyfriend pulled aside the curtain to look, defendant drove away. According to the complaint, "[p]lain[tiff] reports def[endant] did this for the sole purpose of harassing plain[tiff] and attempting to cause strain in plain[tiff]'s present relationship." . . .

In the section of the complaint form that requested identification of prior incidents of domestic violence, plaintiff referred to several. These were: (1) a June 2008 incident in which defendant was outside of the residence taking pictures and asked her boyfriend "how the accommodations were"; (2) an undated incident in which defendant climbed in her window and "attempted to have relations w[ith]" her; (3) an assertion that during "their separation def[endant] would come to the residence at various times"; and (4) an allegation that "[d]uring another occasion pla[intiff] had locked her doors and yet def[endant] was able to gain entry & harass" her.

Based on that complaint, a Temporary Restraining Order (TRO) was issued and a return date was set for the following week. For reasons not apparent from the record, the matter was adjourned and a new return date fixed for a few days later. Plaintiff, accompanied by R.T., and defendant appeared on the adjourned return date.

After administering the oath to plaintiff and defendant, the trial court began to hear testimony from plaintiff about the basis of her complaint. Plaintiff briefly described the events that took place on September 19, explaining that her boyfriend, after emerging from the shower, went to hang a towel at the bedroom window. According to plaintiff, as R.T. was looking out of the window, he told her that he saw defendant outside taking pictures. Plaintiff further testified that she then "went to the window and [defendant] was in his white Dodge, outside the house and you could see flash photography. And he—then my boyfriend proceeded to pull the curtains back and [defendant] pulled away."

After that explanation of the basis for her request for a restraining order, the court inquired further of plaintiff, asking whether there was "[a]nything else you think I should know?" Plaintiff responded by referring to "multiple incidents," none of which had been identified in the complaint as being part of the prior history of domestic violence between the two. The prior incidents that were outside of the complaint have been referred to by the parties as the "videotape," the "lacrosse field," and the "Wawa" incidents. The "videotape" refers to an incident in which defendant left an embarrassing home videotape, created with plaintiff's knowledge and consent, in her mailbox with a message indicating that her new boyfriend should see it. The "lacrosse field" incident refers to a series of verbal arguments between the parties about parenting styles and about one child's missed practice sessions and included one dispute between defendant and R.T. about R.T.'s role in the lives of the children. The "Wawa" incident refers to a conversation between defendant and R.T. in a convenience store parking lot during which plaintiff was not present.

In describing those incidents, plaintiff recited the contents of text messages she asserted she had received and she reported the substance of conversations to which defendant and her boyfriend alone had been parties. . . .

As plaintiff's testimony proceeded, the trial court repeated the earlier inquiry, asking "anything else you think I should know?" In response, plaintiff continued to add to her factual testimony, expanding to include her views that the communications were "threats" and were "annoying" and offering her impression that the conversation between defendant and her boyfriend was defendant's effort to harass him as well.

When plaintiff concluded her series of responses to the trial court's repeated inquiries by saying, "that's basically it," the court offered defendant an opportunity to respond. Defendant immediately said that many of the incidents about which plaintiff had just testified had occurred long ago and asserted that he had not known that plaintiff would be referring to them. As part of that answer, defendant told the court that he "really wasn't prepared." Notwithstanding that, defendant attempted to respond and the court inquired in detail about several of those earlier incidents that had not been identified in the complaint.

After hearing defendant's responses to those questions, the trial court inquired about the early morning photography incident. . . .

Defendant did not deny that he had gone to plaintiff's residence and had taken photographs in the early morning hours, but his response concerning that incident was two-fold. In part, he sought to attack plaintiff's credibility by challenging her testimony that his car was parked while he was taking the photographs. He testified that he was driving slowly by, offering that as evidence in support of his testimony that he intended not to be detected.

Second, defendant attempted to suggest that he had an innocent motive for taking the photographs as proof that he did not intend to harass plaintiff. Although he was reluctant to reveal his motive, it was apparent that defendant had been preparing to file, and on the same day when he was served with the TRO he had filed, a motion seeking to challenge plaintiff's custody of their two children. It was readily apparent from his testimony that he was taking late-night photographs of R.T.'s truck parked outside the home because defendant hoped that gathering photographic evidence that plaintiff's boyfriend was residing there would assist him in his quest to have custody of the two minor children transferred to him. . . . .

The trial court then permitted defendant to inquire of plaintiff briefly. Defendant used that opportunity to try to undercut plaintiff's credibility by focusing on whether he was parked or not. After a time, the trial court concluded that both that line of attack, as well as defendant's assertion that he was only taking photographs for his custody motion and his suggestion that plaintiff was aware of his motive, were irrelevant.

Once the trial court decided that the basis for defendant's credibility challenge was meritless . . . the court found as follows:

> Sir, I've heard enough. You concede to being out there taking pictures and even assuming that it's to build your case to modify the existing order or to modify the custody order, given the history, specifically the videotape, the incident at the lacrosse field, the incident at the Wawa — number one, in and of itself, you being out there, sir, quarter of two in the morning, in my view, qualifies, in and of itself, as harassment. Even assuming that you were trying to build your case, it could not have any other effect but to annoy or alarm [plaintiff]. And especially in light of the prior history, the videotape, which was, at the very least, a dirty trick, sir. And quite frankly, I want to make a comment on your presentation here today. It's not — it just doesn't seem, quite frankly, to be coherent in the sense that you're thinking clearly, sir. . . . Your theory of the case that she somehow knew that you were going to file a custody motion because your stepdaughter had been there, it's simply — those are dots that you can't connect and you concede to being out there at a quarter of two in the morning taking pictures. And that's harassment, sir, regardless of whether you were parked or not.

Defendant pursued an appeal. . . .

New Jersey's Prevention of Domestic Violence Act, N.J.S.A. 2C:25-17 to -35, sets forth the Legislature's purpose and intention in broad and unmistakable language:

> The Legislature finds and declares that domestic violence is a serious crime against society; that there are thousands of persons in this State who are regularly beaten, tortured and in some cases even killed by their spouses or cohabitants; that a

significant number of women who are assaulted are pregnant; that victims of domestic violence come from all social and economic backgrounds and ethnic groups; that there is a positive correlation between spousal abuse and child abuse; and that children, even when they are not themselves physically assaulted, suffer deep and lasting emotional effects from exposure to domestic violence.

. . .

The Act defines domestic violence by referring to a list of predicate acts that are otherwise found within the New Jersey Code of Criminal Justice. It provides that the commission of a predicate act, if the plaintiff meets the definition of a "victim of domestic violence," constitutes domestic violence and authorizes the court to impose restraints and related forms of relief. . . .

Although the restraints imposed pursuant to the Act are essentially civil, they are backed by the threat of enforcement through a contempt proceeding, and are accompanied by the possibility of the imposition of criminal sanctions.

Sadly, in spite of decades of careful and consistent enforcement of the Act by our courts, domestic violence remains a significant problem in our society. In 2009, the most recent year for which statistics were available for inclusion in the statutorily mandated annual report, reports of domestic violence offenses had increased. Although a year-by-year comparison for the period from 2005 though 2009 demonstrates that there had been a slight downward trend in domestic violence incidents through 2008, that trend was reversed for the most recent reporting year, with total reported incidents in most categories exceeding most prior years.

Among the predicate offenses that may serve as the basis for domestic violence purposes, one of the most frequently reported is harassment. In 2009, harassment was not only the most frequently reported of all predicate offenses, but it exceeded its incidence as compared to all prior reporting years. At the same time, however, harassment is the predicate offense that presents the greatest challenges to our courts as they strive to apply the underlying criminal statute that defines the offense to the realm of domestic discord. Drawing the line between acts that constitute harassment for purposes of issuing a domestic violence restraining order and those that fall instead into the category of "ordinary domestic contretemps" presents our courts with a weighty responsibility and confounds our ability to fix clear rules of application.

In part, the decision about which acts constitute domestic violence and which do not can be found not in the analysis of the predicate acts themselves, but in the second inquiry required of courts considering complaints seeking protection pursuant to the Act. Our Appellate Division has ably explained the appropriate approach:

> The second inquiry, upon a finding of the commission of a predicate act of domestic violence, is whether the court should enter a restraining order that provides protection for the victim. . . .

Because all of the arguments raised on appeal rest only on a claimed act of harassment, we begin with a review of the body of law that has developed concerning this most challenging basis for a domestic violence complaint. The predicate act of harassment is defined by statute to be a criminal offense:

> Harassment. Except as provided in subsection e., a person commits a petty disorderly persons offense if, with purpose to harass another, he:
>   a. Makes, or cause to be made, a communication or communications anonymously or at extremely inconvenient hours, or in offensively coarse language, or any other manner likely to cause annoyance or alarm;
>   b. Subjects another to striking, kicking, shoving or other offensive touching, or threatens to do so; or
>   c. Engages in any other course of alarming conduct or of repeatedly committed acts with purpose to alarm or seriously annoy such other person. . . .

Defendant's argument that permitting plaintiff to testify about numerous incidents she asserted were evidence of a prior history of domestic violence, but that were not identified in her complaint, violated his due process rights is a variation of an argument that we have previously addressed. As we have held, ordinary due process protections apply in the domestic violence context, notwithstanding the shortened time frames for conducting a final hearing that are imposed by the statute. What that means is that "[a]t a minimum, due process requires that a party in a judicial hearing receive 'notice defining the issues and an adequate opportunity to prepare and respond.'" More particularly, we held that due process forbids the trial court "'to convert a hearing on a complaint alleging one act of domestic violence into a hearing on other acts of domestic violence which are not even alleged in the complaint.'"

The fact remains, however, that plaintiffs seeking protection under the Act often file complaints that reveal limited information about the prior history between the parties, only to expand upon that history of prior disputes when appearing in open court. And it is frequently the case that the trial court will attempt to elicit a fuller picture of the circumstances either to comply with the statutory command to consider the previous history, if any, of domestic violence between the parties or to be certain of the relevant facts that may give content to otherwise ambiguous communications or behavior.

That reality is not inconsistent with affording defendants the protections of due process to which they are entitled. Instead, ensuring that defendants are not deprived of their due process rights requires our trial courts to recognize both what those rights are and how they can be protected consistent with the protective goals of the Act. To begin with, trial courts should use the allegations set forth in the complaint to guide their questioning of plaintiffs, avoiding the sort of questions that induced plaintiff in this appeal to abandon the history revealed in the complaint in favor of entirely new accusations. That does not mean that trial courts must limit plaintiffs to the precise prior history revealed in a complaint, because the testimony might reveal that there are additional prior events that are significant to the court's evaluation, particularly if the events are ambiguous. Rather, the court must recognize that if it allows that history to be expanded, it has permitted an amendment to the complaint and must proceed accordingly.

To be sure, some defendants will know full well the history that plaintiff recites and some parties will be well-prepared regardless of whether the testimony technically expands upon the allegations of the complaint. Others, however, will not, and in all cases the trial court must ensure that defendant is afforded an adequate opportunity to be apprised of those allegations and to prepare.

When permitting plaintiff to expand upon the alleged prior incidents and thereby allowing an amendment to the complaint, the court also should have recognized the due process implication of defendant's suggestion that he was unprepared to defend himself. Although defendant's assertion that he needed time to prepare was not cloaked in the lawyer-like language of an adjournment request and was made as part of a longer response to a question, it was sufficient to raise the due process question for the trial court and it should have been granted. . . .

This is especially true because there is no risk to plaintiff based on such a procedure; courts are empowered to continue temporary restraints during the pendency of an adjournment, thus fully protecting the putative victim while ensuring that defendant's due process rights are safeguarded as well. . . .

Defendant's final argument relates to the sufficiency of the evidence on which the trial court relied in concluding that he had committed the predicate act of harassment and that plaintiff therefore was entitled to protection under the Act. Our courts have struggled with the proofs needed to support a domestic violence restraining order based on claims of harassment. In part, the challenge comes from litigants, often representing themselves, who use the word "harassment" as it is used in common parlance rather than in the sense meant by either the New Jersey Code of Criminal Justice or the Prevention of Domestic Violence Act. Often, a party's accusation that another's actions are "harassing" is vague and conclusory, making it particularly difficult for a trial court to discern on which side of the line running between domestic violence and ordinary "contretemps" a particular act properly falls.

In our efforts to be faithful to the strong expressions of our Legislature and to protect the rights of both parties we have vested great discretion in our Family Part judges. We have observed that they are judges who have been specially trained to detect the difference between domestic violence and more ordinary differences that arise between couples, and we have recognized that their findings are entitled to deference.

Many published decisions have addressed questions concerning what conduct constitutes harassment and what does not. Our Appellate Division has concluded that sending explicit photographs of plaintiff to her sister and threatening to send them to plaintiff's son and to her workplace was harassment. Similarly, there was sufficient evidence to support a finding of harassment when defendant found plaintiff's new telephone number and sent her a text message that told her that he could see her watching a particular television show. Even though defendant was not in fact watching plaintiff and therefore was unable to see her, the content of the message was such that it was intended to cause her "annoyance, which means 'to disturb, irritate, or bother.'"

A history of domestic violence may serve to give content to otherwise ambiguous behavior and support entry of a restraining order. For example, in part based on the parties' history, a defendant who was angry because plaintiff rebuffed his efforts to talk to her, and who blocked her from leaving in her car, using coarse and vulgar language to express his frustration, committed an act of harassment.

Not all offensive or bothersome behavior, however, constitutes harassment. In the criminal context, our Appellate Division has cautioned against "overextending a criminal statute to rude behavior which is not directed to anyone specifically but only towards an institution in general." That observation convinced the appellate panel that "venting of frustration or irritation" and using obscenities during a 911 call did not demonstrate a purpose to harass, thus making a restraining order inappropriate. . . .

With these principles and these examples of their application to guide us, we turn to a consideration of whether the facts in the record support the court's finding that defendant committed an act or a series of acts of harassment sufficient to entitle plaintiff to issuance of a domestic violence restraining order. Our analysis must begin by restating the findings that the trial court made. Boiled down to its essence, the court first noted that the critical facts were not contested, because defendant conceded that he had been outside of the residence early in the morning taking photographs. Based on that alone, the trial court concluded that "being there . . . at quarter to two in the morning . . . in and of itself, [is] harassment." Supplementing that finding, however, the court relied on three incidents about which plaintiff had testified, none of which had been identified in the complaint. Finally, the court rejected defendant's repeated assurances that his purpose was only to gather evidence for his planned custody motion, concluding instead that he acted with the requisite purpose to harass.

The trial court did not specify which of the two subsections of the harassment statute it was applying to the factual assertions being raised by plaintiff. Although the appellate panel applied subsection c., because the trial court's recitation of findings and conclusions appears to be an alternative analysis that might have been intended to support issuance of the restraining order pursuant to either subsection, we consider each separately.

It is possible that the court meant to apply subsection a., based on the reference to the fact that defendant's presence outside the residence alone sufficed. For purposes of subsection a., a single act can be enough and the act, given that it took place at what could clearly qualify as an "extremely inconvenient hour," could theoretically constitute a predicate act. Nevertheless, it would only qualify as a predicate act if it were both committed with a purpose to harass and if the act was "likely to cause annoyance or alarm."

The evidence in this record, however, is insufficient to support a finding under subsection a. Merely being outside of the home in the early morning hours is not an act of harassment. More to the point, plaintiff's own clear testimony about the incident demonstrates that she was completely unaware that defendant was outside until R.T. walked over to the window and happened to look out. Only then did he notice defendant taking photographs and tell plaintiff what he saw. Plaintiff also conceded that as R.T. pulled aside the curtain, defendant immediately left. Far from a record suggesting that defendant's camera created a series of bright flashes that drew plaintiff's attention and caused her alarm, the undisputed facts are that plaintiff saw nothing until R.T. called to her and that defendant beat a hasty retreat when the curtain moved and he realized that they had seen him.

In the alternative, as the appellate panel surmised, the trial court might have meant to apply subsection c. That test for harassment would require a course of alarming conduct or a series of repeated acts, along with proof of a purpose to alarm or seriously annoy plaintiff. Utilizing the test set forth in subsection c., there is no evidence of a repeated act, with the result that defendant can only be in violation of subsection c. if he engaged in a "course of alarming conduct" within the meaning of the statute.

The trial court did not articulate precise findings of fact and conclusions of law and therefore did not explain what it was in the series of past incidents that led it to conclude that defendant's purpose when he engaged in late-night photography was to harass plaintiff. Certainly, the series of events that plaintiff testified were part of the history between the parties shows that defendant's behavior was hardly praiseworthy. But those events may or may not suffice to demonstrate defendant's intent and absent the trial court's explanation of its reasoning or its analysis, we cannot be confident that they do.

First, the statute requires that the victim, in this instance, the plaintiff, be the target of the harassing intent. Many of the incidents set forth by plaintiff in this record, including defendant's snide remarks to the new beau about the comfort of the accommodations, are ones in which plaintiff was not even present. Those incidents, therefore, could not serve as evidence of an intent to annoy or alarm plaintiff. Moreover, there is nothing in those acts that objectively rises to the level of "alarming" or "seriously annoying" as the statute demands.

Turning to the other past incidents, the trial court placed particular emphasis on defendant's delivery of the videotape to plaintiff. Although referring to it as "a dirty trick," the trial court did not explain how it demonstrated that defendant acted with the purpose to harass plaintiff when he went to take photographs, which is the incident claimed to be the predicate act. Although a purpose to harass can be inferred from a history between the parties, that finding must be supported by some evidence that the actor's conscious object was to alarm or annoy; mere awareness that someone might be alarmed or annoyed is insufficient. The victim's subjective reaction alone will not suffice; there must be evidence of the improper purpose. Moreover, when evaluating whether an individual acted with the requisite purpose, our courts must be especially vigilant in cases involving, as do many domestic violence disputes, the interactions of a couple in the midst of a breakup of a relationship.

It is significant as well that defendant in fact was preparing a motion for a change in custody that was based on plaintiff's cohabitation and the effect he believed that her new relationship was having on his children. That motion, which defendant testified was the reason for his decision to go to the home and take photographs, was filed within hours of the event, and its implications should have been considered and addressed by the court. We do not imply that, in evaluating claims of domestic violence, an individual can have only one motive or intent. On the contrary, domestic violence often presents circumstances in which a party may mask an intent to harass with what could otherwise be an innocent act. But some domestic violence complainants may perceive an entirely innocent act to be a harassing one as well. Our courts must examine the record with care lest an abuser hiding behind an apparently innocent act be overlooked. But they must be equally careful lest a plaintiff be permitted to seize upon what is truly an innocent act in an effort to gain an advantage in litigation between parties.

Finally, although not directly raised by defendant, the record does not include an analysis of "the second inquiry," and thus lacks the required consideration of whether entry of restraints is "necessary" to protect plaintiff from harm. That inquiry serves to ensure that the protective purposes of the Act are served, while limiting the possibility that the Act, or the courts, will become inappropriate weapons in domestic warfare. Although, as our Appellate Division noted, there will be cases in which the risk of harm is so great that the inquiry can be perfunctory, in others, including this one, it is not. In those cases, overlooking that important step in the analysis poses the risk of unfairness and error.

In entering the FRO, the trial court did not sufficiently articulate findings and conclusions consistent with the statutory standards and our independent review of the record leaves us unsure that there is sufficient evidence to sustain the issuance of the order. Therefore, in an abundance of caution, and mindful of the Family Court's "special expertise" and the Act's protective purposes, we are constrained to remand this matter to the trial court for a re-hearing, both to protect defendant's due process rights and to permit the trial court to evaluate the testimony and the evidence in accordance with the principles we have expressed. . . .

NOTES AND QUESTIONS

1. Why did the trial court and appellate court disagree about whether M.D.F. had committed harassment? On remand, what arguments should the parties make about whether the evidence is sufficient to show harassment? To show that an order is necessary to protect J.D.?

The statute in *J.D.* defines domestic violence for purposes of obtaining a restraining order by reference to criminal statutes. The appellate court observes that harassment is one of the most common predicate crimes alleged in petitions for restraining orders and says that it "presents the greatest challenges to our courts as they strive to apply the underlying criminal statute that defines the offense to the realm of domestic discord. Drawing the line between acts that constitute harassment for purposes of issuing a domestic violence restraining order and those that fall instead into the category of 'ordinary domestic contretemps' presents our courts with a weighty responsibility and confounds our ability to fix clear rules of application." Why is it necessary to draw this line? Is the harassment statute's emphasis on the actor's motive a good vehicle for making this distinction?

In other states, restraining order statutes do not incorporate criminal definitions but instead base availability of an order on proof that the respondent has caused or attempted to cause harm to the petitioner or put the petitioner in fear of harm. *See, e.g.*, National Council of Juvenile and Family Court Judges, Model Code on Domestic and Family Violence §§ 102(1), 301; Or. Rev. Stat. § 107.705(1) (2014). What are the advantages and disadvantages of this approach? Would the evidence in *J.D.* have been sufficient for an order in such a jurisdiction?

2. The New Jersey Supreme Court had previously held that issuing a restraining order based on incidents that were not specifically pled in the petition violates the respondent's right to notice, but, as the *J.D.* court says, courts must also consider the context of conduct that is pled to determine whether a restraining order is warranted. At what point does evidence of "context" become allegations of separate conduct that must be pled? If such evidence comes in during a hearing on

the order, what should the court do to protect the respondent's right to notice while also ensuring the safety of the petitioner? The petitioner in this case drafted the petition with the assistance of court personnel, but often petitioners draft petitions alone, and such petitions may be even less complete than this one. Indeed, most states' restraining order statutes create a process that is supposed to be simple enough for a layperson to use without help from an attorney. Do the New Jersey courts strike the right balance between the respondent's right to due process and the petitioner's need to be able to explain her situation to the judge? How important should specific events be in determining whether a petition for a restraining order should be granted?

3. When restraining order statutes were introduced, the provisions allowing ex parte orders were challenged as violating due process, usually without success. For example, in Kampf v. Kampf, 603 N.W.2d 295 (Mich. App. 1999), the court analyzed the issue as follows:

> There is no procedural due process defect in obtaining an emergency order of protection without notice to a respondent when the petition for the emergency protection order is supported by affidavits that demonstrate exigent circumstances justifying entry of an emergency order without prior notice, see, e.g., Mitchell v. WT Grant, 416 U.S. 600 (1974), and where there are appropriate provisions for notice and an opportunity to be heard after the order is issued. Here, subsection 12 permits a court to issue an *ex parte* order only if it clearly appears from specific facts shown by verified complaint, written motion, or affidavit that *immediate and irreparable injury, loss, or damage will result from the delay required to effectuate notice or that the notice will itself precipitate adverse action before a personal protection order can be issued* [emphasis added].
>
> Further, [the statute] gives a respondent the right to bring a motion to rescind a PPO within fourteen days of being served with notice or receiving actual notice of the PPO, and requires the court to schedule a hearing on the motion within five or fourteen days, depending on whether the PPO enjoins the respondent from purchasing and possessing a firearm. Clearly, the procedural safeguards employed under the statute are sufficient to meet respondent's due process challenge.

603 N.W.2d at 299. *See also* State v. Fernando A., 981 A.2d 427 (Conn. 2009) (where statute authorizes restraining order incident to criminal prosecution, due process satisfied by evidentiary hearing conducted after order issued to determine continued necessity of order).

4. Most domestic violence restraining order statutes reach cohabitant or former cohabitant relationships as well as spouses and former spouses. For example, the California Domestic Violence Prevention Act, §§ 6200 et seq., defines "domestic violence" as abuse against a spouse, former spouse, cohabitant, former cohabitant, a person with whom the respondent is having or has had a dating or engagement relationship, a person with whom the respondent has had a child or presumed child, or any other person related by consanguinity or affinity within the second degree. Cal. Fam. Code § 6211 (2014).

A domestic violence statute that covered "persons living as spouses" was challenged as violating the Ohio defense of marriage constitutional amendment, which is drafted broadly to prohibit recognition not only of same-sex marriage but also any other legal status that gives the legal effects of marriage. State v. Carswell,

871 N.E.2d 547 (Ohio 2007), rejected the challenge, holding that the criminal statute does not create or recognize a legal relationship that approximates the designs, qualities, or significance of marriage, but identifies a particular class of persons, who create their own relationships, for purposes of the domestic violence statutes. *See also* In re Ohio Domestic-Violence Statute Cases, 872 N.E.2d 1212 (Ohio 2007). Professor Colker criticizes domestic violence law for basing protections on the extent to which a relationship looks like a marriage, saying that this model fails to protect all those who need protection. She argues that the law of domestic violence should reject the "marriage mimicry" model and examine anew the reasons for having laws that treat certain kinds of violence differently from others. Ruth Colker, Marriage Mimicry: The Law of Domestic Violence, 47 Wm. & Mary L. Rev. 1841 (2006).

5. For information about civil protective order and stalking statutes in all 50 states, *see* American Bar Association Commission on Domestic Violence, Domestic Violence Civil Protection Orders (CPOs) by State, in a link from http://www.americanbar.org/groups/domestic_violence/resources/resources_for_attorneys/civil_protection_orders.html.

6. Despite the widespread availability of protective orders, their usefulness is limited by frequent failure to serve respondents and failure to punish violations. About a fourth of all orders are violated, according to some studies. Diane L. Rosenfeld, Correlative Rights and the Boundaries of Freedom: Protecting the Civil Rights of Endangered Women, 43 Harv. C.R.-C.L. L. Rev. 257, 258 (2008). In Gonzales v. City of Castle Rock, 545 U.S. 748 (2005), the Supreme Court held that there is no constitutional remedy against police officers who fail to enforce a domestic violence restraining order, notwithstanding a state mandatory arrest statute. Jessica Gonzales had obtained a restraining order limiting her husband Simon's contact with her and their daughters, aged ten, nine, and seven. Shortly after the order was issued, the children disappeared from the front of Jessica's home. She suspected (correctly) that her husband had taken the children and called the Castle Rock Police Department. Two officers came to the home, where she showed them a copy of the restraining order and asked that it be enforced and her children returned to her immediately. The officers "stated that there was nothing they could do about the TRO and suggested that Plaintiff call the Police Department again if the children did not return home by 10:00 P.M." Subsequently, Jessica heard from her husband that he was at an amusement park with the children. She called the police, who told her to wait until 8 P.M. At 8 P.M. she was told to wait until 10 P.M., a pattern that continued all evening. At approximately 3:20 A.M., Simon arrived at the Castle Rock police station in his truck. He got out and opened fire on the station with a semi-automatic handgun he had purchased soon after abducting his daughters. He was shot dead at the scene. The police found the bodies of the three girls, who had been murdered by their father earlier that evening, in the cab of the truck.

Jessica Gonzales brought a 1983 action on behalf of herself and her deceased daughters against the City of Castle Rock, Colorado, and three Castle Rock police officers. She claimed her due process rights were violated by the officers' failure to enforce the restraining order against her husband. The district court dismissed the case, holding that there was no violation of either substantive or procedural due process. The Supreme Court ultimately upheld the trial court ruling on the basis of the well-established tradition of police discretion to determine whether to make arrests. The Court rejected the argument that domestic violence statutes calling for arrest are intended by the legislature to be different from other criminal statutes in this regard.

Gonzales then petitioned the Inter-American Commission on Human Rights, alleging that the United States violated several of her rights under the American Declaration on the Rights and Duties of Man. The Commission concluded:

> [T]he [United States] failed to act with due diligence to protect [Gonzales and her daughters] from domestic violence, which violated the State's obligation not to discriminate and to provide for equal protection before the law under Article II of the American Declaration. The State also failed to undertake reasonable measures to protect the life of [the daughters] in violation of their right to life under Article I of the American Declaration, in conjunction with their right to special protection as girl-children under Article VII of the American Declaration. Finally, the Commission finds that the State violated the right to judicial protection of [Gonzales and her daughters], under Article XVIII of the American Declaration.

Lenahan (Gonzales) v. United States, Inter-Am. C.H.R., Report No. 80/11 ¶ 5 (2011). Commentary on *Castle Rock* includes Julie Goldscheid, Rethinking Civil Rights and Gender Violence, 14 Geo. J. Gender & L. 43 (2013); G. Kristian Miccio, The Death of the Fourteenth Amendment: *Castle Rock* and Its Progeny, 17 Wm. & Mary J. Women & L. 277 (2011); Atinuke O. Awoyomi, The State-Created Danger Doctrine in Domestic Violence Cases: Do We Have a Solution in *Okin v. Village of Cornwall-on-Hudson Police Department?*, 20 Colum. J. Gender & L. 1 (2011). The second issue of Volume 21 of the American University Journal of Gender, Social Policy and the Law (2012) is a symposium issue on *Castle Rock*.

NOTE: FEDERAL DOMESTIC VIOLENCE LEGISLATION

The Violence Against Women Act of 1994 (VAWA), Pub. L. No. 103-322, codified as amended in various sections of 8, 18, and 42 U.S.C. (1994), provides federal civil and criminal remedies for victims of violence motivated by gender-based animus. VAWA also requires that states give full faith and credit to and enforce domestic violence restraining orders from other states. 18 U.S.C. § 2265. An order that is valid according to the law of the state that issued it must be enforced, even if it includes terms or applies to parties that the law of the forum state would not permit. For a discussion, *see* Emily J. Sack, Domestic Violence Across State Lines: The Full Faith and Credit Clause, Congressional Power, and Interstate Enforcement of Protection Orders, 98 Nw. U. L. Rev. 827 (2004).

The broadest provision of VAWA, 42 U.S.C. § 13981, declared that all persons have "the right to be free of crimes of violence motivated by gender" and created a federal cause of action, including compensatory and punitive damages, for victims of such offenses. Federal authority for this legislation rested on the commerce clause and Section 5 of the Fourteenth Amendment. In United States v. Morrison, 529 U.S. 598 (2000), the Supreme Court held that Congress lacked authority under the commerce clause or otherwise to enact this remedy. The Court expressed concern about the extent to which the assumption of congressional authority over domestic violence impaired state authority over family law issues. For a discussion of *Morrison* and its implications for VAWA, on the one hand, and state authority over family law matters, on the other, *see* Sally F. Goldfarb, "No Civilized System of Justice": The Fate of the Violence Against Women Act, 102 W. Va. L. Rev. 499 (2000).

State and federal laws also limit the availability of firearms to domestic violence offenders. The federal Gun Control Act prohibits a person who is subject to a domestic violence restraining order from possessing a firearm during the life of the order, and a person convicted of a misdemeanor crime of domestic violence is barred for life from possessing a firearm. 18 U.S.C. § 922(g)(8), (9). In United States v. Hayes, 555 U.S. 415 (2009), the Supreme Court held that this prohibition applies to a person who was convicted of a generic misdemeanor of violence where the victim was the offender's spouse or intimate partner, even if the existence of a domestic relationship between the victim and offender was not an element of the misdemeanor. However, the Court said, in a prosecution for violating the gun law, the prosecution must prove beyond a reasonable doubt that the domestic relationship existed.

Federal law allows states to grant Temporary Assistance to Needy Families (TANF) benefits to victims of domestic violence while exempting them for as long as necessary from the usual limits on welfare recipients, including work requirements, the five-year lifetime limit on benefits, residency requirements, and child support cooperation requirements. 42 U.S.C. § 602(7). Critics argue that generally the states underutilize these options, however. *See, e.g.*, Laurie Pompa, The Family Violence Option in Texas: Why Is It Failing to Aid Domestic Violence Victims on Welfare and What to Do About It, 16 Tex. J. Women & L. 241, 251 (2007); Rachel J. Gallagher, Welfare Reform's Inadequate Implementation of the Family Violence Option: Exploring the Dual Oppression of Poor Domestic Violence Victims, 19 Am. U. J. Gender Soc. Pol'y & L. 987 (2011).

3. Tort Liability

HAKKILA v. HAKKILA

812 P.2d 1320 (N.M. App. 1991)

HARTZ, Judge. In response to the petition of E. Arnold Hakkila (husband) for dissolution of marriage, Peggy J. Hakkila (wife) counter-petitioned for damages arising from alleged intentional infliction of emotional distress. Husband appeals from the judgment entered against him on the tort claim. . . .

Husband and wife were married on October 29, 1975. Each had been married before. They permanently separated in February 1985. Husband filed his petition for dissolution of marriage the following month. Husband, who holds a Ph.D. in chemistry, had been employed at Los Alamos National Laboratory throughout the marriage. Wife, a high school graduate with credit hours toward a baccalaureate degree in chemistry and a vocational degree as a chemical technician, had been employed at the laboratory as a secretary for seven years and as a chemical technician for about seven and one-half years. She voluntarily terminated her employment in December 1979.

The district court found that "[wife's] emotional and mental health, especially since the parties' separation, has been shown to have been characterized by acute depression and one psychotic episode." The district court's findings noted conflicting testimony concerning wife's past and current mental condition. The district court summarized one psychologist's testimony as diagnosing wife "as subject to a borderline personally disorder pre-dating the parties' marriage," and summarized another's as diagnosing her as "an intellectualizing personality in the early years of her marriage and as suffering from acute depression since approximately 1981." Apparently all the experts agreed that wife was temporarily emotionally disabled at the time of the hearing. . . .

a. There was evidence of several incidents of assault and battery. In late 1984 when wife was pushing her finger in husband's chest, he grabbed her wrist and twisted it severely. In 1981 during an argument in their home husband grabbed wife and threw her face down across the room, into a pot full of dirt. In 1978 when wife was putting groceries in the camper, husband slammed part of the camper shell down on her head and the trunk lid on her hands. In 1976 and "sometimes thereafter" during consensual sexual intercourse husband would use excessive force in attempting to stimulate wife with his hands.

b. The one incident in which husband insulted wife in the presence of others was at a friend's Christmas party. At about 11:00 P.M. wife approached husband, who was "weaving back and forth with his hands in his pockets," and suggested that they go home. Husband began screaming, "You f— bitch, leave me alone." Wife excused herself and walked home alone.

c. Wife also testified that when she and husband were home alone he would go into rages and scream at her. There was no evidence of his screaming at her in the presence of others except for the incident described in "b."

d. The locking-out incident occurred after husband returned from a trip. Wife had been at a friend's home where she had eaten dinner and had some wine. During an argument that had ensued when he returned, she grabbed his shirt and popped all the buttons off. She went downstairs and stepped outside. He closed and locked the door. She went across the street to a home of neighbors, who let her in. He then threw his clothes into a camper and drove off for the night. When he returned the next morning, they made up and made love.

e. On several occasions husband told wife that "you prefer women to men." He did not use the word "lesbian." He testified that he meant only that wife preferred the company of other women to his company. She did not testify that his remarks had sexual connotations.

f. Throughout the marriage husband made remarks such as, "You're just plain sick, you're just stupid, you're just insane." . . .

Husband argues that as a matter of public policy one spouse should have no cause of action against the other spouse for intentional infliction of emotional distress. . . .

"New Mexico recognizes the tort of intentional infliction of emotional distress." The tort (also known as the tort of "outrage") is described in Restatement (Second) of Torts Section 46 (1965) (the Restatement):

Outrageous Conduct Causing Severe Emotional Distress

(1) One who by extreme and outrageous conduct intentionally or recklessly causes severe emotional distress to another is subject to liability for such emotional distress, and if bodily harm to the other results from it, for such bodily harm.

(2) Where such conduct is directed at a third person, the actor is subject to liability if he intentionally or recklessly causes severe emotional distress

(a) to a member of such person's immediate family who is present at the time, whether or not such distress results in bodily harm, or

(b) to any other person who is present at the time, if such distress results in bodily harm.

Wife contends that we must recognize the tort when committed by one spouse against the other because New Mexico has abandoned immunity for interspousal torts. Yet the abolition of immunity does not mean that the existence of the marriage must be ignored in determining the scope of liability. After explaining the reasons for abolition of interspousal immunity, the commentary to Restatement Section 895F points out:

> The intimacy of the family relationship may . . . involve some relaxation in the application of the concept of reasonable care, particularly in the confines of the home. Thus, if one spouse in undressing leaves shoes out where the other stumbles over them in the dark, or if one spouse spills coffee on the other while they are both still sleepy, this may well be treated as not negligence.

Id., comment h. The comment refers to Section 895G comment k, which explains that despite abolition of parental immunity:

> The intimacies of family life also involve intended physical contacts that would be actionable between strangers but may be commonplace and expected within the family. Family romping, even roughhouse play and momentary flares of temper not producing serious hurt, may be normal in many households, to the point that the privilege arising from consent becomes analogous.

Thus, the family relationship can be an important consideration in analyzing intrafamilial torts, both negligent and intentional. Despite the abolition of interspousal immunity, we must still evaluate wife's claims in light of the marital context in which they arose. . . .

Considerations that justify limiting liability for intentional infliction of emotional distress to only outrageous conduct also suggest a very limited scope for the tort in the marital context.

Conduct intentionally or recklessly causing emotional distress to one's spouse is prevalent in our society. This is unfortunate but perhaps not surprising, given the length and intensity of the marital relationship. Yet even when the conduct of feuding spouses is not particularly unusual, high emotions can readily cause an offended spouse to view the other's misconduct as "extreme and outrageous." Thus, if the tort of outrage is construed loosely or broadly, claims of outrage may be tacked on in typical marital disputes, taxing judicial resources.

In addition, a spouse's most distressing conduct is likely to be privileged. Partners who are pledged to live together for a lifetime have a right to criticize each other's behavior. Cf. Cole, Intentional Infliction of Emotional Distress Among Family Members, 61 Denv. U. L. Rev. 553, 574 (1984) ("Cole") ("Because the family's functioning depends on open and free communication, even negative give and take is necessary."). Even though one may question the utility of such comments, spouses are also free to express negative opinions of one another. "You look awful" or even "I don't love you" can be very wounding, but these statements cannot justify liability. See Restatement 46 illustration 13 (you look "like a hippopotamus").

Not only should intramarital activity ordinarily not be the basis for tort liability, it should also be protected against disclosure in tort litigation. Although the spouse who raises a claim of outrage has no right to complain of the exposure of matters relevant to the claim, courts must be sensitive to the privacy interests of the defending spouse. Any litigation of a claim is certain to require exposure of the intimacies of married life. . . .

Moreover, largely because so much interspousal communication is privileged (not in the evidentiary sense, but in the sense that it cannot be the basis for liability), a reliable determination of causation is difficult if not impossible when outrage is alleged in this context. The connection between the outrageousness of the conduct of one spouse and the severe emotional distress of the other will likely be obscure. Although the victim spouse may well be suffering severe emotional distress, was it caused by the outrageousness of the conduct or by the implied (and privileged) message of antipathy? What could be more devastating to one's spouse than to say, "I don't love you any more" — a statement that could not form the basis for a cause of action? Rejection alone can create severe emotional distress. Suicides by jilted lovers are legion. Every adult knows individuals who have sunk into disabling depression when a spouse seeks divorce. As a result, litigation of an interspousal claim of outrage could easily degenerate into a battle of self-proclaimed experts performing psychological autopsies to "discover" whether the cause of the emotional distress was some particular despicable conduct or simply rejection by a loved one. . . .

In summary, concerns that necessitate limiting the tort of intentional infliction of emotional distress to "extreme and outrageous" conduct — (1) preventing burdensome litigation of the commonplace, (2) protecting privileged conduct and (3) avoiding groundless allegations of causation — argue strongly in favor of extreme care in recognizing intramarital claims of outrage.

A cautious approach to the tort of intramarital outrage also finds support in the public policy of New Mexico to avoid inquiry into what went wrong in a marriage. New Mexico was the first state to provide for no-fault divorce on the ground of incompatibility. New Mexico apportions community property without regard to fault, and grants alimony without consideration of punishment to either spouse. . . .

Consequently, in determining when the tort of outrage should be recognized in the marital setting, the threshold of outrageousness should be set high enough — or the circumstances in which the tort is recognized should be described precisely enough, e.g., child snatching — that the social good from recognizing the tort will not be outweighed by unseemly and invasive litigation of meritless claims.

Some jurisdictions have apparently set the threshold of outrageousness so high in the marital context as to bar all suits. . . .

We now move to the specifics of the case before us. The merits of wife's claim can be disposed of summarily. Husband's insults and outbursts fail to meet the legal standard of outrageousness. He was privileged to refrain from intercourse. There was no evidence that the other conduct caused severe emotional distress, as opposed to transient pain or discomfort.

Indeed, this case illustrates the risk of opening the door too wide to claims of this nature. Despite the claim's lack of merit, husband was subjected to a six-day trial, to say nothing of discovery and other preparation, surveying the rights and wrongs of a ten-year marriage. Motions for summary judgment should be viewed sympathetically in similar cases. If the potential harms from this kind of litigation are too frequently realized, it may be necessary to reconsider husband's suggestion that the tort of outrage be denied in the interspousal context.

We reverse the decision in favor of wife on her claim of intentional infliction of emotional distress. . . .

NOTES AND QUESTIONS

1. Until the middle of the twentieth century, tort suits between spouses were barred by the doctrine of spousal immunity, which was justified, in part, as protecting marital privacy. The first case abolishing immunity was decided by the Alabama Supreme Court in 1932. Bennett v. Bennett, 140 So. 378 (Ala. 1932). All but four states have abolished or severely limited the doctrine. Bozman v. Bozman, 830 A.2d 450, 465-466 (Md. App. 2003).

2. The Restatement (Second) of Torts says that some conduct that would be tortious between strangers is not actionable between spouses, giving the example of "family roughhousing." Does this principle express a vestige of the family privacy doctrine, or is there another reason for it? Was Mr. Hakkila's conduct, which the court found not to be actionable, of the same variety?

Courts have upheld judgments between spouses or former spouses for the tort of outrage, usually when the evidence shows repeated and sustained physical abuse. *E.g.*, Feltmeier v. Feltmeier, 777 N.E.2d 1032 (Ill. App. 2002); Henriksen v. Cameron, 622 A.2d 1135 (Me. 1993).

3. If one partner can sue the other in tort at the same time that the couple is litigating the breakup of the relationship, complex procedural questions can arise. A concurring judge in *Hakkila* outlined some of the problems:

> The facts in this case, however, illustrate the problems confronting the trial court when a tort claim for intentional infliction of emotional distress is joined and tried together with an action for dissolution of marriage. The problems are compounded where a jury trial is demanded in the trial of the tort claim and where the action for dissolution of marriage also involves a claim of alimony. Here, the trial court granted an award of alimony to the wife, based upon a finding that she was in need of $1,050.00 per month to meet her economic needs. The alimony award appears to duplicate in part the compensatory damage award granted to the wife on her claim of intentional infliction of emotional distress. . . .
>
> In order for a claimant to establish a prima facie claim of intentional infliction of emotional distress, the elements which must be proven are (1) the conduct in question was extreme and outrageous; (2) the conduct of the defendant was

intentional or in reckless disregard of the plaintiff; (3) the plaintiff's mental distress was extreme and severe; and (4) there is a causal connection between the defendant's conduct and the claimant's mental distress. . . . Applying the above requirements to the facts of this case, the continued verbal outbursts and insults of the husband, directed to wife, although patently providing grounds for dissolution of the marriage, did not reach the threshold requirement imposed by the first element of the four-prong test delineated above. Moreover, wife failed to present evidence distinguishing the emotional distress resulting from husband's conduct toward the wife and the accompanying emotional distress resulting from the breakup of the marriage of the parties, as required under the third and fourth elements outlined above. . . .

. . . Because emotional distress, and at times severe emotional distress, is a concomitant factor accompanying the dissolution of many marriages, litigation of a tort claim for intentional infliction of emotional distress at the same time the court is hearing an action for dissolution of marriage improperly injects issues of fault into no-fault divorce proceedings and is destructive of efforts of the trial court to mediate custody and property disputes or to achieve an equitable resolution of the issues between the parties. Moreover, if the tort claim is pursued under a contingent fee agreement, the wife's claim for attorney's fees in the divorce proceeding may become, as in the present case, blurred. The better procedure for the trial judge to follow where a tort claim for outrage is joined with an action for dissolution of marriage is to bifurcate the tort claim from the trial of the divorce proceedings so that the tort claim may be tried separately. . . .

812 P.2d at 1330-1331 (concurring opinion of Judge Donnelly).

4. For in-depth discussions of these issues and other issues regarding liability of spouses and domestic partners for torts against each other, *see* Michelle L. Evans, Wrongs Committed During a Marriage: The Child that No Area of the Law Wants to Adopt, 66 Wash. & Lee L. Rev. 465 (2009); Sarah M. Buel, Access to Meaningful Remedy: Overcoming Doctrinal Obstacles in Tort Litigation Against Domestic Violence Offenders, 83 Or. L. Rev. 945 (2004).

D. REPRODUCTIVE CHOICE

The following materials deal with reproductive decision making by mothers and fathers-to-be during pregnancy. The first section summarizes Supreme Court doctrine recognizing an interest in privacy with respect to procreative choice and defining the extent to which the state can limit that liberty interest. Here, the question is allocation of authority between the state and the mother. The second section addresses the question of who has the authority to make reproductive decisions within the family—that is, between the mother and the father. These materials raise once again difficult problems in conceptualizing the family and in defining its internal relations and its relations with the state.

1. *Reproductive Rights and Interests*

In Griswold v. Connecticut, 381 U.S. 479 (1965), the Supreme Court recognized a constitutionally protected interest in privacy. Appellant Griswold, the

executive director of Planned Parenthood of Connecticut, challenged the constitutionality of a Connecticut statute making it an offense to use, or assist another in
using, "any drug, medicinal article, or instrument for the purpose of preventing
conception." It is impossible to capture the flavor of this case briefly, but for our
purpose it is enough to say that a majority of the Court held the law unconstitutional. Justice Douglas, writing for the Court, concluded that specific
constitutional guarantees generated "penumbras," which, although not mentioned in specific terms by the Constitution, nonetheless were entitled to
constitutional protection. With respect to this case, Justice Douglas found
that a number of specific guarantees — including the First Amendment's protection of speech and belief; the Third Amendment's prohibition against the
quartering during peacetime of soldiers in any house; the Fourth Amendment's
protection of persons, houses, and property against unreasonable search and
seizure; and the Fifth Amendment privilege against self-incrimination — created
zones of privacy that are entitled to constitutional protection. This right to privacy, Justice Douglas concluded, reached the law forbidding the *use* of
contraceptives.

> Such a law cannot stand in light of the familiar principle, so often applied by this
> Court, that a "governmental purpose to control or prevent activities constitutionally
> subject to state regulation may not be achieved by means which sweep unnecessarily
> broadly and thereby invade the area of protected freedoms." NAACP v. Alabama, 377
> U.S. 288, 307. Would we allow the police to search the sacred precincts of marital
> bedrooms for telltale signs of the use of contraceptives? The very idea is repulsive to
> the notions of privacy surrounding the marriage relationship.
>
> We deal with a right of privacy older than the Bill of Rights — older than our
> political parties, older than our school system. Marriage is a coming together for
> better or for worse, hopefully enduring, and intimate to the degree of being sacred. It
> is an association that promotes a way of life, not causes; a harmony in living, not
> political faiths; a bilateral loyalty, not commercial or social projects. Yet it is an
> association for as noble a purpose as any involved in our prior decisions.

Justice Goldberg, joined by Chief Justice Warren and Justice Brennan, concurred. They agreed that the concept of liberty in the Fourteenth Amendment due
process clause was not confined to the specific terms of the Bill of Rights and,
moreover, that it "embraced the right of marital privacy."

Roe v. Wade, 410 U.S. 113 (1973), presented the Court a further opportunity
to define the scope of, and state power with respect to, the privacy right.
The appellant was a single woman residing in Texas who sought a declaratory
judgment that the Texas criminal abortion statutes were unconstitutional on their
face. She alleged that she was unmarried, pregnant, indigent, and could not secure
a legal abortion because her life was not threatened by her pregnancy.

Justice Blackmun's opinion for the Court includes the following elements:
The right to privacy is broad enough to encompass a woman's decision whether or
not to terminate her pregnancy; that right is a "fundamental right" that can be
restricted by the state only when it can show a "compelling interest" and when its
regulations are "narrowly drawn to express only the legitimate state interests at
stake."

Justice Blackmun then applied this analytical framework to the Texas statute. The state had argued that a fetus is a "person" and therefore its protection under the Fourteenth Amendment was a compelling state interest. Justice Blackmun found no consensus in either state laws or other sources for the proposition that the "unborn" are persons in the whole sense and held that Texas could not, by adopting one of the various theories of life, generally override the rights of the pregnant woman.

Justice Rehnquist dissented. He could not agree that the right of privacy recognized in earlier cases included a right to terminate a pregnancy, nor that any liberty interest the mother might have in consensual transactions was entitled to the high level of protection accorded fundamental rights.

Roe v. Wade was followed by a wide variety of statutes seeking to define (or limit) the conditions under which women could obtain abortions. In Planned Parenthood of Southeastern Pennsylvania v. Casey, 505 U.S. 833 (1992), Justice O'Connor announced the judgment of the Court and concluded, after lengthy consideration of the policy embodied in *stare decisis*, that *Roe* should not be entirely abandoned.

Justice O'Connor's opinion holds that the basic decision in *Roe* — that is, recognizing a constitutional liberty to some freedom in deciding whether to terminate a pregnancy — will not be repudiated. In addition, the opinion reaffirms the proposition that, before viability, a woman has the right to choose to terminate her pregnancy. However, the opinion rejects specific tests employed in Roe v. Wade.

> As our jurisprudence relating to all liberties save perhaps abortion has recognized, not every law which makes a right more difficult to exercise is, ipso facto, an infringement of that right. . . . The fact that a law which serves a valid purpose, one not designed to strike at the right itself, has the incidental effect of making it more difficult or more expensive to procure an abortion cannot be enough to invalidate it. Only where state regulation imposes an undue burden on a woman's ability to make this decision does the power of the State reach into the heart of the liberty protected by the Due Process Clause. . . .
>
> A finding of an undue burden is a shorthand for the conclusion that a state regulation has the purpose or effect of placing a substantial obstacle in the path of a woman seeking an abortion of a nonviable fetus. A statute with this purpose is invalid because the means chosen by the State to further the interest in potential life must be calculated to inform the woman's free choice, not hinder it. And a statute which, while furthering the interest in potential life or some other valid state interest, has the effect of placing a substantial obstacle in the path of a woman's choice cannot be considered a permissible means of serving its legitimate ends. To the extent that the opinions of the Court or of individual Justices use the undue burden standard in a manner that is inconsistent with this analysis, we set out what in our view should be the controlling standard. Understood another way, we answer the question, left open in previous opinions discussing the undue burden formulation, whether a law designed to further the State's interest in fetal life which imposes an undue burden on the woman's decision before fetal viability could be constitutional. The answer is no.
>
> Some guiding principles should emerge. What is at stake is the woman's right to make the ultimate decision, not a right to be insulated from all others in doing so. Regulations which do no more than create a structural mechanism by which the State, or the parent or guardian of a minor, may express profound respect for the life of the unborn are permitted, if they are not a substantial obstacle to the woman's exercise of

the right to choose. Unless it has that effect on her right of choice, a state measure designed to persuade her to choose childbirth over abortion will be upheld if reasonably related to that goal. Regulations designed to foster the health of a woman seeking an abortion are valid if they do not constitute an undue burden.

2. *Spousal Consent and Notice*

PLANNED PARENTHOOD OF CENTRAL MISSOURI V. DANFORTH

428 U.S. 52 (1976)

BLACKMUN, J. This case is a logical and anticipated corollary to Roe v. Wade, 410 U.S. 113 (1973), and Doe v. Bolton, 410 U.S. 179 (1973), for it raises issues secondary to those that were then before the Court. Indeed, some of the questions now presented were forecast and reserved in *Roe* and *Doe*. . . .

The spouse's consent. Section 3(3) requires the prior written consent of the spouse of the woman seeking an abortion during the first 12 weeks of pregnancy, unless "the abortion is certified by a licensed physician to be necessary in order to preserve the life of the mother."

The appellees defend § 3(3) on the ground that it was enacted in the light of the General Assembly's "perception of marriage as an institution," and that any major change in family status is a decision to be made jointly by the marriage partners. Reference is made to an abortion's possible effect on the woman's childbearing potential. . . . Reference is made to adultery and bigamy as criminal offenses; to Missouri's general requirement that for an adoption of a child born in wedlock the consent of both parents is necessary; to similar joint-consent requirements imposed by a number of States with respect to artificial insemination and the legitimacy of children so conceived; to the laws of two States requiring spousal consent for voluntary sterilization; and to the long-established requirement of spousal consent for the effective disposition of an interest in real property. It is argued that "(r)ecognizing that the consent of both parties is generally necessary . . . to begin a family, the legislature has determined that a change in the family structure set in motion by mutual consent should be terminated only by mutual consent," and that what the legislature did was to exercise its inherent policymaking power "for what was believed to be in the best interests of all the people of Missouri."

The appellants on the other hand, contend that § 3(3) obviously is designed to afford the husband the right unilaterally to prevent or veto an abortion, whether or not he is the father of the fetus, and that this not only violates *Roe* and *Doe* but is also in conflict with other decided cases. They also refer to the situation where the husband's consent cannot be obtained because he cannot be located. And they assert that § 3(3) is vague and overbroad.

In *Roe* and *Doe* we specifically reserved decision on the question whether a requirement for consent by the father of the fetus, by the spouse, or by the parents, or a parent, of an unmarried minor, may be constitutionally imposed. We now hold that the State may not constitutionally require the consent of the spouse, as is specified under § 3(3) of the Missouri Act, as a condition for abortion during the first 12 weeks of pregnancy. We thus agree with the dissenting judge in the present case, and with the courts whose decisions are cited above, that the State cannot "delegate to a spouse a veto power which the state itself is absolutely and totally prohibited from exercising during the first trimester of pregnancy." Clearly, since the State cannot regulate or proscribe abortion during the first stage, when the physician and his patient make that decision, the State cannot delegate authority to any particular person, even the spouse, to prevent abortion during that same period.

We are not unaware of the deep and proper concern and interest that a devoted and protective husband has in his wife's pregnancy and in the growth and development of the fetus she is carrying. Neither has this Court failed to appreciate the importance of the marital relationship in our society. *See, e.g.,* Griswold v. Connecticut, 381 U.S. 479, 486 (1965); Maynard v. Hill, 125 U.S. 190, 211 (1888). Moreover, we recognize that the decision whether to undergo or to forgo an abortion may have profound effects on the future of any marriage, effects that are both physical and mental, and possibly deleterious. Notwithstanding these factors, we cannot hold that the State has the constitutional authority to give the spouse unilaterally the ability to prohibit the wife from terminating her pregnancy, when the State itself lacks that right.

It seems manifest that, ideally, the decision to terminate a pregnancy should be one concurred in by both the wife and her husband. No marriage may be viewed as harmonious or successful if the marriage partners are fundamentally divided on so important and vital an issue. But it is difficult to believe that the goal of fostering mutuality and trust in a marriage, and of strengthening the marital relationship and the marriage institution, will be achieved by giving the husband a veto power exercisable for any reason whatsoever or for no reason at all. Even if the State had the ability to delegate to the husband a power it itself could not exercise, it is not at all likely that such action would further, as the District Court majority phrased it, the "interest of the state in protecting the mutuality of decisions vital to the marriage relationship."

We recognize, of course, that when a woman, with the approval of her physician but without the approval of her husband, decides to terminate her pregnancy, it could be said that she is acting unilaterally. The obvious fact is that when the wife and the husband disagree on this decision, the view of only one of the two marriage partners can prevail. Inasmuch as it is the woman who physically bears the child and who is the more directly and immediately affected by the pregnancy, as between the two, the balance weighs in her favor.

We conclude that § 3(3) of the Missouri Act is inconsistent with the standards enunciated in Roe v. Wade, and is unconstitutional. It is therefore unnecessary for us to consider the appellants' additional challenges to § 3(3) based on vagueness and overbreadth.

NOTES AND QUESTIONS

1. Could the Court have left *Roe* standing without invalidating the spousal consent provision in *Danforth*? Could, for example, the Court have said that *Roe*

involved only the claim of a single woman and could not, therefore, have considered the claims of her husband?

2. The majority understands the issue in terms of a zero-sum game involving the husband and wife. Is there no intermediate ground? Suppose that the husband brought an action to enjoin his wife from having an abortion. Suppose he conceded that the marriage might not survive his action, but announced a readiness to take sole custody of the child upon delivery, if the mother so desired. Does *Danforth* control the result of that proceeding?

PLANNED PARENTHOOD OF SOUTHEASTERN PENNSYLVANIA V. CASEY

505 U.S. 833 (1992)

Section 3209 of Pennsylvania's abortion law provides, except in cases of medical emergency, that no physician shall perform an abortion on a married woman without receiving a signed statement from the woman that she has notified her spouse that she is about to undergo an abortion. The woman has the option of providing an alternative signed statement certifying that her husband is not the man who impregnated her; that her husband could not be located; that the pregnancy is the result of spousal sexual assault which she has reported; or that the woman believes that notifying her husband will cause him or someone else to inflict bodily injury upon her. A physician who performs an abortion on a married woman without receiving the appropriate signed statement will have his or her license revoked, and is liable to the husband for damages.

The District Court heard the testimony of numerous expert witnesses, and made detailed findings of fact regarding the effect of this statute. These included:

273. The vast majority of women consult their husbands prior to deciding to terminate their pregnancy. . . .

281. Studies reveal that family violence occurs in two million families in the United States. This figure, however, is a conservative one. . . . In fact, researchers estimate that one of every two women will be battered at some time in their life. . . .

298. Because of the nature of the battering relationship, battered women are unlikely to avail themselves of the exceptions to section 3209 of the Act, regardless of whether the section applies to them.

These findings are supported by studies of domestic violence.

The American Medical Association (AMA) has published a summary of the recent research in this field, which indicates that in an average 12-month period in this country, approximately two million women are the victims of severe assaults by their male partners. In a 1985 survey, women reported that nearly one of every eight husbands had assaulted their wives during the past year. The AMA views these figures as "marked underestimates," because the nature of these incidents discourages women from reporting them, and because surveys typically exclude the very poor, those who do not speak English well, and women who are homeless or in institutions or hospitals when the survey is conducted. According to the AMA, "[r]esearchers on family violence agree that the true incidence of partner violence is probably double the above estimates; or four million severely assaulted women per year. Studies suggest that from one-fifth to one-third of all women will be physically assaulted by a partner or ex-partner during their lifetime." AMA Council on Scientific Affairs, Violence Against Women 7 (1991). Thus on an average day in the United States, nearly 11,000 women are severely assaulted by their male partners. Many of these incidents involve sexual assault. . . .

The limited research that has been conducted with respect to notifying one's husband about an abortion, although involving samples too small to be representative, also supports the District Court's findings of fact. The vast majority of women notify their male partners of their decision to obtain an abortion. In many cases in which married women do not notify their husbands, the pregnancy is the result of an extramarital affair. Where the husband is the father, the primary reason women do not notify their husbands is that the husband and wife are experiencing marital difficulties, often accompanied by incidents of violence. . . .

The spousal notification requirement is thus likely to prevent a significant number of women from obtaining an abortion. It does not merely make abortions a little more difficult or expensive to obtain; for many women, it will impose a substantial obstacle. . . .

We recognize that a husband has a "deep and proper concern and interest . . . in his wife's pregnancy and in the growth and development of the fetus she is carrying." *Danforth*, supra. With regard to the children he has fathered and raised, the Court has recognized his "cognizable and substantial" interest in their custody. Stanley v. Illinois, 405 U.S. 645, 651-52 (1972). . . . If this case concerned a State's ability to require the mother to notify the father before taking some action with respect to a living child raised by both, therefore, it would be reasonable to conclude as a general matter that the father's interest in the welfare of the child and the mother's interest are equal.

Before birth, however, the issue takes on a very different cast. It is an inescapable biological fact that state regulation with respect to the child a woman is carrying will have a far greater impact on the mother's liberty than on the father's. . . . The Court has held that "when the wife and the husband disagree on this decision, the view of only one of the two marriage partners can prevail. Inasmuch as it is the woman who physically bears the child and who is the more directly affected by the pregnancy, as between the two, the balance weighs in her favor." *Danforth*. This conclusion rests upon the basic nature of marriage and the nature of our Constitution: "[T]he marital couple is not an independent entity with a mind and heart of its own, but an association of two individuals each with a separate intellectual and emotional makeup. If the right of privacy means anything, it is the right of the *individual*, married or single, to be free from unwarranted governmental intrusion into matters so fundamentally affecting a person as the decision whether to bear or beget a child." . . .

The principles that guided *Danforth* should be our guides today. For the great many women who are victims of abuse inflicted by their husbands, or whose children are the victims of such abuse, a spousal notice requirement enables the husband to wield an effective veto over his wife's decision. Whether the prospect of notification itself deters such women from seeking abortions, or whether the husband, through physical force or psychological pressure or economic coercion, prevents his wife from obtaining an abortion until it is too late, the notice requirement will be tantamount to the veto found unconstitutional in *Danforth*. . . .

NOTES AND QUESTIONS

1. *Casey* held unconstitutional the Pennsylvania requirement that a married woman seeking an abortion inform her husband of her intent and produce a signed statement that she has done so. However, it upheld a parental notification provision in the same statute. The opinion indicates that "[r]egulations which do no more than create a structural mechanism by which the State, or the parent or guardian of a minor, may express profound respect for the life of the unborn are permitted, if they are not a substantial obstacle to the woman's exercise of a right to choose." Why is a regulation that creates a structural mechanism allowing the husband to express his respect for the life of the unborn not permissible?

2. Does the husband of a pregnant woman have any constitutionally cognizable interest deciding whether a fetus will be terminated? If not, on what basis can responsibility after birth be predicated?

3. For discussion of the relationship between the right to abortion and the constitution of the family, *see* Robert Post & Reva Siegel, *Roe* Rage: Democratic Constitutionalism and Backlash, 42 Harv. C.R.-C.L. L. Rev. 373 (2007) (discussing Kristin Luker's work that found widespread opposition to abortion only when it was linked to anxieties about the changing role of women and support for the traditional family); Carol Sanger, Infant Safe Haven Laws: Legislating in the Culture of Life, 106 Colum. L. Rev. 753, 789 (2006) (discussing the relationship between moral panic, abortion, and infant safe haven laws); and Naomi Cahn & June Carbone, Family Classes: Rethinking Contraceptive Choice, 20 U. Fla. J.L. & Pub. Pol'y 361 (2009) (arguing that the two different family systems underlie the tensions between red states and blue states, with red state families entering into marriage and childbearing at younger ages and thus requiring greater social support and structure, and blue states emphasizing contraception and abortion, deferral of family formation until emotional maturity and financial independence, and greater autonomy in family decision making).

4. In 2013 the pregnant former girlfriend of skier Bode Miller moved from California, where Miller lived, to New York after they broke up. When the girlfriend sued Miller for custody in New York, the trial court referee granted his motion to dismiss, finding that the mother's "appropriation" of the child in utero was "reprehensible," warranting an order declining to exercise jurisdiction. The Appellate Division reversed, saying, "the mother's conduct at issue here amounts to nothing more than her decision to relocate to New York during her pregnancy. Further, we reject the Referee's apparent suggestion that, prior to her relocation, the mother needed to somehow arrange her relocation with the father with whom she had only a brief romantic relationship. Putative fathers have neither the right nor the ability to restrict a pregnant woman from her constitutionally-protected liberty (*see* Matter of Wilner v. Prowda, 158 Misc. 2d 579, 601 N.Y.S.2d 518 [(Sup. Ct., N.Y. County 1993)] [refusing the putative father's request to determine custody of the parties' unborn child and restrain his

then-pregnant wife from leaving New York]).” Sara Ashton McK. v. Samuel Bode M., 974 N.Y.S.2d 434, 435-436 (A.D. 2013).

PROBLEM

You are a law clerk to Justice Groat of your state supreme court. The court has taken an appeal in a case arising under a recently adopted state statute, and he would like you to analyze the issues presented.

The facts of the case can be stated relatively simply. Ms. End, the appellant in this case, was pregnant (by her husband) when a long history of marital trouble led to divorce. By the time the divorce action was heard, a child (Ellen) had been born. Mr. End objected to the imposition of any child support obligation for Ellen, citing State Stat. § 400, adopted last year. That statute now provides as follows:

> In cases of divorce, the court shall enter a support order consistent with the [state child support guidelines], unless to do so would be unjust in the circumstances of the case. *It shall be presumed to be unjust to require child support where the mother has intentionally borne a child over the reasonable objection of the father, the father has reasonably sought to avoid conception or birth, and the mother is capable of adequately supporting the child.*

Mr. End testified at the hearing that he did not want to have a child, particularly when it was evident (as it had been for some time) that the marriage was likely to fail. He also testified that his wife had purported to agree and assured him that she was continuing to take birth control pills. Finally, Mr. End testified that, when his wife became pregnant, he immediately and repeatedly asked her to terminate the pregnancy, which she refused to do.

Mr. End called the family physician who delivered Ellen to testify that Ms. End was in good health and that performance of an abortion would not have presented any danger. She further testified that the statistical chances of harm to the mother are greater when bearing the child to term than with an abortion during the first trimester.

Ms. End, testifying as a hostile witness, confirmed Mr. End’s testimony. She conceded that she had not used the pill or any other birth control device around the time she became pregnant, explaining that she “wanted to have a child now, whatever happened to the marriage.” Ms. End also stated that this desire explained her refusal to seek an abortion, against which she has neither religious nor social objections in general. She further testified that she is currently employed as an insurance adjustor, earns an income of $30,000 per year (which is equal to that of Mr. End), and plans to continue working.

On this evidence, the trial judge noted that she ordinarily would be compelled to follow the state child support guidelines, which would have required Mr. End to pay 24 percent of his gross monthly earnings for the support of Ellen. However, she felt that her decision was governed by the italicized portion of § 400, and that no rebuttal evidence had been offered.

Ms. End appeals the trial court decision, arguing that its enforcement is unconstitutional. Please prepare the requested memorandum, analyzing arguments for and against the validity of the italicized portion of the statute.

E. SURROGATE DECISION MAKERS FOR INCOMPETENT ADULTS

If an adult is mentally incapable of making his or her own decisions, or, in the language of the Uniform Probate Code, "incapacitated,"[10] statutes in all jurisdictions create a process that allows a court to appoint a fiduciary, usually called a guardian or guardian of the person, who has the authority and responsibility to make decisions for the incapacitated person. While most of the litigation over guardianship petitions concerns whether the proposed ward is in fact incapacitated and whether a guardianship, rather than some less intrusive mechanism, is necessary to protect the person, the next case concerns who should be appointed as guardian.

IN RE GUARDIANSHIP OF ATKINS

868 N.E.2d 878 (Ind. App. 2007)

BAKER, Chief Judge. Appellant-petitioner Brett Conrad appeals from the trial court's order that, among other things, appointed appellees-cross-petitioners Thomas and Jeanne Atkins (collectively, the Atkinses) as co-guardians of Patrick Atkins and Patrick's estate. . . .

Patrick and Brett met and became romantically involved beginning in 1978 when they attended Wabash College together. Since that time — for twenty-five years — the men have lived together and have been in a committed and loving relationship.

Patrick's family vehemently disapproves of his relationship with Brett. Patrick, however, was able to reconcile his religious faith with his homosexuality and in 2000, Patrick wrote a letter to his family, begging them to accept him and welcome Brett:

> I want you all to know that Brett is my best friend in the whole world and I love him more than life itself. I beg all of you to reach out to him with the same love you have for me, he is extremely special and once you know him you will understand why I love him so much. Trust me, God loves us all so very much, and I know he approves of the love that Brett and I have shared for over 20 years.

Patrick's family, however, has steadfastly refused to accept their son's lifestyle. Jeanne believes that homosexuality is a grievous sin and that Brett and his relatives are "sinners" and are "evil" for accepting Brett and Patrick's relationship. She testified that no amount of evidence could convince her that Patrick and Brett were happy together or that they had a positive and beneficial relationship.

---

10. Uniform Probate Code § 5-102(4) defines an incapacitated person as one who "is unable to receive and evaluate information or make or communicate decisions to such an extent that the individual lacks the ability to meet essential requirements for physical health, safety, or self-care, even with appropriate technological assistance."

Neither Patrick nor Brett earned a degree from Wabash College. In 1982, Patrick began working for the family business, Atkins, Inc. d/b/a Atkins Elegant Desserts and Atkins Cheesecake, and he ultimately became the CEO of that business. Patrick's annual income prior to his incapacitation was approximately $130,000. Brett is a waiter, has been working for Puccini's restaurants for the past ten years, and has an annual income of approximately $31,800. Patrick and Brett pooled their earnings, depositing them into a checking account that was titled solely in Patrick's name but was used as a joint account for payment of living expenses. . . .

Between 1980 and 1992, Brett and Patrick lived together in various apartments. In 1992, they bought a house together in Fishers as joint tenants, and the home is still titled jointly.

On March 11, 2005, Patrick was on a business trip in Atlanta when he collapsed and was admitted to a hospital. Doctors determined that he had suffered a ruptured aneurysm and an acute subarachnoid hemorrhage. Patrick remained in the Intensive Care Unit (ICU) of the Atlanta hospital for six weeks. At some point during his stay in the ICU, Patrick suffered a stroke.

Brett traveled to the Atlanta hospital to be with Patrick; Patrick's family did as well. Patrick's brother testified that Brett's mere presence in the hospital was "hurting" Jeanne and offending her religious beliefs. Jeanne told Brett that if Patrick was going to return to his life with Brett after recovering from the stroke, she would prefer that he not recover at all.

Shortly after Brett's first visit with Patrick in the ICU, Patrick's family restricted the times and duration of Brett's visits. Subsequently, Brett was allowed to see Patrick for only fifteen minutes at a time after the close of regular visiting hours so that Patrick's family would not have to see Brett at all. Eventually, a sign was placed in Patrick's ICU space reading "immediate family and clergy only," purporting to exclude Brett altogether. Nevertheless, hospital staff defied the family's instructions and allowed Brett to continue to visit with Patrick early in the morning and in the evenings, outside of regular visiting hours.

On April 27, 2005, Patrick was moved from the Atlanta hospital to Manor-Care at Summer Trace (Summer Trace), a nursing facility in Carmel. In May and June 2005, Brett visited Patrick daily at Summer Trace, with his visits usually taking place after regular visiting hours so that Patrick's relatives would not see him. Brett was well-received by the Summer Trace staff, who observed that his visits had a positive impact on Patrick's recovery.

On June 20, 2005, Brett filed a guardianship petition, requesting that he be appointed guardian of Patrick's person and property. The Atkinses filed an answer to the petition, a motion to intervene, and a cross-petition requesting that they be appointed co-guardians of Patrick's person and property. Brett eventually voluntarily withdrew his request to be appointed guardian of Patrick's property, seeking only to be named as guardian of Patrick's person.

In mid-August 2005, Patrick was admitted to Zionsville Meadows, another nursing facility, for physical rehabilitation and speech therapy. Brett continued to visit Patrick after regular visiting hours at Zionsville Meadows. Notwithstanding the conclusions of the court-appointed guardian ad litem (GAL) and a neuropsychologist that it would be beneficial to Patrick and his recovery process for Brett to continue to have contact with Patrick, in early November 2005, the Atkinses moved Patrick into their home and have refused to allow Brett to visit with Patrick since that time. The Atkinses have refused phone calls from Brett and requests from Brett and his family members to visit Patrick.

At the time of trial, Patrick was able to walk, dress, bathe, and feed himself with some supervision or prompting, to read printed matter aloud with good accuracy but only 25% comprehension, to engage in simple conversations, to communicate his basic wants and needs, and to answer questions with some prompting. He still required close and constant supervision and had significant problems with short-term memory, attention span, problem-solving, multi-step commands, reacting in urgent situations, and decision-making. The Atkinses took turns supervising or caring for Patrick in their Carmel home and were assisted by a certified home health aide who worked with Patrick daily from 8:30 A.M. until 5:00 P.M. . . .

On January 11, 2006, Brett filed a petition for an order requiring the Atkinses to allow him to visit and have contact with Patrick. At trial, the Atkinses acknowledged that it was "probably true" that if the trial court did not order them to allow visitation between Patrick and Brett, they would not allow any contact between the life partners.

On May 10, 2006, the trial court entered two orders, making very limited findings of fact and disposing of the case by:

- Appointing the Atkinses as co-guardians of Patrick's person and estate;
- Denying Brett's visitation petition and ordering that "it is and shall be the ultimate and sole responsibility of [the Atkinses] to determine and control visitation with and access of visitors to Patrick Atkins in his best interest." . . .

As we consider Brett's challenges to the trial court's judgment, we observe that the trial court is vested with discretion in making determinations as to the guardianship of an incapacitated person. *See* Ind. Code § 29-3-2-4. This discretion extends to both its findings and its order. Thus, we apply the abuse of discretion standard to review the trial court's findings and order. . . .

Brett first argues that the trial court erroneously appointed the Atkinses as Patrick's guardian. . . . The guardianship statutes provide that the following are entitled to consideration for appointment as a guardian . . . in the order listed:

(1) a person designated in a durable power of attorney;
(2) the spouse of an incapacitated person;
(3) an adult child of an incapacitated person;
(4) a parent of an incapacitated person, or a person nominated by will of a deceased parent of an incapacitated person . . . ;
(5) any person related to an incapacitated person by blood or marriage with whom the incapacitated person has resided for more than six (6) months before the filing of the petition;
(6) a person nominated by the incapacitated person who is caring for or paying for the care of the incapacitated person.

I.C. § 29-3-5-5(a). . . . [T]he trial court is authorized to "pass over a person having priority and appoint a person having a lower priority or no priority" if the trial court believes that action to be in the incapacitated person's best interest. The trial court's paramount consideration in making its determination of the person to be appointed guardian is "the best interest of the incapacitated person."

Patrick did not designate Brett for guardianship consideration in a durable power of attorney. Therefore, only if the trial court concluded that it was in Patrick's best interest that Brett be appointed his guardian would his appointment have been proper. Brett makes a sincere and compelling argument that, based on his long-term relationship with Patrick and his heartfelt desire to take care of his life partner, "Patrick's best interest will be served by appointing Brett as guardian over Patrick's person." Under these circumstances, however, our standard of review does not permit us to conduct a de novo analysis of what is in Patrick's best interest. Instead, we must assess whether the trial court abused its discretion when it found that it was in Patrick's best interest that the Atkinses be appointed co-guardians of his person and estate.

The evidence presented established that the Atkinses' home was appropriate for Patrick's care. The Atkinses were actively involved in Patrick's care from the time of his hospitalization in Atlanta until his release to their care, and they have adequately cared for Patrick in their home since November 2005. Other family members are willing and able to assist with Patrick's care as might be necessary in the future. The Atkinses were committed to providing Patrick with the best possible care by applying their own personal efforts, employing outside assistance, and pursuing potentially helpful therapies.

We conclude that there is sufficient evidence in the record supporting a conclusion that the Atkinses and Brett are equally well-equipped to care for Patrick's physical needs. Given the Atkinses' lack of support of their son's personal life through the years and given his mother's astonishing statement that she would rather that he *never recover* than see him return to his relationship with Brett, we are extraordinarily skeptical that the Atkinses are able to take care of Patrick's emotional needs. But we cannot conclude that the record shows that the trial court abused its discretion in denying Brett's guardianship petition. . . .

Brett next argues that the trial court erroneously denied his request for visitation and telephonic contact with Patrick. Turning to the record herein, we note that after observing interactions between Brett and Patrick and between Patrick and his family, the GAL concluded, among other things, as follows:

> . . . It also seems evident that Patrick loves Brett very much and it is evident that Brett loves Patrick.
>
> The challenge in this case seems to be how to provide for all parties to coexist in the best interest of Patrick. It appears that the involvement of *all parties* is paramount to Patrick's continued improvement. . . .
>
> . . . [T]his Guardian Ad Litem strongly believes that an order should be implemented ensuring that *all parties* have regular access to Patrick regardless of who is appointed guardian. All parties to this litigation appear to be truly committed to Patrick's best interest and have no ulterior motives that this Guardian Ad Litem can determine.

The GAL later testified that "cutting back on one of those sources of stimulation or one of those sources of familiarity would just seem to me not to be in Patrick's best interest."

An impartial neuropsychologist who evaluated Patrick testified that people in his profession treating someone with memory problems, such as Patrick, strive to have as many "familiar cues" as possible for the patient "to help try to trigger access to long-term memory as well as to facilitate or try and promote his learning or recognition of new information." The neuropsychologist went on to testify as follows:

A. [A]ssuming that there was a long relationship [between Brett and Patrick] and assuming that . . . that relationship was a significant relationship emotionally and in time it would ordinarily be our objective to reintegrate the patient into that environment so that they can participate in activities and situations with which they're familiar.

Q. Based on your examination and evaluation of Patrick do you have a professional opinion as a neuropsychologist within a reasonable certainty about whether it is appropriate in terms of Patrick's long-term care and rehabilitation and recovery for Patrick's parents to have him continue to live in their home and to prohibit visits from or with Brett?

A. Well, my experience in interacting with the patient and his family were that it seemed that [the Atkinses] were indeed generally interested in his care and were very invested in it. I think, however, that if this relationship [between Brett and Patrick] has persisted as long as you describe that *including Brett in that situation would be at least from a clinical standpoint something that we would recommend. . . .*

Q. Based on what you know and your, of Patrick's background, his family situation, his history, and also on your examination and evaluations of Patrick, do you believe as his neuropsychologist within a reasonable certainty that it would be detrimental to Patrick's health or recovery if he were to see Brett or spend time with Brett outside Patrick's parents' home?

A. I have no reason to believe that it would be detrimental. *I suspect it would be helpful.*

Although the Atkinses argue that there was evidence that "visitation with Brett poses a risk of diminishing Patrick's chance for normalcy of life and possibly causing irreparable psychological harm," they provide no citation in support of this assertion and, indeed, the overwhelming evidence in the record supports a contrary conclusion. . . .

. . . Indeed, the overwhelming wealth of evidence in the record, as well as common sense, establishes that it is in Patrick's best interest that he continue to have contact with Brett, his life partner of over twenty-five years. We cannot conclude, therefore, that the evidence in the record supports the trial court's order denying Brett's request for visitation.

The trial court was required to enter orders to "encourage development of the incapacitated person's self-improvement, self-reliance, and independence" and to "contribute to the incapacitated person's living as normal a life as that person's condition and circumstances permit without psychological or physical harm to the incapacitated person." The trial court was also required to order appropriate relief if it found that the Atkinses were not acting in Patrick's best interest. Ind. Code § 16-36-1-8(d). Given that the evidence overwhelmingly establishes that it is in Patrick's best interest to spend time with Brett and that the Atkinses have made it crystal clear that, absent a court order requiring them to do so, they will not permit Brett to see their son, it was incumbent upon the trial court to order visitation as requested by Brett. Consequently, we reverse the judgment of the trial court on this basis and direct it to amend its order to grant Brett visitation and contact with Patrick as Brett requested. . . .

DARDEN, Judge, dissenting. I would respectfully dissent from the majority's conclusion that the trial court erred when it did not enter an order granting Brett's request for his visitation and contact with Patrick. . . .

NOTES AND QUESTIONS

1. Under the Indiana statutes cited in *Atkins*, if Brett had been Patrick's spouse, he would have been the first choice as guardian. The Indiana statutory priority list is typical. The Uniform Probate Code provides this list:

   (1) a guardian, other than a temporary or emergency guardian, currently acting for the respondent in this State or elsewhere;
   (2) a person nominated as guardian by the respondent, including the respondent's most recent nomination made in a durable power of attorney, if at the time of the nomination the respondent had sufficient capacity to express a preference;
   (3) an agent appointed by the respondent under [a durable power of attorney for health care][the Uniform Health-Care Decisions Act];
   (4) the spouse of the respondent or a person nominated by will or other signed writing of a deceased spouse;
   (5) an adult child of the respondent;
   (6) a parent of the respondent, or an individual nominated by will or other signed writing of a deceased parent; and
   (7) an adult with whom the respondent has resided for more than six months before the filing of the petition.

Uniform Probate Code § 5-310(a) (2010). Under this provision, would Brett have had priority over Patrick's parents? What might explain this preference for an unmarried adult's parents (or adult children) over his or her "life partner"?

2. Under the Indiana statute, Patrick could have executed a durable power of attorney (one that survived his incapacitation) expressing his preference for Brett to be his guardian if that ever became necessary, and Brett would then have had priority over the parents. What might explain Patrick's failure to execute such a document?

3. The court's order allowing Brett to visit Patrick is quite liberal. In a well-known case with facts similar to those in *Atkins*, decided 21 years earlier, the

Minnesota Court of Appeals not only upheld a trial court order appointing an incapacitated adult's father, rather than her life partner, as guardian, but also affirmed the trial court's order giving the father sole authority to determine who could visit her. In re Guardianship of Sharon Kowalski, 382 N.W.2d 861 (Minn. App. 1986). The father had made it quite clear that he would not allow Karen Thompson, Sharon Kowalski's former partner, to see Sharon.

The power of a guardian over an incapacitated person has often been compared to the power of a parent over a child. As we will see in Chapter 9, a parent presumptively has the authority to decide whether other adults will visit a child, and a court can override the parent's choice only upon a showing that the parent's decision is detrimental to the child.

4. The health care facilities in which Patrick was staying allowed Brett to visit, even though he was not part of Patrick's legally recognized family and even though the family objected. Many hospitals and other facilities would not have allowed this, however. In 2009 lawsuits were filed in Florida and Washington when hospitals refused to allow the same-sex partners of patients to see the critically ill patients, even though the patients had executed powers of attorney and other documents nominating their partners as their alternative health care decision makers. Tara Parker-Pope, Kept from a Dying Partner's Bedside, N.Y. Times, May 19, 2009.

5. Most states allow people to execute documents expressing their wishes regarding their own end-of-life care should they become incompetent (living wills), and their choices about who should make health care decisions for them if they are incompetent (powers of attorney for health care). Most people have not executed these documents, however. Nina A. Kohn & Jeremy A. Blumenthal, Designating Health Care Decisionmakers for Patients without Advance Directives: A Psychological Critique, 42 Ga. L. Rev. 979 (2008). Most states have statutes that authorize others to make health care decisions for incompetent patients who have not executed documents expressing their wishes; the priority lists in these statutes are similar to those in guardianship statutes. Id. at 984.

6. As a constitutional matter, family members do not have the right to make health care decisions for their incompetent relatives. In Cruzan v. Director, 497 U.S. 261 (1990), the parents of a woman who was in a persistent vegetative state following an automobile accident sued in state court for an order removing her from life support. The state court denied the order, finding that there was not clear and convincing evidence that she would choose to refuse life support. The Supreme Court rejected the parents' claim that this rule violated due process:

> The Fourteenth Amendment provides that no State shall "deprive any person of life, liberty, or property, without due process of law." The principle that a competent person has a constitutionally protected liberty interest in refusing unwanted medical treatment may be inferred from our prior decisions. . . .
>
> But determining that a person has a "liberty interest" under the Due Process Clause does not end the inquiry; "whether respondent's constitutional rights have been violated must be determined by balancing his liberty interests against the relevant state interests." . . .
>
> . . . [A]n incompetent person is not able to make an informed and voluntary choice to exercise a hypothetical right to refuse treatment or any other right. Such a

"right" must be exercised for her, if at all, by some sort of surrogate. Here, Missouri has in effect recognized that under certain circumstances a surrogate may act for the patient in electing to have hydration and nutrition withdrawn in such a way as to cause death, but it has established a procedural safeguard to assure that the action of the surrogate conforms as best it may to the wishes expressed by the patient while competent. Missouri requires that evidence of the incompetent's wishes as to the withdrawal of treatment be proved by clear and convincing evidence. . . .

. . . The choice between life and death is a deeply personal decision of obvious and overwhelming finality. We believe Missouri may legitimately seek to safeguard the personal element of this choice through the imposition of heightened evidentiary requirements. It cannot be disputed that the Due Process Clause protects an interest in life as well as an interest in refusing life-sustaining medical treatment. Not all incompetent patients will have loved ones available to serve as surrogate decision-makers. And even where family members are present, "[t]here will, of course, be some unfortunate situations in which family members will not act to protect a patient." A State is entitled to guard against potential abuses in such situations. Similarly, a State is entitled to consider that a judicial proceeding to make a determination regarding an incompetent's wishes may very well not be an adversarial one, with the added guarantee of accurate factfinding that the adversary process brings with it. Finally, we think a State may properly decline to make judgments about the "quality" of life that a particular individual may enjoy, and simply assert an unqualified interest in the preservation of human life to be weighed against the constitutionally protected interests of the individual.

In our view, Missouri has permissibly sought to advance these interests through the adoption of a "clear and convincing" standard of proof to govern such proceedings. . . .

Petitioners alternatively contend that Missouri must accept the "substituted judgment" of close family members even in the absence of substantial proof that their views reflect the views of the patient. . . .

No doubt is engendered by anything in this record but that Nancy Cruzan's mother and father are loving and caring parents. If the State were required by the United States Constitution to repose a right of "substituted judgment" with anyone, the Cruzans would surely qualify. But we do not think the Due Process Clause requires the State to repose judgment on these matters with anyone but the patient herself. Close family members may have a strong feeling — a feeling not at all ignoble or unworthy, but not entirely disinterested, either — that they do not wish to witness the continuation of the life of a loved one which they regard as hopeless, meaningless, and even degrading. But there is no automatic assurance that the view of close family members will necessarily be the same as the patient's would have been had she been confronted with the prospect of her situation while competent. All of the reasons previously discussed for allowing Missouri to require clear and convincing evidence of the patient's wishes lead us to conclude that the State may choose to defer only to those wishes rather than confide the decision to close family members. . . .

What assumptions does the Court make about the attitudes, interests, and relationships of families facing the situation in *Cruzan*? For discussion of varying "pictures" of families in judicial discourse, *see* Martha Minow, The Role of Families in Medical Decisions, 1991 Utah L. Rev. 1.

Entering Ceremonial Marriage

3

A. INTRODUCTION

To state the requirements for getting married seems simplicity itself. The parties must agree to marry; they must be generally eligible ("competent") to marry; they must be eligible to marry each other; and they must go through whatever forms are required for marriage in the state where they intend to marry. As we examine the law in this area, what seems simple will come to seem less so. States differ regarding the nature of the requisite agreement. The weight given to compliance with statutory forms for marriage also differs. Laws regarding eligibility to marry differ from state to state and are potentially qualified by constitutional doctrines concerning the power of the state to limit entrance into marriage. Moreover, people in this society tend not to stay put, creating circumstances in which a court in one jurisdiction must pass on the effect to be given marriages contracted in another state or nation.

Finally, whether any given marriage is valid may vary from time to time and from purpose to purpose. As we will see in the course of this chapter, marriage can be — and perhaps ordinarily is — viewed in terms of the social and economic rights and duties of husband and wife for domestic relations purposes. However, that relationship also is as important for determining the various rights, incidents, and benefits that depend on marital or family relationships as it is for its own sake. A variety of social institutions employ familial terms to express the relationships and obligations with which these institutions are concerned; for example, immigration law accords to "spouses of American citizens" a special position, and "spouses" of decedents have an established priority for inheritance purposes and for possible entitlements of workers' compensation and Social Security benefits. To some considerable extent, "one can accurately imagine the family as a hub around which [various intermediate social systems] turn . . . in [their] reliance . . . on family relationships." Lee E. Teitelbaum, Placing the Family in Context, 22 U.C. Davis L. Rev. 801, 818 (1989). Because the various institutional interests that draw on family relationships have their own purposes, however, it is not surprising to find that a marriage may be considered valid for one purpose but not for another.

B. FORMALITIES

The formal requirements for marriage vary somewhat from state to state. Ordinarily, the parties must secure a license. Many states impose a minimum waiting period between the issuance of a license and the marriage celebration, but this can often be waived. A ceremony is also generally required in all states that do not recognize common law marriage. However, the form of ceremony is rarely specified. Statutes typically require that an authorized person conduct the wedding, often with exceptions to recognize the practices of various religious groups or, as in the next case, Native American tribes.

PICKARD V. PICKARD

625 S.E.2d 869 (N.C. App. 2006)

HUDSON, Judge. Carl Glenn Pickard ("plaintiff") appeals from the trial court's order denying the annulment of his marriage to Jane Edwards Pickard ("defendant"). As discussed below, we affirm.

Hawk Littlejohn ("Littlejohn"), a Cherokee Indian, married plaintiff and defendant in the Native American tradition on 7 June 1991. Plaintiff is a physician employed by the University of North Carolina at Chapel Hill ("UNC"). Plaintiff had met Littlejohn at the UNC medical school where Littlejohn lectured as a Cherokee shaman or "medicine man." Littlejohn performed healings and conducted ceremonies in accordance with Cherokee traditions. Littlejohn also possessed a certificate stating that he was ordained as a minister in the Universal Life Church.

Defendant initially desired to be married in a traditional Christian ceremony. Plaintiff persuaded defendant to be married in the Cherokee tradition with Littlejohn performing the ceremony. When Littlejohn performed the wedding ceremony, both the parties believed the ceremony was legally sufficient to bind plaintiff and defendant as husband and wife. Littlejohn conducted the parties' ceremony in accordance with the Cherokee marriage tradition. The parties received a North Carolina license and certificate of marriage on 3 December 2002, which was filed in the Caswell County Register of Deeds office.

After the ceremony, and for the next eleven years, the parties lived together and conducted themselves as husband and wife. In 1998, plaintiff initiated proceedings to adopt defendant's adult biological daughter. In his amended petition for adult adoption, and as a requisite of the adoption, plaintiff provided a sworn statement that he was "the stepfather of the adoptee, having married her natural mother." Plaintiff also listed his marital status as "married." The clerk of superior court in Caswell County filed an amended decree of adoption on 9 November 1998, based on plaintiff's assertions.

On 9 April 2002, the parties separated. On 23 April 2002, plaintiff filed a complaint for annulment of his eleven-year marriage to defendant. On 23 May 2002, defendant answered and denied that plaintiff was entitled to an annulment. After plaintiff presented his evidence, defendant moved for a directed verdict. Counsel for both parties argued and briefed defenses of collateral estoppel and res judicata. . . .

On 27 September 2004, the trial court filed a judgment concluding that the marriage ceremony was not properly solemnized because Littlejohn was not qualified to perform a marriage ceremony. The court denied plaintiff's claim for annulment because plaintiff had asserted under oath, judicially admitted and proved his marriage to defendant in the adoption proceeding. Plaintiff appeals. Defendant argues cross assignments of error. . . .

We begin by noting that the dissent states that Littlejohn was an ordained minister. However, although the trial court found that Littlejohn possessed a certificate stating that he was ordained by the Universal Life Church, "[t]hat at no time was Hawk Littlejohn a minister of the gospel licensed to perform marriages." The court also found and concluded that Littlejohn's ordination was not cured by N.C. Gen. Stat. § 50-1.1. . . .

In its judgment, the trial court concluded as law that although the parties' marriage was not properly solemnized pursuant to statute, plaintiff was estopped from obtaining an annulment on several grounds, including judicial estoppel, quasi-estoppel, collateral estoppel and res judicata. As discussed below, we conclude that judicial estoppel applies here and affirm the trial court's judgment on that basis.

"[J]udicial estoppel seeks to protect courts, not litigants, from individuals who would play 'fast and loose' with the judicial system." In addition, "because of its inherent flexibility as a discretionary equitable doctrine, judicial estoppel plays an important role as a gap-filler, providing courts with a means to protect the integrity of judicial proceedings where doctrines designed to protect litigants might not adequately serve that role." In adopting the framework of the United States Supreme Court as stated in New Hampshire v. Maine, 532 U.S. 742, 121 S. Ct. 1808, 149 L. Ed. 2d 968 (2001), the North Carolina Supreme Court has set forth three factors to be considered in applying judicial estoppel:

> First, a party's subsequent position must be clearly inconsistent with its earlier position. Second, courts regularly inquire whether the party has succeeded in persuading a court to accept that party's earlier position, so that judicial acceptance of an inconsistent position in a later proceeding might pose a threat to judicial integrity by leading to inconsistent court determinations or the perception that either the first or the second court was misled. Third, courts consider whether the party seeking to assert an inconsistent position would derive an unfair advantage or impose an unfair detriment on the opposing party if not estopped.

Here, plaintiff takes the position that his marriage is voidable, a position clearly inconsistent with his sworn statements in the adoption proceedings. The court initially accepted plaintiff's earlier assertion that he was married to defendant in permitting his adoption of defendant's daughter. Although the second adoption order did not explicitly so find, it was based nonetheless on plaintiff's sworn assertion that he was married to defendant. Finally, plaintiff would impose an unfair detriment on defendant by undoing an eleven-year marriage were he allowed to proceed with his inconsistent position here. The trial court's application of judicial estoppel was proper, and we affirm its denial of plaintiff's petition for annulment. . . .

TYSON, Judge, dissenting. The majority's opinion holds plaintiff-husband is judicially estopped from obtaining an annulment and denying his eleven-year marriage to defendant-wife because he asserted in a sworn statement that he and defendant were married during the adoption proceeding of defendant's daughter. Defendant's cross assignments of error and appeal from the trial court's conclusion that the wedding ceremony was not properly solemnized and failed to comply with North Carolina's marriage statutes has merit. That portion of the trial court's order should be reversed, and plaintiff's complaint should be dismissed. I respectfully dissent. . . .

N.C. Gen. Stat. § 51-1 (1977) was the statute governing marriage ceremonies when plaintiff and defendant were married. The statute required the parties to "express their solemn intent to marry in the presence of (1) an ordained minister of any religious denomination, or (2) a minister authorized by his church or (3) a magistrate." . . .

Plaintiff and defendant "express[ed] their solemn intent to marry" in 1991 at a traditional Cherokee wedding ceremony attended by many witnesses before an "ordained minister." The trial court stated in finding of fact number seventeen that the parties' wedding ceremony was "conducted in the 'Cherokee way' and [performed] in accordance with the Cherokee marriage ceremony." The ceremony was held at a location where Cherokee ceremonies and marriages take place. The parties dressed in traditional Cherokee clothing. A ceremonial fire burned throughout the ceremony. Littlejohn conducted a Cherokee spiritual wedding ceremony as he addressed and hailed the Creator and creatures in nature. Plaintiff and defendant exchanged traditional Cherokee marriage symbols. Plaintiff and defendant exchanged wedding rings, and Littlejohn publicly pronounced them to be husband and wife. Littlejohn presented plaintiff and defendant with a marriage stick and a North Carolina marriage license, which was subsequently filed with the Caswell County Register of Deeds. The statute's requirement of the parties to express a solemn intent to marry is satisfied.

North Carolina acknowledges and celebrates the solemnity of a native tribal wedding ceremony and validates the ceremony as a recognized marriage as evidenced in the General Assembly's passage of N.C. Gen. Stat. § 51-3.2 (2003). The statute provides:

(a) Subject to the restriction provided in subsection (b), a marriage between a man and a woman licensed and solemnized according to the law of a federally recognized Indian Nation or Tribe shall be valid and the parties to the marriage shall be lawfully married.

(b) When the law of a federally recognized Indian Nation or Tribe allows persons to obtain a marriage license from the register of deeds and the parties to a marriage do so, Chapter 51 of the General Statutes shall apply and the marriage shall be valid only if the issuance of the license and the solemnization of the marriage is conducted in compliance with this Chapter.

While this statute was enacted after plaintiff and defendant were married, the statute illustrates North Carolina's legislative intent to uphold marriages celebrated and solemnized "according to the law of a federally recognized Indian Nation or Tribe." . . .

Plaintiff entered into evidence a copy of Littlejohn's ordination of ministry from the Universal Life Church. Plaintiff argues these credentials were insufficient to comply with the marriage statute. He asserts Littlejohn did not possess the legal authority to validly perform the parties' wedding ceremony in North Carolina and contends the marriage is voidable.

In *Lynch*, a criminal prosecution for bigamy, our Supreme Court stated:

> "[A] marriage pretendedly celebrated before a person not authorized would be a nullity." A ceremony solemnized by a Roman Catholic layman in the mail order business who bought for $ 10.00 a mail order certificate giving him "credentials of minister" in the Universal Life Church, Inc. — whatever that is — is not a ceremony of marriage to be recognized for purposes of a bigamy prosecution in the State of North Carolina. The evidence does not establish — rather, it negates the fact — that Chester A. Wilson was authorized under the laws of this State to perform a marriage ceremony.

Following the Court's decision in [State v. Lynch, 301 N.C. 479, 487, 272 S.E.2d 349, 354 (1980)], the General Assembly enacted N.C. Gen. Stat. § 51-1.1, which provides:

> Any marriages performed by ministers of the Universal Life Church prior to July 3, 1981, are validated, unless they have been invalidated by a court of competent jurisdiction, provided that all other requirements of law have been met and the marriages would have been valid if performed by an official authorized by law to perform wedding ceremonies.

. . . Here, plaintiff and defendant were married in 1991. Littlejohn was licensed by the Universal Life Church on 4 June 1985 as an "ordained minister." Our Supreme Court stated in *Lynch*, "[i]t is not within the power of the State to declare what is or is not a religious body or who is or is not a religious leader within the body." Unlike the Universal Life minister in the criminal bigamy prosecution in *Lynch*, Littlejohn had performed many wedding ceremonies as a Cherokee Indian in the Cherokee tradition. Littlejohn was known throughout North Carolina as a Cherokee shaman and medicine man who performed various Cherokee rituals, including wedding ceremonies. Littlejohn's death certificate listed his profession as a "craftsman/medicine man." . . .

The trial court erred in holding the parties' wedding was not properly solemnized under our statute. . . . Because plaintiff failed to overcome his burden to show the plain requirements of the statute were not satisfied, it is wholly unnecessary to reach plaintiff's assignments of error, and his complaint should be dismissed.

NOTES AND QUESTIONS

1. If Carl Pickard had not represented in the adoption proceeding that he was married, would he have been judicially estopped from denying the marriage? Would he have been collaterally estopped?

2. What is the purpose of requiring that the wedding ceremony be conducted by a minister, a magistrate, or other authorized person? Was this purpose satisfied in this case?

The statute concerning marriages performed by ministers of the Universal Life Church, enacted after the North Carolina Supreme Court decision in State v. Lynch, validates those that occurred before July 3, 1981. Does this mean that marriages performed after that date are invalid?

According to the dissent in *Pickard*, what was the legal impact of the legislature's enactment of N.C. Gen. Stat. § 51-3.2 regarding marriage ceremonies conducted according to the law of a Native American Nation or Tribe? How, then, could the trial court have concluded that the statute did not "cure" Littlejohn's ordination?

Many jurisdictions recognize the "mock priest" rule, which provides that if either party believed in good faith that the officiant was authorized to perform the wedding, the marriage is valid. In 2012 the North Carolina Supreme Court rejected a claim that a marriage was void as bigamous, based on the husband's claim that the wife had never been divorced from her first husband. The court concluded that the first marriage was invalid because it was performed by a friend who was not proven to be an "ordained minister" or "minister authorized by his church." Mussa v. Palmer-Mussa, 731 S.E.2d 404 (N.C. 2012). The court rejected the view of the intermediate appellate court that the first marriage was merely voidable and, since it had not been annulled, was valid. Is this holding consistent with the mock priest rule?

3. A number of cases concern the validity of weddings conducted without a license, with mixed results. In one of the best known, Carabetta v. Carabetta, 438 A.2d 109 (Conn. 1980), the governing statute provided that "[n]o persons shall be married without a license." However, the Connecticut Supreme Court held that the statutory requirement was "directory" rather than "mandatory" and that the marriage was therefore not "null and void." The court further suggested that it would hold a marriage void only if the legislature expressly required that result. *See also* Vlach v. Vlach, 835 N.W.2d 72 (Neb. 2013); Rivera v. Rivera, 243 P.3d 1148 (N.M. App. 2010) (although parties' Texas license did not authorize marriage in New Mexico, license requirement is only directory, collecting cases from other jurisdictions); Persad v. Balram, 724 N.Y.S.2d 560 (N.Y. Sup. 2001) (parties failed to secure a license for their Hindu marriage or prayer ceremony). *Contra* Estate of DePasse, 118 Cal. Rptr. 2d 143 (Cal. App. 2002) (marriage license requirement is mandatory, and its absence cannot be cured by petition to declare the existence of the marriage after the death of one of the parties); Yaghoubinejad v. Haghighi, 894 A.2d 1173 (N.J. Super. App. 2006) (applying statute that makes any marriage performed without a license "absolutely void").

What value is there in "directory" regulations? What reasons are there for determining that a license requirement is "directory" rather than "mandatory"?

4. Requirements for medical examinations, where they exist, typically have been limited to blood tests for venereal disease. However, the widespread appearance of acquired immunodeficiency syndrome (AIDS) led some states to include HIV testing to identify persons who may develop AIDS. At one time the Illinois Marriage and Dissolution Act Section 204 required all parties to be tested. Notice of a positive result was to be given both parties, but a marriage license could be issued. This statute was repealed in 1989 following criticism directed at the cost and relative inefficiency of AIDS testing. The Utah legislature went further, prohibiting marriage by a person afflicted with AIDS. That statute was held invalid because of inconsistency with the Americans with Disabilities Act, 42 U.S.C. §§ 1201 et seq., in T.E.P. v. Leavitt, 840 F. Supp. 110 (D. Utah 1993).

NOTE: "VOID" AND "VOIDABLE" MARRIAGES

In a simple world, marriages would be either void or valid. This is not, however, a simple world. Analyzing the effect of both the formal and substantive defects in marriage sometimes requires an understanding of one of the genuinely arcane areas of law: the distinction between a "void" and a "voidable" marriage. What makes the distinction difficult is that, while a divorce supposes a valid marriage that is dissolved after some time, an annulment has been understood to declare the *in*validity of the marriage *ab initio*. In point of law, an annulled marriage is one that never existed. One might ask, therefore, how there can be a difference between a void marriage and a voidable marriage, if the result in either case is the nonexistence of the marriage at any time.

The differences between the two kinds of marriage are in substantial respects procedural. A "voidable" marriage has at least potential validity. It is valid unless its nullity has been declared. Moreover, the nullity of a voidable marriage ordinarily can be sought only by one of the parties to the marriage and only during the lifetime of the marriage. If, for example, the parties marry at age 17 when the local law permits marriages only by persons who are 18 years or older, their marriage could be annulled at the instance of at least the underaged spouse, and if the annulment is granted, the formal result is that they were never married. However, the marriage can become a valid marriage, and if the parties never seek its annulment, the marriage will become valid when they continue to live as husband and wife after reaching the age of consent. *See, e.g.*, Powell v. Powell, 86 A.2d 331 (N.J. 1952); Jones v. Jones, 37 S.E.2d 711 (Ga. 1946). *See also* Medlin v. Medlin, 981 P.2d 1087 (Ariz. App. 1999).

A "void" marriage in theory requires no declaration of invalidity. Moreover, the voidness of the marriage can be declared at any time and, generally, at the instance of any interested party. Nor, in principle, can a void marriage ever become a valid marriage.

The distinction between void and voidable marriages has its roots in English ecclesiastical law. Marital disabilities were of two types: civil (which included insanity and prior marriage) and canonical (which included marriages within forbidden degrees of kinship). Civil disabilities rendered a marriage void; canon law disabilities made it voidable. *See* Note, "Void" and "Voidable" Under Marriage Consanguinity Statutes, 17 Iowa L. Rev. 254 (1932). The continued viability of this distinction is doubtful, and it may well be questioned whether any such distinction is worth retaining, since many of the implications of voidness have been eliminated. For example, the children of a void marriage were illegitimate; those of a voidable marriage were legitimate unless the marriage was annulled. *See* Matter of Moncrief's Will, 139 N.E. 550 (N.Y. 1923); 1 Homer H. Clark, Jr., Domestic Relations in the United States 238 (1987). However, modern statutes now generally treat children of an invalid marriage as legitimate under most circumstances.

Similarly, alimony is in principle inconsistent with a void marriage; nonetheless, some states provide for alimony upon annulment—*e.g.*, Conn. Gen. Stat. Ann. § 46b-60 (2013); Or. Rev. Stat. §§ 107.095, 107.105 (2013). Despite such a statute, the Colorado Court of Appeals held that courts still have the ultimate responsibility to issue economic orders that are equitable and that a woman who fraudulently induced a man to marry her was not entitled to a share of the property or to spousal support. In re Marriage of Joel & Roohi, 2012 WL 3127305 (Colo. App. 2012). Other states retain the broader traditional rule that spousal support and property division cannot be ordered if the marriage was invalid. *See, e.g.*, Wright v. Hall, 738 S.E.2d 594 (Ga. 2013).

C. THE AGREEMENT TO MARRY

1. *The Content of the Agreement*

LUTWAK V. UNITED STATES

344 U.S. 604 (1952)

MINTON, J. The petitioners, Marcel Max Lutwak, Munio Knoll, and Regina Treitler, together with Leopold Knoll and Grace Klemtner, were indicted on six counts in the Northern District of Illinois, Eastern Division. The first count charged conspiracy to commit substantive offenses set forth in the remaining five counts and conspiracy "to defraud the United States of and concerning its governmental function and right of administering" the immigration laws and the Immigration and Naturalization Service, by obtaining the illegal entry into this country of three aliens as spouses of honorably discharged veterans. Grace Klemtner was dismissed from the indictment before the trial. . . . The jury acquitted Leopold Knoll and convicted the three petitioners on the conspiracy count. The Court of Appeals affirmed, and we granted certiorari.

We are concerned here only with the conviction of the petitioners of the alleged conspiracy. Petitioner Regina Treitler is the sister of Munio Knoll and Leopold Knoll, and the petitioner Lutwak is their nephew. Munio Knoll had been married in Poland in 1932 to one Maria Knoll. There is some evidence that Munio and Maria were divorced in 1942, but the existence and validity of this divorce are not determinable from the record. At the time of the inception of the conspiracy, in the summer of 1947, Munio, Maria and Leopold were refugees from Poland, living in Paris, France, while Regina Treitler and Lutwak lived in Chicago, Illinois. Petitioner Treitler desired to get her brothers into the United States.

Alien spouses of honorably discharged veterans of World War II were permitted to enter this country under the provisions of the so-called War Brides Act. . . .

The first count of the indictment charged that the petitioners conspired to have three honorably discharged veterans journey to Paris and go through marriage ceremonies with Munio, Leopold and Maria. The brothers and Maria would then accompany their new spouses to the United States and secure entry into this country by representing themselves as alien spouses of World War II veterans. It was further a part of the plan that the marriages were to be in form only, solely for the purpose of enabling Munio, Leopold and Maria to enter the United States. The parties to the marriages were not to live together as husband and wife, and thereafter would take whatever legal steps were necessary to sever the legal ties. It was finally alleged that the petitioners conspired to conceal these acts in order to prevent disclosure of the conspiracy to the immigration authorities.

The conspiracy to commit substantive offenses consisted in that part of the plan by which each of the aliens was to make a false statement to the immigration authorities by representing in his application for admission that he was married to his purported spouse, and to conceal from the immigration authorities that he had gone through a marriage ceremony solely for the purpose of gaining entry into this country with the understanding that he and his purported spouse would not live together as man and wife, but would sever the formal bonds of the ostensible marriage when the marriage had served its fraudulent purpose. . . .

From the evidence favorable to the Government, the jury could reasonably have believed that the following acts and transactions took place, and that the petitioners conspired to bring them about. Lutwak, a World War II veteran, was selected to marry Maria Knoll, his aunt by marriage. He went to Paris where he went through a marriage ceremony with Maria. They traveled to the United States, entering the port of New York on September 9, 1947. They represented to the immigration authorities that Maria was the wife of Lutwak, and upon that representation Maria was admitted. They never lived together as man and wife, and within a few months Munio and Maria commenced living together in this country as man and wife, holding themselves out as such. Lutwak, in the meantime, represented himself to friends as an unmarried man. Lutwak and Maria were divorced on March 31, 1950.

Lutwak and Mrs. Treitler also found two women — Bessie Benjamin Osborne and Grace Klemtner — who were honorably discharged veterans of World War II, and who were willing to marry Munio and Leopold so that the brothers could come to the United States. Bessie Osborne was introduced to Treitler by Lutwak, and went to Paris accompanied by Treitler. There she went through a pretended marriage ceremony with Munio Knoll, and on their arrival at New York City, Munio was admitted on November 13, 1947, on the representation that he was married to Bessie Osborne. The marriage was never consummated and was never intended to be. The parties separated after entering the United States, and they never lived together as husband and wife at any time. Bessie Osborne's suit for divorce from Munio was pending at the time of the trial.

Still later, Grace Klemtner, who was also a World War II veteran and an acquaintance of Regina Treitler, went to Paris and went through a pretended marriage ceremony with Leopold. They then traveled to the United States, where Leopold was admitted on December 5, 1947, upon the representation that he was the husband of Grace Klemtner. They immediately separated after their entry into this country, and they never lived together as husband and wife at any time until about the time Grace Klemtner appeared before the grand jury which returned the indictment. This was approximately April 1, 1950, more than two years after the marriage ceremony in Paris. Bessie Osborne and Grace Klemtner received a substantial fee for participating in these marriage ceremonies. . . .

At the trial, it was undisputed that Maria, Munio and Leopold had gone through formal marriage ceremonies with Lutwak, Bess Osborne and Grace Klemtner, respectively. Petitioners contended that, regardless of the intentions of the parties at the time of the ceremonies, the fact that the ceremonies were performed was sufficient to establish the validity of the marriages, at least until the Government proved their invalidity under French law. They relied on the general American rule of conflict of laws that a marriage valid where celebrated is valid everywhere unless it is incestuous, polygamous or otherwise declared void by statute. Neither side presented any evidence of the French law, and the trial court ruled that in the absence of such evidence, the French law would be presumed to be the same as American law. The court later instructed the jury that "if the subjects agree to a marriage only for the sake of representing it as such to the outside world and with the understanding that they will put an end to it as soon as it has served its purpose to deceive, they have never really agreed to be married at all." The petitioners claim that the trial court erred in presuming that the French law relating to the validity of marriages is the same as American law, and they further contend that even under American law these marriages are valid.

We do not believe that the validity of the marriages is material. No one is being prosecuted for an offense against the marital relation. We consider the marriage ceremonies only as a part of the conspiracy to defraud the United States and to commit offenses against the United States. In the circumstances of this case, the ceremonies were only a step in the fraudulent scheme and actions taken by the parties to the conspiracy. By directing in the War Brides Act that "alien spouses" of citizen war veterans should be admitted into this country, Congress intended to make it possible for veterans who had married aliens to have their families join them in this country without the long delay involved in qualifying under the proper immigration quota. Congress did not intend to provide aliens with an easy means of circumventing the quota system by fake marriages in which neither of the parties ever intended to enter into the marital relationship; that petitioners so believed is evidenced by their care in concealing from the immigration authorities that the ostensible husbands and wives were to separate immediately after their entry into this country and were never to live together as husband and wife. The common understanding of a marriage, which Congress must have had in mind when it made provision for "alien *spouses*" in the War Brides Act, is that the two parties have undertaken to establish a life together and assume certain duties and obligations. Such was not the case here, or so the jury might reasonably have found. Thus, when one of the aliens stated that he was married, and omitted to explain the true nature of his marital relationship, his statement did, and was intended to, carry with it implications of a state of facts which were not in fact true.

Because the validity of the marriages is not material, the cases involving so-called limited purpose marriages,[1] cited by petitioners to support their contention that the marriages in the instant case are valid, are inapplicable. All of those cases are suits for annulment in which the court was requested to grant relief to one of the parties to a marriage on the basis of his own admission that the marriage had been a sham. Where the annulment was denied, one or more of the following factors influenced the court: (1) a reluctance to permit the parties to use the annulment procedure as a quick and painless substitute for divorce, particularly because this might encourage people to marry hastily and inconsiderately; (2) a belief that the parties should not be permitted to use the courts as the means of carrying out their own secret schemes; and (3) a desire to prevent injury to innocent third parties, particularly children of the marriage. These factors have no application in the circumstances of the instant case. . . . In the instant case . . . there was no good faith — no intention to marry and consummate the marriages even for a day. With the legal consequences of such ceremonies under other circumstances, either in the United States or France, we are not concerned. . . .

NOTES AND QUESTIONS

1. If Lutwak had sued for an annulment, rather than a divorce, on the basis that he and Maria did not really intend to take on the rights and duties of marriage, should his petition be granted? The defendants in *Lutwak* cited "limited purpose marriage" cases that reject such claims. One of these is Schibi v. Schibi, 69 A.2d 831 (Conn. 1949), in which the parties married solely for the purpose of legitimating an unborn child. They did not intend to, nor did they, assume the relationship of husband and wife. Subsequently, the husband sought an annulment on the ground that the marriage was void for lack of mutual consent of the parties. The court denied that relief, saying:

> The law is clear that mutual consent is essential to a valid marriage. . . . In his complaint, the plaintiff alleges as the only basis for relief that at the time of the ceremony there was neither consent nor intent to incur the obligations of a marriage contract, and his prayers for relief are that the purported marriage be annulled and declared void. The sole question presented to the court for determination was whether the marriage was void because there was no mutual consent of the parties. That there was such mutual consent is implicit in the court's conclusion that the parties were legally married. Whether this conclusion is supported by the subordinate facts is the question decisive of the appeal.
>
> . . . The result reached is in accord with this general principle relative to the effect of prenuptial agreements: "Once a marriage has been properly solemnized and the obligations of married life undertaken, its validity cannot be affected by an antenuptial agreement not to live together, nor by an agreement previously entered into that the marriage should not be valid and binding, nor because one or even both of the parties did not intend it to be a permanent relation." . . .

---

1. *E.g.*, Schibi v. Schibi, 136 Conn. 196, 69 A.2d 831; Hanson v. Hanson, 287 Mass. 154, 191 N.E. 673. These and other cases cited by petitioners are collected and discussed in a note, 14 A.L.R.2d 624 (1950).

Id. at 832-834. *See also* De Vries v. De Vries, 195 Ill. App. 4 (1915); Bove v. Pinciotti, 46 Pa. D. & C. 159 (Pa. 1942).

2. Why does the majority opinion in *Lutwak* treat the validity of the marriages as a matter of domestic relations law as "immaterial" to the immigration prosecution?

3. Assume that one of the defendants in *Lutwak*, after serving his or her time in prison, married some third person. Would he or she be subject to prosecution for bigamy in New York? If one of the defendants were hospitalized, would the person whom he or she had married in France be responsible for that expense?

4. The validity of a marriage for limited purposes is important in almost any area where marriage confers a benefit or avoids a burden. Consider the following examples:

a. In United States v. Mathis, the defendant's former wife had cooperated with law enforcement authorities. Mathis told her that, if she would remarry him, friends would give her $25,000; if she did not, she and her baby would be killed. She and the defendant remarried after her (inculpatory) grand jury testimony but before trial. At trial, she invoked the husband-wife testimonial privilege, which the court rejected. "It is well established that an exception to the husband-wife privilege exists if the trial judge determines that the marriage is a fraud. Lutwak v. United States, 344 U.S. 604 (1953). . . ." 559 F.2d 294, 298 (5th Cir. 1977). The court in Commonwealth v. Lewis, 39 A.3d 341, 347 (Pa. Super. 2012), found that courts around the country adopt one of three approaches to this issue:

> (1) the privilege is not available if the marriage was collusive, *i.e.*, entered to avoid testifying, *see* United States v. Apodaca, 522 F.2d 568 (10th Cir. 1975) (representing first view that spousal testimony privilege is not available to either spouse in sham or collusive marriages); (2) the privilege applies to events occurring during the marriage but not to pre-marital events or communications, *see* United States v. Clark, 712 F.2d 299 (7th Cir. 1983) (representing second view that spousal testimony privilege does not apply to conduct that took place prior to marriage); and (3) the privilege is available as to all spousal adverse testimony as long as a valid marriage exists, *see* State v. Peters, 213 Ga. App. 352, 444 S.E.2d 609 (1994) (representing position that spousal testimony privilege applies to all spousal testimony where lawful marriage exists when privilege is invoked).

The *Lewis* court adopted the third approach as most consistent with legislative intent.

b. Mpirilis v. Hellenic Lines, Ltd., 323 F. Supp. 865 (S.D. Tex. 1970), involved a wrongful death action under the Jones Act to recover damages by reason of the fatal injuries suffered by the decedent while working on a ship in New York harbor. The plaintiff and the decedent were married on the day of the latter's arrival in the United States, allegedly so that he could gain entry into this country on a preferred basis. Assuming that the parties agreed not to assume any of the normal duties, obligations, or incidents of marriage, should the plaintiff be entitled to wrongful death recovery? Is the case in any way distinguishable from Lutwak v. United States?

5. Should "sham divorces" be legally effective for collateral purposes? In Brown v. Continental Airlines, Inc., 647 F.3d 221 (5th Cir. 2011), the administrator of the airlines' pension plan sued nine pilots and their spouses for

restitution of pension benefits that the plan had paid to the wives pursuant to divorce decrees awarding the benefits to the wives. The terms of the pension plan provided that an employee pilot could not obtain a lump sum payment of his benefits unless he retired, but that if he were divorced and the court awarded pension benefits to his wife, she could elect to take a lump sum even though her ex-husband continued to work. The airline proved that the spouses remarried shortly after the benefits were paid to the wives and that in some cases the spouses continued to live together and never told anyone about their divorce. The airline claimed that the pilots undertook this scheme because they were afraid that they might lose full pension benefits because of financial problems in the airline industry if they waited to claim them until they retired. The court rejected the airlines' claim, saying that there was no requirement that the divorces be obtained in good faith. In contrast, the U.S. Tax Court in Boyter v. Commissioner, 74 T.C. 989 (1981), refused to recognize a Maryland couple's year-end divorce, based upon which they filed as single rather than married and thereby incurred lower income taxes. The couple promptly remarried in January, and at trial the wife testified that they divorced only to obtain the tax advantage.

6. For a discussion of these issues and more, *see* Kerry Abrams, Marriage Fraud, 100 Cal. L. Rev. 1 (2012).

NOTE: MARRIAGE-RELATED IMMIGRATION RULES

A citizen can obtain a K-1 or fiancée visa, allowing a noncitizen to enter the United States for up to 90 days to marry the petitioner. A citizen who marries a noncitizen (either before or after the noncitizen enters the United States) may then petition the Immigration and Naturalization Service (INS) to classify the non-citizen as an "immediate relative." Normally, "immediate relative" status permits a noncitizen to obtain permanent residency and, eventually, citizenship without having to apply and enter the United States as part of his or her country of origin's immigration quota. 8 U.S.C. § 1151(b). In 2012 about 1.03 million people were granted legal permanent-resident status; of these, 273,429, or 27 percent, were spouses of the petitioning citizen. Randall Monger & James Yankay, U.S. Legal Permanent Residents: 2012, Table 2 (Office of Immigration Statistics 2013).

If the citizen spouse dies within the two-year period, legislation enacted in 2009 allows the surviving spouse to pursue permanent residency on his or her own. Kirk Semple, Senate Measure Gives Rights to Widows of Citizens, N.Y. Times, Oct. 20, 2009.

An abused spouse may also file her own petition. 8 U.S.C. § 1151(b)(2)(A)(i). She must prove evidence of physical battery or extreme cruelty, joint residence with the abusive spouse, that she is of good character, and that the marriage was entered into in good faith. 8 U.S.C. § 1154(a)(1). If the couple divorces within the first year after the petition is filed, the noncitizen spouse is still eligible if the divorce was connected to the abuse.

This set of rules creates a tempting opportunity for immigration fraud, as was alleged in *Lutwak*. The most recent legislation designed to smoke out marriages whose only purpose is to obtain advantageous immigration status is the Marriage Fraud Amendments of 1986, 8 U.S.C. §§ 1154(g), (h), 1255(e). This law provides that a foreign national who is not a permanent resident of the United States and who marries a citizen receives only a conditional immigration status, with the bona fides and continuance of the marriage to be reexamined after two years.

Procedures adopted by the INS may include a visit to the couple's residence to see whether they actually reside together and interviews with neighbors, employers, and others to determine the existence of a marital relationship. Regulations interpreting the good faith marriage requirement say that evidence may include but is not limited to documents showing joint ownership of property, joint tenancy of a common residence, commingling of finances, birth certificates of children born to the petitioner and spouse, and affidavits sworn to or affirmed by third parties having personal knowledge of the bona fides of the marital relationship. 8 C.F.R. § 204.2.

Newer legislation addresses a different problem with international marriages, abuse of women who enter the country as "mail order brides." A 1999 government report estimated that a third to a half of the women from other countries who entered the United States on spouse or fiancée visas met their partners through marriage brokers. Eduardo Porter, Law on Overseas Brides Is Keeping Couples Apart, N.Y. Times, Oct. 17, 2006. After two "mail order brides" were murdered by their husbands in the early twenty-first century, Congress enacted the International Marriage Broker Regulation Act (IMBRA), Pub. L. No. 109-162, §§ 831-834, 119 Stat. 2960, 3066-3077 (2006) (codified as §§ 1375a, 1184, and other sections scattered in 8 U.S.C.). An entity or person covered by the law must collect background information about the citizen who is using its services (including any restraining orders, arrests or criminal convictions for violent crimes or prostitution-related offenses, controlled substances or alcohol, any current or previous marriages, the ages of any children younger than 18, and all countries and states in which the citizen has resided within the last 20 years), provide it to the foreign national, and get her consent before disclosing her contact information.

The law applies to any individual or business that charges fees for providing dating, matrimonial, matchmaking, or social referrals and provides personal information or facilitates communication between U.S. residents and foreign nationals. Exemptions are granted for nonprofit, traditional matchmaking organizations of a religious or cultural nature and for organizations whose principal business is not international and that offers U.S. and foreign clients comparable services at comparable rates.

IMBRA also requires all citizens who petition for a fiancée visa to disclose criminal convictions for the offenses listed above, and a citizen will not be granted a fiancée visa more often than once every two years.

For more information, *see* Kerry Abrams, Immigration Law and the Regulation of Marriage, 91 Minn. L. Rev. 1625 (2007); Suzanne H. Jackson, Marriages of Convenience: International Marriage Brokers, "Mail-Order Brides," and Domestic Servitude, 28 U. Tol. L. Rev. 895 (2007); Olga Grosh, Foreign Wives, Domestic Violence: U.S. Law Stigmatizes and Fails to Protect "Mail-Order Brides," 22 Hastings Women's L.J. 81 (2011).

PROBLEMS

1. Virgil and Gretta were an unmarried couple who had sex one time. Several months later, Gretta told Virgil that she was pregnant by him. They decided to

marry in order to "give the baby a name." They also agreed, however, that they would not cohabit after the marriage, that there would be no sharing of incomes or support (except for the child), and that they would get a divorce after the child turned one year old.

They marry and go their separate ways. Virgil has, however, fallen in love with Beatrice in the meantime. Beatrice is Roman Catholic and has serious problems with marrying someone who is divorced. Virgil decides to seek an annulment of his marriage to Gretta rather than a divorce. Will the annulment be granted?

2. Roy and Dale have been friends for some time. At a party one evening, their friends decide to entertain themselves by making fun of Roy and Dale's friendship and whether it will ever "go anywhere." Because they had had a couple of drinks and because they were tired of being teased, Roy and Dale decide to go through a marriage ceremony; but, after a few days, when the joke has worn off, they plan to secure an annulment. They do not intend to cohabit or live together or in any other way act as husband and wife. They go through a marriage ceremony before a justice of the peace. A week later, Roy brings an annulment action. Should the annulment be granted?

2.   *Capacity to Agree*

EDMUNDS V. EDWARDS

287 N.W.2d 420 (1980)

BRODKEY, J. This case involves an action brought in the District Court for Douglas County on May 23, 1977, by Renne Edmunds, guardian of the estate of Harold Edwards (hereinafter referred to as Harold), against Inez Edwards (née Ryan, hereinafter referred to as Inez), to annul the marriage of his ward Harold to Inez, which occurred on May 10, 1975. In his petition, the guardian alleged that the marriage was void for the reason that Harold did not have the mental capacity to enter into a marriage contract on that date, which allegation was specifically denied by Inez. In its order entered on November 27, 1978, following trial of the matter, the District Court found that Harold was mentally retarded, as that phrase is commonly used in medical science, but not to a degree which, under the law of the State of Nebraska, is of such a nature as to render him mentally incompetent to enter into the marriage relation, and that at the time of the marriage between Harold and Inez, Harold had sufficient capacity to understand the nature of the marriage contract and the duties and responsibilities incident to it, so as to be able to enter into a valid and binding marriage contract. The court therefore found that the marriage of Harold and Inez, which occurred on May 10, 1975, was, in fact and in law, a valid marriage and continues to exist as a valid marriage under the laws of the State of Nebraska, and is in full force and effect. The guardian has appealed to this court from that order. We affirm.

Harold was born on August 7, 1918, and was institutionalized at the Beatrice State Home as mentally retarded on September 25, 1939. He was a resident at the Beatrice State Home for a period of approximately 30 years. It was during this period that he first met Inez, who was also a patient of the home, and Bill Lancaster, who lived with Harold in Omaha after their release from the Beatrice State Home, and who has continued to reside with Harold and Inez since their marriage. Harold was placed in Omaha on November 14, 1969, and started a new life under the auspices of the Eastern Nebraska Community Office of Retardation (ENCOR), which was established in 1968 to provide alternatives for institutionalization of retarded persons at the Beatrice State Home and to assist in the normalization of the retarded in local communities. After coming to Omaha, Harold obtained employment as a food service worker in the Douglas County Hospital on February 16, 1970, and lived in a staffed ENCOR apartment from that time until shortly before his marriage in 1975. . . . While under the auspices of ENCOR, Harold and Inez developed a romantic interest in each other and eventually decided to get married. The date of the marriage was postponed in order to afford the couple the opportunity to have premarital sex counseling and marriage counseling from the pastor of their church in Omaha. They were married by Reverend Verle Holsteen, pastor of the First Baptist Church in Omaha, Nebraska, and their friends, staff members of ENCOR, and out-of-state relatives attended the wedding in that church. The guardian did not bring this action to annul the marriage for a period of approximately 2 years after the date of the marriage ceremony. . . .

The guardian first called his medical expert, Dr. Robert Mitchell, a psychologist connected with Creighton University in Omaha. Dr. Mitchell expressed the opinion that he did not believe Harold was competent to enter into a valid marriage, but admitted on cross-examination that being mildly mentally retarded did not automatically preclude a person from marriage. He also testified that he had asked Harold during his examinations and consultations what marriage meant, to which Harold responded "For life," and also "You stay married forever." . . . Dr. Mitchell also testified: "It is much better, I think, to refer to Mr. Edwards as a person who is fifty-nine years of age who is not as bright as most people. But he has had fifty-nine years of experience, and he is an adult, and physiologically he is matured, as well."

The medical expert witness called by the defendant was Dr. Frank J. Menolascino, a psychiatrist specializing in the field of mental retardation, and author of numerous books and articles upon the subject. He was well acquainted with Harold, having first met him in 1959 when he was doing work at the Beatrice State Home, and had seen Harold many times since that time. He had examined Harold in December 1977, and again in July 1978, during the week Dr. Menolascino testified. He testified that Harold was not functioning below the mildly retarded range and that the tests reflected that a great deal of Harold's difficulty appeared to be primarily a lack of training. . . . Dr. Menolascino was asked: "Doctor, do you believe that you have an opinion as to whether Mr. Edwards was capable of understanding the nature of a marriage within the paradigm you have discussed in May of 1975?" and he answered: "Yes, he was able to." . . . On cross-examination Dr. Menolascino was asked: "In your opinion, do you think that Harold Edwards understands the fact that he is liable for Mrs. Edwards' bills if she goes to a store and runs up some bills?" to which he replied: "Yes." He was then asked: "Do you think he understands the fact that if he gets a divorce he might have to pay alimony?" His reply to that question was: "I am not sure. I am not sure. . . ."

In addition to the medical witnesses who testified, there was also evidence adduced from various lay witnesses. Renne Edmunds, the guardian, . . . testified: "It was my conclusion that he [Harold] could not only not manage a fund of thirty thousand, he couldn't manage the small purchases, as well." . . . Harry John Naasz, an adviser for ENCOR, who was Harold's supervisor, testified that he had assisted Harold in making preparations for the marriage including obtaining of blood tests and the marriage certificate. He had discussed the forthcoming wedding with Harold: "Can you tell us what you discussed concerning the marriage? A. We discussed what it would mean, what it would mean living together, sharing their lives. Q. And what did Harold express to you? A. He wanted to get married. Q. What did he say that led you to believe that he might understand marriage? A. He mentioned to me that he understood, too that it was a commitment to each other, that Inez would be living there." Mr. Naasz did admit in his testimony that at the beginning he did have some question in his mind about whether Harold understood marriage. He later referred the couple for marriage counseling. . . .

Also testifying at the trial was Elizabeth Cartwright, an employee of ENCOR, who monitors Harold and Inez's finances. She testified that when Harold gets paid at the Douglas County Hospital he signs his check, takes it to the bank, deposits all the money except $40, and gives Inez $20 and he keeps $20. She does not have to go to the bank with him. Elizabeth Cartwright also testified that Inez is quite a bit sharper than Harold and she helps him around. . . .

We now examine some established rules of law which we believe are applicable to this case. We first consider the nature of the marriage contract. Section 42-101, R.R.S.1943, provides: "In law, marriage is considered a civil contract, to which the consent of the parties capable of contracting is essential." Although by statute, marriage is referred to as a "civil contract," we have held: "That it is not a contract resembling in any but the slightest degree, except as to the element of consent, any other contract with which the courts have to deal, is apparent upon a moment's reflection. . . . What persons establish by entering into matrimony, is not a contractual relation, but a social *status*; and the only essential features of the transactions are that the participants are of legal capacity to assume that *status*, and freely consent so to do." . . .

Another statutory provision of which we must take cognizance in this appeal is section 42-103, R.R.S.1943, which provides: "Marriages are void . . . (2) when either party, at the time of marriage, is insane or mentally incompetent to enter into the marriage relation. . . ." This statute was reiterated, and other applicable rules with reference to competency to enter into a marriage relationship were reviewed in Homan v. Homan, 181 Neb. 259, 147 N.W.2d 630 (1967), wherein we stated: "The petition alleged that the ward was mentally incompetent at the time of the marriage. By statute a marriage is void "when either party is insane or an idiot at the time of marriage, and the term idiot shall include all persons who from whatever cause are mentally incompetent to enter into the marriage relation."

"A marriage contract will not be declared void for mental incapacity to enter into it unless there existed at the time of the marriage such a want of understanding as to render the party incapable of assenting thereto. Mere weakness or imbecility of mind is not sufficient to void a contract of marriage unless there be such a mental defect as to prevent the party from comprehending the nature of the contract and from giving his fee [sic] and intelligent consent to it.

"Absolute inability to contract, insanity, or idiocy will void a marriage, but mere weakness of mind will not unless it produces a derangement sufficient to avoid all contracts by destroying the power to consent. A marriage is valid if the party has sufficient capacity to understand the nature of the contract and the obligations and responsibilities it creates. . . ."

It is the general rule that the existence of a valid marriage is a question of fact. In this case the trier of fact was the court and the court had all the foregoing evidence, summarized above, before it. Concededly, much of the evidence with reference to the capacity of Harold to enter into the marriage contract was conflicting and disputed. . . . However, it is also the well-established rule that where the evidence on material questions of fact is in irreconcilable conflict, this court will, in determining the weight of the evidence, consider the fact that the trial court observed the witnesses and their manner of testifying, and therefore must have accepted one version of the facts rather than the opposite. This rule has been applied both in annulment actions and in divorce actions.

Applying this rule to the present case, we conclude, therefore, that the trial court was correct in dismissing the guardian's petition to annul the marriage of his ward, and that its action in this regard should be and hereby is affirmed.

NOTES AND QUESTIONS

1. Frank Menolascino & Michael L. Egger, Medical Dimensions of Mental Retardation xx-xxii (1978):

The term *mental retardation* refers to the combined diagnostic criteria of impairments in intellectual ability and socially adaptive behavior. The term implies both a symptom of an underlying developmental disorder and an assessment of an individual's potential ability to learn. In brief, retarded persons learn slowly, and at chronological maturity their capacity to understand and adapt to social-vocational challenges will be, to varying degrees, less than average. . . .

The President's Committee on Mental Retardation (1963) has estimated that 3% of our nation's citizens at some time during their lives are diagnosed as being mentally retarded to some degree. By this estimate, some 6-1/2 million children and adults are afflicted with this "developmentally delaying" disorder. . . .

Levels of retardation are usually discussed according to severity and the concomitant expected potentials for learning and general development. The levels of mental retardation are usually classified as mild, moderate, severe, and profound.

The mildly retarded are almost always capable of learning to do productive work. Nearly all can learn academic subjects to varying degrees, and most are capable, as adults, of living independently and becoming self-supporting — *if* they have received appropriate care, training, and other services during childhood, adolescence, and early adulthood.

Moderately retarded persons nearly always can learn to care for themselves, can profit to varying degrees from classroom instruction, and can learn to do simple routine tasks. . . . [M]ost are able to become at least partially self-supporting and may live in the community with some degree of supervision.

Severely retarded persons generally require intensive services at all stages of life. They are capable of learning to care for themselves, and many can become marginally productive as adults, under supervision in a sheltered work setting. . . .

The profoundly retarded nearly always require major medical and/or nursing supervision to remediate physical and medical disabilities and maintain life. . . .

The President's Committee on Mental Retardation in 1973 . . . estimated the percentages of levels of mental retardation among the total population of America's retarded citizens . . . : 89% mildly retarded, 6.0% moderately retarded, 3.5% severely retarded, and 1.5% profoundly retarded. These percentages clearly indicate that the majority of the mentally retarded are more like the normal population than different from it.

2. The action to annul Harold's marriage was brought by the guardian of his estate, also known as a conservator. Persons under a disability may be placed under the care of a conservator, guardian, or both. Although the use of these terms, and the powers that go with them, differ greatly from jurisdiction to jurisdiction, conservators are usually appointed to protect the property of those who are unable to manage their property and affairs effectively — for example, UPC § 5-401 (Official 2010 Text). A conservator has a duty to receive a ward's income, to decide how much of the estate should be used for living expenses, and to prevent loss or waste of the ward's property or business.

Guardianship of the person is a more general notion and, indeed, can mean that the guardian has the same powers, rights, and duties as a parent possesses with respect to an unemancipated child. See UPC § 5-315.

3. Is there any inconsistency between appointment of a guardian of Harold's estate and a decision to permit him to marry? See Ertel v. Ertel, 40 N.E.2d 85 (Ill. App. 1942) ("In Illinois, less mental capacity is required to enable a person to enter into the marriage contract than is required for the execution of ordinary business transactions.").

4. Mental deficiency and disease have always been a concern with respect to the existence of competence to agree to marry. State restrictions on marriage by the developmentally disabled and the mentally ill may also reflect, however, a eugenic concern that found strong support during the late nineteenth and early twentieth centuries. Belief in the hereditary sources of mental illness and faith in scientific solutions to social evils, combined with a growing concern about the health of the American family, seemed to suggest the value of standards for conjugal fitness that would reduce the incidence of "feeble-minded" children.

> Advocates of hereditary restrictions touted them as necessary weapons to defend the nation from degeneration. Feminist and pioneering social scientist Elizabeth Cady Stanton declared in 1879 that the "law of heredity should exclude many from entering the marriage relation." Ten years earlier she had insisted that only those "who can give the world children with splendid physique, strong intellect, and high moral sentiment, may conscientiously take on themselves the responsibility of marriage and maternity." Similarly, sociologist George Howard complained in 1904 that "under pleas of 'romantic love' we blandly yield to sexual attraction in choosing our mates, ignoring the welfare of the race." Appealing for a "higher standard of conjugal choice," he contended that experience "shows that in wedlock natural and sexual selection should play a smaller and artificial selection a larger role." Here, he declared, "the state has a function to perform."

Michael Grossberg, Governing the Hearth: Law and the Family in Nineteenth Century America 148 (1985).

5. In upholding a statute permitting sterilization of "mental defectives," Justice Holmes provided the following justification:

> The attack is not upon the procedure but upon the substantive law. . . . The judgment finds . . . that Carrie Buck "is the probable potential parent of socially inadequate offspring, likewise afflicted, that she may be sexually sterilized without detriment to her general health and that her welfare and that of society will be promoted by her sterilization," and thereupon makes the order. . . . [W]e cannot say as a matter of law that the grounds [for sterilization] do not exist, and if they exist they justify the result. We have seen more than once that the public welfare may call upon the best citizens for their lives. It would be strange if it could not call upon those who already sap the strength of the State for these lesser sacrifices, often not felt to be such by those concerned, in order to prevent our being swamped with incompetence. It is better for all the world, if instead of waiting to execute degenerate offspring for crime, or to let them starve for their imbecility, society can prevent those who are manifestly unfit from continuing their kind. The principle that sustains compulsory vaccination is broad enough to cover cutting the Fallopian tubes. Three generations of imbeciles are enough.

Buck v. Bell, 274 U.S. 200, 207 (1927). Buck v. Bell has never been expressly overruled, although its current vitality has been sharply questioned in light of Skinner v. Oklahoma, 316 U.S. 535 (1942). The accuracy and acceptability of the premises of the eugenic movement have also been widely impeached. *See* Matter of Moe, 432 N.E.2d 712 (Mass. 1982); Elyse Ferster, Eliminating the Unfit — Is Sterilization the Answer?, 27 Ohio St. L.J. 591, 602-604 (1966); Michael Kindregan, Sixty Years of Compulsory Eugenic Sterilization: "Three Generations of Imbeciles" and the Constitution of the United States, 43 Chi.-Kent L. Rev. 123, 134-140 (1966). Most cases now permitting sterilization arise from a request by a parent or guardian for a court order permitting that procedure. *See*, *e.g.*, Matter of Moe, above.

6. The other large category of cases in which competence to marry is challenged involve frail, elderly people who marry those in a position to take advantage of them, often caretakers or others who provide services. An example is Clark v. Foust-Graham, 615 S.E.2d 398 (N.C. Ct. App. 2005), which illustrates the relationship among challenges based on competence and lack of consent.

Goodwin, an 80-year-old man exhibiting signs of dementia and Alzheimer's disease, married Foust-Graham, a 40-year-old real estate broker, about a year after they met when she listed and sold some of his real property. A month before the marriage she became his caretaker when his paid caretaker quit. During the months preceding the marriage, the man had little association with friends or family. The parties married suddenly and without notifying family. Before the ceremony, Goodwin called an acquaintance, asking for help because he was being locked up, and at the wedding the acquaintance believed Goodwin was not taking the event seriously because of how he was acting. Goodwin's daughter filed an action as his guardian ad litem to annul the marriage. The jury found that Goodwin was competent and had consented to the marriage but that Foust-Graham had procured it by undue influence, and the trial court entered an order annulling the marriage.

The appellate court affirmed, recognizing undue influence as a valid basis for granting an annulment, since the state supreme court had previously held that undue influence is a valid basis for invalidation of a will. The court said that here Foust-Graham had exercised "a fraudulent influence over the mind and will of another to the extent that the professed action is not freely done but is in truth the act of the one who procures the result." *See also* Nave v. Nave, 173 S.W.3d 766 (Tenn. Ct. App. 2005); Arnelle v. Fisher, 647 So. 2d 1047 (Fla. Dist. Ct. App. 1995). *See* Hilary Lim, Messages from a Rarely Visited Island: Duress and Lack of Consent in Marriage, 4 Feminist Legal Stud. 195 (1996).

7. Kristine S. Knaplund argues that most cases dealing with similar fact patterns do not provide enough protection for vulnerable elders in the community. On the other hand, she finds that elders who live in care facilities face the problem of too much "protection"—rules and practices that deny residents opportunities for intimacy, not only because facilities fear they will be sued for failing to protect residents with declining competence but also because families don't want to think about grandma or grandpa being sexually active. The Right of Privacy and America's Aging Population, 86 Denv. U. L. Rev. 439 (2009). *See also* Terry L. Turnipseed, How Do I Love Thee, Let Me Count the Days: Deathbed Marriages in America, 96 Ky. L.J. 275 (2007-2008).

3. Fraud and Duress

IN RE MARRIAGE OF RAMIREZ

81 Cal. Rptr. 3d 180 (Cal. App. 2008)

RAMIREZ, P.J. . . . Jorge, an immigrant from the State of Michoacán, Mexico, lived in the United States and sought legal residence here. His mother was a permanent resident and sponsored Jorge in his application for that status. He began his application process in 1994 or 1995 but because his mother was not a citizen herself, the process took many years.

In 1999, Jorge and Lilia were married in a religious ceremony in Moreno Valley, California. The ceremony was performed by a priest or other official from the State of Jalisco, Mexico, and an "Acta de Matrimonio" was issued. No marriage license was issued by the State of California. In 2001, Jorge and Lilia became aware that the 1999 marriage was invalid because Lilia's prior divorce had not been final for 300 days prior to the marriage. Additionally, because it was made to look as though the parties were married in Mexico, the Mexican marriage certificate would prevent Jorge from getting his green card because it would make it appear that he had not been in continuous residence in the United States.

The parties were remarried in 2001 and obtained a confidential marriage license. After the death of Jorge's mother, Lilia assumed the position as Jorge's sponsor to pursue his application for permanent residence and citizenship. In 2004, after she signed a document related to his immigration status, Jorge informed Lilia that it would be the last one. Two weeks later, in May 2004, he took Lilia out to dinner and asked for a divorce because he was in love with someone else and always had been. In June 2004, Jorge moved out.

That same month, Lilia found out who the other woman was when she overheard a conversation between Jorge and Lilia's sister Blanca. Jorge had begun an affair with Blanca prior to the 2001 marriage, and it lasted until 2005. The intercepted conversation occurred in 2005. Lilia asked her teenaged son Victor to call Blanca, who babysat for Jorge and Lilia's daughter, on her cell phone to inquire if she would be joining them for lunch with the child. Blanca, at a restaurant with Jorge, had the cell phone in her purse. Instead of pressing the stop key, she pressed the button to answer the call, so the conversation she was having with Jorge was overheard on Victor's cell phone, which Lilia and Victor listened to by activating the loudspeaker. In this conversation, Jorge professed his love for Blanca, assured her that they would be together once he got his share of money and property from Lilia, and told her that he had only married Lilia to gain permanent resident status. This conversation occurred after Jorge had moved out.

Shortly after the parties separated, an attempt was made to reach an agreement with Jorge as to the disposition of assets. Lilia has a real estate broker's license and she and Jorge had worked together in the realty business during their marriage. Lilia's attorney prepared a proposed settlement agreement listing five parcels of real property as community property, and three as Lilia's separate property. Lilia offered Jorge one of the properties, but he declined. He then filed a petition for dissolution of the marriage on April 21, 2005.

On June 22, 2005, Lilia filed a response to the petition and a request for a judgment of nullity of marriage. At the bifurcated trial relating to the status of the marriage, Jorge demonstrated he had obtained his permanent resident status in 2002. He denied having a relationship with Blanca, although several telephone messages left on Blanca's cell phone and retrieved by a close family friend of Blanca and Lilia — in addition to the conversation overheard by Lilia — belied his protestations.

The trial court concluded the 1999 marriage was void under the laws of Mexico. . . .

The court also found the second marriage was void because Jorge perpetrated a fraud on Lilia by carrying on an extramarital affair with Blanca. The court found that Jorge did not marry Lilia because he was worried about his immigration or work status; instead, the court found Jorge made false statements to Blanca about his reasons for marrying Lilia, including a need for a green card, to string her along and to delay having to make a commitment to her. Thus, the fraud related to Jorge's marrying Lilia while carrying on a sexual relationship with Blanca which he intended to maintain. The court concluded Jorge wanted to "have his cake and eat it too" by carrying on sexual relationships with both women at the same time.

The trial court held that this kind of fraud goes to the heart of the marital relationship and declared the 2001 marriage void on the ground of fraud. . . . Jorge appeals. . . .

A marriage is voidable and may be adjudged a nullity if the consent of either party was obtained by fraud. A marriage may be annulled for fraud only in an extreme case where the particular fraud goes to the very essence of the marriage relation. (In re Marriage of Meagher & Maleki (2005) 131 Cal. App. 4th 1, 3 [31 Cal. Rptr. 3d 663] (*Meagher*).) The fact represented or suppressed to induce consent to marriage will be deemed material if it relates to a matter of substance and directly affects the purpose of the party deceived in entering the marital contract. In other words, the fraud relied upon must be such as directly defeats the marriage relationship and not merely such fraud as would be sufficient to rescind an ordinary civil contract. Fraudulent intent not to perform a duty vital to the marriage state must exist in the offending spouse's mind at the moment the marriage contract is made.

A promise to be a kind, dutiful and affectionate spouse cannot be made the basis of an annulment. (Marshall v. Marshall (1931) 212 Cal. 736, 739-740 [300 P. 816].) Instead, the particular fraudulent intention must relate to the sexual or procreative aspects of marriage. In the absence of this type of fraud, the long-standing rule is that neither party may question the validity of the marriage upon the ground of express or implied representations of the other with respect to such matters as character, habits, chastity, business or social standing, financial worth or prospects, or matters of a similar nature. (*Meagher, supra*, 131 Cal. App. 4th at p. 8.) Concealment of incontinence, temper, idleness, extravagance, coldness or lack of represented fortune will not justify an annulment. (*Marshall, supra*, at p. 740.)

Other decisions demonstrate that to void a marriage, the fraud alleged must show an intention not to perform a duty vital to the marriage, which exists in the mind of the offending spouse at the time of marriage. (Millar v. Millar (1917) 175 Cal. 797 [167 P. 394] [wife concealed from husband at time of marriage that she did not intend to have sexual relations with him]; Hardesty v. Hardesty (1924) 193 Cal. 330 [223 P. 951] [wife concealed from husband at time of marriage that she was pregnant by another man]; Vileta v. Vileta (1942) 53 Cal. App. 2d 794 [128 P.2d 376] [spouse concealed from other spouse known fact of sterility at time of marriage]; In re Marriage of Liu, *supra*, 197 Cal. App. 3d 143 [wife married husband in Taiwan to acquire a green card, and never consummated the marriage].) Thus, historically, annulments based on fraud have only been granted in cases where the fraud relates in some way to the sexual, procreative or child-rearing aspects of marriage.

Here, the trial court specifically found that the fraud was unrelated to the husband's efforts to obtain permanent legal status. Instead, it found the fraud was based on Jorge's intent to continue the ongoing simultaneous sexual relationships with Lilia and Blanca at the time that he and Lilia entered into the 2001 marriage.

In rendering its judgment of nullity, the trial court relied on the decision in Schaub v. Schaub (1945) 71 Cal. App. 2d 467 [162 P.2d 966] (*Schaub*). In that case, a younger woman married an older man to obtain his real property. She had been involved in an intimate relationship with another man for many years, and conspired with her lover to marry the husband, with no intention of fulfilling the obligation of marriage to consummate the marriage. This she did, while continuing her sexual relationship with her lover. The fraud was discovered when an investigator, hired by the husband, found the wife in bed with her lover, both naked.

We read *Schaub* as not standing solely on the intent not to consummate. *Schaub* does not at any point suggest that the intent not to consummate is *the* indicator of fraud. Neither does *Schaub* anywhere indicate that the intent to continue an existing relationship with a third party is enough for a finding of fraud only when accompanied by the intent not to consummate.

Further, the court in *Schaub* points out that "The marriage in itself was a contract under which each of the parties undertook the obligations of mutual respect, *fidelity* and support [citing Civ. Code, former § 155]." The *Schaub* court then concludes that the fraud consisted of the wife's intention not to perform her marriage obligations, including the obligation of fidelity, and the concealment of that from the innocent spouse. That is just what happened here. At the time he entered into the 2001 marriage, Jorge manifestly intended not to perform his marriage obligation of fidelity. That is fraud under Family Code sections 720 and 2210, subdivision (d).

Bolstering this interpretation of *Schaub*, the court in *Meagher* in fact refers to *Schaub* as justifying annulment where one party simply has the "intent to continue in an intimate relationship with a third person." That describes exactly Jorge's intent and actions at the time he and Lilia married in 2001.

Finally, as stated above, historically, annulments based on fraud have only been granted in cases where the fraud relates in some way to the sexual, procreative or child-rearing aspects of marriage. Jorge's actions here, in marrying Lilia while continuing to carry on a sexual relationship with her sister Blanca, directly relates to a sexual aspect of marriage — sexual fidelity. For emphasis, we again quote from Family Code section 720: "Husband and wife contract toward each other obligations of mutual respect, fidelity, and support." At the time of the 2001 marriage, Jorge purposely deceived Lilia into thinking that he would perform one of the central obligations of the marriage contract — the obligation of fidelity. Under Family Code sections 720 and 2210, subdivision (d), and under *Schaub* and *Meagher*, Jorge committed fraud and Lilia is entitled to a judgment of annulment.

The judgment is affirmed. Jorge is directed to pay costs on appeal.

GAUT, J., concurring. I concur with the portion of the decision relating to the nullity of the 1999 marriage. However, regarding the nullity of the 2001 marriage, I dissent. I would reverse the judgment annulling the marriage and direct the entry of a judgment of dissolution of marriage.

The majority holds that infidelity alone, disdainful as it may be, may serve as a basis for annulment on the ground of fraud, relying upon the case of Schaub v. Schaub (1945) 71 Cal. App. 2d 467 [162 P.2d 966]. That case involved a plot by a woman and her longtime lover to cheat an unsuspecting older gentleman out of a half-interest in his real property, while the wife maintained illicit extramarital relations with her lover.

In the 63 years since the *Schaub* case was decided, it has never been cited, until today, for the proposition that the infidelity of a spouse, without more, constitutes a fraud which justifies an annulment. Today's decision could have unintended repercussions in family law practice, leading to unnecessary litigation over title to property acquired by spouses during marriage which may not be considered community property if the marriage is deemed a nullity.

I would reverse the judgment of nullity of marriage and order the entry of a judgment of dissolution of marriage. Annulment should be the exception, not the rule.

NOTES AND QUESTIONS

1. The law of annulment for fraud has been heavily influenced by the law of ecclesiastical courts applied in England until 1857. Even after assumption of civil

jurisdiction over matrimonial affairs, the rule was that a marriage could be annulled only for "error personae," which meant that the wrong person was married. Errors of condition or quality ("error fortunae") were not sufficient to avoid the marriage. *See* Harry W. Vanneman, Annulment of Marriage for Fraud, 9 Minn. L. Rev. 497 (1925), reprinted in Association of American Law Schools, Selected Essays on Family Law 335, 336 (1950). An example of "error personae" (as well as an instance of the remedial effects of polygamy) can be found in the story of Jacob, Leah, and Rachel, Genesis 30:15-28.

2. Although American cases do not go as far as the traditional English view, most have restricted annulment for fraud to misrepresentations going to the "essentials" of marriage. An influential early American case, Reynolds v. Reynolds, 85 Mass. (3 Allen) 605 (1862), expressed the following rationale for this limitation:

> The great object of marriage in a civilized and Christian community is to secure the existence and permanence of the family relation, and to insure the legitimacy of offspring. It would tend to defeat this object, if error or disappointment in personal qualities or character was allowed to be the basis of proceedings on which to found a dissolution of the marriage tie. The law therefore wisely requires that persons who act on representations or belief in regard to such matters should bear the consequences which flow from contracts into which they have voluntarily entered, after they have been executed, and affords no relief for the results of a "blind credulity, however it may have been produced."

Id. at 607. The plaintiff in *Reynolds*, who had never engaged in sexual relations with the defendant prior to marriage, received an annulment based on his wife's undisclosed pregnancy by another. Where is the misrepresentation? And why does this misrepresentation go to the "essentials" of marriage? Under this test, would Lilia Ramirez be entitled to an annulment?

Under the traditional view of fraud, in what sense is agreement necessary to marriage? A cause of action for fraud in an ordinary contracts case involves a representation of fact, known to be false, that is intended to and does deceive the other party to his or her detriment. How does this approach to fraud compare to the way that fraud was defined for purposes of annulling a marriage?

3. The traditional English view of the fraud that will justify annulment stands at one end of the spectrum of possible positions. New York, which sharply restricted divorce until relatively recently, is usually said to stand at the other end:

> [T]he fraud [required for annulment] need no longer "necessarily concern what is commonly called the essentials of the marriage *relation* — the rights and duties connected with cohabitation and consortium attached by law to the marital status. Any fraud is adequate which is 'material, to that degree that, had it not been practiced, the party deceived would not have consented to the marriage' and is 'of such nature as to deceive an ordinarily prudent person.'" Although it is not enough to show merely that one partner married for money and the other was disappointed [citing Woronzoff-Daschkoff v. Woronzoff-Daschkoff, 104 N.E.2d 877, 880 (N.Y. 1952)], and the decisions upon the subject of annulment have not always been uniform, there have been circumstances where misrepresentations of love and affection, with intention to make a home, were held sufficient, likewise in case of fraudulent representations concerning the legitimacy of children of the wife of a supposedly prior marriage,

or concerning prior marital status. Concealment of prior marital status was held to be sufficient in Costello v. Costello; concealment of affliction with tuberculosis in Yelin v. Yelin; failure to reveal treatment of a mental disorder (schizophrenia, catatonic type) was held to be enough in Schaeffer v. Schaeffer; material misrepresentation of age in Tacchi v. Tacchi. . . .

Kober v. Kober, 211 N.E.2d 817, 819 (N.Y. 1965). In *Kober* itself, the New York Court of Appeals held that the husband's fraudulent concealment of his membership in the Nazi party during World War II and fanatical anti-Semitism were sufficient bases for annulment. *Kober* endorses a test similar to that used for ordinary contracts cases. If that is the test applied in New York, why can't false representations regarding wealth or social position suffice? How does this test differ from the test adopted in *Ramirez*, or does it? Under either test, would falsely claiming to be in love with a would-be spouse warrant an annulment?

   4. Duress, like fraud, is usually said to vitiate the consent necessary for marriage. This claim arises only occasionally now. However, the older cases generally held that duress did not exist when a man agreed to marry after being threatened with prosecution for the crimes of seduction or bastardy. Under this approach, to what extent is entrance into marriage a matter of "contract"?

   5. The British Forced Marriage (Civil Protection) Act of 2007 addresses duress in a modern context. The law allows family courts to make Forced Marriage Protection Orders to protect someone from being forced into marriage. An order can also be made to protect someone who has already been forced into marriage, to help remove the person from the situation. Those who fail to obey an order may be found in contempt of court and sent to prison for up to two years. One of the first orders was issued against the father of a 22-year-old woman who tried to force her to go to Pakistan to marry one of his relatives. In another early case, a mother forced her two teenage daughters to marry their first cousins in Pakistan in July 2007. After the girls returned to the UK, they told a teacher, who called the police. The mother was convicted of inciting or causing a child to engage in sexual activity, arranging or facilitating the commission of a child sex offense, and intending to pervert the course of justice. Houriya Ahmed, Landmark Case on Forced Marriage: Mother Jailed (Centre for Social Cohesion blog, May 22, 2009).

PROBLEMS

   1. Plaintiff Elizabeth Princess married the defendant, Kermit, two years ago. Prior to the marriage, Kermit seemed the ideal spouse: handsome, sober, hardworking, and sympathetic. Over the last two years, however, Elizabeth has found that her husband has a serious drinking problem, which he did not reveal; has no genuine interest in seeking a job; and is entirely unconcerned about his physical appearance or his manners. She has filed a complaint seeking an annulment on the ground that he failed to disclose his drinking problem and misrepresented his interest in seeking employment. Kermit has filed a motion to dismiss the bill for failure to state a claim. What arguments would be made by the parties in the hearing on that motion? *See* Johnston v. Johnston, 22 Cal. Rptr. 2d 253

(Cal. App. 1993) (where plaintiff alleged that defendant had "turned from a prince into a frog").

2. Mr. Patel, a native of India now resident in your city, has come to your office for advice. He married his wife, who is also a native of India, nine months ago. Patel is a member of a high caste in Indian society; his wife falsely represented that she is a member of the same caste. He has now learned that she is a member of the lowest ("Untouchable") class. Mr. Patel explains that this marriage violates the Hindu caste system, which is important both religiously and culturally, and embarrasses him and his family. He also tells you that, had he known of his wife's caste, he would not have married her. What advice would you give Patel?

3. Jerry and Nancy had sex once while each was married to someone else; Nancy was also carrying on a long-term affair with a third man, Sam. Nine months later she gave birth to a child, but she did not tell Jerry until three years later that he was the father. At that point, Jerry and Nancy began an affair, got divorces from their spouses, and married. Twenty years later, Nancy filed for divorce, and Jerry cross-petitioned for an annulment on the basis that Nancy had fraudulently induced him to marry her by telling him that he was the father of the baby. DNA testing had proved Nancy's lover Sam to be the actual biological father. If Nancy knew that Jerry was not the biological father, does her misrepresentation amount to fraud going to the essentials of the marriage? What if she honestly thought that Jerry was the father?

4. Angela, a citizen of Colombia, met Raul, an American citizen, through an online dating service. After a brief courtship, they married, and Angela came to the United States. Raul began the process to allow Angela to obtain permanent resident status immediately. As soon as she received final approval for her green card, Angela left Raul and filed for divorce. Raul counterclaimed for annulment, claiming fraud. If the court finds that Angela never loved Raul and married him only to obtain legal residency, should the annulment be granted?

NOTE: NAMES

It is often assumed that, as part of the marriage contract, a married woman assumes her husband's name, and, indeed, this is common practice. However, at common law this practice was a matter of custom rather than a legal requirement. During the late nineteenth and early twentieth centuries, courts in a number of states reinterpreted the precedents to hold that married women must take their husbands' names. Statutes imposed this requirement in other states. Elizabeth F. Emens, Changing Name Changing: Framing Rules and the Future of Marital Names, 74 U. Chi. L. Rev. 761, 771-772 (2007). During the 1970s, a number of cases revisited the common law precedents and held that, in fact, the common law allows a married woman to retain her birth name. *Id.* It is, as well, common for a Latina to adopt a combined name on marriage, retaining her maiden name and adding her husband's name (with or without a hyphen). While legal process can be invoked to change a name, resort to that process is generally not required. One may change one's name by usage, or not. The only general limitation on change (by whatever strategy) is that the name change must not be designed to frustrate creditors or for some other illegitimate purpose. One might not, therefore, be able to change one's name to "State Tax Department."

A more complicated question has to do with naming children, originally and especially after divorce. Three kinds of rules are generally applied when a dispute arises: a presumption favoring maintenance of the child's current name, a "best interests" test, and (more recently) a presumption favoring the choice of the custodial parent. *See* Merle H. Weiner, "We Are Family": Valuing Associationalism in Disputes over Children's Surnames, 75 N.C. L. Rev. 1625, 1630-1631 (1997). Professor Weiner's article suggests that all three standards are flawed in theory or in application because they undervalue the importance of surnames as markers of associations, an approach that better reflects the interests of children and the meaning of divorce. *See also* Emens, discussed above, at 791-803.

D. SUBSTANTIVE RESTRICTIONS ON MARRYING

1. *The Constitutional Framework*

ZABLOCKI V. REDHAIL

434 U.S. 374 (1978)

MARSHALL, J. At issue in this case is the constitutionality of a Wisconsin statute, Wis. Stat. §§ 245.10(1), (4), (5) (1973), which provides that members of a certain class of Wisconsin residents may not marry, within the State or elsewhere, without first obtaining a court order granting permission to marry. The class is defined by the statute to include any "Wisconsin resident having minor issue not in his custody and which he is under obligation to support by any court order or judgment." The statute specifies that court permission cannot be granted unless the marriage applicant submits proof of compliance with the support obligation and, in addition, demonstrates that the children covered by the support order "are not then and are not likely thereafter to become public charges." No marriage license may lawfully be issued in Wisconsin to a person covered by the statute, except upon court order; any marriage entered into without compliance with § 245.10 is declared void; and persons acquiring marriage licenses in violation of the section are subject to criminal penalties. . . .

Appellee Redhail is a Wisconsin resident who, under the terms of § 245.10, is unable to enter into a lawful marriage in Wisconsin or elsewhere so long as he maintains his Wisconsin residency. . . . In January 1972, when appellee was a minor and a high school student, a paternity action was instituted against him in Milwaukee County Court, alleging that he was the father of a baby girl born out of wedlock on July 5, 1971. After he appeared and admitted that he was the child's father, the court entered an order on May 12, 1972, adjudging appellee the father and ordering him to pay $109 per month as support for the child until she reached 18 years of age. From May 1972 until August 1974, appellee was unemployed and indigent, and consequently was unable to make any support payments.

On September 27, 1974, appellee filed an application for a marriage license with appellant Zablocki, the County Clerk of Milwaukee County, and a few days later the application was denied on the sole ground that appellee had not obtained a court order granting him permission to marry, as required by § 245.10. Although appellee did not petition a state court thereafter, it is stipulated that he would not have been able to satisfy either of the statutory prerequisites for an order granting permission to marry. First, he had not satisfied his support obligations to his illegitimate child, and as of December 1974 there was an arrearage in excess of $3,700. Second, the child had been a public charge since her birth, receiving benefits under the Aid to Families with Dependent Children program. It is stipulated that the child's benefit payments were such that she would have been a public charge even if appellee had been current in his support payments. . . .

In evaluating [the statute] under the Equal Protection Clause, "we must first determine what burden of justification the classification created thereby must meet, by looking to the nature of the classification and the individual interests affected." Since our past decisions make clear that the right to marry is of fundamental importance, and since the classification at issue here significantly interferes with the exercise of that right, we believe that "critical examination" of the state interests advanced in support of the classification is required.

The leading decision of this Court on the right to marry is Loving v. Virginia, 388 U.S. 1 (1967). In that case, an interracial couple who had been convicted of violating Virginia's miscegenation laws challenged the statutory scheme on both equal protection and due process grounds. The Court's opinion could have rested solely on the ground that the statutes discriminated on the basis of race in violation of the Equal Protection Clause. But the Court went on to hold that the laws arbitrarily deprived the couple of a fundamental liberty protected by the Due Process Clause, the freedom to marry. The Court's language on the latter point bears repeating: "The freedom to marry has long been recognized as one of the vital personal rights essential to the orderly pursuit of happiness by free men. Marriage is one of the 'basic civil rights of man,' fundamental to our very existence and survival." Id., at 12, quoting Skinner v. Oklahoma ex rel. Williamson, 316 U.S. 535 (1942).

Although *Loving* arose in the context of racial discrimination, prior and subsequent decisions of this Court confirm that the right to marry is of fundamental importance for all individuals. Long ago, in Maynard v. Hill, 125 U.S. 190 (1888), the Court characterized marriage as "the most important relation in life," and as "the foundation of the family and of society, without which there would be neither civilization nor progress." In Meyer v. Nebraska, 262 U.S. 390 (1923), the Court recognized that the right "to marry, establish a home and bring up children" is a central part of the liberty protected by the Due Process Clause, id., at 399, and in Skinner v. Oklahoma ex rel. Williamson, *supra*, 316 U.S. 535 (1942), marriage was described as "fundamental to the very existence and survival of the race," 316 U.S., at 541.

More recent decisions have established that the right to marry is part of the fundamental "right of privacy" implicit in the Fourteenth Amendment's Due Process Clause. In Griswold v. Connecticut, 381 U.S. 479 (1965), the Court observed: "We deal with a right of privacy older than the Bill of Rights — older than our political parties, older than our school system. Marriage is a coming together for better or for worse, hopefully enduring, and intimate to the degree of being sacred. It is an association that promotes a way of life, not causes; a harmony in living, not political faiths; a bilateral loyalty, not commercial or social projects. Yet it is an association for as noble a purpose as any involved in our prior decisions." *Id.*, at 486.

Cases subsequent to *Griswold* and *Loving* have routinely categorized the decision to marry as among the personal decisions protected by the right of privacy. . . .

It is not surprising that the decision to marry has been placed on the same level of importance as decisions relating to procreation, childbirth, child rearing, and family relationships. As the facts of this case illustrate, it would make little sense to recognize a right of privacy with respect to other matters of family life and not with respect to the decision to enter the relationship that is the foundation of the family in our society. . . .

By reaffirming the fundamental character of the right to marry, we do not mean to suggest that every state regulation which relates in any way to the incidents of or prerequisites for marriage must be subjected to rigorous scrutiny. To the contrary, reasonable regulations that do not significantly interfere with decisions to enter into the marital relationship may legitimately be imposed. The statutory classification at issue here, however, clearly does interfere directly and substantially with the right to marry.

Under the challenged statute, no Wisconsin resident in the affected class may marry in Wisconsin or elsewhere without a court order, and marriages contracted in violation of the statute are both void and punishable as criminal offenses. Some of those in the affected class, like appellee, will never be able to obtain the necessary court order, because they either lack the financial means to meet their support obligations or cannot prove that their children will not become public charges. These persons are absolutely prevented from getting married. Many others, able in theory to satisfy the statute's requirements, will be sufficiently burdened by having to do so that they will in effect be coerced into forgoing their right to marry. And even those who can be persuaded to meet the statute's requirements suffer a serious intrusion into their freedom of choice in an area in which we have held such freedom to be fundamental.

When a statutory classification significantly interferes with the exercise of a fundamental right, it cannot be upheld unless it is supported by sufficiently important state interests and is closely tailored to effectuate only those interests. Appellant asserts that two interests are served by the challenged statute: the permission-to-marry proceeding furnishes an opportunity to counsel the applicant as to the necessity of fulfilling his prior support obligations; and the welfare of the out-of-custody children is protected. We may accept for present purposes that these are legitimate and substantial interests, but, since the means selected by the State for achieving these interests unnecessarily impinge on the right to marry, the statute cannot be sustained.

There is evidence that the challenged statute, as originally introduced in the Wisconsin Legislature, was intended merely to establish a mechanism whereby persons with support obligations to children from prior marriages could be counseled before they entered into new marital relationships and incurred further support obligations. Court permission to marry was to be required, but apparently permission was automatically to be granted after counseling was completed. The statute actually enacted, however, does not expressly require or provide for any counseling whatsoever, nor for any automatic granting of permission to marry by the court, and thus it can hardly be justified as a means for ensuring counseling of the persons within its coverage. Even assuming that counseling does take place—a fact as to which there is no evidence in the record—this interest obviously cannot support the withholding of court permission to marry once counseling is completed.

With regard to safeguarding the welfare of the out-of-custody children, appellant's brief does not make clear the connection between the State's interest and the statute's requirements. At argument, appellant's counsel suggested that, since permission to marry cannot be granted unless the applicant shows that he has satisfied his court-determined support obligations to the prior children and that those children will not become public charges, the statute provides incentive for the applicant to make support payments to his children. This "collection device" rationale cannot justify the statute's broad infringement on the right to marry.

First, with respect to individuals who are unable to meet the statutory requirements, the statute merely prevents the applicant from getting married, without delivering any money at all into the hands of the applicant's prior children. More importantly, regardless of the applicant's ability or willingness to meet the statutory requirements, the State already has numerous other means for exacting compliance with support obligations, means that are at least as effective as the instant statute's and yet do not impinge upon the right to marry. Under Wisconsin law, whether the children are from a prior marriage or were born out of wedlock, court-determined support obligations may be enforced directly via wage assignments, civil contempt proceedings, and criminal penalties. And, if the State believes that parents of children out of their custody should be responsible for ensuring that those children do not become public charges, this interest can be achieved by adjusting the criteria used for determining the amounts to be paid under their support orders.

There is also some suggestion that [the statute] protects the ability of marriage applicants to meet support obligations to prior children by preventing the applicants from incurring new support obligations. But the challenged provisions . . . are grossly underinclusive with respect to this purpose, since they do not limit in any way new financial commitments by the applicant other than those arising out of the contemplated marriage. The statutory classification is substantially overinclusive as well: Given the possibility that the new spouse will actually better the applicant's financial situation, by contributing income from a job or otherwise, the statute in many cases may prevent affected individuals from improving their ability to satisfy their prior support obligations. And, although it is true that the applicant will incur support obligations to any children born during the contemplated marriage, preventing the marriage may only result in the children being born out of wedlock, as in fact occurred in appellee's case. Since the support obligation is the same whether the child is born in or out of wedlock, the net result of preventing the marriage is simply more illegitimate children.

The statutory classification . . . thus cannot be justified by the interests advanced in support of it. The judgment of the District Court is, accordingly,

Affirmed.

STEWART, J., concurring in the judgment. I cannot join the opinion of the Court. To hold, as the Court does, that the Wisconsin statute violates the Equal Protection Clause seems to me to misconceive the meaning of that constitutional guarantee. The Equal Protection Clause deals not with substantive rights or freedoms but with invidiously discriminatory classifications. The paradigm of its violation is, of course, classification by race. . . .

The problem in this case is not one of discriminatory classifications, but of unwarranted encroachment upon a constitutionally protected freedom. I think that the Wisconsin statute is unconstitutional because it exceeds the bounds of permissible state regulation of marriage, and invades the sphere of liberty protected by the Due Process Clause of the Fourteenth Amendment.

I do not agree with the Court that there is a "right to marry" in the constitutional sense. That right, or more accurately that privilege, is under our federal system peculiarly one to be defined and limited by state law. A State may not only "significantly interfere with decisions to enter into marital relationship," but may in many circumstances absolutely prohibit it. Surely, for example, a State may legitimately say that no one can marry his or her sibling, that no one can marry who is not at least 14 years old, that no one can marry without first passing an examination for venereal disease, or that no one can marry who has a living husband or wife. But, just as surely, in regulating the intimate human relationship of marriage, there is a limit beyond which a State may not constitutionally go.

The Constitution does not specifically mention freedom to marry, but it is settled that the "liberty" protected by the Due Process Clause of the Fourteenth Amendment embraces more than those freedoms expressly enumerated in the Bill of Rights. And the decisions of this Court have made clear that freedom of personal choice in matters of marriage and family life is one of the liberties so protected [citing Roe v. Wade; Loving v. Virginia; Griswold v. Connecticut; Pierce v. Society of Sisters; Meyer v. Nebraska].

It is evident that the Wisconsin law now before us directly abridges that freedom. The question is whether the state interests that support the abridgment can overcome the substantive protections of the Constitution. . . .

If Wisconsin had said that no one could marry who had not paid all of the fines assessed against him for traffic violations, I suppose the constitutional invalidity of the law would be apparent. For while the state interest would certainly be legitimate, that interest would be both disproportionate and unrelated to the restriction of liberty imposed by the State. But the invalidity of the law before us is hardly so clear, because its restriction of liberty seems largely to be imposed only on those who have abused the same liberty in the past.

Looked at in one way, the law may be seen as simply a collection device additional to those used by Wisconsin and other States for enforcing parental support obligations. But since it operates by denying permission to marry, it also clearly reflects a legislative judgment that a person should not be permitted to incur new family financial obligations until he has fulfilled those he already has. Insofar as this judgment is paternalistic rather than punitive, it manifests a concern for the economic well-being of a prospective marital household. These interests are legitimate concerns of the State. But it does not follow that they justify the absolute deprivation of the benefits of a legal marriage. . . .

The Wisconsin law makes no allowance for the truly indigent. The State flatly denies a marriage license to anyone who cannot afford to fulfill his support obligations and keep his children from becoming wards of the State. We may assume that the State has legitimate interests in collecting delinquent support payments and in reducing its welfare load. We may also assume that, as applied to those who can afford to meet the statute's financial requirements but choose not to do so, the law advances the State's objectives in ways superior to other means available to the State. The fact remains that some people simply cannot afford to meet the statute's financial requirements. To deny these people permission to marry penalizes them for failing to do that which they cannot do. Insofar as it applies to indigents, the state law is an irrational means of achieving these objectives of the State.

As directed against either the indigent or the delinquent parent, the law is substantially more rational if viewed as a means of assuring the financial viability of future marriages. In this context, it reflects a plausible judgment that those who have not fulfilled their financial obligations and have not kept their children off the welfare rolls in the past are likely to encounter similar difficulties in the future. But the State's legitimate concern with the financial soundness of prospective marriages must stop short of telling people they may not marry because they are too poor or because they might persist in their financial irresponsibility. The invasion of constitutionally protected liberty and the chance of erroneous prediction are simply too great. A legislative judgment so alien to our traditions and so offensive to our shared notions of fairness offends the Due Process Clause of the Fourteenth Amendment. . . .

NOTES AND QUESTIONS

1. The majority declares that marriage is a "fundamental liberty" and that state regulations substantially burdening access to marriage will be subject to heightened scrutiny for purposes of the equal protection analysis. There are two issues that this holding raises. The first issue is what justifies heightened judicial scrutiny. It is uncontroversial that scrutiny is increased for laws that classify on a suspect basis; in *Zablocki* the Court used increased scrutiny because of the importance or "fundamental" quality of the interest that was burdened unequally. Disagreement about whether scrutiny should be heightened for the latter reason lies behind the separate analyses of Justices Marshall and Stewart. At the time *Zablocki* was decided, some members of the Supreme Court were still reluctant to use a rigorous substantive due process analysis to test the constitutionality of state action, remembering the excesses of the *Lochner* era. They relied instead on the equal protection clause as a source of authority to protect individual rights.

Assuming the majority's position, that heightened scrutiny of classifications can result from the nature of the interest as well as from the classification involved, the further question is whether a particular interest should be regarded as "fundamental." Justice Marshall concludes that marriage is a fundamental liberty that has long been recognized on the basis of a line of cases beginning with Maynard v. Hill. *Maynard* upheld the right of a state to enact a statute allowing dissolution divorce against a challenge that this remedy constituted an abridgement of the right to contract. Does it support the conclusion that marriage is a fundamental liberty?

2. The majority opinion observes that it will not employ heightened scrutiny for regulations that do not "significantly interfere with decisions to enter into the marital relationship . . . ," thus seeking to distinguish its unanimous decision in Califano v. Jobst, 434 U.S. 47 (1977), earlier in the same term. *Jobst* sustained a section of the Social Security Act that provided for termination of a dependent child's benefits upon marriage to an individual not entitled in his or her own right to benefits under the Act. Jobst himself was dependent because of a disability and married a woman who was also disabled but did not receive benefits under the Act. The Court applied the rational-basis standard, observing that this approach "is not rendered invalid simply because some persons who might otherwise have married were deterred by the rule or because some who did marry were burdened thereby." 434 U.S. at 54. *Compare* the following analyses of the relationship between *Zablocki* and *Jobst*, which appear in the former decision.

> [Justice Marshall (for the Court):] As the opinion for the Court [in *Jobst*] expressly noted, the rule terminating benefits upon marriage was not "an attempt to interfere with the individual's freedom to make a decision as important as marriage." The Social Security provisions placed no direct obstacle in the path of persons desiring to get married, and—notwithstanding our Brother Rehnquist's imaginative recasting of the case . . . —there was no evidence that the laws significantly discouraged, let alone made "practically impossible," any marriages. Indeed, the provisions had not deterred the individual who challenged the statute from getting married, even though he and his wife were both disabled. [Justice Marshall also observed that because of the availability of other federal benefits, total payments to the Jobsts were only $20 per month less than they would have been had Mr. Jobst's child benefits not been terminated.] 434 U.S. at 374, n.12.

> [Justice Stevens (concurring in the judgment):] When a state allocates benefits or burdens, it may have valid reasons for treating married and unmarried persons differently. Classification based on marital status has been an accepted characteristic of tax legislation, Selective Service rules, and Social Security regulations. As cases like *Jobst* demonstrate, such laws may "significantly interfere with decisions to enter into the marital relationship." That kind of interference, however, is not a sufficient reason for invalidating every law reflecting a legislative judgment that there are relevant differences between married persons as a class and unmarried persons as a class.
>
> A classification based on marital status is fundamentally different from a classification which determines who may lawfully enter into a marriage relationship. The individual's interest in making the marriage decision independently is sufficiently important to merit special constitutional protection. It is not, however, an interest which is constitutionally immune from evenhanded regulation. Thus, laws prohibiting marriage to a child, a close relative, or a person afflicted with venereal disease, are unchallenged even though they "interfere directly and substantially with the right to marry." The Wisconsin statute has a different character.
>
> Under this statute, a person's economic status may determine his eligibility to enter into a lawful marriage. . . . This type of statutory discrimination is, I believe, totally unprecedented, as well as inconsistent with our tradition of administering justice equally to the rich and to the poor. 434 U.S. at 403-404.

PROBLEMS

1. Medicaid rules imputing to the recipient all income and assets of a spouse (assuming they are living together) may have the effect of keeping many older couples from marrying. Does *Zablocki* suggest that this deeming provision is unconstitutional?

2. The state in which you live has enacted a statute requiring all persons marrying for the first time to undergo counseling through a state-licensed agency. The agency charges a fee of $50 for two counseling sessions. These sessions address management of finances and interpersonal relations. After attendance at two sessions, persons wishing to marry receive a certificate of compliance with the statutory counseling requirement, and a marriage license will be issued (all other requirements also being satisfied). Will such a statute be upheld against a constitutional challenge?

2. *Different Sexes*

GOODRIDGE v. DEPARTMENT OF PUBLIC HEALTH

798 N.E.2d 941 (2003)

MARSHALL, C.J. Marriage is a vital social institution. The exclusive commitment of two individuals to each other nurtures love and mutual support; it brings stability to our society. For those who choose to marry, and for their children, marriage provides an abundance of legal, financial, and social benefits. In return it imposes weighty legal, financial, and social obligations. The question before us is whether, consistent with the Massachusetts Constitution, the Commonwealth may deny the protections, benefits, and obligations conferred by civil marriage to two individuals of the same sex who wish to marry. We conclude that it may not. The Massachusetts Constitution affirms the dignity and equality of all individuals. It forbids the creation of second-class citizens. In reaching our conclusion we have given full deference to the arguments made by the Commonwealth. But it has failed to identify any constitutionally adequate reason for denying civil marriage to same-sex couples. . . .

Whether the Commonwealth may use its formidable regulatory authority to bar same-sex couples from civil marriage is a question not previously addressed by a Massachusetts appellate court. It is a question the United States Supreme Court left open as a matter of Federal law in Lawrence [v. Texas, 539 U.S. 558 (2003),] at 2484, where it was not an issue. There, the Court affirmed that the core concept of common human dignity protected by the Fourteenth Amendment to the United States Constitution precludes government intrusion into the deeply personal realms of consensual adult expressions of intimacy and one's choice of an intimate partner. The Court also reaffirmed the central role that decisions whether to marry or have children bear in shaping one's identity. The Massachusetts Constitution is, if anything, more protective of individual liberty and equality than the Federal Constitution; it may demand broader protection for fundamental rights; and it is less tolerant of government intrusion into the protected spheres of private life.

Barred access to the protections, benefits, and obligations of civil marriage, a person who enters into an intimate, exclusive union with another of the same sex is arbitrarily deprived of membership in one of our community's most rewarding and cherished institutions. That exclusion is incompatible with the constitutional principles of respect for individual autonomy and equality under law. . . .

In March and April, 2001, each of the plaintiff couples attempted to obtain a marriage license from a city or town clerk's office. . . . In each case, the clerk either refused to accept the notice of intention to marry or denied a marriage license to the couple on the ground that Massachusetts does not recognize same-sex marriage. Because obtaining a marriage license is a necessary prerequisite to civil marriage in Massachusetts, denying marriage licenses to the plaintiffs was tantamount to denying them access to civil marriage itself, with its appurtenant social and legal protections, benefits, and obligations.

On April 11, 2001, the plaintiffs filed suit in the Superior Court against the department and the commissioner seeking a judgment that "the exclusion of the [p]laintiff couples and other qualified same-sex couples from access to marriage licenses, and the legal and social status of civil marriage, as well as the protections, benefits and obligations of marriage, violates Massachusetts law." . . .

The department, represented by the Attorney General, admitted to a policy and practice of denying marriage licenses to same-sex couples. It denied that its actions violated any law or that the plaintiffs were entitled to relief. The parties filed cross motions for summary judgment. . . .

After the complaint was dismissed and summary judgment entered for the defendants, the plaintiffs appealed. . . .

. . . G. L. c. 207, governing entrance to marriage, is a licensing law. The plaintiffs argue that because nothing in that licensing law specifically prohibits marriages between persons of the same sex, we may interpret the statute to permit "qualified same sex couples" to obtain marriage licenses, thereby avoiding the question whether the law is constitutional.

We interpret statutes to carry out the Legislature's intent, determined by the words of a statute interpreted according to "the ordinary and approved usage of the language." The everyday meaning of "marriage" is "[t]he legal union of a man and woman as husband and wife," Black's Law Dictionary 986 (7th ed. 1999), and the plaintiffs do not argue that the term "marriage" has ever had a different meaning under Massachusetts law. This definition of marriage, as both the department and the Superior Court judge point out, derives from the common law. Far from being ambiguous, the undefined word "marriage," as used in G. L. c. 207, confirms the General Court's intent to hew to the term's common-law and quotidian meaning concerning the genders of the marriage partners.

The intended scope of G. L. c. 207 is also evident in its consanguinity provisions. Sections 1 and 2 of G. L. c. 207 prohibit marriages between a man and certain female relatives and a woman and certain male relatives, but are silent as to the consanguinity of male-male or female-female marriage applicants. The only reasonable explanation is that the Legislature did not intend that same-sex couples be licensed to marry. We conclude, as did the judge, that G. L. c. 207 may not be construed to permit same-sex couples to marry. . . .

We begin by considering the nature of civil marriage itself. Simply put, the government creates civil marriage. In Massachusetts, civil marriage is, and since pre-Colonial days has been, precisely what its name implies: a wholly secular institution. No religious ceremony has ever been required to validate a Massachusetts marriage.

In a real sense, there are three partners to every civil marriage: two willing spouses and an approving State. While only the parties can mutually assent to marriage, the terms of the marriage — who may marry and what obligations, benefits, and liabilities attach to civil marriage — are set by the Commonwealth. Conversely, while only the parties can agree to end the marriage (absent the death of one of them or a marriage void *ab initio*), the Commonwealth defines the exit terms. . . .

Marriage also bestows enormous private and social advantages on those who choose to marry. Civil marriage is at once a deeply personal commitment to another human being and a highly public celebration of the ideals of mutuality, companionship, intimacy, fidelity, and family. . . . Because it fulfils yearnings for security, safe haven, and connection that express our common humanity, civil marriage is an esteemed institution, and the decision whether and whom to marry is among life's momentous acts of self-definition.

Tangible as well as intangible benefits flow from marriage. The marriage license grants valuable property rights to those who meet the entry requirements, and who agree to what might otherwise be a burdensome degree of government regulation of their activities. The Legislature has conferred on "each party [in a civil marriage] substantial rights concerning the assets of the other which unmarried cohabitants do not have."

The benefits accessible only by way of a marriage license are enormous, touching nearly every aspect of life and death. The department states that "hundreds of statutes" are related to marriage and to marital benefits. . . .

It is undoubtedly for these concrete reasons, as well as for its intimately personal significance, that civil marriage has long been termed a "civil right." See, e.g., Loving v. Virginia, 388 U.S. 1, 12 (1967) ("Marriage is one of the 'basic civil rights of man,' fundamental to our very existence and survival"). The United States Supreme Court has described the right to marry as "of fundamental importance for all individuals" and as "part of the fundamental 'right of privacy' implicit in the Fourteenth Amendment's Due Process Clause." Zablocki v. Redhail, 434 U.S. 374, 384 (1978). See Loving v. Virginia, supra ("The freedom to marry has long been recognized as one of the vital personal rights essential to the orderly pursuit of happiness by free men").

Without the right to marry — or more properly, the right to choose to marry — one is excluded from the full range of human experience and denied full protection of the laws for one's "avowed commitment to an intimate and lasting human relationship." Because civil marriage is central to the lives of individuals and the welfare of the community, our laws assiduously protect the individual's right to marry against undue government incursion. Laws may not "interfere directly and substantially with the right to marry." Zablocki v. Redhail, supra at 387.

Unquestionably, the regulatory power of the Commonwealth over civil marriage is broad, as is the Commonwealth's discretion to award public benefits. Individuals who have the choice to marry each other and nevertheless choose not to may properly be denied the legal benefits of marriage. But that same logic cannot hold for a qualified individual who would marry if she or he only could.

B

For decades, indeed centuries, in much of this country (including Massachusetts) no lawful marriage was possible between white and black Americans. That long history availed not when the . . . United States Supreme Court . . . held that a statutory bar to interracial marriage violated the Fourteenth Amendment, Loving v. Virginia, 388 U.S. 1 (1967). As . . . *Loving* make[s] clear, the right to marry means little if it does not include the right to marry the person of one's choice, subject to appropriate government restrictions in the interests of public health, safety, and welfare. In this case, as in . . . *Loving*, a statute deprives individuals of access to an institution of fundamental legal, personal, and social significance — the institution of marriage — because of a single trait: skin color in *Perez* and *Loving*, sexual orientation here. . . .

The Massachusetts Constitution protects matters of personal liberty against government incursion as zealously, and often more so, than does the Federal Constitution, even where both Constitutions employ essentially the same language. . . .

The individual liberty and equality safeguards of the Massachusetts Constitution protect both "freedom from" unwarranted government intrusion into protected spheres of life and "freedom to" partake in benefits created by the State for the common good. Whether and whom to marry, how to express sexual intimacy, and whether and how to establish a family — these are among the most basic of every individual's liberty and due process rights. And central to personal freedom and security is the assurance that the laws will apply equally to persons in similar situations. "Absolute equality before the law is a fundamental principle of our own Constitution." The liberty interest in choosing whether and whom to marry would be hollow if the Commonwealth could, without sufficient justification, foreclose an individual from freely choosing the person with whom to share an exclusive commitment in the unique institution of civil marriage. . . .

The plaintiffs challenge the marriage statute on both equal protection and due process grounds. With respect to each such claim, we must first determine the appropriate standard of review. Where a statute implicates a fundamental right or uses a suspect classification, we employ "strict judicial scrutiny." For all other statutes, we employ the "rational basis test." For due process claims, rational basis analysis requires that statutes "bear[] a real and substantial relation to the public health, safety, morals, or some other phase of the general welfare." For equal protection challenges, the rational basis test requires that "an impartial lawmaker could logically believe that the classification would serve a legitimate public purpose that transcends the harm to the members of the disadvantaged class."

The department argues that no fundamental right or "suspect" class is at issue here, and rational basis is the appropriate standard of review. For the reasons we explain below, we conclude that the marriage ban does not meet the rational basis test for either due process or equal protection. Because the statute does not survive rational basis review, we do not consider the plaintiffs' arguments that this case merits strict judicial scrutiny.

The department posits three legislative rationales for prohibiting same-sex couples from marrying: (1) providing a "favorable setting for procreation"; (2) ensuring the optimal setting for child rearing, which the department defines as "a two-parent family with one parent of each sex"; and (3) preserving scarce State and private financial resources. We consider each in turn.

The judge in the Superior Court endorsed the first rationale, holding that "the state's interest in regulating marriage is based on the traditional concept that marriage's primary purpose is procreation." This is incorrect. Our laws of civil marriage do not privilege procreative heterosexual intercourse between married people above every other form of adult intimacy and every other means of creating a family. General Laws c. 207 contains no requirement that the applicants for a marriage license attest to their ability or intention to conceive children by coitus. Fertility is not a condition of marriage, nor is it grounds for divorce. People who have never consummated their marriage, and never plan to, may be and stay married. While it is certainly true that many, perhaps most, married couples have children together (assisted or unassisted), it is the exclusive and permanent commitment of the marriage partners to one another, not the begetting of children, that is the sine qua non of civil marriage.

Moreover, the Commonwealth affirmatively facilitates bringing children into a family regardless of whether the intended parent is married or unmarried, whether the child is adopted or born into a family, whether assistive technology was used to conceive the child, and whether the parent or her partner is heterosexual, homosexual, or bisexual. If procreation were a necessary component of civil marriage, our statutes would draw a tighter circle around the permissible bounds of nonmarital child bearing and the creation of families by noncoital means. The attempt to isolate procreation as "the source of a fundamental right to marry" . . . overlooks the integrated way in which courts have examined the complex and overlapping realms of personal autonomy, marriage, family life, and child rearing. Our jurisprudence recognizes that, in these nuanced and fundamentally private areas of life, such a narrow focus is inappropriate.

The "marriage is procreation" argument singles out the one unbridgeable difference between same-sex and opposite-sex couples, and transforms that difference into the essence of legal marriage. Like "Amendment 2" to the Constitution of Colorado, which effectively denied homosexual persons equality under the law and full access to the political process, the marriage restriction impermissibly "identifies persons by a single trait and then denies them protection across the board." Romer v. Evans, 517 U.S. 620, 633 (1996). In so doing, the State's action confers an official stamp of approval on the destructive stereotype that same-sex relationships are inherently unstable and inferior to opposite-sex relationships and are not worthy of respect.

The department's first stated rationale, equating marriage with unassisted heterosexual procreation, shades imperceptibly into its second: that confining marriage to opposite-sex couples ensures that children are raised in the "optimal" setting. Protecting the welfare of children is a paramount State policy. Restricting marriage to opposite-sex couples, however, cannot plausibly further this policy. "The demographic changes of the past century make it difficult to speak of an average American family. The composition of families varies greatly from household to household." Troxel v. Granville, 530 U.S. 57, 63 (2000).

Massachusetts has responded supportively to "the changing realities of the American family," and has moved vigorously to strengthen the modern family in its many variations. Moreover, we have repudiated the common-law power of the State to provide varying levels of protection to children based on the circumstances of birth. The "best interests of the child" standard does not turn on a parent's sexual orientation or marital status.

The department has offered no evidence that forbidding marriage to people of the same sex will increase the number of couples choosing to enter into opposite-sex marriages in order to have and raise children. There is thus no rational relationship between the marriage statute and the Commonwealth's proffered goal of protecting the "optimal" child rearing unit. Moreover, the department readily concedes that people in same-sex couples may be "excellent" parents. These couples (including four of the plaintiff couples) have children for the reasons others do — to love them, to care for them, to nurture them. But the task of child rearing for same-sex couples is made infinitely harder by their status as outliers to the marriage laws. While establishing the parentage of children as soon as possible is crucial to the safety and welfare of children, same-sex couples must undergo the sometimes lengthy and intrusive process of second-parent adoption to establish their joint parentage. While the enhanced income provided by marital benefits is an important source of security and stability for married couples and their children, those benefits are denied to families headed by same-sex couples. . . . Given the wide range of public benefits reserved only for married couples, we do not credit the department's contention that the absence of access to civil marriage amounts to little more than an inconvenience to same-sex couples and their children. Excluding same-sex couples from civil marriage will not make children of opposite-sex marriages more secure, but it does prevent children of same-sex couples from enjoying the immeasurable advantages that flow from the assurance of "a stable family structure in which children will be reared, educated, and socialized." . . .

No one disputes that the plaintiff couples are families, that many are parents, and that the children they are raising, like all children, need and should have the fullest opportunity to grow up in a secure, protected family unit. Similarly, no one disputes that, under the rubric of marriage, the State provides a cornucopia of substantial benefits to married parents and their children. The preferential treatment of civil marriage reflects the Legislature's conclusion that marriage "is the foremost setting for the education and socialization of children" precisely because it "encourages parents to remain committed to each other and to their children as they grow."

In this case, we are confronted with an entire, sizeable class of parents raising children who have absolutely no access to civil marriage and its protections because they are forbidden from procuring a marriage license. It cannot be rational under our laws, and indeed it is not permitted, to penalize children by depriving them of State benefits because the State disapproves of their parents' sexual orientation.

The third rationale advanced by the department is that limiting marriage to opposite-sex couples furthers the Legislature's interest in conserving scarce State and private financial resources. The marriage restriction is rational, it argues, because the General Court logically could assume that same-sex couples are more financially independent than married couples and thus less needy of public marital benefits, such as tax advantages, or private marital benefits, such as employer-financed health plans that include spouses in their coverage.

An absolute statutory ban on same-sex marriage bears no rational relationship to the goal of economy. First, the department's conclusory generalization — that same-sex couples are less financially dependent on each other than opposite-sex couples — ignores that many same-sex couples, such as many of the plaintiffs in this case, have children and other dependents (here, aged parents) in their care. The department does not contend, nor could it, that these dependents are less needy or deserving than the dependents of married couples. Second, Massachusetts marriage laws do not condition receipt of public and private financial benefits to married individuals on a demonstration of financial dependence on each other; the benefits are available to married couples regardless of whether they mingle their finances or actually depend on each other for support.

The department suggests additional rationales for prohibiting same-sex couples from marrying, which are developed by some amici. It argues that broadening civil marriage to include same-sex couples will trivialize or destroy the institution of marriage as it has historically been fashioned. Certainly our decision today marks a significant change in the definition of marriage as it has been inherited from the common law, and understood by many societies for centuries. But it does not disturb the fundamental value of marriage in our society.

Here, the plaintiffs seek only to be married, not to undermine the institution of civil marriage. They do not want marriage abolished. They do not attack the binary nature of marriage, the consanguinity provisions, or any of the other gate-keeping provisions of the marriage licensing law. Recognizing the right of an individual to marry a person of the same sex will not diminish the validity or dignity of opposite-sex marriage, any more than recognizing the right of an individual to marry a person of a different race devalues the marriage of a person who marries someone of her own race. If anything, extending civil marriage to same-sex couples reinforces the importance of marriage to individuals and communities. . . .

Several amici suggest that prohibiting marriage by same-sex couples reflects community consensus that homosexual conduct is immoral. Yet Massachusetts has a strong affirmative policy of preventing discrimination on the basis of sexual orientation. See G. L. c. 151B (employment, housing, credit, services); G. L. c. 265, § 39 (hate crimes); G. L. c. 272, § 98 (public accommodation); G. L. c. 76, § 5 (public education). . . .

The marriage ban works a deep and scarring hardship on a very real segment of the community for no rational reason. The absence of any reasonable relationship between, on the one hand, an absolute disqualification of same-sex couples who wish to enter into civil marriage and, on the other, protection of public health, safety, or general welfare, suggests that the marriage restriction is rooted in persistent prejudices against persons who are (or who are believed to be) homosexual. "The Constitution cannot control such prejudices but neither can it tolerate them. Private biases may be outside the reach of the law, but the law cannot, directly or indirectly, give them effect." Limiting the protections, benefits, and obligations of civil marriage to opposite-sex couples violates the basic premises of individual liberty and equality under law protected by the Massachusetts Constitution. . . .

SPINA, J. dissenting. . . . 1. *Equal protection.* . . . [T]he marriage statutes do not discriminate on the basis of sexual orientation. As the court correctly recognizes, constitutional protections are extended to individuals, not couples. The marriage statutes do not disqualify individuals on the basis of sexual orientation from entering into marriage. All individuals, with certain exceptions not relevant here, are free to marry. Whether an individual chooses not to marry because of sexual orientation or any other reason should be of no concern to the court. . . .

Unlike the *Loving* and *Sharp* cases, the Massachusetts Legislature has erected no barrier to marriage that intentionally discriminates against anyone. Within the institution of marriage, anyone is free to marry, with certain exceptions that are not challenged. In the absence of any discriminatory purpose, the State's marriage statutes do not violate principles of equal protection. This court should not have invoked even the most deferential standard of review within equal protection analysis because no individual was denied access to the institution of marriage.

Due process. The marriage statutes do not impermissibly burden a right protected by our constitutional guarantee of due process implicit in art. 10 of our Declaration of Rights. There is no restriction on the right of any plaintiff to enter into marriage. Each is free to marry a willing person of the opposite sex.

Substantive due process protects individual rights against unwarranted government intrusion. The court states, as we have said on many occasions, that the Massachusetts Declaration of Rights may protect a right in ways that exceed the protection afforded by the Federal Constitution. However, today the court does not fashion a remedy that affords greater protection of a right. Instead, using the rubric of due process, it has redefined marriage. . . .

SOSMAN, J., dissenting. In applying the rational basis test to any challenged statutory scheme, the issue is not whether the Legislature's rationale behind that scheme is persuasive to us, but only whether it satisfies a minimal threshold of rationality. Today, rather than apply that test, the court announces that, because it is persuaded that there are no differences between same-sex and opposite-sex couples, the Legislature has no rational basis for treating them differently with respect to the granting of marriage licenses. Reduced to its essence, the court's opinion concludes that, because same-sex couples are now raising children, and withholding the benefits of civil marriage from their union makes it harder for them to raise those children, the State must therefore provide the benefits of civil marriage to same-sex couples just as it does to opposite-sex couples. Of course, many people are raising children outside the confines of traditional marriage, and, by definition, those children are being deprived of the various benefits that would flow if they were being raised in a household with married parents. That does not mean that the Legislature must accord the full benefits of marital status on every household raising children. Rather, the Legislature need only have some rational basis for concluding that, at present, those alternate family structures have not yet been conclusively shown to be the equivalent of the marital family structure that has established itself as a successful one over a period of centuries. People are of course at liberty to raise their children in various family structures, as long as they are not literally harming their children by doing so. That does not mean that the State is required to provide identical forms of encouragement, endorsement, and support to all of the infinite variety of household structures that a free society permits.

Based on our own philosophy of child rearing, and on our observations of the children being raised by same-sex couples to whom we are personally close, we may be of the view that what matters to children is not the gender, or sexual orientation, or even the number of the adults who raise them, but rather whether those adults provide the children with a nurturing, stable, safe, consistent, and supportive environment in which to mature. Same-sex couples can provide their children with the requisite nurturing, stable, safe, consistent, and supportive environment in which to mature, just as opposite-sex couples do. It is therefore understandable that the court might view the traditional definition of marriage as an unnecessary anachronism, rooted in historical prejudices that modern society has in large measure rejected and biological limitations that modern science has overcome.

It is not, however, our assessment that matters. Conspicuously absent from the court's opinion today is any acknowledgment that the attempts at scientific study of the ramifications of raising children in same-sex couple households are themselves in their infancy and have so far produced inconclusive and conflicting results. Notwithstanding our belief that gender and sexual orientation of parents should not matter to the success of the child rearing venture, studies to date reveal that there are still some observable differences between children raised by opposite-sex couples and children raised by same-sex couples. Interpretation of the data gathered by those studies then becomes clouded by the personal and political beliefs of the investigators, both as to whether the differences identified are positive or negative, and as to the untested explanations of what might account for those differences. . . . Even in the absence of bias or political agenda behind the various studies of children raised by same-sex couples, the most neutral and strict application of scientific principles to this field would be constrained by the limited period of observation that has been available. Gay and lesbian couples living together openly, and official recognition of them as their children's sole parents, comprise a very recent phenomenon, and the recency of that phenomenon has not yet permitted any study of how those children fare as adults and at best minimal study of how they fare during their adolescent years. The Legislature can rationally view the state of the scientific evidence as unsettled on the critical question it now faces: Are families headed by same-sex parents equally successful in rearing children from infancy to adulthood as families headed by parents of opposite sexes? Our belief that children raised by same-sex couples should fare the same as children raised in traditional families is just that: a passionately held but utterly untested belief. The Legislature is not required to share that belief but may, as the creator of the institution of civil marriage, wish to see the proof before making a fundamental alteration to that institution.

Although ostensibly applying the rational basis test to the civil marriage statutes, it is abundantly apparent that the court is in fact applying some undefined stricter standard to assess the constitutionality of the marriage statutes' exclusion of same-sex couples. . . .

Shorn of these emotion-laden invocations, the opinion ultimately opines that the Legislature is acting irrationally when it grants benefits to a proven successful family structure while denying the same benefits to a recent, perhaps promising, but essentially untested alternate family structure. Placed in a more neutral context, the court would never find any irrationality in such an approach. For example, if the issue were government subsidies and tax benefits promoting use of an established technology for energy efficient heating, the court would find no equal protection or due process violation in the Legislature's decision not to grant the same benefits to an inventor or manufacturer of some new, alternative technology who did not yet have sufficient data to prove that that new technology was just as good as the established technology. That the early results from preliminary testing of the new technology might look very promising, or that the theoretical underpinnings of the new technology might appear flawless, would not make it irrational for the Legislature to grant subsidies and tax breaks to the established technology and deny them to the still unproved newcomer in the field. While programs that affect families and children register higher on our emotional scale than programs affecting energy efficiency, our standards for what is or is not "rational" should not be bent by those emotional tugs. Where, as here, there is no ground for applying strict scrutiny, the emotionally compelling nature of the subject matter should not affect the manner in which we apply the rational basis test.

Opinions of the Justices to the Senate

802 N.E.2d 565 (Mass. 2004)

[On December 11, 2003, the Massachusetts legislature adopted, pending decision by the Massachusetts Supreme Judicial Court, Senate Bill 2175, "An Act Relative to Civil Unions." Section 2 of that bill seeks to "provide eligible same-sex couples the opportunity to obtain the benefits, protections, rights and responsibilities afforded to opposite sex couples by the marriage laws of the commonwealth, without entering into a marriage." The bill includes a new Chapter 207A of the Massachusetts statutes establishing civil unions, open to same-sex couples eligible on grounds of age, non-relationship, and other standard categories, but not to opposite-sex couples. Section 3 of 207A provides that "[p]ersons eligible to form a civil union with each other under this chapter shall not be eligible to enter into a marriage with each other under chapter 207."

A second bill adopted at the same time, Senate Bill 2176, seeks an opinion by the Supreme Judicial Court on the question of whether the pending statute (S.B. 2175) complies with the equal protection and due process requirements of the state constitution.]

... We have now been asked to render an advisory opinion on Senate No. 2175, which creates a new legal status, "civil union," that is purportedly equal to "marriage," yet separate from it. The constitutional difficulty of the proposed civil union bill is evident in its stated purpose to "preserv[e] the traditional, historic nature and meaning of the institution of civil marriage." Senate No. 2175, § 1. Preserving the institution of civil marriage is of course a legislative priority of the highest order, and one to which the Justices accord the General Court the greatest deference. We recognize the efforts of the Senate to draft a bill in conformity with the *Goodridge* opinion. Yet the bill, as we read it, does nothing to "preserve" the civil marriage law, only its constitutional infirmity. ...

The same defects of rationality evident in the marriage ban considered in *Goodridge* are evident in, if not exaggerated by, Senate No. 2175. Segregating same-sex unions from opposite-sex unions cannot possibly be held rationally to advance or "preserve" what we stated in *Goodridge* were the Commonwealth's legitimate interests in procreation, child rearing, and the conservation of resources. Because the proposed law by its express terms forbids same-sex couples entry into civil marriage, it continues to relegate same-sex couples to a different status. The holding in *Goodridge*, by which we are bound, is that group classifications based on unsupportable distinctions, such as that embodied in the proposed bill, are invalid under the Massachusetts Constitution. The history of our nation has demonstrated that separate is seldom, if ever, equal. . . .

The bill's absolute prohibition of the use of the word "marriage" by "spouses" who are the same sex is more than semantic. The dissimilitude between the terms "civil marriage" and "civil union" is not innocuous; it is a considered choice of language that reflects a demonstrable assigning of same-sex, largely homosexual, couples to second-class status. The denomination of this difference by the separate opinion of Justice Sosman (separate opinion) as merely a "squabble over the name to be used" so clearly misses the point that further discussion appears to be useless. If, as the separate opinion posits, the proponents of the bill believe that no message is conveyed by eschewing the word "marriage" and replacing it with "civil union" for same-sex "spouses," we doubt that the attempt to circumvent the court's decision in *Goodridge* would be so purposeful.

NOTES AND QUESTIONS

1. The court in *Goodridge*, like the court in *Zablocki*, analyzes the constitutionality of a limitation on marriage as a matter of equal protection; both courts conclude that the limitation at stake cannot survive, although *Goodridge* relies on the state, rather than the federal, constitution. How does Judge Spina, who dissents, reach the conclusion that the statutes do not deny access to marriage to anyone? During the 1970s, statutes preventing same-sex couples from marrying were challenged in several courts around the country. The courts at that time consistently accepted the argument that Judge Spina makes. *See, e.g.*, Singer v. Hara, 522 P.2d 1187 (Wash. App. 1974); Jones v. Hallahan, 501 S.W.2d 588 (Ky. 1973); Baker v. Nelson, 191 N.W.2d 185 (Minn. 1971). What classification does the *Goodridge* majority interpret the statute as making?

2. In the second opinion above, the Massachusetts Supreme Judicial Court concludes that a statute creating a civil union that would grant same-sex couples all the rights and duties of marriage available under state law would still not satisfy the state constitution. Why not? On the shift in popular and legal perception of civil unions and domestic partnerships, *see* Melissa Murray, Paradigms Lost: How Domestic Partnership Went from Innovation to Injury, 37 N.Y.U. Rev. L. & Soc. Change 291 (2013).

3. While many arguments have been made by supporters of bans on same-sex marriage, the most successful ones have focused on the state's interest in using

marriage to promote childrearing. For example, the New York Court of Appeals wrote the following in its 2006 decision applying rational basis scrutiny and rejecting a challenge to the ban:

> First, the Legislature could rationally decide that, for the welfare of children, it is more important to promote stability, and to avoid instability, in opposite-sex than in same-sex relationships. Heterosexual intercourse has a natural tendency to lead to the birth of children; homosexual intercourse does not. Despite the advances of science, it remains true that the vast majority of children are born as a result of a sexual relationship between a man and a woman, and the Legislature could find that this will continue to be true. The Legislature could also find that such relationships are all too often casual or temporary. It could find that an important function of marriage is to create more stability and permanence in the relationships that cause children to be born. It thus could choose to offer an inducement — in the form of marriage and its attendant benefits — to opposite-sex couples who make a solemn, long-term commitment to each other.
>
> The Legislature could find that this rationale for marriage does not apply with comparable force to same-sex couples. These couples can become parents by adoption, or by artificial insemination or other technological marvels, but they do not become parents as a result of accident or impulse. The Legislature could find that unstable relationships between people of the opposite sex present a greater danger that children will be born into or grow up in unstable homes than is the case with same-sex couples, and thus that promoting stability in opposite-sex relationships will help children more. This is one reason why the Legislature could rationally offer the benefits of marriage to opposite-sex couples only.
>
> There is a second reason: The Legislature could rationally believe that it is better, other things being equal, for children to grow up with both a mother and a father. Intuition and experience suggest that a child benefits from having before his or her eyes, every day, living models of what both a man and a woman are like. It is obvious that there are exceptions to this general rule — some children who never know their fathers, or their mothers, do far better than some who grow up with parents of both sexes — but the Legislature could find that the general rule will usually hold.

Hernandez v. Robles, 855 N.E.2d 1, 7 (N.Y. 2006). Would these arguments succeed if a court concluded that heightened scrutiny applied to the ban?

4. High courts in seven states have, like the Massachusetts Supreme Judicial Court, concluded that denial of access to the benefits of marriage to same-sex couples violates the state constitution; three other states' highest courts have rejected such claims. The state interests asserted in support of the ban are essentially the same in these cases. The difference in outcomes turns on the level of scrutiny the courts apply and the way the courts apply Romer v. Evans.

Cases striking same-sex marriage ban: In re Marriage Cases, 183 P.3d 384 (Cal. 2008) (superseded by constitutional amendment); Kerrigan v. Comm'r Pub. Health, 957 A.2d 407 (Conn. 2008); Baehr v. Lewin, 852 P.2d 44 (Haw. 1993) and Baehr v. Miike, 1996 WL 694235 (Haw. 1st Cir. 1996), aff'd, 950 P.2d 1234 (Haw. 1997) (superseded by constitutional amendment); Varnum v. Brien, 763 N.W.2d 862 (Iowa 2009); Lewis v. Harris, 908 A.2d 196 (N.J. 2006); Griego v. Oliver, 316 P.3d 865 (N.M. 2013); Baker v. Vermont, 744 A.2d

864 (Vt. 1999). The constitutional amendment overriding the California decision was in turn held unconstitutional in Perry v. Brown, 671 F.3d 1052, 1095 (9th Cir. 2012), and the Hawaii legislature enacted a law allowing marriage in 2013. Hawaii SB 1. In contrast, courts in four of these states have held that states must allow same-sex couples to enter the relationship called marriage. *In re Marriage Cases, Kerrigan, Varnum, Griego.* Courts in Vermont and New Jersey disagreed, holding that the relationship can be called something other than marriage, so long as the material benefits are the same. *Baker, Lewis.* However, in both states same-sex couples can now marry. The Vermont legislature enacted a marriage law in 2009, 2009 Vt. Laws No. 3 (S. 115), and in 2013 a trial judge in New Jersey held that, in the wake of United States v. Windsor, 133 S. Ct. 2675 (2013), *infra*, legislation granting all the benefits but not the title of marriage to same-sex couples violated the state constitution, since the legislation did not enable same-sex couples to claim federal marriage benefits (*see* United States v. Windsor, below). Garden State Equality v. Dow, 82 A.3d 336 (N.J. Super. L. 2013). On the day the decision went into effect, the governor of New Jersey withdrew the state's appeal, removing the last impediment to same-sex marriage.

Cases upholding same-sex marriage ban: Conaway v. Dean, 932 A.2d 571 (Md. App. 2007); Hernandez v. Robles, 855 N.E.2d 1 (N.Y. 2006); Andersen v. King County, 138 P.3d 963 (Wash. 2006). In all these states, however, legislation now allows same-sex couples to marry. Md. Fam. Law Code Ann. § 2-201, adopted by initiative in 2012; N.Y. Dom. Rel. Law Ann. § 10-a, enacted in 2011; Wash. Rev. Code § 26.04.010, adopted by initiative in 2012. In addition, intermediate appellate courts in at least two states have rejected constitutional challenges. Standhardt v. Superior Court ex rel. County of Maricopa, 77 P.3d 451 (Ariz. App. 2003); Morrison v. Sadler, 821 N.E.2d 15 (Ind. App. 2005).

Federal district courts in a number of states have held that bans on same-sex marriage violate the federal constitution. The legal developments in this area are occurring so rapidly that it is impossible to report on them accurately here.

5. Five states and the District of Columbia enacted same-sex marriage statutes without the spur of litigation. 79 Del. Laws ch. 19, enacted in 2013; D.C. Religious Freedom and Civil Marriage Equality Amendment Act of 2009, 57 D.C. Reg. 27, enacted in 2009; Illinois Religious Freedom and Marriage Act, HB 5170, enacted 2013; Maine Citizen Initiative, Same-Sex Marriage, Question 1, adopted 2012; 2013 Minn. Laws ch. 74, enacted in 2013; N.H. Rev. Stat. § 457:1-a, enacted in 2012; R.I. Pub. L. 2013-005.

NOTE: STATE DOMESTIC PARTNERSHIPS AND CIVIL UNIONS

As noted above, in response to cases holding that state constitutions forbade denying the benefits of marriage to same-sex couples, legislatures in several states enacted laws creating civil unions or domestic partnerships that granted full rights. Other states enacted such legislation without the threat of litigation. In five of the jurisdictions that originally followed this route, the District of Columbia, Hawaii, Illinois, Washington, and Vermont, marriage legislation has now been enacted.

Civil unions or domestic partnerships remain an alternative in the District of Columbia, Hawaii, and Illinois and, in Washington for couples 62 or older.

Three states only have domestic partnership or civil union laws. The Colorado law gives all the rights of marriage under state law, while those in Nevada and Wisconsin give more limited rights. Colorado Civil Union Act, SB 13-011; Nev. Rev. Stat. §§ 122A.010 et seq.; Wis. 2009 Act 28, § 3218.

Professor Nancy Polikoff has argued that a broadly inclusive domestic partner regime is preferable to marriage:

Almost all domestic partnership models extend eligibility for registration to one of the following three categories of relationships: 1) same-sex couples only; 2) same-sex and opposite-sex couples; and 3) same-sex couples and individuals related to each other to a degree that would prevent them from marrying. Each of these categories is flawed. A small number of jurisdictions extend eligibility to a wider group of relationships and should be considered models for future registration schemes.

The three dominant categories express distinct underlying visions. Allowing only same-sex couples to register validates marriage as the proper norm. Thus, opposite-sex couples, who are permitted to marry, must marry to obtain relationship-based rights and responsibilities. This category does not support alternative family structures; rather it acknowledges the value of gay and lesbian couples and expresses the inequity of denying such couples access to some, or even most, of the incidents accorded spouses. Eligibility criteria customarily eliminate two individuals of the same sex who would be prohibited from marrying were they of opposite sex, thus evidencing marriage as the analogous relationship. Two sisters, or a grandmother and a granddaughter, no matter how emotionally and economically intertwined, cannot register. Conjugal relationships, whether opposite-sex or same-sex, are therefore supported above equally committed relationships between relatives.

The category that includes same-sex couples and relatives unable to marry similarly validates marriage as the proper norm because it excludes opposite-sex couples. This category does, however, recognize the importance of certain familial, non-conjugal, relationships and allows those in such relationships certain benefits.

Extending eligibility to both same-sex and opposite-sex couples validates the choice of heterosexuals to remain unmarried and thus has the potential to chip away at the privileged legal status of marriage. Such regimes, however, are geared toward conjugal relationships, even though engaging in sexual relations is not specified as an eligibility criterion. Intent to recognize only conjugal relationships is evidenced by exclusion from registration of all those who would be unable to marry under state incest laws. . . .

When advocates for same-sex marriage invoke the very two-tiered structure that privileges marriage as a reason why lesbians and gay men must have access to the favored tier, they accept that two-tiered structure as a natural and unquestioned phenomenon. Worse still, advocates often extol marriage as a badge of maturity, commitment, and citizenship. Such arguments place gay and lesbian advocacy on the wrong side of an intense culture war. To be sure, opponents of same-sex marriage populate that side of the culture war as well. But what all on that side share is a conviction that the good of marriage is so profound and basic to a well functioning society that law and policy can single out marriage for "special rights" unavailable to other emotionally and economically interdependent units. On the other side of the culture war are those, like myself, who value equally all family forms and who therefore want just social policies that facilitate maximum economic well-being and emotional flourishing for all, not only for those who marry.

Nancy D. Polikoff, Ending Marriage as We Know It, 32 Hofstra L. Rev. 201, 218-230 (2003). *See also* Nancy Polikoff, Beyond (Straight and Gay) Marriage: Valuing All Families Under the Law (2009); Grace Ganz Blumberg, Legal Recognition of Same-Sex Conjugal Relationships: The 2003 California Domestic Partner Rights and Responsibilities Act in Comparative Civil Rights and Family Law Perspective, 51 UCLA L. Rev. 1555 (2004); Suzanne A. Kim, Skeptical Marriage Equality, 34 Harv. J.L. & Gender 37 (2011); Ruthann Robson, Sappho Goes to Law School (1998).

UNITED STATES v. WINDSOR

133 S. Ct. 2675 (2013)

Justice KENNEDY delivered the opinion of the Court. . . . In 1996, as some States were beginning to consider the concept of same-sex marriage, see, *e.g.*, Baehr v. Lewin, 74 Haw. 530, 852 P.2d 44 (1993), and before any State had acted to permit it, Congress enacted the Defense of Marriage Act (DOMA), 110 Stat. 2419. DOMA contains two operative sections: Section 2, which has not been challenged here, allows States to refuse to recognize same-sex marriages performed under the laws of other States.[2]

Section 3 is at issue here. It amends the Dictionary Act in Title 1, § 7, of the United States Code to provide a federal definition of "marriage" and "spouse." Section 3 of DOMA provides as follows:

> "In determining the meaning of any Act of Congress, or of any ruling, regulation, or interpretation of the various administrative bureaus and agencies of the United States, the word 'marriage' means only a legal union between one man and one woman as husband and wife, and the word 'spouse' refers only to a person of the opposite sex who is a husband or a wife."

The definitional provision does not by its terms forbid States from enacting laws permitting same-sex marriages or civil unions or providing state benefits to residents in that status. The enactment's comprehensive definition of marriage for purposes of all federal statutes and other regulations or directives covered by its terms, however, does control over 1,000 federal laws in which marital or spousal status is addressed as a matter of federal law.

Edith Windsor and Thea Spyer met in New York City in 1963 and began a long-term relationship. Windsor and Spyer registered as domestic partners when New York City gave that right to same-sex couples in 1993. Concerned about Spyer's health, the couple made the 2007 trip to Canada for their marriage, but they continued to reside in New York City. The State of New York deems their Ontario marriage to be a valid one.

---

2. Section 2 of DOMA is considered later in this chapter. — Ed.

Spyer died in February 2009, and left her entire estate to Windsor. Because DOMA denies federal recognition to same-sex spouses, Windsor did not qualify for the marital exemption from the federal estate tax, which excludes from taxation "any interest in property which passes or has passed from the decedent to his surviving spouse." Windsor paid $363,053 in estate taxes and sought a refund. The Internal Revenue Service denied the refund, concluding that, under DOMA, Windsor was not a "surviving spouse." Windsor commenced this refund suit in the United States District Court for the Southern District of New York. She contended that DOMA violates the guarantee of equal protection, as applied to the Federal Government through the Fifth Amendment.

While the tax refund suit was pending, the Attorney General of the United States notified the Speaker of the House of Representatives, pursuant to 28 U.S.C. § 530D, that the Department of Justice would no longer defend the constitutionality of DOMA's § 3. Noting that "the Department has previously defended DOMA against . . . challenges involving legally married same-sex couples," the Attorney General informed Congress that "the President has concluded that given a number of factors, including a documented history of discrimination, classifications based on sexual orientation should be subject to a heightened standard of scrutiny." . . .

Although "the President . . . instructed the Department not to defend the statute in *Windsor*," he also decided "that Section 3 will continue to be enforced by the Executive Branch" and that the United States had an "interest in providing Congress a full and fair opportunity to participate in the litigation of those cases." . . .

In response to the notice from the Attorney General, the Bipartisan Legal Advisory Group (BLAG) of the House of Representatives voted to intervene in the litigation to defend the constitutionality of § 3 of DOMA. . . .

On the merits of the tax refund suit, the District Court ruled against the United States. . . . [T]he Court of Appeals for the Second Circuit affirmed. . . .

When at first Windsor and Spyer longed to marry, neither New York nor any other State granted them that right. After waiting some years, in 2007 they traveled to Ontario to be married there. It seems fair to conclude that, until recent years, many citizens had not even considered the possibility that two persons of the same sex might aspire to occupy the same status and dignity as that of a man and woman in lawful marriage. For marriage between a man and a woman no doubt had been thought of by most people as essential to the very definition of that term and to its role and function throughout the history of civilization. That belief, for many who long have held it, became even more urgent, more cherished when challenged. For others, however, came the beginnings of a new perspective, a new insight. . . .

Slowly at first and then in rapid course, the laws of New York came to acknowledge the urgency of this issue for same-sex couples who wanted to affirm their commitment to one another before their children, their family, their friends, and their community. And so New York recognized same-sex marriages performed elsewhere; and then it later amended its own marriage laws to permit same-sex marriage. New York, in common with, as of this writing, 11 other States and the District of Columbia, decided that same-sex couples should have the right to marry and so live with pride in themselves and their union and in a status of equality with all other married persons. . . .

In order to assess the validity of [DOMA] it is necessary to discuss the extent of the state power and authority over marriage as a matter of history and tradition. State laws defining and regulating marriage, of course, must respect the constitutional rights of persons, see, *e.g.*, Loving v. Virginia, 388 U.S. 1 (1967); but, subject to those guarantees, "regulation of domestic relations" is "an area that has long been regarded as a virtually exclusive province of the States." Sosna v. Iowa, 419 U.S. 393 (1975).

The recognition of civil marriages is central to state domestic relations law applicable to its residents and citizens. The definition of marriage is the foundation of the State's broader authority to regulate the subject of domestic relations with respect to the "[p]rotection of offspring, property interests, and the enforcement of marital responsibilities."

Consistent with this allocation of authority, the Federal Government, through our history, has deferred to state-law policy decisions with respect to domestic relations. . . . In order to respect this principle, the federal courts, as a general rule, do not adjudicate issues of marital status even when there might otherwise be a basis for federal jurisdiction. See Ankenbrandt v. Richards, 504 U.S. 689 (1992).[3] Federal courts will not hear divorce and custody cases even if they arise in diversity because of "the virtually exclusive primacy . . . of the States in the regulation of domestic relations." *Id.*, at 714, 112 S. Ct. 2206 (Blackmun, J., concurring in judgment). . . .

Against this background DOMA rejects the long-established precept that the incidents, benefits, and obligations of marriage are uniform for all married couples within each State, though they may vary, subject to constitutional guarantees, from one State to the next. Despite these considerations, it is unnecessary to decide whether this federal intrusion on state power is a violation of the Constitution because it disrupts the federal balance. The State's power in defining the marital relation is of central relevance in this case quite apart from principles of federalism. Here the State's decision to give this class of persons the right to marry conferred upon them a dignity and status of immense import. When the State used its historic and essential authority to define the marital relation in this way, its role and its power in making the decision enhanced the recognition, dignity, and protection of the class in their own community. DOMA, because of its reach and extent, departs from this history and tradition of reliance on state law to define marriage. "'[D]iscriminations of an unusual character especially suggest careful consideration to determine whether they are obnoxious to the constitutional provision.'" Romer v. Evans, 517 U.S. 620, 633 (1996) (quoting Louisville Gas & Elec. Co. v. Coleman, 277 U.S. 32, 37-38 (1928)).

The Federal Government uses this state-defined class for the opposite purpose — to impose restrictions and disabilities. That result requires this Court now to address whether the resulting injury and indignity is a deprivation of an essential part of the liberty protected by the Fifth Amendment. What the State of New York treats as alike the federal law deems unlike by a law designed to injure the same class the State seeks to protect. . . .

DOMA seeks to injure the very class New York seeks to protect. By doing so it violates basic due process and equal protection principles applicable to the

---

3. *Ankenbrandt* is set out in Chapter 12 of the textbook. — Ed.

Federal Government. The Constitution's guarantee of equality "must at the very least mean that a bare congressional desire to harm a politically unpopular group cannot" justify disparate treatment of that group. In determining whether a law is motived by an improper animus or purpose, "'[d]iscriminations of an unusual character'" especially require careful consideration. DOMA cannot survive under these principles. The responsibility of the States for the regulation of domestic relations is an important indicator of the substantial societal impact the State's classifications have in the daily lives and customs of its people. DOMA's unusual deviation from the usual tradition of recognizing and accepting state definitions of marriage here operates to deprive same-sex couples of the benefits and responsibilities that come with the federal recognition of their marriages. This is strong evidence of a law having the purpose and effect of disapproval of that class. The avowed purpose and practical effect of the law here in question are to impose a disadvantage, a separate status, and so a stigma upon all who enter into same-sex marriages made lawful by the unquestioned authority of the States.

The history of DOMA's enactment and its own text demonstrate that interference with the equal dignity of same-sex marriages, a dignity conferred by the States in the exercise of their sovereign power, was more than an incidental effect of the federal statute. It was its essence. The House Report announced its conclusion that "it is both appropriate and necessary for Congress to do what it can to defend the institution of traditional heterosexual marriage. . . . H.R. 3396 is appropriately entitled the 'Defense of Marriage Act.' The effort to redefine 'marriage' to extend to homosexual couples is a truly radical proposal that would fundamentally alter the institution of marriage." The House concluded that DOMA expresses "both moral disapproval of homosexuality, and a moral conviction that heterosexuality better comports with traditional (especially Judeo-Christian) morality." The stated purpose of the law was to promote an "interest in protecting the traditional moral teachings reflected in heterosexual-only marriage laws." Were there any doubt of this far-reaching purpose, the title of the Act confirms it: The Defense of Marriage.

The arguments put forward by BLAG are just as candid about the congressional purpose to influence or interfere with state sovereign choices about who may be married. As the title and dynamics of the bill indicate, its purpose is to discourage enactment of state same-sex marriage laws and to restrict the freedom and choice of couples married under those laws if they are enacted. The congressional goal was "to put a thumb on the scales and influence a state's decision as to how to shape its own marriage laws." The Act's demonstrated purpose is to ensure that if any State decides to recognize same-sex marriages, those unions will be treated as second-class marriages for purposes of federal law. This raises a most serious question under the Constitution's Fifth Amendment.

DOMA's operation in practice confirms this purpose. When New York adopted a law to permit same-sex marriage, it sought to eliminate inequality; but DOMA frustrates that objective through a system-wide enactment with no identified connection to any particular area of federal law. DOMA writes inequality into the entire United States Code. . . .

DOMA's principal effect is to identify a subset of state-sanctioned marriages and make them unequal. The principal purpose is to impose inequality, not for other reasons like governmental efficiency. Responsibilities, as well as rights, enhance the dignity and integrity of the person. And DOMA contrives to deprive some couples married under the laws of their State, but not other couples, of both rights and responsibilities. By creating two contradictory marriage regimes within the same State, DOMA forces same-sex couples to live as married for the purpose of state law but unmarried for the purpose of federal law, thus diminishing the stability and predictability of basic personal relations the State has found it proper to acknowledge and protect. By this dynamic DOMA undermines both the public and private significance of state-sanctioned same-sex marriages; for it tells those couples, and all the world, that their otherwise valid marriages are unworthy of federal recognition. This places same-sex couples in an unstable position of being in a second-tier marriage. The differentiation demeans the couple, whose moral and sexual choices the Constitution protects, see *Lawrence*, 539 U.S. 558, and whose relationship the State has sought to dignify. And it humiliates tens of thousands of children now being raised by same-sex couples. The law in question makes it even more difficult for the children to understand the integrity and closeness of their own family and its concord with other families in their community and in their daily lives. . . .

This opinion and its holding are confined to those lawful marriages.

The judgment of the Court of Appeals for the Second Circuit is affirmed.

Chief Justice ROBERTS, dissenting. I agree with Justice Scalia that this Court lacks jurisdiction to review the decisions of the courts below. On the merits of the constitutional dispute the Court decides to decide, I also agree with Justice Scalia that Congress acted constitutionally in passing the Defense of Marriage Act (DOMA). Interests in uniformity and stability amply justified Congress's decision to retain the definition of marriage that, at that point, had been adopted by every State in our Nation, and every nation in the world.

The majority sees a more sinister motive, pointing out that the Federal Government has generally (though not uniformly) deferred to state definitions of marriage in the past. That is true, of course, but none of those prior state-by-state variations had involved differences over something — as the majority puts it — "thought of by most people as essential to the very definition of [marriage] and to its role and function throughout the history of civilization." That the Federal Government treated this fundamental question differently than it treated variations over consanguinity or minimum age is hardly surprising — and hardly enough to support a conclusion that the "principal purpose" of the 342 Representatives and 85 Senators who voted for it, and the President who signed it, was a bare desire to harm. . . .

But while I disagree with the result to which the majority's analysis leads it in this case, I think it more important to point out that its analysis leads no further. The Court does not have before it, and the logic of its opinion does not decide, the distinct question whether the States, in the exercise of their "historic and essential authority to define the marital relation," may continue to utilize the traditional definition of marriage.

The majority goes out of its way to make this explicit in the penultimate sentence of its opinion. It states that "[t]his opinion and its holding are confined to those lawful marriages" — referring to same-sex marriages that a State has already recognized as a result of the local "community's considered perspective on the historical roots of the institution of marriage and its evolving understanding of the meaning of equality." Justice Scalia believes this is a "'bald, unreasoned dis-claime[r].'" In my view, though, the disclaimer is a logical and necessary conse-quence of the argument the majority has chosen to adopt. The dominant theme of the majority opinion is that the Federal Government's intrusion into an area "central to state domestic relations law applicable to its residents and citizens" is sufficiently "unusual" to set off alarm bells. I think the majority goes off course, as I have said, but it is undeniable that its judgment is based on federalism. . . .

Justice SCALIA, with whom Justice THOMAS joins, and with whom THE CHIEF JUSTICE joins as to Part I, dissenting. . . . [T]he opinion starts with seven full pages about the traditional power of States to define domestic relations — initially fool-ing many readers, I am sure, into thinking that this is a federalism opinion. But we are eventually told that "it is unnecessary to decide whether this federal intrusion on state power is a violation of the Constitution," and that "[t]he State's power in defining the marital relation is of central relevance in this case quite apart from principles of federalism" because "the State's decision to give this class of persons the right to marry conferred upon them a dignity and status of immense import." But no one questions the power of the States to define marriage (with the concomitant conferral of dignity and status), so what is the point of devoting seven pages to describing how long and well established that power is? Even after the opinion has formally disclaimed reliance upon principles of federalism, mentions of "the usual tradition of recognizing and accepting state definitions of marriage" continue. What to make of this? The opinion never explains. My guess is that the majority, while reluctant to suggest that defining the meaning of "mar-riage" in federal statutes is unsupported by any of the Federal Government's enu-merated powers, nonetheless needs some rhetorical basis to support its pretense that today's prohibition of laws excluding same-sex marriage is confined to the Federal Government (leaving the second, state-law shoe to be dropped later, maybe next Term). But I am only guessing. . . .

Moreover, if this is meant to be an equal-protection opinion, it is a confusing one. The opinion does not resolve and indeed does not even mention what had been the central question in this litigation: whether, under the Equal Protection Clause, laws restricting marriage to a man and a woman are reviewed for more than mere rationality. That is the issue that divided the parties and the court below. . . .

The majority opinion need not get into the strict-vs.-rational-basis scrutiny question, and need not justify its holding under either, because it says that DOMA is unconstitutional as "a deprivation of the liberty of the person protected by the Fifth Amendment of the Constitution," that it violates "basic due process" principles, and that it inflicts an "injury and indignity" of a kind that denies "an essential part of the liberty protected by the Fifth Amendment." . . . The sum of all the Court's nonspecific hand-waving is that this law is invalid (maybe on equal-protection grounds, maybe on substantive-due-process grounds, and perhaps with some amorphous federalism component playing a role) because it is motivated by a "'bare . . . desire to harm'" couples in same-sex marriages. It is this proposition with which I will therefore engage. . . .

. . . [T]he Constitution does not forbid the government to enforce traditional moral and sexual norms. See Lawrence v. Texas, 539 U.S. 558, 599 (2003) (Scalia, J., dissenting). I will not swell the U.S. Reports with restatements of that point. It is enough to say that the Constitution neither requires nor forbids our society to approve of same-sex marriage, much as it neither requires nor forbids us to approve of no-fault divorce, polygamy, or the consumption of alcohol.

However, even setting aside traditional moral disapproval of same-sex marriage (or indeed same-sex sex), there are many perfectly valid — indeed, downright boring — justifying rationales for this legislation. Their existence ought to be the end of this case. For they give the lie to the Court's conclusion that only those with hateful hearts could have voted "aye" on this Act. And more importantly, they serve to make the contents of the legislators' hearts quite irrelevant: "It is a familiar principle of constitutional law that this Court will not strike down an otherwise constitutional statute on the basis of an alleged illicit legislative motive." . . .

To choose just one of these defenders' arguments, DOMA avoids difficult choice-of-law issues that will now arise absent a uniform federal definition of marriage. Imagine a pair of women who marry in Albany and then move to Alabama, which does not "recognize as valid any marriage of parties of the same sex." Ala. Code § 30-1-19(e) (2011). When the couple files their next federal tax return, may it be a joint one? Which State's law controls, for federal-law purposes: their State of celebration (which recognizes the marriage) or their State of domicile (which does not)? (Does the answer depend on whether they were just visiting in Albany?) Are these questions to be answered as a matter of federal common law, or perhaps by borrowing a State's choice-of-law rules? If so, *which* State's? And what about States where the status of an out-of-state same-sex marriage is an unsettled question under local law? DOMA avoided all of this uncertainty by specifying which marriages would be recognized for federal purposes. That is a classic purpose for a definitional provision.

Further, DOMA preserves the intended effects of prior legislation against then-unforeseen changes in circumstance. When Congress provided (for example) that a special estate-tax exemption would exist for spouses, this exemption reached only *opposite-sex* spouses — those being the only sort that were recognized in *any* State at the time of DOMA's passage. When it became clear that changes in state law might one day alter that balance, DOMA's definitional section was enacted to ensure that state-level experimentation did not automatically alter the basic operation of federal law, unless and until Congress made the further judgment to do so on its own. That is not animus — just stabilizing prudence. Congress has hardly demonstrated itself unwilling to make such further, revising judgments upon due deliberation. . . .

. . . As I have said, the real rationale of today's opinion, whatever disappearing trail of its legalistic argle-bargle one chooses to follow, is that DOMA is motivated by "'bare . . . desire to harm'" couples in same-sex marriages. How easy it is, indeed how inevitable, to reach the same conclusion with regard to state laws denying same-sex couples marital status. . . .

By formally declaring anyone opposed to same-sex marriage an enemy of human decency, the majority arms well every challenger to a state law restricting marriage to its traditional definition. Henceforth those challengers will lead with this Court's declaration that there is "no legitimate purpose" served by such a law, and will claim that the traditional definition has "the purpose and effect to disparage and to injure" the "personhood and dignity" of same-sex couples. . . .

I dissent.

Justice ALITO, with whom Justice THOMAS joins as to Parts II and III, dissenting. . . . The Constitution does not guarantee the right to enter into a same-sex marriage. Indeed, no provision of the Constitution speaks to the issue.

The Court has sometimes found the Due Process Clauses to have a substantive component that guarantees liberties beyond the absence of physical restraint. And the Court's holding that "DOMA is unconstitutional as a deprivation of the liberty of the person protected by the Fifth Amendment of the Constitution," suggests that substantive due process may partially underlie the Court's decision today. But it is well established that any "substantive" component to the Due Process Clause protects only "those fundamental rights and liberties which are, objectively, 'deeply rooted in this Nation's history and tradition,'" as well as "'implicit in the concept of ordered liberty,' such that 'neither liberty nor justice would exist if they were sacrificed.'"

It is beyond dispute that the right to same-sex marriage is not deeply rooted in this Nation's history and tradition. . . .

Perhaps because they cannot show that same-sex marriage is a fundamental right under our Constitution, Windsor and the United States couch their arguments in equal protection terms. . . .

In my view, the approach that Windsor and the United States advocate is misguided. Our equal protection framework, upon which Windsor and the United States rely, is a judicial construct that provides a useful mechanism for analyzing a certain universe of equal protection cases. But that framework is ill suited for use in evaluating the constitutionality of laws based on the traditional understanding of marriage, which fundamentally turn on what marriage is. . . .

The first and older view, which I will call the "traditional" or "conjugal" view, sees marriage as an intrinsically opposite-sex institution. BLAG notes that virtually every culture, including many not influenced by the Abrahamic religions, has limited marriage to people of the opposite sex. And BLAG attempts to explain this phenomenon by arguing that the institution of marriage was created for the purpose of channeling heterosexual intercourse into a structure that supports child rearing. Others explain the basis for the institution in more philosophical terms. They argue that marriage is essentially the solemnizing of a comprehensive, exclusive, permanent union that is intrinsically ordered to producing new life, even if it does not always do so. While modern cultural changes have weakened the link between marriage and procreation in the popular mind, there is no doubt that, throughout human history and across many cultures, marriage has been viewed as an exclusively opposite-sex institution and as one inextricably linked to procreation and biological kinship.

The other, newer view is what I will call the "consent-based" vision of marriage, a vision that primarily defines marriage as the solemnization of mutual commitment — marked by strong emotional attachment and sexual attraction — between two persons. At least as it applies to heterosexual couples, this view of marriage now plays a very prominent role in the popular understanding of the institution. Indeed, our popular culture is infused with this understanding of marriage. Proponents of same-sex marriage argue that because gender differentiation is not relevant to this vision, the exclusion of same-sex couples from the institution of marriage is rank discrimination.

The Constitution does not codify either of these views of marriage (although I suspect it would have been hard at the time of the adoption of the Constitution or the Fifth Amendment to find Americans who did not take the traditional view for granted). The silence of the Constitution on this question should be enough to end the matter as far as the judiciary is concerned. . . .

I respectfully dissent.

NOTES AND QUESTIONS

1. Justice Roberts's dissenting opinion says that the majority opinion is based on principles of federalism. The majority, however, says that it uses principles of equal protection applied to the federal government by the due process clause of the Fifth Amendment. What is the significance of this difference?

2. The majority says that the purpose of DOMA is to harm same-sex couples. How does it do so? How does it harm their children? How do Justices Roberts, Scalia, and Alito respond to this claim? How do their responses differ from each other?

3. The federal district court decisions holding that state same-sex marriage bans violate the constitution are based on the reasoning in *Windsor*, as Justice Scalia predicted.

Romer v. Evans, 517 U.S. 620 (1996), discussed extensively in *Windsor*, invalidated "Amendment 2" to the Colorado Constitution, adopted by statewide referendum, which precludes any legislative, executive, or judicial action extending protection against discrimination to homosexuals, homosexual conduct, or homosexual relationships. Justice Kennedy, for a six-member majority, held that the amendment's classification was not rationally related to a legitimate state purpose. He wrote that the breadth of the amendment indicated that its purpose was to express animus to a class, unrelated to any specific state purpose, and held that classifications with the sole aim of generally disadvantaging a group are invalid.

4. What role might Lawrence v. Texas, 539 U.S. 558 (2003), overruled Bowers v. Hardwick, 478 U.S. 186 (1986), which had rejected a constitutional challenge to a Georgia statute criminalizing sodomy (defined as a sexual act involving the sex organs of one person and the mouth or anus of another).

In *Lawrence*, Justice Kennedy, writing for a majority of five, rejected the historical and theoretical premises of the *Bowers* majority. To the extent that the opinion was based on historical grounds, the majority in *Lawrence* found those grounds "not without doubt and, at the very least . . . overstated." To the extent that the opinion rested on a long tradition regarding homosexual conduct as immoral, that "history and tradition are a starting point but not the ending point of the substantive due process inquiry." The Court said:

> The sweeping references by Chief Justice Burger to the history of Western civilization and to Judeo-Christian moral and ethical standards did not take account of other authorities pointing in an opposite direction. A committee advising the British Parliament recommended in 1957 repeal of laws punishing homosexual conduct.

The Wolfenden Report: Report of the Committee on Homosexual Offenses and Prostitution (1963). Parliament enacted the substance of those recommendations 10 years later. Sexual Offences Act 1967, § 1.

Of even more importance, almost five years before *Bowers* was decided the European Court of Human Rights considered a case with parallels to *Bowers* and to today's case. An adult male resident in Northern Ireland alleged he was a practicing homosexual who desired to engage in consensual homosexual conduct. The laws of Northern Ireland forbade him that right. . . . The court held that the laws proscribing the conduct were invalid under the European Convention on Human Rights. Dudgeon v. United Kingdom, 45 Eur. Ct. H.R. (1981) & ¶ 52. Authoritative in all countries that are members of the Council of Europe (21 nations then, 45 nations now), the decision is at odds with the premise in *Bowers* that the claim put forward was insubstantial in our Western civilization.

In our own constitutional system the deficiencies in *Bowers* became even more apparent in the years following its announcement. The 25 States with laws prohibiting the relevant conduct referenced in the *Bowers* decision are reduced now to 13. . . .

Two principal cases decided after *Bowers* cast its holding into even more doubt. In Planned Parenthood of Southeastern Pa. v. Casey, 505 U.S. 833 (1992), the Court reaffirmed the substantive force of the liberty protected by the Due Process Clause. The *Casey* decision again confirmed that our laws and tradition afford constitutional protection to personal decisions relating to marriage, procreation, contraception, family relationships, child rearing, and education. In explaining the respect the Constitution demands for the autonomy of the person in making these decisions, we stated as follows:

> These matters, involving the most intimate and personal choices a person may make in a lifetime, choices central to personal dignity and autonomy, are central to the liberty protected by the Fourteenth Amendment. At the heart of liberty is the right to define one's own concept of existence, of meaning, of the universe, and of the mystery of human life. . . .

> *Bowers* was not correct when it was decided, and it is not correct today. It ought not to remain binding precedent. Bowers v. Hardwick should be and now is overruled.

> The present case does not involve . . . public conduct or prostitution. It does not involve whether the government must give formal recognition to any relationship that homosexual couples seek to enter. The case does involve two adults who, with full and mutual consent from each other, engaged in sexual practices common to a homosexual lifestyle. The petitioners are entitled to respect for their private lives. . . . Their right to liberty under the Due Process Clause gives them the full right to engage in their conduct without intervention of the government.

539 U.S. at 572-578. Dissenting, Justice Scalia wrote, "State laws against bigamy, same-sex marriage, adult incest, prostitution, masturbation, adultery, fornication, bestiality, and obscenity are likewise sustainable only in light of *Bowers*' validation of laws based on moral choices. Every single one of these laws is called into question by today's decision; the Court makes no effort to cabin the scope of its decision to exclude them from its holding." 539 U.S. at 590.

5. As Justice Scalia says, same-sex couples may be married in one state but not in others. In such a situation, if a couple seeks to be recognized as married for purposes of federal law, which state law will control? There is no one answer to this question, since for purposes of some federal laws granting benefits (or imposing

burdens) based on marriage, the law of the state of celebration controls, while for others the law of the claimant's residence or domicile, or that of the state with the most significant connection governs.

6. On the same day that *Windsor* was decided, a different 5-4 majority of the Supreme Court held that the Ninth Circuit opinion striking down California's initiative denying same-sex couples the right to marry should be vacated for lack of justiciability. California state officials declined to defend the law in federal court, and so the official proponents of the ballot measure had been allowed to intervene to support it, consistent with California law, but the Supreme Court held that they lacked Article III standing. Hollingsworth v. Perry, 133 S. Ct. 2652 (2013). Similarly, in *Windsor*, Justices Roberts, Scalia, and Thomas would have held that the case was not justiciable because the United States government would not defend the constitutionality of Section 3 of DOMA. However, the majority found that *Windsor* was justiciable because "the United States retains a stake sufficient to support Article III jurisdiction on appeal and in proceedings before this Court. The judgment in question orders the United States to pay Windsor the refund she seeks. An order directing the Treasury to pay money is 'a real and immediate economic injury,' indeed as real and immediate as an order directing an individual to pay a tax." 133 S. Ct. at 2686.

NOTE: INTERNATIONAL LEGAL RECOGNITION OF SAME-SEX COUPLES

Australia   Same-sex marriage is not allowed in Australia, but all the states have legislation recognizing de facto unions for same-sex as well as opposite-sex couples that have legal consequences similar to marriage. In some states partners can register a de facto union, while in others courts must determine on a case-by-case basis whether a relationship fits the definition. The states vary about whether they allow same-sex couples to adopt. Federal law prohibits discrimination against same-sex couples and their children in many areas.

Canada   In 2005 the Canadian Civil Marriage Act, which authorizes same-sex marriage, went into effect. The legislation was enacted after the supreme courts of several provinces held that denying access to marriage to same-sex couples violated the Canadian Charter of Rights and Freedoms. For a history of the Canadian developments, *see* Christy M. Glass & Nancy Kubasek, The Evolution of Same-Sex Marriage in Canada: Lessons the U.S. Can Learn from Their Northern Neighbor Regarding Same-Sex Marriage Rights, 15 Mich. J. Gender & L. 143 (2008).

Europe   By early in 2014, same-sex couples could marry in ten European countries: Belgium, Denmark, France, Iceland, the Netherlands, Norway, Portugal, Spain, Sweden, as well as the United Kingdom. A number of European countries allow same-sex couples to register as domestic partners, including Andorra, Austria, the Czech Republic, Finland, Germany, Greenland, Hungary, Ireland, Liechtenstein, Luxembourg, Slovenia, and Switzerland. Some of these acts give registrants all the rights of marriage, while others are limited; the most common difference is not allowing registered partners to adopt children. For a review of early developments, *see* Ian Curry-Sumner, Same-Sex Relationships in Europe: Trends Towards Tolerance?, 3(2) Amsterdam Law Forum (2011), available at http://ojs.ubvu.vu.nl/alf/article/view/215/0.

South Africa   In 2005 the Constitutional Court of South Africa held that excluding same-sex couples from marriage constituted unfair discrimination based on sexual orientation, which is forbidden by the national constitution. Minister of Home Affairs v. Fourie and Bonthuys, 2005 SACLR LEXIS 34 (Nos. 60/04, 10/05, Dec. 1, 2005). Legislation enacted in 2006 allows same-sex and opposite-sex couples to enter a marriage or a civil union.

Central and South America   Argentina enacted legislation authorizing same-sex marriage in 2010, and Uruguay did so in 2013. In 2013 the Brazilian National Council of Justice issued a decision that effectively made same-sex marriage available throughout the country. In addition, same-sex couples may enter civil unions, which are similar to marriage. In Mexico same-sex couples may marry in the federal district and the state of Quintana Roo, and the marriages are recognized throughout the country. Civil unions are available in the federal district and the states of Coahuila and Colima. In Colombia same-sex couples can enter de facto unions, registered or unregistered, which grant the rights of marriage, and civil unions in Ecuador provide all the rights of marriage except adoption.

New Zealand   In 2013 the New Zealand parliament enacted legislation authorizing same-sex marriage. In 2005 the parliament had authorized civil unions for same- and opposite-sex couples that gave many of the rights and duties of marriage. Same-sex couples in civil unions can convert them into marriages.

NOTE: DEVELOPMENTS IN TRANSGENDER MARRIAGE

Marriage involving a transgender partner presents the question of how one defines gender. Courts in at least eight states have decided cases involving the marriage of a postoperative transgender person; five states have held that such marriages are not permitted. In re Marriage of Simmons, 825 N.E.2d 303 (Ill. App. 2005); Kantaras v. Kantaras, 884 So. 2d 155 (Fla. Dist. Ct. App. 2d Dist. 2004); In re Marriage License for Nash, 2003 WL 23097095 (Ohio App. 11th Dist.); In re Estate of Gardiner, 42 P.3d 120 (Kan. 2002); Frances B. v. Mark B., 355 N.Y.S.2d 712 (N.Y. App. Div. 1974).

In contrast, M.J. v. J.T., 355 A.2d 204 (N.J. Super. 1976), *cert. denied*, 364 A.2d 1076 (N.J. 1976), permitted transgender marriage, and the Texas appellate courts have recently done an about-face on the issue. In Littleton v. Prange, 9 S.W.3d 223 (Tex. Civ. App. 1999), *cert. denied*, 531 U.S. 872 (2000), the court refused to recognize a marriage between a transgender woman and a male. It held that the "sex" of Littleton (the transgender partner) had been "immutably fixed by our Creator at birth," and that her self-conception as a female and sex reassignment surgery did not alter that initial identity. Fifteen years later, the court in In re Estate of Arguz, 2014 WL 576085 (Tex. Civ. App. 2014), reversed and remanded a trial court order refusing to recognize a marriage between a transgender woman and a man that had occurred before the woman underwent surgery. Observing that the Texas legislature after *Littleton* enacted a statute providing that a court order relating to a sex change established a person's sex for purposes of marriage, the appellate court remanded for determination of the validity of the marriage, given the timing of the operation. The Board of Immigration Appeals recognized a marriage involving a transgender person in In re Lovo-Lara, 23 I. & N. Dec.

746 (B.I.A. 2005), because North Carolina had issued the parties a marriage license and registered their marriage. Similarly, a federal district judge held that the transgender spouse of a pension plan participant was entitled to spousal benefits because their home state, Minnesota, allows transgender people who have undergone surgery to change their birth records and had issued the couple a marriage license. Radtke v. Misc. Drivers & Helpers Union, 867 F. Supp. 2d 1023 (D. Minn. 2012).

The European Court of Human Rights has changed its view on the treatment of transgendered people. In Goodwin v. United Kingdom, (2002) 35 E.H.R.R. 18 ECHR, the court held that U.K. law denying a male-to-female transgendered person the right to change a number of official government records that listed her as male, resulting in her treatment as male for purposes of inter alia Social Security, national insurance, pensions, and retirement age, violated European Convention Articles 8 (guaranteeing respect for one's private life) and 12 (securing the fundamental right of a man and woman to marry and to found a family).

In February 2003, the Family Court of Australia upheld a lower court decision holding valid a marriage by a female-to-male transgendered person with hormone treatment and irreversible surgery and a woman against a challenge by the attorney general. Attorney-General (Cth) v Kevin, 172 FLR 300 (2003). *See also* Attorney General v. Otahuhu Family Court, [1995] 1 NZLR 603.

Most of the decisions allowing marriage by transgendered people seem to restrict their approval to those who have undergone operations. The New Zealand court was plainly troubled by this requirement and decided that while it would not require that sexual function be possible, the couple "must present themselves as having what appear to be the genitals of a man and a woman.'. . ." [1995] 1 NZLR at 612. The appellate court in *Kevin* emphasized the importance of irreversible surgery as an indicator of commitment to the new sexual identity, *see* 172 FLR at 635, thereby avoiding the risk of authorizing what turns out to be a same-sex marriage.

For an extensive analysis of case law and scientific discussion regarding transgender marriage, *see* David B. Cruz, Getting Sex "Right": Heteronormativity and Biologism in Trans and Intersex Marriage Litigation and Scholarship, 18 Duke J. Gender L. & Pol'y 203 (2010); Terry S. Kogan, Transsexuals, Intersexuals, and Same-Sex Marriage, 18 BYU J. Pub. L. 371 (2004).

3. Relationship

STATE v. SHARON H.

429 A.2d 1321 (Del. Super. 1981)

STIFTEL, J. [Sharon H. and Dennis H., who were half-sister and half-brother, were charged with entering a prohibited marriage. They were born to the same mother, but of different fathers. Sharon was adopted at the age of ten days by the W. family; Dennis was raised in various state programs. They met each other after reaching adulthood and were married.]

Title 13 of the Delaware Code, § 101(a)(1) provides:

§ 101. *Void and Voidable Marriages*
   (a) A marriage is prohibited and void between:
   (1) A person and his or her ancestor, descendant, brother, sister, uncle, aunt, niece, nephew or first cousin. . . .

Title 13 of the Delaware Code, § 102 provides:

§ 102. *Entering into a Prohibited Marriage; Penalty*
   The guilty party or parties to a marriage prohibited by § 101 of this title shall be fined $100, and in default of the payment of the fine shall be imprisoned not more than 30 days.

Section 101(a)(1) of Title 13 is what is commonly termed a consanguinity statute. These statutes exist in one form or another in the majority of the states of our nation. In general, a consanguinity statute prohibits marriages between blood relatives in the lineal, or ascending and descending lines. The historical basis for these statutes is rooted in English Canonical Law, which enforced what is considered to be a Biblical prohibition on incestuous relationships.

Another reason advanced for the enactment of incest and consanguinity statutes is a generally accepted theory that genetic inbreeding by close blood relatives tends to increase the chances that offspring of the marriage will inherit certain unfavorable physical characteristics. Even if this theory is accepted, it is unlikely that it was the original basis for consanguinity statutes, given the relative newness of the theory and the ancient history of these statutes; however, it is possible that this theory served as an additional basis for the revision and reenactment of the various statutes.

In any case, it is clear that consanguinity statutes were designed to prohibit marriages between blood relatives. The Delaware consanguinity statute is no exception. Although the language of the statute has been modified over the years, the clear intention of each statute has been the prohibition of marriages between blood relatives.

The present version of Delaware's consanguinity statute, 13 Del. C. § 101(a)(1), expressly prohibits marriages between brother and sister. Although the Delaware Courts have never addressed the issue, other courts which have applied similar statutes have concluded that the policy behind the prohibition of marriages or sexual relations between blood relatives requires the Court to include relatives of half-blood in the prohibition. Given the obvious intent of 13 Del. C. § 101(a)(1) to prohibit marriages between blood relatives, it is clear that a reasonable interpretation of 13 Del. C. § 101(a)(1) would prohibit the marriage between the appellees. . . .

Having concluded that 13 Del. C. § 101(a)(1) would normally prohibit marriage between the appellees, the question becomes whether the effect of 13 Del. C. § 919 is to destroy all ties between an adopted child and the child's natural relatives, including the ties of blood. . . . 13 Del. C. § 919(b) states:

(b) Upon the issuance of the decree of adoption, the adopted child shall no longer be considered the child of his natural parent or parents, and shall no longer be entitled to any of the rights or privileges or subject to any of the duties or obligations of a child with respect to the natural parent or parents. . . .

Appellees contend that the proper interpretation of this statute is that 13 Del. C. § 919 ends all relationships between an adopted child and its natural relatives, including blood relationships, and so the blood relationship prohibited by 13 Del. C. § 101(a)(1). After looking at the plain language of the statute, however, I conclude that the General Assembly did not intend that 13 Del. C. § 919 have such an effect.

NOTES AND QUESTIONS

1. All states prohibit marriage between persons closely related by blood — that is, through a common ancestor — and most states criminalize sexual relationships between close relatives. Moreover, most states — like the court in *Sharon H.* — interpret these prohibitions as applying to persons related by the half as well as the whole blood. *E.g.*, Cal. Fam. Code § 2200 (2013); 750 Ill. Comp. Stat. 5/212 (2013); Tapscott v. Maryland, 684 A.2d 439 (Md. 1996). In fact, attempted marital relationships involving persons so closely related rarely occur. The relationships that do result in domestic relations litigation typically are those between first cousins, uncles and nieces, and aunts and nephews, as well as certain nonconsanguineous relations — that is, between people related by marriage or "affinity" rather than by blood.

2. It is common to dismiss genetic bases for incest restrictions on the ground that taboos against incest are far older than the science of genetics. Certainly genetics as a science is relatively recent; its origins are usually associated with the research of the Austrian monk Gregor Mendel (1822-1884), who discovered the principles of inherited characteristics through painstaking experiments on inheritance in peas. Most of what we know about genetics has developed during the twentieth century. Two things might be said about the relationship of genetic concerns and consanguinity. One is that observations about inheritance might informally have been made by earlier societies and transformed into taboos. The other is that it is quite clear that the mating of closely related persons does present a genuine basis for genetic concern. This concern is particularly strong with respect to the inheritance of harmful recessive alleles (gene forms). A large number of traits in humans have been identified as the result of the expression of recessive alleles. Among these are phenylketonuria (leading to mental retardation), amyotrophic lateral sclerosis (Lou Gehrig's disease), Bloom's syndrome (dwarfism with skin changes and susceptibility to cancer), and cystic fibrosis. These examples are taken from Linda R. Maxson & Charles H. Daugherty, Genetics: A Human Perspective 71-73 (2d ed. 1989).

3. In 2008 a British politician caused an uproar when he claimed that the high rate of birth defects among the UK Pakistani population was caused by the frequency of first-cousin marriage. A biologist and a political scientist reviewed the history of bans on first-cousin marriages and whether they are justified by genetic concerns:

US prohibitions on cousin marriage date to the Civil War and its immediate aftermath. The first ban was enacted by Kansas in 1858, with Nevada, North Dakota, South Dakota, Washington, New Hampshire, Ohio, and Wyoming following suit in the 1860s. Subsequently, the rate of increase in the number of laws was nearly constant until the mid-1920s; only Kentucky (1946), Maine (1985), and Texas (2005) have since banned cousins from marrying. (Several other efforts ultimately failed when bills were either vetoed by a governor or passed by only one house of a legislature; e.g., in 2000, the Maryland House of Delegates approved a ban by a vote of 82 to 46, but the bill died in the Senate.) . . .

The laws must also be viewed in the context of a new, post–Civil War acceptance of the need for state oversight of education, commerce, and health and safety, including marriage and the family. Beginning in the 1860s, many states passed anti-miscegenation laws, increased the statutory age of marriage, and adopted or expanded medical and mental-capacity restrictions in marriage law. Thus, laws prohibiting cousin marriage were but one aspect of a more general trend to broaden state authority in areas previously considered private. And unlike the situation in Britain and much of Europe, cousin marriage in the US was associated not with the aristocracy and upper middle class but with much easier targets: immigrants and the rural poor. In any case, by the late nineteenth century, in Europe as well as the US, marrying one's cousin had come to be viewed as reckless, and today, despite its continued popularity in many societies and among European elites historically, the practice is highly stigmatized in the West (and parts of Asia—the People's Republic of China, Taiwan, and both North and South Korea also prohibit cousin marriage). . . . But is the practice as risky as many people assume?

Until recently, good data on which to base an answer were lacking. . . . In an effort at clarification, the National Society of Genetic Counselors (NSGC) convened a group of experts to review existing studies on risks to offspring and issue recommendations for clinical practice. Their report concluded that the risks of a first-cousin union were generally much smaller than assumed—about 1.7%-2% above the background risk for congenital defects and 4.4% for pre-reproductive mortality—and did not warrant any special preconception testing. In the authors' view, neither the stigma that attaches to such unions in North America nor the laws that bar them were scientifically well-grounded. . . .

. . . Although the report warned against generalizing from (and hence by implication to) more inbred populations, many writers, roughly averaging the statistics for birth defects and pre-reproductive mortality, noted that first-cousin marriage "only" increases the risk of adverse events by about 3%. But for several reasons, any overall calculation of risk is in fact quite complicated.

First, even assuming that the deleterious phenotype arises solely from homozygosity at a single locus, the increased risk depends on the frequency of the allele involved; it is not an immediate consequence of the degree of relatedness between cousins. . . .

Second, children of cousin marriages are likely to manifest an increased frequency of birth defects showing polygenic inheritance and interacting with environmental variation. But as the NSGC report notes, calculating the increased frequency of such quantitative traits is not straightforward, and properly controlled studies are lacking. Moreover, socio-economic and other environmental influences will vary among populations, which can easily confound the effects of consanguinity. . . .

Third, . . . whether first-cousin marriage is an occasional or regular occurrence in the study population matters, and it is thus inappropriate to extrapolate findings from largely outbred populations with occasional first-cousin marriages to populations with high coefficients of inbreeding and vice-versa. Standard calculations, such as the commonly cited 3% additional risk, examine a pedigree in which the ancestors (usually grandparents) are assumed to be unrelated. In North America, marriages between consanguineal kin are strongly discouraged. But such an assumption is unwarranted in the case of UK Pakistanis, who have emigrated from a country where such marriage is traditional and for whom it is estimated that roughly 55%-59% of marriages continue to be between first cousins. . . .

Diane B. Paul & Hamish G. Spencer, "It's OK, We're Not Cousins by Blood": The Cousin Marriage Controversy in Historical Perspective, 6(12) PLoS Biol e320. doi:10.1371/journal.pbio.0060320 (2008).

4. Whatever weight we give to genetic concerns, it is plain that social concerns strongly influence restrictions on sexual relations and marriage between close kin. For one thing, cultural restrictions are not always interpretable in terms that make genetic sense. Historians and anthropologists have long wondered why a number of societies allow marriage between children born to the same father but different mothers but proscribe marriages in the reverse situation. This was the law among the Athenians, where one might marry a half-sister by the father but not by the mother, the Jews (*see* Genesis 20:12), and the Kwakiutl Indians of British Columbia. Claude Lévi-Strauss, On Marriage Between Close Kin, *in* The View from Afar 88-89 (Joachim Neugroschel & Phoebe Hoss trans., 1985). Concern for heredity certainly does not explain an incest prohibition that is stricter on the maternal than on the paternal side.

Lévi-Strauss concludes that the incest prohibition should be regarded not only negatively but positively — that is, as a division of the rights of marriage between families. It arises

only so that families (however defined by each society) could intermingle. . . . As Edward Burnett Tyler understood a century ago . . . man knew very early that he had to choose between "either marrying-out or being killed-out": the best, but not the only, way for biological families not to be driven to reciprocal extermination is to link themselves by ties of blood. Biological families that wished to live in isolation, side by side with one another, would each form a closed group, self-perpetuating and inevitably prey to ignorance, fear, and hatred. In opposing the separatist tendency of consanguinity, the incest prohibition succeeded in weaving the web of affinity that sustains societies and without which none could survive.

Id. at 54-55. Does Lévi-Strauss's location of the deep structure of incest prohibitions in a universal need for social links adopt a particular view of human nature?

5. The Delaware statute involved in State v. Sharon H., like many, also prohibits marriage between uncles and nieces, aunts and nephews, and first cousins. Would those prohibitions survive a constitutional challenge after Zablocki v. Redhail? What arguments would be made for and against the validity of these proscriptions?

6. The European Court of Human Rights held that a British law forbidding marriage between a couple who had been father-in-law and daughter-in-law to each other before they both divorced violated Article 12 of the European Convention on Human Rights. The court held that because the law did not criminalize sexual relationships or cohabitation between former in-laws, the marriage prohibition was not rationally related to the asserted goals of preventing sexual rivalry

between parents and children and preventing harm to minor children who might be adversely affected by such relationships. B and L v. U.K (No. 36536/0s, Judgment Sept. 13, 2005, discussed in Ruth Gaffney-Rhys, The Law Relating to Affinity After B and L v. UK, 2005 Fam. L. 955-957.

7. After *Lawrence*, a number of scholars have argued that the next taboo to be challenged will be incest. *See, e.g.*, Brett H. McDonnell, Is Incest Next?, 10 Cardozo J.L. & Gender 337 (2004); Courtney Megan Cahill, Same-Sex Marriage, Slippery Slope Rhetoric, and the Politics of Disgust: A Critical Perspective on Contemporary Family Discourse and the Incest Taboo, 99 Nw. U. L. Rev. 1543 (2005). The claim was raised but rejected in Muth v. Frank, 412 F.3d 808 (7th Cir. 2005), a criminal conviction of a biological brother and sister who married and had three children. The brother and sister were in and out of foster care as children and were separated for some years. When the sister, who was considerably younger than the brother, reached the age of majority, they reunited and married. They came to the attention of authorities when they abandoned one of the children. *See also* United States v. Dedman, 527 F.3d 577 (6th Cir. 2008) (declining to decide the constitutionality of applying statute that voids marriages between grandparents and grandchildren to adults related by adoption on basis that issue not preserved for appeal). Naomi Cahn has discussed possible constitutional arguments:

> Constitutionally, there are several methods for upholding the incest ban depending on the level of scrutiny applied. First, even if consensual sexual relationships are part of a protected fundamental right and subjected to strict scrutiny, the state may have a compelling interest in banning them. Compelling interests may range from protecting children from abuse to protecting the future offspring of incestuous relationships from increased risk of genetic disorders. If the level of scrutiny is either intermediate or rational basis, then the state's compelling interest certainly justifies the ban.
>
> Second, there is a more fundamental question (as it were) that relates to what types of consensual sexual relationships are included within the right to sexual privacy. If the right is defined to include only partners in non-caretaking, dependency relationships, for example, then the level of scrutiny is irrelevant, and certain incestuous relationships fall outside the scope of the right. The right to sexual privacy could be defined to include relationships between: (1) adults who were never part of a caretaking relationship—this would exclude not just parent-child incest, but also stepparent-child incest, even in the absence of a legally recognized bond between the parent and the child; and (2) adults who are related through affinity or blood as second cousins or further removed—this would exclude uncle/aunt-niece/nephew incest.
>
> Third, even if some incest laws—such as those between comparatively distantly related relatives—might be suspect under a privacy analysis, a nuanced application of constitutional law could help in drawing the right lines both inside and outside of the reproductive technology world. While *Lawrence* may call into question some forms of consensual intra-familial relationships, it still allows for carefully crafted laws banning some forms of incest.

Naomi Cahn, Accidental Incest: Drawing the Line or the Curtain?—for Reproductive Technology, 32 Harv. J.L. & Gender 59, 97-99 (2009).

PROBLEMS

1. Venus and Adonis are adopted sister and brother. They come from different birth families, but were adopted when they were very young and have lived together with their adoptive parents for the last ten years. Venus is now 20 and Adonis 21. They have fallen in love and wish to marry. Would they be barred from doing so under the statute applied in *Sharon H.*? Should they be barred from marrying?

2. Murray was married for many years to Aphrodite, who died last year. Aphrodite brought a daughter, Delilah, to the marriage. Delilah lived and grew up in the home with Murray and Aphrodite. After her mother's death, Delilah moved back into the house to take care of Murray. Murray proposed marriage to Delilah, and she accepted. They sought a marriage license but were turned down by the county clerk, who knows them both. State law prohibits marriage between a father and his "daughter." What arguments might be made in connection with their challenge to the denial of their application to marry?

3. Henry and Fiona are high school sweethearts. Their mothers discover that they conceived the two children with sperm from the same sperm bank, and when they inquire further, they learn that they used the same donor. Thus, Henry and Fiona are half-siblings. If Henry and Fiona nevertheless want to marry, is there any reason to distinguish their situation from that in *Sharon H.*?

4. Age

PORTER V. DEP'T OF HEALTH & HUMAN SERVICES

286 S.W.3d 686 (Ark. 2008)

ROBERT L. BROWN, Justice. [The state filed a petition in juvenile court alleging that Mark Porter and his ex-wife Diana Rolen neglected their two daughters, D.P., age 16, and S.P., age 12, by allowing them to be truant. At the initial hearing on the petition, the state Department of Human Services ("DHS") presented evidence that on August 10, 2007, Porter and Rolen had consented to the marriage of 16-year-old D.P. to Ralph Rodriguez, a 34-year-old man from Mississippi.]

Rolen testified at the hearing that she believed Rodriguez to be twenty-five years old. Rolen also testified that when she returned home from a vacation during the previous weekend, D.P. and Rodriguez had departed for Mississippi. Rolen added that she had given her consent to the marriage because of her fear that D.P. would "run off" otherwise.

Porter testified at the same hearing that he was called at work and asked to consent to D.P.'s marriage to Rodriguez. He left work and signed the necessary documents that provided his consent to the marriage. Although he testified that he was concerned about the marriage, he also testified that he was generally unfamiliar with Rodriguez and had not inquired into Rodriguez's past. At that point, the trial judge asked Porter why he had consented to his sixteen-year-old daughter's marriage to someone about whom he knew so little. Porter replied that he "was afraid

[D.P.] would run off" and he would "never hear from her again." In response, the trial judge said, "Bad answer."

[The juvenile court judge found that there was enough evidence to order the children removed from the parents' home pending further investigation.]

. . . On November 30, 2007, the attorney ad litem for D.P. filed a motion to void the marriage between D.P. and Rodriguez. The attorney ad litem asserted that the marriage should be voided because the parents' consent was given in disregard for the health and safety of D.P. and without knowledge of Rodriguez's true age.

At the adjudication hearing, which was held on December 10, 2007, Porter moved the trial judge to strike the motion to void the marriage. Porter also asked the judge to dismiss the proceedings on the basis that she could not consider his consent to the marriage, which was lawful, as a factor for dependency-neglect. . . . The judge denied all of Porter's motions. . . . [T]he trial judge determined D.P. . . . [was] dependent-neglected. D.P. . . . [was] ordered to remain in DHS. . . . The judge, in addition, voided the marriage of D.P. and Rodriguez on the basis that the parental consent was obtained through coercion and misrepresentation of Rodriguez's age and that D.P. lacked the mental capacity to enter into a contract of marriage. Porter now appeals both the finding of dependency-neglect and the court's order voiding the marriage. . . .

Porter contends that the trial judge's decision to remove the children from his custody was grounded entirely upon his consent to his daughter's marriage. This reliance was in error, he claims, because his consent was lawful under Act 441. Thus, Porter maintains that the trial judge violated his Fourteenth Amendment due-process right to make child-care decisions. . . .

A "dependent-neglected juvenile" is defined by the Juvenile Code as one "who is at substantial risk of serious harm as a result of" abuse, sexual abuse, neglect, or parental unfitness to the juvenile, or a sibling. Ark. Code Ann. § 9-27-303(18)(A) (Repl. 2008). The statute goes on to define "abuse" as "injury to a juvenile's intellectual, emotional, or psychological development as evidenced by observable and substantial impairment of the juvenile's ability to function within the juvenile's normal range of performance and behavior." Ark. Code Ann. § 9-27-303(3)(A)(iii).

The statute also describes "neglect" as: . . .

> (vii) Failure to appropriately supervise the juvenile that results in the juvenile's being left alone at an inappropriate age or in inappropriate circumstances, creating a dangerous situation or a situation that puts the juvenile at risk of harm.

Ark. Code Ann. § 9-27-303(36)(A).

We first address whether the trial judge erred in considering Porter's consent to his daughter's marriage as evidence of dependency-neglect. Parents, of course, have a fundamental right to direct the care and upbringing of their children. But the State of Arkansas has an equally compelling interest in the protection of its children. . . .

The evidence before the trial judge was that D.P.'s parents allowed her, as a fifteen-year-old, to date a thirty-four-year-old man, without appropriate supervision. The evidence showed that D.P. and Rodriguez had inappropriate sexual contact before their marriage, including the posting of sexually exploitative pictures on the internet. Moreover, D.P.'s parents consented to her marriage without inquiring into Rodriguez's age or background and allowed her to drop out of school and move to Mississippi. This easily qualifies as evidence of Porter's "failure to appropriately supervise D.P.," which resulted in her being "left alone . . . in inappropriate circumstances, creating a dangerous situation." The trial judge was correct to consider this factor in determining dependency-neglect.

We turn next to the issue of whether there is sufficient evidence overall to support the trial judge's finding of dependency-neglect. In addition to D.P.'s relationship with Rodriguez, the trial judge placed great weight on the testimony of D.P.'s therapist, Linda VanBlaricom, who testified that she believed D.P. had been neglected. Ms. VanBlaricom stated that D.P.'s problems were 95% to 99% the result of her parents' failure to provide a stable and nurturing environment and her exposure to substance abuse. She further testified that D.P. "perceives that [Porter] had abandoned her a great deal," and that "[g]iven [D.P.'s] long history of being the victim of neglect/trauma, attendance in multiple schools, placement in multiple home settings, her parents' substance abuse and mental illnesses, etc., [D.P.] has developed a lack of trust in most adults and institutions." . . .

. . . There was also sufficient evidence, based on this testimony, to find that Porter's behavior constituted abuse, as it had caused injury to D.P.'s emotional and psychological development. . . .

Even if D.P.'s marriage to Rodriguez is found to be valid, which we hold that it is in this opinion, the result in this case regarding DHS's custody of D.P. will not change. . . .

At the dependency-neglect adjudication hearing, the trial judge declared the marriage between D.P. and Rodriguez void on the following grounds: (1) misrepresentation of Rodriguez's age under § 9-11-104; (2) the marriage was not in D.P.'s best interest and was incompatible with the goal of reunification with her parents; and (3) D.P., a necessary party to the marriage contract, lacked the mental capacity to enter into the marriage. Porter contends that the trial judge had no authority under Arkansas law to declare D.P.'s marriage void. . . .

A. MISREPRESENTATION

It is true that a marriage contract may be set aside and annulled upon the application of a parent or guardian, where there has been a misrepresentation of age by a contracting party. Ark. Code Ann. § 9-11-104 (Repl. 2008). . . .

In the present case, there is no clear and convincing evidence that Rodriguez misrepresented his age or that D.P. misrepresented his age to her parents. Both of D.P.'s parents testified at the FINS hearing that they believed Rodriguez to be in his twenties, but neither asserted that a misrepresentation had taken place. Porter testified, "I had the impression he was in his mid-20s, but when I seen him he looks like he's over 30." Additionally, the marriage certificate that both parents signed listed Rodriguez's true age as thirty-four.

Nor does it appear from the record that either parent relied upon Rodriguez's age in giving his or her consent to the marriage. Porter's ex-wife, Rolen, testified at the FINS hearing that she allowed her daughter to date a thirty-four-year-old man and, again, Porter noted that Rodriguez appeared to be over thirty. Furthermore, Porter testified that he had reservations about allowing his daughter to date a thirty-four-year-old man and had voiced these reservations to D.P. The facts simply do not rise to the level of clear and convincing evidence that either Rodriguez or D.P. misrepresented his age, but rather exhibit extreme carelessness on the part of the parents in supervising D.P.

B. Incompatibility with Reunification and the Best Interests of D.P.

The trial judge's stated ground for declaring the marriage void included her finding that the marriage was incompatible with the goal of reunification of D.P. with her father and that the marriage was not in D.P.'s best interests. This is not a ground for voidance set out by statutory law. Hence, there is simply no statutory basis for granting an annulment on these grounds.

C. Mental Capacity

Arkansas Code Annotated § 9-12-201 (Repl. 2008) provides:

> When either of the parties to a marriage is incapable from want of age or understanding of consenting to any marriage, . . . or when the consent of either party shall have been obtained by force or fraud, the marriage shall be void from the time its nullity shall be declared by a court of competent jurisdiction.

The trial judge found D.P.'s marriage to be void on grounds that D.P. lacked the mental capacity to enter into marriage based on this statute. In support of this finding, the trial judge pointed to the testimony of D.P.'s therapist regarding D.P.'s emotional state and unfitness to make decisions; the fact that D.P. had met Rodriguez on the internet; D.P.'s immaturity based on her testimony that she was ready to have children and was not using contraception; and D.P.'s behavior at trial, which included outbursts, making faces at attorneys, refusal to cooperate, and an inability to control her emotions that was so disruptive that it eventually lead to D.P.'s being handcuffed and placed in a holding cell.

Generally, a party lacks the mental capacity to enter into a contract for marriage if that party is "incapable of understanding the nature, effect, and consequences of the marriage." The relevant inquiry is whether mental incapacity existed at the very time the parties entered into the marriage. As a collateral point, immaturity of the parties is not sufficient to establish a party's inability to consent to marriage. Nor does the mental capacity necessary to enter into marriage require the ability to exercise "clear reason, discernment, and sound judgment."

Here, no inquiry was made by the trial judge into D.P.'s mental capacity at the time the parties entered into the marriage. The trial judge based the majority of her decision upon D.P.'s behavior at trial, which is an insufficient basis for finding mental incapacity. Furthermore, D.P.'s therapist, Linda VanBlaricom, testified that D.P. had a "strong sense of herself," was a "bright girl" and "had learned to make decisions . . . and been responsible for herself in a lot of ways for a long time."

Ms. VanBlaricom added that D.P. was not necessarily able to use the judgment of an adult, but the immaturity of D.P. or her inability to exercise sound judgment are not factors for mental incapacity. As a final point, in response to the question of whether she believed D.P. mature enough to marry, Ms. VanBlaricom responded that she would have a very hard time answering that question about most people.

Taken together, the evidence from the record does not show that D.P. was incapable of understanding the nature, effect, and consequences of marriage. We hold that the trial judge erred in declaring the marriage void on the basis of misrepresentation, best interest of D.P., or mental incapacity. We reverse the trial judge on this point and remand for entry of a judgment in accordance with this opinion. . . .

Affirmed in part. Reversed and remanded in part.

NOTES AND QUESTIONS

1. At common law, the age of consent to marriage for males was 14 and for girls, 12. Early English legislation also required that parents consent to the marriage of a child younger than 21, the age of majority. Vivian E. Hamilton, The Age of Marital Capacity: Reconsidering Civil Recognition of Adolescent Marriage, 92 B.U. L. Rev. 1817, 1825-1828 (2012). The parental consent requirement protected parental and familial interests in controlling family property, which was profoundly affected by marriage. The American colonies adopted statutes that mirrored these provisions, but they frequently did not invalidate marriages by young people over the minimum age of consent who did not have parental permission. *Id.* at 1829.

Today, most state laws still establish a minimum age below which no one may marry, and a window between that minimum age and the age of full consent, during which marriage is allowed only with parental permission. Sometimes statutes also require a court to approve a marriage by someone in the "window" or allow the court to grant permission in lieu of parental permission. In most states, the minimum age for marriage without parental consent is 18, and with parental consent the minimum age in most states is 16. *See* Cornell Legal Information Institute, Marriage Laws of the Fifty States, District of Columbia, and Puerto Rico, available at www.law.cornell.edu/topics/Table_Marriage.htm.

2. What state interests support a law prohibiting teens younger than 18 to marry without parental consent? Why would the law today allow a younger teen to marry with parental permission? What functions does parental consent serve?

Under *Zablocki*, is an age restriction the kind of burden on marriage that invokes heightened scrutiny? If so, could any age restriction survive this level of scrutiny?

3. Considerable evidence shows that teenage marriages are high-risk enterprises, in terms of both the likelihood of divorce and the quality of marital satisfaction. Generally speaking, youthful marriages correlate with the participants' lower educational attainment, lower income, higher unemployment, increased risk of mental health disorders, and poorer physical health. Hamilton, above, 92 B.U. L. Rev. at 1843-1848. Correlation does not prove causation, however, and it is possible that other factors contribute both to the marital instability and unhappiness and to these other social outcomes. What factors might these be?

The riskiness of early marriage has increased over the last 30 years. In 1980 the divorce risk leveled off after the age of 21 so that couples marrying in their early 20s were no more likely to divorce than those who married in their late 20s. By 2000, however, couples experienced greater marital happiness and less divorce risk the older they were, with the improvements continuing all the way into the 30s. Paul R. Amato et al., Alone Together: How Marriage in America Is Changing (2009). Why might age matter more to marital happiness today than it did in 1980?

4. Arkansas Code § 9-11-102 (2013) was amended after *Porter* to provide, "The consent of the parent may be voided by the order of a circuit court on a showing by clear and convincing evidence that: (i) The parent is not fit to make decisions concerning the child; and (ii) The marriage is not in the child's best interest." How would a court determine whether a parent is "fit to make decisions concerning the child"?

5. If a minor's parents are divorced or unmarried, typically the statute provides that either parent or the parent with custody has authority to consent to the child's underage marriage. Kirkpatrick v. Dist. Ct., 64 P.3d 1056 (Nev. 2003), considered the constitutionality of a statute permitting a minor under the age of 16 to marry with the consent of one parent and the district court's authorization. Under that statute, the district court permitted petitioner's 15-year-old daughter to marry her 48-year-old guitar teacher. Although the daughter's mother had provided consent, the father—who had joint legal custody and maintained an ongoing personal and custodial relationship with his daughter—had no knowledge that his daughter was planning to marry. Because he received neither notice nor an opportunity to be heard before his daughter was given judicial permission to marry, he argued that the statute as applied violated his rights to substantive and procedural due process. The Nevada Supreme Court originally ruled in his favor but then withdrew that opinion and issued a new decision, rejecting his claims. It found that the statute appropriately balanced the minor's constitutionally protected interest in access to marriage, "the interest of the mother in her daughter's welfare and happiness," and "the father's interest in the legal control of his daughter for the remainder of her minority." 64 P.3d at 1062.

6. Colorado statutes provide that a person must be at least 18 to marry without parental consent, those between 16 and 18 can marry with parental or judicial consent, and someone younger than 16 can marry only with the consent of both the court and the parents. In re Marriage of J.M.H., 143 P.3d 1116 (Colo. App. 2006), held that, notwithstanding these statutes, the common law rules regarding age apply to common law marriage, so that a girl as young as 12 could enter into a common law marriage. The case involved a 38-year-old man who purportedly entered into a common law marriage with a 15-year-old girl. The man pled guilty to stalking the girl and was serving a four-year prison term when the court issued the decision. In response to the uproar, in July 2006 the Colorado legislature enacted a law that harmonizes the age of consent for common law marriage with the existing law regarding ceremonial marriage. Colo. Rev. Stat. § 14-2-109.5 (2013). A similar sequence of events occurred a few years earlier in Kansas. In re Pace, 989 P.2d 297 (Kan. App. 1999), held that the common law age limits applied to common law marriages, and in 2002 the legislature amended the statute to provide that the minimum age for common law marriage is 18. Kan. Stat. § 23-2502 (2013).

7. In 2005 the Texas legislature amended the family and penal codes to void any marriage in which one party is younger than 16 and to make it a felony for a parent to give consent for a child younger than 16 to marry. The legislature was responding to reports that members of the FLDS church in Texas were regularly consenting to the marriage of their 14- and 15-year-old daughters. (The FLDS church is discussed in the next case.) Rosanne Piatt, Overcorrecting the Purported Problem of Taking Child Brides in Polygamist Marriages: The Texas Legislature Unconstitutionally Voids All Marriages by Texans Younger than Sixteen and Criminalizes Parental Consent, 37 St. Mary's L.J. 753 (2006). In 2007 the legislature again amended the statute to allow a court to grant permission to a minor to marry if it finds this to be in the minor's best interests. Tex. Fam. Code Ann. § 6.205 (2013).

5. One at a Time

STATE V. HOLM

137 P.3d 726 (Utah 2006)

DURRANT, Justice: In this case, we are asked to determine whether Rodney Hans Holm was appropriately convicted for bigamy. . . .

Holm was legally married to Suzie Stubbs in 1986. Subsequent to this marriage, Holm, a member of the Fundamentalist Church of Jesus Christ of Latter-day Saints (the "FLDS Church"),[4] participated in a religious marriage ceremony with Wendy Holm. Then, when Rodney Holm was thirty-two, he participated in another religious marriage ceremony with then-sixteen-year-old Ruth Stubbs, Suzie Stubbs's sister. After the ceremony, Ruth moved into Holm's house, where her sister Suzie Stubbs, Wendy Holm, and their children also resided. By the time Ruth turned eighteen, she had conceived two children with Holm, the second of which was born approximately three months after her eighteenth birthday. . . .

At trial, Ruth Stubbs testified that although she knew that the marriage was not a legal civil marriage under the law, she believed that she was married. Stubbs's testimony included a description of the ceremony she had participated in with Holm. Stubbs testified that, at the ceremony, she had answered "I do" to the following question:

> Do you, Sister [Stubbs], take Brother [Holm] by the right hand, and give yourself to him to be his lawful and wedded wife for time and all eternity, with a covenant and promise on your part, that you will fulfil all the laws, rites and ordinances pertaining to this holy bond of matrimony in the new and everlasting covenant, doing this in the presence of God, angels, and these witnesses, of your own free will and choice?

---

4. The FLDS Church is one of a number of small religious communities in Utah that continue to interpret the early doctrine of the Church of Jesus Christ of Latter-day Saints (the "LDS Church" or "Mormon Church") as supporting the practice of "plural marriage," or polygamy. Though often referred to as "fundamentalist Mormons," these groups have no connection to the LDS Church, which renounced the practice of polygamy in 1890.

Stubbs testified that she had worn a white dress, which she considered a wedding dress; that she and Holm exchanged vows; that Warren Jeffs, a religious leader in the FLDS religion, conducted the ceremony; that other church members and members of Holm's family attended the ceremony; and that photographs were taken of Holm, Stubbs, and their guests who attended the ceremony.

Stubbs also testified about her relationship with Holm after the ceremony. She testified that she had moved in with Holm; that Holm had provided, at least in part, for Stubbs and their children; and that she and Holm had "regularly" engaged in sexual intercourse at the house in Hildale, Utah. Evidence was also introduced at trial that Holm and Stubbs "regarded each other as husband and wife." . . .

Holm appealed his conviction on all charges. . . .

Holm was convicted pursuant to Utah's bigamy statute, which provides that "[a] person is guilty of bigamy when, knowing he has a husband or wife or knowing the other person has a husband or wife, the person purports to marry another person or cohabits with another person." The jury weighing the case against Holm indicated on a special verdict form its conclusion that Holm had both "purported to marry another person" and "cohabited with another person" knowing that he already had a wife. . . .

[The court rejected Holm's argument that the bigamy statute applied only if a defendant purported to enter more than one legally recognized marriage. It concluded that the legislature intended the bigamy statute to cover Holm's religiously but not legally sanctioned marriages and then turned to the constitutional issues.]

It is ironic indeed that Holm comes before this court arguing that the Utah Constitution, despite its express prohibition of polygamous marriage, actually provides greater protection to polygamous behavior than the federal constitution, which contains no such express prohibition. In making this argument, Holm relies on various provisions of our state constitution that protect the freedom of conscience and the exercise of religion, as well as provisions securing liberty interests for the people of this State. While our state constitution may well provide greater protection for the free exercise of religion in some respects than the federal constitution, we disagree that it does so as to polygamy. . . .

. . . [W]e need not address that question here because the Utah Constitution offers no protection to polygamous behavior and, in fact, shows antipathy towards it by expressly prohibiting such behavior. Specifically, article III, section 1, entitled "Religious toleration — Polygamy forbidden," states as follows: "First: — Perfect toleration of religious sentiment is guaranteed. No inhabitant of this State shall ever be molested in person or property on account of his or her mode of religious worship; but polygamous or plural marriages are forever prohibited." Utah Const. art. III, § 1. This language, known commonly as the "irrevocable ordinance," unambiguously removes polygamy from the realm of protected free exercise of religion. . . .

1. THE BIGAMY STATUTE DOES NOT IMPERMISSIBLY INFRINGE HOLM'S FEDERAL FREE EXERCISE RIGHT

Although the United States Supreme Court, in Reynolds v. United States, 98 U.S. 145, (1879), upheld the criminal prosecution of a religiously motivated polygamist as nonviolative of the Free Exercise Clause, Holm contends on appeal that his federal free exercise right is unduly infringed upon by his conviction in this case. Holm argues that *Reynolds* is "nothing more than a hollow relic of bygone days of fear, prejudice, and Victorian morality," and that modern free exercise jurisprudence dictates that no criminal penalty can be imposed for engaging in religiously motivated polygamy. This court recently rejected an identical argument in State v. Green, 2004 UT 76, ¶¶ 18-19, 99 P.3d 820.

As we pointed out in *Green*, *Reynolds*, despite its age, has never been overruled by the United States Supreme Court and, in fact, has been cited by the Court with approval in several modern free exercise cases, signaling its continuing vitality.... As we noted in *Green*, the United States Supreme Court held in Employment Division, Department of Human Resources v. Smith, 494 U.S. 872 (1990) ... that a state may, even without furthering a compelling state interest, burden an individual's right to free exercise so long as the burden is imposed by a neutral law of general applicability. The Court has since clarified that a law is not neutral if the intent of that law "is to infringe upon or restrict practices because of their religious motivation." Church of the Lukumi Babalu Aye, Inc. v. City of Hialeah, 508 U.S. 520, 533 (1993). In *Green*, we concluded that Utah's bigamy statute is a neutral law of general applicability and that any infringement upon the free exercise of religion occasioned by that law's application is constitutionally permissible. . . .

2. HOLM'S CONVICTION DOES NOT OFFEND THE DUE PROCESS CLAUSE OF THE FOURTEENTH AMENDMENT

Holm argues that the State of Utah is foreclosed from criminalizing polygamous behavior because the freedom to engage in such behavior is a fundamental liberty interest that can be infringed only for compelling reasons and that the State has failed to identify a sufficiently compelling justification for its criminalization of polygamy. We disagree and conclude that there is no fundamental liberty interest to engage in the type of polygamous behavior at issue in this case.

In arguing that his behavior is constitutionally protected as a fundamental liberty interest, Holm relies primarily on the United States Supreme Court's decision in Lawrence v. Texas, 539 U.S. 558 (2003). . . .

Despite its use of seemingly sweeping language, the holding in *Lawrence* is actually quite narrow. Specifically, the Court takes pains to limit the opinion's reach to decriminalizing private and intimate acts engaged in by consenting adult gays and lesbians. In fact, the Court went out of its way to exclude from protection conduct that causes "injury to a person or abuse of an institution the law protects." Further, after announcing its holding, the Court noted the following: "The present case does not involve minors. It does not involve persons who might be injured or coerced or who are situated in relationships where consent might not easily be refused. It does not involve public conduct. . . ."

In marked contrast to the situation presented to the Court in *Lawrence*, this case implicates the public institution of marriage, an institution the law protects, and also involves a minor. In other words, this case presents the exact conduct identified by the Supreme Court in *Lawrence* as outside the scope of its holding.

First, the behavior at issue in this case is not confined to personal decisions made about sexual activity, but rather raises important questions about the State's ability to regulate marital relationships and prevent the formation and propagation of marital forms that the citizens of the State deem harmful. . . .

Moreover, marital relationships serve as the building blocks of our society. The State must be able to assert some level of control over those relationships to ensure the smooth operation of laws and further the proliferation of social unions our society deems beneficial while discouraging those deemed harmful. The people of this State have declared monogamy a beneficial marital form and have also declared polygamous relationships harmful. As the Tenth Circuit stated in Potter, Utah "is justified, by a compelling interest, in upholding and enforcing its ban on plural marriage to protect the monogamous marriage relationship." 760 F.2d at 1070 (internal quotation marks omitted); see also *Green*, 2004 UT 76, ¶ 72, 99 P.3d 820 (Durrant, J., concurring) ("[Utah] has a compelling interest in prohibiting conduct, such as the practice of polygamy, which threatens [monogamous marriage].").

Further, this case features another critical distinction from *Lawrence*; namely, the involvement of a minor. Stubbs was sixteen years old at the time of her betrothal, and evidence adduced at trial indicated that she and Holm regularly engaged in sexual activity. Further, it is not unreasonable to conclude that this case involves behavior that warrants inquiry into the possible existence of injury and the validity of consent. *See, e.g., Green*, 2004 UT 76, ¶ 40, 99 P.3d 820 ("The practice of polygamy . . . often coincides with crimes targeting women and children. Crimes not unusually attendant to the practice of polygamy include incest, sexual assault, statutory rape, and failure to pay child support.").

Given the above, we conclude that *Lawrence* does not prevent our Legislature from prohibiting polygamous behavior. The distinction between private, intimate sexual conduct between consenting adults and the public nature of polygamists' attempts to extralegally redefine the acceptable parameters of a fundamental social institution like marriage is plain. The contrast between the present case and *Lawrence* is even more dramatic when the minority status of Stubbs is considered. Given the critical differences between the two cases, and the fact that the United States Supreme Court has not extended its jurisprudence to such a degree as to protect the formation of polygamous marital arrangements, we conclude that the criminalization of the behavior engaged in by Holm does not run afoul of the personal liberty interests protected by the Fourteenth Amendment. . . .

DURHAM, Chief Justice, concurring in part and dissenting in part: I join the majority in upholding Holm's conviction for unlawful sexual conduct with a minor. As to the remainder of its analysis, I respectfully dissent. As interpreted by the majority, Utah Code section 76-7-101 defines "marriage" as acts undertaken for religious purposes that do not meet any other legal standard for marriage—acts that are unlicensed, unsolemnized by any civil authority, acts that are indeed entirely outside the civil law, and unrecognized as marriage for any other purpose by the state—and criminalizes those acts as "bigamy." I believe that in doing so the statute oversteps lines protecting the free exercise of religion and the privacy of intimate, personal relationships between consenting adults. . . .

The majority concludes that Holm may be found guilty of "purport[ing] to marry another person" while already having a wife because he entered a religious union with Ruth Stubbs that the two of them referred to as a "marriage," even though neither believed, represented, or intended that the union would have the legal status of a state-sanctioned marriage. In doing so, the majority deems irrelevant the distinction between the word "marry" when used in a legal context and the same word's idiosyncratic meaning when used as a label for a relationship recognized as significant by a particular individual or group, but not by the state. . . .

The majority's conflation of private relationships with legal unions is also problematic in its analysis of Holm's claim that his bigamy conviction violates the guarantees of individual rights protected by article I of the Utah Constitution. The majority dismisses Holm's claim on the basis that the Utah Constitution "offers no protection to polygamous behavior and, in fact, shows antipathy towards it by expressly prohibiting such behavior" in article III, section 1. However, that provision declares that "polygamous or plural marriages are forever prohibited." Here, as elsewhere in Utah law, I understand the term "marriage" to refer only to a "legal union." Understood in this way, article III, section 1, by its plain language, does not prohibit private individual behavior but instead prevents Utah's state government, to whom the ordinance is addressed, from recognizing a particular form of union as a "marriage." . . .

[The opinion argues that the state constitution provides greater protection for religiously motivated conduct than does the federal constitution and particularly that it guarantees "free exercise of religion to the extent such exercise [is] consistent with public peace and order."]

I agree that the religious freedom provisions in our state constitution were not intended to exempt religious practitioners from criminal punishment for acts that cause injury or harm to society at large or to other individuals. Moreover, I recognize that by defining conduct as criminal, our legislature has signaled its judgment that this conduct generally does harm society or individuals to a degree that warrants criminal punishment.

That this is generally true does not, however, foreclose close scrutiny of the circumstances of a particular case in order to determine whether a prosecution for conduct statutorily defined as criminal is truly directed against the harm the statute was intended to prevent, where the conduct in the particular case is religiously motivated. . . . Given the fundamental nature of the constitutional interest involved and the undeniable burden that criminal penalties impose, heightened scrutiny is warranted. . . .

. . . [T]he burden on the religious conduct at issue must be necessary to serve a strong governmental interest unrelated to the suppression of religious freedom. I do not believe that any of the strong state interests normally served by the Utah bigamy law require that the law apply to the religiously motivated conduct at issue here—entering a religious union with more than one woman.

I note at the outset that the State has not suggested that section 76-7-101 furthers a governmental interest in preserving democratic society. I agree that no such interest is implicated here. . . . [T]he federal government's nineteenth century criminalization of polygamy in the Utah Territory, as construed by the *Reynolds* Court, was intended to address the harm to democratic society that LDS

Church polygamy was thought to embody. However, I do not presume that our modern criminal bigamy statute, enacted in 1973, addresses the same fears—which have since been discounted by many as grounded more in bias than in fact—that propelled Congress' legislation a century earlier.

Indeed, this court previously set forth, in *Green*, a list of state interests served by the modern statute that omits any reference to such a concern. There, we first explained that the modern statute serves the state's interest in "regulating marriage" and in maintaining the "network of laws" that surrounds the institution of marriage. . . . Here, the State has emphasized its interest in "protecting" monogamous marriage as a social institution. I agree that the state has an important interest in regulating marriage, but only insofar as marriage is understood as a legal status. . . .

However, I do not believe the state's interest extends to those who enter a religious union with a second person but who do not claim to be legally married. For one thing, the cohabitation of unmarried couples, who live together "as if" they are married in the sense that they share a household and a sexually intimate relationship, is commonplace in contemporary society. Even outside the community of those who practice polygamy for religious reasons, such cohabitation may occur where one person is legally married to someone other than the person with whom he or she is cohabiting. Yet parties to such relationships are not prosecuted under the criminal bigamy statute, the criminal fornication statute, Utah Code Ann. § 76-7-104 (2003), or, as far as I am aware, the criminal adultery statute, id. § 76-7-103 (2003), even where their conduct violates these laws.

That the state perceives no need to prosecute nonreligiously motivated cohabitation, whether one of the parties to the cohabitation is married to someone else or not, demonstrates that, in the absence of any claim of legal marriage, neither participation in a religious ceremony nor cohabitation can plausibly be said to threaten marriage as a social or legal institution. The state's concern with regulating marriage, as I understand it, has to do with determining who is entitled to enter that legal status, what benefits are accorded, and what obligations and restrictions are imposed thereby. . . . Our state's network of laws may indeed presume a particular domestic structure—whether it be that a man will live with only one woman, that a couple living together will enter a legal union, or that each household will contain a single nuclear family. However, any interest the state has in maintaining this network of laws does not logically justify its imposition of criminal penalties on those who deviate from that domestic structure, particularly when they do so for religious reasons. . . .

Those who choose to live together without getting married enter a personal relationship that resembles a marriage in its intimacy but claims no legal sanction. They thereby intentionally place themselves outside the framework of rights and obligations that surrounds the marriage institution. While some in society may feel that the institution of marriage is diminished when individuals consciously choose to avoid it, it is generally understood that the state is not entitled to criminally punish its citizens for making such a choice, even if they do so with multiple partners or with partners of the same sex. The only distinction in this case is that when Holm consciously chose to enter into a personal relationship that he knew would not be legally recognized as marriage, he used religious terminology to describe this relationship. The terminology that he used—"marriage" and "husband and wife"—happens to coincide with the terminology used by the state to describe the legal status of married persons. That fact, however, is not sufficient for me to conclude that criminalizing this conduct is essential in order to protect the institution of marriage. . . .

The second state interest served by the bigamy law, as recognized in *Green*, is in preventing "marriage fraud," whereby an already-married individual fraudulently purports to enter a legal marriage with someone else, "or attempts to procure government benefits associated with marital status." This interest focuses on preventing the harm caused to the state, to society, and to defrauded individuals when someone purports to have entered the legal status of marriage, but in fact is not eligible to validly enter that status because of a prior legal union. This interest is simply not implicated here, where no claim to the legal status of marriage has been made.

In *Green*, the court cited "protecting vulnerable individuals from exploitation and abuse" as the third state interest served by the bigamy statute. The court concluded that this was a legitimate state interest to which the criminal bigamy statute was rationally related for purposes of our First Amendment Free Exercise Clause analysis. The court rested this conclusion on the idea that perpetrators of other crimes "not unusually attendant to the practice of polygamy"—such as "incest, sexual assault, statutory rape, and failure to pay child support"—could be prosecuted for bigamy in the absence of sufficient evidence to support a conviction on these other charges. . . . However, reviewing this assessment in light of the heightened scrutiny I believe is called for here, I cannot conclude that the restriction that the bigamy law places on the religious freedom of all those who, for religious reasons, live with more than one woman is necessary to further the state's interest in this regard. . . . The State has provided no evidence of a causal relationship or even a strong correlation between the practice of polygamy, whether religiously motivated or not, and the offenses of "incest, sexual assault, statutory rape, and failure to pay child support," cited in *Green*. Moreover, even assuming such a correlation did exist, neither the record nor the recent history of prosecutions of alleged polygamists warrants the conclusion that section 76-7-101 is a necessary tool for the state's attacks on such harms. For one thing, I am unaware of a single instance where the state was forced to bring a charge of bigamy in place of other narrower charges, such as incest or unlawful sexual conduct with a minor, because it was unable to gather sufficient evidence to prosecute these other crimes. The State has suggested that its initial ability to file bigamy charges allows it to gather the evidence required to prosecute those engaged in more specific crimes. Even if there were support for this claim in the record, I would consider it inappropriate to let stand a criminal law simply because it enables the state to conduct a fishing expedition for evidence of other crimes. Further, the State itself has indicated that it does not prosecute those engaged in religiously motivated polygamy under the criminal bigamy statute unless the person has entered a religious union with a girl under eighteen years old. Such a policy of selective prosecution reinforces my conclusion that a blanket criminal prohibition on religious polygamous unions is not necessary to further the state's interests, and suggests that a more narrowly tailored law would be just as effective.

I do not reach this conclusion lightly. I acknowledge the possibility that other criminal conduct may accompany the act of bigamy. Such conduct may even, as was suggested in *Green*, be correlated with the practice of polygamy in a community that has isolated itself from the outside world, at least partially in fear of criminal prosecution for its religious practice. Indeed, the FLDS community in its current form has been likened to a cult, with allegations focusing on the power wielded by a single leader who exerts a high degree of control over followers, ranging from ownership of their property to the determination of persons with whom they may enter religious unions.[5] In the latter regard, reports of forcible unions between underage girls and older men within the FLDS community have recently appeared in the media.[6] Yet, the state does not criminalize cult membership, and for good reason. To do so would be to impose a criminal penalty based on status rather than conduct — long considered antithetical to our notion of criminal justice. *See* Powell v. Texas, 392 U.S. 514, 533 (1968); Robinson v. California, 370 U.S. 660, 666-67 (1962). Moreover, such a criminal law would require that the state make normative judgments distinguishing between communities that are actually "cults" and those that are voluntary associations based on common religious or other ideological beliefs. . . . The State of Utah has criminal laws punishing incest, rape, unlawful sexual conduct with a minor, and domestic and child abuse. Any restrictions these laws place on the practice of religious polygamy are almost certainly justified. However, the broad criminalization of the religious practice itself as a means of attacking other criminal behavior is not. . . .

Because I conclude that Holm's bigamy conviction violates the Utah Constitution's religious freedom guarantees, my dissenting vote is not based on the majority's analysis of Holm's federal constitutional claims. I do, however, wish to register my disagreement with the majority's treatment of Holm's claim that his conviction violates his Fourteenth Amendment right under the Due Process Clause to individual liberty, as recognized by the United States Supreme Court in Lawrence v. Texas, 539 U.S. 558 (2003). . . .

The majority does not adequately explain how the institution of marriage is abused or state support for monogamy threatened simply by an individual's choice to participate in a religious ritual with more than one person outside the confines of legal marriage. Rather than offering such an explanation, the majority merely proclaims that "the public nature of polygamists' attempts to extralegally redefine the acceptable parameters of a fundamental social institution like marriage is plain." It is far from plain to me.

---

5. Media reports suggest that this situation has worsened since Warren Jeffs, the son of Rulon Jeffs, assumed the leadership position in 2002 following his father's death. Polygamous Church May Pull up Roots, Associated Press, Mar. 5, 2005, available at Rick A. Ross Institute, Polygamist Groups, http://www.rickross.com/groups/polygamy.html [hereinafter Ross Institute site]; Lawsuits and Governmental Scrutiny Increase Pressure on Polygamist Sect, Associated Press, Sept. 17, 2004, available at Ross Institute site, *supra*; Authorities Probe Arizona Polygamist Town, N.Y. Times, Jan. 23, 2004, available at Ross Institute site, *supra*.

6. *E.g.*, FLDS Runaways Speak Out on Dr. Phil Show, S.L. Trib., May 4, 2005, available at ReligionNewsBlog.com, http://www.religionnewsblog.com/11129; Polygamists on Utah-Arizona Border Under Scrutiny, All Things Considered, May 3, 2005, available at http://www.npr.org (search term "polygamy"); Allegations Abound: Colorado City's Polygamous Community Comes Under Increasing Scrutiny, Havasu News-Herald, Sept. 25, 2004, available at Ross Institute site, *supra*.

I am concerned that the majority's reasoning may give the impression that the state is free to criminalize any and all forms of personal relationships that occur outside the legal union of marriage. While under *Lawrence* laws criminalizing isolated acts of sodomy are void, the majority seems to suggest that the relationships within which these acts occur may still receive criminal sanction. Following such logic, nonmarital cohabitation might also be considered to fall outside the scope of federal constitutional protection. Indeed, the act of living alone and unmarried could as easily be viewed as threatening social norms.

In my view, any such conclusions are foreclosed under *Lawrence*. Essentially, the Court's decision in *Lawrence* simply reformulates the longstanding principle that, in order to "secure individual liberty, . . . certain kinds of highly personal relationships" must be given "a substantial measure of sanctuary from unjustified interference by the State." Whether referred to as a right of "intimate" or "intrinsic" association, a right to "privacy," a right to make "choices concerning family living arrangements," or a right to choose the nature of one's personal relationships, this individual liberty guarantee essentially draws a line around an individual's home and family and prevents governmental interference with what happens inside, as long as it does not involve injury or coercion or some other form of harm to individuals or to society. . . . The Court determined that when "adults . . . with full and mutual consent from each other" enter into particular personal relationships with no threat of injury or coercion, a state may not criminalize the relationships themselves or the consensual intimate conduct that occurs within them.

In conclusion, I agree with the majority that because Holm's conduct in this case involved a minor, he is unable to prevail on his individual liberty claim under the Due Process Clause. However, I disagree with the majority's implication that the same result would apply where an individual enters a private relationship with another adult. . . .

NOTES AND QUESTIONS

1. Holm and other members of the FLDS church were acutely aware of the state prohibition on plural marriage and made sure that they were not purporting to enter into more than one civil marriage that would be recognized by the state. How, then, did he fall afoul of the criminal prohibition?

2. The majority and dissent disagree about whether Holm's relationships were protected under *Lawrence*. What is the basis for their disagreement?

If a married person left his or her spouse but did not get a divorce and then began living with a new intimate partner, would that violate the Utah statute? Would applying the Utah statute in such a case be unconstitutional under *Lawrence*? If so, why is this different from the situation in *Holm*?

3. More than a decade ago, a leading commentator on the development of the law's treatment of same-sex relationships observed that in many jurisdictions the first liberalizing step was decriminalization of the relationships, followed by antidiscrimination laws, and culminating with legislation recognizing and according rights to partners through civil unions or marriage. Kees Waaldijk, Civil Developments: Patterns of Reform in the Legal Position of Same-Sex Partners in Europe, 17 Canadian J. Fam. L. 62 (2000). As others have observed more recently,

polygamists such as Holm simply seek decriminalization, not affirmative recognition. William N. Eskridge Jr., Backlash Politics: How Constitutional Litigation Has Advanced Marriage Equality in the United States, 93 B.U. L. Rev. 275 (2013); Martin Guggenheim, Texas Polygamy and Child Welfare, 46 Hous. L. Rev. 759 (2009). Do *Goodridge* and *Windsor*, which concern state recognition of same-sex marriage, support Holm's due process claim?

4. Reynolds v. United States, 98 U.S. 145 (1878), is the foundational case addressing whether the constitutional protection for freedom of religion precludes punishing polygamy. A Mormon defendant challenged the constitutionality of federal law making bigamy a crime in the territory of Utah. He introduced evidence that polygamy was the duty of male members of the Church of Jesus Christ of Latter-Day Saints, violation of which duty entailed "damnation in the life to come." The Court sustained the statute and defendant's conviction, saying:

> Polygamy has always been odious among the Northern and Western nations of Europe and, until the establishment of the Mormon Church, was almost exclusively a feature of the life of Asiatic and African people. At common law, the second marriage was always void. 2 Kent, Com. 79, and from the earliest history of England polygamy has been treated as an offense against society.
>
> . . . [W]e think it may safely be said there has never been a time in any State of the Union when polygamy has not been offence against society, cognizable by the civil courts and punishable with more or less severity. In the face of all this evidence, it is impossible to believe that the constitutional guaranty of religious freedom was intended to prohibit legislation in respect to this most important feature of social life. Marriage, while from its very nature a sacred obligation, is nevertheless, in most civilized nations, a civil contract, and usually regulated by law. Upon it society may be said to be built, and out of its fruits spring social relations and social obligations and duties, with which government is necessarily required to deal. In fact, according as monogamous or polygamous marriages are allowed, do we find the principles on which the government of the people, to a greater or less extent, rests. Professor Lieber says, polygamy leads to the patriarchal principle, and which, when applied to large communities, fetters the people in stationary despotism, while that principle cannot long exist in connection with monogamy. . . .

98 U.S. at 164-166.

What did Professor Lieber mean when he said that polygamy is related to despotism, and monogamy to democratic forms of government? Is this simply nineteenth-century parochialism, or might something in the nature of polygamous family life be expected to affect attitudes toward social and political organization?

Justice Durham argues in her dissent in *Holm* that the modern ban on polygamy is not based on these political concerns and suggests that if this argument were used to support the ban today, it might not succeed because the fears expressed in *Reynolds* "have since been discounted by many as grounded more in bias than in fact." Do you agree?

Of the nineteenth-century Mormon style of polygamy, Professor Maura Strassberg has observed, "Polygyny was also fundamentally inegalitarian; it was a practice designed to create a political and religious aristocracy. In a society with relatively equal numbers of men and women, polygyny gives some men significantly greater opportunities to reproduce than others because many wives for some men means no wives for others." Maura I. Strassberg, The Crime of Polygamy, 12 Temp. Pol. & Civ. Rts. L. Rev. 353, 362 (2003). *See also* Maura I. Strassberg, Distinctions of Form or Substance: Monogamy, Polygamy, and Same-Sex Marriage, 75 N.C. L. Rev. 1501 (1997); Shayna M. Sigman, Everything Lawyers Know About Polygamy Is Wrong, 16 Cornell J.L. & Pub. Pol'y 101 (2006).

The first session of the United Nations Commission on the Status of Women in 1947 identified as a principal aim, in the field of marriage, "freedom of choice, dignity of the wife, monogamy, and equal right to dissolution of marriage." Legal Status of Married Women (Reports Submitted by the Secretary-General). Forty-five years later, the United National Committee on the Elimination of Discrimination Against Women said, "Polygamous marriage contravenes a woman's right to equality with men, and can have such serious emotional and financial consequences for her and her dependants that such marriages ought to be discouraged and prohibited." 13th Session, General Recommendation 21: Equality in Marriage and Family Relations (1992), U.N. Doc. A/49/38/UNCEDAW. Why might monogamy be regarded as important to the recognition of equal rights for women?

Is it relevant that women in Utah gained the franchise in 1870 and that the National Woman Suffrage Association (founded by Elizabeth Cady Stanton and Susan B. Anthony) resolved, days after the *Reynolds* decision, that the federal government "should forbear to exercise federal power to disenfranchise the women of Utah, who have had a more just and liberal spirit shown them by Mormon men than Gentile women in the States have yet perceived in their rulers"? *See* Carol Weisbrod & Pamela Sheingorn, Reynolds v. United States: Nineteenth Century Forms of Marriage and the Status of Women, 10 Conn. L. Rev. 828, 850-856 (1978).

5. It may seem odd that *Reynolds* was decided at approximately the same time that serial polygamy — divorce followed by remarriage — became common and the subject of heated controversy. *See generally* William O'Neill, Divorce in the Progressive Era (1967). What relationships might exist between these two issues? *See* Carol Weisbrod, Family, Church and State: An Essay on Constitutionalism and Religious Authority, 26 J. Fam. L. 741, 758-759 (1987-1988).

6. A document prepared by the attorneys general of Utah and Arizona reports that since the 1950s "polygamy laws have not been frequently enforced. However, Utah and Arizona have recently stepped up efforts to enforce laws in polygamous communities involving child abuse, domestic violence and fraud." The Primer: Helping Victims of Domestic Violence and Child Abuse in Polygamous Communities at 6 (2005).

Holm was one of the cases prosecuted under this policy. Numerous reports from Holm's community and other polygamous communities in the West consistently describe girls as young as 13 or 14 being given as plural wives to much older men. The Primer's description of the various strands of modern polygamous practice describes this as well. The Primer at 17-24. Is it necessary to criminalize polygamy to protect young girls from being coerced into sexual relationships and plural marriage? Justice Durham argues that criminal statutes directly targeting these issues are sufficient. On the other hand, some argue that the public licensing and solemnizing of marriages provides an opportunity for coercion to be discovered. Strassberg, The Crime of Polygamy, above, 12 Temp. Pol. & Civ. Rts. L. Rev. at 369. Warren Jeffs, the leader of the group to which Holm belongs, was convicted in Texas of sexually assaulting two minor girls whom he had taken as wives and was sentenced to life in prison. Lindsay Whitehurst, Warren Jeffs Gets Life in Prison for Sex with Underage Girls, Salt Lake Tribune, Aug. 10, 2011. Other adult men in the group were convicted of the same offense in 2009 and 2010.

A 1998 newspaper article reported the average family sizes in Hildale, Utah, and Colorado City, Arizona, to be 8.55 and 7.97, respectively. Average household incomes were, however, half or less than half of the state averages: $21,822 in Hildale (compared with a Utah average of $41,316) and $19,663 in Colorado City (compared with an Arizona average of $35,426). A third of the families in Hildale and 61 percent of the families in Colorado City are reported to be living in poverty; consequently, families in these communities draw far more than their share of welfare benefits and educational subsidies. Polygamy on the Dole, Salt Lake Tribune, June 28, 1998, at A1 et seq. In 2002, 66 percent of Hildale residents received assistance, and 78 percent of the residents of Colorado City received food stamps. The Primer at 18. Do these figures suggest that community members are committing welfare fraud? Or are single mothers simply taking advantage of public benefits to which they are legally entitled?

7. In 2013 a federal district judge ruled that the Utah statute, when applied to criminalize intimate cohabitation among members of the FLDS church, unconstitutionally infringes on freedom of religion and violates substantive due process. Finding that enforcement of the law was limited to and targeted at people who believe in plural marriage as a religious matter, the judge ruled that it was subject to strict scrutiny under Church of the Lukumi Babalu Aye, Inc. v. City of Hialeah, 508 U.S. 520, 531-532 (1993), and that it was not narrowly tailored to advance a compelling state interest. Alternatively, the court agreed with Justice Durham and concluded that the statute fell under *Lawrence* because there is no rational basis for prosecuting religiously motivated polygamy but not other forms of adulterous cohabitation. The opinion specifically rejects the argument that such prosecutions are necessary to protect girls and women from coercion and to prevent fraud. Brown v. Buhman, 947 F. Supp. 2d 1170 (D. Utah 2013). The suit to declare the law unconstitutional was brought by Kody Brown and his plural wives, stars of the reality TV show Sister Wives.

8. A 2007 article estimates that between 500 and 1,000 young men had been expelled, mostly for religious disobedience, from the Hildale/Colorado City, Utah, FLDS settlement. However, social workers providing services to some of the expelled boys believe religious disobedience merely serves as a pretext for removing excess males from the community. The article notes that the increase in the number of disobedient male youth expelled from the community of about 6000 people can be traced to the early 1990s, when Rulon Jeffs, Warren Jeffs's father, married dozens of young wives. The article also notes that, even for behaviors similar to those condemned in their male counterparts, young females are rarely expelled from the group. Erik Eckholm, Boys Cast Out by Polygamists Find Help, N.Y. Times, Sept. 9, 2007. The problem is also discussed in Brieanne M. Billie, Note, The "Lost Boys" of Polygamy: Is Emancipation the Answer?, 12 J. Gender, Race & Just. 127 (2008). The state legislature enacted an emancipation law that is supposed to allow these boys to take independent actions to protect themselves. Utah Code 1953 §§ 78A-6-801 et seq. Billie's note doubts the efficacy of this legislation. Would this concern support the Utah statute?

9. *Holm* concerns the modern-day practice of polygyny among so-called fundamentalist Mormons. Although firm data are lacking, an estimated 30,000 to 50,000 people are engaged in plural marriage in the western part of the United States. For studies of how wives and husbands achieve viable dyadic and communal relationships within plural families, *see* Irwin Altman & Joseph Ginat, Polygamous Families in Contemporary Society (1996); Irwin Altman, Polygamous Family Life: The Case of Contemporary Mormon Fundamentalists, 1996 Utah L. Rev. 367; Irwin Altman, Husbands and Wives in Contemporary Polygamy, 8 J.L. & Fam. Stud. 389 (2006). In the last article Prof. Altman writes:

> The capstone theme of our research is that contemporary polygamous families and their participants display a great variety of profiles in managing their day-to-day lives and interpersonal relationships. They vary considerably in how successful they are in their relationships, exhibit diversity in their coping mechanisms and lifestyles, and continually struggle to maintain viable relationships between husband and wives and between wives. In this respect, they are similar to monogamous families, who also do not exhibit complete uniformity in lifestyle.
>
> Yet many critics of polygamous family relationships portray or think about them as identical in certain qualities, especially negative ones. This pattern of stereotyping was evident in nineteenth century writings and legal opinions. . . . Thus, nineteenth century observers described polygamy among Mormons as despotic, akin to "uncivilized" Asiatic and African cultures, abusive to women and children, contrary to Christianity, barbaric, and a form of prostitution, to name a few depictions. Some of these and other stereotypes and caricatures are still used today, with polygamous men labeled as selfish, controlling, and exploitive of women. Common perceptions of polygamist communities are that all or many young girls marry old men; that women in plural families are hateful and jealous of one another, with no recourse to leaving bad marriages; and that young boys are being thrown out of communities in large numbers. As with many stereotypes, such qualities are applied to whole populations, are often exaggerations, and are based on a limited number of cases. Yet these stereotypes serve to simplify and distort perceptions of others, often of those with whom we have had limited contacts. Such stereotypes are common in portraying ethnic and national groups, and are rampant in times of conflict and war when describing one's enemy.
>
> Although our research confirms individual cases consistent with negative stereotypes in contemporary plural families, the major theme of our findings is that diversity and variation of differences abound in plural family life, and that traditional stereotypes do not apply across the board. In much the same way that one can readily accept the idea that monogamous relationships in contemporary society vary widely in their qualities, so it is that our data reveal the same pattern in polygamous families.

Id. at 392-393. On FLDS communities in Canada, *see* Angela Campbell, Bountiful's Plural Marriages, 6 Int'l J. Law in Context 343 (2010); Martha Bailey, Marriage and Morals, *in* The International Survey of Family Law 2007 Edition, at 53, 58-61.

Although the Mormon fundamentalists are the best known of the American groups that practice polygamy, they are not alone. Nina Bernstein, Polygamy, Practiced in Secrecy, Follows Africans to New York, N.Y. Times, Mar. 23, 2007, describes the practice of polygamy in New York City among recent immigrants from countries that allow polygamy. *See also* Pauline Bartolone, For These Muslims, Polygamy Is an Option, San Francisco Chronicle, Aug. 5, 2007. Although not universal, monogamy is the most common form of marriage. *See* Claude Lévi-Strauss, The Family, *in* The View from Afar 39, 44-45 (J. Neugroschel & P. Hoss trans., 1985). However, a study of 853 cultures found that 83 percent permit polygamy. David M. Buss, The Evolution of Desire: Strategies of Human Mating 178 (1994). For an analysis of Islamic jurisprudence and polygamy, *see* Michele Alexandre, Big Love: Is Feminist Polygamy an Oxymoron or a True Possibility?, 18 Hastings Women's L.J. 3 (2007).

10. Several commentators have pointed out that modern polygamy includes various forms of multi-partner loving relationships, which they broadly term polyamory. An article in Newsweek defined polyamory as "relationships with multiple, mutually consenting partners." It gave the following example:

> Terisa Greenan and her boyfriend, Matt, are enjoying a rare day of Seattle sun, sharing a beet carpaccio on the patio of a local restaurant. Matt holds Terisa's hand, as his 6-year-old son squeezes in between the couple to give Terisa a kiss. His mother, Vera, looks over and smiles; she's there with her boyfriend, Larry. Suddenly it starts to rain, and the group must move inside. In the process, they rearrange themselves: Matt's hand touches Vera's leg. Terisa gives Larry a kiss. The child, seemingly unconcerned, puts his arms around his mother and digs into his meal.
>
> Terisa and Matt and Vera and Larry—along with Scott, who's also at this dinner—are not swingers, per se; they aren't pursuing casual sex. Nor are they polygamists of the sort portrayed on HBO's Big Love; they aren't religious, and they don't have multiple wives. But they do believe in "ethical nonmonogamy," or engaging in loving, intimate relationships with more than one person—based upon the knowledge and consent of everyone involved. They are polyamorous, to use the term of art applied to multiple-partner families like theirs, and they wouldn't want to live any other way.

Jessica Bennett, Only You. And You. And You: Polyamory—Relationships with Multiple, Mutually Consenting Partners—Has a Coming-out Party, Newsweek, July 28, 2009, quoted in Michael Lwin, Big Love: Perry v. Schwarzenegger and Polygamous Marriage, 9 Geo. J.L. & Pub. Pol'y 393, 422 (2011). *See also* Elizabeth F. Emens, Monogamy's Law: Compulsory Monogamy and Polyamorous Existence, 29 N.Y.U. Rev. L. & Soc. Change 277 (2004); Martha M. Ertman, Marriage as a Trade: Bridging the Private/Private Distinction, 36 Harv. C.R.-C.L. L. Rev. 79, 124-125 (2001). Do these relationships pose the same policy problems as the FLDS practices?

11. In almost half the states adultery is still a crime. Gabriele Viator, Note, The Validity of Criminal Adultery Prohibitions After Lawrence v. Texas, 39 Suffolk U. L. Rev. 837, 842-843 (2006). Even more common are statutes making bigamy a criminal offense. A specific exception to criminal liability for bigamy is provided by Enoch Arden statutes (or decisions to the same effect). The situation they address resembles that of the Tennyson poem providing their name: the disappearance for many years—five to seven under most statutes—of a spouse without explanation. Some statutes provide only a defense to the crime of bigamy. *E.g.,* 11 Del. Code § 1002 (2013). Other statutes, however, also provide a procedure for judicial declaration of the death of the absent spouse and, accordingly,

offer protection to a marriage contracted subsequent to the proceeding. *E.g.*, N.Y. Dom. Rel. Law §§ 220, 221 (2013); 23 Pa. Con. Stat. Ann. § 1701 (2013).

Perhaps it should be said that the resemblance between poetry and life is imperfect. Enoch Arden, after a ten-year absence, saw the happiness of his wife Annie, her second husband, and their children, and resolved brokenheartedly that they would not know of his return until after his death.

E.   INTERSTATE RECOGNITION OF MARRIAGE

In re May's Estate

114 N.E. 2d 4 (N.Y. 1953)

Lewis, C.J. In this proceeding, involving the administration of the estate of Fannie May, deceased, we are to determine whether the marriage in 1913 between the respondent Sam May and the decedent, who was his niece by the half blood which marriage was celebrated in Rhode Island, where concededly such marriage is valid is to be given legal effect in New York where statute law declares incestuous and void a marriage between uncle and niece.

The question thus presented arises from proof of the following facts: The petitioner Alice May Greenberg, one of six children born of the Rhode Island marriage of Sam and Fannie May, petitioned in 1951 for letters of administration of the estate of her mother Fannie May, who had died in 1945. Thereupon, the respondent Sam May, who asserts the validity of his marriage to the decedent, filed an objection to the issuance to petitioner of such letters of administration upon the ground that he is the surviving husband of the decedent and accordingly, under section 118 of the Surrogate's Court Act, he has the paramount right to administer her estate. . . .

The petitioner, supported by her sisters Ruth Weisbrout and Evelyn May, contended throughout this proceeding that her father is not the surviving spouse of her mother because, although their marriage was valid in Rhode Island, the marriage never had validity in New York where they were then resident and where they retained their residence until the decedent's death.

The record shows . . . the respondent Sam May had resided in Portage, Wisconsin; that he came to New York in December, 1912, and within a month thereafter he and the decedent both of whom were adherents of the Jewish faith went to Providence, Rhode Island, where, on January 21, 1913, they entered into a ceremonial marriage performed by and at the home of a Jewish rabbi. The certificate issued upon that marriage gave the age of each party as twenty-six years and the residence of each as "New York, N.Y." Two weeks after their marriage in Rhode Island the respondent May and the decedent returned to Ulster County, New York, where they lived as man and wife for thirty-two years until the decedent's death in 1945. Meantime the six children were born who are parties to this proceeding. . . .

We regard the law as settled that, subject to two exceptions presently to be considered, and in the absence of a statute expressly regulating within the domiciliary State marriages solemnized abroad, the legality of a marriage between persons *sui juris* is to be determined by the law of the place where it is celebrated. Van Voorhis v. Brintnall, 86 N.Y. 18, 24....

Incidental to the decision in Van Voorhis v. Brintnall, supra, which followed the general rule that "... recognizes as valid a marriage considered valid in the place where celebrated," this court gave careful consideration to, and held against the application of two exceptions to that rule viz., cases within the prohibition of positive law; and cases involving polygamy or incest in a degree regarded generally as within the prohibition of natural law.

We think the Appellate Division in the case as bar rightly held that the principle of law which ruled Van Voorhis v. Brintnall and kindred cases cited, supra, was decisive of the present case and that neither of the two exceptions to that general rule is here applicable.

The statute of New York upon which the appellants rely is subdivision 3 of section 5 of the Domestic Relations Law which, insofar as relevant to our problem, provides:

§ 5. *Incestuous and Void Marriages*
A marriage is incestuous and void whether the relatives are legitimate or illegitimate between either:
3. An uncle and niece or an aunt and nephew.
If a marriage prohibited by the foregoing provisions of this section be solemnized it shall be void, and the parties thereto shall each be fined not less than fifty nor more than one hundred dollars and may, in the discretion of the court in addition to said fine, be imprisoned for a term not exceeding six months. Any person who shall knowingly and wilfully solemnize such marriage, or procure or aid in the solemnization of the same, shall be deemed guilty of a misdemeanor and shall be fined or imprisoned in like manner....

As section 5 of the New York Domestic Relations Law (quoted supra) does not expressly declare void a marriage of its domiciliaries solemnized in a foreign State where such marriage is valid, the statute's scope should not be extended by judicial construction.... Accordingly, as to the first exception to the general rule that a marriage valid where performed is valid everywhere, we conclude that, absent any New York statute expressing clearly the Legislature's intent to regulate within this State marriages of its domiciliaries solemnized abroad, there is no "positive law" in this jurisdiction which serves to interdict the 1913 marriage in Rhode Island of the respondent Sam May and the decedent.

As to the application of the second exception to the marriage here involved between persons of the Jewish faith whose kinship was not in the direct ascending or descending line of consanguinity and who were not brother and sister, we conclude that such marriage, solemnized, as it was, in accord with the ritual of the Jewish faith in a State whose legislative body has declared such a marriage to be "good and valid in law," was not offensive to the public sense of morality to a degree regarded generally with abhorrence and thus was not within the inhibitions of natural law....

DESMOND, J. (dissenting). . . . The general rule that "a marriage valid where solemnized is valid everywhere" does not apply. To that rule there is a proviso or exception, recognized, it would seem, by all the States, as follows: "unless contrary to the prohibitions of natural law or the express prohibitions of a statute." . . .

. . . Section 5 of the Domestic Relations Law, the one we are concerned with here, lists the marriages which are "incestuous and void" in New York, as being those between parent and child, brother and sister, uncle and niece, and aunt and nephew. All such misalliances are incestuous, and all, equally, are void. The policy, language, meaning and validity of the statute are beyond dispute. It should be enforced by the courts.

NOTES AND QUESTIONS

1. In Catalano v. Catalano, 170 A.2d 726 (Conn. 1961), a resident of Connecticut married his niece, an Italian citizen, in Italy. Their marriage was valid under Italian law. The uncle (Fred) returned to this country immediately; his niece joined him after several years. Fred died shortly thereafter, and his niece sought a widow's allowance from Fred's estate. The Connecticut court, applying Connecticut law, held that her marriage to Fred was contrary to its public policy — a decision based in part on statutory declarations that incestuous marriages are "void" and the existence of a substantial criminal penalty (up to ten years in prison) for incest.

In what respect do the analyses in *May's Estate* and *Catalano* differ? What are the indicia of a "strong public policy" against recognition of marriages that are valid in the state of celebration?

The outcome in *Catalano* is relatively uncommon. *See, e.g.,* Ghassemi v. Ghassemi, 998 So. 2d 731 (La. App. 2008) (first-cousin marriage does not violate strong state policy); Mason v. Mason, 775 N.E.2d 706 (Ind. App. 2002) (same); In re Loughmiller, 629 P.2d 156 (Kan. 1981) (same).

2. Section 283 of The Restatement (Second) of Conflict of Laws provides as follows:

(1) The validity of a marriage will be determined by the local law of the State which, with respect to the particular issue, has the most significant relationship to the spouses and the marriage. . . .

(2) A marriage which satisfies the requirements of the State where the marriage was contracted will everywhere be recognized as valid unless it violates the strong public policy of another State which has the most significant relationship to the spouses and the marriage at the time of the marriage.

According to the reporter for the Second Restatement:

[T]his formulation reflects the three underlying values of (a) State interest, (b) protection of the expectations of the parties and (c) the general policy favouring the validation of marriages. Subsection (2) calls, as a general rule, for the application of the law of the State of celebration provided that the marriage would be valid under that law. . . .

The formulation further makes clear that a marriage good under the law of the State of celebration should not be overthrown unless this is required by the "strong public policy" of the State of most significant relationship.

. . . In making this determination, the forum should first inquire whether the courts of the State of most significant relationship would have invalidated the marriage if the question had come before them. The fact that these courts would not have done so provides, of course, conclusive evidence that no strong policy of this State is involved. If, on the other hand, these courts would have invalidated the marriage . . . the forum would have good reason to do likewise. It would in all probability invalidate the marriage . . . if the parties were still domiciled in the State which was that of most significant relationship at the time of the marriage. The situation would be somewhat different, however, if by the time the action arose the parties had moved to a different State. . . . [A] State will naturally have less interest in having its invalidating rule applied in a case where the parties to the marriage have moved away than it would have if they had remained its local domiciliaries. . . .

Willis L. M. Reese, Marriage in American Conflict of Laws, 26 Int'l & Comp. L.Q. 952, 965-969 (1977).

While there is no comprehensive definition of the "state with the most significant relationship to the spouses and the marriage," it is generally agreed that a state where both parties were domiciled at the time of the marriage (wherever celebrated) would qualify, as would a state in which one of the spouses was domiciled and in which both spouses resided after the marriage.

The Indiana Supreme Court applied the Second Restatement in McPeek v. McCardle, 888 N.E.2d 171 (Ind. 2008). A man and woman who lived in Indiana obtained an Indiana marriage license, participated in a marriage ceremony in Ohio, and recorded the completed marriage license in Indiana. Ten years later, when the woman died, children from her first marriage claimed that the marriage was invalid because the marriage was performed in Ohio without an Ohio license. The trial court ruled that any defect in the formalities made the marriage voidable, not void, and that the children, therefore, lacked standing to raise the issue. The supreme court held that even though the marriage might not be valid according to the law of the Ohio, the state in which the wedding was celebrated (there being no recent decision about whether the license requirement was "mandatory" or "directory"), it was valid under Indiana law and so Indiana would recognize it. *See also* In re Estate of Shippy, 678 P.2d 848 (Wash. App. 1984) (applying law of Washington, the state with the most significant relationship to the issue, to validate a marriage that was void in the state where it was celebrated).

3. *May's Estate* and *Catalano* involve evasionary, or at least migratory, marriages. How does the situation differ when people live and marry in one state, which permits them to do so, and later move to a second state whose laws would not permit them to marry?

. . . [M]any states distinguish between the validity of a marriage and the ability to enjoy its "incidents." There was a time when courts treated marriage as a simple yes-or-no, up-or-down proposition: A marriage was either valid, in which case it was valid for all purposes, or it was not, in which case it was invalid for all purposes. Particularly in this century, however, judges have been willing to draw finer lines, applying the place of celebration rule to the question of validity while saving the public policy exception for particular "incidents" of being married. The right to cohabit, for example, is a usual incident of being married, but not a necessary one. A man married to two wives in India might be able to move to Kansas without being prosecuted for bigamy, but Kansas might forbid the three of them from living together. At the same time, the surviving wives might both be permitted to inherit as spouses under the state's law of succession.

Larry Kramer, Same-Sex Marriage, Conflict of Laws, and the Unconstitutional Public Policy Exception, 106 Yale L.J. 1965, 1971 (1997). *See* In re Dalip Singh Bir's Estate, 188 P.2d 499 (Cal. App. 1948), in which a native of the Punjab province of India legally married two wives. He later moved to California, where he died intestate. Both women sought to inherit as his wives. The California Court of Appeals held that recognition of both marriages for inheritance purposes did not violate strong public policy, but that the result would be different "if the decedent had attempted to cohabit with his two wives in California."

As we will see in Chapter 12, ordinarily a state has jurisdiction to grant a divorce if one of the parties is domiciled there. Therefore, if at least one member of a married same-sex couple moves to another state that also allows same-sex marriage, they can get a divorce in the new state. On the other hand, if the couple moves to a state that does not allow same-sex marriage, will they be able to divorce, since divorcing requires that the state first recognize the marriage?

PORT V. COWAN

44 A.3d 970 (Md. 2012)

HARRELL, J. Appellant, Jessica Port, and Appellee, Virginia Anne Cowan, married in California in 2008. Approximately two years later, Port and Cowan agreed mutually to separate. Port filed ultimately a divorce complaint, on the ground of voluntary separation, in the Circuit Court for Prince George's County (at the time, she was a resident of the County). Cowan answered the complaint in a "no contest" manner. The court denied the requested relief, explaining in its written order that the marriage was "not valid" and "contrary to the public policy of Maryland." Being aggrieved equally, the parties filed appeals timely, asking why an out-of-state, same-sex marriage, valid when and where performed, was not cognizable in Maryland for purposes of the application of its domestic divorce laws.

Putting aside for present purposes whatever may turn out to be the view of the Maryland electorate regarding recognition of the performance in Maryland of domestic same-sex marriages, the treatment given such relationships by the Maryland Legislature (until recently) may be characterized as a case of multiple personality disorder. Exhibit One in this lay diagnosis is the currently effective version of § 2-201 of the Family Law Article of the Maryland Code, defining marriage, for purposes of such ceremonies conducted in Maryland, as being only between a man and a woman.[7] Exhibit Two is a long list of enactments protecting gay persons and same-sex couples from discrimination (by reason of their sexual orientation and relationships) in employment, health care, estate planning, and other areas.

These perceptually mixed legal messages bear directly on resolving the question presented in the present case because they are where we find most often the public policy of Maryland. In order for the parties' foreign same-sex marriage to be recognized in this State for purposes of the application of our domestic divorce laws, that marriage cannot be "repugnant" to Maryland public policy. . . .

. . . Courts deciding whether a foreign marriage is valid in this State, for purposes of divorce or otherwise, employ the common law doctrine of comity, not principally our domestic marriage laws. . . .

Generally, Maryland courts will honor foreign marriages as long as the marriage was valid in the state where performed. There are two exceptions to this rule: the foreign marriage may not be "repugnant" to Maryland public policy and may not be prohibited expressly by the General Assembly.

Maryland recognizes liberally foreign marriages, even those marriages that may be prohibited from being formed if conducted in this State. Research by the parties, amici, and this Court failed to reveal a case, decided by this Court, voiding a valid out-of-state marriage that was prohibited from being formed in Maryland. Liberal recognition of out-of-state marriages promotes "uniformity in the recognition of the marital status, so that persons legally married according to the laws of one state will not be held to be living in adultery in another State, and that children begotten in lawful wedlock in one State will not be held illegitimate in another." Further, the recognition of foreign marriages instills stability in "one of the most important of human relations." Eugene F. Scoles & Peter H. Hay, *Conflict of Laws* 429 (2d ed. 1991); *see also* William M. Richman & William L. Reynolds, *Understanding Conflict of Laws* § 116(a), at 362 (2d ed. 1993). . . .

. . . The parties' California same-sex marriage is valid. Therefore, in order for their marriage to be valid for purposes of whether Maryland will adjudicate its dissolution, it must not run afoul of either exception to *lex loci celebrationis*: that is, it cannot be prohibited by statute or "repugnant" to the public policies of Maryland. For the following reasons, Port's and Cowan's entitlement, on this record, to a Maryland divorce from their California same-sex marriage is not prohibited, as a matter of law and on this record, by these exceptions.

Regarding the statutory prohibition exception, Family Law Article § 2-201 does not forbid expressly valid-where-formed foreign same-sex marriages. The plain wording of § 2-201 provides that "[o]nly a marriage between a man and a woman is valid in this State." It does not preclude from recognition same-sex marriages solemnized validly in another jurisdiction, only those sought-to-be, or actually, performed in Maryland. To preclude the former from being valid, the statute in question must express a clear mandate voiding such marriages and abrogating the common law. Moreover, we note that same-sex marriages are not listed in Family Law Article § 2-202 as among those marriages considered void.

---

7. While this case was pending the Maryland legislature placed an initiative allowing same-sex marriage on the ballot. After it was decided, the voters of Maryland approved the initiative. — Ed.

Other states intending to prevent recognition of valid foreign same-sex marriages have done so expressly and clearly, rather than by implication, subtlety, or indirection. For example, the Pennsylvania Code provides, "A marriage between persons of the same sex which was entered into in another state or foreign jurisdiction, even if valid where entered into, shall be void in this Commonwealth." 23 Pa. Cons. Stat. § 1704. The Virginia Code provides, "Any marriage entered into by persons of the same sex in another state or jurisdiction shall be void in all respects in Virginia and any contractual rights created by such marriage shall be void and unenforceable." Va. Code Ann. § 20-45.2. The Missouri Statute provides, "A marriage between persons of the same sex will not be recognized for any purpose in this state even when valid where contracted." Mo. Rev. Stat. § 451.022(4).[8] The language of § 2-201, by comparison, fails to void for present purposes valid foreign same-sex marriages.

On at least eight occasions, the Maryland General Assembly failed to amend § 2-201 to preclude valid out-of-state same-sex marriages from being recognized in Maryland. . . .

We conclude also that the parties' same-sex marriage is not "repugnant" to Maryland "public policy," as that term is understood properly in applying the doctrine of comity in modern times. Admittedly, "public policy" is an amorphous legal concept. It is agreed, however, that wherever found and identified, that public policy prohibits generally conduct that injures or tends to injure the public good. The primary sources of public policy (and where typically we look to divine it) are the State's constitution, statutes, administrative regulations, and reported judicial opinions. Although courts are not confined to these emanations of public policy in their search, secondary sources are perceived generally as less persuasive.

The bar in meeting the "repugnancy" standard is set intentionally very high, as demonstrated in *Fensterwald* and *Henderson*. In the former case, this Court recognized an uncle-niece marriage solemnized in Rhode Island, despite the fact that it would be void and a misdemeanor had it been attempted to be formed in Maryland. In the latter case, we ruminated, in dictum, that a valid interracial marriage solemnized in another jurisdiction would be deemed invalid in Maryland. The dictum in *Henderson* has been discredited, and the anti-miscegenation statute repealed, 1967 Md. Laws 6. For present purposes, however, the dictum demonstrates how elevated a standard "repugnancy" is. At the time of *Henderson*, interracial marriage was condemned by statute ("an infamous crime") and carried a severe penalty — imprisonment for not less than eighteen months and not more than ten years. By comparison, a same-sex marriage performed in Maryland does not carry for the couple (or the celebrant) a serious criminal penalty. Thus, based on the *Fensterwald-Henderson* line of cases, we cannot conclude logically that valid out-of-state same-sex marriages are "repugnant" to Maryland public policy.

---

8. For additional examples, *see* Ala. Code § 30-1-19(e) ("The State of Alabama shall not recognize as valid any marriage of parties of the same sex that occurred or was alleged to have occurred as a result of the law of any jurisdiction regardless of whether a marriage license was issued."); W. Va. Code Ann. § 48-2-603 (stating that foreign same-sex marriages "shall not be given effect").

With regard to the second exception to *lex loci celebrationis*, recognizing valid foreign same-sex marriages is consistent actually with Maryland public policy. Prior to the Attorney General's opinion surmising that this Court would recognize foreign same-sex marriages (valid where entered), the General Assembly enacted several laws that protect and support same-sex couples, as alluded to earlier in this opinion. An array of statutes prohibit public or private discrimination based on sexual orientation in the areas of employment, public accommodations, leasing commercial property, and housing. Maryland's domestic partner statute extends to same-sex couples, who qualify as domestic partners, certain medical and decision-making rights as regards one another. The General Assembly granted also recordation, transfer, and inheritance tax exemptions to same-sex couples who qualify as domestic partners. Finally, this Court rejected discrimination based on sexual orientation in the context of certain family law situations. In Boswell v. Boswell, we concluded that sexual orientation of a parent ordinarily is irrelevant in a visitation dispute (unless the court finds that the child would be impacted adversely in a demonstrable way because of the parent's conduct with his/her partner in front of the child). . . .

A number of other states with similar comity principles and relevant domestic marriage laws to those of Maryland have recognized foreign same-sex marriages for purposes of their domestic divorce laws. In Christiansen v. Christiansen, a same-sex couple, whose marriage was formed validly in Canada, appealed the denial of their divorce request by the courts of Wyoming. 253 P.3d 153, 154 (Wyo. 2011). Wyoming has a statute limiting marriage to a man and woman, but fails to proscribe by legislation recognition of valid foreign same-sex marriages. It also recognizes foreign marriages pursuant to *lex loci celebrationis* (although the principle is codified, rather than a creature of the common law) and will not validate a foreign marriage "contrary to the policy of [Wyoming] laws." The court, noting that the "policy exception is necessarily narrow, lest it swallow the rule," concluded that recognizing a valid foreign same-sex marriage for purposes of a domestic divorce proceeding "does not lessen the law or policy in Wyoming against allowing the creation of same-sex marriages [in Wyoming]." New York, which prior to enacting a marriage-equality law in 2011 had comity and marriage laws similar to Maryland and Wyoming, recognized foreign same-sex civil unions for purposes of divorce.

Some states have elected not to recognize valid foreign same-sex marriages for purposes of domestic divorce proceedings. *See, e.g.*, In re J.B., 326 S.W.3d 654 (Tex. Ct. App. 2010); Kern v. Taney, 11 Pa. D. & C. 5th 558 (Pa. C.P. Ct. 2010). Those states, unlike Maryland, expressed clear public policies against honoring foreign same-sex marriages. In re J.B., 326 S.W.3d at 665 ("Section 6.204(b) [of the Texas Family Code] declares same-sex marriages void and against Texas public policy."); *Kern*, 11 Pa. D. & C. 5th at 562 ("'A marriage between persons of the same sex which was entered into in another state or foreign jurisdiction, even if valid where entered into, shall be void in this Commonwealth.'" (quoting 23 Pa. Cons. Stat. § 1704)).

. . . A valid out-of-state same-sex marriage should be treated by Maryland courts as worthy of divorce, according to the applicable statutes, reported cases, and court rules of this State.

NOTES AND QUESTIONS

1. How did the court in *Port* decide whether Maryland had a strong public policy against recognizing same-sex marriage? Would it have reached the same conclusion if the legislature had not repeatedly declined to amend the statute to forbid recognition of out-of-state marriages? If the legislature had not enacted statutes that protect gays and lesbians in various legal areas?

Courts in several states have taken the view that they could not assert jurisdiction to end a civil union from another state because civil unions did not exist under state law. *E.g.*, Rosengarten v. Downes, 802 A.2d 170 (Conn. App. 2002). *See also* Burns v. Burns, 560 S.E.2d 47 (Ga. App. 2002) (Vermont civil union not a marriage for purposes of divorce decree that provided that "[t]here shall be no visitation nor residence by the children with either party during any time where such party cohabits with or has overnight stays with any adult to which such party is not legally married. . . ."); Langan v. St. Vincent's Hospital of New York, 802 N.Y.S.2d 476 (App. Div. 2005) (surviving partner from a Vermont civil union could not bring a wrongful death action in New York). Does ending a civil union present a different choice-of-law issue than ending a marriage?

Some states with civil union or domestic partnership laws have enacted statutes such as Or. Laws 2007, ch. 99, § 6(4) to solve this problem:

Each person signing a Declaration of Domestic Partnership consents to the jurisdiction of the circuit courts of Oregon for the purpose of an action to obtain a judgment of dissolution or annulment of the domestic partnership, for legal separation of the partners in the domestic partnership or for any other proceeding related to the partners' rights and obligations, even if one or both partners cease to reside in, or to maintain a domicile in, this state.

2. As discussed above in conjunction with United States v. Windsor, the federal Defense of Marriage Act (DOMA) has a second provision whose constitutionality was not at stake in that case. 28 U.S.C. § 1738C provides:

No State, territory, or possession of the United States or Indian tribe, shall be required to give effect to any public act, record, or judicial proceeding of any other State, territory, possession, or tribe respecting a relationship between persons of the same sex that is treated as a marriage under the laws of such other State, territory, possession, or tribe, or a right or claim arising from such relationship.

Does this statute add anything to the principles discussed in *Port*?

3. Thirty-four states have statutes, state constitutional provisions, or both that limit marriage to opposite-sex couples. (As noted above, federal trial courts have held in several states that excluding same-sex couples from marriage is unconstitutional.) Most of these "mini-DOMAs" explicitly prohibit recognition of a same-sex marriage entered into in another state. Andrew Koppelman, The Difference the Mini-DOMAs Make, 38 Loy. U. Chi. L.J. 265 (2007). Virginia and some other states go further. Va. Code § 20-12.1, enacted in 2004, provides that "the Commonwealth of Virginia is under no constitutional or legal obligation to recognize a marriage, civil union, partnership contract or other arrangement

purporting to bestow any of the privileges or obligations of marriage under the laws of another state or territory of the United States unless such marriage conforms to the laws of this Commonwealth." *See also* Neb. Const., Art. I, §29; Vernon's Tex. Code Ann., Family Code, §6.204. Would these statutes withstand a constitutional challenge based on *Windsor*?

4. Most states that allow same-sex marriage or that have broad domestic partnership or civil union statutes will take jurisdiction to divorce same-sex couples from other states. Robert E. Rains, A Minimalist Approach to Same-Sex Divorce: Respecting States That Permit Same-Sex Marriages and States That Refuse to Recognize Them, 2012 Utah L. Rev. 393, 411. *See, e.g.*, N.J. Stat. Ann. §26:8A-6(c) (2013); Cal. Fam. Code §299.2 (2013); D.C. Code §21-2202 (2013). *See also* Salucco v. Alldredge, 2004 WL 864459 (Mass. Super.) (*Goodridge* and *Opinions of the Justices* require that same-sex couples who enter into a Vermont civil union be given the same rights and responsibilities that opposite-sex married couples have).

5. The courts are divided about whether the full faith and credit clause requires a state to issue an amended birth certificate for a child adopted in another state by a same-sex couple. Finstuen v. Edmondson, 496 F.3d 1139 (10th Cir. 2007), held that an Oklahoma statute that denies legal recognition of out-of-state adoptions by same-sex couples violated the Constitution. The court held that the full faith and credit clause requires interstate recognition of judgments, including adoption decrees, and does not allow a state to assert a public policy exception. Because the court affirmed the district court order on this ground, it did not reach the children's and parents' equal protection and due process arguments. However, the Fifth Circuit sitting en banc in Adar v. Smith, 639 F.3d 146 (5th Cir. 2011), disagreed. Same-sex adoptive parents sued in federal court after a Louisiana official refused to issue an amended birth certificate for the child. The court held that a full faith and credit violation cannot be challenged in a 42 U.S.C. §1983 action and, at any rate, that issuing an amended birth certificate does not constitute "recognition" of another state's decree, but "enforcement" of it, which is not required by the full faith and credit clause. The Supreme Court denied certiorari. 132 S. Ct. 400 (2011). *See also* Miller-Jenkins v. Miller-Jenkins, 637 S.E.2d 330 (Va. App. 2006), which held that Virginia courts had to recognize a Vermont custody order issued incident to the dissolution of a civil union, even though Virginia would not recognize the civil union itself. Vermont had jurisdiction to decide custody, and its order was entitled to full faith and credit.

6. The extensive literature on interstate recognition of marriage, civil unions, and domestic partnerships includes Mary Patricia Byrn & Morgan L. Holcomb, Wedlocked, 67 U. Miami L. Rev. 1 (2012); Brenda Cossman, Betwixt and Between Recognition: Migrating Same-Sex Marriages and the Turn Toward the Private, 71 Law & Contemp. Probs. 153 (Summer 2008); Larry Kramer, Same-Sex Marriage, Conflict of Laws, and the Unconstitutional Public Policy Exception, 106 Yale L.J. 1965 (1997); Linda Silberman, Same-Sex Marriages: Refining the Conflict of Laws Analysis, 153 U. Pa. L. Rev. 2195 (2005); Gary Simon, Beyond Interstate Recognition in the Same-Sex Marriage Debate, 314 U.C. Davis L. Rev. 40 (2006); Joseph William Singer, Same Sex Marriage, Full Faith and Credit, and the Evasion of Obligation, 1 Stan. J. C.R. & C.L. 1 (2005); Lynn D. Wardle, From Slavery to Same-Sex Marriage: Comity versus Public Policy in Inter-Jurisdictional

Recognition of Controversial Domestic Relations, 2008 BYU L. Rev. 1855; Tobias Barrington Wolff, Interest Analysis in Interjurisdictional Marriage Disputes, 153 U. Pa. L. Rev. 2215 (2005).

PROBLEMS

1. John and Susan, a married couple who live in State A, believe in plural marriage. They decide that John should also marry Marie, Susan's younger sister, who is willing. John and Marie travel to Country B, which allows men to have more than one wife, and are married according to that jurisdiction's law. They return to State A after one week and continue to reside together. Two years later, Marie sues John for divorce in State A and asks for spousal support. If John contests the divorce on the ground that there was no marriage, what will be the result?

2. Same facts as problem 1, except that after two years of postmarital residence in State A, John and Susan are killed in an automobile accident. Marie seeks to inherit as his surviving spouse. What result?

3. Suppose that, in both situations above, the parties were originally residents of the country in which John and Marie were married. All three then moved to State A, where they lived together until the events described above. What results?

Legal Recognition of Informal Family Partnerships

4

A. INTRODUCTION

Most of the time we think of marriage as a relationship clearly distinct from others, begun by a formal ceremony and ended by death or formal divorce. However, many people who have not gone through a valid ceremonial marriage live together and share their lives much as people who have been ceremonially married do. While this phenomenon is not new, the rate of cohabitation has increased dramatically over the last 50 years throughout the Western world. This chapter examines legal doctrines that in some circumstances and to varying extents result in the people in these households being treated as members of families.

> ### MARY ANN GLENDON, MARRIAGE AND THE STATE: THE
> ### WITHERING AWAY OF MARRIAGE
>
> 62 Va. L. Rev. 663, 684-687, 692-693 (1976)

Cohabitation, or "living together," is only one aspect of diversity in American marriage behavior, using the word *marriage* broadly. Defining exactly what turns a sexual relation into "marriage" is difficult, but it is useful to follow the lead of the family sociologist Rene Konig, by thinking of the shadow institution of legal marriage as a set of heterosexual unions undertaken with some idea of duration and manifested to the relevant social environment. . . .

Motivations to enter informal rather than legal marriage include economic advantages as in the case of many elderly people,[1] inability to enter a legal

---

1. In many cases, the Social Security system inflicts financial penalties on elderly citizens who remarry. Although individuals who receive old-age assistance by virtue of their own participation are entitled to their full benefits regardless of marital status, 42 U.S.C.

marriage, unwillingness to be subject to the legal effects of marriage, desire for a "trial marriage," and lack of concern with the legal institution. This lack of concern is nothing new among groups accustomed to forming and dissolving informal unions without coming into contact with legal institutions. Among these groups legal marriage is but an aspect of the irrelevance of traditional American family law, law that is viewed as being property-oriented and organized around the ideals of a dominant social group. Lack of concern with marriage law has been growing, however, among many who definitely are not outside the mainstream of American life. Until recently these converts accepted unquestioningly the traditional structures of the enacted law, but they now find that on balance the enacted law offers no advantages over informal arrangements.

. . . In the past our legal response to cohabitation has been to pretend it is marriage and then attribute to it the traditional incidents of marriage. Thus, what in effect were cohabitation cases were disguised as cases involving presumptively legal marriage, estoppels, and implied agreements to pay for service. Because informal marriage exists in every society, every legal system has had to provide some ways to deal with the problems it generates. Professor Walter Weyrauch has convincingly demonstrated that this is the correct way to view not only the institution of common law marriage, but the myriad devices of the law of proof and presumptions that are the functional equivalent of common law marriage in those states that do not recognize it. In this view, naturally, the gradual decline in the number of jurisdictions that recognize the doctrine of common law marriage loses significance because other devices have simultaneously arisen to bring about functionally analogous legal effects, usually through the provision of economic benefits, such as alimony, inheritance rights, wrongful death, or workmen's compensation benefits to members of a de facto family.

The interesting question now becomes whether the increase in, and increased visibility and respectability of, informal marriage will bring about a casting-off of these legal fictions and the direct attribution of economic consequences to de facto dependency.

---

§ 402(a) (1970), widows and widowers who participate only through the earnings of their deceased spouses ordinarily have their benefits cut in half by remarriage. *Id.* § 402(e)(4), (f)(5). Also, the right of a surviving spouse, under some state laws, *e.g.*, N.Y. Estates, Powers & Trusts L. § 5-1.1 (McKinney 1967), as amended (McKinney Pock. Pt. 1975-1976), to elect a statutory share of the decedent spouse's estate despite his will constitutes an obstacle to elderly couples who wish to preserve their separate estates for their individual families by previous marriage. The necessity of an antenuptial agreement to disclaim such rights is, at best, a nuisance and, at worst, an illusion, should the agreement for some reason be invalidated in court.

B.   COMMON LAW MARRIAGE, PRESUMPTIONS ABOUT MARRIAGE, AND THE PUTATIVE SPOUSE DOCTRINE

As Professor Glendon says, the traditional legal treatment of cohabitants was either to regard their relationship as wholly unlawful or to assimilate it into marriage through a variety of doctrines. This section considers three of the most important and widely used of these doctrines: common law marriage, the putative spouse doctrine, and presumptions of marriage validity. Other devices include limitations on standing to attack the validity of marriage (see Chapter 3) and the validity of divorce (see Chapter 12).

1.   Common Law Marriage

American common law marriage derives from English marriage law prior to the Marriage Act of 1753. Ecclesiastical courts did not require that couples marry in church; they also recognized people as married if they exchanged promises to marry in the present tense (*sponsalia per verba de praesenti*) or in the future followed by consummation (*sponsalia per verba de futuro*). However, the 1753 Marriage Act, known as Lord Hardwicke's Act, which provided that only marriages celebrated in church or in a public chapel in the presence of two witnesses would thereafter be valid, officially abolished nonceremonial marriage. Exceptions were made for the royal family, Quakers, and Jews. Nonceremonial marriages were recognized in the English colonies as well.

MICHAEL GROSSBERG, *GOVERNING THE HEARTH*

68-69, 79, 83-84, 86-90, 101 (1985)

[Some colonists deliberately avoided formal marriage as part of their rejection of traditional religious attitudes, while others formed informal unions out of necessity, due to the lack of regular clergy and lay officials empowered to celebrate marriage.] The presence of informal marriage in colonial America may be clear but its legal status was not. . . . In all likelihood, though, the clouded distinction between legality and validity in English law and the uncertainty engendered by the decentralized, informal colonial legal system led to ad hoc, localized solutions. Despite the clear preferences of provincial statutes, informal marriage probably received judicial acquiescence, if not endorsement, and thus the dual nuptial system lingered in the colonies after it had disappeared in the mother country. . . .

[After the American Revolution, judges and legislatures initially endorsed common law marriage.] Republican marriage law made matrimony much easier for a couple to enter, rechristened "irregular marriage" as "common law marriage," and significantly eased the rules governing proof of valid unions.[2] . . .

---

2. Chancellor Kent was a leader in this movement. *See* James Kent, Commentaries on American Law (1827), XXVI (6). — Ed.

The continuing practice of irregular marriage, combined with unreliable public records and laissez faire government, made it difficult for couples to substantiate their marriages. However, judges placed the weight of the law behind those living as husband and wife. They did so by formally receiving into American common law the old rule that marriage could be presumed from the acknowledgements, cohabitation, and reputation of a couple. . . .

At the heart of the judiciary's incorporation of the presumption of marriage lay a persistent inclination to find matrimony whenever a man and a woman lived together. . . . In a clear policy decision favoring practice over form, courts refused to dissolve marriages and break up families for lack of evidence of a wedding ceremony. . . .

The tolerance of informal marriage by jurists . . . evoked growing criticism in mid-century America. By the 1870s an organized reform campaign questioned the intent and methods of American family law. Reformers, legislators, social scientists, journalists, evangelical Protestants, and other interested parties assailed marriage law for its laxity and its failure to protect society from marital instability. . . .

Marriage reform in late nineteenth-century America is an example of what social critic Stan Cohen has labeled a "moral panic." . . . Cohen argues that such mass phenomena erupt when a "condition, episode, person or group of persons emerges to become defined as a threat to societal values and interests; its nature is presented in a stylized and stereotypical fashion by the mass media; the moral barricades are manned by editors, bishops and politicians and other right-thinking people; socially accredited experts pronounce their diagnoses and solution; ways of coping are evolved, or (more often) resorted to; the condition then disappears, submerges or deteriorates." Sometimes panics pass and are forgotten. But other times, he suggests, the panic "has more serious and long term repercussions and it might produce changes in legal and social policy or even in the way in which societies conceive themselves." Such social scares offer a means of expressing deep-seated fears and help focus those concerns on the most visible symbols of the crisis, what Cohen terms "folk devils." In nineteenth-century American domestic relations, panics over family life led to persistent efforts to compel deviant couples to adhere to orthodox republican matrimonial practices. Legal coercion became one of the most trusted weapons of reform. . . .

[One prominent expression of this change was a concerted attack on common law marriage. Once championed as supporting virtue by giving the legal effect of marriage to relationships that functioned as marriage, common law marriage came to be seen as a prime cause of social disintegration and immorality.] . . . [B]y the early twentieth century [common law marriage] met almost universal public condemnation. The 1918 Minnesota Law Review reported that such unions were "becoming quite a rare occurrence, and the instances in which [they are] being presented to the courts are fewer still." But common-law marriage remained a legal option in most jurisdictions.

See also Ariela R. Dubler, Wifely Behavior: A Legal History of Acting Married, 100 Colum. L. Rev. 957 (2000).

IN RE MARRIAGE OF WINEGARD

257 N.W.2d 609 (Iowa 1977)

MASON, J. . . . John and Sally, 53 and 30 years of age respectively at time of trial, first met in 1962, shortly after Sally commenced working in the office of John's Burlington business enterprise, Winegard Company. At the time, Sally was single and John was married and the father of two children. At some time in 1964 or 1965 John's first marriage was dissolved. In May of 1963 John and Sally commenced an erratic relationship which ultimately led to the present controversy.

Five months after John and Sally started seeing one another Sally married one Lonnie Anderkin and moved to Ohio. This union produced a child, Wendy Lynn, who was born in September of 1964. This marriage was apparently subjected to more than its share of marital and financial difficulties. At one point, Sally and Anderkin received a $500 loan from John. Subsequently, Sally returned to Burlington and asked John for financial assistance in order to obtain a dissolution of her marriage to Anderkin. Apparently, John gave her $50 on two different occasions which she used to commence two abortive dissolution actions in Iowa. During this period, which apparently was late 1965 and early 1966, John and Sally dated each other and traveled together.

In October of 1966 John accompanied Sally and her daughter to Las Vegas, Nevada, where Sally intended to commence divorce proceedings against Anderkin. Sally's legal and living expenses were paid by John. On December 7 Sally was granted a divorce from Anderkin, who appeared in the proceedings through counsel. During the six-week interval prior to the divorce decree, John divided his time between Las Vegas and Burlington. On the day the decree was issued, John and Sally returned to Burlington and at some point during the trip marriage was proposed by John and declined by Sally.

Upon their return to the Burlington area, John and Sally dated intermittently until February 1967, when Sally returned to Ohio and began living with her ex-husband Anderkin. A few months later, Anderkin went into military service and Sally moved in with his parents. The record is unclear with respect to Sally's activities in the following 15-18 months, but it is clear she married one Frank Gilvin in Dayton, Ohio, on October 31, 1968.

Sally's second marriage was apparently as troubled as her first and she once again returned to the Burlington area with John's financial assistance. Subsequently, John again accompanied her to Las Vegas, paying all expenses involved, and Sally was granted a default divorce from Gilvin on September 3, 1969.

Evidently, upon the divorce from Gilvin, Sally and John returned to Burlington where their relationship became matrimonially inclined. On April 4, 1970, John and Sally entered into an antenuptial agreement whereby, in essence, Sally waived ". . . all statutory or common law rights that she may have as the wife of John during John's lifetime and/or as the surviving spouse in the property or estate of John. . . ." In exchange for said waiver, John agreed to secure insurance on his life in the face amount of $100,000 and to name Sally as primary beneficiary thereof. The agreement stated its execution was prompted by the fact John and Sally ". . . are contemplating marriage and may be married in the near future. . . ."

Shortly after the execution of said agreement, John and Sally traveled to Hawaii with the intention of being married there. However, upon their arrival in Hawaii, John told Sally he wanted to delay their marriage plans, explaining he had waited until the day before their departure to tell his daughter of their matrimonial intentions and he felt she needed more time to adjust to the situation. John and Sally returned to Burlington unmarried.

In September of 1970, just a few months after her trip to Hawaii with John, Sally returned to Ohio and renewed her living arrangement with her ex-husband Anderkin. Again, Sally's revived relationship with her former husband only lasted for 3-4 months and she returned to the Burlington area in December of that year.

Following Sally's return, her relationship with John was rekindled and on February 14, 1971, he gave her an engagement ring. On March 29 John and Sally reaffirmed the previously executed antenuptial agreement and left for Las Vegas again with the intention to be married upon their arrival in that city. Once again, however, John and Sally returned to Burlington a few days later without having participated in a marriage ceremony. Apparently, abandonment of their plans was at John's request.

Sally testified at trial that on their return flight John asked if she still wanted to get married and she responded she did. At this point, John placed a wedding band on Sally's finger. Confused about his actions, Sally asked John if they were going to be married upon their return to Iowa. John allegedly responded that a marriage ceremony was unnecessary in Iowa and asserted they were "just as much married as anybody else there." Sally expressed concern over what to tell others with respect to their marital status and was directed by John to say they had been married in Las Vegas. In addition, John told Sally she could use his name.

In his version of the events which transpired during their Las Vegas journey, John admitted he intended to be married in that city, but maintained he changed his mind shortly after arriving there. John testified he informed Sally of his decision in their hotel room and there gave her the wedding band. He denied any symbolic significance in the gift of the ring, explaining he was only motivated by the fact he no longer had use for it. In response to Sally's expressed fear of potential embarrassment, John testified he told Sally she could move into his home temporarily and could use his name. He denied telling Sally they were "as much married as anybody else in Iowa," stated he recalled no in-flight conversation concerning their relationship and asserted he clearly told Sally he did not wish to marry her.

Immediately upon her return from Nevada, Sally and her daughter began living with John in his Burlington home. Various individuals were informed by Sally that she and John had in fact been married. John did nothing to deny or dispute his alleged marital relationship with Sally. The couple received wedding gifts from a number of people, including John's mother and brother and John's attorney. John and Sally received mail addressed to and traveled together as Mr. and Mrs. John Winegard. They attended family gatherings and sent out Christmas cards with "John and Sally Winegard" engraved thereon. Sally's picture appeared in the local newspaper and she was referred to therein as Mrs. John Winegard. In addition, Sally was given or had access to numerous credit cards, some of which listed the owner thereof as Mrs. John Winegard.

John and Sally's home life was apparently fairly stable until December 1971, eight months after their Las Vegas trip. At that time, Sally testified she felt John was involved with another woman and confronted him with her suspicions. John confirmed her belief and from that point on the parties' relationship deteriorated. February 6, 1973, Sally's petition for dissolution of marriage was filed. . . .

The trial court concluded John and Sally Winegard were husband and wife by virtue of a common law marriage. However, for purposes of determining the propriety of an order allowing temporary attorney fees in a dissolution proceeding, the marriage relation need not be established by a preponderance. If the proof be such as to make out a fair presumption of the fact of the existence of the marital relationship, then it is sufficient to warrant the court in granting an order for temporary attorney fees. . . .

. . . [W]e turn to some of the decisions of this court which recognize the principles applicable when a common law marital relationship is alleged.

Recently, in In re Marriage of Grother, 242 N.W.2d 1 (Iowa 1976), this court summarized those principles in these words:

"... The burden was on ... (petitioner) as proponent of the marriage to prove it by a preponderance of evidence. . . . A claim of common-law marriage is regarded with suspicion and is closely scrutinized. It was necessary for ... (petitioner) to prove an intent and agreement *in praesenti* to be married by both parties together with continuous cohabitation and public declaration that they were husband and wife. . . ." (Emphasis in original.)

In In re Estate of Dallman, 228 N.W.2d 187, 190 (Iowa 1975), are the following pertinent comments:

"Although, as aforesaid, common-law marriages are recognized in this jurisdiction, one element essential to the proof of such relationship is a general and substantial 'holding-out' or open declaration thereof to the public by both parties thereto. In fact such 'holding-out' or open declaration to the public has been said to be the acid test.

"In other words, there can be no secret common-law marriage."

With respect to the requirement that the parties presently intend to be husband and wife, this court in Gammelgaard v. Gammelgaard, 247 Iowa 979, 980, 77 N.W.2d 479, 480, said:

"... To establish the existence of such a marriage there must be shown a present intent to be husband and wife, followed by cohabitation. Proof of cohabitation is not in itself sufficient. . . . But such proof, as well as evidence of conduct and of general repute in the community where the parties reside, is admissible as tending to strengthen a showing of a present agreement to be husband and wife, and as bearing upon the question of intent."

The following additional comments upon the intent necessary to establish a common law marital relationship are contained in McFarland v. McFarland, 51 Iowa 565, 570, 2 N.W. 269, 273-274:

"... It is true that cohabitation does not of itself constitute marriage. On the other hand, no express form in this State is necessary more than at common law. It is sufficient if the parties cohabiting intend present marriage, and it is immaterial how the intention is evidenced. The woman, indeed, may be entitled to marital rights if she intends present marriage, and the man does not, provided they cohabit and provided his conduct is such as to justify her in believing that he intends present marriage." . . .

The record discloses the following bearing on the existence of the marital relationship: (1) Sally's intent and belief with respect to her relationship with John; (2) opinions of various witnesses that the community generally regarded the parties as married; (3) continuous cohabitation by the parties since April of 1971; (4) John's failure to deny his alleged marriage; (5) John's acquiescence in Sally's use of his name and her representations to the community they were in fact married; (6) Sally's receipt of a wedding band from John; (7) hotel registrations and travel reservations wherein the parties were listed as Mr. and Mrs. John Winegard; (8) receipt of wedding gifts without objection by John; (9) payment by John of retail charge accounts incurred by Sally as Mrs. John Winegard; (10) mail received and sent by the parties as Mr. and Mrs. John Winegard; (11) John's consent to Sally's ownership of and designation as beneficiary under an insurance policy on his life wherein Sally was referred to as "insured's wife"; and (12) checks endorsed by John directing payment to the order of "Sally Winegard." . . .

John contends there is no direct evidence of an intent and agreement *in praesenti* by the parties to be husband and wife. Even assuming, as John maintains, Sally's testimony with respect to John's alleged statements on the return flight from Las Vegas is without credibility, it is well established circumstantial evidence may be relied upon to demonstrate a common law marriage. The record herein regarding the continuous cohabitation of the parties and the declaration or holding out to the public they were in fact husband and wife constitutes circumstantial evidence which tends to create a fair presumption that a common law marital relationship existed.

One final contention advanced by John in an attempt to refute the existence of a marital relationship between him and Sally centers upon the airborne conversation between them wherein John allegedly made reference to the recognition of common law marriages in Iowa. Specifically, John maintains that since that conversation, if it in fact took place, occurred in air space over a state other than Iowa, Sally has not demonstrated, as she must, that said unknown state recognizes common law marriages. John's contention is without merit. The actions of the parties, subsequent to the controverted airborne conversation, are sufficient to create the presumption required.

In light of the foregoing authorities we conclude from our de novo review the proof is sufficient to create a fair presumption of the existence of the marital relationship. Such quantum of evidence meets the standard required to justify the granting of an order for temporary attorney fees under the present factual circumstances.

NOTES AND QUESTIONS

1. At the conclusion of the trial on the merits, the court held that John and Sally were married and awarded Sally $75,000 in lieu of alimony. On appeal the

Iowa Supreme Court affirmed the finding of a common law marriage and raised Sally's award to $140,000. In re Marriage of Winegard, 278 N.W.2d 505 (Iowa 1979). The court also held that John was estopped to attack and lacked standing to attack the validity of Sally's two Nevada divorces from her first two husbands. See Chapter 12, Section B (jurisdiction to grant divorces).

2. What are the elements of common law marriage, according to this court? In principle, the essence of common law marriage is that the parties intended to be married. At what point did Sally form this intent? At what point did John? Whose intent controls?

3. For the most part, the doctrine of common law marriage does not provide a way to avoid the substantive requirements for marriage; it addresses only the issue of formalities. However, appellate courts in Kansas and Colorado have held that common law marriage is not subject to statutory age limits. In re Pace, 989 P.2d 297 (Kan. App. 1999); In re Marriage of J.M.H., 143 P.3d 1116 (Colo. App. 2006). In both cases the courts held that a girl younger than the minimum statutory age for a ceremonial marriage but older than the common law age limit (12 for girls and 14 for boys) could enter a valid common law marriage. In both states the legislature later raised the age limits for common law marriage to match those for ceremonial marriage.

Other substantive limits do apply to common law marriage, though. For example, if John Winegard's first marriage or either of Sally's previous marriages had never been ended and all the other facts were the same, John and Sally could not have had a common law marriage. Yet with surprising frequency people do purport to marry while they are still legally married to someone else, either because they haven't bothered to get a divorce or because the divorce is not yet final. When the parties reside in a state that permits common law marriage, courts typically find that such a marriage commenced if and when the first marriage ended. See, e.g., Hall v. Duster, 727 So. 2d 834 (Ala. Civ. App. 1999). For such situations the Uniform Marriage and Divorce Act (hereinafter UMDA) § 207(b) proposes the following statutory remedy for states that do not generally allow common law marriage: "Parties to a marriage prohibited under this section who cohabit after removal of the impediment are lawfully married as of the date of the removal of the impediment." Under this statute, would John and Sally have been married?

4. In the late 1880s more than half the states allowed common law marriages to be formed within their boundaries, but today only nine states and the District of Columbia do so. The states are Alabama, Colorado, Iowa, Kansas, Montana, Rhode Island, South Carolina, Texas, and Utah. Since 1991, five states — Georgia, Idaho, Ohio, Oklahoma, and Pennsylvania — have abolished common law marriage by statute or judicial decision. A New Hampshire statute provides, "Persons cohabiting and acknowledging each other as husband and wife, and generally reputed to be such, for the period of 3 years, and until the decease of one of them, shall thereafter be deemed to have been legally married." N.H. Rev. Stat. § 457:39 (2013). Under this statute, would the Winegards have been married?

5. Contrary to the trend in other states, in 1987 the Utah legislature enacted a statute providing that a couple is married, even if they have not participated in a valid ceremony, if a court or administrative agency finds that they (a) are capable of giving consent; (b) are legally capable of entering a solemnized marriage under the provisions of this chapter; (c) have cohabited; (d) mutually assume marital rights,

duties, and obligations; and (e) hold themselves out as and have acquired a uniform and general reputation as husband and wife. Utah Stat. § 30-1-4.5 (2013). Under this statute, would the Winegards have been treated as married?

The Utah statute was intended to reduce public assistance to families with children. In Utah stepparents, but not unmarried cohabitants, are obligated to support their stepchildren during their marriage to the children's custodial parent. Accordingly, a family may be eligible for assistance if the custodial parent is living with but not married to a partner, while the family would become ineligible if the cohabitants were married. Does this statute seem likely to accomplish its purpose? Might it be used to increase other public expenditures for family members?

6. Common law marriage is more important than one might conclude from looking only at the number of states in which such marriages can be contracted. Under choice-of-law rules, a state may recognize a common law marriage entered into in another jurisdiction even when the forum state itself does not allow common law marriages. As we saw in Chapter 3, the traditional choice-of-law rule is that a marriage valid where entered into is valid everywhere, but a state may refuse to recognize a marriage entered into in another state if to do so would violate a strong public policy of the forum state. If the parties were actually domiciled in a state that allows common law marriage, other states will generally recognize the parties' common law marriage. The problem arises when the parties were domiciled in a state that does not allow common law marriage but had some level of contact with a state that does.

According to Professor Clark, the states' approaches can be sorted into three groups. Some states do not have a strong policy against common law marriage; they therefore are willing to treat their domiciliaries as having entered into a common law marriage in another state even when the parties' contact with that state was just a short visit. At the other extreme, some states have such a strong policy against common law marriage that they will not recognize an alleged common law marriage between parties not domiciled in the common law marriage state at the time of the alleged marriage. In the third group of states, parties do not have to have been domiciled in the common law marriage state, but they must have established a residence there; visits alone are not sufficient. Homer H. Clark, Jr., The Law of Domestic Relations in the United States § 2.4 at 57-59 (2d ed. 1988).

7. In principle, common law marriage differs from ceremonial marriage only in the way in which it is entered. Consequently, a formal divorce action is necessary to dissolve a common law marriage. However, the Utah statute quoted above provides that a proceeding to establish a common law marriage must be brought within a year after the relationship has ended. Does this statute create a form of common law divorce? *Compare* Texas Family Code § 2.401(b) (2013), which provides that if an action to prove the existence of a common law marriage is not brought within two years of when the parties quit living together, it is rebuttably presumed that the parties did not agree to be married.

PROBLEMS

1. Sandra Renfro and Dave Winfield began dating in 1981, and she became pregnant by him. When Sandra told Dave, they agreed to be informally married,

she says, but Dave didn't want a formal marriage because he believed that his public image would suffer if it were widely known that he had conceived a child outside marriage. They spent the nights of April 11-13 in a Dallas hotel, registering as "Mr. and Mrs. Dave Winfield." Dave says that he never intended to marry Sandra and doesn't remember staying in the hotel. The next week Sandra told her mother that she and Dave had married in Dallas. Her mother believed they were married, although Dave never told her so. Later in April Dave asked Sandra to look for a home for them in Houston. Sandra found a condominium, which Dave bought, telling his secretary that it was for his family. In September the baby was born, and Sandra gave the baby the last name of Renfro. Dave kept his personal belongings in the condominium and stayed there most of the time that fall when he was not traveling for business reasons. Dave's secretary says that over a two-year period Dave spent about one-third of his time at the condominium. When Dave was there, he did errands and worked around the house. The mailbox at the condominium originally had the name Winfield, but that name was taken off and replaced with Renfro.

In October Dave told a friend that he and Sandra had planned to get married after the baby was born but that the wedding had been postponed. In early December 1982 Sandra met with Dave's brother to purchase health insurance. She indicated on the application that she was not married. Dave paid for the insurance. Sandra filed her 1982 and 1983 income tax returns as a single person, at Dave's direction. He paid her taxes. Sandra never used the last name Winfield because Dave told her not to, and neither of them wore a wedding ring.

At Christmas 1982 Dave, Sandra, the baby, and her child from a former marriage visited Dave's family in Minnesota. Dave's mother called both children her grandchildren, and she hung a photograph of the children in her living room.

In the spring of 1983 Sandra at times traveled with Dave, but at other times that spring Dave traveled with Tonya Turner, whom he had been dating since 1981. Throughout this time Dave was seeing other women, as Sandra knew. When Sandra went to Dave's baseball games, at Dave's instruction she did not sit in the section for team members' families, and Dave and Sandra registered in hotels as Dave Winfield and Sandra Renfro. Tonya testified that Dave told her he was not married to Sandra. In the fall of 1983 a neighbor gave a party for Dave and Sandra and introduced them as Mr. and Mrs. Dave Winfield. Dave did not object or correct her.

Sandra filed for a divorce in 1988. Dave replied, alleging that they were not married. During the legal proceedings Dave ceremonially married Tonya Turner. Assuming that Texas allows common law marriage, were Sandra and Dave common law married?

2. In addition to the facts above, assume that Sandra and Dave vacationed for a month in 1983 in Pennsylvania, another state that allows common law marriage. While there, they went to a softball game, and the announcer told the crowd that Dave Winfield and his wife were in the audience. Dave introduced Sandra to a sports writer as his wife, and the writer published a story identifying them as Mr. and Mrs. Dave Winfield. If Dave and Sandra did not enter into a common law marriage in Texas, did they do so in Pennsylvania? If so, would Texas recognize it?

3. Ernest and Irene, who were both widowed and retired, participated in a wedding ceremony performed by a minister, but they did not obtain a marriage license. Irene believed that if she remarried, she would lose her pension benefits as the surviving spouse of her first husband. After the wedding, Ernest and Irene lived together, referred to themselves as husband and wife, and were generally known among their friends as spouses. They filed their income taxes as single people and did not notify the Social Security Administration or the administrators of their private pensions that they were married. Ernest has died, and Irene claims rights as his surviving widow on the theory that they had a common law marriage. Ernest's brother, who is executor of his estate, has denied her claim. What arguments should the parties make?

2. *Presumptions About Marriage and Putative Spouses*

Spearman v. Spearman

482 F.2d 1203 (5th Cir. 1973)

Roney, C.J. At the time of his death, on October 1, 1969, Edward Spearman was insured by Metropolitan Life Insurance Company under Group Policy No. 17000-G in the amount of $10,000. The policy provided that, if no beneficiary were designated, the proceeds were to be paid to the "widow" of the insured. The parties stipulated that the policy designated no beneficiary.

After Spearman's death, both defendants claimed to be his "widow" and claimed the proceeds of his life insurance policy. The first wife, Mary Spearman, is a resident of Alabama and was married to insured on October 2, 1946, in Russell County, Alabama. Two children, twin girls, were born of this marriage, and both carry the surname of Spearman. The second wife, Viva Spearman, a resident of California, married insured on June 7, 1962, in Monterey County, California. This marriage produced no offspring.

Metropolitan filed this interpleader action and paid the proceeds of the policy into the registry of the District Court. . . .

The decision in this case turns on the definition of the term "widow" as used in the life insurance policy. The policy itself does not define "widow," nor does the Federal Employees' Group Life Insurance Act provide any guidance. This question is not however, one of first impression. In Tatum v. Tatum, 241 F.2d 401 (9th Cir. 1957), the Ninth Circuit, by looking to judicial interpretations of an analogous federal statute, the National Service Life Insurance Act, 38 U.S.C.A. §701 et seq., determined that the term "widow" meant "lawful widow." . . .

California law is in accord with the general rule which provides that a second marriage cannot be validly contracted if either spouse is then married.

In a contest between conflicting marriages under California law, once the first wife presents evidence that her marriage has not been dissolved, then the burden of persuasion shifts to the second wife to establish that her spouse's marriage to his first wife had been dissolved. Otherwise, the first wife is deemed to have established her status as the lawful wife. According to the California rule, as in most states, the process of establishing which wife enjoys the status of lawful wife involves these shifting presumptions and burdens of persuasion:

1. Initially, when a person has contracted two successive marriages, a presumption arises in favor of the validity of the second marriage. Absent any contrary evidence, the second wife is deemed to be the lawful wife.

2. The presumption of validity accorded the second marriage is, however, merely a rule of evidence. It is a rebuttable presumption, the effect of which is to cast upon the first wife the burden of establishing the continuing validity of her marriage by demonstrating that it had not been dissolved by death, divorce, or annulment at the time of the second marriage.

3. California formerly required the first wife to prove that her husband had not dissolved their marriage by showing that no record of either divorce or annulment existed in any jurisdiction in which the husband may have resided. This strict burden has now been somewhat relaxed. The current rule is that, to rebut the presumption of validity inuring to the second or subsequent marriage, the first spouse need examine the records of only those jurisdictions in which either she or her husband have been in fact domiciled.

4. If the first wife shows that an examination of the pertinent records of such jurisdictions and all of the available evidence demonstrate that her marriage remains undissolved, the burden of demonstrating the invalidity of the first marriage then shifts to the party asserting its invalidity, the second wife in this case. Unless the second wife then can establish that her husband's first marriage has been dissolved, the first wife qualifies as the "lawful widow." . . .

Even if the second wife cannot qualify as the insured's "widow," she may nevertheless be entitled to one-half of the proceeds of the life insurance policy as insured's "putative spouse."

A putative spouse is one whose marriage is legally invalid but who has engaged in (1) a marriage ceremony or a solemnization, on the (2) good faith belief in the validity of the marriage. According to Estate of Foy, 109 Cal. App. 2d 329, 240 P.2d 685 (1952),

> [t]he term "putative marriage" is applied to a matrimonial union which has been solemnized in due form and good faith on the part of one or of both of the parties but which by reason of some legal infirmity is either void or voidable. The essential basis of such marriage is the belief that it is valid.

109 Cal. App. 2d at 331-332, 240 P.2d at 686.

The theory under which the "putative spouse" is entitled to recover a share of the insurance proceeds is that, as the insured's "putative spouse," she is entitled to share in the property accumulated by the family unit during its existence. The general rule, therefore, is that the "putative spouse" is entitled to the same share in this property as would have been accorded a de jure spouse under the community property laws. . . .

Applying these rules to the facts before it, the District Court first looked to the law of Alabama and concluded that Mary, the first wife, was validly married in Alabama in 1946. The subsequent marriage to Viva in 1962 in California was valid under California law, unless there was a preexisting marriage. At this point, the presumption in favor of the most recent marriage to Viva required Mary to show that her marriage had not been dissolved or annulled at the time of the insured's marriage to Viva. This showing she successfully made by establishing that no petition for annulment or divorce had been filed, by either herself or the insured, in any of their known domiciles since 1946. . . . After Mary had rebutted the presumption of validity initially attaching to Viva's marriage, the burden of persuasion shifted to Viva. This burden failed for want of proof: Viva introduced no credible evidence that either Mary or the insured had ever been a party to any legal proceeding that had annulled or dissolved their marriage. The District Court then correctly ruled that Mary had established the continuing validity of her marriage to the insured and that Viva had failed to establish otherwise.

. . . The District Court found that Viva could not qualify as the insured's "putative spouse" because she could not meet the requirement of a good faith belief in the existence of a valid marriage. . . . The evidence before the District Court showed that Viva knew (1) that the insured had fathered two children by Mary Spearman, (2) that Mary and both children carried the Spearman name, (3) that Mary had secured a support decree against the insured, (4) that the insured returned to Alabama each year on his vacation, and (5) that while on these vacations the insured lived in the same house with Mary and his two children. On these facts, the District Court's finding of an absence of good faith was amply supported. As the District Court stated in its thorough opinion, "Viva admits that she was aware of the possibility, if not the likelihood, of [insured's] prior marriage to Mary, and, yet, she took no steps to perfect her marital status."

Viva contends that the District Court's view of the "bona fide belief requirement rests upon an erroneous interpretation of the California decisions. She argues that these decisions require only that the "putative spouse" have neither actual knowledge of invalidity nor a belief that the marriage was invalid. Under Viva's view, then, so long as she did not actually know of her marriage's invalidity and maintained a belief in its validity, no matter how unreasonable that belief may have been, she qualified as the insured's "putative spouse." We decline to adopt such a test of good faith. Rather, we think that the District Court correctly held that a good faith belief in the validity of the marriage must be posited on a view of the facts known to the spouse in question. . . .

Affirmed.

NOTES AND QUESTIONS

1. *Spearman* invokes the presumption that the most recent of a series of marriages is valid. Another commonly invoked presumption that might apply on facts like these is that a marriage validly entered into continues. Both presumptions are applied in many contexts besides that of *Spearman*. Can you think of any? What factual and policy assumptions underlie these presumptions?

In *Spearman*, Viva benefitted from the presumption that the most recent marriage is valid, while the presumption that a valid marriage continues favored Mary. If both presumptions had been invoked, how should the clash between them have been resolved?

... The Supreme Court of Pennsylvania has specifically instructed courts ... to perform a balancing test by weighing the evidence in the record to determine which of two presumptions, one in favor of continuation of the first marriage and the other in favor of the validity of the second marriage, is more easily sustained by the evidence. ... In adjusting that balance, we think no mechanical rule will suffice. Instead, we think the court should consider the conduct of both parties and their respective contributions to the stability of the family each chose to support or deny in light of the value our society attributes to traditional families and evolving conditions of family life in this nation.

Huff v. Director, 40 F.3d 35, 37 (3d Cir. 1994).

2. *Spearman* allows a first spouse to satisfy the burden of proving that the marriage never ended by a search of divorce records in the state where the parties to the first marriage were domiciled because only states in which one spouse or the other was domiciled may constitutionally assert jurisdiction to divorce them. See Chapter 12. However, not all courts agree that this is sufficient. *See, e.g.,* Yarbrough v. Celebrezze, 217 F. Supp. 943 (M.D.N.C. 1963) (first wife's search of divorce records of various states without finding any divorce obtained by husband did not rebut presumption); Spears v. Spears, 12 S.W.2d 875 (Ark. 1928) (similar). What more could the party alleging the validity of the first marriage possibly do?

3. *Spearman* does not discuss what Mary knew about Edward's relationship with Viva. If evidence showed that Mary knew that Edward and Viva had lived together as spouses for the seven years before his death, should her claim be barred because of her delay in asserting that she, not Viva, was Edward's wife? *See, e.g.,* Rogers v. Office of Personnel Management, 87 F.3d 471 (Fed. Cir. 1996), applying this doctrine to prevent the first wife from asserting a claim to a survivor's annuity. The court held that the second wife was prejudiced because, had the first wife come forward while the man was still alive, the second wife could have taken steps to clarify the situation, to make other financial provision for herself, or both.

4. Applying the putative spouse doctrine, *Spearman* concluded that Viva did not in good faith believe she was married. Even taking an objective view of good faith, as the court does, are there other "reasonable" explanations for Viva's belief that she was married, knowing what she did about Edward's relationship with Mary? The California Supreme Court in Ceja v. Rudolph & Sietten, Inc., 302 P.3d 211 (Cal. 2013), held that under California law, the putative spouse doctrine requires only proof of a subjective good faith belief that the marriage was valid, disapproving of *Spearman* and a number of lower California appellate decisions that applied an objective test. Did Viva have a subjectively good faith belief that she was married?

The putative spouse doctrine derives from Spanish and French law and was first recognized in states, such as California, whose domestic relations law derived from civil law. Finding that one is a putative spouse does not necessarily give that person all the rights of a true spouse. Instead, as *Spearman* indicates, the putative spouse doctrine was originally used to provide marital property rights. For example, the Supreme Court of Nevada recently held that the putative spouse doctrine permits an award of property but not spousal support when the validity of the marriage is successfully challenged. Williams v. Williams, 97 P.3d 1124 (Nev.

2004). *Williams* reports that a majority of states recognize the doctrine in some form.

5. Section 209 of the UMDA creates a remedy for putative spouses, but, unlike the form of the doctrine used in community property states, it does not require that the parties have participated in a wedding ceremony. Xiong v. Xiong, 800 N.W.2d 187 (Minn. App. 2011), applied this section to a traditional Hmong wedding ceremony between a man and a woman who was too young to marry under state law. The two lived together and were regarded as married in the Hmong community, although they knew they were not married under state law. After the woman turned 18, she and her "husband" obtained a marriage license but did not participate in another wedding ceremony. When the couple broke up 15 years later, the court found that the woman was a putative spouse because she believed her "husband" when he told her that obtaining the license constituted a marriage under state law.

6. Both presumptions about the validity of marriage and the putative spouse rule, like common law marriage, are sufficiently indeterminate that courts can apply them flexibly to do justice in individual cases. Why might the court in *Spearman* have favored awarding the insurance proceeds to Mary, rather than to Viva?

7. Application of the presumptions about marriage validity produces a conclusion about which one of two or more marriages is valid. In contrast, the putative spouse doctrine admits of the possibility that two or more people would have spousal rights. In 2013 the South Carolina Supreme Court expressly declined to adopt the putative spouse doctrine because it is inconsistent with state policy prohibiting bigamy. Hill v. Bell, 747 S.E.2d 791 (S.C. 2013). Do you agree? As a result of this decision, Barbara Hill, who had married pro footballer player Thomas Sullivan 16 years before his death, was denied surviving spouse benefits after he died. Sullivan had earlier married Lavona Hill and was never divorced from her; she was, therefore, entitled to the benefits. Hill v. Bert Bell/Pete Rozelle NFL Player Retirement Plan, 2013 WL 6172549 (3d Cir. 2013).

PROBLEM

Irene and Bill were ceremonially married in Texas in 1956 when Irene was 17, a year younger than the minimum marriage age. They lived together until she was 22. Under Texas law their marriage was "ratified" and thus validated by their living together after she became 18. They separated in 1961 without having had children. Bill moved to Pennsylvania. In 1962 Irene filed for divorce from Bill, but the action was dismissed for lack of prosecution. There is no record of their being divorced in the counties in Texas and Pennsylvania in which each of them lived from 1961 until the present.

In 1965 Irene began living with Tom Bennett, with whom she had three children. She is named "Irene Bennett" on the children's birth certificates, even though she was never ceremonially married to Tom.

In 1967 Bill ceremonially married Ethel in Pennsylvania. On the application for the marriage license Bill said that he had never been married. He had told Ethel about his marriage to Irene but said that it had been annulled. Following the wedding ceremony, Bill and Ethel held themselves out and lived as a married couple for 15 years. They had two children. Bill, who was an employee of the federal government, recently died in an automobile accident. Both Irene and Ethel claim benefits as his surviving spouse. What arguments should each make?

C. UNMARRIED COHABITANTS

In the last 50 years unmarried cohabitation has grown from 450,000 couples in 1960 to 7.5 million in 2012. Most young adults will live with an unmarried partner at least once, and more than half of all those who marry live together first, according to the Census Bureau. While cohabitation is not as stable as marriage, it is becoming more stable. In 2013 the Centers for Disease Control reported that the median length of first cohabitation increased between 1995 and 2006 from 13 to 22 months and that 40 percent of women's first cohabitations transitioned to marriage, compared to 32 percent that remained intact or 27 percent that broke up in the first three years. Casey E. Copen et al., First Premarital Cohabitation in the United States: 2006-2010 National Survey of Family Growth 6 (National Health Statistics Reports No. 64, Apr. 4, 2013).

> CYNTHIA GRANT BOWMAN, *SOCIAL SCIENCE AND LEGAL POLICY:*
> *THE CASE OF HETEROSEXUAL COHABITATION*
> _____
>
> 9 J.L. & Fam. Stud. 1, 10-16, 18-20, 23, 31-32 (2007)

As the numbers of cohabitants have skyrocketed, the number of distinct groups from which they come has also increased, as have the types and functions of these unions. . . .

Those most likely to cohabit were persons who had not completed high school or whose families had received welfare, both indicators associated with low income. The connections among low income, low education, and cohabitation remain of continuing importance, leading some scholars to describe cohabitation as the "poor man's marriage." . . .

There are a number of reasons why this might be so. Qualitative research reveals that marriage, although much revered in lower-income communities, is seen by many as appropriate only when a couple's economic situation is secure, a situation that may not happen quickly for some groups, if ever. Interviews with working- and lower-middle-class cohabitants suggest that they believe marriage should not occur until financial stability has been reached, including not only the resources for a large wedding but perhaps also for home ownership.

The economic prospects in some communities are dire. Many Black males, for example, are very loosely connected to the workforce and subject to massive unemployment. In-depth interviews with lower-income women show that they are, not surprisingly, wary of forming permanent connections with men who are not economically productive and who may in fact draw resources away from a woman and her children. As a result, marriage rates among African Americans have fallen much more steeply than among other groups. The Centers for Disease Control (CDC) report that:

> Since 1950, the marital patterns of white and black Americans have diverged considerably. About 91 percent of white women born in the 1950s are estimated to marry at some time in their lives, compared with only 75 percent of black women born in the 1950s. . . .

Social scientists have subjected cohabitants to a great deal of scrutiny about other characteristics — their attitudes to traditional lifestyles, their religiosity, and their political orientation, for example. Although these characteristics were shown in some early studies to correlate with cohabitation behavior, the effect of these determinants has varied over time. As cohabitation has become more common and accepted by most groups within the population, these correlations have faded. . . .

Indeed, even education appears to be disappearing as a predictor of cohabitation among some groups. Brenda Wilhelm's 1998 article analyzing responses from a representative sample of 2,253 U.S. citizens born between 1943 and 1964 showed that, while having less than a high school education increased the odds of cohabitation for those in the oldest cohort, the effect of education disappeared for the youngest cohort. Another scholar working with the 1972 High School dataset found no association between cohabitation and educational attainment.

In fact, education appears to have a much more nuanced relationship to cohabitation than first assumed. There are some indications that educated and high-achieving women may prefer cohabitation, as a lifestyle that allows them to pursue careers and avoid the traditional gender division of labor associated with marriage. On the other hand, wealthier and more educated groups within our society have the highest rates of eventual marriage, which has implications for the transmission of inequality between generations.

In sum, while there are some patterns about cohabitation behavior, those patterns are made up of multiple designs; and many of them are changing with the passage of time. As a result of this demographic research, we do know that multiple and differing groups are included within the aggregate data on cohabitation in the United States, including but not limited to the following:

1. Young "dating" singles, often sharing quarters for reasons of convenience and economy;

2. Young adults cohabiting prior to marriage, either with no plans to marry or as some sort of trial marriage which may succeed or fail;

3. Working-class couples without the resources for a wedding ceremony or home ownership;

4. Low-income mothers making rational use of cohabitation to support themselves and their children;

5. Puerto Rican couples in consensual unions, often with children of the union;

6. Divorced persons either screening candidates for remarriage or seeking an alternative to marriage; and

7. Older persons cohabiting for convenience and economy or because they have no particular reason to marry.

An individual may belong to almost four in ten of these groups at different points in his or her life. There are cross-cutting categories as well — cohabitants with and without children, for example, and unions of longer and shorter duration. . . .

The duration of cohabiting unions is a topic that has attracted a great deal of attention, for a variety of reasons. Duration presumably relates to the quality of these relationships for the partners, and it clearly relates to the stability of living arrangements for any children in their household. Statistics about union length are also important to comparisons between cohabitation and marriage. . . .

The rate of instability in the United States may in fact be increasing. A 2000 article by Larry Bumpass and Hsien-Hen Lu, based on Cycle 5 of the National Survey of Family Growth (1995), found a substantial increase in the instability of cohabiting unions. The change resulted from the decreasing probability of cohabitants' marrying their cohabiting partner; marriages following cohabitation also appeared to have become less stable.

A very important point that can be missed in the aggregate data is that the stability, like the rate, of cohabitation differs by subgroups of the population. The average duration of a cohabiting union is longer, for example, for persons who have previously been married. This is also so for cohabitants who are older. CDC data show that women who are older at the start of a cohabiting union (25 or over) are less likely to experience disruption of the relationship, indicating that at least some of the divorces that statistically would have resulted from early marriage have shifted into the statistics about cohabitation instead. The probability of disruption (under the CDC definition) is also higher in communities with high unemployment: 76% of African American cohabitants in communities of high unemployment break up within ten years, as compared with 57% of non-Hispanic whites living in areas of low unemployment. In addition, the probability that a first cohabitation will transition to marriage within five years is 75% for non-Hispanic white women, 61% for Hispanic women, and 48% for African Americans. In short, if you are older, a member of the dominant racial or ethnic group, and have more money, you are more likely to make a long-term success of either cohabitation or marriage. . . .

Similarly, the generalized finding, oft repeated, that premarital cohabitation increases the rate of subsequent divorce looks different when deconstructed. The conclusion usually drawn from the correlation of cohabitation and subsequent divorce is that cohabitation, touted as a way to try out candidates for marriage, is not a very good screening mechanism. However, the correlation between cohabitation and divorce is not very significant for persons who cohabit only with the person they subsequently marry, as the vast majority do. Other studies confirm that premarital cohabitation with the subsequent spouse is not associated with a higher risk of divorce. The implication is that it is only persons who engage in multiple cohabiting relationships prior to marriage who are a bad risk. . . .

Nonetheless, cohabitation is likely to be shorter in duration on average than marriage and thus more likely to result in disruption of the household unit. Scholars have debated whether the characteristics of persons attracted to cohabitation make them break up (the selection hypothesis), whether the institution itself is inherently unstable, or whether the experience of cohabitation itself leads to instability. For all the paper spent on this debate, there is no definitive answer. . . .

The management of money within cohabiting households is also relevant to their legal treatment. Numbers of early studies concluded that cohabitants did not pool their resources the way married couples did and thus should be treated as separate individuals rather than as an economic unit. . . . More sophisticated recent studies about how cohabitants manage money within their relationships call into question these earlier generalizations and the conclusions drawn from them. It is true that cohabitants are somewhat less likely than married couples to pool their income. However, a majority of both cohabitants and married couples do maintain joint finances. . . .

. . . Bumpass, Sweet, and Cherlin reported that four out of every ten cohabiting couples had children present. . . . The 1990 Census confirmed this 40% figure, comparing it with 46% of married-couple households that include children under 18. . . . In the 2000 Census, these figures had increased to 4.1 million children, or 6.3%. About half of these children are the biological children of the cohabitants, and about half are the children of one of the cohabitants, typically of the woman. . . .

. . . The numbers differ dramatically by race and ethnic group: 8% of Puerto Rican children, 5% of Mexican American and Black children, and 3% of non-Hispanic white children live in cohabiting families. As noted above, cohabitation often has economic benefits for these children, though this of course varies with the resources of the adult partners. But a cohabitant's contribution could be very important to the 25% of children in cohabiting families whose mothers were receiving public assistance. Puerto Rican children born into informal unions appear to benefit the most, with a gain of 51% over the resources that would be available to them in a single-female-parent family. . . .

Traditionally, if a couple lived together without being ceremonially married and were not eligible for or did not satisfy the requirements for a common law marriage or the putative spouse doctrine, their relationship was "meretricious," a word derived from the Latin for "prostitute." Legally, they were at best roommates and at worst outlaws. However, with the dramatic rise in open nonmarital cohabitation, the law has changed. The first part of this section considers judicially created remedies, based on contract and equitable principles, that give the parties some rights against each other. The second part examines statutes and case law solutions recognizing new status relationships between unmarried cohabitants that give them rights and duties between one another, in relation to third parties, or both.

1. *Contractual and Equitable Remedies*

MARVIN V. MARVIN[3]

557 P.2d 106 (Cal. 1976)

TOBRINER, J. Plaintiff avers that in October of 1964 she and defendant "entered into an oral agreement" that while "the parties lived together they

---

3. While actor Lee Marvin and Michelle Triola Marvin lived together, he won an Oscar for *Cat Ballou* in 1965 and starred in other films, including *The Dirty Dozen* in 1967 and *Paint Your Wagon* in 1969. — Ed.

would combine their efforts and earnings and would share equally any and all property accumulated as a result of their efforts whether individual or combined." Furthermore, they agreed to "hold themselves out to the general public as husband and wife" and that "plaintiff would further render her services as a companion, homemaker, housekeeper and cook to . . . defendant."

Shortly thereafter plaintiff agreed to "give up her lucrative career as an entertainer (and) singer" in order to "devote her full time to defendant . . . as a companion, homemaker, housekeeper and cook"; in return defendant agreed to "provide for all of plaintiff's financial support and needs for the rest of her life."

Plaintiff alleges that she lived with defendant from October of 1964 through May of 1970 and fulfilled her obligations under the agreement. During this period the parties as a result of their efforts and earnings acquired in defendant's name substantial real and personal property, including motion picture rights worth over $1 million. In May of 1970, however, defendant compelled plaintiff to leave his household. He continued to support plaintiff until November of 1971, but thereafter refused to provide further support.

On the basis of these allegations plaintiff asserts two causes of action. The first, for declaratory relief, asks the court to determine her contract and property rights; the second seeks to impose a constructive trust upon one half of the property acquired during the course of the relationship.

Defendant demurred unsuccessfully, and then answered the complaint. Following extensive discovery and pretrial proceedings, the case came to trial. Defendant renewed his attack on the complaint by a motion to dismiss. Since the parties had stipulated that defendant's marriage to Betty Marvin did not terminate until the filing of a final decree of divorce in January 1967, the trial court treated defendant's motion as one for judgment on the pleadings augmented by the stipulation.

After hearing argument the court granted defendant's motion and entered judgment for defendant. Plaintiff . . . appealed from the judgment.

2. PLAINTIFF'S COMPLAINT STATES A CAUSE OF ACTION FOR BREACH OF AN EXPRESS CONTRACT . . .

. . . Defendant first and principally relies on the contention that the alleged contract is so closely related to the supposed "immoral" character of the relationship between plaintiff and himself that the enforcement of the contract would violate public policy. . . .

Although the past decisions hover over the issue in the somewhat wispy form of the figures of a Chagall painting, we can abstract from those decisions a clear and simple rule. . . . The fact that a man and woman live together without marriage, and engage in a sexual relationship, does not in itself invalidate agreements between them relating to their earnings, property, or expenses. Neither is such an agreement invalid merely because the parties may have contemplated the creation or continuation of a nonmarital relationship when they entered into it. Agreements between nonmarital partners fail only to the extent that they rest upon a consideration of meretricious sexual services. Thus the rule asserted by defendant, that a contract fails if it is "involved in" or made "in contemplation" of a nonmarital relationship, cannot be reconciled with the decisions. . . .

3. PLAINTIFF'S COMPLAINT CAN BE AMENDED TO STATE A CAUSE OF ACTION FOUNDED UPON THEORIES OF IMPLIED CONTRACT OR EQUITABLE RELIEF

. . . We are aware that many young couples live together without the solemnization of marriage, in order to make sure that they can successfully later undertake marriage. This trial period preliminary to marriage, serves as some assurance that the marriage will not subsequently end in dissolution to the harm of both parties. We are aware, as we have stated, of the pervasiveness of nonmarital relationships in other situations.

The mores of the society have indeed changed so radically in regard to cohabitation that we cannot impose a standard based on alleged moral considerations that have apparently been so widely abandoned by so many. Lest we be misunderstood, however, we take this occasion to point out that the structure of society itself largely depends upon the institution of marriage, and nothing we have said in this opinion should be taken to derogate from that institution. The joining of the man and woman in marriage is at once the most socially productive and individually fulfilling relationship that one can enjoy in the course of a lifetime.

We conclude that the judicial barriers that may stand in the way of a policy based upon the fulfillment of the reasonable expectations of the parties to a nonmarital relationship should be removed. As we have explained, the courts now hold that express agreements will be enforced unless they rest on an unlawful meretricious consideration. We add that in the absence of an express agreement, the courts may look to a variety of other remedies in order to protect the parties' lawful expectations.[4]

The courts may inquire into the conduct of the parties to determine whether that conduct demonstrates an implied contract or implied agreement of partnership or joint venture, or some other tacit understanding between the parties. The courts may, when appropriate, employ principles of constructive trust or resulting trust. Finally, a nonmarital partner may recover in *quantum meruit* for the reasonable value of household services rendered less the reasonable value of support received if he can show that he rendered services with the expectation of monetary reward.

Since we have determined that plaintiff's complaint states a cause of action for breach of an express contract, and, as we have explained, can be amended to state a cause of action independent of allegations of express contract, we must conclude that the trial court erred in granting defendant a judgment on the pleadings.

---

4. We do not seek to resurrect the doctrine of common law marriage, which was abolished in California by statute in 1895. (*See* Norman v. Thomson (1898) 121 Cal. 620, 628, 54 P. 143; Estate of Abate (1958) 166 Cal. App. 2d 282, 292, 333 P.2d 200.) Thus we do not hold that plaintiff and defendant were "married," nor do we extend to plaintiff the rights which the Family Law Act grants valid or putative spouses; we hold only that she has the same rights to enforce contracts and to assert her equitable interest in property acquired through her effort as does any other unmarried person.

The judgment is reversed and the cause remanded for further proceedings consistent with the views expressed herein.

(The concurring and dissenting opinion of Justice Clark is omitted.)

NOTES AND QUESTIONS

1. Could Michelle Marvin have argued that she had a common law marriage? Could she have argued that she was a putative spouse? Was her understanding of her situation significantly different from that of Sally Winegard or Viva Spearman?

If the Marvins had been married, could Michelle have enforced a contract such as that alleged in this case? Why or why not? Does enforcing express agreements between cohabitants give them greater freedom to determine their relationship than married people have?

2. What aspects of relationships such as these are purely economic? In what sense are they severable from the romantic and sexual aspects of the relationship?

3. Courts in at least 26 states and the District of Columbia allow cohabitants to make relational contract claims against each other when the relationship ends, at least in principle. Marsha Garrison, Nonmarital Cohabitation: Social Revolution and Legal Regulation, 42 Fam. L.Q. 309, 315-316 (2008). In three states, statutes require that cohabitants' contracts be in writing to be enforceable. Minn. Stat. §§ 513.075, 513.076 (2014); N.J. Stat. § 25:1-5(h) (2014); Tex. Fam. Code § 1.108 (2014). In addition, in Posik v. Layton, 695 So. 2d 759 (Fla. App. 1997), the court said that an agreement for support between cohabitants is subject to the statute of frauds writing requirement. The New Jersey statute was enacted in 2010 to overturn several judicial decisions liberally interpreting relational contract claims. Maeker v. Ross, 62 A.3d 310 (N.J. Super. 2013) (quoting and discussing legislative history). Besides a writing, it requires that both parties have the advice of counsel before an agreement is enforceable.

4. Courts in Illinois, Georgia, and Louisiana have refused to grant remedies to cohabitants based on relational contracts. Hewitt v. Hewitt, 394 N.E.2d 1204 (Ill. 1979) (reprinted in Chapter 1 at page 13); Rehak v. Mathis, 238 S.E.2d 81 (Ga. 1977); Schwegmann v. Schwegmann, 441 So. 2d 316 (La. App. 1983). Even in these states, though, courts will enforce contracts between cohabitants that the court finds are not founded on the sexual aspects of a relationship. See, e.g., Abrams v. Massell, 586 S.E.2d 435 (Ga. App. 2004) (enforcing contract to make a will for $400,000 at death of first cohabitant).

5. Application of the contract theories varies from state to state. For example, California courts generally interpret the requirements strictly, as illustrated by the outcome of *Marvin* itself. On remand the trial court found no express or implied contract to share property between Lee and Michelle. The court also found that Michelle was not entitled to an equitable trust or a quantum meruit award because she "suffered no damage resulting from her relationship with defendant, including its termination and thus [Lee] did not become monetarily liable to plaintiff at all," that she "actually benefited economically and socially from the cohabitation of the parties," that "a confidential and fiduciary relationship never existed between the parties with respect to property," that Lee "was never unjustly enriched as a result of the relationship of the parties or of the services performed by plaintiff for him or

for them," and that Lee "never acquired any property or money from plaintiff by any wrongful act." Nevertheless, the trial court ordered Lee to pay Michelle $104,000 as rehabilitative support to enable her to get back on her feet. The court relied on footnotes in the supreme court opinion implying that remedies other than those that the court had specifically endorsed might be available on the right facts. 557 P.2d 106, 123, nn.25, 26. The Court of Appeals reversed, saying, "The difficulty in applying either of these footnotes in the manner in which the trial court has done in this case is that . . . there is nothing in the trial court's findings to suggest that such an award is warranted *to protect the expectations of both parties*" (emphasis added). Marvin v. Marvin, 176 Cal. Rptr. 555 (Cal. App. 1981).

In contrast, Alaska courts infer contracts to share "the fruits of the relationship" from parties' commingling their finances to a significant extent. *See, e.g.,* Reed v. Parrish, 286 P.3d 1054 (Alaska 2012) (finding such a contract where parties lived together as a family for 12 years even though they had no joint bank account, did not file joint taxes, and had no joint business venture). *See also* Shuraleff v. Donnelly, 817 P.2d 764, 769 (Or. App. 1991); Wilbur v. DeLapp, 850 P.2d 1151 (Or. App. 1993); Kozlowski v. Kozlowski, 403 A.2d 902 (N.J. 1979); Roccamonte v. Roccamonte, 808 A.2d 838 (N.J. 2002). The last two cases are among those that prompted the New Jersey writing requirement statute discussed above.

6. Where cohabitants have operated a business together outside the home, courts are generally willing to apply partnership principles to determine ownership of the business when the relationship ends. For example, in Bass v. Bass, 814 S.W.2d 38 (Tenn. 1991), a man and woman worked long hours for a number of years in businesses titled in his name. The woman was never paid for her work. When he died, she successfully claimed ownership of half of the business. Similarly, in In re Estate of Thornton, 499 P.2d 864 (Wash. 1972), a man and woman were treated as business partners where they ran a cattle operation together for many years. The administrator of the man's estate argued that the woman was not entitled to compensation because of the familial context. Can a cohabitant make a claim on this theory if she is paid for her work in the business? If she is not an equal manager? *See* Harman v. Rogers, 510 A.2d 161 (Vt. 1986), rejecting a cohabitant's partnership claim under these circumstances.

CATES V. SWAIN

____ So. 3d ____, 2013 WL 1831783 (Miss. 2013) (en banc)

CHANDLER, Justice, for the Court. . . . In 2000, [Elizabeth] Swain and [Mona] Cates met though an online dating service and began a relationship while living in different states. Swain was in the Navy and worked as an oceanographer, and Cates was a commercial airline pilot based in New York, New York, where she maintained a separate residence. During the entirety of her relationship with Cates, Swain was married and estranged from her husband. Swain testified that she remained married so that her husband could remain covered under her medical insurance policy, and so that Swain could claim a larger housing allowance from the Navy than she would have been entitled to as a single individual. Swain divorced after her relationship with Cates had ended.

In late 2000, Swain transferred to Pensacola, Florida, and bought a house there. Cates provided $2,000 in earnest money toward the purchase of the house, residing there and in New York. Swain made the monthly mortgage payments and significantly paid down the principal. The two made improvements to the house.

In 2003, Swain and Cates moved to Seattle, Washington. Cates bought a home in Seattle, where the two cohabitated. Swain sold the Florida home and received $32,000 in equity. Swain testified that she gave Cates a check for $34,000, representing the equity in the Florida home, plus an extra $2,000 from Swain's personal checking account as an investment. Swain testified that Cates used this money for the down payment on the Washington home, which Cates purchased for $191,000. In contrast, Cates testified that the check was repayment for undocumented loans. Swain and Cates made various improvements to the Washington home, and in 2005 the residence sold for $300,000.

In 2005, Cates and Swain moved to Tate County, Mississippi, where Cates bought a home for $350,000, using the equity from the sale of the Washington home. Swain provided Cates a check for $5,000 with "closing costs" written in the memo line. She also paid $4,495 to carpet the home. Again, Cates characterized these expenditures as repayments for undocumented loans to Swain.

Subsequently, the parties' relationship deteriorated, and Swain moved out in March 2006. On June 13, 2006, Swain filed a complaint against Cates, alleging that they had been cohabitants, that they had been involved in several joint ventures together, and that they had entered into an agreement for Swain to invest the proceeds from the sale of her Florida home into future purchases of real property in Washington and Mississippi. Swain requested that the chancery court declare a constructive trust or a resulting trust in the Mississippi home, and that Cates had been unjustly enriched.

The chancellor rejected Swain's claims of a constructive trust or a resulting trust. The chancellor found that Cates had been unjustly enriched by Swain's investment contributions. The chancellor rejected Cates's unsupported assertions that these contributions were merely loan repayments. The chancellor found Swain was entitled to recover the equity from her Florida home. . . . The chancellor also found that Swain was entitled to recover the $5,000 she had tendered to Cates for closing costs on the Mississippi home and the $4,495 she had spent to carpet Cates's Mississippi home. . . .

. . . The Court of Appeals reviewed our prior cases pertaining to unmarried cohabitants, and concluded that "Mississippi does not enforce contracts implied from the relationship of unmarried cohabitants." Therefore, the Court of Appeals held that the chancellor had lacked the authority to grant the remedy of unjust enrichment. This Court granted Swain's petition for certiorari to review the legal question of whether the remedy of unjust enrichment was available to Swain. We find that, in the particular circumstances, the chancellor did not err by granting relief on the basis of unjust enrichment. . . .

Unjust enrichment "applies to situations where there is no legal contract and 'the person sought to be charged is in possession of money or property which in good conscience and justice he should not retain but should deliver to another.'" In these circumstances, equity imposes "a duty to refund the money or the use value of the property to the person to whom in good conscience it ought to belong." The amount of recovery for unjust enrichment is "that to which the claimant is equitably entitled."

The chancellor found that Cates had been unjustly enriched by Swain's contributions to the Mississippi home, which consisted of Swain's proceeds gained from the sale of her Florida home, the $5,000 Swain contributed at closing, and the $4,495 Swain had paid to carpet the Mississippi home. The Court of Appeals concluded that the remedy of unjust enrichment was not available to Swain as an unmarried cohabitant. The Court of Appeals primarily relied upon Davis v. Davis, 643 So. 2d 931 (Miss. 1994), and Estate of Alexander v. Alexander, 445 So. 2d 836 (Miss. 1984), to reach this conclusion.

We find *Davis* and *Alexander* to be distinguishable from this case. In *Davis*, the unmarried parties separated, and the woman, Elvis Davis, sought an equitable distribution of assets. Travis Davis had amassed considerable wealth, and Elvis argued that, by virtue of *her* efforts in her live-in, long-term *relationship* with Travis, she was entitled to an equitable division of assets. The Court disagreed, noting that the Legislature has not extended the rights enjoyed by married people to those who cohabit.

In Estate of Alexander v. Alexander, 445 So. 2d 836 (Miss. 1984), Margie and Sam Alexander had cohabitated for thirty years in a house owned by Sam. When Sam died, Margie petitioned the court for a life estate in the residence. The Court found that the Legislature had made no provision for a person in Margie's situation, and that "a mere 'live-in' relationship . . . cannot be allowed to negate the law of descent and distribution." The Court also found that Margie could not recover under an implied-contract theory because no evidence established the existence of an implied contract between Margie and Sam.

In both *Davis* and *Alexander*, the aggrieved party's claim for recovery was based upon a relationship. Both claims were for equitable division of property. In *Davis*, the Court rightly noted that cohabitation is prohibited as against public policy and that the Legislature has not extended the rights of married persons to cohabitants, nor do we today. In this case, Swain's claim was not one for equitable division. Swain made a claim, *inter alia*, for unjust enrichment based upon her monetary contributions to Cates's purchase of the Washington home and the purchase and improvement of the Mississippi home, which Cates retained after Swain moved from the residence. Ultimately, the chancellor adjudicated the case on that theory of relief, and we find no error in the chancellor's legal conclusion.

True, as Presiding Justice Dickinson indicates in his separate opinion, Swain's unjust-enrichment claim was predicated on her assertion that Swain and Cates had entered into an agreement that Swain would invest the proceeds from the sale of her Florida home toward future home purchases. Thus, as Swain contended at trial, she should be entitled to share in the profits Cates earned from the use of Swain's money.

Swain claimed there was a mutual agreement between her and Cates that her Florida equity proceeds were to be used as an investment in both the Washington and Mississippi homes but offered no written evidence to support her testimony. Cates, who disputed Swain's version, claimed that she considered the funds provided by Swain to be reimbursement money for all the "loans" she had provided Swain, but she offered no written evidence to support her testimony. The only proof offered by either party for her claims was her respective testimony. The chancellor, essentially, accepted neither version. We find no abuse of discretion.

Instead, the chancellor focused on readily identifiable assets (or tangible benefits) each party conferred on the other, which, if retained by that party, would, under the circumstances, inequitably benefit (or unjustly enrich) that party. In essence, these particular benefits spoke for themselves, irrespective of how the parties attempted to characterize them after the fact at trial. The chancellor declined to treat these benefits as either investments or gratuitous gifts, as the Court of Appeals mistakenly construed our caselaw to require. Rather, the chancellor sought, as much as the evidence would allow, to restore the status quo and return the parties to the positions they had occupied before the transaction(s). This Court has held that an unjust-enrichment award may consist of a refund, if that is equitable. . . .

. . . We are mindful that the doctrine of unjust enrichment is not "a roving mandate [for a court] to sort through terminated personal relationships in an attempt to nicely judge and balance the respective contributions of the parties." The chancellor astutely recognized that Swain's unjust enrichment claim did not request that the court undertake such a momentous task. We find that the chancellor did not err in granting Swain recovery under the theory of unjust enrichment.

We affirm the judgment of the Court of Appeals to the extent that it affirmed the chancellor's rejection of the constructive trust or resulting trust claim [and] reverse the judgment of the Court of Appeals regarding the unjust-enrichment award. . . .

[The opinion of Justice Dickinson concurring and dissenting is omitted.]

NOTES AND QUESTIONS

1. Elizabeth Swain claimed a share of the Mississippi property based on constructive trust and resulting trust theories, but, as the Mississippi Court of Appeals explained, she did not prove fraud or the equivalent, which is necessary for a constructive trust in Mississippi, nor that she had purchased the property in Cates's name with the intent to retain beneficial ownership, the basis for a resulting trust. Cates v. Swain, 116 So. 3d 1073 (Miss. App. 2012).

If the house purchased in Washington had been titled in the names of both Swain and Cates, would Cates have had a right to the beneficial interest on a resulting trust theory? Or should it be presumed that she intended that each would own half the house? *Compare* Hofstad v. Christie, 240 P.3d 816 (Wyo. 2010) (man who titled house he purchased jointly with cohabitant was in a family relationship and made a gift of half the value), with Jones v. Graphia, 95 So. 3d 751 (Miss. App. 2012) (on similar facts, rejecting presumption of gift and upholding order giving entire value to man because woman did not contribute to acquisition of property).

2. What made it "unjust" for Cates to retain all of the Mississippi property? Why wasn't it "unjust" for her to retain the increase in value of the properties in Washington and Mississippi rather than sharing it with Swain?

3. *Cates* is consistent with § 28(1) of the Restatement (Third) of Restitution and Unjust Enrichment (2011), which provides:

> If two persons have formerly lived together in a relationship resembling marriage, and if one of them owns a specific asset to which the other has made substantial, uncompensated contributions in the form of property or services, the person making contributions has a claim in restitution against the owner as necessary to prevent unjust enrichment upon the dissolution of the relationship.

Critics of this provision argue that it undermines the goal of rationalizing and taming the field of restitution. *See, e.g.,* Emily Sherwin, Love, Money, and Justice: Restitution Between Cohabitants, 77 U. Colo. L. Rev. 711 (2006). They favor the traditional limits on the remedy, which include: (1) restitution is not available if the claimant intended to make a gift or transferred property under a valid contract, and (2) restitution is not available if the claimant could reasonably have negotiated a payment for the benefit conferred but failed to do so. *Id.* at 724. Those who favor the Restatement view respond that people in intimate relationships should not be expected to protect themselves by arm's-length negotiation. Candace Saari Kovacic-Fleischer, Cohabitation and the Restatement (Third) of Restitution and Unjust Enrichment, 68 Wash. & Lee L. Rev. 1407 (2011). Some courts that do not use this broad unjust enrichment doctrine still apply constructive trust and resulting trust theories to cohabitants. *See, e.g.,* Porter v. Zuromski, 6 A.3d 372 (Md. App. 2010).

4. The states are divided about extending equitable remedies to cohabitants. Among the cases allowing such relief are Boland v. Catalano, 521 A.2d 142 (Conn. 1987); Suggs v. Norris, 364 S.E.2d 159 (N.C. App. 1988); Carol v. Lee, 712 P.2d 923 (Ariz. 1986); Muchesko v. Muchesko, 955 P.2d 21, 24 (Ariz. 1997); and Watts v. Watts, 405 N.W.2d 303 (Wis. 1987). Among the courts that reject this extension are Tapley v. Tapley, 449 A.2d 1218 (N.H. 1982); Carnes v. Sheldon, 311 N.W.2d 747 (Mich. App. 1981); Morone v. Morone, 413 N.E.2d 1154 (N.Y. 1980); Pizzo v. Goor, 857 N.Y.S.2d 526 (App. Div. 2008) (affirming that New York does not recognize as enforceable any claim between cohabitants that is based on one party's providing companionship, platonic or sexual, to the other). For case law throughout the country, *see* George L. Blum, Property Rights Arising from Relationship of Couple Cohabiting Without Marriage, 69 A.L.R.5th 219 (1999 with weekly updates).

5. To prevail on a claim for equitable relief, based on having worked for one's cohabitant, a claimant must prove that the work was not done gratuitously. If the claimant kept the house, cared for the children, and did other kinds of domestic work, should a court presume that the work was gratuitous? What if one cohabitant works in the other's start-up business, with the understanding that neither will be able to take out money unless and until the business becomes successful? For a case denying recovery on such facts on the theory that the woman did not prove that she expected to be paid for her work, *see* Featherston v. Steinhoff, 575 N.W.2d 6 (Mich. App. 1997).

6. Are cohabitants in a confidential relationship with each other, so that fiduciary duties arise between them? If so, what are the legal consequences of such a finding? Williams v. Lynch, 666 N.Y.S.2d 749 (App. Div. 1997), held that the plaintiff's evidence was sufficient to support a finding that the parties' relationship was analogous to that of husband and wife and that as a result "plaintiff

reasonably trusted defendant and relied on him to protect her interests." *Id.* at 751. On the other hand, Maglica v. Maglica, 78 Cal. Rptr. 2d 101 (Cal. App. 1998), held that, although the parties' relationship was like a common law marriage, fiduciary duties do not arise from that relationship alone because to impose them would amount to judicial reinstatement of common law marriage. Unless one party entrusts property to the other, no fiduciary relationship arises, the court said. *See also* Wilcox v. Trautz, 693 N.E.2d 141 (Mass. 1998) (agreement between cohabitants is not governed by the requirements applicable to premarital agreements, including that the terms be fair and reasonable; instead, ordinary rules of contract law apply).

7. The variety in the states' approaches to the rights and duties of cohabitants presents complex choice-of-law problems. For example, if a couple enters into a cohabiting relationship in California and moves to another state that does not recognize equitable remedies before the relationship ends, which state's law applies? Professor William A. Reppy, Jr., who has written extensively on choice-of-law issues when a marriage ends by death or divorce, addresses the choice-of-law problems attendant to cohabitation in Choice of Law Problems Arising When Unmarried Cohabitants Change Domicile, 55 SMU L. Rev. 273 (2002).

PROBLEMS

1. Harry and Margaret engaged in an intimate relationship for seven years but never actually lived together. He was an executive, she an actress. At the end of the relationship she sued, claiming that he expressly promised to support her in return for her acting as his hostess and companion. He defended on the basis that they had never lived together. Is cohabitation necessary under *Marvin*?

What if Harry and Margaret had lived together for four days a week over a long period but Harry maintained a separate dwelling?

2. Fifteen years ago Wendy, who was single, and Max, who was separated but not divorced from his wife, began living together. At the time both worked for Large Construction Co., he as a machine operator and she as a bookkeeper. Within a few months they decided to start an equipment rental business, W & M Rentals. Max provided the start-up money from his savings and maintained the equipment, and Wendy kept the books and managed the rental end. The business license was issued in Wendy's name alone, in the hopes that this would keep Max's wife from having a claim to the business. Max continued to work for Large Construction Co. and worked at W & M nights and on weekends.

After three years W & M had become quite successful, and Max had grown tired of working for Large. He and Wendy agreed that he would quit to work only for W & M and that W & M would expand into the construction business. As the business grew larger and more successful, it demanded more sophisticated accounting than Wendy could provide. She was becoming increasingly busy with volunteer work and entertaining business clients, so eight years ago she quit working for W & M and since then has devoted herself to these other endeavors. Since that time all of the assets of the business have been titled in Max's name. He told Wendy that it was too inconvenient to have her name on anything because she was never in the office.

Five years ago Max's wife died. Wendy and Max discussed getting formally married but never went through with the plans, in part because a number of their business and social acquaintances assumed that they were already married. Wendy has, however, always used her birth surname, and she and Max have never filed a joint income tax return. They have joint bank accounts and charge accounts and own their residence as joint tenants with right of survivorship. They have no children.

Wendy and Max's state recognizes common law marriage, the putative spouse doctrine, and all the *Marvin* remedies, and uses usual business partnership law.

If Wendy becomes ill and is provided emergency medical services, on what theory or theories can the hospital recover the costs of her care from Max? If Max and Wendy are domiciled in a common law property state, on what theory or theories may Wendy claim some or all of the assets of W & M?

2. An Alternative Status?

As described in Chapter 3, a number of European countries enacted legislation creating registered partnerships that give some or, in some cases, all of the rights of marriage, as have several states in the United States. The political impetus for much of this legislation was to allow same-sex couples to enter a relationship that give the family rights, and in a number of jurisdictions only same-sex couples may register as partners. However, registered partnerships are open to opposite-sex couples as well in at least three European countries: the Netherlands, Belgium, and France. In these countries couples have the choice between marriage and registered partnerships, and in both France and the Netherlands the great majority of registered partners are opposite-sex couples. Opposite-sex couples in France often choose a PACS rather than marriage because it offers tax and inheritance advantages while being associated socially and politically with free unions. Edward Cody, Straight Couples in France Are Choosing Civil Unions Meant for Gays, Wash. Post, Feb. 14, 2009.

Most of the civil union and domestic partnership laws in the United States are limited to opposite-sex couples, as we have seen. However, the Hawaii legislation enacted in response to the state supreme court decision favoring gay marriage is quite different.

HAWAII RECIPROCAL BENEFICIARIES LEGISLATION, H.B. 118 (1997), CODIFIED AS HAW. REV. STAT. CH. 572C AND IN OTHER SCATTERED SECTIONS OF THE CODE

Section 572C-4 Requisites of a valid reciprocal beneficiary relationship. In order to enter into a valid reciprocal beneficiary relationship, it shall be necessary that:

(1) Each of the parties be at least eighteen years old;

(2) Neither of the parties be married nor a party to another reciprocal beneficiary relationship;

(3) The parties be legally prohibited from marrying one another under chapter 572;

(4) Consent of either party to the reciprocal beneficiary relationship has not been obtained by force, duress, or fraud; and

(5) Each of the parties sign a declaration of reciprocal beneficiary relationship as provided in section -5.

Section 572C-5 Registration as reciprocal beneficiaries; filing fees; records.

(a) Two persons, who meet the criteria set out in section -4, may enter into a reciprocal beneficiary relationship and register their relationship as reciprocal beneficiaries by filing a signed notarized declaration of reciprocal beneficiary relationship with the director. For the filing of the declaration, the director shall collect a fee of $8, which shall be remitted to the director of finance for deposit into the general fund.

(b) Upon the payment of the fee, the director shall register the declaration and provide a certificate of reciprocal beneficiary relationship to each party named on the declaration. The director shall maintain a record of each declaration of reciprocal beneficiary relationship filed with or issued by the director.

Section 572C-6 Rights and obligations. Upon the issuance of a certificate of reciprocal beneficiary relationship, the parties named in the certificate shall be entitled to those rights and obligations provided by the law to reciprocal beneficiaries. Unless otherwise expressly provided by law, reciprocal beneficiaries shall not have the same rights and obligations under the law that are conferred through marriage under chapter 572.

Section 572C-7 Termination of reciprocal beneficiary relationship; filing fees and records; termination upon marriage.

(a) Either party to a reciprocal beneficiary relationship may terminate the relationship by filing a signed notarized declaration of termination of reciprocal beneficiary relationship by either of the reciprocal beneficiaries with the director. For the filing of the declaration, the director shall collect a fee of $8, which shall be remitted to the director of finance for deposit into the general fund.

(b) Upon the payment of the fee, the director shall file the declaration and issue a certificate of termination of reciprocal beneficiary relationship to each party of the former relationship. The director shall maintain a record of each declaration and certificate of termination of reciprocal beneficiary relationship filed with or issued by the director.

(c) Any marriage license subsequently issued by the department to any individual registered as a reciprocal beneficiary shall automatically terminate the individual's existing reciprocal beneficiary relationship.

(d) If either party to a reciprocal beneficiary relationship enters into a legal marriage, the parties shall no longer have a reciprocal beneficiary relationship and shall no longer be entitled to the rights and benefits of reciprocal beneficiaries.

NOTES AND QUESTIONS

1. Who is eligible to enter into a reciprocal beneficiary relationship in Hawaii? What explains these limitations?

2. The main purpose of the Hawaii reciprocal beneficiaries law was to extend to registrants rights against third parties similar to those that spouses have. *See* Haw. Rev. Stat. §572C-2. For example, the law provides that reciprocal

beneficiaries may be covered by health insurance, have hospital visitation and health care decision-making rights, have the same rights as a spouse in a decedent's estate, and may sue for wrongful death of a partner. *See* Haw. H.B. 118 (1997). The legislation does not address the economic rights of the parties vis-à-vis each other. How might registering affect those rights?

3. How does a couple enter and exit a reciprocal beneficiary relationship? Why are these processes so different from those for marriage?

4. According to the Hawaii State Department of Health, as of January 2009, 1,577 individuals were registered as reciprocal beneficiaries in Hawaii. There had been 188 terminations. Vermont enacted reciprocal beneficiary legislation at the same time it adopted its civil union law. Vt. Stat. Ann. §§ 1301 et seq. However, in 2001 the Vermont Civil Union Review Commission reported that no relationships had been registered with the state office of vital statistics. Report of the Vermont Civil Union Review Commission, Finding 2 (2001).

5. California legislation allows same-sex couples to register as domestic partners and receive virtually all the rights and responsibilities of a married couple available under state law. Opposite-sex couples in which at least one partner is 62 years or older may also register. Cal. Fam. Code § 297(2)(4)(B) (2013). The litigation resulting in extension of the right to marry to California same-sex couples did not change the California legislation on domestic partnerships. California Secretary of State, Domestic Partners Registry, available at www.sos.ca.gov/dpregistry (last accessed October 2013). What might be the reason for this limitation? In contrast, the District of Columbia domestic partnership is open to both same-sex and opposite-sex couples, so long as the parties are at least 18. D.C. Stat. § 32-701(3) (2013).

6. Commentary exploring options for legal recognition of relationships other than marriage includes David L. Chambers, For the Best of Friends and for Lovers of All Sorts, a Status Other Than Marriage, 76 Notre Dame L. Rev. 1347 (2001); Nancy D. Polikoff, Ending Marriage as We Know It, 32 Hofstra L. Rev. 201 (2003); Laura A. Rosenbury, Friends with Benefits?, 106 Mich. L. Rev. 189 (2007); Elizabeth F. Emens, Regulatory Fictions: On Marriage and Countermarriage, 99 Cal. L. Rev. 235 (2011); William N. Eskridge Jr., Family Law Pluralism: The Guided-Choice Regime of Menus, Default Rules, and Override Rules, 100 Geo. L.J. 1881 (2012). *See also* Law Comm'n of Canada, Beyond Conjugality: Recognizing and Supporting Close Personal Adult Relationships (2001).

7. A number of local communities have enacted domestic partner registration ordinances, usually for the purpose of extending benefits to the domestic partners of municipal employees, permitting partners to obtain public recognition of their relationships by registration, or both. The Human Rights Campaign maintains a current list of city and county registries at http://www.hrc.org/resources/entry/city-and-county-domestic-partner-registries.

8. According to Grace Ganz Blumberg, The Regularization of Nonmarital Cohabitation: Rights and Responsibilities in the American Welfare State, 76 Notre Dame L. Rev. 1265, 1282-1283 (2001):

> Independently of any legislation or court action, and for that reason generally less observed, American employers have increasingly been treating nonmarital cohabitants equally with married persons for purposes of employee benefits. The trend is particularly pronounced with large corporations. The significance of this development lies in the central role that employment benefits play in the American welfare

system. By welfare system, I mean not merely "welfare" in the popular sense (public assistance), but rather the entire structure of rights and obligations that secure the welfare of individuals and families in the United States.

After World War II, while other countries were establishing national health systems, American employers increasingly provided health insurance as an employment benefit for workers and their families. Although this approach has been supplemented by relatively limited public provisions for low-income families and the aged, employment has persisted as the dominant source of health coverage, and employment benefits have frequently been expanded to include the full panoply of benefits usually associated with a highly developed welfare state.

When the ALI Principles of the Law of Family Dissolution project turned to the topic of unmarried cohabitants' rights, the *Marvin* line of cases and European statutes creating registered domestic partnerships were available as models. The drafters rejected these approaches and proposed a solution inspired by the law of Canada, Australia, and New Zealand and case law from Washington and Oregon. Principles of the Law of Family Dissolution: Analysis and Recommendations, Chapter 1: Introductory Materials, Topic 1: Summary Overview of the Remaining Chapters. Following is the leading Washington case.

CONNELL V. FRANCISCO

898 P.2d 831 (Wash. 1995) (en banc)

GUY, Justice. Petitioner Richard Francisco and Respondent Shannon Connell met in Toronto, Canada, in June 1983. Connell was a dancer in a stage show produced by Francisco. She resided in New York, New York. She owned clothing and a leasehold interest in a New York apartment. Francisco resided in Las Vegas, Nevada. He owned personal property, real property, and several companies, including Prince Productions, Inc. and Las Vegas Talent, Ltd., which produced stage shows for hotels. Francisco's net worth was approximately $1,300,000 in February 1984.

Connell, at Francisco's invitation, moved to Las Vegas in November 1983. They cohabited in Francisco's Las Vegas home from November 1983 to June 1986. While living in Las Vegas, Connell worked as a paid dancer in several stage shows. She also assisted Francisco as needed with his various business enterprises. Francisco managed his companies and produced several profitable stage shows.

In November 1985, Prince Productions, Inc. purchased a bed and breakfast, the Whidbey Inn, on Whidbey Island, Washington. Connell moved to Whidbey Island in June 1986 to manage the Inn. Shortly thereafter Francisco moved to Whidbey Island to join her. Connell and Francisco resided and cohabited on Whidbey Island until the relationship ended in March 1990.

While living on Whidbey Island, Connell and Francisco were viewed by many in the community as being married. Francisco acquiesced in Connell's use of his surname for business purposes. A last will and testament, dated December 11, 1987, left the corpus of Francisco's estate to Connell. Both Connell and Francisco had surgery to enhance their fertility. In the summer of 1986, Francisco gave Connell an engagement ring.

From June 1986 to September 1990 Connell continuously managed and worked at the Inn. She prepared breakfast, cleaned rooms, took reservations, laundered linens, paid bills, and maintained and repaired the Inn. Connell received no compensation for her services at the Inn from 1986 to 1988. From January 1989 to September 1990 she received $400 per week in salary.

Francisco produced another profitable stage show and acquired several pieces of real property during the period from June 1986 to September 1990. . . . Connell did not contribute financially toward the purchase of any of the properties, and title to the properties was held in Francisco's name individually or in the name of Prince Productions, Inc.

Connell and Francisco separated in March 1990. When the relationship ended Connell had $10,000 in savings, $10,000 in jewelry, her clothes, an automobile, and her leasehold interest in the New York apartment. She continued to receive her $400 per week salary from the Inn until September 1990. In contrast, Francisco's net worth was over $2,700,000, a net increase since February 1984 of almost $1,400,000. In March 1990, he was receiving $5,000 per week in salary from Prince Productions, Inc.

Connell filed a lawsuit against Francisco in December 1990 seeking a just and equitable distribution of the property acquired during the relationship. The Island County Superior Court determined Connell and Francisco's relationship was sufficiently long term and stable to require a just and equitable distribution. The Superior Court limited the property subject to distribution to the property that would have been community in character had they been married. The trial court held property owned by each party prior to the relationship could not be distributed. In addition, the Superior Court required Connell to prove by a preponderance of the evidence that the property acquired during their relationship would have been community property had they been married.

. . . [The Court of Appeals reversed both holdings, and Francisco successfully petitioned the Supreme Court for review.]

A meretricious relationship is a stable, marital-like relationship where both parties cohabit with knowledge that a lawful marriage between them does not exist.[5]

Relevant factors establishing a meretricious relationship include, but are not limited to: continuous cohabitation, duration of the relationship, purpose of the relationship, pooling of resources and services for joint projects, and the intent of the parties.

. . . The Superior Court found Connell and Francisco were parties to a meretricious relationship. This finding is not contested.

Historically, property acquired during a meretricious relationship was presumed to belong to the person in whose name title to the property was placed. "[I]n the absence of any evidence to the contrary, it should be presumed as a matter of

---

5. In Olver v. Fowler, 126 P.3d 69 (Wash. 2006), the Washington Supreme Court announced that it would henceforth use the term *committed intimate relationship*. — Ed.

law that the parties intended to dispose of the property exactly as they did dispose of it." This presumption is commonly referred to as "the *Creasman* presumption."

. . . In 1984, this court overruled *Creasman. Lindsey*, 101 Wash. 2d at 304, 678 P.2d 328. In its place, the court adopted a general rule requiring a just and equitable distribution of property following a meretricious relationship. . . .

In *Lindsey*, the parties cohabited for less than 2 years prior to marriage. When they subsequently divorced, the wife argued the increase in value of property acquired during the meretricious portion of their relationship was also subject to an equitable distribution as if the property were community in character. We agreed, citing former RCW 26.09.080 [which governs property division at divorce].

. . . Francisco contends the Court of Appeals misinterpreted *Lindsey* when it applied all the principles contained in RCW 26.09.080 to meretricious relationships. We agree. A meretricious relationship is not the same as a marriage. . . . As such, the laws involving the distribution of marital property do not directly apply to the division of property following a meretricious relationship. Washington courts may look toward those laws for guidance.

Once a trial court determines the existence of a meretricious relationship, the trial court then: (1) evaluates the interest each party has in the property acquired during the relationship, and (2) makes a just and equitable distribution of the property. The critical focus is on property that would have been characterized as community property had the parties been married. This property is properly before a trial court and is subject to a just and equitable distribution.

While portions of RCW 26.09.080 may apply by analogy to meretricious relationships, not all provisions of the statute should be applied. The parties to such a relationship have chosen not to get married and therefore the property owned by each party prior to the relationship should not be before the court for distribution at the end of the relationship. However, the property acquired during the relationship should be before the trial court so that one party is not unjustly enriched at the end of such a relationship. We conclude a trial court may not distribute property acquired by each party prior to the relationship at the termination of a meretricious relationship. Until the Legislature, as a matter of public policy, concludes meretricious relationships are the legal equivalent to marriages, we limit the distribution of property following a meretricious relationship to property that would have been characterized as community property had the parties been married. This will allow the trial court to justly divide property the couple has earned during the relationship through their efforts without creating a common law marriage or making a decision for a couple which they have declined to make for themselves. Any other interpretation equates cohabitation with marriage; ignores the conscious decision by many couples not to marry; confers benefits when few, if any, economic risks or legal obligations are assumed; and disregards the explicit intent of the Legislature that RCW 26.09.080 apply to property distributions following a marriage.

Francisco argues the Court of Appeals erred in requiring the application of a community-property-like presumption to property acquired during a meretricious relationship. We disagree.

In a marital context, property acquired during marriage is presumptively community property. When no marriage exists there is, by definition, no community property. However, only by treating the property acquired in a meretricious relationship similarly can this court's reversal of "the *Creasman* presumption" be given effect. Failure to apply a community-property-like presumption to the property acquired during a meretricious relationship places the burden of proof on the non-acquiring partner. . . . The Court of Appeals properly rejected the resurrection of "the *Creasman* presumption." . . .

[The dissenting opinion of Justice Utter is omitted.]

Section 6.03 of the ALI Principles of the Law of Family Dissolution recommends the adoption of a new status relationship, the domestic partnership. If the parties have a child together, they will qualify as domestic partners once they have maintained a common household for a particular period of time (to be established by the state; the example given in the commentary is two years). If they do not have a child, they are rebuttably presumed to be domestic partners after they have lived together for a (longer) period of time (e.g., three years). If the relationship is established, the Principles provide that the law applicable at the dissolution of a marriage should apply, unless the couple explicitly agree to the contrary. ALI Principles §§ 6.01, 6.04, 6.05, 6.06.

These provisions have been praised by a number of commentators. *See, e.g.,* Grace Ganz Blumberg, The Regularization of Nonmarital Cohabitation: Rights and Responsibilities in the American Welfare State, 76 Notre Dame L. Rev. 1265, 1282-1283 (2001); Mary Coombs, Insiders and Outsiders: What the American Law Institute Has Done for Gay and Lesbian Families, 8 Duke J. Gender L. & Pol'y 87 (2001); Martha M. Ertman, The ALI Principles' Approach to Domestic Partnership, 8 Duke J. Gender L. & Pol'y 107 (2001); Ira Mark Ellman, "Contract Thinking" Was *Marvin*'s Fatal Flaw, 76 Notre Dame L. Rev. 1365 (2001). However, others have been highly critical.

Lynn D. Wardle, *Deconstructing Family: A Critique of the American Law Institute's "Domestic Partners" Proposal*

2001 BYU L. Rev. 1189, 1200-1201, 1208, 1232-1233

The definition of domestic partners in chapter 6 is so broad that it could include persons who did not intend to intermingle their economic lives or incur any financial support or property sharing obligations. Arguably, it could even include persons who actually and demonstrably intend not to intermingle their economic lives or incur any financial support or property sharing obligations. Any two people unmarried to each other who live together as a couple in a primary residence for a significant time and who do not explicitly and properly agree not to be domestic partners may nevertheless be found to be domestic partners. . . .

The biggest single flaw of chapter 6 is that it fails to create rights and remedies that are customized for domestic partnership; it extends exactly the same economic property interests and compensatory rights to domestic partners as are provided to couples who are in the much more significant, committed, economically interdependent relationship of marriage. Marital property interests are based on the time-verified fact that most parties who marry make a long-term (presumably life-long) commitment to share their lives and their total family and personal interests, and they make significant adjustments in their economic life based on those interdependency commitments. However, it is far from clear that most nonmarital couples have similar expectations and make similar sacrifices in reliance on their expectations. Indeed, the existing social science evidence points in exactly the opposite direction, indicating that parties living in nonmarital cohabitation have very different expectations and characteristics than parties who are married. In the face of the overwhelming evidence of such significant differences, chapter 6 irrationally extends full, equal marital property and compensatory payment rights to domestic partners. . . .

June Carbone & Naomi Cahn, *The Triple System of Family Law*

2013 Mich. St. L. Rev. 1185, 1206-11

[He says,] "I'm not working, thems not my kids." If you're not married to the person you say, "They're not yours? Hit the door then!" But if you're married to them, you say, "Hit the door, please?" You know, you start nagging and they say, "I'm not going nowhere." . . . You're stuck with them just like all the other people stuck with their marriage and stuff. . . . I think it's best not to get married. Unless you're pretty sure that person's going to take care of you.

—A divorced mother of four in Chicago. . . .

Twenty-five years ago, the wariness toward marriage . . . [of] the divorced mother of four living in Chicago was an outlier — thought typical of the African-American underclass and no one else. Today, not only do lower income people echo the same sentiments, so do those closer to the middle. Skepticism about whether marriage is a good thing has become typical of working class American men and women — although they still want to marry, they are wary of someone who will take advantage of them. The legal regulation of the family complicates things further — and mandated sharing of assets, children, and lives can be a threat to those whose lives are unstable and unequal. . . .

Sociologist Linda Burton and her colleagues have studied these contingent relationships among low-income women. The women in the study overwhelmingly bear children outside of marriage and almost all express wariness about men. . . .

In between the top and the marginalized is a working class in transition. Working class conceptions take place the same way as they did in the old days — in the context of courtships that tend to be sexual and brief. These couples may not know each other terribly well at the time of the child's birth. In another era, they would have married, and the dependent mother would have stayed with the father so long as he brought home a paycheck. He could still go out with the boys and she might rely more on her relatives than her husband to care for the children, but his ties to the family would have depended on the strength of his relationship to her. If he refused to marry her or if they divorced, his relationship to the child would typically end. In some parts of the country today, these couples still marry, but those who do also divorce and remarry at high rates. In other parts of the country, the couples cohabit instead and marry only if they secure employment and a measure of financial stability. . . .

The result increases the conviction of lower income women that they will have to look to their own earnings to support themselves and their children. Consider what would happen to Bethenny and Calvin, a young couple with a child in Virginia Beach, if they married and divorced. In *The End of Men*, author Hanna Rosin described how Calvin talked about the jobs he once had and then lost and the ones he was trying to get. Rosin's conclusion was that what Bethenny said she wanted was a traditional model of marriage, but that she recognized:

> Calvin was not going to drive up in a Chevy and take his rightful place at the head of the table one day soon, because Bethenny was already occupying that space, not to mention making the monthly payments on the mortgage, the kitchen renovation, and her own used car. Bethenny was doing too much but she was making it work, and she had her freedom. Why would she want to give all that up?

If their lives continued along the paths they were on at the time of the interview, Bethenny would be the primary wage-earner *and* the primary caretaker. Calvin might provide her with some much needed help with their daughter, and he could contribute financially, if not always reliably. Yet, Calvin could neither assume the "head of the family" role nor was he likely to settle into a subordinate one. If they split, Bethenny could reasonably expect that the courts would equally divide the house, the car, and the bank accounts acquired during the marriage, even if Bethenny had been making the monthly payments on the house, paid for the car out of her earnings, and had put aside the savings for the child's education. . . .

In addition, in a changing sign of the times, Calvin might claim joint custody of the child, and, if Bethenny continued to earn more than he did, spousal or child support. . . . No surprise that Bethenny is not holding her breath in anticipation of a romantic marriage proposal from a man who cannot hold his own in either a financial or a nurturing role.

NOTES AND QUESTIONS

1. What is the basis for finding a "committed intimate relationship" under Washington law? For an argument that the Washington Supreme Court has essentially revived common law marriage through this doctrine, *see* Charlotte K. Goldberg, The Schemes of Adventuresses: The Abolition and Revival of Common-Law Marriage, 13 Wm. & Mary J. Women & L. 483 (2007). Compare the criteria for finding a domestic partnership under the ALI Principles. Would Connell and Francisco's relationship have qualified?

What are the advantages of allowing a court to find that parties are in a familial relationship based on their conduct, rather than requiring them to register as domestic partners? What are the concerns that Professor Wardle identifies? What are the implications of the findings of Professors Carbone and Cahn?

2. Do you think the approach of *Marvin* or that of *Connell* is more consistent with the expectations of most cohabitants? If, as often happens, parties have inconsistent expectations, what principle should govern their property rights?

3. As *Connell* indicates, even though Washington is a community property state, all property acquired by either spouse is subject to equitable division when the parties divorce. Why doesn't the court apply this rule to cohabitants? How would you argue for a contrary rule?

4. Does *Connell* authorize a court to award support to an economically weaker partner at the end of a committed intimate relationship? Does the ALI proposal?

5. The Washington Supreme Court limited some of the expansive language in *Connell* in In re Marriage of Pennington, 14 P.3d 764 (Wash. 2000) (en banc), holding that lower courts had erred in finding meretricious relationships in two cases in which one of the parties had a spouse for at least part of the time they lived together. In each relationship, one of the parties was married to someone else at the outset, though by the time the parties broke up divorces had occurred, and in both cases the parties' relationships were on again–off again to some extent. Based on these facts, the Supreme Court said that the parties' cohabitation was not "continuous" and that they did not have a mutual intent to live in a meretricious relationship. Saying that the meretricious relationship doctrine is still tied to its equitable underpinnings, the court said that its purpose was to prevent the unjust enrichment of one party at the other's expense and found no basis for granting a remedy in either case.

6. Does the committed intimate spouse doctrine give rights to third parties who deal with one or both of the parties? Does the ALI proposal?

FAMILY DISSOLUTION

Divorce Grounds and Procedures

5

A. INTRODUCTION

The idea of divorce involves centuries-old tensions between two conceptions of marriage: marriage as covenant, involving permanent commitments ordained by God, state, or community; and marriage as contract, resting on the consent of husband, wife, and sometimes their families to a set of reciprocal obligations. The division between these two concepts is older than the United States, and the tension between these ideas has shaped much of the history of American family law. Anglo-American law, to the extent it followed canon law and the English ecclesiastical tradition, primarily reflected the former view. Within this tradition, marriage involves permanent obligations beyond the power of the parties to alter or dissolve. At the time the country began, the states that adopted the English tradition, which included all of the southern states, did not recognize the power of the judiciary to grant divorces at all. Yet American law, starting with the New England colonists who came to the Americas to escape the dominance of the Church of England, has also provided some recognition of the contractual aspects of marriage. A number of these early northeastern colonies adopted liberal divorce laws well before England or many American states. This chapter will examine family dissolution in the context of ongoing differences concerning the permissibility and purposes of divorce.

At the time of the settlement of the colonies, English law recognized annulment and separation, which was known as divorce *a mensa et thoro*, or divorce from bed and board. True divorce, which caused the termination of the marital relationship, required an Act of Parliament and was effectively available only to those few persons with enough wealth and influence to secure a private bill of divorce from Parliament.

In the United States, the availability of divorce has always varied by region. Ann Estin observes, "From the earliest periods of American history, the colonies took different approaches to questions of marriage and divorce." Ann Laquer

Estin, Family Law Federalism: Divorce and the Constitution, 16 Wm. & Mary Bill Rts. J. 381, 383-384 (2007). The New England colonies, especially those influenced by various Protestant teachings rather than the traditions of the Church of England, treated divorce as a civil matter and started granting them during the seventeenth century. After the American Revolution, the northern states began to adopt laws providing for judicial divorce, and by 1800 every New England state and many mid-Atlantic states had done so. The southern colonies followed the English ecclesiastical pattern and generally refused to permit complete divorce without an act of the legislature until after the Civil War. Estin concludes that "[t]his diversity and experimentation continued in the years after independence and remains an unusual feature of American divorce law." *Id.* at 384.

Divorce remained a divisive issue throughout much of the nineteenth century and the first half of the twentieth. One legacy of the English tradition was that the authority to regulate divorce resided with the legislature; the judiciary had no equitable jurisdiction regarding divorce. Legislative debates concerned not just whether judicial divorce should be allowed, but on what terms. State differences remained intense, with states also varying in their willingness to recognize out-of-state decrees. The more conservative states were particularly loath to acknowledge divorces from "divorce mill" states, which granted divorces easily and without much regard for marital domicile. The grounds on which divorce should be allowed caused so much turmoil that legislation to enact a constitutional amendment making family law (or least divorce) a federal issue was introduced in almost every session of Congress from 1884 until the late 1940s. *See* Nelson M. Blake, The Road to Reno 145-150 (1977).

After World War II, reform movements focused on eliminating fault as a requirement for divorce. These movements were fueled partly by growing support for the principle that if husband and wife wanted a divorce, the state should not stand in the way, and partly by concern for the integrity of the judicial system as couples colluded to secure divorces the formal law did not allow. In the 20-year period between 1965 and 1985, every state passed legislation recognizing some form of no-fault ground for divorce. The legislation was far from uniform. Some states followed California and the Uniform Marriage and Divorce Act in substituting "irretrievable breakdown" for fault as the exclusive basis for divorce and, as a practical matter, granted a divorce whenever either party wanted one. Other states simply added no-fault grounds, such as irreconcilable differences or a period of separation, without changing the fault provisions. A few states conditioned availability of the no-fault ground on the mutual agreement of the parties or mandated longer periods of separation in cases where the parties disagreed. Other states required that the courts determine whether the alleged differences between the spouses were truly irreconcilable rather than rely on the pleadings alone. In these debates, the tensions between the secular and the religious interpretations of marriage and between private freedom to contract and state responsibility to oversee family well-being reappear and recombine in different ways.

This chapter approaches the issue of divorce by, first, exploring fault-based jurisprudence, elements of which remain good law in the majority of U.S. jurisdictions. Second, it considers the implementation of no-fault provisions. Third, it examines the continuing discussion of divorce reforms and proposals for further change.

B. THE TRADITIONAL DIVORCE SYSTEM

This section examines the grounds for and defenses or bars to divorce under the traditional fault system. Until the last half-century, an action for divorce could be successful only when these conditions were met. The grounds and defenses themselves retain importance in many jurisdictions, where both fault and no-fault grounds may be asserted in a dissolution proceeding. As of 2008, 33 states retained traditional fault grounds for divorce, including the states with a covenant marriage option. Linda D. Elrod & Robert G. Spector, A Review of the Year in Family Law 2006-2007: Judges Try to Find Answers to Complex Questions, chart 4, 41 Fam. L.Q. 661 (2008). The assumptions behind a fault-based system are no less important than the grounds, both in themselves and in assessing the desirability of a return, wholly or in part, to the traditional standards for divorce.

KUCERA V. KUCERA

117 N.W.2d 810 (N.D. 1962)

STRUTZ, J. (on reassignment). The plaintiff brought this action for divorce, alleging extreme mental cruelty. The defendant in his answer denies the material allegations of the plaintiff's complaint and counterclaims on grounds of adultery and extreme cruelty.

The record discloses that the parties were married on September 17, 1955. At the time of the marriage, the plaintiff was pregnant by another man, a certain Mr. K—, and the child who was born to her, less than seven months after the marriage, admittedly is not the child of the defendant. The plaintiff herself, testifying in this case, stated that she had had no sexual relations with the defendant prior to their marriage. She contends, however, that this child, having been born into the family of the defendant after their marriage and the defendant having married the plaintiff with full knowledge of her pregnant condition, should be held to have been adopted at its birth by the defendant and that the defendant is liable for its support as one standing *in loco parentis*.

The record further discloses that the parties themselves were extremely doubtful whether the marriage would be a successful one, even before it was consummated. The plaintiff testified that they had agreed, before marriage, that "if the marriage didn't work out we could get a divorce in a year, but it would give the child a name."

After the birth of this child, a second child was born and, for a period of more than two years before the commencement of this action, the parties ceased to have any marital relations. The defendant testified positively that:

We have had no sexual relations since Robin was born.

The plaintiff does not deny this. There is evidence in the record that the defendant did call the plaintiff names and that, on at least one occasion, he struck her. He also called the first child, who admittedly is not his child, some obscene names.

The differences of the parties finally were brought to a head when the defendant, returning home unexpectedly one evening from the college where he was working on a thesis, discovered Mr. K—, the man who had fathered the plaintiff's first child, in the home with the plaintiff. The plaintiff thereupon admitted that Mr. K— had been calling on her for a period of more than six months, as often as once a week. This was in the month of March 1959. The parties continued to live under the same roof until the end of the school year in June, when this action was commenced by the plaintiff.

On this record the trial court granted to the plaintiff a decree of divorce, and ordered the defendant to make monthly payments for the support of the plaintiff and for the support of the two children born during the marriage. From this judgment the defendant has appealed, demanding a trial de novo. . . .

The plaintiff's cause of action is based on an allegation of extreme cruelty. "Extreme cruelty" is the infliction by one party to a marriage of grievous bodily injury or grievous mental suffering upon the other. Sec. 14-05-05, N.D.C.C.

A divorce may be granted in North Dakota on the grounds of grievous mental suffering, even though such suffering produces no bodily injury.

Does the record disclose conduct on the part of the defendant which would tend to so wound the feelings of the plaintiff that her health was impaired, and were the actions of the defendant such as to destroy the ends of the marriage? We have examined the entire record carefully. The plaintiff did testify to some instances in which the defendant's language and custom was such that she alleges it caused her extreme mental anguish. While the evidence supporting the plaintiff's cause of action is not very strong, the trial court did find that such evidence was sufficient to entitle her to a divorce.

The defendant, however, has counterclaimed for a divorce on grounds of extreme cruelty and on grounds of adultery. On reading the entire record, we believe that the plaintiff also was guilty of conduct which, standing alone, would entitle the defendant to a decree of divorce. For a period of more than six months, the plaintiff was allowing Mr. K—, the man who was the father of her first child, to call on her at the home of the parties. True, the plaintiff contends that he called against her wishes, but the plaintiff does admit that these calls were continued, more or less regularly, for a period of more than six months. The plaintiff must have given some cooperation to Mr. K—, at least to the extent of informing him as to what hours the defendant would be absent from the home.

The plaintiff has denied positively any acts of adultery during the six months of such visits. It is difficult to believe that the man who was the father of her child continued to call on her for more than six months without resuming such relationship as they had had prior to the marriage of the plaintiff and the defendant. While the court, ordinarily, will not require direct evidence on a charge of adultery, the trial court did believe the statements of the plaintiff when she testified that she had had no relations with Mr. K— during these visits. While the evidence is such that it is difficult to believe the plaintiff's testimony on this point, we cannot say that the evidence is so strong that the trial court clearly erred in this finding. . . .

Although the defendant failed to prove his charge of adultery to the satisfaction of the trial court, we do believe that he did prove a cause of action on the ground of extreme cruelty. Here, the defendant had married the plaintiff knowing that she had had previous relations with Mr. K— and that she was pregnant and with child by Mr. K— at the time of the marriage of the parties. Thereafter, he discovered that, for more than six months, the plaintiff was visited by the same Mr. K— in the home of the parties. Certainly that is sufficient evidence to substantiate a charge of extreme cruelty.

But that is not all. The defendant introduced evidence which would have justified a decree of divorce in his favor on grounds of desertion. He testified that "we have had no sexual relations since Robin was born," which was well over two years before the commencement of this action. The plaintiff did not deny this, nor did she try to justify her refusal to have reasonable sexual relations with the defendant, for physical or health reasons. She merely testified, "I couldn't stand to have sexual relations with him," and then admitted that her refusal was not due to physical or health reasons. . . .

Our statute defines "willful desertion" to include "persistent refusal to have reasonable matrimonial intercourse as husband and wife when health or physical condition does not make such refusal reasonably necessary. . . ." Sec. 14-05-06, Subsec. 1, N.D.C.C.

It is true that the defendant alleged only extreme cruelty and adultery as grounds for divorce in his counterclaim. But, under the Rules of Civil Procedure now in force in North Dakota, when issues not raised by the pleadings are tried by express or implied consent of the parties, they shall be tried in all respects as if they had been raised by the pleadings. . . .

Therefore, since the defendant did prove a cause of action for divorce on grounds of desertion as well as on grounds of extreme cruelty, we have a situation where both parties have established a cause of action for divorce.

Section 14-05-10 of the North Dakota Century Code provides:

"Divorces must be denied upon showing: . . .
"4. Recrimination; . . ."

Section 14-05-15 reads:

"Recrimination is a showing by the defendant of any cause of divorce against the plaintiff in bar of the plaintiff's cause of divorce. . . ."

This court repeatedly has held that the above statutes are an absolute bar to divorce in a case where both the plaintiff and the defendant plead and prove facts constituting statutory grounds for divorce against each other.

This court, in these and other cases, pointed out that, where the Legislature has given the same legal effect to every recognized cause for divorce, it is not for the court to determine the gravity of the different causes which are proved.

Thus, where recrimination is proved, as it was in this case, a divorce must be denied to both of the parties. This is true even though we believe the legitimate ends of the marriage have been destroyed and a divorce perhaps would be the better solution for the difficulties facing the parties. The provisions of our statute on recrimination are mandatory, and a divorce "must be denied" upon a showing of recrimination. The court has no discretion in the matter and must follow the mandatory wording of the law.

The judgment of the trial court granting a divorce to the plaintiff must therefore be reversed, and a new judgment shall be entered denying a divorce to either party.

NOTES AND QUESTIONS

1. *Kucera* indicates the content of the most commonly invoked grounds for divorce under the fault system. With the advent of no-fault divorce, many states simply added alternative no-fault grounds, such as a voluntary separation, to the fault grounds, retaining the earlier fault-based law.

a. *Adultery*. Adultery ordinarily is defined as voluntary sexual intercourse by a married person with a person who is not his or her spouse. The element of voluntariness excludes rape from the definition of "adultery." In the traditional view, same-sex relations were not defined as adulterous, but cases seem now inclined to treat them in the same way as extramarital heterosexual relations. *See, e.g.,* Owens v. Owens, 274 S.E.2d 484 (Ga. 1981).

It is one of the oddities of adultery that it typically can be proved by direct evidence only when it did not in fact occur — that is, where one supposedly guilty spouse, typically the husband, agrees to provide the other with manufactured evidence that he has committed adultery so that she can establish a ground for divorce. This practice, which became a cottage industry in New York when adultery was the only available basis for absolute divorce, is discussed later in this section. Absent agreement of this kind, adultery is rarely committed in the presence of others and must be proved by circumstantial evidence. The circumstances that may give rise to an inference that adultery did occur include inclination and opportunity. Whether circumstantial proof actually offered in a divorce case is sufficient is largely a matter for the trial court to decide, as *Kucera*, above, indicates. For a more recent example, *see* Lister v. Lister, 981 So. 2d 340 (Miss. App. 2008), affirming a grant of divorce on the ground of adultery where the husband had an infatuation with his secretary "sufficient to be an adulterous inclination" and there was testimony that the couple "had opportunities to consummate that inclination." *Cf.* Fore v. Fore, 109 So. 3d 137 Miss. App. 2013, (suggesting that in most modern cases of divorce based on adultery, the adultery is admitted and that to show adultery based on circumstantial evidence requires "clear and convincing evidence" and the burden of proof is "a heavy one"); Webb v. Webb, 950 So. 2d 322 (Ala. Civ. App. 2006), reversing a trial court grant of a divorce on grounds of adultery for lack of corroboration. The court had granted the divorce based on the wife's testimony that the husband and his alleged paramour each admitted the adultery. When asked about the affair at the trial, the husband invoked the Fifth Amendment privilege against self-incrimination.

b. *Cruelty*. The definition of "cruelty" was originally developed in connection with divorce *a mensa et thoro*, before absolute divorce was judicially available. The older cases on cruelty required violence or at least intentionally and seriously injurious conduct that reasonably led to fear for life or health.

Although it might reasonably be asked whether the restrictive limitations on the definition of "cruelty" developed in the context of judicial separation or limited divorce should have applied once absolute divorce became available, *see* Lee E. Teitelbaum, Cruelty Divorce Under New York's Reform Act: On Repeating Ancient Error, 23 Buff. L. Rev. 1 (1973), the law in many jurisdictions imported those restrictions, at least initially. Over time, threats to mental as well as physical well-being came to be recognized, more or less generously. However, many courts, while extending the definition of "cruelty," also expressed concern that the definition not be so broad as to reach "mere" incompatibility. Some courts required proof of physical harm to support a divorce based on mental cruelty; some required expert evidence where the effect was emotional rather than physical. Perhaps the most common form of cruelty, at least in reality, may be called general marital unkindness. This includes a variety of forms of misconduct, including ridicule, harassment, false accusations of unfaithfulness, child abuse, relative abuse, and the like. *E.g.*, Stevenson v. Stevenson, 369 P.2d 923 (Utah 1962) (husband falsely accused wife of infidelity, emotional and mental illness, giving him a venereal disease, and—you may think ironically—paranoia). For a collection of cases granting divorce under these circumstances, *see* 2 Homer H. Clark, Jr., Domestic Relations 31-32 (2d ed. 1987).

Ultimately, the law concerning cruel treatment varied substantially at both the formal law and law-in-action levels. Not only did jurisdictions differ considerably in what their appellate decisions required to prove cruelty, but the decisions of trial courts, at least in uncontested cases, seemed to vary from what appellate courts said was needed. Nonetheless, as is evident in *Kucera*, evidentiary decisions by trial courts were often sustained if there was anything to support the trial judge's decision.

New Hampshire's divorce statute, which was adopted in 1840 to provide an easier standard to meet than "extreme cruelty," requires spousal conduct that seriously "injures health" or "endangers reason." The state supreme court, however, affirmed that while the statute "does not require proof of conduct that would have affected an average or reasonable person, it does require proof that the health or reason of the complaining spouse was *actually* affected." Accordingly, the wife's discovery of her husband's sexually suggestive e-mails professing his love to a former girlfriend was not a ground for divorce, where the wife alleged that the discovery made her feel "angry, upset, and distraught." In re Guy, 969 A.2d 373 (N.H. 2009).

c. *Desertion.* This ground, sometimes called "abandonment" and often described in terms of "willful" desertion, requires departure from the home without the consent of the other and without justification. If there has been consent, it is said, there is no marital wrong and therefore no abandonment. What makes out consent is somewhat disputable, but generally failures to object and offers to reconcile may constitute evidence of consent. See 2 Homer H. Clark, Jr., The Law of Domestic Relations in the United States § 14.3 (2d ed. 1987).

Justification for departure from the home is a more complicated business. The strictest view is that departure is justified only when the abandoned spouse has engaged in conduct that would itself provide grounds for divorce. Other jurisdictions view justification more broadly to include conduct that in some way makes cohabitation impossible. See 2 H. Clark, above, at 17-18. See, however,

Brown v. Brown, __ So. 3d __ (Miss. App. 2013) (dismissing divorce action on grounds of desertion because wife's behavior caused husband stress precipitating his departure).

Many statutes, like the New Hampshire law, specify a minimum period, ordinarily between one and five years. And, as in New Hampshire, the period must usually be continuous.

In the ordinary desertion, the offending spouse leaves the marital home. Historically, desertion often involved the husband's failure to support the family. In Gardner v. Gardner, 130 So. 3d 1162 (Miss. App. 2013), the dissent objected to grant of a divorce on grounds of desertion because the husband continued to provide some financial support, primarily contributions to the mortgage payments, even though he did not live with the family. However, some cases, including *Kucera*, recognize a "constructive" abandonment — meaning, as the term *constructive* always does, that no such thing occurred. These cases involve conduct by the offending spouse that amounts to marital misconduct on other grounds, which may or may not statutorily be specified. In Kreyling v. Kreyling, 23 A.2d 800 (N.J. 1942), the husband refused to engage in sexual intercourse without the use of a contraceptive. This refusal was held an unjustified course of conduct by the defendant and an instance of constructive desertion. Is it evident how such a decision permits a judicial expansion of the grounds for divorce?

d. *Impotence*. The New Hampshire statute makes impotence a ground for divorce. Does its inclusion seem logical, given the theory of divorce? However, logical or not, some statutes do include preexisting conditions as a basis for divorce.

2. The fault scheme recognized several defenses to divorce. Ordinarily, these are treated as affirmative defenses that must be specifically pleaded and proved.

a. *Insanity*. In some jurisdictions, incurable insanity is a ground for divorce; it is also generally recognized as a defense to divorce actions founded on adultery or desertion. Is there any reason for doubt to be expressed with respect to the applicability of that defense to divorce based on cruelty? In Simpson v. Simpson, 716 S.W.2d 27 (Tenn. 1986), the wife sought a divorce on the basis of cruelty following a ten-year pattern of abuse in which the husband harassed and belittled her, stockpiled weapons, and physically threatened her and her family. When she attempted to separate from him, he kidnapped her and told her that he was going to kill her. The husband defended the divorce action on the ground of insanity; that is, he argued that he was not responsible for the acts of cruelty because of mental illness. A psychiatrist testified that he was suffering from paranoid schizophrenia, and the trial court dismissed the divorce action on that basis. The Tennessee Supreme Court, noting that the states varied in their treatment of insanity as a bar to divorce, adopted the same standard that would be applicable in a criminal case, *viz.*, that the defendant must establish that, as a result of mental illness, he lacked the capacity to appreciate the wrongfulness of his acts or the volition to prevent them. *See* David Chapus, Insanity as Defense to Divorce or Separate Suit — Post 1950 Cases, 67 A.L.R.4th 277, ¶8b (2014).

b. *Connivance*. The theory of divorce is that the misconduct of one spouse (and only one spouse) has destroyed the marital relationship. One set of circumstances where misconduct otherwise justifying divorce may not suffice arises when the "offending" conduct was in fact agreed to (connived at) by the spouse now seeking the divorce. As a practical matter, this defense is almost entirely limited to adultery, although a similar principle is evident in the requirement that desertion, to support a divorce, must be nonconsensual. For a classic instance, *see* Hollis v. Hollis, 427 S.E.2d 233 (Va. App. 1993). The wife, who wished to divorce her husband, encouraged him to have an affair with someone he met at a Christmas party. In particular, she urged him and the correspondent to rent an apartment for a year and live there as man and wife and, when they did so, sent flowers and a congratulatory note. She then sought a divorce on the grounds of adultery.

Suppose, however, that the petitioning spouse suspects that the other is about to commit adultery and absents him- or herself to permit the gathering of evidence of the wrong. This seems not to be considered connivance. But it has been held connivance where the petitioning spouse simply does not care whether adultery occurs, although he or she does not consent to any such act. *See* 2 H. Clark, Domestic Relations, above, at 55. What is the basis for such a distinction?

c. *Condonation.* Condonation is a defense to most of the grounds of divorce, although its application to cruelty is somewhat unclear. Condonation occurs when the injured spouse, knowing of a marital wrong, continues or resumes marital cohabitation. Although the essence of the defense is said to be forgiveness, that state of mind may be inferred from resumption of marital relations itself.

However, the circumstances in which marital relations are resumed may be important. The New York Supreme Court, Appellate Division, held that an estranged couple's attempt at reconciliation, even where it involves an isolated resumption of cohabitation, or sexual relations, or both, does not, as a matter of law, preclude granting a divorce to a spouse who otherwise had a valid claim for abandonment. "Rather, the trial court should examine the totality of the circumstances surrounding the purported reconciliation, before determining its effect, if any, upon the pending marital proceeding. Among the many factors for the trial court to consider are whether the reconciliation and any cohabitation were entered into in good faith, whether it was at all successful, who initiated it and with what motivation." Haymes v. Haymes, 646 N.Y.S.2d 315, 319 (App. Div. 1996). *See also* Sullivan v. Sullivan, 950 N.E.2d 906 (Mass. App. 2011) (condonation is a "state of mind" that requires an "intent to forgive"). The court relied in part on prior decisions holding that cohabitation, especially if not in good faith, does not condone a course of cruel conduct in the same way it would condone adultery. *See also* Aronson v. Aronson, 691 A.2d 785 (Md. Ct. Spec. App. 1997), *cert. denied and appeal dismissed*, 346 Md. 371, 697 A.2d 111 (1997) (resumption of sexual relations is evidence of condonation); Ware v. Ware, 7 So. 3d 271 (Miss. App. 2008) (no condonation from resumption of sexual relations where the husband did not forgive the wife for her adultery).

In principle, condonation is conditional; it is forgiveness conditioned on the absence of future wrongdoing. An offense, once condoned, may be "revived" if the offending spouse does not treat the condoning spouse properly. Indeed, the initial wrong may be revived even if the offending spouse's subsequent misconduct is not sufficiently grave to constitute an independent basis for divorce.

d. *Recrimination.* The defense of recrimination was raised in *Kucera.* Professor Clark describes recrimination as "a rare combination of silliness, futility and brutality." Homer H. Clark, Jr., Domestic Relations 704 (2d ed. 1979). What is his point?

Some jurisdictions do not recognize recrimination as a bar to divorce but instead look to "comparative rectitude" when both spouses have committed marital fault. *E.g.*, Jenkins v. Jenkins, 55 So. 3d 1094 (Miss. App. 2010) (recrimination is no longer an absolute bar to divorce; instead the court should determine which party's conduct was the proximate cause of the divorce); Alejandro v. Alejandro, 651 S.E.2d 62 (Ga. 2007) (upholding trial court finding that the wife's adultery did not cause the dissolution of the parties' marriage where there was evidence of adultery by both parties, of physical violence by the husband injuring the wife, and that the husband's return to Ohio to work for his father caused the dissolution of the marriage).

3. The doctrine of collusion is often listed as a defense to divorce, but in some sense it is a special doctrine. Unlike the other defenses, collusion need not be pleaded or proved. Rather, for reasons obvious by its nature, this bar is ordinarily raised by the court *sua sponte*. The doctrine of collusion is also the clearest evidence of a public interest in the control of marital dissolution.

This bar arises from an agreement between the parties to frustrate the divorce procedure in some way. It may take the form of an agreement to create the appearance of marital wrongdoing when none has in fact occurred. The industry of supplying fictitious evidence of adultery is a familiar example. The defendant and plaintiff would arrange for one of them, usually the husband, to be in bed in a hotel room with an anonymous woman, partially clothed. A photographer would gain entry and "surprise" the couple in that position, and the photograph would provide evidence of adultery. In England, the practice was even simpler; the hotel bill was sent home by the husband, and witnesses testified that he stayed at the hotel and occupied a bedroom with a woman not his wife. Lawrence M. Friedman, A Dead Language: Divorce Law and Practice Before No-Fault, 86 Va. L. Rev. 1497, 1512-1515 (2000).

Collusion may also arise, or be inferred, from agreements not to defend a case. On the other hand, consent expressed through an agreement to settle the rights of the parties or to grant suit money to the plaintiff is not necessarily improper. The line between illegal and legal agreement has often been unclear, and this uncertainty presented problems in the drafting of separation agreements. Even ordinary provisions that one party will sue and the other not defend may be dangerous to include.

PROBLEMS

1. Colin and Marie married at age 21, when Marie became pregnant. They had a second child three years later. Colin works as a manager in a sporting goods store, Marie as an administrative assistant. After seven years of marriage, Marie feels the spark is gone. They do relatively little together, are too exhausted to go out much, and share few interests. One day Marie comes home and tells Colin she would like a divorce. Two weeks later, she serves him with papers alleging extreme cruelty. Colin is shocked and very angry. At the trial, Marie testifies that Colin drinks alcohol on a daily basis, often consuming six beers a night. On one occasion, he became so intoxicated that he urinated in the parties' closet and then became angry and verbally abusive when she attempted to clean up after him. Since she first

expressed her interest in a divorce, he has criticized and belittled her, provoking arguments. During one of these arguments he threatened to punch her, and during another he slapped her. Marie asserts that she finally left the marital home because she had become afraid of Colin's increasingly uncontrolled anger.

Colin responds that his drinking increased only after Marie told him she wanted a divorce; that he slapped her on only one occasion, after she precipitated an argument with him; that she has relentlessly criticized him and blamed him for their marital difficulties; and that after counseling, he has gained better control over his drinking and anger. He does not want a divorce, but maintains that if the court is to grant one, it should be on the basis of her desertion.

Do grounds exist to grant Marie a divorce? If not, what would be the effect of a counterclaim by Colin on the ground of desertion?

2. A divorce action is brought alleging cruel and inhuman treatment. Plaintiff husband testifies that his wife had for several years repeatedly nagged and scolded him for fancied wrongs on his part and had frequently accused him wrongly of adultery. This, plaintiff says, has resulted in a general decline in his health, loss of sleep, and increased nervousness on his part. Assuming these facts are proved, will a divorce be granted?

3. Plaintiff husband sues for divorce on the ground of adultery. During the trial, he admits that he also had an affair before he left the marital home. Defendant wife denies that she committed adultery and asserts the affirmative defenses of recrimination and condonation. At trial, plaintiff testifies that his wife's alleged paramour had stayed as a guest at their home and when the husband became suspicious, the paramour admitted the affair. He also testifies that the wife had an earlier affair, but that he had forgiven her for that one. He further states that after he learned of the second affair, he and his wife had sexual relations, but he made it clear that he had not forgiven her for this affair.

Will a divorce be granted on these facts?

NOTE: THIRD-PARTY INTERVENTION

As a formal matter, only the spouses are parties to most divorce cases.[1] The state is not a party, nor are children of the marriage. The Michigan Supreme Court, rejecting a suit by four minor children to set aside a divorce granted to their mother against their father on the ground that the divorce was collusive, observed as follows:

> The jurisdiction over divorce is purely statutory, and the legislative authority has not seen fit to allow any but the parties to intervene in such suits. The husband and wife are the only persons recognized as parties.
>
> It is true that the interests of children are in some important respects more nearly affected by such proceedings than by those which merely concern rights of

---

1. There are occasional exceptions, as where a third party claims an interest in property that may be disposed of in the course of a divorce action or, in some states, where grandparents are authorized to intervene with respect to custody issues. For a survey of these exceptions, *see* William David Taylor, Third-Party Practice in Divorce Cases, 26 Fam. L.Q. 5 (1992).

property. . . . But no court in this country has any power to compel discordant husbands and wives to live together, and we do not perceive that any legal rights of these infants have been invaded, however much they may have been affected otherwise.

Baugh v. Baugh, 37 Mich. 59, 61-62 (1877). *See also* Waite v. Waite, 959 So. 2d 610 (Ala. 2006) (where a divorce decree was not invalid on its face, the wife's second husband did not have standing to challenge the validity of the decree ending the wife's earlier marriage, which would have in turn affected the validity of his marriage).

C. THE ADOPTION OF NO-FAULT DIVORCE

LAWRENCE FRIEDMAN, *RIGHTS OF PASSAGE: DIVORCE LAW IN HISTORICAL PERSPECTIVE*

63 Or. L. Rev. 649, 662, 666-667 (1984)

. . . In almost every state, perjury or something close to it was a way of life in divorce court. . . . In theory, a collusive divorce was illegal. Certainly, perjury was a crime, and so was the manufacture of evidence. Judges had to be aware of what was going on in front of their noses. Yet the system flourished, and the divorce rate grew steadily. There were 7,380 divorces in 1860, or 1.2 per 1,000 marriages. There were 167,105 divorces in 1920, or 7.7 per 1,000 marriages. The overwhelming majority were collusive and consensual, in fact if not in theory. The legal system winked and blinked and ignored. . . .

. . . The real divorce revolution, arguably, was not the passage of the no-fault statutes. These statutes were a delayed ratification of a system largely in place; a system that was expensive, dirty, and distasteful, perhaps, but a system that more or less worked. If one asks who created that system, the answer is ordinary people and their lawyers. Their demand for easy divorce, their pressure on the system, led to concrete patterns of legal behavior that flourished for a century. Lower court judges, all over the country, accepted the system, but it was not their idea. The structure of divorce law, as it existed between 1870 and 1970, evolved quietly in obscure places, without disturbing the surface of law or altering official norms.

In its middle period, divorce law was a compromise between the instrumental demand for divorce and the opposing moral postulate. The situation was, by common agreement, a mess: costly, ineffective, destructive. Yet it lasted for generations. . . .

In the middle of the twentieth century, it was clear to everybody that the system of divorce was a fake: "a solemn if silly comic melodrama," "beneath the dignity of the American court"; a system that "cheapens not only the tribunal but the members of the legal profession who are . . . involved." The question was: What to do about it? One suggestion was to increase the role of the court and to reduce the element of sham. It was felt that a judge should have authority to deal with the entire human drama that lay behind a bill of divorce, and that skilled professionals should be attached to the court to help him. The goal was to set up a true "divorce court," a court of family justice.

This was indeed the philosophy of the Report of the Governor's Commission on the Family, issued in California in 1966. The report called for the destruction of the old system, and paved the way for the California no-fault law of 1970. The Commission demanded an end to "dissimulation, hypocrisy, and . . . perjury." A new law was needed to "allow the therapeutic processes of the Family Court to function with full effectiveness." The "standard" the Commission suggested would "permit — indeed . . . require — the Court to inquire into the whole picture of the marriage."

California did change its law in 1970, and in the next decade, so did almost every state. Yet the "therapeutic" path was most decidedly not the one taken. Instead, the whole house of cards collapsed. For divorces at least — child custody of course is a different animal — the judge did not gain more power and discretion. Instead, in practice he lost what little power he had. No-fault reduced divorce to even greater routine. The social-work or family-court ideal faded away. . . .

The no-fault divorce revolution was not solely an American phenomenon, as Mary Ann Glendon observes in Abortion and Divorce in Western Law 66-67 (1987):

> Between 1969 and 1985 divorce law in nearly every Western country was profoundly altered. Among the most dramatic changes was the introduction of civil divorce in the predominantly Catholic countries of Italy and Spain, and its extension to Catholic marriages in Portugal. Other countries replaced or amended old strict divorce laws. . . . The chief common characteristics of all these changes were the recognition or expansion of nonfault grounds for divorce, and the acceptance or simplification of divorce by mutual consent. When California in 1969 became the first Western jurisdiction completely to eliminate fault grounds for divorce, the move was thought by some to pre-figure the direction of reforms in other places. But it soon became clear that the purist approach was not to find wide acceptance. That same year England, too, passed a new divorce law which purported to make divorce available only when marriage had irretrievably broken down. But since the English statute permitted marriage breakdown to be proved by evidence of traditional marital offenses as well as by mutual consent or long separation, it did not really repudiate the old fault system. As it turned out, compromise statutes of the English type (resembling those already in place in Australia, Canada, and New Zealand) became the prevailing new approach to the grounds of divorce.

1. No-Fault Grounds for Divorce: Irretrievable Breakdown

"No-fault" divorce means only that the state recognizes some ground for divorce that does not require finding one (and only one) party at fault. These no-fault grounds can take several forms, and they can constitute either the exclusive grounds for divorce in the state or additional grounds added as an alternative to the traditional fault bases for divorce. First, as the Uniform Marriage and Divorce Act (below) indicates, the legislation can require a finding that that the marriage is "irretrievably broken." Some states alternatively refer to "irreconcilable differences" or "incompatibility." Second, the state can require a period of separation, after which the parties become eligible for divorce. Third, the state can require mutual consent to the divorce, or it can provide for separation periods of different lengths, with a longer period required if the parties do not agree. This section considers irreconcilable differences, and the following section addresses a period of separation when it exists together with fault grounds as alternative bases for divorce.

UNIFORM MARRIAGE AND DIVORCE ACT

§ 302 [Dissolution of Marriage; Legal Separation]

(a) The [_____] court shall enter a decree of dissolution of marriage if:

(1) the court finds that one of the parties, at the time the action was commenced, was domiciled in this State, or was stationed in this State while a member of the armed services, and that the domicil or military presence has been maintained for 90 days next preceding the making of the findings;

(2) the court finds that the marriage is irretrievably broken, if the finding is supported by evidence that (i) the parties have lived separate and apart for a period of more than 180 days next preceding the commencement of the proceeding, or . . .

(ii) there is serious marital discord adversely affecting the attitude of one or both of the parties toward the marriage;

(3) the court finds that the conciliation provisions of Section 305 either do not apply or have been met;

(4) to the extent it has jurisdiction to do so, the court has considered, approved, or provided for child custody, the support of any child entitled to support, the maintenance of either spouse, and the disposition of property; or has provided for a separate, later hearing to complete these matters.

(b) If a party requests a decree of legal separation rather than a decree of dissolution of marriage, the court shall grant the decree in that form unless the other party objects.

§ 305 [Irretrievable Breakdown]

(a) If both of the parties by petition or otherwise have stated under oath or affirmation that the marriage is irretrievably broken, or one of the parties has so stated and the other has not denied it, the court, after hearing, shall make a finding whether the marriage is irretrievably broken.

(b) If one of the parties has denied under oath or affirmation that the marriage is irretrievably broken, the court shall consider all relevant factors, including the circumstances that gave rise to filing the petition and the prospect of reconciliation, and shall:

(1) make a finding whether the marriage is irretrievably broken; or

(2) continue the matter for further hearing not fewer than 30 nor more than 60 days later, or as soon thereafter as the matter may be reached on the court's calendar, and may suggest to the parties that they seek counseling. The court, at the request of either party shall, or on its own motion may, order a conciliation

conference. At the adjourned hearing the court shall make a finding whether the marriage is irretrievably broken.

(c) A finding of irretrievable breakdown is a determination that there is no reasonable prospect of reconciliation.

The following case raises questions about the meaning of "irreconcilable" differences in no-fault provisions. N.H. Rev. Stat. Ann. § 458:7-b provides that no divorce shall be granted when "there is a likelihood for rehabilitation of the marriage" or when "there is a reasonable possibility of reconciliation."

DESROCHERS v. DESROCHERS

347 A.2d 150 (N.H. 1975)

KENISON, C.J. The parties married in September 1970. Their only child, a daughter, was born in January 1973. The parties separated in May of that year and the wife brought this libel for divorce the following September. A month later the parties agreed to and the court approved arrangements for custody, visitation and support. The defendant did not support his wife and child from the time of separation until the temporary decree. He made the payments called for by the decree from its entry until June 1975. In July 1974, the Hillsborough County Superior Court, Loughlin, J., held a hearing and made certain findings of fact. The critical portion of these findings is: "[T]he action was originally brought because the defendant did not work steadily and stated that he, when he learned that the plaintiff was pregnant, wanted a boy instead of a girl; if the plaintiff bore a girl he would like to put the child up for adoption. After the birth of the child [a daughter] the defendant became very attached to the child, has visited the child weekly except on two occasions, and has been faithfully making support payments under the temporary order of $25.00 a week. The defendant claims that he loves his wife, does not want a divorce. The wife claims that she no longer loves her husband, but since the filing of the divorce he has been an industrious worker and is very attached to the child." The superior court transferred without ruling the question "whether, on all the findings of fact, cause exists for granting a divorce under the provisions of RSA 458:7-a." This appeal was argued in September 1975. At the argument, counsel informed the court that the defendant had stopped making support payments and had gone to Nevada in June 1975. At that time he had written to his attorney expressing his desire to remain married. . . .

RSA 458:7-a (Supp. 1973) is the product of a national discussion regarding the proper grounds for divorce. It follows in important respects the California Family Law Act of 1969. . . . A consensus has emerged that a period of separation due to marital difficulties is strong evidence of the irremediable breakdown of a marriage. . . . When asked to interpret a statute similar to

RSA 458:7-a, the Florida court of Appeal stated: "The Legislature has not seen fit to promulgate guidelines as to what constitutes an 'irretrievably broken' marriage. It is suggested that this lack of definitive direction was deliberate and is desirable in an area as volatile as a proceeding for termination of the marital status. Consideration should be given to each case individually and predetermined policy should not be circumscribed by the appellate courts of this State.

"Thus, we are hesitant to set forth specific circumstances which trial courts could utilize as permissible indices of an irretrievable breakdown of the marital status. Were we to attempt to do so, we feel that the basic purpose of the new dissolution of marriage law would be frustrated. Such proceedings would either again become primarily adversary in nature or persons would again fit themselves into tailor-made categories or circumstances to fit judicially defined breakdown situations. It is our opinion that these two problems are the very ones which the Legislature intended to eliminate." Riley v. Riley, 271 So. 2d 181, 183 (Fla. App. 1972).

The existence of irreconcilable differences which have caused the irremediable breakdown of the marriage is determined by reference to the subjective state of mind of the parties. While the desire of one spouse to continue the marriage is evidence of "a reasonable possibility of reconciliation," it is not a bar to divorce. If one spouse resolutely refuses to continue and it is clear from the passage of time or other circumstances that there is no reasonable possibility of a change of heart, there is an irremediable breakdown of the marriage. The defendant may attempt to impeach the plaintiff's evidence of his or her state of mind regarding the relationship. If the trial court doubts plaintiff's evidence that the marriage has irremediably broken down, the court may continue the action to determine if reconciliation is possible. However, if the parties do not reconcile, dissolution should be granted. . . .

The question whether a breakdown of a marriage is irremediable is a question to be determined by the trial court. RSA 458:7-a contemplates the introduction of factual testimony sufficient to permit a finding of irreconcilable differences which have caused the irremediable breakdown of the marriage. Nevertheless there are limits to the inquiry. "In the first place, there is the natural tendency to withhold information of a personal nature from anyone but a trusted and discreet adviser; secondly, any probing into personal matters against the wishes of the party examined would be objectionable . . . ; and thirdly, the parties have come to court for a purpose. Their answers, which may be perfectly honest ones, will inevitably be slanted in the direction of their ultimate goal, which is divorce." Within these limits the trial court must be adequately informed before acting in matters of such importance. But the statute does not contemplate a complete biopsy of the marriage relationship from the beginning to the end in every case. This is a difficult task, but judges face similar problems in other cases.

The separation of the parties for two and one-half years and the plaintiff's persistence in seeking a divorce during that period is evidence from which the trial court could find that this marriage has irremediably broken down.

Remanded.

NOTES AND QUESTIONS

1. In 2010 New York amended its divorce statute to add the following ground for divorce:

> *Dom. Rel. Law § 170. Action for divorce*
>
> (7) The relationship between husband and wife has broken down irretrievably for a period of at least six months, provided that one party has so stated under oath. No judgment of divorce shall be granted under this subdivision unless and until the economic issues of equitable distribution of marital property, the payment or waiver of spousal support, the payment of child support, the payment of counsel and experts' fees and expenses as well as the custody and visitation with the infant children of the marriage have been resolved by the parties, or determined by the court and incorporated into the judgment of divorce.

How does the New York statute differ from the New Hampshire statute? From the UMDA? If one party files an affidavit that the "relationship between husband and wife has broken down irretrievably for a period of at least six months," can the other party contest it? If so, on what ground? *Compare* Strack v. Strack, 916 N.Y.S.2d 759 (Sup. Ct. Essex County 2011) (irretrievable breakdown is a question of fact that may be subject to a jury trial), *with* Vahey v. Vahey, 940 N.Y.S.2d 824 (Sup. Ct. Nassau County 2012) (court can grant divorce on the basis of plaintiff's self-serving declaration of irretrievable breakdown without a trial).

The statute also provides that the court may not issue a divorce decree without addressing the economic and custody issues in the case. What impact do you think it will have on the parties' negotiating positions in a divorce? *See* A.C. v. D.R., 927 N.Y.S.2d 496 (Sup. Ct. Nassau County 2011).

2. In what sense is the marriage broken where one spouse wishes to continue that marriage? Why do the opposing spouses in *Desrochers* wish to prevent divorce? Should it matter?

3. Does a divorce granted on the ground of "irretrievable breakdown" eliminate consideration of fault? In Hadjimilitis v. Tsavliris, [2003] 1 F.L.R. 81, a wife applied for divorce on the ground of her husband's unreasonable behavior. The couple, who lived in Surrey, England, had married in 1990 and had three children. The family was very wealthy, living in a luxurious home with servants and owning other properties, including a yacht. The wife filed for divorce, alleging that the husband was very controlling, routinely subjecting her to public humiliation and undermining her, and had no interest in her viewpoint or mental well-being. The husband defended the divorce, arguing that the marriage could be saved through counseling and criticizing his wife's behavior, accusing her of having affairs and not being a fit wife or mother. The court held that the wife should be granted the divorce, concluding that it was clear that the marriage had irretrievably broken down and that wife could not reasonably be expected to live with husband. The court accordingly granted a divorce to the wife but not the husband.

Should parties alleging irretrievable breakdown be required to allege and prove facts that establish the breakdown? How do such allegations differ from "fault"? *See* Caffyn v. Caffyn, 806 N.E.2d 415 (Mass. 2004) ("The decision that a marriage is irretrievably broken need not be based on any identifiable objective fact; it is sufficient that a party or parties subjectively decide that their marriage is over and there is no hope of reconciliation."). If the New York courts treat "irretrievable breakdown" as a question of fact that is the proper subject of a jury trial, will they invite the type of allegations present in *Hadjimilitis*?

4. Missouri Statute Section 452.320 authorizes a divorce on the ground that a marriage is irretrievably broken only when both parties agree that it is. In Koon v. Koon, 969 S.W.2d 828 (Mo. App. 1998), the wife alleged that she and her husband had "separated on March 19, 1996," and that the marriage was irretrievably broken "because [Husband] has behaved during the marriage in such a way that [Wife] cannot reasonably be expected to live with him." Under the Missouri statute, a finding that the marriage is irretrievably broken, when contested, must be supported by evidence of various kinds of misconduct by the defendant, such that the wife could not be expected to continue to live with the husband. At trial, the wife testified that her husband tried to control everything she did and that they often argued over how and where money should be spent. She also testified that when the husband was working temporarily in Virginia, she was much happier than when he was at home. In her opinion, there was no hope for reconciliation. The husband testified that he did not believe the marriage was irretrievably broken and that he did not want the court to dissolve the marriage.

In rendering judgment, the trial court found that the parties' marriage was irretrievably broken, but also specifically stated it did "not find that [Husband] has behaved in such a way that [Wife] could not reasonably be expected to live with him." On these findings, the appellate court reversed the trial court, holding that no divorce could be granted on these facts.

How is the Missouri statute different from the New Hampshire statute? The one in New York?

2. The Coexistence of Fault and No-Fault Grounds: Voluntary Separation

FLANAGAN V. FLANAGAN

956 A.2d 829 (Md. App. 2008)

HOLLANDER, J. . . . The parties were married on November 23, 1984. It was a second marriage for each, and they have no children together. Ms. Flanagan left the family home on February 2, 2005.

At the time of trial on September 19, 2006, appellant was 68 years old and appellee was 64 years of age.

. . . Appellee recounted that she moved out of the marital home on February 2, 2005, leaving appellant a letter explaining her decision. She and appellant had lived separate and apart since that date, with no hope of reconciliation.

The letter was admitted into evidence. . . . [In the letter] appellee commented:

> On the average, we spend 51 waking hours together a week. When you are sober I admire your intelligence, your wit and enjoy being with you. However, I have to deal

with your varying degree of intoxication every night for a conservative average of 37 hours per week. This isn't the quality of life I expected to be leading at this stage of my life.

Ms. Flanagan added: "I have resolved not to live my life under these conditions any longer. I want peace."

In her testimony, appellee identified two reasons for her departure from the home, which were consistent with her letter. First, she pointed to appellant's alleged excessive drinking, which often led him to be "accusatory, argumentative, you know, all my faults, real and imagined for twenty years would be paraded out in front of me." Second, she complained about appellant's persistent "internet sexual contacts," which she discovered beginning in 2002. They consisted of visits to pornographic websites, which she characterized as "just nasty," as well as participation in "interactive chat rooms" and activity on dating websites. In December 2002, appellee discovered that appellant had made a date with another couple "to set up a sexual encounter with them at a future date. . . ." She contacted the other couple and arranged, without appellant's knowledge, for the two couples to meet in order to confront appellant. According to appellee, appellant denied his online activity "[u]p until that point no matter what I said. . . ." However, appellee noted that when the other woman, Marianne, "was standing in front of [appellant] with her boyfriend . . . then he could no longer deny it because [the other woman] was there in person." Appellee indicated that she believed appellant's behavior had stopped for a time, but resumed in 2004.

In addition, appellee suggested that appellant was "threatening in his manner." But, she described only one incident of physical force, which occurred in January 2003, when appellant "threw a wallet" at appellee after a session of joint counseling.

Appellant stated that on the afternoon of February 2, 2005, as he was driving home from his job as an auctioneer at the Baltimore City tow lot, appellee called his cell phone and asked him to pull the car over. She then told him she was leaving. Claiming that he was "totally flabbergasted," appellant recalled that he "was close to passing out" from the news. When he returned to the marital home, all of the living room furniture and appellee's bedroom furniture were gone, as well as several boxes that he thought had been packed to go to an auction. He found appellee's farewell letter "on the desk next to the computer."

Appellant admitted to "prowling" for women on the internet in order to "add a little spice to [his] sex life." He explained that in 2002 he had a "severe prostatitis attack," which rendered him "dysfunctional." This condition prevented the parties from engaging in a physical relationship, and "stupidly" prompted him to visit online chat rooms, through which he conversed with a woman named Marianne. He arranged to meet her at an area restaurant, and she brought her boyfriend, Ron. Appellant testified: "Marianne's demeanor did not appeal to me. She had tattoos. She was rough. . . . [A]nd I really wasn't planning on having sex with another male." So, appellant "bought them a bucket of clams and a couple of beers and left." Appellant claimed that, a week later, appellee told him she was taking him out to dinner. When they arrived at the restaurant, the other couple was there, and appellee "threw her arms around Marianne as if they were ancient friends. . . ." Appellant testified: "I spun on my heel and walked out of [the restaurant] and spent the next two hours sitting in the parking lot by myself." Appellee remained in the restaurant with appellant's car keys.

Mr. Flanagan insisted that he had no other internet encounter after that incident. He maintained that sometime thereafter appellee "helped [him] solve the [sexual dysfunction] problem." . . .

In addition, appellant categorically denied ever striking appellee at any time during their marriage. . . .

With regard to his alcohol consumption, appellant insisted that his drinking at home was limited to "a couple of cocktails" before or with dinner every other day or so, but that "after dinner I didn't drink anything at all." . . .

On February 27, 2007, the court issued a "Memorandum Opinion," in which it found voluntary separation as the grounds for divorce. However, neither party had advanced the ground of voluntary separation. . . .

In Maryland, the permissible grounds for divorce are governed by statute. . . . F.L. § 7-103(a) provides the permissible bases for an absolute divorce, which include the following:

> (2) desertion, if:
>   (i) the desertion has continued for 12 months without interruption before the filing of the application for divorce;
>   (ii) the desertion is deliberate and final; and
>   (iii) there is no reasonable expectation of reconciliation;
> (3) voluntary separation, if:
>   (i) the parties voluntarily have lived separate and apart without cohabitation for 12 months without interruption before the filing of the application for divorce; and
>   (ii) there is no reasonable expectation of reconciliation; . . .
> (5) 2-year separation, when the parties have lived separate and apart without cohabitation for 2 years without interruption before the filing of the application for divorce[.]

As noted, appellee's complaint alleged constructive desertion, while appellant alleged actual desertion in his counterclaim. In its Memorandum Opinion, the court awarded a divorce on the basis of "mutual and voluntary separation of more than 12 months." It reasoned that, following appellee's departure from the marital home on February 2, 2005, "[n]either party has attempted reconciliation. Insofar as the separation became mutual and voluntary and both parties indicate there is no reasonable expectation of reconciliation." . . .

We addressed the elements of voluntary separation in Aronson v. Aronson, 115 Md. App. 78, 691 A.2d 785, *cert. denied*, 346 Md. 371, 697 A.2d 111 (1997). We began our analysis by reviewing the Court of Appeals's decision in *Wallace*, 290 Md. 265, 429 A.2d 232. . . . We said:

> What the [*Wallace*] Court said is pertinent here:
>
>> In order to establish the existence of the twelve month voluntary separation ground for divorce *a vinculo* . . . three elements must be shown: (i) an express or implied agreement to separate, *accompanied by a mutual intent not to resume the marriage relationship*; (ii) voluntarily living separate and apart without cohabitation for twelve

months prior to the filing of the bill of complaint; and (iii) that the separation is beyond any reasonable hope of reconciliation.

Indeed, the Court of Appeals has consistently held that voluntariness requires an agreement to live separate and apart, coupled with a common intent to terminate the marriage. . . .

In contrast, "[a]cquiescence in or assent to what one cannot prevent does not amount to a voluntary agreement to separate." . . . Nevertheless, the elements of mutuality and separation need not coincide at the inception of the separation. Indeed, an involuntary separation may later be transformed into a voluntary separation. *Wallace*, 290 Md. at 277; *see also* Fader & Gilbert, *supra*, § 3-5(d), at 83. Thus, a separation that begins as a desertion may later achieve "voluntary" status.

We noted in *Aronson* that proof of a *mutually* voluntary separation was lacking. We explained:

[A]ppellee never affirmatively represented that both parties wanted to end the marriage. Instead, in response to a question from her attorney about whether appellant objected to ending the marriage, she merely said: "We really never talked about it, but he never objected." Apart from testimony that appellant agreed to the separation, she failed to describe statements or conduct by appellant that evinced his intent to end the marriage. Moreover, appellee's assertion that the parties agreed that she would move out of the marital home does not distinguish between an agreement to separate, which appellant concedes, and an agreement to separate for the particular purpose of terminating the relationship, which appellant contests. . . .

Appellee's position is at odds with *Wallace* and *Aronson*; there was no evidence below of an agreement to separate that existed for the requisite duration. Specifically, no evidence was presented as to whether or when appellant affirmatively agreed to terminate the relationship. When appellee left the marital home in February 2005, there was no evidence that the parties had a mutual agreement to separate with the intent to end the marriage. To the contrary, the evidence clearly showed that it was a unilateral decision of appellee. . . . Nor was there evidence of such an agreement by April 11, 2005, i.e., one year before appellee filed her Complaint for Absolute Divorce. . . .

Appellee's reliance on the filing by appellant of a Counter-Complaint for Absolute Divorce is also unavailing. That filing, on May 17, 2006, did not demonstrate that appellant agreed to terminate the nuptial bond at the time that is relevant, i.e., at least one year prior to April 11, 2006 — or assuming that appellant's Counter-Complaint established a new date by which the separation could be measured, one year prior to May 17, 2006.

Moreover, appellant's Counter-Complaint based on desertion did not establish his agreement to a no-fault divorce. Voluntary separation is a no-fault ground, while appellant counterclaimed based on desertion, which is a fault-based ground. . . . As we recognized in *Aronson*, the fact that a party seeks to end the marriage on the basis of fault does not establish the party's acquiescence to a no-fault termination. . . .

Accordingly, we agree with appellant that the court erred in granting a divorce on the ground of voluntary separation. Nevertheless, we are equally convinced that any error was harmless. We explain. . . .

The court did not specify a ground in the Divorce Order. Although the Memorandum Opinion found a voluntary separation, we discern no substantial injury that accrued to appellant as a result of that finding, rather than a finding of desertion or constructive desertion. As appellee underscores, appellant clearly wanted a divorce, as evidenced by his counter-complaint, and he obtained the relief he sought, i.e., an absolute divorce.

Moreover, there was an adequate factual basis in the record for an absolute divorce on the grounds of either actual or constructive desertion. In Ricketts v. Ricketts, 393 Md. 479, 487-88, 903 A.2d 857 (2006), the Court explained:

Desertion may be constructive or actual. We have defined actual desertion as

"the voluntary separation of one of the married parties from the other, or the refusal to renew suspended cohabitation, without justification either in the consent or the wrongful conduct of the other party. . . . [Furthermore,] the separation and intention to abandon must concur, and desertion does not exist without the presence of both. The two need not begin at the same time, but desertion begins whenever to either one the other is added."

Here, the record supported a finding of constructive desertion, the ground alleged by appellee. Moreover, the court made factual findings that were consistent with constructive desertion.

We explained the showing required for a divorce based on the basis of constructive desertion in *Lemley, supra*, 102 Md. App. at 281 (emphasis in original; internal citations omitted):

The question, as framed by the Court of Appeals, is whether [one spouse] has engaged in "such conduct as would make a continuance of the marital relationship inconsistent with the health, self-respect and reasonable comfort of the other." There must be "a pattern of persistent conduct which is detrimental to the safety or health of the complaining spouse, *or so demeaning to his or her self-respect as to be intolerable.*" As the italicized language suggests, it is not necessary in every case to show that the safety or physical health of a spouse is threatened; a grave threat to a spouse's self-respect alone may be sufficient.

The findings of the court below were tantamount to a finding of constructive desertion, and were supported by the record. Notably, the court below found that appellee "decided to leave the marital home . . . after years of her husband's soliciting extramarital sexual relationships on the internet, his heavy drinking and verbal abuse." . . .

NOTES AND QUESTIONS

1. Maryland does not recognize irreconcilable differences or irretrievable breakdown as a ground for divorce. Instead, a voluntary separation of 12 months

or a 2-year separation is the only no-fault grounds for divorce. The 12-month separation requires the agreement of the spouses; the 2-year separation does not. What are the advantages and disadvantages of permitting an innocent spouse who does not want a divorce to delay the final decree?

2. The *Flanagan* court recognizes that at some point a unilateral separation may become mutual if the party who initially opposed the separation no longer wants a reconciliation. What standard does the court use for determining when that point occurs?

3. The *Flanagan* court finds that the trial court's erroneous conclusion that the divorce can be granted on the basis of the parties' voluntary separation is "harmless" because the parties met the requirements for a fault divorce: the husband's constructive desertion. How do the elements of desertion, constructive desertion, and a two-year separation differ from each other?

4. By the time the divorce decree was issued, both parties wanted a divorce, but they did not agree on the grounds. The trial court dealt with the issue by choosing a no-fault basis for the divorce; the appellate court insisted on finding that the husband was at fault in part because the parties had not been separated for the two years required in the absence of mutual consent. How would this case have been handled under the UMDA? How does the presence of fault grounds as an alternative basis for divorce change the dynamic of this case?

5. *Compare* Mo. Stat. §452.320, discussed above, which authorizes a divorce on the ground that a marriage is irretrievably broken only when the two parties agree. If one of the parties denies that the marriage is irretrievably broken, a divorce can be granted only on a finding that the respondent has engaged in marital fault or that the parties have lived separate and apart for 12 months by mutual consent, or 24 months without such agreement, prior to the date of the petition. In In re Marriage of Mitchell, 545 S.W.2d 313 (Mo. App. 1976), the court refused to grant a divorce to a husband, although the husband testified that he no longer loved his wife and had had intercourse with another woman, and although efforts at counseling and reconciliation had failed. As a practical matter, the result is the same as provided by the Maryland statute. Given that the parties could agree to an immediate divorce (though not on the grounds), what purpose does the additional period of separation serve?

6. A number of states, like Maryland, mandate periods of separation or cooling-off periods before a divorce. A study in Korea indicated that cooling-off periods can have a substantial impact on the divorce rate, but in Korea the cooling-off period consisted of a change from a few hours to three weeks to ultimately three months. Jungmin Lee, The Impact of a Mandatory Cooling-Off Period on Divorce, 56 J.L. & Econ. 227 (2013). Professor Lee reports that no similar studies test the effects of delay on divorce rates in the United States. What impact do you think the period of separation had on the parties in the *Flanagan* case? Did it have any impact on their inclination to divorce? Did it make dissolution of their marriage any more amicable? Did it affect their likelihood of remarriage? Cohabitation? Hasty remarriage and another divorce?

3. No-Default Divorce Procedure and Collusion

VANDERVORT V. VANDERVORT

134 P.3d 892 (Okla. Civ. App. 2005)

REIF, J. This appeal arises from post-decree proceedings in which Wife, Patricia Vandervort, sought to vacate the parties' divorce decree. . . . Husband and Wife had agreed to divorce and to divest Wife of nearly all her marital property in anticipation of her eventual need for care in a nursing home for multiple sclerosis. Both believed Wife's single status and complete lack of assets would enable her to receive social security disability income and Medicaid to pay for her nursing home care.

In the time period between the divorce and Wife's need for nursing home care, Husband and Wife were to continue living together at their Texas County residence in Guymon. Husband was to care for Wife until she required nursing home care. Not long after the divorce, however, acrimony developed and Wife ended up living with her parents. Wife claims she went to visit her parents and Husband refused to allow her to return; Husband claims Wife "abandoned" her right to live with him. After considering these facts, along with other evidence and contentions of the parties, the trial court vacated the divorce decree.

In announcing the ruling from the bench, the trial court vacated the decree on the ground of fraud, but did not elaborate. . . .

The petition signed by Husband affirmatively represented that incompatibility was the ground upon which divorce should be granted, while the "consent decree" signed by both parties reflected their mutual agreement that incompatibility existed between them. However, at the time the divorce was sought and granted, Husband and Wife intended to return to their Texas County residence where they were to continue living together with Husband providing and caring for Wife. In fact, they did so for a short time after the divorce. These facts belie their claim of incompatibility.

"The statutory ground of incompatibility does not permit the court to dissolve a marriage merely because its termination is desired by one or both parties." "Incompatibility [cannot be] dependent in application upon an agreement or stipulation between the parties, and thus furnish a vehicle for a consensual divorce which the law did not intend."

"Actionable incompatibility is determined to exist when there is such a conflict of personalities as to destroy the legitimate ends of matrimony and the possibility of reconciliation." Incompatibility must be established "by proof, objective in its character, of causes to which marital disharmony is attributed [and cannot be] bottomed on a mere subterfuge or after-thought [without] a substantial foundation."

The State of Oklahoma has constitutional authority "to declare and maintain a policy in regard to marriage and divorce as to persons domiciled within its borders." "The statutory grounds of divorce are exclusive, and the courts have authority in this field to do only that which is prescribed by the legislature."

"The State is a silent third party in every divorce proceeding." The State is an interested party because "the rights of the plaintiff and defendant are not isolated from the general interest of society in preserving the marriage relation as the foundation of the home and the state." To protect the State's interest, a divorce decree is properly vacated where there is conduct that "amounts to a fraud . . . upon the state as represented by the court in the administration of justice."

In cases where parties to a divorce collude to procure a judgment and one party later seeks to vacate that judgment, the law generally "will leave them where it finds them." However, the Oklahoma Supreme Court has also observed that "where the jurisdiction of the court is invoked and obtained by a fraudulent 'concoction' and the fraud is consummated through the instrumentality of a court of justice, it would impeach the moral sense and that of justice that courts be not protected against such fraud." We conclude the case at hand falls under the latter rule rather than the former. The parties here colluded to misrepresent incompatibility as a ground for divorce (when they actually intended to continue cohabitating) and, in turn, used the sham divorce to deceive public agencies concerning Wife's eligibility for public benefits. It not only offends public policy for parties to obtain a divorce on a concocted ground, but it also offends public policy to use such a divorce for financial gain. Rather than leave the parties where we find them, we believe equity and justice require they be returned to the state of matrimony. The trial court's judgment accomplishes that purpose. . . .

GABBARD, J., dissenting. This case is a good example of how bad facts sometimes make bad law.

. . . The parties were dealing with a problem common to many middle-class Americans: How do couples preserve their marital assets in the face of a catastrophic illness? Their solution was to obtain a divorce in which Husband received virtually all the marital property, thereby qualifying Wife for government assistance when her progressive illness caused her health to deteriorate to the point that she needed nursing home care. Husband promised to care for her in the home until that time. Only after Husband allegedly breached his promise of care did Wife move to set aside the decree. That relief should not be granted.

As the majority and the trial court have concluded, this case involves mutual fraud. It is not a case in which one spouse practices fraud upon the other in order to obtain an advantageous divorce settlement. Where both parties have participated in fraud upon the court, 24 Am. Jur. 2d Divorce and Separation §438 (1998) sets forth the general rule:

> [A] spouse who participates in the fraudulent procurement of a divorce decree, and who freely enjoys the fruits of the decree, will be unable to have it set aside under a rule allowing actions for relief from judgments procured by fraud. . . .
>
>   A court of equity will ordinarily refuse to vacate a decree of divorce where its aid is made necessary by the fault or neglect of the applicant. (Emphasis added.)

This rule is based on sound public policy and has been followed by Oklahoma courts since 1910. . . .

Because the majority's decision is contrary to established precedent and public policy, and provides an unnecessary and inappropriate remedy, I dissent.

NOTES AND QUESTIONS

1. If the husband and wife both agreed to the divorce, against whom was the fraud committed? The most obvious answer is the public authorities who would provide the wife with greater benefits. These authorities are not a party to this case, however, and it is not clear that the couple have violated any law or regulation that pertains to those benefits. The second possible answer is that the husband deceived the wife, but the majority and the dissent agree that the wife knew what she was doing when she agreed to the divorce, and that the real problem is that the husband reneged on his promise to provide for her afterward. The third answer is that the couple deceived the court when they maintained that they were "incompatible." Why should that matter? If both parties have their reasons for wanting a divorce and agree that one should be granted, why should it matter to the state what the reasons are (particularly if they do not violate any other law or regulation)? How does the majority respond to this issue? How does the majority justify continuing the marriage at a point where the parties have demonstrated incompatibility?

2. The dissent, in arguing that the divorce should stand, objects that if no divorce is granted, the wife may recover far more than originally agreed. In the original divorce, the husband received all of the marital property, but agreed to care for the wife. If the divorce is vacated, the wife has the opportunity to obtain her share of the marital property. Why might this trouble the dissenting judge?

3. Courts in other states have disagreed about the continuing importance of collusion. In McKim v. McKim, 6 Cal. 3d 673, 493 P.2d 868, 872 (1972), the California Supreme Court held that collusion barred the granting of a no-fault divorce. On the other hand, the Iowa Supreme Court concluded that "collusion is no longer relevant [in divorce proceedings]. In truth, if it were demonstrated the parties were in collusion to bring about a termination of the marriage relationship, it would further evidence the fact of marital breakdown." In re Marriage of Collins, 200 N.W.2d 886, 890 (Iowa 1972). Will the role of collusion in New York depend on that state's determination of whether "irretrievable breakdown" is a factual determination or a matter of pleading in which the court must accept the parties' statement of subjective intent?

4. Jurisdictions vary considerably in the procedures they have adopted for granting no-fault divorce. In Brunges v. Brunges, 587 N.W.2d 554 (Neb. 1998), the Nebraska Supreme Court followed the view, traditional during the fault era, that divorce cases cannot be resolved by stipulation. Both parties filed pleadings stating that the marriage was irretrievably broken. The trial court relied on these pleadings and granted the petition without taking evidence, although the divorce statute requires a hearing at which testimony or deposition evidence is presented. The Nebraska Supreme Court noted that, ordinarily, a court may rely on admissions in pleadings but that, under the dissolution statute, a hearing must be conducted in divorce cases. See also Davis v. Davis, 16 P.3d 478 (Okla. App. 2000) (applying a statute providing that "no divorce shall be granted without proof" and concluding that since neither party testified and no evidence was produced prior to the granting of the divorce, the divorce decree was invalid).

In contrast, the Mississippi Supreme Court has interpreted its divorce statute to require that, for a divorce to be granted on the grounds of irreconcilable differences, the parties must withdraw their allegation of fault grounds and consent in writing to the grant of the divorce on no-fault grounds. In Irby v. Estate of Irby, 7 So. 3d 223 (Miss. 2009), the state supreme court upheld dismissal of a divorce decree, to which both parties had agreed, because of their failure to dismiss the original complaints alleging fault grounds. The court observed that the purpose of the statute "is to provide a less painful alternative to the traditional grounds for divorce which require[s] . . . parties to publicly put on proof of sensitive private matters. The statute expressly permits parties to 'bargain on the premise that reaching an agreement will avoid the necessity of presenting proof at trial.' The cornerstone of the process is mutual consent."

Would the difference in philosophies and procedures underlying the Mississippi and Nebraska statutes have affected the way the court viewed *Vandervort*?

5. *Cf.* § 302 of the Uniform Marriage and Divorce Act, which requires a court to make several findings as a condition of entering a decree of dissolution, including a finding that the marriage is irretrievably broken. In Texas, however, an appellate court has held that where both parties seek a divorce on the basis of irreconcilable differences, the admissions in each party's respective pleadings can be viewed as admissions of fact on which the court can grant a divorce. In re Marriage of Bradley, 2006 Tex. App. LEXIS 338 (2006).

6. Many cases address the issue of whether third parties with a claim against one spouse can reach the assets the other spouse received in a divorce settlement. *See, e.g.*, Commodity Futures Trading Comm'n v. Walsh, 951 N.E.2d 369 (N.Y. 2011). The court distinguished between assets that an innocent spouse acquires in a divorce proceeding "where that spouse in good faith and without knowledge of the fraud gave fair consideration for the transferred property" and "fraudulently-obtained assets in a divorce settlement, where it is demonstrated that the transferee-spouse was aware of or participated in the fraud or otherwise failed to act in good faith." Do these principles create any ground for recovery in *Vandervort*?

7. Several states have adopted summary dissolution procedures *E.g.*, Cal. Fam. Code §§ 2400 et seq. (2011); Or. Rev. Stat. §§ 107.485, 107.490, 107.500 (2008). These procedures, which are often restricted to marriages with no minor children, typically dispense with any requirement of a hearing as long as the parties have agreed to the distribution of any marital property and abandoned spousal maintenance claims. The California version follows:

California Family Code — Summary Dissolution

§ 2400. [Conditions]

(a) A marriage may be dissolved by the summary dissolution procedure provided in this chapter if all of the following conditions exist at the time the proceeding is commenced:

(1) Either party has met the jurisdictional requirements of Chapter 3 . . . with regard to dissolution of marriage.

(2) Irreconcilable differences have caused the irremediable breakdown of the marriage and the marriage should be dissolved.

(3) There are no children of the relationship of the parties born before or during the marriage or adopted by the parties during the marriage, and the wife, to her knowledge, is not pregnant.

(4) The marriage is not more than five years in duration at the time the petition is filed.

(5) Neither party has any interest in real property wherever situated [with the exception of a short-term residential lease].

(6) There are no unpaid obligations in excess of four thousand dollars ($4,000) incurred by either or both of the parties after the date of their marriage, excluding the amount of any unpaid obligation with respect to an automobile.

(7) The total fair market value of community property assets, excluding all encumbrances and automobiles . . . is less than twenty-five thousand dollars ($25,000) and neither party has separate property assets, excluding all encumbrances and automobiles, in excess of twenty-five thousand dollars ($25,000).

(8) The parties have executed an agreement setting forth the division of assets and the assumption of liabilities of the community, and have duly executed any documents, title certificates, bills of sale, or other evidence of transfer necessary to effectuate the agreement.

(9) The parties waive any rights to spousal support.

(10) The parties, upon entry of the judgment of dissolution of marriage . . . irrevocably waive their respective rights to appeal and their rights to move for a new trial.

(11) The parties have read and understand the summary dissolution brochure provided for in Section 2406.

(12) The parties desire that the court dissolve the marriage. . . .

§ 2403. When six months have expired from the date of the filing of the joint petition for summary dissolution, the court may, upon application of either party, enter the judgment dissolving the marriage. The judgment restores to the parties the status of single persons. . . . The clerk shall send a notice of entry of judgment to each of the parties at the party's last known address.

§ 2406. [Brochure supplied by court.] [This section requires courts to supply a brochure, in "nontechnical" English and Spanish language versions, describing summary dissolution proceedings. The brochure summarizes the procedure. It advises that the parties should consult a lawyer, explains the availability of legal aid lawyers, that spousal support will not be available, and that a permanent adjudication of rights will occur.]

PROBLEMS

1. Arthur is a pilot with Centennial Airlines. He has been flying for Centennial for more than two decades and he has accumulated substantial pension benefits, but he is worried about the financial viability of the company. He files for a divorce from Betsy, his wife of 19 years, a full-time homemaker who is two years older than he is. They agree that there are irreconcilable differences between them. They also agree to a settlement that awards Betsy Arthur's pension, and awards Arthur the couple's house and most of their savings. In accordance with federal law, Betsy is to receive the pension benefits immediately in a lump sum payment of $600,000 even though Arthur has no intention of retiring anytime soon.

Centennial suspects that the divorce is a sham that Arthur and Betsy have arranged to secure immediate payment of the pension benefits. If Centennial were to have financial difficulties, the pension would be paid to the Pension Benefit Guarantee Corporation, which would distribute the benefits in lesser sums on an annual basis after Arthur retired. The total value of the pension in that event would likely be less than the lump sum payment.

Centennial would like to intervene in the divorce proceeding to allege that the couple does not in fact have "irreconcilable differences." Does it have standing to do so? If the couple remarry after Betsy receives the pension funds, and Centennial brings the fact to the attention of the court, is there any action the court could take?

2. Walter and Caren have been married for 30 years. Shortly after Caren learned that Walter faced indictment for securities and accounting fraud, she filed for divorce. Walter and Caren have stipulated that their differences are irreconcilable. They have also agreed to a settlement that gives Caren the family home, which Walter arranged to place solely in Caren's name several years ago and which is worth $6 million, as well as bank accounts worth an additional $2 million. Walter is to receive his pension benefits, which he is likely to forfeit; stock options with a face value of $10 million; and an additional $4 million in stocks and bonds. The precise value of Walter's assets, however, is uncertain because the accounting fraud for which he has been indicted has likely distorted the true value of the holdings. In addition, he faces several billion dollars in potential liability as a result of his fraudulent activities and a potential prison sentence of 10 to 15 years. There is no evidence that Caren knew of or engaged in any of Walter's schemes, but the effect of the divorce will be to insulate Caren and the assets she receives in the settlement from Walter's obligations to provide restitution to his victims.

What actions, if any, should the court take to determine whether the differences between Caren and Walter are irreconcilable? To what extent should the court question the settlement to which they have agreed? On what basis could it either refuse to grant the divorce or alter the property division?

D. EVALUATING DIVORCE REFORM

The availability of divorce remains controversial because family values and family stability remain sources of public concern. In the two decades (and counting) since the end of the divorce revolution, the transformation of the American family has been profound. Divorce rates peaked in the era immediately following the adoption of no-fault divorce, and have plateaued at slightly less than 50 percent of all marriages. For many, divorce rates symbolize the broader trend of family-related changes of which they disapprove—and which they attribute to too great an emphasis on individual preferences and personal satisfaction. For others, divorce reform is no more than a small part of a long-overdue transformation of the family. They believe that divorce law did not cause and cannot prevent the changes underlying the redefinition of family, and any effort to restrict divorce is doomed to failure.

This section asks the question whether the law can or should do anything about the larger issue of family stability. As Carol Weisbrod has written, "there is something in family law that makes the matter particularly difficult. The problem is that centrally we care so much, and that law, finally, can do so little." Weisbrod, On the Expressive Functions of Family Law, 22 U.C. Davis L. Rev. 991, 1004-1007 (1989). The response to Weisbrod's challenge of identifying what the law can do involves three debates: First, should family law generally, and divorce law in particular, express moral precepts underlying family conduct? Second, what factors drive the divorce rate, and does the law have any practical impact on them? Third, are there alternatives to no-fault divorce that are worth considering?

1. The American State of Marriage and Divorce

The debate over marriage and divorce often assumes a national set of values and practices. A new round of divorce scholarship, however, suggests that divorce rates may reflect differences rather than similarities, and that divorce rates may reflect the circumstances surrounding marriage as much, if not more, than the legal rules governing divorce.

ANDREW J. CHERLIN, AMERICAN MARRIAGE IN THE EARLY TWENTY-FIRST CENTURY

15 The Future of Children: Marriage and Child Well-Being 33, 43-46 (Fall 2005)

PUTTING U.S. MARRIAGE IN INTERNATIONAL PERSPECTIVE

How does the place of marriage in the family system in the United States compare with its place in the family systems of other developed nations? It turns out that marriage in the United States is quite distinctive.

A GREATER ATTACHMENT TO MARRIAGE

Marriage is more prevalent in the United States than in nearly all other developed Western nations. . . .

Not only is marriage stronger demographically in the United States than in other developed countries, it also seems stronger as an ideal. In the World Values Surveys conducted between 1999 and 2001, one question asked of adults was whether they agreed with the statement, "Marriage is an outdated institution." Only 10 percent of Americans agreed — a lower share than in any [other] developed nation except Iceland. Twenty-two percent of Canadians agreed, as did 26 percent of the British, and 36 percent of the French. Americans seem more attached to marriage as a norm than do citizens in other developed countries.

MORE TRANSITIONS INTO AND OUT OF MARRIAGE

In addition to its high rate of marriage, the United States has one of the highest rates of divorce of any developed nation. Figure 4 displays the total divorce rate in 1990 for [the United States and six other countries]. . . .

Figure 4.

TOTAL DIVORCE RATES, SELECTED EUROPEAN AND ENGLISH-SPEAKING COUNTRIES, 1990

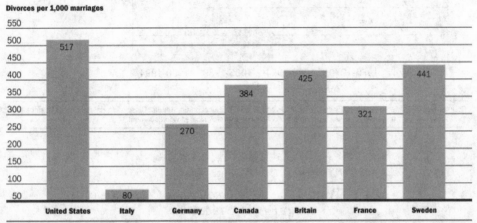

Divorces per 1,000 marriages

United States	517
Italy	80
Germany	270
Canada	384
Britain	425
France	321
Sweden	441

Sources: Monnier and de Guibert-Lantoine, "The Demographic Situation of Europe and the Developed Countries Overseas" (see figure 3); U.S. National Center for Health Statistics, "Advance Report of Final Divorce Statistics, 1989 and 1990," *Monthly Vital Statistics Report* 43, no. 9, supp. (Government Printing Office, 1995).

Both entry into and exit from marriage are indicators of what Robert Schoen has called a country's "marriage metabolism": the number of marriage- and divorce-related transitions that adults and their children undergo. . . . [T]he United States has by far the highest marriage metabolism of any of the developed countries in question. . . . In other words, what makes the United States most distinctive is the combination of high marriage and high divorce rates — which implies that Americans typically experience more transitions into and out of marriages than do people in other countries.

If the United States as a whole has one of the developed world's highest rates of family instability, this rate is not uniform among all groups in the United States. The following chart shows the divergence in divorce rates by wife's educational level, which tends to track income and class. Note that the endpoint for the statistics describes the period between 2000 and 2004, ten years after the marriages between 1990 and 1994.

First Marriages Ending in Divorce Within 10 Years as a Percent
of all First Marriages by Female Educational Attainment

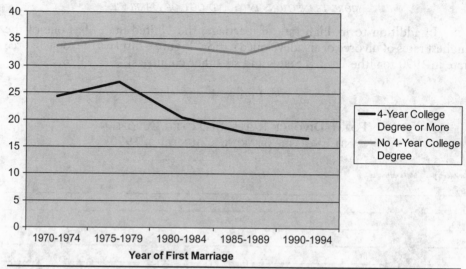

Source: Steven P. Martin, Growing Evidence for a "Divorce Divide"? Education and Marital Dissolution Rates in the U.S. since the
1970s, available at http://www.russellsage.org/publications/workingpapers/divorcedivide/document.

Amy L. Wax, *Engines of Inequality: Class, Race,
and Family Structure*

41 Fam. L.Q. 567, 568-573, 581-582 (2007)

    ... A picture has now emerged of a growing divergence in family life by
social class, income, education, and race. Professional demographers have
known about these trends for some time, and awareness has increased among
social scientists generally. Sara McLanahan, as president of the Population
Association of America, called attention to these developments in a landmark
article in Demography in 2004. Much work in the social sciences literature is
now addressed to documenting these patterns, with efforts directed at
understanding the causes as well as exploring the implications of emerging
family structure disparities along lines of class and race. Legal scholars, in
contrast, have paid relatively little attention to these developments, and few
have probed the implications for family law and policy.
    The segmentation of family forms by class and race is the product of three
interrelated trends. The first is a differential shift in the patterns of marriage,
including its timing and prevalence. The second concerns the incidence of divorce
and remarriage. The third bears on patterns of childbearing and child rearing,
which determine whether children are born within marriage or outside it, and
are raised by both their biological parents, by a single parent, or by some other
combination of adults.

. . . These patterns now vary dramatically by sociodemographic status, and the differences are growing. Despite misconceptions to the contrary, affluent and well-educated whites — society's most privileged group — still marry at very high rates and bear children predominantly within marriage. Although the incidence of divorce increased across the board starting in the 1960s, marriages among the affluent and educated have always been more stable, and divorce has dramatically declined among this group recently. Family "diversity" — and disarray — are now most common among minorities. The traditional family is also declining among less educated whites, including those without a college degree. As summarized recently in a review of family demographics by two economists, "the family trajectories of college graduates have deviated little from the family trajectories of midcentury: almost all children are born within legal marriages, and these marriages are relatively stable. Nonmarital fertility and multipartnered fertility is concentrated among women in the bottom third of the income/education distribution, and the marriages that do take place are relatively early and relatively unstable."

. . . Marriage has long been the foundation for family and child rearing in the United States. . . . Nonetheless, new patterns — called by some demographers the "second transition" — began to emerge "around 1960." One important element of this transition was a change in marital behavior. Age of marriage began to climb for both men and women, and there was a slow but steady decrease in the number of people entering into marriage in all sociodemographic groups.

These overall patterns, however, mask profound differences by race and class — differences that have intensified recently. The relationship of marriage to class has shifted over time. For example, "[h]alf a century ago, Americans, whether poor or well-to-do, all married at roughly the same rate." This uniformity, with some minor variations, continued through this century and into the post-World-War-II period. By the mid-1980s, however, marriage rates began to diverge, with poor women only about three-quarters as likely to marry as more privileged women by the end of that decade. The decline in marriage among the disadvantaged has continued, with poor men and women in 2005 "only about half as likely to be married as those with incomes at three or more times the poverty level."

. . . Class and race have become more strongly correlated not just with the incidence of marriage but also with its persistence. In short, class now predicts marital stability, with more educated persons enjoying longer-lasting relationships.

The correlation between high levels of education and marital longevity has not always been so strong. The incidence of divorce increased generally after World War II, with women at all levels of education ending their marriages in the 1960s and 1970s at about the same rate. Beginning around 1980, however, the incidence of divorce began to diverge. The divorce rate for women without an undergraduate college degree has remained about the same, which is about thirty-five percent. "But for college graduates, the divorce rate in the first [ten] years of marriage has plummeted to just over 16[%] of those married between 1990 and 1994 from 27[%] of those married between 1975 and 1979." Divorce risk has become more sensitive to men's education level as well, with more years of schooling now significantly reducing the odds of divorce. Although better-educated men and women tend to marry later, their reduced divorce risk is only partly explained by the positive association between later marriage and marital stability.

Just as with other demographic trends in marriage and the family over the last fifty years, divorce rates have diverged by race and ethnicity. Blacks have always divorced more often than whites, but blacks have seen a steeper increase since the mid-1980s. As demographers Megan Sweeney and Julie Philips observe, ". . . divorce rates for white women continued to increase during the late 1970s, reaching a peak in 1969, and then stabilized (and even declined somewhat) during the 1980s." In contrast, "[b]eginning in the mid to late 1980s . . . crude divorce rates for blacks appear to drift upward. . . . Indeed the smoothed divorce rate among white women was 9% lower than that of black women in 1980, but by 1993, this difference had expanded to 29%." Although the decline in black marriage rates in recent decades would be expected to decrease the risk of divorce as the population entering into marriage became more selective, in fact the trend has been in the opposite direction. Large differences in the divorce rates of blacks and whites have persisted through the 1990s and into this decade.

. . . In sum, disparities in father absence between well-off children and the less privileged have widened in recent decades and are growing. The gaps in family structure between blacks and whites, especially among educated families, are also pronounced. Class and race differences in family type affect individual children and the wider community. These disparities systematically undermine attempts to create equal opportunity across lines of class and race.

NOTES AND QUESTIONS

1. Paul Amato and his associates find further that the existence of multiple groups of families with different experiences explains one of the mysteries in divorce literature: why measures of marital happiness have dropped even as the unhappiest couples have become less likely to marry. They explain:

> During this period [1980-2000], marriages became more peaceful, with fewer disagreements, less aggression and fewer interpersonal sources of tension between spouses. At the same time, the lives of husbands and wives became more separate, as spouses shared fewer activities. The trend for marital relationships to be less discordant and more individualistic appears to have had few implications for the overall level of satisfaction; spouses were as happy with marriages in 2000 as they were two decades earlier. And with lower levels of conflict and perceived problems, stable marriages were more common in 2000 than in 1980. But somewhat paradoxically, unstable marriages also became more common. People who had *ever* thought that their marriages were in trouble became more likely to progress to advanced stages of instability, such as talking with their spouses about divorce. Presumably, tolerant public attitudes about divorce and the legal ease of getting a divorce have made it easier for individuals with marital problems to think seriously about dissolution. Moreover, because marriages have become more individualistic since 1980, spouses may be less dependent emotionally on one another and hence less likely to invest time and resources in improving their relationship.

Paul Amato et al., Alone Together: How Marriage in America Is Changing 68 (2007). These researchers add that many developments, such as women's greater workforce participation, affect different groups differently — for well-educated women with egalitarian attitudes, employment was associated with an increase in marital stability; for women with more traditional attitudes who preferred to work less, full-time employment was associated with a significant decrease in marital happiness and stability.

How might these factors affect the different racial and class patterns underlying divorce?

2. Scholars are now uniform in acknowledging the class and racial differences in family patterns described above. *Compare*, for example, Charles A. Murray, Coming Apart: The State of White America, 1960-2010 (2012) (documenting the changing family patterns among whites and the class divisions Wax describes), *with* June Carbone & Naomi Cahn, Marriage Markets: How Inequality Is Remaking the American Family (2014) (documenting the same patterns and demonstrating that the same forces affect white and minority families in similar ways). There is less agreement about what causes these patterns. Consider the following possible explanations:

Differences in the age of the marriage: The better educated tend to marry later than others, and marital age, even when researchers control for other factors such as income and education, has a small, though statistically significant, correlation with more stable marriages. *See* Stéphane Mechoulan, Divorce Laws and the Structure of the American Family, 35 Legal Stud. 143 (2006).

Assortative mating: The better off have become increasingly likely to marry the better off. In 2000 levels of assortative mating were higher than they had been at any time since 1940, and they have increased further since then. *See* Christine R. Schwartz, Trends and Variation in Assortative Mating: Causes and Consequences, 39 Ann. Rev. Soc. 451, 460 (2013).

Cultural changes: Less stigma is associated with divorce, nonmarital births, and nonmarital sexuality. The declining stigma has made it easier for mothers to raise children on their own, and women initiate the majority of divorces. Some treat these changes and the no-fault divorce laws associated with them as a symbol of cultural acceptance of greater individualism. *See, e.g.*, James Q. Wilson, The Marriage Problem (2002); Ross Douthat, More Imperfect Unions, N.Y. Times, Jan. 25, 2014, available at http://www.nytimes.com/2014/01/26/opinion/sunday/douthat-more-imperfect-unions.html?ref = rossdouthat (last visited May 1, 2014). Amy Wax concludes that male misbehavior — "men's chronic criminal behavior, drug use, violence, and, above all, repeated and flagrant sexual infidelity" — is a significant factor in explaining poor families' greater instability. Engines of Inequality, 590. She suggests that "single-parent families are, on average, less effective in regulating male behavior" and that better socialization into appropriate norms is part of the answer. *Id*. at 591.

Economic changes: The class-based changes in the incidence of divorce occurred at the same time as an increase in inequality. In addition, male employment instability (the likelihood of changing jobs or being laid off) increased for working class men while staying the same for college graduates through the mid-2000s. Why might these changing economic factors affect divorce rates?

Professors Carbone and Cahn, above, argue that inequality does three things. First, it has increased the gender gap in wages at the top. Looking at the median income of college graduates who work full time, men's wages increased more rapidly than women's wages in the period between 1990 and 2008. Well-educated women used to make a higher percentage of the "male" wage than less educated women; now they make a lower percentage of the male wage than other groups of women. During the same period, well-educated men have come to place greater emphasis on their prospective spouse's earnings. After all, it takes two substantial incomes to live in expensive cities such as New York, San Francisco, or Washington, D.C., where inequality between the top and the middle has grown most rapidly. The result is that the larger group of high-income men seeks to marry spouses from the relatively smaller group of high-income women, and the only group whose marriage rates increased in this period are the top 5 percent of women by income, the group of women who have seen the greatest drop in income parity with men.

Second, greater income inequality has increased the number of men at the bottom who are effectively unmarriageable due to high rates of chronic unemployment, mass incarceration, and to a lesser degree substance abuse. All of these factors tend to be more prevalent in more unequal societies, and they have risen over the last 25 years in American working class communities. A rich literature shows that an increase in the number of marriageable women to marriageable men in a particular community tends to decrease the marriage rates of the entire group (not just the unemployed or the incarcerated) and that differences in the number of available men explain a significant percentage of the racial differences in marriage rates.

Third, the middle consists of those who graduate from high school but not college and cluster near the fiftieth percentile in income. The wage gap has narrowed for this group, with women earning a higher percentage of the male wage than they once did, and income and job stability declining for the men in this group over the last 30 years. Andrew Cherlin finds that white women high school graduates have a higher number of cohabitations — including marriage, remarriage, and nonmarital cohabitations — than any other group. Andrew J. Cherlin, Between Poor and Prosperous: Do the Family Patterns of Moderately-Educated Americans Deserve a Closer Look?, *in* Changing Families in an Unequal Society 68-84 (Marcia J. Carlson & Paula England eds., 2011).

Consider how these different explanations might interact with changes in divorce laws discussed below.

2. *What Role Does the Law Play?*

Many scholars have argued that the principal effect of divorce law on marital stability is its "expressive function," that is, its reinforcement of appropriate societal norms. To what extent should no-fault divorce be held responsible for the increase in family instability? To what extent can legal changes remedy the issue? Although many have advocated greater restrictions on divorce, covenant marriage has been the major innovation to date, and it has had little effect.

A principal shift in divorce discourse over the years, however, has involved identification of the "victims" and "villains" of divorce. In the initial period after the adoption of no-fault divorce, some opponents feared that it would become a "wife-stuffing" measure in which well-off men traded in their long-time wives for younger women, leaving the first wives destitute. More recently, divorce critiques have identified women, who initiate approximately two-thirds of divorces, as the villains, particularly when they end marriages without what (as least in the old days) would be considered good cause. In every era, children, of course, are the real victims, no matter which parent is at fault.

These different perspectives frame divorce discourses. For those who oppose divorce altogether, liberalized divorce laws, which make divorce easier to obtain and express the acceptability of divorce, tend to be seen as the problem. The solution is to make divorce harder to get, deterring (at least in theory) those too quick to file as the solution for temporary setbacks in a marriage. For those who see divorce as facilitating "wife-stuffing," or more neutrally, the ability to renege on obligations to a vulnerable partner, the solution tends to be greater financial obligations. The higher-earning spouse should not be able to cut off a dependent spouse, but should instead be held to a longer period of support. In fact, however, few states, including those that retain fault grounds, directly tie the financial consequences of divorce to fault and there seems to be little sentiment for doing so. Sanford L. Braver & Ira Mark Ellman, Citizens' Views About Fault in Property Division, 47 Fam. L.Q. 419 (2013). For those who blame increased divorce rates on women, the remedy tends to be giving fathers greater custody rights. Fathers' rights advocates argue that men should have an equal say in what happens to their children without necessarily referencing the potential impact on divorce, but the effect is to make marital dissolution more perilous for mothers who wish to control access to their children (see Chapter 9).

As you read through the next set of excerpts, consider how these perspectives shape the arguments and the likely impact of proposed solutions.

ELIZABETH S. SCOTT, *DIVORCE, CHILDREN'S WELFARE, AND THE CULTURE WARS*

9 Va. J. Soc. Pol'y & L. 95, 95-106, 107-108, 111 (2001)

Are children harmed when their parents divorce? If so, should parents' freedom to end marriage be restricted? . . . During the 1970s and 80s, the traditional conviction that parents should stay together "for the sake of the children" was supplanted by a view that children are usually better off if their unhappy parents divorce. By this account, divorcing parents should simply try to accomplish the change in status with as little disruption to their children's lives as possible.

This stance has been challenged sharply by conservative family-values advocates who see divorce and marital instability as the key to societal decline. In their view, children whose parents divorce are damaged in their moral, social, and emotional development, and society ultimately pays a high price through increased teen pregnancy, school drop-outs, poverty, and delinquency. These advocates argue that marriage can only be saved if the government restricts divorce by reinstituting fault grounds and discouraging unhappy spouses from selfishly defecting from their responsibilities. In contrast, liberals and some feminists oppose any restrictions on the freedom of unhappy spouses to divorce, in part because they suspect (correctly for the most part) that the ultimate agenda for many conservatives is a return to the era of traditional marriage and gender roles. Liberals tend to discount concerns about the harm to children of divorce and assume that parents only end marriages that are intolerable. . . .

A growing body of social science research on the impact of divorce on children indicates that the issue is more complex than either conservatives or liberals would have us believe. Among the most important studies of the past decade is a longitudinal study of families conducted by Paul Amato and Alan Booth. Contrary to the conservative line that divorce is always bad for children, Amato and Booth found that children who are exposed to serious conflict in their parents' marriage are better off when conflict is reduced by divorce. On the other hand, we should not reassure ourselves that children generally are better off if their unhappy parents divorce. A surprisingly high percentage of marriages that end in divorce involve low or moderate levels of conflict — what Amato calls "good enough" marriages. Those divorces appear to have quite a negative impact on the long term well-being of the children involved. In short, those children whose parents' marriages are not highly conflictual would be better off if their parents stayed together. . . .

Parents who end low-conflict marriages are an interesting and puzzling group because they seem to choose divorce even though their marriages are not that bad — even by their own reports. In the Amato and Booth study, these spouses reported general happiness, little hostility and indeed expressed affection and respect for their spouses shortly before divorce. They engaged in activities together and generally gave little sign that divorce was likely. So, why did they divorce? The reasons Amato lists are not primarily related to the quality of the marriage. Rather, these individuals left their marriages because (compared to those who remained married) they were less subject to constraints that create barriers to divorce. These constraints include financial costs of divorce, religious beliefs, and close community ties. When asked to explain their decisions, those who left low-conflict marriages reported mid-life crises, dissatisfaction with their spouse's personality, or, in some cases, no reason that they could articulate.

The readiness of parents to leave "good enough" marriages may reflect changing attitudes toward marriage and marital commitment. . . . If this account is accurate, then the attitude that an unsatisfying marriage should be set aside even if it is not miserable, makes some sense. Divorce, on this view, allows each spouse to pursue fulfillment elsewhere. . . .

Whatever its deficiencies, traditional divorce law created barriers that reinforced the initial commitment that most couples have when they get married. By imposing substantial costs on the decision to divorce (the requirement of proving fault), divorce law discouraged unhappy spouses from leaving marriage because of transitory dissatisfaction or routine stresses — boredom, mid-life crises, and the like. Thus, it seems likely that divorces of the kind that seem to be most harmful to children were less common under the fault regime. . . . In general, unhappy spouses likely pursued this option only when continuing in marriage was intolerable and most couples in "good enough" marriages stayed together.

The no-fault reforms removed these legal barriers and made divorce easier. . . . The upshot is that spouses who are not deterred by other barriers (religion, social disapproval, financial constraints), or who have attractive alternatives (other relationships perhaps), are more likely to leave marriage than might have been true a generation ago. . . .

IRA MARK ELLMAN, *THE MISGUIDED MOVEMENT TO REVIVE*
FAULT DIVORCE, AND WHY REFORMERS SHOULD LOOK
INSTEAD TO THE AMERICAN LAW INSTITUTE

11 Int'l J.L. Pol'y & Fam. 216, 219-226 (1997)

Some opponents of pure no-fault divorce believe that no-fault provisions are a cause of rising divorce rates, and that revision of the divorce laws will therefore help reverse that trend. With that goal in mind, some propose a waiting period for a year or more before divorce will be granted, at least for couples with minor children. Even longer waiting periods, up to five years, have been urged before allowing a unilateral no-fault divorce, and some would bar them altogether. Would such proposals work to reduce marital break-up? At one level the claim that the divorce laws affect the rate of divorce seems necessarily true. If divorce were entirely barred, as it was in Ireland until very recently, then there would be no divorces at all. And so it also seems plausible to think that if divorce were allowed, but more difficult to obtain, then the divorce rate would decline. The obvious problem, however, is that while legal barriers can affect the rate of formal divorce, it is far less clear they can affect the rate of actual marital demise. . . .

There are many reasons to think that the law is a minor player in affecting divorce rates. . . .

Of course, it is true that divorce rates are higher today than in the 1960s. The long-term historical pattern of rising divorce rates "is a wide-spread phenomenon in western societies" despite their varying divorce laws. Indeed, divorce laws vary within the United States as well. . . . But while there are marked regional variations in the United States, they are entirely unrelated to regional patterns in divorce laws: the two regions most resistant to pure no-fault divorce laws, the South and the Northeast, have the highest and lowest divorce rates, respectively. Cultural patterns, by contrast, have clear effects on divorce rates. Some religious groups have far lower divorce rates than others, and interfaith marriages, which have increased, have higher divorce rates than intrafaith marriages. . . .

Some no-fault critics are less concerned with deterring divorce than deterring bad marital behaviour. They are therefore less interested in abolishing no-fault grounds for divorce, or imposing lengthy waiting periods, than in making marital fault a factor in allocating marital property or awarding alimony. . . .

. . . If one has in mind the suppression of truly bad behaviour, like interspousal violence, then divorce law seems neither the simplest nor the most effective available tool. The behaviour one seeks to suppress is already a violation of the criminal law and actionable in tort, and in some states the tort claim can even be joined with the dissolution action. Undoubtedly more could be done to improve these remedies. But the claim that the violent actor undeterred by these sanctions will nevertheless cease that violence to avoid its consideration at divorce—a divorce he may not yet even contemplate—seems rather implausible. . . .

STÉPHANE MECHOULAN, *DIVORCE LAWS AND THE STRUCTURE
OF THE AMERICAN FAMILY*

35 J. Legal Stud. 143, 144-147, 165-166 (2006)

Divorce laws have received much attention lately. . . . A commonly expressed claim in support of a return to a fault rule is that the move to no fault caused the divorce rate to rise. . . .

Since the mid-1970's, a vast body of literature has sought to understand the effects of these divorce laws. . . .

The starting point of this analysis rests on the following observations: not only have aggregate divorce rates decreased since most of the legal changes were passed, but the average difference in divorce rates across different divorce regimes has been narrowing. One should then also investigate why, since the early 1980s, divorce rates have decreased faster, on average, in states where fault is not considered for property. . . .

The paper explores the hypothesis that spouses take the law into account and sort themselves differently accordingly to which rule governs their future divorce. . . .

Using cross-sectional micro data . . . (1971-98), the findings first confirm that for couples who married before the changes in the law, there was a significant impact of no fault for property or divorce odds: this is referred to as the "pipeline effect" (that is, the increased divorce rate resulting from the divorces of couples whose marriages were falling apart but who did not divorce until the new law took effect). Most important, among individuals who have not experienced a change in property law since their marriage, the odds of divorce are found not to differ significantly between the two regimes [*i.e.*, fault and no fault]: my interpretation is that the direct effect and the indirect effect (that is, better selection at marriage) cancel out. The law defining divorce grounds, in contrast, has a more limited impact on divorce probabilities. Further, there is evidence of a delay in marriage for women when fault is irrelevant for property decisions, ceterus paribus, a longer search also points toward better matching.

. . . To summarize, this theory says that the divorce law changes introduced in the early 1970's affected the odds of divorce for those couples who married before these laws were passed. Such couples were more likely to divorce after a change in law from fault to no-fault divorce, and the key variable seems to be the law governing property division and spousal support. Once the first legal changes passes, many poorly matched couples who married before the changes in the law broke up, thus boosting the rate of divorce. The legal changes that appeared later still had some impact for those who had married under a fault regime. Most important, the effect of no-fault divorce was mitigated by those couples who reduced their probability of divorce through better sorting upon marriage. The main conclusion of the paper is that this better sorting decreased the probability of divorce by about as much as the institution of no-fault increased it.

This selection effect is apparent since under no fault for property laws on average women marry when they are significantly older than are women in fault states. This work thus provides an explanation for the observed apparent convergence in divorce rates between fault and no-fault states over the last 20 years. It presents a consistent interpretation for the argument that the effects of unilateral divorce laws on divorce rates died out a decade after their introduction. The results also expand on . . . [those scholars] who found that couples married under unilateral divorce regimes are less likely to divorce than those married under mutual consent regimes, all else being equal, despite living in a state with a more liberal regime, which reinforces the theory of selection into marriage. . . .

KATHERINE SHAW SPAHT, *COVENANT MARRIAGE SEVEN YEARS LATER: ITS AS YET UNFULFILLED PROMISE*

65 La. L. Rev. 605, 612-615 (2005)

A Louisiana covenant marriage differs in three principal respects from other legally recognized "standard" marriages: 1) mandatory pre-marital counseling; 2) the legal obligation to take all reasonable steps to preserve the couple's marriage if marital difficulties arise; and 3) restricted grounds for divorce consisting of *fault* on the part of the other spouse or two years living separate and apart. Each of the three components addresses John Witte's observation in *From Sacrament to Contract* that restricting exit rules of marriage by reforming divorce law requires complementary legal restrictions on entry into marriage. Covenant marriage restricts entry into and exit from marriage for those who choose it and attempts to strengthen the marriage itself by imposing a legal obligation upon the covenant spouses which they agree to in advance of their marriage — taking *reasonable* steps to preserve their marriage if difficulties arise.

The mandatory pre-marital counseling under the covenant marriage statute must contain counsel about the seriousness of marriage, the intent of the couple that it be lifelong, and the agreement that the couple will take all reasonable steps to preserve the marriage. Any minister, priest, rabbi, or the secular alternative of a professional marriage counselor is permitted to provide the counseling and sign an attestation form. . . .

At the end of the mandatory pre-marital counseling, the prospective spouses sign a document called a Declaration of Intent that contains the content of their *covenant*, which includes the agreement to seek counseling if difficulties arise. . . . The Declaration of Intent is in essence a special *contract* authorized by the state (Louisiana, Arizona, or Arkansas) that contains legal obligations similar to those in ordinary contracts. Most importantly, it is the agreement of the covenant spouses in advance to take reasonable steps to preserve their marriage. . . . This obligation to take reasonable steps to preserve the marriage begins at the moment the marital difficulties arise and "should continue" until rendition of the judgment of divorce, the one exception being "when the other spouse has physically or sexually abused the spouse seeking the divorce or a child of one of the spouses."

Lastly, a spouse in a covenant marriage may obtain a divorce only if she can prove adultery, conviction of a felony, abandonment for one year, or physical or sexual abuse of her or a child of the parties. Otherwise, the spouses must live separate and apart for two years. A comparison of the grounds for divorce in a Louisiana "standard" marriage reveals that a covenant marriage commits the spouses in advance to a relinquishment of the easy exit rules in favor of more stringent, morally based exit rules. In a "standard" marriage a spouse may seek a divorce for adultery, conviction of a felony, or living separate and apart for *six months* either before *or* after a suit for divorce is filed. There is an enormous difference between living separate and apart for six months versus living that way for two years. . . .

NOTES AND QUESTIONS

1. Compare the different views of these authors on the relationship between legal changes and divorce rates. How do the authors see the role of law? How do the authors describe the moral understandings that make spouses more or less willing to divorce?

How does divorce affect children? Do you accept Professor Scott's views, based on the best sociological work of her era, that divorce hurts children in the vast majority of cases where the parents' "misbehavior" would not constitute fault? For an alternative view, *see* Mark Strasser, Marriage, Cohabitation and the Interests of Children, 3 Ala. C.R.-C.L. L. Rev. 101 (2013).

2. One of the factors that does affect the increase in divorce rates is the changing role of women. Professors Brinig and Allen found in 2000 that two-thirds of those initiating divorce were women, and a factor that affected women's willing to file was custody: women who feared losing their children were less likely to initiate a divorce. Margaret F. Brinig & Douglas W. Allen, "These Boots Are Made for Walking": Why Most Divorce Filers Are Women, 2 Am. L. & Econ. Rev. 126, 128 tbl. 1, 136-137 (2000).

In another study, Professors Betsey Stevenson and Justin Wolfers reported that the adoption of no-fault divorce produced an 8 to 16 percent decline in wives' suicide rates and a 30 percent decline in domestic violence. Betsey Stevenson & Justin Wolfers, Bargaining in the Shadow of the Law: Divorce Laws and Family Distress, 121 Q.J. Econ. 267-288 (2006).

How do these findings affect your view of the arguments made above? What impact do you think covenant marriage is likely to have on despondent women or those who feel trapped? Which groups benefit most from divorce that is easier to obtain?

3. Professor Mechoulan is an economist who attempted to measure the impact of the legal changes by comparing the divorce rates of couples who married in states that allow consideration of fault in the property division with divorce rates in states that do not. He compared women who married before and after the legal change, and found the divorce odds greater for those who married before a change in the law eliminated consideration of fault in the property award. (The addition of no-fault grounds to fault grounds, in contrast, did not produce much effect.) He further found that once he eliminated the "surprise effect" from the change in the law, the divorce rates in the different states tended to be comparable, but the age of marriage increased considerably in the no-fault compared with the fault states. Controlling for education reduced the magnitude of the effect, but it remained statistically significant. Mechoulan concludes that without legal protection, women search longer to find the right mate since compatibility will be what keeps them together. Can you think of other reasons the age of marriage might

be higher in no-fault states than in states that continue to permit consideration of fault?

4. Louisiana was the first state to adopt covenant marriage. Arizona and Arkansas also offer an option of "covenant marriage" either as an initial marital state or through conversion of an earlier marriage to the covenant form. Ariz. Rev. Stat. Ann. §§ 25-901 to 906 (2014); Ark. Code Ann. §§ 9-11-801 to 9-11-811 (2014). The Arizona statute provides for divorce on fault grounds but also on no-fault grounds (separation for at least one year after a separation decree or two years without such a decree or where both spouses agree to the dissolution). Ariz. Rev. Stat. Ann. § 25-903. The Arkansas statute allows dissolution only for fault grounds and where the parties have been separated without reconciliation for two years after entrance of a decree of separation, and also provides that if there is a minor child of the marriage, the waiting period will be two and one-half years from the date of the separation judgment. Ark. Code Ann. § 9-11-808.

5. Participation in covenant marriage has remained low in the states that adopted it — no more than 2 percent of new marriages in Louisiana, and even lower rates in Arizona and Arkansas. Jonathan Mummolo, Va. Foundation Seeks to Reduce Divorces, Wash. Post, July 26, 2007, at B1. Moreover, while the divorce rate has been lower — 8.6 percent of covenant marriage couples in Louisiana were divorced five years after the wedding, in comparison with 15.4 percent of other couples — careful sociological research indicates that the lower divorce rate reflects the characteristics of the individuals who choose this type of marriage. These characteristics include the wife's religiosity, her higher level of education, the lack of previous cohabitation and of children with a different partner, and greater community support — factors that produce lower divorce rates even without covenant marriage. Steven L. Nock, Laura A. Sanchez & James D. Wright, Covenant Marriage: The Movement to Reclaim Tradition in America 3, App. A (2008). Nock and his co-authors indicate that one of the reasons participation in covenant marriage is rare is that relatively few people know about it.

6. The most controversial part of covenant marriage is that it makes it harder to divorce by limiting the grounds. Absent fault of the type specified in the statute, the parties would have to separate for two years, rather than the six months specified for "ordinary" Louisiana marriages. How do the covenant marriage provisions compare with the Maryland divorce statute discussed in *Flanagan*, above?

7. The least controversial part of covenant marriage is the requirement of premarital counseling. While only three states have adopted covenant marriage, more than twice that number now mandate some time type of marriage education. *See* Alan J. Hawkins, Will Legislation to Encourage Premarital Education Strengthen Marriage and Reduce Divorce? 9 J.L. Fam. Stud. 7 (2007). Such programs combine emphasis on commitment, similar to the approach of covenant marriage statutes, with advice about preparation, recognizing the warning signs of domestic violence, harboring realistic expectations about finances, keeping lines of communication open, maintaining mutual respect, and other factors that might be expected to postpone (if not derail) youthful nuptials. Follow-up studies, however, show that most programs have little if any impact on divorce rates. *See, e.g.*, A.J. Hawkins, P.R. Amato & A. Kinghorn, Are Government-Supported Healthy Marriage Initiatives Affecting Family Demographics? A State-Level Analysis, 62

Fam. Rel. 501-513 (2013). For an alternative system promoting reconciliation, *see* Solangel Maldonado, Facilitating Forgiveness and Reconciliation in "Good Enough" Marriages, 13 Pepp. Disp. Resol. L.J. 105 (2013).

8. If parties enter into a covenant marriage, or some other variation (such as a marriage with an extended waiting period when there are children of the marriage or requiring fault grounds if there are children), and one of the spouses seeks a divorce in a jurisdiction that offers pure no-fault divorce grounds, will the restrictions of the state where the marriage was entered into be given effect?

As we will see in Chapter 12, dealing with jurisdiction, divorce can take place in any state in which either of the married parties is domiciled. *See* Williams v. North Carolina, 317 U.S. 287 (1942); Williams v. North Carolina, 325 U.S. 226 (1945). Moreover, the forum state, assuming jurisdiction, may and ordinarily does apply its own rules for divorce, even if they differ substantially from the rules in effect in the place where the parties were married. Consequently, the enforceability in other states of limits on divorce associated with covenant marriage, for example, is doubtful. *See* Brian H. Bix, Choice of Law and Marriage: A Proposal, 36 Fam. L.Q. 255, 259-260 (2002); Katherine Shaw Spaht & Symeon C. Symeonides, Covenant Marriage and the Law of Conflicts of Law, 32 Creighton L. Rev. 1085 (1999).

Property Division and Spousal Support

6

A. OVERVIEW

This chapter and Chapters 7 and 8 concern orders that courts use to allocate the economic rights and obligations of parents and former spouses. This chapter covers property division and spousal support (also called alimony or maintenance) at the time of divorce. Chapter 7 concerns initial child support orders. Chapter 8 deals with modification, termination, and enforcement of support orders and the federal income tax and bankruptcy treatment of obligations.

As we will see, there is debate about whether the justifications and criteria for making these awards differ. As a practical matter, courts and lawyers always consider the relationship among these orders to arrive at a complete picture of the postdivorce economic circumstances of former spouses and their children. On the other hand, practicality also dictates distinguishing and labeling these orders because very important "collateral" consequences of an order — its modifiability and terminability, its tax and bankruptcy consequences — turn on this distinction. Property division orders are not modifiable, but support orders are. Property division and child support have no income tax consequences, while spousal support is deductible to the payor and income to the payee. Support is not dischargeable in bankruptcy, while property division obligations sometimes are.

These issues are the stuff of which a large portion of domestic relations practice is made. This reason alone justifies extended treatment of them. But determination of the economic consequences of divorce is not merely the point at which theoretical and principled understandings about the nature of the family and family law are practically implemented. When courts and legislatures decide what constitutes property and how it should be divided, when and why spousal support is required, and how to divide financial obligations to children between parents who no longer live in the same household, they reexamine fundamental questions about what constitutes a "family," and why and how family membership changes a person's rights and duties.

1. *Historical Justifications of and Criteria for Economic Awards*

A commonly told story of changes in the law of property division and support over the last century assumes that before the no-fault revolution the law sharply distinguished property from support orders. Property was supposed to have been awarded to the spouse who owned it during marriage, and support orders carried the entire burden of providing for dependent women and children. Moreover, the fault theory of divorce shaped the availability of support, for a wife[1] found at fault was not entitled to alimony and was likely to lose custody of the children and so not be entitled to support for them either. As fault-based divorce covertly turned into consensual divorce, according to this story, the presence or absence of formal grounds became bargaining tools used to shape the economic consequences.

Neither the law nor the reality was ever this simple. In some jurisdictions at some times the criteria for property division were not sharply distinct from those for spousal and child support, and scholarly articles written in the early twentieth century debated whether "alimony" was in the nature of support or property division. F. Granville Munson, Some Aspects of the Nature of Permanent Alimony, 16 Colum. L. Rev. 217 (1916). *See also* Chester G. Vernier & John B. Hurlbut, The Historical Background of Alimony Law and Its Present Structure, 6 Law & Contemp. Probs. 197 (1939). Nor were property awards based solely on simple assessments of who owned what during marriage:

> In the nineteenth century, a property settlement apparently was awarded to the wife under the same theory that ongoing support or alimony would be awarded today (i.e., for future needs), rather than as a division of the accumulated assets of the marriage. The legal profession termed this property settlement "alimony," but because the word often was used rather indiscriminately, authority existed for the proposition that "alimony" was meant to include maintenance not only for the wife but also for those children committed to her custody.

Donna Schuele, Origins and Development of the Law of Parental Child Support, 27 J. Fam. L. 807, 827 (1988-1989), citing Schichtl v. Schichtl, 55 N.W. 309, 309-310 (Iowa 1893); Boggs v. Boggs, 49 Iowa 190, 191 (1878); Campbell v. Campbell, 37 Wis. 206 (1875).

It is commonly believed that equitable distribution arose in common law property states only in the latter half of the twentieth century, and that community property states do not permit equitable distribution. In fact, a few common law property states have provided for equitable distribution since the nineteenth century. *See, e.g.*, Gen. Stat. Kan. § 4756 (1889); 43 Okla. Stat. Ann. § 121 (2014) (enacted in 1893). These statutes are discussed in Comment, The Development of Sharing Principles in Common Law Property States, 28 UCLA L. Rev. 1269, 1294-1299 (1981). By the early twentieth century, statutes in all the community property states except Louisiana empowered divorce courts to divide community property "equitably." Harriet S. Daggett, Division of Property upon Dissolution

---

1. Traditionally, men were not entitled to alimony. Orr v. Orr, 440 U.S. 268 (1979), excerpted in Chapter 2, held that this limitation violates equal protection.

of Marriage, 6 Law & Contemp. Probs. 225, 231 (1930), citing McKay, Community Property 39 et seq. (1910). However, today more community property states require title-based distribution, as described in Section B of this chapter.

Thus, the criteria for and purposes of the various types of economic orders in fault-based divorce law overlapped, at least in some jurisdictions, just as they often do today. However, the demise of the fault-based system did generate a conceptual crisis for spousal support and property division orders by eliminating or limiting the effect of a finding of fault on the division of economic resources.

2. Economic Orders in the No-Fault Era

The divorce revolution implied far more than a change in the grounds for marital dissolution. Divorce policy now sought to relieve spouses of a relationship that was "socially dead" so that they might seek new and more satisfying relationships. Given this policy, several propositions initially seemed obvious. One was that judicial decrees should end, as far as possible, all personal and economic ties between the spouses. Second, the abandonment of fault grounds, coupled with the emerging emphasis on gender equality, implied that both spouses should become equal and independent social and economic actors after divorce and that neither spouse should be especially burdened by the divorce decree.

These developments had a number of theoretical and practical implications for economic orders at divorce.[2] Most generally, these orders sought to end the relationship between formerly married parties. Support as a "pension" for the wronged spouse was obviously inconsistent with the new disinterest in fault and with a goal of terminating the previous relationship. Fortunately, an approach to marital property emerged that provided a vehicle for distributing wealth without long-term support. Drawing on social perceptions about the importance of women's work in the (unpaid) domestic economy and the legal theory of community property, legislatures and courts came to regard assets acquired during marriage as the result of the contributions of both spouses. While those contributions differed in kind and in origin, they nonetheless were considered important and, in some approaches, of equal value.

Understood in this new way, the theory that property should be distributed according to spousal contribution, rather than according to title or beneficial ownership in specific items of wealth, did not seem controversial in principle. However, a number of questions presented themselves.

The first part of this chapter introduces some problems of principle and practice in connection with property distributions. Most obvious are questions about the definition and valuation of the parties' contributions to the acquisition of property.

Many of the no-fault era property division statutes permit transfers of wealth from one spouse to the other who is dependent and needy as a qualification of the

---

2. However, Professor Herma Hill Kay has written that the advocates of no-fault divorce did not intend or even contemplate that this change would undermine the traditional bases for economic awards. Herma Hill Kay, Equality and Difference: A Perspective on No-Fault Divorce and Its Aftermath, 56 U. Cin. L. Rev. 1, 62-63 (1987).

"contribution" theory, and spousal support is available for the same reason. A related approach provides support, but only on a limited basis, to allow a spouse who lacks education and training an opportunity to acquire skills. However, the first wave of writing accompanying no-fault divorce provided little theoretical justification for imposing an obligation on one spouse to provide for the other's needs after the marriage had ended. One answer that has developed is to regard support orders at least partially as compensation to the family for contributions that could not adequately be reflected in a property award.

These problems of theory and practice are heightened under current economic circumstances. Until relatively recently, the principal forms of wealth were tangible or intangible property (such as stocks or houses) that could be separated from the activity that generated them (employment). However, the most important forms of modern wealth for many families are directly associated with employment: pension plans and insurance, for example. How should the current forms of wealth be treated within the traditional distinction between property and alimony? And how does one reconcile the current nature of wealth with the desires to end marriage at the point of divorce and at the same time to recognize contributions to the marriage? The third part of this section takes up these questions in some detail.

3. *Criticism of No-Fault Economics*

Less than ten years after the beginning of the "no-fault revolution," critics began to argue that the revolution had caused unprecedented economic disaster for the women and children of divorce. The best known of these critics, Dr. Lenore Weitzman, along with several colleagues, studied divorce awards and the post-divorce economic status of men, women, and children in California in the early 1970s.[3] Virtually no one disagrees with Weitzman's fundamental claim that, on average, women and children suffer badly in their economic position after divorce.[4] In 2009, 13 percent of recently separated men were below the poverty level, compared with 26 percent of recently separated women, and 26 percent of

---

3. Weitzman's book, The Divorce Revolution (1985), collects and analyzes these data. Much of the work was published earlier in a series of articles, including Lenore J. Weitzman & Ruth B. Dixon, Child Custody Awards: Legal Standards and Empirical Patterns for Child Custody, Support and Visitation After Divorce, 12 U.C. Davis L. Rev. 471 (1979); Ruth B. Dixon & Lenore J. Weitzman, Evaluating the Impact of No-Fault Divorce in California, 29 Fam. Rel. 297 (1980); Lenore J. Weitzman & Ruth B. Dixon, The Alimony Myth: Does No-Fault Divorce Make a Difference? 14 Fam. L.Q. 141 (1980); Lenore J. Weitzman, The Economics of Divorce: Social and Economic Consequences of Property, Alimony and Child Support Awards, 28 UCLA L. Rev. 1181 (1981).

4. Perhaps the most widely quoted of Weitzman's statistics is that one year after legal divorce men's standard of living rose 42 percent, while women experienced a 73 percent loss. Weitzman, The Divorce Revolution, at 339. However, others have cast doubt on the accuracy of these numbers. *See, e.g.*, Saul D. Hoffman & Greg J. Duncan, What Are the Economic Consequences of Divorce? 25 Demography 641 (1988); Greg J. Duncan & Saul D. Hoffman, Economic Consequences of Marital Instability, in Horizontal Equity, Uncertainty and Economic Well-Being 427 (M. David & T. Smeeding eds., 1985); Greg J. Duncan & Saul D. Hoffman, A Reconsideration of the Economic Consequences of Marital

recently divorced men or someone in their household received noncash public assistance, compared to 50 percent of recently divorced women or someone in their household. U.S. Census Bureau, Number, Timing, and Duration of Marriages and Divorces: 2009 (2011), at 21.

However, the reasons for the problem are disputed. Weitzman largely blamed the change from fault to no-fault divorce grounds for the poor position of women and children. This change in the law, she said, had two adverse effects. The change in grounds, which essentially was a change from consensual to unilateral divorce (see Chapter 5), deprived women of bargaining power—that is, they could no longer extract favorable economic settlements by refusing to go along with a divorce, and the change gave judges more discretion over economic awards, which they exercised to the disadvantage of women. Weitzman, The Divorce Revolution at 26-28, 63-66.

More recent studies and reanalyses of existing data undermine these claims. Professor Marsha Garrison studied changes in the divorce law of New York and concluded that changes in the law governing spousal support and property division had much more effect than did the changes in grounds. Marsha Garrison, The Economics of Divorce: Changing Rules, Changing Results in Divorce Reform at the Crossroads 1 (S. Sugarman & H. Kay eds., 1990). During the time period that Garrison studied, a spouse in New York could block a divorce because no-fault divorce was available only by mutual consent. The study did not show that no-fault (unilateral) divorce undermines women's bargaining position.[5] The bargaining hypothesis has also been criticized on the basis that it assumes that most of the people who want out of marriage are husbands and that most wives want, or are at least willing, to stay married. Marygold S. Melli, Constructing a Social Problem: The Post-Divorce Plight of Women and Children, 1986 Am. B. Found. Res. J. 759, 770-771; Stephen D. Sugarman, Dividing Financial Interests on Divorce in Divorce Reform at the Crossroads, above, at 130, 135 n.17.

More fundamentally, as several authors have pointed out, changes in the law, especially the law of divorce grounds, do not have a wide-ranging impact on the postdivorce economic position of most divorcing people. As Professor Marygold Melli has written, "The bottom line is that Weitzman's data do not show any substantial changes in the economic situation of women and children under no-fault divorce; it was bad before no fault, and it continues to be bad now." Marygold S. Melli, above, at 770. *See also* Stephen D. Sugarman, above. In fact, most divorcing people do not have much property to divide. In most states the median net value of marital assets is $25,000 or less (in 1994 dollars). Marsha Garrison,

---

Dissolution, 22 Demography 485 (1985); Saul D. Hoffman, Marital Instability and the Economic Status of Women, 14 Demography 67 (1977).

For a more complex analysis, concluding that since the 1950s women's poverty rate increased relative to that of men even though the absolute rate of poor women did not increase, and suggesting explanations for the gender disparity, *see* Sara S. McLanahan, Annemette Sorensen & Dorothy Watson, Sex Differences in Poverty, 1950-1980, 15 Signs 102 (1989).

5. However, Garrison cites work by Elizabeth Peters that "provides some support for the bargaining hypothesis." *Id.* at 80, citing Elizabeth Peters, Marriage and Divorce: Informational Constraints and Private Contracting, 76 Am. Econ. Rev. 437 (1986).

The Economic Consequences of Divorce, 32 Fam. & Conciliation Cts. Rev. 10, 11 (1994). The Census Bureau reported that in 1989 two-thirds of divorced women received no property settlement.[6] Moreover, relatively few divorced women have ever been awarded spousal support, even though all states permit courts to order it. According to Census data collected between 1887 and 1922, only 9 percent to 15 percent of divorced women were awarded alimony.[7] In 1989 only 15.5 percent of divorced or separated women were awarded spousal support.[8] In 2010 the Census Bureau found that only 106,000 people were paying support to a former spouse, down from 142,000 in 2002. Bureau of the Census, Support Providers: 2002 9, Tbl. 5 (Feb. 2005); Bureau of the Census, Support Providers: 2010 Tbl. 10 (June 2012).

Whether the change in divorce grounds caused or aggravated the postdivorce economic position of women and children is of more than theoretical interest. Consistent with her conclusion that no-fault divorce did have such an adverse impact, Weitzman recommended that states not adopt pure no-fault divorce. Weitzman, The Divorce Revolution, ch. 11. In contrast, those who do not believe that the change in grounds significantly affected the economic consequences of divorce reject this solution.

MARYGOLD S. MELLI, *CONSTRUCTING A SOCIAL PROBLEM: THE POST-DIVORCE PLIGHT OF WOMEN AND CHILDREN*, 1986 Am. B. Found. Res. J. 759, 770-772: [T]o the extent that Weitzman lays the blame [for the impoverishment of many divorced women] on the concept of no-fault divorce and gender-neutral rules, she is not only wrong but also may have done us a disservice in our search for a viable solution. There are at least three ways in which this may be the case. First, by emphasizing the bargaining power of innocent spouses under fault divorce,

---

6. Bureau of the Census, Child Support and Alimony: 1989 (Current Population Reports, Series P-60, No. 173), at 2 (1991). The earliest to make this point was William J. Goode, After Divorce 217 (1956). Other studies reporting similar results include Marsha Garrison, Good Intentions Gone Awry: The Impact of New York's Equitable Distribution Law upon Divorce Outcomes, 57 Brook. L. Rev. 621, 660, 9 (1991) (summarizing several studies); The Divorce Revolution, at 57; Lenore J. Weitzman, The Economics of Divorce: Social and Economic Consequences of Property, Alimony and Child Support Awards, 28 UCLA L. Rev. 1181, 1202 (1981); James B. McLindon, Separate but Unequal: The Economic Disaster of Divorce for Women and Children, 21 Fam. L.Q. 351, 381-384 (1987).

7. Lenore J. Weitzman & Ruth B. Dixon, The Alimony Myth: Does No-Fault Divorce Make a Difference?, 14 Fam. L.Q. 141, 180 (1980), citing P. Jacobson, American Marriage and Divorce 126 (1959). A large empirical study conducted in Ohio in 1933 found that divorcing wives asked for some kind of financial award in 2500 of a total of 6586 divorce, annulment, and alimony actions, and that in 23 percent of these 2500 cases they were awarded periodic payments and awards in gross in 10.5 percent of the 2500. John S. Bradway, Foreword, 6 Law & Contemp. Probs. 183 (1939), and Edward W. Cooey, The Exercise of Judicial Discretion in the Award of Alimony, 6 Law & Contemp. Probs. 213, 213-214 (1939), both discussing Leon C. Marshall & Geoffrey May, The Divorce Court—Ohio (1933).

8. Bureau of the Census, Child Support and Alimony: 1989 (Current Population Reports, Series P-60, No. 173) Table L (1991).

Weitzman ignores the fate of mothers who decide to end a marriage and who therefore would suffer the economic hardship of a guilty spouse. . . . Traditional marriage and the role it requires of women can be devastating on the self-confidence and self-esteem of women. For women who are affected in this way, divorce may be seen as the best solution. . . .[9]

Second, Weitzman's preoccupation with the contemporary no-fault-divorce structure and gender-neutral rules . . . leads her to inaccurately credit fault divorce with economic protections for women and children that it in fact never provided. It also results in failure to give sufficient recognition to the efforts now developing in the law to provide more adequate post-divorce economic protection for wives and children. . . .

Finally, by assuming that the disastrous economic consequences of divorce were caused by a change in the law, The Divorce Revolution makes the problem appear to be a simple one: a few more changes in the law and the problems will be rectified. It is undoubtedly true . . . that changes in some laws may incrementally affect the economic status of divorced women and children. . . . But the consequences of divorce for those women who devote their major energies to home-making and the children for whom they care is a problem that has long preceded the current controversies. It defies easy solution and has survived any number of divorce reforms.

MARSHA GARRISON, *THE ECONOMIC CONSEQUENCES OF DIVORCE*, 32 Fam. & Conciliation Cts. Rev. 10, 18-19 (1994): The median income of married couples is more than double that of households headed by women and, when there are children, more than triple that of single mothers. The result is that the poverty rate for single-mother families with children is more than five times that of married couples with children. For Black single mothers, the picture is even more bleak; 69% of these families have incomes below the poverty line.

The economic advantage of marriage is sufficiently great that even male-headed households have a significantly smaller median income than that of married couples. . . .

The economic disadvantage of divorce as compared to marriage is thus clear and inevitable. But this disadvantage does not result from divorce law and cannot be cured by it; no divorce law can provide a standard of living for families that experience divorce that is commensurate with that enjoyed by the marital household. With increasing numbers of two-earner families, the economic disadvantage of divorce as compared to marriage will not abate and will likely grow. We can be confident that divorce will almost always occasion a decline in standard of living as compared to marriage. All that divorce law can accomplish is fair apportionment of that disadvantage.

---

9. A study published in 2006 supports Prof. Melli's argument. It found that domestic violence fell by about one-third in states that enacted unilateral divorce laws between 1976 and 1985, that murder of women by intimates declined by 10 percent, and that women's suicide rates declined 5 to 10 percent. The study found no impact on homicides or suicides of men. Betsey Stevenson & Justin Wolfers, Bargaining in the Shadow of the Law: Divorce Laws and Family Distress, 121 Q.J. Econ. 267, 269-270 (2006). — Ed.

It is thus important to distinguish poverty caused by divorce law, which is preventable, from poverty that flows from divorce (or predates it) and is thus unpreventable. . . . Evidence on this question is still scanty but accumulating.

First, it is now apparent that many women who are poor after divorce were also poor before divorce. Recent Census data suggests that divorce is approximately twice as likely among couples with incomes below the poverty line as compared to others. Among families with children, census researchers have reported that 21% of those that experienced the loss of the father from the household during a 2-year survey period were already poor, a poverty rate generally double that of married-couple households with children. Among mothers living in married-couple families who formed mother-child families within the year, 26% of White mothers and 39% of Black mothers were already poor. Moreover, those mother-child families that were poor before parental separation are most likely to remain poor. One expert has thus estimated that more than 60% of poor Black mothers were poor before forming mother-child families. A large proportion of poor single-mother families thus represent continuing poverty rather than poverty occasioned by family dissolution.

Second, an increasingly large segment of poor mother-child families reflects nonmarriage rather than divorce. . . .

The already poor and the never-married are not the only women represented in the poverty statistics, of course. According to census research from the mid-1980s, almost twice as many mother-child households were poor following divorce as had been during marriage: 35.5% versus 19%. Not all of that increase was preventable, however; for families at the margin of poverty, the increased expenses of two households would likely drive both into poverty under any divorce regime.

Views about the modern role of family and private, rather than public, obligation also substantially affect judgments about how much we should try to use property division and support orders to restructure families' postdivorce lives. Consider the following perspectives.

SUSAN W. PRAGER, *SHARING PRINCIPLES AND THE FUTURE OF MARITAL PROPERTY LAWS*, 25 UCLA L. Rev. 1, 5-6, 12 (1981): Although the views of those favoring separate property and those advocating sharing principles ultimately diverge, both stem from a concern for equality. This preoccupation with equal rights concerns may dangerously skew our vision of marital property policy questions and create a deceptive mode of analysis. The recent literature is dominated by the notion that equality is the critical, perhaps exclusive, factor in *shaping* the property rights of married people. It suggests that to the extent that there is economic inequality a sharing oriented system is required. When inequality is not present, a system based on individual rights is appropriate.

While it is certainly true that in recent years sharing principles have been advanced because of the economic inequalities created by the traditional marriage, it is questionable whether once those inequalities disappear the need for sharing principles will vanish as well. As long as marriage and other similar close personal relationships continue to reflect sharing behavior, there is a place for sharing principles in marital property law. Marital sharing principles are not dependent upon a social structure in which one or the other spouse relinquishes the earner role. Rather the need for the sharing philosophy stems from the dynamics of marriage and similar relationships.

. . . In marriage most of us seek an alliance with another individual who will believe in us, be loyal to us, help us function in a demanding, often hostile world, and who will help make life satisfying. In exchange we will try to do the same. In many senses these needs and the expectations they create shape the frame of mind with which decisions are made during marriage. The expectation of stability and continuity and the desire for a shared life suggest that married people are unlikely to make decisions on an individually oriented basis; rather the needs of each person tend to be taken into account. Thus married people will often make decisions differently than they would if there were no marriage or marriage-like relationship functioning. . . .

. . . The choice of a separate property system may reflect the judgment that, regardless of how the spouses actually make choices, from a societal viewpoint their decisions *ought* to be made on an individual basis. Thus, the marital property law becomes a tool of social engineering, designed to encourage independence. A separate property system encourages each person to function as an earner by refusing to compensate a spouse who remains in the home for some significant period.

The absence of sharing principles can thus be used to discourage the establishment of dependency relationships. But if many couples in fact make decisions with the special exigencies of the marital relationship in mind, a system of property law which assumes decisions ought to be made on an individual basis may produce two quite different ill effects. First, one spouse may ultimately be treated unfairly if the couple does not alter its behavior to conform to the individualistic orientation of the separate property model. Second, if behavior is indeed responsive to a legal structure which dictates putting oneself first, other social values will suffer. By dictating that a married person behave as if unmarried with respect to certain choices or suffer the consequences of subsequent property disadvantage for not doing so, the individually oriented model works to reward self-interested choices which can be detrimental to the continuation of the marriage. At the same time it punishes conduct of accommodation and compromise so important to furthering and preserving the relationship. From a social engineering standpoint, an individualistic property system will begin to produce behavior that is at cross-purposes with other values, such as stability and cooperation in marital relationships.

J. Thomas Oldham, *Putting Asunder in the 1990s*, 80 Cal. L. Rev. 1091, 1125-1126 (1992): Divorce reform is still struggling to respond to the increasing practice of serial marriage in American society. Most divorcing spouses eventually remarry. Indeed, one argument advanced in support of no-fault divorce was that people should be able to establish a happy domestic life; if a first marriage appeared to be a mistake, the spouses should be free to dissolve the first union and initiate another.

Obviously, such a policy is not unrelated to the post-divorce economic problems of women and children. Many divorcing families already are in a difficult economic situation. Once the divorced father remarries, particularly if he establishes a new family, his connections with the first family will probably diminish. . . .

What posture should divorce law take toward the divorced father? Should he be encouraged to remarry, should substantial barriers to remarriage be created, or should the law be neutral? If the father remarries, this may affect his inclination and ability to provide resources to his former spouse and his children. Many, myself included, would find it unfair to burden unduly the noncustodial parent's ability to remarry. Thus, the challenge for the no-fault divorce system is whether it can adequately provide for the custodial parent and the children without placing unreasonable burdens upon the ex-husband's remarriage options. Satisfying both of these goals may require the talents of the magicians Penn and Teller. Many divorcing families already are pressed financially before they divorce. Maintaining two households frequently is quite difficult, even before a divorcing spouse contemplates establishing a new relationship.

It must be recognized that divorce normally will be a financial hardship for both spouses as well as for the children. Marital roles will change and probably become more onerous for most custodial parents, at least until they remarry; this is unfortunate, but given current American family policy it seems inevitable. About 60% of married women living with their spouse work outside the home. In contrast, about 75% of divorced women are in the work force. It is unrealistic to suggest that a divorcing housewife should not be "forced . . . to play multiple roles against her will after the marriage ends." One must strike a fair balance between a desire to use private law to compensate women for roles assumed during marriage and the concern about unduly burdening men's remarriage prospects.

CARL E. SCHNEIDER, *RETHINKING ALIMONY: MARITAL DECISIONS AND MORAL DISCOURSE,* 1991 BYU L. Rev. 197, 243-245: . . . Family law generally, and the law of alimony and marital property particularly, try to regulate two of the most intimate, complex, and consequential things in people's lives—their closest personal relations and their money. People want, and perhaps expect, such a law to make its decisions individually and meticulously, giving its full attention to the whole situation in which the specific parties were acting and to the differences between the specific parties and the rest of the world. Because morality matters deeply to most people, they will consider their moral relations a central part of that full situation and those differences. . . .

Another obstacle to eliminating moral discourse from family law is that there are important reasons for wanting to retain it. The family is a central social institution which affects people in many of the most basic aspects of their lives. The obligations family members assume to each other, then, will have important social consequences, consequences in which the law has a legitimate interest. . . . Thus some people on the right argue in favor of traditional alimony rules partly on the ground that they strengthen the family by enforcing the obligations and the sense of obligation family members are taken to owe each other. And thus some people on the left argue in favor either of restricting alimony (for example, by making alimony available only for rehabilitative purposes) or of expanding alimony . . . as a means of promoting women's moral claims to autonomy and self-sufficiency. . . .

The social interest in alimony which has traditionally had special weight has to do with another of the law's functions — the protective function. It is a basic function of law to protect citizens against harms done them by their fellows. Because spouses do and should be able to depend on each other, and because spouses are for that and other reasons peculiarly vulnerable to each other, spouses can easily and severely injure each other in many ways. Alimony has traditionally been understood to be one way in which the law protects former spouses from the financial component of such injuries. Since those financial injuries can be devastating, this social purpose ought not be easily discarded. And it is a purpose which can be best served where the law undertakes the moral inquiry into whether such an injury has been done.

B. PROPERTY DIVISION AT DIVORCE

In all states, the steps in dividing property at divorce are the same: The first is to determine which property is subject to the court's dispositional authority under state law. Then the property is valued, and the court allocates the divisible party between the spouses according to the governing legal principles. The final order implements the decisions and may provide who gets exactly what assets. The most important issues in principle are those that determine which property is divisible and in what shares. States can be divided into three groups based on how they resolve these issues. A key variable that distinguishes these three systems is the amount of discretion available to the judge.

Title-Based Distribution   Under this type of system, courts have little or no express discretion over property division, for the governing principle is that property is awarded to the spouses as they owned it during the marriage. Thus, distribution at divorce depends on the principles of property ownership discussed in Chapter 2. In a common law property jurisdiction using a pure title system, the spouse in whose name property was titled would receive it at divorce, subject to any claims of the other spouse based on the equitable ownership principles discussed in Chapter 2. A court in a community property jurisdiction using a pure title system would award separate property to the owner and divide the community property equally.

Today, no common law property state relies on title-based distribution. It is used in a limited form in California, Louisiana, and New Mexico, the three community property states that mandate equal division of community property with very few exceptions and require that separate property be awarded to the spouse who owned it during marriage. Cal. Fam. Code § 2550 (2014); La. Civ. Code Ann. art. 1290, 1308, 2336, 2341, 2341.1 (2014); Michelson v. Michelson, 520 P.2d 263, 266 (N.M. 1974). Where community property must be divided equally, division in kind is generally not required. *See, e.g.,* In re Marriage of Fink, 603 P.2d 881 (Cal. 1980).

Pure Equitable Distribution   This type of system is at the opposite end of the discretion spectrum, for the judge has discretion to divide all the property of both spouses as is "just and proper" or through some equivalent formula. Despite the similarity in terminology, "equitable distribution" is very different from the "equitable ownership" principles we examined in Chapter 2. Determining who is the equitable owner of property during marriage is critical to implementing a title-based system of divorce property division, since the equitable owner will prevail over a titleholder who is not the equitable owner. In a state that mandates equitable distribution of all property, which spouse owned property legally or equitably during marriage may be relevant but is not determinative of who will get it at divorce. In 2012 Connecticut, Hawaii, Indiana, Iowa, Kansas, Massachusetts, Michigan, Mississippi, Montana, Oregon, South Dakota, Vermont, West Virginia, and Wyoming allowed courts to divide all the parties' property equitably. Linda D. Elrod & Robert G. Spector, A Review of the Year in Family Law, 46 Fam. L.Q. 471, 536 Chart 5 (2013). In some of these states, however, property is still characterized as marital or separate, and ordinarily only marital property is divided.

Equitable Distribution of Marital or Community Property   This system gives judges more discretion over property division at divorce than does a title system, but less than an equitable distribution system, and it has become the system most commonly used in this country. In most of the community property states — Arizona, Idaho, Nevada, Texas, Washington, and Wisconsin — equitable rather than equal division of community property is mandated. In addition, most common law property states have gone to a form of a "deferred marital property," which was first fully developed in the Nordic countries. In 2012 the common law states using this system were Alabama, Alaska, Arkansas, Colorado, Delaware, D.C., Florida, Georgia, Illinois, Kentucky, Maine, Maryland, Minnesota, Missouri, Nebraska, New Hampshire, New Jersey, New York, North Carolina, North Dakota, Ohio, Oklahoma, Pennsylvania, Rhode Island, South Carolina, Tennessee, Utah, Virginia, and West Virginia. Elrod & Spector, above. Under this system, as long as the marriage lasts, each spouse owns and manages assets that he or she brings into or acquires during the marriage. But when the marriage ends, the assets are shared as if they had been acquired in a community property state.

The current and original versions of Section 307 of the Uniform Marriage and Divorce Act set out alternative approaches to what property is subject to division and on what basis.

UNIFORM MARRIAGE AND DIVORCE ACT § 307

Alternative A (for common law property states)
(a) In a proceeding for dissolution of a marriage . . . the court, without regard to marital misconduct, shall . . . finally equitably apportion between the parties the property and assets belonging to either or both however and whenever acquired, and whether the title thereto is in the name of the husband or wife or both. In making apportionment the court shall consider the duration of the marriage, any prior marriage of either party, any antenuptial agreement of the parties,

the age, health, station, occupation, amounts and sources of income, vocational skills, employability, estate, liabilities, and needs of each of the parties, custodial provisions, whether the apportionment is in lieu of or in addition to maintenance, and the opportunity of each for future acquisition of capital assets and income. The court shall also consider the contribution or dissipation of each party in the acquisition, preservation, depreciation, or appreciation in value of the respective estates, and the contribution of a spouse as a homemaker or to the family unit.

Alternative B (for community property states)

In a proceeding for dissolution of the marriage . . . the court shall assign each spouse's separate property to that spouse. It also shall divide community property, without regard to marital misconduct, in just proportions after considering all relevant factors including:

(1) contribution of each spouse to acquisition of the marital property, including contribution of a spouse as homemaker;

(2) value of the property set apart to each spouse;

(3) duration of the marriage; and

(4) economic circumstances of each spouse when the division of property is to become effective, including the desirability of awarding the family home or the right to live therein for a reasonable period to the spouse having custody of any children.

NOTES AND QUESTIONS

1. As originally drafted, Section 307 of the Uniform Marriage and Divorce Act (UMDA) did not provide different rules for common law and community property states. Instead, like Alternative B, it provided that each spouse was to receive his or her separate property and that the marital property was to be divided "with out regard to marital misconduct, in such proportions as the court deems just after considering" all the factors listed in Alternative B except the duration of the marriage. The original version defined "marital property" as "all property acquired by either spouse subsequent to the marriage" except (1) property acquired by gift, bequest, devise, or descent; (2) property acquired in exchange for property acquired prior to the marriage or in exchange for property acquired by gift, bequest, devise, or descent; (3) property acquired by a spouse after a decree of legal separation; (4) property excluded by valid agreement of the parties; and (5) the increase in value of property acquired prior to the marriage.

This version was initially rejected by the Family Law Section of the American Bar Association, and the version you see above was adopted. However, most common law property states now divide property into marital and nonmarital shares and allow only the former to be distributed at divorce. Linda D. Elrod & Robert G. Spector, A Review of the Year in Family Law, 46 Fam. L.Q. 471, 536 Chart 5 (2013). The American Law Institute Principles of the Law of Family Dissolution, published in 2002 and dealing extensively with the economic consequences of divorce, also recommend this system, with the notable exception that in long-term marriages separate property gradually is converted into marital (and hence divisible) property. ALI, Principles of the Law of Family Dissolution §§ 4.03, 4.12 (2002).

2. Is a deferred marital property system illogical, in that it treats spouses as economic individuals while they are married but as an economic unit when they divorce? If a spouse in a state with a deferred marital property system, seeing divorce coming, begins to give away property, perhaps to children or parents, does the other spouse have any remedy? Should the other spouse be able to avoid these transfers while the parties are still married? Should the divorce court be able to avoid them? Taking economic fault into account when dividing property can sometimes provide a partial solution, as this section discusses below.

3. Courts in common law property states have generally held that a statute providing for equitable distribution of property at divorce does not violate due process, even though it permits a court to award one spouse property that was owned by the other spouse during marriage. For example, in Rothman v. Rothman, 320 A.2d 496, 499, 501 (N.J. 1974), the New Jersey Supreme Court said,

> A state may, in the exercise of the police power, enact a statute to promote the public health, safety, morals or general welfare. Such a state, because of retroactive application or otherwise, may diminish in value or totally destroy an individual's right, whether in property as such or arising out of contract, provided that the public interest to be promoted sufficiently outweighs in importance the private right which is impaired. . . . It has long been well settled and now stands unchallenged that marriage is a social relationship subject in all respects to the state's police power.

However, the Arizona Supreme Court in Hatch v. Hatch, 547 P.2d 1044 (Ariz. 1976) (en banc), suggested that an unequal division of community property would violate due process except in unusual circumstances. The Texas courts have suggested that awarding one spouse's separate property to the other would violate due process. Eggemeyer v. Eggemeyer, 554 S.W.2d 137 (Tex. 1977), *appeal after remand*, 623 S.W.2d 462 (Tex. App. 1981); Cameron v. Cameron, 641 S.W.2d 210 (Tex. 1982). *See also* James R. Ratner, Distribution of Marital Assets in Community Property Jurisdictions: Equitable Doesn't Equal Equal, 72 La. L. Rev. 21, 24 (2011) (criticizing equitable distribution of community property as undermining principles of equal ownership and management of community assets from the time of acquisition and creating risk that fault will be considered).

PROBLEM

Hamilton and Wilma marry when both are 21. Neither brings significant assets into the marriage, and neither inherits or is given property during the marriage. Throughout the marriage Wilma was a homemaker, and Hamilton was a well-paid employee who skillfully invested his excess income in stocks and bonds, always taking title in his name alone. When they divorce, their assets consist of the family home, purchased during the marriage from Hamilton's earnings and titled in joint tenancy, and the securities that Hamilton purchased.

In a common law state using a pure title system, what property would be divisible? In a community property system using a pure title system? In a common law property state that has adopted Alternative A of Section 307, what property would be subject to division? In a community property state that had adopted Alternative B? In a common law property state that had adopted the original version of Section 307?

1.   The Meaning of "Equitable Distribution"

Equitable distribution statutes vary considerably in form but little in substance. Some, like UMDA Section 307, contain lists of factors that judges must consider, while others do not. Appellate courts often interpret the latter kind of statute as requiring consideration of factors similar to those contained in the statutory lists. Lists of factors do not provide much structure, for they do not tell judges what weight or priority to give to the factors.

What these statutes do, then, is to grant judges discretion without providing either governing principles or ultimate goals. However, as a practical matter, judges will probably adopt, consciously or unconsciously, some framework within which to make decisions, either from a sense that such a framework is necessary to ensure a measure of consistency or to achieve efficiency. And good lawyers will construct a theory of their cases so that they can do more than simply present scattered pieces of evidence.

Legislatures and courts are developing principles for property division, as the next cases illustrate. As you study them and the materials that follow, consider what goals are being pursued and to what extent these goals are realistic or even desirable.

ARNEAULT V. ARNEAULT

639 S.E.2d 720 (W. Va. 2006)

DAVIS, Chief Justice. . . . A brief synopsis of the relevant facts shows that the parties were married on July 12, 1969, and now have two adult children. The parties had been married for thirty-three years when Mr. Arneault filed for divorce on March 22, 2002. By agreement of the parties, they denominated December 20, 2002, as their date of separation. By order of the family court, the parties were granted a divorce on July 22, 2004. The parties' marital home was located in Grand Rapids, Michigan. During the marriage, Mrs. Arneault stayed home with the children until 1990, when she returned to work on a part-time basis as a teacher. In 1995, Mrs. Arneault started her own business as a counselor providing college placement and career consulting services to high school students. While there is discord as to the effort Mrs. Arneault applied to her business, there is no dispute that Mrs. Arneault's business did not generate great income.

Mr. Arneault currently holds the same job position as he did at the time of the divorce. Mr. Arneault is Chairman, President, and Chief Executive Officer of MTR Gaming Group, Inc. (hereinafter "MTR"), which owns and controls Mountaineer Park, Inc., and operates video lottery terminals. Since 1995, Mr. Arneault has worked in Chester, West Virginia, away from the marital home. Prior to the divorce, he returned to Michigan on most weekends. There is no dispute that Mr. Arneault has been responsible for MTR's great success. In return for his achievements, Mr. Arneault has received a lucrative income from MTR, as well as MTR stock. . . .

In the bifurcated case below, the family court determined that because Mr. Arneault had contributed significantly to the marital estate, a 50/50 split of the estate would be inequitable. Thus, the family court ordered that the parties' marital estate be divided 35/65, with Mr. Arneault receiving the larger share. . . . Mrs. Arneault now appeals to this Court. . . .

. . . Mrs. Arneault argues that a 50/50 split of the marital estate is appropriate, and that Mr. Arneault has not overcome the presumption of an equal division of the marital property. Conversely, Mr. Arneault avers that his contribution to the marital estate has been so substantial that it would be inequitable to require him to divide the marital estate equally. The family court accepted Mr. Arneault's argument and found that it was unjust to divide equally the vast accumulation of wealth of the marital estate. Therefore, the family court split the marital estate 35/65, and the circuit court affirmed.

In a divorce proceeding, subject to some limitations, all property is considered marital property,[10] which preference is reflected in our case law.

. . . The parties do not contest the lower courts' classification of the estate as marital or separate; thus, we now address the appropriate percentage of the property to be afforded to each party.

With a few exceptions, all of the parties' property constituted marital property and should have been divided equally absent some compelling reason otherwise. Guidance is provided by the mandate that "[e]xcept as otherwise provided in this section, upon every judgment of annulment, divorce or separation, the court shall divide the marital property of the parties equally between the parties. W. Va. Code § 48-7-101 (2001) (Repl. Vol. 2004). . . . Thus, we must presume that the parties' marital estate will be divided equally, subject to the limitations and considerations set forth in W. Va. Code § 48-7-103 (2001) (Repl. Vol. 2004), which provides as follows:

---

10. W. Va. Code § 48-1-233 (2001) (Repl. Vol. 2004) provides as follows:

"Marital property" means:

(1) All property and earnings acquired by either spouse during a marriage, including every valuable right and interest, corporeal or incorporeal, tangible or intangible, real or personal, regardless of the form of ownership, whether legal or beneficial, whether individually held, held in trust by a third party, or whether held by the parties to the marriage in some form of co-ownership such as joint tenancy or tenancy in common, joint tenancy with the right of survivorship, or any other form of shared ownership recognized in other jurisdictions without this state, except that marital property does not include separate property as defined in section 1-238 [§ 48-1-238]; and

(2) The amount of any increase in value in the separate property of either of the parties to a marriage, which increase results from: (A) an expenditure of funds which are marital property, including an expenditure of such funds which reduces indebtedness against separate property, extinguishes liens, or otherwise increases the net value of separate property; or (B) work performed by either or both of the parties during the marriage. . . .

In the absence of a valid agreement, the court shall presume that all marital property is to be divided equally between the parties, but may alter this distribution, without regard to any attribution of fault to either party which may be alleged or proved in the course of the action, after a consideration of the following:

(1) The extent to which each party has contributed to the acquisition, preservation and maintenance, or increase in value of marital property by monetary contributions, including, but not limited to:

(A) Employment income and other earnings; and

(B) Funds which are separate property.

(2) The extent to which each party has contributed to the acquisition, preservation and maintenance or increase in value of marital property by monetary contributions, including, but not limited to:

(A) Homemaker services;

(B) Child care services;

(C) Labor performed without compensation, or for less than adequate compensation, in a family business or other business entity in which one or both of the parties has an interest;

(D) Labor performed in the actual maintenance or improvement of tangible marital property; and

(E) Labor performed in the management or investment of assets which are marital property.

(3) The extent to which each party expended his or her efforts during the marriage in a manner which limited or decreased such party's income-earning ability or increased the income-earning ability of the other party, including, but not limited to:

(A) Direct or indirect contributions by either party to the education or training of the other party which has increased the income-earning ability of such other party; and

(B) Forgoing by either party of employment or other income-earning activity through an understanding of the parties or at the insistence of the other party.

(4) The extent to which each party, during the marriage, may have conducted himself or herself so as to dissipate or depreciate the value of the marital property of the parties: Provided, That except for a consideration of the economic consequences of conduct as provided for in this subdivision, fault or marital misconduct shall not be considered by the court in determining the proper distribution of marital property.

When the issue of the equitable distribution of the marital estate was presented to the family court judge, . . . [t]he judge explained the rationale for the unequal distribution by finding that, under the factors set forth in W. Va. Code § 48-7-103, Mr. Arneault's contributions to the marital estate overwhelmed the contributions made by Mrs. Arneault. Specifically, the family court reasoned as follows:

Having considered the factors enumerated in West Virginia Code § 48-7-103 as above-described, this Court finds that the presumption of equal division has been rebutted. The petitioner's own overwhelming contribution as defined by § 103(2)(E) and § 103(1)(A) make it completely inequitable to divide the marital estate equally.

Equity mandates that the petitioner be awarded a greater percentage of the marital estate. Were subsections 103(2)(E) and (1)(A) the only factors to be considered, the petitioner would be receiving virtually all of the marital estate. However, as [Mrs. Arneault's expert] testified, the respondent engaged in service contributions which gave the petitioner the freedom to focus on his business pursuits. Those contributions and the other factors in § 103 create the respondent's entitlement to a portion of the estate. This Court believes her contributions were substantial, but not as overwhelming as the petitioner's contributions. Thus it is equitable that her share of the estate be less, although still substantial, because of her service contributions, and this Court finds equity to require that she receive thirty-five percent (35%) of the marital estate. It is proper that the petitioner must receive an adequate award for his accomplishments, and, at the same time, the respondent be properly rewarded for her contributions to the environment which permitted him to use his personal talents to amass this fortune.

In that same order, the family court further explained that

[t]he petitioner's intelligence and ability are unique to him and the development of these attributes can not [sic] be attributed equally to the petitioner and respondent, regardless of the environment which the respondent created in order to allow the petitioner to achieve the estate that has been amassed. He must be given some additional weight and credit in equitable distribution for existence of those attributes, intelligence, and abilities, which helped him achieve the marital estate currently in question. This Court looks at these personal attributes as substantial service contributions to the marital estate. There are many persons who have obtained an MBA and become a CPA during their marriage, but they have not accomplished nearly the achievements of the petitioner. These achievements go beyond the acquisition of degrees or experience, and must be given additional consideration in equitable distribution.

In essence, it appears that the family court judge believed Mr. Arneault's intelligence and ability led to his great financial success, and while Mrs. Arneault's homemaking and child-rearing duties were substantial, they did not compare to Mr. Arneault's contribution to the marital estate. . . .

Significantly, we disagree with the family court's undervaluement of the contributions made to the marital estate by Mrs. Arneault. In essence, the family court found that because Mrs. Arneault's contributions were not monetary in nature, they did not count as substantially as Mr. Arneault's contributions to the marital estate. This idea is contrary to West Virginia jurisprudence. We previously have held:

Under equitable distribution, the contributions of time and effort to the married life of the couple — at home and in the workplace — are valued equally regardless of whether the parties' respective earnings have been equal. Equitable distribution contemplates that parties make their respective contributions to the married life of the parties in that expectation.

[Citation omitted.] We likewise have stated that "general contributions, rather than economic contributions [a]re to be the basis for a distribution" of a marital estate. Raley v. Raley, 190 W. Va. 197, 199-200, 437 S.E.2d 770, 772-73 (1993) (per curiam). In *Raley* we recognized that the wife "made a significant monetary contribution to the marriage as well as many other contributions, *i.e.*, homemaker skills, in which she did not receive any sort of financial compensation." Thus, based on the value of her homemaker services, we determined that the wife was entitled to fifty percent of the investment account that was at issue before the Court.

The facts of the present case highlight how important the contributions of both parties were to the marital estate. It was conceded that Mr. Arneault and Mrs. Arneault did not have any unusual fortune at the time of their marriage. Mrs. Arneault had recently received an undergraduate degree, and Mr. Arneault earned his undergraduate degree soon after they married. Mrs. Arneault then earned a master's degree, while Mr. Arneault went on to obtain his CPA license and a master's degree in business administration. The family court found that Mr. Arneault's innate abilities led to the financial wealth of the marital estate. However, the facts illustrate that the opposite is more probable. Mr. Arneault and Mrs. Arneault entered the marriage on fairly equal levels. Mr. Arneault earned a professional license and a graduate degree after the marriage commenced. It is very conceivable that this accumulation of knowledge, after the commencement of the marriage, led to the development of Mr. Arneault's innate abilities.

Even though Mrs. Arneault also had an advanced degree, she abandoned her own career in order to stay home with the couple's children. She also was responsible for the majority of the housework and the maintenance of the marital residence. Her responsibilities were manifestly increased by the fact that Mr. Arneault was completely absent from the marital home during the work week, leaving Mrs. Arneault with even greater responsibilities and household duties than is normally encountered in like circumstances. Rather than the conclusion made by the family court, the facts of this case show it is more likely that Mrs. Arneault's contributions to the marriage are precisely the reason that Mr. Arneault was able to succeed in his work.

While this Court has recognized that there are circumstances in which an unequal distribution of a marital estate is appropriate, this is not one of those cases. . . .

In the present case, there is no allegation that Mrs. Arneault did anything to detract from the value of the marital estate, and no suggestion that she did anything to frivolously dispose of marital money or assets. Thus, we conclude that the family court abused its discretion in fixing a 35/65 split of the marital estate. Mr. Arneault's intelligence and financial prowess is not sufficient justification for straying from the presumption of a 50/50 split. This conclusion is especially true under facts such as these where it is clear that Mr. Arneault's success was due in large part to the contributions made to the marriage by Mrs. Arneault. Accordingly, we find that the marital estate should be split 50/50 and reverse the circuit court's contrary ruling. . . .

STARCHER, J., dissenting. . . . This marriage was *not* a standard fifty/fifty marital partnership, where Mrs. Arneault was the homemaker/support mechanism and Mr. Arneault was the income earner outside the home. Although the couple lived together prior to Mr. Arneault's success (which has resulted in this dispute over the MTR Gaming stock), the Arneaults have lived and worked in separate states for more than a decade.

Since 1995, Mrs. Arneault lived in Michigan and Mr. Arneault spent the bulk of his time in West Virginia. He returned to Michigan a few days a week, being actively involved in various activities with his children, including coaching his son's teams in various sports, such as football, wrestling, basketball, and baseball, and performing household duties, while Mrs. Arneault engaged in her counseling business. Mrs. Arneault only visited West Virginia perhaps three times in ten years. The couple's children are now both emancipated adults and Mrs. Arneault, who received her master's degree in 1971, works in her consulting business, which she has maintained on a full-time basis since 1995. There was no evidence that Mrs. Arneault's choices regarding work were compelled by Mr. Arneault or the couple's circumstances. Rather, since 1995, the couple pursued separate lives in separate states.

There is no evidence to support Mrs. Arneault's assertions that she provided substantial assistance in Mr. Arneault's success with MTR Gaming. For example, there is no evidence of record that Mrs. Arneault was a host for her husband's business functions. When Mr. Arneault accumulated the stock which is the subject of this appeal, Mrs. Arneault lived in Michigan and Mr. Arneault lived and worked in West Virginia. Other than residing in the couple's Michigan home while Mr. Arneault toiled in West Virginia, Mrs. Arneault had nothing to do with MTR Gaming, even long after the children had gone to college.

The record is also undisputed that much of MTR's success was due to Mr. Arneault's considerable efforts. The evidence was undisputed that Mr. Arneault is not merely an employee of MTR. He is president, chief executive officer, and chairman of the board of directors. He is also the spokesman and public persona of the corporation. . . . The family court found that Mr. Arneault nearly single-handedly created the gaming industry in West Virginia. Plainly, Mr. Arneault's role in the success of MTR Gaming has been remarkable.

Essentially, Mrs. Arneault makes a "community property" argument, contending that because she was Mr. Arneault's long-time wife, she is automatically entitled to one-half of the stock of a corporation that Mr. Arneault built irrespective of their relative contributions to the corporation.

West Virginia, however, is *not* a "community property" state. Rather, West Virginia is an "equitable distribution" state in which its legislature has prescribed various factors to be considered in making, not an "equal" distribution of marital property, but an "equitable" distribution, based primarily upon the parties' relative contributions. . . .

As held in the family court judge's order, Mrs. Arneault did almost nothing to refute the substantial evidence presented by Mr. Arneault which supported the thirty-five/sixty-five division of the stock. Consequently, there is a paucity of discussion in the majority opinion regarding her contributions to the marriage or the corporation.

No details are provided about Mrs. Arneault's contributions to MTR Gaming because Mrs. Arneault made no contributions to MTR Gaming. Few details are provided about Mrs. Arneault's contributions to the marital home and child rearing because third parties provided many housekeeping and childcare services, and despite Mr. Arneault's business travel, he shared the parenting duties. There is no evidence that Mrs. Arneault ever sacrificed her career for Mr. Arneault's. Instead, as was noted, Mr. Arneault's career involved great sacrifice on his part in leaving the marital residence to earn a living which allowed Mrs. Arneault to enjoy a comfortable lifestyle and to pursue her far less lucrative business interests. In contrast to the overwhelming evidence of Mr. Arneault's sacrifices, there was *no* evidence of Mrs. Arneault's sacrifices. . . .

Once a litigant, like Mr. Arneault, rebuts the presumption of equal division by demonstrating that the evidence satisfies the statutory criteria for an unequal division, the burden shifts to the other party to adduce evidence that the statutory criteria support an equal division. In this case, rather than presenting any evidence, Mrs. Arneault essentially argued and continues to argue for "judicial nullification" of the equitable distribution statute in favor of fifty/fifty presumption that can never be rebutted. Mrs. Arneault likens a marriage to a law partnership whereby both parties are entitled to share in the good fortune of the other. Law partnerships, however, are governed by written partnership agreements that force whatever division of good or bad fortune the parties decide or other under governing statutory law.

The West Virginia Legislature, however, has not created a "marital partnership" in which each partner, whatever their relative contributions, is always entitled to share equally in the good fortune of the other. Rather, as this Court stated in Burnside v. Burnside, 194 W. Va. 263, 460 S.E.2d 264 (1995), "Thus to be equitable, the division need not be equal, but as a starting point, equality is presumptively equitable." . . .

Even one of Mrs. Arneault's own attorneys, while a Justice on this Court, filed a dissenting opinion in which he advocated that an *unequal distribution of a family farm was appropriate under the circumstances presented. See* Tallman v. Tallman, 183 W. Va. 491, 501, 396 S.E.2d 453, 463 (1990) (Neely, C.J., dissenting); *see also,* Metzner v. Metzner, 191 W. Va. 378, 388, 446 S.E.2d 165, 175 (1994) (Neely, J., concurring in part and dissenting in part) ("Now that the goose is cooked, Mrs. Metzner wants her share, but Mrs. Metzner did not pay for the goose, the fuel to cook it, the sauce to flavor it or even the pot to cook it in. The majority awards Mrs. Metzner the tender breast of the goose merely because the goose happened to wander into Mr. Metzner's yard while Mr. and Mrs. Metzner were still married."). . . .

While married to Mr. Arneault, Mrs. Arneault reaped the benefits of his success and would be a multi-millionaire under the judgment of the Circuit Court of Hancock County. It is simply inequitable for her also to receive fifty percent of the stock in light of her negligible contribution to the success of the company, merely as the result of her status as his wife. MTR is not a "lottery ticket," the cost of which was purchased with marital funds and the equal division of which would be equitable. Rather, the overwhelming evidence was that Mr. Arneault was the heart and soul of MTR and it was his extraordinary personal efforts that built the company into what it is today. . . .

In considering the merits of Mrs. Arneault's appeal, this Court should consider the following factors, used by courts in cases around the country in similar circumstances:

(1) Mrs. Arneault failed to introduce any evidence that she made major contributions to the marital estate as a result of her efforts as a "corporate spouse";

(2) She failed to introduce any evidence that she was a full-time homemaker;

(3) She failed to introduce any evidence that she routinely accompanied Mr. Arneault to conventions and social gatherings of MTR;

(4) She failed to introduce any evidence that she was so involved in the dealings of MTR that for all intents and purposes she was considered an employee;

(5) She failed to introduce any evidence that she entertained MTR customers and other business associates in social and business settings;

(6) She failed to introduce any evidence that she suffered an increased workload and extensive social duties as a result of Mr. Arneault's work at MTR;

(7) She failed to introduce any evidence that she hosted events related to the business of MTR;

(8) She failed to introduce any evidence that her entertainment duties expanded with Mr. Arneault's corporate responsibilities;

(9) She failed to introduce any evidence that she traveled extensively with Mr. Arneault to numerous cities for business purposes;

(10) She failed to introduce any evidence that she in any way was a sounding board for Mr. Arneault, giving advice and guidance to him;

(11) She failed to introduce evidence that during the course of the marriage Mr. Arneault frequently shared information with her about business dealings, daily experiences, and/or asked for advice in a wide variety of circumstances;

(12) She failed to introduce any evidence that she played any role (significant or otherwise) in the financial aspects of MTR or Mountaineer Park, in addition to serving as a "homemaker";

(13) She failed to introduce any evidence that she performed all the typical duties of a wife, parent, and homemaker and still demonstrate that she made an actual economic contribution to the marital estate; and

(14) She failed to introduce any evidence that there is a direct link between her business efforts and the ultimate value of the MTR stock. . . .

What the legislature has instructed is that when the efforts of one spouse are disproportionate to the efforts of another spouse with respect to the acquisition of marital assets, the efforts of the first spouse are *not to be ignored* in the *equitable* distribution of the marital assets; otherwise, slough and neglect would prevail over industry and diligence. The family law judge recognized, based on overwhelming evidence, that Mr. Arneault's contributions to the acquisition and appreciation of the stock were so profound and unique and Mrs. Arneault's contributions were relatively negligible as to justify a relatively unequal distribution of the subject stock. . . .

There are spouses, both husbands and wives, whose contributions to the success of their spouse's businesses are more or less, particularly considering their other contributions to the marriage, such as homemaker services, equal. For those spouses, they absolutely deserve a fifty percent distribution of the value of those businesses. Where one spouse, however, as in the instant case, is so instrumental in building a business, and the other spouse's contributions are relatively insignificant, an unequal distribution of the value of that business is appropriate. Had Mrs. Arneault, in reality, served the role of "corporate spouse" that she alleges, she might be entitled to half of the value of MTR stock.

In most cases, in the ordinary circumstances of divorce—which is that neither party can afford it—a relatively strict application of the presumption of equal distribution may be more appropriate. "Let both parties suffer equally" is not an unreasonable principle. But when the "super rich" start dividing things up, and even a person with the shorter end of the stick will be "rich" after a divorce, then it is less harmful to let the equities have their way. The majority opinion is therefore additionally deficient in its discussion of equitable distribution because it pretends that the enormous wealth that Mr. Arneault has amassed through his work is just like the "house and pension and savings" that ninety-nine percent of us have. . . .

BENJAMIN, J., concurring. It has been said that "[m]otherhood is not a part time job." Yet that is precisely the sentiment the dissenters have expressed in discounting the contributions Ms. Arneault made to the parties' marriage of 35 years—contributions which freed Mr. Arneault of his obligations to home and family and allowed him to make his weekly travels to West Virginia to develop MTR into the successful institution it is today. Because the majority properly considers Ms. Arneault's role in maintaining the marital residence and raising the parties' children during Mr. Arneault's extensive absences and awards her equitable distribution of one-half of the marital estate in recognition of her substantial contributions to the parties' marriage, I respectfully concur with the majority's opinion in this case. . . .

NOTES AND QUESTIONS

1. Much of the reform in property division law in the last 40 years has focused on how to deal with couples in which one partner, usually the woman, stayed out of the labor market to work as a homemaker. In a common law property jurisdiction using the traditional title-based system of property division, a spouse (almost always the wife) who did not work outside the home throughout all or most of the marriage would ordinarily receive little or no property at divorce because her work as a homemaker was not recognized as a financial contribution to the acquisition of property titled in her husband's name. See Chapter 2, Section B.1. Though she might well be in great financial need after a divorce, the only way of providing for her was alimony, where that was available. An important reason that common law property states moved to equitable division of property at divorce was a changed understanding of fairness to homemakers.

In some Southern states the courts developed equitable distribution by expanding resulting and constructive trust remedies to count general economic contributions to the family and then homemaking as a contribution to the acquisition of property. *See, e.g.,* Burgess v. Burgess, 286 S.E.2d 142 (S.C. 1982); Canakaris v. Canakaris, 382 So. 2d 1197 (Fla. 1980); Jenkins v. Jenkins, 278 So. 2d 446 (Miss. 1973). In 1994 the Mississippi Supreme Court officially adopted equitable distribution of all assets, abandoning the resulting trust and lump sum alimony alternatives. Ferguson v. Ferguson, 639 So. 2d 921 (Miss. 1994). Florida and South Carolina have since enacted statutes that provide for equitable distribution of marital assets. Fla. Stat. § 61.075 (2014); S.C. Code Ann. §§ 20-3-620, 20-3-630 (2014).

2. Most jurisdictions today require that homemaking be considered a contribution to the acquisition of property, raising the question of how homemaking should be valued. In wrongful death suits homemaking is broken down into

component jobs, and the market value of each of these jobs is determined. Under this approach, how should the components of homemaking be characterized? Many of the jobs to which a homemaker's work might be compared are very low paying. For example, should the care of young children be compared to baby-sitting or to teaching? Should running the household be compared to housecleaning or to managing a small business? Should the characterization vary from family to family so that a homemaker who takes care of her home herself is compared only to a cleaning person while one who has hired help is compared to a manager? Should this method of analysis be used for purposes of property distribution at divorce?

In Marvin v. Marvin, 557 P.2d 106 (Cal. 1976), set out in Chapter 4, the California trial court on remand found that Lee Marvin's support of Michelle Marvin adequately compensated her for her services. Has the homemaker wife similarly been adequately compensated, so that she should have no claim to property that her husband earned during the marriage? Is the spouse different from the cohabitant? If we take the view that marital support can compensate for home-making, should living a lavish lifestyle be treated as more complete compensation than living simply?

The percentage of families in which one spouse is a full-time homemaker has declined steadily. In 1980, 49.8 percent of all wives were in the labor force; by 2010, the share had grown to 61 percent. Bureau of Labor Statistics, Labor Force Participation Rates by Marital Status, Sex, and Age: 1970 to 2010, Bulletin 2217 and Basic Tabulations, Table 12. This change does not mean, however, that spouses devote themselves equally to career development. Especially when they have children, one spouse may work part time or take a less demanding job that allows flexibility for dealing with issues at home. Should such a spouse be regarded as making homemaker contributions?

3. How does the majority in *Arneault* determine the value of the wife's home-making contributions? Is the state's presumption in favor of an equal division of marital property based on the assumption that the contributions of spouses are ordinarily of equal market value?

In Properties of Marriage, 104 Colum. L. Rev. 75 (2004), Carolyn J. Frantz and Hanoch Dagan assert that the ideal marriage should be understood as "an egalitarian legal community." *Id.* at 77. They argue that contribution should not be the basis for allocating property of spouses because "piercing the veil of marital unity" undermines community. *Id.* at 89. Instead, they argue that for the equal ownership principle as consistent with the principle of a community of equals. *Id.* at 103-104. Under this view, when would an unequal division of property be justified?

4. The *Arneault* court, like many others, analogizes marriage to a partnership. What does it mean here to call marriage a partnership?

When a business partnership is dissolved and the business is ended, all the assets of the partnership are divided equally after returning the "capital investment" of each partner. Only rarely is an unequal division of the remaining assets justified. The rules in the few community property states that require return of separate property to the owner and equal division of community property produce results similar to the business partnership rules. However, when one partner carries on a business, as frequently happens, the withdrawing partner usually may choose between forcing the remaining partner(s) to buy out his/her interest and leaving his/her capital in the business with a right to share future profits. If property division were based on these principles, what would the typical order look like? *See* Cynthia Starnes, Divorce and the Displaced Homemaker: A Discourse on Playing with Dolls, Partnership Buyouts and Dissociation Under No-Fault, 60 U. Chi. L. Rev. 67 (1993). For a critique of the partnership analogy, *see* Ira Mark Ellman, The Theory of Alimony, 77 Cal. L. Rev. 1 (1989).

Sometimes spouses are partners in the conventional business sense, and courts may apply partnership law rather than family law principles to determine ownership of the business assets when the marriage and business partnership both break up. For example, in Leathers and Leathers, 779 P.2d 619 (Or. App. 1989), the court found that the spouses had been partners in an oil business throughout their 22-year marriage and applied partnership law to award a share of the business to the wife. If the court had applied domestic relations principles, it might have been unable to give the wife much or any of the property because of a restrictive premarital agreement the parties had signed. However, because it chose to use business law principles, the court did not fully explore issues of the enforceability and scope of the premarital agreement. For discussion of these issues, see Chapter 10.

5. The dissenting judge in *Arneault* suggests that in a "big money" case in which one spouse was extraordinarily successful at work, the principle of equal sharing no longer applies. Why not? Is the argument of the concurring judge satisfactory? The American cases on this issue are divided; for a discussion, *see* Margaret Ryznar, All's Fair in Love and War: But What About in Divorce? The Fairness of Property Division in American and English Big Money Divorce Cases, 86 N.D. L. Rev. 115 (2010); David N. Hofstein, Scott J.G. Finger & Ellen Goldberg Weiner, Update to Equitable Distribution in Large Marital Estate Cases, 21 J. Am. Acad. Matrimonial Law. 439 (2008).

In White v. White [2001] AC 596, the House of Lords reinterpreted the English statute regarding property division at divorce to include considerations of contribution, including homemaker contributions, as well as need. While the court explicitly declined to say that there is a presumption of an equal division or even that an equal division is a starting point, it said that a court must justify a division that is not equal. Six years later, in Miller v. Miller, McFarlane v. McFarlane [2006] UKHL 24, the House of Lords made clear that an equal division of marital assets was the starting point for property division and that any departure has to be justified. That and later decisions have said that occasions for departure should not be common and that valid reasons include evidence that the spouses deliberately kept their assets separate when both worked and that, in a short-term marriage, significant assets were earned in a business in which only one spouse worked. However, the most discussed criterion for an uneven division is that one spouse made "special contributions" to the marriage.

The English courts borrowed the "special contributions" principle from Australian law, which emphasizes contribution as the main determinant of property division at divorce. The courts are careful to say that special contributions could be in the realm of homemaking and parenting, but the doctrine is usually applied in favor of entrepreneurial spouses who have built up substantial wealth. Patrick Parkinson, The Yardstick of Equality: Assessing Contributions in Australia and England, 19 Int'l J.L. Pol'y & Fam. 163 (2005). Since the Australian courts invented the doctrine, commentators have criticized it for undervaluing the role of the homemaker and parent. As Prof. Parkinson notes, however, in Australia the doctrine is used only in "big money" cases where there is more than enough to go around. He argues that the doctrine is based on the principle of providing spouses with "returns on their investments" rather than valuing their contributions. On the other hand, he admits the difficulty of developing principles to quantify the value of a "special contribution." A 2007 English case suggested that a "special contributor" is likely to get 55 percent to two-thirds of the assets. Charman v. Charman [2007] EWCA Civ 503. However, English courts invoke the special contributions exception infrequently. Ryznar, above, at 143-144.

In 2007 the British Court of Appeal observed, "In big money cases the *White* factor has more than doubled the levels of award and it has been said by many that London has become the divorce capital of the world for aspiring wives. Whether this is a desirable result needs to be considered." AP, British Court Upholds Large Divorce Pact, N.Y. Times, May 24, 2007.

6. The law in many states provides that equitable distribution should be based on each spouse's contributions to the acquisition of assets during the marriage, but that the court should also take into account the economic needs of the parties after the divorce. For example, in Pierson v. Pierson, 653 P.2d 1258 (Or. 1982), the court awarded the husband more than half of the marital assets, applying a statute that required the court to divide the couple's property

> as may be just and proper in all the circumstances. The court shall consider the contribution of a spouse as a homemaker as a contribution to the acquisition of marital assets. There is a rebuttable presumption that both spouses have contributed equally to the acquisition of property during the marriage, whether such property is jointly or separately held. . . .

The court explained its order this way:

> Property division is not a function solely of arithmetic. Absent overriding considerations, marital assets should be divided as equally as practical. . . .
>
> The equation of property division and the entitlement of a party to individually acquired property may be disturbed in order to accomplish broader purposes of a dissolution. There are social objectives as well as financial ones to be achieved and that may result in an uneven financial division. As we said in *Haguewood*, 292 Or. at 206-207:
>
> "Dissolution of a marriage is analogous in many ways to dissolution of a partnership or other joint financial venture. . . . The analogy is not complete, however. Unlike a business dissolution, a marital dissolution often requires the achievement of certain social as well as financial objectives which may be unique to the parties. . . . For example, the parties to a long-term marriage should be awarded the resources for self-sufficient, post-dissolution life apart insofar as possible within the limitations of the capabilities and property of the parties. . . ."
>
> . . . The need in this case is to enable both spouses to emerge from the marriage and recommence life on a sufficient economic footing. Fortunately, there is sufficient property and income to serve that need. Where the income and property of one spouse is greater, the achievement of economic self-sufficiency of both parties is

not necessarily best served by an equal division of the marital assets. In dividing the non-inherited marital assets, we therefore take into account that the wife has greater income and, because of the inheritance, greater financial resources.

However, not all jurisdictions allow courts to alter property divisions resulting from a contribution analysis to account for need. For example, in Fisher v. Fisher, 278 S.W.3d 732 (Mo. App. 2009), the court reversed a trial court order awarding a wife the marital home in lieu of permanent spousal support, applying an earlier Missouri Supreme Court decision abolishing lump sum alimony. The court's rationale was that support orders are always modifiable because of changed circumstances, making an unmodifiable award of property inappropriate. However, the court affirmed that property division is to be "equitable," which does not necessarily mean equal, because the court must consider the economic situation of the spouses at divorce, their contributions to the acquisition of property, the value of nonmarital property each spouse receives, and the conduct of the parties during the marriage. *See also* Wiencko v. Takayama, 745 S.E.2d 168, 175 (Va. App. 2013) (because purpose of property division is only to divide equitably the wealth accumulated during marriage, value of separate property is irrelevant in equitable distribution analysis).

The ALI Family Dissolution Principles recommend a presumption in favor of dividing marital property equally that can be rebutted by a showing that the former spouse is entitled to compensation for reasons that would justify an award of spousal support. ALI, Principles of the Law of Family Dissolution § 4.09 (2002). If need is the controlling factor in property division, a number of questions arise. As this recommendation indicates, questions about the meaning of "need" are more often raised in determining eligibility for and the amount of spousal support, and they are, accordingly, considered in the next section of this chapter.

7. A minority of state statutes list marital fault as a factor that may be considered in property division, and some, like UMDA Section 307, explicitly exclude "marital misconduct" as a factor. The others either call simply for equitable distribution or for equitable distribution with lists of factors that do not include language clearly connoting fault. Most courts today exclude marital fault as a factor in property division, and even where fault can be considered, courts often relegate it to a minor role. This approach to marital fault is consistent with public opinion, as a recent empirical study shows. Researchers surveyed 600 people awaiting jury service in Pima County, Arizona, and found that the great majority of them believe that marital fault should not be considered in dividing property at divorce. In even the most egregious case, where a spouse admits adultery and gives no explanation, 65 percent of the respondents said that fault should not be considered. Sanford L. Braver & Ira Mark Ellman, Citizens' Views About Fault in Property Division, 47 Fam. L.Q. 419, 423, 431 (2013). The survey also included questions designed to reveal the reasons for the respondents' judgments. Discussing the results, the authors wrote:

> [M]ost respondents disagreed with the statement that judges allocating property should consider evidence of fault "because that is fair" (52% disagree, 28% agree). Why don't they think it is fair to consider conduct they condemn? Perhaps they believe the spousal property rights trump — that even though the adulterer did

something wrong, it wasn't wrong enough to deprive him (or her) of a property share. Yet, on further thought, that explanation may not square with the data. The Pew Survey suggests that respondents indeed think adultery is quite wrong, and at least some who supported equal division in the case we gave them would surely still think it "fair" to *consider* adultery in property cases generally. They might believe there are *some* cases, even if not the one we gave them, in which adultery should matter. Yet the "fairness" [survey] suggests a majority reject this view. Why?

. . . [T]hose with experience with divorce, or who would have more at stake in a divorce because they had more property or more income, were all more skeptical of allowing courts to consider fault, as were older and more educated respondents. Perhaps these more seasoned respondents worry that, while it might seem fair in the abstract to consider adultery, allowing its consideration in real cases would actually produce *unfair* outcomes because of problems in the judicial process. . . . This interpretation is supported by our respondents' endorsement of [statements] suggesting just such problems. The . . . statement that received the strongest endorsement — the only one with a mean rating over 5 — was that judges should not consider fault because "deciding which spouse is at fault is so subjective that the decision would just depend on which judge heard the case." That concern could apply even to cases in which the misconduct is clear (as where the adultery is admitted) because one must still decide how large a penalty to impose on the offending spouse. Penalties that fluctuated arbitrarily among cases decided by different judges would not be fair.

Recall as well that it was only the simplest case — where a spouse admits adultery and offers no excuse or justification — in which unequal division received any support at all. In all the other cases, the overwhelming majority of respondents chose equal division. . . . That is, once any factual complication or dispute is present in the case, nearly all our respondents favored equal division. Even most of those sympathetic to considering fault apparently concluded that in these cases they weren't prepared to put all the blame for the marital failure on either spouse. One might guess many would also worry about how well judges would do if they were given that task. Our respondents did, on average, agree with other [statements] offering such prudential reasons for not considering fault: "marital relationships are too complicated for judges to figure out" (mean of 4.85); "courts would end up spending too much time and money" (mean of 4.79); and "divorcing spouses would often end up spending too much money for lawyers and other costs required to make such claims, or to defend [against them]" (mean of 4.87). In other words, though fairness is good in concept, it may be too difficult or expensive to achieve in this context.

47 Fam. L.Q. at 433-435. The researchers found that citizens strongly favor equal division of marital assets at divorce or at the end of a long-term cohabiting relationship, regardless of whether the partners had equal or unequal earnings. Opinions did not vary with the respondents' gender, income, education, marital status, parental status, or political affiliation. Ira Mark Ellman & Sanford L. Braver, Should Marriage Matter?, *in* Marriage at the Crossroads 170 (Elizabeth Scott & Marsha Garrison eds., 2013).

8. In more than 30 states "economic misconduct" is a factor in property division. Linda D. Elrod & Robert G. Spector, A Review of the Year in Family Law, 46 Fam. L.Q. 471, 534 Chart 5 (2013). Under statutes that do not address fault but include lists of factors, courts sometimes justify the consideration of economic fault on the basis that it pertains to the parties' contributions to the

acquisition or dissipation of assets. Most courts have defined economic misconduct as one spouse's use of marital property for his or her own benefit for a purpose unrelated to the marriage after the parties have separated, or at a time where the marriage is in serious jeopardy or undergoing an irreconcilable breakdown, although some courts have held that their divorce statutes do not include this temporal limitation. Finan v. Finan, 949 A.2d 468 (Conn. 2008) (collecting and discussing cases).

While some courts require proof that the at-fault spouse intended to deprive the other of a fair share of the assets, others focus more on economic considerations. Taking the latter approach to determine the effect of a husband's bad investment decisions that resulted in a loss of more than $1 million, the New Hampshire Supreme Court wrote:

> The Court of Appeals of Washington has instructed its trial courts that they may consider "whose negatively productive conduct depleted the couple's assets and . . . apportion a higher debt load or fewer assets to the wasteful marital partner." In re Marriage of Williams, 84 Wash. App. 263, 927 P.2d 679, 683 (1996) (quotation omitted), *review denied*, 131 Wash. 2d 1025, 937 P.2d 1102 (1997). In *Williams*, the court approved the trial court's consideration of various factors to determine that the wife's gambling losses throughout the marriage did not amount to a dissipation of marital assets. *Id.* The factors the trial court considered included: the amount of income the wife brought into the marriage; the nature of the conduct (the court equated legalized gambling to an "entertainment cost[ ]"); and the husband's knowledge of the wife's gambling. *Id.*
>
> The Supreme Judicial Court of Massachusetts adopted a similar view in *Kittredge:* "[D]etermination whether a spouse's expenditures constitute dissipation considers them in the light of that spouse's over-all contribution, including whether the expenditures have rendered the spouse unable to support the other spouse from the much-diminished estate at the time of divorce." *Kittredge*, 803 N.E.2d at 315.
>
> We find these cases persuasive and hold that . . . to support an unequal distribution of assets due to a spouse's conduct which resulted in a diminution in value of property, a trial court must consider factors such as: conduct which contributed to the growth in value of property; the nature of the conduct; the other spouse's knowledge of the conduct; whether the conduct diminished the total marital assets to such an extent that the other spouse is unable to maintain a similar lifestyle following divorce; and any other factor the court deems relevant.
>
> There is evidence in the record before us, and the trial court found, that the respondent contributed the initial start-up funds deposited into the account from the purchase and sale of properties and businesses. The petitioner also testified that she was aware that the respondent had invested money in the stock market and that he managed the account daily. In addition, there is evidence in the record that the parties had other significant marital assets besides the stock account, and that the stock loss allowed the parties to claim a loss on their taxes, contributing to a tax credit of nearly $131,000. The record fails to show that the trial court considered these factors when it found that "the actions of [the respondent] . . . caused the diminution in value of property owned by the parties."

In re Martel, 944 A.2d 975 (N.H. 2008). For further discussion, including a comparison of the approaches to these issues in community property and common law states, *see* J. Thomas Oldham, "Romance Without Finance Ain't Got No Chance":

Development of the Doctrine of Dissipation in Equitable Distribution States, 21 J. Am. Acad. Matrimonial Law. 501 (2008).

9. Tort suits between spouses or recently divorced former spouses have become increasingly common. Most are for the intentional torts of assault or battery, but successful suits have also been brought for intentional infliction of emotional distress, tortious infliction of a venereal disease, negligence, fraud, and on miscellaneous other theories. For a review of the issues and case law, *see* Michelle L. Evans, Note: Wrongs Committed During a Marriage: The Child That No Area of the Law Wants to Adopt, 66 Wash. & Lee L. Rev. 465 (2009).

PROBLEMS

1. Theresa and Nandor lived throughout their married life in a state whose statutory and case law create a rebuttable presumption of equal division of the property and mandate that the court consider "the contributions of each spouse to the acquisition of the property, including the contribution of a spouse as homemaker." Both Theresa and Nandor worked, and they contributed roughly equal amounts of money to running the household, but Theresa has done most of the homemaker work. Is Theresa therefore entitled to more than half the property?

Nandor spent his excess earnings on "toys," and Theresa invested hers in stocks. Has Theresa contributed more to the acquisition of the stocks than has Nandor? Has Nandor committed economic waste?

2. During a time when Betty and Walt were experiencing marital difficulties, Walt gave his son from a prior marriage a very large gift when the son graduated from high school. Betty and Walt divorced six months later. Did Walt's gift amount to "economic misconduct"?

3. Mary and Victor were married four years ago. Before the marriage Victor was a successful psychiatrist earning $50,000 a year; after they were married he quit. Mary is heir to the Johnson & Johnson fortune; she receives more than $1 million annually from a family trust. During the marriage they lived on Mary's income, and they purchased real property worth almost $4 million. At trial Mary presented convincing evidence that Victor was negotiating for her murder. The courts have previously held that the statutes embody a partnership concept of marriage for purposes of property division and that fault is not a factor to be considered in dividing the property. Can Victor's actions be considered in dividing the property?

4. During marriage counseling Wilma admits that she never loved or felt sexually attracted toward her husband, Harry. Soon after, they divorce on grounds of irreconcilable differences. Harry then sues Wilma for fraud, alleging that if she had not professed great love and passion for him while they were courting, he would never have married her or transferred property into her name that he owned before marriage. Wanda moves to dismiss the tort suit on public policy grounds. Should the motion be granted?

5. Cherry and Dave were married in 1996 and separated in April 2001 when Cherry sought a domestic violence restraining order which precluded Dave from owning or possessing a firearm. Dave, who was a deputy sheriff, lost his job because

of the firearm restriction. The court awarded Dave a car and his pension benefits, and Cherry received household goods, a car, and her pension benefits. If the court had divided the pension benefits earned during the relationship equally, Dave would have been ordered to pay Cherry an additional $15,250. To justify the award, the judge made findings that included: "By virtue of the obtaining of the permanent domestic violence protection order, the petitioner's ability to obtain gainful employment or meaningful retirement benefits in the future is severely limited due to his education and training." The judge also commented to Cherry's counsel, "I just don't see that if she's going to put him out of a job, what does she expect him to pay and what does she expect him to do?" Cherry has appealed. Assuming that the law in this state does not allow a judge to take noneconomic fault into account in dividing property, what arguments should the parties make on appeal?

2. *Characterization of Property as Separate or Marital*

In states in which only community or marital property is divisible, characterizing assets as "community/marital" or "separate/nonmarital" is crucial. Even in states that permit division of all property, the principles that underlie characterization may affect how a judge exercises discretion because these principles express commonly held beliefs about fairness and the spouses' expectations. Statutes and case law generally provide that separate property includes (1) property owned by either spouse before marriage, (2) property acquired by a spouse after the marriage by gift or inheritance, and (3) property acquired after the marriage in exchange for separate property. However, many assets cannot readily be characterized on the basis of these rules alone. For example, they do not tell us whether income produced by or the increase in value of separate property is separate or marital, whether separate property that has been mixed ("commingled") with marital property is separate or marital, or whether an asset's character has been changed or "transmuted" by a voluntary act of the owner, such as a change in title, issues with which the next case deals.

Courts in community property states, where characterization has been required for a long time, have more experience with issues of characterization than do those in common law property states. However, the resolutions that these courts have reached should not necessarily be imported into common law property states because community property rules are sometimes shaped by considerations of rights and duties of the spouses during marriage or at death. William A. Reppy, Jr., Major Events in the Evolution of American Community Property Law and Their Import to Equitable Distribution States, 23 Fam. L.Q. 163, 164-165 (1989). Texas and California almost always have different rules for resolving a characterization issue, with California's tending to increase the size of the community estate and Texas's rules tending to decrease it. The other community property states vary in which solution they choose. J. Thomas Oldham, Everything Is Bigger in Texas, Except the Community Property Estate: Must Texas Remain a Divorce Haven for the Rich?, 44 Fam. L.Q. 293, 293-294 (2010). This article details some of the most significant issues and the community property states' solutions.

SIEFERT V. SIEFERT

---

973 N.E.2d 834 (Ohio App. 2012)

TIMOTHY P. CANNON, P.J. Appellant, Susan M. Siefert, appeals the September 23, 2011 judgment of the Trumbull County Court of Common Pleas, Domestic Relations Division. This court must determine whether the trial court abused its discretion in finding that appellant relinquished her separate interest in a 1992 Ford Mustang when she transferred title of the vehicle into the joint names of the parties after their marriage. . . .

The record reveals that appellant purchased the Mustang in 2001, prior to the parties' marriage. The parties testified that, after their marriage on July 13, 2002, they began restoring the vehicle. It is undisputed that the parties spent considerable time, effort, and money during the Mustang's restoration, thereby increasing its value from $7,500 to $27,200, the stipulated appraisal.

At the time of purchase, the Mustang was titled solely in appellant's name. In 2005, however, appellant transferred title of the Mustang from her name to both the parties' names, jointly, with rights of survivorship. . . .

Property is divided into two categories: marital and separate. In this case, it is undisputed that appellant purchased the Mustang prior to the parties' marriage for the sum of $7,500. Although there is evidence that appellant borrowed $500 from appellee, the record demonstrates this amount was paid back to appellee. At the time of purchase, the Mustang was titled solely in appellant's name. As the Mustang was acquired by appellant prior to the marriage, it is deemed separate property.

A spouse, however, may convert separate property to marital property through actions during the marriage. In this case, appellant transferred the title of the vehicle from her name to the parties' joint names in 2005. The trial court found that by transferring the title of the vehicle into the joint names of the parties, appellant converted any separate property claims she may have into a marital asset. As there is a lack of competent, credible evidence to support such a finding, we reverse the trial court's decision.

The most commonly-recognized method for converting separate property into marital property is through an inter vivos gift of the property from the donor spouse to the donee spouse. In Ohio, the elements of an inter vivos gift include: "(1) the intent of the donor to make an immediate gift; (2) the delivery of the property to the donee; and (3) the acceptance of the gift by the donee after the donor has relinquished control of the property." "The donee bears the burden of proving by clear and convincing evidence that the donor made an inter vivos gift."

Based on the findings of fact issued by the trial court, it appears the trial court relied solely on appellant's transfer of the title from her name to the parties' joint names in determining that appellant intended to relinquish by gift to appellee any separate interest she had in the Mustang. The trial court did not cite to any evidence other than the transfer of title; standing alone, this is insufficient to establish an inter vivos gift.

In Frederick v. Frederick, this court found:

> Under prior case law, the presence of both parties' names on a joint title may have given rise to the presumption that appellant had foregone whatever separate

interest [she] had in the property by gifting fifty percent of it to appellee as marital property. Since the enactment of R.C. 3105.171 however, the presumption of a gift has been negated. . . . Rather, a trial court may make such a finding only upon an appropriate factual context.

As the donee, appellee had the burden of showing by clear and convincing evidence that appellant, the donor, made an inter vivos gift. Appellee did not provide any evidence or testimony that appellant intended to make an inter vivos gift when she transferred title of the Mustang. Appellee did submit an exhibit of the certificate of transfer of title illustrating the transfer of title. Appellee also testified this transfer was done in conjunction with the execution of the parties' wills; in the event of both of their deaths, the Mustang was to be bestowed to the Ford Motor Company. Appellant, however, gave no testimony regarding the transfer of the vehicle or the circumstances surrounding the transfer.

Appellee did not meet his evidentiary burden. The title of the Mustang in both parties' names is insufficient to establish an inter vivos gift. This is particularly true where the transfer of the asset has a potential alternate purpose, such as estate planning. Here, the evidence does not indicate that appellant intended to present an immediate possessory interest to appellee; rather, in transferring the title, appellant may simply have been planning for the disposition of the vehicle in the event of her death.

. . . This matter is remanded to the trial court for further proceedings consistent with this opinion.

DIANE V. GRENDELL, J., dissents with a Dissenting Opinion. . . . "[T]he holding of title to property by one spouse individually or by both spouses in a form of co-ownership does not determine whether the property is marital property or separate property." Although "[t]he fact that both parties['] names are on the deed is not determinative of whether the property is marital or separate, . . . such evidence may be considered on the issue."

The issue in the present case is whether there is any evidence in the record, beyond the titling of the vehicle, which supports the lower court's determination that Ms. Siefert's separate interest in the Mustang became a marital interest during the course of the marriage. Because such evidence exists, that determination should be affirmed.

In addition to being titled in the name of both parties, the Mustang's Certificate of Title contains the notation WROS, i.e., with right of survivorship. The right of survivorship, while not determinative of ownership, is evidence of a present ownership interest in each party (both Mr. and Ms. Siefert), which would pass to the other in the event of that party's death.

In connection with this right of survivorship, there was testimony that, at the time the Mustang was re-titled, the parties executed wills to ensure that if anything happened to either one or both of them, the vehicle would pass to the Ford Motor Company rather than Ms. Siefert's daughters. As Mr. Siefert testified: "we had the wills done stating that if anything happened to us, the car would go to Ford Motor Company to a museum because she said that her daughters wouldn't know what to do with it." Again, this is evidence of Ms. Siefert's donative intent, rather than merely an estate planning device. Otherwise, Ms. Siefert could have left the vehicle in her name only and devised it directly to the Ford Motor Company, i.e., there would be no need to provide for the contingency "if anything happened to us."

Lastly, the marital nature of the Mustang is evidenced by the joint effort expended by both parties to restore the vehicle and enter it at car show competitions. The lower court's uncontroverted finding was that "the majority of the restoration work performed on this vehicle was done after the parties' marriage and was done with marital money." Ms. Siefert testified that, during the marriage, they took the Mustang to car shows "together." Mr. Siefert testified that he invested his own time, money, and parts from a separately owned vehicle in the Mustang. The parties agree that Ms. Siefert purchased the Mustang prior to the marriage, in part, with money loaned by Mr. Siefert.

While none of these facts are necessarily determinative of the status of the Mustang as separate or marital property, collectively they corroborate the evidence of the vehicle's Title, and are competent and credible evidence supporting the lower court's determination, which, therefore, must be affirmed. Accordingly, I dissent.

NOTES AND QUESTIONS

1. The owner of property may change or transmute its character by a voluntary act manifesting this intent. Marital or community property can be transmuted into the separate property of one or both spouses, and separate property of one spouse can be transmuted into marital or community property or into separate property of the other spouse. In some community property states transmutation of community property into separate property requires a written agreement.

2. Perhaps the most common situation in which the transmutation issue arises is when the owner of an asset changes how it is titled. The owner of separate property may change the title to both spouses' names, as in *Siefert*, or one spouse may agree that a community asset will be titled only in the name of the other. Often the change in title is not accompanied by a clear expression of intent about whether the asset's character is changing, and the issue only arises later, when the marriage is ending. This problem is essentially the same as a problem discussed in Chapter 2: under what circumstances a change in title establishes that one spouse made a gift of property to the other. Because convincing evidence is often unavailable, many cases are decided based on who has the burden of proof on the intent issue. In *Siefert*, who had the burden? Why?

Absent a statute on point, courts tend to hold that when the owner of separate property jointly titles it, intent to transmute the asset's character is presumed. What arguments support this rule? What arguments would support a presumption that a change in title does not change the character of the asset?

3. In *Siefert* the wife argued that she added her husband's name to the title for estate planning purposes, i.e., so that he would get the car if she predeceased him. This argument is commonly made by a spouse trying to prove that a jointly titled asset remained separate property. The majority and dissent disagree about the sufficiency of this evidence. Why? In a state that presumed a change in title to both names proved the intent to transmute the asset into marital property, would such evidence be enough to rebut the presumption?

4. If one spouse uses his or her separate funds or community/marital funds to buy a gift for the other, should it be presumed that the gift is the recipient's separate property, since gifts during marriage to only one spouse are usually separate property? Or should this rule apply only to gifts from third parties? In California spousal gifts usually remain marital property, except that gifts of clothes and jewelry are separate unless they are "substantial." Other community property states do not necessarily agree. If separate property is used to make a gift, some courts say that the property is transmuted into marital property, and others say that it becomes the separate property of the other spouse. Common law property states are also divided on the effect of interspousal gifts. In some, case law or statutes say that such a gift is marital property, while in others the gift becomes the separate property of the recipient.

5. If a third party makes a gift that increases the value of community or marital property, should the gift be presumed to be community or marital as well? In a number of cases, the parents of one spouse help make the down payment or pay down the mortgage on the couple's home, and at divorce the spouse whose parents made the gift argues that the gift should be his or her separate property. In re Marriage of Krejci, 297 P.3d 1035 (Colo. App. 2013), rejects this position and discusses cases from New York, Florida, Illinois, Missouri, and Washington.

6. Relatively recent jurisdiction-specific discussions of this topic include Sara Craig, Transmutations and the Presumption of Undue Influence: A Quagmire in Divorce Court, 25 Hastings Women's L.J. 81 (2014) (California); Matthew L. Roberts, Transmuting Mississippi's Current Transmutation Doctrines: Establishing Clear and Consistent Precedents to Property Division, 80 Miss. L.J. 709 (2010); Leslie Joan Harris, Tracing, Spousal Gifts and Rebuttable Presumptions: Puzzles of Oregon Property Division Law, 83 Or. L. Rev. 1291 (2004).

O'BRIEN v. O'BRIEN

508 S.E.2d 300 (N.C. App. 1998)

HORTON, Judge. Plaintiff-husband and defendant-wife were married on 24 May 1975, separated on 7 August 1995, and divorced on 24 September 1996. No children were born of the marriage. Following their separation, plaintiff instituted this equitable distribution action on 28 December 1995.

The evidence before the trial court tends to show that in 1986, after receiving an inheritance from her father of approximately $163,000.00, defendant opened an investment account with Wheat First Securities. She deposited about $158,000.00 of her inheritance, as well as a $10,000.00 gift from her Aunt Mabel Dozier Stone (Aunt Mabel), into this investment account. On the advice of her broker, defendant had the investment account listed in the joint names of the parties, with a right of survivorship. From November 1986 until July 1989, the parties deposited a total of $4,550.00 of marital funds into this investment account, and withdrew $38,658.00 from the investment account for marital purposes. This investment account remained with Wheat First Securities until July 1989, at which time it was transferred to Interstate Johnson Lane when the parties' investment broker changed firms. At the time of the transfer, the investment account was valued at $138,161.00 or nearly $30,000.00 less than the initial deposit.

The investment account remained at Interstate Johnson Lane until January 1991, when it again followed the investment broker to his new position at Shearson Lehman. At the time of the transfer to Shearson Lehman, the investment account had depreciated as a result of market forces, and was valued at $119,714.00. Also, during this time Aunt Mabel was in poor health and was attempting to deplete her estate by distributing portions to her intended beneficiaries in order to avoid estate tax consequences. Therefore, Aunt Mabel made gifts to plaintiff and defendant in December 1992 and January 1993 for $10,000.00 each, for a total of $40,000.00. Along with each gift Aunt Mabel included a note describing the purpose of her gifts. The 28 December 1992 note to plaintiff read, in pertinent part, as follows:

> Dear Dick:
>   I have enclosed a check for $10,000 which is part of the inheritance I am leaving Mabel. Since the law allows only $10,000 per family member, I am sending this gift for her in your name to remove assets from my estate that would otherwise be taxed at a very high rate if left in the estate. Please deposit upon receipt.
>   Mabel D. Stone

Aunt Mabel's 15 January 1993 note contained similar language, stating that she had "enclosed a check for $10,000 which is part of the inheritance that I am leaving to Mabel." Of this $40,000.00 in gifts from Aunt Mabel, $24,990.00 was deposited into the investment account at Shearson Lehman, and $9,970.00 was used to purchase a 1993 Volvo 850 automobile for defendant.

In addition to the $24,990.00 in gift money invested in the investment account, the investment account increased in value by approximately $44,000.00 due to dividends, share reinvestment gains and market value gains. Further, approximately $6,500.00 in management fees were charged against the investment account, and $1,035.00 was withdrawn from the investment account. In May 1994, the Shearson Lehman investment account was valued at $181,452.00. The investment account remained at Shearson Lehman until May 1994, when it was transferred to Scott & Stringfellow. While the investment account was at Scott & Stringfellow, defendant received an inheritance from Aunt Mabel's estate totaling $62,841.00, of which she deposited $56,851.00 into the investment account. The investment account remained there until the parties' separation in August 1995. After hearing all of the evidence, the trial court found that the $40,000.00 in gifts from Aunt Mabel were intended to be gifts to defendant in the total amount of $40,000.00, and not gifts to plaintiff. Further, the trial court determined that other than $4,550.00 of marital funds deposited in the investment account when it was with Wheat First Security, all of which was withdrawn and spent for marital purposes, no other marital property or earnings of the parties was ever deposited to or invested in the investment account. Consequently, the trial court determined the investment account to be the separate property of defendant and not subject to distribution. In sum, the trial court found $308,465.12 of the total estate to be the separate property of defendant and $277,578.57 to be marital property. After determining that an equal division of the marital property would be equitable, the trial court awarded plaintiff $158,677.28 of the marital estate, and awarded defendant $118,901.29 of the marital estate. In addition, the trial court ordered plaintiff to pay defendant a distributive award of $19,888.00 in order to equalize the distribution. On appeal, plaintiff contends the trial court erred by (1) classifying the investment account and the gifts from Aunt Mabel as defendant's separate property rather than the marital property of the couple; . . . and (4) failing to award plaintiff an unequal distribution of the marital property and debt.

I.

. . . In an equitable distribution case filed before 1 October 1997, the trial court must undergo a three-step analysis: (1) identify what is marital property and what is separate property; (2) calculate the net value of the marital property; and (3) distribute the marital property in an equitable manner. In this case, we are concerned with the first step, the classification of the investment account as either marital property or separate property.

The main contention raised by plaintiff's appeal is that the trial court improperly classified the investment account as defendant's separate property. According to plaintiff, although the money used to begin the investment account was part of defendant's inheritance, the investment account should nevertheless be classified as marital property for the following reasons: (1) marital funds were commingled with the inherited funds, thus "transmuting" the investment account from separate property to marital property; (2) defendant has failed to "trace out" the $4,550.00 in marital funds which were deposited into the investment account; and (3) plaintiff actively participated with defendant in managing the investment account by making certain decisions which ultimately led to the increased value of the investment account. For purposes of clarity, we will address each of these points separately.

Before addressing plaintiff's contentions, we note that in order to determine the nature of certain property, it is helpful to consult the definitions of martial property and separate property provided in N.C. Gen. Stat. § 50-20(b), which defines the terms as follows:

> (1) "Marital property" means all real and personal property acquired by either spouse or both spouses during the course of the marriage and before the date of the separation of the parties, and presently owned, except property determined to be separate property . . . in accordance with subdivision (2) . . . of this subsection. . . . It is presumed that all property acquired after the date of marriage and before the date of separation is marital property except property which is separate property under subdivision (2) of this subsection. This presumption may be rebutted by the greater weight of the evidence.
>
> (2) "Separate property" means all real and personal property acquired by a spouse before marriage or acquired by a spouse by bequest, devise, descent, or gift during the course of the marriage. . . . Property acquired in exchange for separate property shall remain separate property regardless of whether the title is in the name of the husband or wife or both and shall not be considered to be marital property unless a contrary intention is expressly stated in the conveyance. The increase in value of separate property and the income derived from separate property shall be considered separate property.

N.C. Gen. Stat. § 50-20(b) (Cum. Supp. 1997). Furthermore, in cases such as this there are dual burdens of proof. First, the party seeking to classify the investment as marital property must show by the preponderance of the evidence that the property is presently owned, and was acquired by either of the spouses during the course of the marriage and before the date of separation. Thereafter, the party seeking to classify the investment account as separate property must show by the preponderance of the evidence that the property falls within the statutory definition of separate property. If both parties meet their burdens, "'then under the statutory scheme of N.C.G.S. § 50-20(b)(1) and (b)(2), the property is excepted from the definition of marital property and is, therefore, separate property.'"

A. "TRANSMUTATION" OF SEPARATE PROPERTY INTO MARITAL PROPERTY

According to plaintiff, although the initial deposit into the investment account was without question the separate property of defendant, the subsequent actions by the parties of commingling marital funds with separate funds "transmuted" the nature of the investment account from separate property to marital property. The doctrine of transmutation is well developed in Illinois, where it was first adopted by judicial decision and later by legislative enactment. Under this theory, "the affirmative act of augmenting nonmarital property by commingling it with marital property" creates a rebuttable presumption that all the property has been transmuted into marital property. In re Marriage of Smith, 86 Ill. 2d 518, 56 Ill. Dec. 693, 427 N.E.2d 1239, 1245-46 (Ill. 1981).

However, as plaintiff concedes, this Court has expressly rejected the theory of transmutation. We find, therefore, that the mere commingling of marital funds with separate funds alone does not automatically transmute the separate property into marital property.

B. "TRACING OUT" OF SEPARATE FUNDS

Next, plaintiff contends that regardless of whether the investment account was transmuted into marital property, defendant failed to meet her burden of "tracing out" her separate property. Here, it is clear that the investment account was begun during the marriage and prior to the date of separation. However, it is equally clear that the initial deposit into the investment account was from defendant's separate property, consisting of her inheritance from her father's estate. Therefore, defendant has met her burden of establishing the separate nature of the property.

Despite the fact that defendant has met her burden of proving the separate nature of the investment account, plaintiff contends defendant must also "trace out" her separate property from the $4,550.00 of marital funds which were deposited into the investment account. However, the $4,550.00 of marital funds deposited into the investment account was the only deposit of marital funds into the investment account. Further, soon after this deposit, $38,658.00 was withdrawn from the account.

After considering this evidence, the trial court concluded that the $4,550.00 deposit of marital funds was entirely consumed by the subsequent withdrawal, such that no marital funds remained in the investment account. Since there is competent evidence in the record to support this finding, we are bound by it. Therefore, after these marital funds were removed, the only funds remaining in the investment account were separate funds. This being the case, we find that defendant has met her burden of "tracing out" her separate property.

C. ACTIVE VS. PASSIVE APPRECIATION OF THE INVESTMENT ACCOUNT

Finally, plaintiff contends that he actively participated in the management of the investment account, such that the account should be treated as marital property. It is well recognized that there is a distinction between active and passive appreciation of separate property. Active appreciation refers to financial or managerial contributions of one of the spouses to the separate property during the marriage; whereas, passive appreciation refers to enhancement of the value of separate property due solely to inflation, changing economic conditions or other such circumstances beyond the control of either spouse. Furthermore, the party seeking to establish that any appreciation of separate property is passive bears the burden of proving such by the preponderance of the evidence.

The issue of the characterization of the appreciation of investment accounts, mutual funds, and other stocks or securities, as active or passive has not been previously addressed in North Carolina. . . . Therefore, we will look to other jurisdictions for guidance.

In Deffenbaugh, 877 S.W.2d 186, the Missouri Court of Appeals was presented with the question of whether the appreciated value of 425 shares of a mutual fund was marital or separate property. The evidence tended to show that the shares were originally purchased with the wife's separate property. According to the husband, he regularly looked at the quarterly statements, corresponded with and spoke to the investment broker, and regularly gave advice to his wife. However, the court held that these activities "were within the purview of ordinary and usual spousal duties; and as such, did not transform the increased value of the original shares of the mutual fund into [separate] property." Id. Further, the Missouri Court of Appeals has repeatedly held that several factors must be shown in order for a spouse to be awarded a proportionate share of the increase in value of the other spouse's separate property, including: (1) a contribution of substantial services; (2) a direct correlation between those services and the increase in value; (3) the amount of the increase in value; (4) the performance of the services during the marriage; and (5) the value of the services, lack of compensation, or inadequate compensation.

We believe that the multi-factorial approach of the Missouri Court of Appeals is consistent with the public policy considerations incorporated in our Equitable Distribution Act, and we adopt that approach. We hold, therefore, that if either or both of the spouses perform substantial services during the marriage which result in an increase in the value of an investment account, that increase is to be characterized as an active increase and classified as a marital asset. In making the determination of whether the services of a spouse are substantial, the trial court should consider, among other relevant facts and circumstances of the particular case, the following factors: (1) the nature of the investment; (2) the extent to which the investment decisions are made only by the party or parties, made by the party or parties in consultation with their investment broker, or solely made by the investment broker; (3) the frequency of contact between the investment broker and the parties; (4) whether the parties routinely made investment decisions in accordance with the recommendation of the investment broker, and the frequency with which the spouses made investment decisions contrary to the advice of the investment broker; (5) whether the spouses conducted their own research and regularly monitored the investments in their accounts, or whether they primarily relied on information supplied by the investment broker; and (6) whether the decisions or other activities, if any, made solely by the parties directly contributed to the increased value of the investment account.

Here, the trial court did not find that the actions of the spouses in jointly meeting with the wife's broker and routinely choosing between investment alternatives based on the recommendation of the investment broker rose to the level of substantial activity. The trial court determined that the defendant-wife had established by the preponderance of the evidence that any appreciation of the investment account was purely passive. After careful review, we find that the trial court's findings support its conclusions of law. Therefore, we overrule this assignment of error.

II.

... Next, plaintiff contends the trial court erred by finding the two $10,000.00 checks written by Aunt Mabel to plaintiff were the separate property of defendant. In its 2 April 1997 order, the trial court made the following findings with regard to Aunt Mabel's intent:

> 14. In December [1992] and January [1993], defendant's Aunt Mabel Dozier Stone was in ill health. [Aunt Mabel] was attempting to distribute a portion of her estate to intended beneficiaries prior to her death in order to avoid estate tax consequences. In December [1992], [Aunt Mabel] wrote two $10,000 checks — one payable to defendant individually and one payable to plaintiff individually. In January [1993], [Aunt Mabel] wrote two more $10,000 checks — one to plaintiff individually and one to defendant individually. She also wrote a letter to plaintiff describing her intent and design that the checks payable to plaintiff were in fact gifts for the defendant. [Aunt Mabel's] intention in making the $40,000 in payments was to make a gift to defendant in the total amount of $40,000 and not to make any gift to plaintiff of any of said sum. ... Plaintiff was not an object of [Aunt Mabel's] bounty or gift-giving. He was not the intended recipient of the funds being given. With regard to these checks, plaintiff was merely a conduit for [Aunt Mabel's] gift to defendant.

According to plaintiff, there was no competent evidence in the record to support this finding. Additionally, plaintiff contends that "as a matter of law the aunt's intent is irrelevant given that the aunt had to have been making a gift to [plaintiff] in order to comply with federal gift tax law."

... [T]he trial court's findings in this case are adequately supported by the record evidence, and these findings justify its conclusions. It is clear that plaintiff was not the object of Aunt Mabel's bounty, but was a mere conduit for the gift to defendant. As such, we overrule this assignment of error. Further, we find plaintiff's federal estate tax argument to be without merit. ...

[The court affirmed the trial court order dividing the marital property equally because the husband did not present sufficient evidence to overcome the state's strong policy in favor of equal division.]

NOTES AND QUESTIONS

1. The statute construed in *O'Brien*, like those in many other states, creates a presumption that all property acquired during the marriage is marital. What is the effect of this presumption? What policies underlie it?

2. How did the court determine the character of the gifts from Aunt Mabel? For purposes of the federal estate and gift tax, half of these transfers were gifts to the husband. Why didn't this characterization control who owned the gifts for purposes of the O'Briens' divorce?

3. The wife in *O'Brien* deposited the money she inherited and was given in a joint account with her husband. Why didn't this change in title change the character of the asset?

4. Separate property may be mixed with marital property intentionally, as in *O'Brien*, or when when a separately owned asset is brought into the marriage and is paid off or maintained with marital funds. Commingling of separate and marital property can also occur unintentionally, as when a bank account owned before marriage earns interest in a state that treats the income from separate property as marital. In either situation, the possibility arises that the commingling shows an intent to transmute the separate property into marital property or vice versa. Should commingling create a presumption in favor of transmutation? If so, in which direction?

In *Siefert* the parties restored the wife's vintage Mustang, investing marital funds and effort into the car before its title was changed. Is this commingling evidence that the wife intended to transmute the car into a marital asset?

5. The *O'Brien* court says that it rejects "the doctrine of transmutation." Since the court surely did not mean that the owner of property cannot change its character, just what was it rejecting? In a few states, property cannot be partly separate and partly marital; in these states commingling separate property with marital property automatically converts the separate property into marital property. In most states, it is legally possible to *trace* separate funds in and out of bank accounts and other property. What policy does each approach express? As discussed in *O'Brien*, the Illinois Supreme Court adopted the automatic approach in In re Marriage of Smith, 427 N.E.2d 1239 (Ill. 1981), but *Smith* was overruled by the legislature a few years later. *See* In re Marriage of Malters, 478 N.E.2d 1068 (Ill. App. 1985).

Tracing can be quite difficult, as, for example, when separate and marital funds are mixed in a bank account and then many deposits and withdrawals are made over the years. Ordinarily, the spouse who claims to own separate property carries the burden of tracing the funds. If the spouse cannot carry this burden, commingled property will be entirely marital.

6. In all states, the increase in value of and income from marital/community property is marital/community. Thus, if the court had found that Mrs. O'Brien's

gifts and inheritances had been transmuted into marital property, the increases in value of the assets purchased with them would also have been marital.

However, the court found that the inheritances and gifts remained separate property, requiring it to consider the classification of the increases in value. The governing statute in *O'Brien* said that increases in value of and income from separate property are separate property. The husband argued, though, that the increases in value were "active" and thus marital. What are the difference between active and passive increases? Active increases are always marital; can you see why?

In some other common law property states, all increases in value of separate property, regardless of the reason, are treated as marital, eliminating the need to distinguish between active and passive increases.[11] However, most community property states treat passive increases in value of separate property as separate and active increases as marital.

7. If the increase in value of an asset is partly separate and partly marital, allocating the increase between the two categories can be very complex. For example, this problem could arise in a state that treats passive increases in the value of separate property as separate and active increases as marital. California case law provides the method most widely used in community property states for dealing with an increase in value of separate property that is partly active and partly passive. Two cases, Pereira v. Pereira, 103 P. 488 (Cal. 1909), and Van Camp v. Van Camp, 199 P. 885 (Cal. App. 1921), applied two different methods. Under *Pereira* a reasonable return on the separate investment is calculated and treated as separate property; the remainder of the increase in value is community property. Under *Van Camp* a fair salary for the labor of the spouse is calculated. If the spouse was paid less than this amount, the community receives enough of the increase to make up the difference, and the rest of the increase in value is separate property. While no hard and fast rules determine when each rule should be used, California case law provides that *Van Camp* should be used when the appreciation in value is primarily attributable to community efforts, and *Pereira* should be used when the primary cause is market factors and the like. In re Lopez, 113 Cal. Rptr. 58 (Cal. App. 1974).

8. The ALI Family Dissolution Principles provide that the increase in value of separate property is marital if attributable to a spouse's labor and separate if due to other causes. In mixed cases the Principles recommend an approach similar to that used in *Pereira*. ALI, Principles of the Law of Family Dissolution §§ 4.04, 4.05 (2002).

9. If the principal value of an asset is commingled, partly marital/community and partly separate, characterizing increases in value presents still another allocation problem. Most community property states use the "inception of title" rule, which provides that the character of an asset is determined when it is acquired (unless, of course, the owner transmutes it). Thus, property acquired as separate

---

11. While Section 307 of the UMDA says that increases in value of separate property are separate, one of the reporters for the UMDA has written that the drafters had in mind assets such as bonds, which increase in value without owner effort and for which tracing and identification are easy. Robert J. Levy, An Introduction to Divorce-Property Issues, 23 Fam. L.Q. 147, 154 (1989).

property remains separate property even though community property is invested in it, and vice versa. (Property has a mixed character if it is initially acquired partly with community funds and partly with separate funds.) If the asset's increase is passive, i.e., attributable to market forces, inflation, or the like, the increase in value takes the same character as the original capital investment in the asset. Thus, the separate estate owns all of the increase in value, and the community has no claim to it. If the increase in value of separate property is attributable to the investment of community funds or to the active labor of one of the spouses, the community is entitled to reimbursement for the value of the contribution. The converse is true if separate funds or labor is invested in community property.

Common law property states have not always followed this approach because of its complexity. In states that say that increases due to market forces are separate, many use the "source of funds" rule to allocate market force increases if the principal value of the asset is partly marital and partly nonmarital. Under the source of funds rule, increases in value caused by market or other passive forces are allocated proportionately according to the contributions of separate and marital funds to the principal. Other states grant trial courts substantial discretion to resolve the problem on a case-by-case basis.

10. In all states income produced by marital property—rents, dividends, interest, and the like—is also marital property. The states are divided, though, in their treatment of income from separate property. Four community property states—Idaho, Louisiana, Texas, and Wisconsin—follow the Spanish rule, which treats income from separate property as community property. The other five community property states follow the American rule that such income is separate property. J. Thomas Oldham, Everything Is Bigger in Texas, Except the Community Property Estate: Must Texas Remain a Divorce Haven for the Rich?, 44 Fam. L.Q. 293, 294 (2010).

Equitable distribution statutes that address this issue usually say that income from nonmarital property is nonmarital. The Comment to UMDA Section 307 says that income from nonmarital property is marital property. The ALI Family Dissolution Principles treat income from separate property as they treat appreciation in value: income is marital if attributable to a spouse's labor and separate if due to other causes. ALI Principles, above. For detailed discussion of these issues, *see* the Reporter's Note to §4.04.

11. Property acquired during premarital cohabitation is generally not treated as marital property when the parties divorce. However, some courts have held that property acquired "in anticipation of marriage" is marital property. McCoy v. McCoy, 2013 WL 5925900 (Tenn. App. 2013); Winer v. Winer, 575 A.2d 518 (N.J. App. 1990); In re Marriage of Altman, 530 P.2d 1012 (Colo. App. 1974); Stallings v. Stallings, 393 N.E.2d 1065 (Ill. App. 1979); *contra* Nell v. Nell, 560 N.Y.S. 2d 426 (App. Div. 1990). *See also* Cross v. Cross, 30 S.W.3d 233, 236 (Mo. App. 2000) (debt for wedding acquired in anticipation of marriage is marital debt); *contra* Snacki v. Pederson, 961 N.Y.S.2d 361 (Sup. Ct. 2010).

Treating property acquired in anticipation of marriage as marital property blurs the distinction between the property remedies available to cohabitants and spouses at the break-up of their relationships. Why is this distinction made in the first place? Given the distinction, should property acquired in anticipation of marriage be treated as marital property? What facts would show that property was acquired in anticipation of marriage?

An Ohio statute embraces this blurring; it provides that ordinarily marital property begins to be acquired on the date of the marriage, but the court has discretion to select another date if necessary to do equity. Ohio Rev. Code Ann. § 3105.171(A)(2)(b) (2014). *See* Bryan v. Bryan, 2012 WL 3527120 (Ohio App.) (marital assets began to be acquired six years before wedding where parties had "de facto marriage" during that time); *contra* Ward v. Ward, 2012 WL 6044979 (Ohio App.).

12. A number of legislatures and courts have considered when a marriage ends for purposes of defining "marital property." The possibilities include

(1) The date of separation (*see, e.g.,* Cal. Fam. Code § 771 (2014) (property acquired while parties live separate and apart is separate property); N.C. Gen. Stat. § 50-20 (2014); 23 Pa. Consol. Stat. § 3501(a)(4) (2014); Deitz v. Deitz, 436 S.E.2d 463 (Va. App. 1993); In re Estate of Osicka, 461 P.2d 585 (Wash. App. 1969) (property acquired by either spouse after a permanent separation and separation agreement is separate property)).

(2) The date the petition for dissolution was filed (*see, e.g.,* Fla. Stat. § 61.075 (2014); Sanjari v. Sanjari, 755 N.E.2d 1186, 1192 (Ind. Ct. App. 2001)).

(3) The date the decree is entered (*see, e.g.,* Askins v. Askins, 704 S.W.2d 632 (Ark. 1986); Centazzo v. Centazzo, 509 A.2d 995 (R.I. 1986)).

What are the advantages and disadvantages of each of these rules?

13. A related but different question is when property is valued for purposes of division. Most jurisdictions appear to value assets as of the date of judgment of divorce, though courts in some states have said that the date of valuation is the date of filing or the date of trial, or is to be decided case by case. Toni Hendricks, Comment: Valuation Date in Divorces: What a Difference a Date Can Make, 21 J. Am. Acad. Matrimonial Law. 747 (2008).

NOTE: CHALLENGES TO THE CLASSIFICIATION REGIME—MARITAL PARTNERSHIP THEORY REVISITED

The principles explored in this section for characterizing property as marital/community or nonmarital/separate are based on the economic partnership theory of marriage: parties share the economic fruits of their labors. Under this theory, separate property is any property that does not result from the labor of either spouse during marriage. Some rules, especially the transmutation doctrine, recognize that the parties may choose what to share based on other principles. The ALI Principles of the Law of Family Dissolution modify the transmutation doctrine by adding a new rule: separate property is gradually converted to marital property as it is held over the course of the marriage. ALI Principles § 4.12. The rationale for this proposal is that as the parties' lives grow together over the years, they will increasingly expect and intend to share their economic fortunes fully. Carolyn J. Frantz and Hanoch Dagan support this proposal, regarding the passage of time as a good proxy for intent. Properties of Marriage, 104 Colum. L. Rev. 75, 113-114 (2004). They add, "over time, spouses feel less need and less desire to guard against the possibility of divorce and remarriage." *Id.* at 114. However, unlike the ALI Principles, they argue that in one situation separate property should be transmuted into marital property regardless of intent — when it is used during marriage. The foundation of this proposal is their argument that marriage should be understood as an "egalitarian liberal community" and that property division rules should be based on this understanding. They explain:

> The most common example is the family home, but also included are furniture, automobiles, and other items used by the family. . . . A spouse who has lived in a family home (and quite possibly raised children in it) perceives the property as an aspect of personhood — in constitutive rather than merely instrumental terms. Furthermore, it is not only important to individual identity, but also to identity as a member of the marital community. For the spouse who owns this property separately to claim such property as her own and to treat it as such during marriage would undermine marital sharing, trust and commitment.

Id. at 116-117.

Professor Motro has developed a precise formula for automatically converting separate property into shareable marital or community property as the marriage lengthens. Shari Motro, Labor, Luck, and Love: Reconsidering the Sanctity of Separate Property, 102 Nw. U. L. Rev. 1623 (2008). She rejects the labor theory of marital property as theoretically inconsistent and complicated and unpredictable in practice. In its place she proposes that classification of property as separate or marital be based on the idea that marriage is "a commitment by spouses not only to labor for the unit, but also to share more broadly in the opportunities and vulnerabilities that characterize who they are financially for the duration of their union." *Id.* at 1650. She argues:

> Like the partnership theory, the proposed paradigm ensures that homemakers are compensated for their labor. But unlike the partnership theory, this approach does not impose an artificial fiction. Rather than pretending that monetary and non-monetary contributions have the same value, the proposal matches most people's intuition that husbands' and wives' various contributions to marriage cannot and need not be compared. It also recognizes that spouses often contribute unequally at different points in their relationship as employment and health circumstances change. Indeed, in terms of labor contributed, some marriages are unequal from start to finish. The proposal embodies the notion that matrimony fuses spouses' risks and rewards regardless of their relative contributions of labor.

Id. at 1658-1659. In contrast, Professor Oldham argues that if a spouse does nothing to indicate an intent to transmute separate property into marital or community property, it is not likely that the parties both expected that the property would be shared at divorce. J. Thomas Oldham, Should Separate Property Gradually Become Community Property as a Marriage Continues?, 72 La. L. Rev. 127 (2011). If a state wants to increase the amount of shareable property for policy reasons, he suggests that income from separate property could be classified as community/marital property, that rules for sharing postdivorce income be liberalized, or both. (The latter issue is discussed later in this chapter.)

PROBLEMS

1. Howard is a waiter. A substantial portion of his income comes from tips. Are these gifts from a third party and hence separate property or wages and hence marital property?

2. On Edwin and Julie's wedding day Julie's father gives them $10,000. Is this Julie's separate property or marital property? What if Edwin gives Julie a necklace worth $5000, purchased from his premarital funds? If Julie gives Edwin a valuable painting on their fifth anniversary, purchased from marital funds, does the painting remain marital property or does it become Edwin's separate property?

3. In 1983 Wanda purchased a house, taking title in her own name. She made the down payment and mortgage payments with her own funds. When she married Henry in 1985, the equity in the house was worth $20,000. Two days after the wedding Wanda changed the title of the house to herself and Henry as joint tenants with right of survivorship, and the two began contributing equally to the mortgage payments from their earnings. The equity in the house is now worth $60,000, or $40,000 more than its value when they married. Of this $40,000, $20,000 was attributable to the payoff of principal that they made through their mortgage payments, and $20,000 was attributable to inflation and other market factors. Wanda and Henry are now divorcing. They live in a common law property state where only marital property is divisible at divorce. The statute defines "marital property" as all property acquired by either spouse subsequent to the marriage except (1) property acquired by gift, bequest, devise, or descent and (2) property acquired in exchange for property acquired prior to the marriage or in exchange for property acquired by gift, bequest, devise, or descent. The statute also provides that all property acquired by either spouse subsequent to the marriage is presumed to be marital property regardless of how it is titled and that this presumption may be overcome by showing that the property was acquired in one of the two ways listed above.

Assuming that no cases have interpreted this statute and that Wanda wants as much of the value of the house as possible to be characterized as her separate, nonmarital property, what arguments should she make? How should Henry argue that some or all of the house is marital property?

4. While Herb and Winnie were married and living together, Herb won the lottery. He receives his winnings in annual installments over 20 years. If Herb and Winnie divorce three years after he has won, are the remaining 17 years of payments marital property or Herb's separate property? What if Herb and Winnie had been living separately for two years when Herb won the lottery?

5. W was part owner of a closely held corporation before she married H. After the business H and W worked full time for the business. Each of them drew a salary from the business, and the business paid W dividends. Are assets purchased with the dividends W's separate property or marital property? How about assets the spouses purchased with their wages?

6. Before his marriage to Kathleen, John inherited a small lakeside resort from his first wife, which was and always has been titled in his name alone. He ran the resort throughout his 20-year marriage to Kathleen, and the parties lived in a house that was part of the resort. Kathleen, who worked as a nurse during the marriage, also helped run the resort. John finished paying the mortgage on the

resort with money that it earned during the marriage. The parties had no children, but the wife's ten children from a former marriage lived with the parties and helped run the resort. Over the 20 years, the resort more than doubled in value from $151,000 to $398,000, in part because of market conditions and in part because of improvements that John made over the years. The parties made no attempt to keep their finances separate during the marriage, and each put inherited money, as well as their earnings, into a joint account from which all the bills for the family and for the resort were paid. John's inheritance amounted to $25,000, and Kathleen's to $90,000. The parties dispute the character of the increase in value of the resort property. In this jurisdiction, the passive increase in value of separate property remains separate. What arguments should each party make?

3.   *Choice-of-Law Issues*

When spouses acquire property in one state but are divorced in another, choice-of-law problems may arise. For example, *H* and *W*, who is a homemaker, marry and live for most of their lives in a common law property state. They own $200,000 in personal property, all of which was saved from *H*'s earnings and all of which remains titled in *H*'s name alone. *H* and *W* retire to a community property state and shortly thereafter divorce. Under traditional choice-of-law principles, the court in the community property state will apply its own law to determine what property is subject to division, but it will apply the law of the state where the property was acquired to determine whether it is community or separate property. Thus, the $200,000 will be characterized as *H*'s separate property. (Remember that even in common law states that characterize property as marital or nonmarital at divorce, the common law title system described in Chapter 2 governs ownership during the marriage.) If the state in which they are living at divorce permits division only of community property, *W* will be entitled to none of the assets even though, had the couple been divorced in their original home state, the court could have awarded her some of these assets.

Legislatures in some community property states have solved this problem by enacting "quasi-community property" statutes, which provide that if property would have been community property had it been acquired in the state, it is treated as community property for purposes of property division at divorce. Cal. Fam. Code § 125 (2014); Ariz. Rev. Stat. Ann. § 25-318 (2014); Tex. Fam. Code § 7.002 (2014). In the absence of such legislation, courts in some community property states have solved the problem by applying the substantive property division law of the state in which the property was acquired. Berle v. Berle, 546 P.2d 407 (Idaho 1976); Braddock v. Braddock, 542 P.2d 1060 (Nev. 1975); Hughes v. Hughes, 573 P.2d 1194 (N.M. 1978). This approach creates difficult problems of tracing, apportionment, and determining the effect of a post-acquisition change in the law of the state in which the property was acquired.

Similar issues may arise if spouses acquire property in a community property state and are divorced in a common law property/equitable distribution state. In addition, choice-of-law issues may arise in determining whether property should be characterized as marital or community property or as separate or non-marital property. Consider, for example, a husband and wife who first live in a common law (or community property) state that treats income from separate property as marital property and later move to a state that treats such income as non-marital property. Courts in most common law property states have held that the state's own laws governing characterization as well as division should apply, which eliminates problems of relating inconsistent laws of different jurisdictions. William A. Reppy, Jr., Major Events in the Evolution of American Community Property Law and Their Import to Equitable Distribution States, 23 Fam. L.Q. 163, 191 (1989).

Other articles dealing with these choice-of-law issues include J. Thomas Oldham, What If the Beckhams Move to L.A. and Divorce? Marital Property Rights of Mobile Spouses When They Divorce in the United States, 42 Fam. L.Q. 263 (2008); Eugene F. Scoles, Choice of Law in Family Property Transactions, Hague Academy, 209 Recueil des Cours 13 (1988-II); Russell J. Weintraub, Obstacles to Sensible Choice of Law for Determining Marital Rights on Divorce or in Probate: *Hanau* and the Situs Rule, 25 Hous. L. Rev. 1113 (1988).

For a discussion of jurisdiction to award property located in another state and enforcement of such orders, see Chapter 12.

4. Dividing Debts

Even though many property division statutes do not address division of debts, most courts have assumed that they have authority to allocate responsibility for paying debts. In many families this is, practically speaking, the most important issue.

GELDMEIER V. GELDMEIER

669 S.W.2d 33 (Mo. App. 1984)

REINHARD, J. . . . Husband and wife married in 1963. Their two children, Mark and Kelly, were born in 1964 and 1968, respectively. Husband, a bottler at Anheuser-Busch for the past fifteen years, was the principal breadwinner. His gross income during 1981 was $36,465.00, which included substantial overtime. Husband had worked overtime in each of the past ten years, and testified that he regularly refused overtime work offered to him.

Wife was primarily a homemaker, although she had worked as a secretary at one point during the marriage. Wife completed her master's degree in clinical psychology shortly before the parties' dissolution. Although she was seeking employment in both her chosen profession and other fields, her job search had not proven fruitful at the time of trial.

In its order, the court divided the marital property and awarded wife custody of the two children and support of $80.00 per week, per child. Maintenance was set at $100.00 per month.

On appeal, husband contends that the court "divided the marital property and debts in such a disproportionate manner that the effect of the division of the property was to award property to wife while awarding more debts than property to the husband."

The disposition of marital property is governed by § 452.330 RSMo. 1982:

> The court shall set aside to each spouse his property and shall divide the marital property in such proportions as the court deems just after considering all relevant factors. . . .

The court possesses broad discretion in the division of marital property. Its division must be just and equitable, but an equitable division need not be equal. Moreover, in reviewing this matter, we are bound to sustain the trial court's order unless there is no substantial evidence to support it or it is against the weight of the evidence.

Clearly, the court in its distribution of marital property was aware of the statutory framework within which it was required to act. The marital home, valued at approximately $40,000.00, was the major asset and was encumbered by two separate notes, secured by deeds of trust, for $16,400.00 and $15,000.00. ($16,400.00 was the amount still owed on the parties' original home mortgage; the latter $15,000 was borrowed to pay marital debts.) The court awarded the marital home to wife, who had custody of the minor children. In turn, the court ordered:

> petitioner [wife] [to] execute a note and deed of trust in favor of Respondent [husband] in the amount of Seven Thousand Five Hundred ($7500.00) Dollars, with no interest, payable on the earliest happening of one of the following events: (1) The emancipation of the minor child, Kelly Ann Geldmeier. (2) The marriage of petitioner. (3) The sale of the house by petitioner.

In its decree the court recognized that this note represented husband's interest in the marital home.

As to the other marital property, the court awarded wife the 1973 Cutlass automobile, valued at $800.00; household furniture worth $500.00 and personal property in her possession. Husband received, in addition to his interest in the marital home, a 1974 Chevelle automobile, valued at $450.00; a $500.00 boat; his interest in the Anheuser-Busch pension plan, worth approximately $2,000.00 and including insurance plans connected with the plan; his $1,100.00 interest in a life insurance policy, with directions that the children be named as beneficiaries until their emancipation; $2,500.00 from the recent sale of stock, and the remaining value of his Anheuser-Busch stock fund, worth approximately $3,000.00.

As to the parties' outstanding debts, the court ordered wife to pay the debt to her parents; husband to pay the debt to his parents. Wife was ordered to pay the first note for $16,400.00, secured by a deed of trust, and husband the second note of $15,000.00. By implication, husband is responsible for signature and student loans totalling approximately $6,500.00, for which payments are withheld from his weekly salary. Husband was also ordered to discharge all other debts, which amounted to $600.00, and hold wife harmless.

According to husband, the net result of the property division was that he received no assets, since the debts he was ordered to pay exceeded the property he received. We recognize that, were we to total the balance sheets of each party, husband winds up with a negative balance. However, a balance sheet approach is not necessarily the just approach to distribute marital assets. Here, the court was confronted with a difficult financial situation. By its order, it sought to divide the property in such a manner that the children, placed in wife's custody, would not be wrenched from the security of the family home during their minority. The court's order that husband assume responsibility for the lion's share of outstanding marital debts is supported by the evidence, since only husband at that time possessed the ability to assume those obligations. Moreover, its order concerning the debts does not alter the fact that, consistent with § 452.330, RSMo. Supp. 1982, the court set aside to husband portions of the marital property. Therefore, we can find no abuse of discretion in the court's property division.

KAROHL, P.J. I not only concur in the result I concur in the opinion. However, in order that the opinion not be misunderstood to approve a distribution of marital property of an amount greater than the total value of the marital property before the court at the time of the hearing, I believe the following comments are necessary.

In summary, the total marital assets before the court had a value of $19,450, consisting of: Equity in house — $8,600; automobiles — $1,250; furniture — $500.00; boat — $500.00; pension plan — $2,000; life insurance — $1,100; stock and proceeds of recent stock sale — $5,500, for a total of $19,450. The court awarded the wife a total of $17,400 in marital property summarized as follows:

Marital home	$40,000.00
Less First Deed of Trust	16,400.00
Less Third Deed of Trust in favor of husband	7,500.00
	$16,100.00
1973 Cutlass	800.00
Household furniture	500.00
	$17,400.00

The court awarded the husband marital personal property having a value of $9,550. However he was ordered to pay the $15,000 balance on the second deed of trust on the marital home and received in return a note and third deed of trust for $7,500, for a net deduction of $7,500. Therefore, on balance the husband received $2,050 of marital property. Although both parties were ordered to pay certain general debts they were not debts constituting liens on any of the marital property divided by the court.

In the event the balance due on the second deed of trust had been greater than $17,050, the decree would have so divided the marital property as to give the husband a negative balance. I do not believe that result is authorized by § 452.330, RSMo. Supp. 1982.

NOTES AND QUESTIONS

1. Most state statutes are silent on how to allocate debts at divorce, but most courts conclude that they have jurisdiction to address the issue as part of equitable distribution. Margaret M. Mahoney, The Equitable Distribution of Marital Debts, 79 UMKC L. Rev. 445, 451-452 (2010).

Among the methods discussed in the case law for dividing debts are these:

a. Equitable division of all — treat as distinct issues the division of assets and the division of debts, dividing each "equitably." Relevant factors include ability to pay, which spouse was the principal financial manager or incurred the debt, and so forth.

b. Divide debts proportionately to division of assets — treat division of assets and debts as distinct issues but allocate responsibility for debts in the same proportion that assets are awarded.

c. Total netting out — from the total value of the divisible assets subtract the total amount of divisible debts. Divide the remainder (if any).

d. Netting out of specific assets — when an asset is specifically encumbered, value the asset at the difference between its market value and the debt (sometimes expressed by saying that until the debt is paid, the asset is not yet fully acquired; at the time of divorce the asset is acquired only to the extent that it is free of debt). Some courts extend this method to include debts traceable to the acquisition of a specific asset. Other assets and debts are divided equitably. Some courts say that if an asset is worth less than the amount of the debt incurred in acquiring it, the value of that item is simply reduced to zero; the balance of the debt is not used to reduce the net value of any other item.

Which method is more consistent with a contribution theory of property division? With a need-based theory? Should the choice of theory for purposes of property division govern division of debts? *See* In re Marriage of Fonstein, 552 P.2d 1169, 1175 (Cal. 1976); In re Marriage of Eastis, 120 Cal. Rptr. 861 (Cal. 1975). *See also* Cal. Fam. Code § 2622 (2014) (equal division is not required when marital assets exceed marital debts).

Professor Ratner argues that in a community property state, any rule other than equal division of community debts is inconsistent with the principle that spouses have equal management rights over community property and involves the court in second-guessing how community assets were managed. James R. Ratner, Distribution of Marital Assets in Community Property Jurisdictions: Equitable Doesn't Equal Equal, 72 La. L. Rev. 21, 42-43 (2011).

2. In most states that permit division only of marital property, only marital debts are divisible at divorce. Separate debts are the responsibility of the spouse who incurred them. However, courts that allocate marital debts on an "equitable" basis may take separate debts into account in determining ability to pay. The court in *Geldmeier* seems to have assumed that all of the debts were marital.

Rules for characterizing debts as community or separate were first developed in community property states to determine what assets creditors could reach. Generally, each spouse's separate property is liable for his or her debts, and community property is liable for community debts. The states vary in their treatment of the liability of separate property for community debts and the liability of community property for separate debts.

Ordinarily, a debt is marital if it was incurred for the joint benefit of the parties or in acquiring a marital asset. Some courts have applied this test to characterize debts incurred during periods of separation as marital if they were incurred to pay family living expenses. *Compare* Alford v. Alford, 120 S.W.3d 810 (Tenn. 2003), rejecting the "joint benefit" test as confusing and difficult; marital debt defined consistently with the definition of marital property, that is, "all debts incurred by either or both spouses during the course of the marriage up to the date of the final divorce hearing." *See also* In re Marriage of Scoffield, 852 P.2d 664 (Mont. 1993); In re Marriage of Welch, 795 S.W.2d 640 (Mo. App. 1990).

3. The *Geldmeier* court allocated to each spouse debts owing to his or her parents without discussing their amount. Why?

4. An order or agreement between spouses regarding the allocation of debts does not bind creditors. Why not? *See, e.g.,* Srock v. Srock, 466 P.2d 34, 35-36 (Ariz. App. 1970). For consideration of the consequences to one spouse if the other files bankruptcy, see Chapter 8.

PROBLEM

John and Lois have no substantial debts and have the following marital assets: equity in home — $8,000, 1974 Chevelle — $450, 1973 Cutlass — $800, furniture — $500, boat — $500, pension plan — $2,000, stock and cash — $5,500. John's attorney proposes that Lois, the custodian of three young children, be awarded the equity in the home, the Chevelle, and the furniture, for a total of $8,950; and that husband receive the Cutlass, the boat, the pension plan, and the stock and cash, for a total of $8,800. John works full time and earns $40,000 per year. Lois has a part-time job and earns approximately $600 per month. As attorney for Lois, would you accept this proposal, which gives each spouse property of substantially equal dollar value?

5. *The Marital Home*

The major asset in *Geldmeier* was the family home. It could have been sold to satisfy the debts, but then the children would have been displaced. Even if the parties have no substantial debts, a similar problem arises if their only significant asset is the marital home and an equitable or equal division precludes awarding full ownership of the house to the custodial parent. The *Geldmeier* court sanctioned the common practice of ordering a division of the house but not requiring its immediate sale. Courts and legislatures in some states, however, have significantly limited the authority of trial courts to delay the sale of the family home for a long period of time because of the limitations such an order places on the ability of the spouse not occupying the home to make use of his or her share.

The *Geldmeier* trial court specifically said that the husband, who did not occupy the house, was not entitled to interest on the amount representing his share of the house. Was this fair? If instead of fixing a dollar amount for the spouse who does not occupy the home, a court orders the proceeds of the future sale of the home to be divided according to some formula, the nonoccupying spouse is not ordinarily guaranteed any return.

Instead of awarding ownership of the home to one spouse, with the obligation to pay the other some amount on sale, some courts order continued joint ownership of the house with sale ordered at some future date, and permit the custodial parent to remain in the house until the sale. In such cases, the court should allocate responsibility for the mortgage payments until the house is sold. If the nonoccupying spouse is ordered to pay the mortgage, half the payments might be characterized as spousal or child support.

Empirical studies find that the spouse with physical custody of the children is still likely to be awarded possession of the house, though this tendency decreased over the 1970s and 1980s.[12]

Of course, if the spouse who receives the home does not have enough income to pay the mortgage, taxes, and upkeep, the home will have to be sold anyway.

C. SPOUSAL SUPPORT AT DIVORCE

Spousal support, or alimony, as it was traditionally known, was originally developed by the ecclesiastical courts as an incident of legal separation. The rules regarding it were transferred wholesale to alimony following absolute divorce without much consideration of whether they were appropriate in this different context. The traditional law of alimony and its origins are described in the following excerpt.

---

12. *See* Marsha Garrison, Good Intentions Gone Awry: The Impact of New York's Equitable Distribution Law upon Divorce Outcomes, 57 Brook. L. Rev. 621, 681, Table 24 (1991); Barbara R. Rowe & Alice M. Morrow, The Economic Consequences of Divorce in Oregon After Ten or More Years of Marriage, 24 Willamette L. Rev. 463, 472-473 (1988); James B. McLindon, Separate but Unequal: The Economic Disaster of Divorce for Women and Children, 21 Fam. L.Q. 351 (1987); Alaska Women's Commission, Family Equity at Issue: A Study of the Economic Consequences of Divorce on Women and Children (Research Summary Oct. 1987); Heather R. Wishik, Economics of Divorce: An Exploratory Study, 20 Fam. L.Q. 79 (1986) (Vermont, 1982-1983). *But see* Barbara R. Rowe & Jean M. Lown, The Economics of Divorce and Remarriage for Rural Utah Families, 16 J. Contemp. L. 301 (1990) (women awarded the house outright in 52.7 percent of the cases, joint ownership ordered 32.1 percent of the time, and men received sole ownership the rest of the time; no statistically significant relationship between having custody and getting the house).

CHESTER G. VERNIER & JOHN B. HURLBUT, *THE HISTORICAL BACKGROUND OF ALIMONY LAW AND ITS PRESENT STRUCTURE*

6 Law & Contemp. Probs. 197, 198-200 (1939)

Permanent alimony . . . is an incident of the Ecclesiastical divorce *a mensa et thoro*. . . . Then, as now, pecuniary provision for the injured wife was necessary as a matter of social economy. Inequality of economic opportunity as a fact was not obscured by modern notions of "equal rights." Her technical legal status permitted such relief without resort to novel doctrines. In legal contemplation, the marital tie upon which the husband's legal duty to maintain her rested was not severed by the divorce decree. There were, however, other considerations present. The discriminatory common law scheme of marital property rights was in full bloom. Only very serious and aggravated types of marital transgressions entitled the wife to divorce. It is no wonder that her application for permanent alimony was treated with sympathy, and with liberality when the circumstances permitted liberality.

The primary object of the order for permanent alimony was to provide continuing maintenance for the wife. In form at least there was no pretense of effecting a division of property. The order was invariably for periodic payments, usually commencing at the date of the divorce sentence. The amount of the award rested in broad discretion of the Ecclesiastical judge. The ultimate considerations, of course, were the needs of the wife and the ability of the husband to pay. The marital delinquency of the husband standing established, the amount was usually greater than that given as temporary alimony. While provision for the custody and maintenance of children was without the province of the Ecclesiastical judge, the husband's obligation to support the children was not ignored in fixing the amount which he could appropriately be called upon to pay for the wife's support. Actually, however, the order for permanent alimony involved more than a mere judicial measurement of the husband's legal duty as husband to support the wife. If he acquired wealth from the wife by virtue of the marriage, he could not be compelled to disgorge, but that fact was of influence in fixing the amount of the award. Finally, in the minds of some of the judges at least, the notion of punishment depending upon the degree of the husband's moral delinquency played some part in the process. By balancing the above considerations the wife might be allotted as much as one-half of the combined income of the spouses, and often as much as one-third.[13]

Even though relatively few divorced women have ever been awarded spousal support, the issue has been and continues to be emotionally and symbolically important, as the following passages, written more than 70 years apart, suggest.

---

13. Some courts arrived at the figure of a third of the husband's income as alimony by analogizing to dower. Edward W. Cooey, The Exercise of Judicial Discretion in the Award of Alimony, 6 Law & Contemp. Probs. 213, 221 (1939) (discussing cases). — Ed.

CATHERINE G. PEELE, *SOCIAL AND PSYCHOLOGICAL EFFECTS OF THE AVAILABILITY AND THE GRANTING OF ALIMONY ON THE SPOUSES*

6 Law & Contemp. Probs. 283, 287-290 (1939)

It is not surprising that generally there is much emotion associated with the giving or receiving of alimony. Alimony perpetuates, in most instances, a relationship passionately undesired and in a way that continues and even increases former antagonisms. . . .

. . . [I]n general it may be said that men react in one of two ways to the idea of paying money to a woman from whom they are separated or divorced. If the man believes that his wife was in the wrong and was almost solely to blame for the ensuing separation or divorce, he will often resent having to pay alimony, especially if the woman has means of her own, has no small children, or is thought by him to be capable of earning her own living. . . .

If, on the other hand, the man has a guilty conscience and secretly thinks that he was at fault and that his behavior was the cause of the marital break, the paying of alimony may constitute penance, and may justify him in his own eyes for what he did. Such a man will have a great inner need to pay alimony and may wish to pay more than he can well afford to pay, or may urge a reluctant ex-wife to accept it. It is as if he were saying to the world at large that after all he was willing to do the handsome thing by his former wife, and therefore he can not be greatly blamed for what he did. He thinks, as many people do, that the giving of money should be adequate recompense to anybody for anything that might have been done to them.

Or his guilt may not be involved in the manner in which the marriage tie was broken, but in the knowledge of what has happened to his family since then. One sees instances of men who put aside all thoughts of what is happening to the members of the families of which they were formerly the heads, and as a substitute mail a check. They pride themselves on providing liberal financial support and so hide the fact that they are refusing to assume any other responsibility. Thus, paying alimony, doing all the court requires, may enable a man to feel that he has bought his freedom, when otherwise he would have had to feel that what was happening to his former wife or his children was some concern of his.

. . . On the other hand, to others the making of alimony payments has an opposite meaning, and constitutes for them a reason for maintaining to some extent their former relationship with their families. A man who thinks of money as power and has no sense of guilt in connection with the marital break, may want to pay alimony as a means of retaining his authority in his former home. He may feel that as long as he is contributing regularly to his former wife's support he has the right to demand that he be given a voice in the management of the household of which he formerly was a part. . . .

Thus, the payment of alimony can be a symbol of power to both the man and the woman concerned, and this is probably the usual reason why some women state, as many do, that they will accept support for their children from the children's father, but that they will not under any circumstances take any money for themselves. . . .

On the other hand, a woman may think of alimony as meaning power, not her former husband's power over her, but her power over him. She may cherish this power merely for its nuisance value, hoping that having to pay it constitutes a constant source of annoyance to him. Or she may know that as long as he has to pay alimony he can not afford to marry again, or to live in accordance with the style in which he would like to live. Her desire to punish him may be a much more important factor in her insistence on receiving alimony than is her need for financial support. . . .

Perhaps the wives who are out for vengeance make themselves the most conspicuous, but as a matter of fact a woman may be humiliated by the knowledge that she is receiving support only because of a legal decree as frequently as the man may balk at the threat of compulsion contained in the decree. Anybody who comes into contact with cases of separation and divorce knows that there are many more women who do without what they need rather than take legal means to force their former husbands to support them, than there are women who use the courts to harass their ex-spouses.

Judith G. McMullen, *Alimony: What Social Science and Popular Culture Tell Us About Women, Guilt and Spousal Support After Divorce*

19 Duke J. Gender L. & Pol'y 41, 58 (2011)

Many women who are technically eligible for alimony decline to aggressively pursue it. [I argue] that these divorcing women feel guilt and shame about their divorces and the financial circumstances in which they find themselves at the time of divorce. This guilt comes partly from evolving societal expectations about marriage, parenthood, and divorce, and partly from individual emotional tendencies to accept blame for the end of the marriage. For one thing, there is evidence that women are socially programmed to feel responsible for the success or failure of family relationships. In addition, social pressure to be a perfect mother may lead many women to make risky economic decisions and leave or reduce paid employment to focus on mothering. Later, if this turns out badly, these women may feel guilty or ashamed of having acted imprudently. Additionally, the spouse who initiates the divorce process more acutely experiences guilt, and women are more likely to be the divorce initiators. . . .

1. Spousal Support in the Early No-Fault Era

Consistent with the modern preference for ending spousal obligations at divorce, the law in most states during the 1960s and 1970s disfavored awards of spousal support. When awarded, the spousal support was supposed to facilitate the economic independence of the spouses from each other. The Uniform Marriage and Divorce Act (UMDA) was drafted early in the no-fault era, and it tends to reflect the clean-break perspective that disfavors spousal support. However, it also contains the seeds of change.

Uniform Marriage and Divorce Act § 308

(a) In a proceeding for dissolution of marriage . . . the court may grant a maintenance order for either spouse only if it finds that the spouse seeking maintenance:

(1) lacks sufficient property to provide for his reasonable needs; and

(2) is unable to support himself through appropriate employment or is the custodian of a child whose condition or circumstances make it appropriate that the custodian not be required to seek employment outside the home.

(b) The maintenance order shall be in amounts and for periods of time the court deems just, without regard to marital misconduct, and after considering all relevant factors including:

(1) the financial resources of the party seeking maintenance, including marital property apportioned to him, his ability to meet his needs independently, and the extent to which a provision for support of a child living with the party includes a sum for that party as custodian;

(2) the time necessary to acquire sufficient education or training to enable the party seeking maintenance to find appropriate employment;

(3) the standard of living established during the marriage;

(4) the duration of the marriage;

(5) the age and the physical and emotional condition of the spouse seeking maintenance; and

(6) the ability of the spouse from whom maintenance is sought to meet his needs while meeting those of the spouse seeking maintenance.

NOTES AND QUESTIONS

1. Parts (a) and (b) of Section 308 both refer to the amount of marital property awarded to the claimant spouse, his or her ability to be self-supporting, and minor children in his or her custody. What is the difference between these sections? *See* Commentary to Section 308; In re Marriage of Johnsrud, 572 P.2d 902, 904-905 (Mont. 1977); Farmer v. Farmer, 506 S.W.2d 109 (Ky. 1974).

The UMDA's preference for using property division, rather than spousal support, as the primary vehicle for financial settlement between spouses furthers the goal of providing the parties with a "clean break." Property division awards are final, eliminating subsequent modification problems. Further, property division awards are more advantageous to the recipient than support awards because they do not present continuing enforcement problems (if the award calls for only one lump sum payment or transfer), and to the payors because they provide financial certainty and ability to plan.

Most states have not followed the UMDA in expressly preferring property division over spousal support to satisfy the "need" of one spouse. Instead, their spousal support statutes typically resemble those of part (b) of Section 308, granting the judge discretion in light of a list of factors. The factors vary greatly from state to state, and no state ranks the factors in order of priority. Mary Kay Kisthardt, Re-thinking Alimony: The AAML's Considerations for Calculating Alimony, Spousal Support, or Maintenance, 21 J. Am. Acad. Matrimonial Law. 61 (2008).

2. Even though courts sometimes say that they award spousal support to keep the recipient off the welfare rolls, most courts have held that a person who can earn just enough to subsist is not self-supporting for these purposes, at least if the marital standard of living was substantially higher. *See, e.g.,* In re Marriage of Kuppinger, 120 Cal. Rptr. 654 (Cal. App. 1975); Casper v. Casper, 510 S.W.2d 253, 255 (Ky. 1974); Lepis v. Lepis, 416 A.2d 45 (N.J. 1980).

3. During the 1970s and early 1980s a number of legislatures enacted statutes limiting the duration of spousal support awards. *See, e.g.,* Ind. Code Ann. §§ 31-15-7-1, 31-15-7-2 (2014) (limit of three years unless spouse or child in custody of spouse is physically or mentally incapacitated); Kan. Stat. Ann. § 23-2904 (2014) (limit of 121 months, subject to reinstatement). *See also* Or. Rev. Stat. §§ 107.407, 107.412 (2014) (if after ten years of spousal support payments the recipient has not made a reasonable effort to become financially self-supporting, the payor may petition to terminate support).

4. Studies of spousal support awards beginning in the 1970s found that from one-third to 98 percent were for a limited time; in most of the studies half or more of the awards were of limited duration.[14]

PROBLEM

Donald and Joan divorced after an 11-year marriage. The total value of the marital assets is $112,605.67. The trial court has ordered Donald to pay Joan $50,000 as her share, $25,000 immediately and the rest at $500 a month plus interest until paid off. In determining whether Joan is eligible to receive support under UMDA Section 308, the income that the lump sum payment of $25,000 will produce will be treated as available income. Should she also be expected to invade the principal to support herself? Should the $500 a month that she will receive be treated as income available for her expenses?

---

14. *See, e.g.,* U.S. Dep't of Commerce, Bureau of the Census, Child Support and Alimony: 1983 (Supplemental Report, Current Population Reports, Special Studies, Series P-23, No. 148 (Oct. 1986)); Lenore J. Weitzman & Ruth B. Dixon, The Alimony Myth: Does No-Fault Divorce Make a Difference?, 14 Fam. L.Q. 141, 161-162 (1980); Robert E. McGraw et al., A Case Study in Divorce Law Reform and Its Aftermath, 20 J. Fam. L. 443, 475 (1982); Harriet N. Cohen & Adria S. Hillman, New York Courts Have Not Recognized Women as Equal Marriage Partners, 5 Equitable Distrib. Rep. 93 (1985); Alaska Women's Commission, Family Equity at Issue: A Study of the Economic Consequences of Divorce on Women and Children 17 (Oct. 1987); Heather R. Wishik, Economics of Divorce: An Exploratory Study, 20 Fam. L.Q. 79 (1986); James B. McLindon, Separate but Unequal: The Economic Disaster of Divorce for Women and Children, 21 Fam. L.Q. 351 (1987); Marsha Garrison, Good Intentions Gone Awry: The Impact of New York's Equitable Distribution Law on Divorce Outcomes, 57 Brook. L. Rev. 621, 698, Table 37 (1991); Judith G. McMullen & Debra Oswald, Why Do We Need a Lawyer?: An Empirical Study of Divorce Cases, 12 J.L. Fam. Stud. 57 (2010).

2. *Reconsidering Spousal Support at the End of a Long Marriage*

During the 1980s, views about spousal support began to shift again as the divorce rate rose and the poor economic position of divorced women and their children became more widely known. Realizing that most divorcing people do not have enough property to provide support for dependent spouses and children, courts, commentators, and legislators revisited dividing postdivorce income between spouses. Based on her analysis of cases decided in the mid-1980s, Professor Krauskopf concluded that appellate courts usually uphold awards of indefinite support to women who were homemakers for more than 20, and perhaps more than 15, years. Joan M. Krauskopf, Rehabilitative Alimony: Uses and Abuses of Limited Duration Alimony, 21 Fam. L.Q. 573, 579-580 (1988). The next case is representative of this change.

IN RE MARRIAGE OF LAROCQUE

406 N.W.2d 736 (Wis. 1987)

[The trial court awarded Rosalie LaRocque limited-term spousal support of $1500 per month for 5 months and then $1000 per month for 13 months. The court of appeals affirmed the circuit court's decision on the amount but not on the duration of maintenance, concluding that the circuit court abused its discretion in terminating maintenance at the end of the 18 months. This appeal followed.]

ABRAHAMSON, J. Daniel and Rosalie LaRocque were married in 1959; they filed for divorce in 1982. When the divorce was granted in 1984, Mrs. LaRocque was 46 years old, Mr. LaRocque was 48, and only one of the LaRocques' five children was still a minor (age 17).

Mrs. LaRocque received a bachelor's degree in psychology in June of 1959. During the first two years of the marriage, she held several full-time positions including secretary, clerk and teacher. Thereafter, she worked outside the home sporadically, as a part-time substitute teacher and as a member of the school board. At the time of the divorce she was not certified to teach in a public school. During the marriage, her principal occupation was as a full-time homemaker and caretaker of the parties' five children. She also assisted Mr. LaRocque in his various election campaigns. Her total income from employment outside the home during the marriage amounted to $5660.

Mr. LaRocque received a law degree in 1962. During the marriage he was employed as a lawyer in private practice, an assistant district attorney, a district attorney for Marathon County, and a circuit court judge. In 1984 he was appointed judge of the Wisconsin Court of Appeals. When the divorce action was commenced, his annual income was $49,966; when the divorce was granted, his annual income was $60,000. His earnings during the marriage totaled $548,987. The family annual income had increased from $1763 in 1959 to $50,235 in 1980 and $60,000 at the time of the divorce. . . .

The circuit court divided the property, awarding Mrs. LaRocque the household furniture and appliances ($4043), the family car ($2000), the parties' income tax refund ($3000), and the family home subject to the two mortgages (net value $34,431), for a total value of $43,474. Mrs. LaRocque had foreseeable future expenditures for house repairs, broker's fees and taxes on the sale of the house, 1984 property taxes, and legal fees. Mr. LaRocque was awarded the retirement fund with the vested portion valued at $54,340.

During the separation period Mr. LaRocque paid the family bills of over $1600 per month and paid Mrs. LaRocque $372 every two weeks. Mrs. LaRocque submitted several budgets for expenses in maintaining herself and the children living at home; the budgets ranged from $1654 to $2317 per month. She testified that her standard of living had declined over the two-year separation and that she could not meet her minimum existing expenses on less than $1654 per month, exclusive of property and income taxes and the second mortgage payment. Mr. LaRocque submitted no budget; he listed $225 per month as an apartment rental expense.

In awarding maintenance, the circuit court found that Mrs. LaRocque could work as an elementary school teacher upon certification and that the entry level salary for elementary school teachers in the Wausau district was $12,000 a year and the average salary $25,000 a year. The circuit court further found that Mrs. LaRocque's present earning capacity was between $12,000 and $15,000 per year and her future earning capacity was at least $25,000 per year. The circuit court concluded that the entry level salary upon her certification as a teacher would provide Mrs. LaRocque with a standard of living reasonably comparable to the one enjoyed during marriage inasmuch as the parties' median annual income during the marriage was approximately $18,000 and the average annual income was $20,000 and as many as five children shared that income during the marriage. Thus, according to the circuit court, as an entry level teacher Mrs. LaRocque could earn more than one half of the average annual income during marriage.

The circuit court's memorandum decision explained that the 18 months' maintenance it awarded would enable Mrs. LaRocque to take whatever schooling she deemed appropriate to enhance her earning ability. It went on to say that after the last child reached majority Mrs. LaRocque could sell the house and, with the proceeds from the sale, pursue whatever course she thought would produce an adequate income.

The circuit court also acknowledged that Mr. LaRocque had indicated he would continue to provide for the children who would be going to college and that Mr. LaRocque did not have liquid funds available from the retirement fund.

Thus the circuit court arrived at a maintenance award of $1500 per month for 5 months and then $1000 per month for 13 months. Mrs. LaRocque appealed, arguing that both the amount and duration of the maintenance award were inadequate. . . .

A circuit court determining a maintenance award and an appellate court reviewing a maintenance award must begin with sec. 767.26, Stats. 1985-86, which provides that the court may grant an order requiring maintenance payments to either party for a limited or indefinite length of time after considering:

(1) The length of the marriage.
(2) The age and physical and emotional health of the parties.
(3) The division of property made under 767.255.

(4) The educational level of each party at the time of marriage and at the time the action is commenced.

(5) The earning capacity of the party seeking maintenance, including educational background, training, employment skills, work experience, length of absence from the job market, custodial responsibilities for children and the time and expense necessary to acquire sufficient education or training to enable the party to find appropriate employment.

(6) The feasibility that the party seeking maintenance can become self-supporting at a standard of living reasonably comparable to that enjoyed during the marriage, and, if so, the length of time necessary to achieve this goal.

(7) The tax consequences to each party.

(8) Any mutual agreement made by the parties before or during the marriage, according to the terms of which one party has made financial or service contributions to the other with the expectation of reciprocation or other compensation in the future, where such repayment has not been made, or any mutual agreement made by the parties before or during the marriage concerning any arrangement for the financial support of the parties.

(9) The contribution by one party to the education, training or increased earning power of the other.

(10) Such other factors as the court may in each individual case determine to be relevant.

These factors are the touchstone of analysis in determining or reviewing a maintenance award. They reflect and are designed to further two distinct but related objectives in the award of maintenance: to support the recipient spouse in accordance with the needs and earning capacities of the parties (the support objective) and to ensure a fair and equitable financial arrangement between the parties in each individual case (the fairness objective). . . .

We conclude that the circuit court abused its discretion in this case by misapplying (or failing to apply) several of the statutory factors and by not giving full play to the objectives of maintenance. By construing the support objective too narrowly and disregarding the fairness objective, the circuit court mistook subsistence to be the objective of maintenance and awarded an inadequate amount.

The circuit court offered three principal reasons for concluding that Mrs. LaRocque needed only $1500 per month for 5 months, to be reduced to $1000 per month for 13 months after the minor child graduated from high school: (1) Mrs. LaRocque would eventually have the proceeds of the sale of the house available to her; (2) the award comports with the standard of living of the parties; (3) Mr. LaRocque might pay college expenses for their adult children. Examining each of the circuit court's reasons, we do not find these reasons persuasive.

While the circuit court should consider the property division in awarding maintenance, sec. 767.26(3), we disagree with the circuit court's implication that Mrs. LaRocque use the proceeds from the sale of the house, her share of the property division, to support herself. . . .

It is difficult to understand why, and the circuit court does not explain why, Mrs. LaRocque should liquidate her capital to obtain funds to pay living and retraining expenses, while Mr. LaRocque retains full use of his $60,000 a year salary and keeps his retirement fund (the property he received in the property division) untouched and secure for his retirement years. The property division should provide Mrs. LaRocque as well as Mr. LaRocque with a nest egg for retirement or a reserve for emergencies.

. . . Sec. 767.26(6) requires the circuit court to consider the feasibility of the party seeking maintenance becoming self-supporting at a standard of living reasonably comparable to that enjoyed during the marriage and the length of time necessary to achieve this goal if the goal is feasible. The legislature thus has expressly declared that the standard of living for maintenance is a standard of living comparable to the one enjoyed during the marriage. . . .

The increased expenses of separate households may prevent the parties from continuing at their pre-divorce standard of living, but both parties may have to bear the sacrifices that the cost of an additional household imposes. A court must not reduce the recipient spouse to subsistence level while the payor spouse preserves the pre-divorce standard of living. In this case, while Mrs. LaRocque's budgets were unchallenged, the circuit court implicitly rejected them and awarded limited term maintenance in an amount less than the lowest monthly budget Mrs. LaRocque submitted. . . .

The circuit court's final reason for limiting Mrs. LaRocque's maintenance was that Mr. LaRocque had stated he would help pay the college expenses of the adult children. Apparently the circuit court considered this factor relevant under sec. 767.26(10). We find it difficult to understand why in awarding maintenance the circuit court credited Mr. LaRocque's payment of college expenses for adult children — particularly when such payment is unstipulated and as yet unrealized — but did not consider the expenses Mrs. LaRocque incurred by having adult children live with her. . . .

In regard to fairness, the other objective of a maintenance award, the circuit court appears not to have given any weight at all to this objective of maintenance or to such statutory factors as the length of the marriage, the educational level of each party at the time of the marriage and the time of the divorce, and the contribution by one party to the education, training or increased earning power of the other.

Where a spouse has subordinated his or her education or career to devote time and energy to the welfare, career or education of the other spouse or to managing the affairs of the marital partnership, maintenance may be used to compensate this spouse for these nonmonetary contributions to the marriage. In adopting the 1977 Divorce Reform Act the legislature stated that it intended that "a spouse who has been handicapped socially or economically by his or her contribution to a marriage shall be compensated for such contributions at the termination of the marriage, insofar as this is possible, and may receive additional education where necessary to permit the spouse to become self-supporting at a standard of living reasonably comparable to that enjoyed during the marriage." 1977 Wis. Laws, c. 105, sec. 1.

The LaRocques were married for 25 years. Both parties contributed to the marriage. The record is replete with evidence of Mrs. LaRocque's contributions to Mr. LaRocque's education and increased earning power. Because the wife's contribution in this marriage was as homemaker and the husband's as wage-earner, the husband leaves the marriage with the "asset" of a stream of income which the wife's contributions helped him to develop. The wife, however, does not leave the marriage with a stream of income; a career as homemaker — although of economic value to the family and society — all too frequently does not translate into money-making ability in the marketplace. Because the parties had accumulated some but not a great deal of property during their marriage, the court in this case cannot rely on the property distributed to the wife to "compensate" her for her contribution to the marriage and her loss of a stream of income.

The maintenance award produced a substantial disparity between the post-divorce incomes of the parties. Mrs. LaRocque was granted maintenance for 18 months and probably can earn $1000 per month as long as she can work. Within 18 months of the divorce Mr. LaRocque will have the use of his entire income of $60,000 per year or $5000 per month and his full retirement funds without any further obligation to support Mrs. LaRocque. The circuit court did not consider whether this result satisfied the fairness objective of maintenance. . . .

This court has said that when a couple has been married many years and achieves increased earnings, it is reasonable to consider an equal division of total income as a starting point in determining maintenance.

If the circuit court had considered the fairness objective of maintenance and had applied the *Bahr-Steinke* standard of starting at an equal division of income of the parties in this case, the starting figure of the maintenance award would be $2500 per month, a figure consistent with Mrs. LaRocque's highest budget figure. . . .

. . . We reverse the decision of the court of appeals regarding the amount of maintenance, and we remand this matter to the circuit court.

The circuit court has to consider the statutory factors enumerated in sec. 767.26 to determine whether to award limited or indefinite maintenance. The circuit court's determinations of the amount of maintenance and the duration of maintenance are intertwined. We agree with the court of appeals that the circuit court's judgment terminating maintenance after 18 months is not supported by the record and is an abuse of discretion. . . .

In determining whether to grant limited-term maintenance, the circuit court must take several considerations into account, for example, the ability of the recipient spouse to become self-supporting by the end of the maintenance period at a standard of living reasonably similar to that enjoyed before divorce; the ability of the payor spouse to continue the obligation of support for an indefinite time; and the need for the court to continue jurisdiction regarding maintenance.

Because limited-term maintenance is relatively inflexible and final, the circuit court must take particular care to be realistic about the recipient spouse's future earning capacity. The circuit court must not prematurely relieve a payor spouse of a support obligation lest a needy former spouse become the obligation of the taxpayers.

In this case, in awarding limited-term maintenance the circuit court considered, as it was required to consider under sec. 767.26(5), Mrs. LaRocque's earning capacity and her ability to become self-supporting. The circuit court apparently concluded that the limited-term maintenance award was adequate to enable Mrs. LaRocque to become self-supporting at a standard of living similar to that enjoyed before the divorce.

Mrs. LaRocque acknowledged that she could get a $12,000-per-year job but she believed such a job would not provide advancement or career possibilities. Because $12,000 was inadequate to meet her budget, she asked for maintenance sufficient to retool herself for a job with career potential, job satisfaction and greater earnings so that she could become self-supporting at the pre-divorce standard of living. Although Mrs. LaRocque had expressed interest in a career as a psychologist, the circuit court considered only a career as a teacher.

The circuit court apparently determined the length of time it would take Mrs. LaRocque to acquire certification to teach, the expenses of earning the certification, the likelihood of her obtaining employment in Wausau, and the time it would take her to earn $25,000 per year starting at the low end of the pay scale, but it did so on the basis of conjecture, not facts. Without facts of record, the court assumed that a woman in her mid-forties who had been a full-time homemaker for more than twenty years could readily enter the job market and within 18 months of the divorce support herself at a pre-divorce standard of living.

Like the court of appeals, we conclude that nothing in the record indicates whether Mrs. LaRocque would be certified and employable as a teacher within 18 months, whether teaching jobs were available in Wausau, whether there was a good likelihood she would be hired and, if so, how long it would take her as an entry level teacher to reach the salary of $25,000. Without such facts the circuit court could not appropriately award limited-term maintenance. Accordingly, we conclude, as did the court of appeals, that the circuit court abused its discretion in awarding limited maintenance for 18 months. We therefore affirm that part of the court of appeals decision remanding the issue of the duration of maintenance.

Some legislatures and courts have rejected a preference for limited-term awards or have even created a preference for indefinite awards in some circumstances. *See, e.g.*, Minn. Stat. Ann. § 518.552(3) (2014) (limited-term orders not preferred, if "there is some uncertainty as to the necessity of a permanent award, the court shall order a permanent award leaving its order open for further modification"); Walter v. Walter, 464 So. 2d 538 (Fla. 1985) (rejecting preference for short-term rather than permanent alimony). This trend continued well into the new century. *See, e.g.*, Tenn. Code Ann. § 36-5-121(c)(1), (2) (2014), enacted in 2005 in response to judicial opinions strongly favoring short-term rehabilitative alimony, which "emphasiz[e the] value of family arrangements in which one spouse contributes to the family as a homemaker and/or stay-at-home parent, and underscore[s] the importance of the parties' standard of living during the marriage in determining support." Wiser v. Wiser, 339 S.W.3d 1, 12 (Tenn. App. 2010).

Long-term spousal support to provide for dependent spouses continues to be controversial, as the following readings show.

PAULA ENGLAND & GEORGE FARKAS, *HOUSEHOLDS, EMPLOYMENT AND GENDER*

44-45, 55-56 (1986)

By "human capital" economists refer to the stock of attributes in a person that can be put to use in serving some end. When that end is productivity on the job, attributes such as intelligence, strength, education, and skills are relevant.

Similarly, we can think of those qualities helpful in person-to-person interaction as a form of human capital as well. These include the ability to provide empathy, companionship, sexual and intellectual pleasure, social status, or earnings. Individuals "invest" in human capital whenever they forgo something desirable in the present to develop a personal attribute which will pay off in the future, whether in a job or household relationship.

. . . [M]any of the highest-return investments within the household sector are to relationship-specific rather than general human capital. To call an investment relationship-specific means that it has value only within the current relationship, and would be of no benefit in a different one. . . . Of course, investments may be anywhere along a continuum from those useless in a new relationship to those whose benefits are completely transferable to a new relationship. . . .

Marital investments that transfer poorly to a new relationship include learning what shared leisure activities both partners enjoy, learning what division of labor is most efficient with this partner, decorating the house in a style both partners like, learning to fight and make up with this partner, learning this partner's sexual preferences, and developing relationships with in-laws. In addition, the tremendous investments of time, caring and money that parents make in children bear fruit not only in the children's futures, but also in the satisfaction parents derive from the relationship. Investment in children with one partner contributes relatively little to improving one's relationship with a new partner. . . .

. . . [M]en typically make fewer relationship-specific investments than women, accumulating instead resources which are as useful outside as within their current relationship. Thus, while both men and women work at the relationship-specific issues of learning to get along with the other person, women are usually the expressive-emotional specialists, focusing heavily on personal relationships and empathic understanding. Of course, some of these efforts are potentially useful in future relationships as well — examples include skills at listening, pleasing, and compromising. Yet much of the investment in these emotional skills is by its very nature specific to the particular relationship. In addition, women typically take the major responsibility for child rearing, heavily investing their own time for the future benefit of the children, but also for the benefit of the particular marriage. Thus women's effort is skewed toward investments which are most valuable within the particular relationship.

The relationship-specific nature of learning to get along with a particular husband can be seen by questioning what value such learning has for the woman if she becomes divorced. Furthermore, what good are kin links with the current husband's family (links she has invested time and emotion in) once she is divorced or when she is remarried? And, especially, are the children, in whom she has invested so much, an asset in finding a new partner? More likely they are a hindrance. Of course, the earnings of employed women are something they can transfer out of the relationship. . . . Yet, even women with earnings seldom earn as much as their partners. . . . Thus, whether employed outside the home or not, wives tend to accumulate fewer resources that are of value outside the current relationship.

While women are taking major responsibility for the instrumental and expressive work of the household, men are advancing their careers. Even blue-collar men not getting promotions are accumulating years of seniority that usually increase their earnings. A husband's increased earning power will, of course, benefit the man's wife as long as the relationship persists, but it continues to benefit the husband should he leave the relationship. That is, earning power is "liquid," readily transferable to a new life.

HERMA HILL KAY, *EQUALITY AND DIFFERENCE: A PERSPECTIVE ON NO-FAULT DIVORCE AND ITS AFTERMATH*

56 U. Cinn. L. Rev. 1, 79-85 (1987)

I asked earlier whether, in order to implement equality between the sexes, legal significance should be accorded at the dissolution of the family unit to the consequences of choices made concerning sex roles during the existence of the family relationship. It seems clear that, at least in the short run, the answer to that question must be an affirmative one. It is necessary to take steps to alleviate the situation of those women who are trapped in circumstances neither they nor their husbands anticipated, and that they cannot now avoid. . . .

In the long run, however, I do not believe that we should encourage future couples entering marriage to make choices that will be economically disabling for women, thereby perpetuating their traditional financial dependence upon men and contributing to their inequality with men at divorce. I do not mean to suggest that these choices are unjustified. For most couples, they are based on the presence of children in the family. The infant's claim to love and nurturance is a compelling one both on moral and developmental grounds. Throughout history, the choice of the mother as the primary nurturing parent has been the most common response to the infant's claim. . . . But other choices are possible. . . . Serious discussion of the possibility of shared parenting for children, and for infants in particular, as a way of achieving equality between women and men is very recent. . . .

I do not propose that the state attempt to implement this view of family life by enacting laws requiring mothers to work or mandating that fathers spend time at home with their children. But since, as I noted earlier, Anglo-American family law has traditionally reflected the social division of function by sex within marriage, it will be necessary to withdraw existing legal supports for that arrangement as a cultural norm. No sweeping new legal reforms of marriage and divorce will be required, however, to achieve this end. It will be enough, I think, to continue the present trend begun in the nineteenth century toward the emancipation of married women, and implemented more recently by gender-neutral family laws, as well as the current emphasis on sharing principles in marital property law.

IRA MARK ELLMAN, *THE THEORY OF ALIMONY*

77 Cal. L. Rev. 1, 48-52 (1989)

. . . [M]arital specialization makes sense for most couples, with one spouse concentrating more heavily on the market while the other focuses more heavily on domestic matters. If the spouses view their marriage as a sharing enterprise, they will usually conclude that they are both better off if the lower earning spouse spends more on their joint domestic needs, and allows the higher earning spouse to maximize his or her income. A problem arises only if their mutual commitment to share breaks down, in which case the spouse who has specialized in domestic aspects of the marriage — who has invested in the marriage rather than the market — suffers a disproportionate loss. . . .

[Alimony is intended to compensate for] the "residual" loss in earning capacity that arises from the kind of economically rational marital sharing behavior we have just seen. This is a residual loss in the sense that it survives the marriage. . . . Nonetheless, spouses are not necessarily liable for every loss their former mate incurs. . . . The function of alimony is . . . to reallocate the postdivorce financial consequences of marriage in order to prevent distorting incentives. Because its purpose is to reallocate, it is necessarily a remedy by one spouse against the other. . . . [B]y eliminating any financial incentives or penalties that might otherwise flow from different marital lifestyles, this theory maximizes the parties' freedom to shape their marriage in accordance with their nonfinancial preferences. . . .

A system of alimony that compensates the wife who has disproportionate postmarriage losses arising from her marital investment protects marital decision-making from the potentially destructive pressures of a market that does not value marital investment as much as it values career enhancement.

J. Thomas Oldham, *Putting Asunder in the 1990s*

80 Cal. L. Rev. 1091, 1110-1111 (1992)

Men and women have different earning capacities for many reasons. Although some of these reasons, such as discrimination, education levels, and career choice, are not directly related to roles assumed during marriage, a general argument could be made that all of these factors indirectly stem from society's assumption that women will bear primary child care responsibilities. Discrimination based on this assumption can place women at a considerable economic disadvantage. Employers might be concerned about pregnancy or other leave time, parents might provide less encouragement or education for daughters, and women themselves might choose less "desirable" careers that can more easily accommodate child care responsibilities. . . .

Even if one accepts the view that almost all of the wage gap stems from actual or potential child care responsibilities, it does not follow that the full cost of these employment disabilities should be borne by the divorcing husband. I believe it is fair only to ask the divorcing husband to share the costs of decisions in which he participated and that some mechanism should be found that isolates the effects of decisions made during marriage. It is not fair to ask the husband to compensate the wife for all career damage she incurred on the expectation that one day she would assume child care responsibilities. Even if the husband should be responsible for such damage, a goal of post-divorce equal living standards is not justified by compensation for career damage. Individual spouses have different levels of intelligence and education and have different career interests at the time of marriage; these all would cause income inequalities for reasons largely unrelated to sex. Thus, even a very broad concept of career damage due to child care responsibilities does not justify a goal of post-divorce equal living standards.

JOAN WILLIAMS, *IS COVERTURE DEAD? BEYOND A NEW THEORY OF ALIMONY*

82 Geo. L.J. 2227, 2255-2258 (1994)

Ellman's exclusive focus on reimbursing the wife for losses in her earning capacity presents two separate problems. First, his model for measuring a wife's losses omits the losses typically experienced by lower-status wives. A service-sector or pink-collar worker does not suffer the same direct decrease in earnings as the attorney who leaves the partnership track, but she may well lose opportunities and other employment benefits. Sociological studies show that working-class women who start out in "women's work" often respond to attractive job opportunities; thus, a wife who started out as a clerical worker might have ended up a machinist. Moreover, even working-class wives who reenter the workforce after divorce doing the same job they did before may have sacrificed subtler benefits. For example, informal seniority and flexibility often are granted to valued, long-term workers; these informal benefits can prove extremely important for a mother with a sick child.

Ellman's exclusive focus on *detriment* to the wife also presents a deeper problem: it ignores the *benefits* conferred upon husbands by the dominant family ecology. A wife who shoulders childrearing and other domestic responsibilities allows her husband *both* to perform as an ideal worker *and* to have his children raised according to norms of parental care that Ellman himself explicitly embraces. Husbands receive this benefit regardless of whether or not the wife has received the kind of detriment Ellman is willing to recognize.

Ellman, like other commentators, also overlooks the important fact that divorcing fathers *retain the primary benefit they garner from the domestic ecology even after the marriage has ended*. In the 90 percent of divorces in which mothers are awarded sole physical and legal custody—and even in states such as California where joint custody is favored—mothers typically remain the child's primary caretaker. Thus, even after divorce, noncustodial fathers continue to receive the benefits of the dominant family ecology: they can continue to perform as ideal workers while their children are raised according to norms of parental care. . . .

My analysis of the dominant family ecology suggests an approach to post-divorce entitlements very different from Ellman's. Ellman perpetuates the "he who earns it" rule; I consider it a holdover from coverture. Although the husband clearly owns "his" wage vis-à-vis his *employer*, this does not necessarily determine the issue of whether he owns it vis-à-vis his *family*. My analysis of the dominant family ecology suggests that the wages of the family should be jointly owned. . . . I will argue that the way to accomplish this is by equalizing the incomes of the two post-divorce households.

Twila Perry, *Alimony: Race, Privilege, and Dependency in the Search for Theory*

82 Geo. L.J. 2481, 2483-2484, 2513 (1994)

Statistics indicate that Black women are awarded alimony at a significantly lower rate than white women. . . . It also appears that women in higher income marriages are more likely to receive alimony than women in lower income marriages. In light of this data, it is important that we examine the implications of women scholars devoting substantial attention to an issue that is of practical importance to relatively few women, and especially so few women of color. . . .

. . . [T]he marriage paradigm that has, to a great extent, shaped the discourse on developing a theory of alimony . . . has little relevance to the realities faced by most poor women of color and . . . , accordingly, most of the approaches to alimony based on it have little practical relevance to the lives of these women. I define the issue, however, as more than one of mere irrelevance or exclusion—I argue that the search to develop a theory of alimony may have serious negative implications for poor women of color, especially Black women. Specifically, the paradigmatic model of marriage and divorce has the potential to reinforce the subordination and marginalization of Black women in two ways: first by reinforcing privilege or an image of privilege for middle and upper-middle class white women in both marriage and divorce, and second, by reinforcing a hierarchy among women in which their value is determined by the presence or absence of legal ties to men, particularly affluent men. . . .

Although no-fault divorce has been appropriately criticized for its failure to protect women economically, it has generated one positive result. To some degree, no-fault divorce has served as an equalizer among women. In calling off the bargain that formerly ensured some women compensation for giving up their careers to care for their home, the law, since no-fault, has been sending a similar message to all women: it is not wise to depend on a man for your lifelong economic survival. The privilege of choice, that many middle- or upper-middle class women once may have taken for granted is, more than ever, in jeopardy.

Indeed, it can be said that in some ways the lives of white mothers, either as a result of divorce or because they were never married, are becoming more similar to those of Black mothers. . . . The way that no-fault divorce has pulled the rug out from under women at some of the more comfortable levels of society can be seen as an opportunity for women from different social and economic backgrounds to consider their commonalities. . . . There may be increased connection and cooperation among women of diverse backgrounds if they all see themselves as having to play the multiple roles of parent and worker, without assuming economic dependence on a man.

NOTES AND QUESTIONS

1. What justification does *LaRocque* give for requiring the husband to support his former wife? If the rationale for spousal support is to compensate a spouse who leaves the workplace to be a homemaker, how do we determine the amount of

compensation due? Does the reason that a spouse became a homemaker matter? What if she wanted to work but her spouse asked her to stay home? What if the working spouse encouraged the homemaker to develop a career but she decided not to? What if they simply never discussed the matter?

If spousal support is justified by the contributions of one spouse to the career development of the other spouse, how is this measured? What is the relationship, if any, between this rationale and the marital standard of living? Is dividing the parties' total income equally the same thing as maintaining the marital standard of living, as *LaRocque* suggests? Are there other justifications for dividing the total income?

A survey of 300 people called for jury duty in Pima County, Arizona, found support for awarding alimony when the income of the former spouses is widely disparate, even if both have enough money to live a middle-class lifestyle, particularly if they had lived together six years or more. However, the respondents did not think that compensating a former spouse for being the primary caretaker of children who are now adult was an independently compelling reason to award alimony, although they did think it should be awarded to a former spouse with primary responsibility for children still at home. The amount of awards depended almost entirely on the parties' incomes. Ira Mark Ellman & Sanford L. Braver, Lay Intuitions About Family Obligations: The Case of Alimony, 13 Theoretical Inquiries in Law 209 (2012).

2. In some states limited-term rehabilitative support awards may be modified if a spouse is not able to become self-supporting at the end of the support period. *See, e.g.,* In re Marriage of Deboer, 157 P.3d 1279 (Or. App. 2007); Bentz v. Bentz, 435 N.W.2d 293 (Wis. 1988). In other states limited-term alimony is not modifiable. *See, e.g.,* Self v. Self, 861 S.W.2d 360 (Tenn. 1993). As a practical matter, what is the difference between a limited-term, renewable spousal support award and a modifiable indefinite award of spousal support?

3. You are the trial judge in *LaRocque*. When the case comes back before you on remand, Mr. LaRocque presents credible evidence that Mrs. LaRocque could renew her teaching credentials and get an entry-level teaching job in Wausau within 18 months and that she might expect to reach a salary of $25,000 in another three years. Mrs. LaRocque has decided that she would like to become a psychologist, and she estimates that it will take her seven years to finish her education and begin a practice. For how long should you order Mr. LaRocque to pay support? Why? *See also* Morgan v. Morgan, 366 N.Y.S.2d 977 (1975), *rev'd*, 383 N.Y.S.2d 343 (1976); In re Marriage of Becker, 756 N.W.2d 822 (Iowa 2008). What if Mrs. LaRocque had had no plans and no wish to start a new career?

4. Usually, the early cases on limited-term rehabilitative alimony did not discuss why a divorced person should be required to pay support to enable his or her former spouse to prepare for entry into the workplace. Does the *LaRocque* analysis support an award of limited-term rehabilitative alimony after a short- or medium-term marriage?

5. To be eligible for spousal support, the claimant must "need" assistance. What does it mean to "need" support beyond having enough money for the basics of life? Typically, the parties submit detailed budgets to prove their needs. Must a court take those budgets at face value? In Simmons v. Simmons, 409 N.E.2d 321 (Ill. App. 1980), the wife claimed needs for food and transportation higher than

actual costs during marriage. She explained that she ate out four or five nights a week because she did not like to eat alone at home and that she took a cab to work. On what basis would a judge validly determine whether these were "needs"? Would contributing to a retirement account be a "need"?

6. The ALI Family Dissolution Principles propose that "compensatory spousal payments" be ordered to compensate a spouse for financial losses occasioned by the marriage, rather than to relieve need. ALI, Principles of the Law of Family Dissolution § 5.02 Comment, at 789 (2002). Section 5.03(2) provides for awards to compensate for loss of living standard in long-term marriages and loss of earning capacity caused by undertaking the care of dependents. Section 5.03(3) adds that awards may be made to compensate for "an unfairly disproportionate disparity between the spouses in their respective abilities to recover their pre-marital living standard" after a short marriage.

Commentary on the ALI spousal support provisions includes Cynthia Lee Starnes, Mothers as Suckers: Pity, Partnership, and Divorce Discourse, 90 Iowa L. Rev. 1513 (2005); Tonya L. Brito, Spousal Support Takes on the Mommy Track: Why the ALI Proposal Is Good for Working Mothers, 8 Duke J. Gender L. & Pol'y 151 (2001).

7. Despite the principled importance of indefinite spousal support following long-term marriages, this development affects relatively few people, since the median length of first and second marriages ending in divorce is eight years. U.S. Census Bureau, Number, Timing, and Duration of Marriages and Divorces: 2009 (2011), at 15.

8. The debate over spousal support policy occurs in other countries as well. See, e.g., Belinda Fehlberg, Spousal Maintenance in Australia, 18 Int'l J.L. Pol'y & Fam. 1 (2004) (observing that, notwithstanding the debate, support awards are relatively rare in Australia). In 1992 the Canadian Supreme Court rejected the clean-break approach to spousal support in long-term marriages in favor of an approach like that in *LaRocque*. Moge v. Moge [1992] 43 R.F.L. (3) 345 (S.C.C.). However, seven years later the court upheld a spousal support order where the wife had become too ill to work, even though the marriage was of relatively short duration and the couple had been more or less economic equals during the marriage. The court said that the traditional basis for spousal support based on need and ability to pay survived *Moge*. Bracklow v. Bracklow, (1999) 1 S.C.R. 420, 44 R.F.L. (4th). For analyses, see Carol Rogerson, Spousal Support After *Moge*, 14 Can. Fam. L.Q. 386-387 (1997); Carol Rogerson, Spousal Support Post-*Bracklow*: The Pendulum Swings Again?, 19 Can. Fam. L.Q. 185 (2001); Carol Rogerson, The Canadian Law of Spousal Support, 38 Fam. L.Q. 69 (2004).

PROBLEMS

1. Winnie and Harold are divorcing following an 18-year marriage. Both are 45. Before the marriage and for the first two years after the wedding Winnie taught school. She quit when their first child was born and never went back. The marital property was divided equally. The trial court awarded Winnie sufficient spousal support for two years to enable her to renew her teaching certificate without having to work; at that point the award was to be reduced by 50 percent

and was to continue for an indefinite duration. The judge justified this award as encouraging Winnie to become self-supporting while recognizing that she was unlikely ever to be able to earn enough to enable her to live at the marital standard of living. Winnie has appealed, arguing that this award amounts to a prospective modification of indefinite spousal support without requiring proof of changed circumstances. Can the award be defended?

Two months before the initial two-year period of the award is over, Winnie moves to modify it on the ground that she has not completed the training necessary to renew her teaching certificate and so is not able to be self-supporting at the level expected at the time of divorce. She has been working part time and looking unsuccessfully for full-time work. A vocational expert called by Harold testifies that she has been "minimally involved" in preparing for a career.

Harold first moves to dismiss Winnie's petition on the basis of *res judicata*. What arguments should the parties make?

If Harold loses the *res judicata* argument, what additional arguments should he make, and how should Winnie respond?

2. Hank and Wendy were married for 15 years. Both worked throughout the marriage. During the marriage Hank invented a process to produce wooden parts for curved windows and started his own business based on the invention. By the time of the divorce the business had sales of more than $1 million a year. Wendy was awarded 40 percent of the total marital assets (mostly stock in Hank's company), worth $283,465, as her share of the property. Hank and Wendy did not change their standard of living much when Hank's invention began to pay off, and Wendy earns enough to live at nearly the marital standard of living.

Has Wendy sacrificed education or career opportunities so as to entitle her to spousal support? Does her employment prove that she did not sacrifice? Has a homemaker necessarily made such a sacrifice? Under *LaRocque*'s fairness principle, should Wendy share in Hank's high income through spousal support? If she receives an award on this basis, has she been compensated twice for her contributions, since she received a share of the stock in his company? What if instead of living frugally, Hank and Wendy had had a lavish lifestyle, financed largely by the income from Hank's business?

3. The Emergence of Alimony Guidelines

The widespread adoption of child support guidelines (see Chapter 7) has inspired numerous law reformers and commentators to propose spousal support guidelines to increase consistency in orders, make settlement easier, and reduce the costs of divorce. For example, the ALI Family Dissolution Principles recommend that jurisdictions adopt a formula that will yield presumptive levels and durations of spousal support. ALI, Principles of the Law of Family Dissolution §§ 5.05-5.07 (2002).

However, developing guidelines has been difficult because of lack of agreement on the purposes of spousal support and the large number of factors considered relevant. Soon after the ALI proposal, which would base spousal support on the principle of compensation, the American Academy of Matrimonial Lawyers proposed its own formula, rejecting the compensation principle and based on the income of the spouses and the duration of the marriage. The formula is described in Mary Kay Kisthardt, Re-thinking Alimony: The AAML's Considerations for Calculating Alimony, Spousal Support, or Maintenance, 21 J. Am. Acad. Matrimonial Law. 61 (2008).

In 2011 the Massachusetts legislature made headlines by enacting legislation that limits the duration of alimony obligations based on the length of the marriage, effective in 2012. 2011 Mass. Legis. Serv. Ch. 124 (H.B. 3617), codified at Mass. Gen. Laws Ann. ch. 208 §§ 34, 48-55. The legislation, like statutes in a number of other states, defines several categories of alimony and lists factors that courts must consider in deciding whether to award each type. It goes further than most legislation by setting presumptive limits on the duration and amount of awards, based on the length of the marriage. The key provisions are these:

MASS. GEN. LAWS ANN. CH. 208 (2014)

§ 48. Definitions . . .

"General term alimony," the periodic payment of support to a recipient spouse who is economically dependent. . . .

"Rehabilitative alimony," the periodic payment of support to a recipient spouse who is expected to become economically self-sufficient by a predicted time, such as, without limitation, reemployment; completion of job training; or receipt of a sum due from the payor spouse under a judgment.

"Reimbursement alimony," the periodic or one-time payment of support to a recipient spouse after a marriage of not more than 5 years to compensate the recipient spouse for economic or noneconomic contribution to the financial resources of the payor spouse, such as enabling the payor spouse to complete an education or job training.

"Transitional alimony," the periodic or one-time payment of support to a recipient spouse after a marriage of not more than 5 years to transition the recipient spouse to an adjusted lifestyle or location as a result of the divorce.

§ 49. Termination, suspension or modification of general term alimony . . .

(b) Except upon a written finding by the court that deviation beyond the time limits of this section are required in the interests of justice, if the length of the marriage is 20 years or less, general term alimony shall terminate no later than a date certain under the following durational limits:

(1) If the length of the marriage is 5 years or less, general term alimony shall continue for not longer than one-half the number of months of the marriage.

(2) If the length of the marriage is 10 years or less, but more than 5 years, general term alimony shall continue for not longer than 60 per cent of the number of months of the marriage.

(3) If the length of the marriage is 15 years or less, but more than 10 years, general term alimony shall continue for not longer than 70 per cent of the number of months of the marriage.

(4) If the length of the marriage is 20 years or less, but more than 15 years, general term alimony shall continue for not longer than 80 per cent of the number of months of the marriage.

(c) The court may order alimony for an indefinite length of time for marriages for which the length of the marriage was longer than 20 years.

§ 50. Termination, extension or modification of rehabilitative alimony . . .
(b) The alimony term for rehabilitative alimony shall be not more than 5 years. Unless the recipient has remarried, the rehabilitative alimony may be extended on a complaint for modification upon a showing of compelling circumstances in the event that:

(1) unforeseen events prevent the recipient spouse from being self-supporting at the end of the term with due consideration to the length of the marriage;

(2) the court finds that the recipient tried to become self-supporting; and

(3) the payor is able to pay without undue burden.

§ 51. Termination of reimbursement alimony; modification; applicability of income guidelines
(a) Reimbursement alimony shall terminate upon the death of the recipient or a date certain.

(b) Once ordered, the parties shall not seek and the court shall not order a modification of reimbursement alimony.

(c) Income guidelines in subsection (b) of section 53 shall not apply to reimbursement alimony.

§ 52. Termination of transitional alimony; modification or extension
(a) Transitional alimony shall terminate upon the death of the recipient or a date certain that is not longer than 3 years from the date of the parties' divorce; provided, however, that the court may require the payor to provide reasonable security for payment of sums due to the recipient in the event of the payor's death during the alimony term.

(b) No court shall modify or extend transitional alimony or replace transitional alimony with another form of alimony.

§ 53. Determination of form, amount and duration of alimony; maximum amount; income calculation; deviations; concurrent child support orders
(a) In determining the appropriate form of alimony and in setting the amount and duration of support, a court shall consider: the length of the marriage; age of the parties; health of the parties; income, employment and employability of both parties, including employability through reasonable diligence and additional training, if necessary; economic and non-economic contribution of both parties to the marriage; marital lifestyle; ability of each party to maintain the marital lifestyle; lost economic opportunity as a result of the marriage; and such other factors as the court considers relevant and material.

(b) Except for reimbursement alimony or circumstances warranting deviation for other forms of alimony, the amount of alimony should generally not exceed the recipient's need or 30 to 35 per cent of the difference between the parties' gross incomes established at the time of the order being issued. Subject to subsection (c), income shall be defined as set forth in the Massachusetts child support guidelines. . . .

(e) In setting an initial alimony order, or in modifying an existing order, the court may deviate from duration and amount limits for general term alimony and rehabilitative alimony upon written findings that deviation is necessary. Grounds for deviation may include:

(1) advanced age; chronic illness; or unusual health circumstances of either party;

(2) tax considerations applicable to the parties;

(3) whether the payor spouse is providing health insurance and the cost of health insurance for the recipient spouse;

(4) whether the payor spouse has been ordered to secure life insurance for the benefit of the recipient spouse and the cost of such insurance;

(5) sources and amounts of unearned income, including capital gains, interest and dividends, annuity and investment income from assets that were not allocated in the parties divorce;

(6) significant premarital cohabitation that included economic partnership or marital separation of significant duration, each of which the court may consider in determining the length of the marriage;

(7) a party's inability to provide for that party's own support by reason of physical or mental abuse by the payor;

(8) a party's inability to provide for that party's own support by reason of that party's deficiency of property, maintenance or employment opportunity; and

(9) upon written findings, any other factor that the court deems relevant and material.

(f) In determining the incomes of parties with respect to the issue of alimony, the court may attribute income to a party who is unemployed or underemployed.

(g) If a court orders alimony concurrent with or subsequent to a child support order, the combined duration of alimony and child support shall not exceed the longer of: (i) the alimony or child support duration available at the time of divorce; or (ii) rehabilitative alimony beginning upon the termination of child support.

NOTES AND QUESTIONS

1. Would Mrs. LaRocque be entitled to alimony under the Massachusetts statute? If so, what kind and for how long? How about Wendy, the wife in problem 2 above on page 384?

2. A Boston Globe report on the new alimony law, written 20 months after it went into effect, described its purpose as "replacing an old system marred by inequities and abuses, including, in some cases, alimony payments for life, even for short-term marriages. Critics said the old law discouraged recipients, most of them women, from supporting themselves, and from remarrying." Bella English, New Mass. Alimony Law "Model" — But Is It Working?, Boston Globe, Oct. 20, 2013. *See also* Stephen Hitner, New Law Stops Injustice of Paying Alimony Forever, CNN, Mar. 11, 2012. These articles, like others about alimony reform efforts in other states, emphasize stories of men required to pay indefinite spousal support for long periods of time and say that requiring termination of support obligations at definite points is a primary reform goal. *See, e.g.,* Maddie Hanna, New Jersey Bill Would Set Guidelines for Alimony, Philly.com (Philadelphia Inquirer), Dec. 2,

2013 (describing proposed New Jersey legislation); Colleen O'Connor, New Law Changes Alimony Landscape for Divorcing Colorado Couples, Denver Post, Oct. 18, 2013 (describing Colorado legislation effective Jan. 1, 2014); Kathleen Haughney & Lisa Huriash, Alimony Law in Florida Changes Drastically Under New Bill, Sun Sentinel, Apr. 18, 2013 (proposed Florida legislation).

3. In 2013 Colorado enacted even more radical alimony reform legislation. It establishes presumptive amounts and durations for support awards, based on the length of the marriage and the parties' incomes. Colo. Rev. Stat. Ann. § 14-10-114 (2014). Among the other states with legislation that creates some kind of formula for spousal support are Fla. Stat. Ann. § 61.08 (2014) (limiting duration of various types of alimony based on length of marriage); Me. Rev. Stat. Ann. § 951-A (2014) (eligibility and duration based on duration of marriage); Tex. Fam. Code § 8.054 (2014) (duration limits based on length of marriage); Utah Code Ann. § 30-3-5 (2014) (duration limits based on length of marriage).

4. Canada's spousal support guidelines were promulgated in 2008 and are widely used, although they are not mandatory. Carol Rogerson & Rollie Thompson, The Canadian Experiment with Spousal Support Guidelines, 45 Fam. L.Q. 241 (2011).

4. Fault Revisited

In the era of fault-based divorce a wife's misconduct could either bar her from receiving alimony or limit the amount, and in some places the husband's fault could be a factor in increasing the amount. As of winter 2013, the following states did not permit consideration of marital fault in spousal support awards: Alaska, Arizona, Arkansas, California, Colorado, Hawaii, Illinois, Indiana, Kansas, Kentucky, Maine, Massachusetts, Minnesota, Mississippi, Montana, Nebraska, New Mexico, New York, Oklahoma, Vermont, Washington, and Wisconsin. Linda D. Elrod & Robert G. Spector, A Review of the Year in Family Law, 46 Fam. L.Q. 471, 522 Chart 1 (2013). In a few jurisdictions a person against whom a fault-based divorce is awarded cannot be awarded support, and in some others fault is a factor courts may consider. One of the states that makes fault an absolute bar is North Carolina, as the state court of appeals observed in Romulus v. Romulus, 715 S.E.2d 308, 311 (N.C. App. 2011) ("Our legislature has decreed that even one fleeting incident of 'illicit sexual behavior' by a dependent spouse automatically bars her from an alimony award, even if the supporting spouse has committed serious, indeed criminal, physical abuse against his wife and children throughout the marriage, and we have no authority to question the legislature's widsom in adopting this rule.").

JUNE CARBONE, *THE FUTILITY OF COHERENCE: THE ALI'S PRINCIPLES OF THE LAW OF FAMILY DISSOLUTION, COMPENSATORY SPOUSAL PAYMENTS*

4 J.L. & Fam. Stud. 43, 72-76 (2002)

The most fundamental choice the ALI makes is to deem fault irrelevant to divorce proceedings. . . . The ALI acknowledges that it is possible "to avoid the punitive nature of a fault award by casting it as compensation for the financial costs of splitting one household in two." It then rejects the possibility, however, because of the lack of consensus on what would constitute grounds for divorce, and concludes: "In sum, courts that purport to allocate the unavoidable costs of dissolution by assessing the cause of the marital failure are in fact rewarding failure and punishing sin. They are not compensating one spouse for a harm 'caused' by the other."

I would have preferred that the ALI separate the notion of "sin" from breach of contract. Fault in family law has historically conflated the two, castigating adulterers, for example, both because they have acted shamefully and because they have imposed financial ruin on their families. It is possible to separate the condemnation associated with extracurricular sex, however, from breach of contract. The latter is removed from the moral realm; there is no condemnation comparable to the adulterer's for a party that reneges on a commercial agreement. The obligation is simply to compensate the other party for the consequences of a decision to leave a less than optimal relationship; to compensate one spouse "for a harm 'caused'" by the other's decision to leave. For all that I believe that the two notions are different, however, I would not ultimately come to a different conclusion about the wisdom of the result. Even if breach of contract is defined in terms of the unexcused decision to end a marriage, the ALI is right that it will be difficult to define what constitutes excuse (or, in contract terms, anticipatory breach) and, perhaps more critically, the process of determining breach will impose significant costs of its own. If the financial results turn on the determination, each party will acquire an incentive to charge the other with wrongdoing, the initial charges will inspire anger if not countercharges, and the process of resolution, even if predictable from the outset, will engender more bitterness among parties who under the best of circumstances have difficulty putting anger and bitterness aside. The cost of coherence is simply too high.

If the ALI rejection of fault considerations can be justified, however, then the issue arises whether its decision to protect the interests most associated with breach of contract principles can also be defended. I believe that it can. Consider . . . Carl Schneider's Applebys of Milan, Michigan:

He is fifty-eight; she is fifty-six; they have been married for thirty-five years. He has been a salesman all his life, she is a housewife. Their only child, Meg, is now thirty-two and living in New Mexico. Mrs. Appleby has always spent most of her time at home, in large part because her husband has always insisted on it and because he becomes angry when she does not. Mrs. Appleby consequently has few friends of her own, and what social life the couple has revolves around Mr. Appleby's friends. Mr. Appleby has been spending less and less time at home, and Mrs. Appleby has become more and more distressed. One evening, he tells her that he has fallen in love with his nineteen-year-old secretary and wants a divorce so that he can marry her. . . . Mr. Appleby has never earned much, and they have never saved much. If they are divorced, all his modest income will be consumed supporting his new wife and her twin sons. Mrs. Appleby has a high-school education and hasn't been on the job market for thirty-five years. Now change the facts slightly. Eliminate the child. Give Mr. Appleby some restraint. He's tired of Mrs. Appleby and finds that some of the young women in the office are flirting with him. He takes one to dinner, but stops short of romantic involvement. Instead, the experience heightens his dissatisfaction with his home life, and he requests a divorce. He begins dating after the separation, becomes intimately involved only after the divorce decree becomes final, and marries his nineteen-year-old secretary a year later. Without adultery, his behavior stands on different moral grounds. Yet, in breach of contract terms, the principle is the same: his conduct ends a marriage Mrs. Appleby would prefer to continue. . . .

The Applebys present the classic — and the best continuing — case for an expectation award. Mrs. Appleby's greatest loss is her misguided expectation that the marriage would continue with the status and associations it conferred and the support provided by Mr. Appleby's income. . . . It is Mr. Appleby's breach of the obligation to remain married that disappoints Mrs. Appleby's expectations, and that triggers the duty to provide compensation. Yet, if he is expected to sustain the standard of living she enjoyed while married, he could not also enjoy the same standard of living with his nineteen-year-old second wife and her twin sons. What justifies protection of her expectation interest without protection of his, and without a determination that he, not she, caused the end of the marriage?

The short answer is that the Appleby case . . . represents not only the best case for application of the Principles, but a typical case of those likely to receive a large expectation-based award. While women initiate the majority of divorces, they typically do so after relatively few years of marriage. By age 45, the rate at which men and women initiate divorce evens out. Older women are less likely to initiate divorce than younger women, their opportunities for remarriage decline with age, and the greater their dependence on their husband's income, the less likely they are to seek divorce without what has historically been legally cognizable grounds. The ALI crafts its principles to provide the largest expectation awards for the women most likely to suffer from breach of the promise to remain married. . . .

Finally, in [this case] public policy issues stand alongside the matters of private justice. Even if she were at fault, Mrs. Appleby would be left destitute by the absence of an award, and public policy considerations in every divorce era have suggested that some support be provided. The interests of justice are more complicated than vindication of contract rights might suggest. Providing awards in these cases protects a greater array of interests than denying payment altogether, and at a lower overall price for the divorce system than trying to tailor award to the fault-based equities of each case.

NOTES AND QUESTIONS

1. Many more states allow courts to consider marital fault in making decisions about alimony or spousal support than about property division. What explains this difference?

2. Professors Brinig and Crafton have argued that a regime that does not take marital fault into account for purposes of awarding spousal support encourages people to engage in bad marital behavior, including domestic violence. Margaret F. Brinig & Steven M. Crafton, Marriage and Opportunism, 23 J. Legal Stud. 869 (1994). Professors Ellman and Lohr criticize the methodology of this study and the assumptions upon which the article is based on a variety of grounds, arguing that Brinig and Crafton did not prove their thesis and that use of fault may even produce results contrary to those hypothesized. Ira Mark Ellman & Sharon Lohr, Marriage

as Contract, Opportunistic Violence, and Other Bad Arguments for Fault Divorce, 1997 U. Ill. L. Rev. 719.

3. Even if general fault is not a factor, economic misconduct may be, although some courts reject this approach as well. For example, the Iowa Supreme Court held in In re Marriage of Olson, 705 N.W.2d 312 (Iowa 2005), that a court could not consider the wife's gambling addiction as a negative factor in determining whether to award her alimony. The court cited the overall purpose of the divorce statutes to remove consideration of fault and added, "[W]e should not consider the constraints a payor spouse would like to place on the payee spouse when the payee spouse uses the support in a manner inconsistent with the wishes of the payor spouse. Nor should a court punish a person who is entitled to support because we disapprove of the way the person receiving the support spends the support."

PROBLEM

Throughout Wilma and Fred's 20-year marriage, Wilma worked to support herself and Fred and their two children when the children were young. She was also the children's primary caretaker. Fred drank heavily much of the time and worked only sporadically at unskilled jobs. Wilma has filed for divorce. Fred claims spousal support. On what theories might he be entitled to support? How should Wilma's lawyer argue against an award?

5.   *Spousal Support for the Caregiving Parent?*

PROBLEM

Wanda has filed for divorce from her husband, Herman, alleging incompatibility. They have two children, ages three and six years old. Wanda was employed as a teacher until her older child was born; since then she has remained at home. Wanda has requested spousal support sufficient to enable her to continue caring for her children. Herman opposes any award of permanent alimony and offers evidence that Wanda can obtain employment as a teacher earning $24,000 per year. Herman offers to pay day-care costs for the children, the total cost of which will be $10,000 per year for both children. What arguments should each party make at the hearing on Wanda's request for spousal support? In addition to the materials you have already read, consider the following.

EMPIRICAL DATA ON WORKING PARENTS

In 2012, in about 59 percent of all families with children headed by a married couple, both parents were employed. In 62 percent of married-couple families with children 6 to 17 years old, both parents worked, compared to 55 percent of families with children younger than 6. Bureau of Labor Statistics, Employment Characteristics of Families Summary, Tbl. 4 (Apr. 26, 2013). Another way of looking at this phenomenon is by the labor force participation of mothers. In 2011, about 71 percent of mothers with children under age 18 were employed, compared to 94 percent of fathers. Employment is more common among single mothers than married mothers and among mothers of older than younger children. About 74.9 percent of unmarried mothers were employed, compared to about 69 percent of married mothers. Of mothers with children younger than 6, about 64 percent were employed, compared to about 77 percent with children 6 to 17 years old. Bureau of Labor Statistics, Employment Characteristics of Families, Tbl. 5: Employment status of the population by sex, marital status, and presence and age of own children under 18, 2010-2011 annual averages (2012).

In 40 percent of all households with children younger than 18, mothers are the primary or sole income providers. About a third of this group are married mothers who earn more than their husbands, and the rest are single mothers. The median family income of the first group was $80,000 per year in 2011, while the median income for the single-mother families was $23,000. The married mothers who earn more than their husbands are a little older and disproportionately white and college-educated, while the single mothers are younger, likely to be black or Hispanic, and less likely to have a collge degree. Pew Research Center, Breadwinner Moms (May 29, 2013).

THE GENERAL STATE OF THE LAW

UMDA Section 308(a)(2) provides that a caretaker of children may be eligible for spousal support even though she or he is otherwise capable of self-support,[15] and many cases have held that custodial parents of young children should receive spousal support to enable them to remain at home with the children. When spousal support is awarded because the recipient has custody of the children, it usually terminates at the latest when the youngest child attains the age of majority.

As a practical matter, spousal and child support are often insufficient to provide for the needs of the children and the custodial parent, and so the parent must work anyway. Because of the emphasis on postdivorce self-sufficiency following short- to medium-term marriages, courts rarely approve long-term spousal support for the caretaking parent of young children.

For example, in Berger v. Berger, 747 N.W.2d 336, 352-353 (Mich. App. 2008), the court reversed a child support order based on the wife's relatively low part-time wages, rather than on the $50,000 per year that she could have earned if she worked full-time at jobs for which she was qualified. The appellate court said, "Although it is within the trial court's discretion to consider the children's ages and care needs when considering this issue, this Court still concludes that it is unreasonable and unprincipled to place nearly 100 percent of financial responsibility for the children on [husband] under these circumstances. [Wife] elected to divorce, and she chose to seek custody of the children, i.e., she sought to become a single parent. Moreover, she has a great deal of education and is more than capable of helping to financially support her children. She should not be treated so differently from [husband] simply because she wishes at this point to be essentially a stay-at-home mother."

---

15. Professor Levy initially recommended that child support awards, rather than spousal support, include money for the custodian's maintenance. Robert J. Levy, Uniform Marriage and Divorce Legislation: A Preliminary Analysis 145 (1969).

This approach is not universal, however. In Taylor v. Taylor, 250 S.W.3d 232 (Ark. 2007), the Arkansas Supreme Court approved of permanent spousal support for a stay-at-home mother who home-schooled the couple's children. During the ten-year marriage, the wife did not work outside the home, and she possessed no marketable skills. With the husband's agreement, she had begun home-schooling the children three years before the divorce, and at trial the husband presented no evidence that this arrangement was not in the children's best interests.

THE POLITICS AND SOCIAL VALUE OF CAREGIVING

ANN LAQUER ESTIN, *MAINTENANCE, ALIMONY, AND THE REHABILITATION OF FAMILY CARE,* 71 N.C. L. Rev. 729-738 (1993): In an earlier era, although family care was not compensated, and usually not legally recognized, it was clearly understood to be central to the family's functioning and it was structurally supported through a variety of legal and social devices — devices which have eroded over the past generation. Caregiving is even less recognized today. Despite the language of modern divorce statutes, caregiving is perceived not as an independent contribution to the family, but only as one half of a traditional gender-structured marriage pattern. . . .

Recent years have seen a dramatic polarization of views about family policy issues, and as these issues have become increasingly politicized, the significance of caregiving is further obscured. Women's traditional caregiving roles are either glorified and described as imminently in danger, or treated as the fundamental obstacle to full gender equality. In this debate, private choices around the organization of work and family life take on an added burden of moral and political significance. Those who glorify caregiving have seemed blind to its hazards, and those who demean it have seemed blind to its value. . . .

Despite our often polarized and politicized view of the family, there should be little dispute that caregiving is an essential attribute of family life, worthy of recognition in the law of divorce. . . . Support payments to caregivers would have two benefits: facilitating the care of children in the difficult period after divorce, and allocating to both parents the costs of putting children first *during* marriage. The literature in this area of family law suggests only one disadvantage to caregiver support remedies: the risk that they will foster traditional family roles, economic dependence, and the corresponding gender roles that many men and women find oppressive.

CYNTHIA LEE STARNES, *LOVERS, PARENTS, AND PARTNERS: DISENTANGLING SPOUSAL AND CO-PARENTING COMMITMENTS,* 54 Ariz. L. Rev. 197, 232-236 (2012): A married parent is not simply a participant in two independent relationships, one with the other spouse and another with the child. From both a normative and a practical perspective, children add another dimension to marriage, as adults who are legally committed to each other as spouses undertake a new mutual commitment as parents. This parental commitment runs not only to the child, to whom each parent owes an independent state-imposed obligation, but also to the other parent, both spouses understanding that they will share the physical and financial costs of parenting. The result is a second layer of commitment between married parents — a co-parenting partnership that supplements the marital partnership.

The co-parenting partnership builds on each parent's individual obligation to the child.

Although the co-parenting commitment may be express, more often it is implied, both spouses understanding that the addition of children to their family means a shared commitment to raise those children. The child benefits from the stability of the co-parenting partnership and from the mutuality of the parents' commitment, which at least as a normative matter, makes childcare more dependable, more bountiful, more efficient, and more manageable for parents. . . .

When parents divorce during their child's minority, the marital partnership terminates, but divorce does not so swiftly terminate the co-parenting partnership, which endures at least until its work is complete, i.e., until the couple's children reach majority. Continuation of the co-parenting partnership does not depend on love, intimacy, or friendship between former spouses, but rather on the parents' mutual commitment to take on the economic support and physical labor required to raise shared children.

Divorced parents may coordinate their care for the child or they may refuse to speak to each other. Whatever their inclination toward cooperation, each divorced parent benefits from the other's physical labor on behalf of the child, because what one parent does for the child the other parent need not do. As the ALI observes, while parents "can allocate that responsibility [for children] . . . they cannot avoid it, and the spouse who assumes it discharges a legal obligation of both parents." Simply put, if one parent provides the child with breakfast, the other parent need not; if one parent shops for a winter coat or shoes or crayons, the other need not; if one parent tutors the child, washes her pajamas, transports her to school or soccer practice, the other need not. The point is that labor expended on behalf of the child by one parent frees the other parent from the legal and moral obligation to perform it. While parenting may be pleasant work, it is work nonetheless — a point paid babysitters understand well enough.

As divorced co-parents continue to raise their children, the co-parenting commitment provides a conceptual basis for income sharing between them, and for new default rules that recognize, for the first time, a non-custodial parent's affirmative responsibility to share income not only with his or her child, but also with the other parent who is undertaking the lion's share of the daily labor required to raise joint children. Disentangled from the marital commitment, the co-parenting commitment stands as a distinct undertaking — one the law should encourage parents to honor, and one whose termination the law should police with an exit price. Current law, however, does just the opposite, ignoring the co-parenting commitment and encouraging divorcing partners to assume divorce signals the end of all commitments between them, whether or not they share children. The default rules that produce this result are sticky, nudging spouses to believe this is an appropriate divorce outcome. It is not. Divorce law must be reconceptualized to reflect policy goals more consistent with the best interests of children, their caretakers, and society at large.

Some may object to income sharing for primary caretakers on the grounds that these parents already reap a huge reward in the form of psychic joy stemming from their extensive time with children. This argument is unpersuasive. Most fundamentally, psychic joy is simply not possible of measurement and so cannot be quantified and then offset against a monetary award. Measurement is made more challenging by the fact that time spent with children is a poor proxy for psychic joy. A primary caretaker may spend much time tending to daily chores that produce little joy — cleaning the macaroni and cheese off the floor, laundering, shopping, cooking, and cleaning. The parent who spends less time with children may actually experience more psychic joy than the other parent, especially if that time is devoted more exclusively to child-intensive endeavors — time perhaps at the zoo, the soccer field, the ice cream shop, or the library. Time is a poor proxy for psychic joy. Moreover, the suggestion that psychic joy is time dependent raises uncomfortable questions about the children themselves and their tendency to inspire joy rather than sorrow or worry or frustration or any of the other psychic costs of parenting that are likely to fall disproportionately on the parent with primary residential responsibility.

The partnership metaphor provides an interesting perspective on the argument that income sharing would overcompensate a primary caretaker. Imagine the following exchange between equal partners:

"Did you enjoy your day — working at the office [or the shop, the restaurant, the car wash]?"

"Yes, very much . . ."

"Well then, you have reaped your reward and we will reduce your share of partnership income accordingly."

Psychic joy is a dubious basis for keeping primary caretakers and their children at a lower standard of living than the lesser-time parent.

The co-parenting partnership model I advocate in this Article provides a rationale for new laws that require divorced parents to share the full costs of parenting. Income sharing between parents may assume many forms and levels, and will raise many old and a few new questions, some of them tough ones. So there must be a next conversation, one that builds on the conceptual foundation for income sharing offered here.

D. DIVORCE AND NEW PROPERTY

1. Introduction

Traditionally, interests that may broadly be characterized as "new property," such as pensions and other employment benefits, goodwill in small businesses, professional licenses, and educational degrees were not considered divisible property but as potential sources of income from which spousal support could be paid. Since the 1970s, lawyers have aggressively and often successfully argued that these forms of wealth should be treated as property subject to division.[16]

---

16. In addition to the reasons discussed in the text, a well-known California decision on lawyer malpractice liability has probably motivated lawyers to press these claims as well. In Smith v. Lewis, 530 P.2d 589 (Cal. 1975) (en banc), the court held that an attorney had committed malpractice when he assumed that the husband's retirement benefits were separate property without researching the issue, at a time when the law was not entirely clear. The court awarded damages of $100,000.

As we have seen, former spouses who can be self-supporting often are not entitled to spousal support and so cannot share in employment-related interests through alimony. However, capacity for self-support does not bar property division. In addition, to the extent that an equal division of community or marital property is required or favored, courts that want to award one spouse the family home have often been able to find that the other spouse's interests in pension plans or business goodwill are intangible assets that offset such awards.[17] These circumstances have spurred efforts to expand the pot of interests called "property" for purposes of distribution at divorce.

On the other hand, if wealth associated with employment is treated as divisible property, distributions of pension benefits or professional goodwill will not be modifiable. Sometimes spouses want to characterize these interests as property precisely so that the court orders will not be changeable. However, some courts have been reluctant to deal with the interests in such a final fashion and have for that reason refused to call them "property."

If these interests are to be treated as property, courts ordinarily must assign a present value to them in the course of determining the total property division. However, because these interests typically take the form of a stream of payments of money payable over time, valuing them is difficult. If there were established markets in these interests, valuation could be determined by looking at market price. Often, though, there is no such market, and courts must use other techniques for assigning value. The following explains basic techniques that can be used.

NOTE: VALUING STREAMS OF PAYMENTS

Let's say that you have a goose that lays a golden egg every two weeks. What is it worth? The goose is surely worth more than what its meat and feathers would bring after its death. The meat and feathers constitute the goose's *salvage value*. Assets that produce income are almost always going to be worth more than their salvage value, although their total value includes their salvage value. Most of the assets we will discuss in this chapter are intangibles anyway.

We might try to value the goose by asking how much we paid for it, but what if we paid 59 cents because no one realized that it would lay golden eggs when it grew up? The goose's *book value* would be 59 cents, but this value is historical. It tells us nothing about the changes that have occurred in the goose or in the market for geese and thus has no necessary relationship to the goose's present market value. Besides, some of the assets we will discuss have no book value.

Since we expect that the goose will continue laying a golden egg every two weeks for some indefinite period of time, we are really trying to measure how much that stream of eggs is worth now. If we knew for sure how long the goose would continue to lay eggs and what the price of gold would be, we could easily calculate the total worth of the eggs that the goose will lay. But this sum would not be the

---

17. Professor Herma Hill Kay has suggested that the California cases treating professional goodwill as divisible community property may be merely an effort to raise the total value of the community property to the point that the wife can receive the house as her half and the husband the goodwill as his half. Mary Ann Glendon, The New Family and the New Property 81 n.114 (1981).

value today of those eggs because of the *time value of money*. For example, let's say that the constant profit on one golden egg is $10 (the price we can get for the egg minus the costs of food and other expenses of producing it). A buyer would not pay $10 today for an egg to be delivered in one year because the buyer could invest the same $10 in an interest-bearing account and at the end of the year have $10 plus the interest it earned. Thus, the price today of one egg to be delivered in a year should be an amount that, when invested, will produce $10 in a year. Assuming an interest rate of 8 percent, the amount that must be invested today to earn $10 in one year is $10 divided by 1 plus the interest rate (here, 1.08), or $9.26. (The general formula is Present Value = Future Value divided by 1 + the interest rate. Fortunately, present-value tables are widely available.) This method of determining value is called the *discounted cash flow method*.

The critical choice in determining the present value is deciding what interest rate we assume. The higher the interest rate, the lower the present value will be. The interest rate depends on the current value of money and how uncertain our estimate is of the value of a thing. Valuing the goose is uncertain because we do not and cannot know for certain such critical facts as how long the goose will live, how long it will lay eggs, whether it will continue to lay regularly, and what the price of gold will be. Generally speaking, the more uncertain, or riskier, an investment is, the higher the interest rate will be, since people demand higher rates of return for risky investments. The discussion of assets in this chapter will include how interest rates, or rates of return, are chosen for purposes of valuing them. To the extent that the calculations take into account future uncertainties, they are based on actuarial assumptions for the hypothetical person, which almost always turn out to be inaccurate when applied to the real people involved.

2.   *Pensions and Other Employment-Related Benefits*

Employment-related benefits, provided either by the employer or through public programs such as Social Security, are for many people the most important elements of economic security. Until the 1970s, though, these benefits hardly figured in economic settlements accompanying divorce. Employees' pension rights and other benefits were often very ephemeral; many plans provided that an employee had no absolute right to a pension unless he or she worked for the employer for many years and was employed by that employer at the time of retirement. Courts tended to hold that, under these conditions, pension rights could not be considered property.

Pension rights became more substantial and more common after 1975, the year in which the Employee Retirement Income Security Act (ERISA), 29 U.S.C. §§ 1001 et seq., became effective. Pension plans that are "qualified" under ERISA and related provisions of the Internal Revenue Code provide employers and employees with substantial federal income tax advantages. (The employer's contributions to the plan are deductible as a business expense, and the contributions to the plan and the income they produce are not income to an employee until retirement benefits are paid.) Most important for our purposes, employees covered by qualified plans are guaranteed that even after relatively short periods of employment, their interests in the plan will vest — that is, they will eventually be entitled to receive benefits through the plan. ERISA has made pension rights more substantial and thus more important at divorce, though they are not universal.

Disability payments and workers' compensation are other forms of wage-replacement benefits. Some forms of these benefits may be combined with retirement benefits, as in the next case, which concerns whether to treat these assets as property for purposes of divorce.

MICKEY v. MICKEY

974 A.2d 641 (Conn. 2009)

ZARELLA, J. . . . The marriage of the parties was dissolved on September 21, 2001. At the time of dissolution, the defendant had been employed by the state of Connecticut as a correction officer for approximately fourteen years. Pursuant to his employment with the state, the defendant was enrolled in tier II of the state employees retirement system. Due to the nature of his job, the defendant potentially was eligible for hazardous duty retirement under General Statutes § 5-192n, and, as with all other state employees enrolled in tier II, also was eligible for normal retirement benefits under General Statutes § 5-192*l*, and disability retirement benefits under § 5-192p in the event that he became disabled during the course of his employment.

In its memorandum of decision issued in conjunction with the dissolution of the parties' marriage, the trial court, Dyer, J., ordered that "[t]he plaintiff shall be entitled to, and the defendant's . . . pension plan shall pay to her, 40 percent of the defendant's monthly retirement benefit payment. It is the court's intention that the plaintiff receive 40 percent of the defendant's monthly retirement benefit payment under the contributory hazardous duty retirement plan should he qualify for [the] same, or 40 percent of the defendant's monthly retirement benefit payment under the noncontributory tier II plan should he fail to qualify for a hazardous duty pension." Despite specifically distributing the defendant's potential hazardous duty retirement benefits, however, the trial court did not mention any potential disability benefits that the defendant may have subsequently become entitled to under the plan.

Following the dissolution of the parties' marriage, the defendant suffered an injury in the course of his employment on February 28, 2002, which rendered him disabled and eventually forced him to retire. The defendant began receiving retirement benefits under the state employees retirement system in June, 2005, which was made retroactive to July 1, 2003, in the amount of $990 per month. The defendant's monthly benefit subsequently was increased to $2382.30 in November, 2005, in recognition of the enhanced benefit that he was entitled to receive as a result of the state's certification of his disability under § 5-192p. The plaintiff thereafter continued to receive 40 percent of the defendant's entire monthly benefit payment, including that portion attributable to the defendant's disability benefits.

The defendant subsequently filed a motion for clarification on January 13, 2006, requesting that the trial court clarify that (1) it did not intend to distribute the defendant's disability benefits as part of its original financial orders, and

(2) regardless of its intent, the trial court did not have the statutory authority to distribute those benefits because they were acquired after dissolution. After the trial court, Solomon, J., denied the plaintiff's motion to dismiss the defendant's motion for clarification, the trial court, Dyer, J., subsequently denied the defendant's motion for clarification, concluding, . . . that, because retirement benefits are properly distributable under § 46b-81, the court had the authority to distribute those retirement benefits attributable to the defendant's disability, and that the defendant, therefore, was not entitled to any relief. This appeal followed. . . .

. . . [W]e now address the defendant's principal claim on appeal, namely, that his disability benefits do not constitute distributable marital property and, therefore, that the trial court lacked authority to distribute those benefits under § 46b-81. . . .

With respect to § 46b-81, we previously have determined that the purpose of postdissolution "property division is to unscramble the ownership of property, giving to each spouse what is equitably his." While undertaking this task, we have considered the nature of the marital relationship: "[M]arriage is, among other things, a shared enterprise or joint undertaking in the nature of a partnership to which both spouses contribute — directly and indirectly, financially and non-financially — *the fruits of which* are distributable at divorce." To this end, we generally have taken a liberal view of the term "property," while declaring that "the theme running through this area of our jurisprudence . . . pays mindful consideration to the equitable purpose of our statutory distribution scheme, rather than to mechanically applied rules of property law. In order to achieve justice, equity looks to substance, and not to mere form."

Placing each spouse in an equitable postdissolution position, however, requires a court to consider more than merely how to divide the marital property. Through General Statutes § 46b-82, the legislature has empowered courts to create in either or both spouses an obligation to provide future financial support to the other through continuing alimony payments. We also must examine this companion statute, therefore, in order to understand more completely the inter-relationship between §§ 46b-81 and 46b-82. These two statutes, working together, provide the courts of this state with their primary tools for apportioning the property and income of spouses when a marriage dissolves . . . . Despite their close relationship, however, the purposes and operation of §§ 46b-81 and 46b-82 are distinct and, to an extent, complementary, applying under different circumstances for different reasons. Although the purpose of § 46b-81 is to "unscramble" the spouses' *current* property interests; the purpose of § 46b-82 is to recognize "the obligation of support that spouses assume toward each other by virtue of the marriage." Thus, using both statutes, a court can consider the individual circumstances of each marriage to fashion a fair distribution of *presently* existing marital property as well as ensuring the *future* support of a dependent spouse.

Under § 46b-81, a court has the authority to divide only the *presently* existing property interests of the parties at the time of dissolution, and such division, once made, cannot be altered. An alimony award made at the time of dissolution, on the other hand, *can* be subsequently modified at any time to account for any significant changes in the circumstances of the parties. . . . Thus, §§ 46b-81 and 46b-82 are complementary in that they ensure that courts will consider all of the relevant circumstances in distributing property and establishing future support obligations.

In the event that these circumstances change substantially, for example, if one of the spouses receives a substantial inheritance or becomes unemployed; § 46b-86 provides courts with flexibility to modify an alimony award to reflect these unexpected or uncertain events.

In order to address fully the defendant's claim that his disability benefits are not subject to equitable distribution, it also is important to understand the nature of the disability and retirement plan under which those benefits were granted. General Statutes §§ 5-192e through 5-192x define the state employee tier II retirement plan of which the defendant was a member. The plan is a noncontributory, comprehensive scheme including provisions for normal retirement; hazardous duty retirement; and disability retirement. An employee's eligibility and amount of benefits under the normal retirement plan are based on (1) years of state employment, which are defined as "vesting service"; and (2) various qualified periods of nonstate employment, which together with years of state employment are defined as "credited service. . . ." An employee may retire voluntarily with a retirement benefit upon reaching a certain age with a defined number of years of accrued vesting service. Upon retiring under the normal retirement plan, the eligible employee's actual benefit is computed using formulas that primarily account for the employee's amount of credited service and his average annual earnings.

The disability retirement plan is distinct from, and complementary to, the normal retirement plan. If an employee under this plan is disabled prior to applying for retirement, the formula remains the same, except that § 5-192p(c) provides the employee the benefit of an additional number of years of credited service that "he would have at age sixty-five if he continued to work until that age, but limited to a maximum of thirty years," unless his actual credited service as of his disability retirement date is greater, in which case the formula works exactly the same as in normal retirement. In this way, the acceleration clause of § 5-192p(c) serves to reimburse a disabled employee for those years of compensation forgone due to disability, whereas the amount determined under § 5-192l on the basis of the employee's actual years of credited service operates as a standard pension benefit, representing deferred compensation for those years of service actually completed.

With this background of the relevant statutes in mind, we now turn to a more specific examination of the meaning of the term "property" in § 46b-81. The legislature has not seen fit to define this critical term, leaving it to the courts to determine its meaning through application on a case-by-case basis. . . . As we noted previously, this court has generally taken a rather "broad and comprehensive" view of the meaning of the term "property" for purposes of equitable distribution. We have not erased altogether, however, the limitations inherent in the term. We continue to recognize that "the marital estate divisible pursuant to § 46b-81 refers to interests already acquired, not to expected or unvested interests, or to interests that the court has not quantified."

For instance, in *Krafick*, we addressed the issue of whether a vested[18] but unmatured pension could be classified as marital property subject to equitable

---

18. Black's Law Dictionary defines "vested" as "[h]aving become a completed, consummated right for present or future enjoyment; not contingent; unconditional; absolute. . . ." Black's Law Dictionary (8th ed. 2004). The most important aspect of vesting

distribution pursuant to § 46b-81. The plaintiff in *Krafick* was contesting the trial court's refusal to consider the defendant's pension benefits alongside other assets in distributing the marital estate. The defendant's pension vested at twenty years of service, and the benefit, calculated pursuant to a formula based on the employee's total years of service and an average of the employee's three highest years of earnings, was payable, or matured, upon retirement. At the time of the trial, the defendant in *Krafick* was eligible to retire and represented that he intended to do so in approximately two years.

Analyzing the plaintiff's claim, we first described the nature of the interest in dispute: "Pension benefits represent a form of deferred compensation for services rendered. . . . [T]he employee receives a lesser present compensation plus the contractual right to the future bnefits payable under the pension plan." We then proceeded to place pension benefits in the broader context of the goals of post-dissolution equitable property distribution: "[T]he primary aim of property distribution is to recognize that marriage is, among other things, a shared enterprise or joint undertaking in the nature of a partnership to which both spouses contribute — directly and indirectly, financially and nonfinancially — *the fruits of which* are distributable at divorce." We concluded that vested pension benefits are "an economic resource acquired with the fruits of the wage earner spouse's labors which would otherwise have been utilized by the parties during the marriage to purchase other deferred income assets"; and, thus, distributable as marital property.

We next had to determine whether treating the defendant's vested, but unmatured, pension as property under § 46b-81 violated our understanding of the limitations of the reach of the statute. Recognizing that § 46b-81 "applies only to presently existing property interests, [and] not mere expectancies"; we concluded that *vested* pension benefits are appropriately characterized as a presently existing property interest because they "represent an employee's right to receive payment in the future, subject ordinarily to his or her living until the age of retirement." . . .

There also is a line of cases, at the other end of the spectrum, recognizing that the definition of property interests subject to distribution under § 46b-81, although broad, is not without limits. For instance, in Simmons v. Simmons, 708 A.2d 949, we concluded that a spouse's medical degree is not property within the meaning of § 46b-81. In so holding, we distinguished "presently existing property interest[s]," which are subject to distribution, from "mere expectanc[ies]," which are immune from such treatment; and declared that "the defining characteristic of property for purposes of § 46b-81 is the present existence of the right and the ability to enforce that right." . . .

Our decision in Bender v. Bender, [785 A.2d 197 (2001),] updated this traditional, fairly rigid dichotomy by establishing a more nuanced approach to

---

in the context of pensions is that it immunizes the employee's interest from being unilaterally altered or abolished by the employer. For instance, in the context of statutory pensions, an employee who has a vested pension would be unaffected by legislative changes to the pension plan occurring *after* he has obtained a vested interest in a particular benefit.

A vested interest "matures" when the holder of that interest obtains a right to *present* possession or payment without further precondition.

defining property interests under § 46b-81. In *Bender*, this court "built [on the] foundation" of our prior cases in concluding that the unvested pension of the defendant in that case was property subject to equitable distribution. Consistent with our time-honored approach, we reiterated that presently enforceable rights, based on either property or contract principles, are *sufficient* to cause property to be divisible. Where *Bender* broke new ground was in its recognition that such rights are not the "sine qua non of 'property' under § 46b-81." In building on our prior cases, we expanded our notion of property under § 46b-81, recognizing that there is a spectrum of interests that do not fit comfortably into our traditional scheme and yet should be available in equity for courts to distribute.

If the acquisition of such an "unconventional" interest is contingent on a future event or circumstance, we now examine the contingency to determine if it is overly speculative. Thus, *Bender* created a two step framework that preserved the traditional definition of property while carving out a middle ground, encompassing some inchoate property interests that would have been excluded from the definition of distributable property under the older regime. These interests may now be considered on the basis of the likelihood that a contingency eventually would come to pass. Of course, in order to apply this analytical framework properly, it is critical to categorize the type of contingency being addressed. A contingency on which the mere *enjoyment* of a property interest depends differs from a contingency on which acquisition of the property interest *itself* hinges. The former — e.g., a vested but unmatured pension or an inchoate contractual right — would simply be classified as distributable property under the first step of the *Bender* analysis, whereas the latter would fail the classic test and therefore have to be addressed under *Bender*'s second step.

In *Bender*, we determined that the defendant's unvested pension benefits, although dependent on certain contingencies, were sufficiently certain to constitute divisible property because "these contingencies are susceptible to reasonably accurate quantification." In so concluding, we recognized that the various contingencies that may determine future property interests come in different degrees. Distinguishing the unvested pension benefits at issue in *Bender* from the inheritance interests in Rubin v. Rubin, and Krause v. Krause, we declared that "[u]nvested pension benefits . . . although dependent on certain future contingencies such as length of service and age [i.e., the mere passage of time], are simply not in [the] same *speculative category* [as a potential inheritance]. Moreover, unlike a potential inheritance, pension benefits represent a trade-off for potentially higher wages not earned during the marriage; they often represent . . . the only or principal material asset; and they are treated by employers and employees as property in the workplace."

We conclude that *Bender* stands for the proposition that, even in the absence of a presently enforceable right to property based on contractual principles or a statutory entitlement, a party's expectant interest in property still may fall under § 46b-81 if the conditions precedent to the eventual acquisition of such a definitive right are not too speculative or unlikely. . . .

We turn finally to an application of the *Bender* analysis to the facts of the present case. First, it is clear that, whatever interest the defendant had in potential disability payments under § 5-192p, that interest was not, at the time of dissolution, a presently existing, enforceable right to a future benefit. Although the defendant may have had an abstract statutory entitlement, in the event that he became disabled, to certain defined benefits, he had no concrete, enforceable right to those benefits unless and until an unfortunate accident befell him. Furthermore, the legislature could have modified or terminated the disability retirement program at any time before the defendant suffered a disability. Thus, unlike an interest in a vested pension or a granted but not yet matured stock option, the defendant's interest in his disability benefits was not enforceable prior to the occurrence of the disability. Presumably, the defendant actively was trying to avoid the occurrence of an event triggering an enforceable interest in his disability benefits. We can discern no distinction, for example, between the defendant's interest in his disability benefits and an employee's interest in a potential future workers' compensation claim. To consider these "interests" property in the sense that they could be construed as *presently existing, enforceable* rights to some future asset or income stream is simply to stretch the meaning of these words beyond the breaking point.

Our analysis cannot end here, however, as *Bender* instructs that a presently existing, enforceable right to property, although *sufficient* for purposes of § 46b-81, is not *necessary*. As we noted previously, in light of *Bender*, analyzing an interest that does not become a "right," much less actual, possessory property, prior to the occurrence of some future event or events involves a second step. We must look at the nature of the contingency to determine whether it is so speculative as to be deemed a mere expectancy or, conversely, whether it is "sufficiently concrete, reasonable and justifiable as to constitute a presently existing property interest for equitable distribution purposes." . . .

In the present case, the defendant's receipt of disability benefits under § 5-192p was contingent on his becoming sufficiently disabled prior to sixty-five years of age or completing twenty-five years of credited service. A potential disability is, by its very nature, an accidental event that every employee and employer strives to avoid. It is difficult to perceive how a property interest tied to such an occurrence is "sufficiently concrete, reasonable and justifiable"; to treat any benefits that *might* accrue, *if* the accident eventually occurs *and* is serious enough to cause permanent disability, as a presently existing property interest eligible for equitable distribution at the time of dissolution. We are persuaded that this eventuality is more speculative and far less predictable than the income expected to flow from a medical degree; or the property expected to be acquired through a bequest. As with a testamentary bequest, however, the disability benefits at issue in the present case were terminable at the state's discretion at any time before the defendant suffered a disability. We conclude, therefore, that, consistent with *Bender*, the defendant's interest in future disability benefits is far too speculative to be considered property subject to equitable distribution.

Furthermore, such an interest, even if it was sufficiently concrete to constitute distributable property, could not be classified as distributable under the facts of this case. A benefit derived from an injury occurring years after dissolution, meant solely to compensate for the loss of future wages, simply does not represent the "fruits" of the marital partnership that § 46b-81 is designed to equitably parse. . . .

The difficulty with the present case is that the defendant's "retirement disability" is, in effect, a hybrid of two conceptually distinct interests. We conclude that, as of the date of the parties' dissolution, the portion of the defendant's retirement benefit attributable to his actual years of service — and, therefore, properly characterized as deferred compensation — is distributable as marital property. This conclusion is consistent with our reasoning in *Bender*, as the receipt of regular pension benefits represents, at least in part, deferred compensation earned during the marriage, the value of which is quantifiable at the time of dissolution to a reasonable degree of certainty. On the other hand, we conclude that the portion of the defendant's benefit attributable to the additional amount that he receives as a consequence of being disabled was too speculative at the time of dissolution to be considered distributable property under § 46b-81, and was in no way earned during the course of the marriage. . . .

In the present case, the record indicates that the defendant was entitled to receive $990 per month in regular retirement benefits at the time of his injury. Once his application for disability retirement was approved, that amount increased to $2382.30 per month, reflecting the disability enhancement. Our precedents, together with the policy underlying § 46b-81 and simple common sense, require us to treat the $990 as distributable property, and the difference, $1392.30, as non-distributable property. Therefore, pursuant to the judgment of dissolution, the plaintiff is entitled to 40 percent of the defendant's regular retirement benefits but is not entitled to a percentage of the defendant's disability benefits.

The judgment is reversed and the case is remanded with direction to render judgment granting the defendant's motion for clarification and to issue modified financial orders according to law.

NORCOTT, J., with whom KATZ, J., joins, concurring and dissenting. . . . In my view, . . . our prior precedents and the language of § 5-192p make the defendant's interest in his disability benefits property under the first prong of *Bender* because the defendant had an enforceable and irrevocable right to those benefits as of the first day of his employment with the state, despite the fact that his receipt and future enjoyment of those benefits was contingent on him subsequently becoming disabled. Accordingly, I respectfully dissent.

As an initial matter, I note that I agree with the majority that, under the first prong of the *Bender* analysis, our cases generally have classified property interests by characterizing them as either presently existing and enforceable, and thus distributable, or as mere expectancies that are immune from distribution. My primary disagreement with the majority relates to the analysis that we employ to make that determination, as well as the application of that analysis to the benefits in the present case. Specifically, although our focus under the first prong of *Bender* is to determine whether the right to the benefit is presently existing and enforceable at the time of dissolution; that does not mean that the party must have the right to immediate *receipt* and *enjoyment* of the benefit, or even an unconditional guarantee that the benefit will be received at all. Rather, when the receipt of the benefit associated with a particular interest is contingent on the occurrence of a future event, that interest will nevertheless be considered marital property under our current case law if, at the time of dissolution, the party has an enforceable right to receive the benefit in the event that the condition *does* occur. . . .

Applying the analysis in these precedents to the present case, therefore, I would conclude that the defendant's interest in his disability benefits was distributable property. The language of § 5-192p(a) expressly provides that "[i]f a member of tier II, while in state service, becomes . . . disabled as a result of any injury received while in the performance of his duty as a state employee, he is eligible for disability retirement, *regardless of his period of state service or his age.*" (Emphasis added.) Thus, from the moment the defendant began his employment with the state, he had an enforceable right to receive disability benefits in the event that he subsequently suffered a disabling injury within the scope of his employment. That right was both presently existing and enforceable from that time on, and, had the defendant become disabled on his first day of work, he would have been entitled to receive disability benefits without precondition. . . . Moreover, the fact that the contingency was unlikely to occur is not relevant to our analysis under the first prong of *Bender*, which focuses on whether he had a right to such benefits in the event that the contingency *did* occur. . . .

The majority also concludes that the defendant's interest was not marital property under the first prong of *Bender* because the disability benefit program could have been revoked by the legislature at any time prior to the defendant becoming disabled, implying that the defendant's interest in those benefits did not, and could not, vest until that time. In my view, however, the language of § 5-192p indicates that the defendant's interest had in fact vested as of the first day of his employment with the state, and could not have been revoked by the legislature at any time thereafter. . . .

Finally, I briefly note my disagreement with the majority's conclusion that the defendant's interest in disability benefits did not constitute marital property because the injury occurred postdissolution and represents compensation for future lost wages. We have stated that whether an asset is marital property turns on the time at which an enforceable right to the particular benefit was obtained, and *not* on whether the benefits associated with the interest were received during the marriage. Moreover, we have recognized that "[e]xamining what an asset is intended to reflect is significant . . . only as it relates to whether [an enforceable right to the] asset was earned prior to or subsequent to the date of dissolution. Because in my view the defendant obtained an enforceable interest in his disability benefits under our current case law from the moment he began working for the state, I do not believe that the fact that those benefits were received after the marriage had been dissolved or that they represent, in part, compensation for future lost wages is relevant to our analysis. . . .

NOTES AND QUESTIONS

1. One argument against treating future rights to retirement and disability benefits as property is that they are contingent in many ways. In what ways may the right to receive a pension be contingent? In light of these contingencies, what problems are created if we treat them as property for purposes of divorce? Notwithstanding these problems, virtually all courts and many statutes now treat vested pension rights as property subject to division, and most treat nonvested rights in the same way. Can you see why? This does not mean that the contingencies are ignored; instead, they are addressed in the valuation and methodology of dividing pension rights, as discussed below.

The pension in *Mickey* was a *defined benefit* plan; in this kind of plan, an employee's benefits are determined on the basis of a formula, usually based on years of service and salary, which does not depend on the amount of contributions. Individual accounts are not maintained for each employee. In contrast, in *defined contribution* plans, each employee has a separate account that contains contributions to the plan, interest earned, and any other increase in value of the assets in the account. The amount of the employee's retirement benefit depends on how much is in the account when the employee begins to draw benefits.

Retirement plans can also be categorized according to who puts money into the plan. Both the employer and the employee contribute toward the cost of a *contributory* plan. Only the employer contributes to a *noncontributory* plan. If a plan is contributory, the employee's contributions are immediately vested, so the employee is entitled to them even if he or she quits participating in the plan before retirement. The employee's interest in the amount attributable to the employer's contributions may not vest until the employee has worked for a defined period of time, although ERISA limits how long the employer can delay vesting of pension rights. Both defined benefit and defined contribution plans can be contributory or noncontributory.

An employee is entitled to immediate payment of retirement benefits only if his or her interest is vested and matured. What is the difference between vesting and maturity?

2. If a pension is in payout mode, should it still be treated as property if the employee and his or her spouse divorce? Or at this point should the pension belong to the employee and be treated as a source of income from which spousal support can be paid?

3. Are rights to a disability pension necessarily more contingent than rights to a retirement pension, as the majority in *Mickey* claims?

4. One way that courts divide retirement benefits is to give the entire benefit to the employee and, in lieu of his or her share, give the nonemployee spouse a greater share of other divisible assets. This is known as the "offset" approach and requires the court to determine the value at the time of divorce of the employee spouse's right to receive payments from the pension in the future.

Under the "if, as, and when" approach, each spouse receives a fractional share of each pension payment as it comes due. Originally, courts usually implemented this method by ordering the employee to pay the nonemployee his or her share of each payment as it came in.

What are the advantages and disadvantages of each of these approaches?

5. Many problems associated with the if, as, and when approach could be solved if a court could order the pension plan administrator to pay the non-employee spouse his or her share of the benefits directly. However, as we saw in Chapter 2, pension plans subject to ERISA must provide that benefits are inalienable, and many other plans have the same rule. The Retirement Equity Act of 1984 solves this problem for pensions subject to ERISA by creating an exception to the inalienability requirement. It provides that a court may enter a qualified domestic relations order (QDRO), which directs the pension plan administrator to pay a portion of an employee's benefits to someone other than the employee. 29 U.S.C. § 1056(d). The order can require that payments to the nonemployee begin before the employee actually retires, beginning on or after the earliest date on which the

employee could retire. The nonemployees to whom these payments are made are called "alternate payees."

A QDRO must "relate[ ] to the provision of child support, alimony payments, or marital property rights to a spouse, former spouse, child, or other dependent" of the employee and thus can be used not only to divide a pension as property but also to use pension interests as a fund from which support payments are made. REA imposes seven requirements that an order must meet to be a QDRO. If the order satisfies these requirements, the plan administrator must comply with it; if it does not, ERISA forbids the administrator to comply.

A QDRO divides a defined contribution plan by awarding the nonemployee an amount or percentage of the account balance. Because a defined benefit plan has no account balance, the QDRO uses a flat figure or a formula to designate how much will be paid to the nonemployee.

The Retirement Equity Act applies only to plans governed by ERISA; therefore, QDROs are available only for these plans. The largest group of plans not covered by ERISA are those for federal, state, and local government employees. Some states have legislation allowing QDROs to be used for state and local government pensions.

For more information, *see* Terrence Cain, A Primer on the History and Proper Drafting of Qualified Domestic Relations Orders, 28 T.M. Cooley L. Rev. 417 (2011).

6. Defined contribution and defined benefit plans are assigned present values in fundamentally different ways. Valuing an employee's interest in a defined contribution plan is in principle simple. Since each employee has a separate account, the employee's interest is worth the current fair market value of the assets in the account. If the assets are cash or its equivalent, the value will be the total amount of contributions plus any income they have earned. Valuation is more difficult if the assets are themselves more difficult to value, such as real estate.

Since defined benefit plans do not maintain separate accounts for each employee, valuation of interests in these is more difficult. The problem is similar to valuing the goose that laid the golden eggs. The valuator must estimate the stream of income that the pension will produce, making many assumptions, such as when it will begin and when it will end, and then calculate the value of that stream of income at the time of divorce, making still more assumptions about interest rates and other contingencies.

While a lawyer may well be able to determine the value of benefits in a defined contribution plan alone, most lawyers lack the expertise to value defined benefit plan benefits. Instead, they hire experts. The lawyer's responsibility here is to understand what kinds of analyses various experts perform so that an appropriate one can be chosen. In addition, a lawyer must understand generally the method that the expert uses to value a pension and, specifically, what assumptions about interest rates, mortality, and so on the expert made. These experts do not necessarily know family property law and so may not know that benefits earned after the divorce are not divisible or, in states that permit division only of property acquired during the marriage, that benefits attributable to premarital employment are not divisible. The lawyer must explain these rules to the expert and ensure that the calculations are consistent with them.

For more information, *see* Elizabeth Barker Brandt, Valuation, Allocation, and Distribution of Retirement Plans at Divorce: Where Are We?, 35 Fam. L.Q. 469 (2001). *See also* Marvin Snyder, Challenges in Valuing Pension Plans, 35 Fam. L.Q. 235 (2001).

7. Employees may have a number of other kinds of benefits, which may or may not be intended to provide for retirement. Many of these are treated as defined contribution plans for purposes of property distribution at divorce. They include individual retirement accounts, Keogh plans, profit-sharing plans, stock option plans, employee stock ownership plans, and thrift and savings plans.

8. One of the most valuable employment-related benefits is the right to participate in group health or life insurance, because group insurance may not require proof of insurability and group rates are often substantially lower than the cost of similar coverage under an individual policy. Often an employee's dependents, including a spouse, can participate in the group plan, but those plans typically provide that coverage terminates when a person no longer qualifies as a dependent — for example, when a spouse becomes a divorced former spouse. Federal and state statutes now protect divorced spouses against loss of health insurance coverage. Under federal law, health insurance plans must permit divorced spouses to continue participating in their former spouses' plans for up to 36 months following a divorce. 26 U.S.C. §4980B (2014). Spouses must pay premiums to continue participating. In addition, some states have statutes, some of them pre-dating the federal law, that give divorced people the right to continue participating in group health insurance programs through their former spouses' employment for a limited time.

NOTE: DIVIDING BENEFITS INTO MARITAL AND NONMARITAL SHARES

In jurisdictions that permit only marital property to be divided at divorce, a pension earned in part before or after marriage and in part during marriage must be divided into marital and nonmarital shares. Most courts use the "time rule": the value of the pension rights is multiplied by a fraction whose numerator is the number of years the pension accrued during the marriage and whose denominator is the total number of years the pension accrued. Thus, if at the time of divorce the employee spouse has accrued rights for 20 years and if the spouses have been married for 15 of those years, 15/20, or three-quarters, of the pension rights are marital property.

Some courts use an accrual method to determine the marital share. Under this method the present value of accrued benefits on the date of the marriage is subtracted from the present value of the total accrued benefits on the date of the divorce, and the difference is the value of the benefits earned during marriage. If the pension benefit amounts are linked to the employee's salary, some courts determine the marital share by dividing the total salary the employee received during the marriage by the total salary received throughout the entire period of employment and multiplying this fraction by the total pension benefits. Thus, if an employee earned $150,000 during the marriage and $300,000 throughout his or her employment with the company, $150,000/$300,000, or half, of the pension benefits would be marital property.

In re Marriage of Hunt, 909 P.2d 525 (Colo. 1995), involved husbands' appeals from orders that used the time rule to divide their pension interests. The husbands argued that this method improperly allowed their former wives to share in increases in value of the pensions attributable to increases in the husbands' postdivorce pay raises. After reviewing both the time rule and the accrual rule, the court upheld use of the time rule, particularly where the pension division is deferred. The court said:

> The "time rule" formula recognizes that post-divorce pension benefit enhancements defy easy categorization. Typically, there is commingling of effort undertaken during the marriage and after the marriage which together enhance the value of the future benefit. The employee spouse's ability to enhance the future benefit after the marriage frequently builds on foundation work and efforts undertaken during the marriage. Hence, the theory underlying the "time rule" formula is called the "marital foundation" theory. We agree with the cases . . . that accept the "marital foundation" theory. Thus, we find that although sometimes related to effort, post-dissolution enhancement must be treated identically to passive increases such as cost-of-living increases or increases ascribable to pension plan changes in order to equitably apportion the risks of delay inherent in the deferred distribution and reserve jurisdiction methods for distribution of benefits.

909 P.2d at 534. Further, the court said that the time rule "removes courts from the complicated, time-consuming, inefficient, and hopelessly flawed task of evaluating the enhancement and denominating the enhancement as either marital, separate, passive or some combination thereof." *Id.* at 535. *Contra* Koelsch v. Koelsch, 713 P.2d 1234 (Ariz. 1986).

Why didn't *Mickey* treat disability benefits like pensions and classify them as marital or separate based on when they were earned? Why would the dissent use this methodology? In Holman v. Holman, 84 S.W.3d 903, 906-907 (Ky. 2002), the Kentucky Supreme Court, citing Gragg v. Gragg, 12 S.W.3d 412, 417 (Tenn. 2000), discussed approaches to characterization of disability benefits as marital or separate:

> Those courts which hold that disability benefits constitute marital property have advanced several rationales for this conclusion. Under one approach, which has been referred to as the "mechanistic approach," courts consider whether disability benefits have been specifically excepted from the definition of marital property by statute. Disability benefits will be considered marital property unless there is a statutory provision specifically excluding disability benefits from the marital estate.
>
> Another rationale given in support of the mechanistic approach is that disability benefits should be considered marital property because the policy premiums were paid with marital funds or the marital estate acquired the benefits as a form of compensation for spousal labor during the marriage, much like a pension.
>
> However, the majority of courts considering the proper classification of disability benefits have adopted the analytical approach which focuses on the nature and purpose of the specific disability benefits at issue. Under this approach, benefits which actually compensate for disability are not classified as marital property because such benefits are personal to the spouse who receives them and compensate for loss of good health and replace lost earning capacity. However, where the facts warrant, courts utilizing the analytical approach will separate the benefits into a retirement

component and a true disability component, with the retirement component being classified as marital property and the disability component being classified as separate property. This approach has been applied both to disability benefits paid in connection with insurance coverage maintained by the disabled spouse's employer and to disability benefits paid in connection with a private policy of disability insurance acquired with marital funds during the marriage.

PROBLEMS

1. Wanda was awarded her pension, and Herman received other property as an offset for his share. Wanda's pension has matured, and she is receiving monthly payments from it. Should these monthly payments be considered income to Wanda from which she could be ordered to pay Herman spousal support, or would that allow Herman to double-dip? If the pension was divided by awarding Herman a fractional share of each payment, should these payments be treated as his income in determining spousal support issues?

2. When Winnie and Harold were divorced, Harold was working as a high-level manager at Big Company. Six years later Harold was offered an attractive early retirement package that significantly increased the amount of his retirement benefits. If Winnie had received an increased share of marital property in lieu of an interest in Harold's pension, would she have a claim to some portion of these benefits that were not anticipated when they divorced? If she had been awarded her share in the pension retirement benefits in the form of an "if, as, and when" order, would she be entitled to share in the enhanced package of benefits?

3. During her marriage to Gerald, Mary was awarded stock options. At the time that the options were to expire, the community did not have the funds to exercise the options, and so Mary used her separate funds to exercise the options and purchase the stocks. At the time, the options were worth $50,000, and the purchase price was $40,000. Mary and Gerald are divorcing. The stocks are worth $135,000. What portion of the stocks is community or marital property? What portion, if any, is Mary's separate property?

4. Shirley, a plaintiff's personal injury attorney, and Howard are divorcing. They disagree about whether contingent fees that Shirley hopes to recover for some of the cases she worked on during the marriage are divisible marital property. Case 1 has been settled, but no payments have been made at the time of the divorce. In case 2, Shirley's client won a favorable jury verdict, but the case is on appeal. Case 3 is in the discovery stages. What arguments should Shirley and Howard make regarding the fees in each of these cases?

5. Hank inherited a Christmas tree farm from his parents during his marriage to Wilma. He worked on the farm, which remained his separate property. Wilma had a job in town. At the time of Hank and Wilma's divorce they disagree about whether immature trees, which will be ready to harvest in ten years, are divisible marital property. What arguments should each side make?

6. Virginia's mother created a trust during Virginia's marriage to Alex. Virginia is entitled to one-sixth of the income for her life. At her death her interest goes to her children. When Virginia and Alex divorce, what portion of the trust, if any, is marital property subject to division?

A COMPARISON: SURVIVORSHIP RIGHTS AND DEATH BENEFITS

For pension plans governed by ERISA, employees have the option of receiving their benefits in the form of a joint and survivor annuity, which provides for periodic payments to the retired employee and after the employee's death to the surviving spouse. If an employee divorces before retirement, REA allows the nonemployee former spouse to retain joint and survivor annuity benefits, if the QDRO expressly so provides. A QDRO can also assign *only* survivor benefits to the nonemployee spouse, which means that the nonemployee will receive benefits only at the death of the employee. If the former spouse is the full survivor beneficiary, the employee cannot designate any future spouse as a beneficiary.

Whether an employee's survivors will be entitled to any kind of death benefit if the employee dies before retiring depends on the terms of the plan. To the extent that the funds in the pension were contributed by the employee, there will be a death benefit, and often plans provide a death benefit as to the employee's vested rights based on the employer's contributions. The employee designates who gets the death benefit.

A number of states have enacted statutes that address the frequent failure of holders of insurance policies and pension plans to change the designated beneficiary of their plan or policy after divorce by providing that the designations are automatically revoked by divorce. In Egelhoff v. Egelhoff, 532 U.S. 141 (2001), the Supreme Court held that these statutes are preempted by ERISA. The Court said that the statutes conflict with ERISA because they require plan administrators to determine beneficiaries according to state law rather than the plan documents, which would affect the payment of benefits, a central ERISA concern.

In Kennedy v. Plan Administrator, 555 U.S. 285 (2009), the former wife of a pension plan participant had signed a document waiving any interest in the plan as part of a divorce settlement agreement, but the former husband did not file a change-of-beneficiary form, as required by the plan's governing documents. When he died, the executor of his estate claimed the death benefit, as did the former wife. The Supreme Court ruled that the former wife should prevail, relying on *Egelhoff*.

NOTE: SOCIAL SECURITY, MILITARY, AND OTHER PENSIONS

Approximately 95 percent of all American workers are covered by Social Security. Workers may also be covered by other federal retirement programs, such as the Railroad Retirement Act or a military pension provision. Numerous cases, including several from the Supreme Court, have considered whether these retirement benefits should be treated like the private pension in *Laing*. Typically, state courts have treated federal pensions like other pensions and have applied their marital property law to them. However, the Supreme Court has held that statutory provisions that prevent covered employees from assigning or alienating their pension rights were intended to prevent courts from treating these rights as marital property, and, under the supremacy clause of the Constitution, this federal purpose controls.

The first of these cases was Hisquierdo v. Hisquierdo, 439 U.S. 572 (1979), which dealt with a husband's pension benefits under the federal Railroad

Retirement Act. The Supreme Court concluded that the anti-assignment and anti-alienation provisions are intended to ensure that the benefits actually reach the beneficiary and that treating the benefits as divisible community property conflicts with this purpose. The Railroad Retirement Act applies to relatively few people, but other federal pension statutes also contain anti-assignment and anti-alienation clauses like those in the railroad act.

Military Retirement Benefits   In McCarty v. McCarty, 453 U.S. 210 (1981), the Court held that states could not treat military retirement benefits as marital property, based on the statutes' anti-assignment and anti-alienation clauses and Congress's underlying purposes for creating military retirement benefits. As in *Hisquierdo*, the Court held that a state divorce court could not award the spouse who was not in the military either a share of the retirement benefit itself or an offsetting share of other, divisible property. In 1982, in response to *McCarty*, Congress enacted the Uniformed Services Former Spouses' Protection Act (USFSPA), 10 U.S.C. §§ 1072, 1076, 1086, 1401, 1408, 1447, 1448, 1450, which provides that each state's divorce courts may treat disposable military retired pay or retainer pay according to the state law governing division of marital property.

USFSPA allows former spouses of military personnel to obtain court-ordered payments of property settlements directly from the appropriate military finance center if during the marriage the spouse who was a member of the armed forces performed at least ten years of service credited toward earning the retirement benefits. The former spouse's claim cannot exceed 50 percent of the service member's disposable retired or retainer pay. (When two or more former spouses have claims, direct payments cannot exceed in the aggregate 65 percent.) If the ten-year test is not met, the divorce court can still treat the pension as divisible marital property, but the division can be enforced only by the offset method or by ordering the military spouse to pay a share of pension payments to the former spouse. Similarly, the court can also award the spouse who was not in the military more than 50 percent of the benefits, but amounts above 50 percent cannot be collected directly from the military finance center. Former spouses of military personnel may also receive direct payment of court-ordered spousal or child support regardless of the length of the marriage. Military personnel may designate their former spouses as beneficiaries of death benefits as well.

Military personnel who are disabled may receive disability benefits if they waive a corresponding amount of retirement pay, and it is often to their benefit to do so because disability payments are exempt from federal, state, and local income taxes, while retirement pay is not. In Mansell v. Mansell, 490 U.S. 581 (1989), the Supreme Court considered whether a wife whose former husband made such a waiver after the divorce court had awarded her a share of his military retirement benefits was entitled to a share of his disability benefits. Under California state law, if a former spouse receives disability pay in lieu of retirement benefits, that portion of the disability pay is divisible community property. The California courts applied this rule, interpreting USFSPA as eliminating federal preemption of state law regarding military retirement pay. The Supreme Court, however, held that USFSPA did not completely eliminate federal preemption and concluded that military disability pay is not divisible marital property because the

USFSPA definition of "disposable retired or retainer pay" excludes retirement pay waived to receive disability payments. The effect was that the former wife lost almost 30 percent of the monthly retirement income she would otherwise have received as community property. Justices O'Connor and Blackmun dissented, saying USFSPA should be interpreted as eliminating federal preemption so as to allow states to treat military pensions in the same way that they treat other pensions. Since *Mansell*, many cases concerning military retirees' postdivorce waiver of retirement pay to receive disability benefits have been decided. Most state courts have found a way to protect the retirees' former spouses. Commonly, separation agreements or court orders contain indemnity provisions, which are not considered to violate the USFSPA because the retiree is free to use any assets to satisfy the obligation. Surratt v. Surratt, 148 S.W.3d 761 (Ark. App. 2004), citing and discussing cases. *But see* Halstead v. Halstead, 596 S.E.2d 353 (N.C. App. 2004) (error for court to award spouse an unequal distribution of the military retirement benefits, where the inequality was calculated to replace the amount that spouse lost because of the disability pay election).

Civil Service Pensions   The Civil Service Act allows treatment of civil service benefits as marital property divisible at divorce, 5 U.S.C. §8345(j)(1).

Social Security   Most courts have held that Social Security benefits are not property subject to division and that a court may not divide them indirectly by awarding the other spouse offsetting property of equal value. This conclusion is based on the anti-assignment and anti-alienation provisions of the Social Security Act, 42 U.S.C. §407. The courts are divided about whether the value of benefits may be "considered" in fashioning an equitable division of property, differing on whether this amounts to an offset or not. *See* Olsen v. Olsen, 169 P.3d 765 (Utah App. 2007), for discussion and analysis of the cases. In contrast, the Social Security Act explicitly allows courts to order the Social Security Administration to pay a person's legal obligations to support a spouse, former spouse, or children from his or her benefits. 42 U.S.C. §659.

Further, a divorced spouse is entitled to receive Social Security benefits on the account of a former spouse if the marriage lasted at least ten years. 42 U.S.C. §402(b)(1). The benefit payable to a divorced spouse of a covered worker does not reduce the benefit payable to the worker. 42 U.S.C. §403(a)(3). If a divorced spouse worked and contributed enough to Social Security to be entitled to benefits independently, he or she must choose between these independent benefits and those based on the employment of the former spouse. The maximum that a person may receive on the account of a former spouse who is still living is 50 percent of the latter's benefit. Thus, a person whose independent benefits are greater than the benefits on the account of the former spouse loses the latter altogether. A divorced spouse may apply for dependency benefits when he or she reaches age 62 if the former spouse is also at least 62, even though the latter is not yet collecting Social Security.

A person who collects Social Security on the account of a former spouse must remain single to receive benefits. A person who has been married and divorced more than once may draw benefits on the account of whichever former spouse will provide the greatest benefits. And more than one former spouse may be able to claim benefits on the account of the same earner. For example, assume that Q, a wage earner, and R, a homemaker, were married for 13 years and divorced. Q then married S, who was also a homemaker, and they were divorced after 11 years. R remarried T, another wage earner, and they divorced after 15 years. R, who is not independently entitled to Social Security, may draw benefits on the account of either Q or T, and both R and S may draw benefits on the account of Q.

3. Professional Practices and Other Closely Held Businesses

When one or both spouses own an interest in a small business, either as a sole proprietor, a partner, or a shareholder in a close corporation, dividing this interest may be the most important issue at divorce. Is the business interest divisible property at all? If so, how should this interest be valued (since there will probably not be a readily ascertainable market value) and divided?

When a spouse owns a personal service business, such as a professional practice, the problems are compounded. The practice likely owns some tangible assets — equipment, books, and accounts receivable — but, compared to a hardware store, these assets represent relatively little of the total value of the business. Expertise and services provided by the professional are relatively more important. Thus, there are real problems of defining what constitutes the property in the practice.

McREATH V. McREATH

800 N.W.2d 399 (Wis. 2011)

PATIENCE DRAKE ROGGENSACK, J. . . . Tracy and Tim were married on August 27, 1988. Three children, all of whom were minors at the time the divorce proceedings were initiated, were born of their marriage.[19]

In 1991, Tim received his dental degree, and in 1993, he received a master's degree in orthodontia. Accordingly, most of Tim's dental education was pursued during the marriage. Tim took out student loans to fund his education, all of which were repaid with marital funds.

Upon receiving his masters in orthodontia, Tim worked as an associate at Orthodontic Specialists for two years. Tim then purchased the Baraboo and Portage locations of Orthodontic Specialists from Dr. Grady.

Tim paid approximately $930,000 for the two locations of Orthodontic Specialists. A portion of this purchase price was attributed to a noncompete agreement that Dr. Grady signed and to transitional services that Dr. Grady provided Tim. Specifically, Tim testified that $100,000 was for the physical assets, corporate name, and corporate goodwill. The remaining $830,000 was for, as Tim described, "Dr. Grady's name, the noncompete clause, and the employment agreement that Dr. Grady would stay on to introduce me to his existing patients, [and] to counsel me through the process of learning how to do business."

---

19. The McReaths' eldest child has since reached the age of majority.

With regard to the noncompete agreement, Tim testified that he would not have purchased Orthodontic Specialists for as high of a price as he did without a noncompete agreement because, "[Dr. Grady] could have just opened up a business just down the street and I'm assuming that he would have taken not only the majority of patients with him but the majority of the future patients in the area." Tim also testified that he was not aware of any transaction in the field of orthodontics, for any substantial value, that took place without a noncompete agreement. According to Tim, "the name of the practitioner is always weighted very heavily as opposed to the goodwill or the value of the name of the practice or corporation."

Tim has worked as the sole owner of Orthodontic Specialists since he purchased it from Dr. Grady. Tim has historically averaged a 60-hour work week. This is significantly more than the average orthodontist who works only 35 hours per week. Recently, Tim has reduced the number of hours he works to approximately 45 hours per week. Tim has no plans to sell or dispose of his practice.

Tim has been very successful in operating Orthodontic Specialists. His annual gross business revenues in the five years leading up to the divorce ranged from $1.6 million to in excess of $1.8 million. In the same five years, Tim received an average yearly net cash flow from Orthodontic Specialists of $697,522. Notably, Orthodontic Specialists maintains the only orthodontic offices in Baraboo and Portage.

The success of Orthodontic Specialists has resulted in a relatively high standard of living for the McReath family. They have significant assets and little, if any, personal debt.

Unlike Tim, Tracy does not have a professional degree. She is a high school graduate with some college credits, but no college degree. Tracy worked outside the home while Tim was attending dental school. Throughout much of their marriage, however, Tracy worked as a homemaker and the primary caretaker for the couple's children. Specifically, she was completely out of the workforce from 1993 to 2000. From 2000 to 2008, she performed some financial and clerical duties for Orthodontic Specialists. In this position, she was paid $15,000 to $16,000 per year. The circuit court found Tracy has a current earning capacity of $14.50 per hour, or $30,160 annually. . . .

Regarding the marital property division, with the exception of the value of Orthodontic Specialists, the parties stipulated to the value of their marital assets. They also stipulated to a division of assets with a balancing payment. Hearings were held on the appropriate fair market valuation of Orthodontic Specialists, and resulted in a valuation of $1,058,000. This was the value given by Tracy's expert, Craig Billings (Billings). The court rejected the $415,000 valuation of Tim's expert, Dennis Ksicinski (Ksicinski).

Having valued Orthodontic Specialists at $1,058,000, the court turned to dividing the assets. The court found that there was no reason to deviate from the presumption of equal property division in Wis. Stat. §767.61(3) (2009-10). It then combined the $1,058,000 valuation of Orthodontic Specialists with the other, stipulated-to, assets in the marital estate. Because, among other assets, Tim was the stipulated owner of Orthodontic Specialists, Tim's total assets exceeded Tracy's by $1,593,440. As such, to equalize the property division, the court awarded Tracy $796,720, to be paid at the rate of no less than $80,000 per year plus accrued interest.

Next, to set maintenance, the court used Tim's average annual earnings from Orthodontic Specialists over the preceding five years, i.e., $697,522. However, because the $697,522 salary was based on Tim working 50-70 hours per week, the court adjusted the figure to reflect a 40-hour work week. Consequently, the court set Tim's expected annual income from Orthodontic Specialists at $465,000 (rounded). Next, the court took its finding that Tracy had a current earning capacity of $14.50 per hour, or $30,160 annually. The court then added these income calculations to the other sources of income available to the parties, specifically rental and investment income, and found that Tim's total annual income was $535,806 (or $44,650/month) and Tracy's total annual income was $75,944 (or $6,328/month).

With these figures in hand, the court considered the statutory factors set forth in Wis. Stat. § 767.56 in deciding whether to award maintenance. In considering these factors, the court found that it was unlikely that Tracy would ever have Tim's earning capacity or an income that would allow for a standard of living comparable to that enjoyed during the marriage. The court also underscored that Tracy had contributed to the dental education and increased earning capacity of Tim. Based on these findings, the court awarded Tracy maintenance in the amount of $16,000 per month for a period of 20 years.

Tim appealed and the court of appeals affirmed. . . .

In this case, the issue is whether the entire value of the salable professional goodwill in Orthodontic Specialists is included in the marital estate subject to division under Wis. Stat. § 767.61. . . .

Defining professional goodwill is a necessary starting point. In 1967, we recognized a business's goodwill as a divisible marital asset. Spheeris v. Spheeris, 155 N.W.2d 130 (1967). In doing so, we underscored the difficulty in defining the concept, but set forth the following definition:

> In its broadest sense the intangible asset called good will may be said to be reputation; however, a better description would probably be that element of value which inheres in the fixed and favorable consideration of customers arising from an established and well-conducted business.

. . . As aforementioned, we recognized goodwill as part of the divisible marital estate as early as 1967. In *Spheeris*, in order to calculate Mr. Spheeris's net worth for the divorce judgment, the circuit court included the value of the goodwill attributable to the retail discount store owned by Mr. Spheeris. Mr. Spheeris did not challenge the inclusion of goodwill as a divisible marital asset; rather, he challenged the valuation of the goodwill by use of predictive formulas, absent a sale of the business. In other words, Mr. Spheeris argued that "the only way to establish [goodwill] is through a purchase price agreed upon in a voluntary arm's-length transaction."

We disagreed, holding that there need not be an actual sale in order to determine the existence and value of a business's goodwill. . . .

While *Spheeris* involved a commercial business, subsequent Wisconsin cases have recognized goodwill in professional practices. In *Holbrook*, Mr. Holbrook was a partner in a large law firm. *Holbrook*, 103 Wis. 2d at 330, 309 N.W.2d 343. The court of appeals [held that the circuit court erred in treating the goodwill in Mr. Holbrook's partnership interest as a divisible marital asset]. . . . [T]he court's subsequent discussion focused on its assumption that professional goodwill cannot be sold, and "accrues to the benefit of the owners only through increased salary." For instance, the court compared the professional goodwill in Mr. Holbrook's partnership interest to a professional degree. It opined that "[l]ike an educational degree, a partner's theoretical share of a [law firm's goodwill *cannot be exchanged on an open market: it cannot be assigned, sold, transferred, conveyed or pledged.* . . . In both cases, the 'asset' involved *is not salable* and has computable value to the individual only to the extent that it promises increased future earnings." Moreover, the court underscored that, apart from receiving the value of his capital account, Mr. Holbrook was "[e]thically and contractually . . . prevented from otherwise disposing of his interest" in the firm.

Accordingly, Wisconsin courts considering the valuation of professional goodwill subsequent to *Holbrook* have limited *Holbrook*'s assertion that professional goodwill is not part of the divisible marital estate to situations where the professional goodwill is nonsalable. For example, in *Peerenboom*, the court of appeals concluded that the goodwill in a divorcing spouse's dental practice could be a divisible marital asset. Peerenboom v. Peerenboom, 147 Wis. 2d 547, 552, 433 N.W.2d 282 (Ct. App. 1988). The court distinguished *Holbrook*:

> . . . In contrast, in this case the record shows no ethical or contractual barrier to [Dr. Peerenboom's] disposing of his interest in his dental practice. Accordingly, to the extent that the evidence shows that the goodwill exists, is marketable, and that its value is something over and above the value of the practice's assets and the professional's skills and services, it may be included as an asset in the marital estate and be subject to division.

. . . As aforementioned, the presumption of equal division recognizes the contributions of each spouse to the marriage, including a homemaker spouse's lost earning capacity from being out of the job market. Where the salable professional goodwill is developed during the marriage, it defies the presumption of equality to exclude it from the divisible marital estate. As one court has explained:

> [T]he wife, by virtue of her position of wife, made to that [goodwill] value the same contribution as does a wife to any of the husband's earnings and accumulations during the marriage. She is as much entitled to be recompensed for that contribution as if it were represented by the increased value of stock in a family business.

In sum, pursuant to Wis. Stat. § 767.61, Wisconsin case law and the policy supporting the presumption of equality in the division of the marital estate, we hold that a circuit court shall include salable professional goodwill in the divisible marital estate when the business interest to which the goodwill is attendant is an asset subject to § 767.61.

Tim urges us to require circuit courts to divide professional goodwill into two subgroups, "personal" goodwill and "enterprise" goodwill, and to create a presumption that personal goodwill is excluded from the marital estate. This is an approach taken by some courts and scholars.

When professional goodwill is so divided, enterprise goodwill is characterized as "[g]oodwill in a professional practice ... attributable to the business enterprise itself by virtue of its existing arrangements with suppliers, customers or others, and its anticipated future customer base due to factors attributable to the business." Personal goodwill, on the other hand, is characterized as the goodwill that is "attributable to the individual owner's personal skill, training or reputation," i.e., it is "the goodwill that depends on the continued presence of a particular individual."

Some courts that divide professional goodwill into enterprise and personal goodwill have concluded that enterprise goodwill is included in the divisible marital estate, and personal goodwill is not. This conclusion is based in large part on the belief that enterprise goodwill is salable, while personal goodwill is not. . . .

After reviewing cases that distinguish between personal and enterprise goodwill, we choose not to require circuit courts to draw a distinction between personal and enterprise goodwill when dividing a marital estate that includes professional goodwill. This is so because the premise on which the distinction is grounded — that enterprise goodwill is salable and personal goodwill is not — is mistaken. As evidenced by the facts of the case at hand, Tim testified that when he bought Orthodontic Specialists for $930,000, nearly 90 percent of the sale price was for the professional goodwill. Tim described this goodwill as including elements of "personal" goodwill: "Dr. Grady's name, the noncompete clause, and the employment agreement that Dr. Grady would stay on to introduce me to his existing patients." Therefore, as this case demonstrates, in some situations, personal goodwill is salable. . . .

. . . The second issue presented is whether the circuit court double counted the value of Tim's professional goodwill by basing Tracy's maintenance award on Tim's expected future earnings when the future earnings will arise from Orthodontic Specialists. Under Tim's line of reasoning, the circuit court counted the goodwill once when it treated the goodwill as a divisible marital asset. Tim contends that the court then counted professional goodwill a second time when it awarded maintenance based on his past earnings from Orthodontic Specialists, given that professional goodwill increased those past earnings. . . .

There are two objectives that an award of maintenance seeks to meet. The first objective is support of the payee spouse. LaRocque v. LaRocque, 139 Wis. 2d 23, 33, 406 N.W.2d 736 (1987). This objective may not be met by merely maintaining the payee spouse at a subsistence level. Rather, maintenance should support the payee spouse at the pre-divorce standard. *Id.* This standard should be measured by "the lifestyle that the parties enjoyed in the years immediately before the divorce and could anticipate enjoying if they were to stay married." The second objective is fairness, which aims to "compensate the recipient spouse for contributions made to the marriage, give effect to the parties' financial arrangements, or prevent unjust enrichment of either party." . . .

As is the case here, concerns about double counting sometimes arise when awarding maintenance. . . .

. . . [I]n the typical property division case involving a pension, the trial court may determine the present value of the pension. When the present value of a pension plan is calculated, that present value is based, in part, on projected future benefit payments. Therefore, assuming the employee spouse is awarded the present value of the asset, he or she does not receive the value of the asset at the time of the property division. Rather, the spouse receives that value via future payments. Accordingly, . . . it would be double counting to count the present value of the pension as a divisible asset and also count the future payments as income, since the income, up to the valuation placed on the pension at the time of the division, are one and the same.

Contrarily, when an income earning asset is assigned to one spouse, . . . that spouse, generally, receives the full fair market value of that asset at the time of the property division. Stated otherwise, if the spouse was awarded income property, that spouse could turn around and sell the income property the next day and, thereby, attain the value of the property. The spouse could also elect to keep the property and earn income from it. As the spouse earns income, he or she does not lose the value of the property because he or she always has the option to sell the property for fair market value. Therefore, unlike pension benefit payments (up to the present value placed on the pension at the time of the division), the value of investment property is separate from the income it generates. Consequently, . . . counting income from income earning assets will typically not implicate double counting.

. . . [W]e opined that given the "infinite range of factual situations facing circuit courts in dividing property and determining maintenance and child support," it would be unwise to proscribe inflexible double-counting rules. Instead, we stressed that "the 'double-counting' rule serves to warn parties, counsel and the courts to avoid unfairness by carefully considering the division of income-producing and non-income-producing assets and the probable effects of that division on the need for maintenance and the availability of income to both parents for child support." In short, when analyzing whether there has been double counting, the focus should be on fairness, not rigid double-counting rules. . . .

We now apply the legal principles set forth above to the facts and circumstances of this case. . . .

Pursuant to our conclusion above, the entire amount of *salable* professional goodwill was appropriately included in the marital estate. Here, Tim has not shown that the $1,058,000 value placed on Orthodontic Specialists includes non-salable goodwill. Rather, the facts indicate the contrary. In particular, Tim bought the practice, over a decade ago, for $930,000. Approximately 90 percent of this purchase price was paid for goodwill. Moreover, Tim testified that this goodwill included "Dr. Grady's name, the noncompete clause, and the employment agreement that Dr. Grady would stay on to introduce me to his existing patients, [and] to counsel me through the process of learning how to do business," much of which is included in what Tim classifies as personal goodwill. . . .

Tim argues that the circuit court double counted the value of his professional goodwill when it included the goodwill in the divisible marital estate, and then based Tracy's maintenance award on Tim's expected future earnings. According to Tim, the expected future earnings also included the value of the goodwill because it was calculated using Tim's average income over the preceding five years which was increased by the goodwill. We disagree.

We start by underscoring our directive . . . that the rule against double counting is advisory and not absolute. As set forth above, the double counting rule does not prohibit the inclusion of investment income from assets awarded to a spouse as part of property division when calculating maintenance. This is so because the value of the investment asset is separate from the income it produces. Contrarily, pension benefit payouts (until they reach the amount of the valuation given the pension as an asset at the time of the property division) do not create value separate from the pension as an asset at the time of the property division. Applying these principles to the case at hand, we conclude that the salable professional goodwill in Orthodontic Specialists is similar to an asset that produces income.

As with an income producing asset, the value of Orthodontic Specialists at the time of the property division had a set value, namely, $1,058,000. If Tim so chose, at the time of the property division, he could have sold Orthodontic Specialists and realized this value. Or, he could retain Orthodontic Specialists, earn income from it and sell it at a later time. Consequently, Tim has the option of continuing to generate substantial income from Orthodontic Specialists without diminishing its value. Specifically, the circuit court found that if Tim works 40 hours per week, Tim's income will be $465,000 annually. As with income from an income earning asset, this income is separate from the value of Orthodontic Specialists as it existed at the time of the property division. Consequently, the circuit court did not double count Orthodontic Specialists' professional goodwill and, therefore, did not erroneously exercise its discretion when it awarded Tracy $16,000 per month, for 20 years, in maintenance. . . .

The decision of the court of appeals is affirmed.

NOTES AND QUESTIONS

1. Surely the tangible assets of a business, including a professional practice, may be divisible property, as may intangible assets, such as accounts receivable. In what ways is goodwill so different from these other types of assets that it should not be treated as divisible property? What arguments support treating it as property?

In some other legal contexts, goodwill is treated as property, but in others it is not. For example, under the Internal Revenue Code, goodwill is not subject to depreciation, loss of goodwill is not compensated for in eminent domain proceedings, and its loss does not produce an income tax deduction. However, since 1993 the Internal Revenue Code has provided that goodwill may be amortized over a 15-year period. IRC § 197.

When professionals are associated in practice, their partnership agreement or corporate charter often includes provisions and formulas that permit the partner(s) continuing in the practice to buy out the interest of a partner who dies, resigns, etc. When the formula produces an amount greater than the withdrawing partner's fractional share of the tangible assets and accounts receivable, have the partners in effect acknowledged that the practice has goodwill? When a practice is sold or a partner withdraws, the selling or withdrawing practitioner often signs a covenant not to compete to prevent that partner from continuing to trade on his or her reputation in competition with that of his or her successors. Is this a device that requires the partner to leave his or her share of the goodwill in the business?

What is the relevance of the legal treatment of goodwill in other contexts to the question presented by *McReath*?

2. What is the difference between "enterprise" and "professional" or "personal" goodwill? What arguments support the *McReath* court's holding that all goodwill is divisible at divorce? How would you argue that only enterprise goodwill should be divisible?

The ALI Family Dissolution Principles recommend that goodwill be treated as property, whether it is marketable or not. They also say that to the extent goodwill is not marketable, spousal earning capacity, labor, or skills should not be included in the value. ALI, Principles of the Law of Family Dissolution § 4.07(3) (2002).

3. Some courts say that divisible goodwill can exist only in a partnership and not in a sole practice. *See, e.g.*, Nail v. Nail, 486 S.W.2d 761 (Tex. 1972); Sorensen v. Sorensen, 839 P.2d 774 (Utah 1992). What would be the basis for the distinction? This rule means that a person married to a professional who practices with others may share in goodwill at divorce, while one married to a sole practitioner will not.

4. *McReath* adopts the rule that goodwill must be salable for it to be treated as divisible property. In some states ethical rules forbid lawyers to sell their law practices. In those states a doctor, dentist, or accountant may have professional goodwill while a lawyer would not. Other professions may have ethical limitations that affect the salability of practices. This approach creates the anomaly that some professionals may have goodwill while others may not. What arguments support this position?

Where lawyers are ethically prohibited from selling their practices, the ban is based on a lawyer's obligation to preserve client confidences. Charles Wolfram, Modern Legal Ethics 879-880 (1986); EC 4-6 (a lawyer should not attempt to sell a law practice as a going business because to do so would involve the disclosure of confidences and secrets). In practice, however, this prohibition is sometimes circumvented by inflating the value of other assets or by having the buyer associate with the seller for a few months. Rule 1.17 of the ABA Model Rules of Professional Conduct allows the sale of law practices, including goodwill, but it requires that the seller give actual written notice to each client before the sale. Lawyers are also ethically prohibited from entering into partnership agreements that include covenants not to compete. Charles Wolfram, above, at 885; DR 2-108(A); ABA Model Rules of Professional Conduct, Rule 5.6.

5. If goodwill is divisible property, is it to be characterized as separate or marital, where that distinction matters? Is it separate if "brought into the marriage"? If so, are the profits it produces also separate? How do we distinguish profits attributable to the labor of the working spouse (which is marital property)? How should we account for the decrease in value over time of "old" goodwill while "new" goodwill is built up?

6. *McReath* cites prior cases holding that pension income cannot be the basis for spousal support if the nonemployee spouse received a share of the pension at divorce, but says that the income that a former spouse earns can be considered available to pay spousal support even if his or her professional goodwill was treated

as divisible property, analogizing the goodwill to tangible property. Does the fact that a professional practice and its goodwill can be sold justify this result? Consider that the *McReath* trial court ordered Dr. McReath to pay $80,000 per year in property division installment payments plus $16,000 per month ($192,000 per year) to his ex-wife, a total of $272,000 per year, and it estimated his total annual income to be more than $535,000 per year.

7. Valuation of goodwill (and small businesses generally) is notoriously difficult. If the same or a similar business has recently sold, valuation is not a problem because market value is widely accepted as the gold standard for this issue. Where there is not a ready market for the kind of business being valued, accounting methods are ordinarily used. These methods all look to the flow of income that the business produces and, using a "capitalization rate," calculate what amount of money would have to be invested at that rate of interest to produce the stream of income. The problems with these methods are obvious. Technical issues include how to calculate the income stream that is to be capitalized and what interest rate to choose. More generally, it can be argued that these methods produce figures that have no necessary relationship to what the business person would realize on sale or withdrawal from the business, to the extent that is important.

8. A popular way of dividing pensions is to use a QDRO to divide the pension into separate portions for each spouse. This solution is particularly useful when the spouses do not have enough other property to balance the pension or when valuing the pension is difficult. Since similar problems arise in valuing and dividing small businesses, can a similar solution be employed? That is, can the business be divided in kind by awarding each of the spouses a fraction of it? What problems would be created? Bowen v. Bowen, 473 A.2d 73 (N.J. 1984).

9. In 1990 Professor Grace Ganz Blumberg participated in colloquia in five California cities about treatment of goodwill. The participants were lawyers, judges, and accountants. She observed:

> [A] substantial minority of participants expressed remarkable resistance to the generous [California] appellate law on [goodwill]. Relatively few attorneys or accountants, although rather more trial court judges, totally rejected capitalization measures. Instead, many embraced arguably incorrect valuation practices that tend to down-value goodwill, even practices specifically disapproved by state appellate law.
>
> The sex divide was dramatic. Every one of the few women panelists promoted generous definitions of goodwill and criticized unwarranted and unlawful limiting valuation practices. A fair number of men, particularly accountants, agreed with them. On the other side, only male participants opposed capitalization and sought to limit valuation improperly. Such men were prone to detect "feminist bias" in women participants, including this writer, who did not agree with them. Yet there was only one woman panelist who represented a feminist organization; all the rest could best be described as "successful professional women."
>
> I was struck by this charge of "feminist bias" because the personal bias of any professional would be to oppose goodwill recognition. All colloquia participants, men and women, were "economically male."

Grace G. Blumberg, Identifying and Valuing Goodwill at Divorce, 56 Law & Contemp. Probs. 217, 220-221 (Spring 1993).

10. For more information, *see* Mary Kay Kisthardt, Professional Goodwill in Marital Dissolution Cases: The State of the Law (2008), available at ssrn.com/abstract+1311371; Patrice Leigh Ferguson & John E. Camp, Valuation Basics and Beyond: Tackling Areas of Controversy, 35 Fam. L.Q. 305 (2001); Randall B. Wilhite, The Effect of Goodwill in Determining the Value of a Business in a Divorce, 35 Fam. L.Q. 351 (2001); Ann Bartow, Intellectual Property and Domestic Relations: Issues to Consider When There Is an Artist, Author, Inventor, or Celebrity in the Family, 35 Fam. L.Q. 383 (2001).

PROBLEMS

1. Robert started a State Farm Insurance Agency during his marriage to Linda. His agreement with State Farm provides that he may not sell any brand of insurance except State Farm and that all information about policyholders are trade secrets belonging to State Farm, as are the agency's computer system and business records. If Robert and State Farm ever terminate their relationship, Robert may keep the office and sell other companies' insurance, but he cannot solicit State Farm policyholders for one year. The agency has been the most profitable insurance agency in the state for the last ten years, and Robert works ten to eleven hours a day, seven days a week. The agency pays Robert considerably more than the industry average for insurance agents. Does Robert's agency have goodwill? Why or why not?

2. Vincent and Marilyn are divorcing, and they dispute the value of the Green 'n' Tidy Landscape business, which Vincent founded during the marriage and has operated for 15 years. The business has six employees in addition to Vincent, all of whom do manual labor. He is the only person who deals with clients. Marilyn's expert included a value for goodwill in his calculation of the value of the business, based on the amount by which its earnings exceed a fair salary for Vincent and a fair rate of return on the tangible assets of the business. Vincent's expert's valuation did not include an amount for goodwill, based on the state supreme court's holding in an earlier case that a professional practice of a sole practitioner does not have a goodwill value for purposes of divorce. Should the court find that the business has divisible goodwill? Why or why not?

3. Would a well-known entertainer have professional goodwill that could be divisible marital property? *See* Piscopo v. Piscopo, 557 A.2d 1040 (N.J. Super. 1989) (entertainer Joe Piscopo), discussed in Jay E. Fishman, Celebrity as a Business and Its Role in Matrimonial Cases, 17 Am. J. Fam. L. 203 (2004).

4.   *Degrees, Licenses, Jobs, and Earning Capacity*

PROBLEM

Judith and Phillip were married 17 years ago, when Judith was a second-year medical student and Phillip was beginning his internship. He later did a residency in cardiology, and she did a residency in pediatrics. Both Judith and Phillip took out loans to pay for their medical school expenses, which they have paid off. While

Judith was in medical school, Phillip supported both of them from his very modest salary as a resident.

After completing her residency, Judith was hired as an assistant professor at State University Medical School, and Phillip opened a private cardiology practice with a partner. Judith became a professor rather than entering private practice so that she would have a flexible schedule to care for their three children.

Phillip, who is now 41, earned an average of $150,000 (net) per year during the last three years. Judith, age 40, is an untenured professor with no expectation of tenure in the foreseeable future, although she is widely published and is one of the ten top pediatric geneticists in the nation. She earned $70,000 last year.

Judith and Phillip are now divorcing. They have agreed that Judith will have custody of the three children and that Phillip will pay child support. They disagree, however, about spousal support and property division. Based on the materials that you have already read on property division and spousal support and the materials in this chapter that precede and follow this problem, consider these questions:

1. Is Judith eligible for spousal support?
2. Does Judith or Phillip have "professional goodwill" subject to equitable distribution?
3. Is either Judith or Phillip entitled to compensation for helping the other develop his or her career? If so, why? What is the measure of compensation? Some form of reimbursement is the most common remedy. Is this adequate? If one spouse is awarded periodic payments for helping the other, are the payments terminable on the recipient's remarriage? Are they modifiable? Is a spouse entitled to compensation only when the divorce occurs shortly after one spouse has finished putting the other through school?

As you answer these questions, consider the following materials.

CASE LAW AND STATUTES

MAHONEY V. MAHONEY

453 A.2d 527 (N.J. 1982)

The Court must decide whether the plaintiff's [MBA] degree is "property" for purposes of N.J.S.A. 2A:34-23, which requires equitable distribution of "the property, both real and personal, which was legally and beneficially acquired . . . during the marriage." . . .

[T]his Court has frequently held that an "expansive interpretation [is] to be given to the word 'property.'" . . . This Court, however, has never subjected to equitable distribution of an asset whose future monetary value is as uncertain and unquantifiable as a professional degree or license. . . . A professional license or degree is a personal achievement of the holder. It cannot be sold and its value cannot readily be determined. A professional license or degree represents the opportunity to obtain an amount of money only upon the occurrence of highly uncertain future events. By contrast, [a] vested but unmatured pension entitle[s] the owner to a definite amount of money at a certain future date.

The value of a professional degree for purposes of property distribution is nothing more than the possibility of enhanced earnings that the particular academic credential will provide. In Stern v. Stern, 66 N.J. 340, 345, 331 A.2d 257 (1975), we held that a lawyer's earning capacity, even where its development has been aided and enhanced by the other spouse . . . should not be recognized as a separate, particular item of property within the meaning of N.J.S.A. 2A:34-23. Potential earning capacity . . . should not be deemed property as such within the meaning of the statute.

Equitable distribution of a professional degree would similarly require distribution of "earning capacity" — income that the degree holder might never acquire. The amount of future earnings would be entirely speculative. Moreover, any assets resulting from income for professional services would be property acquired after the marriage; the statute restricts equitable distribution to property acquired during the marriage.

Valuing a professional degree in the hands of any particular individual at the start of his or her career would involve a gamut of calculations that reduces to little more than guesswork. As the Appellate Division noted, courts would be required to determine far more than what the degree holder could earn in the new career. The admittedly speculative dollar amount of earnings in the "enhanced" career [must] be reduced by the . . . income the spouse should be assumed to have been able to earn if otherwise employed. In our view . . . [this] is ordinarily nothing but speculation, particularly when it is fair to assume that a person with the ability and motivation to complete professional training or higher education would probably utilize those attributes in concomitantly productive alternative endeavors.

Even if such estimates could be made, however, there would remain a world of unforeseen events that could affect the earning potential — not to mention the actual earnings — of any particular degree holder. A person qualified by education for a given profession may choose not to practice it, may fail at it, or may practice in a specialty, location or manner which generates less than the average income enjoyed by fellow professionals. The potential worth of the education may never be realized for these or many other reasons. An award based upon the prediction of the degree holder's success at the chosen field may bear no relationship to the reality he or she faces after the divorce.

Moreover, the likelihood that an equitable distribution will prove to be unfair is increased in those cases where the court miscalculates the value of the license or degree. The potential for inequity to the failed professional or one who changes careers is at once apparent; his or her spouse will have been awarded a share of something which never existed in any real sense. The finality of property distribution precludes any remedy for such unfairness. "Unlike an award of alimony, which can be adjusted after divorce to reflect unanticipated changes in the parties' circumstances, a property division may not [be adjusted]." . . .

Even if it were marital property, valuing educational assets in terms of their cost would be an erroneous application of equitable distribution law. As the Appellate Division explained, the cost of a professional degree "has little to do with any real value of the degree and fails to consider at all the nonfinancial efforts made by the degree holder in completing his course of study." Once a degree candidate has earned his or her degree, the amount that a spouse — or anyone else — paid towards its attainment has no bearing whatever on its value. The cost of a spouse's financial contributions has no logical connection to the value of that degree. . . .

This Court does not support reimbursement between former spouses in alimony proceedings as a general principle. Marriage is not a business arrangement in which the parties keep track of debits and credits, their accounts to be settled upon divorce. Rather, as we have said, "marriage is a shared enterprise, a joint undertaking . . . in many ways it is akin to a partnership." But every joint undertaking has its bounds of fairness. Where a partner to marriage takes the benefits of his spouse's support in obtaining a professional degree or license with the understanding that future benefits will accrue and inure to both of them, and the marriage is then terminated without the supported spouse giving anything in return, an unfairness has occurred that calls for a remedy. . . .

To provide a fair and effective means of compensating a supporting spouse who has suffered a loss or reduction of support, or has incurred a lower standard of living, or has been deprived of a better standard of living in the future, the Court now introduces the concept of reimbursement alimony into divorce proceedings. The concept properly accords with the Court's belief that regardless of the appropriateness of permanent alimony or the presence or absence of marital property to be equitably distributed, there will be circumstances where a supporting spouse should be reimbursed for the financial contributions he or she made to the spouse's successful professional training. Such reimbursement alimony should cover all financial contributions towards the former spouse's education, including household expenses, educational costs, school travel expenses and any other contributions used by the supported spouse in obtaining his or her degree or license.

O'BRIEN V. O'BRIEN

489 N.E.2d 712 (N.Y. 1985)

In this divorce action, the parties' only asset of any consequence is the husband's newly acquired license to practice medicine. The principal issue presented is whether that license, acquired during their marriage, is marital property subject to equitable distribution under Domestic Relations Law § 236(B)(5). . . . We now hold that plaintiff's medical license constitutes "marital property" within the meaning of Domestic Relations Law § 236(B)(1)(c) and that it is therefore subject to equitable distribution pursuant to subdivision 5 of that part. . . .

[The court then discussed New York equitable distribution law, which allows division of all marital property, defined as "all property acquired by either or both spouses during the marriage and before the execution of a separation agreement or the commencement of a matrimonial action, regardless of the form in which title is held." The court concluded that "the New York Legislature deliberately went beyond traditional property concepts when it formulated the Equitable Distribution Law. Instead, our statute recognizes that spouses have an equitable claim to things of value arising out of the marital relationship and classifies them as subject to distribution by focusing on the marital status of the parties at the time of acquisition. Those things acquired during marriage and subject to distribution have been classified as 'marital property' although, as one commentator has observed, they hardly fall within the traditional property concepts because there is no common-law property interest remotely resembling marital property."]

The determination that a professional license is marital property is ... consistent with the conceptual base upon which the statute rests. As this case demonstrates, few undertakings during a marriage better qualify as the type of joint effort that the statute's economic partnership theory is intended to address than contributions toward one spouse's acquisition of a professional license. Working spouses are often required to contribute substantial income as wage earners, sacrifice their own educational or career goals and opportunities for child rearing, perform the bulk of household duties and responsibilities and forgo the acquisition of marital assets that could have been accumulated if the professional spouse had been employed rather than occupied with the study and training necessary to acquire a professional license. ...

Plaintiff's principal argument, adopted by the majority below, is that a professional license is not marital property because it does not fit within the traditional view of property as something which has an exchange value on the open market and is capable of sale, assignment or transfer. The position does not withstand analysis for at least two reasons. First, as we have observed, it ignores the fact that whether a professional license constitutes marital property is to be judged by the language of the statute which created this new species of property previously unknown at common law or under prior statutes. Thus, whether the license fits within traditional property concepts is of no consequence. Second, it is an overstatement to assert that a professional license could not be considered property even outside the context of section 236(B). A professional license is a valuable property right, reflected in the money, effort and lost opportunity for employment expended in its acquisition, and also in the enhanced earning capacity it affords its holder, which may not be revoked without due process of law. That a professional license has no market value is irrelevant. Obviously, a license may not be alienated as may other property and for that reason the working spouse's interest in it is limited. The Legislature has recognized that limitation, however, and has provided for an award in lieu of its actual distribution.

Plaintiff also contends that alternative remedies should be employed, such as an award of rehabilitative maintenance or reimbursement for direct financial contributions. ... [N]ormally a working spouse should not be restricted to that relief because to do so frustrates the purposes underlying the Equitable Distribution Law. Limiting a working spouse to a maintenance award, either general or rehabilitative, not only is contrary to the economic partnership concept underlying the statute but also retains the uncertain and inequitable economic ties of dependence that the Legislature sought to extinguish by equitable distribution. Maintenance is subject to termination upon the recipient's remarriage and a working spouse may never receive adequate consideration for his or her contribution and may even be penalized for the decision to remarry if that is the only method of compensating the contribution. As one court said so well, "[t]he function of equitable distribution is to recognize that when a marriage ends, each of the spouses, based on the totality of the contributions made to it, has a stake in and right to a share of the marital assets accumulated while it endured, not because that share is needed, but because those assets represent the capital product of what was essentially a partnership entity." The Legislature stated its intention to eliminate such inequities by providing that a supporting spouse's "direct or indirect contribution" be recognized, considered and rewarded. Turning to the question of valuation, it has been suggested that even if a professional license is considered marital property, the working spouse is entitled only to reimbursement of his or her direct financial contributions. By parity of reasoning, a spouse's down payment on real estate or contribution to the purchase of securities would be limited to the money contributed, without any remuneration for any incremental value in the asset because of price appreciation. Such a result is completely at odds with the statute's requirement that the court give full consideration to both direct and indirect contributions "made to the acquisition of such marital property by the party not having title, including joint efforts or expenditures and contributions and services as a spouse, parent, wage earner and homemaker." If the license is marital property, then the working spouse is entitled to an equitable portion of it, not a return of funds advanced. Its value is the enhanced earning capacity it affords the holder and although fixing the present value of that enhanced earning capacity may present problems, the problems are not insurmountable. Certainly they are no more difficult than computing tort damages for wrongful death or diminished earning capacity resulting from injury and they differ only in degree from the problems presented when valuing a professional practice for purposes of a distributive award, something the courts have not hesitated to do. The trial court retains the flexibility and discretion to structure the distributive award equitably, taking into consideration factors such as the working spouse's need for immediate payment, the licensed spouse's current ability to pay and the income tax consequences of prolonging the period of payment and, once it has received evidence of the present value of the license and the working spouse's contributions toward its acquisition and considered the remaining factors mandated by the statute, it may then make an appropriate distribution of the marital property including a distributive award for the professional license if such an award is warranted. When other marital assets are of sufficient value to provide for the supporting spouse's equitable portion of the marital property, including his or her contributions to the acquisition of the professional license, however, the court retains the discretion to distribute these other marital assets or to make a distributive award in lieu of an actual distribution of the value of the professional spouse's license.

NOTES AND QUESTIONS

1. No state courts follow *O'Brien* in treating a degree as property except two panels of the Michigan Court of Appeals. *See* Postema v. Postema, 471 N.W.2d 912 (Mich. App. 1991); Wiand v. Wiand, 443 N.W.2d 464 (Mich. App. 1989). The ALI Family Dissolution Principles recommend against treating licenses, degrees, and the like as divisible property. ALI, Principles of the Law of Family Dissolution § 4.07(1), (2) (2002).

2. Even though few states treat degrees as property, most are willing to give relief to the spouse who is divorced at or near the end of the other spouse's professional schooling. However, as the following excerpt indicates, the states are far from uniform in the relief they provide.

ANN LAQUER ESTIN, *MAINTENANCE, ALIMONY, AND THE REHABILITATION OF FAMILY CARE*, 71 N.C. L. Rev. 721, 759-762 (1993): In dozens of cases addressing the "diploma dilemma," courts in different jurisdictions have invented new remedies, labeled with titles such as "property division alimony," "reimbursement alimony," "equitable restitution," or "equitable redemption alimony." In some states, reimbursement approaches directed to the diploma problem have been incorporated in maintenance and property division statutes. . . .

Although the restitution and reimbursement cases reflect more willingness to grant compensation to one marital partner, they also reflect deep tension between the economically rooted notion of restitution and the courts' ideal of marriage. Courts determined to compensate the supporting spouse in diploma dilemma cases have come up with theories that allow reimbursement, but they have also wrestled with restitution and family law principles in an effort to identify what types of losses or contributions should be reimbursed. As a result, the cases vary significantly in their definition of the types of marital support for which compensation may be ordered. At a minimum, reimbursement remedies cover the actual costs of a partner's education and professional training: tuition, books, and fees. Some remedies extend further to include payments for the educated partner's living expenses. Most courts specify that compensation is not appropriate for homemaking rather than financial support.

In some jurisdictions, courts compute restitution awards or reimbursement alimony far more broadly, including the lost earnings of the spouse who was educated during the marriage. In others, courts have computed their awards based on the lost opportunities of the spouse who worked instead of attending school. This leads in some cases to an award intended to cover the costs of an "equal educational opportunity" for the supporting spouse. In the most extreme cases, courts have authorized reimbursement remedies based on the present value of the educated spouse's increased future earnings. This method renders the "reimbursement" award indistinguishable from a property division award valuing then "dividing" the degree or license itself. . . .

California Family Code § 2641 (2014)

(a) "Community contributions to education or training" as used in this section means payments made with community or quasi-community property for education or training or for the repayment of a loan incurred for education or training, whether the payments were made while the parties were resident in this state or resident outside this state.

(b) Subject to the limitations provided in this section, upon dissolution of marriage or legal separation of the parties:

(1) The community shall be reimbursed for community contributions to education or training of a party that substantially enhances the earning capacity of the party. The amount reimbursed shall be with interest at the legal rate, accruing from the end of the calendar year in which the contributions were made.

(2) A loan incurred during marriage for the education or training of a party shall not be included among the liabilities of the community for the purpose of division pursuant to this division but shall be assigned for payment by the party.

(c) The reimbursement and assignment required by this section shall be reduced or modified to the extent circumstances render such a disposition unjust, including, but not limited to, any of the following:

(1) The community has substantially benefitted from the education, training, or loan incurred for the education or training of the party. There is a rebuttable presumption, affecting the burden of proof, that the community has not substantially benefitted from community contributions to the education or training made less than 10 years before the commencement of the proceeding, and that the community has substantially benefitted from community contributions to the education or training made more than 10 years before the commencement of the proceeding.

(2) The education or training received by the party is offset by the education or training received by the other party for which community contributions have been made.

(3) The education or training enables the party receiving the education or training to engage in gainful employment that substantially reduces the need of the party for support that would otherwise be required.

(d) Reimbursement for community contributions and assignment of loans pursuant to this section is the exclusive remedy of the community or a party for the education or training and any resulting enhancement of the earning capacity of a party. However, nothing in this subdivision limits consideration of the effect of the education, training, or enhancement, or the amount reimbursed pursuant to this section, on the circumstances of the parties for the purpose of an order for support pursuant to Section 4320.

(e) This section is subject to an express written agreement of the parties to the contrary.

See also Indiana Code § 31-15-7-6 (2014):

If the court finds there is little or no marital property, the court may award either spouse a money judgment not limited to the property existing at the time of final separation. However, this award may be made only for the financial contribution of one (1) spouse toward tuition, books, and laboratory fees for the postsecondary education of the other spouse.

EMPIRICAL DATA— THE VALUE OF EDUCATION

ANTHONY P. CARNEVALE, STEPHEN J. ROSE & BAN CHEAH, *THE COLLEGE PAYOFF: EDUCATION, OCCUPATIONS, LIFETIME EARNINGS 3-4*

Georgetown University Center on Education and the Workforce (2011)

[M]edian lifetime earnings rise steadily for workers with increasing educational attainment. Overall, the median lifetime earnings for all workers are $1.7 million, which is just under $42,000 per year ($20 per hour). Over a 40-year career, those who didn't earn a high school diploma or GED are expected to bring in less than $1 million, which translates into slightly more than $24,000 a year ($11.70 per hour). Obtaining a high school diploma adds 33 percent more to lifetime earnings;

the average annual earnings of people with a high school diploma are $32,600 ($15.67 per hour). Clearly, then, the economic penalty for not finishing high school is steep — almost $9,000 a year.

Having some postsecondary education, even without earning a degree, adds nearly one-quarter of a million dollars to lifetime earnings. Annual earnings rise to $38,700 ($18.69 per hour). Getting an Associate's degree adds another bump of nearly $200,000 in lifetime earnings. At $43,200 a year ($20.77 per hour), those with Associate's degrees earn nearly one-third more than those with just a high school diploma. These numbers demonstrate conclusively the advantage of non-baccalaureate postsecondary education.

Getting a Bachelor's degree adds another large increase in lifetime earnings. With median earnings of $56,700 ($27.26 per hour), or $2.3 million over a lifetime, Bachelor's degree holders earn 31 percent more than workers with an Associate's degree and 74 percent more than those with just a high school diploma. Further, obtaining a Bachelor's is also the gateway to entering and completing graduate education. About one-third of Bachelor's degree holders obtain a graduate degree.

All graduate degree holders can expect lifetime earnings at least double that of those with only a high school diploma. For those with a Master's degree (which includes those with Master's degrees in elementary teaching and in business administration), typical lifetime earnings are $2.7 million ($66,800 a year or $32 per hour). Moreover, earnings rise substantially for those with Doctoral and Professional degrees: Doctoral degree holders have lifetime earnings of $3.3 million ($81,300 per year; $39 per hour) while those with Professional degrees (mainly doctors and lawyers) have the highest earnings, making over $3.6 million over the course of a lifetime ($91,200 per year; $44 per hour). This is a 61 percent increase (nearly 1.4 million) over Bachelor's degree holders.

Parent-Child Support Duties

7

However controversial continuation of spousal support duties after divorce may be, everyone agrees that the parent-child relationship and the need for child support continue after and are in principle unaffected by changes in the relationship between the child's parents. Nonetheless, orders directed to parents inevitably and significantly affect the shape of the household in which children live, and this circumstance raises its own theoretical and practical problems. The following excerpt explains the development of the parents' legal duty to support their children and introduces some of the complexities in implementing that duty.

Leslie Harris, Dennis Waldrop & Lori R. Waldrop, *Making and Breaking Connections Between Parents' Duty to Support and Right to Control Their Children*

69 Or. L. Rev. 689, 692-708 (1990)

At least from the early seventeenth century, the English Poor Laws imposed a legal duty on parents to support their poor children to minimize the financial burden on the community. Well into the nineteenth century, however, the English courts refused to hold parents legally responsible for the support of their children outside this context.[1]

In contrast, during the nineteenth century American courts and legislatures established that under the private law, parents have a legal duty to support their children. The judicial path was not smooth, however. . . . Over the century, though, the judicial trend was to make parents' duty to support their children legally enforceable.

---

1. *See, e.g.*, Shelton v. Springett, 138 Eng. Rep. 549, 550 (1851); Mortimore v. Wright, 151 Eng. Rep. 502, 504 (1840); *see also* 1 W. Blackstone, Commentaries on the Laws of England 446-454 (Christian ed. 1807).

State legislatures also enacted statutes providing that parents had a duty to support their children.[2] The final draft of the New York Field Draft Civil Code declared the existence of such a duty.[3] . . .

The hesitation to make child support a legally enforceable duty did not reflect a belief that parents had no obligation. Blackstone, for example, discussed at length parents' moral duty to maintain and educate their children. Courts feared, however, that if this duty were legally enforceable, parents would lose control over their children to third parties or to the children themselves. . . .

When the courts did impose a legal support duty on parents, they protected parental control by structuring rules regarding the scope of the duty and the means of enforcing it which maximized parental discretion and made legal enforcement difficult. In addition, the expressed justification for requiring parents to support their children seems to have changed. In the eighteenth century Blackstone based parents' moral duty to support their children on their having begotten the children and, by implication, voluntarily undertaken to care for them. In contrast, some nineteenth century courts began to justify requiring parents to support their children as a corollary to their right to custody. Nineteenth century code drafters also grounded the support duty in the parent's right to custody. Custody includes not only physical custody — living with and caring for a child day to day — but also legal custody — the authority to determine how children will live and behave. Thus, such codes effectively linked parents' support duty to their right to exercise control over their children. . . .

The nineteenth century jurists' linkage of support duties and control rights seems consistent with their general inclination to define human relations in contractarian terms. One nineteenth century family law author even conceived parental authority over children as part of a contract between parents and children:

> The parent shows himself ready, by the care and affection manifested to his child, to watch over him, and to supply all his wants, until he shall be able to provide them for himself. The child, on the other hand, receives these acts of kindness; a tacit compact between them is thus formed; the child engages, by acts equivalent to a positive undertaking to submit to the care and judgment of his parent so long as the parent, and the manifest order of nature, shall coincide in requiring assistance and advice on the one side, and acceptance of them, and obedience and gratitude on the other.[4]

While discussions of parent-child relationships today may not use such blunt language, they still are often perceived as being based on exchange. Consider, for example, the claim that one reason absent fathers do not pay child support is that their loss of contact with and control over their children attenuates their

---

2. In 1936, Vernier wrote that all states except Kansas had civil statutes imposing this obligation. 4 C. Vernier, American Family Laws § 234, at 57 (1936).

3. "It is the duty of the father, the mother, and the children, of any poor person who is unable to maintain himself by work, to maintain such persons to the extent of their ability." N.Y. Code Commrs. Draft of a Civil Code for the State of New York § 97 (Final Draft 1865).

4. D. Hoffman, Legal Outlines (1836), quoted in Michael Grossberg, Governing the Hearth 235 (1985).

sense of responsibility to the children. This claim is partly empirical, but it also assumes that people's values and behavior are based on exchange. . . .

Current rationales for parental authority tend to justify it instrumentally as serving the best interests of children and society. Examples include claims that parents are in the best position to know and care about their children's needs, that giving parents authority encourages them to assume and discharge the responsibilities of parenthood, and that diffusing authority over how children will be raised promotes cultural and social diversity. . . .

Making parents' duty to support their children legally enforceable inherently limits the parents' control to some extent. However, in the intact family children cannot sue their parents to enforce this duty, for such suits would interfere too much with parental autonomy.[5] The available common law and statutory enforcement mechanisms — the necessaries doctrine and family expense statutes — protect parental control by making enforcement difficult. In addition, the scope of the support duty is defined by parental choices about their lifestyle and their children's lifestyle.

In the nineteenth century the courts extended the necessaries doctrine, which was originally used to enforce a husband's duty to support his wife, to include parental support.[6] . . .

In approximately twenty states, legislatures have enacted family expense statutes,[7] which, like the necessaries doctrine, permit creditors to sue parents for goods and services supplied to their children without requiring a prior promise by the parents to pay. Parental liability under these statutes is usually broader than under the necessaries doctrine. For example, the creditor may not have to prove that an item was a "necessary." Nevertheless, the statutes preserve some control for parents, since liability exists only for family expenses. Further, the statutes permit only suits by creditors; they do not authorize one family member to sue another for support.

As a practical matter, neither the necessaries doctrine nor a family expense statute is a very effective means of enforcing support obligations. Third parties are likely to be reluctant to rely on these statutes in supplying goods or services to a child, because if a parent refuses to pay, the supplier must bring suit. Thus, both as a matter of substantive law and in practice, the necessaries doctrine and the family expense statute present relatively little threat to parental control. . . .

The most common situation in which courts require parents to support their children, even though they do not have physical or legal custody of them, is when

---

5. J. Madden, The Law of Persons and Domestic Relations 392 (1931); Mandelker, Family Responsibility Under the American Poor Laws: 1, 54 Mich. L. Rev. 497, 499 n.4; Comment, Parent and Child — Child's Right to Sue Parent for Support, 15 N.C. L. Rev. 67 (1936); Comment, Extent of a Parent's Duty of Support, 32 Yale L.J. 825 (1923). Similarly, cohabiting spouses cannot sue each other for support. *See*, *e.g.*, McGuire v. McGuire, 157 Neb. 226, 59 N.W.2d 336 (1953).

6. The necessaries doctrine is covered in Chapter 2. — Ed.

7. 1 Homer Clark, The Law of Domestic Relations in the United States, §7.1, at 433-434 (2d ed. 1987).

the parents are separated or divorced.[8] An essential feature of such orders is that they impose a support duty on a person who no longer has legal authority to control the child.

During the nineteenth century as divorce became more common, the question of whether noncustodial fathers should be required to support their children arose increasingly. . . . Some noncustodial fathers argued that the legal duty to support arose from the right to custody, and that, therefore, they no longer had any such duty. Some fathers also argued that since they no longer had a right to their children's services, they should not be required to support them. Ultimately, courts usually rejected these blanket principles and ordered men who were at fault for the marital breakdown to pay child, as well as spousal, support. To the extent the noncustodial fathers' duty to support their children remained an open question, nineteenth century legislatures often resolved it by enacting separate maintenance and divorce statutes that empowered courts to award child support.

These judicial and statutory developments established that when parents divorce and children live with only one parent, the link between custody and support can be broken as well. Nevertheless, historical judicial reluctance to require divorced fathers to pay adequate sums for their children's support and to enforce support orders may be attributable in part to the lingering belief that support duties should coincide with custodial rights.

The first three parts of this chapter concern how the theoretical and principled issues discussed above play out in the determination of the amount of child support owed by a nonresidential parent. The last two parts consider the boundaries of intrafamilial support duties — when must parents support adult children, and when must adult children support their aging parents?

A. THE CURRENT CHILD SUPPORT MODEL

The extent to which judges' discretion should be limited by a formula or guideline was a recurring issue in the law of spousal support and property division. Not surprisingly, this issue has also arisen for child support. Federal legislation enacted

---

8. Courts also commonly order unmarried fathers not living with their children to pay child support. At least since Elizabethan times the support duty of unmarried fathers has been enforced when a child is receiving public assistance. However, outside this context unmarried fathers had no common law duty to support their children. Simmons v. Bull, 21 Ala. 501 (1852); Nixon v. Perry, 77 Ga. 530, 3 S.E. 253 (1887); Furillio v. Crowther, 16 Eccl. 302 (1826); Cameron v. Baker, 171 Eng. Rep. 1190 (1824); Hard's Case, 91 Eng. Rep. 22 (1795). Nineteenth century statutes also did not impose a support duty on unmarried fathers outside the poor laws. For a discussion of the treatment of nonmarital children in nineteenth century America, see Michael Grossberg, Governing the Hearth ch. 6 (1985).

during the 1980s mandates that all states use child support guidelines. 42 U.S.C. § 667. A Senate report explained the reasons for requiring guidelines:

> Although the child support enforcement program has greatly strengthened the ability of children to have support orders established and collected, there remains a continuing problem that the amounts of support ordered are in many cases unrealistic. This frequently results in awards which are much lower than what is needed to provide reasonable funds for the needs of the child in the light of the absent parent's ability to pay. In some instances, however, there are also awards which are unrealistically high.
>
> Some States have established guidelines to be used by the courts in setting the amount of child support orders. Where these guidelines exist, overall award levels tend to be somewhat higher than where the amount of the order is entirely discretionary with each judge. Moreover, the existence of guidelines tends to assure that there is reasonable consideration given both to the needs of the child and the ability of the absent parent to pay. This provides some protection for both parties.

S. Rep. No. 387, 98th Cong., 2d Sess. 40, reprinted in 1984 U.S. Code Cong. & Admin. News 2397, 2436. Federal regulations provide that child support guidelines must "take into consideration all earnings and income of the absent parent, be based on specific descriptive and numeric criteria and result in a computation of the support obligation." 45 C.F.R. § 302.56. This amount must be rebuttably presumed to be the correct amount of child support, and a deviation must be supported by specific findings based on criteria specified by state law. "Such criteria must take into consideration the best interests of the child. Findings that rebut the guidelines shall state the amount of support that would have been required under the guidelines and include a justification of why the order varies from the guidelines." *Id.*

Early child support guidelines required parents to share the "costs" of raising a child. While this approach has substantial intuitive appeal, no state today bases its guidelines on this approach. The following excerpt explains the difficulties with the cost approach and describes the approaches most widely used in the United States.

ROBERT G. WILLIAMS, *GUIDELINES FOR SETTING LEVELS OF CHILD SUPPORT ORDERS*

21 Fam. L.Q. 281, 287-289, 290-293, 295 (1987)

Why has an equitable level of child support been so difficult to determine by the courts? The root of the problem is that most expenses related to child rearing are commingled with expenditures benefiting all household members. In a recent economic study, Espenshade estimates that over one-half of family expenditures on children fall into just three categories: food, housing and transportation.[9] It is apparent that, on an individual case basis, it is difficult to separate out a child's share of these major household expenses. . . .

---

9. The reference is to T.J. Espenshade, Investing in Children: New Estimates of Parental Expenditures (1984), which was considered the most authoritative study then available. — Ed.

... Since most expenditures made on behalf of children are intertwined with general household expenditures, it is not only virtually impossible to disentangle them reliably, but many costs of children become hidden in the larger pool of spending for the total household. Consequently, the full children's share of expenditures in those categories is generally not recognized, with the result that even parents may underestimate the true costs of bringing up their own children. ...

... What are the costs of children above the minimum level needed for basic subsistence? Economists agree that, above the minimum level, there is no absolute "cost" of rearing a child. Studies of household expenditure patterns make it clear that parents with higher income spend more on their children because they can afford to do so. A more accurate way of posing this question, then, is: What are the normal levels of spending on children within households above the poverty level? Estimating these normal levels of spending is the only method that economists have of estimating costs of children in such households.

The best available evidence on this subject comes from the aforementioned Espenshade study. The study is based on data from 8,547 households drawn from the 1972-1973 Consumer Expenditure Survey, a national survey of household expenditure patterns conducted by the Bureau of Labor Statistics. ...

As can be seen from Espenshade's estimates for three socioeconomic levels, amounts spent on children in intact households go up as family income increases. Based on Espenshade's figures, we have derived estimates for the proportion of net income expended for two children by income level of the parents. These estimates ... show that spending on children can be validly described as proportions of household income, although the proportions decline as household income increases. Thus, spending on one child varies from 26.0 percent of net income at low-income levels to 19.2 percent at the upper end of the income range. Similarly, spending on two children decreases from 40.4 percent at low-income levels to 29.7 percent in high income households.

A third question relevant to determining levels of child support is: How is spending on children affected by the number of children in the family? From Espenshade's findings, we can develop estimates of the proportion of current family consumption devoted to one, two, and three children. ... [E]stimates of expenditures on children as a proportion of current family consumption are 26.2 percent for one child, 40.7 percent for two children, 51.0 percent for three children, and 57.5 percent for four children. ...

There is a common misperception that the declining increments primarily reflect economies of scale in rearing children. Instead, these figures seem to indicate a decreasing level of expenditures for each child as family size increases. Espenshade estimates, for example, that virtually equal amounts are spent on each child in a two-child family, but that the spending level for each represents only about three-fourths the amount that would have been spent on one child alone. ...

A. Flat Percentage Guideline

This simplest type of guideline sets child support as a percentage of obligor income, with the percentage varying according to the number of children. Some percentage guidelines are based on gross income (before tax) while others are based on net income (after mandatory deductions). . . .

The Wisconsin percentage of income standard may be the most well-known example of a flat percentage guideline. Child support orders are determined only on the basis of the obligor's gross income and the number of children to be supported. The percentages of obligor gross income allocated to child support are 17 percent for one child, 25 percent for two children, 29 percent for three children, 31 percent for four children and 34 percent for five or more children. The percentage of income standard is designed to be comparable to a tax in simplicity of structure and ease of application. It is intended for use in conjunction with mandatory income withholding for all child support orders from the date a child support order is established. . . .

Under the percentage of income standard, the child support obligation is not adjusted for the income of the custodial parent. The standard assumes that each parent will expend the designated proportion of income on the child, with the custodial parent's proportion spent directly. There is no adjustment for other factors such as child care expenses, extraordinary medical expenses, or age of child. . . .

B. INCOME SHARES MODEL

. . . The income shares model is based upon the precept that the child should receive the same proportion of parental income that would have been received if the parents lived together. Thus, the income shares model calculates child support as the share of each parent's income estimated to have been allocated to the child if the parents and child were living in an intact household. . . .

Computing child support under the income shares model involves three basic steps:

1. Income of the parents is determined and added together.
2. A basic child support obligation is computed based on the combined income of the parents. This obligation represents the amount estimated to have been spent on the children jointly by the parents if the household were intact. The estimated amount, in turn, is derived from economic data on household expenditures on children. A total child support obligation is computed by adding actual expenditures for work-related child care expenses and extraordinary medical expenses.
3. The total obligation is then pro-rated between each parent based on their proportionate shares of income. The obligor's computed obligation is payable as child support. The obligee's computed obligation is retained and is presumed to be spent directly on the child. This procedure simulates spending patterns in an intact household in which the proportion of income allocated to children depends on total family income.

The income shares model has been specified in both net income and gross income versions. It incorporates a self-support reserve for the obligor, under which the formula is not applied in determining child support until an obligor's income exceeds the poverty level (although a minimum order is set on a case-by-case basis).

C. Delaware Melson Formula

The Delaware Child Support Formula was developed by Judge Elwood F. Melson and was adopted by the Delaware Family Court for statewide use beginning in January 1979. As stated in a recent report of the Delaware Family Court, the basic principles of the Melson child support formula are as follows:

Parents are entitled to keep sufficient income for their most basic needs to facilitate continued employment.

Until the basic needs of children are met, parents should not be permitted to retain any more income than required to provide the bare necessities for their own self-support.

Where income is sufficient to cover the basic needs of the parents and all dependents, children are entitled to share in any additional income so that they can benefit from the absent parent's higher standard of living.

JANE C. VENOHR, *CHILD SUPPORT GUIDELINES AND GUIDELINES REVIEWS: STATE DIFFERENCES AND COMMON ISSUES*

47 Fam. L.Q. 327, 332-336 (2013)

By 1990, thirty-one states had implemented the Income Shares Model, fifteen states had implemented the Percentage of Obligor Income Model, three states had implemented the Melson Formula, and two states had implemented another guidelines model that is no longer in use. Since 1990, nine states have switched guidelines models. With the exception of Montana, all of the states switched to the Income Shares Model. The most common switch was from the Percentage of Obligor Income Model to the Income Shares Model. Most states switched because the Income Shares Model can more readily factor in and address a larger variety of case circumstances than can the traditional Percentage of Obligor Income Model. This includes circumstances in which the custodial parent has more income than the noncustodial parent, shared-parenting time, and other circumstances.

Guidelines award amounts among states using the same guidelines model rarely produce identical amounts. As a consequence, one guidelines model does not consistently result in lower or higher support awards than another guidelines model.

Some Percentage of Obligor Income guidelines apply the same percentage to all obligor incomes, whereas other Percentage of Obligor Income guidelines use a sliding scale. Only about half of state guidelines categorized as Income Shares guidelines resemble the prototype Income Shares Model developed in the 1980s. Several states have developed their own version of the Income Shares Model. . . .

The numbers underlying state guidelines using the same model differ for several reasons. The most obvious difference is that states rely on different measurements of child-rearing expenditures. There are at least eight different studies of child-rearing expenditures that form the basis of current state guidelines. These studies vary in data years, and some of the studies rely on different methodologies to measure child-rearing expenditures. Some consider expenditures made by families surveyed in the early 1970s, whereas others consider expenditures from families surveyed as recently as 2009. When initially developing their guidelines, most states considered one of two economic studies that were available at the time. Since then, new studies that are based on more current expenditure data have become available. Many states have updated their guidelines formulas/ schedules based on the new studies. Some of the studies currently used by states during their guidelines reviews are discussed in more detail later in this article.

There are several other economic assumptions made in the development of guidelines, such as assumptions concerning tax rates, price levels, and some types of child-rearing expenditures. . . . Nonetheless, the classification of a guide-lines income basis as gross or net income is not always definitive because some states develop their own definitions of income available for child support. For example, . . . New York, unlike most gross-income guidelines, actually excludes FICA from income available for child support. New York and Wisconsin both rely on the Percentage of Obligor Income Model and assign essentially the same per-centage of income to determine the support award (i.e., 17% of gross income for one child), but they produce very different guidelines amounts because Wisconsin and New York define guidelines income differently.

Many states with gross-income guidelines also incorporate assumptions about tax filing status and federal and state income tax rates from the year the state last updated its guidelines. In all, the year that the state last updated its guidelines can exacerbate differences because, over time, tax rates change, prices change, and new economic studies on the cost of child rearing become available. . . . [E]ighteen states have updated their guidelines in the last few years, another sixteen states updated sometime between 2005 and 2009, two states updated sometime between 2000 and 2004, seven states updated sometime in the 1990s, and eight states have never updated.

There are several other differences underlying state guidelines formulas/ schedules. Some states with relatively high or low incomes or housing costs make additional adjustments to account for their particular state's economic cir-cumstances. Many state guidelines factor in the actual cost of the child's health insurance and out-of-pocket medical expenses on a case-by-case basis so the core formulas/schedules in these states exclude some or all of these healthcare-related expenses. Many states make a similar adjustment for work-related childcare expenses. In contrast, other states guidelines do not contain similar exclusions to their core formulas/schedules.

The following example of the operation of the Percentage of Obligor Income formula and a generic Income Shares formula, based on parents' gross income, is adapted from Robert G. Williams, Development of Guidelines for Child Support Orders: Advisory Panel Recommendations and Final Report II-106 through II-108 (Office of Child Support Enforcement 1987).

Father lives alone, and the two children live with Mother. Father's gross monthly income is $1,600. Mother has a gross monthly income of $1,200 and spends $150 per month on work-related child care. The children's health insurance and uninsured care cost $200 per month.

INCOME SHARES FORMULA

a) Calculate the parents' total monthly income and each parent's proportionate share of the total:

$$\text{Total} = \$1,600 + 1,200 = \$2,800$$

$$\text{Father's share} = 1,600/2,800 = 57.14\%$$

$$\text{Mother's share} = 1,200/2,800 = 42.86\%$$

b) Calculate the total child support obligation by adding the basic obligations (read applicable tables) to child care costs and extraordinary medical expenses. Here, assume that the applicable table says that the basic support obligation for two children for parents earning a total of $2,800 per month is $646.

$$\text{Total} = \$646 + \$150 + \$200 = \$996$$

c) Calculate noncustodial parent's share by multiplying total child support obligation by his or her proportion from step a.

$$57.14\% \text{ of } \$996 = \$569.11$$

WISCONSIN FORMULA

a) Percent of Obligor's gross income for 2 children = 25%
b) 25% of $1,600 = $400.

NOTES AND QUESTIONS

1. The Percentage of Obligor Income approach is less sensitive to variations in the situations of individual families than the Income Shares approach. Why might a state nevertheless choose it?

2. Noncustodial parents often justify their resistance to paying child support by their claim that the money "isn't really going to the kids." Such a claim raises at least two issues. The first is deciding which expenditures really "go to the kids" and which benefit the custodial parent. The second issue is the form of child support orders. The typical order requires the obligor to pay a fixed sum to the other parent rather than pay specific expenses. Further, if the obligor supplies goods or services directly to the child, the obligor does not usually get an offset for them against the child support ordered. Should courts require the obligor to pay expenses directly rather than bundling everything into a lump sum? Should courts require recipients of child support to account for the money? Or are these kinds of limitations inconsistent with the custodial parents' prerogatives? *See* Krampen v. Krampen,

997 N.E.2d 73 (Ind. App. 2013), reversing an order requiring a mother to account for weekly child support payments of $3000 per week when the father claimed she was diverting some to her start-up veterinary hospital. The father admitted that the children's food, clothing, and housing were adequate, and the mother testified that she was financing the business with loans; the court, therefore, concluded that the evidence did not show that the mother had misappropriated the child support.

3. The Income Shares and Percentage of Obligor Income child support guidelines are based on the principle that parents should share their income with their children, and the size of that share is determined by how much an average intact family (both parents and all children living together) would spend on the children. What arguments support this model, the "continuity of expenditure" approach, as the most appropriate measure of the duty of parents when the family is not intact? Do the Income Shares or the Percentage of Obligor Income formulas, both of which base the child support obligation on the extra amount that parents spend when a child is added to the family, include all the family expenditures that benefit the children? Do they require either parent to contribute more to the child's support than he or she would spend if the family were intact?

4. A study using data from the U.S. Census Survey of Income and Program Participation (SIPP) and the Current Population Survey (CPS) concludes that the family of an average child younger than 6 spends 4.9 percent of after-tax income on child care but that expenditures vary. Families of 63 percent of the children in the study had no child care expenses, while families of 10 percent of the children spent almost 30 percent of their after-tax income on day care. Single-parent families typically spend more than married-couple families, but the researchers could find no relationship between level of expenditures and socio-economic status. Dan T. Rosenbaum & Christopher Ruhm, The Cost of Caring for Young Children (Institute for the Study of Labor (IZA), Bonn, Ger., Nov. 2005). Because of this great variation, most child care formulas do not fold child care costs into the basic formula, but allocate responsibility for this expense separately.

5. Children's medical expenses also vary dramatically, and child support formulas generally do not fold them into the basic obligation but deal with them separately. Federal and state laws require that child support decrees specifically address how children's medical expenses will be paid. For employed parents this can usually be done most economically by ordering a parent whose employer provides insurance to include the children in his or her plan.

B.   CHALLENGES TO THE CONTINUITY OF EXPENDITURES MODEL

States must review their child support guidelines at least once every four years to ensure that they produce "appropriate" orders. In conducting these reviews, the states must consider "economic data on the cost of raising children," and they must analyze case data to determine the extent to which orders deviate from the guidelines. 45 C.F.R. § 302.56. As states have gone through this process, and as more information about the operation of guidelines has become available, critics have challenged both the theoretical assumptions and empirical foundations of existing guidelines. The two most widely discussed alternatives are those proposed by the American Law Institute's Principles of the Law of Family Dissolution and by proponents of the cost-shares approach.

LESLIE JOAN HARRIS, *THE PROPOSED ALI CHILD SUPPORT PRINCIPLES*

35 Willamette L. Rev. 717, 727-733 (1999)

In a memorandum introducing the *Principles*, the reporter explained that existing child support guidelines, "unlike the earlier need-based discretionary rubric, . . . are neither intended nor designed to register and reflect the need of the child in the residential household. They do not, in any meaningful manner, consider the resources independently available to the residential household."[10] Therefore, the combined amount that the parents spent or would spend on the child if all lived in the same household has little directly to do with how much should be spent on the child living with only one parent.

Perhaps the most essential fact the marginal expenditures model fails to take into account is that the costs of the two households together are greater than one household alone because of loss of economies of scale. How this economic burden should be distributed, particularly with regard to its impact on the child, is a critical question that the marginal expenditures model simply does not address.

As it turns out, if the child's parents have equal amounts of income before child support is paid, the marginal expenditures model spreads the loss of economies of scale equally between the households. However, when the parents' incomes are unequal, child support guidelines based on the marginal expenditures model perpetuate, and can exacerbate, the difference in the two households' standards of living. . . .

As in first generation child support formulas, the *Principles* provide that parents will share income with their child or children. Unlike many first generation formulas, the ALI version explicitly acknowledges that each parent's interests sometimes diverge from those of the child, as well as from each other's. It seeks a balance among these interests that can be defended on principle.[11] The *Principles* evaluate the need for and adequacy of child support awards by comparing the economic standard of living in the households of the parents, rather than looking only at the relative income of the parents. Where the household of the residential parent has a lower standard of living, the *Principles* call for increased child support

---

10. Grace G. Blumberg, Reporter's memorandum to the members of the Institute, Mar. 7, 1998, ALI, Principles of the Law of Family Dissolution xxix (Tent. Dr. 3, Pt. II, 1998).

11. See Principles § 3.03.

to narrow the gap; where the residential parent's household has a higher standard of living, child support is lower. . . .

1. THE INTERESTS OF THE CHILD

A common aspiration expressed in judicial opinions and popular discussions concerning child support is that the child should not suffer economically because the parents are not living together. However, the *Principles* do not attempt to achieve this goal because doing so would infringe too greatly on the rights of the nonresidential parent. For the same reason, the *Principles* do not adopt the modest-sounding goal that the child should not suffer disproportionately as compared to other family members. The *Principles* argue that to achieve even this goal, it would be necessary to use an equal living standards formula for child support. The *Principles* reject this formula because of its intrusion on the nonresidential parent's interests. . . .

To avoid this, the *Principles* compromise the child's interests and provide instead that the goals of the child support formula should be to: (1) allow the child to "enjoy a minimum decent standard of living when the resources of both parents together are sufficient to achieve such result without impoverishing either parent"; (2) allow the child to "enjoy a standard of living not grossly inferior to that of the child's higher income parent"; and (3) prevent the child from suffering "loss of important life opportunities that the parents are economically able to provide without undue hardship to themselves or their other dependents."[12]

2. THE INTERESTS OF THE RESIDENTIAL PARENT

The most fundamental interest of the residential parent recognized by the *Principles* is not to bear disproportionately the direct and indirect costs of child rearing.[13] . . .

3. THE INTERESTS OF THE NONRESIDENTIAL PARENT

The *Principles* argue that the marginal expenditure principle, which, as discussed above, is the basis for most child support formulas today, fundamentally expresses a principle of justice for the nonresidential parent: to contribute no more to the support of the children than if the parent were living with the children in a two-parent household.[14] The *Principles* accept this measure as a starting point but do not allow it to prevail in all situations.

> At bottom, the marginal expenditure principle reflects a strong cultural belief in the primacy of the earner's claim to his earnings. . . . It is true that any transfer of income

---

12. This analysis is sent out at Principles § 3.03 and comments thereto. — Ed.
13. Principles § 3.03, comment d at 6.
14. *Id.* at § 3.03, comment e at 7-8.

to the child's residential household may also be enjoyed by other members of the household, including the residential parent. This is an inevitable and unavoidable effect of any child support transfer, and is not itself an adequate reason for limiting or disapproving child support. Nevertheless, the payor parent has an interest in limiting the measure of his child support obligation to his relationship to the child, rather than to the residential household.[15] . . .

[T]his notion of justice arguably overstates the nonresidential parent's claim. The continuity of marginal expenditure measure may be understood to be predicated on the notion that, insofar as he is the dominant earner, the nonresidential parent should be held harmless by divorce, that is, he should be no worse off economically after divorce than he was during marriage. Yet being no worse off suggests, in the alternative, that he should not be heard to complain so long as he does not suffer a decline in his standard of living. To the extent that he will not suffer a decline in his standard of living (using household equivalence measures), there is no persuasive reason he should not pay more than what he would have spent on the children were he living with him. This does not imply equalization of household standards of living. In view of the lost economies of scale, the standard of living in the child's residential household will necessarily drop well below the preseparation standard if the standard of living of the higher income nonresidential parent is held constant.[16]

Although the *Principles* do not use "maintenance of the support obligor's marital standard of living" as the basis for any part of the child support obligation, they use this standard as a touchstone for determining whether the obligor is being treated fairly in particular circumstances. Indeed, to evaluate the fairness of proposed orders, the *Principles* consistently compare the standard of living of each household after payment of child support to the standard of living that the parties would enjoy if they all lived in the same household.

[The Principles begin by establishing a "base amount" of child support, which is the amount that would be required under a well-constructed marginal expenditure formula. When the residential parent's income is lower than the non-residential parent's, as is true in most cases, a supplement is added to the base amount, so as to make the standards of living in the two households closer, though not equal. As the income of the residential parent approaches that of the non-residential parent, the amount of the supplement decreases. When the two parents' households have equal incomes, the supplement is completely eliminated, leaving the base alone as the amount of child support owed. When the income of the residential parent's household is greater than the nonresidential parent's, the ALI Principles call for the child support obligation to be decreased below the base amount. ALI, Principles of Family Dissolution § 3.05.]

The following article describes the cost-shares approach to child support guidelines, whose leading proponent is economist R. Mark Rogers.

---

15. *Id.* at 18.
16. *Id.* § 3.03, Reporters Note to comment e at 18.

JO MICHELL BELD & LEN BIERNAT, *FEDERAL INTENT FOR STATE CHILD SUPPORT GUIDELINES: INCOME SHARES, COST SHARES, AND THE REALITIES OF SHARED PARENTING*

37 Fam. L.Q. 165, 173-174, 177-180 (2003)

. . . The cost shares alternative was developed in the mid-1990s by affiliates of the Children's Rights Council (CRC), a non-profit organization with both national and state chapters "that works to assure children meaningful and continuing contact with both their parents and extended family regardless of the parents' marital status." Its proponents argue that cost shares guidelines are fundamentally different from income shares guidelines, principally in the estimation of child costs and the allocation of these estimated costs between the parents. These differences, in their view, make the model superior to income shares.

While it is true that there are important differences between the prevailing income shares model for child support guidelines and the cost shares model, there are some fundamental similarities as well. Both approaches attempt to establish a clear relationship between child support guidelines and expenditures on children by parents, although the underlying estimates for those expenditures are indeed quite different in the two models. Both approaches base support on the incomes of both parents, with the cost shares model reflecting a Melson-style method of determining each parent's income available for child support. But the cost shares model makes assumptions about expenditure patterns and cost offsets in separated families that income shares models do not routinely make. . . .

The cost shares model borrows several principles from existing income shares guidelines but reflects a very different set of economic assumptions about expenditures on children in separated families. Cost shares guidelines use a Melson formula approach to the determination of income; rely on estimates of expenditures on children in single-parent families after offsets for "tax benefits attributable to the children"; and apply a joint physical custody cross-credit approach to the calculation of the final support obligation. A cost shares order for support is calculated as follows:

(1) Determine each parent's share of their combined income available for child support. As in all three Melson formula states, a cost shares guideline subtracts a self-support reserve from a parent's net income to arrive at his or her income available for child support. The calculation of net income under cost shares includes "an imputed child support order for other biological or adopted children residing with the parent," which is not present in any of the Melson formula states. In addition, the self-support reserve under cost shares is slightly higher than the highest reserve under existing Melson guidelines. . . .

(2) Determine the parents' combined "basic" expenditures on the children. Cost shares guidelines estimate expenditures on the children quite differently than do income shares guidelines. First, cost shares uses estimated single-parent spending as the standard for spending by separated parents. Where the income shares approach adds together the incomes of the parents and estimates what two-parent families with that level of income spend for children's share of housing, food,

transportation, and other pooled expenses, the cost shares approach averages the parents' incomes and estimates what a single-parent family with that level of income spends for these needs. Effectively, this means that the children will be allocated a share of only half the combined income of the parents. Second, "fixed expenses" incurred by either parent (i.e., expenses that do not move with the children between households) are then subtracted from this estimate of single-parent spending on the children. The exact categories of expense in the "fixed expense" component vary with different versions of the cost shares model, but may include expenditures by each parent for housing for the children, medical insurance premiums, and court-ordered life insurance premiums. The remaining amount is considered the "basic child cost" subject to apportionment between the parents.

(3) Determine each parent's "total incurred child cost." The cost shares model also makes very strong assumptions about the way in which children's expenses are distributed between parents who live in separate households. The model assumes that each parent's spending on the children is determined solely by the amount of time the children spend in each household. There is no assumption that custodial parents incur a larger share of the costs by virtue of their status as custodial parents. Consequently, each parent's "total incurred child cost" is calculated as follows:

a. Apportion the basic child cost between the parents according to each parent's percentage of parenting time. The resulting amount is presumed to be the parent's "incurred basic child costs."

b. Add to each parent's incurred basic child costs any other actual expenditures for the children by each parent. Such expenditures include the "fixed expenses" previously subtracted from the estimates of total basic costs (e.g., life insurance premiums, medical insurance premiums, housing), as well as expenses not included in the table of "basic child costs" (e.g., child care, education). The resulting amount for each parent is presumed to be that parent's total expenditures for the children.

c. Calculate the "tax benefit attributable to the children" for each parent and subtract this benefit from the parent's total expenditures for the children to arrive at the parent's "total incurred child costs." Like the definition of "fixed expenses," the definition of "tax benefit attributable to the children" may vary with different versions of the model, but the authors generally describe it as the difference between the after-tax income of the parent after receiving his or her actual child-related tax benefits, and the after-tax income of the parent assuming single taxpayer/no dependents status.

(4) Determine the final order for support through a cross-credit calculation. This step resembles the formula used in some states to establish support for extended parenting time, but without the multiplier that is typically applied to child costs to reflect the increased cost of caring for children in separate households. Each parent's obligation to the other parent is calculated by multiplying the parent's share of their combined monthly income available for child support by the other parent's total incurred child costs. The parent who owes the higher amount to the other parent is the obligor, and pays the difference between the two obligations to the other parent.

NOTES AND QUESTIONS

1. All child support formulas use some kind of standardized measure to determine how much money parents at various levels of income "should" spend on their children. Parents and their attorneys regularly question where these amounts come from, and even experts who understand the economic analysis upon which the measures are founded debate the validity of various methodologies. Since no methodology for determining child support is value-neutral, Professor Ellman argues that drafters of child support guidelines must directly confront these value choices rather than leaving them to the technical experts who have developed the various measures. Ira Mark Ellman, Fudging Failure: The Economic Analysis Used to Construct Child Support Guidelines, 2004 U. Chi. Legal F. 167. What are these choices? How would drafters go about balancing the interests of children and their parents? Would it be desirable to return to the preguideline days when judges decided child support based on individualized assessments of children's needs and parents' ability to pay?

2. Ellman participated in a major effort to revise Arizona's guidelines based on reassessment of these policy choices. The work group's proposal attempted to ameliorate three problems with existing guidelines, which were based on the Income Shares Model:

> First, they specify payment amounts that have very little effect on the child's living standard. If the custodial parent is poor, the custodial household remains poor after receiving the child support payment, even when the support obligor's income is high. Second, children whose parents have the same combined income can find themselves in dramatically different financial circumstances after divorce, if one lives primarily with the higher-earning parent and the other with the lower-earning parent. Third, low-income obligors are expected to pay unreasonably high support amounts to high-income custodial parents, given that in these cases the child enjoys a much higher living standard than the obligor even before any support is paid.

Ira Mark Ellman, A Case Study in Failed Family Law Reform: Arizona's Child Support Guidelines, 54 Ariz. L. Rev. 137, 151-152 (2012). The proposal, like the ALI Principles, focused on the standards of living in the two parents' households after child support was paid, rather than on the additional money that hypothetically would have been spent had the parents and children lived in the same household, which is the basis of the Income Shares Model. However, fathers' rights activists successfully opposed the changes, and the legislature ultimately enacted a law prohibiting adoption of the model that the study committee developed. *Id.* at 155.

3. Other critics of the continuity of expenditure approach also focus on the post-judgment standard of living and advocate for the equal living standards (ELS) model. This approach was proposed in Judith Cassetty, G.K. Sprinkle, Ralph White & Bill Douglass, The ELS (Equal Living Standards) Model for Child Support Awards, *in* Essentials of Child Support Guidelines Development: Economic Issues and Policy Considerations 329 (Women's Legal Defense Fund staff eds., 1986). It provides that the judge should order sufficient child support to equalize the living standards in the households of the child's two parents and

clearly links the nonresidential parent's obligation both to the income of the residential parent and to the living standard in the residential parent's household. *See* Marsha Garrison, The Economic Consequences of Divorce: Would Adoption of the ALI Principles Improve Current Outcomes?, 8 Duke J. Gender L. & Pol'y 119 (2001); Marsha Garrison, An Evaluation of Two Models of Parental Obligation, 86 Cal. L. Rev. 41 (1998). However, the ELS model has been adopted in no state, and the Massachusetts Supreme Judicial Court recently reversed a trial court's child support order equalizing the incomes of the mother's and father's (high-income) households where their child spent equal amounts of time in each home. The court said that the approach was inconsistent with the state guidelines. M.C. v. T.K., 973 N.E.2d 130 (Mass. 2012). What problems do you see that might explain this approach's lack of political acceptance?

4. A group of researchers, including Professor Ellman, have conducted a large-scale study of public opinion about child support, using members of Pima County, Arizona, jury pools. A series of experiements strongly supports the finding that lay people generally do not intuitively find either the Percentage of Obligor Income or the Income Shares approach to determining child support to be the most fair way of setting support. Instead, they choose a method in which the dollar amount of a noncustodial parent's obligation increases with his or her income but the percentage of net income that he or she owes does not vary. They also believed that, the lower the custodial parent's income, the more rapidly the noncustodial parent's obligation should increase. This pattern held true for all demographic groups, even while those groups' judgments varied in other respects (e.g., women generally favored overall higher child support obligations than men). In general, the respondents also believed that the amount of the obligor's child support obligation should be lower if the parents had never married and that an unmarried obligor's child support payment should increase less rapidly as income increased than would a married or formerly married obligor's payment. (The authors explain that if the respondents had supported the Percentage of Obligor Income approach, they would not have said that the obligors' payments should vary with the custodial parents' incomes, and if they had supported the Income Shares approach, they would not have varied the percentage of the total obligation that each parent paid based on their relative incomes.) All of the studies are discussed in Sanford L. Braver, Ira Mark Ellman & Robert J. MacCoun, Public Intuitions About Fair Child Support Obligations: Converging Evidence for a "Fair Shares Rule" 20 Psychol. Pub. Pol'y & L. 146 (2014). *See also* Ira M. Ellman & Sanford L. Braver, Lay Intuitions About Child Support and Marital Status, 23 Child & Fam. L.Q. 465 (2011); Ira Mark Ellman, Sanford Braver & Robert J. MacCoun, Abstract Principles and Concrete Cases in Intuitive Lawmaking, 36 Law & Hum. Behav. 96 (2012).

5. Additional commentaries on the ALI child support proposals include Karen Syma Czapanskiy, ALI Child Support Principles: A Lesson in Public Policy and Truth-Telling, 8 Duke J. Gender L. & Pol'y 259 (2001); Leslie Joan Harris, The ALI Child Support Principles: Incremental Changes to Improve the Lot of Children and Residential Parents, 8 Duke J. Gender L. & Pol'y 245 (2001). *See also* Ira Mark Elllman & Tara O'Toole Ellman, The Theory of Child Support, 45 Harv. J. on Legis. 107 (2008).

6. Several commentators have proposed that households should generally be treated as economic units for purposes of support duties, thus eliminating inter-household support payments altogether in many circumstances. For example, Judge R. Michael Redman suggests that the noncustodial parent should remain financially responsible for the children until the custodial parent remarries. At that point the custodial stepparent would replace the noncustodial parent unless and until the custodial parent remarries somebody else. R. Michael Redman, The Support of Children in Blended Families: A Call for Change, 25 Fam. L.Q. 83, 89 (1991). *See also* Leslie Joan Harris, Reconsidering the Criteria for Legal Fatherhood, 1996 Utah L. Rev. 461. Professor David Chambers has observed:

> ... Without great prodding, most parents who have never lived with their children — most typically, fathers who are the subject of paternity suits — never pay support at all. Even divorced fathers who have lived with their children typically pay regularly for only a short time, then pay less, and then often pay nothing. . . . Neither love nor a sense of moral responsibility induces most absent parents to pay as much as they could.
>
> Current patterns of visitation are similar. Most fathers of children from outside of marriage do not see their children at all. Every study of divorced, noncustodial fathers confirms a pattern somewhat comparable to their patterns of payment of support: visits begin with frequency and then typically taper off within a few years. . . .
>
> Many people attribute noncustodial parents' low rates of payment and visitation to indifference to their children's welfare. It is nonetheless possible to ascribe more sympathetic causes for declining feelings of responsibility over time. Although a minority of divorced, noncustodial fathers sustain a vital relationship with their children years after separation, many fathers who see their children no more frequently than once a week or every other week find the visitation relationship unnatural and unsatisfying. Over time, they feel less and less a part of their children's lives. . . .
>
> If the noncustodial parent remarries, he develops a new center for his life and derives satisfactions from new children with whom he shares life day-to-day. . . .

David Chambers, The Coming Curtailment of Compulsory Child Support, 80 Mich. L. Rev. 1614, 1623-1624 (1982).

What arguments support such a change? What problems can you see, and how would you modify this proposal to deal with them?

C. APPLYING CHILD SUPPORT FORMULAS

TUCKMAN v. TUCKMAN

61 A.3d 449 (Conn. 2013)

EVELEIGH, J. . . . The defendant and the plaintiff . . . were married on November 3, 1990. They have two children, a son, born in 1994, and a daughter, born in 1996. Both parties have substantial income and assets available to them.

In 2005 and 2006, the defendant had an income of $530,000 and $945,000, respectively. The defendant's assets included a one-third stake in BJK Partners (BJK), an investment partnership with her two older brothers, and a one-third ownership interest in Offices Limited, Inc., a family office furniture business. According to the parties' financial affidavits, at the time of trial, the defendant's share of BJK was valued at approximately $2.7 million, while her share of Offices Limited, Inc., was valued at $1.25 million. The defendant also earned well over $2 million through her BJK investment partnership between 1996 and 2007. In 2006 and 2007, the plaintiff, who worked in the commodities division at Merrill Lynch, each year earned a base compensation of $200,000 with a bonus of $1.5 million. In 2008, the plaintiff was set to begin employment at Citicorp, where he was to receive base pay along with a bonus of $1.25 million in 2009 and 2010.

"On September 13, 2006, the plaintiff brought this dissolution action by complaint in which he sought a dissolution of the marriage. . . ."

In its memorandum of decision in the present case, the trial court entered the following order regarding child support: "As a contribution [toward] expenses related to the children when they are with [the defendant], the [plaintiff] shall pay child support to the [defendant] in the amount of $250 per week for each child." The trial court also stated in its memorandum of decision that it "considered the gross and net income of the parties."

Thereafter, the defendant filed a motion for articulation in which, inter alia, she requested that the trial court "articulate and clarify . . . [f]or purposes of the [trial] court's child support orders . . . did the [trial] court accept either parties' child support calculation worksheet and what did the [trial] court find to be the net income of each party" Although the trial court articulated and clarified some issues in its memorandum of decision, it did not address this request. In reviewing the trial court's memorandum of decision, the Appellate Court concluded as follows: "Based on the record before us and the court's memorandum of decision, we cannot conclude that the court properly fashioned its child support order. The court's order failed to follow the guideline's tables, and, more importantly, its memorandum of decision failed to make any reference to the guidelines. . . ."

In Maturo v. Maturo, supra, 296 Conn. at 89-90, 995 A.2d 1, this court considered the impact of the child support statutes, regulations and guidelines on high income families. In doing so, this court recognized that "[t]he legislature has enacted several statutes to assist courts in fashioning child support orders. Section 46b-84 provides in relevant part: '(a) Upon or subsequent to the annulment or dissolution of any marriage or the entry of a decree of legal separation or divorce, the parents of a minor child of the marriage, shall maintain the child according to their respective abilities, if the child is in need of maintenance. . . .

"'(d) In determining whether a child is in need of maintenance and, if in need, the respective abilities of the parents to provide such maintenance and the amount thereof, the court shall consider the age, health, station, occupation, earning capacity, amount and sources of income, estate, vocational skills and employability of each of the parents, and the age, health, station, occupation, educational status and expectation, amount and sources of income, vocational skills, employability, estate and needs of the child.'"

. . .

"The guidelines include a schedule for calculating 'the basic child support obligation' for families that have two minor children and a combined net weekly income ranging from $310 to $4000. The guidelines provide in relevant part that, '[w]hen the parents' combined net weekly income exceeds [$4000], child support awards shall be determined on a case-by-case basis, and the current support prescribed at the [$4000] net weekly income level shall be the minimum presumptive amount.' Id., at § 46b-215a-2b(a)(2). . . . In accordance with the statutory directives set forth in General Statutes § 46b-215b(a), the guidelines emphasize that the support amounts calculated thereunder are the correct amounts to be ordered by the court unless rebutted by a specific finding on the record that such an amount would be inequitable or inappropriate. Any such finding shall include the amount required under the guidelines and the court's justification for the deviation, which must be based on the guidelines' '[c]riteria for deviation. . . .'

"In sum, the applicable statutes, as well as the guidelines, provide that all child support awards must be made in accordance with the principles established therein to ensure that such awards promote 'equity,' 'uniformity' and 'consistency' for children *at all income levels.' . . .* Although the guidelines grant courts discretion to make awards on a 'case-by-case' basis above the amount prescribed for a family at the upper limit of the schedule when the combined net weekly income of the parents exceeds that limit, which is presently $4000; the guidelines also indicate that such awards should follow the principle expressly acknowledged in the preamble and reflected in the schedule that the child support obligation as a percentage of the combined net weekly income should decline as the income level rises. Thus, an award of child support based on a combined net weekly income of $8000 must be governed by the same principles that govern a child support award based on a combined net weekly income of $4000, even though the former does not fall within the guidelines' schedule. Finally, although courts may, in the exercise of their discretion, determine the correct percentage of the combined net weekly income assigned to child support in light of the circumstances in each particular case, including a consideration of other, additional obligations imposed on the noncustodial parent, any deviation from the schedule or the principles on which the guidelines are based must be accompanied by the court's explanation as to why the guidelines are inequitable or inappropriate and why the deviation is necessary to meet the needs of the child."

. . . Although the trial court in the present case stated that it considered the gross and net income of the parties, it never determined the net income of the parties in its memorandum of decision. Without a determination of the net income of the parties, the trial court could not, as required by the guidelines, determine the presumptive amount of support required by the guidelines. . . .

Accordingly, we conclude that the Appellate Court properly determined that the trial court abused its discretion when it awarded $250 per child per week to the defendant without determining the net income of the parties, mentioning or applying the guidelines, or making a specific finding on the record as to why it was deviating from the guidelines.

II

We next address the defendant's claim that the trial court improperly determined that her subchapter S allocated income should be included in her annual net income. Specifically, the defendant asserts that the trial court improperly relied on her personal tax returns showing the taxable income of an S corporation of which she is a shareholder. The defendant claims that the trial court improperly relied on that income in determining alimony and child support, despite the fact that it was not available to her. In response, the plaintiff claims that the trial court did not improperly consider the defendant's gross income and that it properly considered the defendant's subchapter S allocated income under the facts of the present case. We agree with the defendant.

"It is well settled that a court must base child support and alimony orders on the available net income of the parties, not gross income."

In the present case, the trial court stated in its memorandum of decision as follows: "It should be noted that an examination of [the defendant's] tax returns shows that in 2006 her income was approximately $945,000 and the year before approximately $580,000." The trial court further stated in its memorandum of decision, as clarified by a subsequent rectification, "[the defendant] has substantial income available to her (at least $500,000 per annum)."

An examination of the defendant's tax returns demonstrates that a substantial portion of her taxable income for the years 2005 and 2006 was income from her share of the S corporation, Offices Limited, Inc. Because Offices Limited, Inc., is organized as an S corporation, all of its capital gains and losses, for federal income tax purposes, pass through Offices Limited, Inc., to the individual shareholders, and any federal income tax liability on capital gains is the responsibility of the individual shareholder. . . . The trial court did not, however, make any finding as to what portion of the income reported on her tax returns was actually available to the defendant and what portion was merely "[pass] through earnings" of the S corporation. In fact, the defendant's testimony at trial indicated that none of the shareholder taxable income was available to her, but was retained by the corporation for investment. She testified that only her salary of approximately $85,000 was available income.

Although this court has not directly addressed how to treat, for purposes of determining a parent's financial obligations, undistributed earnings of an S corporation that for income tax purposes are attributable to the parent-shareholder, we are persuaded by the Massachusetts Supreme Judicial Court, which addressed this issue in J.S. v. C.C., 454 Mass. 652, 912 N.E.2d 933 (2009). The Massachusetts Supreme Judicial Court while recognizing that courts in a number of other jurisdictions have considered how to treat the retained earnings of an S corporation that are passed through to a shareholder for purposes of measuring and imposing a child support obligation, concluded as follows: "[T]he better reasoned decisions require a case-specific, factual inquiry and determination. . . . We follow the lead of these cases, and similarly conclude that a determination whether and to what extent the undistributed earnings of an S corporation should be deemed available income to meet a child support obligation must be made based on the particular circumstances presented in each case. Such a fact-based inquiry is necessary to balance, inter alia, the considerations that a well-managed corporation may be required to retain a portion of its earnings to maintain corporate operations and survive fluctuations in income, but corporate structures should not be used to shield available income that could and should serve as available sources of child support funds."

The Massachusetts Supreme Judicial Court noted some relevant factors that a trial court judge should weigh in determining what portion of undistributed corporate earnings may be available to a shareholder for a child support obligation, "[f]irst, a shareholder's level of control over corporate distributions — as measured by the shareholder's ownership interest — is a factor of substantial importance. . . . A minority shareholder lacking the power unilaterally to order a distribution may be relatively unlikely to have access to retained income of the corporation. . . . A majority shareholder may be relatively more likely to have access to retained funds and ability to manipulate pass-through income, and a sole shareholder even more so. . . . Second, the judge should evaluate the legitimate business interests justifying retained corporate earnings. . . . Third, the judge should weigh affirmative evidence of an attempt to shield income by means of retained earnings. . . . In that regard, the corporation's history of retained earnings and distributions may be relevant. . . . Finally, it is important to consider the allocation of burden of proof in relation to the treatment of an S corporation's undistributed earnings for purposes of determining income available for child support; this is an issue on which courts in other jurisdictions are split. Some courts shift the burden of proof depending on the shareholder's level of control over the corporation: a minority shareholder is presumed not to have access to retained income and therefore does not carry the burden of proof, while a majority or sole shareholder is presumed to have access to retained income and does carry the burden of proof. . . . Other courts place the burden on the shareholder to present evidence that he or she does not have access to retained income regardless of the shareholder's ownership percentage in the corporation; they reason that the shareholder is the party with greater access to the evidence. . . . We are persuaded that the second approach is more appropriate, because we agree that regardless of the percentage of his or her ownership interest, the shareholder is likely to have greater access to relevant information about the corporation than a party who is not connected to it."

In considering the same issue, the Florida's District Court of Appeal concluded that a majority shareholder's pass through income from an S corporation should not be included in available income for the purposes of determining alimony and child support. Zold v. Zold, 880 So. 2d 779, 781 (Fla. App. 2004). In doing so, it recognized as follows: "When a corporation has more than one shareholder, an officer/shareholder has a fiduciary duty to all shareholders. The corporation is not the personal piggy bank for any one shareholder simply because that shareholder may have a controlling interest in the corporation and is also the chief executive officer. Financial responsibilities to creditors and employees must be satisfied before distributions to shareholders take place if a corporation is to remain viable. Once the distributions are found to be possible, the distributions must be pro-rata in accordance with the percentage ownership of the capital stock of the corporation. Court ordered obligations in marital litigation should not place an ex-marital partner in the position of having to breach a corporate fiduciary obligation in order to avoid the possibility of a court finding that partner contemptuous."

... [T]he record in the present case demonstrates that the trial court looked to the defendant's entire income as measured for income tax purposes as available income for determining the alimony and child support order. The trial court did not make any findings as to the particular facts or circumstances of the S corporation of which the defendant was a shareholder. Accordingly, we conclude that remand is appropriate in the present case for a determination of what portion of the defendant's income was available income for purposes of fashioning alimony and child support orders. ...

The judgment of the Appellate Court is affirmed and the case is remanded to that court with direction to reverse the judgment of the trial court as to the financial orders in their entirety and to remand the case to that court for a new trial in accordance with this opinion.

NOTES AND QUESTIONS

1. A major issue in *Tuckman* is how to set child support when the income of one or both parents is higher than the top amount on the child support scale. By what method did the *Tuckman* trial court resolve this problem? On remand, what will the trial court be required to do? What does the court mean when it says that the guidelines "indicate that such awards should follow the principle expressly acknowledged in the preamble and reflected in the schedule that the child support obligation as a percentage of the combined net weekly income should decline as the income level rises"? In high-income cases, most courts do not simply extrapolate the percentages in the scale to the parents' actual income. Why not?

2. Several courts have remarked that "no child needs three ponies" to explain limits on child suppport in high-income cases. Downing v. Downing, 45 S.W.3d 449 (Ky. App. 2001); Isaacson v. Isaacson, 792 A.2d 525 (N.J. App. Div.), *cert. denied*, 807 A.2d 195 (N.J. 2002); Pearson v. Pearson, 751 N.E.2d 921 (Mass. App. 2001). The origin of the phrase seems to be In re Patterson, 920 P.2d 450, 455 (Kan. App. 1996). What does it mean?

On the other hand, some states' guidelines include a percentage formula that courts must follow in high-income cases. For example, in Florida, if the parents' combined income is more than $10,000 per month, the child support is the highest amount on the scale plus 5 percent for one child, 7.5 percent for two children, 9.5 percent for three children, 11 percent for four children, 12 percent for five children, and 12.5 percent for six children. Fla. Stat. Ann. § 61.30(6)(b) (2014).

In some states the guidelines simply do not apply in very-high-income cases, and courts have discretion to set support under preguideline law. Dyas v. Dyas, 683 So. 2d 971 (Ala. Civ. App. 1995); In re Marriage of Krone, 530 N.W.2d 469 (Iowa App. 1995); Battersby v. Battersby, 590 A.2d 427 (Conn. 1991). In a number of states courts begin with the guideline amount that would apply if the parents' income were equal to the guideline maximum and then determine whether the facts warrant deviating upward. *See*, *e.g.*, Ga. Code Ann. § 19-6-15(i)(2)(a) (2014).

The authors of a recent annual survey of family law developments commented that state child support laws show some of the greatest variation in treatment of child support obligations of high-income parents. Linda D. Elrod & Robert G. Spector, A Review of the Year in Family Law: Working Toward More Uniformity in Laws Relating to Families, 44 Fam. L.Q. 469, 470 (2011); *see also* Lori W. Nelson, High-Income Child Support, 45 Fam. L.Q. 191 (2011).

3. In several high-income cases, including a number involving professional athletes, in which the parent was likely to receive a very high income for only a short time, courts have permitted orders that contemplate or even require that some current child support be saved to provide for the child after the parent's income goes down. *See, e.g.*, Henry v. Beacham, 686 S.E.2d 892 (Ga. App. 2009); Passemato v. Passemato, 427 Mass. 52, 691 N.E.2d 549 (1998); Nash v. Mulle, 846 S.W.2d 803 (Tenn. 1993); Mary L.O. v. Tommy R.B., 544 N.W.2d 417 (Wis. 1996) (allowing a court to order the establishment of an educational trust fund). *See also* Boyt v. Romanow, 664 So. 2d 995 (Fla. Dist. Ct. App. 1995). This approach is not permitted in other states, which say that child support can be ordered only to provide for the child's current needs. *See, e.g.*, Lang v. Koon, 806 N.E.2d 956 (Mass. App. 2004). For further information, *see* Judith G. McMullen, The Professional Athlete: Issues in Child Support, 12 Marq. Sports L.J. 411 (2001).

4. The other major issue in *Tuckman* is how to treat earnings of a subchapter S corporation that are allocated to a parent for purposes of the federal income tax but that are not actually paid out to the parent as a dividend. What arguments generally support including such income in the child support formula calculation? What arguments support a decision not to include it? Should it matter whether the parent is a sole proprietor, a majority shareholder, or a minority shareholder?

The Minnesota Supreme Court interpreted its child support guidelines as requiring inclusion of a parent's share of a subchapter S corporation's income after expenses, regardless of whether it is distributed to or available to him or her. However, the court pointed out, a deviation from the formula amount may be justified if the income is not available to the parent. Haefele v. Haefele, 837 N.W.2d 7903 (Minn. 2013). How is this approach different from that in *Tuckman*? Does the difference matter?

5. The *Tuckman* majority concluded that income that the mother had to report for purposes of the federal income tax was not income for purposes of the child support guidelines. Generally, courts have held that the treatment of an item for purposes of the federal income tax does not determine its treatment for purposes of calculating child support. *See, e.g.*, Asfaw v. Woldberhan, 55 Cal. Rptr. 3d 323 (Cal. App. 2007); Fisher v. Fisher, 171 P.3d 917 (Okla. 2007); Eagley v. Eagley, 849 P.2d 777 (Alaska 1993); Turner v. Turner, 586 A.2d 1182 (Del. 1991); In re Sullivan, 794 P.2d 687 (Mont. 1990). *But see* In re Marriage of Stevenson, 765 N.W.2d 811 (Wis. App. 2009) (under Wisconsin percentage of income formula, if beneficiary of trust must pay taxes on undistributed income, income must be included in child support calculation). Should income and expenses be treated the same for purposes of both income taxes and child support? Why or why not?

6. Child support guideline definitions of income are usually very inclusive, and courts have construed them broadly. Retirement income, lottery winnings, personal injury settlements, and spousal support have been treated as income. *See, e.g.*, Wood v. Wood, 403 S.E.2d 761 (W. Va. 1991); In re Micaletti, 796 P.2d 54 (Colo. App. 1990); Genna Rosten, Consideration of Obligor Spouse's or Parent's Personal Injury Recovery or Settlement in Fixing Alimony or Child Support Award, 59 A.L.R.5th 489 (1998 with weekly updates). The states are divided in

their treatment of inheritances. In some, the total amount of the inheritance is treated as income, while in others only the income that the inheritance generates is counted.

7. On the deduction side, legitimate business expenses are generally deductible for owners of small businesses. Employees cannot usually deduct their expenses, though, because average costs of living are include in parents' self-support reserves.

8. Despite earlier commentary which suggests that parents commonly settle for child support below the presumptive guideline amount, the majority of courts have held that this is not permissible unless a downward deviation is otherwise justified under the state's criteria for rebutting the presumption established by the formula. *See, e.g.,* Cox v. Cox, 776 P.2d 1045 (Alaska 1989); Ching v. Ching, 751 P.2d 93 (Haw. App. 1988); Peerenboom v. Peerenboom, 433 N.W.2d 282 (Wis. Ct. App. 1988). The Department of Health & Human Services has also taken the position that states should require parties who stipulate to child support to justify obligations that deviate from the presumptive amount calculated under the guidelines. 56 Fed. Reg. 22,347 (May 15, 1991).

On the other hand, in general, parents may enter into enforceable contracts for more child support than a court could order or for a longer term, and if the parents agree, courts ordinarily may incorporate such agreements into their orders. *See, e.g.,* Short v. Short, 131 So. 3d 1149 (Miss. 2014).

PROBLEMS

1. Father's employer pays for an apartment and a company car for him. Should the fair market value of these fringe benefits be treated as income for purposes of calculating child support? What about contributions that the employer makes to Father's retirement account?

In a jurisdiction that bases child support on net income, should Father be able to deduct mandatory amounts withheld from his pay to fund his pension? How about extra amounts that he contributes voluntarily to the pension? What if Father is self-employed and regularly contributes to a retirement plan over which he has sole control?

2. Father, a certified public accountant, is a minority shareholder in a closely held accounting firm; the other shareholders are his father and two brothers. Mother, a medical doctor, is a sole practitioner whose practice is incorporated. Last year each business retained some of its earnings rather than paying them out as dividends. Should the retained earnings be included as income?

3. Father and Mother dated briefly in college but broke up when Mother learned she was pregnant. Mother dropped out of school when the baby was born; now, eight years later, she works as a secretary earning $3000 per month. Father graduated from law school four years ago and has just been hired by a major law firm after having completed a prestigious clerkship. At his new firm he earns $14,000 per month. Mother has successfully argued that Father's new job justifies modifying child support, which had been set at $1290. The highest amount on the child support scale is $1437 for one child whose parents' combined income is $10,000 per month. Following *Tuckman*, the court has ordered Father to pay

$2500 per month in child support. Father appeals. What arguments should the parties make?

While the percentage of income model did not include an adjustment for visitation, the income shares and Melson models have always provided for adjustments when each parent has the children for a substantial amount of time, generally defined as at least 25 to 35 percent of the time. Robert G. Williams, Guidelines for Setting Levels of Child Support Orders, 21 Fam. L.Q. 281 (1987). This approach has been criticized, based on the claim that nonresidential parents who spend less time than this with their children still incur substantial expenses. William V. Fabricius & Sanford L. Braver, Non-Child Support Expenditures on Children by Nonresidential Divorced Fathers: Results of a Study, 41 Fam. Ct. Rev. 321 (2003). This claim is also one of the foundations of the argument in favor of the cost-shares formula approach, above. Supporters of the most widely adopted model respond that the study by Fabricius and Braver is methodologically flawed and argue that is it not a good idea to calibrate child support to visitation time because visitation tends to decline over time and because such calibration is likely to promote continuing hostilities between parents over how much visitation should and does occur. Irwin Garfinkel, Sara McLanahan & Judith Wallerstein, Visitation and Child Support Guidelines, 42 Fam. Ct. Rev. 342 (2004). In turn, Fabricius and Braver dispute the substantive accuracy of these claims. William V. Fabricius & Sanford L. Braver, Expenditures on Children and Visitation Time: A Reply to Garfinkel, McLanahan, and Wallerstein, 42 Fam. Ct. Rev. 350 (2004).

Despite this empirical uncertainty, all states' child support rules provided for adjustments for shared parenting time. Linda D. Elrod & Robert G. Spector, A Review of the Year in Family Law, 46 Fam. L.Q. 471, 528 Chart 3 (2013). See also Stephanie Giggetts, Application of Child Support Guidelines to Cases of Joint-, Split-, or Similar Shared-Custody Arrangements, 57 A.L.R.5th 389 (1998 with weekly updates). In the common case where the residential parent's income is lower than the nonresidential parent's, the result is a reduced child support award unless the total amount to be shared is increased to recognize the increased costs of the child being in two households, as the drafters of the Income Shares model recommended. See Williams, above.

While the argument favoring a closer link between parenting time and child support was originally made in support of lowering the support payments of nonresident parents, the next case explores how this principle should be employed when the residential parent's income is substantially higher than that of the nonresidential parent.

COLONNA V. COLONNA

855 A.2d 648 (Pa. 2004)

Justice NEWMAN. . . . Appellant, Mary M. Colonna (Mother), and Appellee Robert J. Colonna (Father), were married in 1983 and separated in 1996. . . . At the time of separation, Father sought primary legal and physical custody of the parties' four children, who at the time ranged in age from nine to three years old. Pending the outcome of Father's custody petition, the parties agreed to a temporary order of shared legal and physical custody, pursuant to which the children lived three and one-half days per week with each parent. . . .

On November 19, 1997, the trial court ordered Father to pay Mother $6,132.00 per month ($73,584.00 per year) in child support and to provide health insurance for Mother and the children. The trial court also ordered Father to pay the interest portion of the mortgage on the marital home; homeowners, personal property and automobile insurance; private school tuition; and other expenses. . . .

By Order dated May 4, 1998, the trial court awarded primary legal and physical custody to father during the school year, and primary legal and physical custody to Mother during the summer. Mother has partial custody of one or more of the children on Tuesday and Thursday during the school year, and Father has partial custody of one or more of the children on Tuesday and Thursday during the summer. The parties alternate holidays and weekends throughout the year, and each parent has two weeks with the children for summer vacation.

On July 24, 1998, Father sought to terminate child support on the basis that he was now the children's primary custodian. . . . A hearing was held before a master in October of 1998, at which time Father introduced his 1997 tax return indicating monthly net income of $16,130.00 ($193,560.00 per year), which was a significant decrease from the monthly net income of $85,942.00 ($1,031,304.00 per year) shown on his 1996 tax return. He presented evidence of living expenses and reasonable needs in the amount of $14,834.23 per month ($178,010.76 per year). The master assessed Mother a net earning capacity of $4,607.00 per month ($55,284.00 per year). Mother presented the same reasonable needs as she did during the 1997 support hearing, namely $28,208.00 per month ($338,496.00 per year) for herself and the children, with $21,106.00 per month ($253,272.00 per year) attributable to the children. She maintained that her expenses were the same as they had been when the parties shared custody equally.[17] The master concluded that Mother's earning capacity was unchanged, but that Father's monthly net income was now $16,130.00 ($193,560.00 per year).

The master determined that Mother had custody 27% of the year, and Father had custody 73% of the year. She was troubled by the disparities in the parties' income and the fact that Mother has certain fixed expenses incident to her alternating weekend and summer custody. . . . [The master recommended that Father be ordered to pay Mother $294 per month in child support, based on the findings that at the level of their combined incomes, the parents' combined child support obligation should be $5868 per month. The master allocated this between the parents proportionately to their incomes and to the amount of time the children spent with each of them.]

Mother and Father both filed exceptions to the master's recommendation. By Order dated April 27, 1999, the trial court sustained Mother's exceptions in part,

---

17. We note that a parent incurs certain fixed costs related to providing the children with a home in which to exercise his or her period of partial custody. Costs such as mortgage or rent payments, insurance, utilities, etc. remain the same whether the children are in a parent's custody or not.

and ordered Father to pay $810.00 per month ($9,720.00 per year) for support of the children. "This order award was calculated using the presumptive minimum under the new guidelines multiplied by the percentage of Mother's custody time." In an Opinion in support of the Order, the trial court stated:

> In this proceeding, the hearing officer recommended a child support amount which was offset by [Mother's] obligation to husband for child support. I agreed with the hearing officer's decision that it was not appropriate in this case to terminate support based solely on the custodial situation. However, [Father] had not filed for child support against [Mother] and I found that it was inappropriate to offset any child support due [Mother] by any amount that she would owe [Father]. Therefore, I awarded [Mother] support based on the guidelines reduced to the percentage of her partial custody time.

Father appealed to the Superior Court, which reversed in a published Opinion. The Superior Court concluded that for purposes of calculating child support, the custodial parent is the obligee and the non-custodial parent is the obligor. Because the children spend 73% of the time with Father and 27% with Mother, the Superior Court determined that Father, as the obligee, does not owe child support to Mother, who is the obligor. . . .

We adamantly disagree with this conclusion. Like the master and the trial court, we are troubled by the disparity in the parties' incomes and are concerned that the refusal to consider this as a factor when fashioning a support order may be contrary to the best interests of the children. We must always be mindful of the fact that the support laws work in conjunction with our custody laws. The General Assembly has declared:

> [I]t is the public policy of this Commonwealth, when in the best interest of the child, to assure a reasonable and continuing contact of the child with both parents after a separation or dissolution of the marriage and a sharing of the rights and responsibilities of child rearing by both parents. . . .

23 Pa. C.S. § 5301. Where the parent who does not have primary custody has a less significant income than the custodial parent, it is likely that he or she will not be able to provide an environment that resembles the one in which the children are accustomed to living with the custodial parent. While a downward adjustment in lifestyle is a frequent consequence of divorce that affects both adults and children, we would be remiss in failing to ignore the reality of what happens when children are required to live vastly different lives depending upon which parent has custody on any given day. To expect that quality of the contact between the non-custodial parent and the children will not be negatively impacted by that parent's comparative penury vis-à-vis the custodial parent is not realistic. Issuing a support order that allows such a situation to exist clearly is not in the best interests of the children.

Therefore, where the incomes of the parents differ significantly, we believe that it is an abuse of discretion for the trial court to fail to consider whether deviating from the support guidelines is appropriate, even in cases where the result would be to order child support for a parent who is not the primary custodial parent. . . .

In a case such as the instant matter, the trial court should inquire whether the non-custodial parent has sufficient assets to provide the children with appropriate housing and amenities during his or her period of partial custody. We specifically note that the term "appropriate" does not mean equal to the environment the children enjoy while in the custodial parent's care, nor does it mean "merely adequate." The determination of appropriateness is left to the discretion of the trial court, upon consideration of all relevant circumstances. . . .

. . . Because we conclude that a parent with primary custody may be ordered to pay child support to a parent with partial custody, we reverse the Order of the Superior Court and remand the case to the trial court for a determination of support for the parent with partial custody.

Chief Justice CAPPY, dissenting. Because I believe that a custodial parent should not be obligated to pay child support to a noncustodial parent, I must respectfully dissent.

The majority has declared that where "the incomes of the parents differ significantly, we believe that it is an abuse of discretion for the trial court to fail to consider whether deviating from the support guidelines is appropriate. . . ." The majority further decrees that "the trial court should inquire whether the noncustodial parent has sufficient assets to provide the children with appropriate housing and amenities during his or her period of partial custody." The majority provides an exceedingly vague definition of "appropriate housing and amenities," stating that "the term 'appropriate' does not mean equal to the environment the children enjoy while in the custodial parent's care, nor does it mean 'merely adequate.'" Finally, the majority specifically states that this ruling is not limited to those high income cases where the combined net income of the parents exceeds $15,000.00 per month, but rather encompasses all situations where there is a "significant disparity in income."

I find this analysis to be troubling for several reasons. First, I can perceive no objective standards within the rule it sets forth. How does a trial court determine what is "appropriate housing and amenities"? Furthermore, what constitutes a "significant disparity" in income? I am concerned that we are providing the trial courts and the practicing bar precious little guidance as to how the majority's rule should be applied.

Second, I find the majority's approach disquieting because I believe it transforms a child support action into a quasi-equitable distribution action. In my view, the majority's new rule is not so much addressing whether the needs of the children are being met (which is a proper subject of a child support action), but rather is focused on augmenting the wealth of the noncustodial parent. While such a focus may be proper in an equitable distribution matter, it has no place in a child support action. A child support action should not be used to jerry-rig a new balance between the respective financial positions of the spouses.

Finally, and most importantly, I am not in accord with the majority's foundational premise concerning the relationships between parents and children. The majority appears to be of the belief that if there is a disparity in income, the parent-child relationship will perforce be corrupted by the wealthier parent's desire to "buy the affection of the children. . . ." The majority goes so far as to state that it is unrealistic to believe that a noncustodial parent's relationship with her child will not suffer where the custodial parent is more wealthy than the noncustodial parent. The majority believes we should capitulate to what it perceives to be a social reality, and redistribute the wealth so that the affections of the child will not be alienated due to a parent's inability to provide the child with material advantages comparable to those provided by the wealthier parent.

I am disturbed by this approach. First, I can find no basis in the law for the proposition that a noncustodial spouse must be enabled, via payments from the custodial parent, to provide material advantages and entertain her children in the same lavish fashion as may the custodial parent. This simply has not been the law of this Commonwealth.

Furthermore, I am disturbed by the philosophy underpinning this rule. Unlike the apparent view of the majority, I do not believe that the health of any given parent-child relationship is measured by a parent's ability to provide a surfeit of expensive possessions or experiences for her child. Rather, the parent-child relationship thrives, or withers, based on the availability of intangibles such as love, attention, and affection. While it may be true that we live in a highly materialistic culture, does this fact stand in contradiction to the timeless realities of parenting? Or, to put it colloquially, *can* money buy love? I think not. And, more importantly, I balk at this court's implication that not only are a child's affections for sale, but also that our judiciary should be in the business of fostering the market for such a "commodity."

For the foregoing reasons, I respectfully dissent.

NOTES AND QUESTIONS

1. In *Colonna*, if the custodial relationship had been reversed, so that the mother had the children 73 percent of the time, the father would surely have been ordered to pay child support. In such a case, should the amount that he spends while the children are with him reduce the amount of support that he pays? If the children live with each parent half the time and the parents' incomes are widely disparate, as in *Colonna*, should child support be ordered from the wealthier to the poorer parent? Does it logically follow that if the residential parent's income is very high, he or she should pay child support to the nonresidential parent for periods of "visitation"? Why or why not?

If the parties had two children, and one lived full time with the mother and the other full time with the father, would the same principles apply that govern in cases of shared custody?

2. In *Colonna*, the father's income was almost four times that of the mother. What if his income had only been twice hers; should the court have ordered him to pay support to her then? By how much must their incomes differ before a court enters an order as in *Colonna?*

NOTE: CHILD SUPPORT OBLIGATIONS OF LOW-INCOME PARENTS

When a parent has little or no income, the first issue that must be considered is whether additional income should be imputed to the parent on the theory that he or she could reasonably be expected to earn more. The question of when income should be imputed to a parent is similar to the question of when a support obligation should be reduced because the obligor's income has decreased, to the extent that both depend on a judgment about whether the obligor parent should be expected to earn more than he or she does. Modification of support based on reduced income is covered in Chapter 8.

Parents with very low incomes who cannot earn more are generally not totally exempt from child support. Many guidelines provide for a minimum child support obligation, such as $25 or $50 per month, since all parents are obligated to support their children. However, the courts in In re Marriage of Gilbert, 945 P.2d 238 (Wash. App. 1997), and Rose ex rel. Clancy v. Moody, 629 N.E.2d 378, 380 (N.Y. 1993), held that a rule that provided for a minimum monthly order violated the federal requirement that amounts determined by a child support formula must be treated as creating a rebuttable presumption.

Most guidelines and courts that have considered the issue have held that public assistance payments, from either Supplemental Security Income (based on disability or old age) or Temporary Assistance to Needy Families, are not "income" from which a parent may be ordered to pay child support. *See* Burns v. Edwards, 842 A.2d 186 (N.J. Super. A.D. 2004) (discussing cases from around the country); Angela E. Epps, To Pay or Not to Pay, That Is the Question: Should SSI Recipients Be Exempt from Child Support Obligations?, 34 Rutgers L.J. 63 (2003). In comparison, most guidelines and courts include Social Security Disability payments received by parent or a child in the calculation of child support, though the states vary in their approaches. *See* Tori R.A. Kricken, Child Support and Social Security Dependent Benefits: A Comprehensive Analysis and Proposal for Wyoming, 2 Wyo. L. Rev. 39 (2002).

A number of courts have held that child support orders should be issued against incarcerated parents, even though the parent has no ability to pay while in prison; the payments become a debt which the parent is expected to pay upon release. *See* Karen Rothschild Cavanaugh & Daniel Pollack, Child Support Obligations of Incarcerated Parents, 7 Cornell J.L. & Pub. Pol'y 531, 532 (1998); Frank J. Wozniak, Loss of Income Due to Incarceration as Affecting Child Support Obligation, 27 A.L.R.5th 540 (1995 with weekly updates).

D. POST-MAJORITY CHILD SUPPORT

LESLIE HARRIS, DENNIS WALDROP & LORI R. WALDROP, *MAKING AND BREAKING CONNECTIONS BETWEEN PARENTS' DUTY TO SUPPORT AND RIGHT TO CONTROL THEIR CHILDREN*

69 Or. L. Rev. 689, 717-720 (1990)

Today we ordinarily think of parents' support duty as terminating when a child attains the age of majority. However, in the nineteenth and into the twentieth century the determination of when parents were no longer required to support their children depended on the child's actual capacity for self-support and submission to parental control.

Older adolescents, especially boys, were considered capable of at least partial self-support and often worked for wages. So long as a minor child lived with or was supported by the parents and had not been emancipated, the father was entitled to the child's earnings. By the same token, a parent was obligated to support a minor child so long as the child remained under the parent's control. A parent might discharge, at least partially, the duty to support a minor child capable of earning wages by giving the child the right to retain the wages. Some authorities went so far as to say that a parent was not required to support a child to the extent that the child could earn money. Further, a parent was not required to support a minor child capable of self-support who left the parent and struck out on his or her own. Some courts expressed this idea by saying that parents were not obligated to support minor children who were emancipated. "Emancipation" is a term with multiple meanings, depending on the context in which it is used. In a formal sense, emancipation means the termination of some or all of the mutual rights and duties of the parent-child relationship, and it could occur by mutual agreement or when one party acted wrongfully, as when a father abandoned or forced a child out. In the latter situation the father was not entitled to the child's earnings. . . .

These rules were formulated in a time when children, especially boys, often attained functional adulthood in late adolescence, even though they were still legally minors. Parents were probably less worried about children remaining dependent for unreasonably long periods than they were that the children would strike out on their own when the parents felt they were still needed at home to work. In this context, the rules can be understood primarily as giving legal effect to circumstances as they actually existed. To some extent the rules also suggested that minors should remain subject to parental authority unless the parents acquiesced in their independence.

In the early 1970s most states lowered the age of majority to 18, the age at which most children are just finishing high school. However, social conditions have changed so that many young people continue in school well into their twenties, remaining economically, and to some extent personally, dependent on their parents. Many parents voluntarily support older children, but the question is whether parents are or should be legally obligated to continue to support them.

STARNES V. STARNES

723 S.E.2d 198 (S.C. 2012)

Justice HEARN: Less than two years ago, this Court decided Webb v. Sowell, 387 S.C. 328, 692 S.E.2d 543 (2010), which held that ordering a non-custodial parent to pay college expenses violates equal protection, thus overruling thirty years of precedent flowing from Risinger v. Risinger, 273 S.C. 36, 253 S.E.2d 652 (1979). . . . Today, we hold that *Webb* was wrongly decided and remand this matter for reconsideration in light of the law as it existed prior to *Webb*.

Kristi McLeod (Mother) and Robert Starnes (Father) divorced in 1993 following five years of marriage. Mother received custody of their two minor children, and Father was required to pay child support in the amount of $212 per week, which was later reduced to $175 per week by agreement, in addition to thirty-five percent of his annual bonus. At the time, Father earned approximately $29,000 per year plus a $2,500 bonus. However, his salary steadily increased to over $120,000 per year and his bonus to nearly $30,000 by 2007. In 2008, his salary was almost $250,000. During the same time period, Mother's income increased and fluctuated from less than $12,000 per year to a peak of approximately $40,000 per year. Despite the rather sizable increases in Father's income, Mother never sought modification of his child support obligation because, as Father admitted, she had no way of knowing about them.

In August 2006, the parties' older child, Collin, reached the age of majority and enrolled as a student at Newberry College.[18] To help take advantage of this opportunity, he sought all scholarships, loans, and grants that he could. Father wholly supported Collin's decision to attend Newberry. Indeed, Father wrote an e-mail in March 2006 agreeing to repay all of Collin's student loans upon graduation. He even co-signed a promissory note for Collin's student loans. Furthermore, in an August 2006 letter, Father agreed to pick up "odd expenses from [Collin]'s education" and told Collin to call him whenever he "needs a little help." Interestingly, Father took it upon himself in that same letter to unilaterally decrease his weekly child support from $175 to $100. Mother later acquiesced in this reduction, apparently in consideration of Father's assurances that he would support Collin while he was in college. However, Father did not uphold his end of the bargain, nor did he regularly pay the percentage of his bonus as required.

Mother brought the instant action in March 2007 seeking an award of college expenses, an increase in child support for Jamie, and attorney's fees and costs. Father counterclaimed, asking that the court terminate: (1) his child support for Collin because he had attained the age of majority and graduated from high school; (2) his support for Jamie upon graduation from high school; (3) and the requirement that he pay a percentage of his annual bonus as child support. He also denied that he should be required to pay any college expenses for Collin. . . .

. . . The court dismissed Mother's claim for college expenses on the ground that it violated the Equal Protection Clause of the United States Constitution.[19] . . .

In *Webb*, we held that requiring a parent to contribute toward an adult child's college expenses violated the Equal Protection Clause. We are not unmindful of the imprimatur of correctness which stare decisis lends to that decision. However, stare decisis is not an inexorable command: "There is no virtue in sinning against light or persisting in palpable error, for nothing is settled until it is settled right. . . . There should be no blind adherence to a precedent which, if it is wrong, should be corrected at the first practical moment." . . .

In *Webb*, we were asked to determine whether requiring a non-custodial parent to pay college expenses was a violation of equal protection. "The *sine qua non* of an equal protection claim is a showing that similarly situated persons received disparate treatment." Absent an allegation that the classification resulting

---

18. Their younger son, Jamie, has autism; although he attained the age of majority in 2008, he is not expected to graduate from high school until he is twenty-one.

19. *Webb* had not yet been decided at this time.

in different treatment is suspect, a classification will survive an equal protection challenge so long as it rests on some rational basis. Under the rational basis test, a classification is presumed reasonable and will remain valid unless and until the party challenging it proves beyond a reasonable doubt that there "is no admissible hypothesis upon which it can be justified." . . .

In *Webb*, the majority viewed the classification created by *Risinger* for equal protection purposes as those parents subject to a child support order at the time the child is emancipated. Without any elaboration, the majority concluded that there is no rational basis for treating parents subject to such an order different than those not subject to one with respect to the payment of college expenses. Upon further reflection, we now believe that we abandoned our long-held rational basis rule that the party challenging a classification must prove there is no conceivable basis upon which it can rest and inverted the burden of proof. By not investigating whether there is any basis to support the alleged classification or refuting the bases argued, we effectively presumed *Risinger*'s reading of what is now section 63-3-530(A)(17) unconstitutional. Our treatment of this issue thus essentially reviewed *Risinger* under the lens of strict scrutiny as opposed to rational basis. . . .

As with any equal protection challenge, we begin by addressing the class *Risinger* created under section 63-3-530(A)(17). Mother argues that the appropriate classification is divorced parents versus non-divorced parents. . . . We accordingly review *Risinger* through the same lens used by the family court: whether it improperly treats divorced parents differently than non-divorced parents.

This State has a strong interest in the outcome of disputes where the welfare of our young citizens is at stake. As can hardly be contested, the State also has a strong interest in ensuring that our youth are educated such that they can become more productive members of our society. It is entirely possible "that most parents who remain married to each other support their children through college years. On the other hand, even well-intentioned parents, when deprived of the custody of their children, sometimes react by refusing to support them as they would if the family unit had been preserved." Therefore, it may very well be that *Risinger* sought to alleviate this harm by "minimiz[ing] any economic and educational disadvantages to children of divorced parents." Kujawinski v. Kujawinski, 71 Ill. 2d 563, 376 N.E.2d 1382, 1390, 17 Ill. Dec. 801 (Ill. 1978); *see also* LeClair v. LeClair, 137 N.H. 213, 624 A.2d 1350, 1357 (N.H. 1993), *superseded by statute on other grounds* ("The legitimate State interest served by these statutes is to ensure that children of divorced families are not deprived of educational opportunities solely because their families are no longer intact."). There is no absolute right to a college education, and section 63-3-530(A)(17), as interpreted by *Risinger* and its progeny, does not impose a moral obligation on all divorced parents with children. Instead, the factors identified by *Risinger* and expounded upon in later cases seek to identify those children whose parents would *otherwise* have paid for their college education, but for the divorce, and provide them with that benefit.

We accordingly hold that requiring a parent to pay, as an incident of child support, for post-secondary education under the appropriate and limited circumstances outlined by *Risinger* is rationally related to the State's interest. While it is certainly true that not all married couples send their children to college, that does not detract from the State's interest in having college-educated citizens and attempting to alleviate the potential disadvantages placed upon children of divorced parents. Although the decision to send a child to college may be a personal one, it is not one we wish to foreclose to a child simply because his parents are divorced. It is of no moment that not every married parent sends his children to college or that not every divorced parent refuses to do so. The tenants (sic) of rational basis review under equal protection do not require such exacting precision in the decision to create a classification and its effect.

Indeed, Father's refusal to contribute towards Collin's college expenses under the facts of this case proves the very ill which *Risinger* attempted to alleviate, for Father articulated no defensible reason for his refusal other than the shield erected by *Webb*. What other reason could there be for a father with more than adequate means and a son who truly desires to attend college to skirt the obligation the father almost certainly would have assumed had he not divorced the child's mother? Had Father and Mother remained married, we believe Father undoubtedly would have contributed towards Collin's education. Collin has therefore fallen victim to the precise harm that prompted the courts in *LeClair*, *Kujawinski*, and *Vrban* — as well as *Risinger* — to hold that a non-custodial parent could be ordered to contribute towards a child's college education. Thus, this case amply demonstrates what we failed to recognize in *Webb*: sometimes the acrimony of marital litigation impacts a parent's normal sense of obligation towards his or her children. While this is a harsh and unfortunate reality, it is a reality nonetheless that *Risinger* sought to address . . . .

We now hold *Risinger* does not violate the Equal Protection Clause because there is a rational basis to support any disparate treatment *Risinger* and its progeny created. In fact, the case before us particularly demonstrates the need for a rule permitting an award of college expenses in certain circumstances in order to ensure children of divorce have the benefit of the college education they would have received had their parents remained together. Accordingly, we reverse the order of the family court and remand this matter for a determination of whether and in what amount Father is required to contribute to Collin's college education under the law as it existed prior to *Webb* . . . .

Children's economic prospects are much improved if they receive advanced training, as the data on the economic value of education in Chapter 6 at page 430 confirms. The economic value of college is particularly great for young men and has been increasing since the 1970s. "[A]mong males ages 24 through 39, the earnings differential between four-year college graduates and high school graduates rose from approximately 18 percentage points in 1979 to 51 percentage points in 2010. While in 1979, the college/high-school differential among young females ages 25 through 39 was substantially higher than among males (32% vs. 18%), the 22 percentage point increase in the college/high-school earnings differential among females was one-third smaller than the 31 percentage point increase among males. Moreover, longer historical evidence suggests that the college premium is higher at present than it has been at any time since 1915, when the first representative data on U.S. earnings by education group became available." David Autor & Melanie Wasserman, Wayward Sons: The Emerging Gender Gap in Labor Markets and Education 24-25 (Third Way Mar. 2013).

A study published in 2011 concludes married parents provide much more financial assistance to their undergraduate children than do divorced or divorced and remarried parents. The study examined the financial information of 2400 undergraduate students drawn from a nationally representative sample of post-secondary students, including supplementary interviews with the parent with whom each child spent the most time. (The researchers excluded children of never-married and widowed parents because they believed that these parents are significantly different from married and divorced parents.) The findings are summarized here:

Ruth N. Lopez Turley & Matthew Desmond, *Contributions to College Costs by Married, Divorced, and Remarried Parents*

32 J. Fam. Issues 762, 776-78, 784 (2011), available at
http://scholar.harvard.edu/mdesmond/publications/contributions-college-costs-married-divorced-and-remarried-parents

Divorced or separated parents contributed significantly less toward their children's college costs than married parents. Compared with married parents, divorced parents contributed only about a third as many dollars toward college costs ($1,500 vs. $4,700 per year). Of course, this was partly because divorced parents tend to have significantly lower incomes. The median income of married parents was about twice as much as the median income of divorced or separated parents ($57,724 vs. $30,546). Remarried parents, however, earned about the same amount as married parents ($57,788 vs. $57,724, a statistically insignificant difference) but contributed considerably less than the latter ($2,490 vs. $4,700). As a proportion of their income, married parents contributed about 8%, divorced parents contributed about 6%, and remarried parents contributed only 5%. All these differences were statistically significant.

But these proportions do not account for students' financial need, which may be lower for children of divorced parents than children of married or remarried parents for the reasons described earlier, including attending lower-cost institutions and qualifying for more financial aid. If the children of divorced parents have less financial need than the children of married or remarried parents, divorced parents may be covering a larger proportion of their children's financial need. . . . [F]inancial need was indeed lower for the children of divorced parents ($4,909) than for the children of married ($6,873) or remarried parents ($5,875). However, despite their children's lower needs, divorced parents covered a significantly smaller proportion of their children's financial need (42%), compared with married parents (77%). The same was true for remarried parents, who covered just a hair above half (53%) of their children's college costs. Divorced or separated parents contributed significantly less than married parents—in absolute dollars, as a proportion of their income, and as a proportion of their children's financial need—and the same was true for remarried parents, even though they had incomes similar to those of married parents. . . .

. . . In aggregate, children whose parents are married must cover about 23% of college expenses themselves, but children with remarried parents must shoulder

47% themselves, and those from divorced households need to come up with a full 58% of the cost. We should stress that these estimates are quite conservative. Because we included loans not only in our measure of financial aid but also in our measure of parental contributions, our measure of unmet financial need does not take into account money that must be repaid, along with interest or loan fees. When we excluded loans from our measure of financial aid, the median student's financial need increased by $1,072. Moreover, the difference between these two measures of need (with and without loans) was smaller among high-income students because they do not take out as many loans as students from low-income families. These findings are troubling for college-bound students with divorced, separated, or remarried parents, especially given the fact that recent shifts in financial aid policy are making it harder for students to qualify for aid and are requiring families to contribute more money toward the cost of college.

WILLIAM V. FABRICIUS, SANFORD L. BRAVER & KENDRA DENEAU, *DIVORCED PARENTS' FINANCIAL SUPPORT OF THEIR CHILDREN'S COLLEGE EXPENSES*

41 Fam. Ct. Rev. 224, 234-236, 238 (2003)

When we took into account divorced mothers' and fathers' financial situations and their ability to pay for college expenses, we found that, by students' reports, mothers and fathers voluntarily contributed remarkably similar proportions of their financial resources to their children's college education. This occurred in a state that has no statute or case law holding parents to a duty to college support. . . .

One dramatic factor [that may have affected parents' contributions] was legal custody arrangements. Equal numbers of students were from joint legal as from sole mother custody. In joint custody families, fathers contributed more than mothers did, and fathers with joint legal custody contributed more than fathers without did. In sole maternal custody families, mothers contributed more than fathers did, and mothers with sole custody contributed more than mothers with joint custody did. A similar result was found for dual or father residential custody. Among mother residential custody families, controlling for legal custody, fathers' contributions steadily increased with the amount of access they had to their children, to the point that they contributed more than mothers, whereas mothers' contributions remained constant. These findings suggest that when either parent feels parentally disenfranchised or that they have "lost" their child, they are likely to contribute less to college expenses. . . .

A potential problem in regarding both of these custody factors as causal for fathers is that "committed" fathers, the kind who requested and/or obtained these custody arrangements, may have been the very ones who would have paid more anyway, regardless of custody arrangements. There are several arguments against this "self-selection" possibility, however. First, the self-selection possibility implies that fathers for the most part had the residential custody arrangements they desired. But we know from previous work on other recent cohorts of this group of students that students reported that fathers wanted more time with their children. This was especially true of fathers who saw their children minimally or not at all, some, and a moderate amount. The percentages of these fathers who their now-adult children judged to have wanted more time with them are 63%, 78%, and 78%, respectively. Second, it is difficult to imagine that fathers who were predisposed to contribute certain amounts sorted themselves into corresponding categories of access arrangements; yet fathers' contributions increased steadily across the categories of increasing time with their children.

NOTES AND QUESTIONS

1. The constitutional challenge in *Starnes* is based on the different legal treatment of married and divorced parents. The data seem to support the conclusion that these groups of parents do respond differently to claims for contribution to their children's post-secondary education. What might explain the difference? Why did the South Carolina Supreme Court do an about-face on the constitutional question after only two years?

In contrast to *Starnes* and the decisions of other state supreme courts, in Curtis v. Kline, 666 A.2d 265 (Pa. 1995), the Pennsylvania Supreme Court held that a statute allowing courts to order divorced parents to pay support for adult children attending school violates the equal protection clause:

> It will not do to argue that this classification is rationally related to the legitimate governmental purpose of obviating difficulties encountered by those in non-intact families who want parental financial assistance for post-secondary education, because such a statement of the governmental purpose assumes the validity of the classification. Recognizing that within the category of young adults in need of financial help to attend college there are some having a parent or parents unwilling to provide such help, the question remains whether the authority of the state may be selectively applied to empower only those from non-intact families to compel such help. We hold that it may not. In the absence of an entitlement on the part of any individual to post-secondary education, or a generally applicable requirement that parents assist their adult children in obtaining such an education, we perceive no rational basis for the state government to provide only certain adult citizens with legal means to overcome the difficulties they encounter in pursuing that end.

In 2009 the New Hampshire Supreme Court ruled that parents' agreements to support their children after the age of majority so that they can continue in school are unenforceable as a matter of law. In re Goulart, 965 A.2d 1068 (N.H. 2009). The court said a statute that provides, "No child support order shall require a parent to contribute to an adult child's college expenses or other educational expenses beyond the completion of high school," N.H. Rev. Stat. § 461-A:14, V, not only prohibits a court from ordering parents to pay post–high school expenses, it also precludes enforcement of parents' efforts to contract around the statute.

2. Should courts ever order parents in "intact families," that is, those in which both parents live with their children, to pay for advanced education?

A national survey of parents of children in grades 6 through 12 found that 91 percent of the students had parents who expected them to continue going to school beyond high school. Of the parents with this expectation, 82 percent reported that the family planned to help pay for this advanced education. Students living in two-parent families were more likely to have family members who expected to help finance higher education (86 percent) than students in single-parent families (76 percent). Laura Lippman et al., Parent Expectations and Planning for College 7, 17-18 (Nat'l Center for Education Statistics, U.S. Dep't Educ. 2008).

3. In states that authorize courts to award post-majority support, the court must still find that the child will benefit from the award and that the parents can afford to pay. How should a court go about determining when a child is benefiting from post–high school education? Whether and how much parents can afford to pay?

4. Requiring parents to help pay for post-secondary education is a politically charged issue, and in recent years the number of states imposing this duty has declined. In 2006 a law review article reported that about half the states allowed courts to order post-majority educational support. Leah duCharme, The Cost of Higher Education: Post-Minority Child Support in North Dakota, 82 N.D. L. Rev. 235, 236 (2006). An article published in 2013 found only 16 states plus the District of Columbia that give courts this authority. Matthew Brandabur, Note: Getting Back to Our Roots: Increasing the Age of Child Support Termination to Twenty-One, 47 Val. U. L. Rev. 169, 171-172 (2012). After this article was written, the Indiana legislature revoked the authority of courts to award support for education beyond the age of 19. Sexton v. Sexton, 970 N.E.2d 707 (Ind. App. 2012), discussing amendments to Ind. Code § 31-14-11-18. The article included South Carolina in the group that does not allow post-majority support orders, but *Starnes* changes that. On the other hand, in 2013 the Alabama Supreme Court overruled a 24-year-old decision authorizing courts to order post-majority support for education on the ground that the earlier decision erroneously interpreted the child suppport statute. Ex parte Christopher, 2013 WL 5506613 (Ala.).

At a minimum most states require support for children older than 18 who are still dependent in the sense of living at home and going to high school. Verna v. Verna, 432 A.2d 630 (Pa. Super. 1981); Ariz. Rev. Stat. § 25-320(f) (2014); Tenn. Code Ann. § 34-1-102(b) (2014); Tex. Fam. Code § 151.001(b) (2014). Some states require child support to continue until a child is 19 or finishes high school or its equivalent, whichever occurs first. Cal. Fam. Code § 3901 (2014); Iowa Code § 252A.3 (2014); S.D. Codified Laws Ann. § 25-5-18.1 (2014).

5. These changes come at a time when costs of higher education are rising and more adult children are living at home and going to school. In 2006, 46 percent of young adults two years out of high school lived with their parents, compared to 39 percent in 1974; 62 percent were taking post-secondary courses, compared to 40 percent in 1974; and 28 percent were working for pay while not in school, compared to 48 percent in 1974. However, of those in school, a higher percentage also worked than in 1974. Steven J. Ingels et al., Trends Among Young Adults over Three Decades, 1974-2006, Executive Summary (Institute of Education Sciences, July 2012).

On the other hand, the efficacy of court orders to support children pursuing advanced education is called into question by the Turley and Desmond study quoted above. The study concluded, "Among divorced/separated parents, living in a state that requires child support for college (postmajority state) did not seem to increase the amount they contributed toward their children's college expenses. And among remarried parents, living in a postmajority state was associated with slightly larger contributions, but these contributions represented neither a higher proportion of their income nor a higher proportion of their children's financial need (since parents in postmajority states had slightly higher incomes and their children had slightly higher financial needs)." 32 J. Fam. Issues at 780.

6. Most child support guidelines do not specifically address parental responsibility for supporting children in college. *See* Linda D. Elrod & Robert G. Spector, A Review of the Year in Family Law, 46 Fam. L.Q. 471, 528 Chart 3 (2013).

7. Courts are divided about whether parents may be ordered to support adult disabled children who are incapable of self-support. The modern trend is to impose a support duty. *See* Riggs v. Riggs, 578 S.E.2d 3 (S.C. 2003) (collecting cases). *See also* Ariz. Rev. Stat. Ann. §25-320(E) (2014); Iowa Code §252A.3 (2014); Mo. Rev. Stat. §452.340(4) (2014). In at least one state, an unmarried father must continue to support an adult disabled child, but married and divorced parents do not have this legal duty. Miss. Code Ann. §43-19-33(3) (2014), discussed in Hays v. Alexander, 114 So. 3d 704, 708 n.5 (Miss. 2013).

Weston v. Weston, 40 A.3d 934 (Me. 2012), discussed one aspect of the relationship between adult children's eligibility for public benefits and parental support duties. The father moved to terminate his child support obligation, arguing that because his 27-year-old son, who had been disabled from infancy, received Supplemental Security Income benefits, he was no longer principally dependent on his parents for support. The court rejected the argument because the son, who lived with his mother, was and would remain dependent on her both financially and for personal care. *See also* Lewis v. Dep't of Soc. Serv., 61 S.W.3d 248 (Mo. App. 2001), holding that a child's SSI benefits should not be considered in calculating child support because they are intended to defray some of the extraordinary expenses associated with caring for a disabled adult.

8. With some frequency, parents who have been ordered to pay support for older children attending school seek reduction or elimination of their obligation because the children are not behaving as the parents think they should. These cases raise starkly the issue of the extent to which support and control should be linked. Some courts hold that, at least if the parent's commands are "reasonable," the child who disobeys has "emancipated" him or herself, meaning that the parent is no longer obliged to pay support. *See, e.g.,* Robles v. Robles, 855 N.E.2d 1049 (Ind. App. 2006); Caldwell v. Caldwell, 823 So. 2d 1216 (Miss. App. 2002); Roe v. Doe, 272 N.E.2d 567 (N.Y. 1971). Other courts ask whether the children's behavior is reasonable; if so, parents must continue to pay the support. *See, e.g.,* Norris v. Pethe, 833 N.E.2d 1024 (Ind. Ct. App. 2005); Newburgh v. Arrigo, 443 A.2d 1031, 1038 (N.J. 1982). Others hold that parents obligated to support their adult children may not condition their payments on their children's behavior. *See, e.g.,* Steele v. Neeman, 206 P.3d 384 (Wyo. 2009); In re Marriage of Miller, 660 P.2d 205 (Or. App. 1983). What are the relative advantages and disadvantages of each of these approaches?

PROBLEMS

1. Molly and Frank's divorce decree requires Frank to pay $450 per month as child support for their two children, Ollie and Terry. The decree is silent about

what happens when Ollie, the older child, becomes 18, which is the age of majority in this jurisdiction. You are Frank's attorney. He has asked you whether he may cut his child support check in half in the month after Ollie becomes 18 without going to court. Molly claims that he cannot reduce his child support until he successfully moves to modify the decree because of Ollie's having attained the age of majority. What advice would you give Frank and why? What course of action would you advise and why?

2. If child support continues for an adult child attending school, should it be paid to the child or to the former custodial parent? Should child support continue during the summer and at other times when school is not in session?

3. Susan's parents' divorce decree requires her father to pay for her tuition, room and board and books while she is in school until age 22 so long as she maintains passing grades. Susan, who is now 19 and who has passing grades, recently moved out of the dorm into an apartment against her father's wishes. Her father, who does not deny that he has the financial ability to pay for Susan's schooling, has moved to terminate his support obligation because of her refusal to live where he believes that she should and because of her general lifestyle, which he regards as irresponsible and immoral. Should his motion be granted?

4. If an adolescent child in the legal custody of one parent moves to the other parent's house following a series of fights with the custodial parent, has the child forfeited a right to child support? Does it matter whether the parent with legal custody "threw the child out"? What if, after leaving, the child refuses to visit or speak to the parent with legal custody? Would the situation be different if the child went to live with a friend's parents?

E. ADULT CHILDREN'S LEGAL OBLIGATION TO SUPPORT PARENTS

Families provide a great deal of support to their adult members. The AARP recently reported that two-thirds of older people with disabilities get all their care from family members, mostly wives and adult daughters, and 26 percent receive a combination of family and paid care. Only 9 percent received only paid help in the home. Lynn Feinberg et al., AARP Pub. Policy Inst., Valuing the Invaluable: 2011 Update on the Growing Contributions and Costs of Family Caregiving 8 (2011). Families also contribute billions of dollars to the financial support of their adult relatives not living in the same household. In 2010 more than two million people helped support adults living outside their homes; almost all of those receiving support were the payors' children, parents, or other relatives. (Most of the rest were spouses or former spouses.) The average annual payment was $6809, while the median was $2400. Bureau of the Census, United States Dep't of Commerce, Support Providers: 2010, Tbl. 1 (June 2012). Does it follow that because adult children often provide support for their parents, they generally should be required to do so?

AMERICAN HEALTHCARE CENTER V. RANDALL

513 N.W.2d 566 (S.D. 1994)

AMUNDSON, J.... Appellant Robert Randall (Robert) is the only child of Harry and Juanita Randall. Although he grew up in Aberdeen, Robert has not resided in South Dakota since 1954. Robert is now a resident of the District of Columbia.

Following an accident which required Juanita's hospitalization, Robert came back to Aberdeen and checked into various nursing homes to place his mother. In the fall of 1990, Juanita was admitted to the Arcadia Unit of Americana Healthcare Center (Americana) in Aberdeen, South Dakota. The Arcadia Unit is specifically designed to deal with individuals who possess mental problems such as Alzheimer's disease. ...

At that time, in view of Juanita's limited income, Robert discussed the possibility of financial assistance from Medicaid with various Americana personnel. Later that month, Robert completed an application for long-term care medical assistance for Juanita. In November, the South Dakota Department of Social Services (DSS) denied this application because Juanita had not exhausted all of her assets. At the time, Juanita's only assets were [the house and mutual funds that had been conveyed to a trust].

Juanita's bill was two months delinquent at the time Americana learned of the rejected Medicaid application. Americana then contacted Robert about his mother's unpaid bills. Because of Juanita's financial position, Robert, as her legal guardian, filed ... a Chapter 7 bankruptcy petition ... and discharged the Americana bill for Juanita individually and Robert, as her guardian, on October 30, 1991. Meanwhile, Americana filed this suit to collect the unpaid bills. ...

In June of 1991, Robert was requested to remove his mother from Americana because of the unpaid bills. Despite this request, Juanita remained at Americana until her death on December 8, 1991. At the time of Juanita's death, the unpaid balance for her care was $36,772.30. ...

Prior to trial, the court granted Robert's motion for summary judgment as to Robert Randall as guardian of the person and estate of Juanita because of the discharge in bankruptcy, but denied summary judgment to Robert Randall individually.... At the summary judgment hearing, Americana raised its claim under SDCL 25-7-27 for the first time.[20]

On September 3, 1992, Robert renewed his motion for summary judgment on the additional ground that SDCL 25-7-27 was unconstitutional and requested a continuance.... The trial court stated that it was premature to rule on the constitutionality of the statute at that time and denied the continuance.

---

20. SDCL 25-7-27 states:

> Every adult child, having the financial ability so to do shall provide necessary food, clothing, shelter or medical attendance for a parent who is unable to provide for himself; provided that no claim shall be made against such adult child until notice has been given such adult child that his parent is unable to provide for himself, and such adult child shall have refused to provide for his parent.

A court trial was held September 22, 1992. At the conclusion of Americana's case, Robert moved for directed verdict on the grounds that Americana had failed to establish either an oral or written contract to act as guarantor for his mother's nursing home bills. . . . The trial court granted Robert's motion for directed verdict on Americana's claims for liability based on an oral or written contract of guarantee. . . . The trial court found in favor of Americana on its SDCL 25-7-27 claim. This appeal followed. . . .

At common law, an adult child was not required to support a parent. Such an obligation could only be created by statute. Such statutes trace their beginnings from the Elizabethan Poor Law of 1601 in England. Swoap v. Superior Court, 10 Cal. 3d 490, 111 Cal. Rptr. 136, 516 P.2d 840, 848 (1973). South Dakota adopted the current version of SDCL 25-7-27 in 1963.

The North Dakota Supreme Court considered a claim premised on a similar statutory provision in Bismarck Hospital & Deaconesses Home v. Harris, 68 N.D. 374, 280 N.W. 423 (1938). That court stated:

> If the person against whom liability is sought to be established refuses to pay for services rendered, an action may be brought against him by such third party. In such action, the plaintiff must establish the kinship of the parties, the financial ability of the person sought to be charged, the indigence of the person to whom relief was furnished, the reasonable value of the services, and that such relief was an immediate necessity. Id. 280 N.W. at 426.

Robert claims SDCL 25-7-27 violates equal protection because it discriminates against adult children of indigent parents. The trial court held that it did not. Any legislative act is accorded a presumption in favor of constitutionality and that presumption is not overcome until the act is clearly and unmistakably shown beyond a reasonable doubt to violate fundamental constitutional principles. Since Robert challenges the constitutionality of the statute, he bears the burden of proving the act unconstitutional.

. . . No quasi-suspect classification or fundamental right has been implicated in this case, thus, a rational basis analysis will be applied to this support statute. . . .

Under the rational basis test, South Dakota uses a two-pronged analysis when determining whether a statute violates the constitutional right to equal protection under the laws. Lyons v. Lederle Laboratories, 440 N.W.2d 769, 771 (S.D. 1989). First, does the statute setup arbitrary classifications among various persons subject to it and, second, whether there is a rational relationship between the classification and some legitimate legislative purpose. Id.

When applying the first prong of the *Lyons* test, it is clear that SDCL 25-7-27 does not make an arbitrary classification. Rather, "it is the moral as well as the legal duty in this state, of every child, whether minor or adult, to assist in the support of their indigent aged parents." An adult child is liable under SDCL 25-7-27 upon the same principle that a parent is liable for necessary support furnished to their child.

Much like the plaintiffs in Swoap v. Superior Court of Sacramento County, Robert argues that the only support obligations which are rational are those arising out of a relationship voluntarily entered into. 10 Cal. 3d 490, 111 Cal. Rptr. 136, 516 P.2d 840, 851 (1973). For instance, the obligation to support a child or spouse is at least initially voluntary, therefore, it is rationally based. Robert argues that, since children do not voluntarily enter into the relationship with their parents, it is arbitrary to force this obligation upon them. Id. The fact that a child has no choice in the creation of a relationship with its parents does not per se make this an arbitrary classification. The fact that an indigent parent has supported and cared for a child during that child's minority provides an adequate basis for imposing a duty on the child to support that parent. Id. . . .

It is certainly reasonable to place a duty to support an indigent parent on that parent's adult child because they are direct lineal descendants who have received the support, care, comfort and guidance of that parent during their minority. If a parent does not qualify for public assistance, who is best suited to meet that parent's needs? It can reasonably be concluded that no other person has received a greater benefit from a parent than that parent's child and it logically follows that the adult child should bear the burden of reciprocating on that benefit in the event a parent needs support in their later years. *Swoap*, 516 P.2d at 851. Consequently, this statute does not establish an arbitrary classification.

The second prong of the test requires a rational relationship between this classification and some legitimate state interest. Clearly, this state has a legitimate interest in providing for the welfare and care of elderly citizens. SDCL 25-7-27 prevents a parent from being thrown out on the street when in need of specialized care. Placing this obligation for support on an adult child is as legitimate as those interests recognized by this court in the past when applying the rational basis test. . . .

The primary purpose of this statute is to place financial responsibility for indigent parents on their adult children when a parent requires such assistance. Although the legislature repealed similar laws in the past, SDCL 25-7-27 has survived. Therefore, SDCL 25-7-27 serves a legitimate legislative interest, especially under the facts of this case, where indigency was voluntarily created by the trust and there would have been sufficient assets to pay for the parent's care had the trust not been created. Robert has not been denied his right to equal protection under the law. . . .

In conclusion, we affirm the trial court's decision in all respects.

SWOAP v. SUPERIOR COURT

516 P.2d 840 (Cal. 1973)

[Children held liable to reimburse the state for public assistance provided to their indigent parents' support argued that the statute imposing the duty on the children was unconstitutional on several grounds. Employing reasoning much like that in *Randall*, the California Supreme Court rejected the challenge.]

TOBRINER, J., dissenting. The majority propose, by the instant opinion, to establish a new constitutional standard for determining when the state may compel some of its citizens to pay for benefits which the state, in its wisdom, decides to provide to other citizens. Under the test proposed by the majority, a state can charge one class of citizens with the costs of providing public programs to another class whenever there is simply some "rational relationship" between the group of benefitted individuals and those who must pay the bill. Applying this "minimal rationality" test in the instant case, the majority hold that since the class of children have generally benefitted from parents, the state can require those children whose parents happen to be poor to reimburse the state for the cost of public old age assistance, regardless of whether a particular child is otherwise legally obligated to provide such support to his parent. . . .

Under the majority's newly propounded "rationality" test, a government intent on reducing the general tax burden could single out insulated minority classes to bear a disproportionate share of the tax burden of a whole range of public services. Thus, for example, the "mere rationality" standard would permit the state not only to charge adult children with the costs of old age benefits but would authorize public savings by charging such children for the costs of subsidized housing projects, medical care, recreational centers, reduced public transportation fares and the various other social programs the state decides to make available to its senior citizens. Although the children of the recipients of such benefits may have had no preexisting obligation to pay for such services, the majority's constitutional test would presumably sanction such charges on the ground that children as a whole have benefitted from parents. Moreover, since the circumstances of the individual case are assertedly irrelevant, the state presumably could require even a child who had been abandoned by his parents to pay the costs of these varied public programs. . . .

It might be possible to understand the reasons for the majority's uprooting of a consistent line of precedent and creation of a novel constitutional ruling if the legislation challenged in the instant case offered the promise of unquestionably beneficial social consequences; under such circumstances one might expect to find the court questioning past decisions that impeded the salutary result. The statutes in question here, however, offer no such beneficent social consequences.

On the contrary, almost all observers agree that the social effects of the challenged relative responsibility provisions are harsh and self-defeating. "[A] large body of social work opinion [has long maintained] that liability of relatives creates and increases family dissension and controversy, weakens and destroys family ties at the very time and in the very circumstances when they are most needed, imposes an undue burden upon the poor . . . and is therefore socially undesirable, financially unproductive, and administratively infeasible." (ten Broek, 17 Stan. L. Rev. at pp. 645-646.) As Justice Friedman, writing for the Court of Appeal in the instant case, observed: "[The challenged provisions] strike most aggressively and harshly at adult children occupying the lower end of the income scale. The enforced shift of subsistence funds from one generation to the other distributes economic desolation between the generations. It galls family relationships. It injects guilt and shame into elderly citizens who have made their contributions to society and have become dependent through life's vicissitudes."

Jenny Baxter, a 75-year-old Californian receiving Old Age Security benefits, eloquently summarized the true effect of the relative responsibility laws: "No one is born into this world with a debt to their parents for their birth and contributions until their maturity. That is the parents' contribution to life and society. When the child reaches maturity, he starts a new separate unit and in turn makes his contribution to life and society as did his parents, carrying on the generation cycle on through eternity. The children should not be saddled with unjust demands that keep them at or near poverty level with no hope to escape it, just because a parent still breathes. And aged parents should not have to live their remaining lives facing the heartbreaking experience of being such a burden to their children. Many would prefer death but are afraid of retribution for taking their own lives. Their grief — a living death."

NOTES AND QUESTIONS

1. Does it follow that, because parents support their children when young, children should support their parents when needy? Is there a general duty of reciprocity, as the court in *Randall* assumes? Are the parents providing some good or service without benefiting themselves? Is there an expectation of reciprocity by parents and children? Do parents generally expect that their children will use their resources to support them?

The view expressed by Jenny Baxter, quoted in Justice Tobriner's dissent, seems to be widely shared. Jane Gross, Adult Children, Aging Parents and the Law, N.Y. Times, Nov. 20, 2008. *See also* Peter Laslett, Is There a Generational Contract? Justice Between Age Groups and Generations 24, 28-29 (Peter Laslett & James S. Fishkin eds., 1992).

2. Are family responsibility laws explained by the notion of the family as an economic unit? Is the family such a unit at the time that support by children is sought? *See* Lee E. Teitelbaum, Intergenerational Responsibility and Family Obligation: On Sharing, 1992 Utah L. Rev. 765, 776-777.

3. At one time 45 states had filial support laws; as of 2013, 29 states had statutes that imposed some kind of duty to support indigent parents on adult children, but only 20 gave the parent standing to sue a child for support. Several states have only laws making it a crime to fail to support an indigent parent under some circumstances. Katherine C. Pearson, Filial Support Laws in the Modern Era: Domestic and International Comparison of Enforcement Practices for Laws Requiring Adult Children to Support Indigent Parents, 20 Elder L.J. 269, 275-277 (2013) (includes a table summarizing all the statutory provisions). Idaho repealed its law in 2011. *Id.* at 277. The author found that most of these states have little or no reported appellate case law within the last 30 or more years that apply the statutes. *Id.* at 279. The exceptions are Pennsylvania and South Dakota. *Id.* at 289-298 (discussing cases).

4. Five years before she entered the nursing home, the mother in *Randall* transferred most of her assets into an irrevocable trust, which named her as the income beneficiary but prevented the trustee from using the corpus of the trust for her benefit. Her son Robert, the appellant in *Randall*, was both trustee and residual beneficiary of the trust. As his mother's guardian, Robert used the income from the trust and his mother's Social Security benefits to pay legal fees incurred by forming the guardianship, the bankruptcy proceedings, and an unsuccessful pursuit of Medicaid benefits instead of paying for her care in the nursing home. While Robert's actions were not illegal or a breach of fiduciary duty, the court expressed its disapproval of his choices and was distinctly untroubled that he would have to pay his mother's bill from the trust assets that he received. 513 N.W.2d at 574.

Presbyterian Medical Center v. Budd, 832 A.2d 1066 (Pa. Sup. 2003), involved similar facts. A daughter had used her power of attorney to transfer her mother's assets to herself, rather than spending them on her mother's care, resulting in the mother neither having the money to pay for her own care nor being eligible for Medicaid (because of the transfer of assets to the daughter). The nursing home sued the daughter for these costs, and the court rejected the claims that the daughter was liable based on contract or fraud, finding that the facts did not support these claims. However, the court held that the daughter was liable under the state relative responsibility statute.

In each case, if the child had not received assets from the parent during the parent's lifetime, would the child still have been liable under the relative responsibility laws? Why or why not?

A more recent Pennsylvania case upheld an order requiring a son to pay his mother's nursing home bill of $93,000, even though he had played no role in accruing the debt and received no money from his mother, who was still alive and living in Greece. Health Care & Retirement Corp. of America v. Pittas, 46 A.3d 719 (Pa. Super. 2012). Professor Pearson says that the case is part of a trend for commercial entities to use filial support laws to recover the costs of providing long-term care. In 2008 she found 15 cases pending in Pennsylvania trial courts in which third parties sued children and spouses under the relative responsibility law. Pearson, above, 20 Elder L.J. at 293-294, 298.

5. In both *Randall* and *Budd* the children attempted to obtain Medicaid benefits to pay for their mothers' custodial care. Medicaid is a public assistance program only for people whose assets and income fall below poverty levels. If Juanita Randall had not transferred her property into the irrevocable trust, she definitely would not have been eligible for Medicaid, and the transfer itself may have disqualified her, or her income may have been too high for her to qualify. In 1993, federal rules that determine whether a person can transfer assets into a trust and still be eligible for Medicaid were substantially tightened. Omnibus Budget Reconciliation Act of 1993 § 13611, codified at 42 U.S.C. § 1396p. Under these rules, if a person gratuitously transfers assets to another outright or in trust within five years of applying for Medicaid, the applicant is disqualified from eligibility for a period of time, as in *Budd*.

6. In determining an unmarried person's eligibility for Medicaid, generally all the applicant's income, including gifts of cash or its equivalent, is considered available to pay for care. This rule limits the ability of a person's children or others to make voluntary contributions to the care of a person. However, trusts created by a Medicaid applicant or by a third party for the benefit of the applicant that provide that none of the money can be used for food, clothing, or shelter but can only be used for other needs, such as transportation, entertainment, and so on, are not considered resources and so do not disqualify the beneficiary from receiving Medicaid. The trusts are called special needs or supplemental needs trusts.

7. For additional perspectives, *see* Seymour Moskowitz, Adult Children and Indigent Parents: Intergenerational Responsibilities in International Perspective, 86 Marq. L. Rev. 401 (2002); Margaret F. Brinig, The Family Franchise: Elderly Parents and Adult Siblings, 1996 Utah L. Rev. 393; Usha Narayanan, The Government's Role in Fostering the Relationship Between Adult Children and Their Elderly Parents: From Filial Responsibility Laws . . . to What? A Cross Cultural Perspective, 4 Elder L.J. 369 (1996).

Modification, Termination, Enforcement, and Tax and Bankruptcy Treatment of Orders

8

A. INTRODUCTION

This chapter examines the policies and rules relating to modification and enforcement of orders and to taxation and bankruptcy treatment of property transfers and obligations imposed incident to family break-up. As we saw in earlier chapters, it is often difficult to distinguish clearly between awards dividing property and those providing for spousal support. The same is true of spousal and child support obligations. However, the classification of an order as property division, spousal support, or child support is centrally important in the issues considered in this chapter.

B. MODIFICATION AND TERMINATION OF SUPPORT

Traditionally and still today in most jurisdictions, support duties terminate at the death of the obligor or the recipient. However, in a number of states, a court may order the obligor's estate to continue to pay spousal support, or the parties may agree in writing to such an extension. In some states, statutes or case law permit child support liability to be imposed on a parent's estate under some circumstances. *See, e.g.,* 750 Ill. Comp. Stat. Ann. 5/510(d) (2014); Nev. Rev. Stat. § 125B.130 (2014); Koidl v. Schreiber, 520 A.2d 759 (N.J. App. 1986); Caldwell v. Caldwell, 92 N.W.2d 356 (Wis. 1958); L.W.K. v. E.R.C., 735 N.E.2d 359 (Mass. 2000). The ALI Principles recommend that state law should not provide for automatic termination of child support upon the death of the obligor; instead, the court should have discretion to modify or terminate the order or commute the obligation to a lump sum. ALI Principles of the Law of Family Dissolution § 325, § 5.07 and commentary (2000). This proposal is derived from the Model Marriage and Divorce Act, which was adopted in Arizona, Colorado, Illinois, Kentucky, Minnesota, Missouri, Montana and Washington. *Id.* at 569, Reporter's Note to comment b.

The traditional rule is that, unlike property awards, spousal support and child support are modifiable upon a showing of a "substantial (or material) change of circumstances." This phrase gives judges considerable discretion to alter previously established support obligations. This section considers generally how courts and legislatures have given meaning to this phrase and the extent to which judicial discretion is narrowed by statute or case law.

As you consider these materials, think about how the problems raised in the cases relate to what you have already learned about the justifications and criteria for imposing support duties in the first place. Are the policies reflected in initial awards carried forward to solve modification problems? Are post-decree changes in circumstances treated the same when spousal support and child support are at stake? Consider, for example, how increases in an obligor's income are treated. Courts typically say that since divorce terminates the marital relationship, an increase in the payor's income alone — that is, without a showing of the recipient's increased need — is not grounds for modifying spousal support because a person is not entitled to share in a former spouse's postdivorce efforts or good fortune. However, divorce does not terminate the parent-child relationship, and therefore a parent's increase in income may be grounds for increasing child support.

1.   *"Foreseeable" Changes in Circumstances*

In many cases a major issue is the tension between the value of rules that promote stability in orders and those that allow courts to respond to changes in individual circumstances. The Uniform Marriage and Divorce Act (UMDA) strongly emphasizes stability; Section 316 provides that to be a ground for modifying a spousal or child support order, a change of circumstances must be "so substantial and continuing as to be unconscionable." Sometimes courts deal with the tension between stability and flexibility by saying that change that was "foreseeable" is not a ground for modification. This test cannot be taken literally, however. Many changes that are widely regarded as sufficient for modifying a support order, such as the increased cost of supporting children as they mature, are also entirely foreseeable.

Indeed, some of these "foreseeable" changes are so predictable that courts and commentators have sought ways to adjust support orders for them automatically. Before widespread use of child support guidelines, cost-of-living adjustments (COLAs) in support orders to adjust for inflation were often proposed. While many courts approved inclusion of COLA provisions, others rejected them because they fail to account for actual changes in income and other factors relevant to need and ability to pay. J. Thomas Oldham, Abating the Feminization of Poverty: Changing the Rules Governing Post-Decree Modification of Child Support Obligations, 1995 BYU L. Rev. 841, 850-853. On the other hand, while it is predictable that parents will spend more to support older children than young ones, courts rarely approve orders automatically increasing child support as children grow older. Instead, they ordinarily require motions to modify previous orders to permit individualized determination of needs and ability to pay. *Id.* at 853-856. However, the Mississippi Supreme Court in a preguidelines case observed:

> James and Marie, like so many couples who divorce, have been at each other's throat almost from the day of the divorce. . . . We add this recurring situation to what we have noted above — and what anyone can reasonably anticipate: That children's expenses generally will increase as they get older, that the father and mother's earning *capacity* will generally increase from year to year, and that inflation will continue at some level and will partially affect both the children's expenses and the parents' earning capacity.
>
> James would have us hold here that, because these things were reasonably foreseeable back in May of 1979 and because the separation agreement makes no reference to them, Marie has "waived" the claims she now makes. Surely, that cannot be the law. By the same token, because we "know" these things, we know that the chancery courts of this state will be swamped more than they already are if every increase in the father's salary, every increase in the inflation rate were to generate a modification hearing (where, to be sure, the first question will always be whether the "change" is enough of a change to be classified as a "material change").
>
> . . . Had James and Marie included in their separation agreement an escalation clause to provide for increases in children's expenses and parents' earning capacities, the agonies of the instant litigation likely could have been avoided. . . . In the child support provisions of their separation agreements, the parties generally ought to be required to include escalation clauses tied to the parents' earnings or to the annual inflation rate or to some factored combination of the two.

Tedford v. Dempsey, 437 So. 2d 410, 419 (Miss. 1983). In 2014 the court reaffirmed this endorsement of escalator clauses. Short v. Short, 131 So. 2d 1149 (Miss. 2014).

The advent of child support guidelines produced a clear difference between modification of child support and alimony. Federal legislation requires states to implement a regular review process that will ensure that child support orders are updated at least every four years. 42 U.S.C. § 667(a). That requirement effectively abrogates the traditional approach under which a child support order, like an alimony order, could be modified only on the initiative of the party who proved a substantial change of circumstances. *See, e.g.,* Morales v. Morales, 984 N.E.2d 748 (Mass. 2013).

2. *"Voluntary" Versus "Involuntary" Decreases in the Payor's Income*

A decrease in an obligor's ability to pay is a commonly asserted ground for modifying support. Involuntary decreases, such as when the obligor is laid off from work, are generally treated as a sufficient reason to decrease support. However, treatment of "voluntary" reductions in income is more complex, as the next case illustrates.

WRENN V. LEWIS

818 A.2d 1005 (Me. 2003)

LEVY, J. . . . David and Cheryl were divorced in April of 1998 (Augusta, Vafiades, J.). They were awarded shared parental rights and responsibilities for their son and daughter, with Cheryl being allocated the primary residential care of the children. At the time of the divorce, David had worked at Carleton Woolen Mills for twenty-three years and was earning $63,000 a year, and Cheryl performed part-time housecleaning earning $4800 a year. The divorce judgment required David to: (1) pay child support in the amount of $228.76 per week (decreasing to $168 when the older child turned eighteen), provide health insurance for the children, and cover 90% of any uninsured health care needs; (2) pay spousal support in the amount of $15,000 per year for two years, and then $16,500 per year for the next three years; and (3) maintain life insurance through his employment with Cheryl as the named beneficiary until both children reach the age of twenty-one years and, if life insurance is no longer available through David's job, to obtain it in an amount sufficient to cover his outstanding child and spousal support obligations. In 2001, the parties' son reached majority, and their then thirteen year old daughter continued to reside with Cheryl.

In late January 2000, David filed a motion to modify the divorce judgment seeking to reduce his child support obligation and eliminate his obligations for spousal support and life and medical insurance. The motion was premised on David's anticipated loss of his job as an assistant plant manager at the Carleton Woolen Mills, which was winding down its operations and was expected to close in April. . . .

From January to April 2000, David earned a total of $8000 from part-time employment at Carleton Woolen Mills. Upon the mill's closing in April, he began to receive unemployment benefits in the amount of $274 per week. The Department of Human Services garnished $127 per week for child support. His total income for the year 2000 was $18,000. David was living with his fiancée in her house in Winthrop at the time of the hearing. Before he lost his job, David had paid $548 per month to his fiancée as his share of her mortgage loan payment.

As a "displaced textile worker," David was eligible to participate in "T.R.A.," a federally funded trade adjustment program, which afforded him eighteen additional months of unemployment benefits conditioned upon his participation in an approved training program. David enrolled in T.R.A. and entered a retraining program to become an airplane pilot, basing his career choice on his interest in aviation and his belief that the textile industry is in decline.[1] David decided not to seek a management position in other manufacturing sectors in Maine.

---

1. David's employment counselor at the Augusta Career Center testified that: the trade adjustment program entitles individuals to retraining if they do not have a marketable skill or cannot easily obtain employment earning at least 80% of what they were earning; when David came in, there were no comparable jobs listed, "so he could not easily jump back into the job market" earning at least 80% of his previous salary; David could have gone to work for another employer and still retained eligibility for the retraining program had he been laid off again as long as his income did not exceed 80% of his former income at

David's unemployment benefits totaled approximately $14,248 a year. Upon being certified as a flight instructor after a year of additional training, David expected to earn $16,000 per year. He estimated he would have to work eighteen months as a flight instructor to accumulate the flight hours required to obtain the licensure necessary to obtain employment as a private pilot.

The court found that David failed to pursue a meaningful employment search. His efforts consisted of contacting "a few people in the [textile] industry," and he made no effort to look for management positions outside of the textile industry because he believed the skills he had learned at the mill were "job-specific" and he would have to "start at entry level and work [his] way up."[2] David testified that he spends his days studying, cutting and "clearing wood, landscaping, . . . and taking care of everything [around the home]" when he is not participating in pilot training. He offered no sound explanation for his failure to pursue full-time employment even though the minimum time he was required to dedicate to his pilot training program was nine hours per week. In addition, in the year following the loss of his job, David liquidated his retirement fund and used the proceeds to pay off all of his debts, including the $7800 owed on his car loan, and his fiancée's student loan. He also received a $3000 tax refund that he chose not to apply toward his support obligations. The court found that "[f]ollowing a job loss which was beyond his control, [David] obtained coverage for his own living expenses and has chosen to train a few hours per week for employment which will not predictably yield more than $16,000 yearly."

Cheryl, who lives in Readfield in the former marital residence, testified that she was forced to spend her savings and most of the retirement money she received in the divorce judgment to pay her bills when David stopped paying the full amount of child support and all of the spousal support. In 2000 Cheryl had earned $11,230 cleaning residential and commercial buildings and working as a cook on weekends. She projected her income for the year 2001 to be $15,000. Cheryl testified that David owed her $22,551 for overdue spousal and child support.

The court made detailed findings of fact in its order dated May 15, 2001. It found that "[a]fter his plant closed, [David] was approached about similar positions at plants in Minnesota, Georgia, North Carolina, and Mexico which would probably pay $40,000 to $50,000 to start. He did not investigate these jobs, testifying that he prefers to remain in Maine to be near his children." The court imputed income to David in the amount of $50,000 per year. Based upon this finding and its finding that Cheryl's income would be $15,000 per year beginning January 1, 2001, the court granted David's motion to modify the child support by ordering a retroactive reduction in his weekly child support obligation from $162.75 per week to $134 per week from January 20, 2000 to December 31, 2000, and $128 per week

---

Carleton Woolen Mills; and the training center did not examine job opportunities for David that would pay less than 80% of his previous salary. The counselor also testified that a requirement of the program is for David to put in a minimum of nine hours of training a week.

2. David's employment counselor testified that there were employment opportunities in Maine for which David might be eligible, including employment with the State Police, the Warden Service, the Department of Corrections, and MBNA, but she did not know the salaries associated with the positions.

from January 1, 2001, forward, but did not modify his life and health insurance obligations. The court denied David's motion to eliminate spousal support, finding that the "[d]efendant may not escape court-ordered obligations by voluntarily earning substantially less than he is able . . . [a]nd under the circumstances, alimony as originally ordered is still appropriate." . . .

David contends that the court committed clear error in its factual findings. He asserts that because the termination of his employment from Carleton Woolen Mills was involuntary and his decision to pursue a training program to become a commercial pilot instead of seeking employment was made in good faith, he is not voluntarily unemployed, and the court should not have imputed income to him apart from his unemployment benefits in the amount of $14,248 per year. He also asserts that the court erred in relying on evidence of distant job opportunities as the basis for imputing an earning capacity of $50,000 per year to him. . . .

A. VOLUNTARY UNEMPLOYMENT OR UNDEREMPLOYMENT

The relationship between a court ordered duty of support and an individual's good faith decision to change careers and pursue additional education or retraining was previously considered in *Harvey v. Robinson*, 665 A.2d 215 (Me. 1995). In *Harvey*, the father, facing the possibility of involuntary retirement, decided to retire voluntarily and pursue a long held dream of attending college and medical school. As a result of this decision, his annual gross income was reduced from $35,500 to $13,840, the amount he was able to earn from part-time employment and an educational grant while attending school. The father sought modification of his child support obligation, and the trial court granted a reduction in the level of support based upon the father's new income of $13,840. As justification for this finding, the trial court found that the father's decision to quit full-time employment to pursue college was made in good faith. The trial court failed, however, to "explain how this accommodation to [the father's] preferences serve[d] the interests of the children in any way."

We held that a parent's good faith decision to voluntarily give up full-time employment to pursue education must be balanced with an evaluation of the long term effect that decision has on the interests of the children for whom the parent had an established duty of support. Accordingly, we vacated the court's decision and "remanded for reconsideration of the child support determination based on [the father's] current earning capacity as a full-time employee."

Here, David's loss of employment from Carleton Woolen Mills was involuntary, but his extended unemployment was not. David failed to conduct a meaningful employment search before deciding to dedicate himself exclusively to pilot training. He testified that he contacted "a few people in the [textile] industry" and that he made little or no effort to look for management positions outside of the textile industry.

The trial court's conclusion that David's "work and spending decisions demonstrate that he mistakenly failed to identify his responsibility for child support and alimony as more important than his personal preferences" is inescapable. As addressed in *Harvey*, an individual's personal preference to pursue education or vocational training cannot, standing alone, justify a reduction in a preexisting support obligation. David failed to meet his burden of establishing that his career decisions following the loss of his job from Carleton Woolen Mills served the interests of his children and his former spouse for whom he owed established duties of support. Indeed, David's career decisions appeared to serve only his self-interest. The court, therefore, did not err in concluding that David was voluntarily unemployed and that his ability to pay child and spousal support should not be premised on the amount of his unemployment benefits.

B. IMPUTATION OF INCOME

Having determined that a payor of support is voluntarily unemployed or underemployed, a court must next determine the appropriate amount of income to impute. Maine's child support and spousal support statutes recognize the propriety of determining an individual's ability to pay support based upon an evaluation of her or his "earning capacity" or "income potential." *See* 19-A M.R.S.A. § 2001(5)(D) (1998) ("Gross income [for purposes of determining child support] may include the difference between the amount a party is earning and that party's earning capacity when the party voluntarily becomes or remains unemployed or underemployed, if sufficient evidence is introduced concerning a party's current earning capacity."); 19-A M.R.S.A. § 951-A(5)(B), (D), (E) (Supp. 2002) ("The court shall consider, [among other things,] the following factors when determining an award of spousal support; . . . [t]he ability of each party to pay; . . . [t]he employment history and employment potential of each party; . . . [and t]he income history and income potential of each party. . . ."). A person's earning or income potential is a product of a variety of factors, including that person's qualifications, income history, and the earning or income opportunities that are reasonably available to that person.

The court imputed an earning capacity of $50,000 to David. In its findings the court expressly cited evidence of employment positions available in Minnesota, Georgia, North Carolina, and Mexico, similar to David's previous position at Carleton Woolen Mills. These positions offered salaries in the range of $40,000 to $50,000 per year.

We have not previously considered the extent to which the determination of an individual's earning potential may be based on evidence of employment opportunities that will require the individual to relocate a great distance. This determination requires a careful balancing of all relevant factors because, as here, it has a direct effect on the financial resources of two households and it has the potential to substantially disrupt the relationship between a parent and his children. People, whether in intact, divorced, or blended families, often forego distant employment opportunities based on their own needs and the needs of their children, spouses, and other family members. A court considering distant employment opportunities in connection with an imputed income determination should be mindful of the legitimate nonfinancial factors that may counsel against an individual's acceptance of such employment.

We conclude that the court erred by relying on evidence of distant employment opportunities in determining David's earning potential without also considering the nonfinancial consequences that would result if he accepted such employment. David has never worked outside of Maine. A court order that would have the effect of compelling him to move from Maine to Minnesota or one of the other distant locations is incongruent with his work and life experience to date. Under these circumstances, the court should consider the effect such a move would have on David's long-established familial and social relationships, and, most importantly, his relationship with his children. When considering evidence of distant employment opportunities as part of the determination of an individual's earning capacity, the evidence should be analyzed not only from the perspective of the financial benefits associated with the opportunities, but also from the perspective of the nonfinancial hardships that will result.

The record evidence reflects that a move by David to accept one of the distant job opportunities would substantially disrupt his relationship with his children. Such a move would also substantially disrupt David's social and community ties because he has worked and resided continuously in Maine for the past twenty-five years. In addition, the court did not find that there are no job opportunities for David in Maine that are commensurate with his experience, qualifications and earning history. Under these circumstances, it was error for the court to base its finding regarding David's earning potential on evidence of the salaries associated with distant job opportunities.

Accordingly, we vacate the court's modification . . . order and remand for its reconsideration of all economic issues. . . . In view of the passage of time, the court should receive additional evidence regarding the parties' current financial circumstances.[3] . . .

NOTES AND QUESTIONS

1. In intact marriages, an income-earning spouse may reduce his or her income. The other spouse may strongly object because of the adverse impact on their lifestyle and future options. Courts will not ordinarily entertain a suit to require a current spouse not to reduce his or her income. How are such disputes resolved? Does the fact that the parties no longer live in the same household justify the different approach to justiciability of the dispute?

2. David's loss of income when the plant closed was involuntary and thus would probably have justified a reduction in his support obligations; the litigated issue was the effect of his decision to go to flight school rather than seeking a management job in another textile mill. Was this decision voluntary? What test does the court adopt to determine whether the resulting loss of income warrants a reduction in support?

Few courts hold that a voluntary loss of income can never be the basis for a reduction in support because of the harsh impact on obligors, and they use various tests for determining when a voluntary reduction can support a reduced order. Some courts require that the obligor have acted in good faith, which may mean

---

3. In arriving at David's earning capacity, the court is not limited to the evidence offered by the parties, but may also consider Department of Labor statistics, and take judicial notice of relevant information "generally known within the territorial jurisdiction of the trial court."

simply that the obligor had reasons other than reducing his or her support obligation, or they may use something closer to what *Wrenn* requires. *See, e.g.*, Busche v. Busche, 272 P.3d 748 (Utah App. 2012) (underemployment when obligor has not made reasonable efforts to earn more income does not justify lower support); Andrews v. Andrews, 719 S.E.2d 128 (N.C. App. 2011) (voluntary loss of income evidencing indifference to or a bad faith disregard for one's child support obligations cannot be the basis for reducing obligation). The Connecticut courts hold that a voluntary loss of income demonstrating extravagance, neglect, misconduct or other fault cannot be the basis for a reduction. Olson v. Mohammadu, 81 A.3d 215 (Conn. 2013).

In In re Marriage of Luty, 263 P.3d 1067 (Or. App. 2011), the parties divorced soon after the husband completed his medical internship, and he was ordered to pay spousal support for 17 years in amounts that increased as his income was expected to increase. Thirteen years later, when the spousal support level had risen to $2500 per month, he moved to terminate the obligation because he had lost his license to practice medicine as a result of his drug abuse. His income dropped from between $16,000 and $21,000 per month to $1200 per month. Was his loss of income voluntary or involuntary? If it was involuntary, but the wife argues that he is underemployed, how should the case be analyzed under *Wrenn*? Under the tests discussed above?

3. Many of the loss of income cases involve the obligor's retirement, either at the normal retirement age or earlier. Is this a voluntary loss of income that should be analyzed under the usual rules? In Marriage of Swing, 194 P.3d 498 (Colo. App. 2008), the court held that retirement or cutting back on employment at a "normal" age is not the kind of voluntary underemployment or unemployment that precludes modification of spousal support. The opinion says that this is the majority rule, citing cases from Minnesota, New Hampshire, North Dakota, and Tennessee. "Retirement is a unique circumstance in support modification cases. Notwithstanding the views of the dissent to the contrary, retirement is simply not like other forms of voluntary underemployment. Because retirement is somewhat of an entitlement, the foreseeability or voluntariness of the retirement decision does not affect the support modification analysis, and the weight given to various considerations is not precisely the same as that given under different circumstances. So long as the retirement is objectively reasonable and taken in good faith, we will not look to the potential income of the retired obligor, and we will give the reduced ability of the retired obligor to pay support at least equal consideration with the need of the receiving spouse." Bogan v. Bogan, 60 S.W.3d 721, 733-734 (Tenn. 2001).

In Pierce v. Pierce, 916 N.E.2d 3310 (Mass. 2009), the court held that there is no presumption that an obligation to pay alimony would terminate upon the payor's reaching full Social Security retirement age. This was a major impetus for the Massachusetts alimony reform legislation of 2011, which does create such a presumption. Charles P. Kindregan, Jr., Reforming Alimony: Massachusetts Reconsiders Postdivorce Spousal Support, 46 Suffolk U. L. Rev. 13 (2013), discussing Mass. Gen. Laws Ann. Ch. 208 § 49.

4. When a parent is unemployed or underemployed, child support guidelines typically require that income be imputed to the parent upon a finding that the parent could reasonably be expected to earn more, and courts may interpret

spousal support statutes as requiring a similar analysis, as in *Wrenn*. This analysis is closely related to the analysis of whether a loss of income justifies a reduction in income, but it may be required when the initial order is made as well as during a modification proceeding. What test does *Wrenn* adopt? How is it different from the test for determining whether a substantial change in circumstances warranting a modification has occurred, or is it?

Support awards are not supposed to be based on "speculative" estimates of earning ability, but rather on actual earning ability. Where the obligor has the qualifications for jobs that are readily available, determining earning ability is not so difficult, but as the match between the obligor's skills and the requirements of available jobs decreases, the line between speculating and legitimate imputation of income is harder to discern. For example, in Hutchinson v. Hutchinson, 69 P.3d 815 (Or. App. 2003) (en banc), at the time of the modification hearing, Husband, who earlier had earned $240,000 per year, had been unemployed for a year. His efforts to find work at a comparable salary had been unsuccessful because of downturns in the economy, his age, and the specialized nature of his experience. He sought a reduction in spousal support from $6000 per month to $250 per month. An expert witness for his former wife testified that Husband was qualified for jobs with actual openings that paid $50,000 to $60,000 per year and that he could probably find work paying $120,000 within a year. The trial court modified the spousal support obligation, based on the assumption that Husband could earn $120,000 per year. The appellate court reversed, characterizing the finding as "speculative" but concluding that he could earn $60,000 per year. Why was the higher figure "speculative"? Because jobs paying that much are scarcer? Because the expert testified that Husband would probably have to look longer to find such a job?

5. When loss of income is involuntary because the obligor becomes disabled, the obligor's children may be eligible for Social Security or other benefits. Most courts give the obligor a dollar-for-dollar credit for the benefits a child receives. In re Marriage of Belger, 654 N.W.2d 902 (Iowa 2002), summarizes case law from other jurisdictions. A minority of courts merely consider the child's receipt of benefits as a change in circumstances that may but does not necessarily justify modification of the child support duty. The New York Court of Appeals in Graby v. Graby, 664 N.E.2d 488 (N.Y. 1996), took this approach, analogizing the child's Social Security benefits to other government benefits such as welfare, which parents do not purchase. The court noted, "In many cases, granting the noncustodial parent a credit for Social Security disability benefits earmarked for dependent children might effectively abolish the child support obligation of that parent, who has regular and consistent income, and at the same time dispropor-tionately reduce the resources available to the children." 664 N.E.2d at 491. *See also* Michael A. DiSabatino, Right to Credit on Child Support Payments for Social Security or Other Government Dependency Payments Made for Benefit of Child, 34 A.L.R.5th 447 (1995 with weekly updates).

6. On these issues generally, *see* Elizabeth Trainor, Basis for Imputing Income for Purpose of Determining Child Support Where Obligor Spouse Is Voluntarily Unemployed or Underemployed, 76 A.L.R.5th 191 (2000 with weekly updates); Karen A. Cusenbary, Decrease in Income of Obligor Spouse Following

Voluntary Termination of Employment as Basis for Modification of Child Support Award, 39 A.L.R.5th 1 (1996 with weekly updates).

PROBLEMS

1. When Martha and Fred were divorced, Fred was awarded custody of their child, and Martha was ordered to pay child support. At the time Martha was an untenured teacher in the local school system. Because of budget cuts she has been laid off work. She could get a job as a secretary, earning half as much as she made as a teacher. However, she expects that the school system will be rehiring in a year or so and has decided to go back to school to get her master's degree because that will move her higher on the rehire list and increase her pay if she is rehired as a teacher. She has moved to eliminate her child support obligation temporarily, until she is rehired. Under the tests discussed in the notes above, how would her motion be analyzed? If the court finds that her motion should be denied, should the court impute income to her at the rate that a secretary would make, or that a teacher would make?

2. Assume instead that Martha decided to go to law school, and that she was not employed during the school year so that she could study hard and make good grades and also spend time with her children. She was a very well-paid summer associate between her first and second and her second and third years of law school at a firm where she had good prospects of being hired after she graduated. If the court modifies her child support obligation, should it impute additional income to her for the months when she is not employed, or should her obligation be based only on the income she actually earns during the summer?

3. Joe Hill was ordered to pay support for his two children, who are in their mother's custody, when he was divorced two years ago. Joe works in a manufacturing plant, and his union has called a strike because wage negotiations with the employer have been stalled for six months. The union does not have a strike fund, so that if Joe goes on strike he will have no income. If he does participate in the strike and then moves to reduce his child support obligation because of his loss in income, should the court grant the motion under the tests discussed above?

3. New Families — Spousal Support, Remarriage, and Cohabitation

Traditionally, as we have seen, alimony was considered a continuation of the support duty imposed by marriage. Therefore, it terminated when the recipient remarried because her new spouse's support duty replaced the former spouse's support obligation. Traditional legal principles had little to say about the effect of cohabitation on alimony because open cohabitation without marriage was not socially acceptable. The following materials consider the impact on spousal support duties of two important changes — the changing justifications and criteria for requiring someone to support a former spouse following divorce, and the high incidence of unmarried cohabitation.

PETERSON V. PETERSON

434 N.W.2d 732 (S.D. 1989)

BRADSHAW, C.J. . . . Janey Peterson (Janey) appeals from a judgment terminating her right to receive alimony from Gregory A. Peterson (Gregory). . . .

Finally, the court decree provided the following language: (Gregory) is ordered to pay to (Janey) as alimony the sum of $1,000 per month for a seven-year period starting with the first month after the entry of judgment herein, . . . after said seven-year period, (Gregory) shall pay to (Janey) $500 per month, . . . for an additional 10 years unless during this last 10-year period (Janey) dies or *remarries*, at which time this portion of the alimony shall cease. (emphasis supplied).

Gregory petitioned the trial court to amend its divorce judgment and extinguish his duty to provide alimony when he learned that Janey had remarried on August 1, 1987. Janey resisted. . . .

The trial judge granted [the motion]. . . . [P]ursuant to our ruling in Marquardt v. Marquardt by Rempfer, 396 N.W.2d 753 (S.D. 1986), his obligation to pay alimony was cancelled.

[Janey appeals.]

Janey seeks an affirmative resolution of this issue by advancing three alternative assertions: (1) That the language of the trial court's alimony award indicates by implication that Gregory's duty to pay alimony would not cease if Janey remarried during the initial seven years following the parties' divorce; (2) That the alimony award was an integral part of the property settlement segment of the divorce decree; and (3) That extraordinary circumstances exist, i.e., Janey's new husband is unable to support her, which require the perpetuation of her alimony payments. These contentions will be addressed seriatim.

In *Marquardt*, supra, we opined that "[p]roof that the spouse receiving spousal support payments has remarried establishes a prima facie case requiring the court to terminate the support payments unless [the recipient of the support payments can show] extraordinary circumstances which justify continuation of the payments." By adopting this stance, we rejected the automatic termination rule espoused in Voyles v. Voyles, 644 P.2d 847 (Alaska 1982), and other cases. These automatic termination jurisdictions have allowed alimony to continue, despite remarriage, if the parties' agreement or the decree of the court expressly provided that the flow of alimony was to remain unimpeded by the recipient spouse's remarriage. Janey urges us to adopt this exception in this case.

We must repeat, in order to fully comprehend the gist of Janey's argument, the succeeding pertinent language of the alimony award: (Gregory) is ordered to pay to (Janey) as alimony the sum of $1,000 per month for a seven-year period starting with the first month after the entry of judgment herein. . . . After said seven-year period, (Gregory) shall pay to (Janey) $500 per month . . . for an additional 10 years unless during this last 10-year period (Janey) dies or remarries, at which time this portion of the alimony shall cease.

Since this language fails to provide that alimony payments will end if Janey remarries during the first seven years, Janey maintains that "it clearly implies that remarriage does not operate to terminate alimony during the first seven years." This assertion is without merit.

Janey's reliance on the *Voyles* exception is misplaced because the *Voyles* exception, by its terms, applies only where there is an express statement that alimony is to survive notwithstanding the remarriage of the recipient spouse. Silence in a divorce decree or a voluntary agreement, as to the occurrence of remarriage, falls short of a specific declaration that alimony will endure in the event the recipient spouse remarries. Thus, the parties to a divorce must, to avail themselves of the *Voyles* deviation, point to either a statement in an agreement or divorce decree which provides that the payor spouse will pay alimony, irrespective of the recipient spouse's remarriage, or evidence that the parties intended that the alimonial obligation would survive past the date of the payee spouse's remarriage. Here, since Janey has shown neither the amount of evidence required nor an agreement that alimony would continue after her remarriage, her argument must collapse.

Next, Janey argues that the alimony award was an intrinsic part of the property settlement segment of the divorce decree. . . . We refuse to countenance this contention on the basis of the facts before us.

In Lien v. Lien, 420 N.W.2d 26 (S.D. 1988) (*Lien II*), we held that payments, though denominated as "support," were, in fact, part of a property division between the parties. As such, they were not terminable under *Marquardt*. We reached that conclusion due to the husband's insistence, at trial, that the payments be labeled "support" so that he could avoid the adverse tax consequences attendant to a total cash award of property.

It is apparent from a reading of *Lien II*, supra, that when deciding whether an award of alimony is, in reality, a portion of a property settlement, a court must scrutinize the language of the divorce decree, the circumstances encompassing it, and the end sought to be achieved by the parties. After conducting this examination in the present case, we are left with the conviction that the alimony award was not a disguised property settlement.

Here, the divorce decree provided that Janey receive the parties' right, title, and interest in and to Karen's, Inc. (a retail store), the family residence, the personal property situated within the home, a 1978 station wagon, and $115,063 to be paid in cash within six months of the date of the decree. This amounted to a total property award of $329,858. The cash award was, in the trial judge's words, necessary to "effectuate the property division."

Based on this language, it is obvious that this money, not the periodically paid alimony, was an integral part of the property settlement necessary to accomplish an equitable division of property. The wording of the divorce decree, coupled with the circumstances of the divorce, indicates that the monthly payments made by Gregory to Janey were for her support and were not meant to accomplish an equitable property division. Thus, this contention of Janey's must also fail. . . .

Janey's final position under this alimony issue is that extraordinary circumstances exist which require the continuation of her alimony payments. Janey argues that since she has not profited economically from her second marriage, she needs the alimony to live in the style to which she had become accustomed prior to her divorce from Gregory. In one of her affidavits, Janey says that "I did marry Timothy W. Johnson on August 1, 1987; however, his income, together with my child support, is not sufficient to provide for me and my two minor children."

The following passage, extracted from the opinion in Nugent v. Nugent, 152 N.W.2d 323, 329 (N.D. 1967), capsulizes our view of Janey's assertion:

> [W]e do not believe that such factors [that the husband's fault caused the divorce, that the wife contributed to the household while the husband obtained a medical degree, and that the wife's new husband was unable to provide for her in the same fashion as her previous mate] constitute extraordinary circumstances as would justify the continuation of the alimony payments in this case, [wife] having voluntarily elected to marry another, who now must assume the responsibility for her support.

Additionally, we have said "it is 'illogical and unreasonable' that a spouse should receive support from a present spouse and a former spouse at the same time." *Marquardt*, supra at 754.

Since Janey has shown no extraordinary circumstances to rebut the prima facie requirement that alimony should terminate, we hold that the trial court was correct and did not abuse its discretion in terminating Janey's alimony.

[The concurring opinions of Justice Morgan and Justice Henderson are omitted.]

NOTES AND QUESTIONS

1. Janey first argued that the language of the decree on its face provided that the payments would not terminate during the first seven years after the divorce. What argument supports this construction of the language? Why do you think the court rejected the argument?

In Simpson v. Simpson, 352 S.W.3d 362 (Mo. 2011) (en banc), the court in a similar case reached the opposite conclusion. It held that an agreement providing that alimony would terminate "only in the event of the death of either party" expressed an agreement that it would not terminate upon the wife's remarriage. The court relied on the use of the word "only" as limiting the events that would terminate the obligation. Would the *Peterson* court have agreed?

Other cases requiring that language very specifically provide that spousal support will survive the recipient's remarriage to be enforceable include Moore v. Jacobsen, 817 A.2d 212 (Md. 2003); Hardesty v. Hardesty, 581 S.E.2d 213 (Ala. App. 2003); Holm v. Holm, 678 N.W.2d 499 (Neb. 2004).

2. Janey's second argument is that the clause requiring Gregory to pay her $1000 a month for seven years was part of the property division and so not modifiable. Ambiguity about the character of an award is commonly found in divorce decrees (and separation agreements). Sometimes this ambiguity is the result of sloppy drafting, and sometimes it is created deliberately so that the obligation will be treated as property division for some purposes and as spousal support for other purposes. As you will see in the rest of this chapter, statutes and courts have created different tests to classify an award as property division or spousal support for purposes of modification and termination, for enforcement, for income taxes, and for bankruptcy. However, as *Peterson* illustrates, ambiguity about these issues often invites subsequent litigation. The alternative is for courts and lawyers to address collateral consequences explicitly.

If the agreement in *Petersen* had also provided, "The agreements of the parties as to the payment of alimony as set forth herein have been made and are given in reciprocal consideration for the agreements of the parties as to equitable distribution and property settlement of the parties," would the outcome of the case have been different? *See* Underwood v. Underwood, 720 S.E.2d 460 (N.C. 2011).

In the face of ambiguous language, the *Peterson* court, like most courts, uses a totality-of-the-circumstances test to determine whether the obligation is spousal support or property division. Which factors suggest that the $1000 a month duty was spousal support? Which suggest that it was property division?

3. Under *Peterson*, spousal support terminates on remarriage absent a showing of "exceptional circumstances." What circumstances did Janey allege, and why did the court find that they were not exceptional? How would the *Peterson* court define "exceptional circumstances"? What rationale today supports a rule that spousal support always terminates on the recipient's remarriage? What justifies the *Peterson* court's approach, which has been adopted in many jurisdictions?

The ALI Family Dissolution Principles provide that periodic payments to a former spouse should automatically terminate at the obligee's remarriage unless "the original decree provides otherwise" or "the court makes written findings establishing that termination of the award would work a substantial injustice because of facts not present in most cases. . . ." ALI, Principles of the Law of Family Dissolution § 5.07 (2000).

4. The Oregon Supreme Court in Bates and Bates, 733 P.2d 1363 (Or. 1989) (en banc), adopted a different formulation for determining when spousal support should terminate on remarriage: when remarriage "supplants the purposes behind the initial award." 733 P.2d at 1366. If this standard had been applied in *Peterson*, would spousal support have been terminated? How does a court faced with a motion to modify ascertain what the purposes behind the initial award were?

In New Jersey, the state supreme court has held that the touchstone for determining the adequacy of a spousal support award is whether it assists "the supported spouse in achieving a lifestyle that is reasonably comparable to the one enjoyed while living with the supporting spouse during the marriage." Lepis v. Lepis, 416 A.2d 45 (N.J. 1980). In Crews v. Crews, 751 A.2d 524 (N.J. 2000), the court held that a motion to modify based on changed circumstances should be decided with reference to this standard. To facilitate that determination, it directed trial courts when setting initial awards to make findings establishing the standard of living during the marriage and evaluating whether the award will enable the parties to enjoy a lifestyle reasonably comparable to the marital standard. In Weishaus v. Weishaus, 849 A.2d 171 (N.J. 2004), the divorcing parties reached a financial settlement but could not agree whether the provisions would enable the former wife to maintain the marital standard of living, and they asked the court to enter a final order consistent with their agreement that did not include the findings that *Crews* calls for. The trial judge refused, and the wife appealed, arguing that the findings should not be required if they stood in the way of settlement. How should the case have been decided and why?

PROBLEMS

1. Wanda and Herbert were divorced after a 30-year marriage. Wanda had quit work two years after the marriage to raise their four children, and she had never worked in the market after that. Herbert was the owner of a successful small business. When Herbert and Wanda divorced, the court awarded Wanda more than half of the marital property other than the business and ordered Herbert to pay her $1500 per month indefinitely as spousal support. Judge Anderson said that the award was partially in recognition of Wanda's claim to an interest in the business. The judge explained that she thought spousal support, which is modifiable, was fairer than property division because it required the parties to share the risk that the business might fall on hard times. The judge said that Wanda's lost earning capacity and the length of the marriage justified the award. Two years later Wanda married Simon, who was disabled in a workplace accident and receives a small disability pension. Herbert has moved to terminate spousal support. Under the *Peterson* rule, how should a court rule on the motion and why? Under *Bates*?

2. When Willow and Harvey divorced, their separation agreement, incorporated into the divorce decree, provided that if Willow "shares a residence with an individual with whom she is having an intimate relationship for over a six-month period," her spousal support would terminate. It continued, "however, if such relationship shall cease, then six months after such cessation, the amount of maintenance will be reinstated." Three years later Willow married Joe, and Harvey quit making spousal support payments. However, the new marriage failed after six months, and Willow successfully sued to have it annulled. Under *Petersen*, would the provision in the separation agreement constitute an agreement that remarriage would not cause spousal support to terminate? If not, would the facts come within the terms of the agreement, so that Harvey's support obligation would be revived?

Absent a statute or agreement to the contrary, most courts hold that spousal support does not automatically terminate because the recipient is cohabiting with someone else. A formal reason is that cohabitation does not create automatic reciprocal support duties, and the rule may also reflect understanding of the relative impermanency of many cohabiting relationships. Proof of cohabitation might, however, be the basis for modification based on changed circumstances. *See, e.g.,* In re Marriage of Dwyer, 825 P.2d 1018 (Colo. Ct. App. 1991). On the other hand, parties may agree to terminate support upon the recipient's cohabitation, and statutes in several statutes establish this rule. *See, e.g.,* Ala. Code § 30-2-55 (2014) ("living openly or cohabiting with a member of the opposite sex"); 750 Ill. Rev. Stat. 5/510(c) (2014) ("cohabits with another person on a resident, continuing conjugal basis"); 23 Pa. Cons. Stat. § 3706 (2014) ("cohabitation with a person of the opposite sex who is not a member of the family of the petitioner within the degrees of consanguinity"); 31 Laws P.R. Ann. § 385 (2014) (wife "lives in public concubinage").

Decisions interpreting such agreements and statutes vary greatly; some of the differences turn on language, but they also reflect different approaches to the underlying policy issues.

In the Matter of Raybeck

44 A.3d 551 (N.H. 2012)

Lynn, J. . . . The parties were divorced in Texas in August 2005 after a forty-two-year marriage. The respondent was awarded property in North Carolina and Texas, and the petitioner was awarded property in Laconia, New Hampshire. The divorce decree, based upon the parties' agreement, obligated the respondent to pay the petitioner alimony of $25,000 per year for ten years, in yearly installments. That obligation would cease, however, if the petitioner "cohabitates with an unrelated adult male."

Approximately three months before the January 2010 alimony payment was due, the petitioner moved out of her Laconia house and rented it to reduce her expenses. She moved into the upper level of a single family home in Plymouth owned by Paul Sansoucie, a man she had met through an online dating service. Sansoucie lived on the lower level and did not charge the petitioner for rent. She did, however, pay about $300 per month for food and often cooked for him. They also shared living space on the middle level of the house. When the respondent learned that the petitioner lived with another man, he stopped paying alimony. In response, the petitioner asked the family division to enforce the alimony agreement and require the respondent to resume his support payments.

After a hearing, the marital master recommended a finding that the petitioner was not cohabiting with Sansoucie under the terms of the divorce decree, and the family division approved the recommendation ordering the respondent to continue his alimony payments. This appeal followed. . . .

Neither the legislature nor this court has had occasion to define "cohabitation" as that term is often used in a divorce decree. Because the divorce decree here reflects the parties' agreement, we will interpret the cohabitation clause according to its common meaning. The trial court applied the following standard:

> [E]vidence of a sexual relationship is admissible, but not necessarily required, for a finding of cohabitation. . . . [T]here must be more to the relationship than just occupying the same living area or sharing some or all of the expenses incurred by both parties. The evidence should reflect a common and mutual purpose to manage expenses and make decisions together about common and personal goals, and a common purpose to make mutual financial and personal progress toward those goals.

Applying this definition, the court concluded that the petitioner and Sansoucie did not cohabit. In support of that decision, the court found, among other facts, that the petitioner was forced to relocate when the respondent first announced that he would discontinue the alimony payments; that she and Sansoucie sleep on different floors of the house although they do share a common living area; that she does not pay rent but pays for food; and that their financial relationship is limited to her paying for food in exchange for shelter. The court also found, however, evidence indicating that there was a personal component to their relationship. They had, for example, shared rooms during their travels together. In a letter to her children, the petitioner stated that she and Sansoucie had discussed marriage but did not marry for "personal and financial reasons." Specifically, the petitioner wrote that "neither of us is sure if we want to remarry. Financial matters become so complicated at our age. . . ." The record also reflected that the petitioner's son-in-law referred to Sansoucie as the petitioner's boyfriend in a Christmas letter. Notwithstanding the evidence of a personal connection, the trial court ruled that the petitioner and Sansoucie did not cohabit in light of their financial situation.

Our common law lacks a definition of cohabitation as that term is used in divorce decrees and separation agreements. Dictionary definitions confirm the trial court's conclusion that to qualify a living arrangement as one of cohabitation there must be a personal connection beyond that of roommates or casual bedfellows. *Black's Law Dictionary*, for example, defines cohabitation as "[t]he fact or state of living together, esp[ecially] as partners in life, usu[ally] with the suggestion of sexual relations." *Black's Law Dictionary* 296 (9th ed. 2009). *The Oxford English Dictionary* defines it as "liv[ing] together as husband and wife, esp[ecially] without legal marriage." 1 *Oxford English Dictionary* 447 (6th ed. 2007). *Ballentine's Law Dictionary* defines it as "a dwelling together of a man and a woman in the same place in the manner of husband and wife." *Ballentine's Law Dictionary* 214 (3d ed. 1967); see also *The New Oxford American Dictionary* 330 (2d ed. 2005) ("live together and have a sexual relationship without being married"); *Webster's Third New International Dictionary* 440 (unabridged ed. 2002) ("[T]o live together as or as if as husband and wife. The mutual assumption of those marital rights, duties and obligations which are usually manifested by married people, including but not necessarily dependent on sexual relations.").

Common law standards from other jurisdictions contain similar articulations. *See, e.g.,* State v. Arroyo, 435 A.2d 967, 970 (1980) ("[Cohabitation] is the mutual assumption of those marital rights, duties and obligations which are usually manifested by married people, including but not necessarily dependent on sexual relations."); Cook v. Cook, 798 S.W.2d 955, 957 (Ky. 1990) (cohabitation is "mutually assum[ing] the duties and obligations normally assumed by married persons"); Fisher v. Fisher, 540 A.2d 1165, 1169 (1988) (cohabitation "envisions at least the normally accepted attributes of a marriage"); Frey v. Frey, 416 S.E.2d 40, 43 (1992) (cohabitation "has been consistently interpreted by courts as encompassing both a permanency or continuity element and an assumption of marital duties"); *see also* Gordon v. Gordon, 675 A.2d 540, 546 n.8 (1996) (rejecting proposition that cohabitation is synonymous with common residence). Similarly, *Corpus Juris Secundum* states: "Generally, where alimony is sought to be modified on the basis of cohabitation with another by the recipient spouse, cohabitation is an arrangement in which the couple reside together on a continuing conjugal basis or hold themselves out as man and wife." 27B C.J.S. *Divorce* § 656, at 334 (2005). The notes of that treatise elaborate: "Where the term 'cohabitation' is used in a divorce decree . . . , court must look to whether the parties have assumed obligations, including support, equivalent to those arising from a ceremonial marriage." *Id.*

After carefully reviewing these authorities, we follow them in defining cohabitation as a relationship between persons resembling that of a marriage. As such, cohabitation encompasses both an element of continuity or permanency as well as an assumption of marital obligations. As the trial court recognized, whether two people are cohabiting will depend on the facts and circumstances of each particular case. Beyond living together on a continual basis, many factors are relevant to the inquiry. Primary among them are the financial arrangements between the two people, such as shared expenses, whether and to what extent one person is supporting the other, the existence and use of joint bank accounts or shared investment or retirement plans, a life insurance policy carried by one or both parties benefiting the other, and similar financial entanglements.

We observe, however, that, in considering the financial arrangements, the age of the putative couple may be an important consideration. Where, as here, the individuals are senior citizens, support of one by the other may have less significance than with younger people not only because older individuals may be more financially secure than their younger counterparts, but also because older individuals may have estate plans in place to benefit children of prior relationships.

Also important is the extent of the personal relationship, including evidence of an intimate connection, how the people hold themselves out to others, the presence of common friends or acquaintances, vacations spent together, and similar signs of an ongoing personal commitment. Evidence of a sexual relationship should also be considered, but is not dispositive. Here too, the age of the couple may be relevant in weighing this factor; for older people, a sexual component to intimacy may not be as significant as it would be for younger couples.

In addition, the shared use and enjoyment of personal property is an indication of cohabitation, such as common use of household rooms, appliances, furniture, vehicles, and whether one person maintains personal items, such as toiletries or clothing, at the residence of the other. So, too, are indications that family members and friends view the relationship as one involving an intimate personal commitment. Taken together, these factors will support a finding of cohabitation if they indicate that two people are so closely involved that their relationship resembles that of marriage.

Because the trial court did not have the benefit of the standard we articulate here for determining whether the relationship between the petitioner and Sansoucie amounted to cohabitation, we vacate and remand the case for the master to reconsider the matter in light of the standard we have established.

Vacated and remanded.

NOTES AND QUESTIONS

1. Assuming that cohabitation does not give rise to a support duty, what arguments support the interpretation of the court in *Raybeck*? If you were representing the first husband, what test would you propose, and how would you argue in support of it?

To the main case, *compare* Paul v. Paul, 60 A.3d 1080 (Del. 2012) (statute defining cohabitation as "regularly residing with another adult . . . if the parties hold themselves out as a couple" satisfied where the parties maintained separate residences, spent two to four nights a week together and pursued different activities during the day), and Lee v. Lee, 721 S.E.2d 53 (W. Va. 2011) (separation agreement providing that wife could live rent-free in marital residence until "she enters into another relationship" means a committed relationship akin to marriage, rather than a dating or sexual relationship).

2. Should spousal support be reduced or eliminated when the recipient becomes platonic roommates with someone else? Should this situation be distinguished from *Raybeck*?

3. Several other states provide that cohabitation may be grounds for modifying or terminating spousal support. *E.g.*, Cal. Fam. Code § 4323 (2014) ("cohabiting with a person of the opposite sex" creates a rebuttable presumption of decreased need for support); Ga. Code Ann. § 19-6-19 (2014) (voluntary cohabitation, defined as "dwelling together continuously and openly in a meretricious relationship with another person, regardless of the sex of the other person"); N.Y. Dom. Rel. Law § 248 (2014) ("wife is habitually living with another man and holding herself out as his wife"); 43 Okla. Stat. § 134(C) (2014) ("voluntary cohabitation," defined as "dwelling together continuously and habitually of a man and a woman who are in a private conjugal relationship not solemnized as a marriage according to law, or not necessarily meeting all the standards of a common-law marriage"); Fla. Stat. § 61.14(1)(b) (2014) (recipient is in a "supportive relationship" with another person; statute provides a nonexclusive list of 11 factors to be considered in determining whether a "supportive relationship" exists: public reputation, length of cohabitation, pooled assets, mutual support, performance of services for one another, performance of services for one another's business or employer, common enterprises, joint contribution to purchase real property, express agreements about property or support, implied agreements about same, and support of one another's children regardless of legal duty). For collected cases, *see* Diane M. Allen, Divorced or Separated Spouse's Living with Member of Opposite Sex as Affecting Other Spouse's Obligation of Alimony or Support Under Separation Agreement, 47 A.L.R.4th 38 (1986 with weekly updates).

4. If state law provides that spousal support does not automatically terminate upon cohabitation or remarriage, but rather is a possible change in circumstances, is it contrary to public policy to enforce an agreement providing for automatic termination? Consider the view of Justice O'Hern, dissenting from a decision upholding the enforceability of such an agreement in Konzelman v. Konzelman, 729 A.2d 7, 17-21 (N.J. 1999):

> When viewed through the Gaussian filter employed by the Court, the anti-cohabitation clause appears as a pleasant piece of bargaining between equals. Although the Court properly declines to presume that all women are passive players in this arena, it fails to afford proper weight to the uneven economic playing field upon which the contest takes place. . . .
>
> The majority downplays the woman's loss of freedom or autonomy by asserting that the case is not about sex, but that it is about money, the freedom of contract, and whether the anti-cohabitation provision entered into was "voluntary, knowing and consensual," and based upon "mutuality, voluntariness and fairness." It offends our intelligence for defendant to suggest that the anti-cohabitation clause in this case is not about sex. If the clause were not about sex, why then is cohabitation with another person of the same sex permitted without a reduction in support? For reasons rooted

in our past, "social conventions [still seek to] . . . deny women the same chance of sexual happiness as men. . . ." Alan Ryan, Cultural Perversions, N.Y. Times Book Review at 16 (Mar. 14, 1999) (reviewing Martha C. Nussbaum, Sex and Social Justice (1999)). There is a double standard at play here that views women as having a lesser need than men for companionship of the opposite sex, "yet . . . universally punishe[s] [women] if they display evidence to the contrary. . . ." Natalie Angier, Men, Women, Sex and Darwin, N.Y. Times Magazine, Feb. 21, 1999, at 51.

The danger against which courts have guarded in the past concerns "the numerous ways in which a spouse can use [economic power associated with spousal support] to exert unjust and inappropriate control over the recipient's personal life." Sara Z. Moghadam, The Maryland Survey: 1995-96: C. Dismissing the Purpose and Public Policy Surrounding Spousal Support, 56 Md. L. Rev. 927, 927 (1997). . . .

Mrs. Konzelman is punished for her choice of companionship while Mr. Konzelman is relieved of the burden to demonstrate that his former partner's financial status is any better because of her new relationship. That approach ignores the economic needs and dependency test that underpins an alimony obligation. The trial court found that Mrs. Konzelman's financial status had improved only to the extent of $170 per week because of her relationship.

Mrs. Konzelman was married for twenty-seven years. The record does not disclose whether she left work to raise her children, thereby decreasing her potential for earnings. That is often the case. . . .

Dependency acquired during the marriage based on the marital roles assumed by the parties is at the heart of an alimony obligation. It is manifestly unfair to relieve Mr. Konzelman of all alimony obligations based upon Mrs. Konzelman's choice of companionship with another man, when economic need is the true measure of alimony. The law is casting this partner of twenty-seven years into poverty for what, a sin? If her relationship ends, she will not even have, from the partners' once-shared earning capacity, a dollar a week to live on while Mr. Konzelman will be permitted to reap the benefits of an increased earning capacity built up during the marriage. . . .

In Melletz, supra, Judge Dreier punctured the hypocrisy attendant to anti-cohabitation clauses by asking the rhetorical question: could a divorced wife obtain a similar promise from her husband in return for less alimony? 271 N.J. Super. at 365-66, 638 A.2d 898. . . .

Finally, the enforcement of anti-cohabitation clauses imposes a needless burden on the judiciary and the matrimonial bar. This trial consumed thirteen days over three months and included twenty-six witnesses. The evidence included the reports and testimony of several private investigators, one of whom watched Mrs. Konzelman's home seven days a week for 127 days. It would not have taken thirteen days or a spy in her yard to determine that Mrs. Konzelman's companion contributed $170 a week to the household. As a result of the Court's ruling, each Konzelman hearing hereinafter will result in an exhaustive (and exhausting) inquiry into whether the situation involved something more than "a mere, romantic, casual or social relationship. . . ." (Does this mean that there is a platonic defense to anti-cohabitation clauses?) Such tasteless inquiries into the private lives of divorced women, when unnecessary, are beneath the dignity of the judiciary.

In addition, by approving anti-cohabitation clauses, the Court will force attorneys and parties to bargain over the fair value of the clause. The Court's holding invites husbands to seek such clauses, perhaps as a bargaining chip. There are only two purposes for the clause, either to eliminate the need to examine changed economic circumstances or to retain control over the divorced spouse. Either way, there will be a price. Wives will not wish lightly to contemplate the kind of surveillance this woman endured. It is regrettably the way of the world that only the wealthy will want to or will be able to buy the clause. I would not add to the already emotionally charged denouement of a marriage this unseemly bit of bargaining. . . .

I would reverse the judgment of the Appellate Division and reinstate that of the trial court reducing Mrs. Konzelman's alimony by $170 per week.

PROBLEM

Helen and Martin were divorced in 1993 after a 31-year marriage. Helen had a GED and had not worked outside the home. Martin was a very successful optometrist. Helen was awarded permanent spousal support because the court found that her employment opportunities were limited to minimum-wage jobs. Martin has filed a motion to terminate spousal support because Helen has been living with Vic for almost three years in the home that she received in the divorce from Martin. The evidence shows that neither Helen nor Vic maintains another residence, that they share household expenses more or less evenly, that they have an exclusive sexual relationship, and that they are open about their relationship and socialize with friends and family as a couple. Vic and Helen do not intend to marry, neither has provided for the other by will, and each has arranged for his or her oldest child to manage things if he or she becomes incompetent. They do not have joint bank accounts, their car titles are not held jointly, and Helen has not put Vic's name on the title to the house. Helen has no income aside from the spousal support she receives from Martin, although she could earn $700 a month if she worked full time at a minimum wage job.

Under the approach in *Raybeck*, how should the court rule on Martin's motion and why? Under the statutes cited in note 3 above?

4. New Families — Child Support

One way of understanding cases and statutes that terminate spousal support when the recipient remarries or cohabits is that the appropriate family unit for allocating economic responsibility is the one that functions as a day-to-day household. On the other hand, rules that do not make termination of spousal support automatic express the view that the economic consequences of a previous marriage are so important that they should continue to have an impact despite the reconfiguring of the family. This section considers the similar, but even more complicated, problems in determining how decisions by parents to remarry or assume financial responsibility for children from a new marriage should affect their child support obligations.

Most divorced adults, including parents with custody, remarry, and never-married parents often marry as well. Almost half of all marriages every year are remarriages for one or both spouses, and in about a third of those remarriages, children from a previous relationship live in the household. Rose M. Kreider, Remarriage in the United States (poster submission to annual meeting of Am. Sociological Ass'n 2006). In 2009, 8 percent of all children lived with a stepparent; about 10 percent of children living with two parents lived with a stepparent. Rose M. Kreider & Renee Ellis, Living Arrangements of Children: 2009 at 7 (U.S. Census Bureau Current Population Reports P70-126, June 2011).

When a parent has children from several relationships, the presumptive child support obligation is calculated separately for each group of full siblings, raising the question of how the parent's obligation to his or her other children is taken into account, if at all.

HARTE V. HAND

81 A.3d 667 (N.J. Super. 2013)

KOBLITZ, J.A.D. This appeal raises the issue of how to properly calculate child support for multiple families. Defendant David Richard Hand appeals from two separate child support orders entered on November 7, 2011. . . .

Defendant has three children, each of whom has a different mother. Defendant's oldest son lives with defendant and his current wife. This child's mother lives in Florida and does not contribute to his support. Defendant's younger son lives with his mother, plaintiff T.B. His youngest child, a girl, lives with defendant's former wife, Harte. Defendant was employed as a concrete layer and finisher before he was seriously injured in a 2003 garage collapse at the Tropicana Casino Hotel in Atlantic City. As a result of this injury, he received a settlement of $1.2 million in 2007. He claims to have netted $533,822 after paying several "obligations." At the time of his personal injury settlement, defendant was married to Harte and paying child support to T.B.

After the settlement, defendant agreed to an imputation of $57,200 in annual income when recalculating child support for T.B. Harte and defendant were divorced in 2008 and defendant again consented to an imputation of $57,200 in annual income as part of their January 2009 final judgment of divorce. In 2011, after a history of enforcement motions by both plaintiffs, defendant unsuccessfully moved to reduce child support for both children, claiming he was unable to obtain through wages and investments the agreed-upon imputed income. The motion judge denied his application, but suggested that if he presented a vocational expert who could demonstrate his lack of ability to earn the imputed income, the judge would consider his application again.

Defendant, representing himself for his re-application, moved again to reduce his support, this time supplying the judge with a vocational expert's report that had been prepared prior to his previous motion, but not provided by his counsel to the judge. Defendant stated on the record at oral argument that his wife supported him. . . .

The judge calculated child support for the two children not living with defendant based on the individual financial circumstances of the mothers as provided in the Child Support Guidelines. In both calculations, the judge entered the undisputed dependent deduction of $177 for the child living with defendant on line 2(d). She determined that it would be unfair to the mothers to designate either order as the initial order, thereby deducting that amount from defendant's available income when calculating the support order for the other child. The judge therefore calculated both support obligations using defendant's imputed annual income of $57,200 as if the only other child defendant supported was the oldest son living with him.

We do not approve the child support calculation method utilized by the motion judge. Equality in treatment for the mothers should not be obtained by requiring the father to pay an inappropriately high level of support for both children. According to Rule 5:6A, the Child Support Guidelines "shall be applied" when a court is calculating or modifying child support. The "guidelines may be modified or disregarded by the court only where good cause is shown. . . ." Although we agree with the judge's concern that the two mothers should not be treated unequally, we do not approve of the method used to achieve equality.

The Guidelines require the court to consider multiple family obligations to obtain an equitable resolution that does not favor any family. The Guidelines also anticipate an adjustment when an obligor must support more than one family. Pursuant to the Guidelines, prior child support orders must be deducted from an obligor's weekly income because such an obligation "represents income that is not available for determining the current child support obligation. . . ." Thus, "the amount of such orders must be deducted from the obligor's total weekly Adjusted Gross Taxable Income." By leaving line 2(b) blank on both the Harte and T.B. worksheets, the judge misapplied the Guidelines.

A later-born child should not be penalized by reducing the obligor's available income by the prior child support obligation. To achieve parity among the children of defendant, we suggest the use of the "prior order" adjustment under the child support guidelines must be modified. For example, here, Guidelines support should be calculated for Harte, first considering her child as having the prior order and listing T.B.'s child as the recipient of the second order; then flipping these positions so the T.B. child is considered the first order and Harte's child considered the recipient of the second order. Similar calculations would be performed in T.B.'s matter, first considering her order as the first entered, then as the second entered. In each calculation, the party receiving the "second" order would have the amount calculated for the "first" order entered on line 2(b) of the worksheet. Then, after the four calculations are prepared, all including defendant's oldest child as another dependent deduction of $177 on line 2(d), the two resulting T.B. worksheet obligations, located at line 27, would be averaged and the two Harte worksheet calculations averaged. Defendant would then be ordered to pay the average of the two support calculations to each plaintiff. This method would ensure that the children were treated fairly regardless of birth order, while not disregarding the father's obligation to pay for all three children. This may well not be the only way to equitably calculate support for multiple families, but we suggest it as one workable method of doing so that is consistent with the Guidelines. We therefore remand for a recalculation of support for the two families. . . .

NOTES AND QUESTIONS

1. What arguments justify a rule that attempts to equalize the support a parent pays for all of his or her children, regardless of when they were born or whether they lived in the same household? What arguments would support the other dominant approach, which provides that earlier born children's support is not reduced because of afterborn children (the first family first approach)? *See* Adrienne Jennings Lockie, Multiple Families, Multiple Goals, Multiple Failures:

The Need for "Limited Equalization" as a Theory of Child Support, 32 Harv. J.L. & Gender 109 (2009).

2. Why shouldn't a parent with children with multiple partners be required to support each set of children as if none of the other children existed, as the trial court in *Harte* decreed?

3. Other jurisdictions have struggled with how to equalize support among different families of children. The Vermont legislature enacted the following statute:

(a) As used in this section, "additional dependents" means any natural and adopted children and stepchildren for whom the parent has a duty of support.

(b) In any proceeding to establish or modify child support, the total child support obligation for the children who are the subject of the support order shall be adjusted if a parent is also responsible for the support of additional dependents who are not the subject of the support order. The adjustments shall be made by calculating an amount under the guidelines to represent the support obligation for additional dependents based only upon the responsible parent's available income, without any other adjustments. This amount shall be subtracted from that parent's available income prior to calculating the total child support obligation based on both parents' available income. . . .

(c) The adjustment for additional dependents shall not be made to the extent that it contributes to the calculation of a support order lower than a previously existing support order for the children who are the subject of the modification hearing at which the adjustment is sought.

15 Vt. Stat. Ann. § 656a (2014). Under this section, would Mr. Hand have received a deduction for the support he provided the child who lived with him? How would his obligations to his two sets of noncustodial children have been calculated?

The ALI Family Dissolution Principles provide for a deduction from the obligor's income of child support actually paid under a prior order or agreement. If the prior child lives with the obligor, the obligor gets a deduction for the amount of support that the parent would pay if the child lived with the other parent. ALI, Principles of the Law of Family Dissolution § 3.14(3) (2000). The Principles give the fact finder discretion to grant a deduction when the obligor has subsequently born children. *Id.* § 3.16(1)(c).

4. A number of states give courts discretion to deviate from the calculated amount because of new support duties. *See, e.g.*, Clark v. Tabor, 830 S.W.2d 873 (Ark. App. 1992); In re C.D., 767 P.2d 809 (Colo. App. 1988); Short v. Short, 577 So. 2d 723 (Fla. Dist. Ct. App. 1991); People ex rel. Browning v. Melton, 536 N.E.2d 133 (Ill. App. 1989); State ex rel. Dix v. Plank, 780 P.2d 171 (Kan. App. 1989); In re Marriage of Ladely, 469 N.W.2d 663 (Iowa 1991). *But see* Gilley v. McCarthy, 469 N.W.2d 666 (Iowa 1991); In re Hall, 798 P.2d 117 (Mont. 1990); Hoover v. Hoover, 793 P.2d 1329 (Nev. 1990); Steuben County Dep't Soc. Serv. ex rel. Padgett v. James, 569 N.Y.S.2d 32 (App. Div. 1991); Ainsworth v. Ainsworth, 835 P.2d 928 (Or. App. 1992).

5. Mary Ann Glendon in The New Family and the New Property 71-72 (1981) notes that much of the problem with child support is that persons of limited means divorce, remarry, and produce new families, incurring more obligations than they can fulfill. She discusses "other, more experienced, polygamous

societies," that is, Muslim countries, but suggests that they have not been more successful in dealing with the economic consequences of multiple families:

> In countries where Muslims are still legally permitted to have more than one wife at a time, they are admonished by religious law not to take more wives than they can afford. At least this is a common interpretation of 4 Koran, Verse 4: "[M]arry of the women who seem good to you, two, or three or four; and if ye fear that you cannot do justice, then one only. . . ." Yet this counsel, like much traditional Western marriage law, seems merely the expression of a moral ideal, with little or no legal sanction.

6. Constitutional challenges to child support schemes that give financial preference to prior children have generally been rejected. In Gallaher v. Elam, 104 S.W.3d 455 (Tenn. 2003), a father argued that the Tennessee child support guidelines, which give obligors a deduction for child support paid pursuant to a court order but not for support paid without an order, including for children living with the obligor, violate equal protection. The state supreme court rejected the argument that strict or heightened scrutiny should be applied to the rule, holding that it did not infringe upon the father's right to be a parent or his right to have a relationship with the children and that the classification made by the statute among children did not justify enhanced scrutiny. The court found the distinction drawn by the rule to be rational. *See also* Kimbrough v. Kentucky Child Support Div. ex rel. Belmar, 215 S.W.3d 69 (Ky. App. 2006); Child Support Enforcement Agency v. Doe, 91 P.3d 1092 (Haw. 2004); Pohlmann v. Pohlmann, 703 So. 2d 1121 (Fla. Dist. Ct. App. 1997); Feltman v. Feltman, 434 N.W.2d 590 (S.D. 1989). After the Tennessee Supreme Court decided *Gallaher*, the legislature enacted a law requiring that the guidelines make an adjustment for additional dependent children. Jane C. Venohr & Tracy E. Griffith, Child Support Guidelines: Issues and Reviews, 43 Fam. Ct. Rev. 415, 425 (2005).

7. Most states adhere to the common law rule that stepparents have no duty to support their stepchildren based on their status alone. A number of states' statutes impose a support duty on stepparents under some circumstances, ordinarily when the child lives in the stepparent's home. *See, e.g.,* N.D. Cent. Code § 14-09-09 (2014); Or. Rev. Stat. § 108.045 (2014); S.D. Laws Ann. § 25-7-8 (2014). A few states make live-in partners of the custodial parent at least secondarily liable for the support of the custodial parent's child. *E.g.,* Haw. Rev. Stat. § 577-4 (2014). In a state that does not impose a legal duty of support on stepparents, should the fact that a stepparent does support a stepchild be a ground for deviating from the amount calculated under the guidelines formula?

Empirical studies show that custodial stepparents almost always support their stepchildren. David Chambers, Stepparents, Biologic Parents, and the Law's Perceptions of "Family" After Divorce, *in* Divorce Reform at the Crossroads 102, at 105 (Stephen D. Sugarman & Herma Hill Kay eds., 1990). Recognizing this economic reality, workers' compensation and unemployment compensation statutes generally cover stepchildren who are dependent on a stepparent. *See, e.g.,* Ariz. Rev. Stat. Ann. § 23-1064 (2014); Conn. Gen. Stat. § 31-234 (2014); Ga. Code Ann. § 34-9-13(a)(1) (2014); Ind. Code Ann. § 22-3-3-19(b) (2014); La. Rev. Stat. § 23:1021(3) (2014); N.C. Gen Stat. § 97-2(12) (2012). *See also* Roush v. Director for the Division of Employment Security, 387 N.E.2d 126 (Mass. 1979) (stepchildren covered by unemployment compensation laws).

Chapter 13 considers the circumstances under which courts impose support duties on stepparents after a marriage between a parent and stepparent ends.

8. Most child support guidelines provide that the income of a parent's new spouse is not income for purposes of calculating the basic obligation. In some community property states, courts have held that half of the earnings of the new spouse, which are community property, belong to the obligated parent and are to that extent considered in calculating the child support obligation. DeTevis v. Aragon, 727 P.2d 558 (N.M. App. 1986). Matherne v. Matherne, 571 So. 2d 888 (La. App. 1990), held that a trial court has discretion to apply the guidelines to the combined income of the payor and new spouse, but in Crockett v. Crockett, 575 So. 2d 942 (La. App. 1991), the court held that where the father was involuntarily unemployed and the new wife's income was not sufficient to meet the expenses of a family, her income should not be included under the guidelines.

Courts in other community property states as well as common law property states have interpreted statutes providing that spouses are not liable for each other's premarital debts to mean that a noncustodial stepparent's income cannot be considered in calculating his or her spouse's child support obligation. Hines v. Hines, 707 P.2d 969 (Ariz. App. 1985); Duffey v. Duffey, 631 P.2d 697 (Mont. 1981). *See also* Van Dyke v. Thompson, 630 P.2d 420 (Wash. 1981) (en banc), and Abitz v. Abitz, 455 N.W.2d 609 (Wis. 1990).

Even though a stepparent's income cannot be considered in calculating the basic support obligation, many cases decided before and after the advent of guidelines have held that courts may consider the extent to which the new spouse's income increases the parent's ability to pay and so may justify an increase in an award. *E.g.*, Spivey v. Schneider, 217 S.E.2d 251 (Ga. 1975); Tedford v. Dempsey, 437 So. 2d 410 (Miss. 1983); Ainsworth v. Ainsworth, 835 P.2d 928 (Or. App. 1992); Shank v. Shank, 444 A.2d 1274 (Pa. Super. 1982); Renaud v. Renaud, 373 A.2d 1198 (R.I. 1977). A California statute provides that the income of a parent's new spouse or nonmarital partner "shall not be considered when determining or modifying child support, except in an extraordinary case where excluding that income would lead to extreme and severe hardship to any child subject to the child support award, in which case the court shall also consider whether including that income would lead to extreme and severe hardship to any child" supported by the parent or the parent's new spouse or nonmarital partner. Cal. Fam. Code § 4057.5 (2014). *See also* Proctor v. Proctor, 2007 WL 2471504 (Tenn. Ct. App.) (former husband's involuntary loss of income was a substantial change in circumstances warranting a modification of his spousal support obligation, but because of financial benefits from his remarriage to a new spouse that improve his ability to pay, the reduction was not as great as would otherwise be expected).

A number of courts have also held that a custodial parent's remarriage can reduce the needs of the children, leading to reduced support from the noncustodial parent. *See, e.g.*, Gardner v. Perry, 405 A.2d 721 (Me. 1979); Beverly v. Beverly, 317 N.W.2d 213 (Mich. App. 1981); Abitz v. Abitz, 455 N.W.2d 609 (Wis. 1990).

What is the practical difference between including a stepparent's income in calculating the basic child support obligation and finding that the custodial parent's ability to pay has increased because of his or her new spouse's income?

PROBLEMS

1. Madelyn and Tom were divorced in 1992. Madelyn was granted primary physical custody of their two children, and Tom was ordered to pay child support. Madelyn married George in 1993. In 1994 Madelyn filed a motion to increase child support. Tom submitted interrogatories seeking extensive information about gifts that Madelyn received from George, including entertainment, travel, restaurant meals, and all amounts that George paid directly or indirectly to third parties on her behalf. Madelyn refused to answer the interrogatories on the grounds that the information sought is irrelevant, and Tom has filed a motion to compel.

The child support guidelines in this state are of the Income Shares type, and they define income as "income from any source including but not limited to salaries, wage, commissions, bonuses, dividends, severance pay, pensions, interest, trust income, annuities, capital gains, social security benefits, workers' compensation benefits, gifts, prizes, and alimony or spousal support received." In this jurisdiction stepparents are not legally obligated to support their stepchildren. Information is discoverable if it is relevant to the subject matter of the litigation. How should the court rule on Tom's motion? Why?

2. When Mary and Fred were divorced, she received sole custody of their child, Carl. Mary married Sam a year ago, and they now have a new baby. Mary has decided to quit work and stay home to care for Carl, the baby, and Amy, Sam's child from a former relationship. Carl goes to kindergarten three hours a day, and Amy is in school six hours a day. Before she quit work, Mary earned $35,000 a year. Fred has asked the court to impute this much income to Mary when it recalculates child support for Carl. What arguments can be made in support of this request? How should Mary respond?

5. *A Comparison: Child Support Duties When the Family Receives Public Assistance*

For centuries Anglo-American societies have imposed duties on family members to support dependent relatives who would otherwise receive or are receiving public assistance. We have already seen two circumstances in which such obligations are imposed today. Chapter 2 considered Medicaid eligibility rules, which sometimes provide that the income of an applicant's spouse is deemed to be available for support of the applicant. The section in Chapter 7 about adult children's duty to support their parents dealt with statutes whose original purpose was reducing or eliminating the public obligation to support needy elders.

Until 1996 public assistance for poor families with children was called Aid to Families with Dependent Children (AFDC), and basic eligibility rules were determined at the national level, just as rules about eligibility for Medicaid still are. The national AFDC standards included a variety of relative responsibility rules. The relative responsibility rules imposed support obligations on families of applicants for public assistance that are not legally enforced for other families. For example, Pub. L. No. 97-35 § 2306(a) (1981), provided that a custodial stepparent's income had to be included in determining a child's eligibility, regardless of whether state law imposed a general obligation on stepparents to support step-children. Pub. L. No. 98-369, § 2640(a) (1984), provided that the income of grand-parents had to be included in determining a child's eligibility if the child's parent was younger than 18 and living in the grandparents' home. These rules typically operated by requiring that income of a responsible relative be deemed available to an applicant for assistance, which could have the effect of making the person ineligible or reducing his or her grant, regardless of whether the relative actually provided financial assistance to the applicant.

In Bowen v. Gilliard, 483 U.S. 587 (1987), the Supreme Court upheld another rule that imposed family support duties on welfare families that are different from those of other families. The Court rejected constitutional chal-lenges to a federal rule that required a parent who lived with children who were half-siblings to include all the children in the family unit that applied for AFDC. Before the rule was adopted, such a parent might choose to exclude a child from the family group when that was financially advantageous. For example, if the parent received child support on behalf of one of three children, the family might be better off financially if the parent applied for assistance as a family consisting of him- or herself and only two children. The challenged rule eliminated this option, and suit was brought alleging a violation of the equal protection clause. Finding no basis for invoking heightened scrutiny, the Court wrote:

> The rationality of the amendment denying a family the right to exclude a supported child from the filing unit is also supported by the Government's separate interest in distributing benefits among competing needy families in a fair way. Given its per-ceived need to make cuts in the AFDC budget, Congress obviously sought to identify a group that would suffer less than others as a result of a reduction in benefits. When considering the plight of two five-person families, one of which receives no income at all while the other receives regular support payments for some of the minor children, it is surely reasonable for Congress to conclude that the former is in greater need than the latter. . . .

483 U.S. at 599. The Court also rejected the argument that the rule violated the takings clause:

> The basic requirement that the AFDC filing unit must include all family members living in the home, and therefore that support payments made on behalf of a member of the family must be considered in determining that family's level of benefits, does not even arguably take anyone's property. . . . Nor does the simple inclusion of the support income in the benefit calculation have any legal effect on the child's right to have it used for his or her benefit. To the extent that a child has the right to have the support payments used in his "best interest," he or she fully retains that right. Of course, the effect of counting the support payments as part of the filing unit's income often reduces the family's resources, and hence increases the chances that sharing of the support money will be appropriate. . . . But given the unquestioned premise that the Government has a right to reduce AFDC benefits generally, that result does not constitute a taking of private property without just compensation.
>
> The only possible legal basis for appellees' takings claim, therefore, is the requirement that an applicant for AFDC benefits must assign the support payments to the State, which then will remit the amount collected to the custodial parent to be

used for the benefit of the entire family. This legal transformation in the status of the funds, the argument goes, modifies the child's interest in the use of the money so dramatically that it constitutes a taking of the child's property. As a practical matter, this argument places form over substance, and labels over reality. Although it is true that money which was earmarked for a specific child's or children's "best interest" becomes a part of a larger fund available for all of the children, the difference between these concepts is, as we have discussed, more theoretical than practical. . . .

483 U.S. at 605-606.

The 1997 Personal Responsibility and Work Opportunity Reconciliation Act (PRWORA), Pub. L. No. 104-193, eliminated AFDC and replaced it with Temporary Assistance to Needy Families (TANF). Among the many changes that PRWORA made was the elimination of many federal eligibility rules, including the relative responsibility rules. States now establish their own eligibility rules, and many continue to use the relative responsibility rules.

Critics have argued that this "dual system of family law" is unprincipled. *See, e.g.*, Jill Elaine Hasday, Parenthood Divided: A Legal History of the Bifurcated Law of Parental Relations, 90 Geo. L.J. 299 (2002); Amy E. Hirsch, Income Deeming in the AFDC Program: Using Dual Track Family Law to Make Poor Women Poorer, 16 N.Y. Rev. Law & Soc. Change 713 (1987-1988); Jacobus ten Broek, California's Dual System of Family Law: Its Origin, Development and Present Status, Parts 1, 2 and 3, 16 Stan. L. Rev. 257, 900 (1964); 17 Stan. L. Rev. 614 (1965). *But see* Thomas P. Lewis & Robert J. Levy, Family Law and Welfare Policies: The Case for "Dual Systems," 54 Cal. L. Rev. 748, 775-776, 779 (1966).

PROBLEMS

1. Joell Sanders and her seven children receive welfare. Vertis Lott is the father of one of her children. The state welfare department, as assignee of that child's support right, sued Lott for child support. The hearing officer, applying the state child support guidelines, found that, based on Lott's income, the presumed amount he owes is $82 per week. Lott showed that an order of $42 per week would reimburse the state in full for its payments on behalf of his child and cover food stamps and incidental expenses. Lott has asked the court to reduce his child support obligation to $42 per week, claiming that the facts constitute "extraordinary circumstances" justifying a deviation from the presumed amount. Should his motion be granted? Why or why not?

2. Under state law, parents do not have a legal duty to support their children 18 years and older, except that they must support children between the ages of 18 and 21 who are living with their parents and receiving welfare. Ellen and John Jones share their home with their 19-year-old daughter, Doris, and Doris's child, Bobby. Ellen and John seek a declaratory judgment that the statute requiring them to support Doris violates equal protection and substantive due process. The state relies on Bowen v. Gilliard to support the rule. Can *Bowen* be distinguished? Why or why not?

C.   ENFORCEMENT

TIMOTHY GRALL, *CUSTODIAL MOTHERS AND FATHERS
AND THEIR CHILD SUPPORT: 2011*

Current Population Reports P60-2246 (U.S. Census Bureau Oct. 2013)

In the spring of 2012, an estimated 14.4 million parents (who are referred to as custodial parents in this report) lived with 23.4 million children under 21 years of age while the other parent lived somewhere else. The 23.4 million children living with their custodial parent represented over one-quarter (28.1 percent) of all 83.4 million children under 21 years old living in families. The proportion of Black children in families who lived with their custodial parent while their other parent(s) lived outside their household (50.6 percent) was more than twice as large as the proportion of White children (24.0 percent). Among children of other races — including American Indian and Alaska Native, Asian, or Native Hawaiian and Other Pacific Islander — 17.2 percent lived in custodial-parent families. About 30.3 percent of Hispanic children, who may be of any race, lived with their custodial parent.

The majority of custodial parents (81.7 percent) were mothers, and 18.3 percent were fathers, proportions that were not statistically different from those in 1994. . . .

The poverty level for custodial-parent families declined between 1993 (33.3 percent) and 2001 (23.4 percent). The 2011 poverty rate of all custodial-parent families (28.9 percent) was higher than 2001 and about twice that of the total population (15.0 percent).

Poverty rates varied greatly among types of custodial-parent families. The poverty rate of custodial-mother families in 2011 (31.8 percent) was about double the poverty rate for custodial-father families (16.2 percent). Some of the highest poverty rates (about 57 percent) were found among custodial-mother families in which the mother had less than a high school education, participated in one or more public assistance programs, or had three or more children. Families in which custodial mothers had full-time, year-round employment or who had a bachelor's degree or higher tended to have much lower levels of poverty (10.0 percent and 9.3 percent, respectively). . . .

The rate of participation in at least one public assistance program has increased for custodial parents in the last few years. Among custodial mothers, 34.9 percent received at least one form of public assistance in 2007. By 2011, this proportion had increased to 42.9 percent. Custodial fathers were less likely than custodial mothers to participate in at least one public assistance program in 2011 (23.3 percent). . . .

Approximately half (48.9 percent) of all 14.4 million custodial parents had a court order or some type of agreement to receive financial support from the non-custodial parent(s) in 2012. The majority (88.8 percent) of the 7.1 million parents with agreements were reported by the custodial parent as formal legal agreements — established by a court or other government entity — while 11.2 percent were informal agreements or understandings.

The percentage of custodial mothers who had child support agreements or awards in 1994 was 59.8 percent and increased to 64.2 percent in 2004. Between 2004 and 2012, the percentage declined to 53.4 percent. The percentage of custodial fathers with child support agreements or awards was 28.8 percent in 2012. Historically, the proportion of custodial fathers with awards has been lower than that of custodial mothers.

Child support award rates varied by other demographic custodial-parent characteristics. Custodial parents who were under 30 years of age, Black, never married, or had less than a high school education tended to have lower rates of child support awards or agreements. Custodial parents who were non-Hispanic White, divorced, married, lived with two or more children from a noncustodial parent in 2012, or had joint physical or legal custody in 2011 had higher rates of child support agreements or awards. . . .

When the 7.9 million custodial parents without any type of legal agreement and those with informal agreements were asked why a legal child support agreement was not established, the reason cited most often was that the other parent(s) provided what he or she could for support (36.8 percent). Other primary reasons given were that the other parent(s) could not afford to pay child support and that the custodial parents did not feel the need to go to court or get legal agreements (about 33 percent each). . . .

About three-quarters (74.1 percent) of custodial parents who were due child support in 2011 received either full or partial child support payments. Approximately 43.4 percent of custodial parents due support received all payments they were due, and 30.7 percent received some, but not all, child support payments due. Approximately one-quarter (25.9 percent) of custodial parents due child support received no payments from their children's noncustodial parent(s).

For the 1.7 million custodial parents below the poverty level and due child support in 2011, 39.6 percent received all support that was due, an increase from 26.4 percent in 1993.

Except for gender, where the proportion of custodial mothers who received full payments in 2011 (43.6 percent) was not statistically different from the proportion of custodial fathers receiving full payments (41.4 percent), the receipt of full child support due differed by the demographic characteristics of the custodial parent. In 2011, some of the lowest rates of receiving all child support that was due belonged to custodial parents who were under 30 years old (36.6 percent), had less than a high school education (36.4 percent), had never been married (35.1 percent), or whose child had no contact with the noncustodial parent(s) (30.7 percent). These rates were not statistically different from each other.

Custodial parents who had at least a bachelor's degree (50.6 percent), whose child had contact with their noncustodial parent(s) (49.1 percent), who were divorced (48.4 percent), or were 40 years or older (48.4 percent) had some of the higher rates of receiving all child support payments that were due in 2011. More than half (56.3 percent) of custodial parents with joint physical or legal child custody situations received the full child support that was due from the noncustodial parent(s).

In 2011, the 6.3 million custodial parents who were due child support under the terms of legal awards or informal agreements were due an annual mean average of $6,050, or approximately $500 per month. The median amount of child support due in 2011 was $4,800, meaning half of custodial parents were due less than that amount and half of them were due more. Among custodial parents who had agreements for child support, a total of $37.9 billion in child support payments was due in 2011.

The mean annual amount of child support received by custodial parents who were due support payments in 2011 was $3,770, or about $315 per month. The median annual amount of child support received was lower, $2,400. About one-quarter (26.4 percent) of custodial parents due support received $5,000 or more in annual child support payments. A total of $23.6 billion of child support due was reported as received, or about 62.3 percent of the $37.9 billion that was due. The 2011 proportion and amounts were not statistically different from 1993, when $24.0 billion of the $36.7 billion (65.3 percent) of child support due was reported as received.

In 2011, custodial mothers received $19.5 billion of the $31.7 billion in support that was due (63.2 percent), and custodial fathers received $2.0 billion of the $3.7 billion that was due (54.6 percent). These proportions of child support received by mothers and fathers were not statistically different from each other.

The mean annual amount of child support received by the 4.6 million custodial parents who received at least some of the support they were due ($5,090) represented 16.1 percent of their mean annual personal income in 2011 ($31,520). Child support represented 10.2 percent of income for the 1.9 million parents who received part of the full support they were due and 19.8 percent for the 2.7 million custodial parents who received all child support that they were due. The poverty rates among these groups were not statistically different from each other (about 24 percent).

Child support represented a higher proportion of income for some lower income parents. For example, among custodial parents below the poverty level who received full payments, the mean average child support received in 2011 represented two-thirds (66.7 percent) of their mean annual personal income. . . .

In 2011, 56.7 percent of all custodial parents received at least one type of noncash support, such as gifts or coverage of expenses, from the noncustodial parent(s) for their children. Custodial fathers were more likely than custodial mothers to receive some type of noncash child support, especially when there was no agreement in place.

About 64.8 percent of custodial fathers and 53.8 percent of custodial mothers without agreements received some noncash support.

The most common type of noncash support received was gifts for birthdays, holidays, or other occasions (53.5 percent), followed by clothes (36.6 percent), food or groceries (27.3 percent), medical expenses other than health insurance (16.5 percent), and full or partial payments for child care or summer camp (8.0 percent).

1. *Private Enforcement Mechanisms—Liens, Trusts, and Insurance*

Under some circumstances judges (and lawyers drafting separation and other agreements) can do much to eliminate or minimize enforcement problems.

For example, if a transfer of property is to take effect at the time the decree or agreement is signed, all the necessary documents should be available at the time of execution so that the transfer can be completed immediately. For executory terms, the decree or agreement should establish definite time limits and procedures for carrying out obligations.

The decree or agreement can also employ devices that preclude or discourage noncompliance and make enforcement easier, such as liens and trusts to secure payment of future money obligations. In some states statutes explicitly authorize courts to order that trusts for dependents be established incident to divorce.

To protect a dependent person against the premature death of a supporting former spouse or parent, some states allow courts to order the obligor to maintain life insurance for the benefit of the obligee in a sufficient amount to provide the ordered support. *E.g.*, Fla. Stat. §61.08(3) (2014); Or. Rev. Stat. §§107.810-107.830 (2014). *See also* Or. Rev. Stat. §107.105(f) (2014) ("If a spouse has been awarded spousal support in lieu of a share of property, the court shall . . . order the obligor to provide for and maintain life insurance in an amount commensurate with the obligation and designating the obligee as beneficiary for the duration of the obligation. . . ."). In other states, though, such an order is considered postmortem alimony and can only be entered with the agreement of the parties.

Federal law provides that if a parent can opt to provide medical insurance to his or her children through an employment-based plan, the employers must allow employees to enroll their children who do not live with them, as well as those who do, and regardless of whether the parent may claim the child as a dependent for income tax purposes. 42 U.S.C. §1396g-1. The insurance plan must allow the child to be enrolled outside limited enrollment seasons, and if the noncustodial parent does not enroll the child, the plan must allow the custodial parent to enroll the child. The insurance plan must provide the child the same documents about the plan that it gives participants, and it must permit the custodial parent to submit claims without the approval of the noncustodial parent. It cannot eliminate coverage for the child unless it receives written evidence that a court order requiring coverage is no longer in effect or that the child is covered by other, comparable health insurance. *Id.*

ERISA requires covered group health plans to honor a qualified medical child support order (QMCSO). 29 U.S.C. §1169. This order creates or recognizes the right of a child to benefits from a parent's group health care plan. QMCSOs, which bear an obvious resemblance to the QDROs (discussed in Chapter 6), must include the following information:

- The name and last known mailing address of the plan participant and each "alternate recipient" covered by the order (an "alternate recipient" is a child entitled by the court order to enroll in the plan);
- A reasonable description of the type of coverage to be provided by the plan, or the method by which coverage is to be determined;
- The period to which the order applies; and
- Each plan to which the order applies.

The QMCSO cannot require the plan to provide a type or form of benefit that it does not otherwise provide. Insurance plans must have procedures for determining the validity of QMCSOs and communicating the decisions to affected parties promptly. Since the QMCSO applies only to the plan named in the order, if the parent employee changes jobs, a new QMCSO must be obtained. The rest of this section considers mechanisms for enforcing duties to transfer property or to pay support when the original decree or agreement did not include enforcement mechanisms or the mechanisms were ineffective.

2. Jailing "Deadbeat" Parents

Both federal and state law provide that in some circumstances failure to pay child support is a crime, and obligors who fail to pay court-ordered support for their dependents may be held in contempt of court and jailed in all states.

Both remedies require proof that the obligor knew of the support duty and willfully refused to pay while having the ability to do so. The following case considers whether an indigent obligor is entitled to a court-appointed attorney in a civil contempt proceeding for failure to pay support.

TURNER v. ROGERS

131 S. Ct. 2507 (2011)

Justice BREYER delivered the opinion of the Court. . . . South Carolina family courts enforce their child support orders in part through civil contempt proceedings. Each month the family court clerk reviews outstanding child support orders, identifies those in which the supporting parent has fallen more than five days behind, and sends that parent an order to "show cause" why he should not be held in contempt. The "show cause" order and attached affidavit refer to the relevant child support order, identify the amount of the arrearage, and set a date for a court hearing. At the hearing that parent may demonstrate that he is not in contempt, say, by showing that he is not able to make the required payments. If he fails to make the required showing, the court may hold him in civil contempt. And it may require that he be imprisoned unless and until he purges himself of contempt by making the required child support payments (but not for more than one year regardless).

In June 2003 a South Carolina family court entered an order, which (as amended) required petitioner, Michael Turner, to pay $51.73 per week to respondent, Rebecca Rogers, to help support their child. (Rogers' father, Larry Price, currently has custody of the child and is also a respondent before this Court.) Over the next three years, Turner repeatedly failed to pay the amount due and was held in contempt on five occasions. The first four times he was sentenced to 90 days' imprisonment, but he ultimately paid the amount due (twice without being jailed, twice after spending two or three days in custody). The fifth time he did not pay but completed a 6-month sentence.

After his release in 2006 Turner remained in arrears. On March 27, 2006, the clerk issued a new "show cause" order. And after an initial postponement due to Turner's failure to appear, Turner's civil contempt hearing took place on January 3, 2008. Turner and Rogers were present, each without representation by counsel.

The hearing was brief. The court clerk said that Turner was $5,728.76 behind in his payments. The judge asked Turner if there was "anything you want to say." Turner replied,

> "Well, when I first got out, I got back on dope. I done meth, smoked pot and everything else, and I paid a little bit here and there. And, when I finally did get to working, I broke my back, back in September. I filed for disability and SSI. And, I didn't get straightened out off the dope until I broke my back and laid up for two months. And, now I'm off the dope and everything. I just hope that you give me a chance. I don't know what else to say. I mean, I know I done wrong, and I should have been paying and helping her, and I'm sorry. I mean, dope had a hold to me."

The judge then said, "[o]kay," and asked Rogers if she had anything to say. After a brief discussion of federal benefits, the judge stated,

> "If there's nothing else, this will be the Order of the Court. I find the Defendant in willful contempt. I'm [going to] sentence him to twelve months in the Oconee County Detention Center. He may purge himself of the contempt and avoid the sentence by having a zero balance on or before his release. I've also placed a lien on any SSI or other benefits." . . .

The court made no express finding concerning Turner's ability to pay his arrearage (though Turner's wife had voluntarily submitted a copy of Turner's application for disability benefits). Nor did the judge ask any followup questions or otherwise address the ability-to-pay issue. . . .

While serving his 12-month sentence, Turner, with the help of *pro bono* counsel, appealed. He claimed that the Federal Constitution entitled him to counsel at his contempt hearing. The South Carolina Supreme Court decided Turner's appeal after he had completed his sentence. And it rejected his "right to counsel" claim. The court pointed out that civil contempt differs significantly from criminal contempt. The former does not require all the "constitutional safeguards" applicable in criminal proceedings. And the right to government-paid counsel, the Supreme Court held, was one of the "safeguards" not required.

Turner sought certiorari. In light of differences among state courts (and some federal courts) on the applicability of a "right to counsel" in civil contempt proceedings enforcing child support orders, we granted the writ. . . .

We must decide whether the Due Process Clause grants an indigent defendant, such as Turner, a right to state-appointed counsel at a civil contempt proceeding, which may lead to his incarceration. This Court's precedents provide no definitive answer to that question. This Court has long held that the Sixth Amendment grants an indigent defendant the right to state-appointed counsel in a *criminal* case. And we have held that this same rule applies to *criminal contempt* proceedings (other than summary proceedings).

But the Sixth Amendment does not govern civil cases. Civil contempt differs from criminal contempt in that it seeks only to "coerc[e] the defendant to do" what a court had previously ordered him to do. A court may not impose punishment "in a civil contempt proceeding when it is clearly established that the alleged contemnor is unable to comply with the terms of the order." Hicks v. Feiock, 485 U.S. 624,

638, n.9 (1988). And once a civil contemnor complies with the underlying order, he is purged of the contempt and is free. *Id.*, at 633 (he "carr[ies] the keys of [his] prison in [his] own pockets" (internal quotation marks omitted)).

Consequently, the Court has made clear (in a case not involving the right to counsel) that, where civil contempt is at issue, the Fourteenth Amendment's Due Process Clause allows a State to provide fewer procedural protections than in a criminal case. *Id.*, at 637-641 (State may place the burden of proving inability to pay on the defendant). . . .

Civil contempt proceedings in child support cases constitute one part of a highly complex system designed to assure a noncustodial parent's regular payment of funds typically necessary for the support of his children. Often the family receives welfare support from a state-administered federal program, and the State then seeks reimbursement from the noncustodial parent. Other times the custodial parent (often the mother, but sometimes the father, a grandparent, or another person with custody) does not receive government benefits and is entitled to receive the support payments herself.

The Federal Government has created an elaborate procedural mechanism designed to help both the government and custodial parents to secure the payments to which they are entitled. These systems often rely upon wage withholding, expedited procedures for modifying and enforcing child support orders, and automated data processing. But sometimes States will use contempt orders to ensure that the custodial parent receives support payments or the government receives reimbursement. Although some experts have criticized this last-mentioned procedure, and the Federal Government believes that "the routine use of contempt for nonpayment of child support is likely to be an ineffective strategy," the Government also tells us that "coercive enforcement remedies, such as contempt, have a role to play." South Carolina, which relies heavily on contempt proceedings, agrees that they are an important tool.

We here consider an indigent's right to paid counsel at such a contempt proceeding. It is a civil proceeding. And we consequently determine the "specific dictates of due process" by examining the "distinct factors" that this Court has previously found useful in deciding what specific safeguards the Constitution's Due Process Clause requires in order to make a civil proceeding fundamentally fair. Mathews v. Eldridge, 424 U.S. 319, 335 (1976). As relevant here those factors include (1) the nature of "the private interest that will be affected," (2) the comparative "risk" of an "erroneous deprivation" of that interest with and without "additional or substitute procedural safeguards," and (3) the nature and magnitude of any countervailing interest in not providing "additional or substitute procedural requirement[s]."

The "private interest that will be affected" argues strongly for the right to counsel that Turner advocates. That interest consists of an indigent defendant's loss of personal liberty through imprisonment. The interest in securing that freedom, the freedom "from bodily restraint," lies "at the core of the liberty protected by the Due Process Clause." And we have made clear that its threatened loss through legal proceedings demands "due process protection."

Given the importance of the interest at stake, it is obviously important to assure accurate decisionmaking in respect to the key "ability to pay" question. Moreover, the fact that ability to comply marks a dividing line between civil and criminal contempt reinforces the need for accuracy. That is because an incorrect decision (wrongly classifying the contempt proceeding as civil) can increase the risk of wrongful incarceration by depriving the defendant of the procedural protections (including counsel) that the Constitution would demand in a criminal proceeding. And since 70% of child support arrears nationwide are owed by parents with either no reported income or income of $10,000 per year or less, the issue of ability to pay may arise fairly often.

On the other hand, the Due Process Clause does not always require the provision of counsel in civil proceedings where incarceration is threatened. And in determining whether the Clause requires a right to counsel here, we must take account of opposing interests, as well as consider the probable value of "additional or substitute procedural safeguards."

Doing so, we find three related considerations that, when taken together, argue strongly against the Due Process Clause requiring the State to provide indigents with counsel in every proceeding of the kind before us.

First, the critical question likely at issue in these cases concerns, as we have said, the defendant's ability to pay. That question is often closely related to the question of the defendant's indigence. But when the right procedures are in place, indigence can be a question that in many — but not all — cases is sufficiently straightforward to warrant determination *prior* to providing a defendant with counsel, even in a criminal case. Federal law, for example, requires a criminal defendant to provide information showing that he is indigent, and therefore entitled to state-funded counsel, *before* he can receive that assistance.

Second, sometimes, as here, the person opposing the defendant at the hearing is not the government represented by counsel but the custodial parent *un*represented by counsel. The custodial parent, perhaps a woman with custody of one or more children, may be relatively poor, unemployed, and unable to afford counsel. . . .

A requirement that the State provide counsel to the noncustodial parent in these cases could create an asymmetry of representation that would "alter significantly the nature of the proceeding." Doing so could mean a degree of formality or delay that would unduly slow payment to those immediately in need. And, perhaps more important for present purposes, doing so could make the proceedings *less* fair overall, increasing the risk of a decision that would erroneously deprive a family of the support it is entitled to receive. The needs of such families play an important role in our analysis.

Third, as the Solicitor General points out, there is available a set of "substitute procedural safeguards" which, if employed together, can significantly reduce the risk of an erroneous deprivation of liberty. They can do so, moreover, without incurring some of the drawbacks inherent in recognizing an automatic right to counsel. Those safeguards include (1) notice to the defendant that his "ability to pay" is a critical issue in the contempt proceeding; (2) the use of a form (or the equivalent) to elicit relevant financial information; (3) an opportunity at the hearing for the defendant to respond to statements and questions about his financial status, (*e.g.*, those triggered by his responses on the form); and (4) an express finding by the court that the defendant has the ability to pay. In presenting these alternatives, the Government draws upon considerable experience in helping to manage statutorily mandated federal-state efforts to enforce child support orders. It does not claim that they are the only possible alternatives, and this Court's cases suggest, for example, that sometimes assistance other than purely legal assistance (here, say, that of a neutral social worker) can prove constitutionally sufficient. But the Government does claim that these alternatives can assure the "fundamental fairness" of the proceeding even where the State does not pay for counsel for an indigent defendant.

While recognizing the strength of Turner's arguments, we ultimately believe that the three considerations we have just discussed must carry the day. In our view, a categorical right to counsel in proceedings of the kind before us would carry with it disadvantages (in the form of unfairness and delay) that, in terms of ultimate fairness, would deprive it of significant superiority over the alternatives that we have mentioned. We consequently hold that the Due Process Clause does not *automatically* require the provision of counsel at civil contempt proceedings to an indigent individual who is subject to a child support order, even if that individual faces incarceration (for up to a year). In particular, that Clause does not require the provision of counsel where the opposing parent or other custodian (to whom support funds are owed) is not represented by counsel and the State provides alternative procedural safeguards equivalent to those we have mentioned (adequate notice of the importance of ability to pay, fair opportunity to present, and to dispute, relevant information, and court findings).

We do not address civil contempt proceedings where the underlying child support payment is owed to the State, for example, for reimbursement of welfare funds paid to the parent with custody. Those proceedings more closely resemble debt-collection proceedings. The government is likely to have counsel or some other competent representative. And this kind of proceeding is not before us. Neither do we address what due process requires in an unusually complex case where a defendant "can fairly be represented only by a trained advocate."

The record indicates that Turner received neither counsel nor the benefit of alternative procedures like those we have described. He did not receive clear notice that his ability to pay would constitute the critical question in his civil contempt proceeding. No one provided him with a form (or the equivalent) designed to elicit information about his financial circumstances. The court did not find that Turner was able to pay his arrearage, but instead left the relevant "finding" section of the contempt order blank. The court nonetheless found Turner in contempt and ordered him incarcerated. Under these circumstances Turner's incarceration violated the Due Process Clause.

We vacate the judgment of the South Carolina Supreme Court and remand the case for further proceedings not inconsistent with this opinion.

[The dissenting opinion of Justice Thomas, joined by Justice Scalia and joined in part by The Chief Justice and Justice Alito, is omitted.]

NOTES AND QUESTIONS

1. If an obligor moves to reduce a child support obligation because he or she lost a job and is unable to find work, we have seen that a court will very likely grant the motion. However, many people do not seek downward modifications of support orders as soon as they have grounds. Instead, they stop paying and wait.

Until the mid-1980s, in some states a court could have retroactively decreased a child support obligation in recognition of these changes. However, federal law now requires states to provide that overdue child support is a final judgment by operation of law. 42 U.S.C. § 666(a)(9).

If a parent who becomes involuntarily unemployed does not seek an immediate modification but also quits paying court-ordered child support, can he or she successfully claim inability to pay in a contempt action? The answer is often no. "Inability to pay" for purposes of a contempt proceeding has a very strict meaning. The obligor must be truly unable to pay in the sense that he or she not only has no money but also has not been able to find work. When an obligor falls behind on support obligations because of loss of employment, courts today typically issue "seek work" orders, which, as their name suggests, require the obligor to look for work and to report on those efforts to the court. *See*, *e.g.*, In re Marriage of Dennis, 344 N.W.2d 128 (Wis. 1984).

Between 2003 and 2014, the amount of child support in arrears in the United States grew from more than $60 million to nearly $120 million. Office of Child Support Enforcement, The Story Behind the Numbers: Major Change in Who Is Owed Child Support Arrears, Fig. at 2 (Mar. 31, 2014). "The driving factor . . . is the underlying characteristics of the individuals who owe arrears. Most arrears are owed by parents who owe substantial amounts of arrears, have little or no income, and have owed arrears for some time. These characteristics make it difficult to collect arrears. One study of nine large states estimated that only 40 percent of the arrears in those states were likely to be collected in 10 years and that arrears were likely to grow by 60 percent during that period unless states took steps to manage arrears growth." *Id.* at 1.

2. Did Michael Turner appear to know that if he was "unable" to pay he would have a defense? If the trial judge had told him this, do you think he would have known how to prove his inability to pay?

3. How important to the decision in *Turner* is the possibility that the petitioner in a civil contempt proceeding may also be unrepresented? Why isn't the solution to this imbalance to provide an attorney to both parties?

Many people anticipated that *Turner* might be the "civil *Gideon*," i.e., the case holding that a person facing the threat of jail, whether the proceeding is civil or criminal, has a constitutional right to counsel, and the unanimous opinion rejecting such a right provoked mixed responses. Supporters of the Court's alternative solution doubted whether a constitutional right to a lawyer would provide much protection, considering the poor qualify of representation provided to many criminal defendants who have overworked public defenders with caseloads much too large to allow them to do good work. From this perspective, the Court's invitation to make contempt proceedings more accessible to lay people could be a much more successful means of providing access to justice. Commentary on the issue includes Stephanos Bibas, Shrinking *Gideon* and Expanding Alternatives to Lawyers, 70 Wash. & Lee L. Rev. 1287 (2013); Russell Engler, Turner v. Rogers and the Essential Role of the Courts in Delivering Access to Justice, 7 Harv. L. & Pol'y Rev. 31 (2013); Elizabeth G. Patterson, Civil Contempt and the Indigent Child Support Obligor: The Silent Return of Debtor's Prison, 18 Cornell J.L. & Pub. Pol'y 95 (2008).

4. The *Turner* opinion suggests that a defendant in a civil contempt action brought by the state child support enforcement agency might be entitled to a court-appointed attorney. The few courts that have addressed the issue are divided. *Compare* State v. Currier, 295 P.3d 837 (Wyo. 2013) (no right to counsel), *with* Crain v. Crain, 2012 WL 6737836 (Ohio App.) (due process requires counsel).

5. As *Turner* says, due process does not require the petitioner in a civil contempt proceeding to prove that the defendant was able to pay, and many states put the burden of proof on the defendant. In a jurisdiction that treats ability to pay as an element of nonsupport that must be proven by the petitioner, what kind of evidence would be sufficient to establish that an obligor was able to pay? In State v. Nuzman, 95 P.3d 252 (Or. App. 2004), the mother testified that when the order was entered, the father was capable of working as a bartender. Over the next 17 years, however, she received small support payments from him on only two occasions, and she had no contact with him or even knowledge of his whereabouts. A clerk who worked for the attorney handling the case testified that the file did not contain any information indicating that the father had a criminal record or that he was receiving disability payments. The clerk also testified that in the usual course of business the office checks criminal records and disability rolls for the names of delinquent obligors every three months. From this, the attorney argued, it should be inferred that the father was not incarcerated or disabled during the time he had not paid support. Would this be enough evidence to prove beyond a reasonable doubt that the father had the ability to pay? Would it make any difference if the file contained 17 years' worth of printouts showing that the father was not incarcerated or receiving disability payments?

6. Defendants in child support contempt proceedings have argued that jailing them for nonpayment violates the Thirteenth Amendment ban on involuntary servitude, state constitutional rules against debtor's prison, or both, but these claims fail. For example, in Moss v. Superior Court, 950 P.2d 59 (Cal. 1998), the court said:

> In its decisions applying the Thirteenth Amendment, the United States Supreme Court has recognized that many fundamental societal obligations involving compelled labor do not violate the proscription of involuntary servitude. It has never held that employment undertaken to comply with a judicially imposed requirement that a party seek and accept employment when necessary to meet a parent's fundamental obligation to support a child is involuntary servitude.
>
> In those decisions in which a Thirteenth Amendment violation has been found on the basis of involuntary servitude, the court has equated the employment condition to peonage, under which a person is bound to the service of a particular employer or master until an obligation to that person is satisfied. A court order that a parent support a child, compliance with which may require that the parent seek and accept employment, does not bind the parent to any particular employer or form of employment or otherwise affect the freedom of the parent. The parent is free to elect the type of employment and the employer, subject only to an expectation that to the extent necessary to meet the familial support obligation, the employment will be commensurate with the education, training, and abilities of the parent. . . .
>
> A parent's obligation to support a minor child is a social obligation that is no less important than compulsory military service, road building, jury service and other constitutionally permissible enforced labor. Even if the necessity of accepting

employment in order to meet this obligation were somehow analogous to those forms of compelled labor, we have no doubt that this form of labor would be recognized as an exception to the ban on involuntary servitude found in the Thirteenth Amendment. . . .

Family support obligations are not ordinary debts subject to the constitutional prohibition of imprisonment for debt. It is held that the obligation to make such payments is not a "debt" within the meaning of the constitutional guaranty against imprisonment for debt.

. . . [A]parent who knows that support is due, has the ability to earn money to pay that support, and still willfully refuses to seek and accept available employment to enable the parent to meet the support obligation acts against fundamental societal norms and fair dealing, and necessarily intentionally does an act which prejudices the rights of his children. This conduct would fall within the fraud exception to the constitutional prohibition of imprisonment for debt.

Is the court's argument convincing? Is a parent free to decline work that he does not enjoy? Could a parent who left a high-paying job for one that provided lower pay and more job satisfaction successfully claim that he or she was "unable" to pay child support at a level based on the original job? For further discussion, *see* Walter W. Klein, Moss v. Superior Court: Enforcing Child Support Orders with New Rules for Contempt Actions, 29 Sw. U. L. Rev. 529 (2000).

7. Sometimes an obligor who fails to pay support attempts to justify this action on the basis that he or she is not receiving access to the child as required by a court order because of the actions of the residential parent, the child or both. Ordinarily, access and child support are independent in the sense that a residential parent's failure to allow the other parent access does not excuse the nonresidential parent from paying child support. Homer H. Clark, Jr., The Law of Domestic Relations in the United States § 16.6 at 682 (2d ed. 1988).

Some courts distinguish visitation interference, which is not a defense to nonpayment of support, from active concealment of a child, which is. The leading case is Damico v. Damico, 872 P.2d 126 (Cal. 1994). The bases for the distinction are that a parent whose child is actively concealed cannot invoke other remedies to gain access and that if the payor does not know where the child is, he or she cannot make payments and the purpose of the order, to provide for the child, is defeated. In Comer v. Comer, 927 P.2d 265 (Cal. 1996), the California Supreme Court limited *Damico*, holding that even if a child has been "actively concealed," the parent deprived of visitation may be required to pay child support arrearages that accrued during the concealment if the concealment ends while the child is still a minor because the child can still benefit from payment of the arrearages. *See* Ira Mark Ellman, Should Visitation Denial Affect the Obligation to Pay Support?, 36 Ariz. St. L.J. 661 (2004).

8. In most jurisdictions, an obligor cannot satisfy an order to pay a specific sum in support by purchasing goods or services instead, and obligors are not entitled to offset the costs of such purchases against the amount they owe. Leslie J. Harris, Dennis Waldrop & Lori R. Waldrop, Making and Breaking Connections Between Parents' Duty to Support and Right to Control Their Children, 69 Or. L. Rev. 689, 712 (1990). However, some courts use their equitable powers to make exceptions, especially when the custodial parent has consented to substituting purchases for payments.

9. Since Elizabethan times, willful failure to support a dependent has been a crime, and many states have criminal nonsupport statutes on the books. *See, e.g.,* Model Penal Code § 230.5. These statutes have fallen into disuse in many places, though they are being used more frequently in some places as a result of current interest in child support enforcement.

People v. Likine, 823 N.W.2d 50 (Mich. 2012), held that the Michigan criminal nonsupport statute imposes strict liability and that the traditional claim of inability to pay is not a defense. However, it also concluded that if was truly impossible for the defendant to pay, he or she had not acted voluntarily and should be acquitted on the basis that the state had not proven the actus reus of the crime. Explaining the meaning of impossibility in this context, the court said:

> [W]e hold that to establish an impossibility defense for felony nonsupport, a defendant must show that he or she acted in good faith and made *all reasonable efforts* to comply with the family court order, but could not do so through no fault of his or her own. In our view, "sufficient bona fide efforts to seek employment or borrow money in order to pay" certainly are expected, but standing alone will not necessarily establish an impossibility defense to a charge under MCL 750.165. Instead, defendants charged with felony nonsupport must make *all reasonable efforts*, and use all resources at their disposal, to comply with their support obligations. For the payment of child support to be truly impossible, a defendant must explore and eliminate all the reasonably possible, lawful avenues of obtaining the revenue required to comply with the support order. Defendants must not only establish that they cannot pay, but that theirs are among the exceptional cases in which it was not reasonably *possible* to obtain the resources to pay. A defendant's failure to undertake those efforts reflects "an insufficient concern for paying the debt" one owes to one's child, which arises from the individual's responsibility as a parent.
>
> To determine whether a defendant has established impossibility in the context of a felony nonsupport case, we provide, for illustrative purposes only, a nonexhaustive list of factors for courts to consider. These should include whether the defendant has diligently sought employment; whether the defendant can secure additional employment, such as a second job; whether the defendant has investments that can be liquidated; whether the defendant has received substantial gifts or an inheritance; whether the defendant owns a home that can be refinanced; whether the defendant has assets that can be sold or used as loan collateral; whether the defendant prioritized the payment of child support over the purchase of nonessential, luxury, or otherwise extravagant items; and whether the defendant has taken reasonable precautions to guard against financial misfortune and has arranged his or her financial affairs with future contingencies in mind, in accordance with one's parental responsibility to one's child. The existence of unexplored possibilities for generating income for payment of the court-ordered support suggests that a defendant has not raised a true impossibility defense, but merely an assertion of inability to pay. A defendant's failure to explore every reasonably possible avenue in order to pay his or her support obligation not only reflects "an insufficient concern for paying the debt he owes to society," it also reflects an insufficient concern for the child. In those instances, the defendant may not invoke the shield of the impossibility defense.

823 N.W.2d at 70-72.

10. Failure to pay child support may be a crime under the federal Child Support Recovery Act. The criminal provision, also known as the Deadbeat

Parents Punishment Act, 18 U.S.C. § 228, authorizes imprisonment for six months for willful failure to pay support for a child who lives in another state for more than a year and for up to two years imprisonment for traveling in interstate commerce with intent to evade a support obligation or for willfully failing to pay support for a child in another state for more than two years. Ability to pay is an element of the crime, but it is rebuttably presumed from proof that a support obligation was in effect at the time of the failure to pay. 18 U.S.C. § 228(b). If this presumption is construed as shifting the burden of persuasion on the issue of ability to pay to the defendant, it is unconstitutional. United States v. Grigsby, 85 F. Supp. 2d 100 (D.R.I. 2000). However, the presumption may be constitutional if it is construed so that the prosecution bears the burden of persuasion on this issue.

11. David Oakley was convicted in Wisconsin of intentionally refusing to pay child support for his nine children as a repeat offender. The trial judge sentenced Oakley to three years in prison the first count, imposed and stayed the execution of an eight-year sentence on two more counts and imposed a five-year term of probation to follow his incarceration; the judge also imposed as a condition of probation that Oakley not have any more children unless he could demonstrate that he was supporting his existing children and had the ability to support another child. Oakley sought postconviction relief, arguing that the condition unconstitutionally limited his right to procreate, citing Skinner v. Oklahoma, 316 U.S. 535 (1942), and Zablocki v. Redhail, 434 U.S. 374 (1978) (page 156 of this text). The divided Wisconsin Supreme Court affirmed in State v. Oakley, 629 N.W.2d 200 (Wis. 2001). The majority, emphasizing that Oakley was convicted of felony intentional refusal to support, scrutinized the probation condition for reasonableness. It found that the condition was not overly broad because it did not eliminate his right to procreate and that it was reasonably related to the goal of rehabilitation. The dissenting justices argued that the means chosen to achieve the state goals here were, as in *Zablocki*, not sufficiently closely tailored to the state goals. In State v. Talty, 814 N.E.2d 1201 (Ohio 2004), the Ohio Supreme Court held unconstitutional an antiprocreation order that did not allow the father to have the order lifted if he became current on his child support obligation. The court expressed no opinion on whether an order with such a provision (like the one upheld in *Oakley*) would be constitutional.

12. Courts are divided about whether contempt proceedings can be used to enforce nonmodifiable property division orders. Some courts say that the constitutional prohibition of debtors' prison precludes this use of contempt. *E.g.*, Stone v. Stidham, 393 P.2d 923 (Ariz. 1964); Bradley v. Superior Court, 310 P.2d 634 (Cal. 1957); McAlear v. McAlear, 469 A.2d 1256 (Md. 1984). Other courts have found no constitutional impediment to the use of the contempt power to enforce monetary obligations in property division. *E.g.*, Harvey v. Harvey, 384 P.2d 265 (Colo. 1963); Haley v. Haley, 648 S.W.2d 890 (Mo. App. 1982); Harris v. Harris, 390 N.E.2d 789 (Ohio 1979); Hanks v. Hanks, 334 N.W.2d 856 (S.D. 1983).

NOTE: CIVIL OR CRIMINAL CONTEMPT?

A defendant facing a criminal contempt action for failure to pay child support is entitled to the constitutional protections generally afforded defendants in criminal proceedings, including the right to have the facts constituting the contempt proven by the prosecution beyond a reasonable doubt, the privilege against self-incrimination, and the right to jury trial. Hicks v. Feiock, 485 U.S. 624, 629 (1988); United Mine Workers of America v. Bagwell, 512 U.S. 821, 826-827 (1994).

In its first case dealing with the distinction between civil and criminal contempt, the U.S. Supreme Court observed, "It may not be always easy to classify a particular act as belonging to either of these two classes." Bessette v. W.B. Conkey Co., 194 U.S. 324, 329 (1904). The problem arises because neither the nature of the proceeding nor the kind of behavior leading to the sanction provides a basis for categorizing. An individual may be held in civil contempt for acts arising out of a criminal case. For example, a witness's refusal to testify may be treated as a civil contempt, even in a murder prosecution. An individual may also be held in criminal contempt for acts arising in a civil matter, as where a plaintiff or her lawyer curses the judge. Nor is the contemnor's behavior a clear indicator of the kind of contempt. Nonpayment of child support may be civil or criminal.

In Hicks v. Feiock, above, an appeal from a California decision holding a child support obligor in contempt for nonpayment, the Supreme Court discussed the test for distinguishing civil from criminal contempt:

> The question of how a court determines whether to classify the relief imposed in a given proceeding as civil or criminal in nature, for the purposes of applying the Due Process Clause and other provisions of the Constitution, is one of long standing, and its principles have been settled at least in their broad outlines for many decades. . . . [T]he labels affixed either to the proceeding or to the relief imposed under state law are not controlling and will not be allowed to defeat the applicable protections of federal constitutional law. This is particularly so in the codified laws of contempt, where the "civil" and "criminal" labels of the law have become increasingly blurred.
>
> Instead, the critical features are the substance of the proceeding and the character of the relief that the proceeding will afford. . . . The character of the relief imposed is thus ascertainable by applying a few straightforward rules. If the relief provided is a sentence of imprisonment, it is remedial if "the defendant stands committed unless and until he performs the affirmative act required by the court's order," and is punitive if "the sentence is limited to imprisonment for a definite period." If the relief provided is a fine, it is remedial when it is paid to the complainant, and punitive when it is paid to the court, though a fine that would be payable to the court is also remedial when the defendant can avoid paying the fine simply by performing the affirmative act required by the court's order. . . .
>
> In repeatedly stating and following the rules set out above, the Court has eschewed any alternative formulation that would make the classification of the relief imposed in a State's proceedings turn simply on what their underlying purposes are perceived to be. Although the purposes that lie behind particular kinds of relief are germane to understanding their character, this Court has never undertaken to psychoanalyze the subjective intent of a State's laws and its courts, not only because that effort would be unseemly and improper, but also because it would be misguided. In contempt cases, both civil and criminal relief have aspects that can be seen as either remedial or punitive or both: when a court imposes fines and punishments on a contemnor, it is not only vindicating its legal authority to enter the initial court order, but it also is seeking to give effect to the law's purpose of modifying the

contemnor's behavior to conform to the terms required in the order. . . . For these reasons, this Court has judged that conclusions about the purposes for which relief is imposed are properly drawn from an examination of the character of the relief itself.

485 U.S. at 631-635.

For purposes of determining whether an indigent person has the right to counsel in a contempt proceeding, many courts have abandoned the civil-criminal distinction. For example, in Mead v. Batchlor, 460 N.W.2d 493 (Mich. 1990), the court held that a person must be afforded the right to counsel, including the right to free counsel if indigent, before he or she can be incarcerated for nonpayment of support, regardless of whether the contempt proceeding is civil or criminal.

PROBLEMS

1. Oliver faithfully complied with an order requiring him to pay $300 per month to his former wife, Paula, for the support of their child, Carlo, until he lost his job as a skilled worker in a plywood mill when the mill closed. While he received unemployment compensation, Oliver looked for work and continued to pay child support. He could not find another mill job, however, and since his unemployment compensation ran out, Oliver has only worked sporadically at odd jobs. He stopped paying child support. Because Oliver was at home much of the time, Carlo, now four, began to spend most of his time at Oliver's house.

A month ago Paula, whose hours at work had just been cut, demanded that Oliver pay her the amounts he owes her for the last five months. She says that she cannot afford to maintain the house for herself and Carlo without this money, and she believes that Oliver could get steady work if he only tried harder. When Oliver refused, Paula angrily told him he could not see Carlo anymore unless he paid up. Oliver has not seen Carlo since, even though the divorce degree provides that he is entitled to visit for eight hours every Saturday.

Two weeks ago Oliver was served with a motion to show cause why he should not be held in (civil) contempt for failing to comply with the child support order. What defenses should his attorney assert on his behalf? How should Paula's attorney respond?

2. Barbara Chadwick filed for divorce in 1992. During pretrial proceedings, her husband Beatty informed the court that he had transferred $2.5 million of marital funds to satisfy an alleged debt to a company in Gibraltar. Barbara's attorney then learned and revealed to the court further information that suggested that the debt might be a sham. The trial judge determined that the transfer was an attempt to defraud Barbara and ordered Beatty to return the $2.5 million to an account over which the court had jurisdiction. Beatty refused to comply, and Barbara moved to have him held in civil contempt. The court found that Beatty had the present ability to comply with the order, held him in civil contempt, and ordered him jailed until he complied with the order. Beatty refused to comply and has been in jail ever since. He has applied eight times to state trial courts and six times to the federal court for release. His latest petition argues that the facts amply demonstrate that there is no possibility that he will ever comply with the order and that, therefore, the action has ceased to be one for civil contempt and has become a

punitive, criminal contempt. He then argues that because he was jailed without being accorded the usual constitutional criminal procedure protections, he must be released or retried. What arguments should the attorneys for Barbara and Beatty make on the issue of whether the contempt action is civil or criminal?

3. The State-Federal Child Support Enforcement Program

Support orders enforced by levying on an obligor's property or by using contempt powers suffer from limitations in addition to the legal ones that we have been examining. As a practical matter, obligees ordinarily need attorneys to draft the appropriate documents and shepherd cases through court. And both kinds of devices are available only to enforce past-due support; neither operates prospectively.

Responding to mounting evidence of problems in child support enforcement, in 1975 Congress enacted Title IV-D of the Social Security Act, Pub. L. No. 93-647, which created the federal Office of Child Support Enforcement. The legislation requires each state to establish a child support enforcement agency, also called a IV-D agency. Additional requirements have been imposed since then. Major provisions are codified at 42 U.S.C. §§ 651-662, 666. A state that does not comply with these requirements loses substantial federal funding for its welfare program. In addition, the federal government pays a percentage of the costs of the states' enforcement programs and provides other financial incentives, which are based in part on the amount of support money collected.

The state IV-D agency must provide certain services, including establishment of support duties, establishment of paternity, and location of absent parents. States cannot charge custodial parents receiving welfare benefits for these services, although they may charge parents who are not receiving welfare a modest application fee. In the mid-1990s it was estimated that at least 60 percent of all child support enforcement actions are brought by IV-D agencies. Paul K. Legler, The Coming Revolution in Child Support Policy; Implications of the 1996 Welfare Act, 30 Fam. L.Q. 519, 522 (1996). In most states the agency attorney who provides these services does not represent the residential parent; instead, like criminal prosecutors, they are said to represent the state. For a discussion of the complex practical and ethical issues that this role presents for attorneys, *see* Barbara Glesner Fines, From Representing "Clients" to Serving "Recipients": Transforming the Role of the IV-D Child Support Enforcement Attorney, 67 Fordham L. Rev. 2155 (1999).

Expedited Processes To expedite the collection of child support, states must have an administrative or quasi-judicial process for obtaining and enforcing support orders in IV-D cases. Some states also handle non-IV-D cases through their administrative processes. Most states that use an administrative process give their courts concurrent original jurisdiction in support cases and provide for appellate judicial review of administrative orders. Federal regulations require that states provide obligors with due process safeguards. Administrative orders must have the same force and effect as court orders, each party must receive a copy of the order, and the state must have written procedures for ensuring that the presiding officers are qualified. 45 C.F.R. § 303.101(c) (1987). Neither the presiding officer nor the parent's advocate must be an attorney. 45 C.F.R. § 303.101(c)(4) (1987).

Enforcement by Wage Withholding   Perhaps the most important enforcement devices are those that allow wage withholding. States must require wage withholding in all child support cases unless a court or administrative agency hearing officer finds good cause, put in writing, not to implement withholding immediately, or the parties agree not to implement withholding immediately. A delinquency equal to one month's amount of support that occurs after one of these exceptions takes effect results in mandatory income withholding, regardless of the good cause finding or parties' agreement. 42 U.S.C. §§ 666(a)(1), 666(b).

Where income withholding is triggered by an alleged arrearage, the obligor is entitled to prior notice and a hearing. The exact procedures for giving notice and allowing contests vary from state to state. The Federal Consumer Credit Protection Act, 15 U.S.C. §§ 1671-1677, limits how much of a person's wages may be withheld. The basic limit is 50 percent of disposable earnings for a noncustodial parent who is not supporting a second family. This amount is much higher than the amount of an obligor's wages that can be withheld to enforce other debts.

Other Enforcement Devices   States must provide a number of other ways to enforce child support, including:

- Judicial authority to impose liens against real and personal property for amounts of overdue support;
- Judicial authority to require obligors to post a bond or give some other guarantee to secure payment of overdue support;
- Allowing failure to pay child support to be reported to consumer credit bureaus;
- Withholding state tax refunds payable to a parent of a child receiving child support services, if the parent is delinquent in making payments; and
- Suspending the driver's licenses and professional, occupational, and recreational licenses of delinquent obligors.

In addition, the IRS must withhold federal tax refunds due to delinquent child support obligors, and parents who owe child support may be denied federal loans.

Efforts to Locate Parents   Federal legislation requires the establishment of a national directory of new hires, which contains employment information about everyone hired in the United States, and of similar state directories. The legislation also requires creation of national and state registries of child support orders. These databases will be linked so that orders can be matched with obligors quickly. States must also have automated, centralized systems for recording the payment and dispersal of child support.

The Program's Effectiveness   The Office of Child Support Enforcement offered the following assessment of the effectiveness of its program.

OFFICE OF CHILD SUPPORT ENFORCEMENT,
FY 2012 PRELIMINARY REPORT

August 2013

Caseload: There were 15.7 million total cases in the IV-D program at the end of FY 2012. This was a small decrease (0.5 percent) from FY 2011. This drop was driven primarily by an 8 percent decrease in the current assistance caseload. There were increases, however, in the former assistance (0.5 percent) and never assistance (0.5 percent) caseloads. Despite small decreases in FY 2011 and FY 2012, the total IV-D caseload is still higher than the pre-recession low in FY 2008. This is primarily due to a 7 percent increase in the never assistance caseload since FY 2008. Since FY 2008, the current assistance caseload is down by 8 percent and the former assistance caseload is down by 4 percent.

Collections: The Child Support Program collections continued to increase for the third year in a row. Total collections increased by 1.4 percent to $31.6 billion in FY 2012 compared to $31.2 billion in FY 2011, as indicated in Chart 2. This was driven primarily by the 1.5 percent increase in IV-D distributed collections that increased to $27.7 billion in FY 2012. Non-IV-D collections remained unchanged at $3.9 billion. The amount of IV-D collections distributed to families increased by 2 percent, but assistance reimbursement decreased by 5 percent.

The overall increase in collections was due primarily to a 3 percent increase in collections from income withholding, particularly payroll-based withholding. . . . [T]hese collections now account for approximately 72 percent of total collections. In FY 2012, collections from the offset of unemployment compensation payments continued to drop. During the recent recession, there was dramatic growth in these collections. The collections increased by more than 4 times over the period between FY 2007 and FY 2010. In FY 2011, these collections decreased by 24 percent, and in FY 2012 they decreased another 24 percent over FY 2011. Even with these significant decreases over the last two years, these collections are still more than twice the amount collected in FY 2007.

While the overall performance picture improved slightly in FY 2012, the data continue to show signs of weakness, particularly among the lowest-income families in the caseload. Although the percentage of "enforcement-ready" cases with support orders that had collections has increased slightly in FY 2012 from 70.4 percent to 71.6 percent, this is still below the FY 2008 pre-recession percentage of 72.2. The sharpest declines are in current and former assistance cases. The percentage of current assistance cases with orders that had collections declined from 59.5 percent in FY 2008 to 57.3 percent in FY 2012 and the percentage of former assistance cases with orders that had collections declined from 68.0 percent to 66.0 percent in FY 2012. The percentage of never assistance cases with orders that had collections has increased slightly from 80.0 percent in FY 2008 to 80.2 percent in FY 2012.

Expenditures: . . . In FY 2012, total administrative expenditures were $5.7 billion, which were essentially unchanged from FY 2011. Program expenditures had steadily declined for the last three years but had a slight increase of .01 percent in FY 2012. During FY 2012, we continued to see a shift in funding from the federal government to states. Also, in FY 2012, federal expenditures decreased by 2 percent, while state expenditures increased by 3 percent. In FY 2011, the federal share of expenditures decreased by 9 percent, as the funding reduction provision included in the Deficit Reduction Act of 2006 went into effect.

4. *The Continuing Challenge of Childhood Poverty*

JANE C. MURPHY, *LEGAL IMAGES OF FATHERHOOD: WELFARE REFORM, CHILD SUPPORT ENFORCEMENT, AND FATHERLESS CHILDREN*

81 Notre Dame L. Rev. 325, 350-352 (2005)

Over the last three decades . . . both the federal and state governments have constructed massive bureaucracies focused on making noncustodial parents — mostly low-income fathers — pay child support. This "revolution" in child support was, for the most part, enthusiastically received by many scholars and policymakers, particularly advocates for women and children. The goals of "legalizing" the father-child relationship for more children of unmarried parents and increasing and enforcing court-ordered child support for all children in single parent households held the promise of reducing child poverty. Thirty years later, however, it is time to reexamine the underlying assumptions driving these reforms as well as the impact of these reforms on low-income families. . . .

The first assumption that needs to be reexamined is that the enhanced child support enforcement scheme is critical to putting food in the mouths of children in poor families. While there has been some success in improving child support collection, the child support regime has largely failed to reduce child poverty. There is some evidence that the receipt of child support may be important for non-welfare custodial households. But the same research shows that aggressive child support enforcement has not reduced poverty for welfare families. The reasons for this are multifaceted but not particularly complex. First, there has been limited success in obtaining child support orders for never married mothers, the population most likely to be receiving welfare benefits. Even for those children who have support orders, custodial mothers receiving welfare obtain no benefit unless the support paid exceeds their welfare benefits. . . . [U]nder the child support distribution scheme for families on welfare, the custodial parent assigns her right to support and the state retains support paid by noncustodial parents as reimbursement for welfare benefits. Thus, the ever-increasing resources devoted to collect child support from low-income fathers have no direct impact on the financial well-being of children on welfare.

In addition to the structural issues in welfare law that redirect child support from families to the state, the desperate economic circumstances of most fathers of children on welfare almost ensures the failure of the child support system to effectively address child poverty. . . .

D. TAXES

The relationship of federal tax policy to family groups, however defined, has posed fundamental questions for both tax policy and family law. One is whether the appropriate unit for imposing taxes is the individual or the family. The other is whether state variations in family law should affect federal tax liability.

The extent to which the tax code treats taxpayers differently, depending on their marital and parental status, has varied, although the current trend is toward differential treatment. For purposes of the most fundamental tax issues — whether people are "married" and whether they are legally "parent and child" — state law generally controls. However, until the Supreme Court struck down Section 1 of the federal Defense of Marriage Act in United States v. Windsor, 133 S. Ct. 2675 (2013) (set out in Chapter 3, above), same-sex couples were not treated as married for purposes of federal taxes, regardless of state law. Now, provided that a couple was validly married in the state of celebration, they will be treated as married for tax purposes. Press Release, U.S. Dep't of the Treasury, All Legal Same-Sex Marriages Will Be Recognized for Federal Tax Purposes (Aug. 29, 2013), available at http://www.treasury.gov/press-center/press-releases/Pages/jl2153.aspx. Same-sex couples in domestic partnerships or civil unions often continue to be treated as unmarried for purposes of federal law, even where they have all the rights and duties of married people under state law. See Deborah A. Widiss, Leveling Up After DOMA, 89 Ind. L.J. 43 (2014). However, registered domestic partners in California, Nevada, and Washington must each report half the combined income of the couple as earned income on their federal income tax returns. IRS Pub. No. 17, at 5 (rev. Nov. 26, 2013).[4]

Partly in response to the controversy over the tax treatment of same-sex relationships, a number of legal scholars have challenged the conventional idea that family membership should affect a person's federal tax liability, arguing that the individual should be the unit for taxation regardless of his or her family status. Stephanie Hunter McMahon, To Have and to Hold: What Does Love (of Money) Have to Do with Joint Tax Filing?, 11 Nev. L.J. 718 (2011), discusses these arguments but cautions that during the era when individuals were the unit of taxation, wealthy people developed many strategies to avoid taxes and that the change to taxing family units was motivated in no small part by the desire to defeat these strategies. She argues that a return to a tax system based on the individual would increase the complexity of the tax code and opportunities for tax avoidance, and would very likely reduce the overall equity of the system.

---

4. Employer-provided health insurance for family members of their employees is not taxable income if the recipients are the spouses or legal children of the employees. Since the last quarter of the twentieth century, a number of employers have also provided such benefits to the domestic partners of employees and to those partners' children. These benefits are typically taxable income to the employees. For a discussion of the principled and practical issues, see Patricia A. Cain, Taxation of Domestic Partner Benefits: The Hidden Costs, 45 U.S.F. L. Rev. 481 (2010).

1. Taxation of the Ongoing Family

Originally, the income tax code implicitly assumed that the individual was the tax-paying unit. Married and unmarried people were taxed at the same rates, and the income from children's property was taxed at the children's rates rather than at their parents' rates. Because tax rates are progressive — that is, the rates increase as income goes up — a system that treats the individual as the taxing unit is likely to extract a different amount of tax from a family with two income earners than a family earning the same amount with one income earner.

To illustrate, imagine two families, the Joneses and the Smiths. Mr. Jones is employed in the marketplace, earning $60,000 per year, and Mrs. Jones is a homemaker. Both Mr. and Mrs. Smith work in the marketplace, each earning $30,000 per year. Further, assume that the income tax rate is 20 percent on the first $20,000 of income, 33 percent on income between $20,000 and $50,000, and 50 percent on income over $50,000. The tax owed by the Joneses (ignoring exemptions, deductions, and the like) is 20 percent of $20,000 ($4,000), 33 percent of $30,000 ($10,000), and 50 percent of $10,000 ($5,000), for a total of $19,000. The Smiths owe 20 percent of $20,000 ($4,000) each, plus 33 percent of $10,000 ($3,333) each, for a total of $14,666.

The first major challenge to this regime arose in response to two Supreme Court decisions that interpreted the Internal Revenue Code (IRC) as making state law rules about marital property ownership determinative of married people's income tax liability. Both cases involved couples in which the husband worked in the paid labor force and the wife was a homemaker.

In Lucas v. Earl, 281 U.S. 111 (1930), the spouses, who lived in a common law property state, entered into a contract providing that they would share equally all their income during their marriage. They therefore claimed that each of them owed taxes on half the husband's wages. If they had prevailed, their total tax bill would have been lower than if he had been taxed on all the income. However, the Supreme Court ruled against them, holding that income is taxed to the person who earned it by labor or investment of capital, regardless of whether it is validly assigned to someone else.[5] Since only the husband really earned the money, he was taxable on all of it. A few months later the Court decided Poe v. Seaborn, 282 U.S. 101 (1930), which involved a similar married couple who lived in a community property state and who also claimed that each of them owned half the husband's income and was taxable on it. The Court ruled in their favor because their state's marital property law treated them as equal owners of the income.

As word of the tax advantages of living in community property states got out, six common law property jurisdictions enacted community property legislation between 1939 and 1949. Carolyn C. Jones, Split Income and Separate Spheres: Tax Law and Gender Roles in the 1940s, 6 Law & Hist. Rev. 259, 266-274 (1988); Stephanie Hunter McMahon, To Save State Residents: States' Use of Community Property for Federal Tax Reduction, 1939-1947, 27 Law & Hist. Rev. 585 (2009); Dennis J. Ventry, Saving *Seaborn*: Ownership as the Basis of Family Taxation, 86 Ind. L.J. 1459 (2011); Judith Younger, Marital Regimes: A Story of Compromise

---

5. This principle has been generalized as the "assignment-of-income" doctrine, which has a substantial impact throughout the income tax code.

and Demoralization, Together with Criticism and Suggestions for Reform, 67 Cornell L. Rev. 45, 69-70 (1981).[6] Some feminist scholars have argued that more states did not adopt community property, despite the tax savings for citizens, because of philosophical hostility to the idea that a wife might have a property interest in a husband's earnings and because of the difficulty of combining community property principles with common law property rules. *E.g.*, Jones at 269-270. Professor McMahon argues that the difference in the state responses to *Lucas* and *Poe* is more complex. She says that the public rhetoric in the states that temporarily enacted and then repealed community property focused much more on tax equity than on marital property rights, and that a major motivator for states that enacted the legislation was fear of losing wealthy residents, who could easily move to nearby community property states.

Congress eliminated the advantage enjoyed by residents of community property states in the Revenue Act of 1948, Pub. L. No. 471, ch. 168, §301, which provided for joint returns and thus for income splitting between married couples, regardless of the underlying marital property regimes. The effect of the joint return is to treat married couples as an economic unit, at least for this purpose. As soon as the legislation was enacted, Congress had to deal with questions of tax rates—should married people be taxed at the same rate as single taxpayers? If they are taxed at a different rate, should it be higher or lower? Congress has not settled on answers to these questions, as variations in relative tax rates over the last 50 years demonstrate. *See generally* Boris I. Bittker, Federal Income Taxation and the Family, 27 Stan. L. Rev. 1389 (1975); Pamela B. Gann, Abandoning Marital Status as a Factor in Allocating Income Tax Burdens, 59 Tex. L. Rev. 1 (1980); Lawrence Zelenak, Marriage and the Income Tax, 67 S. Cal. L. Rev. 339 (1994).

The same legislation that created the joint income tax return also introduced the marital deduction and splitting of estates and gifts for purposes of the federal estate and gift tax. Younger, above. These changes introduced treatment of married people as an economic unit into these wealth transfer taxes. Today, this process has been completed; under IRC §§2056 and 2523, spouses can now transfer unlimited amounts of property to each other without federal gift or estate tax consequences.

The taxation of income from property belonging to young children also results in the family (parent and child) rather than the individual (child) being treated as the taxable unit. Rules regarding taxation of trusts make it difficult for parents to shift income to children for short periods of time, and the unearned income of children younger than 14 is taxed at the higher of the parents' rate or the child's rate. IRC §1(g). For a description and critique, *see* Samuel D. Brunson, Grown-Up Income-Shifting: Yesterday's Kiddie Tax Is Not Enough, 59 U. Kan. L. Rev. 457 (2011).

Ordinarily, spouses are jointly and severally liable for the full amount of tax that either owes. However, under IRC §6015 in circumstances an "innocent spouse," that is, a spouse who did not know or have reason to know that the amount of tax stated on a joint return was understated, may be exempt from liability for

---

6. The states were Michigan, Nebraska, Oklahoma, Oregon, Pennsylvania, and the territory of Hawaii. Colorado, Illinois, Kansas, Massachusetts, New Jersey, New York, South Dakota, and Wyoming considered but did not enact such legislation. Jones, 6 Law & Hist. Rev. at 268-269.

errors attributable to his or her spouse. *See* Stephanie Hunter McMahon, What Innocent Spouse Relief Says About Wives and the Rest of Us, 37 Harv. J.L. & Gender 141 (2014); J. Abraham Gutting, The "Price" Is Right: An Overview of Innocent Spouse Relief and the Critical Need for a Uniform Approach to Interpreting the Knowledge Requirement of Internal Revenue Code § 6015, 2 Charleston L. Rev. 751 (2008).

2.   *Taxation of the Family After Divorce*

For some families, the income tax consequences of financial transfers incident to divorce are of substantial importance. Knowledgeable lawyers can do much good for families earning enough income to make tax planning important. Proper structuring of financial arrangements can reduce the amount of taxes that all the members collectively pay, leaving more money to support the former spouses and their children.

Two basic principles of tax law are at the heart of tax planning: (1) As previously mentioned, the income tax is progressive, so that people with higher incomes pay tax at a higher rate; (2) Property division and child support payments have no income tax consequences, but spousal support is a deduction for the payor and income for the recipient. Taken together, these principles generally make it more desirable from the perspective of income taxes for payments to be treated as alimony if the payor's income is significantly higher than the recipient's. In return for taking on the tax burden that spousal support imposes, the recipient can be given a greater absolute number of support dollars.

Even though child support is tax neutral, the personal exemption for a child is of substantial value. Thus, allocation between divorced parents of the exemptions for children is also an important tax issue.

Implicit in this structure is a major issue that we have already examined in other contexts: Is there a meaningful difference among the three major types of orders incident to divorce — property division, spousal support, and child support? If so, how do we distinguish among the types of orders? When the tax code provisions were first adopted, fewer states had equitable distribution laws, and spousal support, if ordered, was typically indefinite. As we have seen, though, under the modern law of equitable distribution of property and new forms of spousal support, such as rehabilitative and reimbursement alimony, it is debatable whether these types of orders are sharply distinct. Nevertheless, the tax code makes distinctions, but parties (or courts in litigated cases) may determine the tax consequences of postdivorce transfers — within limits. Other perennial issues in the tax treatment of postdivorce financial transfers are the same as those that arise in taxation of ongoing families — whether variations in state law should have an impact on federal income tax liability and what the basic taxing unit should be.

a.   Property Division — IRC § 1041

Before 1984, if the property of one spouse was transferred to the other, the property had increased in value from the time of its acquisition, and the spouses lived in a common law property state, the original owner was required to pay income taxes on the increase in value. United States v. Davis, 370 U.S. 65 (1962). The *Davis* rule often worked a real hardship, because the transferor spouse had to dip into other assets to pay the taxes. Because of this and because of ignorance, the rule was widely disobeyed. Moreover, the rule did not apply in community property states when community property was divided equally at divorce because this distribution was not considered a transfer of property owned by one spouse to the other. *See, e.g.,* Carrieres v. Commission, 64 T.C. 959 (1975), *acq.* 1976-2 C.B. 1, *aff'd per curiam,* 552 F.2d 1350 (9th Cir. 1977); Wren v. Commissioner, 24 T.C.M. (CCH) 290 (1965); Davenport v. Commissioner, 12 T.C.M. (CCH) 856 (1953); Walz v. Commissioner, 32 B.T.A. 718 (1935).

In 1984 Congress amended IRC § 1041 to provide that, just as spouses may transfer unlimited amounts of property to each other during marriage and at death without estate or gift tax consequences, their property may also be divided at divorce without income tax consequences. If property was owned by one spouse during the marriage and transferred to the other at divorce, the transferee takes the basis of the original owner. This means that when the property is sold, the transferee spouse will owe income taxes on the capital gain in value of the property that accrued while the property was owned by the original owner as well as after the divorce.

More specifically, IRC § 1041 eliminates income tax consequences for property transfers "incident to divorce." A transfer falls in this category if it occurs within one year of the termination of the marriage, or within six years of termination of the marriage if made pursuant to a divorce decree or separation agreement. Other transfers are presumed not to be incident to divorce, but the taxpayer can rebut the presumption.

Section 1041 also provides for no income tax consequences if one spouse transfers property to a third party for the benefit of a former spouse if (1) the transfer is required by the decree or separation agreement, (2) the transfer is made pursuant to a written request from the former spouse, or (3) the transferor receives written consent or ratification from the former spouse.

Property transfers between former spouses incident to divorce are also free from gift tax under IRC § 2516.

Transfers of Pensions and Related Assets As you recall from earlier chapters, if an employee's pension rights are covered by the Employee Retirement Income Security Act (ERISA), some or all of those rights can be transferred to a former spouse by a Qualified Domestic Relations Order (QDRO). An alternate payee under a QDRO is treated as the recipient of benefits under the plan for tax purposes. This means that the alternate payee pays any income taxes owing on benefits as they are paid. The payments have no tax consequences for the employee; they are not income, and they are not deductible. IRC § 402. The code also permits transfers of Individual Retirement Accounts (IRAs) between former spouses under a divorce decree or written separation agreement without tax consequences. IRC § 408(d)(6). When such a transfer is made, the IRA becomes the IRA of the transferee.

Sale of Principal Residence If married taxpayers sell their principal residence, up to $500,000 of capital gains is not recognized as income. Single taxpayers may exclude from recognition up to $250,000 in capital gains. IRC § 121. To qualify for this exclusion, the taxpayer must have owned and lived in the residence for two of the five years before the date of sale. The exclusion can be claimed every two years, but only once during each two-year period. For divorced spouses, the former spouse who occupies the residence is entitled to the exclusion, and so is the former spouse who does not occupy the residence, as long as the former spouse who occupies the residence is entitled to use the residence under a divorce or settlement agreement. Thus, if at the time of divorce both parties remain owners but one is granted the right to occupy the house until the youngest child is 18, and the house is then sold, both parties are entitled to the capital gains exclusion.

b. Spousal Support — IRC §§ 71 and 215

The character of the payments under state law does not determine their treatment for purposes of the federal income tax. Payments will be treated as alimony for tax purposes if they satisfy the objective test set out in IRC §§ 71 and 215, unless the separation agreement or divorce decree provides to the contrary. The five requirements of the test are:

(1) Payments must be in cash or cash equivalent to or for the benefit of a former spouse.
(2) Payments must be required by a
    a. written separation agreement, or
    b. divorce or separate maintenance decree, or
    c. other support decree such as an order of temporary support.
(3) If the payments are made after a final decree of divorce or legal separation, the payor and payee cannot live in the same household. The parties have a one-month grace period to establish separate households.
(4) Payments must end at the payee's death, and the payor cannot be required to make substitute payments to the payee's estate or third parties after the payee's death.
(5) The payments may not be treated as child support.

These requirements do not depend on the form of payment, and therefore lump sum as well as periodic payments may be treated as alimony.

However, if the size of payments treated as alimony declines precipitously in the first three years, the payor will owe income taxes under the recapture rules. These rules express the judgment that there is a real and significant difference between spousal support and property division and that spouses should not be able to disguise property division as spousal support. The recapture rules discourage front-end loading of payments. If recapture is required, the party who paid alimony must declare the recaptured amount as income and pay taxes on it. The recipient is entitled to a corresponding deduction.[7]

---

7. A recapture calculation must be done only once, in the third year after payments begin. The recapture formula requires comparison of the total amount paid during the

Even if payments are originally set up so that no amounts will be recaptured, the calculations are based on actual payments, not obligations. Thus, if a payor falls into arrears in the first or second year and then catches up in the third year, a recapture may be created that would reverse the intended tax consequences of the payments. The risk of recapture also makes modification of payments tricky within the first three years.

In some circumstances amounts will not be recaptured, even though the calculation discussed here apparently calls for recapture:

(1) If the payments cease within the three years because of the death of either party or the remarriage of the payee.
(2) If payments are made under temporary support orders.
(3) If the payments are to be made for at least three years and the amount is a fixed portion of the income from a business or property or from employment rather than a fixed dollar amount.

See generally Stephen P. Comeau, An Overview of the Federal Income Tax Provisions Related to Alimony Payments, 38 Fam. L.Q. 111 (2004).

c. Child Support

Child support payments are tax-free to the payee and not deductible to the payor. Where obligations are clearly designated as child support, applying this principle is easy. However, it is common for separation agreements to provide that one parent will pay a certain amount to the other as "family support," without designating explicitly how much is for child support.

Under IRC § 71(c)(2), amounts are treated as child support if they are clearly associated with a contingency relating to a child. This makes it difficult to obtain alimony treatment for undifferentiated spousal and child support. For example, say

---

second year to the total paid in the third year and then comparison of the amount paid in the first year to the amounts paid in the second and third years in the following way:

(I) Subtract [the amount paid in Year 3 plus $15,000] from the amount paid in Year 2 to get R1.
(II) Average [the amount paid in Year 2 plus the amount paid in Year 3 minus R1]. Add $15,000 to this amount, and subtract all from the amount paid in Year 1. This is R2.
(III) Total R1 and R2 to get the amount to be recaptured, if any.

For example, say that A pays B alimony of $30,000 in Year 1, $30,000 in Year 2, and $5,000 in Year 3. The amount of recapture is calculated this way:

(I) $30,000 - (5,000 + 15,000) = 10,000 = R1$.
(II) $30,000 - [(30,000 + 5,000 - 10,000)/2 + 15,000] = 30,000 - [12,500 + 15,000] = 2,500 = R2$.
(III) $\$10,000 + \$2,500 = $ Amount to be recaptured in Year 3.

If either R1 or R2 is negative, it is treated as 0 for purposes of the rest of the calculations, so one negative number does not fully or partially cancel a positive number.

that *A* pays *B*, the custodian of the two children, $1000 per month as family support, to be reduced by $200 per month when the first child turns 18 and by $200 per month when the second child turns 18. Only $600 per month would be treated as alimony.

Internal Revenue Service Reg. § 1.71-1T provides that a contingency is presumed to be related to a child if:

(1) payments are to be reduced not more than six months before or after the date the child is to attain the age of 18, 21, or the local age of majority, or

(2) payments are to be reduced on two or more occasions which occur not more than one year before or after a different child of the payor spouse attains a certain age between the ages of 18 and 24, inclusive.

The presumption that payments are clearly related to a child contingency can be rebutted by showing that the timing of a change was calculated independently of considerations relating to children.

d.   Dependency Exemptions, Child Tax Credits, Child Care Credits, Earned Income Credits, and Children's Medical Expenses

The parent who has custody may claim the dependency exemption for the child, as well as the child tax credit of $1000 per child. IRC §§ 152, 24. If the parents have joint custody, the parent with whom the child lives for a longer period of time is entitled to the exemption and the credit. If the child spends an equal amount of time with both parents, the parent with the higher adjusted gross income receives the exemption. Both the dependency exemption and the tax credit are phased out for higher-income taxpayers, although the credit is phased out at a lower income level than the exemption. The majority of courts have held that a domestic relations court may order that the custodial parent assign the dependency exemption to the other parent. Leseberg v. Taylor, 78 P.3d 201 (Wyo. 2003). However, a court order is not effective to shift the exemption to the noncustodial parent; only a written document signed by the custodial parent is. The child credit is partially refundable for low-income families. If a family does not owe any income tax, it will be entitled to a refund equal to the lesser of the family's child credit or 15 percent of their earnings that exceed $10,000, an amount regularly adjusted for inflation.

Only the parent entitled to the dependency exemption is entitled education-related benefits, the Hope Scholarship and the lifetime learning credits. IRC § 25A.

The custodial parent alone is entitled to claim two other kinds of credits, both of which are phased out for higher-income taxpayers: the child care credit and the earned income credit. Neither of these credits can be assigned to the other parent, and if the parents have joint custody, the parent with physical custody for a longer time gets the credits. The child care credit reduces taxes for parents with earned income who must pay for child care to enable themselves to work. IRC § 21. Low-income custodial parents are also entitled to the earned income credit if they have earned income.

Allocation of one tax benefit associated with children—the deduction for medical expenses—depends only upon who pays. Regardless of who has custody, whichever parent pays a child's medical expenses may deduct them. IRC § 213(d)(5).

PROBLEMS

1. When Harold and Wanda separated, Harold agreed to give Wanda $800 per month to support her and the children. They were separated, and Harold made the payments for eight months. At that point the court entered a final divorce decree, which required Harold to pay $535 per month as "child support" and $300 per month as "spousal support." The spousal support payments terminate when the youngest child becomes 21.

How much, if any, of the payments that Harold made while he and Wanda were separated may he deduct as alimony? Which of the two streams of payments required by the divorce decree may Harold deduct as alimony? If you were Harold's attorney and wanted to ensure that the $300 per month would be treated as alimony, what additional or different terms in the decree would you ask for?

2. When Millie and David were divorced, they agreed to hold their house as tenants in common, and that Millie and the children would have the right to occupy the house for ten years. At that point the house is to be sold and the proceeds divided equally. They have also agreed that David will make the mortgage payments on the house. How much of each payment is alimony for purposes of income taxes? If the divorce decree provided that Millie owned the house and that David was to pay the mortgage, how much of each payment would be treated as alimony for tax purposes?

E. BANKRUPTCY

An empirical study conducted in 2001 found that the families who are in the worst financial trouble and most likely to declare bankruptcy are families with children. "Our study showed that married couples with children are more than twice as likely to file for bankruptcy as their childless counterparts. A divorced woman raising a youngster is nearly three times more likely to file for bankruptcy than her single friend who has no children." Elizabeth Warren, The Growing Threat to Middle Class Families, 69 Brook. L. Rev. 401, 402 (2004); *see also* Elizabeth Warren, The New Economics of the American Family, 12 Am. Bankr. Inst. L. Rev. 1 (2004).

> Personal bankruptcy often follows a serious economic reversal. About two-thirds of all bankruptcies occur after one or both adults in a household have had a serious interruption in income, such as a layoff, cutback in hours, downsizing, outsourcing, or some other euphemism that means income has been cut sharply. Nearly half of all families file for bankruptcy in the aftermath of a serious medical problem. Divorce has hit more than one in five families in bankruptcy. In the 2001 sample, nearly nine

out of ten filers listed at least one of these three reasons in explaining their bankruptcy petitions.

Elizabeth Warren, Bankrupt Children, 86 Minn. L. Rev. 1003, 1022 (2002). The financial strains that lead to bankruptcy may undermine the marriage too, or the costs of divorce may force either or both former spouses into bankruptcy shortly after the divorce is final.

The fundamental purpose of bankruptcy law is to give debtors a fresh start by freeing them from pre-bankruptcy debts while equitably dividing their assets among creditors. Individuals may undergo either of two kinds of bankruptcy proceedings. In a Chapter 7 proceeding, the debtor's nonexempt assets are liquidated under the supervision of a trustee to pay off creditors to the extent possible. People with a regular income may instead go through Chapter 13 proceedings, which allow the debtor to remain in control of his or her assets and to set up a reorganization plan to pay off some or all of the debts over three or five years. In other words, a Chapter 13 proceeding allows the debtor to rehabilitate him- or herself and repay at least some debts.

The Bankruptcy Abuse Prevention and Consumer Protection Act of 2005 (BAPCPA) made the most substantial changes to the bankruptcy code in many decades. Under the Act, it is much more difficult for debtors to file bankruptcy under Chapter 7 and obtain a complete discharge of all debts. This change has resulted in fewer complete discharges under Chapter 7 and more cases being resolved under Chapter 13 than under the prior law.

For purposes of a Chapter 7 proceeding, spousal and child support and property division obligations are all nondischargeable in bankruptcy. 11 U.S.C. § 523(a)(15), (c). However, for actions brought under Chapter 13, only "domestic support obligations" (DSOs) — that is, orders for spousal or child support, obligations in lieu of a support order, and obligations assigned to the government, as in welfare recovery cases — are not dischargeable. 11 U.S.C. §§ 101(14A), 523(c). Property division orders are dischargeable. 11 U.S.C. § 1328(a)(2). "If the debtor manages to propose and complete a Chapter 13 plan, the debtor could successfully discharge a divorce-related, non-domestic support obligation. This, indeed, remains the debtor's only pawn to play to renegotiate the terms of a divorce decree or separation agreement in a bankruptcy case. The ability of the debtor to discharge the non-DSO in Chapter 13 is the reason why clearly differentiating between support and non-support obligations in a divorce decree or separation agreement is still necessary." Shayna M. Steinfeld, The Impact of Changes Under the Bankruptcy Abuse Prevention and Consumer Protection Act of 2005 on Family Obligations, 20 J. Am. Acad. Matrimonial Law, 251, 278 (2007).

IN RE EARNEST

___ B.R. ___, 2013 WL 6504359 (Bankr. N.D. Fla.)

KAREN K. SPECIE, United States Bankruptcy Judge. . . . The parties were married in 2005, and have two children together. When their youngest was only two months old, the Debtor left the marital home and moved into an apartment with his girlfriend and her child; at some point during the parties' separation the Debtor had a child with his "paramour." After the Debtor left the marital home, Ms. Dodson worked two jobs at times and paid all expenses related to the home and the children's daycare with no contribution from the Debtor. The Debtor filed the dissolution of marriage action on March 10, 2009, a little over two years after the parties separated. The original Final Judgment of Dissolution of Marriage was entered on May 12, 2010, after a contested evidentiary hearing at which the State Court heard testimony of the parties and their witnesses; it is the original Final Judgment that determined the amounts due from the Defendant to Ms. Dodson. . . .

At the time of the dissolution in May of 2010 the marital home had negative equity, so the parties agreed to put it on the market and attempt a "short sale." In between the Debtor moving out and the final dissolution hearing, Ms. Dodson had paid a total of $61,461.14 toward the mortgage to prevent foreclosure of the home while she and the children lived there; the Debtor had paid nothing. Ms. Dodson and the parties' children stayed in this very home because after the couple divorced the Debtor successfully blocked her from moving with the children to Mississippi with her then-fiancé.

At the conclusion of the evidentiary hearing the State Court ordered the Debtor to reimburse Ms. Dodson half of the amount she had paid on the mortgage during the separation ($30,730.57), awarded continued, exclusive possession of the home to Ms. Dodson, and ordered each party to pay half of the mortgage payments from the dissolution (June 1, 2010) until the home was sold. The State Court found that the parties had comparable incomes at the time of the dissolution. Because it found that the Debtor had "received more debt than the Wife," the State Court denied Ms. Dodson's request for the Debtor to pay half of the children's daycare expenses for the twenty-two months of their separation and ordered Ms. Dodson to pay for the children's health insurance and all childcare expenses going forward. Each party retained an automobile with a loan on it, the Debtor retained the couple's boat with a loan on it, and Ms. Dodson retained the furniture and the loan on it. Finding that the couple's assets and liabilities, with the exception of the house, had been equitably divided by the parties, the State Court ordered:

> [I]t is equitable for the Wife to be reimbursed by the Husband for one-half (1/2) of all mortgage payments made by her since the separation, for a total of $30,730.57. The Husband should begin one-half (1/2) payment of the mortgage on June 1, 2010, and the Wife shall pay one-half (1/2) of the mortgage until the home is sold. . . . Upon sale of home, Husband shall continue to pay one-half (1/2) of mortgage payment directly to Wife until the entire sum of $30,730.57 is paid in full.

. . .

Both parties agree that the Debtor's obligations to pay half of the home mortgage payments, both the past due sum of $30,730.57 and the payments from June 1, 2010, through the present, are marital obligations that would be non-dischargeable in a Chapter 7 under 11 U.S.C. § 523(a)(15). Because the Debtor filed a Chapter 13, the issue before the Court is whether the sums the Debtor owes Ms. Dodson constitute domestic support obligations that are in the nature of alimony, maintenance, or support under 11 U.S.C. § 523(a)(5), thus making them non-dischargeable in Chapter 13.

Section 1328(a) of the Bankruptcy Code provides a debtor in Chapter 13 a "super discharge" of some debts, including certain marital obligations that would otherwise be non-dischargeable in Chapter 7. Section 1328 does not allow a debtor to discharge a marital obligation that is a "domestic support obligation" under § 523(a)(5). A "domestic support obligation" is defined in § 101(14A) as one that is "*in the nature of* alimony, maintenance, or support . . . of such spouse, former spouse, or child of the debtor . . . without regard to whether the debt is expressly so indicated." The critical issue for this Court to decide is whether the Debtor's obligations, both past and ongoing, to pay half of the mortgage payments are "in the nature of" alimony, maintenance, or support.

"[C]ourts have ruled that exceptions from discharge for . . . spousal support deserve a liberal construction. . . ." Pagels v. Pagels (In re Pagels), Adv. No. 10-07070-SCS, 2011 WL 577337, at *9 (Bankr. E.D. Va. Feb. 9, 2011). Bankruptcy courts are not bound by labels placed on marital settlement awards in state court, so this Court must consider the substance of the State Court's ruling in order to determine whether the Debtor's obligations are "in the nature of" alimony, maintenance, or support. The Plaintiff has the burden of proof based on a preponderance of the evidence; the Court is to make a "simple inquiry as to whether the obligation can legitimately be characterized as support, that is, whether it is in the *nature* of support." Harrell v. Sharp (In re Harrell), 754 F.2d 902, 906 (11th Cir. 1985). One factor is whether the award "grossly favored" one spouse over the other or left one spouse with virtually no income. Other factors include whether one spouse had custody of the minor children, the circumstances surrounding the dissolution ("the context in which the obligation arises" and "who was at fault in the marriage"), and whether the award served to provide basic necessities, such as "shelter." The Eleventh Circuit has held that an "equitable distribution" by a state court can function as support. *See* Cummings v. Cummings, 244 F.3d 1263, 1266 (11th Cir. 2001) ("Although the divorce court labeled the [award] an 'equitable distribution,' the language used by the court suggests that it intended at least some portion of the equitable distribution to function as support."). "[A]ll evidence, direct or circumstantial," that tends to lead to subjective intent is relevant. *Id.*

In *Cummings*, the Eleventh Circuit vacated a bankruptcy court's decision that a divorce court's "equitable distribution" of $6.3 million to the debtor's former wife was dischargeable as a "property settlement" that the debtor was unable to pay. In vacating this ruling, the Eleventh Circuit held that the bankruptcy court should have examined the intent of the divorce court before making its ruling and remanded the case for a determination of what portion, if any, of the "equitable distribution" the divorce court intended as support for the wife.[8]

---

8. In many states, including Florida, failure to pay alimony or child support may be punishable by contempt. In our case, like in *Cummings*, no court below ever determined whether the payments were enforceable by contempt. Although Ms. Dodson moved for contempt against the Debtor, she withdrew that motion and the State Court never ruled on it, making this case distinguishable from *In re Benson*, cited by the Debtor, in which the husband's obligation to pay the mortgage was held not to be a support obligation because it

Following *Cummings* and focusing on the factors listed in the cited cases, this Court must discern the intent of the State Court as of the date it entered its original Final Judgment dissolving the marriage, awarding Ms. Dodson the $30,730.57, and ordering the Debtor to pay half of the monthly mortgage payments from June 1, 2010 through the sale of the home. . . .

Focusing on whether one spouse had custody of the minor children and the circumstances surrounding the dissolution (who was at fault in the marriage), the State Court seemed most troubled by what the Debtor did to create the situation before it. In both the original and amended final judgments, the State Court emphasized that the Debtor left while the younger of the parties' two children was only two months old to move in with his "paramour" with whom he had a child "out of wedlock." In short, the State Court focused on the fact that the Debtor just walked away and left Ms. Dodson holding the bag — two young children, two jobs, the house underwater, the mortgage payments, the furniture and car loans, and all of the other household and child care expenses. By the time of the evidentiary hearing in May of 2010, this situation had continued for twenty-two months. The State Court also placed emphasis on the fact that Ms. Dodson had custody of the couples' young children and that she was far more sensitive to the children's needs than was the Debtor.

The awards by the State Court were clearly to help provide shelter to Ms. Dodson and the young children, did not grossly favor one party over the other, and did not leave one spouse with virtually no income. Although the Debtor disputed the accuracy of Ms. Dodson's State Court financial affidavit at the trial in this Court, the State Court's finding that the parties' incomes were "comparable" in May of 2010 is supported by the record in the State Court. . . .

The State Court's award of half of the mortgage payments cannot, under any circumstance, be considered property settlement. As to the house, there was no "property" to divide between the parties because the house had no value over the mortgage and was "under water." Even if the State Court's allocation of the debt on the home constituted "equitable distribution" of debt, rather than of property, the award can still be, and in this case was, in the nature of support. The State Court had already divided all of the parties' other property and debts as evenly as possible There was nothing left for the State Court to "equitably divide" other than the debt on the house.

The Defendant cites In re Wood, No. 11-006583-8-JRL, 2012 WL 14270 (Bankr. E.D.N.C. Jan. 4, 2012) in support of his position that his obligations to Ms. Dodson are dischargeable and not "in the nature of support." In *Wood*, a North Carolina bankruptcy court held a debtor's obligation to pay a mortgage was not in the nature of support. *Wood* is distinguishable: the obligation in *Wood* was established by agreement rather than by court order after a contested hearing; the opinion does not discuss whether there was equity in the property to which the mortgage debt was attached; and the former wife in *Wood* "did not present any evidence" that the parties intended the debtor's obligations to be in lieu of alimony. In the trial before this Court, the Wife's testimony was that the Debtor's obligation

---

was not enforceable by contempt. Also, in *Benson*, the parties' division of tax exemptions for the children was evidence of support — here, the parties agreed to split tax exemptions for the children, just like they split the mortgage payments.

to pay half of the mortgage payments was to help keep a roof over her head and those of their children; the Debtor presented no evidence to the contrary. In *Wood*, both parties "forever [gave] up any right to spousal support." Here there was no such waiver; in fact, Ms. Dodson asked the State Court to enforce the Debtor's failure to pay the one-half mortgage payments by contempt but later withdrew that request upon the parties' agreement on other matters.

The Defendant's argument that the State Court has already determined dischargeability of its awards is without merit. The record is totally devoid of any evidence that the State Court ever considered dischargeability of debt under the Bankruptcy Code.

In *Cummings*, the Eleventh Circuit instructed the bankruptcy court to determine how much of an award to a former spouse was "in the nature of support" and therefore non-dischargeable. Here there are two awards: one is the past due sum of $30,730.57 and the other is the one-half monthly mortgage payments since June 1, 2010. Using the Eleventh Circuit's standard in *Cummings*, and considering all of the testimony and evidence, this Court concludes that the State Court's intent in ordering the Debtor to pay Ms. Dodson half of the mortgage payments until the house sold was to force the Debtor to help provide a roof over the heads of the Plaintiff and their two young children, which he had not done through the date of the dissolution. At trial Ms. Dodson testified that she is now a debtor in her own Chapter 13 case and is attempting to refinance the mortgage on and keep the home. It is unclear whether Ms. Dodson is keeping the home because she wants to or because she was unable to sell it. Because the State Court intended the Debtor's obligation to continue making one half of the mortgage payments on the home to be temporary until the home sold, further proceedings are necessary for a determination as to when this obligation should end. . . .

Because this Court and the State Court have concurrent jurisdiction over dischargeability of marital obligations, the parties may ask this Court or the State Court to determine an end date for the Debtor's obligation to make the one-half mortgage payments from and after June 1, 2010.

NOTES AND QUESTIONS

1. The *Earnest* court, like most bankruptcy courts, treats the parties' or the court's intent at the time of divorce as determining the character of an order. What factors in this case support the finding that the obligation was in the nature of support? What would have to change to result in a finding that the order was a division of property? For a discussion of the intent test, *see* Shayna M. Steinfeld & Bruce R. Steinfeld, A Brief Overview of Bankruptcy and Alimony/Support Issues, 38 Fam. L.Q. 127 (2004).

2. When a bankruptcy proceeding is filed, all creditors' efforts to collect against the debtor are automatically stayed. 11 U.S.C. § 362(a). A creditor may move to lift the stay, and the motion will be granted if lifting the stay will not be detrimental to the debtor's estate and if the creditor's rights are otherwise adequately protected. When the bankrupt person's assets are distributed in the bankruptcy, secured creditors generally are preferred to unsecured ones, though by statute certain unsecured creditors have priority over other unsecured creditors.

Once the bankruptcy proceeding is concluded, the debtor starts anew with the exempt property that he or she retained, and any debts that were not paid from the bankruptcy estate are discharged. *See generally* Shayna M. Steinfeld & Bruce R. Steinfeld, A Brief Overview of Bankruptcy and Alimony/Support Issues, 38 Fam. L.Q. 127 (2004).

The automatic stay applies to property division and measures to enforce judgments against property that is in the bankruptcy estate. Almost all other family law–related actions are exempt from the stay. Therefore, even if a bankruptcy petition has been filed, a court can proceed with domestic violence matters and with actions to grant a divorce; establish paternity; establish or modify a support order; and establish, modify, or enforce custody and related rights. 11 U.S.C. § 362(b)(2)(A). The stay also does not apply to various types of child support enforcement actions, including income withholding, driver's license suspensions, tax intercepts, and credit reporting, or to enforcement of medical support obligations. 11 U.S.C. § 362(b)(2).

3. In a Chapter 7 liquidation proceeding, if the bankruptcy estate actually has funds to distribute to unsecured creditors, domestic support orders are at the top of the priority list for payment, behind only the claim of the trustee for fees and expenses. 11 U.S.C. § 507(a)(7). Throughout the duration of a Chapter 13 proceeding, domestic support orders must be paid in full. 11 U.S.C. § 1322(a). If they are not, the debtor will not be granted a discharge in the Chapter 13 proceeding.

4. Some assets, such as a homestead interest in real property, may be exempt from bankruptcy and will not be taken to satisfy the debtor's creditors. 11 U.S.C. § 522. In addition, if exempt assets are encumbered by judicial liens, under certain circumstances the liens will be avoided (that is, eliminated) as well. Most important for our purposes, a lien on exempt property that secures an obligation characterized as part of the property division and that attaches to property that the debtor owned before the lien was created is avoided by the bankruptcy proceeding. However, if the underlying debt secures a duty to pay support, the lien is not avoided. 11 U.S.C. § 522(f).

This rule creates a risk for obligees of property division debts, as illustrated in Farrey v. Sanderfoot, 500 U.S. 291 (1991). Gerald and Jeanne Sanderfoot were divorced in Wisconsin. Gerald was awarded the family home, and he was ordered to pay his former wife an equalizing judgment. To secure this award, the decree also gave Jeanne a lien against the property to secure the debt. Less than a year after the divorce, Gerald filed for Chapter 7 bankruptcy and claimed the home as exempt property. He also moved under § 522 to avoid Jeanne's lien on the ground that it was a judicial lien that impaired his exemption. Jeanne ultimately prevailed in the Supreme Court.

The Court interpreted § 522 as avoiding only those judicial liens that attach to property interests that the debtor owns before the lien attaches. 500 U.S. at 296. Gerald had conceded for purposes of argument that the divorce decree gave him a wholly new interest in the home rather than adding his former wife's share to his pre-existing share. 500 U.S. at 294. The Court therefore held that § 522 did not apply and that Jeanne's lien survived Gerald's bankruptcy. If Gerald had not made this concession, though, would Gerald's interest in the property have been characterized as pre-existing the divorce decree or as newly created by the decree? This is a question of state law, which differs from state to state.

5. If a former spouse successfully discharges obligations under a divorce decree by declaring bankruptcy, may the domestic relations court modify its decree to provide relief to the other spouse? In such cases, the obligee is often successful in modifying support obligations in the family law court, though it is improper for the domestic relations court to reinstate the discharged obligation in effect. Alyson F. Finkelstein, A Tug of War: State Divorce Courts Versus Federal Bankruptcy Courts Regarding Debts Resulting from Divorce, 18 Bankr. Dev. J. 169 (2001). Some courts have even held that the property division provisions of the divorce decree may be revised under such circumstances. *See, e.g.*, Birt v. Birt, 96 P.3d 544 (Ariz. App. 2004), holding that a lower court erred when it refused to set aside a divorce judgment on the wife's motion after the husband obtained a discharge in bankruptcy of his obligations under the decree. The effect of the bankruptcy order was to leave the wife liable for all of the couple's substantial debts, rather than for only half as provided in the divorce decree, while allowing the husband to keep his share of property awarded in the decree. The appellate court ruled that the trial court correctly refused to reopen the divorce case on the ground that the bankruptcy action was newly discovered evidence or that the debt division provisions of the divorce decree were prospective in their application. However, it said, the trial court should have granted wife's motion to vacate the judgment for "any other reason justifying relief from the operation of the judgment," Ariz. R. Civ. Pro. 60(c)(60). The court said, "Husband's filing of bankruptcy, which he concedes was to avoid the terms of the dissolution decree, creates such a substantial injustice that it overrides the commitment to finality of judgments. . . ." 96 P.3d at 550. The opinion cites cases from North Dakota, New Mexico, Kansas, Minnesota, and Alabama that modify divorce decree provisions regarding property division or spousal support following one former spouse's successful declaration of bankruptcy.

6. Volume 41, No. 2 (2007) of the Family Law Quarterly covers the effect of BAPCPA on family law obligations in depth.

Child Custody

9

A. INTRODUCTION

During the colonial period in this country, and in England during the same time, custody disputes rarely came before the courts. Common law doctrine assigned to fathers sole custody of their legitimate children. A father not only had the sole right to custody while he lived, he could determine custody after death by appointing a testamentary guardian. The following excerpt describes the transition from a clear rule of paternal custody to judicial superintendence in the United States.

MICHAEL GROSSBERG, *GOVERNING THE HEARTH:*
LAW AND THE FAMILY IN NINETEENTH CENTURY AMERICA

235-239 (1985)

Prerepublican Anglo-American law granted fathers an almost unlimited right to the custody of their minor legitimate children. Moored in the medieval equation of legal rights with property ownership, it assumed that the interests of children were best protected by making the father the natural guardian and by using a property-based standard of parental fitness. Custody law held children to be dependent, subordinate beings, assets of estates in which fathers had a vested right. Their services, earnings, and the like became the property of their paternal masters in exchange for life and maintenance. Literary critic Jay Fliegelman summarized the stark reality of the traditional law of parent and child: "[T]he debt is owed nature not nurture." These assumptions lingered on in the new republic. The influential University of Maryland law professor David Hoffman explained the dual nature of paternal authority in his 1836 Legal Outlines. First was "the injunction imposed on parents by nature, of rearing, and carefully watching over the moral, religious, and physical education of their progeny, and

547

the impracticality of advantageously discharging that duty, unless children yield implicit obedience to the dictates of parental concern, seeing that they are not of sufficient age and discretion to limit the measure of their submission or obedience." Second was "the presumed consent of the offspring." . . .

Professor Hoffman also emphasized that these parental rights conferred authority primarily on the father:

> If parental power arose not in truth from these principles, but from some fancied property given to the parent in his offspring, by the act of propagation, it would seem to follow . . . that this authority would appertain in the largest degree to the mother, since she not only has the pains and deprivations incident to gestation and parturition, but is the principal sharer in the cares which succeed the birth. Yet it is the father who holds and exercises the principal authority. . . .

In 1809 a South Carolina equity court heard Jennette Prather's demand for a separation from her husband and the custody of her children. She charged her mate with living openly in adultery. The judges easily complied with her first request, but hesitated in granting the second. Chancellor Henry De Saussure was mindful, he said, of the father being the children's "natural guardian, invested by God and the law of the country with reasonable power over them. Unless his parental power has been monstrously and cruelly abused, this court would be very cautious in interfering with the execution of it." The court finally denied the errant husband his full parental rights. It gave the custody of an infant daughter, though not of the older children, to Jennette. In doing so, the judges acknowledged that they were treading on uncertain legal ground.

The ambivalence of the South Carolina court reveals the conflicting pressures on the post-Revolutionary bench generated by custody disputes between mothers and fathers. Traditional male authority over the family remained a fundamental tenet of family law. But a growing concern with child nurture and the acceptance of women as more legally distinct individuals, ones with a special capacity for moral and religious leadership and for child rearing, undermined the primacy of paternal custody rights. . . .

The judicial disposition to emphasize child welfare in determining custody began to refashion the preferences of the common law. The "best interests of the child" became a judicial yardstick used to measure all claims for children. Its dramatic impact is most apparent in the resolution of disputes between the natural parents for their children.

B. STANDARDS FOR CUSTODY DETERMINATION

1. An Introduction to the "Best Interests" Standard

Professor Grossberg describes the transition in the American law of custody as a movement from paternal patriarchy to judicial patriarchy, by which he means (at least in part) the replacement of virtually unbounded paternal authority by virtually unbounded judicial authority (exercised, of course, by male judges). The doctrinal vehicle conveying that judicial power was the "best interests" doctrine. In many situations family law uses "standards" rather than rules to govern the exercise of official authority, and, plainly, the "best interests" doctrine falls in the "standards" category.

Although moving from a nearly absolute and therefore clear rule of paternal custody to a best-interest standard enhanced judicial authority over child custody decisions, the breadth of the latter standard creates problems of management for judges and parties alike. The difference between rules and standards is between an approach to legal decision making that employs apparently mechanical formulae (rules) and one that proceeds by the individualized application of generally stated social policies (standards).

The tension between rules and standards runs throughout the law of custody, but the fault lines change with each generation. When the best-interest standard first took hold, the courts were convinced that custody needed to be awarded to one, and only one, parent. Under the best-interest rubric, the determination of which parent gradually changed from a preference for fathers to a presumption, at least for children of "tender years," in favor of mothers. Under either approach, the participation of the other parent then depended on the cooperation of the custodial parent. Certainty in decision-making authority was considered essential.

More recently, with greater acceptance of shared parenting and more egalitarian gender roles, legislatures and courts have authorized joint custody awards that acknowledge both parents' contribution to child rearing. In some jurisdictions, the preference for the continuing involvement of both parents has become a rule creating a legal presumption in favor of shared custody; in all jurisdictions, the law favors the continuing inclusion of both parents in the child's life and makes it difficult to deny a parent access to a child altogether.

The presumption of both parents' continuing involvement, in turn, places greater emphasis on disqualifying conduct—and determinations of unfitness. The U.S. Constitution recognizes "fit" parents as having a fundamental liberty interest in the care, custody, and management of their children, limiting the courts' discretion to award custody or visitation to others. *See* Troxel v. Granville, 530 U.S. 57 (2000). Chapters 13 and 14 explore the increasingly contentious law regarding how legal parenthood is determined. The materials in this chapter assume that legal parenthood has been decided and address custody and visitation disputes between a child's legal parents or between a legal parent and a third party. The first part of this section introduces the meanings and application of the "best interests" standard, and the second examines joint custody. As we will see, both of these standards permit and sometimes even require courts to judge parents' conduct to determine their "fitness" to parent. The remainder of this section concerns the legal issues that arise from this inquiry.

PAINTER v. BANNISTER

140 N.W.2d 152 (Iowa), *cert. denied*, 385 U.S. 949 (1966)

STUART, J. . . . The custody dispute before us in this habeas corpus action is between the father, Harold Painter, and the maternal grandparents, Dwight and

Margaret Bannister. Mark's mother and younger sister were killed in an automobile accident on December 6, 1962 near Pullman, Washington. The father, after other arrangements for Mark's care had proved unsatisfactory, asked the Bannisters to take care of Mark. They went to California and brought Mark to their farm home near Ames in July, 1963. Mr. Painter remarried in November, 1964 and about that time indicated he wanted to take Mark back. The Bannisters refused to let him leave and this action was filed in June, 1965. Since July 1965 he has continued to remain in the Bannister home under an order of this court staying execution of the judgment of the trial court awarding custody to the father until the matter could be determined on appeal. For reasons herein-after stated, we conclude Mark's better interests will be served if he remains with the Bannisters.

Mark's parents came from highly contrasting backgrounds. His mother was born, raised and educated in rural Iowa. Her parents are college graduates. Her father is agricultural information editor for the Iowa State University Extension Service. The Bannister home is in the Gilbert Community and is well kept, roomy and comfortable. The Bannisters are highly respected members of the community. Mr. Bannister has served on the school board and regularly teaches a Sunday school class at the Gilbert Congregational Church. Mark's mother graduated from Grinnell College. She then went to work for a newspaper in Anchorage, Alaska, where she met Harold Painter.

Mark's father was born in California. When he was 2-1/2 years old, his parents were divorced and he was placed in a foster home. Although he has kept in contact with his natural parents, he considers his foster parents, the McNelly's, as his family. He flunked out of a high school and a trade school because of a lack of interest in academic subjects, rather than any lack of ability. He joined the navy at 17. He did not like it. After receiving an honorable discharge, he took examinations and obtained his high school diploma. He lived with the McNelly's and went to college for 2-1/2 years under the G.I. bill. He quit college to take a job on a small newspaper in Ephrata, Washington in November 1955. In May 1956, he went to work for the newspaper in Anchorage which employed Jeanne Bannister. . . .

We are not confronted with a situation where one of the contesting parties is not a fit or proper person. There is no criticism of either the Bannisters or their home. There is no suggestion in the record that Mr. Painter is morally unfit. It is obvious the Bannisters did not approve of their daughter's marriage to Harold Painter and do not want their grandchild raised under his guidance. The philosophies of life are entirely different. As stated by the psychiatrist who examined Mr. Painter at the request of the Bannisters' attorneys: "It is evident that there exists a large difference in ways of life and value systems between the Bann-isters and Mr. Painter, but in this case, there is no evidence that psychiatric insta-bility is involved. Rather, these divergent life patterns seem to represent alternative normal adaptations." . . .

The Bannister home provides Mark with a stable, dependable, conventional, middle-class, middle-west background and an opportunity for a college education and profession, if he desires it. It provides a solid foundation and secure atmosphere. In the Painter home, Mark would have more freedom of conduct and thought with an opportunity to develop his individual talents. It would be more exciting and challenging in many respects, but romantic, impractical and unstable. . . .

Our conclusion as to the type of home Mr. Painter would offer is based upon his Bohemian approach to finances and life in general. We feel there is much evidence which supports this conclusion. His main ambition is to be a free lance writer and photographer. He has had some articles and picture stories published, but the income from these efforts has been negligible. At the time of the accident, Jeanne was willingly working to support the family so Harold could devote more time to his writing and photography. In the 10 years since he left college, he has changed jobs seven times. . . .

There is general agreement that Mr. Painter needs help with his finances. Both Jeanne and Marilyn, his present wife, handled most of them. Purchases and sales of books, boats, photographic equipment and houses indicate poor financial judgment and an easy come easy go attitude. He dissipated his wife's estate of about $4300, most of which was a gift from her parents and which she had hoped would be used for the children's education.

The psychiatrist classifies him as "a romantic and somewhat of a dreamer." An apt example is the plan he related for himself and Mark in February 1963: "My thought now is to settle Mark and myself in Sausalito, near San Francisco; this is a retreat for wealthy artists, writers, and such aspiring artists and writers as can fork up the rent money. My plan is to do expensive portraits ($150 and up), sell prints ($15 and up) to the tourists who flock in from all over the world. . . ."

The house in which Mr. Painter and his present wife live, compared with the well kept Bannister home, exemplifies the contrasting ways of life. In his words, "it is a very old and beat up and lovely home. . . ." They live in the rear part. The interior is inexpensively but tastefully decorated. The large yard on a hill in the business district of Walnut Creek, California, is of uncut weeds and wild oats. The house "is not painted on the outside because I do not want it painted. I am very fond of the wood on the outside of the house."

The present Mrs. Painter has her master's degree in cinema design and apparently likes and has had considerable contact with children. She is anxious to have Mark in her home. Everything indicates she would provide a leveling influence on Mr. Painter and could ably care for Mark.

Mr. Painter is either an agnostic or atheist and has no concern for formal religious training. He has read a lot of Zen Buddhism and "has been very much influenced by it." Mrs. Painter is Roman Catholic. They plan to send Mark to a Congregational Church near the Catholic Church, on an irregular schedule. . . .

Were the question simply which household would be the most suitable in which to raise a child, we would have unhesitatingly chosen the Bannister home. We believe security and stability in the home are more important than intellectual stimulation in the proper development of a child. There are, however, several factors which have made us pause.

First, there is the presumption of parental preference, which though weakened in the past several years, exists by statute. We have a great deal of sympathy for a father, who in the difficult period of adjustment following his wife's death, turns to the maternal grandparents for their help and then finds them unwilling to return the child. There is no merit in the Bannister claim that Mr. Painter permanently relinquished custody. It was intended to be a temporary arrangement. A father should be encouraged to look for help with the children from those who love them without the risk of thereby losing the custody of the children permanently. This fact must receive consideration in cases of this kind. However, as always, the primary consideration is the best interest of the child, and if the return of custody to the father is likely to have a seriously disrupting and disturbing effect upon the child's development, this fact must prevail.

Second, Jeanne's will named her husband guardian of her children and if he failed to qualify or ceased to act, named her mother. The parent's wishes are entitled to consideration.

Third, the Bannisters are 60 years old. By the time Mark graduates from high school they will be over 70 years old. Care of young children is a strain on grandparents and Mrs. Bannister's letters indicate as much.

We have considered all of these factors and have concluded that Mark's best interest demands that his custody remain with the Bannisters. Mark was five when he came to their home. The evidence clearly shows he was not well adjusted at that time. He did not distinguish fact from fiction and was inclined to tell "tall tales" emphasizing the big "I." He was very aggressive toward smaller children, cruel to animals, not liked by his classmates and did not seem to know what was acceptable conduct. As stated by one witness: "Mark knew where his freedom was and he didn't know where his boundaries were." In two years he made a great deal of improvement. He now appears to be well disciplined, happy, relatively secure and popular with his classmates, although still subject to more than normal anxiety.

We place a great deal of reliance on the testimony of Dr. Glenn R. Hawks, a child psychologist. The trial court, in effect, disregarded Dr. Hawks' opinions stating: "The court has given full consideration to the good doctor's testimony, but cannot accept it at full face value because of exaggerated statements and the witness's attitude on the stand." We, of course, do not have the advantage of viewing the witness's conduct on the stand, but we have carefully reviewed his testimony and find nothing in the written record to justify such a summary dismissal of the opinions of this eminent child psychologist.

Dr. Hawks is head of the Department of Child Development at Iowa State University. However, there is nothing in the record which suggests that his relationship with the Bannisters is such that his professional opinion would be influenced thereby. Child development is his specialty and he has written many articles and a textbook on the subject. He is recognized nationally, having served on the staff of the 1960 White House Conference on Children and Youth and as consultant on a Ford Foundation program concerning youth in India. He is now education consultant on the project "Head Start." He has taught and lectured at many universities and belongs to many professional associations. He works with the Iowa Children's Home Society in placement problems. Further detailing of his qualifications is unnecessary.

Between June 15th and the time of trial, he spent approximately 25 hours acquiring information about Mark and the Bannisters, including appropriate testing of and "depth interviews" with Mark. Dr. Hawks' testimony covers 70 pages of the record and it is difficult to pinpoint any bit of testimony which precisely summarizes his opinion. He places great emphasis on the "father figure" and discounts the importance of the "biological father." "The father figure is a figure that the child sees as an authority figure, as a helper, he is a nurturant figure, and one who typifies maleness and stands as maleness as far as the child is concerned."

His investigation revealed: ". . . the strength of the father figure before Mark came to the Bannisters is very unclear. Mark is confused about the father figure prior to his contact with Mr. Bannister." Now, "Mark used Mr. Bannister as his father figure. This is very evident. It shows up in the depth interview, and it shows up in the description of Mark's life given by Mark. He has a very warm feeling for Mr. Bannister."

Dr. Hawks concluded that it was not for Mark's best interest to be removed from the Bannister home. He is criticized for reaching this conclusion without investigating the Painter home or finding out more about Mr. Painter's character. He answered: "I was most concerned about the welfare of the child, not the welfare of Mr. Painter, not about the welfare of the Bannisters. In as much as Mark has already made an adjustment and sees the Bannisters as his parental figures in his psychological makeup, to me this is the most critical factor. . . ."

It was Dr. Hawks' opinion "the chances are very high (Mark) will go wrong if he is returned to his father." This is based on adoption studies which "establish that the majority of adoptions in children who are changed, from ages six to eight, will go bad, if they have had a prior history of instability, some history of prior movement. When I refer to instability I am referring to where there has been no attempt to establish a strong relationship." . . .

Mark has established a father-son relationship with Mr. Bannister, which he apparently had never had with his natural father. He is happy, well adjusted and progressing nicely in his development. We do not believe it is for Mark's best interest to take him out of this stable atmosphere in the face of warnings of dire consequences from an eminent child psychologist and send him to an uncertain future in his father's home. Regardless of our appreciation of the father's love for his child and his desire to have him with him, we do not believe we have the moral right to gamble with this child's future. He should be encouraged in every way possible to know his father. We are sure there are many ways in which Mr. Painter can enrich Mark's life.

For the reasons stated, we reverse the trial court and remand the case for judgment in accordance herewith.

ANNA FREUD, *PAINTER V. BANNISTER: POSTSCRIPT BY A PSYCHOANALYST*

7 The Writings of Anna Freud 247, 247-255 (1966-1970)

I can imagine plaintiff and defendants, father and grandparents of Mark, in spite of their tug of war, being sufficiently united in their concern for the child to seek expert advice concerning him instead of bringing the matter to the court. If the clinic to which they turned were the Hampstead one (or the Yale Child Study Center), the advice given would be based on psychoanalytic reasoning. The main difference between the legal and the clinical situation then would be that in the first instance the warring partners would have a solution imposed on them, while in the second instance they would be left free either to adopt or to reject the solution with which they are presented.

MARK'S PROBLEM

I do not think that we would find Mark's problem easier to handle than either the trial judge or Mr. Justice Stuart. . . . Mark was lucky enough to live in normal family circumstances until he was five. There is no reason to suspect that during these decisive years his father did not play the usual important role for him. This "normal" life came to an end only with the disastrous accident which, for reason of their deaths, deprived him of mother and sister and, for other reasons, soon there-after deprived him of the presence of his father.

Disturbing as the accident was, it does not alter the fact that Mark grew up with parents of his own. We take it for granted that the sudden loss of mother and sibling coupled with the separation from his father, was deeply upsetting for him. There is no evidence to show how his relations with mother, father, and sister had developed, or how his personality had been shaped before the traumatic moment intervened. That he showed signs of maladjustment after the events, i.e., when he arrived at the grandparents, is not surprising, nor is this necessarily connected with mismanagement on the part of the father or other influences derived from the father's personality. Children frequently react with overt behavior problems to shocks, upsets, and disruptions in their lives, i.e., to events following which adults withdraw into a lengthy mourning process.

MARK'S PAST

In the absence of any other surviving member of the immediate family, the clinic would have to enlist the father's help for clarifying questions concerning Mark's past. We would want to know whether developmental progress was satisfactory or unsatisfactory until age five; whether Mark was in good affectionate contact with his mother, or his father, or with both; whether they considered him a clinging or an independent child; whether before losing his mother, he had reached the stage of obvious preference for her, accompanied by rivalry with and jealousy of his father; whether at this time he had impressed people as a manly or as an unmanly little boy; whether the parents considered him to be a "good" child, age adequately in control of his impulses, or whether they found him self-indulgent and difficult to manage. Data of this kind would give a clue whether or not the disruption of the family had caused him to undergo a change of personality.

Other relevant information concerning Mark would have to be elicited in the clinic's usual manner from the boy himself. The investigator would have to piece together in particular the residues of his infantile love life. What methods did Mark adopt to cope with his losses? Has he forgotten, denied, or repressed all memories of events before the accident? How far is the image of his dead mother still alive in his mind? Does it or does it not play an important role in his conscious fantasies or, perhaps inaccessible to consciousness, in his unconscious? To what extent has he transferred the feelings for his mother to his grandmother? If he has done so in an intense way, how would he react to a further separation, this time from her? Are there signs to be noted that he would be able to shift his affections, this time to a stepmother who is, so far, unknown to him? . . .

As regards Mark, we have no evidence so far to show what happened in his case. There is the contention that the boy's allegiance to his father has been transferred in its entirety to the grandfather. If this were proved to be true, inquiry would still be needed whether this shift was a wholly positive one or whether it was prompted, at least in part, by the boy's anger with the absent father, an anger which may well be smoldering under the surface and may burst out some time to the detriment of his development.

THE WARRING ADULTS

Since in the clinical situation both parties in the dispute have consulted us of their own free will, we can also count on their cooperation in investigating their own respective attitudes toward the child. . . .

With Mark's father and grandparents it is difficult to foresee the result of our investigations. In the father, there are signs of obvious, object-directed feelings for the child, alternating with periods of detachment, which may or may not be attributable to the man's immediate reaction to his tragic losses. On the other hand, there are also indications that, as a father, he is not disinclined to use his son selfishly, i.e., for his own aggrandizement as an author, a figure on TV, etc.

As for the grandparents, we are prepared to find that for them Mark represents the daughter whom they have lost and mourn. There is also the suspicion that in claiming Mark, they reclaim symbolically their daughter from the son-in-law, who from the start was unwelcome to them for many reasons. There also is little doubt that the grandparents love Mark himself, are attentive to his needs, and sacrifice for him some of the peace and quiet of their home life to which every elderly couple is entitled.

The weight and truth of any of these pronouncements remain tentative until they are confirmed or disputed by probing interviews with the three adults in question.

LEGAL V. PSYCHOANALYTIC ASPECTS

Unlike the two courts, we are in the lucky position not to have to pronounce judgment. We merely formulate advice. When doing so, we disregard or minimize the importance of some of the facts which swayed the courts.

In disagreement with the trial judge, and in agreement with his expert, Dr. Hawks, we discount the importance of the "biological father" as such. The "blood ties" between parent and child as well as the alleged paternal and maternal "instincts" are biological concepts which, only too often, prove vague and unreliable when transferred to the field of psychology. Psychologically speaking, the child's "father" is the adult man to whom the child attaches a particular, psychologically distinctive set of feelings. When this type of emotional tie is disrupted, the child's feelings suffer. When such separations occur during phases of development in which the child is particularly vulnerable, the whole foundation of his personality may be shaken. The presence of or the reunion with a biological father to whom no such ties exist will not recompense the child for the loss which he has suffered. Conversely, the biological father's or mother's unselfish love for their child is by no means to be taken for granted. It happens often enough that biological parents fail in their duty to the child, while other adults who are less closely related to him, i.e., who have no "instinctive" basis for their feelings, successfully take over the parental role.

We place less emphasis than Mr. Justice Stuart on benefits such as a "stable, dependable background" with educational and professional opportunities. Important as such external advantages are, we have seen too often that they can be wasted unless they are accompanied by the internal emotional constellations which enable the children to profit from them. Children are known to thrive in socially and financially unstable situations if they are firmly attached to their parents, and to come to grief under the best social conditions when such emotional security is missing. . . .

FORMULATION OF ADVICE

It is not possible at this point to foretell whether, after investigation, our advice will be in line with the judgment of the trial court or with Mr. Justice Stuart. What can be promised is that it will be based not on external facts but on internal data. We shall advise that Mark had better stay with his grandparents provided that the following facts can be ascertained:

> that the transfer of his attachment from the parents to the grandparents is fairly complete and promises to be permanent during his childhood; i.e., that they have become the central figures toward whom his feelings are directed and around whom his emotional life revolves . . . that, given this new attachment, a further change is not advisable . . . ; that the grandparents, on their part, cherish Mark for his own sake, not only as a replacement for the daughter who was killed, nor as a pawn in the battle with their son-in-law.

Conversely, we shall advise that Mark had better be returned to his father if the following facts emerge:

> that Mr. Painter still retains his place as "father" in Mark's mind and that in spite of separation and new experiences the child's feelings and fantasies continue to revolve around him; that anger about the "desertion" (and perhaps blame for the mother's death) have not succeeded in turning this relationship into a predominantly hostile one; that the father cherishes Mark for his own sake; that it can be shown that Mr. Painter's using the child for publicity purposes was not due to lack of paternal consideration on his part but happened owing to the bitterness and resentment caused by the fight for possession of his son.

Provided that Mr. Painter, Mr. and Mrs. Bannister, and Mark would allow the clinic two or three weeks' time for investigation, I am confident that we should be able to guide them toward a potentially helpful solution of their difficult problem.

NOTES AND QUESTIONS

1. The court in *Painter* notes the existence of a presumption favoring custody by a child's parents against all others. Who bore the burden of overcoming that presumption? What kind of factual showing did the court require to overcome the presumption? Did the court's use of the best-interest standard effectively eliminate the parental presumption? The *Painter* court noted that the presumption of parental preference had been "weakened in the past several years." In 2000, however, in Troxel v. Granville, 530 U.S. 57 (2000) (*see* Chapter 13), the U.S. Supreme Court found the court-ordered grandparent visitation to be an unconstitutional infringement of a parent's fundamental right to make decisions concerning the custody, care, and control of the child. Subsequent decisions have added real teeth to the presumption in favor of parents' custody and visitation preferences, and a number of courts require either a showing of parental unfitness or detriment to the child to overcome the presumption that parents will act in their children's best interests. If Painter v. Bannister were decided today, do you think the case would come out differently? Do you think constitutional protection is necessary to protect parents from the type of subjective judgments made in *Painter*? If you represented the Bannisters in an action today, is there additional evidence you would try to present? Would you characterize the existing evidence differently?

2. The *Painter* court treated the custody determination as a de novo proceeding although Mark had lived with his grandparents, with his father's consent, for almost two years when the action was filed. Had the grandparents secured a custody award when Mark initially moved in with them, in most states, the father would have had to establish a substantial change in circumstances to justify a custody transfer. Such a change would ordinarily need to involve something that affected Mark directly, rather than merely an improvement in the father's circumstances. *See* Rennels v. Rennels, 257 P.3d 396 (Nev. 2011) (where parent consented to grandparent visitation order, acrimony grew, and parent changed his mind, presumption in favor of deference to parental views no longer controls and parent was required to show a substantial change in circumstances that justified modification or termination of the order); Lovlace v. Copley, 814 S.W.3d 1 (Tenn. 2013) (custodial parents seeking modification or termination of a grandparent visitation order must show a material change in circumstances); In re Welfare of B.R.S.H., 169 P.3d 40 (Wash. App. 2007) (father's constitutional rights were taken into account during an initial custody hearing that awarded custody to the grandparents, and in a motion to modify, father must show change in the child's circumstances with the grandparents, not just an improvement in the father's ability to care of the child). *But see* Hunter v. Hunter, 771 N.W.2d 694 (Mich. 2009) (even where parents consented to a guardianship by the children's uncle and aunt because of the parents' drug abuse, the parental presumption still prevails over the presumption in favor of an established custodial environment, and the parental presumption can be rebutted only by clear and convincing evidence that custody with the natural parent is not in the best interests of the child); In re K.I., 903 N.E.2d 453 (Ind. 2009) (although a parent must show a significant change of circumstances to change an initial custody award from a grandparent to a parent, the necessary showing was a "modest" one because the presumption in favor of custody with the parent over a third party did not end with

the initial order). The characterization of the existing custody arrangement and the differing burdens of proof come up as potential issues in most of the cases in this chapter. Consider whether you think the characterization changes the outcome of these cases.

3. Judgments regarding a child's best interests inevitably involve social scientific propositions. It is not surprising, therefore, that expert witnesses commonly play an important role in contested custody matters, as Dr. Hawks did in Painter v. Bannister. Their role is the subject of much controversy. Must the trier of fact give any weight to expert testimony? If one party produces expert evidence and the other does not, does it follow that the former will succeed? If not, why not? Could the grandparents have overcome a presumption in favor of the parent in a case like this without expert testimony? Should the courts appoint an independent expert and if so, who should be expected to pay for the expert?

4. Mark later chose to return to his father. Is this fact instructive in any way?

5. An extensive literature addresses children's adjustment to divorce. It finds that:

Divorce is a process: Joan Wexler emphasized that divorce "is not a single stressful event confined to a certain moment," but rather something that changes over time, beginning prior to the formal divorce with a state of family dissolution and ending some time as the parties experiment with ways to cope and adjust over time. She notes that research finds that:

> Indeed, during that first year [following the divorce], family conflict escalates rather than declines. On almost every measure of parental behavior, divorced parents during the first twelve months after divorce were coping far less well than non-divorced parents. Divorced parents made fewer maturity demands on their children, were less consistent in their discipline, were less apt to reason with their children, communicated less well, and were less affectionate. The authors described a cycle of negative parent-child interaction, with the most notable effect on the mother-son relationship. Only after that first year of heightened tension did an increased sense of well-being begin to emerge. At the two-year follow-up, the most debilitating effects of the divorce on both parents and children had abated.

In this process, the children's well-being is linked to the well-being of the custodial parent (or parents), and the custodial parent's coping mechanisms and parenting skills typically improve over time. Joan G. Wexler, Rethinking the Modification of Child Custody Decrees, 94 Yale L.J. 757, 784-788 (1985).

Conflict harms children in all families: Sociologist Paul Amato found that children in high-conflict marriages show signs of distress even before a divorce occurs, and the children in the highest-conflict marriages do better if their parents divorce even though children generally do better if their parents stay together. Paul R. Amato, Good Enough Marriages: Parental Discord, Divorce, and Children's Long Term Well-Being, 9 Va. J. Soc. Pol'y & L. 71, 71-94 (2001); Solangel Maldonado, Facilitating Forgiveness and Reconciliation in "Good Enough" Marriages, 13 Pepp. Disp. Resol. L.J. 105 (2013). High conflict following divorce also impedes children's adjustment, while cooperative parenting facilitates that adjustment. Janet R. Johnston, High Conflict Divorce, *in* 4 The Future of the Child 165, 174 (Spring 1994).

Resources matter: Two parents typically have both more money and more time to spend on their children and the differences between children in divorced and intact families narrow significantly (but do not disappear) once researchers account for the difference in resources. Sara McLanahan & Gary Sandefur, Growing Up with a Single Parent: What Hurts, What Helps (1994).

Stress is cumulative: Divorce, in addition to challenging parental well-being and reducing family resources, typically introduces other stresses such as residential moves and changes in school, friendships, and extended family relationships. Kyle Crowder & Jay Teachman, Do Residential Conditions Explain the Relationship Between Living Arrangements and Adolescent Behavior?, 66 J. Marriage & Fam. 721, 721-738 (2004).

Two parents are better than one — when they reinforce each other's parenting: Children generally benefit from the involvement of both parents, and divorce typically involves a substantial loss of contact with the noncustodial parent. E. Mavis Hetherington & Joan B. Kelly, For Better or Worse: Divorce Reconsidered (2002); Joan B. Kelly & Robert E. Emery, Children's Adjustment Following Divorce: Risk and Resiliency Perspectives, 52 Fam. Rel. 352-362 (2003). Moreover, the loss of parental contact following divorce may have a greater impact on young children. R. Chris Fraley & Marie E. Heffernan, Attachment and Parental Divorce: A Test of the Diffusion and Sensitive Period Hypotheses, 39 Pers. Soc. Psychol. Bull. 1199 (2013); Pamela S. Ludolph & Milfred D. Dale, Attachment in Child Custody: An Additive Factor, Not a Determinative One, 46 Fam. L.Q. 1 (2012). Other studies show, however, that it is the quality of parental involvement, not the amount of time that a parent spends with a child, that matters most. Paul R. Amato & Joan G. Gilbreth, Nonresident Fathers and Children's Well-being: A Meta-analysis, 61 J. Marriage & Fam. 557 (1999). For a compilation of social science research related to custody, *see* Parenting Plan Evaluations: Applied Research for the Family Court 540 (Kathryn Kuehnle & Leslie Drozd eds., 2012).

2. *The Primary Caretaker*

Entirely predictably, courts faced with the dilemma between regimes of rules and standards have sought a middle ground through the use of what might be called intermediate rules. The following materials present one of the most important bases for decision making in custody cases. Does it solve the problems created by intermediate standards such as "the child's best interests"?

BURCHARD v. GARAY

724 P.2d 486 (Cal. 1986)

BROUSSARD, J. This case concerns the custody of William Garay, Jr., age two and one-half at the date of trial. Ana Burchard, his mother, appeals from an order of the superior court awarding custody to the father, William Garay.

As a result of a brief liaison between Ana and William, Ana became pregnant. Early in her term she told William that she was pregnant with his child, but he refused to believe that he was the father. William, Jr., was born on September 18, 1979.

After the birth, Ana undertook the difficult task of caring for her child, with the help of her father and others, while working at two jobs and continuing her training to become a registered nurse. William continued to deny paternity, and did not visit the child or provide any support.

In the spring of 1980 Ana brought a paternity and support action. After court-ordered blood tests established that William was the father, he stipulated to paternity and to support in the amount of $200 a month. Judgment entered accordingly on November 24, 1980. In December of that year William visited his son for the first time. In the next month he moved in with Ana and the child in an attempt to live together as a family; the attempt failed and six weeks later he moved out.

William asked for visitation rights; Ana refused and filed a petition for exclusive custody. William responded, seeking exclusive custody himself. The parties then stipulated that pending the hearing Ana would retain custody, with William having a right to two full days of visitation each week.

At the onset of the hearing Ana requested a ruling that William must prove changed circumstances to justify a change in custody. William opposed the motion, arguing that the court need only determine which award would promote the best interests of the child. The court deferred ruling on the motion. The evidence at the hearing disclosed that William, Jr., was well adjusted, very healthy, well mannered, good natured, and that each parent could be expected to provide him with adequate care.

. . . Applying the "best interests" test, [the court] awarded custody to William. Its decision appears to be based upon three considerations. The first is that William is financially better off — he has greater job stability, owns his own home, and is "better equipped economically . . . to give constant care to the minor child and cope with his continuing needs." The second is that William has remarried, and he "and the stepmother can provide constant care for the minor child and keep him on a regular schedule without resorting to other caretakers"; Ana, on the other hand, must rely upon babysitters and day care centers while she works and studies. Finally, the court referred to William providing the mother with visitation, an indirect reference to Ana's unwillingness to permit William visitation. . . .

. . . [A]lthough we conclude that the trial court correctly ruled that the case was governed by the best-interest standard, we find that it erred in applying that standard. The court's reliance upon the relative economic position of the parties is impermissible; the purpose of child support awards is to ensure that the spouse otherwise best fit for custody receives adequate funds for the support of the child. Its reliance upon the asserted superiority of William's child care arrangement suggests an insensitivity to the role of working parents. And all of the factors cited by the trial court together weigh less to our mind than a matter it did not discuss — the importance of continuity and stability in custody arrangements. We therefore reverse the order of the trial court. . . .

The trial court's decision referred to William's better economic position, and to matters such as homeownership and ability to provide a more "wholesome environment," which reflect economic advantage. But comparative income or economic advantage is not a permissible basis for a custody award. "[There] is no basis for assuming a correlation between wealth and good parenting or wealth and happiness." If in fact the custodial parent's income is insufficient to provide proper care for the child, the remedy is to award child support, not to take away custody.

The court also referred to the fact that Ana worked and had to place the child in day care, while William's new wife could care for the child in their home. But in an era when over 50 percent of mothers and almost 80 percent of divorced mothers work, the courts must not presume that a working mother is a less satisfactory parent or less fully committed to the care of her child. A custody determination must be based upon a true assessment of the emotional bonds between parent and child, upon an inquiry into "the heart of the parent-child relationship . . . the ethical, emotional, and intellectual guidance the parent gives to the child throughout his formative years, and often beyond." It must reflect also a factual determination of how best to provide continuity of attention, nurturing, and care. It cannot be based on an assumption, unsupported by scientific evidence, that a working mother cannot provide such care—an assumption particularly unfair when, as here, the mother has in fact been the primary caregiver.

Any actual deficiency in care, whether due to the parent's work or any other cause, would of course be a proper consideration in deciding custody. But the evidence of such deficiencies in the present case is very weak—the testimony of William, disputed by Ana, that on one occasion Ana left the child alone briefly while she cashed a support check, and that sometimes the child was delivered for visitation in clothes that were shabby or too small. But these matters are trivial. The essence of the court's decision is simply that care by a mother who, because of work and study, must entrust the child to daycare centers and babysitters, is per se inferior to care by a father who also works, but can leave the child with a step-mother at home. For the reasons we have explained, this reasoning is not a suitable basis for a custody order.

The trial court recited other grounds for its order. One was that William was "better equipped psychologically" to care for the child. Ana has had emotional problems in the past, and reacted bitterly to the separation, but William's conduct has not been a model of emotional maturity. After they separated, Ana objected to William seeing the child and did not communicate about matters involving the child. But after William obtained custody pursuant to the trial court's order, he proved equally obdurate to Ana's visitation rights, leading the court to amend its order to spell out those rights.

All of these grounds, however, are insignificant compared to the fact that Ana has been the primary caretaker for the child from birth to the date of the trial court hearing, that no serious deficiency in her care has been proven, and that William, Jr., under her care, has become a happy, healthy, well-adjusted child. We have frequently stressed, in this opinion and others, the importance of stability and continuity in the life of a child, and the harm that may result from disruption of established patterns of care and emotional bonds. The showing made in this case is, we believe, wholly insufficient to justify taking the custody of a child from the mother who has raised him from birth, successfully coping with the many difficulties encountered by single working mothers. We conclude that the trial court abused its discretion in granting custody to William, Sr., and that its order must be reversed.

We acknowledge the anomalous position of an appellate court, especially a supreme court, in child custody appeals. Over four years have passed since the trial court awarded custody to William. Our decision reversing that order returns the case to the trial court which, in deciding the child's future custody, must hold a new hearing and determine what arrangement is in the best interests of the child as of the date of that hearing. Thus, the effect of our decision is not to determine finally the custody of William, Jr., but is to relieve Ana of the adverse findings of the trial court and of the burden of proving changed circumstances since the trial court order, and to make clear that in deciding the issue of custody the court cannot base its decision upon the relative economic position of the parties or upon any assumption that the care afforded a child by single, working parents is inferior.

The order is reversed.

BIRD, C.J., concurring. I write separately to underscore that the trial court's ruling was an abuse of discretion not only in its failure to give due weight to the importance of continuity and stability in custody arrangements but in its assumption that there is a negative relation between a woman's lack of wealth or her need or desire to work and the quality of her parenting. As this case so aptly demonstrates, outmoded notions such as these result in harsh judgments which unfairly penalize working mothers. . . .

Read in light of the record, the court's findings amount to "outmoded notions of a woman's rule being near hearth and home." In an era where over 50 percent of mothers and almost 80 percent of divorced mothers work, this stereotypical thinking cannot be sanctioned. When it is no longer the norm for children to have a mother at home all day, courts cannot indulge the notion that a working parent is ipso facto a less satisfactory parent. Such reasoning distracts attention from the real issues in a custody dispute and leads to arbitrary results. . . .

Stability, continuity, and a loving relationship are the most important criteria for determining the best interests of the child. Implicit in this premise is the recognition that existing emotional bonds between parent and child are the first consideration in any best-interests determination. . . .

. . . [T]here is no accepted body of expert opinion that maternal employment per se has a detrimental effect on a child. On the contrary, one recent study on maternal employment and child development has concluded that "[maternal] employment status had no negative relation to children's development over a 5-year period. . . . Thus, the trial court's presumption lacks any expert support. . . .

Yet, under the trial court's rationale, it is the mother—and not the father—who would be penalized for working out of the home. She and she alone would be placed in this Catch-22 situation. If she did not work, she could not possibly hope to compete with the father in providing material advantages for the child. She would risk losing custody to a father who could provide a larger home, a better neighborhood, or other material goods and benefits.

If she did work, she would face the prejudicial view that a working mother is by definition inadequate, dissatisfied with her role, or more concerned with her own needs than with those of her child. This view rests on outmoded notions of a woman's role in our society. Again, this presumption is seldom, if ever, applied even-handedly to fathers. The result—no one would take an unbiased look at the amount and quality of parental attention which the child was receiving from each parent.[1]

The double standard appears again when, as here, the father is permitted to rely on the care which someone else will give to the child. It is not uncommon for courts to award custody to a father when care will actually be provided by a relative, second wife, or even a babysitter. However, the implicit assumption that such care is the equivalent of that which a nonworking mother would provide "comes dangerously close to implying that mothers are fungible — that one woman will do just as well as another in rearing any particular children." This is scarcely consistent with any enlightened ideas of childrearing. . . .

NOTES AND QUESTIONS

1. The California Supreme Court in *Burchard* agreed with the trial court that the award to William was an initial custody determination to be determined in accordance with a best-interest standard. Ana, in contrast, had argued that the court should treat the parties' earlier stipulation giving her custody as a court order, and William's subsequent request for custody as a motion to modify subject to a changed-circumstances standard.

In a divorce proceeding, courts ask the parties to list children of the marriage and address custody of the children in the divorce decree. With unmarried parents, no court order arises unless one of the parties chooses to go to court. When the parents do not live together and one parent has acted as the child's "primary caretaker," the court may take this into account as part of a best-interest determination, but the other party has no burden to show changed circumstances. For discussion of the tension between the parents' equal standing in a de novo custody determination and deference to the child's interest in the continuity of parental relationships, *see* Harrison v. Tauheed, 256 P.3d 851 (Kan. 2011). In this case, the father objected that the trial court's emphasis on the mother's role as the child's primary caretaker amounted to "a demand that he demonstrate a compelling reason to have [his son's] living arrangement changed" and that such a standard was inappropriate for an initial custody determination. The Kansas

---

1. *See also* In re Marriage of Estelle (Mo. App. 1979) 592 S.W.2d 277, in which the court affirmed a custody award to a working father, not remarried, as against an equally fit working mother. The reviewing court made no negative comments about the child's placement in day care, but rather emphasized that the father often prepared the child's breakfast and dinner and picked her up from the day care center himself. *Id.*, at p.278. It is difficult to imagine a mother's performance of these chores even attracting notice, much less commendable comment. . . .

See also Masek v. Masek (1975) 89 S.D. 62[,228 N.W.2d 334], in which a mother who taught music part-time lost custody to a father who worked full-time. The trial court noted that the mother slept until 9 A.M. on Saturdays, failed to prepare breakfast for her husband, who left for work at 7 A.M., and on occasion had run out of jam and cookies. It concluded from these facts that she was unfit for custody because her "primary interests are in her musical career and outside of the house and family."

Supreme Court agreed with the mother, however, that the trial court's choice to "place great weight" on the length of time the child had spent with each parent and his successful adjustment to the mother's home, the school she chose, and the community in which she was living with the son was an appropriate part of a multi-factor best-interest determination.

In light of these standards, how would you advise Ana and William, respectively, if they had asked you how to preserve each of their interests in securing custody of the child at the time of the child's birth?

2. What role does gender play in determining children's interests? Historically, courts recognized a maternal preference and presumed that children of "tender years" would be better off with their mothers. Many courts have declared such presumptions unconstitutional. *See, e.g.*, Pusey v. Pusey, 728 P.2d 117 (Utah 1986). Even if gender is not an express or exclusive consideration, however, the traits associated with caretaking mothers and wage-earning fathers may continue to influence custody decisions. The Supreme Court of Wyoming concluded that its governing statute prohibits use of gender as the "sole" basis for a custody award, but does not prohibit all consideration of gender. It refused to overturn an award that described the parents' activities in stereotypical ways, referring to the stay-at-home mother as the "need" provider and the employed father as the "wants" provider. Donnelly v. Donnelly, 92 P.3d 298 (Wyo. 2004).

3. Burchard v. Garay looks to the primary caretaker as the preferred custodian. Is that more than a socially acceptable strategy for reaching the same result produced by the maternal preference? Is the appropriate solution to replace notions of "mothers" and "fathers" with that of "parents"? For an analysis of the implications of gender neutralization, *see* Martha A. Fineman, The Neutered Mother, the Sexual Family, and Other Twentieth Century Tragedies Part 2 (1995). For an argument that the law should actively promote a norm of nurturing fatherhood that encourages noncustodial fathers to remain involved with their children, *see* Solangel Maldonado, Beyond Economic Fatherhood: Encouraging Divorced Fathers to Parent, 153 U. Pa. L. Rev. 921 (2005). For an examination of the role of gender stereotypes in custody decisions involving gay fathers and lesbian mothers, *see* Clifford J. Rosky, Like Father, Like Son: Homosexuality, Parenthood, and the Gender of Homophobia, 20 Yale J.L. & Feminism 257, 343 (2009).

As a statistical matter, men have increased their involvement in childrearing, but women still overwhelmingly take on more of the primary caretaker role. Between 2000 and 2012, for example, the number of stay-at-home dads doubled, but that meant an increase from a paltry .04 percent of all married couples to a still paltry .08 percent. During the same time period, the number of stay-at-home moms increased from approximately 20 percent of all married households to approximately 23 percent. Philip Cohen, Exaggerating Gender Changes (Aug. 13, 2012), available at http://familyinequality.wordpress.com/2012/08/13/exaggerating-gender-changes/ (last visited Oct. 31, 2013). Public attitudes, however, strongly support the continued involvement of both parents following divorce irrespective of each parent's involvement with the child during the marriage and the existence of conflict between the parents during the divorce. *See* Sanford L. Braver, Ira M. Ellman, Ashley M. Votruba & William V. Fabricius, Lay

Judgments About Child Custody After Divorce, 17 Psychol. Pub. Pol'y & L. 212 (2011).

4. While most states continue to consider the primary caretaker role, its importance is limited by two factors. First, these states use the primary care-taker role the way the court did in *Burchard v. Garay*, that is, as part of a finding that placement of a child with his or her primary caretaker will serve the "best interests of the child," psychologically understood. Thought of this way, the primary caretaker standard simply becomes one of a number of unweighted factors that contribute to a holistic best-interest determination. A primary care-taker *presumption*, in contrast, assumes that the child's best interest lies with an award of custody to the primary caretaker, absent a demonstration to the contrary. The presumption makes the primary caretaker role central to the definition of the child's best interest, giving it precedence over other consid-erations. Second, most states give much more weight today to the continuing involvement of both parents in the child's life, rather than the selection of one parent over the other as the child's sole custodian. This shift, discussed throughout the rest of the chapter, has substantially changed the nature of custody decision making.

NOTE: VISITATION AND PARENTING PLANS

A court that awards primary custody to one parent may still allocate substantial parenting time to the other parent. Indeed, denial of visitation is an extreme remedy, and in the past has rarely been approved. Visitation may be regarded as a basic human right. In 2008 the House of Lords in the United Kingdom held, in EM (Lebanon) v. Secretary of State for the Home Depart-ment, [2008] UKHL 64, that a Lebanese woman should have been granted asylum in England because deporting her to Lebanon would infringe the right to respect for family life under Article 8 of the European Convention on Human Rights. She was divorced from her husband, and Sharia law provides that he is entitled to custody and has the absolute right to decide whether the mother will have any contact with the child, despite the fact that the father had seen the child only once, on the day of his birth.

States may nevertheless restrict visitation by a party who has been convicted of child abuse. *See, e.g.*, Mo. Rev. Stat. § 452.400 (2009). Cannon v. Cannon, 280 S.W.3d 79 (Mo. 2009), upholds the constitutionality of the statute against a challenge from a father who had been convicted of sexually abusing his stepdaugh-ter, and as a result was limited to supervised visitation with his children when he was released from prison. The courts, however, have reversed visitation orders where there is no showing of harm to the child or where the court's concerns could be addressed through less restrictive means. *See* Sharp v. Keeler, 256 S.W.3d 528 (Ark. App. 2007); R.B.O. v. Jefferson County Dep't of Human Resources, 70 So. 3d 1286 (Ala. App. 2011).

Both courts and parents have been moving away from the "visitation" label, which appears to create "winners" and "losers" in custody battles. Consider the provision below for "parenting plans" as a way to avoid such determinations. The courts can use these plans to allocate both residential time with the child and decision-making authority.

AMERICAN LAW INSTITUTE, *PRINCIPLES OF THE LAW OF
FAMILY DISSOLUTION*

§ 2.05 Parenting Plan: Proposed, Temporary, and Final (2002)

(1) An individual seeking a judicial allocation of custodial responsibility or
decision making responsibility . . . should be required to file with the court a proposed parenting plan. . . .

(2) Each parenting plan filed under Paragraph (1) should be required to be
supported by an affidavit containing . . . [the names and addresses of involved
individuals, a description of the past allocation of caretaking and other parenting
functions, the child's and caretakers' schedules, a description of the known areas of
agreement and disagreement, and other relevant information].

(5) . . . [T]he court should order a parenting plan that is consistent with the
custody provisions of §§ 2.08-2.12 [favoring continuation of the division of responsibility that existed during the marriage] and contains the following provisions:

(a) a provision for the child's living arrangements and for each parent's
custodial responsibility, which should include either

(i) a custodial schedule that designates in which parent's home each
minor child will reside on given days of the year; or

(ii) a formula or method for determining such a schedule in sufficient
detail that, if necessary, the schedule can be enforced in a subsequent
proceeding.

(b) an allocation of decision making responsibility as to significant matters
reasonably likely to arise with respect to the child; and

(c) a provision . . . for resolution of disputes that arise under the plan, and a
provision establishing remedies for violations of the plan.

NOTES AND QUESTIONS

1. The ALI approach moves away from the use of labels (*e.g.*, "sole custody,"
"joint custody," and "visitation") to allocate decision-making power in favor of
more detailed plans that define the respective responsibilities of each parent.
A parenting plan might specify, for example, that the mother, who coaches the
child's soccer team, shall have physical custody on the days of every soccer game
and practice, and sole decision-making power over team-related issues, whereas
the father shall attend parent-teacher conferences and have primary decision-
making responsibility for homework disputes. Are more detailed plans likely to
generate conflict as circumstances change (*e.g.*, the child joins a more competitive
team that practices more frequently and travels during the period the other parent
is supposed to have custody) or prevent conflict by eliminating some of the ambi-
guity and discretion in more traditional awards?

2. The ALI Principles of Family Dissolution provide that "a court may modify a court-ordered parenting plan if it finds, on the basis of facts that were not
known or have arisen since the entry of the prior order and were not anticipated
therein, that a substantial change has occurred in the circumstances of the child or
of one or both parents and that a modification is necessary to the child's welfare."
§ 2.15(1). The Principles also permit modifications in the child's best interest if the

parents agree, the modification reflects a de facto change already in place for at least six months, the change is necessary to accommodate an older child's preferences, and other circumstances. § 2.16.

3. Consider how you would draft a parenting plan in the following case: Father would ideally like joint legal decision-making power and time with the two children, ages 7 and 9, three weekends a month and one day during the week. Mother prefers an award of sole decision-making power to her, and visitation for the father every other weekend and on rotating days during the week that change with her work schedule. If you represented the father, what kind of plan would you propose, and how might you try to persuade the mother to accept it? How would the result be different from an award of sole legal or physical custody to the mother, with visitation for the father?

4. If the parents cannot agree on a parenting plan, the ALI Principles propose the following approach:

AMERICAN LAW INSTITUTE, PRINCIPLES OF THE LAW OF FAMILY DISSOLUTION

§ 2.08 Allocation of Custodial Responsibility (2002)

(1) Unless otherwise resolved by agreement of the parents . . . , the court should allocate custodial responsibility so that the proportion of custodial time the child spends with each parent approximates the proportion of time each parent spent performing caretaking functions for the child prior to the parents' separation . . . except to the extent required under § 2.11 [where there is credible evidence of abandonment, domestic abuse, or other serious misconduct by a parent] or necessary to achieve one or more of the following objectives:

(a) to permit the child to have a relationship with each parent which, in the case of a legal parent or a parent by estoppel who has performed a reasonable share of parenting functions, should be not less than a presumptive amount of custodial time set by a uniform rule of statewide application;

(b) to accommodate the firm and reasonable preferences of a child who has reached a specific age, set by a uniform rule of statewide application;

(c) to keep siblings together when the court finds that doing so is necessary to their welfare;

(d) to protect the child's welfare when the presumptive allocation under this section would harm the child because of a gross disparity in the quality of the emotional attachment between each parent and the child or in each parent's demonstrated ability or availability to meet the child's needs;

(e) to take into account any prior agreement . . . ;

(f) to avoid an allocation of custodial responsibility that would be extremely impractical or that would interfere substantially with the child's need for stability . . . ;

(g) [to deal with a parent's proposed relocation] . . . ;

(h) to avoid substantial and almost certain harm to the child.

NOTES AND QUESTIONS

1. In identifying the "primary caretaker," courts look to various factors. One list of relevant considerations appears in Garska v. McCoy, 278 S.E.2d 357, 363 (W. Va. 1981):

> While it is difficult to enumerate all of the factors which will contribute to a conclusion that one or the other parent was the primary caretaker parent, nonetheless, there are certain obvious criteria to which a court must initially look . . . : (1) preparing and planning of meals; (2) bathing, grooming and dressing; (3) purchasing, cleaning, and care of clothes; (4) medical care, including nursing and trips to physicians; (5) arranging for social interaction among peers after school, i.e., transporting to friends' houses or, for example, to girl or boy scout meetings; (6) arranging alternative care, i.e., babysitting, daycare, etc.; (7) putting child to bed at night, attending to child in the middle of the night, waking child in the morning; (8) disciplining, i.e., teaching general manners and toilet training; (9) educating, i.e., religious, cultural, social, etc.; and (10) teaching elementary skills, i.e., reading, writing, and arithmetic.

West Virginia became the first state to adopt a version of the American Law Institute (ALI) draft provision on custodial responsibility. W. Va. Code § 48-11-201 (1999). To what extent do the ALI Principles change the approach in Garska v. McCoy? How does § 2.08 seek to reconcile these factors, and is it likely to be more or less successful than the approach in *Garska*?

2. How does one measure the past caretaking functions that form the basis for postdivorce custodial responsibility under the ALI Principles? Section 2.03(6) of the Principles defines caretaking functions as tasks involving "interaction with the child or direct[ing] the interaction and care provided by others." Those functions resemble the functions described in Garska v. McCoy, and include feeding, bedtime and wake-up routines, care of the child when sick or hurt, bathing, grooming, personal hygiene, educational activities, disciplinary and training activities, arrangements for and communication with schools and teachers, moral guidance, and arrangement of alternative care. Caretaking functions are distinguished from "parental functions," which include provision of economic support, decision-making regarding the child's welfare, maintenance of the family home, financial planning, and "other functions . . . that are important to the child's welfare, and development."

The allocation described in the Principles takes only caretaking, and not parental, functions into account. Only time spent on caretaking activities is relevant; the degree of initiative or investment is not ordinarily to be considered.

Where the parents' time commitments to caretaking have changed over time, the Comment indicates that the longer (rather than the more recent) arrangement should be given priority on the ground that a different result would inadequately recognize the caretaking functions likely to have been most significant to the child and would provide an incentive for strategic behavior in anticipation of divorce. A substantial change that had endured for some time, however, should be given precedence. For criticism that the approximation rule undermines the purposes of a primary caretaker preference, *see* Pamela Laufer-Ukeles, Selective Recognition of Gender Difference in the Law: Revaluing the Caretaker Role, 31 Harv. J.L. &

Gender 1 (2008). For an evaluation of the social science data underlying the approximation rule and criticism that it will neither reduce litigation nor better serve children's interests, *see* Richard A. Warshak, Punching the Parenting Time Clock: The Approximation Rule, Social Science, and the Baseball Bat Kids, 45 Fam. Ct. Rev. 600 (2007).

PROBLEMS

1. Bryan and Shannan were married and had two young children. After the birth of their youngest child, Shannan became depressed and began taking medication and drinking heavily. Shannan entered a rehabilitation program and remained there for five and a half months. After four years of marriage, while Shannon was still in the rehabilitation program, Bryan filed for dissolution of the marriage. The trial court awarded Bryan sole physical custody. Five months later, Shannan asked for and received alternating weekend and holiday visitation.

A year after the initial custody award, Shannan moved to modify the custody award to grant her physical custody. Because Bryan worked long hours, the children were spending many hours with day care providers and Bryan's parents. Shannan had remarried and had another child. She was a full-time homemaker who could care for the children in her home during the day, and she argued that being with her would be in the child's best interests.

The trial court found that Shannan's recovery efforts had been successful and that she had been sober for more than a year. The judge ruled that it would be in the children's best interests to live with Shannan, since she could provide personal care for them. Bryan was granted visitation.

Bryan appeals, citing Burchard v. Garay. What arguments should the parties make?

2. This custody dispute involves the mother, Jennifer, and the child's unmarried father, Steve. Jennifer gave birth to her daughter in 1993, when she was 15 years of age and a sophomore in high school. Steve was three months older, and also in school. He acknowledged paternity immediately and now seeks sole custody.

Jennifer initially considered terminating her pregnancy, but ultimately decided to have the child and to raise her in her mother's house. Both parties are still in school. Jennifer has been the custodial parent during the child's life. The evidence indicates that, due to Jennifer's immaturity, the maternal grandmother and Jennifer's sister have raised the child virtually from its infancy. They have supplied almost all of the child's necessities, since neither parent has the earning capacity to provide support.

Jennifer is intelligent and has received a scholarship from the University of Michigan. She plans to live in resident housing during the period required for a bachelor's and, perhaps, a master's degree. She contemplates living at the university and placing the child in appropriate day care or schooling and in off-school times would return to her mother's home.

Steve resides with his parents and, in the early days, exercised visitation with his mother participating in caring for the child. He has a good relationship with his daughter. He is currently a student at the local community college and maintains part-time employment. Steve's mother is not employed outside the home and would welcome the opportunity to spend her entire time raising the child when the father is at school or work. She is in good health and is 39 years old. What custodial order should be entered?

3. Marie and James are divorcing after a 20-year marriage. They have three minor children, ages 14, 13, and 8. For the last 17 years, James worked as a public school teacher and Marie stayed at home with the children. Three years before their separation, the youngest child began attending kindergarten and Marie began a nine-month course in computing at a local community college. This training led to her employment as a computer programmer in a bank. Her education and employment have occupied much of Marie's time, and James has assumed responsibility for after-school caretaking of their children. Marie and James agree that the children should have one primary home, and each wants primary custody. How should custody be allocated under the primary caretaker presumption and under the ALI Principles?

3. Joint Custody

We have already considered a number of areas of substantial change in family law doctrine and procedure. The grounds for divorce, the theory of alimony, the principles of property distribution at divorce, and the process for dissolving families have all changed dramatically over the last several decades. The shift from recognition of a sole parent with decision-making power to encouragement of the continuing involvement of both parents in the child's life may also be counted as a significant development.

Currently, the justifications for most custodial rules reflect empirical claims. The maternal preference initially proceeded not from a natural right but from a judicial belief that mothers were, for social or other reasons, better suited than fathers to care for children. Today, shared parenting similarly follows from a deep conviction that children benefit from continuing contact with both parents. It is reasonable to wonder about the bases for these claims about how the world works.

Until relatively recently, courts generally agreed that all children of a family should be placed with a single custodial parent. Shared custody arrangements were disfavored or simply rejected on a number of grounds, including the notion that a single parent with primary responsibility provided consistency in discipline and moral education. Joint legal custody also seemed to threaten a continuation of the spousal conflict leading to divorce — a conflict that would now directly involve the children. Rejection of joint custodial arrangements was so general that Professor Clark's 1968 hornbook on domestic relations does not even mention joint custody. Homer H. Clark, Jr., The Law of Domestic Relations ch. 17 (1968).

Over the last 30 years, however, attitudes and legal rules concerning joint custody have changed. Central among the changes is the conviction, in an era of greater family instability, that children's interests are best served by custody orders that facilitate continuing contact with both parents, and that designation of one parent as the "custodian" and the other as a "visitor" contributes to acrimony underlying custodial disputes and the weakening of the children's ties to the noncustodial parent. As we will see, some states now articulate a preference for joint custody, and most permit it in appropriate cases. The most contentious remaining issue is not whether joint custody should be allowed, but when, and to what extent the courts use it to avoid having to choose between two otherwise fit parents.

IN RE MARRIAGE OF HANSEN

733 N.W.2d 683 (Iowa 2007)

APPEL, Justice. In this case, we review physical care and property issues related to the parties' dissolution of marriage. The district court granted joint legal custody and joint physical care of the two children to Lyle and Delores Hansen. . . .

Lyle and Delores were married on September 4, 1987. The marriage lasted approximately eighteen years. At the time of trial, Lyle was forty-five years of age and Delores was forty-six. Two children were born of the marriage, Miranda, who was twelve years old at the time of the district court proceedings, and Ethan, who was eight.

At all times prior to the filing of the divorce petition, Delores was the primary caregiver. Lyle, alternatively, was the main breadwinner. For example, during the course of the marriage Delores attended parent teacher conferences on a regular basis, while Lyle did not. The vast majority of the time, it was Delores who helped the children with their homework. Lyle admits that she was better at it, particularly math. During the marriage, Lyle missed important childhood events because of social activities or work-related assignments. When the children were in infancy, Delores opened a day care center in their home. Later, when family finances became an issue, she held full-time employment outside the home. After the parties' separation, however, Lyle has become more involved in the lives of the children.

The record developed at trial reveals serious marital stress. The record demonstrates a history of recurrent arguments, excessive consumption of alcohol, allegations of infidelity and sexual misconduct, and allegations of domestic abuse. Unfortunately, at least some of these contretemps were in front of the children. It was not a pleasant proceeding. As part of our de novo review, we have reviewed thoroughly all of these matters, which need not be described in detail here.

The record further reveals that Delores tended to acquiesce to Lyle when there were disagreements. For example, when Delores was pregnant with Miranda, she wanted to attend child-birthing classes, but Lyle stated that *he* had already undergone training and that, as a result, the classes were not needed. When Delores began operating a child care center out of their home, Lyle insisted on reviewing applicant backgrounds and controlled which children could utilize the service. He further demanded that parents or custodians pick up their children by 5:00 P.M. sharp. Delores did not agree with these practices, but felt she had no choice but to acquiesce. In addition, Delores asked Lyle if he would participate in marital counseling, but he refused, stating that he did not believe in counseling. Delores testified that she agreed to temporary joint physical care prior to trial only because she did not feel she could stand up to her husband. Delores expressed concern that if she disagrees with Lyle, he becomes angry and intimidating.

The parties appear to have different approaches to child rearing. Delores wants the children to be active in the Methodist church and other extracurricular activities. While not being overtly resistant, during the course of the marriage, Lyle did not encourage these kinds of activities. The parties also have different approaches to discipline. Lyle claims to have been the disciplinarian in the marital home. The record reveals that there are occasions when Lyle believed that discipline needed to be more severe than Delores was willing to impose. Lyle acknowledged that, at times, he is overprotective. As Lyle admitted, there are some things that he might let the children do that [sic] Delores might not, and vice versa.

At trial, Lyle expressed concern that Delores will expose their children to her family, which he finds highly dysfunctional. Delores testified that her father abused her as a child, but they have reconciled sufficiently to maintain an ongoing relationship. Lyle's concern, however, extends beyond the father, as other members of Delores' family have been convicted of child endangerment and drug offenses. Delores counters that when the children visit her family, it is always under her supervision.

Prior to trial, the parties were apparently able to work out the scheduling issues inherent in a joint physical care arrangement. There was not always agreement, however, on matters related to the children. For instance, when one child experienced unexpected academic difficulties, Delores believed professional counseling would be of help. Lyle disagreed, once again stating that he did not believe in professional counseling. Delores acquiesced, and counseling was not obtained. On another occasion, the kids called their mother and asked to be picked up because Lyle was angry that they had not cleaned their rooms, and had slammed the kitchen door, breaking its glass pane. Moreover, Delores testified that Miranda told her she desired a more stable living arrangement with a home base.

While much of the record in this case is unattractive, it is clear that both Lyle and Delores love their children. They are both capable of making substantial contributions to their lives. The record further reveals that the children are bright and generally well-adjusted. . . .

On November 15, 2004, Lyle filed a petition for dissolution of marriage. The district court entered an order on December 30, 2004 which granted temporary physical care and legal custody to both parents. . . . The matter came to trial on November 2, 2005. Each party requested physical care. Only Lyle sought joint physical care as a secondary alternative. . . .

The district court granted "joint legal custody" and "joint physical care" of the minor children to Lyle and Delores. The district court order, however, established a schedule where "physical care" would alternate between Lyle and Delores for six-month periods beginning on January 1, 2006, with liberal visitation for the spouse not currently having physical care. . . .

On appeal, no party contests the district court's award of joint legal custody. With respect to the children, Delores seeks to overturn the district court's ruling awarding joint physical care to both parties. She seeks physical care. Lyle, however, seeks physical care, but in the event this does not occur, is willing to accept joint physical care in the alternative.

At the outset, it is important to discuss the differences between joint legal custody and joint physical care. "Legal custody" carries with it certain rights and responsibilities, including but not limited to "decisionmaking affecting the child's legal status, medical care, education, extracurricular activities, and religious instruction." Iowa Code § 598.1(3), (5) (2005). When joint legal custody is awarded, "neither parent has legal custodial rights superior to those of the other parent." A parent who is awarded legal custody has the ability to participate in fundamental decisions about the child's life.

On the other hand, "physical care" involves "the right and responsibility to maintain a home for the minor child and provide for routine care of the child." *Id.* § 598.1(7). If joint physical care is awarded, "both parents have rights to and responsibilities toward the child including, but not limited to, shared parenting time with the child, maintaining homes for the child, [and] providing routine care for the child. . . ." *Id.* § 598.1(4). The parent awarded physical care maintains the primary residence and has the right to determine the myriad of details associated with routine living, including such things as what clothes the children wear, when they go to bed, with whom they associate or date, etc.

If joint physical care is not warranted, the court must choose a primary caretaker who is solely responsible for decisions concerning the child's routine care. Visitation rights are ordinarily afforded a parent who is not the primary caretaker.

. . . In In re Marriage of Burham, 283 N.W.2d 269 (Iowa 1979), this court outlined reasons against "divided custody." Specifically, the court cited Iowa precedent for the proposition that divided custody is destructive of discipline, induces a feeling of not belonging to either parent, and in some instances can permit one parent to sow seeds of discontent concerning the other. Although *Burham* referred to "divided custody," later cases made it clear that the underlying rationale regarding the best interest of children applied to cases involving "joint physical care."

These cases have generally emphasized that the best interest of children is promoted by stability and continuity. Although a child's best interests will be served by associating with both parents, "an attempt to provide equal physical care may be harmfully disruptive in depriving a child of a necessary sense of stability." In re Marriage of Muell, 408 N.W.2d 774, 776 (Iowa Ct. App. 1987). As a result, Iowa appellate courts have stated divided physical care is "strongly disfavored" as not in the best interest of children except in the most unusual of circumstances. . . .

In 2004, the legislature again revisited the issue of joint physical care by amending Iowa Code section 598.41(5) to read, in relevant part:

> If joint legal custody is awarded to both parents, the court may award joint physical care to both joint custodial parents upon the request of either parent. . . . If the court denies the request for joint physical care, the determination shall be accompanied by specific findings of fact and conclusions of law that the awarding of joint physical care is not in the best interest of the child.

. . . In In re Marriage of Ellis, 705 N.W.2d 96 (Iowa Ct. App. 2005), . . . the court of appeals rejected the claim that the new statutory provisions created a *presumption* in favor of joint physical care. On the other hand, the court of appeals came to the conclusion that the amendments had the effect of reversing the traditional disfavor against joint physical care by Iowa courts. . . . We agree with the court of appeals that the . . . legislation did not create a presumption in favor of joint physical care. . . .

We disagree, however, with the court of appeals as to whether the . . . amendments have affected any change in substantive law. While the amendments clearly require that courts consider joint physical care at the request of any party and that it make specific findings when joint physical care is rejected, the legislation reiterates the traditional standard — the best interest of the child — which appellate courts in the past have found rarely served by joint physical care. . . .

. . . [W]e nonetheless believe that the notion that joint physical care is strongly disfavored except in exceptional circumstances is subject to reexamination in light of changing social conditions and ongoing legal and research developments. Increasingly in Iowa and across the nation, our family structures have become more diverse. While some families function along traditional lines with a primary breadwinner and primary caregiver, other families employ a more undifferentiated role for spouses or even reverse "traditional" roles. A one-size-fits-all approach in which joint physical care is universally disfavored is thus subject to serious question given current social realities.

In addition, the social science research related to child custody issues is now richer and more varied than it was in the past. In the past, many scholars and courts rejected joint physical care based on the influential writings of Joseph Goldstein, Anna Freud, and Albert J. Solnit. These scholars utilized attachment theory to emphasize the need to place children with a single "psychological parent" with whom the children had bonded. Joseph Goldstein, Anna Freud, & Albert J. Solnit, Beyond the Best Interests of the Child 98 (1979). Although the research upon which the "psychological parent" attachment theory was based rested upon studies of infants, it was also thought to apply throughout the life cycle of a child. . . .

Attachment theory that emphasizes primary relationships continues to have strong advocates. The validity of the parent-child dyad or monotropic view of attachments, however, has been subject to substantial question. Many scholars now view infants as capable of attaching to multiple caregivers and not simply one "psychological parent." Michael E. Lamb, Placing Children's Interest First: Developmentally Appropriate Parenting Plans, 10 Va. J. Soc. Pol'y & L. 98, 109-13 (2002). Further, a growing body of scholarship suggests that the continued presence and involvement of both parents is often beneficial to the lives of children and not necessarily detrimental as believed by many adherents of the "psychological parent" theory. Id. at 100 (citing disadvantages of children growing up in fatherless families, including psychological adjustment, behavior and achievement at school, educational attainment, employment trajectories, and income generation); Michael T. Flannery, Is "Bird Nesting" in the Best Interest of Children?, 57 SMU L. Rev. 295, 302 (2004) (most commentators agree that, generally, children benefit from continued contact with both parents after a divorce).

As a result, a substantial body of scholarly commentary now challenges the blanket application of the monotropic psychological parent attachment theory to avoid joint physical care. . . . Thomas M. Horner & Melvin J. Guyer, Prediction, Prevention, and Clinical Expertise in Child Custody Cases in Which Allegations of Child Sexual Abuse Have Been Made, 25 Fam. L.Q. 217, 248 (1991). Some academic observers suggest that joint physical care may be a way to encourage continued involvement of both spouses in the lives of the children. Matthew A. Kipp, Maximizing Custody Options: Abolishing the Presumption Against Joint Physical Custody, 79 N.D. L. Rev. 59 (2003); Stephanie N. Barnes, Strengthening the Father-Child Relationship Through a Joint Custody Presumption, 35 Willamette L. Rev. 601 (1999). They cite a wide range of studies to suggest that children may be better off with joint physical care than other arrangements.

The current social science research cited by advocates of joint custody or joint physical care, however, is not definitive on many key questions. To begin with, there are substantial questions of definition and methodology. Such criticisms include: samples that only examine parents who voluntarily choose joint custody, the use of small and homogeneous groups, the skewing of samples toward middle class parents with higher incomes and education, the lack of control groups, the lack of distinction between "joint custody" arrangements and traditional sole custody with visitation, and the failure to differentiate the effects of preexisting parental characteristics from the effects of custody type. Jana B. Singer & William L. Reynolds, A Dissent on Joint Custody, 47 Md. L. Rev. 497, 507 (1988); *see also* Diane N. Lye, What the Experts Say: Scholarly Research on Post-Divorce Parenting and Child Wellbeing, Report to the Washington State Gender and Justice Commission and Domestic Relations Commission 4-2 (1999) (research fraught with methodological difficulties and severe limitations) [hereinafter Lye, Report]; Daniel A. Krauss & Bruce D. Sales, Legal Standards, Expertise, and Experts in the Resolution of Contested Child Custody Cases, 6 Psychol. Pub. Pol'y & L. 843, 850 (2000) (noting myriad of conceptual and methodological problems).

Further, the data is conflicting or ambiguous. As noted by one recent academic observer, the research to date on the benefits of joint physical care is inconclusive and has produced mixed results. Stephen Gilmore, Contact/Shared Residence and Child Well-Being: Research Evidence and Its Implications for Legal Decision Making, 20 Int'l J.L. Pol'y & Fam. 344, 352-53 (2006); *see also* Krauss & Sales, 6 Psychol. Pub. Pol'y & L. at 857-58 (recent empirical studies of joint custody have not been able to demonstrate a substantial positive effect on postdivorce child adjustment when joint physical care is compared with other custodial arrangements).

An exhaustive review commissioned by the Washington State Supreme Court Gender and Justice Commission and the Domestic Relations Commission examined the many studies related to child custody issues. The review concluded that the available research did not reveal any particular postdivorce residential schedule to be most beneficial to children. While the review concluded that the research did not demonstrate significant advantages to children of joint physical care, the research also did not show significant disadvantages.

While it seems clear that children often benefit from a continuing relationship with both parents after divorce, the research has not established the amount of contact necessary to maintain a "close relationship." Preeminent scholars have noted that "surprisingly, even a fairly small amount of close contact seemed sufficient to maintain close relationships, at least as these relationships were seen from the adolescents' perspective." Eleanor E. Maccoby et al., Postdivorce Roles of Mothers and Fathers in the Lives of Their Children, 7 J. Fam. Psychol. 24, 24

(1993); *see also* Michael E. Lamb, Noncustodial Fathers and Their Impact on the Children of Divorce, in The Postdivorce Family: Children, Parenting, and Society 105, 111 (Ross A. Thompson & Paul R. Amato eds., 1999) (causal link between frequency of father-child contact and child's adjustment to parental divorce "much weaker than one might expect").

There is thus growing support for the notion that the quality, and not the quantity, of contacts with the non-custodial parent are the key to the well-being of children. Quality interaction with children can, of course, occur within the framework of traditional visitation and does not occur solely in situations involving joint physical care.

At present, the available empirical studies simply do not provide a firm basis for a dramatic shift that would endorse joint physical care as the norm in child custody cases. Nonetheless, in light of the changing nature of the structure of families and challenges to the sweeping application of psychological parent attachment theory, we believe the joint physical care issue must be examined in each case on the unique facts and not subject to cursory rejection based on a nearly irrebuttable presumption found in our prior cases.

Any consideration of joint physical care, however, must still be based on Iowa's traditional and statutorily required child custody standard—the best interest of the child. Physical care issues are not to be resolved based upon perceived fairness to the *spouses*, but primarily upon what is best for the *child*. The objective of a physical care determination is to place the children in the environment most likely to bring them to health, both physically and mentally, and to social maturity.

We recognize that the "best interest" standard is subject to attack on the ground that it is no standard at all, that it has the potential of allowing gender bias to affect child custody determinations, and that its very unpredictability increases family law litigation. On the other hand, the advantage of the standard is that it provides the flexibility necessary to consider unique custody issues on a case-by-case basis. We believe the best approach to determining difficult child custody matters involves a framework with some spine, but the sufficient flexibility to allow consideration of each case's unique facts.

In Iowa, the basic framework for determining the best interest of the child has long been in place. In the context of *custody decisions*, the legislature has established a nonexclusive list of factors to be considered. Iowa Code § 598.41(3) (citing nonexclusive factors including suitability of parents, whether psychological and emotional needs and development of child will suffer from lack of contact with and attention from both parents, quality of parental communication, the previous pattern of caregiving, each parent's support of the other, wishes of the child, agreement of the parents, geographic proximity, and safety). Although Iowa Code section 598.41(3) does not directly apply to *physical care* decisions, we have held that the factors listed here as well as other facts and circumstances are relevant in determining whether joint physical care is in the best interest of the child.

In considering whether to award joint physical care where there are two suitable parents, stability and continuity of caregiving have traditionally been primary factors. . . . Stability and continuity factors tend to favor a spouse who, prior to divorce, was primarily responsible for physical care. We continue to believe that stability and continuity of caregiving are important factors that must be considered in custody and care decisions. As noted by a leading scholar, "past care taking patterns likely are a fairly reliable proxy of the intangible qualities such as parental abilities and emotional bonds that are so difficult for courts to ascertain." Bartlett, 35 Willamette L. Rev. at 480. While no postdivorce physical care arrangement will be identical to predissolution experience, preservation of the greatest amount of stability possible is a desirable goal. In contrast, imposing a new physical care arrangement on children that significantly contrasts from their past experience can be unsettling, cause serious emotional harm, and thus not be in the child's best interest.

As a result, the successful caregiving by one spouse in the past is a strong predictor that future care of the children will be of the same quality. Conversely, however, long-term, successful, joint care is a significant factor in considering the viability of joint physical care after divorce.

Stability and continuity concepts have been refined in the recent literature and expressed in terms of an approximation rule, namely, that the caregiving of parents in the postdivorce world should be in rough proportion to that which predated the dissolution. Elizabeth S. Scott, Pluralism, Parental Preference, and Child Custody, 80 Cal. L. Rev. 615, 617 (1992). Recently, the American Law Institute's Principles of Family Law, published in 2000, adopted the general rule that custodial responsibility should be allocated "so that the proportion of custodial time the child spends with each parent approximates the proportion of time each parent spent performing caretaking functions for the child prior to the parents' separation. . . ." Principles § 2:08, at 178. A reporter of the ALI Project on Family Dissolution that produced Principles suggests that the ALI approximation rule is gender neutral, focuses on historical facts rather than subjective judgments, and is, in most cases, likely to provide an environment that is in the best interest of the child. Bartlett, 35 Willamette L. Rev. at 480-82.

We do not, however, adopt the ALI approximation rule in its entirety. Iowa Code section 598.41(3) and our case law requires a multi-factored test where no one criterion is determinative. Any wholesale adoption of the approximation rule would require legislative action. Nonetheless, we believe that the approximation principle is a factor to be considered by courts in determining whether to grant joint physical care. By focusing on historic patterns of caregiving, the approximation rule provides a relatively objective factor for the court to consider. The principle of approximation also rejects a "one-size-fits-all" approach and recognizes the diversity of family life. Finally, it tends to ensure that any decision to grant joint physical care is firmly rooted in the past practices of the individual family.

There may be circumstances, of course, that outweigh considerations of stability, continuity, and approximation. For example, if a primary caregiver has abandoned responsibilities or had not been adequately performing his or her responsibilities because of alcohol or substance abuse, there may be a strong case for changing the physical care relationship. In addition, the quality of the parent-child relationship is not always determined by hours spent together or solely upon past experience.

All other things being equal, however, we believe that joint physical care is most likely to be in the best interest of the child where both parents have historically contributed to physical care in roughly the same proportion. Conversely, where one spouse has been the primary caregiver, the likelihood that joint physical care may be disruptive on the emotional development of the children increases.

A second important factor to consider in determining whether joint physical care is in the child's best interest is the ability of spouses to communicate and show mutual respect. A lack of trust poses a significant impediment to effective co-parenting. Evidence of controlling behavior by a spouse may be an indicator of potential problems. Evidence of untreated domestic battering should be given considerable weight in determining custody and gives rise to a presumption against joint physical care.

Third, the degree of conflict between parents is an important factor in determining whether joint physical care is appropriate. Joint physical care requires substantial and regular interaction between divorced parents on a myriad of issues. Where the parties' marriage is stormy and has a history of charge and counter-charge, the likelihood that joint physical care will provide a workable arrangement diminishes. It is, of course, possible that spouses may be able to put aside their past, strong differences in the interest of the children. Reality suggests, however, that this may not be the case.

In short, a stormy marriage and divorce presents a significant risk factor that must be considered in determining whether joint physical care is in the best interest of the children. The prospect for successful joint physical care is reduced when there is a bitter parental relationship and one party objects to the shared arrangement. As noted in the Washington state review, there is evidence that high levels of child contact with a nonresidential father are beneficial to children in low conflict families, but harmful to children in high conflict families.

Conflict, of course, is a continuum, but expressions of anger between parents can negatively affect children's emotions and behaviors. Even a low level of conflict can have significant repercussions for children. Courts must balance the marginal benefits obtained from the institution of a joint physical care regime as compared to other alternatives against the possibility that interparental conflict will be exacerbated by the arrangement, to the detriment of the children.

Because of the perceived detrimental impact of parental conflict on children, some commentators have urged that joint physical care should be encouraged only where both parents voluntarily agree to it. Frank F. Furstenberg, Jr. & Andrew J. Cherlin, Divided Families: What Happens to Children When Parents Part 75-76 (1991); see Or. Rev. Stat. § 107.169(3) (2007) (joint custody only upon agreement of parents); Vt. Stat. Ann. tit. 15, § 665(a) (2007) ("When parents cannot agree to divide or share parental rights and responsibilities, the court shall award parental rights and responsibilities primarily or solely to one parent."). Iowa Code section 598.41(5)(a), however, requires the court to consider joint physical care upon the request of either party. While we, therefore, reject the notion that one spouse has absolute veto power over whether the court grants joint physical custody, the lack of mutual acceptance can be an indicator of instability in the relationship that may impair the successful exercise of joint physical care. See Iowa Code § 598.41(3)(g) (court should consider whether one or both spouses agree or are opposed).

A fourth important factor in determining whether joint physical care is in the best interest of the children, particularly when there is a turbulent past relationship, is the degree to which the parents are in general agreement about their approach to daily matters. It would be unrealistic, of course, to suggest that parents must agree on all issues all of the time, but in order for joint physical care to work, the parents must generally be operating from the same page on a wide variety of routine matters. The greater the amount of agreement between the parents on child rearing issues, the lower the likelihood that ongoing bitterness will create a situation in which children are at risk of becoming pawns in continued post-dissolution marital strife. While the above factors are often significant in determining the appropriateness of joint physical care, we do not mean to suggest that they are the exclusive factors or that these factors will always be determinative. This court has stated, despite application of a multi-factored test, that district courts must consider the total setting presented by each unique case. The above factors present important considerations, but no iron clad formula or inflexible system of legal presumptions.

Once it is decided that joint physical care is not in the best interest of the children, the court must next choose which caregiver should be awarded physical care. The parent awarded physical care is required to support the other parent's relationship with the child. In making this decision, the factors of continuity, stability, and approximation are entitled to considerable weight. The court should be alert, however, to situations where the emotional bonds between children and a parent who has not been the primary caregiver are stronger than the bonds with the other parent.

In making decisions regarding joint physical care and, if joint physical care is not appropriate, in choosing a spouse for physical care, courts must avoid gender bias. There is no preference for mothers over fathers, or vice versa. The preference is to advance gender neutral goals of stability and continuity with an eye toward providing the children with the best environment possible for their continued development and growth. . . .

In light of the above principles, and after our de novo review of the entire record, we agree with the court of appeals that joint physical care is not in the best interest of the children under the unique facts presented in this case. For most of the marriage, Delores has been the primary caregiver. The concepts of continuity, stability, and approximation thus cut strongly against joint physical care as a quality alternative least disruptive to the children and most likely to promote their long-term physical and emotional health.

The record also shows that the parties have significant difficulties in communication. Lyle has strong beliefs, and Delores tends to attempt to avoid conflicts with him by simply acquiescing. Further, the divorce proceedings demonstrated considerable mutual distrust and a high level of conflict between the parties, complete with allegations of sexual improprieties and domestic abuse. It is noteworthy that while Lyle disputed most of the alleged incidents of physical abuse, he admitted that he and Delores engaged in "pushing matches." Furthermore, there was substantial evidence in the record that Lyle has a controlling personality that could extend into the postdivorce world. In light of this record, there is a distinct danger that flare-ups in the relationship could disrupt the children's lives in a joint physical care context.

The record also demonstrates differences in parenting styles. Lyle admits to being "overly protective." Their discipline styles are also different, with Lyle recognizing that there are some things that he would allow, but Delores would not, and vice versa. Additionally, Lyle and Delores have different views on the potential role of counseling in helping the children through the difficulties created by divorce. While the parties were able to handle the logistics of joint physical care pursuant to the district court's temporary order, this factor is not dispositive. Over the long haul, we believe there is a high potential for conflict if joint physical care were to continue. . . .

. . . We conclude that the best interest of the children will be advanced by awarding physical care to Delores rather than to award joint physical care.

At the same time, Lyle has an important role to play in his children's lives. No one questions his devotion to them and their need for his guidance and support. A responsible, committed, nonresident parent, with good parenting skills, has the potential to engage in a high-quality relationship with his or her child and to positively impact the child's adjustment.

Because the district court ordered the parties to share joint legal custody, Lyle will continue to be involved in major decisionmaking for his children. In order to promote the desirable level of physical contact, on remand, the district court should establish liberal visitation for Lyle. . . .

NOTES AND QUESTIONS

1. The Iowa Supreme Court distinguishes between "joint legal custody" and "joint physical care," giving definitions for each. Most other states use the term joint physical *custody* rather than joint physical *care*. Increasingly, advocates also use the terms *shared custody* or *shared parenting* sometimes as a synonym with joint legal and physical custody and sometimes to mean approximately equal shares of the child's time. *See* Jennifer E. McIntosh, Legislating for Shared Parenting: Exploring Some Underlying Assumptions, 47 Fam. Ct. Rev. 389 (2009).

States vary considerably in the definitions they use to describe joint physical custody. The majority of states have adopted the Iowa approach, which defines joint physical care to mean that "both parents have rights to and responsibilities toward the child including, but not limited to, shared parenting time with the child, maintaining homes for the child, [and] providing routine care for the child." This definition does not tie joint physical custody to a particular allocation of time, but rather to joint assumption of responsibility for the child. For similar definitions, *see* Mo. Ann. Stat. § 452.375 (2011); Cal. Fam. Code § 3004 (2014); Haw. Rev. Stat. § 571-46.1 (2009); Idaho Code Ann. § 32-717B(2) (2014); Mass. Ann. Laws ch. 208 § 31 (2014); Miss. Code Ann. § 93-5-24(5) (2014). Other states set minimum requirements before the courts can use the joint physical custody label. *See, e.g.,* N.H. Rev. Stat. Ann. 461-A:20 (2014) (unless the parties had agreed that they would each have 50 percent of the residential responsibility, only one of them could be the "custodial parent"); Okla. Stat. Ann. tit. 43 § 118(10)(a) (2009) ("shared parenting time" means that "each parent has physical custody of the child or children overnight for more than one hundred twenty (120) nights each year"); Tenn. Code Ann. § 36-6-402(4) (2014) ("primary residential parent" means "the parent with whom the child resides more than fifty percent (50%) of the time," reserving joint physical custody only for those cases with an equal division of parenting time); Utah Code Ann. § 78B-12-102 (14) (2014) ("joint physical custody" means "the child stays with each parent overnight for more than 30% of the year, and both parents contribute to the expenses of the child in addition to paying child support"); W. Va. Code § 48-1-239 (2014) (distinguishing between "basic shared parenting," which "means an arrangement under which one parent keeps a child or children overnight for less than thirty-five percent of the year," and "extended shared parenting," which means "an arrangement under which each parent keeps a child or children overnight for more than thirty-five percent of the year"). In many of the latter states, the definitions are tied to child support calculations. In 2013 Arkansas amended its custody statute to redefine "joint custody" to mean the "approximate and reasonable equal division of time with the child by both parents individually as agreed to by the parents or as ordered by the court." Ark. Code § 9-13-101(a)(5).

Aside from the child support calculations, what difference does the label make? Suppose that a custody order provides that the child spends less than 30 percent of the time with one of the parents. What is the difference between joint custody in such a case and sole custody with visitation?

The Supreme Court in *Hansen* held that the father should have "liberal visitation," which includes

> visitation every other weekend, commencing at 6:00 P.M. on Friday night and concluding at 6:00 P.M. Sunday evening and every Wednesday night commencing at 6:00 P.M. and ending at 8:00 A.M. Thursday morning. Lyle shall have visitation on his birthday and Father's Day every year. Delores, conversely, shall have physical custody of the children on her birthday and Mother's Day each year. In addition, Lyle shall have visitation on every other holiday including New Year's Day, Easter, Memorial Day, Fourth of July, Labor Day, Thanksgiving Day, Christmas Eve, Christmas, New Year's Eve. Holiday visitation shall be from 9 A.M. to 9 P.M. Lyle shall have visitation on the children's birthdays on odd numbered years, while Delores shall have even numbered years. In addition, Lyle shall have visitation of the children in the summer for a total of four weeks at two two-week intervals. These two-week intervals shall be separated by at least one week. Lyle shall give Delores written notice no later than April 15 of each year of the times at which he wishes to exercise these vacation periods. During one of those two-week intervals, Lyle shall have uninterrupted visitation. Delores is also entitled to exercise one two-week period of visitation exclusive of Lyle's rights each summer. Delores shall provide Lyle written notice no later then April 30 of each year of the weeks she has selected. Each party is further entitled to uninterrupted visitation during alternating spring breaks. Delores shall have visitation in even numbered years and Lyle shall have visitation in odd numbered years. Finally, the parties shall alternate visitation during Christmas break. In odd numbered years, Delores shall have visitation the first half and Lyle the second. The reverse is true in even numbered years. Lyle is further entitled to any additional visitation that can be agreed upon by the parties.

How would joint physical care be different from what the court ordered? How would an award under the ALI "approximation" standard discussed above be different? How does *Hansen* explain the relationship between the ALI approximation approach and joint physical care?

2. In *Hansen*, the court addresses the propriety of joint physical care, but not joint legal custody. Are the reasons the court gives for rejecting joint physical care also reasons for disputing the propriety of joint legal custody?

3. The Iowa statute construed in *Hansen* states:

> If joint legal custody is awarded to both parents, the court may award joint physical care to both joint custodial parents upon the request of either parent. . . . If the court denies the request for joint physical care, the determination shall be accompanied by specific findings of fact and conclusions of law that the awarding of joint physical care is not in the best interest of the child.

Do you agree with the court that the legislation did not intend to create a presumption in favor of joint physical care?

4. The ALI reports that a number of state statutes have a presumption or preference favoring joint custody, although the states differ considerably as to what such preferences require. The most common preference, adopted in California, Connecticut, Maine, Mississippi, Nevada, and Oregon, is one favoring joint custody where both parents agree. As a practical matter, all that this presumption means is that the court should ordinarily award joint custody where both parents want it—something that courts routinely do in any case absent a showing that what the parents want is not in the child's interest. An additional six states — Idaho, Iowa, Kansas, Michigan, New Mexico, and Missouri — along with the District of Columbia, have a preference for joint custody that can be overcome by showing by a preponderance of the evidence that the child's best interests call for an alternative award. These states have a presumption in favor of some form of joint custody even where the parents disagree. Florida has a presumption favoring shared parental responsibility, which can be overcome only by a showing that shared responsibility would be detrimental to the child. Florida defines "shared parental responsibility" as "a court-ordered relationship in which both parents retain full parental rights and responsibilities with respect to their child and in which both parents confer with each other so that major decisions affecting the welfare of the child will be determined jointly." Fla. Stat. § 61.043(17). It does not, however, create a preference for any particular time sharing arrangement. ALI Principles § 2.08 reporter's notes, at 211. Arizona has also adopted a preference for shared custody, providing that "the court shall adopt a parenting plan that provides for both parents to share legal decision-making regarding their child and that maximizes their respective parenting time." Ariz. Rev. Stat. § 25-403.02(B) (2013). A District of Columbia court has extended the legislative policy favoring joint custody by divorcing parents to a custody action between unmarried parents. Ysla v. Lopez, 684 A.2d 775 (D.C. App. 1996); Hutchins v. Compton, 917 A.2d 680 (D.C. App. 2007).

Should there be a presumption in favor of joint custody? In favor of an alternative standard such as primary caretaker? Or should the best-interest standard depend entirely on the circumstances of the individual case?

5. Some fathers' rights groups argue for a presumption favoring not only joint physical custody, but also equal shares of the child's time for mothers and fathers. Is such a presumption practical? *See* Margaret F. Brinig, Penalty Defaults in Family Law: The Case of Child Custody, 33 Fla. St. U. L. Rev. 779 (2006); David D. Meyer, The Constitutional Rights of Non-Custodial Parents, 34 Hofstra L. Rev.

1461, 1461 (2006). Arkansas enacted such a statute in 2013. *See* Ark. Code § 9-13-101(a)(1)(A) (2013).

In *Hansen*, the trial court attempted to ensure equal time for the parents by having the children spend six months with each parent. What are the advantages and disadvantages of such an approach from the children's perspective? *See* Ireland v. Ireland, 914 S.W.2d 426, 429 (Mo. Ct. App. 1996) (invalidating change of custody every two months); In re Custody of D.M.G., 951 P.2d 1377, 1387 (Mont. 1998) (reversing two-year alternating custody order). *But see* Kaloupek v. Burfening, 440 N.W.2d 496, 498-499 (N.D. 1989) (affirming trial court order alternating custody on six-month basis).

6. *Hansen* reviews the empirical research on joint custody, but concludes that it "is not definitive on many key questions." The initial studies, which tended to be based on small, not necessarily representative samples, focused on self-selected couples who were joint custody enthusiasts. These studies were designed to show that joint custody could work, overcoming the long-standing judicial reluctance to what was then called "divided parenting." In that era, courts sometimes refused to approve joint custody awards even when both parties favored it.

The second round of research documented the implementation of joint custody in those jurisdictions that embraced it. The two most influential studies were Marygold S. Melli et al., Child Custody in a Changing World: A Study of Post-Divorce Arrangements in Wisconsin, 1997 U. Ill. L. Rev. 773, and Eleanor E. Maccoby & Robert R. Mnookin, Dividing the Child (1992). Both studies found that dual-resident families fell into two distinct groups: those experiencing relatively amicable divorces in which the parties agreed to shared parenting early in the process, and more hostile parents, who agreed to a joint custody arrangement only after substantial conflict. The Wisconsin study found that the first group, which represented a little more than half of the joint physical custody total, produced approximately equal divisions of time between the two parents. The remaining cases resembled joint custody with visitation, with the mother assuming primary custody of the child in over 80 percent of these cases. 1997 U. Ill. L. Rev. at 780. The study concluded that "[c]ases where the outcome is equal shared custody had generally low levels of dispute, while those with an unequal shared custody award were the most contentious. This suggests that parents with equal shared time are very different from those who negotiate or are given an unequal shared custody award." *Id.* at 788. Maccoby and Mnookin, in what they termed the "most disturbing" result of their study, similarly found that 40 percent of the later settling (and presumably higher-conflict) cases resulted in joint physical custody, typically with primary mother residence, compared with 25 percent of the cases resolved earlier. Dividing the Child, at 58. This suggests that courts may be using the joint physical custody label to paper over the most difficult disputes. A more recent Wisconsin study, which found that shared custody had increased overall, still found that the cases of equal custody settled more quickly, reflecting parental agreement, while the more contested cases continued to produce shared custody with the mother as the primary custodial parent. Patricia Brown & Steven T. Cook, Children's Placement Arrangements in Divorce and Paternity Cases in Wisconsin 27 (rev. ed. 2012), available at http://www.irp.wisc.edu/research/childsup/cspolicy/pdfs/2009-11/Task4A_CS_09-11_Final_revi2012.pdf (last visited Dec. 10, 2013).

Maccoby and Mnookin also found that dual-residence arrangements proved to be unstable. While only 19 percent of children in the mother's residence at the outset of the study were living with their fathers or in dual-residence by its end, more than one-half of the children who lived initially in dual residences (or with their fathers) had moved into some different residential arrangement by two years after the divorce. Dividing the Child, at 167-170. *See* John R. Gardner, Custody and Visitation: Where's the Morph? Joint "Custody" vs. the Changed Circumstances Rule, 16 J. Contemp. Legal Issues 277 (2007) (arguing that parents often end up in court arguing "changed circumstances" when in fact what is taking place is the failure to agree on the implementation of shared custody).

A third round of studies, described in greater detail in *Hansen*, focused on the benefits of including both parents in the child's upbringing. These studies concluded that the child did not benefit from continuing contact with both parents in high-conflict cases, and in other cases the results did not depend on either the quantity of contacts or the form of the award. Instead, the quality of the interaction between the parents (did the two support each other?) and between parent and child (was the interaction consistent and did it establish close emotional bonds?) mattered most. In a recent test of the impact of these "good divorces" with close parental cooperation and strong parent-child interactions, a team of sociologists still found mixed results. They reported that in comparison with a single parent control group, the children of these "good" divorces had closer ties with their fathers and fewer behavior problems (as reported by the resident parents) than the control group. Yet, the two groups were about the same in adolescent self-esteem, school grades, liking school, substance use, and life satisfaction, and the "young adults in the good divorce cluster were no better off than were young adults in the single parenting cluster with respect to substance use, early sexual activity, number of sexual partners, cohabiting or marrying as a teenager, and closeness to mothers." Paul R. Amato, Jennifer B. Kane & Spencer James, Reconsidering the "Good Divorce," 60 Fam. Rel. 511-524 (2011). For other evaluations of this third round of studies and additional critiques of joint custody, *see* Honorable Arnold F. Blockman, Survey of Illinois Law: Joint Custody Dilemmas and Views from the Bench, 31 S. Ill. U. L.J. 941 (2007); Christy M. Buchanan & Parissa L. Jahromi, A Psychological Perspective on Shared Custody Arrangements, 43 Wake Forest L. Rev. 419 (2008); Cynthia C. Siebel, Fathers and Their Children: Legal and Psychological Issues of Joint Custody, 40 Fam. L.Q. 213 (2006).

7. Split physical custody occurs when each parent has physical care of at least one child. Many states recognize a presumption that siblings should not be separated on the ground that such an arrangement "deprives children of the benefit of constant association with one another." In re Marriage of Pundt, 547 N.W.2d 243, 245 (Iowa App. 1996); In re Marriage of Smiley, 518 N.W.2d 376, 380 (Iowa 1994). As is true of most custody rules, however, disapproval of split custody is not ironclad, and "circumstances may arise which demonstrate that separation may better promote the long-range best interests of children. Good and compelling reasons must exist for a departure." In re Marriage of Pundt, 547 N.W.2d 243, 245 (Iowa App. 1996); In re Marriage of Williams, 90 P.3d 365, 370 (Kan. Ct. App. 2004); In re Murphey, 207 S.W.3d 679 (Mo. App. 2006); In re Marriage of Morales, 159 P.3d 1183, 1189 (Or. Ct. App. 2007). *See also* Johns v. Cioci, 865 A.2d 931, 943

(Pa. Super. Ct. 2004) (refusing to apply presumption in favor of keeping siblings together to half-siblings because it would be "blatantly unfair" to parent who is not related to both children); MBB v. ERW, 100 P.3d 415, 420 (Wyo. 2004) (holding that Wyoming law did not authorize sibling visitation where the siblings had been placed in different homes). For a comprehensive review of the law's failure to protect sibling ties, *see* Jill Elaine Hasday, Siblings in Law, 65 Vand. L. Rev. 897 (2012).

Some courts have sought to avoid the difficulties involved in choosing between parents or between sole or joint custody by adopting "parenting plans" that specify each parent's responsibility without labeling the result. Could a parenting plan be used to address siblings' interests in visitation with each other? If so, how would it differ from existing practices?

LOMBARDO v. LOMBARDO

507 N.W.2d 788 (Mich. App. 1993)

HOLBROOK, Jr., J. . . . The parties were divorced on May 14, 1985, and awarded "joint custody, care, control and education" of their children Michael, Erin, and Robert. The original divorce judgment awarded physical custody of the children to plaintiff, but the judgment was amended later to transfer physical custody to defendant. Plaintiff was awarded visitation rights.

On the Traverse City school district's third-grade placement test, the parties' son Robert ranked fourth of nine hundred students. Robert completed a fourth-grade curriculum as a third grader at the Old Mission School. Robert was selected to attend the school district's talented and gifted program, which selects children from home schools and places them with other gifted children for education.

The parties disagree over whether to enroll Robert in the program for gifted children. Plaintiff thinks that Robert's attendance in the program is essential for him to reach his scholastic potential. After watching Robert's brother Michael go through the program, defendant believes that Robert would experience difficulty adjusting to the program and might narrow his focus on academics only. Unable to agree with regard to the issue, plaintiff filed a motion to order Robert into the program. Following a hearing regarding the matter, the trial court entered its order denying plaintiff's motion. The trial court found that an established educational environment was in place and that Robert was doing well in that environment. The trial court noted the problem of transporting Robert to the school and the segregated nature of the program. In the absence of any law regarding the subject, the trial court determined that the parent who is the primary physical custodian should make the decision. The trial court concluded that if a different standard of review was applicable, then there had not been a showing that keeping Robert at his current school was not in his best interest. . . .

. . . [P]laintiff argues that the trial court erred in determining that the parent who is the primary physical custodian of a child should decide where the child goes to school when the parents are joint custodians of the child and cannot agree concerning that issue. Plaintiff further argues that to the extent that the trial court considered the best interests of the child, it erred in its determination of the best interests of Robert under these circumstances. . . .

Defendant has primary physical custody of the children, and plaintiff has physical custody of the children for not less than 128 days each year. When a child resides with a parent, that parent decides all routine matters concerning the child. MCL 722.26a(4); MSA 25.312(6a)(4). Because the parties in this case were awarded joint custody of their children, they share the decision-making authority with respect to the "important decisions affecting the welfare of the child." MCL 722.26a(7)(b); MSA 25.312(6a)(7)(b). This Court has held that a trial court properly denies joint custody in a proceeding to modify the custody portion of a divorce judgment where the parties cannot agree on basic childrearing issues, in light of the state's interest in protecting the child's best interests. Unfortunately, the Legislature has not provided guidance concerning how to resolve disputes involving "important decisions affecting the welfare of the child" that arise between joint custodial parents. Citing Griffin v. Griffin, 699 P.2d 407 (Colo. 1985), defendant argues that the parent who has primary physical custody of a child has the power to decide the type of educational program the child will experience. In *Griffin*, the divorce decree awarded custody of the parties' child to the petitioner mother. The petitioner and the respondent agreed in the divorce decree that they were to select jointly the child's schools. When the parties were unable to agree about the choice of schools for their child, the respondent father moved to enforce the education provision of the decree. Noting that the agreement did not provide a means of resolving deadlocks over school selection, the Colorado Supreme Court ruled that the agreement was unenforceable because the court has no power to force the parties to reach agreement. The *Griffin* court determined that "any attempt to enforce the agreement by requiring the parents to negotiate and reach a future agreement would be not only futile, but adverse to the interests of the child as well." The court in *Griffin* further determined that the power to control the child's education remained with the mother as the custodial parent in accordance with a Colorado statute that authorizes the custodial parent to make child-rearing decisions in the absence of an enforceable agreement concerning the child's education.

Griffin is similar to the present case where the parties have agreed through the use of joint custody to share the decision-making authority with respect to decisions concerning the welfare of the children. However, *Griffin* is distinguishable by the existence of the Colorado statute that authorizes the custodial parent to make child-rearing decisions in the absence of an enforceable agreement concerning the child's education.

We are mindful of the fact that a court is usually ill-equipped to fully comprehend and act with regard to the varied everyday needs of a child in these circumstances, because it is somewhat of a stranger to both the child and the parents in a marital dissolution proceeding. We also recognize that requiring the parent to meet and resolve the issue "exposes the child to further discord and surrounds the child with an atmosphere of hostility and insecurity." However, joint custody in this state by definition means that the parents share the decision-making authority with respect to the important decisions affecting the welfare of the child, and where the parents as joint custodians cannot agree on important matters such as education, it is the court's duty to determine the issue in the best interests of the child.

We believe the trial court in this case clearly erred in determining that the parent who is the primary physical custodian has the authority to resolve any disputes concerning the important decisions affecting the welfare of the children. MCL 722.27(1)(c); MSA 25.312(7)(1)(c), provides that a court shall change a previous custody order only if there is clear and convincing evidence that it is in the best interests of the children. . . .

The controlling consideration in child custody disputes between parents is the best interests of the children. Parties to a divorce judgment cannot by agreement usurp the court's authority to determine suitable provisions for the child's best interest. Similarly, the court should not relinquish its authority to determine the best interests of the child to the primary physical custodian. Accordingly, we conclude that a trial court must determine the best interests of the child in resolving disputes concerning "important decisions affecting the welfare of the child" that arise between joint custodial parents.

We agree with plaintiff that the trial court did not make specific findings concerning the best interests of Robert. A trial court must consider, evaluate, and determine each of the factors listed at MCL 722.23; MSA 25.312(3), in determining the best interests of the child. The trial court in this case merely determined that plaintiff had failed to show that keeping Robert at his current school was not in his best interest. Consequently, we remand this case to the trial court to determine the best interests of Robert according to the relevant factors contained in MCL 722.23; MSA 25.312(3). . . .

NOTES AND QUESTIONS

1. The Michigan Supreme Court, in another case involving schools, suggested that the courts should apply a two-step analysis:

> To summarize, when considering an important decision affecting the welfare of the child, the trial court must first determine whether the proposed change would modify the established custodial environment of that child. In making this determination, it is the child's standpoint, rather than that of the parents, that is controlling. If the proposed change would modify the established custodial environment of the child, then the burden is on the parent proposing the change to establish, by clear and convincing evidence, that the change is in the child's best interests. Under such circumstances, the trial court must consider all the best-interest factors because a case in which the proposed change would modify the custodial environment is essentially a change-of-custody case. On the other hand, if the proposed change would not modify the established custodial environment of the child, the burden is on the parent proposing the change to establish, by a preponderance of the evidence, that the change is in the child's best interests.

Pierron v. Pierron, 782 N.W.2d 480, 487 (Mich. 2010). *Compare* Brzozowski v. Brzozowski, 625 A.2d 597 (N.J. Super. Ct., Ch. Div. 1993). The father and mother had joint legal custody but the mother was the physical custodian. Their separation agreement defined "joint" custody as "mutual cooperation and decision making regarding the child's health, education, and welfare." The agreement also provided for equal sharing of unreimbursed medical expenses and barred both parents from incurring non-emergency major medical expenses without the other's knowledge and consent.

After a bicycle accident, a doctor recommended elective surgery to correct an obstruction to their daughter's nose. The father secured two "second opinions" concluding that surgery at that time was neither necessary nor risky. The chancery court held that it was unwilling to interfere with the decision making of the residential parent and denied the father's application to prevent the operation in question.

> The contrary holding will produce applications, emergent and otherwise, to the court whenever the parties cannot reach agreement. *Cf.* Novak v. Novak, 446 N.W.2d 422, 15 FLR 1622 (Minn. Ct. App. 1989), in which it was held that, where joint legal custodians disagree on the choice of schooling for the child, the trial court must resolve the dispute consistent with the child's best interests. Putting aside the real questions regarding judicial administration posed by this situation, any court should be reluctant to substitute whatever limited expertise it may have for the empirical knowledge and day-to-day experience of the parent with whom the child lives, except where there is a clear showing that an act or omission will contravene the best interests of the child. Here, no such showing has been made.

See also Debenham v. Debenham, 896 P.2d 1098 (Kan. App. 1995). Parents with joint custody disagreed over whether to send their child to private school. Although it affirmed the trial court order that the child should attend the private school chosen by the parent with primary physical custody, the Kansas Court of Appeals rejected a per se rule favoring decisions by the primary custodian. The appellate court also went out of its way to regret that the "legislature has declared joint custody and equal decisional rights as the public policy of this state." 896 P.2d at 1101.

2. How is the trial court to decide whether it is in Robert's best interest to be in the gifted or regular school program?

What meaning does joint legal custody have under the approach taken in *Brzozowski?*

PROBLEM

As clerk to Justice Austin of the state supreme court, you have been asked to prepare an analysis of Andersen v. Andersen, pending before the court. The trial judge awarded joint legal and physical custody of the parties' two daughters. Neither party requested joint custody, but the court below found that arrangement met the statutory standard that custody orders should be in the best interests of the children.

The record indicates that the children, who are 8 and 10 years of age, desire to remain with their mother but expressed love for their father and wanted to spend substantial time with him. The trial judge found both parents to be fit, and that they wished equally to have close contact with their children. She also found Ms. Andersen to be sensible but somewhat bitter about the divorce and more partisan than Mr. Andersen; Mr. Andersen she found to be a rather "relaxed" person. Ms. Andersen resisted joint custody because she did not think she could cooperate with her former husband; Mr. Andersen did not object to joint custody, although he also did not seek it.

Please advise Justice Austin.

4.   *Judging Parenthood: What Makes Parents Unfit?*

How do we "judge" parents? If custody decisions reflect shared norms that fathers should ordinarily have custody (the presumption in the nineteenth century), that mothers should ordinarily have custody (the presumption in the middle of the twentieth century), or that custody should ordinarily be shared (the presumption in some states today), individualized judgments may not be necessary. But if a custody decision involves choosing between fit parents, value judgments are inevitable. And if the parents' relationship with each other is so contentious they cannot agree on a custody arrangement, the parents might also be quite willing to believe the worst about the other parent and to allege parental misconduct in court. Historically, the courts often considered the factors that determined fault-based divorce, particularly adultery and abandonment, as factors in the subsequent custody award. With no-fault divorce, the custody award is often the only time in a dissolution proceeding that the court passes judgment on adult behavior. How should courts approach these determinations? Should the standards focus on commitment to the child or the qualities of the parent? This section explores the role of the courts in evaluating parental behavior that may influence custody determinations. The materials specifically consider the contentious issues of sexual behavior, race, religion, spousal abuse, and "unfriendly co-parenting" as they relate to the best interests of children.

a.   New Partners

MOIX v. MOIX

___ S.W.3d ___ (Ark. 2013)

CLIFF HOOFMAN, Associate Justice. Appellant John Moix appeals from the circuit court's visitation order, which contained a provision prohibiting his long-term, domestic partner from being present during any overnight visitation with appellant's minor child. On appeal, appellant argues that the circuit court's order violated his state and federal constitutional rights to privacy and equal protection, and that the circuit court erred by finding that such a non-cohabitation restriction was required in the absence of any finding of harm to the child. . . . We reverse and remand.

John and Libby Moix were divorced in 2004. The divorce decree incorporated the parties' settlement agreement, which provided that the parties would share joint custody of their three sons, with appellee serving as the primary custodian and appellant receiving reasonable visitation.

The settlement agreement also stated that neither party was to have overnight guests of the opposite sex.

In May 2005, appellee filed a petition to modify visitation, alleging that since the entry of the divorce decree, appellant had been having a romantic relationship with a live-in male companion and that the children had been exposed to that relationship on multiple occasions. Appellee asserted that appellant and his partner had recently separated after they were involved in a physical altercation in which appellant was seriously injured, although they had since resumed their relationship and were again residing together. Appellee requested that, due to this change in circumstances, the circuit court grant her sole custody of the children and limit appellant's visitation in such a way as to limit the children's exposure to the illicit relationship and to the danger caused by the volatility of his companion. Appellant agreed to the entry of an order of modification, filed on July 18, 2005, which provided that the existing custody arrangement would continue with the two older twin boys, but that appellee would receive full custody of R.M., who was five years old at the time. The order also restricted appellant to visitation with R.M. on every other weekend and every Wednesday, with no overnight visitation.

Despite the agreed order modifying visitation, it is undisputed by the parties that the order was not followed and that appellant had liberal overnight visitation with R.M. until late 2009 or early 2010, when he became addicted to prescription drugs and sought inpatient treatment after being involved in a hit-and-run accident. After he completed his treatment, appellant was limited to daytime visitation at the discretion of appellee. In May 2012, appellant filed a motion for modification of visitation and child support, in which he alleged that appellee had remarried in 2010 and that she had informed him that R.M. had a new father and no longer needed him. Appellant asserted that the severe reduction in his visitation coincided with appellee's remarriage and that his son had expressed the desire to spend more time with him. Because there had been a material change in circumstances based on appellee's remarriage, her new husband usurping his role as father of R.M., and the fact that R.M. was now twelve years old and wished to spend more time with his father, appellant requested that the circuit court modify visitation to allow overnight visits, as well as holiday and extended summer visitation. . . .

At the hearing held on October 9, 2012, appellant testified that he had been a pharmacist for twenty-three years and that he had had previous problems with a prescription-drug addiction in 1993, although he had completed treatment and remained sober until his recent relapse subsequent to his divorce. He testified that he gradually relapsed from 2004 until February 2010, when he was arrested for a DWI after being involved in a hit-and-run accident. Appellant completed several months of inpatient treatment and testified that he had completely abstained from alcohol and prescription drugs since February 2010. He further testified that he was now under a ten-year contract with the pharmacy board, pursuant to which he had been able to regain his pharmacist license, and that he has to call every morning to see if he must undergo a drug screen. So far, appellant stated that he had undergone fifty-nine random drug screens, all of which had been negative. He testified that he has also been regularly attending AA and NA meetings as required under the contract.

With regard to his relationship with his partner, Chad Cornelius, appellant testified that they had been in a committed, monogamous relationship for at least seven years and that they had applied for a marriage license in Iowa. Appellant stated that he had enjoyed overnight visitation with R.M. for five years before appellee forbade it and that even though Chad had been present, R.M. had never been exposed to any type of romantic behavior between them. Appellant testified that he and Chad had never slept in the same bed during any of R.M.'s previous visits and that if overnight visitation were again allowed, he would continue to abstain from bed sharing or other romantic behavior in the presence of his son. Appellant stated that Chad has a son from his previous marriage who often stays overnight at their home and that R.M. and Chad's son have a close relationship that would be greatly hindered if Chad were not allowed to be present during any overnight visits. According to appellant, he and Chad had not had any altercations since the one in 2005, which did not occur in the presence of R.M., and he stated that Chad is a positive role model for his son. . . .

Chad also testified and stated that he was a registered nurse at a hospital focusing on children and adolescents with behavioral-health issues. Chad testified that he has had to pass multiple state and federal background checks as a condition of his employment. He agreed that he and appellant had been in a committed relationship since 2005 and that they would like to get married. . . .

Chad's ex-wife, Robyn Cornelius, also testified on behalf of appellant and Chad. She stated that Chad is a loving and supportive father to their two children and that they share custody of their son, who is still a minor. Robyn testified that she had never witnessed Chad being verbally or physically abusive. . . . According to Robyn, after having seen R.M. around appellant and Chad, she believed it was in R.M.'s best interest to have overnight visitation and that he would be negatively affected if he were not allowed to spend more time with his father.

The final witness to testify was appellee. She testified that she had obtained the 2005 modification order after she became concerned about appellant's and Chad's relationship and how it would affect R.M. She stated that appellant's relationship was not the sole reason why she was contesting his attempt to increase visitation. According to appellee, appellant had complained to her about Chad acting in a threatening and controlling manner, and she indicated that their relationship was unstable and unhealthy. She also indicated that she had found needles and vials of steroids in a guest bedroom of appellant's home while cleaning it in 2009 and that appellant had told her that Chad had a past history of steroid use. . . . She admitted that R.M. had a loving relationship with his father and that it was important that they spend time together, but testified that it was not in R.M.'s best interest to have overnight or extended visitation at the present time due to his recent drug issues and his relationship with Chad.

In rebuttal testimony, appellant responded to appellee's allegation about finding needles and steroids in his home. He testified that he was not aware of these items, that he had never used intravenous drugs at any point, and that he was not aware that Chad had ever used them.

The circuit court entered an order on November 14, 2012, granting appellant's motion for modification of visitation. . . . However, the court found that it was required by the public policy of this state to impose a non-cohabitation restriction preventing Chad from being present during any overnight visits. The court noted that appellant and Chad were in a long-term committed relationship, that they had resided together since at least 2007, and that Chad posed "no threat to the

health, safety, or welfare" of R.M. Other than the prohibition on unmarried cohabitation with a romantic partner in the presence of a minor child, the circuit court
found no other factors present to militate against overnight visitation in this
case. . . .

With regard to visitation, the primary consideration is the best interest of the
child. Important factors for the court to consider in determining reasonable visitation are the wishes of the child, the capacity of the party desiring visitation to
supervise and care for the child, problems of transportation and prior conduct in
abusing visitation, the work schedule or stability of the parties, and relationship
with siblings and other relatives. We have held that fixing visitation rights is a
matter that lies within the sound discretion of the circuit court.

In his first two points on appeal, appellant argues that the non-cohabitation
agreement imposed by the circuit court violates his federal and state constitutional
rights to privacy and equal protection. However, because we find merit in appellant's final argument, there is no need to address these constitutional
arguments. . . .

In his third and final point on appeal, appellant argues that, contrary to the
circuit court's belief, our prior cases do not require the imposition of non-
cohabitation provisions in the absence of any finding of evidence of harm to the
minor child. . . .

As the circuit court in this case recognized, under the long-standing public
policy of the courts in this state, a parent's extramarital cohabitation with a
romantic partner in the presence of children, or a parent's promiscuous conduct
or lifestyle, has never been condoned. In Campbell v. Campbell, 336 Ark. 379, 985
S.W.2d 724 (1999), this court made it clear that the purpose of non-cohabitation
provisions are to promote a stable environment for the children and not merely to
monitor a parent's sexual conduct.

We have also repeatedly held, however, that the primary consideration in
domestic relations cases is the welfare and best interest of the children and that all
other considerations are secondary. Therefore, we have emphasized in more recent
cases that the policy against romantic cohabitation in the presence of children must
be considered under the circumstances of each particular case and in light of the
best interest of the children. For example, in Taylor [v. Taylor, 353 Ark. 69, 80, 110
S.W.3d 731, 737 (2003)], we reversed the trial court's modification of custody
where the finding of a material change in circumstances was based on the trial
court's concern about protecting the children from future harm based on public
misperception. In that case, the evidence showed that the custodial parent resided
with a lesbian woman and that the two sometimes shared a bed, although they
denied a romantic or sexual relationship. We cited cases from other states in
support of the proposition that there must be concrete proof of likely harm to
the children from the parent's living arrangement before a change in custody can
be made. We held that "evidence-based factors must govern," rather than stereotypical presumptions of future harm.

We further discussed the issue of non-cohabitation agreements in Arkansas
Department of Human Services v. Cole, 2011 Ark. 145, 380 S.W.3d 429. In Cole,
we held that the Arkansas Adoption and Foster Care Act of 2008 (Act 1), which
prohibited an individual from adopting or serving as a foster parent if that

individual was cohabiting with a sexual partner outside of marriage, was unconstitutional because it violated the fundamental right to privacy implicit in the
Arkansas Constitution. In response to the appellants' argument in that case that
our holding would render non-cohabitation agreements in custody or
dependency-neglect cases unenforceable, we stated the following:

> We strongly disagree with the State and FCAC's conclusion that if this court finds
> that the categorical ban on adoption and fostering for sexual cohabitors put in
> place by Act 1 violates an individual's fundamental right to sexual privacy in one's
> home, state courts and DHS will be prohibited henceforth from considering and
> enforcing non-cohabitation agreements and orders in deciding child-custody and
> visitation cases as well as dependency-neglect cases. That simply is not the case.
> The overriding concern in all of these situations is the best interest of the child.
> To arrive at what is in the child's best interest, the circuit courts and state agencies
> look at all the factors, including a non-cohabitation order if one exists, and make
> the best-interest determination on a case-by-case basis. Act 1's blanket ban pro-
> vides for no such individualized consideration or case-by-case analysis in adoption
> or foster-care cases and makes the bald assumption that in all cases where adoption
> or foster care is the issue it is always against the best interest of the child to be
> placed in a home where an individual is cohabiting with a sexual partner outside of
> marriage.

But in addition to case-by-case analysis, there is another difference between
cohabitation in the child-custody or dependency-neglect context and cohabiting
sexual partners who wish to adopt or become foster parents. Third-party strangers
who cohabit with a divorced parent are unknown in many cases to the circuit court
and have not undergone the rigorous screening associated with foster care or
adoption. By everyone's account, applicants for foster care must comply with a
raft of DHS regulations that include criminal background checks, home studies,
family histories, support systems, and the like. Adoption, under the auspices of the
trial court, requires similar screening. Unsuitable and undesirable adoptive and
foster parents are thereby weeded out in the screening process. The same does not
pertain to a third-party stranger who cohabits with a divorced or single parent.

Thus, we agree with appellant that the public policy against romantic cohabitation is not a "blanket ban," as it may not override the primary consideration for
the circuit court in such cases, which is determining what is in the best interest of
the children involved.

In the present case, the circuit court found from the evidence presented that
appellant and his partner are in a long-term, committed romantic relationship and
that "Mr. Cornelius poses no threat to the health, safety, or welfare of the minor
child." The court further found that, "[o]ther than the prohibition of unmarried
cohabitation with a romantic partner in the presence of the minor child, there are
no other factors that would militate against overnight visitation." However,
because the circuit court also stated that the mandatory application of our public
policy against unmarried cohabitation required it to include a non-cohabitation
provision, it made no finding on whether such a provision was in the best interest of
R.M. Therefore, we reverse and remand for the circuit court to make this
determination. . . .

KAREN R. BAKER, Justice, dissenting.

Because I believe that the majority errs in its disposition of this case, I must dissent. . . .

Courts impose a more stringent standard for modifications in visitation. The reasons for requiring these more stringent standards are to promote stability and continuity in the life of the child, and to discourage the repeated litigation of the same issue. Based on these more stringent standards, none of the changes alleged by John or upon which the circuit court based its ruling constitute a material change in circumstances.

The circuit court focused on the fact that Libby had stopped allowing John overnight visitation. However, I do not agree that this constituted a material change in circumstances. Libby had the authority to deny John overnight visitation with R.M. from the time the agreed order was entered in 2005. The fact that she began to exercise that authority is not a material change in circumstances. Further, Libby should not be punished now for allowing John more visitation than was provided for in the agreed order. . . .

For these reasons, the circuit court clearly erred in finding that there had been a material change in circumstances. Normally, this would be grounds for reversal, however, that is not the relief that Libby seeks. Libby does not ask us to modify the circuit court's visitation order. Instead, it is John who asks us to modify the order and strike the noncohabitation provision, by arguing that there was no finding of harm to the child or analysis of the child's best interest. However, the best-interest analysis is not reached when there has been no material change in circumstances. As there has been no material change in circumstances, we should not reach John's arguments. Therefore, I would affirm the circuit court's order. . . .

COURTNEY HUDSON GOODSON, Justice, dissenting.

The majority in this case finds error in the circuit court's conclusion that the restriction on overnight visitation was in the best interest of the child. I must dissent.

Arkansas's appellate courts have steadfastly upheld chancery court orders that prohibit parents from allowing romantic partners to stay or reside in the home when the children are present. This court has gone so far as to say that "a parent's unmarried cohabitation with a romantic partner, or a parent's promiscuous conduct or lifestyle, *in the presence of a child* cannot be abided." Taylor v. Taylor, 353 Ark. 69, 80, 110 S.W.3d 731, 737 (2003) (emphasis supplied). This rule has been applied regardless of whether the parent is heterosexual or homosexual. . . .

In our 2001 decision in *Taylor*, this court affirmed the circuit court's requirement that the mother's female sexual companion move out of the home as a condition of retaining custody of her children. There was no showing of harm occasioned by the companion's presence, as the circuit court expressed the willingness to allow the companion to babysit when the mother was at work. Nonetheless, we held that the circuit court acted within its authority and was not clearly erroneous in determining that it was not in the children's best interests for the mother to continue cohabitating with another adult with whom she was romantically involved. This court said,

As emphasized by our court's earlier decisions, the trial court's use of the non-cohabitation restriction is a material factor to consider when determining custody issues. Such a restriction or prohibition aids in structuring the home place so as to reduce the possibilities (or opportunities) where children may be present and subjected to a single parent's sexual encounters, whether they be heterosexual or homosexual.

Taylor, 345 Ark. at 304-305, 47 S.W.3d at 225.

... The primary consideration regarding visitation is the best interest of the child. In its oral ruling from the bench, the circuit court recognized this guiding principle. The court also recognized the settled law permitting the imposition of a restriction on overnight visitation in the presence of sexual partners. Contrary to the majority's assertion, the circuit court did not neglect to make a determination that the restriction was in the best interest of the child. The court quite plainly stated that "the best interest dictates that that be the continued policy of the Court" to not permit overnight visitation in the presence of the child. I would affirm the circuit court's decision in keeping with our time-tested law. The court acted well within in its authority to conclude that the restriction promoted the best interest of this child.

NOTES AND QUESTIONS

1. Given the emphasis in most states on the continued involvement of both parents in the child's life, most custody orders provide for time with both parents. As a practical matter, therefore, one parent can seek to limit the involvement of the other parent only upon a showing of misconduct or circumstances that are harmful to the child. Upon what factors does the mother, Libby Moix, rely in claiming the child should not be allowed more extended contact with his father? How do the trial and appellate opinions treat these allegations?

2. In 1980 custody law did not vary widely across the United States in its attitude toward nonmarital cohabitation. Indeed, that year a Utah court cited a New York case in holding that overnight visitation should be conditioned on a prohibition on nonmarital cohabitation in the presence of the child. *See* Kallas v. Kallas, 614 P.2d 641, 645 (Utah 1980). Today, courts in some parts of the country reject requests for non-cohabitation orders out of hand (*see* Logan v. Logan, 763 A.2d 587, 589 (R.I. 2000), dismissing request for non-cohabitation order as frivolous), while courts in other parts of the country still grant them. Until the *Moix* decision, Arkansas would have been in the latter category, although the Arkansas courts had been moving away from a categorical prohibition on the presence of nonmarital cohabitants to more individualized case-by-case determinations. What kind of showing does the *Moix* court anticipate will be necessary to justify such orders in the future?

In 2005 the Arkansas Supreme Court upheld a trial court decision changing custody from the mother to the father at least in part because of the mother's nonmarital cohabitation, even though the mother married her boyfriend before the trial court decision and the father had also remarried after cohabiting with a new partner. The court in Alphin v. Alphin, 219 S.W.3d 160 (Ark. 2005), observed that while the trial court emphasized the mother's nonmarital relationship, it could have also based the change of custody on the mother's lack of stability and multiple nonmarital partners. The dissent, however, attacked the court's double standard, because the father had married his current wife only when she was three months pregnant and his lack of support had left the mother dependent on her new partners. *See also* Roberts v. Roberts, 402 S.W.3d 833 (Tex.-App.-San Antonio 2003) (rejecting father's equal protection challenge to a non-cohabitation clause that was not also imposed on the mother); McGriff v. McGriff, 99 P.3d 111 (Idaho 2004); Moses v. King, 637 S.E.2d 97 (Ga. App. 2006), *cert. denied*, King v. Moses, 2007 Ga. LEXIS 84 (Ga. Jan. 8, 2007); June Carbone & Naomi Cahn, Judging Families, 77 UMKC L. Rev. 267 (2008). Would a showing that the father had lived with multiple cohabitants have changed the outcome in *Moix*?

3. The *Moix* opinion refers to the Arkansas Supreme Court's decision in Arkansas Department of Human Services v. Cole, 380 S.W.3d 429 (Ark. 2011). Arkansas voters had passed a proposition, targeting gay and lesbian adoptive couples, that prohibited an individual living with an unmarried cohabitant from adopting or serving as a foster parent, and the *Cole* court had declared the act unconstitutional. Responding to concerns that had been raised in *Cole*, the *Moix* court agreed that unmarried cohabitants in custody cases pose different risks from unmarried cohabitants in adoption and foster care cases because adoptive and foster parents undergo background checks while other cohabitants do not. Consider how the testimony in *Moix* was orchestrated to address this issue, particularly in light of the allegations of domestic violence and drug use in the case.

Robin Wilson has argued that the presence of unrelated males in a household as a general matter increases the risk of child abuse and is a factor counseling hesitation in the extension of parental rights. Robin Fretwell Wilson, Limiting the Prerogatives of Legal Parents: Judicial Skepticism of the American Law Institute's Treatment of De Facto Parents, 25 J. Am. Acad. Matrimonial L. 477 (2013). What is the best way to address such concerns?

4. One of the effects of cohabitation orders is to change the issue from the trial court's assessment of the effect of cohabitation on the child's interests to the parent's defiance of the court. While *Moix* addressed the issue in terms of a motion to modify, in other cases the issue arises when the other parent brings a contempt action. In a contempt action, the ability of the cohabiting parent to contest the validity of the order may be more limited. For an example of how an existing non-cohabitation order can change the dynamic of custody modifications, *see* Holmes v. Holmes, 2007 Ark. App. LEXIS 251 (Apr. 11, 2007). While such orders apply to both heterosexual and homosexual cohabitation, they may disproportionately affect gay and lesbian cohabitants who cannot marry. For criticism of judicial orders conditioning parental contact on the absence of same-sex partners, *see* Nancy G. Maxwell & Richard Donner, The Psychological Consequences of Judicially Imposed Closets in Child Custody and Visitation Disputes Involving Gay or Lesbian Parents, 13 Wm. & Mary J. Women & L. 305 (2006).

5. *Moix* involved the father's motion to modify an existing custody order. The majority and minority opinions agreed that the appellate courts review the evidence in such determinations de novo. The majority nonetheless emphasized that it would not

reverse the circuit court's findings unless they are clearly erroneous. We also give special deference to the circuit court's superior position in evaluating the witnesses, their testimony, and the child's best interest. Because a circuit court maintains continuing jurisdiction over visitation, it may modify or vacate a prior visitation order when it becomes aware of a material change in circumstances since the previous order. The party seeking modification has the burden of demonstrating such a material change in circumstances.

In contrast, Justice Baker's dissent observed that the court could "review the record and the evidence presented to determine whether a material change in circumstances has occurred." How did the majority and dissent differ in the way that they framed the standard for modification and the standard for review on appeal? Do you believe that the difference in framing the standards affected their resolution of the case?

6. Apart from cohabitation, the majority of courts consider a parent's sexual orientation only in accordance with a nexus test that requires evidence of harm to the child. *See* Kim H. Pearson, Sexuality in Child Custody Decisions, 50 Fam. Ct. Rev. 280 (2012); Maxwell v. Maxwell, 382 S.W.3d 892 (Ky. App. 2012) (court cannot simply assume that mother's same-sex relationship is not in the child's interest). The impact of sexual orientation on parenting has nonetheless been the subject of numerous studies and much debate. For a summary of the social science literature concluding that "the empirical evidence showing the lack of an association between parental sexual orientation and the psychological and social functioning of children is so conclusive and uniform that there is no conceivable factual basis for suggesting otherwise," *see* Carlos A. Ball, Social Science Studies and the Children of Lesbians and Gay Men: The Rational Basis Perspective, 21 Wm. & Mary Bill Rts. J. 691 (2013). For a critique of these studies' methodological limitations, *see* Loren Marks, Same-Sex Parenting and Children's Outcomes: A Closer Examination of the American Psychological Association's Brief on Lesbian and Gay Parenting, 41 Soc. Sci. Res. 735 (2012). Most studies of gay and lesbian parenting examine children raised by same-sex couples from birth or after adoption. Yet, the majority of children with gay and lesbian parents were born into heterosexual relationships like that in *Moix*. For a study of children whose parents ever engaged in same-sex relationships, *see* Mark Regnerus, How Different Are the Adult Children of Parents Who Have Same-Sex Relationships? Findings from the New Family Structures Study, 41 Soc. Sci. Res. 752 (2012). The Regnerus study, which found more negative outcomes associated with adult children raised by gay and lesbian parents than the earlier studies, selected its sample by including any adult who indicated that a parent had engaged in a same-sex relationship during his or her childhood and comparing these adults to adults who reported that they have been raised by exclusively heterosexual parents. The study has been criticized for using an overly broad definition of gay and lesbian parents that included parents who may have engaged in a single same-sex encounter over the 18 years of the adult child's minority and noncustodial parents who spent little or no time with the child during the period in which they were engaged in same-sex relationships. For critiques of the Regnerus study, *see* Paul R. Amato, The Well-Being of Children with Gay and Lesbian Parents, 41 Soc. Sci. Res. 771, 773 (2012), and Gary J. Gates et al., Letter to the Editors and

Advisory Editors of Social Science Research, 41 Soc. Sci. Res. 1350, 1351 (2012) (the Regnerus study "fails to distinguish, for children whose parents ever had a same-sex relationship experience, the associations due to family structure from the associations due to family stability. However, [Regnerus] does attempt to distinguish family structure from family instability for the children of different-sex parents by identifying children who lived in an intact biological family.").

b. Race

PALMORE V. SIDOTI

466 U.S. 429 (1984)

BURGER, C.J. We granted certiorari to review a judgment of a state court divesting a natural mother of the custody of her infant child because of her remarriage to a person of a different race.

When petitioner Linda Sidoti Palmore and respondent Anthony J. Sidoti, both Caucasians, were divorced in May 1980 in Florida, the mother was awarded custody of their 3-year-old daughter.

In September 1981 the father sought custody of the child by filing a petition to modify the prior judgment because of changed conditions. The change was that the child's mother was then cohabiting with a Negro, Clarence Palmore, Jr., whom she married two months later.

After hearing testimony from both parties and considering a court counselor's investigative report, the court noted that the father had made allegations about the child's care, but the court made no findings with respect to these allegations. On the contrary, the court made a finding that "there is no issue as to either party's devotion to the child, adequacy of housing facilities, or respectability of the new spouse of either parent."

The court then addressed the recommendations of the court counselor, who had made an earlier report "in [another] case coming out of this circuit also involving the social consequences of an interracial marriage. Niles v. Niles, 299 So. 2d 162." From this vague reference to that earlier case, the court turned to the present case and noted the counselor's recommendation for a change in custody because "[t]he wife [petitioner] has chosen for herself and for her child, a lifestyle unacceptable to the father and to society. . . . The child . . . is, or at school age will be, subject to environmental pressures not of choice."

The court then concluded that the best interests of the child would be served by awarding custody to the father. The court's rationale is contained in the following: "The father's evident resentment of the mother's choice of a black partner is not sufficient to wrest custody from the mother. It is of some significance, however, that the mother did see fit to bring a man into her home and carry on a sexual relationship with him without being married to him. Such action tended to place gratification of her own desires ahead of her concern for the child's future welfare. This Court feels that despite the strides that have been made in bettering relations between the races in this country, it is inevitable that Melanie will, if allowed to remain in her present situation and attains school age and thus becomes more vulnerable to peer pressures, suffer from the social stigmatization that is sure to come."

The judgment of a state court determining or reviewing a child custody decision is not ordinarily a likely candidate for review by this Court. However, the court's opinion, after stating that the "father's evident resentment of the mother's choice of a black partner is not sufficient" to deprive her of custody, then turns to what it regarded as the damaging impact on the child from remaining in a racially mixed household. This raises important federal concerns arising from the Constitution's commitment to eradicating discrimination based on race. . . .

The court correctly stated that the child's welfare was the controlling factor. But that court was entirely candid and made no effort to place its holding on any ground other than race. Taking the court's findings and rationale at face value, it is clear that the outcome would have been different had petitioner married a Caucasian male of similar respectability.

A core purpose of the Fourteenth Amendment was to do away with all governmentally imposed discrimination based on race. Classifying persons according to their race is more likely to reflect racial prejudice than legitimate public concerns; the race, not the person, dictates the category. Such classifications are subject to the most exacting scrutiny; to pass constitutional muster, they must be justified by a compelling governmental interest and must be "necessary . . . to the accomplishment" of their legitimate purpose, McLaughlin v. Florida, 379 U.S. 184, 196 (1964). *See* Loving v. Virginia, 388 U.S. 1, 11 (1967).

The State, of course, has a duty of the highest order to protect the interests of minor children, particularly those of tender years. In common with most states, Florida law mandates that custody determinations be made in the best interests of the children involved. The goal of granting custody based on the best interests of the child is indisputably a substantial governmental interest for purposes of the Equal Protection Clause.

It would ignore reality to suggest that racial and ethnic prejudices do not exist or that all manifestations of those prejudices have been eliminated. There is a risk that a child living with a stepparent of a different race may be subject to a variety of pressures and stresses not present if the child were living with parents of the same racial or ethnic origin.

The question, however, is whether the reality of private biases and the possible injury they might inflict are permissible considerations for removal of an infant child from the custody of its natural mother. We have little difficulty concluding that they are not. The Constitution cannot control such prejudices but neither can it tolerate them. Private biases may be outside the reach of the law, but the law cannot, directly or indirectly, give them effect. . . .

Whatever problems racially mixed households may pose for children in 1984 can no more support a denial of constitutional rights than could the stresses that residential integration was thought to entail in 1917. The effects of racial prejudice, however real, cannot justify a racial classification removing an infant child from the custody of its natural mother found to be an appropriate person to have such custody.

The judgment of the District Court of Appeal is reversed.

NOTES AND QUESTIONS

1. What interests are at stake in this case? Do the child's interests include identification with a racial group?

2. *Palmore* discusses the potential impact of peer and community reaction on children. The same might be said of the child in *Moix*. Indeed, in an earlier case, an Arkansas trial court observed:

> It would seem likely that if it is generally known by friends and acquaintances that defendant resides with and also sleeps with an admitted lesbian that most will conclude sex is involved. This assumption on the part of the public would subject the children to ridicule and embarrassment and could very well be harmful to them. Therefore, it is the conclusion of this Court that residence of Kelli Tabora [the "admitted lesbian"] with defendant and the children even without sex is inappropriate behavior and is a circumstance that justifies changing of custody from defendant to plaintiff. It is at least poor parental judgment on the part of defendant to allow a well known lesbian to both reside with defendant and the children and sleep in the same bed with defendant.

The Supreme Court of Arkansas reversed, finding that a change of custody could not be based on "perceptions and appearances rather than concrete proof of likely harm." Taylor v. Taylor, 110 S.W.3d 731 (Ark. 2003). But what if there had been evidence that the children were being teased and they were distressed by the reaction of peers and community? Would *Palmore* be relevant to cases about sexual orientation? How might it be distinguished?

3. Palmore v. Sidoti has been distinguished in a number of cases. In Jones v. Jones, 542 N.W.2d 119 (S.D. 1996), the father was an enrolled member of the Sisseton-Wahpeton Dakota Nation who was adopted at age 7; the mother was a Caucasian. The father was employed on a family farm and earned about $22,000 per year, and the mother was a homemaker and nursing student. The father was a recovering alcoholic, and the mother suffered from depression and low self-esteem. They had three children, all of whom have Native American features. In its findings, the trial court noted the father's arguments that the children would be discriminated against if they moved from their home and the family farm and that he wished to continue to make the children aware of their culture and heritage. The trial court indicated that this was an example of the father's concern for "the totality of the upbringing of his children," but also stated that its decision had to be "made on a racially neutral basis." On appeal, this decision was affirmed against the mother's claim that race was impermissibly taken into account:

> While the trial court was not blind to the racial backgrounds of the children, we are satisfied that it did not impermissibly award custody on the basis of race. As noted, [the father] showed a sensitivity to the need for his children to be exposed to their ethnic heritage. All of us form our own personal identities, based in part, on our religious, racial and cultural backgrounds. To say, as [the mother] argues, that a court should never consider whether a parent is willing and able to expose to and educate children on their heritage, is to say that society is not interested in whether children ever learn who they are. *Palmore* does not require this. . . .

See also Davis v. Davis, 658 N.Y.S.2d 548 (App. Div. 1997); In re Marriage of Gambla, 853 N.E.2d 847 (Ill. App. Ct. 2006); David D. Meyer, *Palmore* Comes of Age: The Place of Race in the Placement of Children, 18 U. Fla. J.L. & Pub. Pol'y 183 (2007).

4. A case in 2004 raised the issue of whether it is appropriate to allow testimony about racial attitudes. In that case, the mother had married a man described as "biracial" and the trial court had allowed extensive testimony about the father's and other witnesses' "reservations [about] raising a non-interracial child in an inter-racial marriage." The mother's attorney had not objected to the testimony. The state supreme court held that the issue had not been preserved for appeal, but it reversed the award of custody to the father on the ground that it went against the weight of the evidence. The concurrence, however, raised the question whether, given the holding, the trial court should have cut off the testimony about the witnesses' reactions (and objections) to interracial marriage *sua sponte*. Tipton v. Aaron, 87 Ark. App. 1 (2004).

In In re Marriage of Olson, 194 P.3d 619 (Mont. 2008), the mother objected to consideration of the guardian ad litem's observation that the father "should serve as the primary parent because he is American and could integrate [the child] into the community better than [the mother], who is Mexican." Is this statement similarly objectionable and should it not be allowed into testimony?

PROBLEMS

1. Isabel and Ian Wright are divorcing and disagree about the proper custodian for their two children, a boy age 4 and a girl age 7. The couple have long disagreed about many issues, including those related to racial matters. Ian Wright has made disparaging remarks about minorities generally, and African Americans particularly, that offend Isabel. To make matters more acute, Isabel has admitted that she has fallen in love with Richard Addison, who is African American, and intends to divorce her husband in order to marry Richard. Ian offers the testimony of a qualified psychologist that their children have adopted their father's view of African Americans and would hate living with their mother and her new husband. What weight, if any, should the trial court place on this evidence?

2. Judith Fox received custody of her son, Reynard, age 7, after a bitterly contested divorce. She has married a Mexican American, and they are the only ethnically mixed couple in the neighborhood in which they reside. Allen Fox has sought custody and has offered the evidence of school teachers and school children that Reynard has been teased unmercifully by the Anglo children in the school and that he is not invited to birthday parties by their parents. Is this evidence relevant to the assignment of custody? Would the testimony of a psychologist that the child faces a significant risk of emotional distress as a result of the behavior of other children and parents in the community be relevant? Is it in a child's best interest to grow up without conflict or unusual discomfort?

c. Religion

The meanings of terms such as *fitness* or *best interests* change with time and place. At one time the parents' religion may be a central concern. At other times the emphasis may be on sexual behavior, physical characteristics and qualifications, or general commitments to mainstream values. Challenges to the center may come from the social and political left or right. In some cases, religious beliefs are founded on, or at least are related to, beliefs about sexual behavior, race, and the like, or religious beliefs themselves may be expressly at issue.

IN RE MARRIAGE OF HADEEN

619 P.2d 374 (Wash. App. 1980)

CALLOW, C.J. Judith N. Hadeen, petitioner below . . . appeals from the trial court's award of custody of four of the Hadeens' five daughters to Mr. Hadeen. The trial court awarded Mr. Hadeen custody of Lisa, age 15, Lynn, age 13, Lila, age 11, and LaVon, age 8. Mrs. Hadeen was awarded custody of the Hadeens' oldest daughter, Lori, age 17. . . .

In the fall of 1977, a person who had previously been the Hadeens' minister returned from Canada and activated a Bellingham branch of the First Community Churches of America. The First Community Church is a fundamentalist Christian sect which demands much of its members' time, their total loyalty, and a subservience to the teachings of the church. The church teaches a strict code of discipline as a means of gaining parental control of children. Mrs. Hadeen admitted that on one occasion she had her other children hold her daughter Lisa while she spanked her with a Ping-Pong paddle for 2 hours. Mrs. Hadeen testified that usually only a few spankings were necessary. It is unclear whether Mr. Hadeen sanctioned Mrs. Hadeen's disciplinary practices. Witnesses testified that the church teaches enforced isolation and fasting as another means of discipline. The church also teaches that there are essentially two classes of people: "natural people" and "spirit filled people" who have repented, been baptized and received the Holy Spirit. There was testimony that children were taught to use foul language when speaking to other children who were "natural people," and that there was nothing wrong with lying to "natural people." Mrs. Hadeen denied that church members were taught not to associate with "natural" people. . . .

Mr. Hadeen testified that the church exercised control over its members to whatever extent possible. He said that he never treated his children violently, but had slapped and kicked Mrs. Hadeen in the children's presence following their separation. He did so, he testified, because on one occasion she would not talk to him and on another she cursed him and began "speaking in tongues."

Mrs. Hadeen's sister-in-law testified that the parties' religion had not had bad effects on the children and that their conduct was exemplary. Others testified similarly. Mr. Hadeen's sister-in-law testified that the church taught parents to spank their children until they stopped screaming. She further testified that ex-members were shunned. Another church member testified that ex-members were ostracized, and that some parents beat their children while others did not. According to this witness, the church came before family for Mrs. Hadeen.

The trial court interviewed three of the Hadeens' daughters in chambers. Lori testified that her grades are excellent and that she is active in basketball. She testified that the church did not force her or others to do anything. She said she did not visit her father because of the way he had treated her mother and tried to buy the children's affection. Lisa testified that her mother would not talk to her because she would not go to church. She left her mother because she beat her to force her to go to church. Lynn testified that she was in the seventh grade, played sports, had high grades, and did not like her father because he tried to bribe her. . . .

When the taking of testimony was complete, the trial court appointed a psychiatrist as an independent expert to evaluate (a) the children's interrelationship; (b) the parents' and children's interrelationship; (c) whether the children had personality problems; and (d) the problems, effects and desirability of split custody. . . .

Based on the records before it, the trial court entered the following findings of fact respecting custody:

a) That the four youngest children of the parties maintain strong emotional bonds with both parents.

b) That the Petitioner provides proper physical care for the children.

c) That the children are reasonably well adjusted with the exception of Lisa, who is having difficulties adjusting to the dissolution.

d) That both of the parties were members at one time in the First Community Churchs [sic] of America. The Respondent has subsequently removed himself from the church.

e) That the Petitioner, Judith Hadeen, is in complete submission to the First Community Church of America, to the exclusion of other reasonable relationships.

f) That the Petitioner's first fidelity is to the church, as is evidences [sic] by the Petitioner's rejection of the parties' minor child Lisa, and as evidenced by the Petitioner's move to Seattle with only a short time remaining in school and the subsequent move made in Seattle, all of which are not in the best interest of the parties' minor children.

g) That [the psychiatrist] recommends the children's custody be with the Petitioner, provided the problems caused by the Petitioner's religious involvement with the First Community Churches of America are satisfactorily resolved.

h) To award custody to the Petitioner, Judith Hadeen, would effectively cut Glen Hadeen off from his involvement with the children, and that the children need to have continued contact with both parents. That Lori Hadeen, the oldest of the parties' minor children, is deeply involved with the First Community Church of America, and she had close associations with her mother and the church. Because of her age Lori should be placed in the custody of her mother.

i) The best interest of the parties' other minor children is served by placing those children in the custody of the Respondent, Glen Hadeen, subject to reasonable rights of visitation for the Petitioner. Mrs. Hadeen assigns error to the last five of the findings. . . .

The best interests and welfare of the children are paramount in custody matters. The trial court must consider all relevant factors, including the parents' and children's wishes; the interrelationship of the children with their parents and others who may affect their best interests; the child's adjustment to his or her home, school, and community; and the mental and physical health of all concerned. . . . Whether the trial court considered and premised its decision upon considerations violative of the First Amendment's provision respecting religion requires our consideration of the principles used in determining the scope and application of the First Amendment's provision respecting religion.

The First Amendment provides in pertinent part, "Congress shall make no law respecting an establishment of religion, or prohibiting the free exercise thereof. . . ." This clause applies through the Fourteenth Amendment to the states, including the states' judiciary. The dual nature of the First Amendment's provision respecting religion encompasses the establishment clause, which guarantees government neutrality in matters touching upon religion, and the free exercise clause, which recognizes the individual's liberty in religious matters. The overall purpose respecting freedom of religion is to insure that no religion is advanced or favored, commanded or inhibited. . . .

Wisconsin v. Yoder considered whether compulsory school attendance laws past the eighth grade violated the right of Amish parents to exercise their religious beliefs. Noting that parents have the right to direct the religious upbringing of their children, Wisconsin v. Yoder, supra at 233-34, added: To be sure, the power of the parent, even when linked to a free exercise claim, may be subject to limitation . . . if it appears that parental decisions will jeopardize the health or safety of the child, or have a potential for significant social burdens. . . . The Court held that Amish parents could not be penalized for a violation of the compulsory attendance laws, but noted that the case before it was not a case in which "any harm to the physical or mental health of the child . . . has been demonstrated or may be properly inferred." Cases involving religion as an aspect of a custody dispute generally comport with the language of Wisconsin v. Yoder, regarding a showing that the parental decisions will jeopardize the child's health or safety. The showing that must be made and the test involved in the determination of when the jeopardy must arise are, however, subject to significant dispute.

We glean from . . . [prior] cases that religious decisions and acts may be considered in a custody decision only to the extent that those decisions or acts will jeopardize the temporal mental health or physical safety of the child. The question remains whether jeopardy to a child must be one of actual present impairment of the child's physical and/or mental well-being or a reasonable and substantial likelihood of impairment. We conclude that the . . . requirement of actual impairment is improvident and could lead a trial court to ignore a child's present welfare. We hold that the requirement of a reasonable and substantial likelihood of immediate or future impairment best accommodates the general welfare of the child and the free exercise of religion by the parents.

The trial court's finding that Mrs. Hadeen is in complete submission to the church to the exclusion of other "reasonable" relationships is a subjective conclusion which should have played no part in the trial court's decision unless Mrs. Hadeen's submission posed a substantial threat of endangering the children's mental or physical welfare. There was no evidence that Mrs. Hadeen neglected her children or did not provide them with her companionship because of her membership in the church. In fact, the trial court expressly found that the children were adjusted reasonably well.

Also unsupported by substantial evidence is the finding that the psychiatrist's recommendation of custody being with the mother was conditioned upon the mother's resolution of her involvement with the church. The psychiatrist stated that it was in the children's best interests to maintain contact with the father if that could be done without having the mother and father fight. He recommended that if the children were uncomfortable with visitation, then it would be in their best interests not to be forced to visit either parent. . . .

Reversed and remanded.

NOTES AND QUESTIONS

1. The "rejection" discussed by the *Hadeen* court is related to shunning or excommunication. More generally, it is an instance of the practice of exclusion, which is a conventional sanction used by religious and social groups. How should this exclusion be dealt with in the custody context? Will entrance of a court decree ordering visitation with the parent to be shunned avoid the effects of rejection? What if the custodial parent takes the child to a church that teaches that non-believers cannot be saved, will roast in hell, or are in some way "unclean"?

2. In Kendall v. Kendall, 687 N.E.2d 1228 (Mass. 1997), *cert. denied*, 524 U.S. 953 (1998), the Massachusetts Supreme Judicial Court considered a case in which a trial court restricted a father, who had joint legal custody, from exposing his children to fundamentalist Christian doctrine. At the time of their marriage, the mother was Jewish and the father Catholic. Before marriage, the parties agreed that any children (they ultimately had three) would be raised in the Jewish faith. Several years after their marriage, the husband joined the Boston Church of Christ, a fundamentalist Christian church, and shares his church's belief that those of other faiths are "damned to go to hell." He has stated that he would like his children to accept Jesus Christ as their savior and that he would "never stop trying to save his children." The mother adopted Orthodox Judaism subsequently, and the oldest child began studying and adhering to Orthodox principles.

The trial court awarded the parents joint legal custody, with the mother having sole physical custody. The court also found it substantially damaging to the children to leave each parent free to expose the children without limitation to his or her religion and ordered both parents not to indoctrinate the children in a way that alienated them from the other parent. The father was further ordered not to take the children to his church or Sunday school or engage the children in prayer or Bible study that would promote rejection of their mother or their own Jewish self-identity. The order allowed, for example, the father to have pictures of Jesus Christ on the wall but did not allow taking the children to religious services where they would receive the message that those who do not accept Jesus Christ as their savior would burn in hell.

The court analyzed the issue as follows:

"[P]arents together have freedom of religious expression and practice which enters into their liberty to manage their familial relationships." Those individual liberties may be restricted where there is compelling interest. A parent's right to practice religion may be restricted only where limited exposure to that parent's beliefs is necessary to further the child's best interests. To do so, there must be an affirmative showing of harm caused by exposure to the conflicting religious teachings.

The determinative issue is whether the harm found to exist in this case to be so substantial so as to warrant a limitation on the defendant's religious freedom. . . .

[P]roof of substantial harm "by implication" could be derived from testimony as to the child's general demeanor, attitude, school work, appetite, health or outlook. [This] court also opined that the "wholly uncorroborated testimony" of a parent was insufficient to demonstrate harm. By implication, the court suggested that a plaintiff should consult "church, school, medical or psychiatric authorities" to support a charge that a child has been harmed by exposure to the parent's religious beliefs. Moreover, the court specifically recommended the appointment of [a guardian ad litem]. . . .

Other states [addressing these issues] have struggled to define what constitutes substantial harm. Very few have actually ruled that substantial harm had been demonstrated.

We adhere to the line of cases requiring clear evidence of substantial harm. Application of the strict requirements in those cases comports with the protections of religious freedoms historically preserved under the Massachusetts Constitution.

The harm found to exist in this case presents more than . . . generalized fears. . . . Among the factors the judge cited to support her conclusion that substantial harm to the children had been demonstrated are the following findings: [that Jeffrey threatened to cut off the fringe of his son's religious clothing; that church services to which the children were taken included teaching that non-members would be damned to hell; that the oldest son may experience choosing a religion as choosing between his parents, which would likely cause him significant emotional distress; and that all three children are now emotionally distressed].

Whether the harm found to exist amounts to the "substantial harm" required to justify interference with the defendant's liberty interest is a close question, especially because there is considerable value in "frequent and continuing contact" between the child and both parents, and "contact with the parents' separate religious preferences." . . .

. . . [W]e conclude that the judge's findings support her order. . . .

Where, as here, the judge has found demonstrable evidence of substantial harm to the children, we reject the defendant's argument that the divorce judgment burdens his right to practice religion under the free exercise clauses of the Massachusetts and United States Constitution. Both . . . permit limitations on individual liberties where there exists a compelling interest. Promoting the best interests of the children is an interest sufficiently compelling to impose a burden on the defendant's right to practice religion and his parental right to determine the religious upbringing of his children. . . .

See also Johns v. Johns 918 S.W.2d 728 (Ark. App. 1996) (upholding trial court order to noncustodial parent requiring him to ensure church attendance over his free exercise objection); Shepp v. Shepp, 906 A.2d 1165, 1166-1168 (Pa. 2006) (reversing trial court order prohibiting the husband from teaching his daughter about polygamy, plural marriage, or multiple wives because even though polygamy is illegal, there was no evidence of that advocating the prohibited conduct would jeopardize the physical or mental health of the child). Professor Jeffrey Shulman objects that the harm requirement subverts the best interest standard and subjects children to behavior that would not be tolerated in other contexts. What *Yoder* Wrought: Religious Disparagement, Parental Alienation and the Best Interests of the Child, 53 Vill. L. Rev. 173 (2008).

3. A much discussed and sometimes litigated aspect of the relationship of religious belief to custody is presented in Osier v. Osier, 410 A.2d 1027 (Me. 1980).

The trial court had granted custody to the father, largely on the basis of the mother's testimony that she would withhold her consent to a blood transfusion for her son even if it became medically necessary to safeguard the child's health. The court concluded "that the [mother's] religious beliefs are such that they would endanger the physical well-being or life of their child." The Maine Supreme Court reversed.

> [I]n approaching a case of this sort the divorce court should make a preliminary determination of the child's best interest, without giving any consideration to either parent's religious practices, in order to ascertain which of them is the preferred custodial parent. Where that preliminary determination discloses that the religious practices of only the nonpreferred parent are at issue, any need for the court to delve into a constitutionally sensitive area is avoided.
>
> If, on the other hand, that preliminary determination discloses a preference for the parent whose religious practices have been placed in issue, the divorce court, in fashioning an appropriate custody order, may take into account the consequences upon the child of that parent's religious practices. Because of the sensitivity of the constitutional rights involved, however, any such inquiry must proceed along a two-stage analysis designed to protect those rights against unwarranted infringement. To summarize that analysis briefly: first, in order to assure itself that there exists a factual situation necessitating such infringement, the court must make a threshold factual determination that the child's temporal well-being is immediately and substantially endangered by the religious practice in question and, if that threshold determination is made, second, the court must engage in a deliberate and articulated balancing of the conflicting interests involved, to the end that its custody order makes the least possible infringement upon the parent's liberty interests consistent with the child's well-being. . . .
>
> If and only if the court is satisfied that an immediate and substantial threat to the child's well-being is posed by the religious practice in question, need it proceed to the second stage of the inquiry, requiring it to engage in an explicit balancing of the conflicting interests. In fashioning the appropriate order, the court should adopt a means of protecting the best interests of the child that makes the least possible intrusion upon the constitutionally protected interests of the parent. This balancing process requires the judge to conduct an evidentiary hearing on the alternative remedies available. . . . Although this court is not now willing to say that an order completely denying custody may never be appropriate where the temporal welfare of the child is genuinely threatened by a religious practice of the parent seeking custody, the divorce court should explore every reasonable alternative before resorting to such a drastic solution.

Compare Harrison v. Tauheed, 256 P.3d 851 (Kan. 2011) (distinguishing between religious belief including a belief in the impermissibility of transfusions, which may not be considered, and religiously motivated conduct, which can be considered to the extent it affects the best interest of the child).

4. In the context of medical decision making based on a parent's religious objection, do we know how the group would receive a child healed by a procedure contrary to the group's beliefs but ordered by a court? Should the answer matter?

5. How do the approaches to parental religious beliefs and practices in *Hadeen* and *Osier* differ?

6. Can the parties address the children's religious beliefs in a settlement agreement? In Rownak v. Rownak, 288 S.W.3d 672, 674-675 (Ark. App. 2008),

the Arkansas court of appeals held valid an agreement, incorporated into a divorce decree, that the parties would not promote a religion other than Protestantism to the minor children. The father later converted to the Latter-Day Saints faith and promoted that faith to the children, and the court found the father in contempt and ordered him to cease such conduct. In its decision, the court of appeals found that "the injunction about which appellant complains has for its basis a valid contract between the parties and does not violate appellant's constitutional rights." *Id.* at 674-675.

7. In *Hadeen*, the trial judge interviewed three of the daughters in chambers. This procedure is commonly authorized, sometimes by statute and sometimes by practice. Ohio Rev. Code Ann. § 3109.04(B)(1) and (2) (2011) illustrate the former. It provides that "the court, in its discretion, may and, upon the request of either party, shall interview in chambers any or all of the involved children regarding their wishes and concerns with respect to the allocation." In exercising that discretion, the legislature replaced an earlier requirement tied to the age of the child with a requirement that the "court first shall determine the reasoning ability of the child." The court also has discretion to appoint a guardian ad litem fore the interests of the child. What weight should be given to the child's preferences, and why?

STEPHEN WIZNER & MIRIAM BERKMAN, *BEING A LAWYER FOR A CHILD TOO YOUNG TO BE A CLIENT: A CLINICAL STUDY*

68 Neb. L. Rev. 330 (1989)

The widespread adoption of [appointing lawyers for children] has generated considerable professional and scholarly debate over the role of the child's legal representative in divorce litigation, especially in cases involving young children. This debate encompasses diverse views, which include: (1) a child's lawyer in a custody case should play the classic advocate's role of employing all legal means to advance the child's expressed preference, regardless of the child's age or the lawyer's view of what would be in the child's best interests; (2) an attorney should refuse to represent a child who is too young to express a meaningful preference; (3) the attorney for the child has a duty to advocate her independent, professional judgment of the child's best interests, even if it is inconsistent with the child's expressed preference; (4) the child's attorney should act as a mediator, not an advocate, assisting the parents to negotiate a settlement of their dispute that may, or may not, give substantial weight to the child's preferences or the attorney's view of the best interests of the child; (5) the child's legal representative should act as a neutral, objective investigator, fact gatherer, and reporter, assisting the court in making a fully informed assessment of the needs of the child and how those needs can best be met; (6) counsel for the child should not act as a lawyer, but should serve only as a professional companion for the child, protecting her from the process, explaining the process to her, answering her questions, and influencing or "orchestrating" the conduct of the process so that the child is damaged as little as possible by the legal proceedings; (7) the appointment of independent legal counsel for a child disempowers the parents and undermines their ability to act in their child's best interests; and (8) a child's attorney should act to make the custody determination process more formal and public, to diminish the influence of mental health experts, and to advocate the abolition of the "best interest" standard in favor of a "primary caretaker" standard.

Some have argued that the child advocate in a divorce case must assume a variety of roles including confidante, counselor, investigator, negotiator, mediator, "orchestrator," and advocate. Depending on the age, maturity, intelligence, and emotional state of the child, as well as the circumstances of the case, some argue that the advocate should assume several or all of these roles simultaneously or at different times in a given case. Even those who hold this view may disagree on how to balance the various roles, how to evaluate and weigh the child's preferences, and what to do when a child is too young to state a meaningful preference. Others have argued that *none* of these roles are appropriate professional roles for lawyers, and that young children ought not have their own legal representatives in custody disputes.

For further discussion of the challenges of representing, interviewing, and counseling children, *see* Laura Cohen & Randi Mandelbaum, Kids Will Be Kids: Creating a Framework for Interviewing and Counseling Adolescent Clients, 79 Temp. L. Rev. 357 (2006); Linda D. Elrod, Client-Directed Lawyers for Children: It's the "Right" Thing to Do, 27 Pace L. Rev. 869 (2007); Donald N. Duquette & Julian Darwall, Child Representation in America: Progress Report from the National Quality Improvement Center, 46 Fam. L.Q. 87 (2012); Marcia M. Boumil, Cristina F. Freitas & Debbie F. Freitas, Legal and Ethical Issues Confronting Guardian Ad Litem, 13 J.L. & Fam. Stud. 43 (2011); David A. Martindale, Reporter's Foreword to the Association of Family and Conciliation Courts' Model Standards of Practice for Child Custody Evaluation, 45 Fam. Ct. Rev. 61 (2007); Amy Russell, Best Practices in Child Forensic Interviews: Interview Instructions and Truth-Lie Discussions, 28 Hamline J. Pub. L. & Pol'y 99 (2006); Marvin Ventrell, The Practice of Law for Children, 28 Hamline J. Pub. L. & Pol'y 75 (2006).

PROBLEMS

1. Frank and Irene Jones are divorcing. They have two children. Irene is a devout member of a religious sect led by her father. Among this sect's principal tenets, shared by Irene, are beliefs that government is a manifestation of Satan and that all persons who are not members of the sect are God's enemies. Sect members also believe that they may ignore all acts of government, including tax laws and hunting and fishing regulations. There is no evidence that the children have been harmed, and they maintain a close bond with their mother.

What arguments will be made by either Frank or Irene? To what extent, if any, should the court consider the religious views of the sect and Irene?

2. Juan and Anita Chavez are seeking a divorce. Both identify as Roman Catholics. The evidence indicates that Juan Chavez is highly observant, has participated in church-related activities, and believes that the children should attend

parochial school. Anita is less observant and attends church infrequently, has no interest in church-related activities, and prefers that the children go to public school. Both wish primary custody of their children. May and should the trial judge take the relative religious commitments of the parents into account? If so, in what way? If Juan asks for custody of the children on all major religious holidays including Christmas and Easter so that he can ensure that they attend services, how should the judge respond?

3. How, if at all, would your answer to each of the preceding problems change if two of the children were 8 and 10, the 10-year-old strongly preferred that the nonreligious parent receive custody, and the 8-year-old believed that he would go to hell if he did not follow the observances of the more religious parent?

4. Cheryl and Elsey lived in a committed relationship for 11 years. They adopted a child from China; after being informed by a social worker that same-sex couples were not permitted to adopt, they filed the adoption proceedings in Cheryl's name alone. Nonetheless, both women went to China together to pick up the 6-month-old, and both participated equally in her upbringing. Six years after the adoption, the couple separated. The court awarded Cheryl primary physical custody and recognized Elsey as a psychological parent who was entitled to substantial visitation. After the separation, Cheryl became more religious, and she and her daughter now regularly attend church. The trial court specified in the custody award that Cheryl "make sure that there is nothing in the religious upbringing or teaching that the minor child is exposed to that can be considered homophobic." Discuss any grounds that Cheryl might have to challenge the condition.

5. The mother and father in this case have one son, M. Mother received custody of the child at the time of the divorce, when M was 4, but Father obtained custody when M was 9. M is now 12. Mother seeks a change in custody on the ground that Father is planning to have M circumcised. Mother is a member of the Russian Orthodox Church, and the parties originally raised M as a member of the church. After the divorce, Father converted to Judaism, and he has been teaching M about Judaism, having him learn Hebrew, and attend classes at the synagogue. Father would like M to convert also, and for M to do so in Father's conservative synagogue requires circumcision. Mother recently learned about the planned circumcision and believes that M objects. She has filed an emergency petition asking the court to enjoin the planned circumcision, which is scheduled for that evening, and to transfer custody to her. What arguments should Father make in opposition to Mother's motion?

d. Domestic Violence

Niemann v. Niemann

746 N.W.2d 3 (N.D. 2008)

VandeWalle, C.J. . . . In 1998, Lyle Niemann and Heidi Wolf divorced and Heidi Wolf was granted custody of their son and daughter. Both remarried. By agreement in June 2004, their daughter moved in with Lyle Niemann. In August

2005, Lyle Niemann brought a motion to gain custody of their son and the district court ordered an evidentiary hearing.

... The parties, prior to the hearing, stipulated to the physical change in custody of their daughter from Heidi Wolf to Lyle Niemann. However, the parties could not agree on a custodial arrangement for their son. ...

A custody investigator was appointed and interviewed Lyle Niemann, Heidi Wolf, their spouses, the two children and several friends and family members of both parties. The custody investigator recommended in her affidavit and at the hearing that custody of the son be awarded to Lyle Niemann, citing concerns about domestic violence, alcohol abuse, lack of structure and arguments with vulgar, inappropriate language in front of the children at the Wolf home.

The domestic violence concerns stem from two alleged incidents. First, in June 2002, the daughter spoke with a social worker at her school about a fight between her mother and stepfather. According to the daughter, after Heidi Wolf locked her keys in her car, her husband yelled and swore at her in front of the children, then "trashed" the house when they arrived home. The daughter stated she wanted to call the police and her stepfather chased them when they left the house.

The second incident occurred in May 2005, when the children indicated to their school social worker that their stepfather came home drunk, yelled, swore and pushed their mother. A report was filed with Social Services. The custody investigator interviewed several of the Wolfs' friends regarding the incident. Two friends said Heidi Wolf and her husband were "in each other's faces" and yelling but saw no physical violence. A third friend said he took his child and Heidi Wolf's son out of the house and was told by Heidi Wolf's husband to leave. The parties' daughter said she saw her stepfather yell, swear and push her mother. She said she grabbed her half-brother and snuck out of the house through a construction area.

Heidi Wolf admits she left with the children that night and her husband admitted to yelling, swearing and name-calling when angry. Heidi Wolf said she left the confrontation rather than dealing with it. She denied any domestic violence but admitted to the involvement of Social Services. A Social Services note indicates the case was closed after Heidi Wolf said she was leaving her husband and would obtain counseling for herself and the children. Heidi Wolf never obtained such counseling and disputes Social Services' note.

... The judge, ruling from the bench, found no material change of circumstances and denied Lyle Niemann's motion.

II.

A court may modify a prior custody order after the two-year period following the date of entry of an order establishing custody if the court finds either a) on the basis of facts that have arisen since the prior order or which were unknown to the court at the time of the prior order, a material change has occurred in the circumstances of the child or the parties, and b) modification is necessary to serve the best interest of the child. ...

A material change of circumstances includes important new facts unknown at the time of the prior custodial decree. A material change of circumstances can occur if a child's present environment may endanger the child's physical or emotional health or impair the child's emotional development. Improvements in a noncustodial parent's situation, coupled by a general decline in the condition of the children with the custodial parent over the same period may constitute a significant change in circumstances. The party seeking to modify the custody order bears the burden of proof.

Lyle Niemann argues the incident in May of 2005 was domestic violence and constitutes a material change of circumstances. Section 14-07.1-01, N.D.C.C., defines domestic violence to include "physical harm, bodily injury, sexual activity compelled by physical force, assault, or the infliction of fear of imminent physical harm, bodily injury, sexual activity compelled by physical force, or assault, not committed in self-defense." The district court stated, "The court does not find that credible domestic violence or a pattern of domestic violence exists." But the language used by the district court suggests the domestic violence must rise to the level of the standard used to invoke the domestic violence presumption in N.D.C.C. § 14-09-06.2(1)(j) for purposes of determining whether a material change of circumstances occurred. Under that section the presumption is invoked if the court finds credible evidence that domestic violence has occurred and there exists one incident of domestic violence resulting in serious bodily injury, or "there exists a pattern of domestic violence within a reasonable time proximate to the proceeding."

. . . Insofar as the district court believed there must be serious bodily injury or a pattern of domestic violence to justify a change in custody, we conclude the district court made a mistake of law by applying the standard necessary to invoke the domestic violence presumption to determine whether a change in circumstances justifying a change in custody occurred.

The incident in May 2005 comports with the definition of domestic violence. . . . Domestic violence is not confined to instances where the parent is the direct victim of the violence. Even if Heidi Wolf did not fear imminent physical harm during the fight with her husband, it is obvious the children were afraid. The parties' son was removed from the house by his stepfather's friend. Their daughter's fear of imminent physical harm is evident in her testimony regarding that night and in her current refusal to have contact with her stepfather.

The new split-custody arrangement also appears to be a material change in circumstances. After living together with Heidi Wolf since the divorce in 1998, the children were separated when the daughter went to live with Lyle Niemann in 2005. Although split custody is not flatly prohibited, as a general rule we do not look favorably upon separating siblings in custody cases. . . .

Lyle Niemann argues the language of the district court order suggests the district court went through the best interest analysis and found in favor of him. The judge stated in his ruling from the bench, "If this was first round, Lyle would get custody." However, in a best interest analysis, the trial court's findings of fact should be stated with sufficient specificity to enable us to understand the factual basis for the court's decision. There are not sufficient findings of fact in the record regarding the best interest analysis to conclude the district court found in favor of Lyle Niemann on this part of the test. . . .

We reverse and remand for further proceedings in accordance with this opinion.

MARING, J., dissenting in part and concurring in part. I respectfully dissent from parts I and IIA. I would affirm the order of the trial court in its entirety. . . .

I disagree with the majority's statement of the "two-step" test. The statute specifically requires a material change in the circumstances of the child or the parties and that "modification is *necessary* to serve the best interest of the child." I also disagree with the majority's implication that the trial court misapplied or misapprehended the law with regard to domestic violence. The trial court considered the mother Heidi Wolf's version of what happened in May 2005 and the minor daughter's version and found the mother's explanation credible. In the trial court's September 20, 2006, Order Denying Motion for Reconsideration, the court stated:

> This incident did not rise to the level of domestic violence but rather is an isolated domestic disagreement. While such disagreements and conduct should be avoided, it surely is not the basis for a material change of circumstances.

In the parties' Stipulation to Correct and Supplement the Record, the trial court's findings included a sentence left out by the majority:

> *If there is no domestic violence, and only strong words, that is not good, but the incidents in 2002 and then in 2005 don't rise to the level of domestic violence as we recognize it.* The court does not find that credible domestic violence or a pattern of domestic violence exists.

(Emphasis added.) This Court has never held that loud words or domestic disagreements amount to domestic violence.

The trial court did not find any credible evidence of domestic violence. It did not find "physical harm, bodily injury, sexual activity compelled by physical force, assault, or the infliction of fear of imminent physical harm, bodily injury, sexual activity compelled by physical force, or assault, not committed in self-defense, on the complaining family or household members." *See* N.D.C.C. § 14-07.1-01(2).

The majority makes a finding that the testimony of the daughter is evidence of the daughter's fear of imminent physical harm. The daughter said in her affidavit about the incident in May 2005, "It was really scary." In her testimony, she said she was afraid of Vance Wolf and when asked why she said, "[h]e just scares me." There is no evidence she was in fear of imminent physical harm, and the trial court did not make any such finding. The majority is reweighing the evidence, thereby ignoring precedent and applying a de novo standard of review. This Court has held that when two parties present conflicting testimony on issues of fact, we will not redetermine the trial court's findings based upon that testimony. Here, the trial court found the mother's version of what occurred credible and impliedly did not find the testimony of the daughter that there was physical violence credible.

Although the majority is correct that we have held that domestic violence does not need to be directed to a child to have a harmful effect on the child, there is no finding of domestic violence in this case, only a loud and strongly worded domestic disagreement. Such a finding is not a material change in circumstances necessitating a modification of custody in the best interest of the minor son, who was the only child left at issue.

The majority, at P 16, goes on to find "the new split-custody arrangement also appears to be a material change in circumstances" as a matter of law. The parties stipulated to this split after the parties' minor daughter stated a preference to live with her father. If this amounts to a material change as a matter of law, it will discourage parties from settling custody disputes such as this. There is little, if any, evidence in this record about the relationship between the minor daughter and the minor son. What is there is lacking in detail and substance. There is no evidence they spend a substantial amount of time together or share any activities or interests. . . .

NOTES AND QUESTIONS

1. Substantial empirical evidence shows that children may be harmed by exposure to domestic violence even when that violence is directed against other family members and the children themselves are not at risk of physical abuse. Joan Kelly and Michael Johnson observe:

> The effects of intimate partner violence on children's adjustment have also been well documented. . . . Violence has an independent effect on children's adjustment and is significantly more potent than high levels of marital conflict. . . . Behavioral, cognitive, and emotional problems include aggression, conduct disorders, delinquency, truancy, school failure, anger, depression, anxiety, and low self-esteem. Interpersonal problems include poor social skills, peer rejection, problems with authority figures and parents, and an inability to empathize with others. Preschool children traumatized by the earlier battering of their mothers had pervasive negative effects on their development, including significant delays and insecure or disorganized attachments. School-age children repeatedly exposed to violence are more likely to develop post-traumatic stress disorders, particularly when combined with other risk factors of child abuse, poverty, and the psychiatric illness of one or both parents. . . .

Joan B. Kelly & Michael P. Johnson, Domestic Violence: Differentiation Among Types of Intimate Partner Violence: Research Update and Implications for Interventions, 46 Fam. Ct. Rev. 476, 489-490 (2008). *See also* Jeffrey L. Edelson, Children's Witnessing of Adult Domestic Violence, 14 J. Interpersonal Violence 839, 845 (1999) (reviewing 31 studies of children who witnessed domestic violence between their parents but who were not abused themselves, and concluding among other things that children who witness violence are more likely to engage in violent behavior as adults); Gregory K. Moffatt & Savannah L. Smith, Childhood Exposure to Conjugal Violence: Consequences for Behavioral and Neural Development, 56 De Paul L. Rev. 879 (2007) (exposure to domestic violence during childhood may have lifelong impact on children's developing brains); Report of the Attorney General's National Task Force on Children Exposed to Violence, Defending Childhood: Protect Heal Thrive (2012) (summarizing evidence).

In a little less than a decade, the courts shifted from viewing domestic violence as a private matter between the parents to seeing it as a critical consideration in child custody decisions. Today, all jurisdictions mandate consideration of domestic violence as a factor in custody decision making, and many have enacted presumptions against an award of custody to a parent who has engaged in domestic violence. 1-10 Nat'l Council of Juvenile & Family Court Judges, Family Violence: Legislative Update (1995-2004). For a summary of the different state approaches, *see* Erin Bajackson, Best Interests of the Child—A Legislative Journey Still in Motion, 25 J. Am. Acad. Matrimonial L. 311, 330-339 (2013). For an assessment of these changes, *see* Leigh Goodmark, A Troubled Marriage: Domestic Violence and the Legal System (2012); Leslie Joan Harris, Failure to Protect from Exposure to Domestic Violence in Private Custody Contests, 44 Fam. L.Q. 169 (2010); Suzanne Reynolds & Ralph Peeples, When Petitioners Seek Custody in Domestic Violence Court and Why We Should Take Them Seriously, 47 Wake Forest L. Rev. 935 (2012).

Despite the legal changes, researchers find that:

> In our studies of custody-litigating families, domestic violence was alleged in the large majority of cases (two thirds to three fourths), and parental abuse of drugs and alcohol was alleged on average in about one half of cases. . . . To date, findings indicate that the majority of domestic violence and substance abuse allegations (one half to three fourths) and a large minority of child neglect and abuse allegations (one fourth to one half) in family law matters can be subsequently substantiated in some manner.

Janet Johnston, Vivienne Roseby & Kathryn Kuehnle, In the Name of the Child: A Developmental Approach to Understanding and Helping Children of Conflicted and Violent Divorce 308 (2d ed. 2009).

2. The ALI defines domestic violence as "the infliction of physical injury, or the creation of a reasonable fear thereof, by a parent or a present or former member of the child's household, against the child or another member of the household. Reasonable action taken by an individual for self-protection, or the protection of another individual, is not domestic violence." Principles of the Law of Family Dissolution § 2.03(7). How does this definition compare to the definition in *Niemann*? Would use of the ALI definition have affected the approach of either the majority or the dissent?

3. The ALI provides that if a parent is found to have engaged in domestic violence, "the court should not allocate custodial responsibility or decisionmaking responsibility to that parent without making special written findings . . . that the child, other parent, or other household member can be adequately protected from harm. . . ." A parent found to have engaged in domestic violence "should have the burden of proving that an allocation of custodial responsibility or decisionmaking responsibility to that parent will not endanger the child, other parent, or other household member." Principles of the Law of Family Dissolution § 2.11(3). Protecting family members from harm may involve a range of measures from supervised visitation to anger management classes to denial of custodial or decision-making responsibility. North Dakota, in contrast, creates a statutory presumption against granting custody to a parent who has committed acts of domestic violence:

> If the court finds credible evidence that domestic violence has occurred, and there exists one incident of domestic violence which resulted in serious bodily injury or involved the use of a dangerous weapon or there exists a pattern of domestic violence

within a reasonable time proximate to the proceeding, this combination creates a rebuttable presumption that a parent who has perpetrated domestic violence may not be awarded residential responsibility for the child. This presumption may be overcome only by clear and convincing evidence that the best interests of the child require that parent have residential responsibility.

N.D. Cent. Code § 14-09-06.2(1)(j) (2013). The North Dakota statute accordingly combines a stricter definition of domestic violence with a strong presumption against an award of custody, while the ALI has a broader definition of domestic violence and a range of possible consequences that follow from such a finding. Which approach do you prefer? Would the analysis in *Niemann* have been different under the ALI standards?

The majority in *Niemann* indicates that even if the behavior at issue does not constitute domestic violence within the definition of the statute, it may constitute changed circumstances, allowing the court to reconsider the appropriate custody award. Does this approach give adequate notice to the custodial parent of what may constitute conduct justifying a change in custody? On what basis does the dissent object to the approach of the majority to the issue of violence?

Once the majority concludes that changed circumstances exist, what role does domestic violence play in its determination of the child's best interest?

Would the result be different in an initial award of custody? In Law v. Whittet, 844 N.W.2d 885 (N.D. 2014), the mother had been arrested for hitting her own mother in front of the children on an evening in which she was very drunk, and later escaped from the police car. She eventually pled guilty to disorderly conduct and escape. The trial court awarded the unmarried mother and father joint residential responsibility for the child, but the North Dakota Supreme Court reversed and awarded primary residential responsibility for the child to the father. The court opined:

> Even if the evidence of domestic violence does not trigger the statutory presumption under N.D.C.C. § 14-09-06.2(1)(j), the violence must still be considered as one of the factors in deciding primary residential responsibility, and when credible evidence of domestic violence exists it "dominates the hierarchy of factors to be considered" when determining the best interests of the child.

Is this consistent with the approach in *Niemann*?

4. Chapter 2 describes research defining different types of domestic violence and comparing them in terms of severity. Researchers emphasize that the studies documenting the harmful effects of domestic violence on children do not necessarily distinguish among these types of violence. Jaffe et al. suggest that whether or not domestic violence should preclude shared custody depends on the nature of the violence involved, and that mild incidents of domestic violence (*e.g.*, separation-related violence involving isolated incidents uncharacteristic of the relationship) need not prevent development of a parenting plan in which parents share continued involvement with the child. They describe a continuum of shared parenting measures any of which might be appropriate depending on the level of violence. These measures include:

- Co-parenting, generally involving joint custody in which both parents are involved in making cooperative decisions about the child's welfare;
- Parallel parenting with both parents involved, but including arrangements designed to minimize contact and conflict between the parents;
- Supervised exchanges of the child from parent to parent in a manner that minimizes the potential for parental conflict or violence;
- Supervised access, when one or both parents pose a temporary danger to the child, provided under direct supervision in specialized centers and/or by trained personnel with the hope that the conditions that led to supervised access will be resolved and the parent can proceed to a more normal relationship with the child.
- Prohibition of all contact with the child, in the most serious cases, in which a parent poses an ongoing risk to the child.

Peter G. Jaffe, Janet R. Johnston, Claire V. Crooks & Nicholas Bala, Custody Disputes Involving Allegations of Domestic Violence: Toward a Differentiated Approach to Parenting Plans, 46 Fam. Ct. Rev. 500, 516 (2008). Under what circumstances would each measure they propose be appropriate?

5. How should the court deal with a case in which credible evidence existed that both parents had engaged in domestic violence? Would your answer change if state law included a presumption against awarding custody to either of them? *See* Owan v. Owan, 541 N.W.2d 719 (N.D. 1996); Leigh Goodmark, When Is a Battered Woman Not a Battered Woman? When She Fights Back, 20 Yale J.L. & Feminism 75, 96-113 (2008). How should a court deal with a case in which one parent engaged in domestic violence and the second parent, after the first relationship ended, entered in a new relationship where domestic violence occurred?

6. For a discussion of the use of mediation in cases involving domestic violence, see Chapter 11.

PROBLEMS

1. Sandra and Jerome are African Americans in their mid-20s with a 4-year-old son. On several occasions, neighbors called the police when they heard screams or shouts coming from their house. On other occasions, Jerome initiated the calls, alleging that Sandra had attacked him. Each time, Jerome told police his version of the events, but Sandra refused to talk to them. She was arrested as the perpetrator more than once and was charged with resisting arrest, even though the police report stated that Jerome had beaten her and that she was injured and bleeding at the time of the arrest. Prosecutors eventually dropped the charges against her without explanation. Sandra sought legal protection from Jerome for the first time only after they had broken up and he was arrested for assaulting and injuring her outside a shopping mall — an incident that resulted in his conviction for battery. After the incident, Sandra went to family court and asked for an award of sole physical and legal custody, and a civil restraining order limiting his contact with her and the child. Jerome responded by also seeking sole legal and physical custody, and asking the court to limit Sandra's contact with their son to supervised

visitation. At the family court hearing, Sandra testified that Jerome had beaten her at least once a month over the five years they were together, but that she was too afraid of him to tell the police. Jerome testified that they often quarreled when they were together and that Sandra had initiated most of the violence by cursing, pushing, or slapping him. At the time of the hearing, Sandra had been employed as a clerk in a professional office for seven years while Jerome is unemployed.

What arguments might Sandra and Jerome raise if the case is heard in North Dakota? Would your answer change under the ALI Principles? Is the continuing involvement of both parents with the child appropriate in this case? If so, what measures should be taken to protect the child from exposure to violence? If you were an attorney for either Sandra or Jerome, would you be concerned that racial stereotypes might affect the outcome of the case? If so, in what way? *See* Elizabeth L. MacDowell, Theorizing from Particularity: Perpetrators and Intersectional Theory on Domestic Violence, 16 J. Gender Race & Just. 531, 537-538 (2012) (describing a case involving similar facts).

2. Charlotte and Gary lived together for a short time after their son was born. When the child was 5, Charlotte moved to another town to live with her new boyfriend, David. Four years later, Charlotte called Gary and asked him to come and get her and their son because she was leaving David. Charlotte, Gary, and their son moved in together, but Charlotte reconciled with David and filed for custody.

At trial, Gary argued that Charlotte should not have custody because of domestic violence that had occurred between her and David in the presence of the child. The testimony included descriptions of two occasions when Charlotte had fled with the boy because of fear of David's behavior, and other occasions in which David pushed the boy or exposed him to marijuana use. Charlotte minimized the violence and denied that the child had been exposed to it. She also testified that when she and Gary were together, Gary had been convicted of assaulting her. The 9-year-old boy testified that he wanted to live with his mother, but Gary argued that the boy's views reflected the fact that Charlotte had continually denigrated him to the boy and interfered with their relationship.

The trial court awarded primary physical custody to Gary and visitation to Charlotte, finding that Charlotte, who was still living with David, had failed to protect their son from exposure to domestic violence. What arguments would you make on Charlotte's behalf on appeal? What alternatives were available to the trial judge if he concluded that the boy would be better off remaining with Charlotte, but that her relationship with David posed a risk of exposure to domestic violence?

3. Susan and Walter married ten years ago, shortly after graduating from college. They have a 7-year-old and a 9-year-old. Susan has been the primary caretaker, but Walter has been actively involved with the children. One day, shortly after he returned home from work, Susan told Walter she was leaving him for his best friend, Arthur. Susan moved out the next day, taking the children with her. Walter, who had no idea that Susan was dissatisfied with their relationship, was devastated. He tried to talk Susan into returning, to no avail. Several weeks later, Susan came by unexpectedly to pick up some of her belongings. She and Walter quarreled. Walter, who had been drinking, struck her, knocking her across the room and breaking her nose. Susan quickly obtained a restraining order keeping Walter away from her and the children. He has not seen the children in the

intervening six months. At trial, Susan testifies that Walter has been controlling and verbally abusive during the marriage and that she is afraid of him. The guardian ad litem for the children testified that Walter was actively involved with the children's homework and extracurricular activities, but he was moody and inconsistent, sometimes berating them and other times surprising them with gifts or spur-of-the-moment activities. She also testifies that the children are deeply distressed about the conflict between their parents; they witnessed their father breaking their mother's nose and have often been present when they quarreled. How should custody be allocated under the principles set out in the principal case and cases discussed in the notes?

e.   Unfriendly Co-parenting

IN THE MATTER OF MILLER

20 A.3d 854 (N.H. 2011)

HICKS, J. . . . Miller and Todd met in 1999 over the internet and established a relationship. At that time, Miller lived in Michigan and Todd lived in New Hampshire. Although they never married, their relationship produced two daughters, Laurel born in 2002 and Lindsay born in 2003. During 2002 and 2003, the parties spent some time living together in Michigan, Todd and the children spent some time alone in New Hampshire living with Todd's parents, and the parties all spent some time together at Todd's parents' house in New Hampshire.

Toward the end of 2003, the parties' relationship broke down. On December 23, 2003, Miller obtained an *ex parte* order in the circuit court in Michigan granting him sole temporary legal and physical custody of his daughters. That same day, Todd took the children to her parents' home in Hampton, New Hampshire. On January 6, 2004, Todd was served with the Michigan custody order. . . .

Sometime in January, Todd's mother told her that, four months earlier, she saw Miller molest Laurel by inserting his forefinger into her. On January 27, on the advice of her attorney, Todd took the children to the emergency department at Exeter Hospital and requested a "well baby check." The physician's report states: "[P]atient here for well child check-up; told by Lawyer to have evaluated for custody issue." There is no evidence in the record that Todd notified the hospital staff of any concerns regarding sexual abuse. The physical exam indicated the children's condition was good. Todd then transferred the children to Miller's custody.

On February 5, 2004, a report was filed with the Family Independence Agency of Michigan, Child Protective Services, alleging that maternal grandparents recalled an incident that occurred in New Hampshire between 10/03/03 and 10/05/03 when father was rubbing diaper cream on Laurel because she had a diaper rash. Maternal grandmother states she did not have [a] diaper rash. Maternal grandmother stated father inserted his forefinger inside of Laurel. This was never reported to anyone. The agency investigated the report, including having pelvic examinations of both children administered. No indications of sexual abuse of either child were found and the investigation was closed.

In November 2004, the Rockingham County Superior Court issued a temporary decree awarding the parties joint legal custody of the children. In that order, the trial court questioned the credibility of both parties. Regarding Todd, the court found "most troubling" the allegations of sexual abuse raised by her. As the court stated, "It is simply far too convenient to believe the testimony put forth by [Todd]: that her mother [chose] not to reveal the allegations of [Miller's] alleged sexual assault until custody of the minor children was awarded to [Miller]." The court noted that neither party "appears to care to whom they lie so long as they achieve favorable results."

In June 2005, Todd's father reported to the Hampton police that while he was lying in bed with Lindsay and Laurel watching a movie, Laurel tried to "straddle" him on his chest and stated, "I'm f——— you." When the grandfather asked Laurel where she heard that she said nothing. When the grandfather then asked, "from your father," Laurel said "yes." The police noted the report as a "possible disclosure" of sexual abuse, but took no action.

In September 2005, a friend of Todd's made a statement to the police that Laurel had reported that Miller had spanked her in the groin area. Todd filed an *ex parte* petition for temporary stay of visitation between Miller and the children alleging that the children reported being spanked by Miller and a third party in the groin area and that Laurel had displayed "other alarming behavior of a sexual nature," referring to the grandfather's report to the police in June. As a result of these allegations, the court issued an order prohibiting Miller from having any contact with the children "until this matter is duly investigated and any and all allegations of abuse are deemed unfounded." After an investigation that included a second pelvic examination of Laurel, the New Hampshire Division for Children, Youth, and Families (DCYF) closed the matter as unfounded. . . .

In November 2005, Todd and the children's therapist reported to DCYF that Laurel had stated that Miller took "pictures of her with her clothes off," made her "eat his pee pee" and "panks her in the front." On January 30, 2006, DCYF sent a letter to Miller stating that it had determined that he was "the individual responsible for the abuse" and that his name would be entered "on its central registry of founded child abuse and neglect reports." Miller appealed the finding and, on February 24, 2006, DCYF rescinded its initial determination. In a letter to Todd, DCYF informed her that new evidence had come to its attention and that "the assessment regarding your children has been closed **unfounded**." DCYF stated that "[t]here has been a concern that Laurel has been coached with the information that she has been disclosing. Please understand that this . . . type of coaching, if proven, is equally as abusive to a child as if the abuse had actually occurred." . . .

In July 2006, the parties agreed to be evaluated by psychologist Peggie Ward. . . . On December 18, 2007, Dr. Ward issued an eighty-eight page report in which she considered several hypotheses. First, Dr. Ward posed the hypothesis that "Laurel was not sexually abused by her father or anyone else." Dr. Ward noted that both children were subjected to multiple examinations and questioning and that Laurel's statements to the Child Advocacy Center "do not appear to be consistent with her initial statement nor do they have a good deal of context." Dr. Ward opined that "this hypothesis may be supported by the data" in that "Laurel's presentation is less consistent with a child who has been repeatedly sexually abused."

Second, Dr. Ward posed the hypothesis that "Laurel was sexually abused or inappropriately touched by Mr. Miller." Dr. Ward noted that "Laurel's statements and behaviors are less consistent with child sexual abuse than they are of premature focus on the genital area followed by a good deal of anxiety and distress about sexual abuse from both Janet Todd as well as [Todd's mother]." Due to the "lack of context and the lack of memory regarding abusive behavior, combined with multiple physical exams and multiple interviews," it was "impossible to determine whether Laurel was sexually abused by her father." Dr. Ward's opinion was that "Laurel's presentation is less consistent with a child sexually abused by her father and more consistent with other hypotheses."

Third, Dr. Ward posed the hypothesis that Todd "has deliberately coached the children in what to say and scripted their responses." It was Dr. Ward's opinion that "this hypothesis is not the hypothesis best supported by the data."

Fourth, Dr. Ward posed the hypothesis that "Todd came to believe that Laurel, not Lindsay, was sexually abused by Mr. Miller." It was Dr. Ward's opinion that this hypothesis "is the most likely hypothesis supported by the data. That is, that Ms. Todd, after experiencing her parent's concerns about Mr. Miller and after having experienced her own negative interactions with Mr. Miller, became increasingly convinced that Mr. Miller was harming Laurel." Referring to a psychological report on Todd that was prepared in August 2007 by Dr. David Medoff, Dr. Ward noted that

> [p]sychological testing shows that Ms. Todd has a "serious impairment in her ability to accurately process the information she takes in from her surroundings and the degree of misperception she demonstrates has major implications for her adaptive functioning. . . . These data indicate that Ms. Todd will not only fail to recognize or foresee the consequences of her actions at times, but that she will also become confused at times in separating fantasy from reality."

As Dr. Ward explained,

> Ms. Todd has the liability of distortion of information and failure to accurately identify intentions, motivations and behavior of others. Ms. Todd's emotional state placed her at risk for misinterpreting information that she gained from her environment, adamantly believing that Laurel was sexually abused, and acting with full force on this information.

Dr. Ward thus concluded that "the hypothesis that Ms. Todd unintentionally but clearly caused Laurel to come to believe that she has been sexually abused by her father is the hypothesis best supported by the data."

In making her recommendations, Dr. Ward cautioned that "[w]hile it is unlikely that Mr. Miller has sexually abused Laurel, it is not possible to say with an absolute certainty that he did not." She concluded, however, that while it is "likely that Janet Todd did influence her children with her negative beliefs about Mr. Miller, from her psychological profile, it is most likely that her feelings colored her perceptions and that she not only came to see Mr. Miller as harmful to Laurel but also did not protect the children from her feelings." In addition, Dr. Ward noted that "Ms. Todd's parents appear to have wholly and adamantly accepted that

Mr. Miller is a pervasive negative influence on his children. Mrs. Todd in particular is active in helping her daughter prove that Mr. Miller sexually abused the children." Finally, Dr. Ward noted that "Laurel's therapist is convinced that Laurel has been sexually abused, and may have inadvertently reinforced the abuse by making a 'book' with Laurel about her abuse." . . .

On January 7, 2008, the trial court . . . expressed its intent

> to set a course for the **immediate** *therapeutic* reunification of the children with their father. Too much time has already passed and too much opportunity has been lost. The children certainly deserve better. [Todd] asserts that she accepts the goal of reunification, but wants it to proceed at a slow pace. The court is convinced that [Todd's] pace for reunification is far too slow and is premised on assertions which may not be true.

. . . The court found "that the children's best interests require that they 'normalize' their relationship with their father. It is extraordinarily harmful to them to deprive them of a relationship with one parent, especially when the reasons for doing so appear to be wholly unjustified." . . .

On March 6, 2008, following a hearing, the trial court issued an order stating that its "hope that progress could be made in [Miller's] reunification with the parties' minor children was misguided." The January 7, 2008 order setting forth a plan for restoring the relationship "failed in relatively short order." The court attributed responsibility for its failure to both parties: "[Miller] because of his insistence and belligerence with the reunification therapist" and Todd "because of her fanciful concern about the therapist's 'fraudulent billing' of insurance." The court ordered that the parties enroll in reunification counseling with a new therapist and that they develop a schedule which gives Miller "some increasingly longer periods of parenting time" during the reunification process. The court stated that it was "growing increasingly convinced that [Todd's] insistence that [Miller] sexually abused the children is the single biggest obstacle to restoring [Miller's] relationship with them. If her insistence continues to be so intractable, [it] may be left with no alternative short of modifying the children's primary residence." . . .

. . . In October 2008, Miller filed an *ex parte* motion again seeking modification of residential responsibility "made necessary due to the fact that [he] ha[d] not had any contact with his children since August 14, 2008." . . . The "uncontroverted evidence" demonstrated that Miller had not seen the children since August "for reasons entirely unclear to the court," that Todd had offered parenting time to Miller for a couple of days in August "but then reneged," and that Todd neither met Miller in New Hampshire when he came to pick up the children, nor did she bring the children to New York. The court noted that Miller was not blameless in that he "unreasonably insists that his reunification with the children be done on his terms, and his impatience with the process has now caused the second reunification therapist to withdraw from this case. He chose both therapists, but his conduct has made their work nearly impossible." Concluding that only a specific schedule of parenting time would guarantee Miller's contact with the children, the court set forth a visitation schedule.

In March 2009, the guardian ad litem filed an *ex parte* motion to cancel the custodial time the children were scheduled to have with their father during the weekend beginning March 20, 2009. The motion indicated that "[o]n 3/18/09 Janet Todd told the GAL that the children disclosed to her inappropriate touching by their father . . . during their last custodial time with [him]." In response, the trial court scheduled a hearing and, in the interim, ordered that the "father shall *not* have parenting time." At the hearing, the guardian stated that Todd claimed Lindsay reported that "daddy touched her pee-pee. She told him not to and he did it anyway, and that there was also a threat in there that if they told anyone, he would kill their mother." Following the hearing, the court ordered that Miller's parenting time was not suspended but ordered the guardian ad litem and Todd to report the disclosures to DCYF "immediately." DCYF investigated and closed the matter as unfounded. In a letter to the parties, DCYF recommended that both Laurel and Lindsay engage in individual therapy and that the parents participate in a Child Impact Seminar to understand "the impact it has on children to have a relationship with both parents." . . .

In April 2009, the guardian ad litem filed a statement with the court indicating that Laurel's first grade teacher had reported that on April 20 Laurel began to cry in class and disclosed that during her most recent visit with her father he said that he was going to hurt her mother and there was nothing she could do to stop him. In response, Miller filed a motion to modify custody of the children due to new acts of child abuse. Following a hearing, the court denied the motion. The court noted that it understood

> that [Miller] fears that this new allegation, when combined with previous ones and the recent one in March, is a "slippery slope" spiraling into new and more serious ones. The court will carefully consider all that has happened before March and since. The Final Hearing is scheduled in July, only two months away. Until then, the court does not find a risk of imminent harm to justify the uprooting of the children, especially so close to the end of the school year.

. . . [T]he master found that they have lived primarily with their mother in New Hampshire for nearly five years, where they have attended school. He found that they have friends in New Hampshire and a close relationship with their maternal grandparents. In addition, he found that although they have reestablished a healthy bond with their father, have made friends in New York, and enjoy their time with their father's brother and mother, a move to New York would be a drastic change requiring them to leave most of what they have known during their formative years and would not be in their best interest. Accordingly, the master concluded that "the girls' best interests require that they continue living primarily with their mother in New Hampshire."

. . . The trial court has wide discretion in matters involving custody and visitation. . . .

"When determining matters of child custody, a trial court's overriding concern is the best interest of the child." In the Matter of Martin & Martin, 160 N.H. 645, 647, 8 A.3d 60 (2010), *cert. denied,* ___ U.S. ___, 131 S. Ct. 1046, 178 L. Ed. 2d 865 (2011). RSA chapter 461-A, the Parental Rights and Responsibilities Act, states that "children do best when both parents have a stable and meaningful involvement in their lives." Accordingly, it is the policy of this state to "[s]upport frequent and continuing contact between each child and both parents" and to "[e]ncourage parents to share in the rights and responsibilities of raising their children." The Act codifies the "best interests of the child" criteria, setting forth twelve factors that the court must consider, including:

> (e) The ability and disposition of each parent to foster a positive relationship and frequent and continuing physical, written and telephonic contact with the other parent, except where contact will result in harm to the child or to a parent.
> (f) The support of each parent for the child's contact with the other parent as shown by allowing and promoting such contact.
> (g) The support of each parent for the child's relationship with the other parent.

RSA 461-A:6, I(e)-(g) (Supp. 2009) (amended 2010).

"Across the country, the great weight of authority holds that conduct by one parent that tends to alienate the child's affections from the other is so inimical to the child's welfare as to be grounds for a denial of custody to, or a change of custody from, the parent guilty of such conduct." Renaud v. Renaud, 168 Vt. 306, 721 A.2d 463, 465-66 (1998). "[A] child's best interests are plainly furthered by nurturing the child's relationship with both parents, and a sustained course of conduct by one parent designed to interfere in the child's relationship with the other casts serious doubt upon the fitness of the offending party to be the custodial parent." As we have recognized, "the obstruction by a custodial parent of visitation between a child and the noncustodial parent may, if continuous, constitute behavior so inconsistent with the best interests of the child as to raise a strong possibility that the child will be harmed." Webb v. Knudson, 133 N.H. 665, 673, 582 A.2d 282 (1990).

In addition, many courts have held that unfounded allegations of sexual abuse made by one parent can be grounds for granting custody to the other parent.

In Beekman v. Beekman, 96 Ohio App. 3d 783, 645 N.E.2d 1332, 1336 (1994), the court reasoned:

> Although a court grants one parent custody and the other visitation, the children need to know that they are loved by both parents regardless of the antagonism the parents might feel for each other. It is the duty of each parent to foster and encourage the child's love and respect for the other parent, and the failure from that duty is as harmful to the child as is the failure to provide food, clothing, or shelter. Perhaps it is more harmful because no matter how well fed or well clothed, a child cannot be happy if he or she feels unloved by one parent.
>
> When a court makes a custodial decision, it makes a presumption that the circumstances are such that the residential parent will promote both maternal and paternal affection. The residential parent implicitly agrees to foster such affection, not out of any good feeling toward the nonresidential parent, but out of the need of the child for both parent's love. Where the evidence shows that after the initial decree the residential parent is not living up to the court's presumption and is attempting to poison the relationship between the ex-spouse and the child, this is a change of circumstances that warrants a modification of the prior custody decree. Unsubstantiated allegations of abuse are the worst kind of poisoning of the relationship.

The trial court's order in the case before us does not cite RSA chapter 461-A, nor does it mention the application of the statutory factors to the specific facts before it. . . .

Based upon the record before us, the negative ramifications of Todd's unfounded belief that Miller has sexually abused his children, and continues to do so, are several and serious. First and foremost, the false allegations of abuse significantly interfered with Miller's visitation and deprived him of any relationship with his children for years. Further, as a result of the false allegations, both children have been subjected repeatedly to invasive physical examinations, they have been interviewed by DCYF and law enforcement, they have been evaluated by Dr. Ward, they have had two guardians ad litem and they have twice participated in reunification therapy. These actions were not in the children's best interests. . . .

The trial court awarded custody to Todd primarily because the children have spent the majority of their lives with her and that is where they are most comfortable. However, it was because of the unfounded allegations of sexual abuse that Miller was denied *any* contact with his children for over two years and had little opportunity to establish a home life with them between 2004 and 2009. This raises the question whether Todd has benefitted from her misbehavior. In Begins v. Begins, 168 Vt. 298, 721 A.2d 469, 470-71 (1998), the children's relationship with their mother deteriorated following the parents' separation due to the fact that the father unfairly blamed her for the parties' marital problems and made disparaging remarks about her lifestyle. The trial court concluded that the boys' hostility toward their mother, encouraged and fueled by their father, precluded an award of custody to mother. Although the court found that father did not "deserve to win custody," it concluded that it had no choice but to award custody to him. The Vermont Supreme Court rejected such reasoning. As the court stated:

> Although obviously well intended, the court's decision effectively condoned a parent's willful alienation of a child from the other parent. Its ruling sends the unacceptable message that others might, with impunity, engage in similar misconduct. Left undisturbed, the court's decision would nullify the principle that the best interests of the child are furthered through a healthy and loving relationship with both parents.

Dr. Ward's report, characterized by the master as "thorough and extraordinarily perceptive," contains several conclusions particularly relevant to Todd's inability to foster a positive relationship with Miller and to support the children's contact with him. . . .

We conclude that the award of parental rights and responsibilities must be vacated and the case remanded for reconsideration in light of this opinion.

NOTES AND QUESTIONS

1. In the early 1990s, psychologist Richard Gardner argued that "parental alienation syndrome" should be recognized as a divorce phenomenon in which one parent, typically the mother, attempts to maintain the psychological bond with the child by undermining the child's relationship with the other parent. He recommended a transfer of custody to the non-alienating parent in egregious cases. The Parental Alienation Syndrome: A Guide for Mental Health and Legal Professionals (1992, 2d ed. 1998). Critics have noted that parental alienation syndrome is not a recognized diagnosis in the Diagnostic and Statistical Manual IV (DSM-IV)

and that Gardner's work did not appear in peer-reviewed journals. Sandra Berns, Parents Behaving Badly: Parental Alienation Syndrome in the Family Court— Magic Bullet or Poisoned Chalice?, 15 Austl. J. Fam. L. 191 (2001); Carol Bruch, Parental Alienation Syndrome and Parental Alienation: Getting It Wrong in Child Custody Cases, 35 Fam. L.Q. 527 (2001); Robert E. Emery, Reader Commentary, Parental Alienation Syndrome: Proponents Bear the Burden of Proof, 43 Fam. Ct. Rev. 8, 9 (2005). Courts, however, can consider parental willingness to cooperate without a formal diagnosis of a psychiatric "syndrome." See, e.g., C.J.L. v. M.W.B., 879 So. 2d 1169 (Ala. 2003), discussing the distinction between expert testimony establishing parental alienation syndrome and a custody evaluation documenting the mother's efforts to undermine the children's relationship with their father through, among other things, false accusations of child abuse. Today, many courts use the term *parental alienation* to describe such conduct without reference to a "syndrome." In addition, the Diagnostic and Statistical Manual V (DSM-V), which came out in 2013, added a broader category of "child psychological abuse," defined as "non-accidental verbal or symbolic acts by a child's parent or caregiver that result, or have reasonable potential to result, in significant psychological harm to the child." The description states that the abuse "may include negative attributions of the other's intentions, hostility toward or scapegoating of the other, and unwarranted feelings of estrangement." See Joan S. Meier, A Historical Perspective on Parental Alienation Syndrome and Parental Alienation, 6 J. Child Custody 232, 237-238 (2009), and Note, Allison M. Nichols, Toward a Child-Centered Approach to Evaluating Claims of Alienation in High-Conflict Custody Disputes, 112 Mich. L. Rev. 663 (2014).

Moreover, many states, like New Hampshire, have a custody preference for the parent who will facilitate a positive relationship and the child's continuing contact with the other parent. See, e.g., California's "friendly parent" provision, Cal. Fam. Code § 3040(a)(1) (2014) ("the court shall consider, among other factors, which parent is more likely to allow the child frequent and continuing contact with the non-custodial parent"); Va. Code Ann. § 20-124.3(6) (2012) (directing the courts to consider, in determining the child's best interests, "[t]he propensity of each parent to actively support the child's contact and relationship with the other parent, including whether a parent has unreasonably denied the other parent access to or visitation with the child"). The usual indicia of willingness to foster post-divorce relationships between the other parent and the child include willingness to permit visitation; provide information about the child's health, education, and activities; and avoid unfounded allegations and other negative comments regarding the other parent. See, e.g., Bingham v. Bingham, 167 P.3d 14 (Wyo. 2007); Puddicombe v. Dreka, 167 P.3d 73 (Alaska 2007). The unwillingness to allow the other parent's relatives to visit with the child can also be regarded as a sign of "unfriendliness" even though other cases recognize parents as having a constitutional right to deference with respect to such issues. See Nancy M. v. John M., 308 P.3d 1130 (Alaska 2013).

In *Miller*, the New Hampshire Supreme Court chided the trial court for its failure to cite the state's "friendly parent" statute and to apply "the statutory factors to the specific facts" of the case. How would you expect the trial court to rule on remand? If the court wished to keep its previous parenting plan in place, would you recommend that the court make additional findings?

2. False charges of spousal or child abuse are perhaps the most dramatic instances of bad relations between parents, and they pose a particularly intense

dilemma for the courts and the parents. Compare the approach of the trial court in *Miller* with that of a Missouri court in Holmes v. Holmes, ___ S.W.3d ___ (Mo. App. 2014). The dissent in that case observed:

> Acknowledging the deference that is due the trial court in one of the most disturbing dissolution cases that I have reviewed, I believe the trial court erred in awarding Father sole custody of the four-year-old child. I note that, at the end of the evidence, the guardian ad litem ("GAL") who represented the child suggested that a neutral therapist meet with all of the parties. That never happened. Instead, the trial court decided that Father had not sexually abused the child and, by inference, that Mother was at fault for the allegations. That decision stemmed from the work of a licensed psychologist, Dr. Frederick Nolen. Although the court claimed it "rejected other parts of the [trial] testimony as not credible" and referred to Dr. Nolen's report twice in its judgment as the "flawed report by Fred Nol[e]n . . . ," it is clear in reviewing the evidence that it was not possible to separate Dr. Nolen's influence . . . in the trial.
>
> Dr. Nolen did something that no reputable therapist would do. He stated with absolute certainty that the child's statements were false. Then, . . . he came to the conclusion that there was absolutely no possibility that Father had abused the child. That is an important conclusion and one that is disturbing. But more disturbing is the manner in which Dr. Nolen arrived at his conclusions. He reasoned that if the child's statements were false, then Mother must have been at fault for the child making the statements. Dr. Nolen indicated, in an absolutely bizarre report, that he must "rule out for factitious disorder of [Mother] in [his] report of her." As a result of his conclusions in his report to the juvenile office, the child was taken into foster care. . . .
>
> [T]he GAL addressed the new allegations being raised at trial and asked that the child be interviewed again by Dr. Ann Duncan-Hively, the purported expert in parental alienation. Mother testified that the new allegations, since January 26, 2011, are that the child said Father "still plays bad games. She says that they hurt. She says that sometimes he touches her with his tongue, sometimes he touches her with his hand, sometimes he touches her with this part. She's not—she's just showing me, she's pointing." There was no interview by Dr. Ann Duncan-Hively. Despite the overwhelming probative evidence contrary to the proposition that Mother coached the child into making allegations that she had been sexually abused by her father, the judgment awarded Father sole legal [and physical] custody. I believe the judgment is against the weight of the evidence and should not stand.

The differences between these two cases illustrate the difficult issues at the core of sexual abuse cases.

First, can sexual abuse be disproven with certainty? The overwhelmingly answer is no. In *Miller*, the court observed that none of the investigations validated the charges, but neither could they establish that the abuse had not occurred. In contrast, in *Holmes*, the court stated categorically that the abuse did not happen. These are very different conclusions. It is not unusual for there to be no physical evidence of the alleged abuse and absent that, the determination may rest on the evaluation of the child. If the child is very young (Laurel was 2 and the child in *Holmes* was 3 at the time of the initial allegations), her account of what took place may not be reliable and once the allegations have been made, investigators fear that the child's later accounts may be influenced by the investigation itself. In *Miller*, for example, the court relied on an expert report that observed that "Laurel's therapist is convinced that Laurel has been sexually abused, and may have inadvertently reinforced the abuse by making a 'book' with Laurel about her abuse." In *Miller*, this leads to a conclusion that the allegations can neither be substantiated nor disproved; in *Holmes*, the lack of proof leads to a conclusion that the abuse did not happen. Setting standards to determine whether the abuse occurred is a routine (if often contested) judicial determination. What evidence should be required to determine that abuse did not occur? What approach should a court take if it concludes, as the court did in *Miller*, that allegations of abuse can neither be substantiated nor disproved with certainty?

Second, irrespective of the strength of the corroborating evidence, the child and the custodial parent may believe the allegations. How should that affect the custodial ruling? In *Miller*, the court relies on expert testimony that "Ms. Todd, after experiencing her parent's concerns about Mr. Miller and after having experienced her own negative interactions with Mr. Miller, became increasingly convinced that Mr. Miller was harming Laurel." The court accordingly concluded both that Ms. Todd's allegations were probably false *and* that it was likely that she sincerely believed them and that the child's statements were not necessarily the product of coaching. In contrast, in *Holmes*, once the expert concluded that the abuse had not happened, he also concluded that the child's allegations were the result of coaching and the trial court stated that the mother's insistence on pursuing the unsubstantiated allegations "raise[d] questions as to her ability to properly raise the minor child." Think about how it can be simultaneously true that the abuse was unlikely to have occurred and that the custodial parent genuinely believes that it occurred. The cases suggest the following possibilities:

a. The custodial parent had negative experiences with the other parent and projects those experiences on the other parent's interactions with the child. For example, in Allen v. Farrow, 197 A.D.2d 327 (N.Y. App. Div. 1994), Mia Farrow alleged that Woody Allen abused their 7-year-old adopted daughter, Dylan. The relationship between Farrow and Allen had ended when Farrow discovered that Allen was having an affair with Soon Yi Previn, a daughter Farrow had adopted with Andre Previn. Is Woody's relationship with Soon Yi, who was an adult at the time they began their intimate relationship, relevant to the allegation that he abused 7-year-old Dylan? Is it relevant to Mia's conclusion that Woody did so?

b. The custodial parent may have psychological issues that make it more difficult for her to assess the truth of abuse allegations accurately. The experts in both *Miller* and *Holmes* reached such a conclusion. Moreover, the trial court in *Holmes* placed considerable weight on the mother's testimony that she would continue to believe her daughter's statements that she had been abused even if the factual allegations could be shown to be false. In that case, for example, the daughter gave a graphic account of how she had been abused on a trampoline. The mother acknowledged that the father had never been on the trampoline with the child, yet still asserted that she believed the child's allegations. Should this testimony affect the court's ruling on custody?

c. A parent, in the face of ambiguous or inconclusive evidence, may err on the side of protecting the child. For example, *Miller* referred to the case of Renaud v. Renaud, in which the Vermont Supreme Court concluded that the mother's initial concerns may have been warranted and she may have been justified in reporting them, but once an official investigation concluded that the allegations could not be substantiated, the mother should have dropped the issue, but she failed to do so. Is this realistic if the child is continuing to express concerns about possible abuse? What should a parent do in such circumstances?

Third, how should the court advance the best interests of the child in these cases? In *Miller*, the trial court placed considerable emphasis on the children's ties to the mother and the community in which the mother was living. Yet, the appellate court seems to suggest that if the children's ties to the mother, as opposed to the father, were the result of unfounded allegations, the court should switch custody. In *Holmes*, the trial court did precisely that, first putting the 4-year-old in foster care and then transferring custody from the mother to the father because of the mother's persistent allegations of sexual abuse. If the child bonds more closely with one parent than the other because of unfounded allegations of abuse, how should the courts evaluate the child's interests?

Fourth, how can the courts resolve individual cases without creating incentives that will negatively affect other cases? If the courts allow parents to influence custody decisions through unfounded accusations, they will create incentives to make such allegations. In *Miller*, for example, the abuse allegations were the primary basis for changing the Michigan court's temporary award of custody to the father to what eventually became an award of custody to the mother. On the other hand, once a parent reports a child's statements that indicate abuse to a doctor, teacher, or other professional, that professional is bound to report them, triggering an investigation. Should a custodial parent not report such statements, particularly if there does not seem to be evidence sufficient to corroborate a finding of abuse, for fear of undermining the child's relationship with the other parent?

Some research indicates that raising hard-to-prove allegations of child abuse increases the likelihood that the accused abuser will receive custody. *See* Joan S. Meier, Understanding Judicial Resistance and Imagining the Solutions, 11 Am. U. J. Gender Soc. Pol'y & L. 657, 677-678 (2003) (discussing, inter alia, preliminary California study finding that 90 percent of the alleged abusers received full or partial unsupervised visitation while 50 percent of the parents charging child sexual abuse received no contact or supervised visitation with the child). *See also* Joan Meier, Parental Alienation Syndrome and Parental Alienation: A Research Review, Harrisburg, PA: VAWnet, a project of the National Resource Center on Domestic Violence (2013), available at http://www.vawnet.org (last visited Dec. 19, 2013); Michele A. Adams, Framing Contests in Child Custody Disputes: Parental Alienation Syndrome, Child Abuse, Gender, and Fathers' Rights, 40 Fam. L.Q. 315 (2006).

3. Parental alienation and friendly parent provisions may be considerations in the initial award of custody, but they often arise as grounds to modify custody when two parents do not get along. In K.T.D. v. K.W.P., 119 So. 3d 418 (Ala. Civ. App. 2012), for example, the mother was 16 and the father was 21 at the child's birth. The father established paternity and received visitation when the child was 9 months old. Four years later, the parents, who could not communicate and agreed on little, both moved to modify custody, with the mother seeking to restrict the father's visitation rights and the father seeking a larger share of the child's time. Finding that the mother had shown poor judgment toward the father and his family and sought to undermine his relationship with the child, the court changed the mother's sole custody award to joint legal and physical custody of the child and provided that the child would spend approximately half of his time with the father. The dissenting judge argued that the mother's conduct might be a basis for contempt, but did not constitute the type of "changed circumstances" necessary for a modification of custody. *See also* Sharp v. Keeler, 256 S.W.3d 528 (Ark. App. 2007) (changing custody of 3-year-old from mother to father because of parental alienation).

4. Montana law makes "parenting interference" a felony. State v. Young, 174 P.3d 460 (Mont. 2007). *See* Nancy Levit, Matrimonial Torts and Crimes: An Annotated Bibliography, 19 J. Am. Acad. Matrimonial L. 117, 181 (2004) (describing criminal and civil remedies for interference with custodial rights).

5. One solution to abuse allegations is to make a therapist, rather than a custodial parent, the gatekeeper for reunification efforts with an estranged parent. In Allen v. Farrow, for example, the court conditioned Woody Allen's continued visitation rights with Dylan on participation in therapy. Dylan objected to seeing her father because of his relationship with her sister, and in a subsequent proceeding the court denied Woody's request for therapeutic visitation. Neither the court nor the therapist based the denial of visitation on the abuse allegations, relying instead on Dylan's preferences and the potential impact of visitation on her well-being. The order was upheld on appeal. Allen v. Farrow, 215 A.D.2d 137, 626 N.Y.S.2d 125 (1995). What roles did the various therapists play in *Miller*?

June Carbone, *From Partners to Parents: The Second Revolution in Family Law*

193-194 (2000)

Custody battles have become ground zero in the gender wars because they are among the few remaining family law disputes where courts judge adult behavior. . . . Maintaining parental ties is the new sine qua non of responsible parenthood — and a possible lever in the effort to exact revenge on the other spouse. The emphasis on parental cooperation then increases the importance of potentially disqualifying conduct: domestic violence, child abuse, and parental alienation carry greater significance as they become the limited exceptions to the principle of shared parenting. And, in this context, the courts still pass judgment. While neither the *Allen* nor the *Renaud* courts considered the father's infidelity to their partners, they ruled that Woody's behavior with Soon Yi . . . had harmed his children, and that Gail Renaud's baseless allegations against her faithless ex-husband were bad parenting. Custody decisions — and the connections between parents and children — hold the new moral center of family law.

PROBLEM

Michael and Renae began living together in Homer, Alaska, in April 2002. Their daughter, Ella, was born on June 22, 2003. The couple married in September 2003 but separated two years later. Upon separation, the parties were unable to reach a formal agreement on a custody schedule for Ella. At first, Ella spent two nights of each week with Michael and five nights of each week with Renae. Michael spent a substantial amount of time with Ella during the day while Renae was working. For most of the time after separation, the parties had approximately equal time with Ella during the child's waking hours.

Renae obtained permission from the trial court in April 2006 to relocate to pursue her nurse practitioner career. In June 2006 the trial court entered an interim custody order providing for shared custody while Renae was in Anchorage. Specifically, the court ordered that "[d]uring alternate weeks, the child shall be with plaintiff Michael Yourkowski from Sunday at 10:00 A.M. to Friday at 10:00 A.M." and "[d]uring the remaining period of each two-week cycle, the child shall be with defendant Renae Blanton." The order also provided that "[d]uring the time that the child is with Renae . . . , Michael . . . shall be entitled to reasonable, non-overnight visitation with the child whenever he travels to Anchorage. This shall include the right to care for the child while Renae . . . is at work." Thereafter, Michael made numerous trips to Anchorage for extra visitation. The "reasonable visitation" provision in the order caused disagreement between Renae and Michael. Michael alleges that Renae interfered with his efforts to spend time with Ella every time he came to Anchorage. Renae responds that "Michael abused his privilege of visitation by making it a point of being in Anchorage every week that Ella was with Renae" in order to "bully Renae into agreeing to a week on—week off schedule." She testified that she did not comply with Michael's requests upon advice of counsel.

After a three-day trial, the court granted Michael's motion for a change of custody, citing three factors:

- The ability and willingness to foster a good relationship between the child and the other parent, finding that "Ms. Blanton is consistently unwilling to foster a good relationship between the father and the child, and does so by attempting to limit his time with the child and frustrating his efforts to see the child."
- The ability to meet Ella's needs, observing that "Michael would be able to take care of Ella most of the time, 'rather than relying on babysitters,' while Renae would have to utilize childcare more often."
- The need for continuity, pointing to "Michael's long residence in Homer and the social network and supportive friends that surrounded him and Ella there."

What arguments would you make if you represented Renae in an appeal of the trial court order? How would you argue on behalf of Michael? If you were appointed as a guardian ad litem for Ella, how would you approach the determination of the child's best interests?

C. VISITATION AND ITS ENFORCEMENT

MORGAN V. FORETICH

546 A.2d 407 (D.C. Cir. 1988)

STEADMAN, J. The formal parties to this appeal are the divorced parents of a daughter, H, the ultimate real party in interest. She was born in 1982. On November 8, 1984, appellant Morgan was awarded custody of H and appellee Foretich was given liberal visitation. Almost continuously since that date, the parties have been in litigation on these issues. . . . Now before us is an appeal from an order of August 19, 1987, granting Foretich a two-week summer visitation with *H* and a subsequent order of civil contempt and imprisonment of Morgan for refusal to comply with the August 19 order.

. . . In January 1985, within two months of the custody and visitation order of November 8, 1984, Morgan began to make accusations that Foretich was sexually abusing *H* during visitation. . . .

Matters first came to a head in February 1986, when Morgan refused to allow *H* to visit Foretich in accordance with the court-ordered visitation schedule. Hearings were held in June and July of 1986 on several motions, including Foretich's motions to hold Morgan in contempt and for change of custody and Morgan's motions for temporary suspension of visitation and to compel discovery. On July 17, 1986, Judge Dixon orally announced his finding that Morgan had failed to prove by a preponderance of the evidence that Foretich had abused *H*, and that Morgan had disobeyed the visitation orders without lawful justification or excuse. A series of further hearings and orders then ensued, resulting in a finding of contempt and order of incarceration in August 1986. . . . On appeal, we upheld the closure of the contempt hearings and affirmed the judgment of contempt.

Meanwhile, Judge Dixon had ordered that visitation be resumed. When Morgan again failed to comply, Judge Dixon found her in contempt and ordered her incarcerated on February 17, 1987. Morgan was released from jail on February 19, 1987, and on February 24, 1987, visitations resumed for the first time in over a year. From February 24 through April 1, 1987, the visits were supervised and lasted one hour. On April 1, Judge Dixon ordered that the visits be extended to four hours.

On April 6, 1987, Judge Dixon began a series of hearings on a motion by Foretich for a change of custody and termination of Morgan's parental rights and on Morgan's cross motion to suspend visitation, or, in the alternative, to require supervised visitation. . . .

During the course of the hearings on the motions, Judge Dixon entered several orders continuing to gradually expand the visitation schedule. On April 21, 1987, he ordered the first overnight unsupervised weekend visitations. Pursuant to further orders, *H* spent nine or ten weekends with Foretich. Several emergency stays of the weekend visitation orders sought by Morgan and *H*'s guardian were denied by this court. *H*'s guardian played some part in most of these weekend visits and submitted reports of her observations to Judge Dixon.

Then on August 19, 1987, with the hearings still not completed, Judge Dixon entered an order providing for an extended visitation from August 22 through September 6, 1987. In his six-page order, he noted, inter alia, that since *H* was scheduled to return to school on September 8, "[w]hatever the court's ultimate ruling may be on the pending motions, to further delay the defendant-father's entitlement to summer visitation with his child until that ultimate ruling results in a denial of said summer visitation by default."

Morgan appealed this visitation order that same day. Her emergency motion for stay pending appeal filed the following day was denied by this court on August 21. Morgan failed to comply with the visitation order. She secreted the child and refused to reveal her whereabouts. (To this day, *H* remains hidden.) On August 24, Judge Dixon issued an order to show cause why Morgan should not be held in contempt. . . .

After a hearing held on August 26, Judge Dixon held Morgan in contempt and ordered her incarcerated, effective August 28. He also ordered that the security posted one year earlier pursuant to this court's order be forfeited at the rate of $5,000 per day. On August 27, Morgan appealed the contempt judgment and sought a stay pending appeal. The stay was denied and Morgan was incarcerated on August 28, where she remains.

A principal issue before us is whether the record supports the trial court's action in ordering a two-week summer visitation. Our standard of review is well established. Trial court decisions as to visitation rights are reversible only for clear abuse of discretion. . . . [A] trial court judgment may not be set aside except for errors of law, unless it appears the judgment is "plainly wrong or without evidence to support it." Thus, to the extent that such decisions rest on factual foundations, such findings are binding unless clearly erroneous. Such is particularly the case where, as here, the findings rest in significant part on considerations of credibility. . . .

The critical factual determination challenged by Morgan was that sexual abuse of *H* by her father had not been proven, or, as the court put it, the evidence was "in equipoise." That finding, asserts Morgan, was "plainly wrong." . . .

A review of the record shows that there was probative evidence on both sides of the issue of abuse. The ultimate question, however, is not how we weigh the evidence but rather whether a finder of fact, fully and personally knowledgeable of not only the evidence presented in the April to August hearings but also the entire history of these proceedings from November 1985 forward, would be clearly erroneous in concluding that the alleged sexual abuse had not been proven and would commit a clear abuse of discretion in allowing a two-week visitation. We cannot so conclude. . . .

In this litigation, neither party can conclusively speak for *H*. She has her own champion, a court-appointed guardian. Although the guardian states that she is in clear disagreement with the trial court's order for the extended summer visitation, we think correct her assessment that she "cannot argue that the order was without evidence to support it or an abuse of Judge Dixon's discretion." . . .

Probably neither our courts nor any courts anywhere in the world can deal in a perfect way with matters so intimately linked to a family unit formed and dissolved. We can but try. The little girl *H* grows older day by day. It is she, first and foremost, to whom the courts must seek to render justice as the process moves on.

. . . [T]he orders appealed from are affirmed.

NOTES AND QUESTIONS

1. An empirical study of abuse allegations found that fewer than half are substantiated. It also found that while mothers were more likely to allege abuse, the proportion of the allegations that could be substantiated were about the same for men and women. Janet R. Johnston et al., Allegations and Substantiations of Abuse in Custody-Disputing Families, 43 Fam. Ct. Rev. 283, 286 (2005).

What options did the court have in *Morgan* in the absence of proof by a preponderance of the evidence that abuse had occurred? The *Morgan* court held that the evidence was "in equipoise," which presumably means that it was equally likely that the abuse did or did not occur. Under these circumstances, could the court take the possibility into account that abuse might be occurring? Could it take into account the child's alienation from her father or the hostility between the parents?

In Volodarsky v. Tarachanskaya, 916 A.2d 991 (Md. App. 2007), a 3-year-old girl testified in such graphic sexual detail that the court concluded that, at the very least, she had been exposed to sexual material. One expert testified that it was likely that her father had abused her, that ongoing contact between daughter and father would be "psychologically and potentially physically dangerous to the child," and that the child suffered from post-traumatic stress disorder and would protest any visitation with her father. The second expert concluded that sexual abuse had not occurred; the child feared losing her mother and had discovered that sexual abuse allegations elicited a strong response. The court concluded that the abuse allegations had not been substantiated. The intermediate court of appeals reversed, holding that the governing statute required only "reasonable grounds to believe" that abuse had occurred. The Maryland Court of Appeals reversed, concluding that the reference to "reasonable ground to believe" abuse had occurred still required a preponderance of the evidence to restrict custody. The result, however, was to affirm the trial court opinion, in which the judge:

> recognized that she was dealing with a child who, at the time, was totally alienated from her father, which constituted a change in circumstances since the last (2004) custody order. Given that the parents were unable to communicate or reach shared decisions, joint custody was not an option. The court therefore entered an order placing Greta in the legal and physical custody of Kira, requiring Greta to continue in regular therapy with a goal of providing a plan to repair the damage to her relationship with Mikhail, requiring both parents to participate in counseling to reduce parental conflict, and precluding visitation with Mikhail other than in a therapeutic setting.

Id. at 998. Would such an order have been appropriate in Morgan? Is this result similar to the order in Allen v. Farrow, in which the court did not find that abuse had occurred, but restricted visitation in light of the trauma to the children?

2. What weight should trial judges give to the child's expressed preference regarding visitation? Should that preference be given more weight than in the determination of custody, or less weight? Although interference with visitation often is attributed to hostile custodial parents, children themselves may be unwilling to cooperate in visitation arrangements. A study of 59 children between the ages of 5 and 12 in Toronto, Ontario, who were involved in custody or visitation disputes reports that some 60 percent of the children held generally negative attitudes toward visitation, but only 10 percent completely refused to see a parent. Older children more often held negative attitudes toward visitation, and a history of parental violence was often present. Negative feelings were related to the quality of their own interactions with the parents (such as punitive or restrictive parenting) and to negative personality traits they associated with parents (lying, selfishness). Since the sample for this study came from high-conflict families, it is quite plausible that attitudes were influenced by stories from the custodial parent or by interparental behavior. Helen Radovanovic et al., Child and Family Characteristics

of Children's Post-Separation Visitation Refusal, 25 J. Psychiatry & L. 33 (1997). *See also* Benjamin D. Garber, Conceptualizing Visitation Resistance and Refusal in the Context of Parental Conflict, Separation, and Divorce, 45 Fam. Ct. Rev. 588 (2007). Courts, however, hold custodial parents responsible for failure to comply with a visitation order even when the child is older and does not want to see the other parent. Sisk v. Sisk, 711 N.W.2d 203 (N.D. 2006).

What do you think would have happened in *Morgan* if the court had conditioned the father's visitation on both parties' cooperation with therapy and the therapist's conclusion that the child was ready to accept renewed visitation? In the case of Eric Foretich's older daughter by another woman, who had also alleged that her father abused her, the therapist opposed reestablishing regular visitation for several years. As the child became old enough to form her own opinions, she became adamant that she did not want to reestablish contact with her father, and the Virginia court with jurisdiction over that case deferred to her views.

3. If, as in the *Morgan* case, the court believes that one or both of the parents may leave the country, how should the court respond? In Sutton v. Flores, 2010 WL 2006243 (Ariz. Ct. App. 2010), Flores, a Mexican citizen, sought a restraining order against Sutton when the child was a few months old, and then left Arizona for Mexico, taking the child with her. Sutton filed a paternity action in Arizona and when the mother did not respond, he received a default order establishing his paternity and awarding him custody. Sutton and Flores attempted to reconcile five years later and Flores and the child, who had not seen her father during most of the intervening five years, returned to Arizona. When the reconciliation failed, Flores attempted to return to Mexico with the child, but could not do so because of the earlier custody ruling. During the period the child lived with Sutton, he had traveled to Australia with her, but the court confiscated the child's passport in order to prevent him from leaving without the permission of the court. In a de novo custody proceeding, the court vacated the earlier default order, but then issued a new order again awarding the father custody, finding that Sutton was the parent whose travel with the child "the court could most control." The court awarded Flores supervised parenting time.

What argument would you make in an appeal of this case? Are there other measures the court could have taken to prevent Flores from taking the child to Mexico? The court was particularly concerned that it could not control the child's travel with Flores because the child had dual citizenship and therefore did not need a passport to enter Mexico. Is this an appropriate basis for a custody ruling? Would the arguments in this case change if Flores were not in the United States legally?

4. Dr. Morgan arranged for her parents to take the child abroad, convinced that if the U.S. courts regained jurisdiction, they would not just insist on unsupervised visitation, but transfer custody to Dr. Foretich. *See* June Carbone & Leslie J. Harris, Family Law Armageddon: The Story of Morgan v. Foretich, *in* Family Law Stories (Carol Sanger ed., 2007). Indeed, that is the almost inevitable result in a case in which parents have fled with their children in order to prevent court-ordered visitation. *See, e.g.,* D.C. v. D.C., 988 So. 2d 359 (Miss. 2008).

In Schultz v. Schultz, 187 P.3d 1234 (Idaho 2008), however, the Idaho Supreme Court reversed a lower court order requiring that the mother return from Oregon, where she had fled to following a domestic violence incident, or else surrender custody of the daughter. The mother fled immediately following a physical assault and sought and obtained a restraining order against the father, who eventually pled guilty to criminal charges. After she left, the husband filed for divorce and received an order granting supervised visitation. The mother, however, refused to return from Oregon, and the trial court granted the father's petition requiring the mother to return to Idaho or relinquish custody of the child. The Idaho Supreme Court reversed on the ground that the trial court had not made specific findings about the child's best interest.

5. Could custodial parents be granted a necessity defense in contempt proceedings such as Morgan v. Foretich when they believe in good faith that violating the court order is necessary to protect a child from further harm? Susan B. Apel, Custodial Parents, Child Sexual Abuse, and the Legal System: Beyond Contempt, 38 Am. U. L. Rev. 491 (1989). The Ohio courts have recognized such a defense if the custodial parent has "a reasonable, good faith belief that she must deny visitation to protect the safety of the child." See McClead v. McClead, 2007 Ohio 4624; cf. Morehard v. Snider, 2009 Ohio 5674 (Ohio App. 2009) (overturning grant of unsupervised visitation to alleged abuser but upholding contempt conviction for mother's failure to comply with visitation order).

Would recognition of such a defense have made any difference in the *Morgan* case?

6. The court in *Morgan* used the contempt sanction in an effort to secure compliance with its visitation order. Dr. Morgan remained in jail for just over two years and was released only when President George H. W. Bush signed a bill limiting the period of incarceration for contempt to one year. Congress passed the bill expressly to deal with Elizabeth Morgan's situation.

Eric Foretich continued to search for Hilary (i.e., *H*). He finally located her in New Zealand, living with her maternal grandparents, and sought custodial rights there. However, the New Zealand courts ruled that it was in Hilary's best interest to remain with her grandparents rather than being put in the custody of a father she feared and had not seen in two years.

In September 1996, Congress passed the Elizabeth Morgan Act, which allowed Dr. Morgan to return with Hilary to the United States without being subject to the outstanding visitation order, and without the possibility of a new order being entered without Hilary's consent. In December 2003, the Act was declared to be an unconstitutional bill of attainder that applied to only one person. By then, however, Hilary had reached the age of majority. See Foretich v. United States, 351 F.3d 1198 (2003). (For a fuller account of Hilary's flight to New Zealand and the aftermath of the trial, *see* Carbone and Harris, above.)

Was Congress right to intervene in this case at any time? Is there some sanction other than incarceration that might have been effective in dealing with Morgan's refusal to comply with the court order? What should the system do if the child herself refuses to participate in court-ordered visitation? For a review of the use of contempt sanctions in the context of custody and visitation disputes, *see* Margaret M. Mahoney, The Enforcement of Child Custody Orders by Contempt Remedies, 68 U. Pitt. L. Rev. 835 (2007).

7. Dr. Morgan's father had been in the OSS (the forerunner to the CIA) during World War II, and he orchestrated the departure from Virginia of himself,

his wife, and Hilary. The family traveled on their own passports, largely using their own names. Carbone and Harris, above. Such a flight would be harder today. A much larger number of countries, including the United States (1988) and New Zealand (1991), have ratified the Hague Convention on International Child Abduction. Had the convention been in effect between New Zealand and the United States when Dr. Foretich discovered that his daughter was in New Zealand, he could have sought her return to Washington, D.C., and New Zealand would have been obliged to comply with the request unless it concluded that the United States was no longer Hilary's "habitual residence" or that there was a grave risk of harm if she were returned. Linda Silberman, Interpreting the Hague Abduction Convention: In Search of a Global Jurisprudence, 38 U.C. Davis L. Rev. 1049, 1053-1057 (2005). Moreover, in 1993 Congress passed the International Parental Kidnapping Crime Act, which makes it a federal offense wrongfully to take a child outside of the United States. If the Act had been in effect when Morgan's parents took Hilary to New Zealand, they could have been prosecuted upon their return, whether or not New Zealand recognized the Hague Convention. Deborah M. Zawadzki, Note, The Role of Courts in Preventing International Child Abduction, 13 Cardozo J. Int'l & Comp. L. 353, 360-361 (2005); Catherine F. Klein, Leslye E. Orloff & Hema Sarangapani, Border Crossings: Understanding the Civil, Criminal and Immigration Implications for Battered Women Fleeing Across State Lines with Their Children, 39 Fam. L.Q. 109, 110-111 (2005). In addition, the U.S. State Department has tightened passport controls; minors under 14 must apply for a passport in person, and issuance may be conditioned on both parents' consent. The airlines have also become stricter about allowing children to travel without both parents' consent.

<h2 style="text-align:center">BURGESS v. BURGESS</h2>

913 P.2d 473 (Cal. 1996)

MOSK, Justice. . . . Paul D. Burgess (hereafter the father) and Wendy A. Burgess (hereafter the mother), were married and had two children, Paul and Jessica. Both parents were employed by the State Department of Corrections at the state prison in Tehachapi and owned a home in a suburb. They separated in May 1992, when the children were four and three years old. The mother moved with the children to an apartment in Tehachapi; the father remained in their former home, pending sale of the property. The mother petitioned for dissolution shortly thereafter.

In July 1992, the trial court entered a "Stipulation and Order" dissolving the marriage and providing for temporary custody and visitation in accordance with a mediation agreement between the parties. The parents agreed that they "shall share joint legal custody of the children. The mother shall have sole physical custody of the children."

The mediation agreement expressly identified as "[a]t [i]ssue" the visitation schedule for the father "if the mother leaves Kern County." The parents agreed to a detailed schedule for weekly visitation by the father, as well as an alternative schedule for biweekly weekend visitation, depending on his work schedule.

At a hearing concerning custody in February 1993, the mother testified that she had accepted a job transfer to Lancaster and planned to relocate after her son's graduation from preschool in June. She explained that the move was "career advancing" and would permit greater access for the children to medical care, extracurricular activities, and private schools and day-care facilities. The travel time between Lancaster and her home in Tehachapi was approximately 40 minutes. The father testified that he would not be able to maintain his current visitation schedule if the children moved to Lancaster; he wanted to be their primary caretaker if the mother relocated.

The trial court issued a ruling providing that the father and the mother would share joint legal custody, with the mother to have sole physical custody. It retained the present visitation schedule, but provided that after June 1993, "the father will have visitation with the children, assuming the wife moves to Lancaster, on alternate weekends . . . with at least one three hour midweek visitation. . . ."

The father moved for reconsideration and for a change in custody. . . .

In July 1993, the trial court denied the motion for reconsideration. . . . Shortly thereafter, it held a hearing on the motion for change in custody. . . . [The father] again testified that if his children relocated with the mother he would not be able to maintain his current visitation schedule; he sought a custody arrangement under which each parent would have the children for "[a]bout a month and a half." He also testified that he regularly traveled to Lancaster on alternate weekends, to shop and visit friends; he characterized the trip to Lancaster from his home as "an easy commute."

The mother testified that she had been working in Lancaster for four months and planned to move there. She identified several advantages to the children to living in Lancaster, including proximity to medical care and increased opportunities to participate in extracurricular activities. She also testified that the father objected to her move, at least in part, in order to retain control of her and the children. To her understanding, he did not want to change his work shift "because it keeps me in Tehachapi." She expressed her willingness to accommodate weekend visitation with the father as well as extended visitation in the summers.

In August 1993, the trial court issued an order on custody and visitation to the following effect. "The court finds that it is in the best interest of the minor children that the minors be permitted to move to Lancaster with the petitioner and that respondent be afforded liberal visitation. Due to the complexity of the work schedules of both of the parties, who are employed by the California Department of Corrections, the court requests that a four-way meeting be held by the parties within ten days from the date of this order to work out a mutually agreed upon visitation schedule. In the event that such a schedule cannot be worked out, then the parties are to attend mediation. The court suggests that during the summertimes and if school is on a year round basis, that respondent father be provided with 'large block of time' visitations."

The father appealed from both the order denying reconsideration and the order denying change in custody; the appeals were consolidated.

The Court of Appeal reversed. . . .

. . . In an initial custody determination, the trial court has "the widest discretion to choose a parenting plan that is in the best interest of the child. . . ."

In addition, in a matter involving immediate or eventual relocation by one or both parents, the trial court must take into account the presumptive right of a custodial parent to change the residence of the minor children, so long as the removal would not be prejudicial to their rights or welfare. (Fam. Code, §7501 ["A parent entitled to custody of a child has a right to change the residence of the child, subject to the power of the court to restrain a removal that would prejudice the rights or welfare of the child."].) Accordingly, in considering all the circumstances affecting the "best interest" of minor children, it may consider any effects of such relocation on their rights or welfare. . . .

No abuse of discretion appears. After extensive testimony from both parents, the trial court not unreasonably concluded that it was in the "best interest" of the minor children that the father and the mother retain joint legal custody and that the mother retain sole physical custody, even if she moved to Lancaster.

The trial court's order was supported by substantial evidence concerning the "best interest" of the minor children. First, and most important, although they had almost daily contact with both parents during the initial period after the separation, the minor children had been in the sole physical custody of the mother for over a year at the time the trial court issued its order concerning permanent custody. Although they saw their father regularly, their mother was, by parental stipulation and as a factual matter, their primary caretaker. As we have repeatedly emphasized, the paramount need for continuity and stability in custody arrangements—and the harm that may result from disruption of established patterns of care and emotional bonds with the primary caretaker—weigh heavily in favor of maintaining ongoing custody arrangements (Burchard v. Garay, supra, 42 Cal. 3d at p. 541, 229 Cal. Rptr. 800, 724 P.2d 486).

From the outset, the mother had expressed her intention to relocate to Lancaster. The reason for the move was employment related; the mother evinced no intention to frustrate the father's contact with the minor children. Moreover, despite the fact that the move was, as the Court of Appeal observed, primarily for the mother's "convenience," her proximity to her place of employment and to the children during the workday would clearly benefit the children as well. A reduced commute would permit increased and more leisurely daily contact between the children and their primary caretaker. It would also facilitate the children's participation, with their mother, in extracurricular activities. In the event of illness or emergency, the children could more promptly be picked up and treated, if appropriate, at their regular medical facility, which was also located in Lancaster.

Although it would be more convenient for the father to maintain a daily visitation routine with the children if they remained in Tehachapi, he would still, even under his present work schedule, be able to visit them regularly and often. The trial court's order of "liberal visitation" included overnight visits on alternative weekends and additional weekday visits each month. The father conceded that he regularly traveled to Lancaster and that he considered it an "easy commute." . . .

The Court of Appeal concluded that the trial court abused its discretion in ordering that the mother should retain physical custody, on the ground that her relocation to Lancaster was not "necessary. . . ."

. . . The Court of Appeal relied on Family Code section 3020: "The Legislature finds and declares that it is the public policy of this state to assure minor children frequent and continuing contact with both parents after the parents have separated or dissolved their marriage, and to encourage parents to share the rights and responsibilities of child rearing in order to effect this policy, except where the contact would not be in the best interest of the child, as provided in [Family Code] [s]ection 3011." . . .

The Family Code specifically refrains from establishing a preference or presumption in favor of any arrangement for custody and visitation. Thus, Family Code section 3040, subdivision (b), provides: "This section establishes neither a preference nor a presumption for or against joint legal custody, joint physical custody, or sole custody, but allows the court and the family the widest discretion to choose a parenting plan that is in the best interest of the child." Similarly, although Family Code section 3020 refers to "frequent and continuous contact," it does not purport to define the phrase "frequent and continuous" or to specify a preference for any particular form of "contact." Nor does it include any specific means of effecting the policy, apart from "encourag[ing] parents to share the rights and responsibilities of child rearing."

Moreover, construing Family Code section 3020 by implication to impose an additional burden of proof on a parent seeking to relocate would abrogate the presumptive right of a custodial parent to change the residence of the minor child. It has long been established that . . . the "general rule [is that] a parent having child custody is entitled to change residence unless the move is detrimental to the child."

As this case demonstrates, ours is an increasingly mobile society. Amici curiae point out that approximately one American in five changes residences each year. Economic necessity and remarriage account for the bulk of relocations. Because of the ordinary needs for both parents after a marital dissolution to secure or retain employment, pursue educational or career opportunities, or reside in the same location as a new spouse or other family or friends, it is unrealistic to assume that divorced parents will permanently remain in the same location after dissolution or to exert pressure on them to do so. It would also undermine the interest in minimizing costly litigation over custody and require the trial courts to "micromanage" family decisionmaking by second-guessing reasons for everyday decisions about career and family.

More fundamentally, the "necessity" of relocating frequently has little, if any, substantive bearing on the suitability of a parent to retain the role of a custodial parent. A parent who has been the primary caretaker for minor children is ordinarily no less capable of maintaining the responsibilities and obligations of parenting simply by virtue of a reasonable decision to change his or her geographical location.[2]

---

2. An obvious exception is a custodial parent's decision to relocate simply to frustrate the noncustodial parent's contact with the minor children. "Conduct by a custodial parent designed to frustrate visitation and communication may be grounds for changing custody." (Burchard v. Garay, supra, 42 Cal. 3d at p. 540, fn. 11, 229 Cal. Rptr. 800, 724 P.2d 486; In re Marriage of Ciganovich, supra, 61 Cal. App. 3d at p. 294, 132 Cal. Rptr. 261 ["a custodial parent's attempt to frustrate the court's order has a bearing upon the fitness of that parent"].)

Accordingly, we decline to interpret Family Code section 3020, in the absence of express statutory language, to impose a burden of proof on a parent seeking to relocate with the minor children to establish "necessity." . . .

Although this matter involved an initial order of custody and visitation, the same conclusion applies when a parent who has sole physical custody under an existing judicial custody order seeks to relocate: the custodial parent seeking to relocate, like the noncustodial parent doing the same, bears no burden of demonstrating that the move is "necessary."

Ordinarily, after a judicial custody determination, the noncustodial parent seeking to alter the order for legal and physical custody can do so only on a showing that there has been a substantial change of circumstances so affecting the minor child that modification is essential to the child's welfare. . . .

We conclude that the same allocation of the burden of persuasion applies in the case of a custodial parent's relocation as in any other proceeding to alter existing custody arrangements: "[I]n view of the child's interest in stable custodial and emotional ties, custody lawfully acquired and maintained for a significant period will have the effect of compelling the noncustodial parent to assume the burden of persuading the trier of fact that a change [in custody] is in the child's best interests." Similarly, the same standard of proof applies in a motion for change in custody based on the custodial parent's decision to relocate with the minor children as in any other matter involving changed circumstances: "[O]nce it has been established [under a judicial custody decision] that a particular custodial arrangement is in the best interests of the child, the court need not reexamine that question. Instead, it should preserve the established mode of custody unless some significant change in circumstances indicates that a different arrangement would be in the child's best interest."

The showing required is substantial. We have previously held that a child should not be removed from prior custody of one parent and given to the other "unless the material facts and circumstances occurring subsequently are of a kind to render it essential or expedient for the welfare of the child that there be a change." In a "move-away" case, a change of custody is not justified simply because the custodial parent has chosen, for any sound good faith reason, to reside in a different location, but only if, as a result of relocation with that parent, the child will suffer determent rendering it "essential or expedient for the welfare of the child that there be a change."

This construction is consistent with the presumptive "right" of a parent entitled to custody to change the residence of his or her minor children, unless such removal would result in "prejudice" to their "rights or welfare." The dispositive issue is, accordingly, not whether relocating is itself "essential or expedient" either for the welfare of the custodial parent or the child, but whether a change in custody is "essential or expedient for the welfare of the child."

At the same time, we recognize that bright line rules in this area are inappropriate: each case must be evaluated on its own unique facts. Although the interests of a minor child in the continuity and permanency of custodial placement with the primary caretaker will most often prevail, the trial court, in assessing "prejudice" to the child's welfare as a result of relocating even a distance of 40 or 50 miles, may take into consideration the nature of the child's existing contact with both parents — including de facto as well as de jure custody arrangements — and the child's age, community ties, and health and educational needs. Where appropriate, it must also take into account the preferences of the child. . . .

For the reasons discussed, we reverse the judgment of the Court of Appeal.

NOTES AND QUESTIONS

1. Limitations on movement, especially interstate movement, by a custodial parent to protect custodial rights present obvious federal and state constitutional issues. The Indiana Supreme Court summarized the various views, observing that

[n]o Supreme Court case has addressed the interaction between a parent's right to travel and a child custody order, but several state courts have considered how [the constitutional right to travel recognized in Shapiro v. Thompson, 394 U.S. 618, 629, 631 (1969),] applies in the child custody context. One state reads *Shapiro* as weighing the scale in favor of the parent's right to travel. Others view the child's best interests as trumping the parent's right to travel. And yet others balance the relocating parent's right to travel with two other important interests — the best interests of the child and the nonrelocating parent's interest in the care and control of the child. We agree with those courts that take *Shapiro* as recognizing that a chilling effect on travel can violate the federal Constitution, but also acknowledging that other considerations may outweigh an individual's interest in travel. We think it clear that the child's interests are powerful countervailing considerations that cannot be swept aside as irrelevant in the face of a parent's claimed right to relocate. In addition, it is well established that the nonrelocating parent's interest in parenting is itself of constitutional dimension. In short, we agree with the recent well-reasoned opinion of the Colorado Supreme Court that the trial court is to balance these considerations.

Baxendale v. Raich, 878 N.E.2d 1252, 1250 (Ind. 2008). The mother in the *Baxendale* case was a lawyer who had been laid off. After a year of searching for new employment, she found a job in Minneapolis and proposed to move from Valparaiso, Indiana, an area near Chicago. She argued that if the move were not approved, she would be unable to take out-of-state employment "for fear that the state will take her child." The court, however, held that under the terms of the final custody order, which transferred custody to the father if the mother moved, the mother still retained significant involvement with the child through visitation and joint legal custody. *Cf.* Ferrante v. Geisler, 915 N.E.2d 568 (Ind. App. 2009) (unpublished/noncitable) (permitting a custodial father to move in order to take advantage of better job opportunities, but providing the mother with additional time with the children).

The courts do not ordinarily rule on whether the parents can move. Usually, the issue arises when a custodial parent wishes to relocate, and the noncustodial parent seeks to change custody on the basis of the move. The *Baxendale* opinion is typical in treating the issue as one involving custody modification, not permission to travel, but many custodial parents will not move if the result is to transfer custody to the other parent. Does the court's framing of the issue affect its resolution of the constitutional issue?

Compare the approach of the Wyoming Supreme Court in Testerman v. Testerman, 193 P.3d 1141 (Wyo. 2008). The trial court in that case found that the mother was the primary caretaker, the father had relatively little involvement with the child, and the parties did not communicate well or cooperate in the child's upbringing. The mother wished to return to California, where she had family and had lined up employment. The trial court thought that the move would effectively end the father's involvement with the child, and it included a provision in the parenting plan indicating that relocation would trigger consideration of a change in custody. The Supreme Court reversed that provision, observing that

> [i]t is unrealistic to assume that divorced parents will remain in the same location after dissolution of the marriage *or to exert pressure on them to do so.* The "parenting plan" imposed by the district court did exert pressure on Ms. Testerman to remain in the same location. It was meant to do so. This was an improper restraint on Ms. Tester-man's protected constitutional rights.

Id. at 1146. Which approach do you prefer? How do you think the Wyoming court would respond to an argument by the father that his constitutional rights would be undermined by the failure to consider the move to be a change in circumstances?

2. In the original *Burgess* decision, the move was only 40 miles and within the state. Subsequent cases suggest that where the move involves longer distances that will necessarily alter the children's relationship with the noncustodial parent, the courts may engage in more searching review. In re Marriage of Condon, 73 Cal. Rptr. 2d 33 (Cal. App. 1998), involved a mother's desire to take her two sons back to her native Australia. The court noted that allowing relocation to a foreign country, given the problems of distance, cost, cultural differences, and the difficulties of enforcing visitation rights, would often effectively raise problems distinct from problems raised by interstate and intrastate moves, including introduction to cultural conditions far different from those experienced in this country and the greater distance and associated additional, perhaps prohibitive, costs of visitation ordinarily implicated by international relocation. A third concern is the difficulty of enforcing local custody and visitation orders in a foreign country. The appellate court considered this case to test the outer limits of the *Burgess* principle allowing relocation absent a showing that the move was inconsistent with the child's best interest, and suggested that in foreign relocation cases, the court should ordinarily consider such a move a termination of visitation rights and require a showing by the relocating parent that termination would be in the child's best interests. It also suggested the importance of flexibility and imagination in devising ways to deal with the various problems of international relocation.

The California Supreme Court revisited the move-away issue more generally in In re Marriage of LaMusga, 88 P.3d 81 (Cal. 2004), a case that involved a cross-country move and the conclusion that relocation would undermine the children's tenuous relationship with their father. In *LaMusga*, the court rejected the conclusion that a custodial parent with "a good faith reason to move . . . cannot be prevented directly or indirectly, from exercising his or her right to change the child residence" absent a "substantial showing" by the noncustodial parent that a change of custody is "essential" to prevent detriment to the child. Instead, the court indicated that a "noncustodial parent opposing such a change of residence bears the initial burden of showing that the move will cause some detriment to the children." Once this showing of detriment has been made, the trial court must then "weigh the likely effects on the child's welfare from moving with the custodial parent, against the likely effects from a change in custody" in accordance with a best interest analysis. While many courts have concluded that the move itself cannot be the factor constituting detriment, the *LaMusga* court permitted consideration of the impact of the move on the relationship with the noncustodial parent as the principal factor establishing detriment in the case. The *LaMusga* court, in otherwise restraining too great a deference to the custodial parent's decision to move, cited *Condon* with approval.

3. With the increase in divorce rates and a more mobile society, the courts found themselves addressing moves more frequently. *Burgess* was one of a number of decisions to reconsider what has been judicial hostility to moves and to make it easier for custodial parents, overwhelmingly mothers, to move. Since then, joint or shared custody orders have become significantly more common. Does the *Burgess* standard depend on whether the moving parent has sole or joint physical custody? The *Burgess* court observed in footnote 12:

> A different analysis may be required when parents share joint physical custody of the minor children under an existing order and in fact, and one parent seeks to relocate with the minor children. In such cases, the custody order "may be modified or terminated upon the petition of one or both parents or on the court's own motion if it is shown that the best interest of the child requires modification or termination of the order." . . . The trial court must determine de novo what arrangement for primary custody is in the best interest of the minor children.

Cf. Maynard v. McNett, 710 N.W.2d 369 (N.D. 2006) (parent with joint legal and physical custody may not be granted permission to relocate with the parties' child unless the trial court first determines that the best interests of the child require an award of primary custody to that parent); Singletary v. Singletary, ____ S.W.3d ____ (Ark. 2013) (where court order specified that mother and father would have "joint custody," but named the mother as the "primary physical custodian," the appellate court affirmed a trial court ruling that the order, which gave each parent approximately equal time with the child, was a joint custody award and therefore the mother's proposed move from Arkansas to Texas with her new husband constituted "changed circumstances" that justified a change in custody to the father).

4. The states vary considerably in the standards they apply to parental moves, irrespective of the nature of the custody award. *Burgess* is one of a number of state appellate decisions to reconsider that presumption in light of increasing societal mobility and the disproportionate impact on women, who are more likely to be custodial parents. Professor Linda Elrod places the current state approaches to postdivorce relocation into three categories:

> 1. Relocation alone is not a change. These states find that a proposed relocation alone is not a change in circumstances, resulting in a presumption in favor of relocation by the custodial or residential parent.
> 2. Relocation is a sufficient change for a hearing. . . . If a hearing is held, the court may use shifting presumptions so the residential parent has the initial burden to show that the move is in good faith and is in the child's best interest; the burden then shifts to the nonresidential parent to show the move is not in the child's best interests.

3. Relocation may be a change of circumstances, but both parents bear the burden of proving the child's best interests. A move may be a change of circumstances, but the court uses no presumptions. Each party bears the burden of showing why being with him or her is in the child's best interests.

Linda D. Elrod, States Differ on Relocation: A Panorama of Expanding Case Law, Fam. Advoc., Spring 2006, at 8. How would you characterize *Burgess* in accordance with these categories? *LaMusga*? Would the significance of sole or joint physical custody vary with each standard?

5. A comprehensive review of law and policy concerning relocation appears in Carol S. Bruch & Janet M. Bowermaster, The Relocation of Children and Custodial Parents: Public Policy, Past and Present, 30 Fam. L.Q. 245 (1996). For evaluation of the empirical research on moves, *compare* Carol S. Bruch, Sound Research or Wishful Thinking in Child Custody Cases? Lessons from Relocation Law, 40 Fam. L.Q. 281, 291-312 (2006) (emphasizing the importance of continuity of care and the potential negative impact of changes in custody), *with* William G. Austin, Effects of Residential Mobility on Children of Divorce, 46 Fam. Ct. Rev. 137 (2008), and William G. Austin, Relocation, Research, and Forensic Evaluation, Part II: Research in Support of the Relocation Risk Assessment Model, 46 Fam. Ct. Rev. 347 (2008) (emphasizing the importance of stability and the potential negative impact of relocations). The dissent in *LaMusga* observed:

> Here, the trial court's explanation for its ruling shows that it properly considered how relocation to Ohio might detrimentally affect the children — including the impact on their tenuous relationship with their father. But the trial court was also required to weigh this detriment against the detriment that would result from removing the boys from the mother's custody. This the court did not do. In its statement of reasons, the court said: "So I don't think that I have any real question as to the qualifications or competence of either parent, that is not the issue before me. *The issue is the effect on these children of relocating, and the effect of the relationship with their father if they are permitted to relocate.*" (Italics added.) But the effect of the relocation on the children's relationship with the father was not *the* issue before the court. Rather, it was just one of the potential detriments shown by the evidence that the trial court was required to consider. Equally important was the potential detriment from disrupting the existing custodial arrangement by transferring custody from the mother to the father.

In re Marriage of LaMusga, 88 P.3d 81, 102 (Cal. 2004) (Kennard, J., dissenting). Does this difference in perspectives also explain the different approaches to the empirical literature, which shows that separated parents move more than intact families and that greater residential stability benefits children?

6. Relocation cases require the courts to balance the opportunities available to one spouse from the move, which often include remarriage to an out-of-state spouse, greater family support, or increased employment opportunity, with prejudice to the noncustodial spouse's opportunity for visitation. Given that mothers are more likely to be custodial parents, the balancing issues are often framed in terms of gender equality. Professor Tom Oldham writes:

> For many custodial parents, it is very important to have the right to relocate with their minor child. For non-primary custodians, it is similarly important to have the right to

change careers, even if the change will reduce their income for a period or permanently. The trends in the law regarding relocation and income imputation are inconsistent. The prevailing view regarding relocation (and the ALI view) reflects a philosophy that the primary custodian should have substantial freedom. The lack of significant barriers to moving suggests a wish not to impede the parent's autonomy due to the fact of parenthood.

In contrast, child support rules seem to be moving in the other direction. A rule consistent with the prevailing relocation approach would give the obligor significant freedom to structure his life and career as he in good faith would choose. This rule would allow an obligor the right to have his child support obligation reduced if he made a good faith career change that reduced his income. However, most courts ignore voluntary reductions in income by an obligor, with the justification that parenthood substantially limits one's choices.

J. Thomas Oldham, Limitations Imposed by Family Law on a Separated Parent's Ability to Make Significant Life Decisions: A Comparison of Relocation and Income Imputation, 8 Duke J. Gender L. & Pol'y 333, 339-340 (2001). For a study of the impact of such rulings on mothers, *see* Patrick Parkinson & Judy Cashmore, When Mothers Stay: Adjusting to Loss After Relocation Disputes, 47 Fam. L.Q. 65 (2013). For a study of children's views, *see* Megan Gollop & Nicola J. Taylor, New Zealand Children and Young People's Perspectives on Relocation Following Parental Separation, *in* 14 Law and Childhood Studies: Current Legal Issues 219 (Michael Freeman ed., 2012).

Professor Merle Weiner responds that this analysis leaves out an important potential factor in the equation: the ability of the noncustodial spouse to move. Just as the courts now expect custodial parents to contribute financially to their children's upbringing even if they have been long-term homemakers, shouldn't the courts also consider the possibility of a parallel move in evaluating the impact on the noncustodial spouse's relationship with the child? Merle H. Weiner, Inertia and Inequality: Reconceptualizing Disputes Over Parental Relocation, 40 U.C. Davis L. Rev. 1747 (2007). Weiner observes that some cases and statutes already take the possibility into account.

7. The American Law Institute Principles of the Law of Family Dissolution note that the basic principle of awarding custody in a way reflecting the time spent by each parent in caretaking functions may be affected by a parent's relocation. Section 2.08(1)(g) provides that when this is so, the court should apply the principles of § 2.17(4), dealing with modification of an existing order. Those principles would justify an award of custody, with permission to relocate, to a parent who has been exercising a significant majority of the caretaking responsibility as long as the relocation is in good faith, for a legitimate purpose, and to a location that is reasonable in light of that purpose. Legitimate purposes for relocation include closeness to significant family or other support networks, significant health reasons, protecting the child's safety, pursuing a significant employment opportunity, and being with a spouse or partner.

If neither parent has exercised a significant majority of caretaking responsibilities, custody should be allocated according to the child's best interests in general.

PROBLEMS

1. Alma is the custodial parent for three children, ages 4, 6, and 9. She is a sales executive. Her employer has decided to close its Atlanta office, where Alma has worked for the past several years, and has offered to promote Alma to a more senior position, with a substantial raise, in San Francisco. Alma has looked and found nothing comparable to her current job in Atlanta. Her former husband, Ralph, is employed at a job that does not allow him to make lengthy trips. He is very much opposed to any arrangement that will interfere with his continuing visitation (which he has carried out faithfully). Alma plans to accept the transfer and seeks your advice regarding her custodial situation. Advise Alma what arguments she should make in opposition if Ralph seeks a change in custody in response to her plans to move, and the arguments Ralph is likely to make in response.

2. Suppose that Alma is not currently employed but has decided to enroll in law school. She has been accepted at an ABA-accredited law school in her home state of Georgia and at Stanford. Alma would greatly prefer to study at Stanford. Ralph, who has visited the children regularly, seeks an order prohibiting Alma from moving with the children to any location more than 180 miles from Atlanta. Should that order be granted?

3. In problem 2, Ralph also offers the testimony of a psychologist that the children's best interests would be served by continuing regular contact with him. Should this affect the outcome?

4. Does the availability of other relatives to assist with child care affect the result? Suppose that in problem 1, Alma grew up in the Bay Area and her sisters and their children still live there. Suppose as well that Ralph's elderly parents, who are close to the children, live in Atlanta. How might these factors affect the analysis?

BERSANI V. BERSANI

565 A.2d 1368 (Conn. 1989)

FREEDMAN, J. On October 3, 1988, the plaintiff wife instituted an action against the defendant husband for dissolution of marriage. On November 11, 1988, the court awarded custody pendente lite of the parties' two minor children to the plaintiff and specific visitation rights pendente lite to the defendant.

On March 7, 1989, under an agreement of the parties, approved by the court, the plaintiff was required to give the defendant thirty days written notice of her intent to leave the country. After a hearing on May 9, 1989, the court denied a motion filed by the plaintiff in which she sought a court order permitting her to return to Spain with the children pending the final hearing in the dissolution action.

In early June, the defendant learned that the plaintiff had moved out of the house that she was occupying with the children. The defendant sought information concerning the whereabouts of the plaintiff and the children from the plaintiff's attorney. While the plaintiff's attorney acknowledges that she possesses the requested information, she has declined to disclose it on the ground that to do so would violate her obligation to maintain confidential information imparted to her by a client.

By motion dated June 7, 1989, the defendant seeks an order to compel the plaintiff's attorney to reveal the information claiming that the attorney-client privilege must yield to assure that a judicial determination is made and enforced respecting the best interests of the children.

On June 8, 1989, the court found the plaintiff in wilful contempt, ordered her to return to Connecticut and awarded temporary custody of the two children to the defendant.

On July 14, 1989, after a hearing that the plaintiff did not attend but at which she was represented by counsel, the marriage was dissolved and the court ordered, inter alia, that custody of the minor children was to be with the defendant.

The defendant acknowledges in his memorandum in support of his motion to compel that Rule 1.6 of the Rules of Professional Conduct precludes, except as specifically authorized, disclosures by an attorney of confidential information imparted to the attorney by a client in the course of the attorney's representation. He argues, however, that sustaining the privilege in the present circumstances would "tend to immunize a flagrant violation of this court's orders and to inflict an unjustifiable harm to the interests of the defendant and of the children."

The plaintiff argues in her memorandum of law in opposition to the defendant's motion to compel that, while the court has an obligation to apply the best interests of the child standard in custody disputes, "the issue presently before this court does not involve custody, it involves disclosure of privileged information." The plaintiff further argues that the "best interests of the child" does not provide an exception to the confidentiality rule. . . .

"The common-law rule of privileged communications has been stated as follows: 'Where legal advice of any kind is sought from a professional legal adviser in his capacity as such, the communications relating to that purpose, made in confidence by the client, are at his instance permanently protected from disclosure by himself or by the legal adviser, except the protection be waived.' 8 Wigmore, Evidence at 2292, p.554 (McNaughton Rev. 1961). . . ." Connecticut has not altered the rule by statute, as have some states. "The privilege is designed to remove client apprehension as to compelled disclosure by the attorney, and thereby encourage freedom of full disclosure by the client of all the facts relating to the subject matter of inquiry or litigation." C. Tait & J. LaPlante, Connecticut Evidence sec. 12.5 (1976).

Subsection (c)(2) of Rule 1.6 of the Rules of Professional Conduct provides that a lawyer may reveal information relating to the representation of a client to the extent that the lawyer believes that it is necessary to "[r]ectify the consequence of a client's criminal or fraudulent act in the commission of which the lawyer's services had been used." Rule 3.3(a)(2) of the Rules of Professional Conduct states that "[a] lawyer shall not knowingly . . . fail to disclose a material fact to a tribunal when disclosure is necessary to avoid assisting a criminal or fraudulent act by the client. . . ."

It is the opinion of this court that the plaintiff's wilful contempt in leaving the country in violation of the court's order constitutes a fraud on the court, a fraudulent act under Rule 1.6(c)(2). While it is clear to this court that the plaintiff's attorney did not assist or advise the plaintiff to violate the court's order, the attorney's present refusal to disclose her client's whereabouts does serve to assist the plaintiff in her ongoing violation of the court's order.

The New Jersey Supreme Court in *Fellerman v. Bradley*, 99 N.J. 493, 503, 493 A.2d 1239 (1985), stated that in the context of the "crime or fraud" exception to the attorney-client privilege, "our courts have generally given the term 'fraud' an expansive reading." In *Fellerman*, the failure of the defendant's attorney to disclose the whereabouts of his client prevented the court from enforcing a provision of the final judgment in a dissolution action, to which the defendant had previously agreed, requiring the defendant to pay an expert's fee. The court stated that "the client, through his attorney, attempted to perpetrate a fraud on the court — to 'mock' justice — by consenting to and subsequently flouting a judgment that obligated him to bear the costs of an accountant."

The situation in the present case presents more compelling facts than those in *Fellerman* to justify the expansion of the meaning of fraud in Rule 1.6(c)(2) beyond traditional tort or criminal law definitions to include those which constitute "a fraud on the court." The court in *Fellerman* concluded that the defendant's attempt to escape payment of a court ordered expense constituted a fraud on the court. The plaintiff's deliberate violation of the court's order in the instant case has extended ramifications because it impedes the court's ability to implement its subsequent orders regarding custody, orders made in the best interests of the two minor children. . . .

This court, mindful of the importance of the attorney-client privilege and the function it serves in our adversary system, must nevertheless weigh the benefits of that privilege against the state's vital interest as parens patriae in determining the best interests of the minor children. While the plaintiff would have this court hold that the issue before it does not involve custody, the issue of custody here is inextricably intertwined with the issue of attorney-client privilege. The facts reveal: (1) that the plaintiff has left the country with the children in direct violation of a court order; (2) that the plaintiff's attorney knows the precise whereabouts of her client and declines to disclose that information; (3) that the failure to disclose that information assists the plaintiff in her ongoing contempt of the court's order; and (4) that the court's ability to effectuate subsequent orders issued in the best interests of the children has been thwarted.

It is this court's opinion, that, under the circumstances, the attorney-client privilege does not apply to information imparted to an attorney by a client in the course of perpetrating a fraud on the court. Moreover, any claim of privilege must yield in these circumstances to the best interests of the children. Accordingly, the defendant's motion to compel counsel to reveal the whereabouts of the plaintiff and the children is granted.

NOTES AND QUESTIONS

1. Two related issues are presented in this case. One has to do with the scope of the lawyer-client privilege, which is defined by local rules of evidence. Many states have adopted Proposed Rule 503 of the Federal Rules of Evidence, which provides in subsection d(1) that there is "no privilege under this rule. . . . If the services of the lawyer were sought or obtained to enable or aid anyone to commit or plan to commit what the client knew or reasonably should have known to be a crime or fraud."

The most obvious instance occurs when a client engages a lawyer to provide legal assistance in connection with contemplated illegal activity. People v. Chappell, 927 P.2d 829 (Colo. 1996), involved the disbarment of an attorney who helped her client flee after the attorney learned that a custody evaluator was going to recommend that the husband receive custody of their son and as-yet-unborn baby, and that the court was likely to follow the recommendation. The client stated that the attorney advised her "as her attorney to stay, but as a mother to run." The lawyer also informed her client about a network of safe houses for people in her situation and helped her to liquidate her assets and empty her bank accounts. The lawyer contacted a friend of the client, asked the friend to pack her client's belongings from the marital home and to put them into storage, let the friend into the home with a key, gave the friend money from the client to pay for moving and storage, and retained the storage locker key. The client fled in violation of a court order that had awarded her temporary custody but prohibited either parent from taking the child from Colorado. After the client left the jurisdiction, but before the husband realized that she had fled, the attorney appeared in court and accepted the husband's offer to continue paying support and maintenance without informing him or the court of the client's actions, which under the court's existing order would produce a change in custody. The Colorado courts concluded that the attorney's conduct contributed to a fraud, violating R.P.C. 1.2(d) (a lawyer "shall not counsel a client to engage, or assist a client, in conduct that the lawyer knows is criminal or fraudulent"), R.P.C. 3.3(a)(2) (a lawyer shall not knowingly fail to disclose a material fact to a tribunal when disclosure is necessary to avoid assisting a criminal or fraudulent act by the client), R.P.C. 8.4(b) (it is professional misconduct for a lawyer to commit a criminal act by aiding the lawyer's client to commit a crime), and R.P.C. 8.4(c) (it is professional misconduct for a lawyer to engage in conduct involving dishonesty, fraud, deceit or misrepresentation). When the client later returned to Colorado, she was charged with a felony for violation of the court order, and the husband obtained custody of both children.

At the hearing in which the attorney accepted the husband's offer to continue paying support, the attorney also invoked the attorney-client privilege in refusing to disclose her client's whereabouts. Did the attorney have any basis on which to do so? If the attorney reported that her client had left the state, but refused to disclose the location, would she have had any better basis for withholding the information?

If, without advice from the attorney, the client had said, "I plan to leave the state with the child in violation of the court order and I want you to represent me in any ensuing legal action," would that change the likelihood of prevailing on a claim of confidentiality?

2. The second issue concerns the reach of rules of professional conduct. Model Rule 1.6 provides that

> [a] lawyer shall not reveal information relating to representation of a client unless the client consents after consultation. . . . A lawyer may reveal such information to the extent the lawyer reasonably believes necessary . . . to prevent the client from committing a criminal act that the lawyer believes is likely to result in imminent death or substantial bodily harm. . . .

The language of this Rule does not make explicit the relationship between the evidentiary privilege and ethical requirements. If information received by the lawyer *is* subject to the attorney-client evidentiary privilege, its disclosure over the objection of the client cannot be ordered. If, however, the information is not subject to the lawyer-client privilege, it may still be confidential as an ethical matter. Indeed, all information received by an attorney that relates to representation is subject to the general expectation of confidentiality set out in Rule 1.6. However, if confidential information is not privileged, it is subject to *involuntary* disclosure when ordered by a court. *See* Comment to Rule 1.6.

With this background, how would you characterize plaintiff wife's communication to her lawyer about her whereabouts? To whom, and under what circumstances, can that communication be disclosed?

3. Other cases requiring attorneys to disclose information in similar circumstances include Matter of Jacqueline F., 391 N.E.2d 967 (N.Y. 1979); Kerman v. Jafarian-Kerman, 424 S.W.2d 333 (Mo. App. 1967). *Cf.* Taylor v. Taylor, 359 N.E.2d 820 (Ill. App. Ct. 5th Dist. 1977) (upholding claim of confidentiality with respect to a client's address in a case where husband had been convicted of violence and wanted the address for service of process to initiate a new action). *See generally* Leigh Goodmark, Going Underground: The Ethics of Advising a Battered Woman Fleeing an Abusive Relationship, 75 UMKC L. Rev. 999 (2007).

4. A duty to disclose may also arise when an attorney learns after the event that his or her client has committed a fraud on the court, usually through perjury or other false statements. Model Rule 3.3(a) provides that "[a] lawyer shall not knowingly: . . . (2) Fail to disclose a material fact to a tribunal when disclosure is necessary to avoid assisting a criminal or fraudulent act by the client." Subsection (4) provides that "[i]f a lawyer has offered material evidence and comes to know of its falsity, the lawyer shall take reasonable remedial measures." The Comment to this Rule indicates that the lawyer's duty to take remedial steps includes remonstrating with the client, seeking to withdraw, or ultimately disclosing the fraudulent conduct.

5. Different ethical issues arise for lawyers who may represent children in cases in which the children's wishes differ from their parents. Such attorneys may often be appointed by the courts. In these cases, should the attorney always advocate for the child's wishes? Or does the attorney have an independent duty to determine what is in the child's best interests? Does it matter how old the child is? Does it matter whether the attorney believes that the child is capable of reaching an informed judgment about what the child wants in the case? For a discussion of these issues, *see* Barbara A. Atwood, Representing Children Who Can't or Won't Direct Counsel: Best Interests Lawyering or No Lawyer at All?, 53 Ariz. L. Rev. 381 (2011); Linda D. Elrod, Client-Directed Lawyers for Children: It Is the "Right" Thing to Do, 27 Pace L. Rev. 869 (2007); Katherine Hunt Federle, Lawyering in Juvenile Court: Lessons from a Civil *Gideon* Experiment, 37 Fordham Urb. L.J. 93 (2010) (comparing the child representation with representation of marginalized groups); Martin Guggenheim, The AAML's Revised Standards for Representing Children in Custody and Visitation Proceedings: The Reporter's Perspective, 22 J. Am. Acad. Matrimonial L. 251 (2009) (examining AAML's decision to limit children's representatives to children's expressed objectives); and LaShanda Taylor, A Lawyer for Every Child: Client-Directed Representation in Dependency Cases, 47 Fam. Ct. Rev. 605 (2009) (explaining commitment to client-directed representation in proposed ABA Model Act Governing the

Representation of Children in Abuse, Neglect, and Dependency Proceedings); Note, Jamie Rosen, The Child's Attorney and the Alienated Child: Approaches to Resolving the Ethical Dilemma of Diminished Capacity, 51 Fam. Ct. Rev. 330 (2013).

PROBLEMS

1. Suppose that the custodial mother has taken the children away because she believes the father is sexually abusing the children. The children are too young to testify, and, while there is some circumstantial evidence to support the mother's belief, you have advised her that a court is unlikely to find the evidence sufficient to eliminate the father's visitation rights. Should disclosure of the children's location be required in these circumstances?

2. During a deposition, your client states that he has no property or wealth other than that set out in interrogatories completed prior to the deposition. You have just learned that, six months prior to separating from his wife, your client opened a bank account in the neighboring state in which he has deposited $60,000 in cash proceeds from his business. What obligations, if any, do you have in this situation?

3. Your client, Alena Martinez, is in the middle of a hotly contested custody dispute. While it is agreed that Alena will have custody, Juan Martinez wants joint legal custody and extensive visitation. Alena Martinez opposes both, in part because she resents Juan's repeated adulteries, which provoked the divorce. Efforts to negotiate a specific visitation schedule have failed. Opposing counsel has proposed that the parties agree simply that Juan have "reasonable visitation." You know that Alena will not make it easy for Juan to see their children. Can you agree to this provision?

4. Your client is a 9-year-old girl. Her mother has alleged that the father has abused her. The girl tells you that she feels a great deal of pressure to say that the father did so. She also tells you that she is terrified of her father and does not want to see him again. Your client has told you things that you know to be untrue, and you believe that she had difficulty distinguishing between what she has been told and what she personally experienced. What are your obligations to your client?

Family Contracts

10

A. INTRODUCTION: STATUS AND CONTRACT REVISITED

The expression *family contracts* may refer to a wide variety of agreements. In addition to the agreement to marry, contracts affecting family relationships may include agreements between the spouses regarding religious upbringing of children, ownership of wealth during the marriage, and settlements in contemplation of divorce, or an agreement between the spouses and some third person to bear a child. A contract can also be an important vehicle for analyzing the rights and duties of unmarried cohabitants. (See Chapter 4.) In these and many other instances, a central problem is the fit between legal contract principles — designed to deal with arm's-length, usually commercial, transactions — and family relationships.

Despite the ubiquity of contract ideas and vocabulary in family law, that fit seems uncomfortable on its face. The tension between contracts and family relationships is long-standing and has been variously expressed. Toennies's distinction between *gesellschaft* (principles of exchange) and *gemeinschaft* (principles of community) and Hegel's comment that rights in the family do not exist until the family dissolves both reflect that tension.[1]

This sense of tension between rights defined in terms of economic exchange and the more complex, communitarian relationships we associate with family life continues in a more modern idiom. As Milton Regan has written:

---

1. "The right which the individual enjoys on the strength of the family unit and which is in the first place simply the individual's life within this unity, takes on the form of right (as the abstract moment of determinate individuality) only when the family begins to dissolve." Georg W. F. Hegel, Philosophy of Right § 159, at 110-111 (Knox trans., 1952). *Cf.* Ferdinand Toennies on Sociology: Pure, Applied, and Empirical 160-169 (Werner Cahnman & Rudolf Herbele eds., 1971).

Appreciation of the social significance of marriage as a constitutive relationship, however, leads to some skepticism about claims that contract should be privileged over status as the source of obligations at divorce. First, the interdependence and vulnerability that characterize intimate relationships systematically create unique opportunities for overreaching. The cultivation of a relational sense of identity by definition indicates a disposition inclined to regard the parties' interests as largely coterminous. Such an attitude may undermine the willingness to engage in self-interested bargaining that normally makes us confident that a contract accurately reflects each party's preferences. The party who has a more individuated sense of self is likely to be the one to propose a contract in the first place, to distinguish more sharply the resources belonging to each party, and to seek to limit the other partner's access to assets. Yet this is not the sense of self that the law should necessarily privilege in family matters.

Milton Regan, Family Law and the Pursuit of Intimacy 149 (1993).

For an overview of many of the complex themes involved in the question of contracts and the family, *see* Elizabeth S. Scott, Rational Decisionmaking About Marriage and Divorce, 76 Va. L. Rev. 9 (1990); Brian Bix, Bargaining in the Shadow of Love: The Enforcement of Premarital Agreements and How We Think About Marriage, 40 Wm. & Mary L. Rev. 145 (1998); Howard Fink & June Carbone, Between Private Ordering and Public Fiat: A New Paradigm for Family Law Decision-Making, 5 J.L. & Fam. Stud. 1 (2003); Judith T. Younger, Lovers' Contracts in the Courts: Forsaking the Minimum Decencies, 13 Wm. & Mary J. Women & L. 349 (2007); J. Thomas Oldham, With All My Worldly Goods I Thee Endow, or Maybe Not: A Reevaluation of the Uniform Premarital Agreement Act After Three Decades, 19 Duke J. Gender L. & Pol'y 83, 84-88 (2011); Barbara A. Atwood, Marital Contracts and the Meaning of Marriage, 54 Ariz. L. Rev. 11 (2012); Marital Agreements and Private Autonomy in Comparative Perspective (Jens M. Scherpe ed., 2012).

Why, then, do we continue to use contract language in connection with families? Part of the answer is that there are economic aspects to family relationships, perhaps now more than before. Moreover, contracts are important for other than economic transactions. We talk routinely about church covenants and the social contract. In this broader view, it is natural that relationships as important as those involved in marriage and the family should invoke the idea of contract. We may also note that the *idea* of contract (or promise, or agreement, or covenant) is not the same as a legal contract enforceable in court. The Uniform Commercial Code, for example, distinguishes between the agreement made in fact by the parties and the contract enforceable in court. The word *contract*, then, may be understood as referring to an image or metaphor, or even to a piece of paper useful in framing the expectations of the parties as an educational or counseling device but not intended to be legally enforceable.

It may also be that the difference between status and contract is overstated. The role of the courts and the state is evident in both. And, as Corbin noted many years ago, an overly strong emphasis on an agreement between strangers misses much of contract law.

The legal relations consequent upon offer and acceptance are not wholly dependent, even upon the reasonable meaning of the words and acts of the parties. The law determines these relations in the light of subsequent circumstances, these often being totally unforeseen by the parties. In such cases it is sometimes said that the law will create that relation which the parties would have intended had they foreseen. The fact is, however, that the decision will depend upon the notions of the court as to policy, welfare, justice, right and wrong, such notions often being inarticulate and subconscious.

Arthur L. Corbin, Offer and Acceptance, and Some of the Resulting Legal Relations, 26 Yale L.J. 169, 206 (1917).

However, ignoring the contractual aspects of relationships presents similar dangers. Martha Ertman emphasizes:

[C]ontract allows regulation akin to a dimmer switch that can recognize a range of roles. . . . Public law, in contrast, tends to work like a conventional light switch. . . . If law's function is to provide certainty and a measure of justice to social and economic relations, the dimmer switch performs this function better than the rigid on/off switch of public law. In this light, we see that contract not only answers the functional needs of particular parties in particular relationships, but it also provides law and society at large a view of how public law can and should change.

Martha M. Ertman, Mapping the New Frontiers of Private Ordering: Afterword, 49 Ariz. L. Rev. 695, 700 (2007).

B. PREMARITAL AGREEMENTS

At least since the sixteenth century, spouses have used premarital agreements to alter the legal regimes for marital property ownership and management. The English Statute of Frauds of 1677 dealt with such contracts, requiring them to be in writing to be enforceable. Today, in the United States, they are still with us, but their acceptability waxes and wanes. As marital regimes ossify, contract offers a more flexible way to order individual relationships. As marriage laws seek to protect the vulnerable, premarital contracts may become more associated with the rich and powerful. The headlines belong to the famous; the premarital agreements of a baseball player or a still young technology billionaire receive disproportionate attention, but their most common use may well be to keep the assets of a first marriage separate from the arrangements of a second one.

To be enforceable, premarital agreements must satisfy the usual contract requirements: They must be entered into voluntarily, supported by consideration, and satisfy the statute of frauds. Traditionally, and still today in most states, premarital agreements must also satisfy additional procedural requirements and are subject to greater judicial supervision of their substantive terms than are commercial contracts. The cases and statutes regulating premarital agreements can be divided into two broad categories: the Uniform Premarital Agreement Act (UPAA) and a number of state court decisions such as Simeone v. Simeone proceed from the belief that the parties should be relatively free to reach whatever agreements they like, and be able to rely on the enforceability of such contracts at separation or divorce. The ALI Principles and the decisions in other states place greater weight on the fairness of the result at the time of enforcement, even if that makes the result less predictable. A new Uniform Premarital and Marital Agreement Act, approved in 2012, is in between. The following materials first consider the common law decisions and then compare the UPAA and the ALI Principles. As you study these materials, consider whether the resolution of individual issues, such as the importance of representation by counsel, reflects different approaches to the enforceability of these agreements, and whether the traditional justifications for treating these agreements differently from commercial contracts still ring true.

SIMEONE V. SIMEONE

581 A.2d 162 (Pa. 1990)

FLAHERTY, J. At issue in this appeal is the validity of a prenuptial agreement executed between the appellant, Catherine E. Walsh Simeone, and the appellee, Frederick A. Simeone. At the time of their marriage, in 1975, appellant was a twenty-three year old nurse and appellee was a thirty-nine year old neurosurgeon. Appellee had an income of approximately $90,000 per year, and appellant was unemployed. Appellee also had assets worth approximately $300,000. On the eve of the parties' wedding, appellee's attorney presented appellant with a prenuptial agreement to be signed. Appellant, without the benefit of counsel, signed the agreement. Appellee's attorney had not advised appellant regarding any legal rights that the agreement surrendered. The parties are in disagreement as to whether appellant knew in advance of that date that such an agreement would be presented for signature. Appellant denies having had such knowledge and claims to have signed under adverse circumstances, which, she contends, provide a basis for declaring it void.

The agreement limited appellant to support payments of $200 per week in the event of separation or divorce, subject to a maximum total payment of $25,000. The parties separated in 1982, and, in 1984, divorce proceedings were commenced. Between 1982 and 1984 appellee made payments which satisfied the $25,000 limit. In 1985, appellant filed a claim for alimony pendente lite. A master's report upheld the validity of the prenuptial agreement and denied this claim. . . .

There is no longer validity in the implicit presumption that supplied the basis for Estate of Geyer, 533 A.2d 423 (Pa. 1987) and similar earlier decisions. Such decisions rested upon a belief that spouses are of unequal status and that women are not knowledgeable enough to understand the nature of contracts that they enter. Society has advanced, however, to the point where women are no longer regarded as the "weaker" party in marriage, or in society generally. Indeed, the stereotype that women serve as homemakers while men work as breadwinners is no longer viable. Quite often today both spouses are income earners. Nor is there viability in the presumption that women are uninformed, uneducated, and readily subjected to unfair advantage in marital agreements. Indeed, women nowadays quite often have substantial education, financial awareness, income, and assets.

Accordingly, the law has advanced to recognize the equal status of men and women in our society. Paternalistic presumptions and protections that arose to shelter women from the inferiorities and incapacities which they were perceived as having in earlier times have, appropriately, been discarded. . . . It would be inconsistent, therefore, to perpetuate the standards governing prenuptial agreements that were described in *Geyer* and similar decisions, as these reflected a paternalistic approach that is now insupportable.

Further, *Geyer* and its predecessors embodied substantial departures from traditional rules of contract law, to the extent that they allowed consideration of the knowledge of the contracting parties and reasonableness of their bargain as factors governing whether to uphold an agreement. Traditional principles of contract law provide perfectly adequate remedies where contracts are procured through fraud, misrepresentation, or duress. Consideration of other factors, such as the knowledge of the parties and the reasonableness of their bargain, is inappropriate. . . . Prenuptial agreements are contracts, and, as such, should be evaluated under the same criteria as are applicable to other types of contracts. . . . Absent fraud, misrepresentation, or duress, spouses should be bound by the terms of their agreements.

Contracting parties are normally bound by their agreements, without regard to whether the terms thereof were read and fully understood and irrespective of whether the agreements embodied reasonable or good bargains. Based upon these principles, the terms of the present prenuptial agreement must be regarded as binding, without regard to whether the terms were fully understood by appellant. *Ignorantia non excusat.*

Accordingly, we find no merit in a contention raised by appellant that the agreement should be declared void on the ground that she did not consult with independent legal counsel. To impose a per se requirement that parties entering a prenuptial agreement must obtain independent legal counsel would be contrary to traditional principles of contract law, and would constitute a paternalistic and unwarranted interference with the parties' freedom to enter contracts.

Further, the reasonableness of a prenuptial bargain is not a proper subject for judicial review. *Geyer* and earlier decisions required that, at least where there had been an inadequate disclosure made by the parties, the bargain must have been reasonable at its inception. *See Geyer*, 516 Pa. at 503, 533 A.2d at 428. Some have even suggested that prenuptial agreements should be examined with regard to whether their terms remain reasonable at the time of dissolution of the parties' marriage.

By invoking inquiries into reasonableness, however, the functioning and reliability of prenuptial agreements is severely undermined. Parties would not have entered such agreements, and, indeed, might not have entered their marriages, if they did not expect their agreements to be strictly enforced. If parties viewed an agreement as reasonable at the time of its inception, as evidenced by their having signed the agreement, they should be foreclosed from later trying to evade its terms by asserting that it was not in fact reasonable. . . .

Further, everyone who enters a long-term agreement knows that circumstances can change during its term, so that what initially appeared desirable might prove to be an unfavorable bargain. Such are the risks that contracting parties routinely assume. Certainly, the possibilities of illness, birth of children, reliance upon a spouse, career change, financial gain or loss, and numerous other events that can occur in the course of a marriage cannot be regarded as unforeseeable. If parties choose not to address such matters in their prenuptial agreements, they must be regarded as having contracted to bear the risk of events that alter the value of their bargains. . . .

The present agreement recited that full disclosure had been made, and included a list of appellee's assets totaling approximately $300,000. Appellant contends that this list understated by roughly $183,000 the value of a classic car collection which appellee had included at a value of $200,000. The master, reviewing the parties' conflicting testimony regarding the value of the car collection, found that appellant failed to prove by clear and convincing evidence that the value of the collection had been understated. The courts below affirmed that finding. . . . Appellant's contention is plainly without merit.

Appellant's final contention is that the agreement was executed under conditions of duress in that it was presented to her at 5 P.M. on the eve of her wedding, a time when she could not seek counsel without the trauma, expense, and embarrassment of postponing the wedding. The master found this claim not credible. The courts below affirmed that finding, upon an ample evidentiary basis.

Although appellant testified that she did not discover until the eve of her wedding that there was going to be a prenuptial agreement, testimony from a number of other witnesses was to the contrary. . . . And the legal counsel who prepared the agreement for appellee testified that, prior to the eve of the wedding, changes were made in the agreement to increase the sums payable to appellant in the event of separation or divorce. He also stated that he was present when the agreement was signed and that appellant expressed absolutely no reluctance about signing. It should be noted, too, that during the months when the agreement was being discussed appellant had more than sufficient time to consult with independent legal counsel if she had so desired. Under these circumstances, there was plainly no error in finding that appellant failed to prove duress.

Hence, the courts below properly held that the present agreement is valid and enforceable. Appellant is barred, therefore, from receiving alimony pendente lite.

Order affirmed.

PAPADAKOS, J., concurring. . . . I cannot join the opinion authored by Mr. Justice Flaherty, because, it must be clear to all readers, it contains a number of unnecessary and unwarranted declarations regarding the "equality" of women. Mr. Justice Flaherty believes that, with the hard-fought victory of the Equal Rights Amendment in Pennsylvania, all vestiges of inequality between the sexes have been erased and women are now treated equally under the law. I fear my colleague does not live in the real world. If I did not know him better I would think that his statements smack of male chauvinism, an attitude that "you women asked for it, now live with it." If you want to know about equality of women, just ask them about comparable wages for comparable work. Just ask them about sexual harassment in the workplace. Just ask them about the sexual discrimination in the Executive Suites of big business. And the list of discrimination based on sex goes on and on.

I view prenuptial agreements as being in the nature of contracts of adhesion with one party generally having greater authority than the other who deals in a subservient role. I believe the law protects the subservient party, regardless of that party's sex, to insure equal protection and treatment under the law.

McDERMOTT, J., dissenting. Let me begin by setting forth a common ground between my position in this matter and that of the majority. There can be no question that, in the law and in society, men and women must be accorded equal status. I am in full agreement with the majority's observation that "women nowadays quite often have substantial education, financial awareness, income, and assets." However, the plurality decision I authored in Estate of Geyer, 516 Pa. 492, 533 A.2d 423 (1987), as well as the Dissenting Opinion I offer today, have little to do with the equality of the sexes, but everything to do with the solemnity of the matrimonial union. . . .

The subject of the validity of pre-nuptial agreements is not a new issue for this Court. A pre-nuptial agreement is the reservation of ownership over land, money and any other property, acquired in the past, present or future, from the most unique of human bargains. A pre-nuptial agreement may also prove an intention to get the best out of a marriage without incurring any obligation to do more than be there so long as it suits a purpose. Certainly, a prenuptial agreement may serve many purposes consistent with love and affection in life. It may answer obligations incurred prior to present intentions, obligations to children, parents, relatives, friends and those not yet born. . . . Moreover, society has an interest in protecting the right of its citizens to contract, and in seeing the reduction, in the event of a dissolution of the marriage, of the necessity of lengthy, complicated, and costly litigation. Thus, while I acknowledge the long-standing rule of law that pre-nuptial agreements are presumptively valid and binding upon the parties, I am unwilling to go as far as the majority to protect the right to contract at the expense of the institution of marriage. Were a contract of marriage, the most intimate relationship between two people, not the surrender of freedom, an offering of self in love, sacrifice, hope for better or for worse, the begetting of children and the offer of effort, labor, precious time and care for the safety and prosperity of their union, then the majority would find me among them.

In my view, one seeking to avoid the operation of an executed pre-nuptial agreement must first establish, by clear and convincing evidence, that a full and fair disclosure of the worth of the intended spouse was not made at the time of the execution of the agreement. This Court has recognized that full and fair disclosure is needed because, at the time of the execution of a pre-nuptial agreement, the parties do not stand in the usual arm's length posture attendant to most other types of contractual undertakings, but "stand in a relation of mutual confidence and trust that calls for the highest degree of good faith. . . ." In addition to a full and fair disclosure of the general financial pictures of the parties, I would find a pre-nuptial agreement voidable where it is established that the parties were not aware, at the time of contracting, of existing statutory rights which they were relinquishing upon the signing of the agreement. It is here, with a finding of full and fair disclosure, that the majority would end its analysis of the validity of a pre-nuptial agreement. I would not. An analysis of the fairness and equity of a pre-nuptial agreement has long been an important part of the law of this state. . . .

At the time of dissolution of the marriage, a spouse should be able to avoid the operation of a pre-nuptial agreement upon clear and convincing proof that, despite the existence of full and fair disclosure at the time of the execution of the agreement, the agreement is nevertheless so inequitable and unfair that it should not be enforced in a court of this state. . . . The majority holds to the view, without waiver, that parties, having contracted with full and fair disclosure, should be made to suffer the consequences of their bargains. In so holding, the majority has given no weight to the other side of the scales: the state's paramount interest in the preservation of marriage and the family relationship, and the protection of parties to a marriage who may be rendered wards of the state, unable to provide for their own reasonable needs. . . .

It is also apparent that, although a pre-nuptial agreement is quite valid when drafted, the passage of time accompanied by the intervening events of a marriage, may render the terms of the agreement completely unfair and inequitable. While parties to a pre-nuptial agreement may indeed foresee, generally, the events which may come to pass during their marriage, one spouse should not be made to suffer for failing to foresee all of the surrounding circumstances which may attend the dissolution of the marriage. Although it should not be the role of the courts to void pre-nuptial agreements merely because one spouse may receive a better result in an action under the Divorce Code to recover alimony or equitable distribution, it should be the role of the courts to guard against the enforcement of pre-nuptial agreements where such enforcement will bring about only inequity and hardship. It borders on cruelty to accept that after years of living together, yielding their separate opportunities in life to each other, that two individuals emerge the same as the day they began their marriage.

At the time of the dissolution of marriage, what are the circumstances which would serve to invalidate a pre-nuptial agreement? This is a question that should only be answered on a case-by-case basis. However, it is not unrealistic to imagine that in a given situation, one spouse, although trained in the workforce at the time of marriage, may, over many years, have become economically dependent upon the other spouse. In reliance upon the permanence of marriage and in order to provide a stable home for a family, a spouse may choose, even at the suggestion of the other spouse, not to work during the marriage. As a result, at the point of dissolution of the marriage, the spouse's employability has diminished to such an extent that to enforce the support provisions of the pre-nuptial agreement will cause the spouse to become a public charge, or will provide a standard of living far below that which was enjoyed before and during marriage. In such a situation, a court may properly decide to render void all or some of the provisions of the pre-nuptial agreement.

I can likewise conceive of a situation where, after a long marriage, the value of property may have increased through the direct efforts of the spouse who agreed not to claim it upon divorce or death. In such a situation, the court should be able to decide whether it is against the public policy of the state, and thus inequitable and unfair, for a spouse to be precluded from receiving that increase in the value of property which he or she had, at least in part, directly induced. I marvel at the majority's apparent willingness to enforce a pre-nuptial agreement in the interest of freedom to contract at any cost, even where unforeseen and untoward illness has rendered one spouse unable, despite his own best efforts, to provide reasonable support for himself. I would further recognize that a spouse should be given the opportunity to prove, through clear and convincing evidence, that the amount of time and energy necessary for that spouse to shelter and care for the children of the marriage has rendered the terms of a pre-nuptial agreement inequitable, and unjust and thus, avoidable.

NOTES AND QUESTIONS

1. The landmark case of Posner v. Posner, 233 So. 2d 381 (Fla. 1970), *rev'd on other grounds*, 257 So. 2d 530 (1972), held that contracts concerning property division and spousal support at divorce are not inherently contrary to public policy. Most courts faced with the issue since then have taken the same view, concluding that no-fault divorce laws express a legislative policy of neutrality toward divorce and that, in an era of frequent divorce, public policy favors settling disputes amicably. Nonetheless, *Simeone* remains one of the watershed cases embracing the right of married couples to reach their own agreements. Part of the reasoning of the case stems from its declaration that "the law has advanced to recognize the equal status of men and women in our society." What does the court mean by "equal status," and how do the concurrence and dissent differ in their consideration of gender equality?

2. The Pennsylvania cases prior to *Simeone* required full disclosure or fair and adequate provision before a premarital agreement would be enforced. What is the relationship between disclosure, a matter of the bargaining process, and fair and adequate provision, which pertains to the substance of the agreement? The Supreme Court of Nebraska explained the reasoning this way:

> At least three principles support our interpretation of the [disclosure] rule. First, . . . an agreement to marry gives rise to a confidential relationship. As a result, the parties to an antenuptial agreement do not deal at arm's length and must exercise candor and good faith in all matters bearing upon the contract.
>
> Secondly, parties to an antenuptial agreement are very often ill-matched in terms of bargaining power. As one court put it, "candor compels us to raise to a conscious level the fact that, as in this case, prenuptial agreements will almost always be entered into between people with property or an income potential to protect on one side and people who are impecunious on the other." Gant v. Gant, 329 S.E.2d 106, 114 (W. Va. 1985). Thus, a rule requiring full disclosure or independent knowledge serves to level the bargaining field for the party in the weaker position.
>
> Finally, unlike other private commercial contracts, the State has an interest and is a party to every marriage. . . . In the absence of antenuptial agreements, state laws govern the division of marital property and the awarding of alimony in the event of divorce. Often, antenuptial agreements alter the rights parties otherwise would have under those state laws. Consequently, it is altogether appropriate that parties entering into antenuptial agreements do so with knowledge of the holdings to which they are waiving any claim under state law. . . .

Randolph v. Randolph, 937 S.W.2d 815 (1996).

None of these requirements applies to ordinary contracts. Why should they apply to agreements between people about to be married? Should parties who are *engaged* to be married have fiduciary obligations to each other? Many states agree with *Randolph*, but California distinguishes between spouses, who do have such fiduciary obligations, and those contemplating marriage, who do not. In re Bonds, 5 P.3d 815 (Cal. 2000).

3. All of the opinions in the case associate the historical reluctance to enforce premarital agreements with the historic role of gender in the assignment of marital roles and women's dependence (and weaker bargaining power) because of their gender. How do the various opinions describe women's roles today? What relationship does each opinion see between the status of women and the enforceability of the *Simeone* agreement? How do they view the wife's assumption of a very traditional homemaking role in this case? How do they view the nature of marriage? Would the justices come to the same conclusions if the roles of husband and wife were reversed?

LANE V. LANE

202 S.W.3d 577 (Ky. 2006)

LAMBERT, Chief Justice. Three days before their marriage on November 24, 1990, Appellant, Paula O. Lane, and Appellee, David L. Lane, entered into an ante-nuptial agreement. Appropriate asset disclosures were made and the underlying validity of the agreement is not at issue herein. What is at issue is whether events subsequent to the nine and a half year marriage and the birth of two children render enforcement of the agreement unconscionable. . . .

At the time of their marriage, Appellant was working as a night desk clerk in a hotel earning $19,000 a year. She was twenty-nine years of age. Despite his youthful age of twenty-six, Appellee was already a successful stockbroker at Edward D. Jones and Company, earning $166,000 per year. Appellee was a college graduate while Appellant had only a high school education. Two children were born of the marriage, after which Appellant did not work outside the home as she was the primary caregiver for the children. By the time the marriage was dissolved, Appellee had achieved great financial success. He was earning approximately one million dollars per year and he was a partner in a regional brokerage firm.

According to the agreement, the parties waived their rights under the law to claim maintenance in the event the marriage was dissolved. The parties further agreed that the separate property of each would be deemed nonmarital in the event of divorce. The agreement explicitly identified certain items as Appellee's separate property. These items were two parcels of real estate (not relevant here), a partnership interest in Edward D. Jones, and Appellee's pension plan, profit sharing plan and voluntary profit sharing plan through Edward D. Jones. The agreement further provided that should either party default in or breach any obligations contained therein, the defaulting party would be responsible for attorney's fees, court costs, costs of depositions, transportation, lodging, and other related expenses. As there was a dramatic difference in the parties' economic circumstances when enforcement of the agreement was sought, we must determine whether the doctrine of unconscionability allows relief to Appellant. . . .

This Court has embraced the view that ante-nuptial agreements are not per se invalid as against public policy. However, courts retain the right to analyze such agreements for unconscionability at the time of enforcement. . . .

From the time this Court first recognized the validity and enforceability of ante-nuptial agreements, we have included the following qualification:

> The ingenuity of persons contemplating marriage to fashion unusual agreements, particularly with the assistance of counsel, cannot be overestimated. We will observe the tradition whereby the law develops on a case by case basis. It should be recognized, however, that trial courts have been vested with broad discretion to modify or invalidate ante-nuptial agreements.

Thus, it is beyond reasonable dispute that a trial court may modify or invalidate all or part of an ante-nuptial agreement where enforcement is unconscionable in its application. This includes cases where "the facts and circumstances changed since the agreement was executed so as to make its enforcement unfair and unreasonable." On this basis, the trial court modified the agreement and ordered Appellee to pay maintenance of $12,000.00 per month for three years.

* * *

In the case at bar, this was the first marriage for both Appellant and Appellee and both parties were in their twenties. Two children were born of the marriage and Appellant quit her job to care for the children while Appellee rapidly progressed in his career. While a significant disparity in the parties' incomes existed at the time of the marriage, this disparity grew exponentially during the marriage in large part because the husband was able to concentrate on his career while the wife stayed home to care for the children and the home. Contrary to the dissent's contention, Appellant's discontinuance of employment to rear the children and maintain the household is not of nominal value and should in fairness be considered a substantial factor in this case, along with the affluent lifestyle maintained during their marriage, towards rendering the maintenance waiver provision unconscionable.

Parties who contemplate entering into ante-nuptial agreements have a duty to appropriately consider their circumstances and whether such an agreement is right for them. The more one-sided an agreement appears at the time it is made, the more likely courts are to invalidate the agreement at the time enforcement is sought. Bare-knuckle bargaining is not an appropriate practice. As this was a first marriage between younger persons, it is curious that these parties even wanted an ante-nuptial agreement. Their situation differed vastly from the customary and proper ante-nuptial agreement circumstances where parties desire to preserve their assets for their children and grandchildren. But they made their agreement and it will be enforced, subject to judicial scrutiny for unconscionability.

. . . [O]n the maintenance issue, we reinstate the judgment of the trial court. . . .

GRAVES, Justice, concurring.

I concur with the majority but write separately to express some additional thoughts in this case. Entering such an antenuptial agreement during the period of excitement on the eve of a wedding evokes questions about the sufficiency of the parties' consent and indicates that Appellee likely had serious mental reservations about marriage. . . . Perhaps, an *anti*-nuptial agreement would be a more apt description as KRS 402.005 defines marriage as a union for life.

The intimate partnership of life and love which constitutes the married state is rooted in the conjugal covenant of irrevocable personal consent. In the eyes of society, marriage receives its stability from the human act by which the partners mutually surrender themselves to each other without any hesitation or reservation whatsoever. While there is no single definitive explanation for the breakdown of the sacred institution of marriage, the casual attitude expressed in this antenuptial agreement is no doubt a facilitating factor contributing to a disturbing trend.

. . . Since 1916, it was the declared public policy of this Commonwealth that antenuptial agreements contemplating divorce and separation were void as they tended to promote (or at least predict) marital instability. Yet, the . . . Court nonetheless overruled [the 1916 decision] explaining that the policy declared therein was no longer necessary or pertinent as it was designed primarily to protect women, who were "decidedly second class" citizens at the time. Edwardson v. Edwardson, 798 S.W.2d 941, 944 (Ky. 1990). Unfortunately, the great strides made by both women and children, as a class, have done nothing to validate the majority's reasoning in *Edwardson, supra*.

While anecdotal, but sadly not surprising, it was the husband and not the wife who scored the commercial deal of the century in this fateful contract. Perhaps the wife felt lucky to receive the scraps she did obtain, as she was granted the ultimate privilege of being this man's wife and bearing his children for at least the duration of her youth. Or perhaps as behavioral studies have continually demonstrated, the wife never believed that her incredibly bad bargain would ever come to fruition. *See* Reviewing Premarital Agreements to Protect the State's Interest in Marriage, 91 Va. L. Rev. 535, 543 (2005) (citing one study demonstrating "that although most people accurately estimated the country's overall divorce rate at fifty percent, they assessed their own chances of divorce at zero").

Our current case law nevertheless mandates that brides and grooms-to-be must be held to their bad bargains, no matter how foolish, last minute, or ill-conceived they may be, unless such bargains rise to the level of being unconscionable. . . .

It is indeed chauvinistic for one to contend that the agreement in this case is somehow fair since the wife was merely some lowly hotel clerk[2] while the husband was a youthful and successful stockbroker. Perceiving these positions as vastly disparate on life's socioeconomic ladder, some would suggest that the wife's nine and a half years of living beyond her assigned socioeconomic rung with her stockbroker husband was more than enough consideration for her (1) discontinuance of employment; (2) her bearing of two children; (3) her caring for those two children; (4) her maintenance of the household; and (5) her role as her husband's consort, hostess, and social liaison. Indeed, the record demonstrates that the wife held numerous and lavish parties for her husband's associates and held positions in several high-profile community organizations for the purpose of benefiting her husband's reputation and promoting his career.

Yet, as the majority rightly acknowledges, the varied contributions of a homemaker is not of nominal value in this Commonwealth. . . . [Kentucky statutes reflect the concept that] marriage is a partnership that both spouses contribute to

---

2. Who, apparently, was past her prime at the ripe old age of 29.

in equal, yet differing ways, and that children and the accumulation of financial assets is a corresponding result or byproduct of that partnership.

In the case of homemaker spouses, the division of labor in a family is compartmentalized. One spouse focuses time, talents, and experience to the marketplace while the other spouse focuses equal time, talents, and experience to the family. In such a system, the partnership strives to achieve maximum output and return in two essential areas of life — one spouse will have more time and energy to develop greater skill and earnings potential in the marketplace while the other will have more time and energy to ensure that the children and the household thrive and grow. This system is nothing new and has always been valued as a meaningful and successful model for maintaining both a marriage and a family.[3]

However, when homemaker spouses find themselves in the midst of family breakdown through either separation or divorce, they are prematurely forced to abandon their chosen callings and start anew in the marketplace. These spouses are understandably ill-equipped to compete in such an arena as they are frequently impaired by the loss of youth and lack of skills. Years spent homemaking are viewed by potential employers as years of "unemployment." Contacts and relevant experience are almost always lacking on a homemaker's resume and many are simply regarded as too old for entry-level employment. Rehabilitative alimony for homemaker spouses is therefore not a gift, but something these hardworking spouses have earned after years of toiling outside the marketplace on behalf of their families. This is analogous to an on-the-job anatomical injury in workers' compensation and the resulting functional impairment.

The antenuptial agreement in this case is fundamentally unfair in large part because it accords almost no consideration for the wife's contributions as a homemaker in this marriage. Were we to hold as the dissent suggests it would be foolish, indeed, to continue investing in a marriage through the role of a homemaker as such a contribution would be accorded diminished status under the laws of Kentucky and hence, this Court would be contributing to the feminization of poverty.

Fortunately for the children and families in this Commonwealth, the majority continues to respect and protect the partnership theory of marriage, the sanctity of the family, and the important contributions of homemaker spouses as such concepts are codified in our statutory law.

McANAULTY, Justice, dissenting. Respectfully, I dissent from that portion of the Majority's Opinion affirming the trial court's determination that the provision of the agreement regarding waiver of maintenance was unconscionable. . . . I believe that the trial court, and now a Majority of this Court, set aside the provisions of the waiver of maintenance clause because it constituted a bad — not unconscionable — bargain for Paula at the time of divorce. I agree with the reasoning of the Court of Appeals that considered the lack of evidence to suggest that the marriage caused Paula to forego the completion of her education so that now her

---

3. This division of labor concept has also been very successful in our modern industrial society, to wit: the assembly line.

decision to forego joining the work force to pursue her education somehow makes the agreement unfair and unreasonable.

The highest number that Paula agrees that she received in the trial court's division of marital property is $233,593.12. I do not disagree that David is in a significantly better financial position with his monthly income, as found by the trial court, of $95,728.33, but I cannot agree with Paula that the amount that she received will not support her while she sensibly and responsibly pursues her career interests. Nor can I agree that an affluent lifestyle as opposed to a comfortable lifestyle (which I believe Paula and her children can enjoy with her property award plus $3,000.00 per month child support) should necessarily render the maintenance provision unconscionable.

I believe the trial court abused its discretion in declaring the waiver of maintenance provision unconscionable when David and Paula had disparate incomes from the start of the marriage; they signed the antenuptial agreement; they signed the agreement with the assistance and advice of independent counsel and with full knowledge that the agreement substantially altered their marital and property rights, claims, or interests that they would have had but for the execution of the agreement; and they were married for 9-1/2 years.

NOTES AND QUESTIONS

1. *Lane* was decided 16 years after *Simeone*. How would you describe the differences between *Lane* and *Simeone* in their evaluation of the status of women, their identification of the purposes of marriage, and their articulation of the reasons for validating or invaliding the respective agreements? Has the passage of time changed the justices' evaluation of the homemaking role?

2. What is the relationship between "equal status" and equal bargaining power? Barbara Atwood and Brian Bix report that:

> Notwithstanding the persistence of economic inequality along gender lines, the relative value of marriage for men and women has been shifting since the original UPAA was enacted. Women have exceeded men in education and income growth over the last four decades and have almost reached parity as a percentage of the workforce. In almost a quarter of marriages, wives are now the higher wage earners, and in a majority of marriages, wives have an equal or higher education level than their husbands. If these trends continue, marriage will carry greater economic value for men than for women, giving women new leverage in this form of intimate contract.

Barbara A. Atwood & Brian H. Bix, A New Uniform Law for Premarital and Marital Agreements, 46 Fam. L.Q. 313, 316 (2012). Atwood and Bix also point out that increasing acceptance of same-sex marriage "renders assumptions about gender dynamics in marital contracting somewhat dated." *Id.* How should the courts take such changes into account?

There are no published empirical studies of premarital agreements, but empirical studies show that while the differences in income between men and women who work full time have narrowed overall since 1990, the gap has *grown* for those with the highest incomes and, indeed, for college graduates overall. Median Annual Income, by Level of Education, 1990-2009, InfoPlease, http://www.infoplease.com/ipa/A0883617.html#ixzz1JFxpOxL9 (last visited Mar. 12, 2013). Men's income is most likely to exceed women's among couples with the highest incomes—the couples most likely to have premarital agreements. In addition, premarital agreements are most common in second marriages, which frequently involve men quite a bit older and wealthier than the women they are marrying. Judith Younger's review of appellate cases since 2000 indicates that this may still be true. Judith T. Younger, Lovers' Contracts in the Courts: Forsaking the Minimum Decencies, 13 Wm. & Mary J. Women & L. 349 (2007). How should these developments affect judicial willingness to uphold marital agreements?

3. Courts and commentators disagree as to whether the courts should police the contracting process (*e.g.*, by mandating disclosure, requiring legal representation for each party, and ensuring voluntariness), review the substantive fairness of the agreement, or both. Courts differ in their approaches in a number of ways, with some holding that:

a. if the parties reached their agreement through an appropriate process, the court will not review the substantive fairness of the agreement at all;

b. the court will invalidate an unconscionable agreement only if the parties did not have (and did not waive) full disclosure at the time it was signed;

c. the court will determine unconscionability only in terms of the facts that existed at the time the contract was signed; or

d. the court will consider the fairness of the agreement in light of the facts that exist at the time of enforcement even if the agreement was otherwise fair and enforceable at the time it was signed.

See Gail F. Brod, Premarital Agreements and Gender Justice, 6 Yale J.L. & Feminism 229, 283-284, 286 (1994). What approach do each of the *Simeone* and *Lane* opinions take in determining the enforceability of the agreement?

4. The justices in the varying opinions in *Simeone* and *Lane* disagree in their evaluations of the substantive fairness of each premarital agreement. One of the factors they address that affects the perceived fairness of each agreement is the difference in income between the spouses at the beginning of each marriage. In 1975, at the time of the marriage in *Simeone*, it was not unusual for a man to marry a spouse who had less education and income than he did. Since then, sociologists find that couples have become much more likely to marry someone with similar education and income and that both men and women place greater emphasis on a prospective spouse's income than they did a half century ago. The sociologists call this "assortative mating." Christine R. Schwartz & Robert D. Mare, Trends in Educational Assortative Marriage from 1940 to 2003, 43 Demography 621-646 (2011); Philip Cohen, College Graduates Marry Other College Graduates Most of the Time, The Atlantic, Apr. 4, 2013, http://www.theatlantic.com/sexes/archive/2013/04/college-graduates-marry-other-college-graduates-most-of-the-time/274654/; David M. Buss, Todd K. Shakelford, Lee A. Kirkpatrick & Randy J. Larsen, A Half Century of Mate Preferences: The Cultural Evolution of Values, 63 J. Marriage & Fam. 491 (2001).

In both *Simeone* and *Lane*, the differences in income motivate the premarital agreement. How should such disparities affect the evaluation of the validity of the premarital agreement? What views do the justices express about the purposes of marriage and the relationship between those purposes and their willingness to enforce a premarital agreement? If disparities such as those in *Lane* have become less common over time, should that make the premarital agreement more likely or less likely to be enforced?

5. A second issue that affects the evaluation of the fairness of premarital agreements is the change in the parties' position after the marriage. The single most common change is the birth of children, particularly when one spouse decreases workforce participation in response to the child's needs. The assumption of childcare responsibilities continues to affect women disproportionately, though such responsibilities may also affect men to a greater degree today than in the past. *See e.g.*, Marianne Bertrand, Claudia Goldin & Lawrence F. Katz, Dynamics of the Gender Gap for Young Professionals in the Financial and Corporate Sectors, 2 Am. Econ. J.: Applied Econ. 228-255 (2010). For couples who plan to have children, these changes are predictable and where the disparities between the two spouses are as great as they are in *Lane*, it is also predictable that the lower-earning spouse will be the one who cuts back workforce participation more. Should such changes always be grounds to refuse to enforce a premarital agreement? Should they constitute appropriate grounds only where the parties could not be reasonably be expected to foresee the changes?

A factor that sometimes affects the evaluation of an agreement is the impact on children. On the one hand, courts sometimes note that the child support award may provide the custodial parent with a substantial sum that contributes to expenses such as housing. On the other hand, courts may consider the impact of large disparities as a factor in itself. *See, e.g.*, Ware v. Ware, 748 A.2d 1031, 1047 (Md. App. 2000) (in citing the substantial effect that large income disparities have on the children of a marriage, the court stated that "[t]here is a child involved, who will undoubtedly go back and forth between the father, who can afford to live in luxury, and the mother, who cannot"). Should the courts address such considerations by invalidating the agreement rather than by awarding higher amounts of child support?

6. The other set of issues that affect the validity of premarital agreements involves the bargaining process. In *Simeone*, for example, the wife claimed that the husband first presented her with the premarital agreement on the eve of the wedding and therefore she entered into it under duress. Why does the court reject the wife's argument in *Simeone*? *Compare* In re Yannalfo, 794 A.2d 795 (N.H. 2002) (upholding a premarital agreement presented one day before the wedding), *with* In re Estate of Hollett, 834 A.2d 348 (N.H. 2003) (invalidating agreement presented two days before the wedding in a case in which the wife had rejected a similar agreement two years earlier). In In re Bonds, 5 P.3d 815 (Cal. 2000), Barry Bonds and his fiancée had rushed to the lawyer's office to complete an antenuptial agreement in time to make a flight to Las Vegas, where the wedding was scheduled for the following day. Despite the fact that Sun Bonds saw the agreement for the first time that afternoon, the California Supreme Court upheld the trial court's finding that "the temporal proximity of the wedding to the signing of the agreement was not coercive, because under the particular circumstances of the case, including the small number of guests and the informality of the wedding

arrangements, little embarrassment would have followed from postponement of the wedding." *Id.* at 825-836.

7. If spouses are required to make full disclosure to each other, what must be disclosed? Must each spouse know the details of the other's holdings, or is having a general idea sufficient? The *Randolph* court required that "the spouse seeking to enforce an antenuptial agreement must prove, by a preponderance of the evidence, either that a full and fair disclosure of the nature, extent, and value of his or her holdings was provided to the spouse seeking to avoid the agreement, or that disclosure was unnecessary because the spouse seeking to avoid the agreement had independent knowledge of the full nature, extent, and value of the proponent spouse's holdings." 937 S.W.2d at 821. California, in contrast, places the burden of proof on the party challenging the premarital agreement. Connecticut has held that disclosure need not be tailored to the capacity of the spouse to understand the significance of the disclosure provided. Friezo v. Friezo, 914 A.2d 533, 551 (Conn. 2007). If you were advising a party on how to ensure sufficient disclosure to validate an agreement in a state following *Randolph*, what would you suggest? How would your answer differ in a state following *Simeone*? In Mallen v. Mallen, 622 S.E.2d 812 (Ga. 2005), the wife challenged the premarital agreement on the ground of lack of disclosure. At the time of the marriage, husband had a net worth of approximately $8.5 million and wife, $10,000. When the parties divorced 18 years later with four children, the husband's assets had increased to over $22 million. In accordance with the premarital agreement, the husband was to pay alimony of $2900 per month for four years and retain all of the assets he had before the marriage as well as all of those accumulated during the marriage. The wife alleged that, although the husband revealed his holdings in an attachment to the premarital agreement, the agreement said nothing about his income, which was over $500,000 per year. The Georgia Supreme Court nonetheless upheld the agreement, observing that the couple lived together before the marriage, and the wife should have been aware of her husband's substantial resources. In contrast, the Georgia Supreme Court invalidated a different agreement in which the husband, a truck driver with a relatively modest income, did not disclose that he had saved $150,000 to build a house on the land that was the subject of the premarital agreement. Blige v. Blige, 656 S.E.2d 822 (Ga. 2008). Justice Sears, who wrote the court's opinion in *Blige*, had dissented in *Mallen*. She nonetheless distinguished the two cases, observing that the two parties had lived together in *Mallen* but not in *Blige* before signing the agreement, and the agreement in *Mallen* had included an attachment listing all of the husband's assets (though not his income). Do you find the differences persuasive?

8. Must each party's legal rights absent an agreement be disclosed, as the wife in *Simeone* argued? If so, does this mean as a practical matter that each person must have independent legal advice? Many courts suggest that independent legal advice is the best means of ensuring that an agreement is enforceable, but no statutes impose a requirement of counsel in all cases. California, in response to the *Bonds* case described above, enacted one of the strictest statutes in the country. It provides, inter alia, that

>   (c) . . . it shall be deemed that a premarital agreement was not executed voluntarily unless the court finds in writing or on the record all of the following:

(1) The party against whom enforcement is sought was represented by independent legal counsel at the time of signing the agreement or, after being advised to seek independent legal counsel, expressly waived, in a separate writing, representation by independent legal counsel.

(2) The party against whom enforcement is sought had not less than seven calendar days between the time that party was first presented with the agreement and advised to seek independent legal counsel and the time the agreement was signed.

(3) The party against whom enforcement is sought, if unrepresented by legal counsel, was fully informed of the terms and basic effect of the agreement as well as the rights and obligations he or she was giving up by signing the agreement, and was proficient in the language in which the explanation of the party's rights was conducted and in which the agreement was written. The explanation of the rights and obligations relinquished shall be memorialized in writing and delivered to the party prior to signing the agreement. The unrepresented party shall, on or before the signing of the premarital agreement, execute a document declaring that he or she received the information required by this paragraph and indicating who provided that information.

Cal. Fam. Code § 1615 (2004).

As a lawyer drafting a premarital agreement for one party, would you advise the other party to seek independent counsel? If the other party has representation, the agreement is more likely to be upheld. Some lawyers, concerned about potential malpractice charges if the agreement is invalidated, routinely recommend that counsel be provided for the other party.

If you were asked to represent the wife in a case like *Simeone* or *Lane*, would you agree to do so? What would you do if you concluded that the only impact your participation would have was to make it more likely that the agreement would be upheld? What is your obligation in a case in which you believe that the agreement is one-sided or unfair and the client intends to sign the agreement over your objections?

BRIAN BIX, *BARGAINING IN THE SHADOW OF LOVE: THE ENFORCEMENT OF PREMARITAL AGREEMENTS AND HOW WE THINK ABOUT MARRIAGE*

40 Wm. & Mary L. Rev. 145, 182, 188 (1998)

When the court in *Simeone* and certain commentators advocated applying the standards from contract law to premarital agreements, they intended the agreements to be subject to minimal scrutiny. That perspective seems to depend, however, on a view of contract law that is decades behind the developments in contractual doctrine and commentary. A modern approach to contract law might reach results that, by enforcing some premarital agreements but not others, better reflect the intuitions of most people regarding the fair result in different cases. . . .

The court in *Simeone*, when it relegated premarital agreements to a contractual approach, seemed to have in mind some classical conception of contract encompassing caveat emptor, naïve "plain meaning" enforcement, and little attention to the relationship between the parties or the larger context within which the agreement was signed. If one could apply "contract principles" to premarital agreements, why not apply, by analogy, the quite different principles underlying Article 2 of the U.C.C.?

The U.C.C. obligates parties to exercise good faith in performing and enforcing the obligation of an agreement, construes contractual terms in light of the parties' course of performance and course of dealing and in light of trade usage, and implies various warranties unless they are expressly excluded. For contracts of indefinite duration, a party may terminate only after reasonable notice, and courts sometimes have held actions apparently authorized by the express wording of a contract to be bad faith actions in breach of the agreement. These changes from classical contract thinking are by no means limited to U.C.C. cases.

If courts apply *these* types of contract principles to premarital agreements, there will be far less reason for complaint. Perhaps courts could interpret the terms of premarital agreements that appear to be one-sided in more reasonable ways by using the tools of modern contract law, or by disallowing the strict enforcement of the express terms of some agreements as contrary to "good faith." . . .

A growing body of literature has discussed whether contracts governing long-term commercial relations should be considered, either by the law or at least by legal commentators, in a way significantly different from other contracts. Advocates of . . . different treatment argue that "beyond a certain point, contracts governing long-term relations come to appear less like individual bargains, in which all the terms can be discerned from the intentions of the parties at the time of formation, and more like *constitutions* governing polities — requiring similar modes of ongoing interpretation." Courts should understand the agreement between the parties — in particular, any *written* agreement between the parties — *in light of the* ongoing relationship, they argue, and the presumptive purpose of court (or arbitrator) intervention should be to maintain that relationship, even if slight deviation from or supplementation to the precise terms of the contract is required.

Those who oppose different treatment assert that with long-term agreements, as in most places, it is better to enforce terms strictly as written, as this will reflect better the choices and preferences of the parties. Such a method of interpretation, they argue, is more efficient and avoids the "freedom of contract" problem of foisting contractual obligations on parties who never consented to them. More subtle arguments for this position maintain that agreements that appear to be "incomplete" are so because of an asymmetry of information between the parties, or because of a fear that more "complete" provisions would encourage strategic behavior by one of the parties. . . .

[However,] one must distinguish legal standards that may in fact help to maintain the relationship from those that will have no such effect because they will be applied only in endgame situations. Premarital agreements — at least the vast majority of those subject to court action and academic commentary — purport to control the endgame situation: they affect the disposition of property upon separation, divorce and death. Though the enforceability of such provisions may have indirect effects on maintaining the relationship at earlier points, the terms of such agreements become relevant only when the marriage relationship is already over.

Though it appears, therefore, that the flexible approaches suggested by some courts and commentators for long-term agreements may have a place in understanding the modern approach to contract law, they are not applicable to divorce-centered premarital agreements, which do not govern the day-to-day maintenance of the marriage relationship. The approaches to long-term agreements aimed at maintaining relationships would, however, be highly relevant if and when states start enforcing agreements focused on the actions and obligations of parties *during* marriage.

Although both the traditional theories justifying contract law and the ideas underlying the influential economic analysis of law assume that people act rationally to protect their own interests, recent work in psychology has begun to question that assumption. There are particular situations and circumstances in which parties are particularly unlikely to act in a rational way, and the law—especially contract law—should respond to that reality.

Premarital agreements are good examples of contracts that illustrate problems with rational judgment, as they involve long-term planning and the consideration of possible negative outcomes at a time when the parties are most likely to be optimistic that no such negative outcomes will occur. Parties need protection in this situation because they are unlikely to be able to think clearly for themselves regarding the consequences of divorce at any time, and certainly not immediately before marriage. . . . [E]ven those who are well educated in such matters, e.g., law students in a family law course, carry an unduly optimistic view about the chances that their marriage will last. More general studies in psychology have confirmed that people tend to evaluate causal theories in a self-serving manner; though people may know that fifty percent of marriages end in divorce, they convince themselves—with little grounding for their conclusions—that they have characteristics that will put them in the portion that will endure. People who assume that they will not divorce will not work hard to maintain a fair deal contingent on divorce occurring, just as parties do not bargain for reasonable terms on the failure of installment payments, as they do not expect to ever fail in their payments. Additionally, parties may have some sense of the consequences of failure one year from now, but it may be harder to foresee and plan for the consequences of failure fifteen years from now—after one or both partners have made sacrifices in their careers and perhaps after children have been born.

JUDITH T. YOUNGER, *LOVERS' CONTRACTS IN THE COURTS: FORSAKING THE MINIMUM DECENCIES*

13 Wm. & Mary J. Women & L. 349, 419-420 (2007)

Enforcing premarital agreements is consistently justified as enhancing the parties' autonomy by allowing them freedom to contract and tailor settlements on breakup to their own situations and satisfactions, exemplary goals. Anyone who disputes the benefits of breakup planning may be accused of antiquarian paternalism. Yet it is perfectly clear from the cases that it is always one member of the couple, the one with the assets, whose autonomy is preserved and whose satisfactions are achieved by execution and enforcement of these agreements. Similarly the reformers in this field have stated their goals in theoretically unexceptionable terms, for example, to eliminate "uncertainty" and "lack of uniformity," thought to be the product of a "spasmodic, reflexive response to varying factual circum-stances at different times," rather than of basic policy conflicts among the states, and to achieve "consensus . . . on the appropriate rules to apply" to premarital agreements and the rationales to explain them.

Although it may be too soon to assess the effect, if any, of the proposed A.L.I. reforms [see below], the accomplishments of the Uniform Act, now adopted in twenty-six jurisdictions, are clear. The Act has facilitated enforcement of an increasing number of these contracts. Interestingly, enforcement philosophy has been contagious; it has slipped over state borders and infected non-ULA jurisdictions as well. Thus, premarital agreements, one-sided by definition, are being enforced more frequently than ever across American jurisdictions. This increased enforcement would be tolerable as long as courts respected "minimum decencies" in the process. Three disconcerting trends suggest that courts are not meeting these standards: conflicting decisions on similar facts within the same jurisdiction, and other judicial errors in resolving these cases; removal of substance from substantive fairness reviews at both execution and enforcement with a concomitant disregard for dependent spouses; and mythifying procedural fairness by upholding agreements entered under subtle coercion, without independent representation or concern for legal ethics or proper disclosure.

The National Conference of Commissioners on Uniform State Laws (NCCUSL) drafts proposed uniform acts in an effort to promote more consistent state legislation. These acts become law if enacted by the individual state legisla-tures. NCCUSL accordingly attempts to draft acts of broad applicability and acceptability. The Uniform Premarital Agreement Act (UPAA) was adopted by roughly half the states between the mid-1980s and the late 1990s. In 2012 NCCUSL approved a new Uniform Premarital and Marital Agreement Act (UPMAA) intended to replace the UPAA and address marital as well as premarital agreements. Two states (Colorado and North Dakota) have adopted the Act, and it is pending before other state legislatures. These Acts are discussed below.

The UPMAA and UPAA are set forth first with detailed questions that take you through the interaction of its various provisions. The ALI Principles that address premarital agreements follow, with commentary from Professor Younger and problems at the end of this section that will help to recognize the differ-ences. In examining these provisions, consider whether they reflect *Simeone*'s embrace of freedom of contract in marital bargaining, or some of the criticisms from Professors Bix and Younger.

Uniform Premarital and Marital Agreements Act (UPMAA)
SECTION 9. ENFORCEMENT.
(a) A premarital agreement or marital agreement is unenforceable if a party against whom enforcement is sought proves:

(1) the party's consent to the agreement was involuntary or the result of duress;

(2) the party did not have access to independent legal representation under subsection (b);

(3) unless the party had independent legal representation at the time the agreement was signed, the agreement did not include a notice of waiver of rights under subsection (c) or an explanation in plain language of the marital rights or obligations being modified or waived by the agreement; or

(4) before signing the agreement, the party did not receive adequate financial disclosure under subsection (d).

(b) A party has access to independent legal representation if:

(1) before signing a premarital or marital agreement, the party has a reasonable time to:

(A) decide whether to retain a lawyer to provide independent legal representation; and

(B) locate a lawyer to provide independent legal representation, obtain the lawyer's advice, and consider the advice provided; and

(2) the other party is represented by a lawyer and the party has the financial ability to retain a lawyer or the other party agrees to pay the reasonable fees and expenses of independent legal representation.

(c) A notice of waiver of rights under this section requires language, conspicuously displayed, substantially similar to the following, as applicable to the premarital agreement or marital agreement:

"If you sign this agreement, you may be:

Giving up your right to be supported by the person you are marrying or to whom you are married.

Giving up your right to ownership or control of money and property.

Agreeing to pay bills and debts of the person you are marrying or to whom you are married.

Giving up your right to money and property if your marriage ends or the person to whom you are married dies.

Giving up your right to have your legal fees paid."

(d) A party has adequate financial disclosure under this section if the party:

(1) receives a reasonably accurate description and good-faith estimate of value of the property, liabilities, and income of the other party;

(2) expressly waives, in a separate signed record, the right to financial disclosure beyond the disclosure provided; or

(3) has adequate knowledge or a reasonable basis for having adequate knowledge of the information described in paragraph (1).

(e) If a premarital agreement or marital agreement modifies or eliminates spousal support and the modification or elimination causes a party to the agreement to be eligible for support under a program of public assistance at the time of separation or marital dissolution, a court, on request of that party, may require the other party to provide support to the extent necessary to avoid that eligibility.

(f) A court may refuse to enforce a term of a premarital agreement or marital agreement if, in the context of the agreement taken as a whole[:]

[(1)] the term was unconscionable at the time of signing[; or

(2) enforcement of the term would result in substantial hardship for a party because of a material change in circumstances arising after the agreement was signed].

(g) The court shall decide a question of unconscionability [or substantial hardship] under subsection (f) as a matter of law.

SECTION 10. UNENFORCEABLE TERMS.

(a) In this section, "custodial responsibility" means physical or legal custody, parenting time, access, visitation, or other custodial right or duty with respect to a child.

(b) A term in a premarital agreement or marital agreement is not enforceable to the extent that it:

(1) adversely affects a child's right to support;

(2) limits or restricts a remedy available to a victim of domestic violence under

law of this state other than this [act];

(3) purports to modify the grounds for a court-decreed separation or marital dissolution available under law of this state other than this [act]; or

(4) penalizes a party for initiating a legal proceeding leading to a court-decreed

separation or marital dissolution.

(c) A term in a premarital agreement or marital agreement which defines the rights or

duties of the parties regarding custodial responsibility is not binding on the court.

Uniform Premarital Agreements Act (UPAA)

§ 3. Content (a) Parties to a premarital agreement may contract with respect to:

(1) the rights and obligations of each of the parties in any of the property of either or both of them whenever and wherever acquired or located; . . .

(4) the modification or elimination of spousal support; . . .

(8) any other matter, including their personal rights and obligations, not in violation of public policy or a statute imposing a criminal penalty.

(b) The right of a child to support may not be adversely affected by a premarital agreement. . . .

§ 5. Amendment, Revocation After marriage, a premarital agreement may be amended or revoked only by a written agreement signed by the parties. The amended agreement or the revocation is enforceable without consideration.

§ 6. Enforcement (a) A premarital agreement is not enforceable if the party against whom enforcement is sought proves that:

(1) that party did not execute the agreement

(2) voluntarily; or

(3) the agreement was unconscionable when it was executed and, before execution of the agreement, that party:

(i) was not provided a fair and reasonable disclosure of the property or financial obligations of the other party;

(ii) did not voluntarily and expressly waive, in writing, any right to disclosure of the property or financial obligations of the other party beyond the disclosure provided; and

(iii) did not have, or reasonably could not have had, an adequate knowledge of the property or financial obligations of the other party.

(b) If a provision of a premarital agreement modifies or eliminates spousal support and that modification or elimination causes one party to the agreement to be eligible for support under a program of public assistance at the time of separation or marital dissolution, a court, notwithstanding the terms of the agreement, may require the other party to provide support to the extent necessary to avoid that eligibility.

(c) An issue of unconscionability of a premarital agreement shall be decided by the court as a matter of law.

Professors Barbara Atwood and Brian Bix, the reporters for the UPMAA, summarize their approach and the comparison with the UPAA as follows:

> The enforcement standards for premarital and marital agreements, set out in Section 9 of the Act, reflect the Committee's goals of protecting vulnerable parties and promoting informed decision-making without placing all agreements under a cloud of uncertainty. Like the UPAA, the Act starts from a presumption of validity, placing the burden of proof on the party seeking to avoid enforcement. The standards for enforceability, however, diverge significantly from the UPAA. Under UPMAA's Section 9, an agreement is unenforceable if a party proves any one of four independent showings: that the agreement was involuntary or the result of duress; that the party lacked access to independent legal representation; that the party, if unrepresented by counsel, received neither an explanation of the rights being waived nor a safe-harbor warning in the agreement; or that adequate financial disclosure was not made. Each of these showings represents an independent requirement for validity; two are newly-formulated versions of similar requirements in the UPAA, and two are new requirements. Importantly, a court may refuse to enforce an agreement if it finds a term to have been unconscionable at the time of signing or, as a bracketed alternative, if enforcement would result in substantial hardship because of a material change in circumstance since the signing of the agreement.

Barbara A. Atwood & Brian H. Bix, A New Uniform Law for Premarital and Marital Agreements, 46 Fam. L.Q. 313, 339 (2012).

NOTES AND QUESTIONS

1. Under the UPAA, what is the relationship between disclosure (or the lack thereof) and the fairness of the terms? How does this differ, if it does, from traditional law? From the approach adopted in *Simeone*? From the approach in the

UPMAA? Under the UPAA, what is the relationship between voluntariness and disclosure? *See* Penhallow v. Penhallow, 649 A.2d 1016 (R.I. 1994) (a finding of unconscionability by itself would not render a premarital agreement unenforceable because the UPAA requires proof of both involuntary execution and nondisclosure and/or waivers in addition to unconscionability). What do Atwood and Bix mean when they describe the four showings the UPMAA requires as "independent" requirements?

2. What is the test for voluntariness under the UPAA? Most interpretations of the UPAA reject any requirement of independent counsel. *See, e.g.*, Penhallow v. Penhallow, 649 A.2d 1016 (R.I. 1994). How does the UPMAA differ? What does it mean to have access to legal representation under the Act? Are there circumstances in which an agreement will be enforceable even without legal representation? If the UPMAA applied and you represented the husband in *Simeone*, what would you suggest he do to make sure that the agreement is enforceable under the UPMAA?

3. The UPAA, like a number of recent cases, provides that under certain circumstances an agreement is unenforceable if it is "unconscionable." This term is borrowed from the commercial context. Both the Uniform Commercial Code (UCC) and the Restatement of the Law of Contracts 2d provide that unconscionable contracts are not enforceable.[4] The UCC uses the term without defining it. *See* Arthur A. Leff, The Emperor's New Clause, 115 U. Pa. L. Rev. 485 (1967). What does it mean? Consider Melvin A. Eisenberg, The Bargain Principle and Its Limits, 95 Harv. L. Rev. 741, 752 (1982):

> When the concept of unconscionability was first made explicit by the Uniform Commercial Code, the initial effort was to reconcile it with the bargain principle. A major step in this direction was a distinction, drawn in 1967 by Arthur Leff, between "procedural" and "substantive" unconscionability. Leff defined procedural unconscionability as fault or unfairness in the bargaining *process*; substantive unconscionability as fault or unfairness in the bargaining *outcome* — that is, unfairness of terms. The effect (if not the purpose) of this distinction, which influenced much of the later analysis, was to domesticate unconscionability by accepting the concept insofar as it could be made harmonious with the bargain principle (that is, insofar as it was "procedural"), while rejecting its wider implication that in appropriate cases the courts might review bargains for fairness of terms. Correspondingly, much of the scholarly literature and case law concerning unconscionability has emphasized

---

4. **UCC § 2-302. Unconscionable Contract or Clause** If the court as a matter of law finds the contract or any clause of the contract to have been unconscionable at the time it was made, the court may refuse to enforce the contract, or it may enforce the remainder of the contract without the unconscionable clause, or it may so limit the application of any unconscionable clause as to avoid any unconscionable result.

When it is claimed or appears to the court that the contract or any clause thereof may be unconscionable the parties shall be afforded a reasonable opportunity to present evidence as to its commercial setting, purpose and effect to aid the court in making the determination.

Restatement of the Law of Contracts 2d § 208, Unconscionable Contract or Term If a contract or term thereof is unconscionable at the time the contract is made, a court may refuse to enforce the contract, or may enforce the remainder of the contract without the unconscionable term, or may so limit the application of any unconscionable term as to avoid any unconscionable result.

the element of unfair surprise, in which a major underpinning of the bargain principle — knowing assent — is absent by hypothesis.

Over the last fifteen years, however, there have been strong indications that the principle of unconscionability authorizes a review of elements well beyond unfair surprise, including, in appropriate cases, fairness of terms.

Can each term be assessed separately, or must the agreement be viewed in terms of its fairness as a whole? *See* In re Marriage of Ikeler, 161 P.3d 663 (Colo. 2007), invalidating a clause precluding attorneys' fees as unconscionable in an otherwise enforceable agreement. Compare the different approaches to unconscionability in the UPMAA and the UPAA. Some commentators have argued that the UPAA made it easier to enforce a premarital agreement than a commercial contract. Do you see why? One of the purposes of the UPMAA was to address that anomaly. Under the UPMAA, is the standard for unconscionability the same as the standard that applied to commercial contracts, or does it make premarital agreements harder or easier to enforce? What does it mean for a uniform act to contain a "bracketed alternative"?

4. What does Section 3(b) of the UPAA, pertaining to child support, mean? How does it differ from Section 10 of the UPMAA? What latitude for bargaining do the two Acts give the parties? Traditionally, parties' agreements regarding arrangements for children have not been enforceable, on the theory that the court must always have authority to act in the best interests of children. What does this principle suppose about the way parents negotiate agreements? About the capacity of courts?

> *Principles of the Law of Family Dissolution*
> ### § 7.04 Procedural Requirements
> (1) An agreement is not enforceable if it is not set forth in a writing signed by both parties.
>
> (2) A party seeking to enforce an agreement must show that the other party's consent to it was informed and not obtained under duress.
>
> (3) A premarital agreement is rebuttably presumed to satisfy the requirements of Paragraph (2) when the party seeking to enforce the agreement shows that
>
> > (a) it was executed at least 30 days before the parties' marriage;
> >
> > (b) both parties were advised to obtain independent legal counsel, and had reasonable opportunity to do so, before the agreement's execution; and
> >
> > (c) in the case of agreements concluded without the assistance of independent legal counsel for each party, the agreement states, in language easily understandable by an adult of ordinary intelligence with no legal training,
> >
> > > (i) the nature of any rights or claims otherwise arising at dissolution that are altered by the contract, and the nature of that alteration, and
> > >
> > > (ii) that the interests of the spouses with respect to the agreement may be adverse.
>
> ### § 7.05 When Enforcement Would Work a Substantial Injustice
> (1) A court should not enforce a term in an agreement if, pursuant to Paragraphs (2) and (3) of this section,

(a) the circumstances require it to consider whether enforcement would work a substantial injustice; and

(b) the court finds that enforcement would work a substantial injustice.

(2) A court should consider whether enforcement of an agreement would work a substantial injustice if, and only if, the party resisting its enforcement shows that one or more of the following have occurred since the time of the agreement's execution:

(a) more than a fixed number of years have passed, that number being set in a rule of statewide application;

(b) a child was born to, or adopted by, the parties, who at the time of execution had no children in common;

(c) there has been a change in circumstances that has a substantial impact on the parties or their children, but when they executed the agreement the parties probably did not anticipate either the change, or its impact.

(3) The party claiming that enforcement of an agreement would work a substantial injustice has the burden of proof on that question. In deciding whether the agreement's application to the parties' circumstances at dissolution would work a substantial injustice, a court should consider all of the following:

(a) the magnitude of the disparity between the outcome under the agreement and the outcome under otherwise prevailing legal principles;

(b) for those marriages of limited duration in which it is practical to ascertain, the difference between the circumstances of the objecting party if the agreement is enforced, and that party's likely circumstances had the marriage never taken place;

(c) whether the purpose of the agreement was to benefit or protect the interests of third parties (such as children from a prior relationship), whether that purpose is still relevant, and whether the agreement's terms were reasonably designed to serve it;

(d) the impact of the agreement's enforcement upon the children of the parties.

JUDITH T. YOUNGER, *A MINNESOTA COMPARATIVE FAMILY LAW SYMPOSIUM: ANTENUPTIAL AGREEMENTS*

28 Wm. Mitchell L. Rev. 697, 716-720 (2001)

California was the first state to adopt the Uniform Premarital Agreement Act, although it, like a number of other jurisdictions, modified it to conform more closely to its own prior law. Since California's adoption in 1985, twenty-five states followed suit. . . . As the California Supreme Court pointed out in the *Bonds* case, the Act was intended to enhance the enforceability of antenuptial agreements. To that end, it specifically included spousal support as a permissible subject for antenuptial agreement and attempted to circumscribe courts in their reviews of these agreements for procedural and substantive fairness. . . . The Act also limited the review at enforcement to provisions waiving or modifying spousal support rights which, if enforced, would result in making a spouse eligible for public assistance. It has been roundly criticized, of course, and whether it has accomplished its goals in the adopting jurisdictions is hard to determine. . . .

Enter then, the American Law Institute, with its new Principles of Family Dissolution. The Principles provide procedural requirements for antenuptial agreements of the sort already required by most, if not all, states. These requirements are a signed writing, financial disclosure and a showing of informed consent not obtained under duress. The latter is the rough equivalent of the common law and Uniform Act requirements of voluntariness. The Reporters justify the new language by stating their desire to focus the courts' attention on the tactics of the proponent of the agreement rather than on the state of mind of the challenger; however, the change seems little more than a misguided example of "elegant variation." The Principles raise a presumption of informed consent and the absence of duress if the agreement was executed at least thirty days before the parties' marriage, both parties were advised to obtain legal counsel and had opportunity to do so. In an important departure from existing law, the Principles put the burden of proving the lack of duress and the presence of consent on the party who is trying to enforce the agreement. The Reporters hope that this change in the usual contract rule will "caution the stronger party against overreaching tactics that would make this burden of proof more difficult to meet." . . . In cases where one party did not have independent counsel, for the presumption to arise, the agreement must contain understandable language explaining the significance of its terms and the fact that the parties' interests may be adverse with respect to them.

It is on the subject of substantive fairness that the Principles are most remarkable. They depart from the Uniform Act and the common law by omitting any requirement of substantive fairness at the time of execution of an antenuptial agreement. If contained in a signed writing and entered with disclosure, without duress and with informed consent, the agreement satisfies the test at execution no matter how one-sided or unfair its terms. At enforcement, however, the Principles call for a wider substantive review of these agreements than called for by the Uniform Act. . . . The Principles would prohibit enforcement of antenuptial agreements whenever enforcement would "work a substantial injustice." Here, again, the Principles opt for new language abandoning the old standard of unconscionableness at enforcement. They lay out guidelines to help courts in applying the new language. Before making any inquiry into the effects of enforcement, under the Principles, one of three prerequisites must be present: the passage of a certain number of years after execution; or the birth or adoption of a child to parties who had no children at execution; or a significant, unexpected change in circumstances since execution. If one of these events has occurred the court can consider whether the enforcement of the agreement would work a substantial injustice. Again, in an attempt to help courts with the inquiry, the Principles lay out a number of factors which courts already consider: the disparity of outcome under the agreement and under the marital property regime; the likely circumstances of the party challenging the agreement had the marriage never taken place; whether the agreement was designed to benefit or protect the interests of third parties; and the impact of its enforcement on post-execution children. Overall, the Principles are to be applauded for incorporating the best practices of the courts and trying to tread a middle ground between those who would refuse to enforce antenuptial agreements altogether and those who would enforce them as ordinary business contracts.

NOTES AND QUESTIONS

1. Many attorneys are wary of drafting premarital agreements because of potential liability for malpractice in the event that the agreements are found to be unenforceable. Would adoption of the ALI Principles make such attorneys more or less willing to draft premarital agreements?

2. Contract law and the UPAA determine unconscionability at the time the agreement is signed. The ALI Principles and a number of non-UPAA state court rulings determine validity at the time of enforcement. Which approach makes more sense?

3. Professor Younger refers to the ALI Principles' emphasis on procedural requirements such as "a signed writing, financial disclosure and a showing of informed consent not obtained under duress" that she describes as already required by a number of states. Is the approach of the ALI on financial disclosure and a showing of informed consent similar to or different from the UPAA's?

4. Professor Younger also emphasizes the limited review of the substance of the agreement at the time it is signed and the far more extensive review contemplated at the time of enforcement. What does this mean for the validity of a one-sided agreement? Is it possible for it to be valid when signed, but not enforceable 20 years later?

5. The ALI's procedural requirements refer to the "reasonable opportunity" to "obtain independent legal counsel." In Friezo v. Friezo, 914 A.2d 533 (Conn. 2007), the trial court concluded that the wife did not have such an opportunity, as required by Connecticut law, because the wife consulted an attorney, suggested by her husband's sister, who charged her no fee, met with her only briefly, and did not explain the agreement to her or provide her with significant advice. The Connecticut Supreme Court reversed the trial court decision, finding that she had the opportunity to meet with any attorney she chose, signed a conflict-of-interest waiver permitting the attorney to represent her, and never sought additional representation or legal advice. *Id.* at 557-558.

PROBLEMS

1. On the day of Hank and Wanda's wedding they signed a premarital agreement providing that if they divorced, Hank would give Wanda a house and $500,000 or half his assets, whichever value was greater. Hank and Wanda divorced eight months later. Hank has attacked the agreement as violating public policy because it encourages divorce. How should the court rule and why? If you learned that Hank and Wanda are immigrants and that such agreements are common in the country of their birth, would you change your answer?

2. When Carl and Jill were married, Jill was 18, pregnant, and unemployed. Carl, who was 25, had graduated from college and worked on his family's farm. Their premarital agreement, drafted by Carl's family attorney, provided that if the

parties divorced, neither would be entitled to the property of the other, and neither would be entitled to spousal or child support. Carl told Jill that if she would not sign the agreement, he would not marry her. Jill, who was not represented by counsel, reluctantly agreed. Their baby was born six months after the wedding, and ten months later Carl moved out of the house. Jill filed for divorce and sought spousal and child support. Carl responded with the premarital agreement. In a jurisdiction that has adopted the UPAA, what arguments should Jill's attorney make in support of her position that the agreement is not enforceable? How should Carl's attorney respond? How would the analysis change if the parties live in a jurisdiction that follows traditional legal principles about the enforceability of premarital agreements? In a jurisdiction that followed the ALI Principles? In a jurisdiction that adopted the UPMAA?

3. Harriet and Wynona were married 14 years ago. Each had previously been married and has children from the former marriage. At the time of their wedding, Harriet, then 32 years old, was part owner of her family's successful business. Wynona, who was 27, worked as a secretary in the business. When they married, Wynona owned property worth $5000, and Harriet's interest in the family business was worth $550,000. After fully disclosing their assets and income to each other, they signed a premarital agreement, which provided that all of the property Harriet owned before marriage, along with increases in value and income from it, would remain her separate property. The agreement also limited Wynona's claim to spousal support to $200 per month for 10 years. During their marriage Harriet gave birth to another child, using Wynona's egg and sperm from an anonymous donor. After the child's birth, Wynona did not work outside the home, and Harriet continued to work in the family business, which grew rapidly. At the time of divorce Harriet's interest in the business was worth $8 million, and her income was $250,000 per year. Wynona's property had tripled in value (to $15,000), but she had no income and only 14-year-old skills as a secretary. Under traditional rules, would the agreement be enforceable? Under *Simeone*? Under *Lane*? Under the UPMAA? Under the UPAA? Under the ALI Principles?

4. Susan was 50 and John was 78 when they married four years ago. Susan, who was divorced and had two children and three grandchildren, owned her own home and worked as a real estate agent. John lived on his 30-acre farm. He had never married before and had no children or living siblings. On the day of their wedding they signed a premarital agreement drafted by Susan's attorney. The agreement did not include a written disclosure of their assets, but the attorney explained the agreement in detail to both parties and asked if they had any questions. Neither did, and both affirmed that they wanted to sign the agreement. The agreement provided that all Susan's property would remain her separate property, that John would transfer all his real property into tenancy by the entireties, and that he would transfer all his cash and personal property into joint tenancy with Susan. The agreement also said that if Susan initiated a divorce, she would have to return to John all property she had acquired under the agreement, but that if he initiated a divorce, Susan would retain the property she had acquired. After the wedding the couple lived on John's farm.

Three months ago Susan filed a domestic violence complaint against John and obtained a restraining order requiring him to move out and to stay away from her. He went to stay with neighbors, who filed a complaint with the local senior services agency alleging that Susan was abusing and financially exploiting John. A state social worker investigated the complaint and made a written report that it was "founded," but no further action was taken.

John has now filed a petition for divorce, which requests that the premarital agreement be invalidated. Under the traditional law would the agreement be enforceable? Under *Simeone*? Under the UPAA? Under the ALI Principles?

5. George was 55 and Martha was 50 when they married four years ago. Martha had a teenage daughter from a prior marriage, for whom she received child support, and George had no children. Before the wedding, George and Martha signed a premarital agreement providing that "neither one shall have or acquire any right, title or claim to the property of the other" and that "neither party, in the case of a divorce, shall have a right to division of property or support from the other." Neither was represented by an attorney, but both knew the nature and extent of the other's property. At the time of the wedding, George owned little property, had taken early retirement, and received pension income of $1247 per month. Martha owned a home worth $60,000 and other assets worth $5500. Martha was employed and earned $30,000 per year, but during the marriage she became very disabled and had to quit her job. She cannot work and has no source of income, though she may be eligible for Social Security Disability benefits. She still owns the home, which together with her other assets is now worth $70,000. George has petitioned for divorce and asked the court to enforce the premarital agreement. Should the agreement be enforced under the UPAA?

C. SPOUSAL CONTRACTS DURING MARRIAGE

BORELLI V. BRUSSEAU

16 Cal. Rptr. 2d 16 (Cal. App. 1993)

PERLEY, J. . . . On April 24, 1980, appellant and decedent entered into an antenuptial contract. On April 25, 1980, they were married. Appellant remained married to decedent until the death of the latter on January 25, 1989.

In March 1983, February 1984, and January 1987, decedent was admitted to a hospital due to heart problems. As a result, "decedent became concerned and frightened about his health and longevity." He discussed these fears and concerns with appellant and told her that he intended to "leave" the following property to her.

1. "An interest" in a lot in Sacramento, California.
2. A life estate for the use of a condominium in Hawaii.
3. A 25 percent interest in Borelli Meat Co.
4. All cash remaining in all existing bank accounts at the time of his death.
5. The costs of educating decedent's stepdaughter, Monique Lee.

6. Decedent's entire interest in a residence in Kensington, California.
7. All furniture located in the residence.
8. Decedent's interest in a partnership.
9. Health insurance for appellant and Monique Lee.

In August 1988, decedent suffered a stroke while in the hospital. "Through-out the decedent's August, 1988 hospital stay and subsequent treatment at a reha-bilitation center, he repeatedly told [appellant] that he was uncomfortable in the hospital and that he disliked being away from home. The decedent repeatedly told [appellant] that he did not want to be admitted to a nursing home, even though it meant he would need round-the-clock care, and rehabilitative modifications to the house, in order for him to live at home."

"In or about October, 1988, [appellant] and the decedent entered an oral agreement whereby the decedent promised to leave to [appellant] the property listed [above]. . . . In exchange for the decedent's promise to leave her the property . . . [appellant] agreed to care for the decedent in his home, for the duration of his illness, thereby avoiding the need for him to move to a rest home or convalescent hospital as his doctors recommended. . . .

Appellant performed her promise but the decedent did not perform his. Instead his will bequeathed her the sum of $100,000 and his interest in the resi-dence they owned as joint tenants. The bulk of decedent's estate passed to respondent, who is decedent's daughter.

Discussion

"It is fundamental that a marriage contract differs from other contractual relations in that there exists a definite and vital public interest in reference to the marriage relation. . . ."

"The laws relating to marriage and divorce have been enacted because of the profound concern of our organized society for the dignity and stability of the marriage relationship. This concern relates primarily to the status of the parties as husband and wife. The concern of society as to the property rights of the parties is secondary and incidental to its concern as to their status." . . .

In accordance with these concerns the following pertinent legislation has been enacted: Civil Code section 242 — "Every individual shall support his or her spouse. . . ." Civil Code section 4802 — "[A] husband and wife cannot, by any contract with each other, alter their legal relations, except as to property. . . ." Civil Code section 5100 — "Husband and wife contract toward each other obliga-tions of mutual respect, fidelity, and support." Civil Code section 5103 — "[E]ither husband or wife may enter into any transaction with the other . . . respecting prop-erty, which either might if unmarried." Civil Code section 5132 — "[A] married person shall support the person's spouse while they are living together."

The courts have stringently enforced and explained the statutory language. "Although most of the cases, both in California and elsewhere, deal with a wife's right to support from the husband, in this state a wife also has certain obligations to support the husband."

"Indeed, husband and wife assume mutual obligations of support upon marriage. These obligations are not conditioned on the existence of community property or income." "In entering the marital state, by which a contract is created, it must be assumed that the parties voluntarily entered therein with knowledge that they have the moral and legal obligation to support the other."

Moreover, interspousal mutual obligations have been broadly defined. "[Husband's] duties and obligations to [wife] included more than mere cohabitation with her. It was his duty to offer [wife] his sympathy, confidence [citation], and fidelity." When necessary, spouses must "provide uncompensated protective supervision services for" each other.

Estate of Sonnicksen (1937) [73 P.2d 643] and Brooks v. Brooks (1941) [119 P.2d 970] each hold that under the above statutes and in accordance with the above policy a wife is obligated by the marriage contract to provide nursing-type care to an ill husband. Therefore, contracts whereby the wife is to receive compensation for providing such services are void as against public policy; and there is no consideration for the husband's promise.

Appellant argues that *Sonnicksen* and *Brooks* are no longer valid precedents because they are based on outdated views of the role of women and marriage. She further argues that the rule of those cases denies her equal protection because husbands only have a financial obligation toward their wives, while wives have to provide actual nursing services for free. We disagree. The rule and policy of *Sonnicksen* and *Brooks* have been applied to both spouses in several recent cases arising in different areas of the law. . . .

Vincent v. State of California (1971) [99 Cal. Rptr. 410], held that for purposes of benefit payments spouses caring for each other must be treated identically under similar assistance programs. In reaching such conclusion the court held: "Appellants suggest that one reason justifying denial of payment for services rendered by ATD attendants who reside with their recipient spouses is that, by virtue of the marriage contract, one spouse is obligated to care for the other without remuneration.

"Such preexisting duty provides a constitutionally sound basis for a classification which denies compensation for care rendered by a husband or wife to his spouse who is receiving welfare assistance. . . . But insofar as one spouse has a duty created by the marriage contract to care for the other without compensation when they are living together, recipients of aid to the aged, aid to the blind and aid to the disabled are similarly situated."

These cases indicate that the marital duty of support under Civil Code sections 242, 5100, and 5132 includes caring for a spouse who is ill. They also establish that support in a marriage means more than the physical care someone could be hired to provide. Such support also encompasses sympathy, comfort, love, companionship and affection. Thus, the duty of support can no more be "delegated" to a third party than the statutory duties of fidelity and mutual respect. Marital duties are owed by the spouses personally. This is implicit in the definition of marriage as "a personal relation arising out of a civil contract between a man and a woman." (Civ. Code, sec. 4100.)

We therefore adhere to the long-standing rule that a spouse is not entitled to compensation for support, apart from rights to community property and the like that arise from the marital relation itself. Personal performance of a personal duty created by the contract of marriage does not constitute a new consideration supporting the indebtedness, alleged in this case. . . .

Speculating that appellant might have left her husband but for the agreement she alleges, the dissent suggests that marriages will break up if such agreements are not enforced. While we do not believe that marriages would be fostered by a rule that encouraged sickbed bargaining, the question is not whether such negotiations may be more useful than unseemly. The issue is whether such negotiations are antithetical to the institution of marriage as the Legislature has defined it. We believe that they are.

The dissent maintains that mores have changed to the point that spouses can be treated just like any other parties haggling at arm's length. Whether or not the modern marriage has become like a business, and regardless of whatever else it may have become, it continues to be defined by statute as a personal relationship of mutual support. Thus, even if few things are left that cannot command a price, marital support remains one of them. . . .

POCHE, J., dissenting. A very ill person wishes to be cared for at home personally by his spouse rather than by nurses at a health care facility. The ill person offers to pay his spouse for such personal care by transferring property to her. The offer is accepted, the services are rendered and the ill spouse dies. Affirming a judgment of dismissal rendered after a general demurrer was sustained, this court holds that the contract was not enforceable because — as a matter of law — the spouse who rendered services gave no consideration. Apparently, in the majority's view she had a preexisting or precontract nondelegable duty to clean the bedpans herself. Because I do not believe she did, I respectfully dissent.

The majority correctly read Estate of Sonnicksen (1937) [73 P.2d 643] and Brooks v. Brooks (1941) [119 P.2d 970] as holding that a wife cannot enter into a binding contract with her husband to provide "nursing-type care" for compensation. . . . It reasons that the wife, by reason of the marital relationship, already has a duty to provide such care, thus she offers no new consideration to support an independent contract to the same effect. The logic of these decisions is ripe for reexamination.

Sonnicksen and Brooks are the California Court of Appeal versions of a national theme. Excerpts from several of these decisions reveal the ethos and mores of the era which produced them.

"It would operate disastrously upon domestic life and breed discord and mischief if the wife could contract with her husband for the payment of services to be rendered for him in his home; if she could exact compensation for services, disagreeable or otherwise, rendered to members of his family; if she could sue him upon such contracts and establish them upon the disputed and conflicting testimony of the members of the household. To allow such contracts would degrade the wife by making her a menial and a servant in the home where she should discharge marital duties in loving and devoted ministrations, and frauds upon creditors would be greatly facilitated, as the wife could frequently absorb all her husband's property in the payment of her services, rendered under such secret, unknown contracts."

"A man cannot be entitled to the services of his wife for nothing, by virtue of a uniform and unchangeable marriage contract, and at the same time be under obligation to pay her for those services. . . . She cannot be his wife and his hired servant at the same time. . . . That would be inconsistent with the marriage relation, and disturb the reciprocal duties of the parties." . . .

Statements in two of these cases to the effect that a husband has an entitlement to his wife's "services" smack of the common law doctrine of coverture which treated a wife as scarcely more than an appendage to her husband. . . . One of the characteristics of coverture was that it deemed the wife economically helpless and governed by an implicit exchange: "The husband, as head of the family, is charged with its support and maintenance in return for which he is entitled to the wife's services in all those domestic affairs which pertain to the comfort, care, and well-being of the family. Her labors are her contribution to the family support and care." But coverture has been discarded in California, where both husband and wife owe each other the duty of support.

Not only has this doctrinal base for the authority underpinning the majority opinion been discarded long ago, but modern attitudes toward marriage have changed almost as rapidly as the economic realities of modern society. The assumption that only the rare wife can make a financial contribution to her family has become badly outdated in this age in which many married women have paying employment outside the home. A two-income family can no longer be dismissed as a statistically insignificant aberration. Moreover today husbands are increasingly involved in the domestic chores that make a house a home. Insofar as marital duties and property rights are not governed by positive law, they may be the result of informal accommodation or formal agreement. If spouses cannot work things out, there is always the no longer infrequently used option of divorce. For better or worse, we have to a great extent left behind the comfortable and familiar gender-based roles evoked by Norman Rockwell paintings. No longer can the marital relationship be regarded as "uniform and unchangeable." . . .

No one doubts that spouses owe each other a duty of support or that this encompasses "the obligation to provide medical care." There is nothing found in *Sonnicksen* and *Brooks*, or cited by the majority, which requires that this obligation be *personally* discharged by a spouse except the decisions themselves. However, at the time *Sonnicksen* and *Brooks* were decided — before World War II — it made sense for those courts to say that a wife could perform her duty of care only by doing so personally. That was an accurate reflection of the real world for women years before the exigency of war produced substantial employment opportunities for them. . . .

However the real world has changed in the 56 years since *Sonnicksen* was decided. Just a few years later with the advent of World War II Rosie the Riveter became not only a war jingle but a salute to hundreds of thousands of women working on the war effort outside the home. We know what happened thereafter. Presumably, in the present day husbands and wives who work outside the home have alternative methods of meeting this duty of care to an ill spouse. Among the choices would be: (1) paying for professional help; (2) paying for nonprofessional assistance; (3) seeking help from relatives or friends; and (4) quitting one's job and doing the work personally.

A fair reading of the complaint indicates that Mrs. Borelli initially chose the first of these options, and that this was not acceptable to Mr. Borelli, who then offered compensation if Mrs. Borelli would agree to personally care for him at home. To contend in 1993 that such a contract is without consideration means that if Mrs. Clinton becomes ill, President Clinton must drop everything and personally care for her.

According to the majority, Mrs. Borelli had nothing to bargain with so long as she remained in the marriage. This assumes that an intrinsic component of the marital relationship is the *personal* services of the spouse, an obligation that cannot be delegated or performed by others. The preceding discussion has attempted to demonstrate many ways in which what the majority terms "nursing-type care" can be provided without either husband or wife being required to empty a single bedpan. It follows that, because Mrs. Borelli agreed to supply this personal involvement, she was providing something over and above what would fully satisfy her duty of support. That personal something — precisely because it was something she was not required to do — qualifies as valid consideration sufficient to make enforceable Mr. Borelli's reciprocal promise to convey certain of his separate property.

Not only does the majority's position substantially impinge upon couples' freedom to come to a working arrangement of marital responsibilities, it may also foster the very opposite result of that intended. For example, nothing compelled Mr. Borelli and plaintiff to continue living together after his physical afflictions became known. Moral considerations notwithstanding, no legal force could have stopped plaintiff from leaving her husband in his hour of need. Had she done so, and had Mr. Borelli promised to give her some of his separate property should she come back, a valid contract would have arisen upon her return. Deeming them contracts promoting reconciliation and the resumption of marital relations, California courts have long enforced such agreements as supported by consideration. Here so far as we can tell from the face of the complaint, Mr. Borelli and plaintiff reached largely the same result without having to endure a separation. There is no sound reason why their contract, which clearly facilitated continuation of their marriage, should be any less valid. . . .

BEDRICK v. BEDRICK

17 A.3d 17 (Conn. 2011)

McLACHLAN, J. This appeal involves a dissolution of marriage action in which the defendant, Bruce L. Bedrick, seeks to enforce a postnuptial agreement.[5]

---

5. A postnuptial agreement is distinguishable from both a prenuptial agreement and a separation agreement. Like a prenuptial agreement, a postnuptial agreement may determine, inter alia, each spouse's legal rights and obligations upon dissolution of the marriage. As the name suggests, however, a postnuptial agreement is entered into during marriage — after a couple weds, but before they separate, when the spouses "plan to continue their marriage"; A.L.I., Principles of the Law of Family Dissolution: Analysis and Recommendations (2002) § 7.01(1)(b), p. 1052; and when "separation or divorce is not imminent." Black's Law Dictionary (9th Ed. 2009).

Today we are presented for the first time with the issue of whether a postnuptial agreement is valid and enforceable in Connecticut.

The defendant appeals from the trial court's judgment in favor of the plaintiff, Deborah Bedrick. The defendant claims that the trial court improperly relied upon principles of fairness and equity in concluding that the postnuptial agreement was unenforceable and, instead, should have applied only ordinary principles of contract law. We conclude that postnuptial agreements are valid and enforceable and generally must comply with contract principles. We also conclude, however, that the terms of such agreements must be both fair and equitable at the time of execution and not unconscionable at the time of dissolution. Because the terms of the present agreement were unconscionable at the time of dissolution, we affirm the judgment of the trial court. . . .

I

The defendant contends that the trial court improperly applied equitable principles in determining whether the postnuptial agreement was enforceable and, instead, should have applied only principles of contract law. . . . Although we agree with the defendant that principles of contract law generally apply in determining the enforceability of a postnuptial agreement, we conclude that postnuptial agreements are subject to special scrutiny and the terms of such agreements must be both fair and equitable at the time of execution and not unconscionable at the time of dissolution. . . .

The standard applicable to postnuptial agreements presents a question of law, over which our review is plenary. We begin our analysis of postnuptial agreements by considering the public policies served by the recognition of agreements regarding the dissolution of marriage, including prenuptial, postnuptial and separation agreements.

Historically, we have stated that "[t]he state does not favor divorces. . . . Its [public] policy is to maintain the family relation[ship] as a life status." McCarthy v. Santangelo, 137 Conn. 410, 412, 78 A.2d 240 (1951). Accordingly, prenuptial agreements were generally held to violate public policy if they promoted, facilitated or provided an incentive for separation or divorce. Similarly, a separation agreement is not necessarily contrary to public policy unless it is made to facilitate divorce or is concealed from the court.

More recently, our court has acknowledged that the government has an interest in encouraging the incorporation of separation agreements into decrees for dissolution. Postnuptial agreements may also encourage the private resolution of family issues. In particular, they may allow couples to eliminate a source of emotional turmoil — usually, financial uncertainty — and focus instead on resolving other aspects of the marriage that may be problematic. By alleviating anxiety over uncertainty in the determination of legal rights and obligations upon dissolution, postnuptial agreements do not encourage or facilitate dissolution; in fact, they harmonize with our public policy favoring enduring marriages.

Postnuptial agreements are consistent with public policy; they realistically acknowledge the high incidence of divorce and its effect upon our population. . . . "[R]ecent statistics on divorce have forced people to deal with the reality that many marriages do not last a lifetime. As desirable as it may seem for couples to embark upon marriage in a state of optimism and hope, the reality is that many marriages end in divorce. There is a growing trend toward serial marriage; more people expect to have more than one spouse during their lifetime." T. Perry, Dissolution Planning in Family Law: A Critique of Current Analyses and a Look toward the Future, 24 Fam. L.Q. 77, 82 (1990). "[B]oth the realities of our society and policy reasons favor judicial recognition of prenuptial agreements. Rather than inducing divorce, such agreements simply acknowledge its ordinariness. With divorce as likely an outcome of marriage as permanence, we see no logical or compelling reason why public policy should not allow two mature adults to handle their own financial affairs. . . . The reasoning that once found them contrary to public policy has no place in today's matrimonial law." Brooks v. Brooks, 733 P.2d 1044, 1050-51 (Alaska 1987). Postnuptial agreements are no different than prenuptial agreements in this regard.

Having determined that postnuptial agreements are consistent with public policy, we now must consider what standards govern their enforcement. Neither the legislature nor this court has addressed this question. To aid in our analysis of the enforceability of postnuptial agreements, we review our law on the enforceability of prenuptial agreements.[6] . . .

Prenuptial agreements entered into on or after October 1, 1995, are governed by the Connecticut Premarital Agreement Act, General Statutes § 46b-36a et seq. The statutory scheme provides that a prenuptial agreement is unenforceable when: (1) the challenger did not enter the agreement voluntarily; (2) the agreement was unconscionable when executed or enforced; (3) the challenger did not receive "a fair and reasonable disclosure of the amount, character and value of property, financial obligations and income of the other party" before execution of the agreement; or (4) the challenger did not have "a reasonable opportunity to consult with independent counsel." . . .

Although we view postnuptial agreements as encouraging the private resolution of family issues, we also recognize that spouses do not contract under the same conditions as either prospective spouses or spouses who have determined to dissolve their marriage. The Supreme Judicial Court of Massachusetts has noted that a postnuptial "agreement stands on a different footing from both a [prenuptial agreement] and a separation agreement. Before marriage, the parties have greater freedom to reject an unsatisfactory [prenuptial] contract. . . .

"A separation agreement, in turn, is negotiated when a marriage has failed and the spouses intend a permanent separation or marital dissolution. . . . The circumstances surrounding [postnuptial] agreements in contrast are pregnant with the opportunity for one party to use the threat of dissolution to bargain themselves into positions of advantage. . . .

---

6. We do not review our law on the enforceability of separation agreements, which are distinct from both prenuptial and postnuptial agreements and are entered into when spouses have determined to dissolve their marriage. We merely note that their enforcement is governed by General Statutes § 46b-66(a), which provides in relevant part that "where the parties have submitted to the court an agreement concerning . . . alimony or the disposition of property, the court shall . . . determine whether the agreement of the spouses is fair and equitable under all the circumstances. . . ."

"For these reasons, we join many other [s]tates in concluding that [postnuptial] agreements must be carefully scrutinized." Ansin v. Craven-Ansin, supra, 457 Mass. at 289-90, 929 N.E.2d 955. The Appellate Division of the New Jersey Superior Court has also recognized this "contextual difference" and has noted that a wife "face[s] a more difficult choice than [a] bride who is presented with a demand for a pre-nuptial agreement. The cost to [a wife is] . . . the destruction of a family and the stigma of a failed marriage." Pacelli v. Pacelli, 319 N.J. Super. 185, 190, 725 A.2d 56 (App. Div.), cert. denied, 161 N.J. 147, 735 A.2d 572 (1999). A spouse who bargains a settlement agreement, on the other hand, "recogniz[es] that the marriage is over, can look to his or her economic rights; the relationship is adversarial." Thus, a spouse enters a postnuptial agreement under different conditions than a party entering either a prenuptial or a separation agreement.

Other state courts have not only observed that spouses contract under different conditions; they have also observed that postnuptial agreements "should not be treated as mere 'business deals.'" Stoner v. Stoner, 572 Pa. 665, 672-73, 819 A.2d 529 (2003). They recognize that, just like prospective spouses, "parties to these agreements do not quite deal at arm's length, but rather at the time the contract is entered into stand in a relation of mutual confidence and trust. . . ."

. . .

Because of the nature of the marital relationship, the spouses to a postnuptial agreement may not be as cautious in contracting with one another as they would be with prospective spouses, and they are certainly less cautious than they would be with an ordinary contracting party. With lessened caution comes greater potential for one spouse to take advantage of the other. This leads us to conclude that postnuptial agreements require stricter scrutiny than prenuptial agreements. In applying special scrutiny, a court may enforce a postnuptial agreement only if it complies with applicable contract principles,[7] and the terms of the agreement

---

7. The defendant also argues that the trial court improperly concluded that the postnuptial agreement at issue failed to comply with contract principles because it lacked adequate consideration. Because we conclude that the trial court properly found that the present agreement was unenforceable, we need not address whether the agreement also could have failed for lack of consideration.

General Statutes § 46b-36c, however, expressly provides that prenuptial agreements are enforceable without consideration. Because no similar statute exists for postnuptial agreements, and because such agreements generally must comply with contract principles, the present agreement would require adequate consideration to be enforceable.

. . . In the present case, the plaintiff released, *inter alia*, her right to alimony and her interest in the defendant's car wash business, in exchange for, *inter alia*, the defendant's right to alimony and his release of the plaintiff's liability for the defendant's personal and business loans. Although the trial court found that the present agreement lacked adequate consideration, the agreement would not fail for lack of consideration.

In the present case, the defendant does not argue that a promise to remain married constitutes adequate consideration, and the postnuptial agreement does not refer to any promise to remain married or right to dissolution of marriage. Thus, for purposes of the present dispute, it is irrelevant whether a spouse's forbearance from bringing a claimed dissolution action and the continuation of the marriage provides adequate consideration for a postnuptial agreement.

are both fair and equitable at the time of execution and not unconscionable at the time of dissolution.

We further hold that the terms of a postnuptial agreement are fair and equitable at the time of execution if the agreement is made voluntarily, and without any undue influence, fraud, coercion, duress or similar defect. Moreover, each spouse must be given full, fair and reasonable disclosure of the amount, character and value of property, both jointly and separately held, and all of the financial obligations and income of the other spouse. This mandatory disclosure requirement is a result of the deeply personal marital relationship.[8]

Just as "[t]he validity of a [prenuptial] contract depends upon the circumstances of the particular case"; McHugh v. McHugh, supra, 436 A.2d 8; in determining whether a particular postnuptial agreement is fair and equitable at the time of execution, a court should consider the totality of the circumstances surrounding execution. A court may consider various factors, including "the nature and complexity of the agreement's terms, the extent of and disparity in assets brought to the marriage by each spouse, the parties' respective age, sophistication, education, employment, experience, prior marriages, or other traits potentially affecting the ability to read and understand an agreement's provisions, and the amount of time available to each spouse to reflect upon the agreement after first seeing its specific terms . . . [and] access to independent counsel prior to consenting to the contract terms." Annot., 53 A.L.R.4th 85, 92-93, § 2[a] (1987). . . .

Unfairness or inequality alone does not render a postnuptial agreement unconscionable; spouses may agree on an unequal distribution of assets at dissolution. . . . Unforeseen changes in the relationship, such as having a child, loss of employment or moving to another state, may render enforcement of the agreement unconscionable.

II

Now that we have set forth the applicable legal standards for postnuptial agreements, we turn to the present case and address the question of whether the trial court properly concluded that the parties' postnuptial agreement should not be enforced. . . .

Although the value of the parties combined assets is $927,123, the last addendum to the agreement, dated May 18, 1989, provides that the plaintiff will receive a cash settlement of only $75,000. This addendum was written prior to the initial success of the car wash business in the early 1990s, the birth of the parties' son in 1991, when the parties were forty-one years old, and the subsequent deterioration

---

8. The defendant also argues that the trial court improperly determined that the agreement was unenforceable because the plaintiff did not consult with an attorney. The record, the defendant argues, establishes that the plaintiff had ample time to consult with an attorney, as stated in the text of the agreement itself. Because we conclude that the trial court properly found that the agreement was unenforceable, we do not address this argument beyond noting that, in evaluating the circumstances surrounding a particular agreement, the court should examine the parties' knowledge of their rights and obligations and whether they had a reasonable opportunity to confer with independent counsel.

of the business in the 2000s. At the time of trial, the parties were both fifty-seven years old. Neither had a college degree. The defendant had been steadily employed by the car wash business since 1973. The plaintiff had worked for that business for thirty-five years, providing administrative and bookkeeping support, and since approximately 2001, when the business began to deteriorate, the plaintiff had managed all business operations excluding maintenance. In 2004, the plaintiff also had worked outside of the business in order to provide the family with additional income. Since approximately 2007, when the plaintiff stopped working for the business, the defendant had not been able to complete administrative or bookkeeping tasks, and had not filed taxes.

The trial court found that "[t]he economic circumstances of the parties had changed dramatically since the execution of the agreement" and that "enforcement of the postnuptial agreement would have worked injustice." It, therefore, concluded that the agreement was unenforceable. Although the trial court did not have guidance on the applicable legal standards for postnuptial agreements, which we set forth today, we previously have determined that the question of whether enforcement of a prenuptial agreement would be unconscionable is analogous to determining whether enforcement would work an injustice. Thus, the trial court's finding that enforcement of the postnuptial agreement would work an injustice was tantamount to a finding that the agreement was unconscionable at the time the defendant sought to enforce it. We review the question of unconscionability as a matter of law. The facts and circumstances of the present case clearly support the findings of the trial court that, as a matter of law, enforcement of the agreement would be unconscionable. . . .

NOTES AND QUESTIONS

1. Contracts by married women were generally unenforceable at common law. As the opinions in *Borelli* indicate, several grounds have been advanced to support that view. For Blackstone, the myth of marital unity was a sufficient bar to recognition of agreements between spouses. "A man cannot grant any thing to his wife, or enter into covenant with her: for the grant would be to suppose her separate existence; and to covenant with her, would be only to covenant with himself." 1 William Blackstone, Commentaries on the Laws of England *430. The author of the first treatise on marital relations in the United States took a more sophisticated view: "The law considers the wife to be in the power of the husband; it would not, therefore, be reasonable that she should be bound by any contract she makes during the coverture. . . ." Moreover, execution upon contracts included arrest and confinement in prison; these remedies imposed upon a wife would deprive the husband of her household and other services. Tapping Reeve, Baron and Femme 98 (1970). Marylynn Salmon provides a third explanation:

> In one way or another, everything women owned before marriage became their husbands' afterwards. A significant result of this social policy was the inability of femes coverts to contract. No agreement a woman made could be enforced against her because she owned nothing the court could seize to meet a judgment. Even a woman's contract to provide services was unenforceable. According to common law

rules, a woman's services belonged to her husband. They could not be given to another unless he consented.

Marylynn Salmon, Women and the Law of Property in Early America 41 (1986).

A fourth, perhaps more modern, rationale for the refusal of courts to enforce spousal agreements is found in the classic case of Balfour v. Balfour, L.R. 2 K.B. 571 (C.A. 1919). Plaintiff wife sued her husband for money she claimed to be due from an agreed allowance of £30 a month. They made the agreement while on a visit to England from their home in Ceylon. The wife was unable for medical reasons to return with her husband, and she testified that Mr. Balfour agreed to send her £30 per month until she returned. Subsequently, she decided not to return, and her husband said he would send her £30 a month for maintenance until he returned. Mrs. Balfour later sued for divorce, and the court order enforced the support agreement. Mr. Balfour appealed, and the Court of Appeals reversed.

> . . . [I]t is necessary to remember that there are agreements between parties which do not result in contracts within the meaning of that term in our law. The ordinary example is when two people agree to take a walk together. . . . [O]ne of the most usual forms of agreement which does not constitute a contract appears to me to be the arrangements which are made between husband and wife. It is quite common, and it is the natural and inevitable result of the relationship of husband and wife, that the two spouses should make arrangements between themselves — agreements such as are in dispute in this action — agreements for allowances, by which the husband agrees that he will pay to his wife a certain sum of money per week, or per month, or per year, to cover either her own expenses or the necessary expenses of the household and of the children of the marriage. . . .
>
> To my mind it would be the worst possible example to hold that agreements such as this resulted in legal obligations which could be enforced in the Courts. . . . All I can say is that the small Courts of this country would have to be multiplied one hundredfold if these arrangements were held to result in legal obligations. They are not sued upon, not because the parties are reluctant to enforce their legal rights when the agreement is broken, but because the parties, in the inception of their arrangement, never intended that they should be sued upon. . . . The terms may be repudiated, varied or renewed as performance proceeds or as disagreements develop, and the principles of the common law as to exoneration and discharge and accord and satisfaction are such as find no place in the domestic code. The parties themselves are advocates, judges, Courts, sheriff's officer and reporter. In respect of these promises each house is a domain into which the King's writ does not seek to run, and to which his officers do not seek to be admitted.

The court held that the wife failed to prove that the promise was intended to carry legal consequences.

2. In *Bedrick*, the Connecticut Supreme Court treats the enforceability of a postnuptial (or marital) agreement as one of first impression. After concluding that such agreements may be enforceable, the opinion nonetheless emphasizes that agreements entered during marriage are different from ones entered into before marriage and should be subject to stricter review. What differences does the Connecticut court see between the two types of agreements? Does the UPMAA also draw a distinction between the enforceability of the two types of agreements?

For an example of a statutory scheme with different requirements for premarital and marital agreements, *compare* Minn. Stat. §519.11, Subd. 1 (2010 & Supp. 2011) (premarital agreements) *with id.*, Subd. 1a (marital agreements). Under Minnesota law, a marital agreement must meet all the requirements of premarital agreements, *plus* both parties must be represented by counsel, and it is presumed unenforceable if either party seeks a divorce within two years of its signing (subject to the party seeking enforcement showing the agreement to be fair). Ohio is even stricter, suggesting that contracts that alter the terms of marriage are not enforceable at all. Ohio Rev. Code Ann. §3103.06 (West 2012). For a most supportive view of postnuptial bargaining, *see* Sean Hannon Williams, Postnuptial Agreements, 2007 Wis. L. Rev. 827.

3. Would the agreement in *Borelli* have been enforced under the standards adopted in *Bedrick*? Under the UPMAA? Atwood and Bix, the UPMAA reporters, observe that:

> Consistent with the consensus among states, the Act requires that agreements be in writing and signed by both parties. Similarly, states and commentators have generally taken the position that premarital agreements should be enforceable, without consideration other than the marriage itself, and the Act endorses that position.
>
> The issue of consideration, however, is not a dead letter in the context of marital agreements, with some state courts requiring a showing that agreements between spouses rest on valid consideration. An inquiry into the adequacy of consideration may engage courts in an assessment of the mutuality of the spouses' exchanges, or a determination of whether a delay in filing for divorce constitutes valid consideration. The Committee chose to avoid such inquiries, . . . in holding that marital agreements cannot be invalidated on the basis of an absence of consideration. As elsewhere in contract law, questions about consideration often serve as a vehicle for effectuating general policies of fair dealing. Rather than requiring a showing of consideration, the Act provides such protections more directly through other provisions.

Barbara A. Atwood & Brian H. Bix, A New Uniform Law for Premarital and Marital Agreements, 46 Fam. L.Q. 313, 338 (2012). In Bratton v. Bratton, 136 S.W.3d 595 (Tenn. 2004), the court held that a postnuptial agreement entered into while the husband was in medical school lacked consideration and was unenforceable. The wife requested the agreement soon after the marriage, while she was supporting the husband through medical school; it provided that she was entitled to half his salary for the rest of her life. When the wife sought to enforce the agreement at the time of the divorce 17 years later, the court held that the wife's promise to forgo dental school was illusory because she had made the decision before the agreement was signed.

4. It might seem that Ms. Brusseau would have had a greater chance of success in enforcing her contract if she had not been married to Mr. Borelli and thus not subject to the assumption that her services were already due because of her marriage. Consider, however, the other traditional contract doctrines that might have been at issue in the case: the Statute of Frauds ordinarily applies to contracts to make a will, Mr. Borelli's capacity to contract might have been questioned on the basis of the stroke he suffered, and, if he had changed his will, his daughter might have questioned the result on the basis of undue influence. Indeed, American

courts have generally regarded with suspicion contractual efforts to induce or acknowledge support by non–family members. They may impose heightened evidentiary standards for enforcement, such as the requirement of writing for any recovery beyond quantum meruit. *See, e.g.*, Uniform Probate Code §2-514 (requiring written evidence of contract to devise) and comment; Frances H. Foster, The Family Paradigm of Inheritance Law, 80 N.C. L. Rev. 199, 215-216 (2001). Even if evidentiary requirements for proving the contract are met, contractual caregiving provisions may be challenged by "natural" objects of a decedent's bounty on grounds of fraud, duress, and undue influence. If nonmarital sexual relations with the caregiver were also involved, courts may occasionally invalidate the contract on the ground that it rests on "illegal consideration." *See* Foster, *supra* at 217.

5. Borelli and Brusseau also had a premarital agreement that was enforced. Why are the two contracts treated differently?

D. SEPARATION AGREEMENTS

In contrast to the relative rarity of premarital agreements, separation agreements are the norm. The great majority of divorce cases are uncontested, and a high percentage of these are settled against the background provided by statutes and case law, with the settlement expressed in a separation agreement. Robert H. Mnookin & Lewis Kornhauser, Bargaining in the Shadow of the Law: The Case of Divorce, 88 Yale L.J. 950, 951 n.3 (1979) (probably less than 10 percent of divorce cases are resolved by litigation); Homer C. Clark, Jr., The Law of Domestic Relations in the United States 755 (2d ed. 1988) (90 percent of all divorces are uncontested and well over 50 percent settled by separation agreement).

Separation agreements must satisfy basic contract law requirements to be enforceable. They sometimes raise issues under the statute of frauds because they concern real property or their terms cannot be performed within one year, although judicial approaches limit the significance of the stationary requirement of a writing. *See* E. Allan Farnsworth, Contracts 286 (1995); Stewart Macauley et al., Contracts 265 (1995).

1. *The Permissible Scope of the Agreement*

Just as the law of premarital agreements has moved in the last 20 or so years from a position that officially limited the parties' ability to determine by contract the legal consequences of marriage, the law of separation agreements has also moved toward a contractual freedom model. Agreements routinely address issues of spousal and child support and child custody and visitation. However, traditionally, and still officially in some states, parties may not enter into binding contracts with regard to support, custody, and visitation that tie the hands of the court.

TESS WILKINSON-RYAN & DEBORAH SMALL WINTER, *NEGOTIATING DIVORCE: GENDER AND THE BEHAVIORAL ECONOMICS OF DIVORCE BARGAINING*

26 Law & Ineq. 109, 111-112 (2008)

Family law has become increasingly dependent on private contracts to determine the allocation of entitlements before, during, and after marriage. Ideally, prenuptial contracts, divorce settlements, and child custody agreements each require the parties involved to negotiate effectively in order to maximize the joint welfare of the spouses, ex-spouses, and children. Evidence suggests, however, that this contractarian ideal is not borne out by the current reality in which women are at a financial disadvantage to their male counterparts after divorce. Women, with or without children, experience an average decline in standard of living of about one-third upon divorce. Men experience a slight increase in standard of living because their family size decreases while they maintain their personal income.

Both legal scholars and economists have posited a link between negative outcomes for women and the current system of divorce bargaining. Legal scholars have couched this in terms of women's preference for cooperation or an "ethic of care." Thus, even if private ordering is theoretically desirable, questions remain. Are private negotiations an effective means to attain a mutually beneficial contract? What background legal rules might support such a regime? Why do women fare worse in these private negotiations? . . .

[W]e consider three trends in modern family law . . . and discuss research on the psychology of gender and negotiation that relate to each trend. While there are a number of different potential bargaining situations, we focus here on divorce settlement agreements, though it is clear that many of the issues raised in that context would apply to prenuptial agreements or custody arrangements. The first trend we review is the increasing preference for private, face-to-face negotiations rather than judge-made settlements. We review literature suggesting that women and men may bring different goals to the bargaining table, which may produce different behavior and outcomes for men and women in these negotiations. The second trend is that modern family laws are often quite vague, using standards like "equitable distribution" and "best interest of the child." Since gender differences are typically larger when situations are ambiguous, indeterminate legal standards may provide a context where gender is most likely to matter. Finally, we discuss the trend toward complete financial separation at the time of divorce, which decreases the possibility of alimony. Research indicates that women are more comfortable asking for things than negotiating for things. Alimony involves transfers from one party to another, whereas a financial settlement involves a division of resources between two parties; the former seems like more of an ask situation and the latter more of a negotiate situation.

Uniform Marriage and Divorce Act § 306

(a) To promote amicable settlement of disputes between parties to a marriage attendant upon their separation or the dissolution of their marriage, the parties may enter into a written separation agreement containing provisions for disposition of any property owned by either of them, maintenance of either of them, and support, custody, and visitation of their children.

(b) In a proceeding for dissolution of marriage or for legal separation, the terms of the separation agreement, except those providing for the support, custody, and visitation of children, are binding upon the court unless it finds, after considering the economic circumstances of the parties and any other relevant evidence produced by the parties, on their own motion or on request of the court, that the separation agreement is unconscionable.

(c) If the court finds the separation agreement unconscionable, it may request the parties to submit a revised separation agreement or may make orders for the disposition of property, maintenance, and support.

ALI Principles of the Law of Family Dissolution § 7.09

(2) Except as provided in the last sentence of this Paragraph, the terms of a separation agreement providing for the disposition of property or for compensatory payments are unenforceable if they substantially limit or augment property rights or compensatory payments otherwise due under law, and enforcement of those terms would substantially impair the economic well-being of a party who has or will have

(a) primary or dual residential responsibility for a child or

(b) substantially fewer economic resources than the other party. Nevertheless, the court may enforce such terms if it finds, under the particular circumstances of the case, that enforcement of the terms would not work an injustice.

Robert H. Mnookin & Lewis Kornhauser, *Bargaining in the Shadow of the Law: The Case of Divorce*

88 Yale L.J. 950, 954-956 (1979)

In families with minor children, existing law imposes substantial doctrinal constraints. For those allocational decisions that directly affect children — that is, child support, custody, and visitation — parents lack the formal power to make their own law. Judges, exercising the state's parens patriae power, are said to have responsibility to determine who should have custody and on what conditions. Private agreements concerning these matters are possible and common, but agreements cannot bind the court, which, as a matter of official dogma, is said to have an independent responsibility for determining what arrangement best serves the child's welfare. Thus, the court has the power to reject a parental agreement and order some other level of child support or some other custodial arrangement it believes to be more desirable. Moreover, even if the parties' initial agreement is accepted by the court, it lacks finality. A court may at any time during the child's minority reopen and modify the initial decree in light of any subsequent change in circumstances. The parties entirely lack the power to deprive the court of this jurisdiction.

On the other hand, available evidence on how the legal system processes undisputed divorce cases involving minor children suggest that parents actually have broad powers to make their own deals. Typically, separation agreements are rubber stamped even in cases involving children. A study of custody in England suggests, for example, that courts rarely set aside an arrangement acceptable to the parents. Anecdotal evidence in America suggests that the same is true here.

The parents' broad discretion is not surprising for several reasons. First, getting information is difficult when there is no dispute. The state usually has very limited resources for a thorough and independent investigation of the family's circumstances. Furthermore, parents may be unwilling to provide damaging information that may upset their agreed arrangements. Second, the applicable legal standards are extremely vague and give judges very little guidance as to what circumstances justify overriding a parental decision. Finally, there are obvious limitations on a court's practical power to control the parents once they leave the courtroom. For all these reasons, it is not surprising that most courts behave as if their function in the divorce process is dispute settlement, not child protection. When there is no dispute, busy judges or registrars are typically quite willing to rubber stamp a private agreement, in order to conserve resources for disputed cases.

NOTES AND QUESTIONS

1. If the parties have agreed to no spousal support or to spousal support for a limited term, should a court have authority to order support beyond that provided for in the agreement if the dependent spouse will otherwise become a "public charge"? *See, e.g.,* O'Brien v. O'Brien, 623 N.E.2d 485 (1993). *Compare* the UMDA *with* the ALI Principles.

2. Should the parties be able to agree to child support below the presumptive amount calculated under the child support guidelines and agree to a correspondingly greater amount of spousal support? Why might the parties desire this agreement? What problems can you see with it? The ALI Principles provide that terms of a separation agreement altering child support or custodial responsibilities are not enforceable, but allow such agreements if approved and adopted by the court. *Compare* § 7.09(5) *with* §§ 3.13 and 2.06. *See also* Kraisinger v. Kraisinger, 928 A.2d 333 (Pa. Super. 2007).

3. Courts generally hold that the parties may agree to take on more extensive obligations than a court could impose on them. For example, in a jurisdiction that does not allow courts to order parents to support their children after the age of majority, an agreement to support an adult child attending school is usually enforceable. *See, e.g.,* Shortt v. Damron, 649 S.E.2d 283 (W. Va. 2007).

4. In most jurisdictions, if a court does not award spousal support at the time of the decree, it does not have jurisdiction to award it later. Therefore, in some jurisdictions parties may agree that a separation agreement that would not otherwise provide for spousal support will include a requirement that one spouse pay the other $1 per year. The idea is that if spousal support is needed later, the court can "modify" this provision. In other states, though, this tactic is not permitted.

2. Post-Decree Attacks on Agreements and Decrees Based on Them

Courts often do not scrutinize the terms of separation agreements closely at the time of divorce. Some time after the divorce decree has been entered, however, one of the parties may find fault with the agreement and the negotiating process that produced it. A successful attack at this point requires setting aside not only the agreement but also the decree.

HRESKO V. HRESKO

574 A.2d 24 (Md. App. 1990)

ALPERT, J. . . . During the spring or early summer of 1985, James and Marie Hresko decided to terminate their 24-year marriage. The parties agreed to and signed a separation and property settlement agreement on July 10, 1985. According to terms of the settlement agreement, James (appellant) agreed to pay $400 per month in child support, to pay the total costs of the minor child's college education, and to assume payment of certain family consumer debts. The agreement further provided that Marie (appellee) had the option of buying out appellant's interest in the family home three years from the date of the settlement agreement.

On August 4, 1987, appellee filed a Complaint for Absolute Divorce against appellant in the Circuit Court for Anne Arundel County. On October 5, 1987, appellant filed an answer to the complaint which did not contest the divorce. A hearing before Master Malcolm M. Smith was held on December 7, 1987, with only appellee and her counsel present. Based on the master's findings, the Honorable James A. Cawood, Jr. entered an order of divorce *a vinculo matrimonii* on December 23, 1987. A voluntary separation agreement that the parties had executed two years earlier was incorporated but not merged into the order.

In the summer of 1988, appellee exercised her option to buy out appellant's interest in the family home and on the day of settlement, August 4, 1988, paid appellant $30,000 in cash for his one-half interest. Appellant had assumed that appellee would require a mortgage to purchase his interest in the house and claimed that he was "stunned" when she fulfilled her obligation with cash. He then became convinced that a fraud had been perpetrated against him during the 1985 negotiations that led to the property settlement. This alleged fraud involved the concealment, by appellee, of at least $30,000 in cash at the time of the agreement. As a result of this belief, appellant filed a Motion to Revise Judgment and to Rescind Separation and Property Settlement Agreement, together with a memorandum of law and an affidavit. Appellee responded by filing a motion to dismiss appellant's motion. Judge Cawood held a hearing on appellee's motion on June 7, 1989. After briefly holding the matter sub curia, the judge issued a written opinion on June 13, 1989, granting appellee's motion to dismiss appellant's motion to revise judgment. . . .

In an action to set aside an enrolled judgment or decree, the moving party must initially produce evidence sufficient to show that the judgment in question was the product of fraud, mistake or irregularity. Furthermore, it has long been black letter law in Maryland that the type of fraud which is required to authorize the reopening of an enrolled judgment is extrinsic fraud and not fraud which is intrinsic to the trial itself.

Appellant contends that appellee concealed from him an unknown, but apparently sizable, sum of money at the time the two parties were negotiating the subject separation and property settlement agreement. In an affidavit accompanying his motion, appellant alleges that during negotiations between the parties prior to the agreement, appellee represented and constantly reiterated to him that she had no money in any account or investment except for a small reserve account used for her expenses during the summer when she was not working or receiving a salary from her public school teaching job. . . . Appellant claims that, based on these incidents and appellee's frequent assertions that she was not hiding money, he entered into the subject agreement.

Assuming without deciding that appellant has produced facts and circumstances sufficient to establish fraud, we will address whether this alleged fraud is extrinsic or intrinsic to the trial itself. We hold, based on appellant's claims and verified statements, that appellee's alleged concealment of funds is an example of, at most, intrinsic fraud.

Intrinsic fraud is defined as "[t]hat which pertains to issues involved in the original action or where acts constituting fraud were, or could have been, litigated therein." Black's Law Dictionary (5th ed. 1979). Extrinsic fraud, on the other hand, is "[f]raud which is collateral to the issues tried in the case where the judgment is rendered." *Id.*

Fraud is extrinsic when it actually prevents an adversarial trial. Fleisher, 483 A.2d 1312. In determining whether or not extrinsic fraud exists, the question is not whether the fraud operated to cause the trier of fact to reach an unjust conclusion, but whether the fraud prevented the actual dispute from being submitted to the fact finder at all. *Id.* In Schwartz v. Merchants Mortgage Co., 322 A.2d 544 (1974), the Court of Appeals, quoting from United States v. Throckmorton, 98 U.S. 61 (1878), provided examples of what would be considered extrinsic fraud:

> Where the unsuccessful party has been prevented from exhibiting fully his case, by fraud or deception practiced on him by his opponent, as by keeping him away from court, a false promise of a compromise; or where the defendant never had knowledge of the suit, being kept in ignorance by the acts of the plaintiff; or where an attorney fraudulently or without authority assumes to represent a party and connives at his defeat; . . . or where the attorney regularly employed corruptly sells out his client's interest in the other side — these, and similar cases which show that there has never been a real contest in the trial or hearing of the case, are reasons for which a new suit may be sustained to set aside and annul the former judgment or decree, and open the case for a new and a fair hearing.

Schwartz, 322 A.2d 544.

Appellant contends that appellee's alleged fraudulent representations were extrinsic to the subsequent divorce action because they took place over two years before its inception and served to prevent appellant from taking advantage of his right to an adversarial proceeding. He argues that appellee's concealment is a "fraud or deception practiced upon the unsuccessful party by his opponent as by keeping him away from court or making a false promise of a compromise."

As stated above, the issue of whether appellee's alleged fraudulent concealment of assets during pre-separation agreement negotiations is intrinsic or extrinsic to the divorce litigation is one of first impression in Maryland courts. Upon looking to other jurisdictions for guidance, we find conflict among our sister states.

California courts have uniformly recognized that the failure of one spouse to disclose the existence of community property assets constitutes extrinsic fraud. In re Marriage of Modnick, 663 P.2d 187 (Cal. 1983). The principle underlying these cases is that each spouse has an obligation to inform the other spouse of the existence of community property assets. This duty stems in part from the confidential nature of the marital relationship and from the fiduciary relationship that exists between spouses with respect to the control of community property. . . .

Other courts have found extrinsic fraud holding, as appellant would have us do, that a spouse's concealment or misrepresentation of assets can be classified as an intentional act by which the one spouse has prevented the other spouse from having a fair submission of the controversy and thus amounts to extrinsic fraud. Pilati v. Pilati, 592 P.2d 1374, 1380 (Mont. 1979).

Other jurisdictions have reached the opposite result, determining that the fraudulent concealment of assets by one spouse during a property settlement agreement is intrinsic to the divorce litigation. Recently, in Altman v. Altman, 150 A.D.2d 304, 542 N.Y.S.2d 7, 9 (1989), the New York Supreme Court, Appellate Division, held that alleged fraud in the negotiations of the separation agreement involves the issue in controversy and is not a deprivation of the opportunity to make a full and fair defense. The court reasoned that the alleged misrepresentations of financial status are in essence no different from any other type of perjury committed in the course of litigation and thus constitute intrinsic fraud.

Similarly, in Chapman v. Chapman, 591 S.W.2d 574, 577 (Tex. Civ. App. 1979), the Texas court refused to overturn on the basis of fraud a property settlement agreement incorporated into a divorce decree. The court stated that the fraud alleged at most related to untruths which misled the wife into acquiescence and approval of an unjust division of property. Because these misrepresentations bore only on issues in the trial (or which could have been at issue in the trial), they, therefore, amounted to no more than intrinsic fraud. . . .

We are persuaded that these latter cases are the better reasoned ones. Misrepresentations or concealment of assets made in negotiations leading to a voluntary separation and property settlement agreement later incorporated into a divorce decree represent matters intrinsic to the trial itself. In fact, a determination of each party's respective assets, far from being a collateral issue, would seem to be a central issue in a property settlement agreement. . . .

No "extrinsic fraud" prevented appellant from seeking trial and this court will not, therefore, reopen the decree in the present case. To rule otherwise would be to subject every enrolled divorce decree that includes a property settlement to revision upon discovery of alleged fraud in the inducement of the settlement. Public policy of this state demands an end to litigation once the parties have had an opportunity to present in court a matter for determination, the decision has been rendered, and the litigants afforded every opportunity for review.

NOTES AND QUESTIONS

1. For purposes of attacks made on an agreement after the parties have signed it, what difference does it make that the agreement has been the basis for a divorce decree? Should it make a difference? Why or why not? Should a decree that was

based on a separation agreement be given the same amount of protection from collateral attack that a decree entered at the close of a trial has? Why or why not?

Courts have historically been reluctant to reopen litigated judgments because of their desire to promote finality, and a number of cases hold, for example, that perjury constitutes intrinsic fraud that will not support a collateral attack on the judgment. *See, e.g.*, Shih Ping Li v. Tzu Lee, 62 A.3d 212, 237 (Md. App. 2013). In some jurisdictions, however, the courts have become more willing to provide relief from judgments procured through an intentional effort to conceal assets. *See, e.g.*, Ray v. Ray, 647 S.E.2d 237 (S.C. 2007). In *Ray*, the husband and wife sold a pharmacy they jointly owned to CVS. The wife, however, arranged separately to sign an agreement not to compete with CVS for an additional $130,000, but delayed the payment until after the divorce became final and concealed the agreement from her husband. The majority found that the deliberate effort to structure the agreement to take effect only after the divorce constituted "extrinsic" fraud while the dissent characterized it as a classic case of "intrinsic" fraud. Would the majority have reached the same conclusion if, instead of going to trial, the husband had reached a settlement incorporated into the divorce decree without knowledge of the contract with CVS?

2. As a matter of contract law, would Mrs. Hresko's concealment of assets (assuming for these purposes that she did hide them) be a basis for setting aside the agreement? On what ground?

3. Are parties in the process of negotiating a divorce in a confidential relationship so that they have a duty of full disclosure to each other? Is this situation distinguishable from that of engaged people negotiating a premarital agreement? If each party is represented by counsel, are they in a confidential relationship? What duties of disclosure do the parties have then? How can a lawyer ensure that the other spouse is not hiding assets? Must the value of property be disclosed? Would you as a lawyer rely on the opposing party's representations about value? *See, e.g.*, Gainey v. Gainey, 675 S.E.2d 792 (S.C. App. 2009); In re Marriage of Conrad, 81 P.3d 749, 751 (Or. App. 2003); In the Matter of the Marriage of Auble, 866 P.2d 1239 (Or. App. 1993).

4. The UMDA adopts an unconscionability standard for determining the validity of settlement agreements. If the agreement is incorporated into the decree, can a party challenge the agreement as unconscionable after the divorce has become final?

PROBLEMS

1. Jack and Marian separated five years ago, and they have lived in different cities since then. During their marriage Jack had purchased a business, and their original plan was that Marian and their two children would join him once the business was well established. However, Jack always reported that the business was struggling, and Marian and the children never made the move. When Jack moved away, Marian went back to work, since the children were in school, and she has been self-supporting since Jack left. Jack has sent Marian $400 per month as support for the children. Last year Jack and Marian agreed to divorce, and they negotiated a separation agreement by themselves without a lawyer. Jack told

Marian that his business was nearly bankrupt and that he could not afford to pay spousal support but would continue to pay the same amount of child support. He offered to let Marian take the house (and its mortgage payments) and told her there was not much else to share. Jack then took the agreement to a lawyer, who drafted a petition for divorce. Marian consented to entry of a decree consistent with the terms of the agreement. After the time for appeal had passed, Marian learned that in fact Jack's business has been very successful and that he has become a wealthy man. Under the approach of *Hresko*, can Marian successfully reopen the divorce on the grounds of fraud? In a jurisdiction that presumes that married people are in a confidential relationship, will Marian have greater success? Why or why not?

2. Hal and Wilma live in a state in which the appreciation in value of pre-marital property is marital property unless the increase is attributable purely to market factors or inflation. Wilma had purchased a house before marriage, and she never added Hal's name to the title to the house during the marriage. During the marriage they made mortgage payments on the house, paying an additional $3500 in principal. They also did some remodeling, at a cost of $4500, which increased the house's value by $11,000. During the marriage the housing market was generally rising as well. At the end of the marriage the fair market value of the house was $24,000 greater than it had been at the beginning of the marriage. Wilma was the family bookkeeper, and only she knew this information during the marriage. If Hal and Wilma live in a jurisdiction that imposes a duty of disclosure on spouses who are negotiating a separation agreement without attorneys, how much of the information about the house must Wilma disclose and why?

3. *Modification of Agreements*

Support awards are ordinarily modifiable; property awards are not. If a divorce agreement provides that a support award is not modifiable, does the agreement supersede the power of the court to modify the agreement? In child support cases, the answer is no because the right belongs to the child, who is not a party to the agreement. In spousal support cases, jurisdictions have taken different approaches. The following case summarizes the cases, although the majority and dissent interpret them differently. At the heart of the differences between the majority and the dissent is the role of the courts in policing the fairness of agreements for the protection of more vulnerable parties.

TONI v. TONI

636 N.W.2d 396 (N.D. 2001)

VANDE WALLE, C.J. . . . Conrad and Sheila Toni were married from July 9, 1971, until May 10, 1999. The couple had three children during the marriage, and one of them was a minor at the time of the divorce. Both parties are employed in Fargo: Conrad as a urologist, and Sheila as a clerk at Barnes & Noble Bookstore.

Before their divorce was granted, the parties entered into a "Custody and Property Settlement Agreement" which comprehensively addressed all divorce issues. The agreement stated that, although Conrad had been represented by counsel, Sheila "has not been represented by counsel and has been informed that Maureen Holman does not represent her interests in this matter but has not sought such independent counsel and enters into this custody and property settlement agreement of her own free will." The agreement also stated, "both parties agree that each has made a full disclosure to the other of all assets and liabilities and is satisfied that this custody and property settlement agreement is fair and equitable," and "each party has entered into this custody and property settlement agreement intending it to be a full and final settlement of all claims of every kind, nature, and description which either party may have or claim to have, now or in the future, against the other and, except as is expressly provided herein to the contrary, each is released from all further liability of any kind, nature or description whatsoever to the other."

The agreement provided for "joint physical custody" of the couple's minor daughter, who was expected to graduate from high school in May 1999. The agreement divided the parties' real property, stocks and retirement accounts, but did not disclose the value of those assets. The agreement also contained the following provision on spousal support:

> Commencing May 1, 1999, Conrad shall pay to Sheila the sum of $5,000 per month as and for spousal support. Said payments will continue on the first day of each month thereafter until the death of either party, Sheila's remarriage, or until the payment due on April 1, 2002 has been made. It is intended that the spousal support payable to Sheila shall be included in Sheila's gross income for income tax purposes and shall be deductible by Conrad. The court shall be divested of jurisdiction to modify in any manner whatsoever the amount and term of the spousal support awarded to Sheila immediately upon entry of the judgment and decree herein. The court shall retain jurisdiction to enforce Conrad's obligation to pay spousal support to Sheila.

At the divorce hearing, Conrad appeared with his attorney, but Sheila . . . did not personally appear. The trial court granted the divorce and, finding the parties' agreement to be "a fair, just and equitable settlement," incorporated its provisions into the divorce decree.

In November 2000, Sheila moved under N.D.C.C. § 14-05-24 to modify the spousal support award. Sheila claimed in an affidavit that Conrad earned $14,000 per month in "take-home pay" when they married and she believed he continued to earn a "similar" amount per month, while she earns $1,000 per month working full-time as a clerk at Barnes & Noble Bookstore. Sheila further alleged, although income from assets she received in the divorce had paid her about $2,700 per month, the "return on those assets this year has been almost nothing." Sheila estimated her monthly expenses to be $5,340, and said her accountant informed her she could convert a retirement account into an annuity producing $2,000 per month in additional income, but she is "afraid to convert this to an annuity because I believe I need it for my retirement." Sheila claimed she has a "neurological condition" that causes her trouble sleeping, and she stayed home with the children during her marriage to Conrad rather than pursuing her own career. Sheila also stated:

> I met Bob Boman after I separated from my husband. I had agreed to a reduced three-year term for spousal support because Dr. Boman was in his residency following medical school. Once he finished, we had agreed that he would pay the family expenses. Conrad and I had decided to divorce in August and I met Bob in October. Bob and I planned to marry after the divorce. Bob and I are no longer together and I do not receive any money from him.

The parties agreed to submit to the trial court the sole issue whether the provision of the parties' agreement divesting the court of jurisdiction to modify spousal support was valid under North Dakota law. . . . The trial court dismissed Sheila's motion, ruling "the parties entered into a binding contract which was incorporated into the judgment and . . . the court now lacks jurisdiction to modify spousal support."

II

We assume, for purposes of argument only, that Sheila's claims of lowered investment yields and a failed relationship are sufficient to constitute a material change of circumstances to support a motion to modify spousal support. . . . The legal question in this case is whether the parties' divorce stipulation regarding spousal support can divest the trial court of its statutory authority to modify the amount and duration of support. . . .

. . . Under N.D.C.C. § 14-05-24, the trial court generally retains continuing jurisdiction to modify spousal support, child support, and child custody upon a showing of changed circumstances. This Court has construed the statute, however, to not allow a trial court continuing jurisdiction to modify a final property distribution, and we have held when a trial court makes no initial award of spousal support and fails to expressly reserve jurisdiction over the issue, the court subsequently lacks jurisdiction to award spousal support. Sheila argues N.D.C.C. § 14-05-24 gives a trial court the unconditional right to modify a spousal support award, regardless of any agreement by divorcing parties purporting to divest the court of that power.

We encourage peaceful settlements of disputes in divorce matters. . . . It is the promotion of the strong public policy favoring prompt and peaceful resolution of divorce disputes that generates a judicial bias in favor of the adoption of a stipulated agreement of the parties. We have also noted a person may waive "all rights and privileges to which a person is legally entitled, whether secured by contract, conferred by statute, or guaranteed by the constitution, provided such rights and privileges rest in the individual who has waived them and are intended for his benefit."

In line with these principles, this Court has held a trial court has continuing jurisdiction to modify child support notwithstanding parental divorce settlement agreements prohibiting or limiting the court's modification powers, because the right to child support belongs to the child rather than to the parent, rendering such agreements violative of public policy and invalid. On the other hand, we have encouraged spousal support awards based on agreements between the divorcing parties, and noted those agreements "should be changed only with great reluctance by the trial court." Although this Court has often said a spousal support award based on an agreement between the parties can be modified upon a showing of material change of circumstances, we have not been confronted with a contractual settlement clause, adopted by the trial court and incorporated into the divorce decree, attempting to divest the court of its continuing jurisdiction to modify the amount and term of the spousal support award.

Jurisdictions differ over their treatment of agreements between divorcing couples seeking to limit a court's ability to modify spousal support arrangements. Some jurisdictions, by statute, specifically allow parties to enter into nonmodifiable spousal support agreements. *See, e.g.*, In re Marriage of Ousterman, 46 Cal. App. 4th 1090, 54 Cal. Rptr. 2d 403, 405 (Cal. App. 1996) (construing Cal. Family Code § 3651(d) and predecessor statute); In re Marriage of Chalkley, 99 Ill. App. 3d 478, 426 N.E.2d 237, 240, 55 Ill. Dec. 262 (Ill. App. 1981) (construing 750 Ill. Comp. Stat. Ann. 5/502(f)); Bair v. Bair, 242 Kan. 629, 750 P.2d 994, 997 (Kan. 1988) (construing Kan. Stat. Ann. § 60-1610(b)(3)); Hamilos v. Hamilos, 52 Md. App. 488, 450 A.2d 1316, 1320 (Md. App. 1982) (construing Md. Code Ann., Family Law § 8-103(c)(2)); Santillan v. Martine, 560 N.W.2d 749, 750 (Minn. App. 1997) (construing Minn. Stat. § 518.552); Lueckenotte v. Lueckenotte, 34 S.W.3d 387, 392 (Mo. 2001) (construing Mo. Rev. Stat. § 452.325.6); In re Marriage of Pearson, 1998 MT 236, 965 P.2d 268, 274, 291 Mont. 101 (Mont. 1998) (construing Mont. Code Ann. § 40-4-201(6)); Pendleton v. Pendleton, 22 Va. App. 503, 471 S.E.2d 783, 784 (Va. App. 1996) (construing Va. Code Ann. § 20-109); Yearout v. Yearout, 41 Wn. App. 897, 707 P.2d 1367, 1369 (Wash. App. 1985) (construing Wash. Rev. Code § 26.09.070(7)). *See also* Uniform Marriage and Divorce Act § 306(f), 9A U.L.A. 249 (1998). Other jurisdictions, by statute, specifically prohibit nonmodifiable spousal support agreements. *See, e.g.*, Vorfeld v. Vorfeld, 8 Haw. App. 391, 804 P.2d 891, 897 (Haw. App. 1991) (construing Haw. Rev. Stat. §§ 572-22 and 580-47).

Several jurisdictions, by judicial decision, have allowed contractual waivers of the right to seek spousal support modification. *See, e.g.*, Beasley v. Beasley, 707 So. 2d 1107, 1108 (Ala. Civ. App. 1997); Rockwell v. Rockwell, 681 A.2d 1017, 1021 (Del. Super. 1996); Kilpatrick v. McLouth, 392 So. 2d 985, 986 (Fla. App. 1981); Ashworth v. Busby, 272 Ga. 228, 526 S.E.2d 570, 572 (Ga. 2000); Voigt v. Voigt, 670 N.E.2d 1271, 1280 (Ind. 1996); Staple v. Staple, 241 Mich. App. 562, 616 N.W.2d 219, 223 (Mich. App. 2000); Karon v. Karon, 435 N.W.2d 501, 503-04 (Minn. 1989) (upholding right to waive modification before right was legislatively established); Moseley v. Mosier, 279 S.C. 348, 306 S.E.2d 624, 627 (S.C. 1983); Nichols v. Nichols, 162 Wis. 2d 96, 469 N.W.2d 619, 623 (Wis. 1991). Other jurisdictions, through court decisions, have disallowed contractual waivers of the right to seek modification of spousal support. *See, e.g.*, Norberg v. Norberg, 135 N.H. 620, 609 A.2d 1194, 1196 (N.H. 1992); Matter of Marriage of Eidlin, 140 Or. App. 479, 916 P.2d 338, 341 (Or. App. 1996).

We think the reasoning of the current trend of jurisdictions which allow divorcing couples to agree to make spousal support nonmodifiable is persuasive.

This result is consistent with our prior caselaw on spousal support. In *Becker*, 262 N.W.2d at 484, this Court held, unless a trial court makes an initial award of spousal support or expressly reserves jurisdiction over the issue, the court lacks jurisdiction under N.D.C.C. § 14-05-24 to subsequently modify its decision and award spousal support. The original divorce decree in *Becker* stated, "'neither party shall pay alimony to the other,'" and that language was incorporated from the parties' stipulation and property settlement agreement found to be "fair and equitable" by the trial court. This Court ruled the contract provision was unambiguous, and the "parties are bound by their contract provision for no alimony even if the court is not." We see no valid distinction between a stipulation to waive all spousal support at the time of the initial divorce decree and a waiver of future modification. If a spouse can waive all right to spousal support, it logically follows that a spouse can waive the right to modification.

In response to the argument that contracting parties cannot divest a court of its jurisdiction under a statute similar to N.D.C.C. § 14-05-24, the court in *Karon*, 435 N.W.2d at 503, reasoned:

> It is not the parties to the stipulation who have divested the court of ability to relitigate the issue of maintenance. The court had the authority to refuse to accept the terms of the stipulation in part or *in toto*. The trial court stands in place and on behalf of the citizens of the state as a third party to dissolution actions. It has a duty to protect the interests of both parties and all the citizens of the state to ensure that the stipulation is fair and reasonable to all. The court did so here and approved the stipulation and incorporated the terms therein in its decree. Thus, the decree is final absent fraud. . . .

Our caselaw invalidating parental divorce stipulations prohibiting or limiting a court's modification powers over child support is governed by public policy principles entirely different from those present when reviewing an agreement concerning spousal support. While a spousal support agreement "serves primarily to determine the interests of the contracting parties themselves," a child support agreement "directly affects the interests of the children of the marriage, who have the most at stake as a result of such an agreement but who have the least ability to protect their interests." "Put simply, the parties to a [spousal support] agreement are both grown-ups, free to bargain with their own legal rights." Freedom to contract on terms not specifically prohibited by statute, is the major public policy question presented here.

Permitting parties to determine the future modifiability of their spousal support agreements maximizes the advantages of careful future planning and eliminates uncertainties based on the fear of subsequent motions to increase or decrease the obligations of the parties. In *Staple*, 616 N.W.2d at 228, the court relied on public policy reasons identified by the American Academy of Matrimonial Lawyers (AAML) for validating agreements to waive future modification of spousal support awards:

> The AAML comments that "recognizing and enforcing" the parties' waiver of modification "does no violence to public policy, and is consistent with the reasonable expectancy interests of the parties." The AAML also offers five public policy reasons

why courts should enforce duly executed nonmodifiable alimony arrangements: (1) Nonmodifiable agreements enable parties to structure package settlements, in which alimony, asset divisions, attorney fees, postsecondary tuition for children, and related matters are all coordinated in a single, mutually acceptable agreement; (2) finality of divorce provisions allows predictability for parties planning their post-divorce lives; (3) finality fosters judicial economy; (4) finality and predictability lower the cost of divorce for both parties; (5) enforcing agreed-upon provisions for alimony will encourage increased compliance with agreements by parties who know that their agreements can and will be enforced by the court.

(footnote omitted). It has been noted that honoring and enforcing nonmodification agreements will "discourage former spouses from using the modification process 'repeatedly for vexatious purposes only.'" In *Karon*, 435 N.W.2d at 504, the court also found "compelling" amicus curiae's argument that setting aside the parties' spousal support agreement incorporated into the divorce decree would be "insulting and demeaning to women," because it would mean "the state must protect them in the manner it protects children in the role of parens patriae," resulting "in chaos in the family law field and declining respect for binding agreements as well." . . .

The divorce court found the agreement to be "a fair, just and equitable settlement" of the parties' divorce action and incorporated the provisions of the agreement into the divorce decree. We conclude the trial court correctly ruled it had no jurisdiction under N.D.C.C. § 14-05-24 to entertain Sheila's motion to modify the spousal support award. . . .

The trial court's order is affirmed.

MARING, J., dissenting. . . . We have consistently concluded trial courts have the power to modify spousal support awards regardless of what the parties may have agreed to in their stipulation. . . . The majority opinion deviates from these holdings today. The principle of finality has never applied to spousal support or child support. If parties need finality and freedom to agree to a definitive spousal support, then we should not modify their agreement for any reason. Parties, however, should not be able to bind themselves in advance to an amount and duration regardless of what circumstances arise because the right to seek modification of a judgment for spousal support is not only given for the protection of persons obligated to pay and the persons who are entitled to support, but also for the benefit of society. If a spouse becomes destitute, then society will bear the burden of support.

We are not dealing with contract law in these cases; we are dealing with family law matters. When, as in this case, a trial court wholly incorporates a settlement agreement into a divorce judgment, the settlement agreement merges with the judgment and "ceases to be independently viable or enforceable." "Consequently, when a stipulation is incorporated into a divorce judgment, we are concerned only with interpretation and enforcement of the judgment, not with the underlying contract." "As such, the court retains management and control over the incorporated stipulation, and remedies can be sought in the divorce action rather than starting afresh with another lawsuit based on the stipulation as a contract." A court dealing with family law matters and exercising powers granted by the Legislature cannot divest itself of the power to modify a judgment contrary to legislative will. . . .

In Norberg v. Norberg, 135 N.H. 620, 609 A.2d 1194, 1196 (N.H. 1992), the Supreme Court of New Hampshire reached this very conclusion in construing a statute similar to N.D.C.C. § 14-05-24. In *Norberg*, the plaintiff argued the defendant's express agreement to abstain from seeking modification of spousal support deprived the trial court of its power to modify the spousal support payments under section 458:14, N.H. Rev. Stat. Ann. (1992). . . . In rejecting the plaintiff's argument, the court concluded:

> Whether the parties expressly agreed to waive their rights to seek modification of the agreement is irrelevant. RSA 458:14 grants the court the authority to revise any order made by the court. This statute is to be liberally construed. *To rule as the plaintiff suggests would allow the parties to circumvent the statute and defeat its evident purpose.* We will not allow the parties to effectively divest the court of its statutory authority to modify a decree by merely agreeing that no modification of their agreement shall be sought. Thus, regardless of the language in the stipulation, the court retains the power to modify orders concerning alimony upon a proper showing of changed circumstances.

Norberg, at 1196 (citation omitted) (emphasis added).

The majority declines to follow the reasoning of *Norberg* and instead abrogates the will of the Legislature and concludes a court can divest itself of the power conferred by statute to modify decrees of spousal support. However, a number of the decisions relied on by the majority are distinguishable from the case at hand and directly conflict with our statutes and prior case law.

In Beasley v. Beasley, 707 So. 2d 1107, 1108 (Ala. Civ. App. 1997), the parties' agreement stated it could not be modified unless the parties consented in writing. However, the decision in *Beasley* turned on whether the property rights and the alimony rights were integrated in the agreement. *Id.* The court never even addressed the portion of the agreement regarding modification. . . .

The next decision cited by the majority is Rockwell v. Rockwell, 681 A.2d 1017 (Del. 1996). *Rockwell* is distinguishable from the case at hand in that the parties never stipulated to divest the court of jurisdiction at all. At issue in *Rockwell* was whether the statutory standard for modification of alimony applied when parties stipulated to an alimony award. In concluding that it did not apply, the court reasoned "with regard to alimony awards, the stipulation, merger, or incorporation of the parties' voluntary agreement into a court order does not divest that agreement of its contractual nature." Thus, the court held "unlike a prior judicial determination of alimony, the Family Court cannot modify an agreement between the parties regarding alimony, pursuant to the 'real and substantial change' statutory standard." *Id.* In contrast, we have stated "once the settlement agreement is merged into the divorce decree, it is interpreted and enforced as a final judgment of the court, not as a separate contract between the parties." *Sullivan*, 506 N.W.2d at 399. . . .

Relying on Voigt v. Voigt, 670 N.E.2d 1271, 1279 (Ind. 1996), the majority lists Indiana as a jurisdiction which, by judicial decision, has allowed contractual waivers of the right to seek spousal support modification. However, the decision in

Voigt turned on a statute which provided: "The disposition of property settled by such an agreement and incorporated and merged into the decree shall not be subject to subsequent modification by the court except as the agreement itself may prescribe or the parties may subsequently consent." *Id.* at 1278 (quoting Ind. Code Ann. § 31-1-11.5-10(c) (West 1979)). . . .

In *Karon*, the stipulation at issue expressly stated: "Except for the aforesaid maintenance, each party waives and is forever barred from receiving any spousal maintenance whatsoever from one another, and this court is divested from having any jurisdiction whatsoever to award temporary or permanent spousal mainte-nance to either of the parties." 35 N.W.2d at 502. Unlike the stipulation in *Karon*, the stipulation at issue in this case contained no express waiver of the statutory right to modification. . . . Furthermore, *Karon*, which was a four to three decision, has been superseded by statute. . . . Under the current Minnesota statute, nonmodifiable spousal support agreements are only enforceable "if the court makes specific findings that the stipulation is fair and equitable, is supported by consideration described in the findings, and that full disclosure of each party's financial circumstances has occurred." Minn. Stat. § 518.552, subd. 5 (1996).

The decision of the Supreme Court of Wisconsin in Nichols v. Nichols, 162 Wis. 2d 96, 469 N.W.2d 619 (Wis. 1991), can also be distinguished. The Wisconsin Supreme Court decided to recognize an exception to its general rule that maintenance is always subject to modification. It concluded a party is estopped from seeking modification if:

> both parties entered into the stipulation freely and knowingly, . . . the overall settle-ment is fair and equitable and not illegal or against public policy, and . . . one party subsequently seeks to be released from the terms of the court order on the grounds that the court could not have entered the order it did without the parties' agreement.

Therefore, the Wisconsin Supreme Court will enforce a waiver of modification only if the requirements of the doctrine of estoppel are established.

. . . The majority reasons, "If a spouse can waive all right to spousal support, it logically follows that a spouse can waive the right to modification." I do not agree with this logic. When a trial court orders spousal support, it does so to accomplish a variety of objectives; i.e., rehabilitation, economic parity, equalization of the burden of divorce, etc. It logically follows that if spousal support is not ordered, the need to attain these objectives did not exist. If the need did not exist, modi-fication under N.D.C.C. § 14-05-24 is not necessary because there is no objective the modification would further. However, when spousal support is ordered ini-tially, trial courts must have the power to modify the spousal support award in order to accomplish the objective for which it was originally ordered.

Like this Court, Oregon courts recognize that "when no spousal support was awarded in the original decree, the court cannot modify the decree to provide spousal support." At the same time, however, Oregon courts recognize the rule that "specific language in the decree or in an underlying property settlement incor-porated in the decree does not bar the court from modifying the decree as it relates to spousal support." The reason for this rule and the reason we should not travel down the path taken by the majority opinion was well summarized by the Supreme Court of Oregon in Prime v. Prime, 172 Or. 34, 139 P.2d 550 (Or. 1943).

The right to alimony is, therefore, based upon the statute and not upon any contractual obligations. The law is designed for the protection of the parties and to promote the welfare of society. How, then, can parties, by any private agreement, oust the court of jurisdiction to regulate the payment of alimony when the status of the parties justifies a modification? Any agreement of the parties in reference to the payment of alimony was made in view of the statute authorizing the court to modify the same. The mere fact that the court incorporated in the decree the stipulation concerning alimony is immaterial. It is entirely possible that, while the court undoubtedly considered the stipulation of the parties fair and equitable at the time the decree was rendered, it might, upon a showing of subsequent changed conditions, deem it unjust. To hold otherwise would defeat the very purpose and spirit of the statute.

Prime, at 554-55 (quoting Warrington v. Warrington, 160 Or. 77, 83 P.2d 479 (Or. 1938)).

II

Sheila also argues that, even if nonmodifiable spousal support agreements are enforceable, the particular spousal support agreement at issue in this case does not prevent a trial court from modifying the spousal support award under N.D.C.C. § 14-05-24. . . .

The parties to this agreement were married for 28 years. They had three children, one of whom was a minor at the time of the divorce. Conrad was 53 years old at the time of the divorce and employed as a urologist making $14,000 per month in take home pay. Sheila was 51 years old and is employed as clerk at a bookstore making $1,000 per month. The property division did not reveal any valuations of the assets of the parties. On these facts, the trial court found the agreement to be "fair, just, and equitable."

Although we favor prompt and peaceful settlements of divorces, we must not sacrifice our responsibility to ensure they are fair and equitable. . . .

. . . Our statutes and case law certainly set the stage for permanent spousal support under the facts of this case, which include a long-term marriage, forgone career opportunities, and a huge disparity in earning capacity and standard of living.

The majority argues a person can waive their statutory right to seek modification of spousal support. However, "for a waiver to be effective, it must be a voluntary and intentional relinquishment and abandonment of a known existing right, advantage, benefit, claim or privilege which, except for such waiver, the party would have enjoyed." . . . Nowhere in this agreement does Sheila acknowledge she is voluntarily and intentionally waiving that right. Furthermore, Sheila was not represented by counsel according to the agreement. Under these circumstances, I am of the opinion Sheila did not effectively waive her right to seek modification of spousal support.

. . . Unfortunately, the trial court's mere recitation that the agreement is "a fair, just and equitable settlement" is a far cry from the Uniform Marriage and Divorce Act's requirement that the trial court make a finding whether the agreement is unconscionable, a standard which "includes protection against overreaching, concealment of assets, and sharp dealing" and inquiry into "the conditions

under which the agreement was made, including the knowledge of the other party."
Id. The risk of overreaching in divorce stipulations where one party is unrepresented is significant, and without a requirement that the trial court actively engage
in determining the conditions under which the agreement was entered, the risk
increases tremendously. The decision reached by the majority today provides no
protection whatsoever against these risks.

I am also concerned that there is nothing in the record of this case to indicate
the trial court took an active role in determining the stipulation was fair and
equitable. The Minnesota Supreme Court has stated the trial court "stands in
place and on behalf of the citizens of the state as a third party to dissolution
actions . . . to protect the interests of both parties and all the citizens of the
state to ensure that the stipulation is fair and reasonable to all."

I, therefore, respectfully dissent and would reverse and remand.

NOTES AND QUESTIONS

1. *Toni* discusses the substantive issue of whether North Dakota law permits
the parties to agree to limit the courts' jurisdiction to modify support awards.
Other cases, including some of those discussed in *Toni*, turn on the technical
issue of whether the agreement has been "merged" into the decree, making it
part of a judicial order, or whether the court merely "approved," "ratified," or
"incorporated" the agreement into the decree, making it enforceable only as a
contract. The court in In re Estate of Hereford, 250 S.E.2d 45 (W. Va. 1978),
explained:

> A great deal of incomprehensible domestic relations law in the State of West Virginia
> hinges upon the technicality of whether a property settlement has been "ratified and
> confirmed" by a court, in which case the parties are left to contract remedies for the
> enforcement of the settlement or, alternatively, whether provisions of a property
> settlement are "merged" into the divorce decree. If the provisions are "merged"
> they become subject to the continuing jurisdiction of the court which may extinguish
> or enlarge rights to periodic payments (alimony) initially provided by the property
> settlement agreement.
>
> We have held that where a property settlement agreement is merely "ratified
> and confirmed" the property settlement agreement does not become part of the
> decree and any periodic payments (alimony) provided for in such property settlement
> agreement can be neither enlarged nor diminished by the circuit court. Where,
> however, a property settlement agreement providing for alimony or periodic pay-
> ments is merged or made a part of the decree, we have held that the circuit court may
> increase or decrease the amount of payments in subsequent proceedings in the same
> way that it could if it had awarded alimony after a contest without any property
> settlement agreement.

In *Hereford* the wife, who was in a nursing home and dependent on the
support payments, survived the husband. If the support award were merged into
the divorce decree, the court could order support only until the death of the payor.
On the other hand, the agreement provided that support was to continue until the
wife's death or remarriage, and as a contract term, it could be enforced against the

payor's estate. The court mused, "We dream today of inaugurating a system of domestic relations law in this State which is not dependent upon the use of words of art." The opinion speculated that the lawyers who drafted the agreement used the "so-called 'words of art' . . . without intending or implying any particular legal consequences," and it concluded that the one clear (and equitable) intent was to have the support continue until the wife's death.

2. For a review of the aftermath of *Hereford* and of the abundant and confusing case law in this area, *see* Doris Del Tosto Brogan, Divorce Settlement Agreements: The Problem of Merger or Incorporation and the Status of the Agreement in Relation to the Decree, 67 Neb. L. Rev. 235 (1988). *See also* Sally B. Sharp, Semantics as Jurisprudence: The Elevation of Form over Substance in the Treatment of Separation Agreements in North Carolina, 69 N.C. L. Rev. 319 (1991). In *Toni*, would the distinction between merger into the decree versus ratification and confirmation by the court make any difference to the outcome of the case? The dissent observes, "We are not dealing with contract law in these cases; we are dealing with family law matters. When, as in this case, a trial court wholly incorporates a settlement agreement into a divorce judgment, the settlement agreement merges with the judgment and 'ceases to be independently viable or enforceable.'" If the trial court had ratified and confirmed the agreement, but not incorporated it into the decree, would the dissent reach a different conclusion about its modifiability? Does the dissent suggest that substantially different policies underlie the exercise of judicial authority from those addressing enforcement of private agreements? If so, is the distinction between merger into the decree and ratification and confirmation a substantive policy matter? Or is the real problem the failure of trial courts to police agreements more carefully?

3. If the court ratifies but does not incorporate the separation agreement into the divorce decree, may either party be held in contempt for failing to comply with the terms of the agreement? Why or why not?

4. As the two opinions indicate, states vary substantially in their treatment of a court's ability to modify an order based on a separation agreement. For example, in Rockwell v. Rockwell, 681 A.2d 1017 (Del. 1996), the court rejected the distinction between incorporation and merger and concluded that the underlying agreement retains its nature as a contract, and, therefore, that a court cannot modify an agreement regarding support according to the standard normally used for court-ordered support. In contrast, in Massachusetts even if the agreement survives the decree as an independently enforceable contract, the court has power to modify the spousal support terms in the decree, though in deciding whether to do so a court is to consider the parties' expressed desire that the support terms not be modifiable. Bercume v. Bercume, 704 N.E.2d 177 (Mass. 1998). In Idaho, if the agreement is merged into the decree, support terms may be modified without consent of the parties unless the court finds that the agreement is integrated. This means that the parties agreed that the property division and support terms were "reciprocal consideration" and thus that the support provisions are "necessarily part and parcel of a division of property." Keeler v. Keeler, 958 P.2d 599 (Idaho App. 1998). The courts have held, however, that child support, as opposed to spousal support, agreements cannot limit the courts' ability to modify them. In re Marriage of Damschen, 265 P.3d 1245 (Mont. 2011).

5. The distinction between a contract and a decree may affect the power of the court to grant relief. In Alabama, for example, the court does not have the authority to order alimony payments to a party who remarries. The couple, however, may agree contractually to provide for such payments. In Ex parte Murphy, 886 So. 2d 90 (Ala. 2003), the Supreme Court of Alabama accordingly held that when the parties petitioned the court to incorporate an alimony agreement into the decree in light of one of the parties' remarriage, the court lost the authority to order continuing alimony payments. *See* ALI Principles of Family Dissolution § 7.10, which provides that contract terms unenforceable as terms of a decree survive as independent contracts even if the rest of the agreement is incorporated into the decree.

6. If a court incorporates a separation agreement into a divorce decree and the agreement and decree allow for modification of spousal support upon the happening of certain events, if the parties agree to reduce support but do not move the court to modify the decree, is the payor obligated to pay the amount in the decree or the amount in the modified agreement? Could the payor be held in contempt for failing to pay the full amount required by the decree? Why or why not? Could the breaching party be ordered to pay damages? Why or why not?

7. If a court incorporates a separation agreement into a divorce decree, and the agreement and the decree do not provide for modification of spousal support, are there any circumstances in which the court can nonetheless modify the award? In Richardson v. Richardson, 218 S.W.3d 426 (Mo. 2007), the Missouri Supreme Court held that where the separation agreement had been incorporated into the divorce decree and expressly provided for nonmodifiable alimony, the court had no discretion to modify the payments even where the ex-husband alleged that his former wife had attempted to have him murdered.

8. Uniform Marriage and Divorce Act (UMDA) Section 306 deals with the relationship between the agreement and the decree in the following way:

> (d) If the court finds that the separation agreement is not unconscionable as to disposition of property or maintenance, and not unsatisfactory as to support:
> (1) unless the separation agreement provides to the contrary, its terms shall be set forth in the decree of dissolution or legal separation and the parties shall be ordered to perform them, or
> (2) if the separation agreement provides that its terms shall not be set forth in the decree, the decree shall identify the separation agreement and state that the court has found the terms not unconscionable.
> (e) Terms of the agreement set forth in the decree are enforceable by all remedies available for enforcement of a judgment, including contempt, and are enforceable as contract terms.
> (f) Except for terms concerning the support, custody, or visitation of children, the decree may expressly preclude or limit modification of terms set forth in the decree if the separation agreement so provides. Otherwise, terms of a separation agreement set forth in the decree are automatically modified by modification of the decree.

If an agreement is incorporated into the divorce decree, can one of the parties later challenge it as unconscionable? *Compare* In re Marriage of Nilles, 955 N.E.2d 611 (Ill. App. 2011) (rejecting unconscionability challenge to nonmodifiable support award on the grounds that the agreement must be determined to be unconscionable when signed, not in light of financial circumstances ten years later) *with* Stewart v. Stewart, 41 A.3d 401 (Del. 2012) (holding that lifetime award that was not modifiable even in the event of the wife's marriage or cohabitation was unconscionable). *See also* In re Marriage of Callahan, 984 N.E.2d 531 (Ill. App. 2013) (permitting post-judgment attack on settlement as unconscionable and procured through fraud because unrepresented wife relied on husband's attorney's inaccurate description of the implications of the agreement).

PROBLEM

When Judy and Richard were divorced in 1985, Richard was a surgeon earning $100,000 per year, and he had unearned income of $15,000 per year and property worth $600,000. Judy was a homemaker who received property worth $400,000, consisting mostly of the marital home. Their separation agreement provides that Richard will pay Judy one-third of his annual gross earned income until his death, her death, or her remarriage. The agreement also provided that the parties intended it to survive entry of a divorce decree and that it would not be modifiable "even though future events might occur that would alter the position of either party as it exists [at the time of the divorce]." Richard, who is now 55 years old, has recently retired. He has no earned income and is living on unearned income of $50,000, and his property has increased in value to $1 million. Judy, who is 57, earns $97 per week as a museum tour guide, and she has unearned income of $104 per month. Richard has stopped paying Judy spousal support, saying that he no longer has any earned income. Judy has filed a petition to modify the decree, seeking one-third of Richard's gross unearned income, notwithstanding the separation agreement. What arguments should each side make? How should the court rule and why?

Would your answer change if Richard had been represented by counsel and Judy had not been? What if Judy testified further that Richard's counsel told her that the agreement ensured that she would be taken care of "for life"? If you were Richard's counsel and believed that the settlement agreement you had negotiated was a good one for your client, what steps might you take to protect the settlement from a later claim of unconscionability?

Lawyers and Family Dispute Resolution

11

A. INTRODUCTION

Family law cases involve not only substantive and procedural law but also the activities of lawyers and other professionals who participate in marital dissolutions. In the aftermath of divorce liberalization, the courts were overwhelmed. Jessica Pearson and Nancy Thoennes reported in the 1980s that "[o]ver half of the cases filed in all trial courts are concerned with matrimonial actions." Mediation and Litigating Custody Disputes: A Longitudinal Evaluation, 17 Fam. L.Q. 497, 497-498 (1984). Since then, family dispute resolution has become even more complex, with an expansion in the range of services family courts provide or require, and a change in the characteristics of the litigants and the complexity of the issues they present. John Lande, The Evolution in Family Law Dispute Resolution, 24 J. Am. Acad. Matrimonial Law. 411, 415 (2012).

Moreover, with the growth in the sheer number of cases came the growing conviction that the process itself escalated conflict. One writer argued that "the adversarial system encourages 'dog and cat fights' that run counter to the best interests of the child." Others criticized the courts for failing to encourage cooperation, communication, or healing. Still others attacked the "twin dragons" of cost and delay. Pearson and Thoennes, above. It became increasingly clear that there had to be a better way.

The result has been what Jana Singer has termed a "paradigm shift" that "replaced the law-oriented and judge-focused adversary model with a more collaborative, interdisciplinary, and forward-looking family dispute resolution regime. It has also transformed the practice of family law and fundamentally altered the way in which disputing families interact with the legal system." Jana B. Singer, Dispute Resolution and the Postdivorce Family: Implications of a Paradigm Shift, 47 Fam. Ct. Rev. 363 (2009). This has led to redefinition of the role of lawyers and the family law litigation process.

717

This chapter addresses that shift. The first two sections deal with aspects of the lawyer-client relationship that present special issues in family law cases. The last part of the chapter considers proposals to change the method by which family disputes are resolved and the role of lawyers in alternative approaches to dispute resolution.

B.   THE LAWYER'S DUTIES TO CLIENTS AND THE COURT

IN RE THE DISCIPLINE OF ORTNER

699 N.W.2d 865 (S.D. 2005)

GILBERTSON, C.J. . . .

Throughout their marriage David and Jami Reaser lived on David's family ranch where he worked. For twenty years Ortner helped the family with branding. When David initiated divorce proceedings in 1999 he retained Ortner to represent him. Jami did not have a lawyer. Ortner was aware that Jami's mother and stepfather were South Dakota lawyers and he assumed that they were assisting her.

Ortner prepared a stipulation regarding child custody, child support, alimony and property division which David and Jami signed. Pursuant to this stipulation David received custody of the children and relieved Jami of any child support obligation. Jami waived alimony. Ortner was aware of Circuit Judge Kern's policy to require child support in divorce decrees because when he presented the stipulation and decree of divorce to Judge Kern, he specifically "advised her there was something unusual about this particular stipulation for this divorce and that was that there was no provision in it for child support." Judge Kern refused to grant the divorce due to the omission of any provision for child support.

Ortner advised David that whoever did not have primary custody of the children would have to pay child support. Since David was receiving custody, Ortner advised him that he could simply tear up any checks he received for child support. David discussed the proposal with Jami who, according to Ortner, definitely wanted something in writing.

Ortner revised the stipulation to include a provision for child support:

> [Jami] is required to pay child support for the minor children in the total amount of $250.00 per month, except during those summer months when she has the children for visitation. During those summer months, [David] shall pay $250.00 per month for support of the minor children. Said support shall continue until the younger child graduates from high school or turns 19 years of age, whichever is earlier.

The judgment decreeing dissolution of marriage that Ortner drafted incorporated the stipulation, "it being the intention of this court that all of the terms and conditions of said Stipulation be made an express part of this Decree of Dissolution."

At the time Ortner drafted these documents he also drafted a "Private Contractual Agreement Between Parties" which provided:

> It is hereby stipulated and agreed by and between David R. Reaser, the Plaintiff, and Jami D. Reaser, the Defendant, subject to the approval of the above-named Court, that in the event the Court does see fit to grant [David] hereto a dissolution as prayed for in his Complaint, the same shall be upon the terms and conditions as set forth in the Stipulation and Agreement, except that the parties further privately stipulate and agree between themselves as follows:
>
> I. That [David] agrees that he will not seek to collect the Two Hundred Fifty Dollars ($250.00) per month child support ordered to be paid by [Jami].
>
> II. [Jami] stipulates and agrees that during those times when she has custody of the minor children for visitation purposes in the summer for one month or longer that she will not seek to collect child support from [David].
>
> III. Both parties stipulate and agree and contract as set forth above even though the Court itself has ordered payment of child support. The basis of the agreement for the dissolution of the marriage was that no child support be paid and this agreement carries out that earlier agreement reached by the parties.

On March 29, 1999 Jami came to Ortner's office and signed the revised stipulation and the private contractual agreement. David signed the documents the next day. Judge Kern signed the judgment decreeing dissolution of marriage which incorporated the revised stipulation on April 1. It was filed on April 6, 1999. At no time did Ortner advise Judge Kern of the private contractual agreement.

In May 2002 Jami moved for a change in custody and sought child support. Circuit Judge Thomas Trimble heard the motions and learned of the existence of the private contractual agreement. He denied the motion for a change of custody and advised David that he was free to seek child support from Jami.

In the fall of 2002 David initiated a child support action against Jami. The child support referee's recommendations that Jami pay current child support and arrearages were adopted by the circuit court. Jami's motions to set aside the interim order of support and eliminate the arrearages were heard by Judge John J. Delaney. Judge Delaney learned about the private contractual agreement and expressed serious concerns about the deception created by it. During this proceeding Ortner filed an "Affidavit Regarding Motion to Deny Claim for Arrears" which was dated April 1, 2003.

[Ortner's affidavit described what took place, including that "Affiant informed [Ms. Twiss] that even though the private agreement should be binding on the parties themselves it would not be binding upon the Court."] Judge Delaney filed findings of fact, conclusions of law and an order vacating judgment in regard to child custody, visitation, alimony and property settlement on November 18, 2003. Judge Delaney did so essentially sua sponte, because of the private contractual agreement and the court's findings of fraud upon the court.

[David appealed.] In Reaser v. Reaser we examined Ortner's conduct in light of Judge Delaney's findings:

> Here, under Judge Delaney's findings, the actions of these parties and the attorney are egregious conduct involving corruption of the judicial process itself. Considering those findings, this fraudulent conduct may have violated a criminal

statute, and it certainly violated the Rules of Professional Conduct for attorneys. . . .

This Court's opinion in Reaser v. Reaser was handed down on October 13, 2004. Six days later, on October 19, 2004, Ortner wrote to Judge Kern:

Dear Judge Kern:

As hollow as it may seem at this late date, I cannot adequately express how deeply I apologize to you for the way I mishandled the Reaser divorce five and one-half years ago.

My heart and emotions totally got in the way of my brain and legal training. I had been going to brandings with David Reaser and his father for nearly twenty years at that time, and David was so adamant about not accepting any child support from his wife that I went ahead and prepared the private agreement for them to sign. I had no intent to defraud the Court or violate any laws. While trying to help a client I have totally jeopardized twenty-six years of law practice and nearly forty years of public service and service to the public.

You had always treated me with total honesty and fairness and that is what makes me so sick and ashamed about the way I handled this matter.

When this came to light in April 2003, I did an affidavit admitting to everything that had occurred. Since that date I have not had a decent night of sleep.

In twenty-six years there has been one private reprimand from the Disciplinary Board and two investigations in criminal cases which were found to be frivolous and were sealed.

What I did in this case clearly violated the Rules of Professional Responsibility, and I am ready to accept whatever action is recommended by the Disciplinary Board.

Respectfully submitted,

/s/

MICHAEL P. ORTNER

LAWYER

. . . On February 15, 2005 the Disciplinary Board entered its findings of fact, conclusions of law, recommendations, and formal accusation. The Board . . . recommended, in part:

1. Michael Ortner be censured for his violation of the Rules of Professional Conduct.

. . . The purpose of the disciplinary process is to protect the public from fraudulent, unethical or incompetent practices by attorneys. It is also intended to deter like conduct by other attorneys. The disciplinary process is not conducted to punish the lawyer. . . .

Rather than advising David concerning child support obligations, Ortner followed his client's directive and drafted the original stipulation and divorce decree which omitted the payment of ongoing child support. When Ortner submitted the documents to Judge Kern, she refused to enter a decree that provided no support.

Ortner advised David of Judge Kern's position and suggested that the stipulation and decree provide for support. He then advised David that he could tear up the support checks, thereby thwarting the intention of the child support obligation. When David advised Ortner that Jami insisted on a written agreement waiving child support Ortner did not advise him that parties cannot make a valid irrevocable contract relieving them of the duty to support their minor children. Rather, he prepared a revised stipulation providing for child support and a private contractual agreement where each party agreed to "not seek to collect child support" from the other. Ortner advised Jami, who was unrepresented, that the private contractual agreement bound the parties.

When Ortner presented the revised stipulation providing for child support and the decree incorporating its terms to Judge Kern she signed the decree. As the Disciplinary Board found, "Ortner did not advise Judge Kern of the parties' intent to not actually collect child support from each other, nor did he inform her of the existence of their written agreement to that effect." Moreover, Ortner admitted at the Disciplinary Board hearing that in one other case he had prepared a similar type of secret agreement in an attempt to avoid paying child support. . . .

The Disciplinary Board also found, however, that "Ortner's conduct toward Judge Kern was not based on an intent to defraud the trial court, nor did he intend to violate any laws." This language . . . is not consistent with Ortner's admission that when he initially sought approval of the decree without child support, he specifically called that matter to Judge Kern's attention as he knew it was her policy to require child support. The Board's finding also fails to appropriately consider the fact that Judge Delaney found that the "secret agreement purports to do precisely what the court had specifically refused to approve" and was "contrary to the court's previous direction to counsel." It is not consistent with Judge Delaney's conclusion that the divorce was obtained by fraud upon the court. It is also at odds with this Court's conclusion in Reaser v. Reaser that Ortner was dishonest in his representation and disclosures to Judge Kern, circumvented Judge Kern's express direction and engaged in "egregious conduct that corrupted the judicial process through the involvement of an officer of the court."

. . . Without question Ortner has led a life of public service. His disciplinary history is minimal. Custer and Fall River County attorneys have found him honest and ethical in legal matters. The judge he deceived views his deception as an isolated act that will not be repeated. Weighing against this, however, is that Ortner's conduct in this matter was a direct fraud on the court which corrupted the delicate balance of judicial fact finding, went to the heart of legal decision making and constituted egregious conduct by an officer of the court that corrupted the judicial process. . . .

. . . This was an issue involving child support. While Jami and David protected their respective interests, the trial court which properly protected the best interests of the children by refusing to waive child support at the outset, was ultimately duped by Ortner's actions. This made the trial court's already difficult duty to provide for the interests of the children, now impossible. . . .

In some cases we have examined an attorney's misrepresentation and have determined that public censure was the appropriate discipline. . . . We warned, however, "public censure in this type of case has been the penalty of the past, but whether it will be in the future is debatable and the whole Bar should take note of this." . . .

The Disciplinary Board concluded that "no public interest or professional purpose would be served by suspending Ortner's privilege to practice law." Its recommendation of a public censure cannot be accepted by this Court. . . .

It is difficult to conceive of a more blatant act of fraud than that committed in Ortner's drafting of the private contractual agreement and his participation in its execution which were directly contrary to the trial court's express direction after reviewing the first stipulation. This cannot be viewed as accidental or an honest mistake as Ortner has conceded that he knew prior to this case that it was Judge Kern's policy to require child support in divorce cases involving minor children. This private agreement did exactly what the trial court refused to approve after Ortner previously called the proposed no-support provision to the court's attention. The subsequent execution of the decree of dissolution was predicated on the revised stipulation's provision providing for meaningful child support. Ortner failed to self report for approximately six years. It was only after Judges Trimble and Delaney discovered the private contractual agreement that Ortner admitted his conduct. His apology to Judge Kern came only after the release of our decision in Reaser v. Reaser where his conduct became public. Moreover, he admitted he prepared a similar "secret agreement" on another occasion.

Lawyers must guard against conduct that diminishes public confidence in the legal system. . . . It is clear from the frequency of this type of misconduct that public censure is not providing sufficient deterrence to adequately protect the public in the future.

Had there been a history of violations by Ortner or if we suspected he was likely to repeat such acts in the future, for the protection of the public our only appropriate course of action would be to enter an order of disbarment. . . . Our review of the record indicates that such does not appear to be the case.

. . . After reviewing this record we conclude that Ortner's conduct was of such egregious professional nature that it is in the best interests of the public and the legal profession to suspend him from the practice of law for a period of nine months. . . .

Prior to any application for reinstatement Ortner must take and pass the Multistate Professional Responsibility Examination. He must also reimburse the State Bar of South Dakota and the Unified Judicial System for expenses allowed under SDCL 16-19-70.2. . . .

NOTES AND QUESTIONS

1. The secret agreement Ortner drafted was clearly a fraud on the court. Can you think of other ways to reach a resolution that would have satisfied the parties in this case that would not subject the attorney to disciplinary proceedings?

2. The court articulates two types of harm arising from Ortner's deception. The first is that it undermines confidence in the bar and the judiciary. The second is that it interferes with the court's ability to protect the interests of the children, who were not represented in this litigation. What do you think the court had in mind when it observed that the parties' actions "made the trial court's already difficult duty to provide for the interests of the children, now impossible . . ."?

3. Ortner represented David in the divorce while Jami acted pro se. Did Ortner have any obligations to Jami? Did she have a basis for objecting to David's

actions in drafting the agreement and presenting it to her? ABA Model Rule of Professional Conduct 4.3 states:

> In dealing on behalf of a client with a person who is not represented by counsel, a lawyer shall not state or imply that the lawyer is disinterested. When the lawyer knows or reasonably should know that the unrepresented person misunderstands the lawyer's role in the matter, the lawyer shall make reasonable efforts to correct the misunderstanding. The lawyer shall not give legal advice to an unrepresented person, other than the advice to secure counsel, if the lawyer knows or reasonably should know that the interests of such a person are or have a reasonable possibility of being in conflict with the interests of the client.

What arguments might Jami make that Ortner violated this obligation to her in this case?

4. The facts in *Ortner* state that "[t]hroughout their marriage David and Jami Reaser lived on David's family ranch where he worked. For twenty years Ortner helped the family with branding." Could Ortner's personal relationship with the Reasers have given rise to a conflict of interest that made his representation of David inappropriate? Does it matter that Ortner had never previously represented either David or Jami? Would your answer change if Jami had spoken to David about the possibility of hiring him to represent her, but then decided not to do so?

C. CONFLICTS OF INTEREST

ABA MODEL RULE OF PROFESSIONAL CONDUCT 1.7, CONFLICT OF INTEREST: CURRENT CLIENTS

(a) Except as provided in paragraph (b), a lawyer shall not represent a client if the representation involves a concurrent conflict of interest. A concurrent conflict of interest exists if:

(1) the representation of one client will be directly adverse to another client; or

(2) there is a significant risk that the representation of one or more clients will be materially limited by the lawyer's responsibilities to another client, a former client or a third person or by a personal interest of the lawyer.

(b) Notwithstanding the existence of a concurrent conflict of interest under paragraph (a), a lawyer may represent a client if:

(1) the lawyer reasonably believes that the lawyer will be able to provide competent and diligent representation to each affected client;

(2) the representation is not prohibited by law;

(3) the representation does not involve the assertion of a claim by one client against another client represented by the lawyer in the same litigation or other proceeding before a tribunal; and

(4) each affected client gives informed consent, confirmed in writing.

Dual Representation   In *Ortner*, David and Jami appear to have agreed on the divorce settlement, and both wanted the side agreement that Ortner drafted for them. Yet Ortner represented only David while Jami did not have legal counsel. Could Ortner have represented both of them? Clients with a common purpose (such as establishing a partnership or concluding a real estate transaction) often retain a single lawyer to carry out that purpose. Could an attorney ever represent both parties in a divorce? Rule 1.7 above was modified in 2002 to add Section (b)(3). How does this addition affect the possibility of joint representation in a divorce?

In Klemm v. Klemm, 142 Cal. Rptr. 509 (Cal. App. 1977), an attorney who knew the husband and the wife agreed to represent them both, without fee, in an uncontested dissolution. Neither party could afford an attorney, both consented in writing to the joint representation, and the consent was filed with the court. The wife, however, was receiving Aid for Dependent Children payments from the county, and the county recommended that the husband be required to pay child support to reimburse the county for the payments. The attorney objected in writing to the recommendation on behalf of the wife (who had custody of the children in accordance with the divorce agreement), but appeared at the hearing on behalf of the husband. Even after the attorney appeared with both the husband and wife and their written consent to the joint representation, the trial court refused to permit the attorney to represent both parties in opposing the county's recommendation. The court of appeals disagreed and explained:

> As a matter of law a purported consent to dual representation of litigants with adverse interests at a contested hearing would be neither intelligent nor informed. . . .
>
> However, if the conflict is merely potential, there being no existing dispute or contest between the parties represented as to any point in litigation, then with full disclosure to and informed consent of both clients there may be dual representation at a hearing or trial.
>
> In our view the case at bench clearly falls within the latter category. The conflict of interest was strictly potential and not present. The parties had settled their differences by agreement. There was no point of difference to be litigated. The position of each inter se was totally consistent throughout the proceedings. The wife did not want child support from the husband, and the husband did not want to pay support for the children. The actual conflict that existed on the issue of support was between the county on the one hand, which argued that support should be ordered, and the husband and wife on the other, who consistently maintained the husband should not be ordered to pay support.
>
> While on the face of the matter it may appear foolhardy for the wife to waive child support,[1] other values could very well have been more important to her than such support — such as maintaining a good relationship between the husband and the children and between the husband and herself despite the marital problems — thus avoiding the backbiting, acrimony and ill will which the Family Relations Act

---

1. It is to be noted that the parties' agreement that the children should not receive support would not prevent the court from awarding child support either at the hearing or at some time subsequent thereto. Therefore, the children's rights are not in issue nor are they jeopardized.

of 1970 was, insofar as possible, designed to eliminate. It could well have been if the wife was forced to choose between A.F.D.C. payments to be reimbursed to the county by the husband and no A.F.D.C. payments she would have made the latter choice. . . .

The conclusion we arrive at is particularly congruent with dissolution proceedings under the Family Law Act of 1970, the purpose of which was to discard the concept of fault in dissolution of marriage actions, to minimize the adversary nature of such proceedings and to eliminate conflicts created only to secure a divorce. It is contrary to the philosophy of that act to create controversy between the parties where none exists in reality. . . .

The attorney in *Klemm*, like Michael Ortner, was involved in a case where neither parent sought to have the other pay child support, and both wished to oppose a third party who preferred a different result. The courts treat the two cases very differently. At least part of the reason is that the attorney in *Klemm* did not in any way conceal the attorney's or the clients' actions. Is that the only difference?

While *Klemm* has never been repudiated, joint representation in a divorce is unusual. Can you think of circumstances where it might be appropriate? In Olson v. Olson, ___ So. 3d ___ (La. App. 2014), a Louisiana Court of Appeals upheld a postnuptial agreement, approved by the trial court, where a single attorney represented both spouses. The couple later divorced, and the husband challenged the validity of the agreement on the grounds that the joint representation violated the Rules of Professional Conduct. The court of appeals disagreed, emphasizing that the attorney had informed the couple at the time that their interests might be adverse, and the husband had signed a verification certifying to the court that the matrimonial agreement was in his best interest and that he understood the principles involved. Would the result have been different if the agreement had not been presented to a court with such verifications?

Many jurisdictions prohibit joint representation in family law proceedings altogether. The American Academy of Matrimonial Lawyers takes the position in Goal 3.1 that "[a]n attorney should not represent both husband and wife even if they do not wish to obtain independent representation." The comments observe that "[e]ven a seemingly amicable separation or divorce may result in bitter litigation over financial matters or custody. A matrimonial lawyer should not attempt to represent both husband and wife, even with the consent of both." In Ware v. Ware, 687 S.E.2d 382, 389 (W. Va. 2009), the West Virginia Court of Appeals held that the "likelihood of prejudice is so great with dual representation so as to make adequate representation of both spouses impossible, even where the separation is 'friendly' and the divorce uncontested." The court further extended the per se rule against joint representation to premarital agreements, observing that "the parties' interests are fundamentally antagonistic to one another" and that the very purpose of a prenuptial agreement is to prevent a spouse "from obtaining that to which he or she might otherwise be legally entitled."

In re Gamino, 753 N.W.2d 521 (Wis. 2008), provides a catalogue of the things that can go wrong with joint representation. In *Gamino*, the attorney claimed that the parties had come to him to finalize a settlement agreement that they had reached while represented by other attorneys. The disciplinary proceedings against the lawyer, however, included allegations that:

- The parties were confused about when the attorney began and ended his representation of each party.
- He failed to communicate the same information at the same time to each of the parties, including information about scheduled hearings.
- He prepared a financial statement without independently ascertaining the value or accuracy of the assets listed to the disadvantage of one of the parties.
- He failed to turn over records on a timely basis to a new attorney for one of the parties because of the other party's lack of consent.
- He did not address the unequal status between the two parties in a case in which one of the spouses had been a victim of domestic violence, was in poor health, and had less education and financial experience than the other spouse.
- He drafted a settlement that was later determined to be patently unfair to one of the parties and did so without a knowing waiver, undermining the ability of the other party to enforce it.
- He failed to inquire about a possible claim with respect to dissipation of assets.

Wisconsin suspended Gamino's license to practice law for 18 months. *See also Klemm*, above, observing that:

> Attorneys who undertake to represent parties with divergent interests owe the highest duty to each to make a full disclosure of all facts and circumstances which are necessary to enable the parties to make a fully informed decision regarding the subject matter of the litigation, including the areas of potential conflict and the possibility and desirability of seeking independent legal advice. Failing such disclosure, the attorney is civilly liable to the client who suffers loss caused by lack of disclosure. In addition, the lawyer lays himself open to charges, whether well founded or not, of unethical and unprofessional conduct. Moreover, the validity of any agreement negotiated without independent representation of each of the parties is vulnerable to easy attack as having been procured by misrepresentation, fraud and overreaching. It thus behooves counsel to cogitate carefully and proceed cautiously before placing himself/herself in such a position.

Limited Scope Representation   Gamino claimed to play a "scrivener's role" in representing the parties to the divorce. That is, he attempted to limit his representation to drafting a final settlement agreement and presenting it to the court. In characterizing his representation this way, he argued that he should be held responsible only for a limited scope of representation (the drafting of the settlement to which the parties had already agreed) rather than a full duty to investigate his clients' circumstances and look out for their best interests even when they were not asking him to do so. Gamino, however, had no written understanding with the clients, not even an oral agreement in which he explained the implications of such limited representation and secured a waiver of the clients' rights. The Wisconsin Supreme Court accordingly held him responsible for his failure to recognize the conflicts between the parties' respective positions and to look out for their broader interests. *Gamino* leaves open the question, however, of whether attorneys can ever agree to limited representation of their clients' interests. This issue arises regularly in two contexts.

In the first context, a husband and wife voluntarily enter mediation, reach an agreement, and then ask the mediator (who is also an attorney) to set forth their agreement in writing. Is the mediator permitted to do so? Does it matter if the attorney-mediator who drafts the agreement does not sign the papers and does not enter an appearance for either of the parties, each of whom appears pro se in the divorce proceeding? The Illinois State Bar says no. The State Bar concluded that it would violate Rule 1.7(a) above for a mediator to represent both sides in a divorce, because the proceeding involves parties with adverse interests, and that preparing a proposed dissolution agreement constitutes representation even if the mediator does not enter an appearance in the case. Illinois State Bar Ass'n Comm. on Professional Ethics, Op. 04-03, 4/05, 31 Fam. L. Rptr. 1319 (2005). *See also* Utah State Bar Ethics Advisory Op. Comm., Op 05-03, 5/6/05, 31 Fam. L. Rptr. 1321 (2005). California, which as noted above, permits lawyers to represent both sides in an uncontested divorce, and Virginia, which defines the scrivener's role (in which a mediator simply writes down those terms to which the party have agreed) as outside of the practice of law, would appear to permit the practice. *See* N.Y. State Bar Ass'n, Ethics Op. 01-736 (2001); Paula M. Young, A Connecticut Mediator in a Kangaroo Court? Successfully Communicating the "Authorized Practice of Mediation" Paradigm to the "Unauthorized Practice of Law" Disciplinary Bodies, 49 S. Tex. L. Rev. 1047 (2008) (citing Va. State Bar Standing Comm. on Legal Ethics, Op. 1368, at 1-2); Avi Braz, Note, Out of Joint: Replacing Joint Representation with Lawyer-Mediation in Friendly Divorces, 78 S. Cal. L. Rev. 323 (2004). The ABA Model Rules of Professional Conduct recognize the lawyer's role in alternative dispute resolution as a "third-party neutral," whether as mediator, arbitrator, conciliator, or evaluator. Model Rule 2.4 states that a lawyer serves that role when he or she assists two or more persons *who are not clients of the lawyer* to reach a resolution of some dispute or issue between them. Rule 2.4(b) requires a lawyer in this capacity to inform unrepresented parties that the lawyer is not representing them and, if it appears necessary, to explain the difference between a lawyer's role as a third-party neutral and the role of a lawyer who represents a client.

The second issue involves what is called "unbundled" legal services. Divorcing parties who cannot afford to hire an attorney to handle the entire proceeding might nonetheless like to retain an attorney to advise them about a particular issue (*e.g.*, the tax aspects of a settlement) or to draft a particular pleading or agreement. May an attorney provide such limited representation without investigating the rest of the client's case or considering other arguments the client might raise? The Illinois ethics opinion above again said no. It concluded that the mediator could not limit the scope of representation to preparation of the proposed documents, *id.* at 1320, but Illinois, like many states, has since altered its position to permit some forms of limited scope representation, including the preparation of documents. Ill. Rule of Professional Conduct 1.2(c) (2010); Supreme Court Rule 137 (2013). The Illinois changes do not address the issue of dual representation and some jurisdictions that allow representation to review a proposed settlement may limit the representation to one of the parties. *See* Michael Millemann, Reporter, ABA Handbook on Limited Scope Legal Assistance (2003), available at http://www.abanet.org/litigation/taskforces/modest/report.pdf (last visited May 3, 2014).

Limited scope representation has gained increasing use in family law representation more generally. Clients may wish to consult an attorney with respect to a particularly complex legal matter, such as division of a closely held business, or with respect to specific language in an agreement without retaining the lawyer to handle the case as a whole. In addition, new companies, such as Legal Zoom and Wevorce, offer a different business model. Wevorce, for example, assists divorcing couples in managing their own divorces by providing the necessary computerized forms, assistance in filling them out, a financial advisor, and a mediator for a fixed price. Website available at http://www.wevorce.com/ (last visited May 3, 2014). The goal of the company is to help couples reach a settlement without litigation.

Use of limited scope representation in the context of litigation raises other issues. While some individuals do not hire attorneys because they wish to keep control of their own divorces, many simply cannot afford attorneys. This raises questions about effectiveness. Empirical studies tend to find that limited scope representation is not as effective as full representation in protecting the client's interests. Others have been concerned about attorney accountability, particularly where attorneys engage in "ghostwriting" and help clients prepare documents to be filed in court that do not bear the attorney's name or signature. *See* Michele N. Struffolino, Taking Limited Representation to the Limits: The Efficacy of Using Unbundled Legal Services in Domestic-Relations Matters Involving Litigation, 2 St. Mary's J. Legal Mal. & Ethics 166 (2012); Jessica K. Steinberg, In Pursuit of Justice? Case Outcomes and the Delivery of Unbundled Legal Services, 18 Geo. J. on Poverty L. & Pol'y 453 (2011).

ABA Model Rule of Professional Conduct Rule 1.9, Duties to Former Clients

(a) A lawyer who has formerly represented a client in a matter shall not thereafter represent another person in the same or a substantially related matter in which that person's interests are materially adverse to the interests of the former client unless the former client gives informed consent, confirmed in writing. . . .

(c) A lawyer who has formerly represented a client in a matter or whose present or former firm has formerly represented a client in a matter shall not thereafter:

(1) use information relating to the representation to the disadvantage of the former client except as these Rules would permit or require with respect to a client, or when the information has become generally known; or

(2) reveal information relating to the representation except as these Rules would permit or require with respect to a client.

Representation Adverse to a Former Client   Conflicts of interest are troublesome because they create concerns about the loyalty of the lawyer to his or her client. These concerns in turn arise from two sources. One has to do with whether a lawyer will fully advise or zealously represent a party if that same lawyer owes an identical duty to an opposing party. The other source of concern is the lawyer's duty to preserve a client's confidences.

Simultaneous representation of two clients in a common matter as in *Klemm* and *Gamino* presents both of these sets of concerns. However, a conflict reflecting the second concern may also arise when a lawyer clearly represents only one party and the other is independently represented if the lawyer representing one party *has previously* represented the other. The critical question is whether there is reason to believe that that lawyer acquired confidential information during the first representation that would be relevant to the present matter. If it appears that the lawyer may have done so and the former client has not consented to the lawyer's current representation, the lawyer maybe disqualified on motion of the former client. *See* Rule 1.9 of the ABA Model Rules of Professional Conduct; Bergeron v. Mackler, 623 A.2d 489 (Conn. 1993).

Rule 1.9 uses the "substantial relationship" test, which focuses on whether the scope of the prior representation is such that information relating to the current case would have been pertinent to the earlier representation. Courts differ on the specificity with which they examine similarities between the former and current matters, but most require a particularized inquiry into scope of representation, as opposed to information actually transmitted:

> Essentially, then, disqualification questions require three levels of inquiry. Initially, the trial judge must make a factual reconstruction of the scope of the prior legal representation. Second, it must be determined whether it is reasonable to infer that the confidential information allegedly given would have been given to a lawyer representing a client in those matters. Finally, it must be determined whether that information is relevant to the issues raised in the pending case against the former client.

Westinghouse Electric Corp. v. Gulf Oil Corp., 588 F.2d 221, 225 (7th Cir. 1978). The courts have held that "[d]oubts should be resolved in favor of disqualification." In re Kennedy, 2008 Bankr. LEXIS 1108. Thus, where lawyers in the same firm as an attorney who represented the wife in a divorce proceeding later represented the husband in a bankruptcy action, the court disqualified the law firm. Even though the wife was not an adverse party in the bankruptcy and no confidential information appeared to be involved, the court observed that the bankruptcy addressed the dischargeability of the husband's obligations in the divorce decree and thus might adversely affect the wife. In Gabel v. Gabel, 955 N.Y.S.2d 171 (App. Div. 2012), the attorney had previously represented the wife in the formation of a corporation, but the appellate division nonetheless reversed the trial court's disqualification on the ground that the attorney did not have any information about the corporation other than that contained in the public filings about the business. How can the court be sure that no confidential communications were involved?

Representation Adverse to a Prospective Client   Model Rule 1.18(c) provides that "[a] lawyer . . . shall not represent a client with interests materially adverse to those of a prospective client in the same or a substantially related matter if the lawyer received information from the prospective client that could be significantly harmful to that person in the matter. . . ." "Prospective clients" include those who discuss the possibility of forming an attorney-client relationship with the lawyer even if no such relationship ever comes into existence. In In re Z.N.H., 280 S.W.3d 481 (Tex. App. 2009), a prospective client had a 35- to 40-minute consultation with an attorney but did not hire him. The attorney later agreed to represent the prospective client's ex-wife, a custodial parent who wished to move over the ex-husband's objections. The attorney did not remember that he had met the ex-husband, nor did he remember anything about the interview. The trial court concluded that no conflict existed and a multi-day trial ensued. The Texas appellate court reversed and remanded for a new trial with another attorney. It held that under the Texas Rules of Evidence the term *client* includes one "who consults a lawyer with a view to obtaining professional legal services from that lawyer," Tex. R. Evid. 503(a)(1), and thus the husband was entitled to a conclusive presumption that he had imparted confidential information to the lawyer. *See also* In re Conduct of Knappenberger, 108 P.3d 1161 (Or. 2005) (attorney-client relationship existed on the basis of a two-hour interview because the attorney provided advice, billed client for the interview, and led him to believe the interview was confidential). In other jurisdictions, however, the courts do not use the term *client* to include those who consult with an attorney for the purpose of deciding whether to retain that attorney. Instead, they place the burden on the party seeking disqualification to show that the attorney had access to confidential information adverse to the consulting party. Where the party cannot establish the transmission of confidential information, the attorney can represent another party in the same litigation. In In re Marriage of Perry, 293 P.3d 170 (Mont. 2013), for example, the court allowed the attorney to represent the husband, even though the wife testified that she had revealed confidential information during a number of phone calls with the attorney. The attorney testified that it was her practice not to engage in confidential communications over the phone before an attorney-client relationship had been established and that her notes of the communications and office records did not contain any indication that the wife had transmitted confidential information. *See also* State ex rel. Thompson, 346 S.W.3d 390, 396 (Mo. App. 2011).

Representation by a Firm That Had Represented Other Family Members In general, any conflict of interest affecting a member of a firm and any confidential information received by a firm member are imputed to all members of the firm. Thus, in the *Kennedy* case above, lawyers from the law firm that represented the wife in a divorce could not later represent the husband in a bankruptcy even though different lawyers were involved and there did not appear to be confidential communications at issue. In addition, some courts have disqualified firms even where the family members they represented in earlier litigation were not the same family members as those involved in the new litigation. In Kennedy v. Eldridge, 135 Cal. Rptr. 3d 545 (Cal. App. 2011), for example, the litigation involved unmarried parents disputing custody and support. The father in the case retained his own father (the child's grandfather) to represent him. The attorney and his wife (the child's grandmother), who were in practice together, had represented the mother's father in an earlier divorce action. The trial court disqualified the firm and the court of appeals affirmed. The grandfather/attorney, who doted on the grandchild, had many interactions with the mother of the child apart from the firm's earlier representation of her father. Would the courts have disqualified him solely because of those interactions had his firm not been involved in the earlier divorce action?

The ABA Model Rules of Professional Conduct suggest that lawyers employed in the same unit of a legal services organization constitute a firm, but the same is not necessarily true of lawyers employed in separate units. What constitutes a separate unit apparently depends on "the particular rule that is involved, and on the specific facts of the situation." Comment 2 to Rule 1.10. If the lawyers are in the same unit, whatever that means, the categorical rule of disqualification set out in Rule 1.10(a) seemingly applies.

Perhaps the most rapidly growing group of conflict of interest cases between lawyers and clients are those involving sexual relationships. This issue is discussed below at page 745.

PROBLEMS

1. Alma and Gustav Mahler have been married for ten years and now have agreed to divorce. Gustav is employed as a mechanic by an aircraft company, making about $30,000 a year; Alma has not worked outside the home for several years. They have been discussing matters for some time and have agreed that Alma will have custody of their two children (ages 2 and 5). Gustav will have visitation for one day each weekend and will pay child support according to the state child support guidelines. Alma will seek employment. Their real and personal property consists of a house, in which they have $28,000 equity, two cars worth approximately $8000 each, and about $10,000 in personal property (mostly household furnishings). Alma will keep the house, the furnishings, and one car.

Alma and Gustav have both come to your office for assistance in securing the divorce. They want you to represent both of them, and they do not want a second attorney, who would, in their view, add unnecessarily to the expense of the divorce and perhaps create problems. Would you and should you represent Alma and Gustav?

2. Assume Alma comes to you two years after receiving a divorce. She and her former husband, Gustav, had reached an agreement between themselves, identical with the agreement described in problem 1. Arnold Becker, an experienced divorce lawyer, represented both. Last week, however, Alma was talking with a friend of hers, also divorced, who mentioned that she has received an interest in her ex-husband's pension plan. Alma was not aware that she might have some interest in Gustav's pension plan and wants to know if she can still receive something for it. How would you advise her?

3. Jean and Taylor Smith are divorcing. Taylor Smith is represented by Haddock & Carp, a law firm that has previously represented him in connection with his business interests. The firm also represented both Jean and Taylor when they challenged a lien on their home initiated by an electrician who charged what they considered, and the court agreed, to be an exorbitant amount for replacing the

wiring in their home. Jean Smith now seeks to disqualify Haddock & Carp from representing Taylor. Should she succeed?

4. Suppose that, in problem 3, Taylor's lawyer had previously represented him in a bankruptcy proceeding. Would that affect your analysis?

5. Harold schedules a consultation for the purpose of deciding whether to retain you with respect to a custody dispute he is having with his ex-wife. You discover that a woman with the same last name already has an appointment to see you, also about a custody matter. You have never met or spoken to either party. What steps should you take to avoid any conflicts of interest and to keep open the possibility that at least one of the parties can hire you if they are in fact involved in the same dispute?

NOTE: FEE ARRANGEMENTS

Most courts take the view that contingent fees are not allowed in domestic relations cases. The court in Meyers v. Handlon, 479 N.E.2d 106 (Ind. App. 1985), summarizes the usual justifications for this prohibition:

> . . . [W]e discern at least five reasons for the traditional disapproval of contingent fee contracts. They are: 1) the public policy favoring marriage; 2) disapproval of giving attorneys a financial incentive to promote divorce; 3) the statutory availability of attorney fee awards making contingent fees unnecessary; 4) the potential for over-reaching or undue influence in a highly emotional situation; and 5) a need for the court to make an informed distribution of property which includes the obligation of attorney fees. . . .
>
> The reason cited in virtually every case dealing with this issue is the State's interest in preserving the marital relationship and discouraging divorce. It is thought that a contingent fee contract in contemplation of divorce gives an attorney some incentive to actually promote the divorce or hinder possible reconciliation. Such a financial interest in derogation of marriage offends public policy. . . .
>
> . . . The evolution away from restrictive divorce laws occurred, in our opinion, not because of a diminished societal interest in preserving the marriage relationship but in recognition that society's interest was rarely served by prolonging the agonies of a dying marriage. This does not, however, lessen the impropriety of an attorney having a financial stake in promoting a hostile, adversarial atmosphere between the parties. . . .
>
> The fourth reason . . . is potential for overreaching and undue influence. . . . Divorce and the resulting division of the marital property creates an emotional atmosphere in which distraught parties are especially vulnerable to agreeing to a contract which turns out to be oppressive. . . .
>
> The final reason . . . is the concern that the trial court's duty to provide an equitable property settlement and establish support for minor children or a disabled spouse may be thwarted by the existence of a contingent fee arrangement—especially where the court has not been informed of its existence. . . .

Id. at 109-111. *See also* Maxwell Schuman & Co. v. Edwards, 663 S.E.2d 329 (N.C. App. 2008) (finding contingent fee agreement with Canadian law firm in child custody and support action to be void as against public policy). Rule 1.5(d)(1) of the ABA Model Rules of Professional Conduct also prohibits "any fee in a domestic relations matter, the payment of which is contingent upon the securing of a divorce or upon the amount of alimony or support, or property settlement in lieu thereof. . . ." Comment [6] of Section 1.5 provides that the prohibition does not apply to "legal representation in connection with the recovery of post-judgment balances due under support, alimony, or financial orders because such contracts do not implicate the same policy concerns." The Comments provide no explanation for the prohibition generally. Why don't the policy concerns present in the initial divorce proceeding also present in post-judgment actions? For a discussion of this issue, *see* Ethics Opinion: How Far Can You Go in a Divorce?, 29 Mont. Law. (2004) (allowing a contingent fee agreement to investigate the possibility that one of the parties to a divorce concealed assets in the completed dissolution). *See also* Ballesteros v. Jones, 985 S.W.2d 485 (Tex. App. 1998), upholding a contingent fee arrangement in a divorce case. The arrangement was for counsel to receive one-third of the settlement recovery; the resulting claim was for $90,000. The court noted that contingent fee arrangements are rarely justified in divorce actions, but held that the issues here — including need for proof of a common law marriage — were sufficiently complex and the outcome sufficiently uncertain that a contingent fee was permissible and that there was in this case no glaring or flagrant disparity between the fee paid and the value of the services rendered.

As noted above, courts often shift responsibility for fees in divorce cases from one party to another. Such awards are usually entered and/or upheld when the party lacks sufficient funds to pay the agreed (reasonable) fee in whole or in part, or where the spouse seeking relief will have substantially fewer resources than the other. An allowance of attorneys' fees will be overturned only when there is an abuse of discretion, that is, when it appears that the trial court could not reasonably have concluded as it did. *Compare* In re Marriage of Robinson and Thiel, 35 P.3d 89 (Ariz. App. 2001) (abuse of discretion to spouse with far fewer resources), *with* In re Marriage of Duncan, 108 Cal. Rptr. 2d 833 (Cal. App. 2001) (no abuse of discretion where both parties had sufficient financial resources to pay for their litigation, even though husband had substantial earned income and wife had none). "Performance" or "value-added" fees — fees that reflect the outcome reached rather than the amount or kind of work done — have become common in many legal settings. A New York court has considered the extent to which such fees are "contingent" and therefore improper where contingent fees are prohibited in domestic relations cases. The wife had agreed to pay her attorney a "bonus" of $2 million in light of the favorable results achieved in the divorce action — an agreement by the husband to pay her $15 million in property and alimony after his initial offer of $750,000. The wife sought to avoid a $1 million payment and rescind the performance agreement because it was executed 24 hours before the husband signed the separation agreement, which provided for an uncontested divorce. The trial court entered summary judgment in favor of the client, finding the agreement amounted to a contingent fee on the property and alimony arrangement and was violative of the disciplinary rule barring such arrangements. The Appellate Division reversed the summary judgment and remanded, noting that the separation agreement was complete at the time the fee agreement was made and that the issue was whether any contingency remained after that point. Weinstein v. Barnett, 640 N.Y.S.2d 77 (App. Div. 1996). The issue remains unresolved in Michigan. In 2013 the Michigan Supreme Court refused to bar such an agreement but instead invited the Attorney Grievance Commission to file a proposal with the court "for amending the Michigan Rules of Professional Conduct so as to clarify whether the use of a 'results obtained' or 'value added' provision in the calculation of attorney fees in a divorce case makes the fee 'contingent' and thus impermissible." In re Fryhoff, 838 N.W.2d 873 (Mich. 2013). *See* Denise Fields, Risky Business or Clever Thinking? An Examination of the Ethical Considerations of Disguised Contingent Fee Agreements in Domestic Relations Matters, 75 UMKC L. Rev. 1065 (2007).

Given the difficulty of financing divorces, some third-party lenders have begun to help divorcing parties get through their divorce. They provide loans that can be used to pay for expenses during the litigation, with repayment tied to a judgment or settlement. The loans are designed, in particular, for lower-earning parties who stand to gain a sizeable share of a marital estate. There is almost no regulation of these practices. *See* Note, Kingston White, A Call for Regulating Third-Party Divorce Litigation Funding, 13 J.L. & Fam. Stud. 395 (2011).

PROBLEMS

1. Martha Allen visits your office to discuss her divorce action, which has been in negotiation for some time. She has been married for 18 years, and a considerable amount of property is involved. Her husband's attorney is a well-known, aggressive divorce lawyer. Martha Allen has lost confidence in her current attorney because "he just doesn't seem interested in my problems and isn't willing to take on my husband's lawyer." She tells you that she has heard good things about you but wants to be quite sure that you are really committed to her success. Accordingly, she would prefer a fee arrangement in which you receive an initial retainer of $15,000, a fee of $100 per hour (substantially less than your normal hourly rate) for any work you perform after the first 100 hours on the case, a bonus of $10,000 if she receives spousal support for a period longer than two years (she is currently employed and self-supporting, and her prior attorney told her she is unlikely to receive more than minimal support), 20 percent of any amount her husband agrees to provide toward the children's college education (a contribution the court has no power to award in this jurisdiction), and one-third of any property she receives greater than a 50 percent interest in the house, car, and bank accounts jointly titled in her and her husband's names. May you enter into the proposed fee arrangement? Would you?

2. In the same situation as that in problem 1, Martha Allen tells you that she settled the divorce action and the final decree was entered two years ago. She received relatively little property because most of what the court identified was tied up in her husband's law practice and was not subject to division at divorce. In addition, the court decided that she did not need alimony because she had a good job, which she has held for the last several years. Martha has recently heard, however, that her ex-husband concealed extensive assets that should have been part of the property division. She also tells you that she believes her last lawyer took her

for a ride, collecting large fees while doing very little to assist her, and that she does not have much in the way of savings because of the divorce and the fact she is supporting two children in college without much assistance from her husband. She would like to enter into a contingent fee agreement in which you receive a percentage of any assets you are able to obtain. May you enter into the proposed fee arrangement? Would you?

D. COUNSELING, NEGOTIATION, AND CLIENT RELATIONS

The allocation of authority between lawyers and their clients is both important and complex. Rule 1.2(a) of the ABA Model Rules of Professional Conduct provides as follows:

> (a) Subject to paragraphs (c) and (d), a lawyer shall abide by a client's decisions concerning the objectives of representation and, as required by Rule 1.4, shall consult with the client as to the means by which they are to be pursued. A lawyer may take such action on behalf of the client as is impliedly authorized to carry out the representation. A lawyer shall abide by a client's decision whether to settle a matter. . . .

In principle, it seems that the client should have the authority to decide whether to pursue a potentially available legal remedy, whether to propose a settlement, and whether to accept an offered settlement, while clients should ordinarily "defer to the special knowledge and skill of their lawyer with respect to the means to be used to accomplish their objectives, particularly with respect to technical, legal and tactical matters." Comment to Rule 1.2.

The practical difficulty in distinguishing between the responsibilities of clients and lawyers, however, is reflected in theoretical disagreement regarding those roles. One view maintains that the primary duty of lawyers is to assist their clients' expressions of their own dignity and autonomy, rather than deciding for the client what is good and wise. *E.g.*, Monroe H. Freedman, Understanding Legal Ethics 43-64 (1990); Charles J. Fried, The Lawyer as Friend: The Moral Foundations of the Lawyer-Client Relationship, 85 Yale L.J. 1060, 1071 (1976); Monroe H. Freedman, Client-Centered Lawyering — What It Isn't, 40 Hofstra L. Rev. 349 (2011). The other urges lawyers to take responsibility for acts on behalf of clients and be guided by their own senses of both client interests and just conduct. *E.g.*, David Luban, Lawyers and Justice: An Ethical Study (1988); William W. Simon, Ethical Discretion in Lawyering, 101 Harv. L. Rev. 1083, 1113-1119 (1988).

What is not disputed is that lawyers act as advisors to their clients, however their respective responsibilities are defined and allocated. A broader counseling role has been increasingly recognized over the last several decades. Model Rule 2.1 provides that "[i]n representing a client, a lawyer shall exercise independent professional judgment and render candid advice. In rendering advice, a lawyer may refer not only to law but to other considerations such as moral, economic, social and political factors that may be relevant to the client's situation."

AMERICAN ACADEMY OF MATRIMONIAL LAWYERS, *BOUNDS OF ADVOCACY*

Family law disputes occur in a volatile and emotional atmosphere. It is difficult for matrimonial lawyers to represent the interests of their clients without addressing the interests of other family members. Unlike most other concluded disputes in which the parties may harbor substantial animosity without practical effect, the parties in matrimonial disputes may interact for years to come. In addition, many matrimonial lawyers consider themselves obligated to consider the best interest of children, regardless of which family member they represent. . . .

Matrimonial lawyers should recognize the effect that their words and actions have on their client's attitudes about the justice system, not just on the "legal outcome" of their cases. As a counselor, a problem-solving lawyer encourages problem solving in the client. Effective advocacy for a client means considering with the client what is in the client's best interest and determining the most effective means to achieve that result. The client's best interests include the well being of children, family peace, and economic stability. Clients looks to attorneys' words and deeds for how they should behave while involved with the legal system. Even when involved in a highly contested matter, divorce attorneys should strive to promote civility and good behavior by the client toward the parties, the lawyers and the court. . . .

1. Competence and Advice

. . .

1.2 An attorney should advise the client of the emotional and economic impact of divorce and explore the feasibility of reconciliation.

1.3 An attorney should refuse to assist in vindictive conduct and should strive to lower the emotional level of a family dispute by treating all other participants with respect.

1.4 An attorney should be knowledgeable about different ways to resolve marital disputes, including negotiation, mediation, arbitration and litigation.

1.5 An attorney should attempt to resolve matrimonial disputes by agreement and should consider alternative means of achieving resolution.

Comment

The litigation process is expensive and emotionally draining. Settlement may not be appropriate or workable in some cases due to the nature of the dispute or the animosity of the parties. Litigation is the best course in those cases.

In matrimonial matters, a cooperative resolution is highly desirable. Matrimonial law is not a matter of winning or losing. At its best, matrimonial law should result in disputes being solved fairly for all parties, including children. Major tasks of the matrimonial lawyer include helping the client develop realistic objectives and attempting to attain them with the least injury to the family. The vast majority of cases should be resolved by lawyers negotiating settlements on behalf of their clients.

Parties are more likely to abide by their own promises than by an outcome imposed on them by a court. When resolution requires complex trade-offs, the parties may be better able than the court to forge a resolution that addresses their individual values and needs. An agreement that meets the reasonable objectives of the parties maximizes their autonomy and their own priorities. A court-imposed resolution may, instead, maximize legal principles that may seem arbitrary or unfair within the context of the parties' family. An agreement may establish a positive tone for continuing post-divorce family relations by avoiding the animosity and pain of court battles. It may also be less costly financially than a litigated outcome. Parents who litigate their custody disputes are much more likely to believe that the process had a detrimental effect on relations with the divorcing spouse than parents whose custody or support disputes are settled. These issues should be discussed with the client. . . .

6. Children

One of the most troubling issues in family law is determining a lawyer's obligations to children. The lawyer must competently represent the interests of the client, but not at the expense of the children. The parents' fiduciary obligations for the well being of a child provide a basis for the attorney's consideration of the child's best interests consistent with traditional advocacy and client loyalty principles. It is accepted doctrine that the attorney for a trustee or other fiduciary has an ethical obligation to the beneficiaries for whom the fiduciary's obligations run. Statutory law and decisional law in most jurisdictions imposes a fiduciary duty on parents to act in their children's interests. For this analysis to be of benefit to practitioners, however, a clearer mandate must be adopted as part of the ethical code or its interpretations.

6.1 An attorney representing a parent should consider the welfare of, and seek to minimize the adverse impact of the divorce on, the minor children.

6.2 An attorney should not permit a client to contest child custody, contact or access for either financial leverage or vindictiveness. . . .

NOTES AND QUESTIONS

1. Does a lawyer's role as counselor conflict with the lawyer's traditional role as litigator? Do the principles in the AAML *Bounds of Advocacy* conflict with your understanding of the attorney's role in other disputes? If so, how would you manage these conflicts? How do you understand the obligation of a lawyer to settle in a routine divorce case? Does it matter whether there are children involved? Is this obligation different from the obligation of a lawyer in a torts action? Why? For discussion of the Bounds of Advocacy, *see* John M. Burman, Ethics in Child Custody Proceedings: Changing From Client-Centered to Family-Centered Representation, 33 Wyo. Lawyer 40 (2010).

2. In a classic study of family law negotiations, Austin Sarat and William B. Felstiner, Law and Strategy in the Divorce Lawyer's Office, 20 Law & Soc'y Rev. 93 (1986), the authors observed one side of family law negotiations in forty divorce cases in Massachusetts and California, attending court proceedings, recording lawyer-client sessions, and interviewing the participants about their perception of the events. While many of the clients tended to view the legal system as a formal, rule bound, relatively predictable process, the lawyers emphasized uncertainty—

the outcome might depend on the judge, the persuasiveness of witnesses who might be nervous or uncertain of their recollections, or the occurrence of events the lawyers might not be able to foresee, such as a change in a child's school performance. The study focused in particular on how lawyers deal with clients' emotions in the conduct of negotiations. The authors described in detail a divorce case that turned on the division of the couples' one major asset: their house. Although the parties had initially indicated a willingness to try mediation, that ended when the husband secured an ex parte restraining order that barred the wife from setting foot on the property. In the negotiations, the wife's first priority was rescinding the restraining order, but her lawyer tried to persuade her to focus instead on a global settlement resolving the divorce. She wanted vindication. She described the lawyer as her "knight in shining armor." She saw him as someone who would protect her and do battle for her. The lawyer tried to shift her attention from the restraining order, which was an all or nothing side issue, to her objectives in the property settlement, where compromise was possible. The negotiation between lawyer and client was as, if not more, complex than the negotiation between the two sides. The lawyer had to manage to retain the client's trust, even as he counseled compromise, and to defend himself against "a kind of emotional transference" in which "the client makes the lawyer into a kind of husband substitute." The authors emphasized the importance for both lawyer and client of separating the "legal self" and the "emotional self" and describe the lawyer's role in assisting the client in maintaining the separation between the two.

This particular example involved a male lawyer and a female client. The client acknowledged having sexual fantasies about the lawyer, and the authors emphasize that these demands, including the need to establish trust with someone who has experienced betrayal from an intimate and the need to police lawyer-client boundaries, "typify the kind of environment in which divorce lawyers work."

Consider how you would handle such a client and whether the *Bounds of Advocacy* suggest principles that would be helpful in doing so. How does a lawyer persuade a client to negotiate who wants vindication more than she wants a particular outcome? Would your answer change if the issue involved child custody rather than a property division? Does the answer depend on what legal outcome you would predict from litigation or on your assessment of the clients' long term interests? How should you proceed if your view of the clients' interests is different from hers? For an alternative view of the lawyers' role that places weight on the importance of empathy, *see* Douglas O. Linder and Nancy Levit, *The Good Lawyer: Seeking Quality in the Practice of Law* (2014).

PROBLEM

Fred's softball team wins the division championships and has a wild party to celebrate. His teammates hire prostitutes for the celebration and Fred indulges. His wife, Maria finds out about it, and she is furious. She tells him she wants a divorce. A couple of weeks later, Fred stops by the house to apologize. He had been drinking earlier in the evening. He and Maria argue and Fred grabs Maria and shakes her in an effort to stop her from yelling at him. Maria calls the police. Although their two young children had been asleep during the argument, Maria obtains an ex parte order barring Fred from the residence and limiting his contact to the children to supervised visitation.

Fred is your client. He feels humiliated by the order. He had been very involved with the children and had coached the older child's T-ball team. His argument with Maria had been the first time anything like this had happened between them and while Maria told the judge that Fred had hit her and terrified her, he feels all he did was to try to get her attention. Fred wants you to do everything you can to eliminate the restraining order. He would also like to fight for as much time as he can with the children. He feels he has been the more involved parent and Maria's response to the party with the prostitutes, which Fred didn't organize and didn't know about in advance, was entirely disproportionate to what really happened. He is convinced that the marriage is over and his first priority is to protect his relationship with the children.

You are convinced that the best way to approach the restraining order is to ignore it for now. If the judge sees that Fred is cooperative, no further incidents occur and you reach a settlement on custody, the court will lift the order anyway. You also wonder if reconciliation is possible, though Fred rejected the idea when you mentioned it.

What obligations do you have under the *Bounds of Advocacy* to promote reconciliation between Fred and Maria? To what extent should you accept Fred's insistence on trying to lift the restraining order before trying to settle the custody issue? If Maria were to propose lifting the order in exchange for a custody order giving her sole legal and physical custody with once a week visitation for Fred, how would you respond? If you are convinced you could do better in court, but Fred wants to accept the proposal, how would you advise him?

Timothy Hedeen & Peter Salem, *What Should Family Lawyers Know? Results of a Survey of Practitioners and Students*

44 Fam. Ct. Rev. 601, 605-606, 608-611 (2006)

Presented with a list of twenty-two skills, generated through consultation with law faculty and a review of the MacCrate Report, the respondent pool was asked to rank each skill as "extremely important," "moderately important," or "not important at all." Fully ninety-seven percent (97.0%) indicated that listening was extremely important, while more than nine in ten identified setting realistic expectations for clients (93.6%), involving clients in decision making (93.1%), and identifying clients' interests (91.3%) as extremely important. These responses suggest that today's family law practitioner should be equipped with strong interpersonal, collaborative, and negotiation skills. While some of the most frequently identified skills reflect traditional expectations of lawyers as drivers of cases — setting expectations, keeping clients informed, client counseling — the preponderance of interactive, joint decision-making skills indicates the need for training in other areas as well. The interpersonal skills of listening, working with clients in emotional crisis, and conveying empathy are important for contemporary practice. . . .

We examined whether students placed the same level of importance on the skills, knowledge, and attributes of family lawyers as did law professors and practicing lawyers. There was considerable agreement as to what skills, knowledge, and attributes were considered extremely important, including listening (law professors 100%; lawyers 100%; law students 97.1%), identifying clients' interests (law professors 96.3%; lawyers 95.4%; law students 94.1%), family court procedure (law professors 96.2%; lawyers 78.8%; law students 88.2%), governing law (law professors 92.3%; lawyers 86.2%; law students 91.2%), and preparedness (law professors 88.5%; lawyers 91.2%; law students 87.9%). It is interesting to note that family court procedure was ranked higher among both law professors and law students than it was among practicing lawyers.

There were also some noteworthy differences. Of the skills considered extremely important, law students tended to place a greater emphasis than their professors, lawyers, and indeed, virtually all of those surveyed, on the traditional legal skills of courtroom advocacy (law students 61.8%; lawyers 52.3%; law professors 33.3%), ability to question witnesses (law students 55.9%; lawyers 44.0%; law professors 44.4%), and persuasive writing (law students 44.1%; lawyers 39.8%; law professors 33.3%). . . .

Moreover, fewer law students (79.4%) than professors (100%) and lawyers (94%) responded that involving clients in decision making was extremely important, and fewer students (67.6%) than professors (88.9%) and lawyers (80.3%) considered the ability to work with clients in emotional crisis to be an extremely important skill (see [figure]).

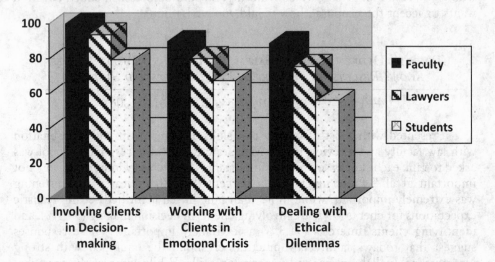

Law students in this survey were not as concerned with the ethics of family law practice as were the lawyers and law professors who responded to the survey. Knowledge of the ethical dimensions of family law was extremely important for 88.5% of law professors, 80.7% of lawyers, and 67.6% of law students. Consistent with these findings, ethical behavior was extremely important for 100% of law professors, 90% of lawyers, and 72.7% of law students. Further, while 88.9% of law professors and 75.7% of lawyers responded that recognizing and resolving ethical dilemmas was extremely important, this was the case with only 55.9% of law students. Finally, 76.0% of law professors, 64.5% of lawyers, and 54.5% of law students reported that they believed fair-mindedness to be extremely important.

ANDREA KUPFER SCHNEIDER & NANCY MILLS, *WHAT FAMILY LAWYERS ARE REALLY DOING WHEN THEY NEGOTIATE*

44 Fam. Ct. Rev. 612 (2006)

In 1976, Professor Gerald Williams studied lawyers' approaches to negotiation through a mail survey to about 1,000 attorneys in Phoenix. His seminal study found two kinds of styles — cooperative and competitive. Twenty-five years later, this research seeks to revisit these two approaches and determine whether there may be more than just two negotiation styles. The methodology used was similar to Williams' study — sending surveys to attorneys and asking them to describe and evaluate the lawyer with whom they had most recently negotiated — whether or not that particular dispute was settled. . . .

The survey was sent to 1,000 attorneys in Milwaukee, Wisconsin, and 1,500 attorneys in the Chicago area. The surveys were completely anonymous with an overall response rate of 29%. Although more than 30% of the respondents were women, higher than the actual female population, less than 18% of the evaluated attorneys were female. . . .

. . . There are a few notable differences between the lawyers of 25 years ago and those of today. First, the number of adversarial lawyers as a percentage of the bar has gone up from 27% to 36%. Second, the number of ineffective lawyers — as reported by their peers — has also gone up from 12% to 22%. Finally, the adversarial lawyers as a group have gotten more negative and nastier. Twenty-five years ago, the effective competitive lawyers still had plenty of positive adjectives describing them, including convincing and experienced. Today, that situation is quite different — the top seven adjectives describing adversarial lawyers are stubborn, headstrong, arrogant, assertive, irritating, argumentative, and egotistical. . . .

The difference between the ethically and unethically adversarial lawyers can be found in four areas. First, the ethically adversarial lawyers still are considered trustworthy (i.e., rated highly in ethical behavior) while the unethical lawyers are highly rated in being manipulative, conniving, and deceptive — not at all trustworthy. Second, unethically adversarial lawyers are also not trustful, rated highly in being suspicious of the other side. Third, while the ethically adversarial lawyers are tough and firm, unethically adversarial lawyers are generally considered to be rude and angry. Finally, the only group of lawyers not viewed as experienced is the unethically adversarial lawyers who are also missing the adjective of deliberate, perhaps reflecting a lack of preparation or thoughtfulness about their case. The bipolar behavior ratings further differentiate between the ethically and unethically adversarial attorneys, describing the unethical group as untrustworthy, unpleasant, inflexible, and not understanding of or caring to understand the other side. It should be of little surprise that only 2.6% of these unethically adversarial lawyers were perceived as effective by their peers. . . .

II. FAMILY LAW IS DIFFERENT

... Family law had the highest percentage of unethically adversarial law-yers — 14.8% — as compared to all other practice areas. Civil law attorneys were less unethically adversarial at 13.6%, as were criminal lawyers at 8.5%, and commercial lawyers at 5.9%. The average of all other practice areas was seen as less unethically adversarial at 11.8%, as compared to 14.8% for family law attorneys. For those of us from outside the family law field, this seems shocking. Family law and alternative dispute resolution (ADR) texts discuss how fitting ADR is for the field of family law with so many long-term and emotional issues at stake. Collaborative law has its genesis among family lawyers. Both the FLER Report and the FLER Survey emphasize that family lawyers require skills in listening, handling emotional conflict, communicating with child clients, working with clients in emotional crisis, recognizing and resolving ethical dilemmas, and the use of ADR processes and problem solving in general. More typically, it is the Rambo-type civil litigator assailed for a scorch-and-burn policy of litigation that would seem to be represented by the unethically adversarial approach. In fact, that is not the case.

The proportion of family lawyers rated as adversarial (including both ethical and unethical) is higher than that of any other practice group (this means that, correspondingly, family law has the lowest percentage — just over 60% — of problem-solving attorneys). In comparing family law attorneys to civil attorneys, 39.4% of family law attorneys were adversarial as compared to 32.5% of the civil law attorneys. Commercial law attorneys were only 38.3% adversarial, and criminal law attorneys were 28.8% adversarial. Total comparison of adversarial family law attorneys to all other attorneys was a significant 39.4% to 33.3% (and problem solving was 60.7% for family law attorneys compared to 66.8% for all lawyers). Despite the fact that the very nature of family law — at least when children are involved — virtually assures a long-term relationship between the parties, more attorneys in this practice area engage in the very behavior that destroys that relationship. ...

In part, a review of what is actually happening within the family law bar should trouble those who think that family law disputes should be resolved as quickly and as amicably as possible. Clearly, that is not actually happening, at least compared to other practice areas. This disconnect between what we think *should* be happening and what is *actually* happening leads to a number of reflections about lawyers and lawyer training.

NOTES AND QUESTIONS

1. How does the lawyer's role as described in the AAML's Bounds of Advocacy compare with the lawyer's role described in the Hedeen and Salem surveys? Do the surveys suggest that lawyers will need new skills and perhaps a different type of training to live up to the role described in the Bounds of Advocacy? What are the implications for legal education? What are the implications for the structure of law practice? Do innovations such as Wevorce, which provide financial counseling and channel clients into mediation, offer a better

way to address client's needs? How would you expect family law practice to change in accordance with these prescriptions?

2. The Hedeen and Salem survey asks the participants to describe the skills that are important to family law practice. What do you think accounts for the differences among lawyers, law professors, and students? When these groups differed about the importance of ethical knowledge and behavior, do you think they were making a positive statement (i.e., describing what was important to being a successful lawyer) or a normative statement (i.e., stating what they thought successful lawyers *should* be)?

3. Are the Schneider and Mills studies consistent or inconsistent in the way they describe family law practice? To the extent that they are inconsistent, do you think the different time periods might explain some of the differences?

4. International studies suggest that lawyers abroad react similarly to family law practice, emphasize settlement over litigation, and try to restrain aggressive behavior. *See, e.g.,* John Griffiths, What Do Dutch Lawyers Actually Do in Divorce Cases?, 20 Law & Soc'y Rev. 135, 163-167 (1986). A study of lawyers in the Australian legal system likewise found that: ". . . [L]ess than 8 percent of a sample of 812 cases resulted in a hearing and judicial decision, and three-quarters of the cases were resolved before a pre-hearing conference. It may be that lawyer negotiations are more successful at producing full settlements than is mediation." Rosemary Hunter, Adversarial Mythologies: Policy Assumptions and Research Evidence in Family Law, 30 J.L. Soc'y 156, 159-162 (2003). Margo Melli, Howard Erlanger and Elizabeth Chambliss emphasize, however, that settlement is not the same thing as agreement. They write:

> . . . Divorcing couples are usually in a major life crisis and one or both are bitter; the resulting "settlement" does not represent genuine agreement but a "best I can get" solution. In other words, true agreement between the parties is much less common than the frequency of settlements might indicate. We have data on satisfaction with the settlement for 41 of the 44 parties interviewed. Twenty of these were satisfied; six said they were satisfied but nonetheless felt that the settlement was unfair to them, while 15 were very dissatisfied. The following are typical comments from the latter 21 parties, who constituted half the group for which we have data; clearly their settlements do not represent consensual agreements.
>
> > Well, I was worn down. . . . I cried through the whole thing, I could hardly say yes, I could hardly sign. [But I did and] I walked out of there and cried for probably two weeks straight. . . .
>
> This characteristic of divorce negotiation — that it often results in settlements which are not agreeable to one or both of the parties — may help explain a current problem in the divorce courts: the high volume of post-divorce litigation.

Marygold S. Melli, Howard S. Erlanger & Elizabeth Chambliss, The Process of Negotiation: An Exploratory Investigation in the Context of No-Fault Divorce, 40 Rutgers L. Rev. 1133, 1142 (1988). Australia has responded to these concerns by creating Family Relationship Centres in which parents with children are encouraged to provide for their children in a nonadversarial way, no lawyers permitted. The goal is to encourage greater shared parenting after a break-up. *See* Joan B. Kelly, Getting It Right for Families in Australia: Commentary on the April 2013

Special Issue on Family Relationship Centres, 51 Fam. Ct. Rev. 278 (2013); Patrick Parkinson, The Idea of Family Relationship Centres in Australia, 51 Fam. Ct. Rev. 195 (2013). Why might Australia conclude that the inclusion of lawyers exacerbates conflict?

5. In the United States, mediators have a different view of the role of lawyers in family law disputes than the lawyers do of themselves. A study of mediators' views of the obstacles they face included lawyers among the obstacles. The study found that:

> Family law attorneys may have conflicting thoughts about the value of mediation, particularly mandatory mediation, and may feel "caught in the crossfire" when they must "suddenly shift out of a litigation mindset and into the delicate role of conciliator; a role, which some otherwise competent litigants are ill equipped and/or loath to play." They may have a win-lose or zero-sum view of the matrimonial case and project that bias onto the client in advance of the mandatory mediation process. Further, if the parties come to a successful mediated child custody or visitation agreement, the parties' attorneys may believe they cannot properly advise their clients whether the agreement is fair and therefore cannot provide proper protection because the attorneys have not "witness[ed] the give-and-take of the negotiations that created them and lack access to the information needed to evaluate properly alternatives to settlement."

Sandra J. Perry, Tanya M. Marcum & Charles R. Stoner, Stumbling Down the Courthouse Steps: Mediators' Perceptions of the Stumbling Blocks to Successful Mandated Mediation in Child Custody and Visitation, 11 Pepp. Disp. Resol. L.J. 441, 450-451 (2011). How do you reconcile these views with those of the other studies?

6. In principle the client is entitled to make the substantive decisions about the conduct of his or her case. The client may decide whether to seek, or accept, sole or joint custody; what to seek by way of property distribution; whether to ask for or forgo alimony. If, after advising the client, the lawyer is profoundly dissatisfied with the client's position, he or she may withdraw *if* that can be accomplished without a materially adverse effect on the client's interests or if, among other things, the client insists on a criminal or fraudulent course of action or one that the lawyer considers repugnant or with which he or she has a fundamental disagreement. Model Rule 1.16(b). How ready should a lawyer be to withdraw? Some lawyers try to anticipate conflicts with the client by establishing a reputation for a certain type of lawyering or by describing to a client at the beginning of the representation how he or she plans to handle the divorce. For example, some lawyers clearly state a belief that the continuing involvement of both parents is in the children's interest and that the law creates a presumption in favor of such involvement absent egregious conduct. How should a lawyer respond if the client later insists an seeking sole legal and physical custody and excluding the other parent from the child's life without what the lawyer feels is adequate justification?

7. The common law of fraud, of course, applies to lawyers and imposes a minimum standard of conduct for negotiations. *See* Russell Korobkin, Michael Moffitt & Nancy Welsh, The Law of Bargaining, 87 Marq. L. Rev. 839 (2004). Similarly, Rule 4.1 of the Model Rules of Professional Conduct provides that "[i]n the course of representing a client a lawyer shall not knowingly: (a) make a false

statement of material fact or law to a third person." Model Rule 8.4 has language that suggests an even broader set of restrictions. These obligations may become particularly difficult to apply when the other party is not represented by counsel. In Barrett v. Virginia State Bar, 611 S.E.2d (Va. 2005), a lawyer was suspended from practice for giving his wife "unauthorized legal advice" in the midst of their divorce. In a split opinion, the Virginia Supreme Court reversed. Rule 4.3(b) provides that a lawyer "shall not give advice to a person who is not represented by a lawyer . . . if the interests of such person are or have a reasonable possibility of being in conflict with the interest of the client." Barrett had expressed to his wife his views about the strength of his legal position in their matrimonial disputes. How can attorneys in cases in which the other party is unrepresented by a lawyer protect themselves from alleged violations of this rule?

8. Sarat and Felstiner discuss the phenomenon of transference. In some instances, that may lead to opportunities for sexual relations between clients and attorneys. ABA Model Rule 1.8(j) prohibits a lawyer from having sex with a client unless a consensual sexual relationship existed prior to the beginning of professional representation. Standard 3.3 of the American Academy of Matrimonial Lawyers Standards of Conduct provides: "An attorney should not simultaneously represent both a client and a person with whom the client is sexually involved." Standard 3.4 prohibits a lawyer from having sex with a client unless a consensual sexual relationship existed prior to the beginning of professional representation.

Rule 3-120(B) of the California Rules of Professional Conduct provides that a lawyer shall not "(1) Require or demand sexual relations with a client incident to or as a condition of any professional representation; or (2) Employ coercion, intimidation, or undue influence in entering into sexual relations; or (3) Continue representation of a client with whom the member has had sexual relations if such sexual relations cause the member to perform legal services incompetently. . . ."

Standard 2.16 of the American Academy of Matrimonial Lawyers Standards of Conduct states that "[a]n attorney should never have a sexual relationship with a client or opposing counsel during the time of the representation." *See* Disciplinary Counsel v. Detweiler, 936 N.E.2d 498 (Ohio 2010); Attorney Grievance Comm'n of Maryland v. O'Leary, 69 A.3d 1121 (Md. App. 2013); Linda Fitts Mischler, Personal Morals Masquerading as Professional Ethics: Regulations Banning Sex Between Domestic Relations Attorneys and Their Clients, 23 Harv. Women's L.J. 1 (2000).

PROBLEMS

1. During a hotly contested custody litigation, you realize that you, the other attorney, and the parents are not going to reach any interim or permanent settlement. You are also convinced that the children are undergoing terrible emotional strain because of the conduct of their parents. You feel the best recourse is to ask the court to appoint a guardian ad litem for the children. Must you discuss this step with your client? If your client directs you not to seek such an appointment, may you do so anyway? Are there any other actions you might take? Is there any action

you could have taken at the beginning of the action to lay the foundation for the resolution of this type of dispute with a client?

2. You represent the wife in a petition for an increase in child support. You have negotiated a deal for an amount above the state child support guidelines and feel you will not do any better in court. You so inform the wife, but she still wants more and refuses to settle. Can you accept the offer on your client's behalf? If not, should you seek to withdraw, and can you properly do so?

3. Your client, Anthony Ciulla, has told you that he feels very guilty about the end of his marriage, and he is willing to give his wife all the marital property except for one automobile and is willing to pay her substantial alimony, even though she has been employed throughout the marriage. You have advised him that, under the circumstances, a court is unlikely to require more than an equal distribution of marital property and would almost surely not award spousal maintenance. Nonetheless, Anthony does not want any contest with his wife and instructs you to accept any offer that leaves him an automobile and provides alimony of not more than $1000 per month.

Opposing counsel opens negotiations by saying, "My client wants to be reasonable. She thinks that 80 percent of the marital property will suffice. But she really does not want to fight about this, and there is some flexibility. Will your client give her the 75 percent?" How do you answer?

E.   ALTERNATIVE DISPUTE RESOLUTION

JANA B. SINGER, *DISPUTE RESOLUTION AND THE POSTDIVORCE FAMILY: IMPLICATIONS OF A PARADIGM SHIFT*

47 Fam. Ct. Rev. 363 (2009)

Over the past two decades, there has been a paradigm shift in the way the legal system handles most family disputes — particularly disputes involving children. This paradigm shift has replaced the law-oriented and judge-focused adversary model with a more collaborative, interdisciplinary, and forward-looking family dispute resolution regime. It has also transformed the practice of family law and fundamentally altered the way in which disputing families interact with the legal system. . . .

The paradigm shift in family dispute resolution encompasses a number of related components. The first component is a profound skepticism about the value of traditional adversary procedures. An overriding theme of recent divorce reform efforts is that adversary processes are ill suited for resolving disputes involving children. Relatedly, social science suggests that children's adjustment to divorce and separation depends significantly on their parents' behavior during and after the separation process: the higher the levels of parental conflict to which children are exposed, the more negative the effects of family dissolution. Armed with these social science findings, academics and court reformers have argued that family courts should abandon the adversary paradigm, in favor of approaches that help parents manage their conflict and encourage them to develop positive postdivorce co-parenting relationships. . . .

A second element of the paradigm shift in family dispute resolution is the belief that most family disputes are not discrete legal events, but ongoing social and emotional processes. This de-legalization of family disputes began with the shift from fault-based to no-fault divorce; more recently, it has become one of the basic tenets of the movement for unified family courts. Thus recharacterized, family disputes call *not* for zealous legal approaches, but for interventions that are collaborative, holistic, and interdisciplinary, because these are the types of interventions most likely to address the family's underlying dysfunction and emotional needs. Understanding family conflict as primarily a social and emotional process, rather than a legal event, also reduces the primacy of lawyers in handling these disputes and enhances the role of nonlegal professionals in the family court system.

Third, this new understanding of family disputes has led to a reformulation of the goal of legal intervention in the family. Traditionally, legal intervention was a backward-looking process, designed primarily to assign blame and allocate rights; under the new paradigm, by contrast, judges assume the forward-looking task of supervising a process of family reorganization. As Andrew Schepard has noted, family court judges no longer function primarily as fault finders or rights adjudicators, but rather as ongoing conflict managers. . . .

Fourth, to achieve these therapeutic goals, family courts have adopted systems that deemphasize third-party dispute resolution in favor of capacity-building processes that seek to empower families to resolve their own conflicts. Consistent with this philosophy, jurisdictions across the country have instituted mandatory divorce-related parenting education and other programs designed to enhance litigants' communication and problem-solving skills. Similarly, the American Law Institute's (ALI) Principles of the Law of Family Dissolution endorses individualized parenting plans as an alternative to judicial custody rulings and urges the adoption of court-based programs that facilitate these voluntary agreements. . . . More recently, a number of family courts have added parenting coordinators to their staffs; these quasi-judicial officials assist high-conflict families to develop concrete parenting plans and to resolve ongoing parenting disputes that arise under these plans.

A fifth component of the paradigm shift is an increased emphasis on pre-dispute planning and preventive law. Familiar examples include the increased acceptance and enforceability of prenuptial agreements and domestic partnership contracts. Parenting plans that include a mechanism for periodic review or a process for resolving future disagreements are similarly designed to minimize the need for future court intervention. More recently, a number of commentators have advocated a similar, preventive approach to determining, prior to a child's birth, the parental status of a non–biologically related adult who anticipates caring for the child. Perhaps more ambitiously, a few states have considered broad-based premarriage education requirements as a prerequisite for obtaining a marriage license, and the federal government has invested substantial resources in public and private marriage education programs aimed especially at low-income partners. More generally, scholars and advocates of preventive law have urged individuals to use legal mechanisms to anticipate and plan for family transitions such as the formation and dissolution of intimate partnerships. . . .

Interest in "alternative dispute resolution" arises from a variety of sources: academic commentary, the legal and other "helping" professions, and the popular media. *See, e.g.*, Thomas E. Carbonneau, Alternative Dispute Resolution: Melting the Lances and Dismounting the Steeds (1989). In its 1991 Standards of Conduct, the American Academy of Matrimonial Lawyers added its support through Standard 1.4, providing that "[a]n attorney should be knowledgeable about alternate ways to resolve matrimonial disputes." The comment has been revised since then to suggest that

> [m]any clients favor a problem-solving model over litigation. It is essential that matrimonial lawyers have sufficient knowledge about alternative dispute resolution to understand the advantages and disadvantages for a particular client and to counsel the client appropriately concerning the particular dispute resolution mechanism selected. Professor Andrew Schepard argues that the obligation should extend beyond "sufficient knowledge" to mandate that a lawyer "should have an affirmative obligation to advise his or her client about mediation and about other alternatives to litigation — an 'ADR discussion requirement,'" at least in cases in which children are involved. *Kramer vs. Kramer* Revisited: A Comment on the Miller Commission Report and the Obligation of Divorce Lawyers for Parents to Discuss Alternative Dispute Resolution with Their Clients, 27 Pace L. Rev. 677, 677 (2007). *See also* Gerald F. Phillips, The Obligation of Attorneys to Inform Clients About ADR, 31 W. St. U. L. Rev. 239 (2004) (summarizing history of efforts to persuade the ABA to adopt such a rule for all cases).

The phrase "alternative dispute resolution" itself refers to a variety of methods of handling disputes that are considered alternatives to adversarial litigation. Negotiation, which as noted above has always been part of litigation, is one alternative. So is arbitration, a long-established practice in a number of fields. As perceptions of the costs, dangers, and ineffectiveness of litigation have become more acute, increasing attention has turned to mediation and collaborative practice. The rest of the chapter will consider arbitration, mediation, and collaborative practice in terms of their ability to defuse the tensions litigation appears to inflame.

1. Arbitration

Arbitration typically involves a contractual agreement to designate a third party to resolve a dispute without the formality and expense of litigation. The agreement to submit a dispute to arbitration can be set forth in a premarital agreement, as part of a divorce settlement, or at any time the dispute arises. Arbitration allows the parties to choose a decision maker who shares their values. It also allows the parties to control the timing and the form of the hearing. Arbitration is typically much faster than litigation and the arbitrator's decision is final. The speed and informality of the process make it much less expensive than litigation. On the other hand, arbitration generally does not involve discovery, it lacks the procedural protections of formal litigation, and the arbitrator's decision may be subject to greater review in many jurisdictions if it affects children's interests. Allan R. Koritzinsky, Robert M. Welch & Stephen W. Schlissel, The Benefits of Arbitration, 14 Fam. Advoc. 45 (1992); George K. Walker, Family Law Arbitration: Legislation and Trends, 21 J. Am. Acad. Matrimonial Law. 521 (2008).

FAWZY v. FAWZY

973 A.2d 347 (N.J. 2009)

LONG, J. . . . Plaintiff, Christine Saba Fawzy, and defendant, Samih M. Fawzy, were married on September 28, 1991, and have two children born in 1996 and 1997, respectively. On September 13, 2005, Mrs. Fawzy filed a complaint for divorce. . . .

On January 22, 2007, the day on which the trial on all issues was to take place, the parties apparently notified the judge that they had agreed to arbitrate in place of proceeding to trial. . . . The judge stated that he would delay issuing the judgment of divorce until March 5, 2007, which would give the parties six weeks to complete the arbitration proceedings.

During the same proceeding, . . . the attorney for Mr. Fawzy asked that the parties be sworn and place on the record their agreement to submit the case to arbitration. The following colloquy ensued:

> [*The Court:*] Both of you need and want closure as do your children. Arbitration is unappealable. . . . You can never — neither you nor she can ever return to court, except in one or two circumstances. And here's how you can return.
>
> If there's a change of circumstances, you can return. Now, a change of circumstances is a legal term of art. . . .
>
> . . . If down the road, you or your wife believe that — that circumstances have changed and that the best interests of your children will be served by a modification of Mr. Busch's order, which again as the arbitrator he's — he'll be deciding parenting time, not recommending it. He'll be deciding it. . . .
>
> Let's assume there's a child support obligation, and I assume there will be. If someone's financial circumstances change, you can return to court. Child support can always be revisited. . . .
>
> I think the incomes are, again, about $80,000.00 and $40,000.00. If, hypothetically, someone's income doubles . . . or if someone loses their job, someone can say we need a modification of the financial obligations.
>
> Here's what you can't do. You can't come back to me and say I don't like the award or I think Mr. Busch was partial or I think he was unbalanced. Neither side could do that.

| | . . . There's one other instance in which you can return to court. To enforce the award. If Mr. Busch's award says X dollars in child support and someone's not paying it, you can come back to court to enforce that. But you can't come back to court because you've said I don't like Mr. Busch's decision. |

	Okay. Now, before either side is questioned by their attorney, Mrs. Fawzy, do you understand and agree to everything I just said?
Mrs. Fawzy:	Yes, I do.
The Court:	Sir, do you?
Mr. Fawzy:	Yes, I do.
The Court:	Okay. Thank you. . . .

On March 6, 2007, judgment of divorce was entered, including reference to the agreement to arbitrate. . . .

[The arbitrator] issued a custody and parenting-time award on April 4, 2007, which granted the parties joint legal custody with primary physical custody to Mrs. Fawzy; designated Mrs. Fawzy as the parent of primary residence; and granted Mr. Fawzy weekday, weekend, vacation, and holiday parenting time. . . .

Mr. Fawzy appealed. . . .

We begin with some brief observations regarding arbitration, which is "'a method of dispute resolution involving one or more neutral third parties who are usu[ally] agreed to by the disputing parties and whose decision is binding.'" . . .

"Although arbitration is traditionally described as a favored remedy, it is, at its heart, a creature of contract." It is for that reason that binding arbitration cannot be imposed by judicial fiat. . . .

In 2003, the Legislature adopted the Arbitration Act, which in most respects mirrors the Uniform Arbitration Act. L. 2003, c. 95. Under the Act, a court will vacate an arbitration award only if:

(1) the award was procured by corruption, fraud, or other undue means;

(2) the court finds evident partiality by an arbitrator; corruption by an arbitrator; or misconduct by an arbitrator prejudicing the rights of a party to the arbitration proceeding;

(3) an arbitrator refused to postpone the hearing upon showing of sufficient cause for postponement, refused to consider evidence material to the controversy, or otherwise conducted the hearing contrary to section 15 of this act, so as to substantially prejudice the rights of a party to the arbitration proceeding;

(4) an arbitrator exceeded the arbitrator's powers;

(5) there was no agreement to arbitrate, unless the person participated in the arbitration proceeding without raising the objection pursuant to subsection c. of section 15 of this act not later than the beginning of the arbitration hearing; or

(6) the arbitration was conducted without proper notice of the initiation of an arbitration as required in section 9 of this act so as to substantially prejudice the rights of a party to the arbitration proceeding. . . .

As can be seen from those provisions and, as might be expected, the scope of review of an arbitration award is narrow. Otherwise, the purpose of the arbitration contract, which is to provide an effective, expedient, and fair resolution of disputes, would be severely undermined.

We note that there is no express bar to the arbitration of family law matters in the Arbitration Act. Further, in Faherty v. Faherty, we long ago approved the arbitration of some family law issues, alimony and child support in particular. 97 N.J. 99, 108-09, 477 A.2d 1257 (1984). There we reserved decision on the issue of arbitration of child-custody questions. . . . Today, the issue left open in *Faherty* — whether child-custody and parenting-time issues can be resolved by arbitration — is before us.

The legal landscape across the country has changed in the quarter century since *Faherty*, which was decided at a time when few, if any, jurisdictions allowed arbitration of child-custody disputes. Indeed, the majority of our sister states that have addressed the issue have concluded that parents are empowered to submit child-custody and parenting-time issues to arbitration in the exercise of their parental autonomy.

We note as well that that conclusion has been urged by the bulk of scholarly writing on the subject. *See, e.g.*, Christine Albano, Comment, Binding Arbitration: A Proper Forum for Child Custody?, 14 J. Am. Acad. Matrimonial Law. 419 (1997); Joan F. Kessler et al., Why Arbitrate Family Law Matters?, 14 J. Am. Acad. Matrimonial Law. 333 (1997); Janet Maleson Spencer & Joseph P. Zammit, Mediation-Arbitration: A Proposal for Private Resolution of Disputes Between Divorced or Separated Parents, 1976 Duke L.J. 911 (1976); E. Gary Spitko, Reclaiming the "Creatures of the State": Contracting for Child Custody Decisionmaking in the Best Interests of the Family, 57 Wash. & Lee L. Rev. 1139 (2000); Aaron E. Zurek, Note, All the King's Horses and All the King's Men: The American Family After *Troxel*, the Parens Patriae Power of the State, A Mere Egghsell Against the Fundamental Right of Parents to Arbitrate Custody Disputes, 27 Hamline J. Pub. L. & Pol'y 357 (2006).

Such scholarly support for child-custody arbitration recognizes that it has the potential to minimize the harmful effects of divorce litigation on both children and parents. As Professor Linda Elrod explained:

> Unlike a tort action where the issue is liability and the litigants may never cross paths again, a divorce legally ends a relationship between people who may not have separated emotionally and who must continue to interact as long as there are minor children. . . . The win/lose framework [of child-custody litigation] encourages parents to find fault with each other rather than to cooperate. . . .
>
> In addition, unlike tort cases that end with a money judgment, issues regarding children remain modifiable throughout a child's minority, giving parents more opportunities to carry on a dispute. . . . The entire process becomes negative and expensive.

[Linda D. Elrod, Reforming the System to Protect Children in High Conflict Custody Cases, 28 Wm. Mitchell L. Rev. 495, 501-502 (2001).]

On the other hand, "arbitration conducted in a less formal atmosphere, often in a shorter time span than a trial, and always with a fact-finder of the parties' own choosing, is often far less antagonistic and nasty than typical courthouse litigation." Kessler et al., *supra*, 14 J. Am. Acad. Matrimonial Law. at 343. In sum, the benefits of arbitration in the family law setting appear to be well established. . . .

As the arguments of the parties make clear, although the stated issue before us is whether we should permit arbitration of child-custody issues, the case is really about the intersection between parents' fundamental liberty interest in the care, custody, and control of their children, and the state's interest in the protection of those children. . . .

Indeed, the primary role of parents in the upbringing of their children is now established beyond debate as an enduring tradition to which we have unflinchingly given voice. *See, e.g., Yoder,* supra, 406 U.S. at 232-34, 92 S. Ct. at 1541-43, 32 L. Ed. 2d at 35-36 (holding state could not force Amish child to remain in formal high school until age sixteen); Pierce v. Soc'y of Sisters, 268 U.S. 510, 534-35, 45 S. Ct. 571, 573, 69 L. Ed. 1070, 1078 (1925) (holding state could not require children to attend public school); *Meyer,* supra, 262 U.S. at 400-03, 43 S. Ct. at 626-28, 67 L. Ed. at 1045-47 (holding state could not criminalize teaching of German language to pupils who had not yet passed eighth grade); Watkins v. Nelson, 163 N.J. 235, 256, 748 A.2d 558 (2000) (holding in custody dispute between non-custodial father and parents of deceased custodial mother, non-custodial parent awarded custody unless harm shown).

Deference to parental autonomy means that the State does not second-guess parental decision making or interfere with the shared opinion of parents regarding how a child should be raised. Nor does it impose its own notion of a child's best interests on a family. Rather, the State permits to stand unchallenged parental judgments that it might not have made or that could be characterized as unwise. That is because parental autonomy includes the "freedom to decide wrongly."

Nevertheless, "[t]he right of parents to the care and custody of their children is not absolute." . . .

Indeed, the state has an obligation, under the *parens patriae* doctrine,[2] to intervene where it is necessary to prevent harm to a child. . . .

The question then becomes whether the right to parental autonomy subsumes the right to submit issues of child custody and parenting time to an arbitrator for disposition. We think it does. As we have said, the entitlement to autonomous family privacy includes the fundamental right of parents to make decisions regarding custody, parenting time, health, education, and other child-welfare issues between themselves, without state interference. That right does not evaporate when an intact marriage breaks down. It is for that reason, as the parties conceded, that when matrimonial litigants reach a settlement on issues regarding child custody, support, and parenting time, as a practical matter the court does not inquire into the merits of the agreement. It is only when the parents cannot agree that the court becomes the default decision maker.

Indeed, Mr. Fawzy does not suggest otherwise. He recognizes that parental autonomy subsumes all child-custody and parenting-time questions and that so long as the parties agree, they can make decisions on those subjects between themselves without state interference. The only decision that he appears to carve out of that right to parental autonomy is the decision to submit child-custody and parenting-time matters to arbitration.

---

2. "*Parens patriae*" means "parent of his or her country," and refers to "the state in its capacity as provider of protection to those unable to care for themselves," such as children. Black's Law Dictionary 1144 (8th ed. 2004). . . .

We see no basis for that exception. For us, the bundle of rights that the notion of parental autonomy sweeps in includes the right to decide how issues of custody and parenting time will be resolved. Indeed, we have no hesitation in concluding that, just as parents "choose" to decide issues of custody and parenting time among themselves without court intervention, they may opt to sidestep the judicial process and submit their dispute to an arbitrator whom they have chosen. . . .

Under *Faherty*, the review of an arbitration award is to take place within the confines of the Arbitration Act, unless there is a claim of adverse impact or harm to the child. . . .

Mere disagreement with the arbitrator's decision obviously will not satisfy the harm standard. The threat of harm is a significantly higher burden than a best-interests analysis. Although each case is unique and fact intensive, by way of example, in a case of two fit parents, a party's challenge to an arbitrator's custody award because she would be "better" is not a claim of harm. Nor will the contention that a particular parenting-time schedule did not include enough summer vacation time be sufficient to pass muster. To the contrary, a party's claim that the arbitrator granted custody to a parent with serious substance abuse issues or a debilitating mental illness could raise the specter of harm. Obviously, evidential support establishing a prima facie case of harm will be required in order to trigger a hearing. Where the hearing yields a finding of harm, the court must set aside the arbitration award and decide the case anew, using the best-interests test.

We recognize that some other jurisdictions have approached the standard of review issue differently. For example, Pennsylvania has adopted a pure best-interests test for judicial review of an arbitrated custody award. We decline to adopt that model, which allows a court to substitute its judgment regarding the child's best interests for that of the arbitrator chosen by the parents and fails to accord the constitutionally required deference to the notion of parental autonomy. . . .

In our view, the hybrid model we have adopted at once advances the purposes of arbitration by providing a final, speedy, and inexpensive resolution of the dispute; affords deference to parental decision making by allowing the parents to choose the person who will resolve the matter; and leaves open the availability of court intervention where it is necessary to prevent harm to the child.

. . . The question of how a harm claim can be advanced within the arbitration matrix is a more difficult one in light of the fact that the Arbitration Act does not require a full record to be kept of arbitration proceedings. . . . Because we do not discern that an empty arbitration record can supply any basis on which to evaluate a party's claim that the award threatens harm to the child, and in order to avoid a complete replay of the arbitration proceedings, we will require more than that in child-custody cases.

We therefore direct that . . . in respect of child-custody and parenting-time issues only, a record of all documentary evidence shall be kept; all testimony shall be recorded verbatim; and the arbitrator shall state in writing or otherwise record his or her findings of fact and conclusions of law with a focus on the best-interests standard. It is only upon such a record that an evaluation of the threat of harm can take place without an entirely new trial. Any arbitration award regarding child-custody and parenting-time issues that results from procedures other than those that we have mandated will be subject to vacation upon motion. . . .

We turn finally to the question of how parents may exercise their rights and bind themselves to arbitrate a child-custody dispute. Reflecting the fact that arbitration "is, at its heart, a creature of contract," the Arbitration Act provides that: "[a]n agreement contained in a record to submit to arbitration any existing or subsequent controversy arising between the parties to the agreement is valid, enforceable, and irrevocable except upon a ground that exists at law or in equity for the revocation of a contract," N.J.S.A. 2A:23B-6(a).

The Act defines a record necessary to establish an agreement to arbitrate as "information that is inscribed on a tangible medium or that is stored in an electronic or other medium and is retrievable in perceivable form." N.J.S.A. 2A:23B-1. . . . In addition, it must state in clear and unmistakable language: (1) that the parties understand their entitlement to a judicial adjudication of their dispute and are willing to waive that right; (2) that the parties are aware of the limited circumstances under which a challenge to the arbitration award may be advanced and agree to those limitations; (3) that the parties have had sufficient time to consider the implications of their decision to arbitrate; and (4) that the parties have entered into the arbitration agreement freely and voluntarily, after due consideration of the consequences of doing so.

It goes without saying that parties are not bound to arbitrate on an all-or-nothing basis, but may choose to submit discrete issues to the arbitrator. The arbitration agreement should reflect, with specificity, which issues are to be subject to an arbitrator's decision. . . .

Applying the standards we have enunciated to the facts of this case, we are satisfied that the agreement to arbitrate was insufficient to bind the parties. Although both Mr. and Mrs. Fawzy responded affirmatively to questions regarding their agreement, the nature of what was spread upon the record was inadequate to assure that they fully understood the consequences of removing their custody dispute from the judicial arena and into binding arbitration.

. . . Although the judge fully explained "changed circumstances," . . . he did not as fully explain the parties' statutorily limited ability to challenge the award without such a change. Nor did he allude to the particular standards under which modification or vacation of the award would be allowed, or what other standards would warrant judicial intervention. Further, he erred in suggesting that bias on the part of the arbitrator would not be a basis for challenge under the Arbitration Act.

To be fair, the judge, who did not have the benefit of this opinion, most likely thought that all the details of the arbitration had been worked out and explained by the lawyers, and indeed, they might have been. We simply cannot tell from the record whether that is so. Thus, lacking a basis on which to conclude that the Fawzys understood what they were relinquishing by opting for arbitration, we cannot say that they agreed to arbitrate their custody dispute. . . .

NOTES AND QUESTIONS

1. Judicial enforcement of arbitration clauses and acceptance of arbitration decisions have varied widely, particularly in the child custody context. Compare *Fawzy* with Kelm v. Kelm, 749 N.E.2d 299 (Ohio 2001), which held that "[t]he trial

court has a continuing responsibility . . . to protect the best interests of the children. . . . [T]he parties' agreement to arbitrate custody and visitation disputes impermissibly interferes with the court's ability to carry out this responsibility." The Ohio court acknowledged that the decisions from other states permit arbitration of custody and visitation, but noted:

> Typically, these decisions protect the courts' role as *parens patriae* by making the arbitrator's decision subject to *de novo* review and modification by the courts. . . . While this approach preserves the court's role as *parens patriae*, we believe that, ultimately, it advances neither the children's best interests nor the basic goals underlying arbitration.
>
> A two-stage procedure consisting of an arbitrator's decision followed by *de novo* judicial review "is certain to be wasteful of time and expense and result in a duplication of effort." Clearly, it does not seem advantageous to the best interests of children that questions of custody be postponed "'while a rehearsal of the decisive inquiry is held.'"
>
> The protracted two-stage process adopted by some courts also frustrates the very goals underlying arbitration. "'Arbitration is favored because it provides the parties thereto with a relatively expeditious and economical means of resolving a dispute . . . [and] ". . . has the additional advantage of unburdening crowded court dockets.""" A two-stage process consisting of both arbitration and judicial review achieves none of these goals.
>
> Furthermore, "if an issue is to be arbitrated, the expectation [of the parties] is that an award will not be disturbed." *De novo* review destroys this expectation. Thus, there is an inevitable tension between the court's traditional responsibility to protect the best interests of children and the parties' expectation that an arbitration award will be final.

Id. at 302. *See also* Tuetken v. Tuetken, 320 S.W.3d 262 (Tenn. 2010). Does *Fawzy* address the Ohio court's concerns about duplicative proceedings?

2. The discussion of divorce contrasted the idea of marriage as a contract, that is, an expression of the agreement of the parties, and as a covenant, that is, a status determined by the relationship between the couple, the state, and the community. In determining the enforceability of arbitration agreements, the New Jersey and Ohio courts also disagree about the extent to which custody should be resolved by the parties, and the extent to which the state has an independent duty to determine children's well-being. The New Jersey and Ohio courts both use the term *parens patriae* as part of their analysis of the proper allocation of decision-making responsibility. Do the two courts use it to mean the same thing? What are the implications of their use of the term for the enforceability of arbitration agreements?

3. The New Jersey court refers to an article on arbitration by Professor Gary Spitko. Professor Spitko argues that couples who fear that judges may reflect majoritarian values hostile to their own may wish to use arbitration to select decision makers who share their values. E. Gary Spitko, Gone but Not Conforming: Protecting the Abhorrent Testator from Majoritarian Cultural Norms Through Minority-Culture Arbitration, 49 Case W. Res. L. Rev. 275 (1999). He develops his analysis in the context of will contests, but the same principles could be applied to divorce or custody disputes. A lesbian couple, for example, raising children together could specify that any dispute over custody, visitation, or

child support will be subject to mandatory arbitration, with the arbitrators to be chosen from a group of gay- and lesbian-friendly arbitrators.

Professor Ayelet Shachar, however, questions the practice to the extent it is intended to result in decision makers who are not just more in sync with the parties' values or cultural perspectives, but expected to apply different legal standards. He asks:

> [S]hould a court be permitted to enforce a civil divorce contract that also has a religious aspect, namely a promise by a Jewish husband to remove all barriers to remarriage by granting his wife the religious *get* (Jewish divorce decree)? Is it legitimate to establish private religious tribunals — as alternative dispute resolution (ADR) forums — in which consenting adults arbitrate family law disputes according to the parties' religious personal laws in lieu of the state's secular family laws? And, is there room for considerations of culture, religion, national-origin, or linguistic identity in determining a child's best interests in cases of custody, visitation, education, and so on? None of these examples are hypothetical. They represent real-life legal challenges raised in recent years by individuals and families who are seeking to redefine the place of culture and religion in their own private ordering, and, indirectly, in the larger polity as well.

Ayelet Shachar, Privatizing Diversity: A Cautionary Tale from Religious Arbitration in Family Law, 9 Theoretical Inquiries L. 573, 576 (2008). Professor Shachar notes, for example, the uproar over an announcement by the Canadian Society of Muslims (a small, relatively conservative religious group) that it intended to rely on the Canadian Arbitration Act to establish a Sharia tribunal that "would have permitted consenting parties not only to enter a less adversarial, out-of-court, dispute resolution process, but also to use the Act's *choice of law* provisions to apply religious norms to resolve family disputes, according to the 'laws (*fiqh*) of any [Islamic] school, e.g. Shiah or Sunni (Hanafi, Shafi'i, Hambali, or Maliki).'" Id. at 577-578. Canada has since amended the Act to preclude the application of religious principles in conflict with secular law. See Arbitration Act, 2006 S.O., ch. 1, §1(2) (incorporated into Section 2.2 of the 1991 Arbitration Act). What would happen if a couple in the United States stipulated in a premarital agreement that any dispute between them was to be resolved through mandatory arbitration, and the arbitrator was to be chosen from a list of arbitrators who had agreed to decide the dispute in accordance with Islamic laws and customs? Would New Jersey and Ohio differ in their approaches to child custody arbitration in such circumstances? See, e.g., Schechter v. Schechter, 881 N.Y.S.2d 151 (App. Div. 2009) (rejecting child custody arbitration by religious tribunal); Evan M. Lowry, Note, Where Angels Fear to Tread: Islamic Arbitration in Probate and Family Law: A Practical Perspective, 46 Suffolk U. L. Rev. 159 (2013).

4. Suppose the parties include a provision in their separation agreement stating that the noncustodial spouse need not pay child support if visitation provisions are violated. The agreement also includes an arbitration provision. State court decisions hold that noncompliance with visitation orders does not affect the child support obligation. What should the result be if an arbitrator finds repeated interference with the noncustodial parent's visitation rights? Would judicial review be effective?

5. Although arbitration of custody disputes remains unusual, use of another third party to aid decision making is not: the child custody evaluator often plays a significant role in custody decision making. Professors Kelly and Ramsay explain that the child custody evaluator may take one of three forms:

> *Source 1: Court-Appointed Private-Sector Forensic Evaluator*, the judge orders an evaluation unilaterally or as part of a stipulation agreed to by the parties and appoints the evaluator from the pool of available private mental health professionals.
>
> *Source 2: Court-Appointed Public-Sector Forensic Evaluator* is the same as Source 1, with the exception that the evaluator comes from a publicly financed agency or program, which normally, but not always, is associated with the court.
>
> . . . *Source 3: Party-Paid Mental Health Expert Testimony*, has fallen into disfavor. Under this model, one or both parties unilaterally commission a custody investigation with the implicit expectation that the report will favor the commissioning party.

Robert F. Kelly & Sarah H. Ramsey, Child Custody Evaluations: The Need for Systems-Level Outcome Assessments, 47 Fam. Ct. Rev. 286 (2009). In each case, the evaluation is submitted to the court, and the judge remains the ultimate decision maker. Nonetheless, the recommendations, particularly in situations where the judge appoints the evaluator, tend to be influential. This process is similar to arbitration in that a neutral third party evaluates the circumstances, and does so in accordance with a less formal, less adversarial process. It differs from arbitration in the following respects:

- Although in some cases the parties initiate the evaluation and jointly choose an evaluator, the court typically initiates the process and may select a professional without input from the parties.
- The judge remains the ultimate decision maker in accordance with the best-interest-of-the-child standard.
- The evaluator's recommendations are not ordinarily binding on the court or the parties (although the parties can agree to follow the evaluator's recommendations).
- The standards behind the evaluators' recommendations generally reflect mental health practices rather than legal rules, with the court bearing the ultimate responsibility for determining how the evaluation adheres to the best-interest-of-the-child legal standard.

Kelly and Ramsey emphasize that while there is an extensive literature on the substance of child custody evaluations, there is relatively little empirical research assessing their use, influence, or effectiveness. The evaluations may, however, influence not only judicial decisions, but also negotiation, mediation, and settlement of custody disputes. *See also* Association of Family and Conciliation Courts, Model Standards of Practice for Child Custody Evaluation, 45 Fam. Ct. Rev. 70 (2007); Robert E. Emery, Randy K. Otto & William T. O'Donohue, A Critical Assessment of Child Custody Evaluations: Limited Science and a Flawed System, 6 Psychol. Sci. Pub. Int. 16 (2005); T.M. Tippins & J.P. Wittmann, Empirical and Ethical Problems with Custody Recommendations: A Call for Clinical Humility and Judicial Vigilance, 43 Fam. Ct. Rev. 45 193 (2005).

PROBLEM

You are a law clerk to Judge Wilson, who sits on the Family Court of your county. Pending before her is the case of Mr. and Ms. Feld, an orthodox Jewish couple with six children. The Felds decided to divorce and voluntarily submitted their custody dispute for arbitration to a Beth Din (a religious court). The Beth Din divided custody between the parents, with the three oldest placed with the father and the three youngest with the mother. The father has filed a divorce petition in Judge Wilson's court. The petition seeks incorporation of the religious court's decree in the civil order, relying on a state statute providing generally for judicial enforcement of decisions reached by an arbitrator to whom a dispute has been submitted by the parties. Judge Wilson asks for your analysis of the father's request.

2. Mediation

The most widespread institutionalized form of alternative dispute resolution is mediation. The Model Standards of Practice for Family and Divorce Mediation define mediation as

> [a] process in which a mediator, an impartial third party, facilitates the resolution of family disputes by promoting the participants' voluntary agreement. The family mediator assists communication, encourages understanding and focuses the participants on their individual and common interests. The family mediator works with the participants to explore options, make decisions and reach their own agreements.[3]

The increase in divorce rates increased interest in alternative mechanisms that could resolve disputes more quickly, less expensively, and with less judicial involvement. At the same time, the move away from fault-based decision making increased the need for an alternative foundation for resolving disagreements. Law professor Jay Folberg, an early advocate of mediation, argued that:

> Mediation can help the parties learn how to solve problems together . . . and recognize that cooperation can be of mutual advantage. Mediation is bound neither by rules of procedure and substantive law nor by other assumptions that dominate the adversary process. The ultimate authority in mediation belongs to the parties. . . . The emphasis is not on who is right and who is wrong . . . but on establishing a workable resolution that best meets the needs of the participants.

Jay Folberg, Mediation of Child Custody Disputes, 19 Colum. J.L. & Soc. Probs. 413, 414-418 (1985).

The cornerstone of mediation is self-determination. The parties negotiate and resolve disputes on their own. Several decades of research has produced impressive arguments for the value of mediation. Psychologist Robert Emery,

---

3. Model Standards of Practice for Family and Divorce Mediation, Overview and Definitions (2000), available at http://www.nh.gov/family-mediator/documents/model-standards-of-practice.pdf, last visited June 1, 2014.

for example, persuaded the court in Charlottesville, Va., to assign divorcing couples randomly to mediation and litigation groups. Emery and his colleagues then tracked the families for 15 years. They found that those assigned to the mediation group were more likely to settle their disputes, and to do so earlier in the process. They reported some evidence of greater compliance with child support orders, and compelling evidence of greater satisfaction with the process. The increase in satisfaction was particularly striking for fathers, while some mothers were happier with the results of litigation. In a follow-up study, Emery and his colleagues found that:

> . . . [B]eing randomly assigned to mediation versus adversary settlement did indeed make a substantial difference in nonresidential parent-child contact twelve years later. Thirty percent of nonresidential parents who mediated saw their children once a week or more twelve years after the initial dispute in comparison to only 9% of parents in the adversary group. At the opposite extreme, 39% of nonresidential parents in the adversary group had seen their children only once or not at all in the last year compared to 15% in the mediation group. These differences are both substantively important and statistically significant.

The study also reported no increase in conflict between parents despite greater contact. Instead, the researchers said that "when parents mediated rather than continuing with the legal action over their children, twelve years later the residential parent reported that the nonresidential parent was (statistically and substantively) significantly more likely to discuss problems with the residential parent" and "the nonresidential parent had a greater influence on childrearing decisions, and was more involved in the children's discipline, grooming, moral training, errands, holidays, significant events, school or church functions, recreational activities, and vacations." These improvements, with long-lasting effects, came after an average mediation session of five hours. Robert E. Emery, David Sbarra & Tara Grover, Divorce Mediation: Research and Reflections, 43 Fam. Ct. Rev. 22 (2005).

Mediation, however, also has its critics. The following except summarizes the principal objections.

SUZANNE REYNOLDS, CATHERINE T. HARRIS & RALPH A. PEEPLES, BACK TO THE FUTURE: AN EMPIRICAL STUDY OF CHILD CUSTODY OUTCOMES

85 N.C. L. Rev. 1629, 1631 (2007)

As a nation, indeed, as a world, we are not satisfied with how we resolve disputed issues of child custody. In this country, for example, we continue to experiment with different processes and different personnel as we search for better ways to serve that elusive goal, "the best interests of the child." While there is a consensus that we should resolve custody disputes in the best interests of the child, the statutory standard that most states articulate, there certainly is no consensus on the processes that will achieve it.

At one stage of our national experiment, we appeared to conclude that mediation offered the most promise for resolving custody disputes. Mediation proponents insisted that the adversary process and the lawyers who practiced it created acrimony between the parents, acrimony that decreased the chances that parents would cooperate in post-separation parenting. No sooner had proponents focused on mediation, however, than its detractors warned that mediation posed a dangerous threat to the custody process. These detractors, the most vocal of whom were feminist scholars, found that mandatory mediation posed the most serious peril.

Most of all, opponents feared that mandatory mediation created artificial incentives for parties to agree to joint physical custody, or the significant sharing of parenting time by both parents. While commentators generally applauded joint physical custody for parents committed to it, opponents of routine use of mediation argued that it would force equal parenting on parents in inappropriate cases. Circumstances might advise against joint physical custody, for example, for parents whose high conflict made it difficult to coordinate the child's living arrangements in two households. Also, for parents whose approaches to discipline varied dramatically, joint physical custody might confuse an already troubled child. Most dramatically, domestic violence might make joint custody not only ill-advised but dangerous. For any number of reasons, joint physical custody might be inappropriate in a particular case.

Opponents feared that mediators and the mediation process would push joint physical custody and that in those cases in which it was inappropriate, mothers and the children for whom they had been primary caretakers would be the losers. To stem the tide of mandatory mediation, opponents argued that power imbalances in the parents' relationship, whether from domestic violence or other factors, would carry over to mediation. Opponents feared that mediators, committed to neutrality, would not redress the imbalances. Moreover, opponents argued that mediators demonstrated a bias favoring joint physical custody. According to opponents, with this bias and mediators' natural tendency to promote settlements, mediators would pressure mothers to agree to joint physical custody even when mothers thought that equal parenting time would not further the best interests of the child.

IN RE LEE

411 S.W.3d 445, 447-467 (Tex. 2013)

Justice LEHRMANN announced the Court's decision and delivered the opinion of the Court with respect to Parts I, II, III, V, and VII, in which Justice JOHNSON, Justice WILLETT, Justice GUZMAN, and Justice BOYD joined, and delivered an opinion with respect to Parts IV and VI, in which Justice JOHNSON, Justice WILLETT, and Justice BOYD joined. . . .

I. BACKGROUND

Relator Stephanie Lee and Real Party in Interest Benjamin Redus are the parents . . . of their minor daughter. Stephanie has the exclusive right to designate the child's primary residence under a 2007 order adjudicating parentage. Benjamin petitioned the court of continuing jurisdiction to modify that order, alleging that the circumstances had materially and substantially changed because Stephanie had relinquished primary care and possession of the child to him for at least six months. Benjamin sought the exclusive right to determine the child's primary residence and requested modification of the terms and conditions of Stephanie's access to and possession of the child, alleging that Stephanie's "poor parenting decisions" had placed the child in danger. He also sought an order requiring that Stephanie's periods of access be supervised on the basis that she "has a history or pattern of child neglect directed against" the child. Additionally, Benjamin sought an order enjoining Stephanie from allowing the child within twenty miles of Stephanie's husband, Scott Lee, a registered sex offender, and requiring Stephanie to provide Benjamin with information on her whereabouts during her periods of access so that Benjamin could verify her compliance with the twenty-mile restriction.

Before proceeding to trial, the parties attended mediation at which they were both represented by counsel. The mediation ended successfully with the parties executing a mediated settlement agreement modifying the 2007 order. The MSA gives Benjamin the exclusive right to establish the child's primary residence, and it gives Stephanie periodic access to and possession of the child. Among the terms and conditions of Stephanie's access and possession, the MSA contains the following restriction concerning Scott:

> At all times[,] Scott Lee is enjoined from being within 5 miles of [the child]. During [Stephanie]'s periods of possession with [the child,] Scott Lee shall notify [Benjamin] through Stephanie Lee by e-mail or other mail where he will be staying . . . [a]nd the make and model of the vehicle he will be driving. This shall be done at least 5 days prior to any visits. [Benjamin] shall have the right to have an agent or himself monitor Mr. Lee's location by either calling or driving by the location at reasonable times.

The introductory paragraph of the MSA explains that "[t]he parties wish to avoid potentially protracted and costly litigation, and agree and stipulate that they have carefully considered the needs of the child[ ] . . . and the best interest of the child." The MSA also contains the following language in boldfaced, capitalized, and underlined letters:

THE PARTIES ALSO AGREE THAT THIS MEDIATION AGREEMENT IS BINDING ON BOTH OF THEM AND IS NOT SUBJECT TO REVOCATION BY EITHER OF THEM.

The MSA was signed by both Stephanie and Benjamin, as well as their attorneys.

Benjamin appeared before an associate judge to present and prove up the MSA. During Benjamin's testimony in support of the MSA, the associate judge inquired about the injunction regarding Scott. Benjamin informed the judge that Scott was a registered sex offender, and he testified that Scott "violated conditions of his probation with [Benjamin's] daughter in th[e] house" and that he "sle[pt] naked in bed with [Benjamin's] daughter between [Scott and Stephanie]." Stephanie did not attend the hearing and therefore was not able to respond to these allegations.[4] Based on this testimony, the associate judge refused to enter judgment on the MSA. . . .

II. THE NEED FOR MEDIATION IN HIGH-CONFLICT CUSTODY DISPUTES

Encouragement of mediation as an alternative form of dispute resolution is critically important to the emotional and psychological well-being of children involved in high-conflict custody disputes. Indeed, the Texas Legislature has recognized that it is "the policy of this state to encourage the peaceable resolution of disputes, *with special consideration given to disputes involving the parent-child relationship, including the mediation of issues involving conservatorship, possession, and support of children*, and the early settlement of pending litigation through voluntary settlement procedures." Tex. Civ. Prac. & Rem. Code § 154.002 (emphasis added). This policy is well-supported by, *inter alia*, literature discussing the enormous emotional and financial costs of high-conflict custody litigation, including its harmful effect on children. Children involved in these disputes — tellingly, referred to as "custody battles" — can face perpetual emotional turmoil, alienation from one or both parents, and increased risk of developing psychological problems. All the while, most of these families have two adequate parents who merely act out of fear of losing their child. For the children themselves, the conflict associated with the litigation itself is often much greater than the conflict that led to a divorce or custody dispute. The Legislature has thus recognized that, because children suffer needlessly from traditional litigation, the amicable resolution of child-related disputes should be promoted forcefully. With the Legislature's stated policy in mind, we turn to the statute in question.

III. STATUTORY INTERPRETATION

The sole issue before us today is whether a trial court presented with a request for entry of judgment on a validly executed MSA may deny a motion to enter judgment based on a best interest inquiry. . . .

B. SECTION 153.0071

Consistent with the legislative policy discussed above regarding the encouragement of the peaceable resolution of disputes involving the parent-child relationship, the Legislature enacted section 153.0071 of the Family Code, which provides in pertinent part as follows: . . .

---

4. Stephanie was represented by substitute counsel at the hearing, but neither Stephanie nor her attorney who signed the MSA was present and therefore could not respond to any allegations made by Benjamin at the hearing. Benjamin appeared personally and, although his attorney who signed the MSA did not appear with him, he was accompanied by alternate counsel. Finally, the Attorney General was represented by counsel at the hearing, although the Attorney General was not a party to either the MSA or the mediation.

(c) On the written agreement of the parties or on the court's own motion, the court may refer a suit affecting the parent-child relationship to mediation.

(d) A mediated settlement agreement is binding on the parties if the agreement:

(1) provides, in a prominently displayed statement that is in boldfaced type or capital letters or underlined, that the agreement is not subject to revocation;

(2) is signed by each party to the agreement; and

(3) is signed by the party's attorney, if any, who is present at the time the agreement is signed.

(e) If a mediated settlement agreement meets the requirements of Subsection (d), a party is entitled to judgment on the mediated settlement notwithstanding Rule 11, Texas Rules of Civil Procedure, or another rule of law.

(e-1) Notwithstanding Subsections (d) and (e), a court may decline to enter a judgment on a mediated settlement agreement if the court finds that:

(1) a party to the agreement was a victim of family violence, and that circumstance impaired the party's ability to make decisions; and

(2) the agreement is not in the child's best interest.

Tex. Fam. Code § 153.0071(a)-(e-1). . . .

D. ANALYSIS OF SECTION 153.0071

Section 153.0071(e) unambiguously states that a party is "entitled to judgment" on an MSA that meets the statutory requirements "notwithstanding Rule 11, Texas Rules of Civil Procedure, or another rule of law." Subsection (e-1) provides a narrow exception, allowing a trial court to decline to enter judgment on an MSA when three requirements are all met: (1) a party to the agreement was a victim of family violence, *and* (2) the court finds the family violence impaired the party's ability to make decisions, *and* (3) the agreement is not in the child's best interest. By its plain language, section 153.0071 authorizes a court to refuse to enter judgment on a statutorily compliant MSA on best interest grounds *only* when the court also finds the family violence elements are met. Stated another way, "[t]he statute does not authorize the trial court to substitute its judgment for the mediated settlement agreement entered by the parties unless the requirements of subsection 153.0071(e-1) are met." . . .

Section 153.0071(b), governing arbitration of child-related disputes, is also instructive. In stark contrast with subsection (e), subsection (b) explicitly gives trial courts authority to decline an arbitrator's award when it is not in the best interest of the child. This distinction between arbitration and mediation makes sense because the two processes are very different. Mediation encourages parents to work together to settle their child-related disputes, and shields the child from many of the adverse effects of traditional litigation. On the other hand, arbitration simply moves the fight from the courtroom to the arbitration room. If the Legislature had intended to authorize courts to inquire into the child's best interest when determining whether to render judgment on validly executed MSAs, as it did in section 153.0071(b) with respect to judgments on arbitration awards, it certainly knew how to do so.

Benjamin argues that, despite section 153.0071's plain language, "[n]othing precludes the court from considering the best interests of the child, including a request for entry on a mediated settlement agreement." Benjamin and the State are correct that the Family Code provides that "[t]he best interest of the child shall always be the primary consideration of the court in determining the issues of conservatorship and possession of and access to the child." However, section 153.0071(e) reflects the Legislature's determination that it is appropriate for parents to determine what is best for their children within the context of the parents' collaborative effort to reach and properly execute an MSA. This makes sense not only because parents are in a position to know what is best for their children, but also because successful mediation of child-custody disputes, conducted within statutory parameters, furthers a child's best interest by putting a halt to potentially lengthy and destructive custody litigation. . . .

IV. A Trial Court's Duty to Take Protective Action

. . . [W]e hold today that a trial court may not deny a motion to enter judgment on a properly executed MSA [mediated settlement agreement] . . . based on a broad best interest inquiry. But we certainly do not hold that a child's welfare may be ignored. Rather, we recognize that [the] mandatory duty to report abuse or neglect [under state law], the numerous other statutes authorizing protective action by the trial court, and the safeguards inherent in the mediation process fulfill the need to ensure that children are protected. And they do so without subjecting MSAs to an impermissible level of scrutiny that threatens to undermine the benefits of mediation. The trial court's authority to continue an MSA hearing and to take protective action under the various statutes discussed above is triggered not by a determination that an MSA is not in a child's best interest, but by evidence that a child's welfare is in jeopardy. Thus, the mediation process and its benefits are preserved, and, most importantly, children are protected.

GUZMAN, J., concurring.

. . . Despite discord on other issues, the opinions make several matters apparent. First, the Court holds that section 153.0071 of the Family Code prohibits a trial court from conducting a broad best-interest inquiry at a hearing for the purpose of entering judgment on a properly executed MSA. Second, a different majority of the Court would hold that a trial court does not abuse its discretion by refusing to enter judgment on an MSA that could endanger the safety and welfare of a child—an issue on which the remaining four justices express no opinion. Third, no Justice disputes that trial courts possess a number of mechanisms to protect children from endangerment, such as issuing temporary orders and contacting the Texas Department of Family and Protective Services. Finally, a majority of the Court agrees that if there is evidence of endangerment, an additional mechanism the trial court possesses to protect the child is to refuse to enter judgment on the MSA.

I write separately because although I agree with Court that section 153.0071 precludes a broad best-interest inquiry, I also believe that it does not preclude an endangerment inquiry. . . . The trial court sustained a hearsay objection to the only statement at the hearing that could have demonstrated the mother might not comply with the MSA (a statement from the father that the mother informed him after signing the MSA that she did not have to inform him of her and her husband's whereabouts). Thus, this record is sparse and does not establish the threshold I believe must be met before a trial court may disregard legislative policy concerning the deference to which MSAs are entitled. . . . If on remand the trial court considers evidence and finds that entry of judgment on the MSA could endanger the child, I am certain the trial court will take appropriate action.

GREEN, J. joined by Chief Justice JEFFERSON, Justice HECHT, and Justice DEVINE, dissenting.

. . . Although the Court tries to distinguish between this case — in which the trial court stated on the record that it was not in the best interest of the child to approve the MSA — and a case in which modification pursuant to an MSA could endanger a child, here it is a distinction without a difference. Whether the trial court calls its grounds "best interest" or "endangerment," the bottom line is the same — the trial court, having heard testimony of the parties, refused to adopt the parents' agreed modification that it believed would subject the child to exposure to a registered sex offender. The Legislature has made the policy of this state clear: "The best interest of the child *shall always be the primary consideration* of the court in determining the issues of conservatorship and possession of and access to the child." (emphasis added). I would hold that a trial court has discretion to refuse to enter judgment on a modification pursuant to an MSA that could endanger the child's safety and welfare and is, therefore, not in the child's best interest. To suggest that the Legislature intended otherwise is, I believe, absurd. I respectfully dissent.

NOTES AND QUESTIONS

1. Reynolds et al. conducted an empirical test of the criticisms of mediation in one district in North Carolina and found that:

> [T]he comparison of the three types of custody resolution events — mediation, set-tlement, and litigation — reveals that in this mandatory mediation jurisdiction, mothers did not receive less physical custody in mediation. On the contrary, in our study, in a comparison of those three types of custody resolution events, mothers received primary physical custody more often in mediation than they did in either settlements or litigation.
>
> The findings belie another widely-held belief about the prevalence of joint physical custody. . . . Again, to the contrary, in our study, custody disputes ended in joint physical custody in less than 16% of the cases. Moreover, joint physical custody appeared more often in lawyer-negotiated settlements than it did either in mediation or litigation.

Id. at 1633.

In explaining the results, Professor Reynolds and her colleagues emphasize that mediation is no longer a single process, and the way it is implemented in North Carolina may be different from its implementation in other parts of the country. The researchers note, in particular, that:

- In the early days of custody mediation, the mediator was also the evaluator who made recommendations to the court on how to resolve the custody dispute when the mediation failed to result in agreement. This practice, which is now disfavored, never took hold in North Carolina.
- Custody mediation in North Carolina guarantees confidentiality, the parties are free to reject the mediator's suggestions, and the custody mediator does not participate in later proceedings other than to inform the court that the parties participated in the mediation.
- Mediators in North Carolina encourage the parties to consult with lawyers before the parties execute an agreement and, to a greater degree than the norm elsewhere, in a high percentage of the North Carolina cases, one or both parents were represented by counsel.

Id. at 1634.

2. Professor Reynolds and her colleagues review the criticisms of mediation. The two most influential feminist critics have been Trina Grillo, The Mediation Alternative: Process Dangers for Women, 100 Yale L.J. 1545, 1551-1555 (1991), who focused on the combination of mandatory mediation with a emerging emphasis on joint custody in California; and Martha A. Fineman, Dominant Discourse, Professional Language, and Legal Change in Child Custody Decisionmaking, 101 Harv. L. Rev. 727, 756, 765 (1988).

Conversely, the North Carolina study found that representation by counsel and the ability to resort to litigation in the absence of a satisfactory proposal helped resist pressures to settle. Is the role of lawyers in the North Carolina study consistent with or different from the role of lawyers discussed above? Is the adversarial nature of litigation, with the ability to present the case for each side, a protection for less powerful family members or a source of victimization? Or do the results have more to do with the substantive law? For a view of mediation in Israel concluding that mediation does not disadvantage women, but the influence of the rabbinical courts has a greater effect, *see* Bryna Bogoch & Ruth Halperin-Kaddari, Divorce Israeli Style: Professional Perceptions of Gender and Power in Mediated and Lawyer-Negotiated Divorces, 28 Law & Policy 137-163 (2006).

3. The most controversial aspect of mediation, especially mandatory mediation in custody disputes, is the role of domestic violence. William Howe and Hugh McIsaac insist that:

Whenever there is significant or persistent domestic violence and significant issues of mental health on the part of one or both parties, or significant levels of chemical abuse, generally the adversarial model is preferable because of procedural and other safeguards it provides to the victim or less capable party. Essentially, non-adversarial decision-making models presuppose rational actors, that is, parties who are generally capable of accurately perceiving their self-interest and acting upon it. Most jurisdictions using alternative means in dispute resolution, such as mediation, private arbitration or any of the models discussed above, have developed elaborate safeguards to filter inappropriate cases, assuring that those requiring the control and muscle of the court are directed to the conventional litigation track.

William Howe & Hugh McIsaac, Finding the Balance: Ethical Challenges and Best Practices for Lawyers Representing Parents When the Interests of Children Are at Stake, 46 Fam. Ct. Rev. 78, 84 (2008). In contrast, Judge Mary Ann Grilli, an experienced and well-respected family law judge in the California Superior Court, County of Santa Clara, states:

> After years of experience in cases involving parents, domestic violence, and child custody, I have concluded that if properly designed and operated, mediation provides a safe, effective way of resolving these custody disputes. What many people forget is that the court process does not offer a better environment for the resolution of these cases. The parties have to appear together in the same courtroom, and there is much less time for the judge to hear evidence and understand the family dynamics. Moreover, in the courtroom there will be no opportunity for the parties to exchange proposals and to have some level of control over what happens to their children.

Leonard Edwards, Comments on the Miller Commission Report: A California Perspective, 27 Pace L. Rev. 627, 663-664 (2007). Professor Nancy Ver Steegh offers a third perspective:

> In order to make informed decisions about participation in mediation, families should consider factors such as the following: the pattern of domestic violence; the frequency and severity of the violence; the health and mental health status of the parties; the likely response of the primary perpetrator; the quality of the mediation process actually available; whether the parties are represented; the presence of children; relative financial resources; and preferred decision making approach. If it occurs, mediation should be conducted by an experienced and specially trained mediator who institutes tailored safety precautions and procedures. At a minimum, these should include written ground rules, inclusion of lawyers and support persons; separate arrivals and departures, and use of separate caucusing.

Nancy Ver Steegh, Family Court Reform and ADR: Shifting Values and Expectations Transform the Divorce Process, 42 Fam. L.Q. 659, 665-666 (2008).

Can you reconcile these perspectives? Ver Steegh, like the North Carolina researchers, emphasizes the inclusion of lawyers in the process. What role should lawyers be expected to play in a case in which domestic violence is an issue and the state mandates custody mediation as a precondition to litigation?

4. To provide protection from the concerns raised about domestic violence, the Texas statute in *Lee* specifically gave the courts the ability to review mediated agreements reached where domestic violence — and only domestic violence — was a concern. Should the statute have authorized the courts to consider the interests of children more broadly, as the dissent suggests?

5. In *Lee*, the father, who had agreed to the MSA, raised issues before the court about the adequacy of the agreement in a proceeding that the wife may not have expected to be adversarial and did not attend. How should a court respond to such allegations?

6. Can parents involved in mediation be expected to take the children's interests into account? How do assumptions about the parents' ability and willingness to do so influence the different opinions in *Lee*?

7. The majority opinion in *Lee* specifically contrasts the statutory approach to arbitration, which expressly gives the court the power to consider the best interest of the child, with the approach to mediation, which limits judicial review to a greater degree. Do you find the distinction persuasive? Professor Reynolds and her colleagues compare mediation in North Carolina with mediation elsewhere. Are the factors elsewhere — court-ordered rather than voluntary mediation, lack of representation by counsel, the ability of mediators to report or make recommendations to the court — similar to the reasons that the Texas courts treat arbitration differently from mediation? Should the form of mediation matter to the courts' willingness to review it?

8. Mediation, as these different perspectives illustrate, may take different forms. It may be voluntary or mandatory. It may be comprehensive or limited to a single issue, such as custody. The parties may be represented by lawyers who provide advice before, during, or after the sessions, or they may be acting pro se. They may (or may not) have "coaches" who help them to prepare. The mediator may be a lawyer, a professional with multi-disciplinary training, or none of the above. Depending on the jurisdiction, the mediator may be able to report to the court if the mediation fails, or may be precluded from disclosing any part of the mediation sessions or any recommendation for a resolution. *See* Russell M. Coombs, Noncourt-Connected Mediation and Counseling in Child-Custody Disputes, 17 Fam. L.Q. 469 (1984).

While mediation once served as the primary alternative to litigation, some courts now offer greater assistance to struggling litigants. Mediator Peter Salem writes:

> The proliferation of services for separating and divorcing families since the early 1970s has been nothing short of remarkable. . . . Over the years this movement — combined with the growing number of challenges families bring with them to the court — has unleashed the creativity of professionals worldwide, resulting in literally dozens of distinct dispute resolution processes for separating and divorcing parents. These include multiple models of mediation; psycho-educational programs; collaborative law; interdisciplinary arbitration panels; parenting coordination; and early neutral custody evaluation to name just a few. . . . Many jurisdictions have court-connected family court service agencies and offer a continuum of services, e.g., parent education, mediation, custody evaluation, judicially moderated settlement conference and high conflict interventions. These services are traditionally offered in a linear or tiered fashion, where families begin with the least intrusive and least time consuming service and, if the dispute is not resolved, proceed to the next available process, which is typically more intrusive and directive than the one preceding it. Under a tiered service model, virtually all parents participate in mediation and in many jurisdictions are required by statute or administrative rule to do so.
>
> In recent years, a handful of family court service agencies, including those in Connecticut, Arizona and British Columbia, have begun to explore variations of triage, or differentiated case management, as an alternative service delivery model. Triage proponents suggest a departure from the common practice of referring all parents to mediation. Instead, they contend that identifying the most the appropriate service on the front end may result in a reduced burden on families, more effective provision of services, and more efficient use of scarce court resources.

Peter Salem, The Emergence of Triage in Family Court Services: The Beginning of the End for Mandatory Mediation?, 47 Fam. Ct. Rev. 371 (2009). How are Salem's suggestions likely to be implemented in an era of budget cuts that affect the services courts are able to offer? For alternative approaches that combine mediation and arbitration under the guidance of a single professional, *compare* Allan Barsky, "Med-Arb": Behind the Closed Doors of a Hybrid Process, 51 Fam. Ct. Rev. 637 (2013), *with* Yishai Boyarin, Court-Connected ADR—A Time of Crisis, a Time of Change, 95 Marq. L. Rev. 993 (2012). Would the adoption of a "triage" approach help deal with issues such as domestic violence? With protection of the child in *Lee*? Would a "med-arb" approach provide more or less protection for victims of domestic violence or sexual abuse? As the variety of services available changes, how does the availability of these services change the lawyer's role? Should basic definitions of competence include an obligation to

- know what services are available in each court in which the attorney appears?
- have the training to advise the client which services may be appropriate for that client's personality, circumstances, and needs?
- recognize the warning signs of domestic violence or mental illness?
- discourage the client from pursuing alternatives for which the client may not be suited even if they save the client money or reduce the attorneys' fees?

For discussion of the complex ethical issues underlying family representation, *see* Barbara Glesner-Fines, Ethical Issues in Family Representation (2009).

9. Some commentators have suggested that family law mediation can occur on-line. What do you see as the advantages and disadvantages of a system in which the parties are not present in the same room? *See* Rebecca Brenna, Mismatch.com: On-Line Dispute Resolution and Divorce, 13 Cardozo J. Conflict Resol. 197 (2011).

10. Should children or their representatives be included in child custody mediation? *See* Jennifer E. McIntosh et al., Child-Focused and Child-Inclusive Divorce Mediation: Comparative Outcomes from a Prospective Study of Post-separation Adjustment, 46 Fam. Ct. Rev. 105, 105 (2008).

PROBLEMS

1. Michael and Sue Heikkonen are ending their 20-year marriage. Both express resistance to hiring individual lawyers for all of the usual reasons. During the interview, Michael does most of the talking; Sue speaks only when spoken to and always agrees with her husband. Michael is a salesman for a computer company; Sue has not been employed since their youngest child (now age 8) was born. She was previously a secretary in the company for which Michael then worked. Michael thinks that each should keep his or her own separate property, which accounts for most of the parties' wealth in this case. He has inherited a substantial amount of money; his wife has inherited none. Sue wants custody of their two children; Michael wants joint legal custody (although his travel schedule makes physical custody impossible). Michael is willing to pay child support according to state guidelines and is opposed to alimony that will discourage Ms.

Heikkonen from finding employment. Sue does not want to find employment outside the home until the children are out of high school. Accordingly, she thinks alimony is necessary. How will you approach this mediation?

Would your answer change if, in the course of discussions, Sue tells you that she will give up on her alimony claim and seek work if Michael abandons any claim to joint custody?

2. You are a lay leader in your local church as well as a prominent attorney. Your church strongly discourages divorce. Two members of that church come to you for counseling and assistance in connection with their marriage, which has been weak for some time. They know you as a religious leader and as a leader of the bar, where you have specialized in trusts and estates for many years. Is there any reason why you should not serve as an intermediary?

3.   *Collaborative Practice*

As Professor Jana Singer explained above, alternative dispute resolution, with its emphasis on family conflict as a social and emotional process rather than a legal event, "reduces the primacy of lawyers in handling these disputes and enhances the role of nonlegal professionals in the family court system." Many lawyers, however, have sought to redefine the legal role rather than cede the field to other professionals. Notable among these efforts has been the advent of collaborative practice.

> Collaborative law ("CL") . . . is a dispute resolution process that relies on negotiation and puts aside the prospect of litigation. . . .
>
> CL's most novel — and controversial — feature is the "four-way" agreement that divorcing spouses and their lawyers sign at the outset, thereby committing themselves to collaborate in a good-faith effort to reach a marital dissolution agreement without resort to litigation. To motivate all four participants to put the prospect of litigation aside and focus on reaching an agreement, a "disqualification" provision limits the scope of the lawyers' engagements. Each lawyer not only agrees with her client, but also promises the other spouse, that the lawyer's engagement will end if negotiations fail and litigation is necessary. Should either spouse choose to end the process and litigate, both will have to retain new counsel or litigate pro se, and neither collaborative lawyer will earn any additional fees in the matter. Thus, each spouse has the power to terminate the other spouse's lawyer-client relationship by ending the process.

Ted Schneyer, The Organized Bar and the Collaborative Law Movement: A Study in Professional Change, 50 Ariz. L. Rev. 289, 290-291 (2008).

Schneyer explains that collaborative practice arose in response to demand from both lawyers and clients. Some long-time family law practitioners tired of "the growing contentiousness and incivility they were encountering, and even found themselves exacerbating." Some clients in turn wished to maintain an amicable postdivorce relationship and avoid the expense, hostility, and invasion of privacy that litigation might encourage. *Id.* at 293-294. He concludes that:

> . . . [I]n order to gain broad acceptance and a meaningful share of the market for divorce representation, CL requires an ethical or regulatory infrastructure that the

mainstream bar is ill-equipped to provide. That infrastructure must (1) enable collaborative lawyers to develop reliable reputations for trustworthiness, (2) clarify through explicit norms the conduct expected of all the participants in the CL process, including the clients, and (3) promote adequate compliance with those norms.

Id. at 292-293.

To establish that ethical infrastructure, a number of groups are establishing ethical and legal principles to guide the development of collaborative practice. The discussion starts with the issue of whether collaborative agreements can be reconciled with attorneys' more general ethical obligations. A 2007 ABA ethics opinion finds collaborative practice to be an acceptable form of limited scope representation. The committee explained:

When a client has given informed consent to a representation limited to collaborative negotiation toward settlement, the lawyer's agreement to withdraw if the collaboration fails is not an agreement that impairs her ability to represent the client, but rather is consistent with the client's limited goals for the representation. A client's agreement to a limited scope representation does not exempt the lawyer from the duties of competence and diligence, notwithstanding that the contours of the requisite competence and diligence are limited in accordance with the overall scope of the representation. Thus, there is no basis to conclude that the lawyer's representation of the client will be materially limited by the lawyer's obligation to withdraw if settlement cannot be accomplished. In the absence of a significant risk of such a material limitation, no conflict arises between the lawyer and her client under Rule 1.7(a)(2).

ABA Comm'n on Ethics and Prof'l Responsibility, Formal Op. 07447 (Aug. 9, 2007). The opinion nevertheless underscores the importance of clear communication to the client of the nature of collaborative practice and the client's knowing consent to the terms of the agreement.

In July 2009 the Uniform Law Commission approved the first Uniform Collaborative Law Act. In 2010 the Uniform Law Commission adopted amendments that created an explicit mechanism for the Act to be adopted by rule rather than by statute and included an option for the states to limit collaborative law to family law matters. The Act would not take the place of state bar ethics oversight. It nonetheless establishes some benchmarks for ethical conduct. Among them are screening requirements. Given that a collaborative agreement "fails" if the parties cannot negotiate a settlement, screening out those for whom such an approach is inappropriate is an important component to its success.

Collaborative law also depends on establishing trust between the parties and their attorneys. Accordingly, confidence that both parties have disclosed relevant information and that the information cannot be used to the detriment of either party in subsequent litigation is critical to the process. The proposed Uniform Collaborative Practice Act provides that each party "shall make timely, full, candid, and informal disclosure of information related to the collaborative matter without formal discovery, and shall update promptly information that has materially changed" (Section 12). The Act also states that collaborative law communications are confidential and privileged from disclosure in subsequent litigation.

NOTES AND QUESTIONS

1. An increasing number of states have statutes expressly regulating collaborative law. Ohio defines a "collaborative family law process" as "a procedure intended to resolve a matter without intervention by a court in which parties sign a collaborative family law participation agreement and are represented by collaborative family lawyers." Ohio Rev. Code § 3105.41(C) (eff. 3-22-13) (Baldwin's 2014). *See also* D.C. Code Ann. § 16-4002(3) (eff. 5-9-12) (West 2014) (a procedure intended to resolve a collaborative matter without intervention by a tribunal); Ala. Code 1975 § 6-6-26.01(eff. 1-1-2014) (same); Cal Fam. Code § 2013 (eff. 1-1-07) (West 2014) (a "process in which the parties and any professionals engaged by the parties to assist them agree in writing to use their best efforts and to make a good faith attempt to resolve disputes . . . on an agreed basis without resorting to adversary judicial intervention"); N.C. Gen. Stat. § 50-72 (eff. 1-1-03) (2013) ("A collaborative law agreement must be in writing, signed by all the parties to the agreement and their attorneys, and must include provisions for the withdrawal of all attorneys involved in the collaborative law procedure if the collaborative law procedure does not result in settlement of the dispute."); Tex. Fam. Code Ann. § 15.109 (eff. 9-1-11) (Vernon 2014).

2. For empirical studies of collaborative practice, *see* Julie Macfarlane, The Emerging Phenomenon of Collaborative Family Law (CFL): A Qualitative Study of CFL Cases 13-15 (June 2005) (Can.) (describing methodology), available at http://canada.justice.gc.ca/en/ps/pad/reports/2005-FCY-1/2005-FCY-1.pdf; William H. Schwab, Collaborative Lawyering: A Closer Look at an Emerging Practice, 4 Pepp. Disp. Resol. L.J. 351 (2004); John Lande, Practical Insights from an Empirical Study of Cooperative Lawyers in Wisconsin, 2008 J. Disp. Resol. 203. Lande compares collaborative lawyers with "cooperative" lawyers, who commit themselves to cooperative practices without the agreement to withdraw if the case does not settle.

3. Should the duty to screen clients in order to determine an appropriate approach to family dispute resolution be limited to collaborative law? How should attorneys assess whether the client "has a history of a coercive or violent relationship with another party" if the client does not disclose the information? Are the terms in Section 15(c) for the treatment of a party who has been the victim of domestic violence also appropriate for mediation or are the circumstances different? For a discussion of the importance of such screening and the available tools, *see* Nancy Ver Steegh, Differentiating Types of Domestic Violence: Implications for Child Custody, 65 La. L. Rev. 1379 (2005). Some commentators nonetheless worry that many attorneys are not prepared to screen adequately for domestic violence and its cycle of coercion and control and that the collaborative process is uniquely vulnerable to manipulation. For discussion of the particular dangers, *see* Margaret B. Drew, Collaboration and Coercion, 24 Hastings Women's L.J. 79 (2013).

4. For further discussion of the ethics of collaborative practice, *see* Barbara Glesner Fines, Note, Ethical Issues in Collaborative Lawyering, 21 J. Am. Acad. Matrimonial Law. 141 (2008); Scott R. Peppet, The Ethics of Collaborative Law, 2008 J. Disp. Resol. 131; Christopher M. Fairman, Growing Pains: Changes in

Collaborative Law and the Challenge of Legal Ethics, 30 Campbell L. Rev. 237 (2008).

PROBLEMS

1. Paul and Maria are divorcing. Maria accused Paul of sexually abusing their 2-year-old daughter, Amy, but the court-ordered evaluation found no evidence of abuse, and the judge has threatened to switch custody to Paul if Maria persists in the allegations. Maria, who does not want Paul to be alone with Amy, is very frustrated with the judicial proceedings; and Paul, who has exhausted most of his savings defending the abuse allegations, feels that he cannot afford continued litigation. Maria's parents have helped pay her legal fees, and she has recently hired a new lawyer, who has suggested a collaborative approach. Paul has come to you for a consultation about representing him in a collaborative proceeding. What problems do you foresee? How would you go about determining whether Paul is a suitable client for a collaborative approach? If you enter into discussions with Paul, Maria, and Maria's attorney about a collaborative practice arrangement, but the discussions fall through without signing a collaborative practice agreement, are you free to represent Paul in subsequent litigation? Does it matter that Paul communicated confidential information to you? Does it matter that Maria's attorney also communicated confidential information to you during the initial meetings? *See* Mandell v. Mandell, 949 N.Y.S.2d 580 (Sup. Ct. 2012).

2. You, Paul, Maria, and Maria's attorney sign a collaborative practice agreement. During the negotiations you learn that Paul had a brief affair during the marriage that Maria never knew about. Since the separation Paul and the girlfriend have become closer, and Paul recently moved in with her. She earns considerably more than Paul does. In the jurisdiction in which Paul and Maria live, the girlfriend's income would not affect any determination of spousal or child support unless she and Paul marry. Nonetheless, soon after the separation Paul fell behind in his child support payments and told Maria that it was because all of his money had been going toward rent and legal fees. Maria has not pressed him to make up the arrears. Do you have any obligation to inform Maria of the relationship or to encourage Paul to do so? *See* H.K. v. A.K., 950 N.Y.S.2d 723 (Sup. Ct. 2012) (fact that husband, without the wife's knowledge, had entered into a new relationship during the collaborative negotiations did not in and of itself void the agreement).

3. Maria continues to insist that Paul be limited to supervised visitation with Amy. Paul, who claims that he has been wrongly accused of sexual abuse, is incensed. The negotiations break up over the issue, and Maria—who has since moved a short distance away, but across the state line—decides to discontinue the collaborative process. Maria would like the attorney who participated in the collaborative agreement to continue to represent her. He is also licensed in the other state. Paul has told you and Maria that he doesn't care, and that he doesn't have enough money to hire another attorney, so he will appear in any continuing litigation on a pro se basis. You would like to oppose Maria's attorney's continuing participation in the case. Do you have standing to do so? Are you in privity with the attorney by virtue of the four-way collaborative agreement the four of you signed

such that you can claim that the attorney breached his contractual obligations to you? If you cannot do so on behalf of yourself, can you do so on Paul's behalf?

4. During the collaborative sessions, Paul shared with Maria the results of a psychological evaluation prepared by a psychiatrist Paul had consulted. The report indicates that after Maria accused Paul of sexually abusing Amy, he became deeply depressed and took an overdose of sleeping pills. Paul's girlfriend found him and rushed him to the hospital in time to revive him. The psychiatrist concluded that while Paul suffered from clinical depression at the time of the incident, he had since overcome the depression and did not constitute a threat to himself or others. No one but Paul, Paul's girlfriend, the psychiatrist, and the parties to the collaborative practice session know about the overdose of sleeping pills. If Maria continues to litigate the custody issue, will she be able to introduce the psychiatrist's report or call the psychiatrist as a witness?

Jurisdiction

12

A. INTRODUCTION

John and Harriet Haddock were married in New York in the summer of 1868. The marriage was never consummated, however, because John—feeling that he had been tricked into the marriage—left New York the same day. Harriet remained in New York, while John drifted about the country, finally settling in Connecticut nine years later. Thirteen years after the wedding, in 1881, John sought a divorce from Harriet, mailing notice to her last known address in New York and publishing in the local Connecticut newspaper. John obtained his divorce and remarried.

In 1891, 23 years after the wedding and 10 years after the divorce action, John inherited considerable property from his father. Harriet, from whom John had not heard since their wedding day, sued John for a legal separation in New York. She received a default separation decree and an award of alimony but could not recover because of lack of personal service on John. Five years later, John returned to New York. Harriet obtained personal service in New York and refiled her suit for legal separation and alimony.

John's defense to Harriet's suit, of course, was his prior Connecticut divorce. The New York court refused to recognize the sister-state decree because Harriet had not been subject to the jurisdiction of the Connecticut court when the decree was rendered. Holding that, as far as New York courts were concerned, John and Harriet were still married, the court awarded Harriet her legal separation and $780 a year in maintenance.[1]

Variations of this story provide the basis for a vexing set of jurisdictional problems peculiar to matrimonial issues. The case itself arises out of desertion, in this case, the husband's, which was the primary ground for divorce in nineteenth-century America. Norma Basch, The Victorian Compromise: Divorce

---

1. These are the facts of Haddock v. Haddock, 201 U.S. 562 (1906).

in New York City, 1787-1870, at 20 (unpublished paper delivered at the 1985 Annual Meeting of the Organization of American Historians), quoted in Neal R. Feigenson, Extraterritorial Recognition of Divorce Decrees in the Nineteenth Century, 34 Am. J. Legal Hist. 119, 123 (1990). Because desertion was the most common basis for divorce, most nineteenth-century suits, like John Haddock's Connecticut action, were uncontested (although it would have been more usual for the deserted spouse to prosecute the suit). As a practical matter, service of process did not notify the defendant of the pending divorce because his or her whereabouts were usually unknown at the time of the suit. And a decree issued by one state, even though relied on by the plaintiff, was often refused recognition by a sister state.

The questions presented by this situation were many. Could Harriet, had she wished, have sought a divorce from John in New York? Was John's Connecticut divorce valid? If the Connecticut divorce was invalid, was John a bigamist? If either Harriet or John could secure a divorce without the presence of the other, would that mean that the defendant could be required to pay or lose any entitlement to property or support she might have claimed had she participated?

The answers to these questions depend on whether a court in one state would, or would be required to, recognize a divorce decree issued in another state. And the answer to that question, in turn, depends on when and to what extent a state court has jurisdiction to enter a decree of divorce. The next section of this chapter discusses this question. The following two sections look at jurisdiction to award support and to divide property and inter jurisdictional enforcement of these orders. The fifth section considers jurisdiction over child custody disputes, and the chapter concludes with materials on federal court jurisdiction over domestic relations litigation.

B. DIVORCE JURISDICTION

A principal benefit of absolute divorce is the possibility of remarriage, and a party seeking a divorce wants assurance that any future alliance will be immune from attack on the ground that it is invalid because of a prior subsisting marriage. Jurisdiction is the key to any such assurance.

The basis for saying so lies in two principles: *res judicata* and full faith and credit. *Res judicata* provides that a matter that has been, or could have been, litigated in an action brought before a court and decided on the merits cannot be relitigated in a subsequent action, at least between the same parties. This is obviously a rule seeking finality of judgments, designed to establish stable relations by denying endless opportunities for harassment and to protect courts from repeated litigation of the same matter. However, a court that lacks jurisdiction over a defendant cannot issue a decision that binds her. Absent jurisdiction, she would be free to ignore the decision and, if need be, could litigate the issues in a second case if the plaintiff were to bring another action. In short, there can be no *res judicata* if there was no jurisdiction.

Full faith and credit becomes important when two or more states deal with issues related to a divorce. Suppose, for example, that Arthur sues Bernice in Florida for breach of contract, and both are present at the time of the suit. Bernice loses and then moves to New York. Arthur writes Bernice asking her to pay up, and Bernice replies, "Nuts" (or words to that effect). Arthur sues Bernice in New York based on the judgment entered in Florida. Bernice says in the New York court, "I shouldn't have to pay this. I have a good defense, and the Florida judge was wrong and silly." Bernice's claim will not be heard, however, because the Florida judgment, which would be *res judicata* in that state, is entitled to recognition in New York under the full faith and credit clause of Article IV, §1 of the federal Constitution. This clause states:

> Full Faith and Credit shall be given in each state to the public acts, Records, and judicial Proceedings of every other State.

By virtue of the full faith and credit clause, the New York court must say something like this:

> Arthur has a valid final judgment against Bernice rendered by Florida, which is, of course, a sister state. The full faith and credit clause requires that we accept this judgment as if it were our own. Thus, Arthur is entitled to recover on the basis of the Florida judgment, without retrying the case here.

Matters would be different if Florida did not have jurisdiction over Bernice. Full faith and credit must be given only to orders that the court had power to enter. Thus, the court in New York could refuse to recognize the Florida order. Indeed, New York *cannot* enforce the Florida order. To do so would violate Bernice's right to due process because she did not participate voluntarily, and Florida had no authority to require her participation.

Thus far, we have been talking about jurisdiction in actions to determine personal liability. But jurisdiction is not the same in all actions. Actions to determine personal liability are called "transitory" precisely because jurisdiction depends on the location of the parties rather than on any other fact. There are some cases, however, where it is not enough that the parties are before the court. When land, for example, is involved, a different jurisdictional requirement appears.

Suppose Arthur sues Bernice over title to a piece of land located in New York. The suit is brought in Florida, where Arthur has served Bernice with process during one of her business trips to that state. Presumably, the Florida court would decline jurisdiction. Although service of process on Bernice creates personal jurisdiction over her as the defendant, the court does not have jurisdiction over the subject matter of this action, the land. And because the court does not have jurisdiction over the subject matter, it cannot enter an order touching the land. Jurisdiction over land depends not on the location of the parties but on the location of the land. This power over land, as you will recall, is called *in rem* jurisdiction — jurisdiction over things. An *in rem* order speaks not simply to the relationships between the parties, but to the world at large.

The question then becomes, what is jurisdiction for purposes of divorce? Courts sometimes talk of marriage as a "civil contract," and if it were only that, the answer would be simple. Personal jurisdiction over the parties would be both necessary and sufficient. It would be necessary in the sense that, generally speaking, a court cannot make a binding determination without jurisdiction over the person of the defendant. It would be sufficient in that, if both parties were actually before the court, that circumstance alone would allow the court to render a binding decision concerning the marriage. In practice, this would mean that divorces could be rendered wherever both parties are present. If Arthur wished to sue Bernice, he would have to find her and sue her there. Similarly, if Bernice had moved from the state where Arthur lived and wished to get a divorce, she would have to go back to the state of Arthur's residence, or to any state where Arthur might be found, and bring the divorce action there. (Long-arm statutes can, of course, change this scheme.)

Here, as elsewhere, however, marriage is not viewed as a simple matter of contract. The relationship is the concern not solely of the two parties but, so it is said, of the world at large. The *status* aspect of marriage (or better, the public aspect) is important, and courts sometimes seem to take the same view concerning marriage as they do regarding land — that is, they tend to view it as an *in rem* action. Accordingly, one looks for a forum that has some interest in the marriage relationship, not simply for a court that happens to have power over the litigants. This is done by reifying the marital status into a fictional situs. What is such a situs? In many cases, the answer is simple. If the parties have always lived in State *X*, were married there, raised their children in *X*, and seek to get divorced there, surely State *X* is the forum with an interest in determining whether the marriage should come to an end. Moreover, it is the only state with such an interest and therefore with jurisdiction to end the marriage. No other state may take jurisdiction to divorce the parties. If another state purports to do so, its decree is not entitled to recognition under the full faith and credit clause.

To this point, determining the jurisdiction with authority over the "res" — the marital status — has been easy enough. Suppose, however, that Albert is physically abusive to his wife, Donna. Donna leaves Albert to live with her mother, a resident of the neighboring state. She intends to remain in that state and wishes to be relieved of her vows to Albert. Can she bring a divorce action in her new residence?

The answer depends on whether the domicile of one spouse (but not the other) is sufficient to give that state jurisdiction over that spouse's marital status. A married woman can acquire a separate domicile "whenever it is necessary or proper that she should do so." *E.g.*, Cheever v. Wilson, 76 U.S. (9 Wall.) 108, 124 (1869). *See also* Barber v. Barber, 62 U.S. (21 How.) 582, 599-600 (1858). To say that the wife can establish her own domicile, however, does not answer the question of whether the domicile of only one spouse provides jurisdiction to terminate a marital relationship. This issue was much disputed during the nineteenth century but was resolved for some time in Haddock v. Haddock, 201 U.S. 562 (1906), the facts of which are described above. Although some courts had taken the view that, where the parties were domiciled in different jurisdictions, each state had sufficient interest in the subject matter of the relationship to issue a divorce, *Haddock* decided otherwise. An ex parte divorce (that is, one in which only one spouse participates) could be obtained only in the state of the "matrimonial domicile," meaning the last state in which both parties were domiciled as husband and wife. Accordingly, John Haddock's Connecticut decree, which we know was obtained ex parte with service by mail and publication, was not entitled to recognition in New York.

In 1942, however, the Supreme Court reconsidered and overruled *Haddock* in Williams v. North Carolina, 317 U.S. 287 (1942) (*Williams I*). After some 20 years of marriage to their respective spouses in North Carolina, Mr. Williams and Mrs. Hendrix decamped together to Las Vegas, Nevada, where they each obtained a divorce and then married each other. The North Carolina spouses received notice of the divorce proceedings but were not served with process in Nevada, nor did they appear in the divorce proceedings. Upon their return from Nevada, the newlyweds were prosecuted for bigamy. They were convicted on the basis that their Nevada divorces were not entitled to recognition in North Carolina.

Although this conclusion would follow from *Haddock*, the Supreme Court held that every state has a "rightful and legitimate concern" in the marital status of persons domiciled in that state, which is sufficient to justify termination of the marital status even though the other spouse is not present. Moreover, such an assertion of jurisdiction is entitled to full faith and credit by other states. Thus, if Nevada were the domicile of Mr. Williams and Mrs. Hendrix, North Carolina must recognize their divorces. North Carolina's interest in the integrity of its divorce laws, of such concern in *Haddock*, was now dismissed as "part of the price of our federal system." 317 U.S. at 302. In recent cases left-at-home spouses have argued, without success, that permitting a state to grant a divorce or legal separation based on the domicile of the spouse who left violates procedural due process, relying on the minimum contacts test of International Shoe Co. v. Washington, 326 U.S. 310 (1945). *See, e.g.,* Henderson v. Henderson, 818 A.2d 669 (R.I. 2003).

Williams I held that Nevada could exercise divorce jurisdiction *over its domiciliaries.* In the first prosecution, there seemed to be no need for challenging the domicile of Mr. Williams and Mrs. Hendrix. The persistent North Carolina prosecutor retried the defendants for bigamy, claiming that they had never intended to reside indefinitely in Nevada and therefore had never been domiciliaries of that state. The defendants were again convicted and again appealed to the Supreme Court. This time the Court upheld the conviction, holding that, under the full faith and credit clause, the Nevada finding of the jurisdictional fact of domicile incorporated in the original divorce decree did not bind North Carolina (which did not participate in the Nevada proceeding). That finding, therefore, was subject to reexamination by the North Carolina court. Williams v. North Carolina, 325 U.S. 226 (1945) (*Williams II*).

One of the implications of *Williams II* is that domicile is not only a sufficient, but a necessary, condition for full faith and credit recognition of divorce decrees. Another is that Mrs. Williams, the left-at-home spouse, could also have challenged the ex parte divorce decree for lack of jurisdiction. If she had never appeared in the foreign divorce action, she did not have the opportunity to be heard on the jurisdictional issue and thus was not precluded from challenging that jurisdictional basis at a later time. But that is all that she could challenge. If a second court determines that the court issuing the divorce decree did have jurisdiction because the plaintiff was a domiliciary of the forum state at the time the decree was entered, the left-at-home spouse cannot then litigate the existence of adequate grounds for the divorce. And while that spouse can attack the jurisdictional finding if she did not participate, she will carry the burden of proving the absence of domicile. *See* Homer H. Clark, Jr., Domestic Relations 718-719 (2d ed. 1987). Of course, if she prevails on the jurisdictional issue, then the divorce is invalid and has no effect. The following case considers the consequences if both spouses participate in the divorce action.

Professor Ann Estin places the *Williams* cases in the context of a national debate about whether divorce laws should be relaxed and argues that when differences among the states could not be resolved through the political process, the court "was eventually unwilling to allow the policies of a few states to block a more workable national compromise. . . . In the process of this transition, the Supreme Court set family law on a new course. After these cases, marital fault was no longer relevant to the determination of divorce jurisdiction, and states were free to grant unilateral ex parte divorces. Married couples gained a greater measure of freedom to come to terms together for the dissolution of their marriages. And while these developments spelled the end of strict controls over the grounds for divorce, they also ushered in a new era of greater attention to its custodial and financial incidents." Ann Laquer Estin, Family Law Federalism: Divorce and the Constitution, 16 Wm. & Mary Bill Rts. J. 381, 431-432 (2007).

Today, divorce jurisdiction has re-emerged as a hotly contested issue, since some states allow same-sex couples to marry while the law of other states not only prevents their residents from marrying but also prevents the state from recognizing same-sex marriages entered into in other states. Courts in some states that forbade same-sex marriage nevertheless recognized such marriages from other jurisdictions for purposes of granting a divorce. *See, e.g.,* Port v. Cowan, 44 A.3d 970 (Md. 2012) (reproduced above at page 219); Christiansen v. Christiansen, 253 P.3d 153 (Wyo. 2011); Beth R. v. Donna M., 853 N.Y.S.2d 501 (Sup. Ct. N.Y. Cty. 2008). However, other courts have refused to take jurisdiction to divorce same-sex couples domiciled within their borders who were validly married in another state, on the basis that granting a divorce inherently entails recognizing the marriage, which state law prevents. *See, e.g.,* In re Marriage of J.B. and H.B., 326 S.W.3d 654 (Tex. App. 2010), *rev. granted,* Aug. 23, 2013); Chambers v. Ormiston, 935 A.2d 956 (R.I. 2007).

SHERRER V. SHERRER

334 U.S. 343 (1948)

VINSON, C.J. [Mr. and Mrs. Sherrer lived in Massachusetts during their marriage. In April 1944 Mrs. Sherrer went to Florida, ostensibly for vacation. In July she filed for divorce on the ground of extreme cruelty, alleging that she was domiciled in Florida. Mr. Sherrer was notified by mail of the proceedings and appeared generally through counsel. He denied his wife's jurisdictional allegations and the grounds for divorce, but the Florida court granted Mrs. Sherrer a divorce, specifically finding that she was domiciled there. Mr. Sherrer did not appeal. In December Mrs. Sherrer married Mr. Phelps. They lived together in Florida for two months and then returned to Massachusetts. In June 1945 Mr. Sherrer filed an action in Massachusetts predicated on the claim that he was still married to (the former) Mrs. Sherrer. She defended on the grounds that the Florida divorce was valid and that the parties were no longer married. The Massachusetts court reexamined the Florida court's basis for asserting jurisdiction, found that Mrs. Sherrer had not been domiciled there, and granted Mr. Sherrer the relief he sought.]

At the outset, it should be observed that the proceedings in the Florida court prior to the entry of the decree of divorce were in no way inconsistent with the requirements of procedural due process. We do not understand the respondent to urge the contrary. . . . It is clear that respondent was afforded his day in court with respect to every issue involved in the litigation, including the jurisdictional issue of petitioner's domicile. Under such circumstances, there is nothing in the concept of due process which demands that a defendant be afforded a second opportunity to litigate the existence of jurisdictional facts. . . .

That the jurisdiction of the Florida court to enter a valid decree of divorce was dependent upon petitioner's domicile in that State is not disputed. . . . But whether or not petitioner was domiciled in Florida at the time the divorce was granted was a matter to be resolved by judicial determination. Here, unlike the situation presented in Williams v. North Carolina, 325 U.S. 226 (1945), the finding of the requisite jurisdictional facts was made in proceedings in which the defendant appeared and participated. The question with which we are confronted, therefore, is whether such a finding . . . may be subjected to collateral attack in the courts of a sister State. . . .

The question of what effect is to be given to an adjudication by a court that it possesses requisite jurisdiction in a case, where the judgment of that court is subsequently subjected to collateral attack on jurisdictional grounds has been given frequent consideration by this Court over a period of many years. Insofar as cases originating in the federal courts are concerned, the rule has evolved that the doctrine of *res judicata* applies to adjudications relating either to jurisdiction of the person or of the subject matter where such adjudications have been made in proceedings in which those questions were in issue and in which the parties were given full opportunity to litigate. . . .

This Court has also held that the doctrine of *res judicata* must be applied to questions of jurisdiction arising in state courts involving the application of the Full Faith and Credit Clause where, under the law of the state in which the original judgment was rendered, such adjudications are not susceptible to collateral attack. . . .

Applying these principles to this case, we hold that the Massachusetts courts erred in permitting the Florida divorce decree to be subjected to attack on the ground that petitioner was not domiciled in Florida at the time the decree was entered. . . . It has not been contended that respondent was given less than a full opportunity to contest the issue of petitioner's domicile or any other issue relevant to the litigation. There is nothing to indicate that the Florida court would not have evaluated fairly and in good faith all relevant evidence submitted to it. . . .

If respondent failed to take advantage of the opportunities afforded him, the responsibility is his own. . . .

It is urged . . . however, that because we are dealing with litigation involving the dissolution of the marital relation, a different result is demanded from that which might properly be reached if this case were concerned with other types of litigation. It is pointed out that under the Constitution the regulation and control of marital and family relationships are reserved to the States. . . .

But the recognition of the importance of a State's power to determine the incidents of basic social relationships into which its domiciliaries enter does not resolve the issues of this case. This is not a situation in which a State has merely sought to exert such power over a domiciliary. This is, rather, a case involving inconsistent assertions of power by courts of two States in the Federal Union and thus presents considerations which go beyond the interests of local policy, however vital. In resolving the issues here presented, we do not conceive it to be a part of our function to weigh the relative merits of the policies of Florida and Massachusetts with respect to divorce and related matters. . . .

It is one thing to recognize as permissible the judicial reexamination of findings of jurisdictional facts where such findings have been made by a court of a sister State which has entered a divorce decree in ex parte proceedings. It is quite another thing to hold that the vital rights and interests involved in divorce litigation may be held in suspense pending the scrutiny by courts of sister States of findings of jurisdictional fact made by a competent court in proceedings conducted in a manner consistent with the highest requirements of due process and in which the defendant has participated. . . . That vital interests are involved in divorce litigation indicates to us that it is a matter of greater rather than lesser importance that there should be a place to end such a litigation. And where a decree of divorce is rendered by a competent court under the circumstances of this case, the obligation of full faith and credit requires that such litigation should end in the courts of the State in which the judgment was rendered.

NOTES AND QUESTIONS

1. The practical effect of *Sherrer* is that a bilateral divorce—one in which both parties appear—cannot be attacked collaterally. Justice Frankfurter dissented vigorously, arguing that the Court's decision largely vitiates the domicile requirement, since it prevents attack on the decree where the defendant appeared and the court makes a finding of domicile, even though subsequent events plainly establish that the finding was erroneous. Is this problem more severe in divorce than in other kinds of litigation?

2. Would the *Sherrer* rule apply to a same-sex couple who sought a divorce in a state that does not recognize same-sex marriages from other states? In O'Darling v. O'Darling, 188 P.3d 137 (Okla. 2008), one member of a married lesbian couple obtained an ex parte divorce without disclosing that her spouse was also a woman. When a newspaper reporter contacted the court to learn if it had in fact granted the divorce, the court vacated the judgment. In the years following *Sherrer*, some but not all courts held that its rule does not apply if the parties

colluded to present a fraudulent claim of domicile. Homer H. Clark, Jr., The Law of Domestic Relations in the United States § 13:2, at 727 (2d ed. 1987).

3. The Court emphasizes that principles of *res judicata* and full faith and credit require that sister states give a decree as much finality as the forum state provides. It follows that no state is required to give greater finality to a decree than does the rendering state and that challenges that would be available to the jurisdictional finding in the forum might be available in a collateral attack brought in a sister state. The requirement of full faith and credit thus depends on the rules of *res judicata* and collateral attack of the state granting the divorce.

This approach provides part of the answer to one of the questions left open by *Sherrer*: the position of third parties who might wish to challenge the validity of the divorce. Suppose that Mr. and Mrs. Lear marry in New York and have two children. The husband receives an ex parte Nevada divorce. He then marries a second wife, who is also a divorcee with three children and a great deal of money. The second wife dies intestate. Can the children of the second Mrs. Lear attack the validity of their stepfather's divorce on the grounds that he was not domiciled in Nevada, and argue therefore that his marriage to their mother was invalid because he was still married? In Johnson v. Muelberger, 340 U.S. 581 (1951), the Court held that where the law of the forum did not permit a child to collaterally attack her parent's divorce decree, the full faith and credit clause prevented such an attack in any other state. To the same effect is Cook v. Cook, 342 U.S. 126 (1951) (second husband cannot attack wife's divorce from her first husband). *See* Note, Stranger Attacks on Sister-State Decrees of Divorce, 24 U. Chi. L. Rev. 376 (1957).

4. In today's increasingly mobile society, does it make sense to base divorce jurisdiction on the domicile of one of the parties? How does one even determine a person's domicile if he or she moves frequently? *See* Black v. Black, 968 N.Y.S.2d 722 (App. Div. 2013), holding that a woman who grew up, was married, and lived in New York until she was 38 and then relocated with her husband 6 times over 16 years retained her domicile in New York (even though the parties lived for 7 years in France).

Professor Courtney Joslin discusses the problem same-sex couples face when their marriage breaks down and they are domiciled in a state that will not recognize their marriage from another state, in Modernizing Divorce Jurisdiction: Same-Sex Couples and Minimum Contacts, 91 B.U. L. Rev. 1669 (2011). She argues that the domicile rule should be replaced by the typical minimum contacts rule and recommends that states amend their long-arm statutes to provide that by marrying in the state, the parties submit to jurisdiction for purposes of dissolving the marriage and that they require parties who marry in the state to consent to jurisdiction for purposes of a later dissolution and to use of the forums law for the issue of dissolution. *Id.* at 1716-1717. She notes that Louisiana covenant marriage law, which restricts the grounds for divorce, requires the parties to agree that Louisiana law will govern dissolution of their marriage, regardless of the state in which they file for divorce. La. Rev. Stat. § 9:273(A)(1) (2014). This law has not been tested in a published opinion, however. Joslin, above, at 1719. *See also* Rhonda Wasserman, Divorce and Domicile: Time to Sever the Knot, 39 Wm. & Mary L. Rev. 1 (1997).

5. When restrictive divorce laws were prevalent in the United States, some foreign countries — most notably Mexico — conducted a substantial business in

matrimonial dissolutions. "Mail-order" Mexican divorces, which could be obtained without the presence of either party in Mexico at any time, were among the most notorious strategies, particularly favored in New York at one time. The validity of foreign divorces is not governed by the full faith and credit clause, which speaks only to the judicial acts of sister states. Rather, recognition is a matter of comity. Although there is no constitutional obligation to grant comity recognition to a foreign decree, it is regarded as a matter of international duty that should be discharged as long as the foreign court had jurisdiction of the subject matter and acceptance of that judgment will not offend domestic public policy. *See, e.g.*, Kugler v. Haitian Tours, Inc., 293 A.2d 706, 709 (N.J. Super. 1972).

What issues are relevant to determining whether an American jurisdiction should recognize a unilateral foreign divorce? A bilateral divorce? *Compare* Rosenstiel v. Rosenstiel, 209 N.E.2d 709 (N.Y. 1965), *cert. denied*, 384 U.S. 971 (1966), *and* Hyde v. Hyde, 562 S.W.2d 194 (Tenn. 1978) (recognizing bilateral Dominican Republic divorce), *with* Warrender v. Warrender, 190 A.2d 684 (N.J. App. 1963) (bilateral Mexico divorce "absolutely void on its face"), *and* Everett v. Everett, 345 So. 2d 586 (La. App. 1977).

6. The doctrine of equitable estoppel may prevent attack on divorces that would otherwise be subject to collateral challenge. This doctrine prevents a party from challenging a decree that one has obtained or has led another to rely on. The most obvious case of estoppel arises when the party who obtained the divorce later claims that it is invalid. The defendant may also be estopped if he or she participated collusively in securing the divorce, perhaps through Haitian Tours, or if he or she acquiesces for a long time in the divorce, knowing of its jurisdictional defect. Acceptance of benefits associated with the divorce may have the same result. Third parties may also be subject to estoppel if they actively participate in securing a defective divorce for another. Analysis and rationalization of estoppel in this setting is one of the many contributions of Professor Clark's treatise on Domestic Relations. *See* 1 Homer H. Clark, Jr., Domestic Relations § 13.3, at 732-755 (2d ed. 1987) (proposing that usual minimum contacts rules apply to dissolution jurisdiction).

PROBLEMS

1. Harold and Wendy were domiciled in State *A*. Harold went to State *B* on vacation. While there he sought and was granted a divorce. The State *B* court erroneously found that he was domiciled there. Wendy in no way participated in the State *B* proceedings. Harold then returned to State *A*. Wendy collaterally attacked the State *B* divorce in a State *A* court. Harold claimed that State *A* must give the State *B* decree full faith and credit. Must it?

2. Hiram and Wilma were domiciled in State *A*. Hiram moved to State *B* to go to college. Six months later Hiram sued Wilma for a divorce in State *B*, relying on a State *B* statute that says that State *B* has jurisdiction to grant a divorce if either spouse has been resident there for six months. Wilma, who remained in State *A*, was served by mail, but she did not appear or participate in any way in the State *B* action. The State *B* court granted the divorce. Wilma collaterally attacked the

decree in State *A*. Hiram claimed that State *A* must give the State *B* decree full faith and credit. Must it?

3. Hank and Willa were domiciled in State *A*. Hank went to State *B* and sued Willa for divorce, serving her in State *B*. Willa entered an appearance by her attorney, but the divorce was granted. Willa collaterally attacked the State *B* divorce in State *A*, claiming that State *B* lacked jurisdiction to grant the divorce since neither she nor Hank was domiciled there. What should Hank argue in response? What if Willa was personally served in State *B* but elected not to appear?

4. Hinkley and Wren were domiciled in State *A*. Hinkley went to Mexico and sued Wren for divorce, serving her in State *A*. Wren did not appear or participate in any way in the Mexican proceedings, but the divorce was granted anyway. Hinkley returned to State *A*. Wren, who remained in State *A*, remarried. Her new husband died, and Wren claimed the rights of a surviving spouse in his estate. Her new husband's executor rejected her claim on the basis that her divorce from Hinkley was not valid and that therefore she was not the surviving spouse of her "new husband." What are the arguments of Wren and the executor? If instead Wren claimed rights as Hinkley's surviving spouse, what arguments should the executor of Hinkley's estate make in opposition to Wren's claim?

C. DIVISIBLE DIVORCE

We have seen that jurisdiction to grant a divorce or legal separation is viewed, after *Williams I* and *Williams II*, as an *in rem* matter. The *res* is the marriage relationship itself, embodied in the domicile of one of the parties to the marriage. Accordingly, the state in which one of the parties is domiciled has jurisdiction to adjudicate the divorce action.

The *Williams* cases hold not only that the state of domicile of one party may adjudicate the marital status of its domiciliary but that the state's judgment, even if ex parte, is entitled to extraterritorial effect through the full faith and credit clause. However, the Supreme Court expressly reserved judgment regarding the extraterritorial effect of ex parte orders about the parties' financial interests. This matter was addressed in Estin v. Estin, 334 U.S. 541 (1948), and in the next case.

VANDERBILT V. VANDERBILT

354 U.S. 416 (1957)

BLACK, J. Cornelius Vanderbilt, Jr., petitioner, and Patricia Vanderbilt, respondent, were married in 1948. They separated in 1952 while living in California. The wife moved to New York, where she has resided since February 1953. In March of that year the husband filed suit for divorce in Nevada. This proceeding culminated, in June 1953, with a decree of final divorce which provided that both husband and wife were "freed and released from the bonds of matrimony and all the duties and obligations thereof. . . ."[2] The wife was not served with process in Nevada and did not appear before the divorce court.

In April 1954, Mrs. Vanderbilt instituted an action in a New York court praying for separation from petitioner and for alimony. The New York court did not have personal jurisdiction over him, but in order to satisfy his obligations, if any, to Mrs. Vanderbilt, it sequestered his property within the State. He appeared specially and, among other defenses to the action, contended that the Full Faith and Credit Clause of the United States Constitution compelled the New York court to treat the Nevada divorce as having ended the marriage and as having destroyed any duty of support which he owed the respondent. While the New York court found the Nevada decree valid and held that it had effectively dissolved the marriage, it nevertheless entered an order, under Section 1170-b of the New York Civil Practice Act, directing petitioner to make designated support payments to respondent. The New York Court of Appeals upheld the support order. Petitioner then applied to this Court for certiorari contending that Section 1170-b, as applied, is unconstitutional because it contravenes the Full Faith and Credit Clause.

In Estin v. Estin, 334 U.S. 541, this Court decided that a Nevada divorce court, which had no personal jurisdiction over the wife, had no power to terminate a husband's obligation to provide her support as required in a pre-existing New York separation decree. . . . Since the wife was not subject to its jurisdiction, the Nevada divorce court had no power to extinguish any right which she had under the law of New York to financial support from her husband. It has long been the constitutional rule that a court cannot adjudicate a personal claim or obligation unless it has jurisdiction over the person of the defendant. Here, the Nevada divorce court was as powerless to cut off the wife's support right as it would have been to order the husband to pay alimony if the wife had brought the divorce action and he had not been subject to the divorce court's jurisdiction. Therefore, the Nevada decree, to the extent it purported to affect the wife's right to support, was void and the Full Faith and Credit Clause did not obligate New York to give it recognition. . . .

Affirmed.

[The dissenting opinion of Justice Frankfurter is omitted.]

NOTES AND QUESTIONS

1. Is the majority's primary concern the rights of the states or the due process interests of the parties?

2. Suppose New York law did *not* allow the wife to prosecute a suit for support if her marital status had been validly terminated. Would this mean that the wife could not pursue a right to spousal maintenance following a valid ex parte divorce in Nevada? Would such a rule be constitutional?

---

2. It seems clear that in Nevada the effect of this decree was to put an end to the husband's duty to support the wife — provided, of course, that the Nevada courts had power to do this. Sweeney v. Sweeney, 42 Nev. 431, 438-439, 179 P. 638, 639-640; Herrick v. Herrick, 55 Nev. 59, 68, 25 P.2d 378, 380. *See* Estin v. Estin, 334 U.S. 541, 547.

A Louisiana appellate court has affirmed that divorce does not require minimum-contacts personal jurisdiction, even if it is possible that the decree will adversely affect the economic rights of the left-at-home spouse in another state, relying on the *Williams* line of cases. Watkins v. Watkins, 862 So. 2d 464 (La. App. 2003).

3. In Simons v. Miami Beach First National Bank, 381 U.S. 81 (1965), the Court indicated that there is at least one situation in which a spouse's economic interests can be affected by an ex parte divorce. The husband, who had lived with his wife in New York, went to Florida and secured an ex parte Florida divorce with constructive service. He continued to pay support to her under a New York judicial separation order until his death. After he died, his "widow" appeared in probate proceedings in Florida, claiming dower rights under Florida law. The respondent bank opposed the dower claim. The petitioner brought an action to set aside the divorce decree and to obtain a declaration that the divorce, even if valid with regard to her marital status, did not affect her claim to dower. The Florida courts dismissed her action. The Supreme Court affirmed, rejecting her argument that Florida could not extinguish her dower right without personal jurisdiction:

> Insofar as petitioner argues that since she was not subject to the jurisdiction of the Florida divorce court its decree could not extinguish any dower right existing under Florida law, Vanderbilt v. Vanderbilt, 354 U.S. 416, 418, the answer is that under Florida law no dower right survived the decree. The Supreme Court of Florida has said that dower rights in Florida property, being inchoate, are extinguished by a divorce decree predicated upon substituted or constructive service.
>
> It follows that the Florida courts transgressed no constitutional bounds in denying petitioner dower in her ex-husband's Florida estate.

The majority assumed that its decision is consistent with *Estin* and *Vanderbilt*. Is this because dower rights are in some way different from the kinds of rights the Court had previously protected? If dower is inchoate, why does that matter? For a consideration of this explanation, *see* Note, Divorce ex Parte Style, 33 U. Chi. L. Rev. 837 (1966).

If *Simons* is consistent with prior decisions, is it because the property interest asserted here arose under the law of the divorcing state rather than the nonparticipating spouse's domicile? What if New York law eliminated dower interests upon divorce?

Suppose that Florida had replaced dower with a forced spousal share upon death. Would that be extinguished as well by an ex parte divorce? If a forced share can be thus terminated, what about the wife's interest in property that she might receive through an "equitable distribution"? If the parties originally lived in and the wife still resides in a community property state, what about community property interests? What about Social Security benefits tied to marriage? Workers' compensation benefits?

4. The principle underlying *Estin* and *Vanderbilt*, that there are different jurisdictional bases for divorce and for support orders, is commonly called "divisible divorce." As you will see in the remainder of the chapter, the principle goes even further, as still different criteria are used to establish jurisdiction to decide property division and custody.

NOTE: PROPERTY DIVISION—JURISDICTION AND FULL FAITH AND CREDIT

As discussed earlier, only a court in the state in which real property is located has *in rem* jurisdiction to determine its ownership and thus to enter property division orders. The Supreme Court applied this principle in Fall v. Eastin, 215 U.S. 1 (1909), holding that a Washington divorce decree awarding real property in Nebraska to a wife was not entitled to full faith and credit. However, many courts today will recognize property division orders from courts in states in which the property is not located if the court validly asserted *in personam* jurisdiction over the parties. *E.g.*, Ivey v. Ivey, 439 A.2d 425 (Conn. 1981); Weesner v. Weesner, 95 N.W.2d 682 (Neb. 1959); McElreath v. McElreath, 345 S.W.2d 722 (Tex. 1961); Roberts v. Locke, 304 P.3d 116 (Wyo. 2013); Russo v. Russo, 714 A.2d 466 (Pa. Super. 1998).

A concomitant of the traditional rule is that a court in a state in which real property is located may constitutionally assert jurisdiction to divide the property even though the defendant has no other contact with the state. Homer H. Clark, Jr., Domestic Relations § 13.4 at 763-764, discussing Shaffer v. Heitner, 433 U.S. 186, 207-208 (1977); In re Ramsey's Marriage, 526 P.2d 319 (Colo. App. 1974); Harrod v. Harrod, 526 P.2d 666 (Colo. App. 1974); Hodge v. Hodge, 422 A.2d 280 (Conn. 1979); Gelkop v. Gelkop, 384 So. 2d 195 (Fla. App. 1980).

PROBLEMS

1. Hank and Winifred were domiciled in State *A*. Winifred moved to State *B* and established a domicile. She sued Hank for divorce in State *B*, serving him in State *A*. Hank did not appear or in any way participate in the State *B* proceedings. The State *B* court granted Winifred a divorce, ordered Hank to pay her $200 per month in spousal support, and found that Hank was not entitled to spousal support from Winifred. Winifred took the decree to State *A* and asked the State *A* court to enforce the order to Hank to pay her support. Hank cross-claimed for spousal support from Winifred. Winifred argued that the State *A* court must give full faith and credit to the State *B* decree. What should Hank argue in response? Who wins and why?

2. Homer and Wanda were domiciled in State *A*. Homer moved to State *B* and established his domicile there. He sued Wanda for divorce in State *B*, serving her in State *A*. Wanda did not appear or in any way participate in the State *B* proceedings. The State *B* court granted Homer a divorce. The decree was silent on the issue of spousal support. Homer returned to State *A*, and Wanda sued him in State *A* for spousal support, serving him personally in State *A*. Under the law of State *A*, if a divorce decree makes no provision for spousal support, a court cannot later grant it. How should the court rule on Wanda's motion for support?

3. Holden and Wilma were divorced in State *A*, where they are both domiciled. The State *A* court awarded their vacation home, located in State *B*, to Wilma. After the order was entered, Holden did nothing to comply with the decree, and the State *B* title continued to show that Holden and Wilma owned the vacation home as joint tenants with right of survivorship. Wilma died. The executor of her estate claimed that Wilma owned the State *B* vacation home, relying on

the divorce decree. Holden claimed that it is his because he is the surviving joint tenant. If this dispute were litigated in State *B*, would the State *B* court have to give full faith and credit to the State *A* order?

NOTE: JURISDICTION TO ENTER DOMESTIC VIOLENCE PROTECTIVE ORDERS

May a court issue a domestic violence protective order even though it lacks *in personam* jurisdiction over the respondent? In several recent cases, an alleged victim of domestic violence left home and fled to another state, where she sought a protective order. The alleged batterers moved to dismiss for lack of jurisdiction because they had had no contacts with the forum state. In Caplan v. Donovan, 879 N.E.2d 117 (Mass. 2008), the court rejected the respondent's argument, analogizing the case to ones involving divorce. The court, therefore, concluded that a trial court could properly exercise jurisdiction to prohibit the respondent from abusing or approaching the plaintiff. *See also* Rios v. Ferguson, 978 A.2d 592 (Conn. 2008) (man living in North Carolina who posted a video on YouTube threatening his girlfriend in Connecticut committed a tortious act in Connecticut, supporting jurisdiction to issue protective order); Bartsch v. Bartsch, 636 N.W.2d 3 (Iowa 2001); Spencer v. Spencer, 191 S.W.3d 14 (Ky. App. 2006); Hemenway v. Hemenway, 992 A.2d 575 (N.H. 2010); Shah v. Shah, 875 A.2d 931 (N.J. 2005). *Contra*, T.L. v. W.L., 820 A.2d 506 (Del. Fam. Ct. 2003); Becker v. Johnson, 937 So. 2d 1128 (Fla. App. 2006); Anderson v. Deas, 632 S.E.2d 682 (Ga. App. 2006). States agree that a lack of *in personam* jurisdiction precludes orders that require affirmative action by the respondent, such as paying child support and not possessing a firearm. For further discussion, *see* Jessica Miles, We Are Never Ever Getting Back Together: Domestic Violence Victims, Defendants, and Due Process, 35 Cardozo L. Rev. 141 (2013).

The federal Violence Against Women Act, discussed in Chapter 2, requires states to give full faith and credit to and enforce domestic violence restraining orders from other states. 18 U.S.C. §2265. An order that is valid according to the law of the state that issued it must be enforced, even if it includes terms or applies to parties that the law of the forum state would not permit. *See* Emily J. Sack, Domestic Violence Across State Lines: The Full Faith and Credit Clause, Congressional Power, and Interstate Enforcement of Protection Orders, 98 Nw. U. L. Rev. 827 (2004).

D. JURISDICTION AND FULL FAITH AND CREDIT FOR SUPPORT DUTIES

Estin and *Vanderbilt* confirm that *in personam* jurisdiction is required for orders that establish parties' rights and duties regarding spousal and child support. In other words, jurisdiction to decide these rights must satisfy the minimum-contacts test of International Shoe Co. v. Washington, 326 U.S. 310, 316 (1945), and its successors. In Burnham v. Superior Court, 495 U.S. 604 (1990), the Supreme Court addressed the constitutional sufficiency of "tag jurisdiction" — that is, jurisdiction asserted over a defendant who is served while physically present in the state but has no other substantial connection to the state. Burnham, a New Jersey resident, was served with process in a suit for divorce and determination of support and property issues while he was in California to take care of business and visit his children. The Court unanimously agreed that the defendant was subject to California's jurisdiction, although the Justices differed significantly as to the theory supporting jurisdiction.

The next case considers the extent to which long-arm statutes may constitutionally be used to assert jurisdiction over obligors or obligees who are not physically present in the jurisdiction. *Estin* and *Vanderbilt* were, of course, cases concerning interstate enforceability of support orders under the full faith and credit clause, but since the lower courts' assertion of jurisdiction violated due process, the cases do not actually address when courts must recognize and enforce support orders from other jurisdictions. The second part of this section addresses these issues.

1. Long-Arm Jurisdiction in Support Cases

KULKO v. SUPERIOR COURT

436 U.S. 84 (1978)

[Ezra and Sharon Kulko, then both New York domiciliaries, were married in 1959 in California during Ezra's three-day stopover while he was en route to overseas military duty. After the wedding, Sharon returned to New York, as did Ezra following his tour of duty. In 1961 and 1962 a son and daughter were born in New York. The family lived together in New York until March 1972, when Ezra and Sharon separated. Sharon moved to California. The spouses entered into a separation agreement in New York, which provided that the children would live with Ezra during the school year and visit Sharon in California during specified vacations. Ezra agreed to pay Sharon $3000 per year in child support for the periods when the children were with her. Sharon obtained a divorce in Haiti, which incorporated the terms of the separation agreement, and returned to California. In December 1973 the daughter asked to move to California to live with her mother. Ezra consented. Without Ezra's consent Sharon arranged for the son to join her in California about two years later. Sharon then sued Ezra in California to establish the Haitian divorce decree as a California judgment, to modify the judgment to award her full custody of the children, and to increase Ezra's child support obligation. Ezra, resisting the claim for increased support, appeared specially, claiming that he lacked sufficient "minimum contacts" with California under International Shoe Co. v. Washington, 326 U.S. 310, 316 (1945), to warrant the state's assertion of personal jurisdiction over him. The California Supreme Court upheld lower-court determinations adverse to Ezra.]

MARSHALL, J. The issue before us is whether, in this action for child support, the California state courts may exercise *in personam* jurisdiction over a nonresident, nondomiciliary parent of minor children domiciled within the State. For reasons set forth below, we hold that the exercise of such jurisdiction would violate the Due Process Clause of the Fourteenth Amendment. . . .

The Due Process Clause of the Fourteenth Amendment operates as a limitation on the jurisdiction of state courts to enter judgments affecting rights or interests of nonresident defendants. *See* Shaffer v. Heitner, 433 U.S. 186, 198-200 (1977). It has long been the rule that a valid judgment imposing a personal obligation or duty in favor of the plaintiff may be entered only by a court having jurisdiction over the person of the defendant. Pennoyer v. Neff, 95 U.S. 714, 732-733 (1878); International Shoe Co. v. Washington, 326 U.S., at 316. The existence of personal jurisdiction, in turn, depends upon the presence of reasonable notice to the defendant that an action has been brought, Mullane v. Central Hanover Trust Co., 339 U.S. 306, 313-314 (1950), and a sufficient connection between the defendant and the forum State to make it fair to require defense of the action in the forum. In this case, appellant does not dispute the adequacy of the notice that he received, but contends that his connection with the State of California is too attenuated, under the standards implicit in the Due Process Clause of the Constitution, to justify imposing upon him the burden and inconvenience of defense in California.

The parties are in agreement that the constitutional standard for determining whether the State may enter a binding judgment against appellant here is that set forth in this Court's opinion in International Shoe Co. v. Washington, supra: that a defendant "have certain minimum contacts with [the forum State] such that the maintenance of the suit does not offend 'traditional notions of fair play and substantial justice.'" . . . [A]n essential criterion in all cases is whether the "quality and nature" of the defendant's activity is such that it is "reasonable" and "fair" to require him to conduct his defense in that State. . . .

In reaching its result, the California Supreme Court did not rely on appellant's glancing presence in the State some 13 years before the events that led to this controversy, nor could it have. . . . To hold such temporary visits to a State a basis for the assertion of *in personam* jurisdiction over unrelated actions arising in the future would make a mockery of the limitations on state jurisdiction imposed by the Fourteenth Amendment. Nor did the California court rely on the fact that appellant was actually married in California on one of his two brief visits. We agree that where two New York domiciliaries, for reasons of convenience, marry in the State of California and thereafter spend their entire married life in New York, the fact of their California marriage by itself cannot support a California court's exercise of jurisdiction over a spouse who remains a New York resident in an action relating to child support.

Finally, in holding that personal jurisdiction existed, the court below carefully disclaimed reliance on the fact that appellant had agreed at the time of separation to allow his children to live with their mother three months a year and that he had sent them to California each year pursuant to this agreement. . . . [T]o find personal jurisdiction in a State on this basis, merely because the mother was residing there, would discourage parents from entering into reasonable visitation agreements. Moreover, it could arbitrarily subject one parent to suit in any State of the Union where the other parent chose to spend time while having custody of their offspring pursuant to a separation agreement. As we have emphasized: "The unilateral activity of those who claim some relationship with a nonresident defendant cannot satisfy the requirement of contact with the forum State. . . . [It] is essential in each case that there be some act by which the defendant purposefully avails [him]self of the privilege of conducting activities within the forum State. . . ." Hanson v. Denckla.

The "purposeful act" that the California Supreme Court believed did warrant the exercise of personal jurisdiction over appellant in California was his "actively and fully [consenting] to Ilsa living in California for the school year . . . and . . . [sending] her to California for that purpose." We cannot accept the proposition that appellant's acquiescence in Ilsa's desire to live with her mother conferred jurisdiction over appellant in the California courts in this action. A father who agrees, in the interests of family harmony and his children's preferences, to allow them to spend more time in California than was required under a separation agreement can hardly be said to have "purposefully availed himself" of the "benefits and protections" of California's laws.

Nor can we agree with the assertion of the court below that the exercise of *in personam* jurisdiction here was warranted by the financial benefit appellant derived from his daughter's presence in California for nine months of the year. This argument rests on the premise that, while appellant's liability for support payments remained unchanged, his yearly expenses for supporting the child in New York decreased. But this circumstance, even if true, does not support California's assertion of jurisdiction here. Any diminution in appellant's household costs resulted, not from the child's presence in California, but rather from her absence from appellant's home. . . .

The circumstances in this case clearly render "unreasonable" California's assertion of personal jurisdiction. . . . The cause of action herein asserted arises, not from the defendant's commercial transactions in interstate commerce, but rather from his personal, domestic relations. It thus cannot be said that appellant has sought a commercial benefit from solicitation of business from a resident of California that could reasonably render him liable to suit in state court; appellant's activities cannot fairly be analogized to an insurer's sending an insurance contract and premium notices into the State to an insured resident of the State. Furthermore, the controversy between the parties arises from a separation that occurred in the State of New York; appellee Horn seeks modification of a contract that was negotiated in New York and that she flew to New York to sign. As in Hanson v. Denckla, the instant action involves an agreement that was entered into with virtually no connection with the forum State.

Finally, basic considerations of fairness point decisively in favor of appellant's State of domicile as the proper forum for adjudication of this case, whatever the merits of appellee's underlying claim. It is appellant who has remained in the State of the marital domicile, whereas it is appellee who has moved across the continent. . . . Appellant has at all times resided in New York State, and, until the separation and appellee's move to California, his entire family resided there as well. As noted above, appellant did no more than acquiesce in the stated preference of one of his children to live with her mother in California. This single act is surely not one that a reasonable parent would expect to result in the substantial financial burden and personal strain of litigating a child-support suit in a forum 3,000 miles away, and we therefore see no basis on which it can be said that appellant could reasonably have anticipated being "haled before a [California] court." To make jurisdiction in a case such as this turn on whether appellant bought his daughter her ticket or instead unsuccessfully sought to prevent her departure would impose an unreasonable burden on family relations, and one wholly unjustified by the "quality and nature" of appellant's activities in or relating to the State of California.

In seeking to justify the burden that would be imposed on appellant were the exercise of *in personam* jurisdiction in California sustained, appellee argues that California has substantial interests in protecting the welfare of its minor residents and in promoting to the fullest extent possible a healthy and supportive family environment in which the children of the State are to be raised. These interests are unquestionably important. . . .

California's legitimate interest in ensuring the support of children resident in California without unduly disrupting the children's lives, moreover, is already being served by the State's participation in the Revised Uniform Reciprocal Enforcement of Support Act of 1968. This statute provides a mechanism for communication between court systems in different States, in order to facilitate the procurement and enforcement of child-support decrees where the dependent children reside in a State that cannot obtain personal jurisdiction over the defendant. California's version of the Act essentially permits a California resident claiming support from a nonresident to file a petition in California and have its merits adjudicated in the State of the alleged obligor's residence, without either party's having to leave his or her own State. New York State is a signatory to a similar Act. Thus, not only may plaintiff-appellee here vindicate her claimed right to additional child support from her former husband in a New York court . . . but also the Uniform Acts will facilitate both her prosecution of a claim for additional support and collection of any support payments found to be owed by appellant. . . .

Reversed.

NOTES AND QUESTIONS

1. One standard for determining the permissible extent of state court jurisdiction asks whether the defendant purposely availed him- or herself of the protection and benefits of California law. Didn't the defendant in *Kulko* do so? The court seems to distinguish between commercial undertakings (for example, where an insurance company sends a policy to a California insured) and the father's sending his daughter to California. Doesn't that distinction mean that commercial agreements will be more easily enforced than child support obligations?

2. The court also addresses the question of whether it is fair to require Kulko to participate in a California adjudication. Is fairness a categorical question? For example, is asking a defendant to participate in a proceeding in another state with which he or she has minimal contacts always unfair? Suppose in *Kulko* that the wife and children were living in New Jersey. What factors influence the meaning of "fairness" and "inconvenience"? *See* Terry S. Kogan, Geography and Due Process: The Social Meaning of Adjudicative Jurisdiction, 22 Rutgers L.J. 627 (1991).

3. The Uniform Interstate Family Support Act (UIFSA), which all states have adopted in some form, deals with all aspects of interstate support orders, including

personal jurisdiction. Section 201 is a long-arm statute providing that a court may exercise personal jurisdiction over a nonresident to establish, enforce, or modify a support order or to determine parentage if

1) the individual is personally served with [citation, summons, notice] within this State;
2) the individual submits to the jurisdiction of this State by consent in a record, by entering a general appearance, or by filing a responsive document having the effect of waiving any contest to personal jurisdiction;
3) the individual resided with the child in this State;
4) the individual resided in this State and provided prenatal expenses or support for the child;
5) the child resides in this State as a result of the acts or directives of the individual;
6) the individual engaged in sexual intercourse in this State and the child may have been conceived by that act of intercourse;
7) the individual asserted parentage of a child in the [putative father registry] maintained in this State by the [appropriate agency]; or
8) there is any other basis consistent with the constitutions of this State and the United States for the exercise of personal jurisdiction.

Is this statute constitutional under *Kulko*? UIFSA also creates special procedures that a court may use to invoke the assistance of courts in other states to obtain evidence and discovery in the other states. UIFSA §§ 316, 318.

4. Statutes and case law in many states provide that a court that validly asserts personal jurisdiction to determine a person's support duties has continuing jurisdiction for purposes of modification, even after the person has moved from the state. *See* Annot., E. H. Schopler, Necessity of Personal Service Within State upon Nonresident Spouse as Prerequisite of Court's Power to Modify Its Decree as to Alimony or Child Support in Matrimonial Action, 62 A.L.R.2d 544, 546 (1958 with weekly updates). What are the outer constitutional limits on such an assertion of jurisdiction? A number of courts have upheld claims of continuing jurisdiction even after *both* parties have moved away. Compare the continuing-jurisdiction provisions of UIFSA, which are discussed in the next section.

PROBLEMS

1. Herb and Wilma were married and lived in State *A* for the first years of their marriage. Four years ago they separated, and Wilma moved to State *B*, where the couple together purchased a condo for her, titled in her name. Herb has paid the mortgage but has never been to the condo. He has also leased a car for Wilma in State *B*. Wilma has filed for divorce in State *B* and asks the court to award her ownership of the condo and to require Herb to pay her spousal support. State *B*'s long-arm statute allows its courts to assert *in personam* jurisdiction over a person outside the state who has transacted business within the state; made a contract within the state; committed a tort within the state; owns, uses, or possesses real estate within the state; or has "lived in lawful marriage" within the state. Under this

statute, may a State *B* court assert jurisdiction to determine ownership of the condo and to award Wilma spousal support? Would such assertions of jurisdiction be consistent with due process?

2. Harley and Wendy were married in New York, and their children were born there. After 15 years of marriage, they separated, and Harley moved to California. Wendy brought a divorce action 18 months later, seeking child support. Would New York have jurisdiction to order child support under UIFSA? Would it be constitutional for New York to assert this jurisdiction? What if it were five years later?

3. Hudson and Wanda were married and had two children in California. Ten years later they moved to New York, where they lived for three months before moving overseas. They lived in Mali for three years, and then Wanda returned to California with the children. Could California assert jurisdiction under UIFSA to determine Hudson's child support obligation? If Wanda and the children returned to New York instead, would New York have jurisdiction under UIFSA over Hudson to decide child support?

4. Mary and Fred were married in Texas. Fred was very violent toward Mary, abusing her physically and mentally. He eventually threatened to kill her, and she left that night, moving in with a friend. Fred stalked Mary at work and where she was living, and when Mary reported all these events to the police, they recommended that she move to a battered women's shelter. Fred continued to stalk her, and friends saw him with guns at the house where she had lived. He also called her father in Colorado to threaten her. Fearful for her life, she finally fled to Colorado, where her father lived. In Colorado she sued Fred for divorce and child support. Fred moved to dismiss the child support action on the basis that UIFSA does not support jurisdiction on these facts and that if a court tried to assert jurisdiction to award child support here, due process would be violated. Should the court grant Fred's motion?

2. *Interstate Modification and Enforcement of Support*

Sharon Horn could have pursued her action for child support against Ezra Kulko by traveling to New York and filing suit there. For many people, though, the costs of such a suit would be prohibitive. Further, even if a New York court had ordered Ezra to pay child support, if he refused to pay, Sharon might have had to return to New York or at least retain New York counsel to enforce the order.

If Ezra moved to a third state and refused to pay, Sharon would have had still more difficulties. Besides the practical ones, under traditional legal principles the third state might not have recognized her New York order because states did not have to give full faith and credit to modifiable support orders. Sistare v. Sistare, 218 U.S. 1 (1910); Barber v. Barber, 62 U.S. (21 How.) 582 (1858). While other states might have enforced nonfinal orders as a matter of comity, the practical difficulties of interstate enforcement of support remained. Worthley v. Worthley, 283 P.2d 19 (Cal. 1955); Restatement 2d of Conflicts § 109 (1971). Moreover, due process requires that obligors be given an opportunity to present defenses and arguments for modification in such cases. Griffin v. Griffin, 327 U.S. 220 (1946). The Uniform Reciprocal Enforcement of Support Act (URESA), referred to in *Kulko*, was intended to solve the practical and legal problems of interstate support enforcement. Most American jurisdictions adopted one version or another of the Act, but state law was never uniform because of inconsistencies in the versions adopted by the various states.

To provide a truly uniform set of laws and to resolve ambiguities created by URESA, the Uniform Law Commissioners in 1992 proposed a replacement, the Uniform Interstate Family Support Act (UIFSA), which was amended in 1996, 2001, and 2008. Congress has required that the states enact the 1996 or later version of UIFSA. Personal Responsibility and Work Opportunity Reconciliation Act (PRWORA), Pub. L. No. 104-193, 110 Stat. 2105 (1996). The 1996 version of UIFSA was adopted in every state, the District of Columbia, Puerto Rico, and the U.S. Virgin Islands, and the 2001 amendments were enacted in at least 22 jurisdictions. By 2014 Florida, Georgia, Maine, Missouri, Nevada, New Mexico, North Dakota, Rhode Island, Tennessee, Utah, and Wisconsin had adopted the 2008 amendments. Legislative Fact Sheet—Interstate Family Support Act Amendments (2008), available at the Uniform Law Commission website, http://www.uniformlaws.org/.

To complement UIFSA, Congress enacted the Full Faith and Credit for Child Support Orders Act (FFCCSOA), 28 U.S.C. § 1738B, which implements the full faith and credit clause and requires states to recognize, enforce, and not modify child support orders from other states. Its principles track those of UIFSA.

UIFSA applies to orders to establish, modify, or enforce child or spousal support, including income withholding, and to proceedings to determine parentage. UIFSA § 301. Its fundamental concept is simple: only one state at a time may exercise jurisdiction to determine the amount of support owed, and all other states must enforce without modifying a support order that was issued by the state exercising jurisdiction consistent with the act. UIFSA §§ 205, 603. Under UIFSA a support order issued in one state may be enforced in other states through state agency administrative processes, which obligees can invoke personally without having to go through their home state agencies. Interstate judicial enforcement is also governed by the Act and is initiated by registering a support order from one state in the state where enforcement is sought. UIFSA §§ 601-608. Procedures for contesting the validity or enforceability of a registered order are provided in UIFSA §§ 605-607. A registered order continues to be the order of the issuing state but can be enforced in the same way that an order from a court in the registering state would be enforced. A party seeking to modify an order from one state in the court of another must register it and petition to modify it, but the court in the second state may assert jurisdiction to modify only if the conditions of UIFSA § 611 or § 613 are satisfied. UIFSA §§ 609, 610. If these conditions are not satisfied, the court does not have jurisdiction to modify and may only enforce the order. The next case discusses a potentially complex issue, the difference between orders that modify prior support orders and new orders.

OCS/Pappas v. O'Brien

67 A.3d 916 (Vt. 2013)

Dooley, J. . . . Mother and father were married in Oklahoma in 1979. They had two sons, P.P. and A.P. The couple moved to New York in 1983, where they lived until they separated in 1985. The parties were divorced in Los Angeles County, California, in October 1986. Pursuant to the California divorce order, the parties were awarded joint legal custody of the children, then ages three and five. Primary physical custody was awarded to mother, and father was ordered to pay child support in the amount of $237 per month for each child. Eventually, father returned to Oklahoma, and mother moved with the children to Atlanta, Georgia. In October 1994, the Superior Court of Gwinnett County, Georgia, issued an order domesticating the California divorce order and modifying the child support obligation. Finding that father's financial condition had improved and that the needs of the children had increased, the court ordered father to pay $350 per month for each child, as well as a percentage of any bonuses father should receive in addition to his salary. This order stated that child support would cease if "custody is changed by a Court of competent jurisdiction." In 1996, mother moved with the children to New York.

Beginning in July 1998, the younger child, P.P., moved from his mother's home in New York to his father's home in Oklahoma. In November 1998, the older child, A.P. turned eighteen years of age. In April 1999, father filed documents to initiate a child custody proceeding in Oklahoma under the Uniform Child Custody Jurisdiction and Enforcement Act (UCCJEA). Father initially petitioned to have custody of P.P. transferred to him and to have his child support obligation for both children ended — for A.P. because he had attained the age of majority and for P.P. because he was residing with father. Mother moved to bifurcate the issues of custody and child support. A hearing was held in October 1999, at which mother attempted to make a limited appearance for the purposes of the child custody determination. During the hearing, father requested an order obligating mother to pay him child support for P.P. in addition to changing the child's custody. The Oklahoma court awarded custody to father and retroactively relieved him of any child support obligation as of April 22, 1999, the date he moved for a change of custody. Furthermore, the court ordered mother to pay child support to father in the amount of $338.50 per month, retroactive to April 22, including an arrearage of $2724.00. Mother made two motions for new trials in the Oklahoma court raising jurisdictional concerns. The court denied the first, and mother withdrew the second, after P.P. returned to her custody. She did not appeal either the initial Oklahoma order or the denial of her motion for a new trial.

In early July 2000, P.P. returned to live with mother in Georgia. At that time, father sought enforcement of the child support judgment for the time when P.P. had been in his custody. On July 18, 2000, an Oklahoma Administrative Law Judge issued an administrative order awarding judgment to father in the amount of $2369.50 for child support for the period from January through July of 2000. When this amount was added to the previous judgment, the total arrearage became $5093.50. . . .

Mother is now a resident of Vermont; father continues to reside in Oklahoma. In 2008, the Oklahoma Department of Human Services sought to collect the outstanding child support from mother. These enforcement efforts were transferred to Vermont, and, on September 4, 2009, Vermont's Office of Child Support (OCS) filed a petition to register the Oklahoma support order in Vermont, pursuant to UIFSA. Mother responded on October 16, 2009, by filing a motion to set aside the Oklahoma order, contesting inter alia the subject matter jurisdiction . . . in the Oklahoma proceedings. After three days of hearings, a magistrate issued an order registering the Oklahoma support order and granting judgment against mother in the amount of $7611.30. Mother appealed the magistrate's order to the Chittenden Superior Court, Family Division, pursuant to Vermont Rule for Family Proceedings 8(g). On September 15, 2010, the superior court affirmed, concluding that collateral estoppel barred mother from challenging the Oklahoma court's subject matter jurisdiction. . . .

Mother also responded to father's enforcement action by pursuing her own enforcement. She filed three documents simultaneously on April 21, 2010, within thirty days from the date of the magistrate's decision: (1) an appeal of the magistrate's decision to the family court; (2) a request for a stay of the magistrate's decision; and (3) an application to register and enforce the Georgia child support order to collect support owed by father to mother under that order. The stay request argued that father owed back child support to mother and it would be inequitable for father to collect back child support owed to him, without paying the child support he owed to mother. The application to enforce the Georgia order was to have the Vermont court determine the amount of back support owed to mother. She claimed that the amount due under the Georgia order, with interest, amounted to $34,093.50. On May 12, before the application was accepted as a separate case, the court denied the stay saying: "If [mother] is entitled to collect past due child support from [father], she may seek appropriate enforcement."

Mother served father with the application, and, in addition, the court notified OCS of the filing. OCS intervened and moved to dismiss. On August 11, 2010, the magistrate granted OCS's motion and dismissed mother's petition, concluding that Vermont courts lacked personal jurisdiction over father under UIFSA. . . .

Mother appeals from both adverse decisions — one allowing registration of the Oklahoma order and one denying her attempt to register and enforce the Georgia order. We have consolidated these matters on appeal. In both cases, the primary question is whether Vermont has the authority under UIFSA to register and enforce an out-of-state child support order. . . .

Before we address the legal issues, we make one observation to explain, in part, the length and coverage of this opinion. Although the facts may seem commonplace at first, they are not when understood in the context of the applicable law. The combination of three factual elements complicates the analysis of the legal issues: (1) at the time that father sought child support, neither he nor mother nor either of the children resided in the state in which the original child support order was created — California — or in the state in which it was domesticated and modified — Georgia; (2) one of the children moved from the custody of one parent to the custody of the other; and (3) each party alleges that the other party owes back child support. . . .

The three elements of factual complexity are combined with an element of particular legal complexity. There are two legal regimes governing interstate enforcement and modification of child support orders and each, read in isolation from the other, would not likely produce the same result on some of the legal issues in this case. The two are UIFSA, 15B V.S.A. §§ 101-904, and the Full Faith and Credit for Child Support Orders Act (FFCCSOA), 28 U.S.C. § 1738B. . . .

We begin by considering the validity of the Oklahoma child support order, which mother contests on several grounds under UIFSA. In considering mother's arguments, we focus primarily on UIFSA, only occasionally touching upon the application of FFCCSOA,[3] because this is how the parties framed the issues. Mother's first and major argument is that the Oklahoma court lacked subject matter jurisdiction to issue the order. . . .

Father, through OCS, responds that the Georgia order "terminated automatically" when custody was changed due to language in the order stating that "monthly payments shall be made on the first (1st) day of each consecutive month thereafter until . . . custody is changed by a Court of competent jurisdiction." It is

---

3. There is a significant question concerning whether FFCCSOA preempts UIFSA, which we note here, but do not decide. FFCCSOA has many of the same purposes as UIFSA, particularly "to establish national standards under which the courts of the various States shall determine their jurisdiction to issue a child support order and the effect to be given by each State to child support orders issued by the courts of other States," and "to avoid jurisdictional competition and conflict among State courts in the establishment of child support orders." FFCCSOA and UIFSA "are for the most part 'complementary or duplicative and not contradictory.'" . . . [H]owever, that where it applies, FFCCSOA "preempts any inconsistent provision of state law."

In this case, the UIFSA prohibition on modifying the Georgia child support order on motion of a resident of Oklahoma, see 43 Okla. Stat. Ann. § 601-611A (describing requirements for modifying child support order from another state including either nonresidence of the petitioner or residence of the child and consent of all parties); see also U.L.A. Unif. Interstate Family Support Act, Refs & Annos, Prefatory Note II.D.2 (1996) ("Except for modification by agreement or when the parties have all moved to the same new state, the party petitioning for modification must submit himself or herself to the forum state where the respondent resides."), is arguably in tension with FFCCSOA, 28 U.S.C. § 1738B. The UIFSA section provides that the forum court "may modify" the foreign order only if the petitioner is a nonresident of the forum state or obtains written consent. FFCCSOA has a provision that covers the same subject, listing three requirements for when "a State may modify" a child support order from another state, none of which require nonresidency of the petitioner. In short, FFCCSOA does not require the same preconditions for modification as UIFSA — in particular, it does not include the nonresidency requirement that mother argues father failed to meet in the Oklahoma court.

A number of courts have addressed this tension and have split on its consequence. Some courts have refused to find preemption on the grounds that Congress almost certainly did not intend that FFCCSOA preempt UIFSA. See Hamilton v. Hamilton, 914 N.E.2d 747, 751 (Ind. 2009); Basileh v. Alghusain, 912 N.E.2d 814, 818-20 (Ind. 2009); LeTellier v. LeTellier, 40 S.W.3d 490, 497 (Tenn. 2001). Other courts have found preemption, concluding that the nonresidency requirement is inconsistent with the purposes of FFCCSOA and the FFCCSOA cannot be read to accommodate it. See Draper v. Burke, 450 Mass. 676, 881 N.E.2d 122 (2008); Bowman v. Bowman, 82 A.D.3d 144, 917 N.Y.S.2d 379 (2011). This issue was not raised or briefed by either party and we do not decide it here.

the position of father and OCS, therefore, that there was no longer anything to modify — that the Georgia order had expired. . . .

Nevertheless, we reject mother's attempt to contest the validity of the Oklahoma order on the basis that the Oklahoma court lacked subject matter jurisdiction. Her argument fails for two reasons. First, we conclude that mother is precluded from challenging subject matter jurisdiction because she thoroughly litigated that issue in the Oklahoma proceeding. Second, mother's argument fails on the merits insofar as we conclude that the Oklahoma court's child support order was not a modification for the purposes of UIFSA.

The superior court concluded that mother is collaterally estopped from raising subject matter jurisdiction. We affirm the court's conclusion. Because the issue of subject matter jurisdiction was decided by the Oklahoma court after having been litigated there, we must give that determination full faith and credit. . . .

Even if we were to conclude that mother could renew her jurisdictional challenge in this Court, we are not convinced that the UIFSA jurisdictional requirements were violated in this case. The UIFSA requirement that the petitioner not reside in the forum state applies only to modifications of prior [support] orders. Thus, mother's contention that the Oklahoma court lacked subject matter jurisdiction to issue its support order is premised on the notion that father was seeking a modification of the prior Georgia support order. We conclude that the Oklahoma order was not a modification of the preexisting Georgia order for the purposes of UIFSA.

As noted, the Georgia order explicitly stated that child support would cease if "custody is changed by a Court of competent jurisdiction." Here, there is no dispute that custody was changed by a court of competent jurisdiction. As a result, father's ongoing support obligation expired. This does not mean that the Georgia support order no longer exists or cannot form the basis for an arrearage or other claim. But though the Georgia order still governs the parties' support obligations from before the change of custody, it has expired in the sense that it has no prospective effect with respect to support obligations. Once the Oklahoma court, a court of competent jurisdiction, entered an order transferring custody of the only remaining minor child from mother to father, father's support obligation expired under the terms of the Georgia support order. Having modified custody, and with the Georgia support obligation no longer in effect by its own terms, the Oklahoma court had jurisdiction to address father's new and independent request for child support.

In short, by its own terms, the Georgia order expired when father obtained custody of P.P., thereby ending both parents' prospective child support obligations under the order. Absent the automatic termination provision of the Georgia order, father's obligation to pay mother child support would have continued — even after he was awarded custody of the child — until the Georgia order was modified by court decision. Thus, without a provision automatically terminating child support upon change of custody, an award of child support to the new custodian would have been a modified order necessarily terminating the former custodian's right to child support under the preexisting order and would therefore have been subject to the jurisdictional requirements for modification under UIFSA. This case is different, however, because, for the reasons stated above, the Georgia support order expired when the Oklahoma court transferred custody to father.

This case is not controlled by the line of cases culminating in Spencer v. Spencer, 10 N.Y.3d 60, 853 N.Y.S.2d 274, 882 N.E.2d 886 (2008), a decision that is factually very different, but provides some context and a basis for comparison. *Spencer* was the final resolution of a series of New York cases where the prospective obligation to pay child support had reached an end point because the child covered by the order had reached the age of majority in the state where the order was issued. Some New York courts had held that in the case of an order from another state that had expired due to the age of the minor, they could extend the duration of the previous obligation at the request of the obligee because the age of majority was higher in New York than in the state where the order was issued. They held that such an extension was not a modification of the initial order because that order had expired by its terms.

The "only issue" in *Spencer*, however, was whether the New York child support petitions that were filed after the termination of the initial out-of-state child support obligation "because the child reached the issuing state's age of majority [sought] a 'modification' of the issuing state's order." The *Spencer* court answered in the affirmative for three reasons. First, the New York orders fit within FFCCSOA's broad definition of "modification" because they changed the amount, scope, and most particularly the duration of the out-of-state order. [S]ee 28 U.S.C. § 1738B(b) (defining "modification" as "a change in a child support order that affects the amount, scope, or duration of the order and modifies, replaces, supersedes, or otherwise is made subsequent to the child support order"). Second, drafters of UIFSA made explicit in comments and amendments to the model act that subsequent orders extending the duration of initial support orders that had expired because of the original issuing state's lower age limit on such orders should be considered a modification of the original order for purposes of UIFSA. [S]ee U.L.A. Unif. Interstate Family Support Act § 611(c) cmt. (1996); *id.* § 611(d) (2001). Third, allowing New York courts to enter support orders extending the duration of support beyond the age limit in the original issuing courts' orders undermined the principle of comity critical to the policies underlying FFCCSOA and UIFSA.

This case is plainly distinguishable. In the cases governed by *Spencer*, the New York orders were inconsistent with, and therefore a modification of, the original issuing courts' support orders. In contrast, the Oklahoma order in this case was entirely consistent with the expired Georgia order, which, by its own terms, ended father's ongoing child support obligations upon a change of custody, which occurred before the Oklahoma court issued its support order. This is not a situation in which one court extended the duration of the original child support obligation. In this case, the support obligation no longer had any prospective effect based on the original order's own terms following a change of custody. Thus, as explained above, the Oklahoma court's order was a new and independent order rather than a modification of the expired Georgia order.

We do not consider this result to be at odds with UIFSA's one-order philosophy. The primary aim of UIFSA is to ensure that states do not second-guess the support orders of other states, thereby opening the door to forum shopping and the proliferation of conflicting orders. That is not what occurred in this case.

Allowing father to proceed in Oklahoma also makes practical sense. Having obtained custody of P.P., father was in no different position than a custodial parent who was seeking a support order for the first time against the other parent residing in another state. In general, if there is no child support order in place, then the custodial parent can initiate a proceeding in his or her state of residence — assuming the custodian has personal jurisdiction over the noncustodial parent under UIFSA's liberal personal jurisdiction rules — and then seek an enforcement order in the state of the noncustodial parent. In the present case, when father obtained custody of P.P., there was no order in effect providing child support for the ongoing costs of P.P.'s living expenses. If we define the Oklahoma court's action as a modification of the Georgia order in this case, father is denied the normal UIFSA avenue to obtain child support through the courts of his home state. Father would have fewer options for obtaining child support essentially because he was previously a noncustodial parent.

This additional hurdle may have practical significance for parents like father. Given the age of the child and the temporary nature of father's custody, the cost of pursuing establishment and enforcement of a support order in Vermont, or Georgia if jurisdiction there is still available, is likely prohibitive in relation to the amount of support to be obtained. Thus, the consequence of accepting mother's argument is very likely no support order at all for a period in which the child is undeniably entitled to support from the noncustodial parent. While we have become consumed by jurisdictional challenges, mother has no apparent defense to a claim that she should pay some amount of child support during the period father was the custodial parent.[4] We cannot view there being no support order for that period as consistent with the intent of UIFSA. . . .

We turn now to mother's appeal from the superior court's denial of her separate attempt to register and enforce the Georgia child support order. Mother contends that, if father is able to register and enforce the Oklahoma order against her in Vermont, then she should be able to register and enforce the Georgia order against him in Vermont. OCS responded on father's behalf, arguing that Vermont lacks personal jurisdiction over father for the purposes of collecting child support. The magistrate accepted this assessment, and the superior court affirmed the magistrate.

As we understand mother's petition, there are three components to her child support claim. First, mother alleges that father failed to pay child support under the Georgia order for the period when P.P. was living with father but before father moved to modify custody. Second, mother alleges that father failed to pay support under the order from the date when P.P. moved back to live with mother until he reached the age of majority. Third, mother alleges that father failed to pay the child support amount with respect to the oldest son, A.P., in part of 1996 and for one month in 1998.

Mother's central argument is that, by choosing to register the Oklahoma order in Vermont, father thereby subjected himself to the personal jurisdiction

---

4. Indeed, to the extent we can determine why this conflict has escalated over a relatively small amount of money, it is because mother believes she is owed child support in an amount at least as great as the amount claimed by father. As we hold *infra*, the reasonable response is to allow mother to litigate all her claims against father at the same time his are litigated against her in the hope that the whole dispute can finally be resolved.

of Vermont. She contends that the Oklahoma order incorporates the Georgia order, that father therefore necessarily registered the Georgia order alongside the Oklahoma order, and that he has therefore waived any objection to personal jurisdiction. Father's argument is that, under UIFSA, mother is required to bring an enforcement action not in her home state but in his home state. The superior court concluded that father was entitled to a limited immunity under UIFSA affording him the ability to petition to enforce child support without submitting to personal jurisdiction "in another proceeding." . . .

We conclude the trial court erred in ruling that mother's application could not go further because of lack of personal jurisdiction over father. Two provisions of Vermont's UIFSA potentially establish personal jurisdiction. Section 201 grants personal jurisdiction over a nonresident where "the individual submits to the jurisdiction of this state by consent or by filing with the tribunal a responsive document having the effect of waiving any contest to personal jurisdiction," and also where "there is any other basis consistent with the constitutions of this state and the United States for the exercise of personal jurisdiction." It is well established that initiating a legal proceeding in a state is sufficient to waive any challenge to personal jurisdiction for the purposes of a countersuit. . . .

The waiver of personal jurisdiction here is somewhat complicated by the fact that Vermont OCS has been litigating this case on father's behalf. It was OCS, not father, who filed the request to register the Oklahoma order. UIFSA explicitly fails to resolve whether the relationship between a state enforcement agency and a petitioner constitutes legal representation.

We need not decide this question. Irrespective of whether the relationship between OCS and a nonresident obligee is one of attorney and client, we hold that father's initiation of the present enforcement action is sufficient to constitute a waiver of personal jurisdiction. Technically, father is the plaintiff in the present action. Furthermore, UIFSA authorizes OCS involvement only "upon request." In this sense, the rationale for finding waiver in the traditional context—namely, that a petitioner has deliberately availed himself of the forum state's courts—applies just as well when litigation is carried out by an enforcement agency that is acting at the request of the petitioner. Finally, UIFSA's limited immunity provision grants immunity for "[p]articipation by a petitioner in a proceeding before a responding tribunal, whether in person, by private attorney, or *through services provided by the support enforcement agency*," presupposing that participation through OCS would waive personal jurisdiction normally.

Implicitly accepting that there would otherwise be personal jurisdiction over father, the superior court held that the UIFSA immunity provision prevented finding personal jurisdiction in this case. UIFSA's immunity provision entitles father to appear specially for the purpose of enforcing child support without submitting to personal jurisdiction "in another proceeding." Father's initiation of this UIFSA proceeding would not, for example, create personal jurisdiction in an unrelated dispute about marital property—the marital property dispute is "another proceeding." Nor would it create jurisdiction over a dispute over child custody or jurisdiction. . . . The superior court ruled that mother's attempt to raise father's alleged child support arrearage was similarly barred.

We conclude that this determination was incorrect. We hold that the UIFSA immunity provision does not operate to prevent personal jurisdiction over a claim of outstanding child support between the same parties. That is, we read UIFSA's grant of immunity "in another proceeding" as not including immunity regarding claims of child support that are sufficiently connected with the proceeding initiated by the petitioner. This includes, as here, not only claims involving the same parents and the same child, but also claims involving the same parents and a different child. This reading is based on the understanding that a dispute concerning outstanding support obligations is not a collateral issue, which the official comment describes as "[t]he primary object of this prohibition."

For two reasons, we conclude that mother's claim in this case is not collateral and therefore that adjudicating it would not involve the kind of proceeding cognized by the immunity provision. First, the child support obligation ultimately exists for the benefit of the child, not the obligee. Even in a case like this where the children have long ago reached the age of majority and only an arrearage is involved, it is important to create the expectation for parents who share an unfair burden of the costs of supporting children that they will be able eventually to obtain reimbursement for the other parent's share of those costs. That expectation inures to the benefit of the children.

In this light, father's obligations under the Georgia order and mother's obligations under the Oklahoma order both relate to the parents' joint duty to ensure that the needs of their children are met. That is, both orders established ways to discharge partially the overarching shared duty to the children. Mother has not paid her share of what was allocated under the Oklahoma order. Mother is entitled to have this failure balanced against previous or later stretches during which father allegedly failed to pay his share and she was forced to pick up the financial slack. This is because, in the broader picture, any dispute over arrearages is a dispute over equitably allocating the burdens of a shared obligation to the child. "[I]t makes more sense, and on balance is fair to both parties, to resolve both matters in the registering court. Support is support . . . and one would reasonably expect to air and resolve all support claims in a single forum." As a result, father's alleged arrearages are not an issue collateral to mother's arrearages—in the way that a separate marital obligation or contractual liability would be—and they are therefore not the subject of "another proceeding" for the purposes of UIFSA's immunity provision.

Second, at least in a case where the only amounts in issue are arrearages, it is in everyone's interest to resolve all related claims in one proceeding in one location. The underlying purpose of UIFSA is "to cure the problem of conflicting support orders entered by multiple courts." It is wholly inconsistent with this purpose for father to pursue his arrearage in one jurisdiction while mother pursues her arrearage in another jurisdiction. In a controversy where it is likely that the transactional costs have already greatly exceeded the amount in controversy, the need for an efficient, final, and complete resolution is compelling. Thus, the policy considerations behind the limited immunity provision of §314 are entirely different when we are dealing with disputes over child support arrearages involving the same parents. Introducing other issues into a child support proceeding interferes with the compelling purpose that the children have the protection of a child support order and it is enforced. There is no interference when all issues involve child support. . . .

NOTES AND QUESTIONS

1. UIFSA and the FFCCSOA *forbid* a state court from modifying a support order from another state if the issuing state has continuing, exclusive jurisdiction. *Pappas* holds that the Oklahoma child support order was not a modification but a new order. What distinguishes the two?

2. The mother in *Pappas* argued that this case was similar to *Spencer*, the New York case holding that if a child support obligation terminates because the child attains the age of majority under the law of the state that issued the initial order, New York courts cannot issue new orders requiring payment of child support until the child reaches the age of 21, which is the New York age of majority. *Spencer* said that such orders are modifications, not new orders. Do you agree with how the *Pappas* court distinguished *Spencer*?

UIFSA Section 303 provides that the tribunal ordinarily will use forum law rather than the law of another jurisdiction. Important exceptions are set out in Section 604, which provides that if a support order from one state is registered in another, the law of the issuing state governs the nature, extent, amount, and duration of current payments, and other obligations of support and the payment of arrearages for so long as the issuing state remains the residence of the obligor, the obligee, or the child for whose benefit the support is ordered. However, the applicable statute of limitations is that of the statute providing the longer time period.

3. A court that issues an initial order but then loses jurisdiction to modify continues to be able to assert enforcement jurisdiction. Sometimes parties dispute whether an action by a court that did not issue the initial order is a modification or an enforcement. For example, in Philippe v. Stahl, 798 A.2d 83 (N.J. 2002), after Georgia issued the initial child support order, New Jersey courts issued orders changing who had responsibility to pay for the children's medical expenses and the travel costs when the children visited their father, who remained in Georgia, as well as changing the father's obligation from paying $500 per month for each child to $1000 per month for both children. Reversing the intermediate appellate court, the New Jersey Supreme Court held that these changes were not modifications but were instead required to implement and enforce custody changes.

4. Ordinarily, a court with personal jurisdiction over an obligor must enforce a valid support order from another state, but in Sidell v. Sidell, 18 A.3d 499 (R.I. 2011), the court held that this jurisdiction is permissive and that a trial court could decline to enforce a support order that was part of a larger case involving possible modification of custody and visitation orders and that had to be tried in another state.

5. If the state that issued a child support order no longer has continuing, exclusive jurisdiction to modify, another state may acquire jurisdiction to modify the order under the provisions of Section 611 or 613.

Section 611. Modification of Child-Support Order of Another State

(a) If Section 613 does not apply, upon [petition] a tribunal of this state may modify a child-support order issued in another state which is registered in this state if, after notice and hearing, the tribunal finds that:

(1) the following requirements are met:

(A) neither the child, nor the obligee who is an individual, nor the obligor resides in the issuing State;

(B) a [petitioner] who is a nonresident of this State seeks modification; and

(C) the [respondent] is subject to the personal jurisdiction of the tribunal of this State; or

(2) this State is the residence of the child, or a party who is an individual is subject to the personal jurisdiction of the tribunal of this State, and all of the parties who are individuals have filed consents in a record in the issuing tribunal for a tribunal of this State to modify the support order and assume continuing, exclusive jurisdiction. . . .

Section 613. Jurisdiction to Modify Child-Support Order of Another State When Individual Parties Reside in This State

(a) If all of the parties who are individuals reside in this State and the child does not reside in the issuing State, a tribunal of this State has jurisdiction to enforce and to modify the issuing state's child-support order in a proceeding to register that order. . . .

Could New Jersey properly have asserted jurisdiction over the mother's motion to modify under either of these provisions?

As footnote 3 in *Pappas* discusses, the FFCCSOA provision on this issue is slightly different. 28 U.S.C. § 1738B(i) provides: "If there is no individual contestant or child residing in the issuing State, the party or support enforcement agency seeking to modify, or to modify and enforce, a child support order issued in another State shall register that order in a State *with jurisdiction over the nonmovant* for the purpose of modification" (emphasis added). The courts are divided as to the effect of this difference. Some courts hold that the FFCCSOA language refers to personal and subject matter jurisdiction, making it consistent with UIFSA. Others say that it refers only to personal jurisdiction, and that, therefore, the FFCCSOA may sometimes authorize the state to assert jurisdiction even though the petitioner resided in the state; the FFCCSOA provision would prevail under the supremacy clause. In addition to the cases cited in the footnote above, *see* Pulkkinen v. Pulkinnen, 127 So. 3d 738 (Fla. Dist. Ct. App. 2013).

6. UIFSA provides that the state that issued a spousal support order has "continuing, exclusive jurisdiction over a spousal-support order *throughout the existence of the support obligation.*" UIFSA § 211. That section further provides, "A tribunal of this State may not modify a spousal-support order issued by a tribunal of another State or a foreign country having continuing, exclusive jurisdiction over that order under the law of that State or foreign country." The commentary explains this difference in treatment on the basis that state law regarding spousal support orders varies from state to state much more than does the law regarding child support. Recent cases enforcing this provision, even though neither party still lived in the issuing state, include Midyett v. Midyett, 2013 Ark. App. 291 (2013); O'Neil v. O'Neil, 724 S.E.2d 247 (Va. App. 2012).

7. UIFSA Section 204 governs simultaneous proceedings in two states and provides that if either state is the home state, i.e., the state in which the child has

resided for at least six months, the action in its court should proceed and the action in the other court should be stayed. If neither state is the home state, the first action filed should proceed, and the other court should stay its proceeding. The purpose of this rule is to ensure that conflicting orders will not be issued, and the rule requires courts to seek information to determine whether support actions have been filed in other states and to cooperate with each other in determining which action has priority. Section 311 imposes pleading and related requirements so that courts will have the necessary information.

8. UIFSA Section 305(d) provides that visitation interference cannot be raised as a defense to child support enforcement.

9. Each state and the federal government have parent locator services to facilitate interstate support enforcement. 42 U.S.C. §§ 653, 654(8). The federal Parent Locator Service also maintains a national directory of new hires and a registry of child support orders, which will contain an abstract of every child support order that is part of the IV-D system. The goal of these provisions is to enable the federal Parent Locator Service to match orders in the registry with information in the new hires directory to track down parents quickly.

PROBLEMS

1. Harry and Winifred were domiciled in and divorced in State *A*. Their divorce decree provides that Harry must pay Winifred $250 per month in child support and $150 per month in spousal support. Harry moved to State *B* and stopped paying. Winifred registered the State *A* decree in State *B* and asked the State *B* court to order Harry to pay the past-due amounts and to enforce the decree without modifying as to future payments. Harry asked the State *B* court to modify downward both the past-due amounts and the future award on the grounds that his income has decreased. States *A* and *B* have enacted UIFSA. May the State *B* court take jurisdiction to modify the State A order?

2. In addition to the facts in problem 1, assume that Winifred and the children moved from State *A* to State *C* and that Harry again quit paying support. Winifred registered the State *A* decree in State *C* and asked the court to enforce the overdue amounts and to modify the decree to increase the amount of child and spousal support Harry owes in the future. State *C* has also enacted UIFSA. May the State *C* court take jurisdiction to modify the State *A* order?

3. Mary and Fred were divorced in State *A*; the divorce decree provided that Fred would pay Mary child support of $750 per month. Mary and the children moved to State *B*, and Fred moved to State *C*. Mary registered the support order in State *C* and asked the court to modify the amount of child support upward, alleging changed circumstances under the law of State *C*. Fred responded that the court should use the law of the issuing state, State *A*, to determine the amount of child support. Should the court use the law of State *A* or State *C*? Why?

NOTE: INTERNATIONAL SUPPORT ENFORCEMENT

Negotiations to establish the Hague Convention on the Recovery of Child Support and Other Forms of Family Maintenance were completed in 2007.

The full text and an official explanatory document are available at http://
www.hcch.net/index_en.php?act=conventions.text&cid=131. As was true of earlier
treaties on the subject, the Convention does not propose uniform rules regarding
assertion of jurisdiction. Some countries permit jurisdiction to be asserted in the state
in which the creditor is located, and others, including the United States, require that a
state have minimum contacts with the obligor to assert jurisdiction. The Convention
is in force among Albania, Bosnia and Herzegovina, the European Union, Norway,
and Ukraine. While the United States has signed the Convention, it cannot take
effect here until the states and Congress pass implementing legislation. The federal
legislation is expected to include a reservation against enforcing orders that do not
comply with U.S. due process principles. Such legislation has been introduced but
not enacted. The National Conference of Commissioners on Uniform State Laws
has revised UIFSA to comply with the Convention. UIFSA Art. 7 (2008).
The amendments also address international child support cases involving countries
that are not signatories to the Convention, relying on principles of comity.
For additional information, *see* Eric M. Fish, The Uniform Interstate Family Support
Act (UIFSA) 2008: Enforcing International Obligations Through Cooperative Federalism, 24 J. Am. Acad. Matrimonial L. 33 (2011).

E. CHILD CUSTODY JURISDICTION

Determining which state may decide a custody dispute is perhaps the most difficult
jurisdictional issue of all. The traditional view was that only the state where the
child was domiciled had jurisdiction to grant a custody order. Restatement, Conflict of Laws § 117 (1934). Custody was regarded as a status, and only the state of
the child's domicile had sufficient interest to regulate that status. *Id.* §§ 119, 144.
The benefit of that approach is simplicity: Only one state can have custody jurisdiction at any given time. However, the rule was sharply criticized on the ground
that it was too simple, because it failed to recognize that states other than that of
domicile may have substantial interests in the child's care and welfare and may be in
a better position than the state of domicile to determine what action would serve
the child's welfare. *See, e.g.*, Albert Ehrenzweig, Interstate Recognition of Custody
Decrees, 51 Mich. L. Rev. 345 (1953); Leonard Ratner, Child Custody in a Federal
System, 62 Mich. L. Rev. 795 (1964); Sampsell v. Superior Court, 197 P.2d 739
(Cal. 1948) (Traynor, J.). Over time, the rigidity of the Restatement view was
replaced by a more flexible approach, recognizing that several states may have
significant interests in determining the child's custody. In the only Supreme
Court case that addresses constitutional limits on custody jurisdiction, May v.
Anderson, 345 U.S. 528 (1953), the Court held that Ohio did not have to give
full faith and credit to a Wisconsin order granting custody to the father that was
issued ex parte by a court that did not have personal jurisdiction over the mother,
who lived in Ohio. The Court said:

> . . . [W]e have before us the elemental question whether a court of a state, where a
> mother is neither domiciled, resident nor present, may cut off her immediate right to

the care, custody, management and companionship of her minor children without having jurisdiction over her *in personam*. Rights far more precious to appellant than property rights will be cut off if she is to be bound by the Wisconsin award of custody. "It is now too well settled to be open to further dispute that the 'full faith and credit' clause and the act of Congress passed pursuant to it do not entitle a judgment *in personam* to extra-territorial effect if it be made to appear that it was rendered without jurisdiction over the person sought to be bound." Baker v. Baker, Eccles & Co., 242 U.S. 394.

Justice Frankfurter concurred in the judgment, interpreting the lead opinion as not requiring Ohio to recognize the decree but also as not holding that Wisconsin's assertion of jurisdiction to decide custody violated due process.

At the time May v. Anderson was decided, custody disputes between parents living in different states were comparatively rare. By the mid-1960s, however, the number of cases had increased significantly and continued to grow through the 1970s. Brigitte Bodenheimer, Progress Under the Uniform Child Custody Jurisdiction Act and Remaining Problems: Punitive Decrees, Joint Custody, and Excessive Modifications, 65 Cal. L. Rev. 978 (1977). Parents dissatisfied with unfavorable custody decisions were sorely tempted to take their children and run to other states to seek modification of the decrees. The flexible law of child custody jurisdiction combined with other factors to facilitate interstate child snatching. Once states other than that of a child's domicile could claim an interest in regulating custody, the only substantial obstacle to awards favoring the petitioning (and often snatching) parent was the obligation to give full faith and credit to a prior custody decree. However, as we have seen, courts of one state are required to give judgments of another state only such finality as the rendering forum grants. Child custody orders, as we know, are routinely considered modifiable on a showing of changed circumstances and thus were not traditionally considered to be entitled to full faith and credit. *Cf.* Kovacs v. Brewer, 356 U.S. 604 (1958); Halvey v. Halvey, 330 U.S. 610 (1947).

By the mid-1960s the indeterminacy of child custody jurisdiction law prompted the National Conference of Commissioners on Uniform State Laws to develop the Uniform Child Custody Jurisdiction Act (UCCJA), which was adopted, sometimes with modifications, by all 50 states and the District of Columbia. The National Conference recommended replacement of the UCCJA with the Uniform Child Custody Jurisdiction and Enforcement Act (UCCJEA) in 1997. The UCCJEA is available on the website of the Uniform Law Commission, http://www.uniformlaws.org/. As of 2014 the UCCJEA had been enacted in all states except Massachusetts. Legislative Fact Sheet — Child Custody Jurisdiction and Enforcement Act, available at the Law Commission website.

The UCCJEA, which applies to a broad range of custody proceedings, including actions regarding visitation, *see* UCCJEA § 102(3) and (4), prescribes when a state may take jurisdiction in the first instance to decide a custody dispute, when a state must enforce custody orders from other states, and when a state may and may not take jurisdiction to modify a custody order from another state. Under the UCCJEA, only one state at a time has jurisdiction to decide custody disputes, and once a state obtains jurisdiction, it retains exclusive jurisdiction to modify until statutory conditions for losing that jurisdiction occur.

Just as the UIFSA is complemented by the federal FFCCSOA, the UCCJEA is complemented by the federal Parental Kidnapping Prevention Act (PKPA), which was enacted in 1980. The PKPA implements the full faith and credit clause and prescribes when states must recognize (enforce) custody and visitation decrees from other states and when they must refuse to modify such decrees. Most courts hold that the PKPA does not itself grant jurisdiction; instead state law does that.

The first part of this section deals with subject matter jurisdiction to make an initial custody order, and the second considers interstate enforcement and modification. The third part addresses jurisdiction in adoption cases, and the last part deals with international custody disputes.

1. Initial Jurisdiction

EX PARTE SIDERIUS

___ So. 3d ___ (Ala. 2013)

MOORE, Chief Justice. . . . From September 2006 to July 2009, [Caroline M. Siderius and Kenneth V.] Fordham lived together as husband and wife in Mobile with their minor children, L.F. and M.F. Siderius worked as a prosecutor in Mobile. Fordham is a retired Coast Guard officer and is involved in several business enterprises. In June 2009, Siderius accepted an appointment with the Social Security Administration's Office of Disability Adjudication and Review ("ODAR") to serve as an administrative law judge in the Portland, Oregon ODAR office. In July 2009, Siderius moved with L.F. and M.F. to Portland to begin her new job. Fordham thereafter joined the family in Portland.

The family lived in Portland until March 2010. . . . In February 2010, Siderius sought a hardship transfer to the Spokane, Washington, ODAR office. The hardship transfer was approved, and in March 2010 the whole family relocated to Washington. . . .

In May 2011, the parties retained a court-approved mediator to assist with the dissolution of their marriage and custody of the minor children. . . . Fordham does not dispute that the parties agreed that M.F. would be in Alabama from June 17 to July 7 or 8, 2011, and would then return to Washington. Likewise, Fordham does not dispute that the parties agreed that L.F. would be in Alabama from July 21 to August 6, and would then return to Washington. M.F. and L.F. traveled to Alabama as planned, and remained there with Fordham.

. . . Siderius purchased a plane ticket for M.F. to return to Spokane on August 11, 2011. However, on September 6 and 7, Fordham transferred the school registration of both children, who had remained in Alabama, from Spokane to schools in Mobile.

On August 11, 2011, Fordham filed a child-custody petition and complaint for divorce in the Mobile Circuit Court. Fordham also filed an emergency motion seeking immediate custody of the children. The next day, the Mobile Circuit Court signed an order granting Fordham's emergency motion and awarding him custody of the children pendente lite. On August 15, 2011, Siderius filed a petition in

Spokane seeking dissolution of the marriage and custody of the minor children. The same day, the Spokane trial court issued an ex parte restraining order ordering Fordham to return the minor children to Washington. The Spokane trial court also scheduled initial divorce, custody, contempt hearings, and a telephone conference with the Mobile Circuit Court pursuant to the Uniform Child Custody Jurisdiction and Enforcement Act, § 30-3B-101, et seq., Ala. Code 1975 ("the UCCJEA"). Also on August 15, 2011, Siderius filed a limited appearance in Fordham's Mobile proceeding to challenge personal and subject-matter jurisdiction.

On August 30, 2011, the Spokane and Mobile courts held a telephone conference as required by the UCCJEA. The Mobile court also held an evidentiary hearing on that day on the question of which state had jurisdiction and held a follow-up hearing on October 4, 2011. . . .

On October 7, 2011, the Mobile court issued an order finding that it had jurisdiction over Siderius on the basis of her minimum contacts with Alabama. The court did not rule on the applicability of the UCCJEA to the proceeding. . . .

On February 10, 2012, the Spokane court issued an order awarding custody of the children to Siderius and finding, among other things, that Washington had jurisdiction under the UCCJEA because the minor children had lived with their parents in Washington for 17 months before the commencement of the child-custody proceeding in Alabama. . . . On February 24, 2012, Siderius registered the Spokane court's custody determination and a motion for enforcement with the Mobile court. In March 2012, the Mobile court held a hearing on Siderius's motion. On July 12, 2012, the Mobile court issued a brief order denying Siderius's motion to enforce the Spokane court's custody determination.

Siderius again petitioned the Court of Civil of Appeals for a writ of mandamus, seeking review of the Mobile court's July 2012 order. The Court of Civil Appeals denied Siderius's petition on January 11, 2013. . . .

Siderius thereafter filed this petition with this Court, together with the transcript of the Alabama trial court's September and October 2011 hearings and relevant supporting evidence. . . .

For this Court to issue a writ of mandamus, Siderius must demonstrate that she has a clear legal right to an order dismissing Fordham's custody proceeding in Alabama. The controlling issue is which state — Alabama or Washington — has jurisdiction to make an initial child-custody and visitation determination under § 30-3B-201, Ala. Code 1975.

A. Home-State Jurisdiction Under the UCCJEA

Alabama and Washington have both adopted the UCCJEA.

The relevant parts of Washington's and Alabama's respective versions of the UCCJEA are substantially the same. Section 30-3B-201 governs jurisdiction of Alabama courts to make an initial child-custody determination:

(a) Except as otherwise provided in Section 30-3B-204, a court of this state has jurisdiction to make an initial child custody determination only if:

(1) This state is the home state of the child on the date of the commencement of the proceeding, or was the home state of the child within six months before the

commencement of the proceeding and the child is absent from this state but a
parent or person acting as a parent continues to live in this state;

. . .

(b) Subsection (a) is the exclusive jurisdictional basis for making a child custody
determination by a court of this state.

(c) Physical presence of a child is not necessary or sufficient to make a child
custody determination.

The UCCJEA defines the term "home state" as follows:

The state in which a child lived with a parent or a person acting as a parent for at least
six consecutive months immediately before the commencement of a child custody
proceeding. In the case of a child less than six months of age, the term means the state
in which the child lived from birth with any of the persons mentioned. A period of
temporary absence of the child or any of the mentioned persons is part of the period.

§ 30-3B-102(7), Ala. Code 1975. Alabama adopted the UCCJEA to achieve the
following purposes:

(1) Avoid jurisdictional competition and conflict with courts of other states in matters
of child custody which have in the past resulted in the shifting of children from state
to state with harmful effects on their well-being;
(2) Promote cooperation with the courts of other States to the end that a custody
decree is rendered in that State which can best decide the case in the interest of the
child;
(3) Discourage the use of the interstate system for continuing controversies over child
custody;
(4) Deter abductions of children;
(5) Avoid relitigation of custody decisions of other states in this state;
(6) Facilitate the enforcement of custody decrees of other states.

Official Comment to § 30-3B-101, Ala. Code 1975.

B. Two Definitions of "Home State" in the UCCJEA

Section 30-3B-201(a)(1) provides that a state has jurisdiction in a child-
custody matter if the state "was the home state of the child *within six months before*"
the commencement of the child-custody proceeding. Section 30-3B-102(7), Ala.
Code 1975, defines "home state" as "[t]he state in which a child lived with a
parent . . . for at least *six consecutive months immediately before*" the proceeding commenced (emphasis added). On their face, it appears that § 30-3B-201(a)(1) and the
definition of "home state" in § 30-3B-102(7) are in conflict.

In this case the children had lived in Washington for 17 months, nearly a year
beyond the required "six consecutive months," before Fordham filed the child-
custody proceeding in Alabama. The children's stay in Washington, however, was
interrupted in June 2011, as to M.F., and in July 2011, as to L.F., when the children
went to Alabama temporarily for either vacation or visitation. On August 11, 2011,
Fordham filed his petition for divorce and custody in Alabama. On August 15,
2011, Siderius filed her petition in Washington.

It is undisputed that the children did not live in Alabama for "six consecutive months immediately before" Fordham filed his custody proceeding in Alabama. Thus, Alabama cannot be the "home state" under § 30-3B-102(7). The children also did not live in Washington in the "six consecutive months *immediately before*" the mother filed for divorce and custody. Thus, Washington cannot be the "home state" under § 30-3B-102(7). However, under § 30-3B-201(a)(1), Washington was the home state of the children "within six months before" Fordham's August 11 filing for divorce and custody in Mobile.

Because the description of "home state" in § 30-3B-201(a)(1) is broader than the definition in § 30-3B-102(7), we resolve the apparent conflict between the two sections, in keeping with the purposes of the UCCJEA, by applying the construction that finds the existence of a home state, rather than the one that finds that the children had no home state. We interpret the UCCJEA in order to "[a]void jurisdictional competition and conflict with courts of other states in matters of child custody which in the past resulted in the shifting of children from state to state with harmful effects on their well-being." Official Comment to § 30-3B-101, Ala. Code 1975. There are two ways to resolve the apparent lack of "home state" jurisdiction under § 30-3B-201(a)(1), which is the "exclusive jurisdictional basis for making a child custody determination."

1. *TEMPORARY ABSENCES ARE INCLUDED IN CALCULATING THE SIX-MONTH PERIOD*

First, "[a] period of temporary absence of the child or any of the mentioned persons is part of the period" of six consecutive months immediately before the custody proceeding commences. § 30-3B-102(7), Ala. Code 1975. . . .

In addition, "[c]ourts have found that 'temporary absences include court-ordered visitations, and *vacations* and business trips.'" "[W]here both parents intend a child's absence from a state to be temporary, the duration of that absence must be counted toward the establishment of a home state pursuant to the UCCJEA. . . ." 175 Wash. App. at 489-90, 307 P.3d at 728. "[T]emporary absences do not interrupt the six-month pre-complaint residency period necessary to establish home state jurisdiction." Ogawa v. Ogawa, 125 Nev. 660, 662, 221 P.3d 699, 700 (2009). . . .

Based on the facts before us, the children's absence from Spokane appears to have been only temporary, i.e., for the purpose of vacation or visitation. This temporary absence from Spokane is thus part of the "six consecutive months immediately before" the custody proceeding commenced. When the children's temporary absences are factored in, therefore, the Spokane court clearly has home-state jurisdiction to make an initial child-custody and visitation determination under the UCCJEA. Conversely, Alabama does not.

2. *THE SIX-MONTH "EXTENDED HOME STATE PROVISION"*

Second, Washington's home-state jurisdiction continued for an extended period of up to six months *after* the children had been removed to Alabama by Fordham, because Siderius continued to reside in Washington, the home state. In determining the legislative intent of the UCCJEA, "we must examine the statute as a whole and, if possible, give effect to each section." . . .

One purpose of the UCCJEA is to "[p]romote cooperation with the courts of other States to the end that a custody decree is rendered in that State which can best decide the case in the interest of the child." Official Comment to § 30-3B-101, ¶ 2. The UCCJEA "prioritizes home state jurisdiction" "over other jurisdictional bases," such as personal jurisdiction obtained through sufficient minimum contacts. The Official Comment to Section 30-3B-201 provides:

> "The six-month *extended home state provision* of subsection (a)(1) has been modified slightly from the UCCJA [Uniform Child Custody Jurisdiction Act]. The UCCJA provided that home state jurisdiction continued for six months when the child had been removed by a person seeking the child's custody or for other reasons and a parent or a person acting as a parent continues to reside in the home state. Under this Act, it is no longer necessary to determine why the child has been removed. The only inquiry relates to the status of the person left behind."

(Emphasis added.) The comment to the model Uniform Child Custody Jurisdiction Act, the predecessor to the UCCJEA, explained the six-month extended home-state provision:

> "Subparagraph (ii) of paragraph (1) extends the home state rule *for an additional six-month period in order to permit suit in the home state after the child's departure.* The main objective is to protect a parent who has been left by his spouse taking the child along."

In order to give effect to the legislative purpose of the UCCJEA, § 30-3B-201(a)(1) must be construed to extend home-state jurisdiction under § 30-3B-102(7) for an additional six months. Thus, the "home state" is not limited to *only* the "six consecutive months *immediately before*" the custody proceeding commences. The applicable six-consecutive-month period may also be determined "within" an extended or additional six-month period before the commencement of the proceeding under the second prong of § 30-3B-201(a)(1).

This construction of the UCCJEA avoids the absurd result here of the minor children's having no home state because they did not live in Washington, the home state, for the full six months "immediately before" the proceeding commenced. This construction prioritizes home-state jurisdiction "over other jurisdictional bases," and carries forward the clear intent of the UCCJEA that expressly incorporated the "six-month extended home state provision" from the UCCJA.

Finally, our construction of this apparent conflict in the UCCJEA comports with the construction given the UCCJEA by other state courts (citations omitted). Thus, the Washington trial court in this case properly exercised jurisdiction under the UCCJEA because it was the "home state" of the children *within six months before* the commencement of the child-custody proceeding under the "six-month extended home state provision" of § 30-3B-201(a)(1). Because Washington is the home state under the "extended home state provision" of the UCCJEA, the Alabama trial court lacks home-state jurisdiction over Fordham's custody proceeding. . . .

Siderius's petition for a writ of mandamus is granted and we direct the Mobile Circuit Court to dismiss Fordham's child-custody proceeding.

NOTES AND QUESTIONS

1. Many of the cases involving disputes over initial jurisdiction under the UCCJEA arise when a parent files for custody in the midst of or shortly after a major move, as in *Siderius*. The practical issue is whether the custody litigation will occur in the state from which the children moved or in the state of their new residence. The starting point of the analysis is determining which state, if either, has home state or extended home state jurisdiction. In *Siderius* the court concluded that Washington had jurisdiction under both criteria by applying the rule that temporary absence from a state does not break the required six months. What would have happened if the home state and extended home state analyses conflicted?

Consider, for example, this adaption of the facts of Powell v. Stover, 165 S.W.3d 322 (Tex. 2005):

> In February 2001, Russell Powell moved from Texas to Tennessee to accept a new position with his employer. In May 2001, his wife, Sonia Powell, sold her house in Texas, closed her Texas bank accounts, and moved with the couple's son, D.B.P., to Tennessee to join Russell. There, the couple leased a house with an option to buy. Within a week of her arrival in Tennessee, Sonia obtained a Tennessee driver's license, opened a checking account with a Tennessee bank, and began applying for jobs. She and Russell enrolled D.B.P. in kindergarten. Five months later, Sonia took D.B.P. and returned to to Texas.

Assume that Russell, who remained in Texas, filed suit seeking custody a month later, i.e., six months after Sonia and D.B.P. first moved to Texas, and that a few days later Sonia filed a similar suit in Tennessee. Is Texas D.B.P.'s home state, based on the argument that his absence for the last month is "temporary"? Or is Tennessee his home state, either because the five months he spent in Texas constituted a "temporary absence" or because Tennessee was his home state within the last six months?

In *Powell* the child was actually in Tennessee for six months before his mother took him back to Texas and filed for custody. The Texas Supreme Court rejected her argument that he had only been temporarily absent from Texas and that Texas therefore remained his home state. It held that where the child lives is determined by his or her physical location, and that therefore Tennessee was the home state. This interpretation, the court said, was necessary to further the purposes of the UCCJEA. Do you agree? *See also* Chick v. Chick, 596 S.E. 303 (N.C. App. 2004); Marriage of McDermott, 307 P.3d 717 (Wash. App. 2013).

In a more recent Texas case the never-married mother and father were separated, and the father, along with his pregnant wife and the child from his former relationship, moved from Georgia to Texas in late May. After about two weeks in Texas, the family returned to Georgia so that the baby could be born there. They remained in Georgia until late July and then moved all their belongings to Texas. The child's mother at all times remained in Georgia. In November (six months after the first trip to Texas), the father filed for custody in Texas. Did Texas have home state jurisdiction? Was the time that the child spent in Georgia over the summer a temporary absence? *See* In re Walker, 428 S.W.3d 212 (Tex.

App. 2014); *see also* Caruso v. Caruso, 2013 WL 6808608 (Ohio App. 2013). If the child's mother filed for custody in Georgia in January (six months after the July move), would Georgia still have had extended home state juridiction?

2. For a state to have extended home state jurisdiction, a parent or person acting as parent must still live in the state. UCCJEA § 201(a)(1). If this condition is not satisfied, or if a child has simply moved around a great deal, the child may not have a home state. In that case, a state may claim jurisdiction if "the child and the child's parents, or the child and at least one parent or a person acting as a parent, have a significant connection . . . other than mere physical presence" with the state, and "substantial evidence is available concerning the child's care, protection, training, and personal relationships" is available in the state. UCCJEA § 201(a)(2). In the rare case where no state has home state, extended home state, or significant connection jurisdiction, another state may take jurisdiction. UCCJEA § 201(a)(4).

3. The UCCJEA provides that if a child is less than six months old, the state in which the child has lived from birth is the home state. UCCJEA § 102(7). Courts have consistently held that the UCCJEA does not provide jurisdiction over a custody proceeding involving an unborn child. Gray v. Gray, ___ So. 3d ___ (Ala. App. 2013); Arnold v. Price, 365 S.W.3d 455, 461 (Tex. App. 2012); B.B. v. A.B., 916 N.Y.S.2d 920 (Sup. Ct. 2011); In re Custody of Kalbes, 733 N.W.2d 648 (Wis. App. 2007).

4. UCCJEA Section 204 provides that a court may take emergency jurisdiction if the child has been abandoned in the state or if action is necessary to protect the child or the child's sibling or parent from mistreatment or abuse, regardless of whether a prior custody order exists or not. The section also makes explicit that the orders of a court acting on this jurisdictional basis last only until a court with jurisdiction under other provisions of the UCCJEA takes charge. *See*, *e.g.*, In re Brode, 566 S.E.2d 858 (N.C. App. 2002). The emergency jurisdiction provision of UCCJA Section 3 has generally been interpreted narrowly and as allowing a court to enter temporary custody orders only to protect the child until a court with jurisdiction under another provision of the statute can step in.

5. The commentary to UCCJA Section 13 indicates that the Act's drafters assumed that Frankfurter's concurrence in May v. Anderson, above, employs the due process test to determine when a state may assert personal jurisdiction over an absent parent or other person claiming rights to custody. Based on this assumption, the UCCJEA does not require that the state have minimum-contacts jurisdiction over all the parties, though notice "reasonably calculated to give actual notice" is required. UCCJEA § 108. Any person who claims a right to the child's custody must be given notice. UCCJEA § 205. Participation in a custody suit does not in and of itself give a court jurisdiction over a person with regard to other matters. UCCJEA § 109. Professor Russell Coombs has argued that in some extreme circumstances, a state's assertion of jurisdiction to determine the custody rights of a person with no contacts with the state would violate due process. Russell M. Coombs, Interstate Child Custody: Jurisdiction, Recognition and Enforcement, 66 Minn. L. Rev. 711 (1982).

6. The drafters of the UIFSA borrowed major substantive principles from the UCCJA. The purpose, according to the drafters, was to consolidate jurisdiction over support and custody issues in the same state. Unofficial Annotation to UIFSA § 207; John J. Sampson, Unofficial Comment to § 801, Uniform Interstate

Family Support Act, reprinted at 27 Fam. L.Q. 93, 123 (1993). The jurisdictional provisions of the UCCJEA in many cases enhance the chances that the same state will have jurisdiction over both custody and child support. However, jurisdiction under the UIFSA and the UCCJEA is not always consolidated. For example, under the UCCJEA, a court in a state that is the child's home state has exclusive jurisdiction to determine custody, but it may not have jurisdiction to award child support if the defendant parent does not have sufficient contacts with the state to satisfy due process, as interpreted in *Kulko. See, e.g.*, Coleman v. Coleman, 864 So. 2d 371 (Ala. Civ. App. 2003).

2.   *Interstate Enforcement and Modification Jurisdiction*

The UCCJEA and PKPA both provide that a court must enforce a custody order from another state if the first state exercised jurisdiction in substantial conformity with the Act or under factual circumstances meeting the jurisdictional standards of the Act. UCCJEA §303, PKPA 28 U.S.C. §1738A(a); *see also* UCCJA §13. A custody order is made consistently with the PKPA or the UCCJA if the court issuing the order had jurisdiction under its own state laws. 28 U.S.C. §1738A(c)(1). In addition, one of five conditions enumerated in Section 1738A(c)(2) must be met. They are:

> (A) such State (i) is the home State of the child on the date of the commencement of the proceeding, or (ii) had been the child's home State within six months before the date of the commencement of the proceeding and the child is absent from such State because of his removal or retention by a contestant or for other reasons, and a contestant continues to live in such State;
> (B) (i) it appears that no other State would have jurisdiction under subparagraph (A), and (ii) it is in the best interest of the child that a court of such State assume jurisdiction because (I) the child and his parents, or the child and at least one contestant, have a significant connection with such State other than mere physical presence in such State, and (II) there is available in such State substantial evidence concerning the child's present or future care, protection, training, and personal relationships;
> (C) the child is physically present in such State and (i) the child has been abandoned, or (ii) it is necessary in an emergency to protect the child because he has been subjected to or threatened with mistreatment or abuse;
> (D) (i) it appears that no other State would have jurisdiction under subparagraph (A), (B), (C), or (E), or another State has declined to exercise jurisdiction on the ground that the State whose jurisdiction is in issue is the more appropriate forum to determine the custody of the child, and (ii) it is in the best interest of the child that such court assume jurisdiction; or
> (E) the court has continuing jurisdiction pursuant to subsection (d) of this section.

The UCCJEA provides that the mechanism for obtaining enforcement of a custody order from another state is by registration. A court receiving an order for registration must give notice to the parties, give them an opportunity to contest on the basis that the court lacked jurisdiction or that the order has been modified, or that the person contesting did not receive notice. If the registration is not contested or if objections are overruled, the order is to be enforced to the same extent as custody orders issued by courts in the state. UCCJEA § 305.

The UCCJEA and the PKPA strictly limit the jurisdiction of a court to modify a custody order from another state. The statutory provisions are, for the most part, quite unambiguous. UCCJEA Section 202 provides that a court that has validly asserted jurisdiction has exclusive, continuing jurisdiction until a court in that state "determines that neither the child, the child and one parent, nor the child and a person acting as a parent have a significant connection with this State and that substantial evidence is no longer available in this State concerning the child's care, protection, training and personal relationships," or until "the child, the child's parents, and any person acting as a parent do not presently reside in this State."

BRANDT v. BRANDT

268 P.3d 406 (Colo. 2012) (en banc)

Justice HOBBS delivered the Opinion of the Court. . . . Petitioner Christine Brandt and Respondent George Brandt were divorced in Montgomery County, Maryland on May 25, 2006. At that time, the terms of the parties' Voluntary Separation and Property Settlement Agreement were incorporated into the divorce decree. The agreement provided that the couple would have joint custody of their child, C.B., with Christine Brandt having primary physical custody. . . .

In 2008, the Army transferred George Brandt to Fort Carson, Colorado Springs, Colorado. The parties divided time with C.B. equally during the summer of 2008, and C.B. returned to Maryland for the 2008-09 school year. George Brandt served at Fort Carson until 2010 when he retired, re-married, and settled with his new wife in Littleton, Colorado.

Christine Brandt was commissioned into the Army in 2009, serving in the Nursing Corps. Following training, she was stationed at Fort Hood, Texas, where she moved with C.B. from Maryland in March of that year. C.B.'s 2009 summer was also split between his parents. Christine Brandt was deployed to Iraq on active duty in April 2010. The parties mutually agreed that, while she was in Iraq, C.B. would live with George Brandt in Colorado. Christine Brandt returned from Iraq on October 10, 2010, and was reassigned to Fort Hood, Texas. She and George Brandt agreed to let C.B. complete the remainder of the 2010-11 school year in Colorado at which point George Brandt would return C.B. to Christine Brandt.

On April 26, 2011, Christine Brandt received military orders to return to Maryland and finish her active duty in a non-deployable position at Fort Meade. Her orders required her to report there no later than August 1, 2011, and authorized her to report there on July 15, 2011. As previously agreed between the parties, C.B. returned on May 22, 2011, to live with Christine Brandt, who was still at Fort Hood.

Meanwhile, on May 6, 2011, George Brandt filed a petition in the Arapahoe County district court to register the Maryland custody order pursuant to section 14-13-305, C.R.S. (2011), and to request that the court assume jurisdiction to modify the custody order pursuant to section 14-13-203, C.R.S. (2011) ("May 6

Petition"). Christine Brandt was served in Texas on May 18 with the May 6 Petition and a Notice of the Registration of the Maryland decree. On May 25, the district court entered its order registering the Maryland decree and assuming jurisdiction to modify it ("May 25 Order"). The court based its assumption of modification jurisdiction on the fact that C.B. had resided in Colorado for more than one year and neither Christine Brandt nor George Brandt nor their child "currently reside[d]" in Maryland.

On June 1, within the time allowed to contest the petition following service upon her, Christine Brandt filed a pro se motion to dismiss the petition George Brandt had filed. On June 8, Christine Brandt and C.B. returned to her home in Maryland pursuant to her military orders. On June 13, George Brandt simultaneously filed a petition to modify parenting time in the Arapahoe County District Court, together with an emergency motion for issuance of a writ of habeas corpus and writ of assistance in order to secure the return of C.B. In the latter motion, George Brandt claimed that Christine Brandt abducted C.B. to Maryland without his consent because he and Christine Brandt had previously agreed that C.B. would spend the second half of the summer (commencing on June 25) with him in Colorado. The district court issued both requested writs on June 16.

On June 20, Christine Brandt traveled back to Texas to out-process from Fort Hood, during which time she left C.B. in Maryland with his maternal grandmother. At some point during the next week, C.B. and his grandmother traveled to Pennsylvania. George Brandt, with the help of local law enforcement, exercised the Colorado writ, taking C.B. into his physical custody and returning to Colorado, where C.B. has resided with him since June 26.

In the meantime, Christine Brandt obtained counsel in Colorado and, on June 22, filed a motion for reconsideration and motion to dismiss the May 25 Order. She also filed an emergency motion for a telephone conference in Maryland, pursuant to which Judge Quirk in Montgomery County, Maryland held three teleconferences with Judge Russell in Arapahoe County during which both parties were represented by counsel.

On July 29, during the final teleconference, our district court said that: (1) Maryland had lost exclusive continuing jurisdiction due to Christine Brandt's presence in Texas, not Maryland; (2) under the UCCJEA, the preferred forum is where a child has lived for six months; and (3) Colorado was the most convenient forum to hear this case. Judge Quirk explicitly disagreed and reiterated his position from earlier teleconferences that Maryland retained exclusive continuing jurisdiction over the custody order:

> [I]t would still be my decision that continuing exclusive jurisdiction is proper here because residence, quite frankly, within the meaning of our Maryland law, of Ms. Brandt has never been anywhere but Maryland, and has continued here, and there is a connection. That connection exists, as well as the connection of the child to Maryland.

The Maryland judge lamented that both states were now asserting jurisdiction, the very result the legislatures in both states had intended to avoid in enacting the uniform statute.

Christine Brandt petitioned us for a rule to show cause, which we issued. She claims that the district court erred in finding that she no longer resided in Maryland for purposes of determining modification jurisdiction under the UCCJEA. . . .

2. Exclusive Continuing Jurisdiction

Once a state enters an initial child custody determination, that state has exclusive jurisdiction to modify the determination provided that initial jurisdiction was proper. Exclusive jurisdiction continues until:

> (a) A court of [the issuing] state determines that the child, the child's parents, and any person acting as a parent do not have a significant connection with [the issuing] state and that substantial evidence is no longer available in [the issuing] state concerning the child's care, protection, training, and personal relationships; or
> (b) A court of [the issuing] state or a court of another state determines that the child, the child's parents, and any person acting as a parent *do not presently reside* in [the issuing] state.

§ 14-13-202(1)(a)–(b) (emphasis added).

It is clear from the statute that only a court of the issuing state can decide that it has lost jurisdiction due to erosion of a "significant connection" between the child and the state. However, it is equally clear that a court in either the issuing state or any other state may divest the issuing state of jurisdiction by making a determination that the child and both parents do not "presently reside" there.

Thus, although a child's home state may change within the meaning of the UCCJEA provision regarding jurisdiction to enter an initial custody order, the issuing state nevertheless may not be divested of exclusive continuing jurisdiction by any other state unless no party presently resides in the issuing state. This provision tracks the PKPA and helps ensure that parents do not have an incentive to take their child out-of-state in order to re-litigate the issue of custody.

3. Modification

A state may modify the custody order of another state only if it would have jurisdiction to make an initial determination, and either:

> (a) The court of the [issuing] state determines that it no longer has exclusive, continuing jurisdiction under [section 14-13-202] . . . or that a court of the [new] state would be a more convenient forum . . . ; *or*
> (b) A court of the [issuing] state or a court of the [new] state determines that the child, the child's parents, and any person acting as a parent *do not presently reside* in the [issuing] state.

The issue of modification thus tracks the issue of exclusive continuing jurisdiction: the new state may modify only if it has jurisdiction to make an initial custody order, *and* if the issuing state decides that it has lost exclusive continuing jurisdiction pursuant to section 14-13-202 or either state determines that no party presently resides in the issuing state. The issuing state may also decline to exercise its jurisdiction on the grounds that the new state would be a more convenient forum to hear a modification proceeding. If a new state enters a modification order, that state then assumes exclusive continuing jurisdiction over determinations of child custody.

4. THE APPROPRIATE PROCEDURE FOR DETERMINING WHERE THE PARENTS AND THE CHILD "PRESENTLY RESIDE"

Although there is no Colorado case on point, cases from other jurisdictions strongly suggest that more than a perfunctory determination of residence is required to divest an issuing state of jurisdiction. In a 2006 New Mexico case, the court affirmed that the UCCJEA "specifically requires action" by the state of potential modification before exclusive continuing jurisdiction in the issuing state ceases. State of N.M. ex rel. CYFD v. Donna J., 139 N.M. 131, 129 P.3d 167, 171 (2006). The court held that "[a]n automatic loss of jurisdiction, without any factual determination, would add uncertainty, diminish oversight ability of the courts, and increase conflicts between the states." . . .

The UCCJEA requires a "clear end-point to the decree state's jurisdiction." Only a state that has made a child custody decree "consistent" with § 14-13-201 (the provision for initial jurisdiction) or -203 (the provision for modification jurisdiction) is entitled to exclusive continuing jurisdiction. Therefore, it is imperative that an out-of-state court tasked with enforcing a custody order has a clear factual record, either by stipulation or from the taking of evidence, on which to assess whether jurisdiction was properly asserted by the court which entered the order.

A plaintiff typically "bears the burden of proving that the trial court has jurisdiction to hear the case." Because, under the UCCJEA, a new state may not modify an out-of-state child custody order unless it properly finds that the issuing state has been divested of jurisdiction (or declined to exercise it), the parent petitioning the new state to assume jurisdiction bears the burden of proving, not only that the new state would have jurisdiction to enter an initial child custody order, but that the issuing state has lost or declined to exercise jurisdiction as well.

Communication between the courts as authorized in sections 14-13-110 to -112 is exceedingly beneficial in this type of proceeding. Inter-court communication facilitates an understanding between sister states regarding whether the issuing state has lost jurisdiction pursuant to section 14-13-202(1)(a)–(b) or -203(1)(a)–(b), or declined to exercise jurisdiction in favor of a more convenient forum pursuant to section 14-13-207. Such communication alerts the issuing state to a potential loss of exclusive continuing jurisdiction, based on residence, before the new state assumes jurisdiction to modify the issuing state's child custody order. It also alerts the new state to any pending actions in the issuing state and helps to develop a factual record in the matter of jurisdiction.

We therefore determine that, before a court of this state may assume jurisdiction to modify an out-of-state custody order, the court must communicate with the issuing state pursuant to sections 14-13-110 to -112, conduct a hearing at which both sides are allowed to present evidence if there is a factual dispute on the residency issue, with the burden of proof being on the parent who has petitioned for the court to assume jurisdiction, following which the district court in our state makes its findings of fact, conclusions of law, and order.

5. TOTALITY OF CIRCUMSTANCES TEST FOR "PRESENTLY RESIDE"

We interpret sections 14-13-202 and -203, the provisions of the UCCJEA upon which the court below will determine whether it has jurisdiction to modify the Maryland child custody order. . . .

. . . [W]hile the UCCJEA for some purposes does prioritize the "home state"—the state where the child lived for the six months prior to the custody determination—this preference pertains only to jurisdiction to enter an initial child custody order, not jurisdiction to modify an order that has already been entered by another state. "Home state" preference at the modification stage would defeat the purposes of exclusive continuing jurisdiction, which are to ensure that custody orders, once entered, are as stable as possible and to discourage parents from establishing new "home states" for their children so as to re-litigate the issue of custody in a friendlier forum.

Absent action by Maryland disclaiming exclusive continuing jurisdiction or declining to exercise it, the only basis for Colorado to divest Maryland of jurisdiction is to determine that "the child, the child's parents, and any person acting as a parent do not presently reside" there.

Unfortunately, comment 2 to section 14-13-202 has confused construction of the operative statutory term "presently reside" and has led to a split among states in applying the act. This comment states, in part:

> Continuing jurisdiction is lost when the child, the child's parents, and any person acting as a parent no longer reside in the original decree State. . . . It is the intention of this Act that [the phrase, "do not presently reside"] means that the named persons *no longer continue to actually live within the State.* . . . [W]hen the child, the parents, and all persons acting as parents *physically leave the state to live elsewhere*, the exclusive continuing jurisdiction ceases.
>
> The phrase "do not presently reside" is *not used in the sense of technical domicile.* The fact that the original determination State still considers one parent a domiciliary does not prevent it from losing exclusive, continuing jurisdiction after the child, the parents, and all persons acting as parents have moved from the state.

§ 14-13-202, cmt. 2 (emphasis added). Based on this commentary, some states take the view that a person resides only where physically present when a petition for assumption of modification jurisdiction is filed. In Staats v. McKinnon, the Tennessee court of appeals concluded that the "sole question is whether the relevant individuals 'continue to actually live within the state' or have 'physically left the state to live elsewhere.'" 206 S.W.3d 532, 549 (Tenn. Ct. App. 2006). Relying on the same language, the Tennessee court also held in a separate case that, although one of the litigants maintained a residence, nursing license, driver's license, and voting registration in Arkansas and paid Arkansas state taxes, she nonetheless did not "presently reside" in Arkansas because she was, albeit temporarily, physically residing in Tennessee on the date the action commenced. Highfill v. Moody, 2010 WL 2075698, at *12 (Tenn. Ct. App. May 25, 2010).

A Pennsylvania court has defined "residence" as "living in a particular place, requiring only physical presence." Wagner v. Wagner, 887 A.2d 282, 287 (Pa. Super. Ct. 2005). The court held that, for UCCJEA purposes, a parent presently resided in New Jersey, where she had been assigned by the Army, notwithstanding that she retained a Florida mailing address, driver's license, and voter registration.

However, cases from other jurisdictions disagree that "presently reside" means only physical presence. In 2009, a California court of appeal found that the relevant question under the UCCJEA was "not whether Husband 'resided' in Pakistan, but whether he *stopped* residing in California." In re Marriage of Nurie, 98 Cal. Rptr. 3d at 219. Additionally, the court rejected the wife's construction of the word "presently":

> Wife insists that the term "presently" must be given effect in the statute, and that it means continuing jurisdiction may be lost based on where the parties are "actually living" regardless of their volition or intent. *We perceive a different significance to the word "presently,"* namely that the determination of relocation must be made during the period of nonresidence in the decree state.

The court concluded that, because it is well established that a party may have more than one residence, the husband could have "presently resided" in Pakistan at the time the Pakistan court asserted jurisdiction while "still maintaining a 'present residence' in California." The court held that, since the husband maintained a functioning home, car, telephones, and fax in California and was employed there, he continued to "presently reside" there. Thus, California (the issuing state) retained jurisdiction.

Similarly, in Russell v. Cox, a South Carolina court was tasked with determining whether South Carolina had jurisdiction to modify a Georgia custody decree where the mother resided in Florida and the father and child resided in South Carolina. 383 S.C. 215, 678 S.E.2d 460 (App. 2009). The court concluded that Georgia had not lost jurisdiction because the father, "notwithstanding significant evidence that he currently resided in South Carolina, was still a resident of Georgia as well." Underlying the court's reasoning was evidence that the father owned real estate in Georgia, was registered to vote there, held a Georgia driver's license, was paid as a Georgia resident, and paid Georgia state taxes.

We agree that, for UCCJEA purposes, the term "presently reside" does not equal "technical domicile." The reference to "technical" domicile suggests that "presently reside" means something other than meeting the technical requirements of domicile for specific purposes, including, for example, the obligation to pay state taxes. Instead, "presently reside" necessitates a broader inquiry into the totality of the circumstances that make up domicile — that is, a person's permanent home to which he or she intends to return to and remain. *Black's Law Dictionary* at 558 (9th ed. 2009).

Residency provisions contained in other Colorado statutes provide guidance for what factors should be considered in making the totality of the circumstances determination. . . . While those statutes do not specifically address the term "presently reside" in section 14-13-202(1)(b), which itself contains no definition, we conclude that factors to be weighed in making the residency determination under section 14-13-202(1)(b) and -203(1)(b), a mixed question of fact and law, include but are not limited to the length and reasons for the parents' and the child's absence from the issuing state; their intent in departing from the state and returning to it; reserve and active military assignments affecting one or both parents; where they maintain a home, car, driver's license, job, professional licensure, and voting registration; where they pay state taxes; the issuing state's determination of residency based on the facts and the issuing state's law; and any other circumstances demonstrated by evidence in the case.

The statutory language of sections 14-13-202(1)(b) and -203(1)(b) is clear that, before a new state can divest the issuing state of jurisdiction, the new state must "*determine[ ]* that the child, the child's parents, and any person acting as a parent *do not presently reside*" in the issuing state. (Emphasis added). This statutory requirement for determination is consistent with the UCCJEA's emphasis on the primacy of exclusive continuing jurisdiction as a means to ensure the stability of custody orders and to discourage parental kidnapping. To hold that the term "presently reside" means only physical presence would undercut the actual statutory language and purpose that centers on exclusive continuing jurisdiction remaining in the issuing state unless that jurisdiction has been clearly divested, enabling the new state to assume jurisdiction.

In addition, such a construction of the statute would allow Parent A to move out of the issuing state with the child, establish a new home state for the child, and engage in a "race to the courthouse" by simply filing a petition for the new state to assume jurisdiction as soon as Parent B leaves the issuing state to physically live elsewhere for any length of time. Under this construction, the issuing state would lose jurisdiction if Parent B were temporarily out-of-state on vacation, in a hospital, or on military assignment. . . .

In the case before us, residency is a hotly contested issue. Christine Brandt alleges that she has constantly maintained a home, driver's license, nursing license, and voting registration in Maryland and pays Maryland state taxes. Indeed, under both federal and Colorado law, she cannot gain or lose residence for purposes of taxation and voting registration by virtue of her service in the armed forces. Moreover, she received her orders to transfer back to Maryland on April 26, ten days *before* George Brandt filed the May 6 Petition. At that point, she contends, her return to Maryland was not just a matter of her intention; it was certain to occur.

The portion of the May 25 Order divesting Maryland of jurisdiction reads, in its entirety, as follows: "the Court finds that neither the child nor the child's parents currently reside in Maryland and the child has resided in Colorado for more than a year before the filing of the petition. As a result, this Court assumes jurisdiction for purposes of modifying the Maryland child-custody determination."

While George Brandt argues that he and the child have significant contacts with Colorado, it is clear that the district court did not have the benefit of the legal test we articulate in this opinion. Its order assuming jurisdiction to modify Maryland's custody decree cannot stand because that order appears to be based solely on Christine Brandt being out of Maryland on military assignment. . . .

. . . On remand, as the petitioning party, George Brandt bears the burden of proving that Maryland has lost exclusive continuing jurisdiction and that Colorado may assume it. If the facts are still in dispute, the district court should afford the parties an opportunity to present additional evidence and argument in light of our decision, and engage in additional consultation with the Maryland court regarding the factual and legal issues concerning Maryland residency and the Maryland court's jurisdiction. . . .

NOTES AND QUESTIONS

1. As we have seen, in determining whether a state has home state jurisdiction for an initial order, most courts' interpretations tend to send the case back to the state from which a child came if a parent remains there. Do the same arguments support expansive findings on the issue of whether a parent still "resides" in the issuing state for purposes of determining whether that state has lost jurisdiction to modify? Would a test that looked exclusively to where the parent maintained a physical residence be more or less favorable to a parent who wanted the court to find that the issuing state had not lost jurisdiction? How about a test based on the parent's intent? The parent's phsyical presence? Do "living" and "residing" mean the same thing? Can a person have more than one residence? *See* Kevin Wessel, Comment, Home Is Where the Court Is: Determining Residence for Child Custody Matters Under the UCCJEA, 70 U. Chi. L. Rev. 1141 (2012).

2. Even if a child or parent still resides in the issuing state, a court in that state may find that it no longer has continuing jurisdiction because the case no longer has a significant connection with the state and because substantial evidence is no longer available in the state. UCCJEA § 202. Section 203 complements this section, providing that a court may not modify a child custody determination made by a court of another state unless the court in the state determines it no longer has exclusive, continuing jurisdiction. The meaning of this provision is typically contested when the children moved away from the original state some time ago and return infrequently for visits, if at all. The fundamental question is whether the "significant connection" provision should be interpreted broadly, which favors retention of jurisdiction in the issuing state, or narrowly. What policies support a broad interpretation? A narrow one? For discussion, *see, e.g.,* In re Forlenza, 140 S.W.3d 373 (Tex. 2004).

3. Recall that, for purposes of initial jurisdiction, if no state has home state jurisdiction, the next choice is a state with a "significant connection" to the case and in which "substantial evidence is available concerning the child's care, protection, training, and personal relationships." UCCJEA § 201(a)(2). Should interpretations of this language from initial jurisdiction cases be used when the issue is continuing jurisdiction, and vice versa?

4. The UCCJA allowed the "significant connnection" issue to be litigated in either the issuing state or the state that was asked to assume jurisdiction if the issuing state had lost it. The UCCJEA, as you see in *Brandt*, requires the question to be determined by the issuing state. What is the significance of the change?

5. A court that validly asserts initial jurisdiction or jurisdiction to modify has discretion to decline to exercise it on the ground that a court in another state would be a more convenient forum. UCCJEA § 207. In deciding whether to grant a

motion to decline jurisdiction on the basis of *forum non conveniens*, the court should consider

a) Whether domestic violence has occurred and is likely to continue in the future and which state could best protect the parties and the child;

b) The length of time that the child has resided outside this state;

c) The distance between the court in this state and the court in the state that would assume jurisdiction;

d) The relative financial circumstances of the parties;

e) Any agreement of the parties as to which state should assume jurisdiction;

f) The nature and location of the evidence required to resolve the pending litigation, including testimony of the child;

g) The ability of the court of each state to decide the issue expeditiously and the procedures necessary to present the evidence; and

h) The familiarity of the court of each state with the facts and issues in the pending litigation.

6. UCCJEA Section 208 says that a court with initial or modifying jurisdiction shall decline to exercise that authority on the basis that the petitioner "has engaged in unjustifiable conduct" unless the parties agree to the court's exercise of jurisdiction, the court with jurisdiction determines that the state is a more appropriate forum, or no other state has jurisdiction. The commentary to the UCCJEA section notes,

> Most of the jurisdictional problems generated by abducting parents should be solved by the prioritization of home State in Section 201; the exclusive, continuing jurisdiction provisions of Section 202; and the ban on modification in Section 203. . . . Nonetheless, there are still a number of cases where parents, or their surrogates, act in a reprehensible manner, such as removing, secreting, retaining, or restraining the child. This section ensures that abducting parents will not receive an advantage for their unjustifiable conduct. If the conduct that creates the jurisdiction is unjustified, courts must decline to exercise jurisdiction that is inappropriately invoked by one of the parties.

7. If a court learns that another custody proceeding regarding the child is ongoing, UCCJEA Section 206 provides that the court may not exercise its jurisdiction if the other court's assumption of jurisdiction is "substantially in conformity with this Act, unless the proceedings has been terminated or is stayed by the court or the other State because a court of this State is a more convenient forum under Section 207."

8. Several sections of the UCCJEA provide that a court may find that it lacks jurisdiction or that it will not exercise jurisdiction on the assumption that a court in another state will have and will take jurisdiction. The sections presuppose a high degree of cooperation among courts in the various states, and the Act includes several sections that facilitate this cooperation. First, the parties must state under oath in its first pleading "the child's present address or whereabouts, the places where the child has lived during the last five years, and the names and present addresses of the persons with whom the child has lived during that period." Each

party must also provide information about prior custody proceedings affecting the child and whether anyone not already named has physical custody of the child or claims rights to legal custody of the child. UCCJEA § 209(a). Courts may communicate with each other and ask that courts in other states take testimony and hold hearings, forward the records to the state in which litigation is occurring, order custody evaluations, and forward records. UCCJEA §§ 110-112. Judges from different states are encouraged to confer with each other before deciding whether to accept jurisdiction in particular cases.

9. Custody orders from foreign countries are to be treated like orders from other states if they were made "under factual circumstances in substantial conformity with the jurisdictional standards of the Act." UCCJEA § 105. UCCJEA Section 104 is a similar provision that applies to custody determinations made by Native American tribal courts. The Indian Child Welfare Act (ICWA) provides for tribal court jurisdiction in child welfare and adoption cases and requires state recognition of tribal decrees. However, it does not apply to custody disputes at divorce. 25 U.S.C. §§ 1903, 1911(d). The ICWA is considered in Chapter 14.

10. The same legislation that created the PKPA provides that the federal Parent Locator Service, established to facilitate interstate child support enforcement, may also be used to search for people who have taken children in violation of custody decrees in some circumstances. 42 U.S.C. § 663. The PKPA also amended the Federal Fugitive Felony Act, 18 U.S.C. § 1073, to allow its use in cases of parent child snatching. The act had previously been interpreted to exclude these cases. The effect is to allow FBI involvement in cases of interstate child snatching if a state statute makes parental kidnapping a felony.

NOTE: DOMESTIC VIOLENCE CASES AND THE UCCJEA

A number of interstate custody cases involve claims that a custodial parent, almost always a mother, left the state in which she, the father and the children were living to escape domestic violence. This asserted circumstance may affect determinations under the UCCJEA, particularly the application of the home state preference and the *forum non conveniens* analysis.

In one of the best-known examples, Stoneman v. Drollinger, 64 P.3d 997 (Mont. 2003), the mother obtained several domestic abuse restraining orders against the father in Montana, but he repeatedly violated them. The parties were divorced in Montana in 1998, and the mother then moved to Washington. The Montana trial court ordered her to return the children to Montana every other weekend for unsupervised visits with their father, despite the recommendations of a GAL that unsupervised visits not be allowed; the Montana Supreme Court reversed, holding that it was an abuse of discretion to order unsupervised visitation. The mother then moved the Montana court to decline to exercise its continuing jurisdiction over custody on the basis that Washington was a more convenient forum. The trial court denied her motion, and the Montana Supreme Court again reversed. It explained,

> The UCCJEA places domestic violence at the top of the list of factors that courts are required to evaluate when determining whether to decline jurisdiction as an

inconvenient forum for child custody proceedings. Since domestic violence was not raised by the now-repealed UCCJA as a factor for court consideration, the NCCUSL, which drafted the UCCJEA, offered the following guidance to assist courts in applying this factor:

> For this purpose, the court should determine whether the parties are located in different States because one party is a victim of domestic violence or child abuse. If domestic violence or child abuse has occurred, this factor authorizes the court to consider which State can best protect the victim from further violence or abuse.

9 U.L.A. 683. The NCCUSL explicitly recognized that past abuse or a continuing threat of violence might compel a battered spouse or parent of an abused child to relocate to another state. The NCCUSL further directed courts to proceed with an evaluation of which forum can provide the greater safety whenever domestic violence or child abuse has occurred. . . .

Given the high propensity for recidivism in domestic violence, we hold that when a court finds intimate partner violence or abuse of a child has occurred or that a party has fled Montana to avoid further violence or abuse, the court is authorized to consider whether the party and the child might be better protected if further custody proceedings were held in another state. While this factor alone is not dispositive under § 40-7-108, MCA, we urge district courts to give priority to the safety of victims of domestic violence when considering jurisdictional issues under the UCCJEA.

The court held that the trial court abused its discretion when it failed to consider which forum could better protect the mother and children, given the well-documented history of domestic violence in the case. *See also* Foster v. Foster, 664 S.E.2d 525 (Va. App. 2008) (trial court did not abuse discretion in declining to make inconvenient forum finding despite evidence of domestic violence); Huege v. Huege, 2013 WL 2286102 (Ariz. App. 2013) (upholding inconvenient forum finding where mother testified that she would not have a safe place to stay if required to return to Arizona to litigate custody).

New York courts have held that when a parent takes a child from the forum to escape domestic violence, the general rule that a wrongful removal is treated as a temporary absence for purposes of the home state analysis does not apply. Felty v. Felty, 882 N.Y.S.2d 504 (App. Div. 2009).

PROBLEMS

1. Mona and Frank, an unmarried couple, had a child, Cynthia, while they were living in State X. When Cynthia was three months old, Mona left Frank and moved to State Y, where Mona's mother lived. After she left him, Mona refused to let Frank visit Cynthia. Frank sued Mona in State X, seeking custody or visitation. Mona moved to dismiss, alleging that State X lacked jurisdiction under the UCCJEA. How should the court rule and why?

2. Mary and Fred lived with their two children in State A. They were divorced three years ago and were awarded joint physical and legal custody. Two years ago Mary took the children and left the state without telling Fred. She moved to State B and obtained an order granting her full legal and physical custody of the children. To obtain the order she falsely said that she did not know where Fred was, and he

was served only by publication in a small newspaper in State *B*. Eight months ago Mary and the children moved to State *C*. Fred recently found Mary and the children in State *C*, and he has brought the State *A* custody order to a State *C* court, asking the State *C* court to recognize the State *A* order and modify it to give him full custody. Mary has asked the State *C* court to enforce the State *B* order and argues that State *C* does not have jurisdiction to hear the motion to modify. Fred continues to live in State *A*. Under the UCCJEA, must the court in State *C* enforce either of the prior orders? May it take jurisdiction to decide the motion to modify custody?

3. Harold and Wanda lived in State *A* with their daughter, Connie. When Connie was two years old, a court in State *A* granted Wanda a divorce and awarded her custody of Connie. Harold moved to State *B* shortly after the divorce, where he still lives. Wanda and Connie moved to State *C* four months ago. Wanda sent Connie to visit Harold in State *B* for two weeks, and he has refused to return her. Wanda went to State *B* and registered the custody order, asking State *B* to enforce it. Harold counterclaimed, asking the State *B* court to modify the order to give him custody. Wanda moved the court to dismiss the counterclaim, alleging that State *B* lacks jurisdiction to modify the order. How should the court rule and why?

4. Travis and Rachel were divorced in State *A*; the divorce decree awarded custody to Travis, with visitation to Rachel. Shortly thereafter, Travis, the children, and Travis's mother Dorothy, who lived with them, moved to State *B*. Four years later Dorothy, believing that Travis was abusing the children, left home with the children over his objection and moved across town. Dorothy then filed a motion in State *B*, seeking sole custody of the children. Rachel was served but did not enter an appearance. Travis moved to dismiss, arguing that under the UCCJEA State *B* does not have jurisdiction. How should the court rule and why?

If instead Dorothy had returned to State *A* and asked the court to find that it had no jurisdiction or that it should decline to exercise its jurisdiction, what arguments should she make? How should the court rule? (Assume again that Rachel is served but does not appear.)

3. *Adoption Jurisdiction*

The UCCJEA applies to cases of neglect, abuse, dependency, wardship, guardianship, termination of parental rights, and protection from domestic violence. UCCJEA § 102(4). It does not apply to adoption cases but instead defers to the Uniform Adoption Act (UAA). UCCJEA § 103. The jurisdictional provisions of the UAA are fundamentally consistent with those of the UCCJEA and the PKPA, but they are modified to fit the adoption context. UAA Section 3-101(a)(1) includes "prospective adoptive parents" among those people whose relationship with a child may give rise to a basis for jurisdiction. The following alternative criteria for asserting jurisdiction over an adoption matter are provided by Sections 3-101(a)(1)–(c)(2):

> (a) (1) immediately before commencement of the proceeding, the minor lived in this State with a parent, a guardian, a prospective adoptive parent, or another person acting as parent, for at least six consecutive months, excluding periods of temporary

absence, or, in the case of a minor under six months of age, lived in this State from soon after birth with any of those individuals and there is available in this State substantial evidence concerning the minor's present or future care;

(2) immediately before commencement of the proceeding, the prospective adoptive parent lived in this State for at least six consecutive months, excluding periods of temporary absence, and there is available in this State substantial evidence concerning the minor's present or future care;

(3) the agency that placed the minor for adoption is located in this State and it is in the best interest of the minor that a court of this State assume jurisdiction because:

(i) the minor and the minor's parents, or the minor and the prospective adoptive parent, have a significant connection with this State; and

(ii) there is available in this State substantial evidence concerning the minor's present or future care;

(4) the minor and the prospective adoptive parent are physically present in this State and the minor has been abandoned or it is necessary in an emergency to protect the minor because the minor has been subjected to or threatened with mistreatment or abuse or is otherwise neglected; or

(5) it appears that no other State would have jurisdiction under prerequisites substantially in accordance with paragraphs (1) through (4), or another State has declined to exercise jurisdiction on the ground that this State is the more appropriate forum to hear a petition for adoption of the minor, and it is in the best interest of the minor that a court of this State assume jurisdiction.

(b) A court of this State may not exercise jurisdiction over a proceeding for adoption of a minor if at the time the petition for adoption is filed a proceeding concerning the custody or adoption of the minor is pending in a court of another State exercising jurisdiction substantially in conformity with [the UCCJA] or this [act] unless the proceeding is stayed by the court of the other State.

(c) If a court of another State has issued a decree or order concerning the custody of a minor who may be the subject of a proceeding for adoption in this State, a court of this State may not exercise jurisdiction over a proceeding for adoption of the minor unless:

(1) the court of this State finds that the court of the State which issued the decree or order:

(i) does not have continuing jurisdiction to modify the decree or order under jurisdictional prerequisites substantially in accordance with [the Uniform Child Custody Jurisdiction Act] or has declined to assume jurisdiction to modify the decree or order; or

(ii) does not have jurisdiction over a proceeding for adoption substantially in conformity with subsection (a)(1) through (4) or has declined to assume jurisdiction over a proceeding for adoption; and

(2) the court of this State has jurisdiction over the proceeding.

In several termination of parental rights cases parents have argued minimum-contacts jurisdiction is necessary for these proceedings, with mixed results. Cases that require minimum contacts include In the Interest of Doe, 926 P.2d 1290, 1296 (Haw. 1996); Matter of Laurie R., 760 P.2d 1295, 1297 (N.M. App. 1988); In re Trueman, 99 S.E.2d 569, 570 (N.C. App. 1990). Other courts have found that the "status exception" based on May v. Anderson, above, applies to terminations. J.D. v. Tuscaloosa County Dep't of Human Resources, 923 So. 2d 303 (Ala. App. 2005); S.B. v. State, 61 P.3d 6 (Alaska 2002); Matter of Interest of M.L.K.,

768 P.2d 316, 319 (Kan. App. 1989); Div. Youth & Fam. Serv. v. M.Y.J.P., 823 A.2d 817 (N.J. Super. A.D. 2003); In re Williams, 563 S.E.2d 202, 205 (N.C. App. 2002); In re Adoption of Copeland, 43 S.W.3d 483, 487 (Tenn. App. 2000); In the Interest of M.S.B., 611 S.W.2d 704, 706 (Tex. App. 1980); State ex rel. W.A., 63 P.3d 100 (Utah 2002); In re Thomas J.R., 663 N.W.2d 734 (Wis. 2003); In re R.W., 39 A.3d 682 (Vt. 2011).

In addition, under some circumstances interstate adoptions are subject to the requirements of the Interstate Compact on the Placement of Children, which has been adopted in all U.S. jurisdictions except New Jersey, the District of Columbia, and Puerto Rico. The Compact applies to interstate placements of children for foster care or "preliminary to a possible adoption" except for placements of children made by their parents, stepparents, grandparents, adult brothers, sisters, uncles, aunts, or guardians. Interstate Compact Art. III, VIII(a). The Compact requires that interstate placements be coordinated through public authorities. A revised version of the Compact, which will, among other changes, apply to some placements by parents, will go into effect as soon as 35 states have adopted it. More information is available at http://icpc.aphsa.org/Home/home_news.asp.

4. International Enforcement of Custodial Rights

Child abduction is an international problem as well. The Hague Convention on the Civil Aspects of International Child Abduction is an international treaty intended to solve these problems. The Convention does not grant or withhold jurisdiction to determine custody disputes. Jurisdiction continues to be determined by state law, therefore. However, the Convention limits the application of state law because it requires that children wrongfully removed from the country of their "habitual residence" be returned to that country. If the Convention applies, the responding country is supposed to order return of the child without addressing the merits of the custody dispute and without making value judgments about the culture of and conditions in the child's country of habitual residence. The following case considers the meaning of some of the core provisions of the Convention.

MOZES v. MOZES

239 F.3d 1067 (9th Cir. 2001)

KOZINSKI, Circuit Judge. . . . Arnon and Michal Mozes are Israeli citizens. Married in 1982, they have four children, ranging in age from seven to sixteen years. Until 1997, parents and children lived in Israel, as they had their entire lives. In April 1997, with Arnon's consent, Michal and the children came to Los Angeles. Michal had long wanted to live in the United States, and both parents agreed that the children would profit from a chance to attend school here, learn English and partake of American culture. Accordingly, Michal moved with the children to Beverly Hills, where she leased a home, purchased automobiles and enrolled the children in school. Arnon remained in Israel, but he paid for both the house and the automobiles used by his family, and stayed with them at the house during his visits to Los Angeles. The parties agree that Arnon consented to have Michal and the children remain in the United States for fifteen months, though they disagree as to what understanding existed beyond that. What we know for certain is that on April 17, 1998, a year after they arrived in the United States, Michal filed an action in the Los Angeles County Superior Court seeking dissolution of the marriage and custody of the children. The court granted temporary custody to Michal, and entered a temporary restraining order enjoining Arnon from removing the children from southern California. Less than a month later, Arnon filed a petition in federal district court, seeking to have the children returned to Israel under the Hague Convention. The oldest child elected to return to Israel, and did so by mutual agreement of the parents. Arnon now appeals the district court's denial of his petition with regard to the three younger children.

Adopted in 1980, the Hague Convention on the Civil Aspects of International Child Abduction ["Convention"] is intended to prevent "the use of force to establish artificial jurisdictional links on an international level, with a view to obtaining custody of a child." Despite the image conjured by words like "abduction" and "force," the Convention was not drafted in response to any concern about violent kidnappings by strangers. It was aimed, rather, at the "unilateral removal or retention of children by parents, guardians or close family members. Such an abductor "rarely seeks material gain; rather, he or she will aspire to the exercise of sole care and control over a son or daughter in a new jurisdiction." . . .

The Convention seeks to deter those who would undertake such abductions by eliminating their primary motivation for doing so. Since the goal of the abductor generally is "to obtain a right of custody from the authorities of the country to which the child has been taken," the signatories to the Convention have agreed to "deprive his actions of any practical or juridical consequences." To this end, when a child who was habitually residing in one signatory state is wrongfully removed to, or retained in, another, Article 12 provides that the latter state "shall order the return of the child forthwith." Further, Article 16 provides that "until it has been determined that the child is not to be returned under this Convention," the judicial or administrative authorities of a signatory state "shall not decide on the merits of rights of custody."

The key operative concept of the Convention is that of "wrongful" removal or retention. In order for a removal or retention to trigger a state's obligations under the Convention, it must satisfy the requirements of Article 3:

The removal or the retention of a child is to be considered wrongful where—

a) it is in breach of rights of custody attributed to a person, an institution or any other body, either jointly or alone, under the law of the State in which the child was habitually resident immediately before the removal or retention; and

b) at the time of removal or retention those rights were actually exercised, either jointly or alone, or would have been so exercised but for the removal or retention.

Convention, art. 3, 19 I.L.M. at 1501. A court applying this provision must therefore answer a series of four questions: (1) When did the removal or retention at issue take place? (2) Immediately prior to the removal or retention, in which state was the child habitually resident? (3) Did the removal or retention breach the rights of custody attributed to the petitioner under the law of the habitual residence? (4) Was the petitioner exercising those rights at the time of the removal or retention?

. . . The district court denied Arnon's petition based on its answer to the second question: It found that as of that date, the children's "habitual residence" was in the United States, not Israel. Our central task is to review this finding, which we do immediately below. . . .

. . . [W]e are mindful that Congress has emphasized "the need for uniform international interpretation of the Convention." 42 U.S.C. § 11601(b)(3)(B). The Perez-Vera Report describes "habitual residence" as "a well-established concept in the Hague Conference, which regards it as a question of pure fact, differing in that respect from domicile." In seeking to understand this "well-established concept," we discover that although the term "habitual residence" appears throughout the various Hague Conventions, none of them defines it. As one commentary explains, "this has been a matter of deliberate policy, the aim being to leave the notion free from technical rules which can produce rigidity and inconsistencies as between different legal systems." . . .

Perhaps the most straightforward way to determine someone's habitual residence would be to observe his behavior. . . . Under this approach, we might say that if we observe someone centering his life around a particular location during a given period, so that every time he goes away from it he also comes back, we will call this his habitual residence.

This approach, while intuitively appealing, suffers from a fatal flaw: It may yield strikingly different results depending on the observer's time frame. . . . The absence of an objective temporal baseline however, requires that we pay close attention to subjective intent when evaluating someone's habitual residence. . . .

. . . [T]he first step toward acquiring a new habitual residence is forming a settled intention to abandon the one left behind. . . .

Having concluded that a settled intention to abandon one's prior habitual residence is a crucial part of acquiring a new one, we confront an additional problem: Whose settled intention determines whether a *child* has abandoned a prior habitual residence? One obvious response would be, the child's. It is, after all, the child whose habitual residence we are out to determine. And indeed we sometimes find courts declaring the intentions of the parents to be irrelevant. There is an obvious problem with this approach, however. Children, particularly the ones whose return may be ordered under the Convention, normally lack the material and psychological wherewithal to decide where they will reside. This leads to the conclusion that, "in those cases where intention or purpose is relevant — for example, where it is necessary to decide whether an absence is intended to be temporary and short-term — the intention or purpose which has to be taken into account is that of the person or persons entitled to fix the place of the child's residence."

Difficulty arises, of course, when the persons entitled to fix the child's residence no longer agree on where it has been fixed — a situation that, for obvious reasons, is likely to arise in cases under the Convention. In these cases, the representations of the parties cannot be accepted at face value, and courts must determine from all available evidence whether the parent petitioning for return of a child has already agreed to the child's taking up habitual residence where it is. The factual circumstances in which this question arises are diverse, but we can divide the cases into three broad categories.

On one side are cases where the court finds that the family as a unit has manifested a settled purpose to change habitual residence, despite the fact that one parent may have had qualms about the move. Most commonly, this occurs when both parents and the child translocate together under circumstances suggesting that they intend to make their home in the new country. When courts find that a family has jointly taken all the steps associated with abandoning habitual residence in one country to take it up in another, they are generally unwilling to let one parent's alleged reservations about the move stand in the way of finding a shared and settled purpose.

On the other side are cases where the child's initial translocation from an established habitual residence was clearly intended to be of a specific, delimited period. In these cases, courts have generally refused to find that the changed intentions of one parent led to an alteration in the child's habitual residence.

In between are cases where the petitioning parent had earlier consented to let the child stay abroad for some period of ambiguous duration. Sometimes the circumstances surrounding the child's stay are such that, despite the lack of perfect consensus, the court finds the parents to have shared a settled mutual intent that the stay last indefinitely. When this is the case, we can reasonably infer a mutual abandonment of the child's prior habitual residence. Other times, however, circumstances are such that, even though the exact length of the stay was left open to negotiation, the court is able to find no settled mutual intent from which such abandonment can be inferred. . . .

While the decision to alter a child's habitual residence depends on the settled intention of the parents, they cannot accomplish this transformation by wishful thinking alone. First, it requires an actual "change in geography." Second, home isn't built in a day. It requires the passage of "[a]n appreciable period of time," one that is "sufficient for acclimatization." When the child moves to a new country accompanied by both parents, who take steps to set up a regular household together, the period need not be long. On the other hand, when circumstances are such as to hinder acclimatization, even a lengthy period spent in this manner may not suffice.

A more difficult question is when evidence of acclimatization should suffice to establish a child's habitual residence, despite uncertain or contrary parental intent. Most agree that, given enough time and positive experience, a child's life may become so firmly embedded in the new country as to make it habitually resident even though there be lingering parental intentions to the contrary. The question is how readily courts should reach the conclusion that this has occurred. . . .

The Convention is designed to prevent child abduction by reducing the incentive of the would-be abductor to seek unilateral custody over a child in another country. The greater the ease with which habitual residence may be shifted without the consent of both parents, the greater the incentive to try. The question whether a child is in some sense "settled" in its new environment is so vague as to allow findings of habitual residence based on virtually any indication that the child has generally adjusted to life there. Further, attempting to make the standard more rigorous might actually make matters worse, as it could open children to harmful manipulation when one parent seeks to foster residential attachments during what was intended to be a temporary visit — such as having the child profess allegiance to the new sovereign. The function of a court applying the Convention is not to determine whether a child is happy where it currently is, but whether one parent is seeking unilaterally to alter the status quo with regard to the primary locus of the child's life. . . .

Recognizing the importance of parental intent, some courts have gone off in the other direction, announcing a bright line rule that "where both parents have equal rights of custody no unilateral action by one of them can change the habitual residence of the children, save by the agreement or acquiescence over time of the other parent. . . ." While this rule certainly furthers the policy of discouraging child abductions, it has been criticized as needing to be "carefully qualified if it [is] not to lead to absurd results." The point is well taken: Habitual residence is intended to be a description of a factual state of affairs, and a child *can* lose its habitual attachment to a place even without a parent's consent. Even when there is no settled intent on the part of the parents to abandon the child's prior habitual residence, courts should find a change in habitual residence if "the objective facts point unequivocally to a person's ordinary or habitual residence being in a particular place." The question in these cases is not simply whether the child's life in the new country shows some minimal "degree of settled purpose," but whether we can say with confidence that the child's relative attachments to the two countries have changed to the point where requiring return to the original forum would now be tantamount to taking the child "out of the family and social environment in which its life has developed."

[Because the trial court applied a different standard for determining habitual residence than the one set out in this opinion, the court remanded to allow a decision under the correct standard.]

Given the need to resolve these regrettably prolonged proceedings as expeditiously as possible, judicial economy counsels that we address certain issues the district court may confront on remand. Should the district court, after considering our discussion of the applicable principles, reaffirm its holding that the children's habitual residence had shifted to the United States by April 17, 1998, the case should end there. If, on the other hand, the district court decides that the facts do not warrant such a finding, it will have to resolve a series of additional questions. The first of these is whether the retention breached rights of custody attributed to Arnon under Israeli law. Only if this is the case is the retention wrongful under Article 3 of the Convention.

Article 14 of the Convention provides that we may take direct judicial notice of the law of the habitual residence in order to answer this question. The applicable Israeli law, in turn, states that "[i]n any matter within the scope of their guardianship the parents shall act in agreement." By seeking sole custody over the children outside their state of habitual residence, then, Michal "disregarded the rights of the other parent which are also protected by law, and . . . interfered with their normal exercise." Nor is there any doubt that Arnon was exercising his parental rights and responsibilities up until the time Michal sought custody. As the district court noted, he had remained in regular contact with his family, visited them several times, and "provided all finances needed to support his wife and children in

California." This means that if the children's habitual residence was still in Israel on April 17, 1998, their retention here would be wrongful under the Convention, and the United States would be required under Article 12 to order their return forthwith so that an Israeli court may consider the question of custody.

Article 13 of the Convention, however, provides certain exceptions to the duty to return a wrongfully retained child to its state of habitual residence. Because the district court decided that there was no wrongful retention under Article 3, it had no occasion to examine whether any of these exceptions were applicable. Unlike Article 3, which restricts a court's inquiry to the state of affairs prevailing immediately prior to the retention or removal alleged to be wrongful, two of the exceptions in Article 13 — namely, the risk of physical or psychological harm and objection by a mature child to its return — depend on circumstances at the time a child's return is to be ordered. Should the district court find a wrongful retention to have occurred, it must make a prompt determination as to whether either of these exceptions is applicable and, if not, order the return of the children to Israel forthwith.

REVERSED and REMANDED.

NOTES AND QUESTIONS

1. What test for "habitual residence" does *Mozes* adopt? Most circuits use the *Mozes* approach to determine where a child is habitually resident. However, the Sixth Circuit uses a different test; the habitual residence is the nation where, at the time of their removal, the child has been present long enough to allow acclimatization, and where this presence has a "degree of settled purpose from the child's perspective." Robert v. Tesson, 507 F.3d 981, 993 (6th Cir. 2007). How would you describe the difference in the two tests? Would the tests result in different conclusions on the facts of *Mozes*?

2. Article 12 creates an exception to the obligation to return a child who was wrongfully removed or retained. It applies only if the proceedings for return of the child were commenced more than one year after the wrongful removal or retention and grants the court discretion to deny the petition if the child is "well settled" in the new environment. How is this analysis different from consideration of whether the child has become "acclimatized" to the new environment, which bears on the finding of habitual residence? *See* Hoffman v. Sender, 716 F.3d 282, 294 n.5 (2d Cir. 2013) ("We note that the second prong of the [habitual residence] analysis seems to address the same concerns as the 'now-settled' defense found in Article 12 of the Hague Convention. Hypothetically, these ostensibly parallel analyses could allow for a finding that a child has become well settled in its new country before the one year time limit in Article 12 has elapsed."). In Lozano v. Montoya Álvarez, 134 S. Ct. 1224 (2014), the Supreme Court held that the one-year period in which the well-settled exception applies is not tolled even though the abductor conceals the child from the person entitled to custody. The unanimous Court concluded that tolling was inconsistent with the intent of the drafters of the Convention and that the well-settled provision allows a court to consider the child's interests.

3. A person is entitled to return of the child under the Hague Convention only if he or she was exercising rights of custody, an issue decided under the law of

the habitual residence. A parent who does not have custody but who has visitation rights is not entitled to the remedy of return of the child, but the Convention protects visitation rights without specifying a particular remedy. Hague Convention Arts. 12 and 21.

Sometimes a court couples an order granting custody or visitation with an order prohibiting a parent from taking the child out of the jurisdiction without the consent of the other parent or a court; the latter provision is called a *ne exeat* clause in international law. The Supreme Court held in Abbott v. Abbott, 560 U.S. 1 (2010), that a parent with visitation rights protected by a *ne exeat* clause has a form of joint custody for purposes of the Hague Convention. Therefore, if the child is taken from the country without that parent's permission, the parent may claim the return remedy under the Convention. Most foreign courts have held that a right to visitation protected by a *ne exeat* clause is a custody right under the Hague Convention. *Abbott*, 560 U.S. at 16.

4. As *Mozes* says, the Convention provides affirmative defenses to return of a child who has been wrongfully removed. The first, created by Article 13b, says that a child should not be returned if there is a grave risk of harm to the child. Hirst v. Tiberghien, 947 F. Supp. 2d 578, 595 (D.S.C. 2013), summarizes the courts' interpretation of this clause:

> Some courts have held that demonstrating grave risk requires a showing that the child would be returned to an environment in which the child would experience war, famine or disease, or that there exists the serious threat of abuse where the court in the country of habitual residence could not protect the child. *See Friedrich II*, 78 F.3d at 1060. Other cases have held that a respondent must establish by clear and convincing evidence a pattern of sexual or physical abuse of child or parent in order to invoke the Article 13(b) grave risk exception. *See, e.g.*, Danaipour v. McLarey, 386 F.3d 289 (1st Cir. 2004). The Third Circuit Court of Appeals has held the grave risk exception applies only if the respondent shows "that the alleged physical or psychological harm is a great deal more than minimal [and] something more than would normally be expected on taking a child away from one parent and passing him to another." Baxter v. Baxter, 423 F.3d 363, 373 n.8 (3d Cir. 2005). All courts agree that an Article 13(b) defense "may not be used as a vehicle to litigate (or relitigate) the child's best interests." Danaipour v. McLarey, 286 F.3d 1, 14 (1st Cir. 2002) (quoting Hague International Child Abduction Convention: Text and Legal Analysis, 51 F.R. 10,494, 10,510 (Dep't of State Mar. 26, 1986)).

> In *Miller*, the Fourth Circuit held that the grave risk exception was not applicable where the "courts in the abducted-from country are as ready and able as we are to protect children." The court further stated:

>> If return to a country, or to the custody of a parent in that country, is dangerous, we can expect that country's courts to respond accordingly. . . . When we trust the court system in the abducted-from country, the vast majority of claims of harm — those that do not rise to the level of gravity required by the Convention — evaporate.

> *Miller*, 240 F.3d at 402 (quoting *Friedrich*, 78 F.3d at 1068).

In addition, a state may also refuse to return the child if doing so would contravene "fundamental principles . . . relating to the protection of human rights and fundamental freedoms." Art. 20. For analyses of this provision and how it relates to "grave risk," *see* Merle Weiner, Strengthening Article 20, 38 U.S.F. L. Rev. 701 (2004); Merle Weiner, Using Article 20, 38 Fam. L.Q. 583 (2004).

5. Another affirmative defense arising under Article 13 of the Hague Convention, the child's objection clause, allows a court to consider the objection of a child of sufficient age and maturity to being returned to the country of habitual residence. American courts rarely refuse to order return based on the child's objection alone, however. For a discussion of the clause, *see* Anastacia M. Green, Seen and Not Heard?: Children's Objections Under the Hague Convention on International Child Abduction, 13 U. Miami Int'l & Comp. L. Rev. 105 (2005).

6. The final affirmative defense is that the person seeking the child's return consented or acquiesced in the child's removal to the jurisdiction where he or she is alleged to be wrongfully held. Art. 13(b). *See* Darín v. Olivero-Huffman, 746 F.3d 1 (1st Cir, 2014); Mota v. Castillo, 692 F.3d 108 (2d Cir. 2012) (conditional consent does not bar return if condition does not occur); Hoffman v. Sender, 716 F.3d 282 (2d Cir. 2013) (same); Nicholson v. Pappalaardo, 605 F.3d 100 (1st Cir. 2010) (applying law to close facts).

7. In 2013 the State Department reported that it had closed 487 cases initiated by people in other countries seeking the return of children in the United States and 1250 cases initiated by people in the United States seeking children in other countries. For both groups, by far the largest number of cases involved Mexican residents. U.S. Dep't of State, Bureau of Consular Affairs, 2013 Outgoing and Incoming Case Closings. In the same year, 702 cases of alleged abduction of children from the United States and 364 alleging abduction to the United States were reported. U.S. Dep't of State, Bureau of Consular Affairs, CY 2013 New Reported Outgoing Cases, New Reported Incoming Cases. These cases are from countries that have not acceded to the Hague Convention as well as those that have. The reports are available at http://travel.state.gov/content/childabduction/english/legal/compliance/statistics.html.

8. If a Hague claim is raised in state court litigation regarding the child's custody, a federal court is expressly barred from relitigating the issue. 42 U.S.C. §11603(g). What, though, if the Hague claim is not raised in the state court? Should a parent be barred by principles of *res judicata* or principles of abstention from later seeking return of the child in federal court? In Holder v. Holder, 305 F.3d 854 (9th Cir. 2002), the Ninth Circuit held that *res judicata* should not be applied to bar the federal court litigation, saying that to apply preclusion would undermine the purposes of the Hague Convention. Further, the court said, the issues in a Hague petition are not substantially similar to the issues in state custody litigation, even though there might be some overlap between the Hague "habitual residence" and the state court "home state" issues.

Article 16 of the Hague Convention provides that if a Hague proceeding is pending, other proceedings regarding the child's custody should be stayed until the Hague issue is resolved. Thus, if the issue is raised in federal court, state court proceedings should be stayed. However, the petitioner may choose to raise the Hague issue in state court; in such a situation, any federal proceeding should be stayed. Yang v. Tsui, 416 F.3d 199 (3d Cir. 2005). *See also* Mozes v. Mozes, 239 F.3d 1067 (9th Cir. 2001); Silverman v. Silverman, 338 F.3d 886 (8th Cir. 2003).

9. Removing a child from the United States or retaining a child who has been in the United States outside the United States with intent to obstruct the lawful

exercise of parental rights is a federal felony punishable by up to three years in prison. 18 U.S.C. §1204, enacted as Pub. L. No. 103-173 §2(a), Dec. 2, 1993. The statute creates three affirmative defenses: (1) the defendant had been granted custody or visitation by a court acting pursuant to the UCCJA; (2) the defendant was fleeing from an incident or pattern of domestic violence; and (3) the defendant had physical custody consistent with a custody order and failed to return the child because of circumstances beyond the defendant's control, provided that the defendant made reasonable attempts to notify the other parent or lawful custodian within 24 hours after the visitation period had expired. *Id.*

NOTE: THE HAGUE CONVENTION AND DOMESTIC VIOLENCE

Contrary to some expectations, many, perhaps most, international abductors of children are mothers, and many of the relationships that these mothers left were marked by domestic violence. Geoffrey L. Freig & Rebecca L. Hega, When Parents Kidnap 18-19 (1993); Lord Chancellor's Dep't, Child Abduction Unit, Report on the Third Meeting of the Special Commission to Discuss the Operation of the Hague Convention on the Civil Aspects of International Child Abduction, Apr. 8, 1997, at 1.

The Sixth Circuit in Simcox v. Simcox, 511 F.3d 594 (6th Cir. 2007), discussed how to analyze a claim that domestic violence directed toward the abducting parent constitutes a grave risk of physical or psychological injury to the children so that return is not required:

[W]e believe that Hague Convention cases dealing with abusive situations can be placed into three broad categories. First, there are cases in which the abuse is relatively minor. In such cases it is unlikely that the risk of harm caused by return of the child will rise to the level of a "grave risk" or otherwise place the child in an "intolerable situation" under Article 13b. In these cases, undertakings designed to protect the child are largely irrelevant; since the Article 13b threshold has not been met, the court has no discretion to refuse to order return, with or without undertakings. Second, at the other end of the spectrum, there are cases in which the risk of harm is clearly grave, such as where there is credible evidence of sexual abuse, other similarly grave physical or psychological abuse, death threats, or serious neglect. See, e.g., *Van De Sande*, 431 F.3d at 571; *Walsh*, 221 F.3d at 220 (both rejecting undertakings in the face of such evidence). In these cases, undertakings will likely be insufficient to ameliorate the risk of harm, given the difficulty of enforcement and the likelihood that a serially abusive petitioner will not be deterred by a foreign court's orders. Consequently, unless "the rendering court [can] satisfy itself that the children will in fact, and not just in legal theory, be protected if returned to their abuser's custody," the court should refuse to grant the petition. Third, there are those cases that fall somewhere in the middle, where the abuse is substantially more than minor, but is less obviously intolerable. Whether, in these cases, the return of the child would subject it to a "grave risk" of harm or otherwise place it in an "intolerable situation" is a fact-intensive inquiry that depends on careful consideration of several factors, including the nature and frequency of the abuse, the likelihood of its recurrence, and whether there are any enforceable undertakings that would sufficiently ameliorate the risk of harm to the child caused by its return. Even in this middle category, undertakings should be adopted only where the court satisfies itself that the parties are likely to obey them. Thus, undertakings would be particularly inappropriate, for example, in cases where the petitioner has a history of ignoring court orders. Where a grave risk of harm has been established, ordering return with feckless undertakings is worse than not ordering it at all. . . .

511 F.3d at 607-608.

An analysis of published judicial opinions in 47 cases in which a claim of domestic violence was raised found that a respondent successfully raised a defense in only 18 cases. In 22 cases the petition was denied or dismissed, in 20 cases the children were returned to the country of habitual residence, and 5 cases were remanded to the lower court with an unknown outcome. In 3 cases domestic violence was successfully used to support the claim that children were not habitual residents of the petitioners' country because the petitioner coerced the mother into remaining in the country. Grave risk was argued in 80 percent of the cases but was successful in only a quarter of them; in almost all the successful cases the court found evidence of child maltreatment. In 10 of the 12 successful grave risk cases the court found that the child(ren) witnessed domestic violence between the parents, and in the same number of successful cases experts testified that a child might suffer if returned to the habitual residence. In 8 of the 12 successful grave risk cases, the child had a diagnosis of PTSD. Typically, a parent needed to have multiple factors to have a successful grave risk claim, and in no case was proof of battering alone sufficient. Most of the cases (35) were from federal courts. In the cases in which the fathers' citizenship was identified, most (32 of 40) were not U.S. citizens, and the mothers usually were U.S. citizens (25 of 39 cases). William M. Vesneski, Taryn Lindhorst & Jeffrey L. Edleson, U.S. Judicial Implementation of the Hague Convention in Cases Alleging Domestic Violence, 62 Juv. & Fam. Ct. J. 1 (2011).

F. FEDERAL COURT JURISDICTION OVER DOMESTIC RELATIONS

ANKENBRANDT V. RICHARDS

504 U.S. 689 (1992)

WHITE, J. . . . Petitioner Carol Ankenbrandt, a citizen of Missouri, brought this lawsuit on September 26, 1989, on behalf of her daughters L. R. and S. R. against respondents Jon A. Richards and Debra Kesler, citizens of Louisiana, in the United States District Court for the Eastern District of Louisiana. Alleging federal jurisdiction based on the diversity of citizenship provision of § 1332, Ankenbrandt's complaint sought monetary damages for alleged sexual and physical abuse of the children committed by Richards and Kesler. Richards is the divorced father of the children and Kesler his female companion. On December 10, 1990, the District Court granted respondents' motion to dismiss this lawsuit. Citing In re Burrus, 136 U.S. 586, 593-594 (1890), for the proposition that "[t]he whole subject of the domestic relations of husband and wife, parent and child, belongs to the laws of the States and not to the laws of the United States," the court concluded that this case fell within what has become known as the "domestic relations" exception to diversity jurisdiction, and that it lacked jurisdiction over the case. . . .

We granted certiorari limited to the following questions: (1) Is there a domestic relations exception to federal jurisdiction? (2) If so, does it permit a district court to abstain from exercising diversity jurisdiction over a tort action for damages? . . .

The domestic relations exception upon which the courts below relied to decline jurisdiction has been invoked often by the lower federal courts. The seeming authority for doing so originally stemmed from the announcement in Barber v. Barber, 21 How. 582 (1859), that the federal courts have no jurisdiction over suits for divorce or the allowance of alimony. In that case, the Court heard a suit in equity brought by a wife (by her next friend) in federal district court pursuant to diversity jurisdiction against her former husband. She sought to enforce a decree from a New York state court, which had granted a divorce and awarded her alimony. The former husband thereupon moved to Wisconsin to place himself beyond the New York courts' jurisdiction so that the divorce decree there could not be enforced against him; he then sued for divorce in a Wisconsin court, representing to that court that his wife had abandoned him and failing to disclose the existence of the New York decree. In a suit brought by the former wife in Wisconsin Federal District Court, the former husband alleged that the court lacked jurisdiction. The court accepted jurisdiction and gave judgment for the divorced wife.

On appeal, it was argued that the District Court lacked jurisdiction on two grounds: first, that there was no diversity of citizenship because although divorced, the wife's citizenship necessarily remained that of her former husband; and second, that the whole subject of divorce and alimony, including a suit to enforce an alimony decree, was exclusively ecclesiastical at the time of the adoption of the Constitution and that the Constitution therefore placed the whole subject of divorce and alimony beyond the jurisdiction of the United States courts. Over the dissent of three Justices, the Court rejected both arguments. After an exhaustive survey of the authorities, the Court concluded that a divorced wife could acquire a citizenship separate from that of her former husband and that a suit to enforce an alimony decree rested within the federal courts' equity jurisdiction. . . . [T]he Court also announced the following limitation on federal jurisdiction:

> Our first remark is — and we wish it to be remembered — that this is not a suit asking the court for the allowance of alimony. That has been done by a court of competent jurisdiction. The court in Wisconsin was asked to interfere to prevent that decree from being defeated by fraud.
>
> We disclaim altogether any jurisdiction in the courts of the United States upon the subject of divorce, or for the allowance of alimony, either as an original proceeding in chancery or as an incident to divorce a vinculo, or to one from bed and board. . . .

The statements disclaiming jurisdiction over divorce and alimony decree suits, though technically dicta, formed the basis for excluding "domestic relations" cases from the jurisdiction of the lower federal courts, a jurisdictional limitation those courts have recognized ever since. . . .

Counsel argued in *Barber* that the Constitution prohibited federal courts from exercising jurisdiction over domestic relations cases. An examination of Article III, *Barber* itself, and our cases since *Barber* makes clear that the Constitution does not exclude domestic relations cases from the jurisdiction otherwise granted by statute to the federal courts. . . .

Subsequent decisions confirm that *Barber* was not relying on constitutional limits in justifying the exception. . . .

The Judiciary Act of 1789 provided that "the circuit courts shall have original cognizance, concurrent with the courts of the several States, *of all suits of a civil nature at common law or in equity, where the matter in dispute exceeds*, exclusive of costs, the sum or value of *five hundred dollars*, and . . . an alien is a party, or the suit is *between a citizen of the State where the suit is brought, and a citizen of another State.*" Act of Sept. 24, 1789, § 11,1 Stat. 73, 78. (Emphasis added.) The defining phrase, "all suits of a civil nature at common law or in equity," remained a key element of statutory provisions demarcating the terms of diversity jurisdiction until 1948, when Congress amended the diversity jurisdiction provision to eliminate this phrase and replace in its stead the term "all civil actions."

The *Barber* majority itself did not expressly refer to the diversity statute's use of the limitation on "suits of a civil nature at common law or in equity." The dissenters in *Barber*, however, implicitly made such a reference, for they suggested that the federal courts had no power over certain domestic relations actions because the court of chancery lacked authority to issue divorce and alimony decrees. . . .

We have no occasion here to join the historical debate over whether the English court of chancery had jurisdiction to handle certain domestic relations matters. . . . We thus are content to rest our conclusion that a domestic relations exception exists as a matter of statutory construction not on the accuracy of the historical justifications on which it was seemingly based, but rather on Congress's apparent acceptance of this construction of the diversity jurisdiction provisions in the years prior to 1948, when the statute limited jurisdiction to "suits of a civil nature at common law or in equity." . . . Considerations *of stare decisis* have particular strength in this context, where "the legislative power is implicated, and Congress remains free to alter what we have done." . . .

In the more than 100 years since this Court laid the seeds for the development of the domestic relations exception, the lower federal courts have applied it in a variety of circumstances. Many of these applications go well beyond the circumscribed situations posed by *Barber* and its progeny. *Barber* itself disclaimed federal jurisdiction over a narrow range of domestic relations issues involving the granting of a divorce and a decree of alimony, and stated the limits on federal-court power to intervene prior to the rendering of such orders:

> It is, that when a court of competent jurisdiction over the subject-matter and the parties decrees a divorce, and alimony to the wife as its incident, and is unable of itself to enforce the decree summarily upon the husband, that courts of equity will interfere to prevent the decree from being defeated by fraud. The interference, however, is limited to cases in which alimony has been decreed; then only to the extent of what is due, and always to cases in which no appeal is pending from the decree for the divorce or for alimony. Id., at 591.

The *Barber* Court thus did not intend to strip the federal courts of authority to hear cases arising from the domestic relations of persons unless they seek the granting or modification of a divorce or alimony decree. The holding of the case itself sanctioned the exercise of federal jurisdiction over the enforcement of an alimony decree that had been properly obtained in a state court of competent jurisdiction. . . .

Subsequently, this Court expanded the domestic relations exception to include decrees in child custody cases. . . .

Not only is our conclusion rooted in respect for this long-held understanding, it is also supported by sound policy considerations. Issuance of decrees of this type not infrequently involves retention of jurisdiction by the court and deployment of social workers to monitor compliance. As a matter of judicial economy, state courts are more eminently suited to work of this type than are federal courts, which lack the close association with state and local government organizations dedicated to handling issues that arise out of conflicts over divorce, alimony, and child custody decrees. Moreover, as a matter of judicial expertise, it makes far more sense to retain the rule that federal courts lack power to issue these types of decrees because of the special proficiency developed by state tribunals over the past century and a half in handling issues that arise in the granting of such decrees.

By concluding, as we do, that the domestic relations exception encompasses only cases involving the issuance of a divorce, alimony, or child custody decree, we necessarily find that the Court of Appeals erred by affirming the District Court's invocation of this exception. This lawsuit in no way seeks such a decree; rather, it alleges that respondents Richards and Kesler committed torts against L. R. and S. R., Ankenbrandt's children by Richards. Federal subject-matter jurisdiction pursuant to § 1332 thus is proper in this case. . . .

JUDITH RESNIK, *"NATURALLY" WITHOUT GENDER: WOMEN,*
JURISDICTION, AND THE FEDERAL COURTS

66 N.Y.U. L. Rev. 1682, 1742-1744, 1750-1757 (1991)

The assumption of lack of federal judicial power over personal relations has been eroded by litigation over the course of this century about reproduction and federal benefits, both of which structure relations "among different members of private families in their domestic intercourse." Further, that assertion ignored nineteenth century federal efforts to control polygamy and sexual relations, which in turn affect family relations, albeit nontraditional ones. In 1862, 1882, and 1887, Congress outlawed polygamy. Fragments of these laws still remain. While this legislation was directed at federal governance of the territories and was implemented by the federal courts in their capacity as "territorial courts" (thus acting as "state courts" for these purposes), other federal legislation did bring the federal courts into the governance of multiple marriages in the states. The "Mann Act" — involving federal regulation of sexual activity — was used in prosecutions of individuals who transported women in "interstate commerce." In one of the cases prosecuted under the Mann Act, the Court expressly endorsed

Congress's authority to "defeat what are deemed to be immoral practices; the fact that the means used may have the 'quality of police regulations' is not consequential." Despite a claim of noninvolvement in interpersonal relations (some of which might bear the title "family"), federal law and federal courts have, on selected occasions, taken on these issues. . . .

Pointing out links between federal law and families raises a question, traditional for federal courts scholars. While not discussed by federal courts jurisprudence, a complex mosaic of federal regulation of economic and social relations now overlays state laws on divorce, alimony, and child support. What is to be made of this fact of joint governance of the field? Because I hope scholars of federal courts will take seriously the topic of federal family law, it is appropriate to consider how doctrinal developments — shaped by different images of what is on the national agenda that federal courts implement and adjudicate — might take federal courts' authority over family life into account. The central question is what "business is the federal business," and it is time to answer this question by recognizing that there already is joint federal and state governance of an array of issues, from land use and torts to families. Once understood as a joint endeavor, the next issue is how to allocate authority.

A first possibility is that federal court involvement in family life is bad, per se, at a structural level. This claim takes seriously the arguments made in the many cases espousing (slight pun intended) state control over family life and fearing that the federal courts would become hopelessly "enmeshed" in family disputes. Under this vision, the states (and Indian tribes) as smaller units of government are closer to "the people" and thus a more appropriate level of government to determine matters affecting intimate life.

Possible justifications for this view exist. Contemporary invocations of the domestic relations exception discard arguments based on ecclesiastical authority, the alleged lack of jurisdictional diversity between married couples, and the claim that divorces lack monetary value — all in favor of a "modern view that state courts have historically decided these matters and have developed both a well-known expertise in these cases and a strong interest in disposing of them." . . . Holding aside the ever-present question of boundaries, doctrine might shift in a variety of ways when ideological claims about the relationship between federal courts and family are revised.

First, one could insist that, despite recognition of federal laws of the family, the claim of deference to state governance remains strong and, as a matter of doctrine, complete abstention (a form of reverse preemption) is desirable. To the extent recent federal law in bankruptcy, pensions, and benefits law points in the other direction, that erosion should be stopped — by legislation or judicial interpretation. But were one to really press this claim — that states are specially situated and should be controlling family life — one would not seek only to cabin the federal courts. This position would also require urging Congress and agencies to avoid defining families by rewriting statutes and regulations to incorporate state law, so as to permit state governance of interpersonal relations. An array of federal statutes would have to incorporate state definitions of families, and what would be lost in uniformity and national norms would be gained in recognition of the special relationship of states in defining family life. . . .

Yet a problem remains. The current hierarchy stipulates the federal courts as most powerful; the supremacy clause confirms that sense of authority. Further, federal courts theorists might affirmatively argue that federal courts are needed in this area — either because of their special capacity to protect the politically disfavored or because federal sovereign and administrative interests are at stake. While neither the appeal to the community envisioned by the claim of closeness of the state to the family nor the concern about attitudes and knowledge of federal judges should be discounted, the "inevitability of federal involvement" in family life remains, as does a sense that the rejection of that role by federal courts reconfirms the marginalization of women and families from national life.

Federal involvement emerges here, as it does in torts, land use, health regulation, criminal law, and other areas, because of the wealth of interactions that make the imagined coherence of the very categories "federal" and "state" themselves problematic. Whether looking at the problem from the top down, and seeing "joint governance" or considering the issue from the perspective of individuals and speaking of "membership in multiple communities," the point is the same: an interlocking, enmeshed regulatory structure covers the host of human activity in the United States. There is no a priori line one can invoke to separate legal regulation into two bounded boxes "state" and "federal." Uniform state laws demonstrate the limits of state court borders and the need for regulatory structures that bridge them. State and federal court interpretations of "family" are unavoidable.

NOTES AND QUESTIONS

1. As *Barber* and *Ankenbrandt* both make clear, and as Professor Resnik also emphasizes, the domestic relations exception does not preclude federal courts from hearing all cases involving family law issues. For example, the courts have held that tort suits based on interference with custody and visitation are not within the exception. *See, e.g.*, Drewes v. Ilnicki, 863 F.2d 469 (6th Cir. 1988); MacIntyre v. MacIntyre, 771 F.2d 1316 (9th Cir. 1985); Bennett v. Bennett, 682 F.2d 1039 (D.C. Cir. 1982). In Lannan v. Maul, 979 F.2d 627 (8th Cir. 1992), the court held that a child's suit to enforce a separation agreement term for her benefit was not within the exception either. However, framing a claim in terms of breach of contract or tort does not automatically mean that the domestic relations exception does not apply.

> The proper inquiry focuses on the type of determination the federal court must make in order to resolve the claim. If the federal court is called upon to decide those issues regularly decided in state court domestic relations actions such as divorce, alimony, child custody, or the support obligations of a spouse or parent, then the domestic relations exception is applicable.

Vaughan v. Smithson, 883 F.2d 63, 65 (10th Cir. 1989). In 2014 a federal district court described the division of authority over application of *Ankenbrandt* in just one circuit:

> The scope of the domestic relations exception has been the subject of conflicting interpretations in the Sixth Circuit. In Catz v. Chalker, 142 F.3d 279

(6th Cir. 1998), *overruled on other grounds as stated in* Coles v. Granville, 448 F.3d 853, 859 n.1 (6th Cir. 2006), a former husband brought civil rights actions against his former wife and her attorneys alleging that the procedures in the state divorce trial violated his due process rights. The Sixth Circuit narrowly construed *Ankenbrandt* as holding that the domestic relations exception applies "only where a plaintiff positively sues in federal court for divorce, alimony, or child custody." *Id.* at 292; *see also* Callahan v. Callahan, 247 F. Supp. 2d 935, 944 (S.D. Ohio 2002) (post-divorce action brought by ex-wife seeking to hold ex-husband in contempt of divorce decree due to his failure to transfer all of his interest in his ERISA pension plan to her was not an action specifically for divorce and domestic relations exception did not apply).

However, a year later, another panel of the Sixth Circuit took a broader view of the domestic relations exception in McLaughlin v. Cotner, 193 F.3d 410 (6th Cir. 1999). That case involved a former wife's claim for breach of a separation agreement for the sale of real estate. This agreement had been incorporated into the divorce decree, and was also the subject of a pending state court action. Plaintiff argued that the domestic relations exception did not apply because she was merely suing for breach of contract and tortious interference with contract. The court rejected this argument, noting that plaintiff was "attempting to disguise the true nature of the action by claiming that she is merely making a claim for damages based on a breach of contract." The court concluded that because the alleged contract was incorporated into the divorce decree, the case "involve[d] issues arising out of conflict over a divorce decree" and fell within the domestic relations exception. The court went on to hold that the federal court lacked jurisdiction, "as this case is not a tort or contract suit that merely has domestic relations overtones, but is one seeking a declaration of rights and obligations arising from marital status."

The Sixth Circuit in *McLaughlin* noted that the case before it was similar to Allen v. Allen, 518 F. Supp. 1234 (E.D. Pa. 1981), where, despite the pendency of divorce proceedings and other state court actions concerning the marital property at issue, the husband filed another state court action for breach of monetary obligations contained in a separation agreement, which the wife removed to federal court. Although the husband pleaded claims for breach of contract and fraud, the court in *Allen* noted that these claims and the pending state court actions "contain overlapping factual and legal matrices" with "a multiplicity of intertwined suits, the dominant theme of which is a dispute over the ownership of marital property." The *Allen* court also stated that the case before it was one in which "the parties are attempting to play one court system off against the other." The *Allen* court granted the husband's motions to dismiss and for remand, concluding that "this is a clear case for the application of the domestic relations exception." The *McLaughlin* court observed that a similar rationale applied to the case before it, as the property at issue was also the subject of a pending state court action.

The *McLaughlin* panel also cited with approval the Sixth Circuit's previous decision in *Firestone*. *Firestone* involved an action brought by the former Mrs. Firestone against her ex-husband and the trustee of his trust assets, alleging that Mr. Firestone failed to meet his support obligations under the divorce settlement, and seeking to compel him to use his trust income to meet his support obligations. The *Firestone* court held that the district court acted properly in declining jurisdiction. The *Firestone* court noted that none of the sums claimed had been reduced to judgment in the Florida state court, and that the district court would have to hear extensive evidence concerning the parties' needs and finances, and would have to interpret and apply the provisions of the divorce decree to determine what sums were due. While the *Firestone* case was pending, the Florida state court found that Mrs. Firestone was in contempt of the divorce decree and relieved

Mr. Firestone of his obligation to pay alimony. The *Firestone* court observed that any declaratory and injunctive relief compelling Cleveland Trust to pay Mr. Firestone's support obligations from trust income would have interfered with the pending state court proceedings and conflicted with the Florida contempt order.

In Chambers v. Michigan, the ex-wife filed an action for declaratory and injunctive relief against Michigan state officials, challenging the constitutionality of the state court's decision to consider certain assets and property in calculating the ex-husband's income, upon which the payment of alimony was based. Plaintiff requested that the state court be enjoined from using property she characterized as her "federally protected ERISA, marital and personal property" to determine the amount of alimony owed. Plaintiff argued that the domestic relations exception did not apply because she was not seeking a divorce, alimony, or child custody decree. The Sixth Circuit rejected this argument, concluding that because plaintiff's complaint revolved around a state court order involving alimony, jurisdiction was lacking under the domestic relations exception.

In United States v. MacPhail, 149 Fed. Appx. 449, 455-56 (6th Cir. 2005), the Sixth Circuit concluded that cross-claims filed by ex-spouses seeking to recover the amount of a refund erroneously paid to the husband by the Internal Revenue Service for the tax year immediately preceding the year their divorce decree became final fell within the domestic relations exception. The court noted that resolution of the indemnification cross-claims required allocation of the refund into some combination of separate or marital property in accordance with Ohio domestic relations law. *Id.* The court concluded that the "division of property as either separate or marital raises exactly the kind of 'delicate issue[ ]' that is more 'appropriate for the federal courts to leave . . . to the state courts.'" *Id.* at 456 (quoting Elk Grove Unified Sch. Dist. v. Newdow, 542 U.S. 1, 13 (2004)).

Chevalier v. Barnhart, 2014 WL 198494 (S.D. Ohio Jan. 15, 2014). How would you create the line between federal and non-federal jurisdiction? Or should the domestic relations exception simply be abandoned? In addition to Professor Resnik's analysis, *see* Naomi R. Cahn, Family Law, Federalism, and the Federal Courts, 79 Iowa L. Rev. 1073 (1994); Emily J. Sack, The Domestic Relations Exception, Domestic Violence, and Equal Access to Federal Courts, 84 Wash. U. L. Rev. 1441 (2006).

2. If the domestic relations exception is difficult to justify on a purely historical basis, why is it retained in *Ankenbrandt*? Is there any inconsistency between the result in *Ankenbrandt* and the arguably increased constitutional review of restrictions on marriage and the adoption of federal legislation governing child support and child custody awards?

3. In Marshall v. Marshall, 547 U.S. 293 (2006), the Supreme Court clarified the circumstances in which federal courts that would otherwise have jurisdiction must decline to exercise it under the "probate exception" to federal jurisdiction, a judicially created doctrine closely related to the domestic relations exception. In *Marshall* the scope of the exception determined whether a federal bankruptcy court could resolve a conflict between a bankrupt person, Anna Nicole Smith (whose real name was Vickie Lynn Marshall), and her creditor (Pierce Marshall, son of Anna Nicole's octogenarian deceased husband, J. Howard Marshall). J. Howard, who died after 14 months of marriage to the 1993 Playmate of the Year, left a will and trust that gave the entire estate to Pierce. Vickie asserted that he had intended to take care of her by amending the living trust, in fulfillment

of his promise to give her half his estate if she would marry him. J. Howard did not make these amendments, and a Texas probate court jury found that he had not made that promise to her. While the Texas probate was pending, Vickie, who was facing an unrelated tort judgment, filed for bankruptcy in California. Pierce Marshall filed a proof of claim in the bankruptcy proceeding stating that Vickie had defamed him by alleging he had engaged in forgery, fraud, and overreaching to gain control of his father's assets. He wanted a declaration that the claim was not dischargeable in bankruptcy. Vickie counterclaimed for tortious interference with an expectancy. The bankruptcy court granted Vickie summary judgment with regard to Pierce's claims against her and, after a trial on the merits, entered judgment for her on her counterclaim. Vickie promptly voluntarily dismissed her claims in the Texas probate proceeding. The bankruptcy court awarded her more than $449 million in compensatory damages and $25 million in punitive damages. Pierce appealed. When the case reached the Supreme Court, it interpreted the probate exception narrowly, as it had narrowed the domestic relations exception in *Ankenbrandt*. The Court said that the exception prevents federal courts only from taking jurisdiction over "the probate or annulment of a will and the administration of a decedent's estate" and from "endeavoring to dispose of property that is in the custody of a state probate court." 547 U.S. at 312. Because Vickie sought a tort judgment that would impose personal liability on Pierce, the Court said that the case was not within the probate exception to federal jurisdiction.

4. Since *Ankenbrandt* was decided, the Fourth, Fifth, and Ninth Circuits have held that the domestic relations exception does not apply when federal jurisdiction is based on a federal question rather than on diversity of the parties. United States v. Bailey, 115 F.3d 1222 (5th Cir. 1997); United States v. Johnson, 114 F.3d 476 (4th Cir. 1997); Atwood v. Fort Peck Tribal Court Assiniboine, 513 F.3d 943 (9th Cir. 2008). *See also* Elk Grove Unified School Dist. v. Newdow, 542 U.S. 1, 13 (2004) ("Thus, while rare instances arise in which it is necessary to answer a substantial federal question that transcends or exists apart from the family law issue, *see, e.g.,* Palmore v. Sidoti, 466 U.S. 429, 432-434 (1984), in general it is appropriate for the federal courts to leave delicate issues of domestic relations to the state courts."). *But see* Jones v. Brennan, 465 F.3d 304 (7th Cir. 2006) (probate exception to federal jurisdiction applies in federal question cases). For discussion of this issue, *see* Meredith Johnson Harbach, Is the Family a Federal Question?, 66 Wash. & Lee L. Rev. 131 (2009).

5. A party may also be barred from seeking relief in federal court if the relief sought is "unnecessary" or "inappropriate" because an adequate remedy exists within the state divorce proceedings, or if the federal claim is inconsistent with a claim asserted in the state court. For example, in Atwood v. Fort Peck Tribal Court Assiniboine and Sioux Tribes, above, the court dismissed Atwood's federal claim because he had failed to exhaust his remedies in tribal court. *See also* Mooney v. Mooney, 471 F.3d 246 (1st Cir. 2006) (federal district court properly abstained because plaintiff husband's claim in state court seeking modification of a divorce decree either made the requested federal relief unnecessary or was inconsistent with that relief, depending on interpretation of the claim).

6. In Thompson v. Thompson, 484 U.S. 174 (1988), the Supreme Court held that Congress did not intend to create an implied federal cause of action when it

enacted the PKPA. Had the court ruled to the contrary, the effect would have been to open the federal courts to litigation over the validity of conflicting custody orders from different states. In California v. Superior Court, 482 U.S. 400 (1987), Louisiana asked California to extradite a father and grandfather who were charged with kidnapping. The men took the father's children from Louisiana in violation of a Louisiana custody order. They argued, in effect, that Louisiana had not charged them with a crime because the Louisiana order violated the PKPA. The Supreme Court held, however, that in an extradition proceeding California could not inquire into the merits of a jurisdictional dispute.

CHILDREN, PARENTS, AND THE STATE

Determining Legal Parenthood: Marriage, Biology, and Function

13

As recently as the 1970s, about 90 percent of all children were born to married mothers. A married woman's husband was (and still is) presumed to be the father of her children, and blood tests then available were so primitive that they were unlikely to exclude a man as the biological father even if he were not. As a result, the legal father of most children was also the social father, the man who functioned as their father—their mother's husband. This man was usually also their biological father, but even when he was not, few people were likely to know for sure. Children born to unmarried mothers usually did not have a social father, but they also did not have legal fathers because paternity was rarely legally established. In these circumstances, the law simply did not need to choose between children's biological and social fathers for purposes of determining their legal fathers. For all practical purposes, social fathers were legal fathers.

Over the last 40 years, major advances in genetic testing, the development of an aggressive national child support program, and dramatic changes in adults' marriage, divorce, and cohabitation practices have shaken the traditional law of parent-child relationships to its foundations.

Today, many more parents with children divorce, and many more children are born outside marriage. In 2013, 5.25 million children lived with their divorced mothers, compared to 2.3 million in 1970, and 1.3 million lived with their divorced fathers in 2013, compared to 177,000 in 1970.[1] In 2011, 41 percent of all births in the United States were nonmarital.[2] Nonmarital childbearing, which used to be confined largely to the very poor, is becoming the norm for much of the middle

---

1. U.S. Bureau of the Census, Living Arrangements of Children Under 18 Years Old: 1960 to Present, Ch-1 through Ch-5 (2004). Internet release date: September 15, 2004; U.S. Bureau of the Census, Living Arrangements of Children Under 18 Years Old and Marital Status of Parents, 2008; U.S. Bureau of the Census, Living Arrangements of Children Under 18 Years Old: Table C-3 (2013).

2. Joyce A. Martin et al., Births: Final Data for 2011, Nat'l Vital Stat. Rep., June 28, 2013, at 3, 11, available at http://www.cdc.gov/nchs/data/nvsr/nvsr62/nvsr62_01.pdf.

class as well. In contrast, well-educated upper middle and middle class women rarely bear children outside marriage.[3] These class distinctions are also associated with racial and ethnic distinctions. In 2011, 17 percent of births to Asian/Pacific Islander mothers were nonmarital, compared to 29 percent to non-Hispanic white mothers, 53 percent to Hispanic mothers, 66 percent to American Indian/Alaska Native mothers, and 72 percent to non-Hispanic black mothers.[4] Unmarried parents on average are also younger and poorer than married parents.[5]

One consequence of these changes is that many more children spend portions of their lives living in households with a parent and the parent's partner, since single parents ordinarily do not remain single but enter new relationships. These new adults are not the children's biological parents but may function as parents.

At the same time, the rise in divorce and in nonmarital births has increased the occasions for questions about a child's biological paternity to arise. In the 1980s, the federal-state child support enforcement program began to emphasize identifying the fathers of nonmarital children as the first step in establishing and collecting child support. Between 1992 and 2012, paternity establishment increased from 516,000 to more than 1.2 million children per year.[6] One result is that many men today are identified as legal fathers and are required to support children with whom they may never have lived or developed a parent-child relationship.

Today, when someone becomes suspicious that a child's legal father may not be the biological father, whether that man is the mother's husband or a man to whom she was never married, genetic testing can readily resolve the question. By the 1990s, the science of genetic testing had advanced to the point that in most cases a test can not only exclude a man falsely identified as the biological father but can also positively identify a biological father to near-certainty. Home paternity testing kits, which may not even require a sample from the mother, are readily available.

---

3. *See* Sara McLanahan, Fragile Families and Children's Opportunities (CRCW & Fragile Families Publ'n Collection, Working Paper No. WP12-21-FF, 2012), available at http://crcw.princeton.edu/workingpapers/WP12-21-FF.pdf; *see also* Andrew J. Cherlin, American Marriage in the Early Twenty-First Century, Future of Child, Fall 2005, at 33, 37-38.

4. Martin et al., *supra* note 2, at 12. *See also* Gretchen Livingston & Kim Parker, Pew Research Ctr., A Tale of Two Fathers: More Are Active, but More Are Absent 1, 8 (2011), available at http://www.pewsocialtrends.org/files/2011/06/fathers-FINAL-report.pdf (finding that 37 percent of white fathers have at least one nonmarital child, and 77 percent have at least one marital child; 72 percent of black men have a nonmarital child, and 48 percent have one in marriage; 59 percent of Hispanic men have a nonmarital child, and 58 percent have one in marriage).

5. Child Trends, Births to Unmarried Women: Indicators on Children and Youth 2, 4 (2013), available at http://www.childtrends.org/wp-content/uploads/2012/11/75_Births_to_Unmarried_Women.pdf.

6. FY 1998 Annual Report — Appendix H: Fact Sheets and News Releases, Off. Child Support Enforcement (June 24, 1998), http://www.acf.hhs.gov/programs/css/resource/fy1998-annual-report-appendix-h; Child Support Enforcement FY 2012 Preliminary Report Tbl. P-31, Off. Child Support Enforcement (Aug. 15, 2013), http://www.acf.hhs.gov/programs/css/resource/fy2012-preliminary-report.

All these changes create complex issues of which adults should be regarded as children's legal parents, both for purposes of having rights of access to the children and duties to support them.

This chapter first examines the constitutional rights of those designated as legal parents in relationship to others who might play a parental role. The rest of the chapter explores the legal designation of parenthood, examining its relationship to marriage, biological ties, stepparent status, and same-sex partnership. It concludes with proposals to divide parental rights and responsibilities among more than two parents. Chapter 14 considers alternative means of establishing parental status, including adoption and assisted reproduction.

A.   THE CONSTITUTIONAL RIGHTS OF PARENTS

One way of approaching the definition of family is to ask what difference the definition makes. The issue in the following case is what degree of deference the Constitution guarantees for parental decision making. In reading the following case, consider how the Supreme Court's decision might affect the importance of who fits the definition of a legal parent and who does not in other cases. Consider as well how the definition of "parent" may affect the extent of constitutional protection afforded to "families."

TROXEL v. GRANVILLE

530 U.S. 57 (2000)

Justice O'CONNOR announced the judgment of the Court and delivered an opinion, in which THE CHIEF JUSTICE, Justice GINSBURG, and Justice BREYER join. . . . Tommie Granville and Brad Troxel shared a relationship that ended in June 1991. The two never married, but they had two daughters, Isabelle and Natalie. Jenifer and Gary Troxel are Brad's parents, and thus the paternal grandparents of Isabelle and Natalie. After Tommie and Brad separated in 1991, Brad lived with his parents and regularly brought his daughters to his parents' home for weekend visitation. Brad committed suicide in May 1993. Although the Troxels at first continued to see Isabelle and Natalie on a regular basis after their son's death, Tommie Granville informed the Troxels in October 1993 that she wished to limit their visitation with her daughters to one short visit per month.

In December 1993, the Troxels . . . [petitioned for visitation under Washington law]. Section 26.10.160(3) [of the Wash. Rev. Code] provides: "Any person may petition the court for visitation rights at any time including, but not limited to, custody proceedings. The court may order visitation rights for any person when visitation may serve the best interest of the child whether or not there has been any change of circumstances." . . . In 1995, the Superior Court issued an oral ruling and entered a visitation decree ordering visitation one weekend per month, one week during the summer, and four hours on both of the petitioning grandparents' birthdays.

Granville appealed, during which time she married Kelly Wynn. Before addressing the merits of Granville's appeal, the Washington Court of Appeals remanded the case to the Superior Court for entry of written findings of fact and conclusions of law. On remand, the Superior Court found that visitation was in Isabelle and Natalie's best interests. . . .

The Washington Supreme Court granted the Troxels' petition for review and, after consolidating their case with two other visitation cases, affirmed. . . .

The demographic changes of the past century make it difficult to speak of an average American family. The composition of families varies greatly from household to household. While many children may have two married parents and grandparents who visit regularly, many other children are raised in single-parent households. In 1996, children living with only one parent accounted for 28 percent of all children under age 18 in the United States. . . . Understandably, in these single-parent households, persons outside the nuclear family are called upon with increasing frequency to assist in the everyday tasks of child rearing. In many cases, grandparents play an important role. For example, in 1998, approximately 4 million children — or 5.6 percent of all children under age 18 — lived in the household of their grandparents.

The nationwide enactment of nonparental visitation statutes is assuredly due, in some part, to the States' recognition of these changing realities of the American family. Because grandparents and other relatives undertake duties of a parental nature in many households, States have sought to ensure the welfare of the children therein by protecting the relationships those children form with such third parties. The States' nonparental visitation statutes are further supported by a recognition, which varies from State to State, that children should have the opportunity to benefit from relationships with statutorily specified persons — for example, their grandparents. The extension of statutory rights in this area to persons other than a child's parents, however, comes with an obvious cost. For example, the State's recognition of an independent third-party interest in a child can place a substantial burden on the traditional parent-child relationship. Contrary to Justice Stevens' accusation, our description of state nonparental visitation statutes in these terms, of course, is not meant to suggest that "children are so much chattel." Rather, our terminology is intended to highlight the fact that these statutes can present questions of constitutional import. . . .

The liberty interest at issue in this case — the interest of parents in the care, custody, and control of their children — is perhaps the oldest of the fundamental liberty interests recognized by this Court. More than 75 years ago, in Meyer v. Nebraska, we held that the "liberty" protected by the Due Process Clause includes the right of parents to "establish a home and bring up children" and "to control the education of their own." Two years later, in Pierce v. Society of Sisters, we again held that the "liberty of parents and guardians" includes the right "to direct the upbringing and education of children under their control." We explained in Pierce that "[t]he child is not the mere creature of the State; those who nurture him and direct his destiny have the right, coupled with the high duty, to recognize and prepare him for additional obligations." We returned to the subject in Prince v. Massachusetts, and again confirmed that there is a constitutional dimension to the right of parents to direct the upbringing of their children. "It is cardinal with us that the custody, care and nurture of the child reside first in the parents, whose primary function and freedom include preparation for obligations the state can neither supply nor hinder."

Section 26.10.160(3), as applied to Granville and her family in this case, unconstitutionally infringes on that fundamental parental right. The Washington nonparental visitation statute is breathtakingly broad. According to the statute's text, "[a]ny person may petition the court for visitation rights *at any time*," and the court may grant such visitation rights whenever "visitation may serve *the best interest of the child*." § 26.10.160(3) (emphases added). That language effectively permits any third party seeking visitation to subject any decision by a parent concerning visitation of the parent's children to state-court review. Once the visitation petition has been filed in court and the matter is placed before a judge, a parent's decision that visitation would not be in the child's best interest is accorded no deference. Section 26.10.160(3) contains no requirement that a court accord the parent's decision any presumption of validity or any weight whatsoever. Instead, the Washington statute places the best-interest determination solely in the hands of the judge. Should the judge disagree with the parent's estimation of the child's best interests, the judge's view necessarily prevails. Thus, in practical effect, in the State of Washington a court can disregard and overturn any decision by a fit custodial parent concerning visitation whenever a third party affected by the decision files a visitation petition, based solely on the judge's determination of the child's best interests. The Washington Supreme Court had the opportunity to give § 26.10.160(3) a narrower reading, but it declined to do so. . . .

Turning to the facts of this case, the record reveals that the Superior Court's order was based on precisely the type of mere disagreement we have just described and nothing more. The Superior Court's order was not founded on any special factors that might justify the State's interference with Granville's fundamental right to make decisions concerning the rearing of her two daughters. To be sure, this case involves a visitation petition filed by grandparents soon after the death of their son — the father of Isabelle and Natalie — but the combination of several factors here compels our conclusion that § 26.10.160(3), as applied, exceeded the bounds of the Due Process Clause.

First, the Troxels did not allege, and no court has found, that Granville was an unfit parent. That aspect of the case is important, for there is a presumption that fit parents act in the best interests of their children. . . .

Accordingly, so long as a parent adequately cares for his or her children (i.e., is fit), there will normally be no reason for the State to inject itself into the private realm of the family to further question the ability of that parent to make the best decisions concerning the rearing of that parent's children.

The problem here is not that the Washington Superior Court intervened, but that when it did so, it gave no special weight at all to Granville's determination of her daughters' best interests. More importantly, it appears that the Superior Court applied exactly the opposite presumption. In reciting its oral ruling after the conclusion of closing arguments, the Superior Court judge explained:

"The burden is to show that it is in the best interest of the children to have some visitation and some quality time with their grandparents. I think in most situations a commonsensical approach [is that] it is normally in the best interest of the children to spend quality time with the grandparent, unless the grandparent, [sic] there are some issues or problems involved wherein the grandparents, their lifestyles are going to impact adversely upon the children. That certainly isn't the case here from what I can tell."

The judge's comments suggest that he presumed the grandparents' request should be granted unless the children would be "impact[ed] adversely." In effect, the judge placed on Granville, the fit custodial parent, the burden of disproving that visitation would be in the best interest of her daughters. The judge reiterated moments later: "I think [visitation with the Troxels] would be in the best interest of the children and I haven't been shown it is not in [the] best interest of the children."

The decisional framework employed by the Superior Court directly contravened the traditional presumption that a fit parent will act in the best interest of his or her child. In that respect, the court's presumption failed to provide any protection for Granville's fundamental constitutional right to make decisions concerning the rearing of her own daughters. . . . In an ideal world, parents might always seek to cultivate the bonds between grandparents and their grandchildren. Needless to say, however, our world is far from perfect, and in it the decision whether such an intergenerational relationship would be beneficial in any specific case is for the parent to make in the first instance. And, if a fit parent's decision of the kind at issue here becomes subject to judicial review, the court must accord at least some special weight to the parent's own determination.

Finally, we note that there is no allegation that Granville ever sought to cut off visitation entirely. Rather, the present dispute originated when Granville informed the Troxels that she would prefer to restrict their visitation with Isabelle and Natalie to one short visit per month and special holidays. In the Superior Court proceedings Granville did not oppose visitation but instead asked that the duration of any visitation order be shorter than that requested by the Troxels. . . .

Considered together with the Superior Court's reasons for awarding visitation to the Troxels, the combination of these factors demonstrates that the visitation order in this case was an unconstitutional infringement on Granville's fundamental right to make decisions concerning the care, custody, and control of her two daughters. The Washington Superior Court failed to accord the determination of Granville, a fit custodial parent, any material weight. . . . As we have explained, the Due Process Clause does not permit a State to infringe on the fundamental right of parents to make childrearing decisions simply because a state judge believes a "better" decision could be made. Neither the Washington nonparental visitation statute generally—which places no limits on either the persons who may petition for visitation or the circumstances in which such a petition may be granted—nor the Superior Court in this specific case required anything more. Accordingly, we hold that § 26.10.160(3), as applied in this case, is unconstitutional. . . .

Justice SOUTER, concurring in the judgment. I concur in the judgment affirming the decision of the Supreme Court of Washington, whose facial invalidation of its own state statute is consistent with this Court's prior cases addressing the substantive interests at stake. I would say no more. The issues that might well be presented by reviewing a decision addressing the specific application of the state statute by the trial court, are not before us and do not call for turning any fresh furrows in the "treacherous field" of substantive due process.

Justice THOMAS, concurring in the judgment. . . . I agree with the plurality that this Court's recognition of a fundamental right of parents to direct the upbringing of their children resolves this case. . . . I would apply strict scrutiny to infringements of fundamental rights. Here, the State of Washington lacks even a legitimate governmental interest—to say nothing of a compelling one—in second-guessing a fit parent's decision regarding visitation with third parties. On this basis, I would affirm the judgment below.

Justice STEVENS, dissenting. . . . In response to Tommie Granville's federal constitutional challenge, the State Supreme Court broadly held that Wash. Rev. Code § 26.10.160(3) (Supp. 1996) was invalid on its face under the Federal Constitution. Despite the nature of this judgment, Justice O'Connor would hold that the Washington visitation statute violated the Due Process Clause of the Fourteenth Amendment only as applied. I agree with Justice Souter that this approach is untenable.

We are . . . presented with the unconstrued terms of a state statute and a State Supreme Court opinion that, in my view, significantly misstates the effect of the Federal Constitution upon any construction of that statute. . . .

In my view, the State Supreme Court erred in its federal constitutional analysis because neither the provision granting "any person" the right to petition the court for visitation, nor the absence of a provision requiring a "threshold . . . finding of harm to the child," provides a sufficient basis for holding that the statute is invalid in all its applications. I believe that a facial challenge should fail whenever a statute has "a 'plainly legitimate sweep.'" Under the Washington statute, there are plainly any number of cases—indeed, one suspects, the most common to arise—in which the "person" among "any" seeking visitation is a once-custodial caregiver, an intimate relation, or even a genetic parent. Even the Court would seem to agree that in many circumstances, it would be constitutionally permissible for a court to award some visitation of a child to a parent or previous caregiver in cases of parental separation or divorce, cases of disputed custody, cases involving temporary foster care or guardianship, and so forth. As the statute plainly sweeps in a great deal of the permissible, the State Supreme Court majority incorrectly concluded that a statute authorizing "any person" to file a petition seeking visitation privileges would invariably run afoul of the Fourteenth Amendment.

The second key aspect of the Washington Supreme Court's holding—that the Federal Constitution requires a showing of actual or potential "harm" to the child before a court may order visitation continued over a parent's objections—finds no support in this Court's case law. While, as the Court recognizes, the Federal Constitution certainly protects the parent-child relationship from arbitrary impairment by the State, we have never held that the parent's liberty interest in this relationship is so inflexible as to establish a rigid constitutional shield, protecting every arbitrary parental decision from any challenge absent a threshold finding of harm. The presumption that parental decisions generally serve the best interests of their children is sound, and clearly in the normal case the parent's interest is paramount. But even a fit parent is capable of treating a child like a mere possession.

Cases like this do not present a bipolar struggle between the parents and the State over who has final authority to determine what is in a child's best interests. There is at a minimum a third individual, whose interests are implicated in every case to which the statute applies — the child. . . .

. . . A parent's rights with respect to her child have thus never been regarded as absolute, but rather are limited by the existence of an actual, developed relationship with a child, and are tied to the presence or absence of some embodiment of family. These limitations have arisen, not simply out of the definition of parenthood itself, but because of this Court's assumption that a parent's interests in a child must be balanced against the State's long-recognized interests as parens patriae, and, critically, the child's own complementary interest in preserving relationships that serve her welfare and protection. . . .

. . . [P]resumptions notwithstanding, we should recognize that there may be circumstances in which a child has a stronger interest at stake than mere protection from serious harm caused by the termination of visitation by a "person" other than a parent. The almost infinite variety of family relationships that pervade our ever-changing society strongly counsel against the creation by this Court of a constitutional rule that treats a biological parent's liberty interest in the care and supervision of her child as an isolated right that may be exercised arbitrarily. . . . It seems clear to me that the Due Process Clause of the Fourteenth Amendment leaves room for States to consider the impact on a child of possibly arbitrary parental decisions that neither serve nor are motivated by the best interests of the child.

Accordingly, I respectfully dissent.

Justice SCALIA, dissenting. In my view, a right of parents to direct the upbringing of their children is among the "unalienable Rights" with which the Declaration of Independence proclaims "all Men . . . are endowed by their Creator." And in my view that right is also among the "othe[r] [rights] retained by the people" which the Ninth Amendment says the Constitution's enumeration of rights "shall not be construed to deny or disparage." The Declaration of Independence, however, is not a legal prescription conferring powers upon the courts; and the Constitution's refusal to "deny or disparage" other rights is far removed from affirming any one of them, and even farther removed from authorizing judges to identify what they might be, and to enforce the judges' list against laws duly enacted by the people. Consequently, while I would think it entirely compatible with the commitment to representative democracy set forth in the founding documents to argue, in legislative chambers or in electoral campaigns, that the state has no power to interfere with parents' authority over the rearing of their children, I do not believe that the power which the Constitution confers upon me as a judge entitles me to deny legal effect to laws that (in my view) infringe upon what is (in my view) that unenumerated right. . . .

Judicial vindication of "parental rights" under a Constitution that does not even mention them requires (as Justice Kennedy's opinion rightly points out) not only a judicially crafted definition of parents, but also — unless, as no one believes, the parental rights are to be absolute — judicially approved assessments of "harm to the child" and judicially defined gradations of other persons (grandparents, extended family, adoptive family in an adoption later found to be invalid, long-term guardians, etc.) who may have some claim against the wishes of the parents. If we embrace this unenumerated right, I think it obvious — whether we affirm or reverse the judgment here . . . — that we will be ushering in a new regime of judicially prescribed, and federally prescribed, family law. . . .

Justice KENNEDY, dissenting. . . . The first flaw the State Supreme Court found in the statute is that it allows an award of visitation to a non-parent without a finding that harm to the child would result if visitation were withheld; and the second is that the statute allows any person to seek visitation at any time. In my view the first theory is too broad to be correct, as it appears to contemplate that the best interests of the child standard may not be applied in any visitation case. I acknowledge the distinct possibility that visitation cases may arise where, considering the absence of other protection for the parent under state laws and procedures, the best interests of the child standard would give insufficient protection to the parent's constitutional right to raise the child without undue intervention by the state; but it is quite a different matter to say, as I understand the Supreme Court of Washington to have said, that a harm to the child standard is required in every instance.

Given the error I see in the State Supreme Court's central conclusion that the best interests of the child standard is never appropriate in third-party visitation cases, that court should have the first opportunity to reconsider this case. I would remand the case to the state court for further proceedings. . . .

My principal concern is that the holding seems to proceed from the assumption that the parent or parents who resist visitation have always been the child's primary caregivers and that the third parties who seek visitation have no legitimate and established relationship with the child. That idea, in turn, appears influenced by the concept that the conventional nuclear family ought to establish the visitation standard for every domestic relations case. . . . As we all know, this is simply not the structure or prevailing condition in many households. For many boys and girls a traditional family with two or even one permanent and caring parent is simply not the reality of their childhood. This may be so whether their childhood has been marked by tragedy or filled with considerable happiness and fulfillment. . . .

NOTES AND QUESTIONS

1. Troxel v. Granville produced a fractured decision with a plurality opinion by Justice O'Connor in which three other Justices joined. What differences do you see among the Justices? Are there any principles that can be said to command a majority of the Court?

2. At the time that *Troxel* was decided, all 50 states had statutes that permitted grandparent visitation in at least some circumstances. The *Troxel* decision generated a wave of litigation, with some cases upholding and other cases invalidating the state statutes. Professor Sonya Garza surveyed state court responses to *Troxel* in 2009:

After *Troxel*, the majority of states waited for the challenges to visitation statutes to play out in court. Either through appellate court or supreme court decisions, twenty-one states found their third-party visitation statutes to be constitutional. Only six states found their third-party statutes facially unconstitutional. Nine states found their third-party statutes unconstitutional as applied, and fourteen states made no court determination regarding their third-party visitation statutes. Even in those instances where courts found third-party visitation statutes to be unconstitutional on their face, state legislatures did not always subsequently respond.

The variety among the individual third-party visitation statutes is even more apparent after *Troxel*. While most states limit third-party visitation to grandparents, many include great-grandparents, stepparents, siblings, and third parties who have a significant relationship with the child. For those states that permit third-party visitation, only some states define what is necessary to establish the significant or existing relationship required. Further, some states do not rely on third-party visitation statutes to award visitation; instead, they use the common law doctrines of de facto parenthood, in loco parentis, or psychological parenthood. In addition, even though part of the ultimate holding in *Troxel* articulated a longstanding constitutional presumption that a parent is fit and acts in a child's best interests, twenty-one states do not have such a presumption via statute or common law. Most statutes use a "best interests of the child" standard in third-party visitation cases, but only some states provide factors to be considered by the court, leaving the best interests standard open to interpretation by individual courts. In addition, only a few states require a showing of harm as discussed in *Troxel*.

Sonya C. Garza, The *Troxel* Aftermath: A Proposed Solution for State Courts and Legislatures, 69 La. L. Rev. 927, 940-942 (2009). *See also* George L. Blum, Grandparents' Visitation Rights Where Child's Parents Are Living, 71 A.L.R.5th 99 (1999 with weekly updates); George L. Blum, Grandparents' Visitation Rights Where Child's Parents Are Deceased, or Where Status of Parents Is Unspecified, 69 A.L.R.5th 1 (1999 with weekly updates); Wendy Evans Lehmann, Award of Custody of Child Where Contest Is Between Natural Parent and Stepparent, 10 A.L.R.4th 767 (1981 with weekly updates).

3. If third parties requesting visitation must overcome a presumption that the parent's decision is in the child's best interest, what kind of showing would they need to make? What kind of evidence would you advise the grandparents to develop in *Troxel? Compare* Harrold v. Collier, 836 N.E.2d 1165 (Ohio 2005), *cert. denied*, 547 U.S. 1004 (2006) (upholding visitation to grandparents after giving "special weight" to unmarried father's opposition in case where mother, who had been living with the 5-year-old and her own parents, died and father claimed that grandparents were undermining his relationship with the child), *and* Smith v. Wilson, 90 So. 3d 51 (Miss. 2012) (upholding grandparent visitation, noting that the Mississippi statute, in contrast with the Washington law at issue in *Troxel*, conferred standing to grandparents as a distinct class, and that in this case, the mother had died and father cut off all visitation with the mother's parents after they reported a bruise on the child to the authorities that had resulted from a spanking from the father), *with* In re R.L.S., 844 N.E.2d 22 (Ill. 2006), which concluded that grandparents, with whom the mother and child had been living at the time of the mother's death in an automobile accident, lacked standing to sue for custody unless they overcame the presumption that the father was willing and able to make

day-to-day childcare decisions. The court concluded that if the father, who had been living in another state, "is a fit person who is competent to transact his own business, he is entitled to custody."

4. The *Troxel* decision potentially affects not just the issue of grandparent visitation, but the question of whether the courts can recognize the interests of any nonparent over the parent's objection. *See* David D. Meyer, What Constitutional Law Can Learn from the ALI Principles of Family Dissolution, 2001 BYU L. Rev. 1075; Rebecca L. Scharf, Psychological Parentage, *Troxel*, and the Best Interests of the Child, 13 Geo. J. Gender & L. 615 (2012). The most contested applications involve stepparents and unmarried partners, which will be discussed later in the chapter.

PROBLEMS

1. Consider the facts of Painter v. Bannister on page 549. On the facts of that case, would the ruling pass constitutional muster under *Troxel*? Why or why not?

2. Kira and Terry, who have never married, have a daughter, Dakota. Kira and Terry broke up after Terry was arrested and sent to prison while Dakota was still less than a year old. Terry's mother, Brenda, helped take care of Dakota during the period immediately after Dakota's birth when Kira was suffering from post-partum depression, and she has remained close to Dakota ever since. Dakota is now 2. After one of her visits to Brenda's home, Dakota broke out in hives. Kira believes that Brenda was not sufficiently attentive to Dakota's lactose intolerance, and refuses to permit Dakota to stay at her grandmother's house, though she permits Brenda to visit Dakota at her house. Brenda, who states that Dakota did not receive milk products during the visit in which she broke out in hives, seeks a court order requiring visitation. She introduces evidence that she has had a close relationship with Dakota since her birth, that Kira's new husband has encouraged Kira to cut off visitation, and that numerous complaints have been filed about Kira's parenting skills with Social Services. What would be the result in a state that requires a showing of detriment to the child to award grandparent visitation? Parental unfitness? Extraordinary circumstances?

B. FATHERS' CUSTODIAL RIGHTS AND SUPPORT DUTIES

LESLIE JOAN HARRIS, *REFORMING PATERNITY LAW TO ELIMINATE GENDER, STATUS AND CLASS INEQUALITY*

2013 Mich. St. L. Rev. 1295, 1299-1302

From very early in English history, the law of paternity sharply distinguished between children born to married and unmarried women, strongly privileging father-child relationships within marriage. This pattern prevailed well into the twentieth century until the Supreme Court began using the Equal Protection Clause to dismantle the distinction. . . .

The husband of a married woman has long been presumed to be the father of her children, a presumption that at common law could be rebutted only by showing that the husband had been out of the kingdom of England for more than nine months.[7] This rule presumed the existence of a biological relationship between the legal father and child at a time when biological truth was often very uncertain, but it also excluded highly reliable evidence that no biological relationship existed (e.g., the mother's testimony), protecting the social relationship between a child and the functional father, as well as the integrity of the marriage. The marital presumption continues to be the law in all states, although in all states it is rebuttable, at least in some circumstances.

In contrast, at common law nonmarital children were bastards, the children of no one,[8] although by the early nineteenth century, these children were recognized as legally related to their mothers in most American states.[9] During the twentieth century, many states revised their laws, allowing nonmarital children to inherit from their fathers in some circumstances, but many states clung to the old rule that nonmarital children had no right to inherit from their fathers, to receive other financial benefits at the deaths of their fathers, or to be supported during their fathers' lives.[10] And in many states unmarried fathers had no legal right to custody or visitation.

This regime began to change in the late 1960s . . . as the Supreme Court started applying the Equal Protection Clause to state statutes that discriminated against nonmarital children and their parents. The first cases held that nonmarital children could not be denied the right to inherit from their parents and receive other death benefits in circumstances when marital children would inherit and receive benefits.[11] Another early case held that if parents of a child born in marriage could sue for the wrongful death of their child, this right had to be extended to nonmarital parents too.[12] In 1972, the Court first considered the custodial rights of

---

7. 1 William Blackstone, Commentaries on the Laws of England 457 (Thomas M. Cooley ed., 2d ed. 1872). Lord Mansfield's Rule, first articulated in 1777, prevented either spouse from giving testimony that casts doubt on the husband's biological paternity. Goodright v. Moss, (1777) 98 Eng. Rep. 1257 (K.B.) 1258; 2 Cowp. 591, 592-94.

8. Blackstone at 454, 459.

9. Michael Grossberg, Governing The Hearth: Law And The Family In Nineteenth-Century America 198-200, 207-15 (1985).

10. *See id.* at 228-33.

11. The Constitution does not bar all distinctions, but it does prohibit distinctions if there is no means by which a nonmarital child can become entitled to the rights of a child born in marriage. Levy v. Louisiana, 391 U.S. 68, 71-72 (1968) (statute limiting inheritance rights to legitimate children unconstitutional because it posed an insurmountable barrier to inheritance); Labine v. Vincent, 401 U.S. 532, 539-40 (1971) (statute denying nonmarital child right to inherit from father who had legitimated her violated equal protection); Weber v. Aetna Cas. & Sur. Co., 406 U.S. 164, 165, 175-76 (1972) (statute denying right of nonmarital children to receive worker's compensation benefits on death of their father violated equal protection); Trimble v. Gordon, 430 U.S. 762, 773-76 (1977) (state law denying nonmarital children right to inherit from father violated equal protection).

12. Glona v. Am. Guarantee & Liab. Ins. Co., 391 U.S. 73, 76 (1968).

nonmarital fathers, ruling in Stanley v. Illinois that a biological father who had lived with his children and their mother over a period of years and acted as a father was entitled to be recognized as the children's legal father in a custody matter.[13]

Today, some states have eliminated all *legal* differences based on parents' marital status. For example, § 202 of the 2002 Uniform Parentage Act provides: "A child born to parents who are not married to each other has the same rights under the law as a child born to parents who are married to each other."

However, legal distinctions continue to be made for some purposes in some jurisdictions, as you will see. In addition, even in states that have eliminated legal distinctions, marital and nonmarital children are still in significantly different positions as a matter of practicality. In all states a child born to a married woman is at least rebuttably presumed to be the child of her husband. This means that if no one challenges the presumption, the husband is the legal parent of the child. However, other processes are required to establish the paternity of children born to unmarried women. The first part of this section concerns procedures for establishing legal paternity. The second part examines the custodial and related rights of unmarried fathers, as well as their duties to support their children.

1. Establishing Paternity

Today, marriage is still the most common way that a child's legal father is determined, since about 60 percent of children are born to married women, whose husbands are presumed to be the fathers. In most cases, no one tries to rebut the presumption. Traditionally, and still in many states, if unmarried parents marry after their child's birth, the marital presumption also applies to that family. In addition, in many states the marital presumption covers children when the husband dies or the marriage is terminated during the pregnancy. For example, § 204(a)(2) of the 2002 Uniform Parentage Act extends the marital presumption to births within 300 days of a divorce or the husband's death.

At common law, the only way that an unmarried father's paternity could be legally established (if he and the mother did not marry) was through a quasi-criminal judicial proceeding called a bastardy action. Its limited purpose was to establish the father's responsibility to support the child when the child would otherwise become dependent on the people of the parish.[14] Today, the modern successor of the bastardy action, called a paternity suit or a filiation suit, is an option in all states, but other procedures are much more commonly used.

In at least 19 states a man who is not married to a child's mother may nevertheless be presumed to be the father when he has lived with and held out the child

---

13. 405 U.S. 645, 646, 658 (1972).

14. *See* R.H. Helmholz, Support Orders, Church Courts, and the Rule of Filius Nullius: A Reassessment of the Common Law, 63 Val. U. L. Rev. 431 (1977).

as his own.[15] These states are Alabama, California, Colorado, Delaware, Hawaii, Indiana, Massachusetts, Minnesota, Montana, Nevada, New Mexico, Oklahoma, North Dakota, New Hampshire, New Jersey, Pennsylvania, Texas, Washington, and Wyoming. For details on the statutes, *see* Leslie Joan Harris, above, 2013 Mich. St. L. Rev. at 1318-1319.

However, even these provisions are much less important than they might seem because all states, in compliance with federal law, have statutes that allow mothers and alleged fathers to file signed documents with the state identifying the man as a child's legal father. 42 U.S.C. §666(a)(5). Once filed, a voluntary acknowledgment of paternity (VAP) becomes final unless one of the parties rescinds it within 60 days, and it must be given the legal effect of a judicial determination of paternity. 42 U.S.C. §666 (a)(5)(D)(ii). After 60 days a VAP can be challenged only on the ground of fraud, duress, or material mistake of fact. *Id.* §666 (a)(5)(D)(ii). States may not require blood testing as a precondition to signing a VAP,[16] and they must give full faith and credit to VAPs signed in other states. *Id.* §666 (a)(5)(C)(iv).

VAPs have become easily the most common way to establish the legal parentage of unmarried fathers. In 2012, 1.6 million children were born outside marriage.[17] In the same year, paternity was established by a VAP for almost 1.2 million children, compared to 588,000 cases in which paternity was established by adjudicative processes.[18] VAPs are most commonly signed at the time of birth at the hospital or other birthing facility. The man's name can appear on the birth certificate only if a VAP has been filed, or a court or administrative agency has ruled that the man is the father. 42 U.S.C. §666 (a)(5)(D)(i). Recent sociological studies show that most unmarried parents are emotionally committed to each other and are living togther at birth and want to raise their child together; the high rate at which they sign VAPs at the time of birth reflects such attitudes. *See* Leslie Joan Harris, Voluntary Acknowledgments of Parentage for Same-Sex Couples, 20 Am. U. J. Gender Soc. Pol'y & L. 467, 476-478 (2012); Leslie Joan Harris, Questioning Child Support Enforcement Policy for Poor Families, 45 Fam. L.Q. 157, 166-171 (2011).

Paternity or filiation suits are usually brought as part of child support enforcement proceedings, which are by definition adversarial in form and very often are initiated because the mother and child are receiving public assistance. If a case is contested, the most important evidence, except in very unusual cases, is genetic testing evidence. State law must require that the results of a genetic test to establish paternity will be admitted into evidence if the test is "of a type generally

---

15. Sections 201 and 204 of the 2002 Uniform Parentage Act create such a presumption and require that the man have lived with the child during the first two years of the child's life.

16. 45 C.F.R. §302.70 (a)(5)(vii) (2009); Sherri Z. Heller, U.S. Dep't of Health and Human Servs., Policy Interpretation Question 03-01: Paternity Disestablishment (2003).

17. Joyce A. Martin et al., Nat'l Vital Stat. Sys., Births: Final Data for 2012 at 8 (2013).

18. Off. Child Support Enforcement, Child Support Enforcement FY 2012 Preliminary Report Fig. 3, (Aug. 15, 2013), http://www.acf.hhs.gov/programs/css/resource/fy2012-preliminary-report.

acknowledged as reliable by accreditation bodies designated by the Secretary [of HHS]" and performed by an accredited laboratory. 42 U.S.C. § 666(a)(5)(F). State law must create a rebuttable presumption, or at the option of the state, a conclusive presumption of paternity "upon genetic testing results indicating a threshold probability that the alleged father is the father of the child." 42 U.S.C. § 666(a)(5)(G).

Many paternity or filiation suits are resolved without genetic testing. In compliance with federal requirements, state laws allow paternity suits to be resolved by a default judgment, and, even if both parties appear, cases can be settled without genetic testing. Alleged fathers who believe that they are in fact biological fathers can be motivated by finances to forgo testing, since a state may recover the costs of testing from the man if paternity is established.

The complexity of paternity law creates many possibilities for uncertainty about the identity of a child's legal father. Consider, for example, the possibilities under the provisions of the Uniform Parentage Act, some of which are considered in the next case.

Uniform Parentage Act (2002)

Section 201. Establishment of Parent-Child Relationship

(b) The father-child relationship is established between a man and a child by:

(1) an unrebutted presumption of the man's paternity of the child under Section 204;

(2) an effective acknowledgment of paternity by the man under [Article] 3, unless the acknowledgment has been rescinded or successfully challenged;

(3) an adjudication of the man's paternity;

. . .

Section 204. Presumption of Paternity

(a) A man is presumed to be the father of a child if:

(1) he and the mother of the child are married to each other and the child is born during the marriage;

(2) he and the mother of the child were married to each other and the child is born within 300 days after the marriage is terminated by death, annulment, declaration of invalidity, or divorce[, or after a decree of separation];

(3) before the birth of the child, he and the mother of the child married each other in apparent compliance with law, even if the attempted marriage is or could be declared invalid, and the child is born during the invalid marriage or within 300 days after its termination by death, annulment, declaration of invalidity, or divorce[, or after a decree of separation];

(4) after the birth of the child, he and the mother of the child married each other in apparent compliance with law, whether or not the marriage is or could be declared invalid, and he voluntarily asserted his paternity of the child, and:

(A) the assertion is in a record filed with [state agency maintaining birth records];

(B) he agreed to be and is named as the child's father on the child's birth certificate; or

(C) he promised in a record to support the child as his own; or

(5) for the first two years of the child's life, he resided in the same household with the child and openly held out the child as his own.

Section 505. Genetic Testing Results; Rebuttal

(a) Under this [Act], a man is rebuttably identified as the father of a child if the genetic testing complies with this [article] and the results disclose that:

(1) the man has at least a 99 percent probability of paternity, using a prior probability of 0.50, as calculated by using the combined paternity index obtained in the testing; and

(2) a combined paternity index of at least 100 to 1.

(b) A man identified under subsection (a) as the father of the child may rebut the genetic testing results only by other genetic testing satisfying the requirements of this [article] which:

(1) excludes the man as a genetic father of the child; or

(2) identifies another man as the possible father of the child.

GREER EX REL. FARBO V. GREER

---

324 P.3d 310 (Kan. App. 2014)

ARNOLD-BURGER, J. . . . Jack and Dana married in 2009. After a time, the couple began to experience marital discord, and in August 2011 they separated. Dana moved in with her father, and Jack obtained a divorce attorney and filed for divorce in Missouri.

Shortly after the separation, Dana contacted her long-time acquaintance John and the two entered into a dating relationship. Although John discovered early in the relationship that Dana was married, Dana assured John that she and Jack planned on divorcing. As the relationship progressed, John and Dana discussed a variety of long-term plans, including living together as a family unit with Dana's daughter from a previous relationship. John moved from Illinois to Kansas during this time. But in February 2012, Jack and Dana reconciled, and Dana ended her relationship with John.

A few weeks later, in March 2012, Dana contacted John and informed him that she was pregnant. John assumed the child was his and informed Dana that he wished to be part of the child's life and help support the child financially.

The child, Emily, was born in October 2012. John discovered the fact of Emily's birth a few weeks later, as his contact with Dana during her pregnancy was inconsistent and Dana had not informed him of Emily's birth. In January 2013, John, Dana, and Emily underwent genetic testing that determined there was a 99.99% probability that Emily was in fact John's biological child. Based on the genetic testing, John filed a paternity suit in Franklin County to establish Emily's legal paternity. In his petition, he asked the court, pursuant to In re Marriage of Ross, 245 Kan. 591, 783 P.2d 331 (1989), "for a hearing to determine it is in the best interests of the minor child to determine paternity [and] to make a finding that petitioner is the natural father." In his proposed findings of fact, he enumerated the nonexclusive factors under *Ross* that the court should consider in deciding the case.

He proposed findings of fact which corresponded to the *Ross* factors. He proposed that the court conclude:

"Pursuant to the *Ross* case, the Court has determined it is in the best interests of the minor child for the evidence of the genetic testing in this case to be received into court, which establishes with a 99% certainty that the Petitioner is the biological father of the minor child, Emily Greer."

The district court scheduled a *Ross* hearing to determine Emily's best interests prior to establishing paternity.

The *Ross* hearing occurred on June 3, 2013. John, Dana, and Jack each testified. Although other relevant facts will be added as needed, a brief overview of the hearing is as follows:

John testified that, in the time between Emily's birth and the hearing, he had seen Emily approximately 22 times. These visits occurred during time periods in which Jack was temporarily living away from the Greer residence. John explained that during visits he had helped Dana and Dana's older daughter care for Emily and had attempted to establish a parental bond with the baby. John also testified that he had purchased a number of items for Emily and set up a room for Emily in his home. He gave Dana a few items, such as a stroller and car seat, to help her care for the baby. John further stated that he bought formula and diapers for Emily and paid for at least one doctor's visit, although he admitted he never sent Dana money.

Dana did not counter John's version of events in her testimony. However, Dana noted that she felt pressured by her family and John to involve John in Emily's life. Dana acknowledged that she blocked John's phone number because he continued to contact her even after she asked him to stop. Regarding her marriage to Jack, Dana testified that although she and Jack were estranged twice after Emily's birth, they had started seeing a marriage counselor to work on their relationship. Dana emphasized that Jack coparented Emily with her and that, since Emily's birth, Emily and Jack had formed a strong father-child bond. Dana also stated that although she believed Jack's relationship with Emily would not suffer if Emily knew her biological parentage, she worried that forcing a relationship between John and Emily might confuse Emily unnecessarily.

Jack briefly testified, explaining that most people in the community and his personal life understand Emily to be his child. Jack explained that he wanted Emily to grow up in his home as his child and that he wanted John to stop "interfering" with his family. However, he also acknowledged that his feelings about Emily would not change were John part of her life.

After John's attorney closed his argument, the district judge asked the following question:

"The briefs which I received, which were good, were on the issue of the *Ross* hearing, which we're having today, which is whether it's in the best interest of the child for the court to admit the evidence of the genetic testing. I would determine that it is in the best interest of the child to admit the genetic testing, don't we need to have another hearing or at least—maybe not any additional evidence, but another determination by the court as to which presumption, the presumption of that the child was born during the course of the marriage of the Greers or the presumption that the child, you know, that is 97 percent plus genetically the child of Mr. Farbo. Don't I need to resolve those presumptions at some point in time? There hasn't been any really authority or evidence presented on that."

The attorneys appeared to agree that the district court first needed to determine whether consideration of the genetic testing was in Emily's best interests and then, if such consideration was in her best interests, decide which man should be adjudged her legal father.

When the district court reconvened on June 6, 2013, to issue its decision, it began by considering the factors traditionally applied to a *Ross* hearing. After determining that the factors balanced equally between Jack and John, the district judge explained:

> "[B]ased on the evidence that's been presented in this case and the snapshot I have of the situation and my judgment, and judging the demeanor and the evidence and so forth and the testimony of everybody involved, I would think that the overall best interest is that—the guardian ad litem I think had a good point that although if I would grant the petition for paternity and moving forward the child would have, Emily would have two fathers, that that might start out as a normal situation or that that would be her paradigm of being normal, that she doesn't really need to have two fathers, and I think I agree with that rationale. A lot of these cases come up, as counsel knows, that we don't—we either have just one strong candidate or no candidates; we're trying to find somebody to be a father. In this case, we've got two strong candidates."

However, the district court ultimately found that, based on both the evidence and Kansas caselaw, considering the genetic test results was not in Emily's best interests. Based upon that finding, the district court went on to find that all the court was "left with is the presumption of paternity that this child was born of the marriage of Dana Greer and Jack Greer. So that will be the finding and order of the court." The district court then dismissed the paternity action. . . .

THE ROSS HEARING AND ADMISSION OF GENETIC TEST RESULTS

John contends that the district court erred in conducting a *Ross* hearing. John bases this contention on the premise that because the genetic test establishing him as Emily's biological father existed prior to the paternity action, it also established a presumption in his favor. John acknowledges that under the Kansas Parentage Act (KPA), K.S.A. 2013 Supp. 23-2201 *et seq.*, a presumption exists in Jack's favor as well however, John argues that the proper procedural mechanism was not to conduct a *Ross* hearing and exclude the genetic test results but rather to weigh the conflicting presumptions as provided in K.S.A. 2013 Supp. 23-2208(c). . . .

WE EXAMINE THE LAW REGARDING PRESUMPTIONS OF PATERNITY

A paternity proceeding determines who a child's legal father is and, therefore, who will enjoy the rights and responsibilities of legal parenthood. Presumptions of paternity may simultaneously arise in favor of different men. In family law, "[t]here is a strong presumption that a woman's husband is the father of any child born during the marriage." This presumption exists both at common law and statutorily. In Kansas, the statute specifically reads: "A man is presumed to be the father of a child if . . . [t]he man and the child's mother are, or have been, married to each other and the child is born during the marriage." K.S.A. 2013 Supp. 23-2208(a)(1). However, this presumption — also sometimes referred to as the presumption of legitimacy — can, like any other presumption, be rebutted.

But the presumption of legitimacy is not the only statutory presumption in Kansas. In fact, five other presumptions exist in Kansas, including those that arise when "[t]he man notoriously or in writing recognizes paternity of the child" and when "[g]enetic test results indicate a probability of 97% or greater that the man is the father of the child." Additionally, many of the criteria that tend to establish these presumptions overlap, meaning that "[m]ore than one man may be presumed to be the father." Therefore, in the case of conflicting presumptions, "the presumption which on the facts is founded on the weightier considerations of policy and logic, including the best interests of the child, shall control." K.S.A. 2013 Supp. 23-2208(c). A presumption "may be rebutted only by clear and convincing evidence, by a court decree establishing paternity of the child by another man," or as provided by the section of the statute regarding conflicting presumptions.

WE EXAMINE THE ROSS *CASE*

Because the district court relied on the *Ross* case to find that admission of the genetic test establishing John as the biological father of Emily was not in Emily's best interests and, therefore, the only remaining presumption was the legitimacy presumption, it is important to review the *Ross* case.

During the marriage of Sylvia and Robert Ross, a child was born. When the couple subsequently divorced, Sylvia was given custody of the child, and Robert was given visitation rights and ordered to pay child support. He was later given joint custody. Sylvia subsequently remarried and was interested in her new husband adopting the child. Two years after her divorce from Robert, Sylvia filed a paternity action under the KPA claiming that Charles, a man she had a sexual relationship with around the time of the child's conception, was the father. Charles had no interest in parenting the child, and he and Sylvia had already discussed whether he would be amenable to relinquishing his parental rights and allowing Sylvia's new husband to adopt the child if it was determined that he was the father. After filing her action, Sylvia asked that genetic testing be ordered by the court. A guardian ad litem was appointed, and the guardian filed a separate paternity action on behalf of the child. The district court dismissed Sylvia's action, apparently on the basis of res judicata and equitable estoppel related to the prior divorce decree, but the court allowed the action to proceed through the guardian ad litem. The court then sustained the guardian ad litem's request for a blood test without a hearing.

The court subsequently conducted a hearing to determine paternity but only allowed evidence regarding the child's biological parentage. The court did not accept any evidence regarding the best interests of the child. Charles was determined, by clear and convincing evidence, to be the biological father of the child.

Charles was ordered to pay child support, but the court maintained joint custody of the child between Sylvia and Robert, finding that Robert stood in loco parentis.

The Kansas Supreme Court found that the district court abused its discretion by admitting the blood test results without first having a hearing as to whether such testing was in the child's best interests. The court specifically rejected the notion that if blood testing proves the presumed father to be the biological father, the issue of parentage is closed and the necessity for extended evidence as to the child's best interests is precluded. The Supreme Court reversed the district court's order for blood tests and restored the parties to their positions before the tests were ordered. It ordered the district court to conduct a hearing purely based upon the best interests of the child and not to consider the blood tests "until such consideration is determined to be in [the child's] best interest."

A review of the statute in effect at the time of *Ross* is critical to understanding the court's analysis. The statute listed several presumptions of a paternity. Applicable to the *Ross* case was the presumption of legitimacy contained at K.S.A. 38-1114(a)(1) (Ensley 1986) and the fact that Robert had notoriously or in writing recognized his paternity under K.S.A. 38-1114(a)(4) (Ensley 1986). The *Ross* court noted that not only were the parties married, but Robert

> "acknowledged his paternity of the child in writing; with his consent, he was named as the father on the child's birth certificate; he willingly became obligated to support the child in the divorce decree; and he notoriously and in writing recognized his paternity of the child to the district court."

The statute went on to state that these presumptions were rebuttable by clear and convincing evidence. There were no conflicting presumptions in *Ross*. There were only two presumptions, both favoring Robert.

Although genetic testing was allowed and could be offered into evidence at the time, it had not yet been elevated to the level of a presumption. The statutes did require a court, either on its own motion or on the motion of any party, to order blood tests "[w]henever the paternity of a child is in issue." But because the shifting of paternity from the presumed father to the biological father could easily be detrimental to the emotional and physical well-being of any child, the Kansas Supreme Court found that prior to ordering a paternity test the court must conduct a hearing to determine the best interests of the child, including the child's physical, mental, and emotional needs. *Ross*, 245 Kan. 591, Syl. ¶ 5, 783 P.2d 331.

We note that "the best interests of the child" standard did not appear anywhere in the KPA at the time of the *Ross* decision. Instead, the court found that "[t]he Uniform Parentage Act clearly was designed to provide for the equal, beneficial treatment of children. In this regard, it requires courts to act in the best interests of the child when imposing legal obligations or conferring legal rights on the mother/child relationship and the father/child relationship."

WE EXAMINE THE STATUTORY SCHEME SINCE ROSS

The applicable provisions of the KPA have changed dramatically since *Ross* and, perhaps in part, in response to it. In 1994, the legislature elevated genetic test results to a presumption of paternity. It also included the "best interests of the child" as a consideration when weighing competing presumptions. The 1994 legislature also specifically provided that "[p]arties to an action may agree to conduct genetic tests prior to or during the pendency of any action for support of a child." The legislative changes further required that the written report of genetic test results be admitted into evidence without the need for further foundation if there is not an objection lodged in the manner provided in the statute. . . .

Based upon the current statutes and caselaw, if there is not a genetic test in place at the time the action is filed and a party requests that one be performed, the order for genetic testing must be based on a determination, after a hearing, that such a test is in the best interests of the child. But if the testing is completed before the case is filed, the presumption is elevated to a legal, albeit rebuttable, presumption. These statutory changes remain in the law to this day and are codified at K.S.A. 2013 Supp. 23-2208(a)(5) (genetic test results can create a presumption of paternity), K.S.A. 2013 Supp. 23-2208(c) (best interests of child considered when weighing two or more presumptions), and K.S.A. 2013 Supp. 23-2212 (genetic tests may be conducted prior to filing case, and report of results must be admitted unless timely objection lodged). It is because of these changes that the decision in *Ross* does not control the procedure required of the district court in this case — or, more importantly, the outcome of this case.

Since *Ross* was decided, most cases invoking a *Ross* hearing also involve facts very similar to *Ross*: a party attempts to challenge a long-standing presumption *prior* to any genetic testing of the parties by filing a paternity action. Only one Kansas case involves genetic testing that predated the filing of the paternity action; there, the district court refused to admit the testing based on its lack of scientific validity, not based on the *Ross* factors. . . .

In summary, our Supreme Court's mandate in *Ross* continues to be good law. But the caselaw and statutory changes since *Ross* make it clear that a *Ross* hearing is only required in two very specific situations: when (1) there is not a genetic test resulting in a presumption of paternity performed prior to the filing of the paternity action, or (2) a genetic test was completed prior to the filing of the paternity action but the result is inadmissible due to a proper statutory objection being lodged. In addition, *Ross* would only apply when one man's presumption is at risk of rebuttal; when "no credible evidence exists that child has a presumed father," a *Ross* hearing in advance of admitting a genetic test results is not required.

WE APPLY THE LAW TO THE FACTS

Under the current statutory scheme, and the one in place at the time of this paternity action, the district judge was faced with two competing presumptions: legitimacy and genetic. Both presumptions were in place prior to the filing of the paternity action. The court was required to admit and consider the genetic test results because no objection was lodged as required by K.S.A. 2013 Supp. 23-2212(c). In addition, . . . the parties agreed to genetic testing, and a copy of the report was filed with the court at the same time as the petition to determine paternity. During the hearing, no one disputed the test results and the fact that John was Emily's biological father. A *Ross* hearing to determine whether to *consider* the test results was not required because, given the posture of the case and the lack of objection, the court was required to consider the test results as one of the presumptions of paternity. The court did not disregard the test results due to any concerns about its validity; its validity was not in question. Instead, the court disregarded the test results totally on a *Ross* "best interests of the child" analysis. By not considering the genetic test results, the district court committed an error of law.

Additionally, the district court was required to weigh the competing presumptions and find in favor of the presumption "founded on the weightier considerations of policy and logic, including the best interests of the child." K.S.A. 2013 Supp. 23-2208(c). The district court failed to weigh competing presumptions because it refused to even consider one of the presumptions. This is also an error of law. . . .

At the conclusion of the *Ross* hearing, the district court found that upsetting Jack's presumption of legitimacy was not in Emily's best interests and, accordingly, dismissed the paternity action without considering the genetic test results. Although the court spoke to Emily's best interests, the judge's failure to recognize both competing presumptions, legitimacy and genetic, and then conduct the weighing of presumptions was the cause of the error we have found here.

Accordingly, we reverse the decision of the district court and remand the case for a hearing for the district court to weigh the two competing presumptions as required by K.S.A. 2013 Supp. 23-2208(c).

WE PROVIDE GUIDANCE IN WEIGHING THE CONFLICTING PRESUMPTIONS AND THE BEST INTERESTS OF THE CHILD

Because this is a matter of first impression in Kansas, there are no cases guiding a court in weighing competing presumptions, although there is some guidance in determining the best interests of the child. We briefly review those factors here to provide future guidance when courts are faced with competing presumptions.

THE WEIGHTIER CONSIDERATIONS OF POLICY AND LOGIC

The KPA does not designate any one presumption as conclusive, and K.S.A. 2013 Supp. 23-2208(c) requires that when presumptions conflict, "the presumption which on the facts is founded on the *weightier considerations of policy and logic*, including the best interests of the child, shall control." (Emphasis added.)

A few courts around the country have tried to parse the *considerations of policy and logic* language. The Wyoming Supreme Court noted that this language is not only limited to legal policy but "clearly implies that a court should consider the broader sociological and psychological ramifications of its decision as to which man should be adjudicated the legal father." See GDK v. State, Dept. of Family Services, 92 P.3d 834, 839 (Wyo. 2004). The Minnesota Court of Appeals observed that the statutory language embraces "the policy of not unnecessarily impairing blood relationships" and requires that the outcome be "logically based on the facts." In re Paternity of B.J.H., 573 N.W.2d 99, 103 (Minn. App. 1998). Appropriately, the *policy and logic* portion of the inquiry appears in part to be heavily based on a state's individual caselaw and policy. See Ex parte C.A.P., 683 So. 2d 1010, 1011-12 (Ala. 1996) (weighing presumptions by relying heavily on Alabama precedent).

Several courts, including those in Kansas, have specifically referred to the strength of the presumption of legitimacy. The *Ross* court emphasized that if a blood test proves the presumed father is the biological father, the issue of parentage is not closed. "Though such reasoning promotes judicial economy, it is contrary to our longstanding public policy that a child born during a marriage should not be bastardized." The district court is still required to consider the best interests of the child.

Our Supreme Court has also recognized, in an adoption proceeding, the important rights of biological fathers who promptly assert their rights by taking affirmative steps to show they are fully committed to accepting parenting responsibilities.

> "A natural parent's right to the companionship, care, custody, and management of his or her child is a liberty interest. The liberty interest of a natural parent has its origin in the biological connection between the parent and child, but a biological relationship does not guarantee the permanency of the parental rights of an unwed natural father. Rather, the significance of the biological connection is that it offers the natural father an opportunity that no other male possesses to develop a relationship with his offspring. The opportunity is lost, however, if the natural father does not come forward to demonstrate a full commitment to the responsibilities of parenthood."

The West Virginia Supreme Court noted that *both* marriage to the child's mother and "factual, biological parentage" are weighty factors. State ex rel. v. Michael George K., 207 W. Va. 290, 299, 531 S.E.2d 669 (2000).

Interestingly, K.S.A. 60-415 is the only other place in Kansas statutes where this language is used, and it states:

> "If two presumptions arise which are conflicting with each other the judge shall apply the presumption which is founded on the weightier consideration of policy and logic. If there is no such preponderance both presumptions shall be disregarded."

In the case of a paternity action, if both *presumptions* were disregarded, the child would be left without a presumptive father at all, defeating the entire purpose of the KPA. Accordingly, the judge in a paternity action must make the difficult choice while always including the overarching consideration of the best interests of the child in the equation.

THE BEST INTERESTS OF THE CHILD

Over the years, courts have distilled the best interests of the child consideration present in paternity cases to include approximately 10 factors. These factors have been summarized as including: (1) whether the child thinks the presumed father is his or her father and has a relationship with him; (2) the nature of the relationship between the presumed father and child and whether the presumed father wants to continue to provide a father-child relationship; (3) the nature of the relationship between the alleged father and the child and whether the alleged father wants to establish a relationship and provide for the child's needs; (4) the possible emotional impact of establishing biological paternity; (5) whether a negative result regarding paternity in the presumed father would leave the child without a legal father; (6) the nature of the mother's relationships with the presumed and alleged fathers; (7) the motives of the party raising the paternity action; (8) the harm to the child, or medical need in identifying the biological father; (9) the relationship between the child and any siblings from either the presumed or alleged father; and (10) whether there have been previous opportunities to raise the issue of paternity.

"Time may be a major factor" in determining best interests, as well as "the notoriety of the child's situation in the community," the stability of the home in which the child will reside, the child's uncertainty regarding the paternity issue, "and any other factors that will maximize the child's opportunities for a successful life."

However, most courts also recognize that a best interests analysis is incredibly fact-specific and rarely limited to a narrow number of factors. In N.A.H. v. S.L.S., 9 P.3d at 363, the Colorado Supreme Court observed that "the whole paternity proceeding [is intended] to be about the best interests of the child." This focus is in part because "[t]he outcome of a paternity action irrevocably alters a child's current family situation and her future." Accordingly, it is clear that courts weighing two or more conflicting presumptions may consider a wide array of nonexclusive factors when deciding which presumption serves the child's best interests.

Because we reverse the district court's decision and remand for a hearing for the district court to properly determine which presumption "is founded on the weightier considerations of policy and logic, including the best interests of the child," we need not address the balance of the issues presented.

NOTES AND QUESTIONS

1. The presumption of paternity based on genetic testing uses biology as the determinant of legal paternity. Why does biological parenthood support a claim to be a legal parent? Is the presumption that a married woman's husband is the father of her child an inference of biological fact? Does it express other policies? How about the presumption of paternity based on living with and holding out a child as one's own?

2. *Greer* holds that when two or more men are presumed to be a child's father, based on conflicting presumptions, the trial court should "find in favor of the presumption founded on the weightier considerations of policy and logic, including the best interests of the child." In most jurisdictions the usual rule for resolving the problem of conflicting presumptions is to prefer the one best supported by policy and logic; Kansas added "best interests of the child." Upon what basis should the court make this choice? How should a court decide which presumption expresses the more important policy? What role should factual considerations play? If Dana and Jack Greer had divorced instead of reconciling, how would the analysis have been different?

3. Note that if the parties had not agreed to genetic testing and if the trial court had not ordered it, only the presumption favoring the husband would have been at play in the case. Under the *Ross* case, before ordering genetic testing, the

trial court would have to have found that this was in the child's best interests. What arguments would support ordering the testing in *Greer*? What arguments would support denying tests?

Recognizing the overarching legal and human importance of genetic testing, Uniform Parentage Act § 608(a) allows a court to deny an order for testing if the wife or the husband is estopped from denying the husband's paternity and the court finds by clear and convincing evidence that it would be inequitable to disprove the father-child relationship. When deciding whether to order the tests, the court must also consider the child's best interests. Under these provisions, should a court have ordered genetic testing on the facts of *Greer*?

4. States that recognize same-sex marriage, civil unions, or domestic partnerships that are the equivalent of marriage extend the marital presumption to same-sex couples. What does the presumption mean in the context of two partners who could not possibly both be genetic parents? What grounds, if any, should be recognized as a basis for rebutting the presumption? Will two men who arrange for the birth of child genetically related to one of the two men through use of a surrogate mother necessarily be entitled to the benefit of the marital presumption on the same terms as two lesbians, where one of the two women gives birth? *See* Susan Frelich Appleton, Presuming Women: Revisiting the Presumption of Legitimacy in the Same-Sex Couples Era, 86 B.U. L. Rev. 227 (2006).

5. Until 1980 the California marital presumption was conclusive as against all the world if the spouses were cohabiting and the husband was not impotent or sterile. In Michael H. v. Gerald D., 491 U.S. 110 (1989), the Supreme Court upheld this statute against due process challenges brought by a child's undisputed biological father, Michael. He sought to establish paternity because the mother, Carole, and her husband, Gerald, had reconciled and cut off Michael's contact with the child. A majority of the Court rejected Michael's procedural and substantive due process claims, based on earlier cases protecting the custodial rights of biological fathers in some circumstances. The case, which is discussed further in the next section of this chapter, did not produce a majority opinion. The plurality opinion by Justice Scalia denied that Michael had any constitutional right:

> In an attempt to limit and guide interpretation of the [Due Process] Clause, we have insisted not merely that the interest denominated as a "liberty" be "fundamental" (a concept that, in isolation, is hard to objectify), but also that it be an interest traditionally protected by our society. As we have put it, the Due Process Clause affords only those protections "so rooted in the traditions and conscience of our people as to be ranked as fundamental." . . . Thus, the legal issue in the present case reduces to whether the relationship between persons in the situation of Michael and Victoria has been treated as a protected family unit under the historic practices of our society, or whether on any other basis it has been accorded special protection. We think it impossible to find that it has. In fact, quite to the contrary, our traditions have protected the marital family (Gerald, Carole, and the child they acknowledge to be theirs) against the sort of claim Michael asserts. . . .
>
> We have found nothing in the older sources, nor in the older cases, addressing specifically the power of the natural father to assert parental rights over a child born into a woman's existing marriage with another man. Since it is Michael's burden to establish that such a power (at least where the natural father has established a relationship with the child) is so deeply embedded within our traditions as to be a

fundamental right, the lack of evidence alone might defeat his case. But the evidence shows that even in modern times — when, as we have noted, the rigid protection of the marital family has in other respects been relaxed — the ability of a person in Michael's position to claim paternity has not been generally acknowledged. . . .

491 U.S. at 122-125. In 1980 the California legislature amended the statute to permit the husband to introduce blood test evidence to rebut the presumption within two years of the child's birth, and in 1981 amended it to give the mother the same opportunity, provided that the biological father files an affidavit acknowledging paternity. These rules are now codified at Cal. Fam. Code §§ 7540 and 7541 (2014). These amendments did not give Michael the ability to contest the marital presumption over Gerald and Carole's objections.

At least two state supreme courts have held that their state constitutions, unlike the federal constitution as interpreted in *Michael H.*, may protect an unwed father's interest in establishing paternity even though the child's mother is married to another. In the Interest of J.W.T., 872 S.W.2d 189 (Tex. 1994); Callender v. Skiles, 591 N.W.2d 182 (Iowa 1999) (finding denial of standing to biological father unconstitutional). In C.C. v. A.B., 550 N.E.2d 365 (Mass. 1990), the Massachusetts Supreme Judicial Court avoided the constitutional issue, holding that on facts like those in *Michael H.*, the presumption that the husband is the father no longer exists as a matter of common law, leaving the way open for the putative father to bring a paternity suit.

LESLIE JOAN HARRIS, *REFORMING PATERNITY LAW TO ELIMINATE GENDER, STATUS AND CLASS INEQUALITY*

2013 Mich. St. L. Rev. 1295, 1312-1316

While the statutes regarding challenges to the marital presumption . . . vary in their specifics, they generally protect father-child relationships formed within marriage against disruption by the spouses themselves, outsiders, or both. . . . [M]ost of the statutes that address rebuttal of the presumption provide special protection to husband-child relationships. Moreover, while many of these statutes are gender neutral in the sense that they provide the same authority to husbands and wives to invoke the protections of the marital presumption, a number protect only a husband's desires about whether to remain the legal father or privilege his views over those of the mother . . . .

Recent cases about the marital presumption that are not governed by clear statutory rules also tend to protect the legal relationship between the husband and the child where the husband wants to maintain his legal paternity, and they are less likely to preserve the marital presumption where a mother seeks to prevent her husband from rebutting it. Often the cases describe the purpose of the presumption, at least in part, as protecting the child by protecting the caring relationship between the husband and the child. When the husband does not want to preserve the presumption, the reasoning goes, this goal cannot be served.

Several recent cases rejecting efforts to rebut the marital presumption explicitly invoke the special protections for parenthood that marriage provides. In 2012, the Maryland Court of Appeals in Mulligan v. Corbett confirmed and applied a line of cases which hold that if a husband's paternity is challenged, the parentage provisions of the state estates and trusts code govern, while if the child's mother is unmarried, parentage challenges are governed by the family law code.[19] The significance of the distinction is that a finding of legal paternity under the family law code must be set aside based on genetic tests unless the man acknowledged the child, knowing he was not the biological father.[20] The child's interests are irrelevant.[21] In contrast, under the estates and trusts code, the court considers the child's best interests in determining whether to allow the marital presumption to be rebutted.[22] The leading Maryland cases explain that when a child is born to a married woman and two men claim paternity, it is "'more satisfactory' and 'less traumatic'" to use the trusts and estates code than the family law code.[23] . . .

Courts in a number of other states have adopted more straightforward strategies that allow protection of husbands who want to retain their parental status, such as precluding rebuttal when contrary to the child's best interests[24] or using estoppel to prevent a party from rebutting the presumption.[25] In theory, estoppel could be invoked against any party, but it is most often successfully asserted against mothers who seek to terminate their husbands' paternal status . . . .

Federal law requires that states have "procedures ensuring that the putative father has a reasonable opportunity to initiate a paternity action." 42 U.S.C.

---

19. 45 A.3d 243, 252-61 (Md. 2012).

20. Md. Code Ann., Fam. Law § 5-1038(a)(2) (LexisNexis 2013).

21. *Id.* § 5-1038(b). The statute was enacted to overrule Tandra S. v. Tyrone W., 648 A.2d 439, 449-50 (Md. 1994), which held that a man could not have a judgment of paternity set aside because of res judicata. *See also* Langston v. Riffe, 754 A.2d 389, 392 (Md. 2000) (interpreting the statute as absolute and not allowing consideration of the child's best interests).

22. The leading case for this proposition is Turner v. Whisted, 607 A.2d 935, 938, 940 (Md. 1992). More recent cases are Evans v. Wilson, 856 A.2d 679 (Md. 2004); and Kamp v. Dep't of Human Servs., 980 A.2d 448 (Md. 2009) (holding a court should make the best interests determination before ordering genetic tests; genetic tests are not in a child's best interests when the husband filed when he had acted as a father for at least thirteen years, also estopped to deny paternity).

23. *Turner*, 607 A.2d at 938 (quoting Thomas v. Solis, 283 A.2d 777, 781 (Md. 1971)).

24. *See, e.g.*, Williamson v. Williamson, 690 S.E.2d 257, 258-59 (Ga. Ct. App. 2010); Dep't of Revenue *ex rel.* Garcia v. Iglesias, 77 So. 3d 878 (Fla. Dist. Ct. App. 2012) (citing Dep't of Health & Rehabilitative Servs. v. Privette, 617 So. 2d 305 (Fla. 1993)); J.T.J. v. N.H., 84 So. 3d 1176, 1178 (Fla. Dist. Ct. App. 2012) (citing *Privette*, 617 So. 2d at 305). Less often, the best interests criterion is used to prevent a husband from rebutting the marital presumption. *See, e.g., In re* Marriage of Betty L.W. v. William E.W., 569 S.E.2d 77 (W. Va. 2002).

25. *See, e.g.*, K.E.M. v. P.C.S., 38 A.3d 798 (Pa. 2012); *In re* Marriage of K.E.V. & M.L.V., 883 P.2d 1246, 1250 (Mont. 1994).

§ 666(a)(5)(L). Does application of the best-interest rule and estoppel principles described above violate this requirement?

For more on the marital presumption, *see* June Carbone & Naomi Cahn, Marriage, Parentage and Child Support, 45 Fam. L.Q. 219 (2011); Theresa Glennon, Somebody's Child: Evaluating the Erosion of the Marital Presumption of Paternity, 102 W. Va. L. Rev. 547 (2000); Melanie Jacobs, Overcoming the Marital Presumption, 50 Fam. Ct. Rev. 289 (2012); Jana Singer, Marriage, Biology, and Paternity: The Case for Revitalizing the Marital Presumption, 65 Md. L. Rev. 246 (2006); Robin Fretwell Wilson, Evaluating Marriage: Does Marriage Matter to the Nurturing of Children?, 42 San Diego L. Rev. (2005).

PROBLEM

Margaret was married to Frank and having an affair with Harry. When she was three months pregnant she divorced Frank, and she and Harry were married a month before her child, Carol, was born. Throughout her marriage to Harry, Margaret told him that he was Carol's biological father. When Carol was six weeks old, blood tests were done to determine whether Harry was the biological father, but they were inconclusive. Harry was a loving father who supported Margaret and Carol and provided much personal care to Carol as well. Margaret and Carol had nothing to do with Frank after Margaret divorced him. When Carol was 5 Margaret and Harry divorced.

(a) Seeking to avoid paying child support, Harry offers evidence to rebut the presumption that he is Carol's biological father. In a state that follows the rule that the presumption can be rebutted only if it is in the child's best interest, should the court allow the presumption to be rebutted? How should the court rule in a state that has adopted the rule that says a person may be estopped from denying paternity?

(b) Margaret seeks to introduce evidence that Harry is not Carol's biological father because she does not want him to have visitation rights. In a state that follows the best-interest rule, should the evidence be admitted? Should it be admitted in a state that has adopted the estoppel doctrine?

(c) Would your answers to (a) or (b) change if Harry and Margaret separated when Carol was 5, Harry learned at that time that he was not Carol's biological father, the divorce hearing did not occur until two years later, and by that time Carol was 7 and had not seen Harry in the intervening two years?

2. Unmarried Fathers' Rights — Adoption and Custody

The U.S. Supreme Court held for the first time that the Constitution protects unmarried fathers' custodial rights, at least in some situations, in Stanley v. Illinois, 552 U.S. 866 (1972). In that case, Illinois law provided that, upon the death of an unmarried mother, her children became wards of the state and the state granted custody to a court-appointed guardian. The father, who had lived intermittently with the mother and children for 18 years, received no legal recognition. The Court declared the statute, which gave no recognition to any unwed father however devoted to his children, an unconstitutional violation of due process. Chief Justice Burger issued a strong dissent, observing that:

> ... I believe that a State is fully justified in concluding, on the basis of common human experience, that the biological role of the mother in carrying and nursing an infant creates stronger bonds between her and the child than the bonds resulting from the male's often casual encounter. This view is reinforced by the observable fact that most unwed mothers exhibit a concern for their offspring either permanently or at least until they are safely placed for adoption, while unwed fathers rarely burden either the mother or the child with their attentions or loyalties. Centuries of human experience buttress this view of the realities of human conditions and suggest that unwed mothers of illegitimate children are generally more dependable protectors of their children than are unwed fathers. While these, like most generalizations, are not without exceptions, they nevertheless provide a sufficient basis to sustain a statutory classification whose objective is not to penalize unwed parents but to further the welfare of illegitimate children in fulfillment of the State's obligations as *parens patriae*.

The *Stanley* majority rejected Burger's approach. Consider, however, how the courts in the next two cases deal with the different positions of mother and father when their child is born outside marriage.

LEHR V. ROBERTSON

463 U.S. 248 (1983)

STEVENS, J. . . . Jessica M. was born out of wedlock on November 9, 1976. Her mother, Lorraine Robertson, married Richard Robertson eight months after Jessica's birth. On December 21, 1978, when Jessica was over two years old, the Robertsons filed an adoption petition in the Family Court of Ulster County, New York. The court heard their testimony and received a favorable report from the Ulster County Department of Social Services. On March 7, 1979, the court entered an order of adoption. In this proceeding, appellant contends that the adoption order is invalid because he, Jessica's putative father, was not given advance notice of the adoption proceeding.

The State of New York maintains a "putative father registry." A man who files with that registry demonstrates his intent to claim paternity of a child born out of wedlock and is therefore entitled to receive notice of any proceeding to adopt that child. Before entering Jessica's adoption order, the Ulster County Family Court had the putative father registry examined. Although appellant claims to be Jessica's natural father, he had not entered his name in the registry.

In addition to the persons whose names are listed on the putative father registry, New York law requires that notice of an adoption proceeding be given to several other classes of possible fathers of children born out of wedlock — those who have been adjudicated to be the father, those who have been identified as the father on the child's birth certificate, those who live openly with the child and the child's mother and who hold themselves out to be the father, those who have been identified as the father by the mother in a sworn written statement, and those who were married to the child's mother before the child was six months old. Appellant admittedly was not a member of any of those classes. He had lived with appellee prior to Jessica's birth and visited her in the hospital when Jessica was born, but his name does not appear on Jessica's birth certificate. He did not live with appellee or Jessica after Jessica's birth, he has never provided them with any financial support, and he has never offered to marry appellee. Nevertheless, he contends that the following special circumstances gave him a constitutional right to notice and a hearing before Jessica was adopted.

On January 30, 1979, one month after the adoption proceeding was commenced in Ulster County, appellant filed a "visitation and paternity petition" in the Westchester County Family Court. In that petition, he asked for a determination of paternity, an order of support, and reasonable visitation privileges with Jessica. Notice of that proceeding was served on appellee on February 22, 1979. Four days later appellee's attorney informed the Ulster County Court that appellant had commenced a paternity proceeding in Westchester County; the Ulster County judge then entered an order staying appellant's paternity proceeding until he could rule on a motion to change the venue of that proceeding to Ulster County. On March 3, 1979, appellant received notice of the change of venue motion and, for the first time, learned that an adoption proceeding was pending in Ulster County.

On March 7, 1979, appellant's attorney telephoned the Ulster County judge to inform him that he planned to seek a stay of the adoption proceeding pending the determination of the paternity petition. In that telephone conversation, the judge advised the lawyer that he had already signed the adoption order earlier that day. According to appellant's attorney, the judge stated that he was aware of the pending paternity petition but did not believe he was required to give notice to appellant prior to the entry of the order of adoption.

. . . On June 22, 1979, appellant filed a petition to vacate the order of adoption on the ground that it was obtained by fraud and in violation of his constitutional rights. The Ulster County Family Court . . . denied the petition. . . .

The Appellate Division of the Supreme Court affirmed. . . .

The New York Court of Appeals also affirmed by a divided vote. . . .

THE DUE PROCESS CLAIM

. . . This Court has examined the extent to which a natural father's biological relationship with his illegitimate child receives protection under the Due Process Clause in precisely three cases: Stanley v. Illinois, 405 U.S. 645 (1972), Quilloin v. Walcott, 434 U.S. 246 (1978), and Caban v. Mohammed, 441 U.S. 380 (1979).

Stanley involved the constitutionality of an Illinois statute that conclusively presumed every father of a child born out of wedlock to be an unfit person to have custody of his children. The father in that case had lived with his children all their lives and had lived with their mother for eighteen years. There was nothing in the record to indicate that Stanley had been a neglectful father who had not cared for his children. . . . [T]he Court held that the Due Process Clause was violated by the automatic destruction of the custodial relationship without giving the father any opportunity to present evidence regarding his fitness as a parent.

Quilloin involved the constitutionality of a Georgia statute that authorized the adoption of a child born out of wedlock over the objection of the natural father. The father in that case had never legitimated the child. It was only after the mother had remarried and her new husband had filed an adoption petition that the natural father sought visitation rights and filed a petition for legitimation. The trial court found adoption by the new husband to be in the child's best interests, and we unanimously held that action to be consistent with the Due Process Clause.

Caban involved the conflicting claims of two natural parents who had maintained joint custody of their children from the time of their birth until they were respectively two and four years old. The father challenged the validity of an order authorizing the mother's new husband to adopt the children; he relied on both the Equal Protection Clause and the Due Process Clause. Because this Court upheld his equal protection claim, the majority did not address his due process challenge. The comments on the latter claim by the four dissenting Justices are nevertheless instructive, because they identify the clear distinction between a mere biological relationship and an actual relationship of parental responsibility.

Justice Stewart correctly observed: "Even if it be assumed that each married parent after divorce has some substantive due process right to maintain his or her parental relationship, cf. Smith v. Organization of Foster Families, 431 U.S. 816, 862-863 (opinion concurring in judgment), it by no means follows that each unwed parent has any such right. Parental rights do not spring full-blown from the biological connection between parent and child. They require relationships more enduring." 441 U.S., at 397.[26]

In a similar vein, the other three dissenters in *Caban* were prepared to "assume that, if and when one develops, the relationship between a father and his natural child is entitled to protection against arbitrary state action as a matter of due process." Caban v. Mohammed, 441 U.S. 380, 414.

The difference between the developed parent-child relationship that was implicated in *Stanley* and *Caban*, and the potential relationship involved in *Quilloin* and this case, is both clear and significant. When an unwed father demonstrates a full commitment to the responsibilities of parenthood by "com[ing] forward to

---

26. In the balance of that paragraph Justice Stewart noted that the relation between a father and his natural child may acquire constitutional protection if the father enters into a traditional marriage with the mother or if "the actual relationship between father and child" is sufficient. The mother carries and bears the child, and in this sense her parental relationship is clear. The validity of the father's parental claims must be gauged by other measures. By tradition, the primary measure has been the legitimate familial relationship he creates with the child by marriage with the mother. By definition, the question before us can arise only when no such marriage has taken place. In some circumstances the actual relationship between father and child may suffice to create in the unwed father parental interests comparable to those of the married father. *Cf.* Stanley v. Illinois, supra. But here we are concerned with the rights the unwed father may have when his wishes and those of the mother are in conflict, and the child's best interests are served by a resolution in favor of the mother. It seems to me that the absence of a legal tie with the mother may in such circumstances appropriately place a limit on whatever substantive constitutional claims might otherwise exist by virtue of the father's actual relationship with the children. Ibid.

participate in the rearing of his child," *Caban*, 441 U.S., at 392, his interest in personal contact with his child acquires substantial protection under the due process clause. At that point it may be said that he "act[s] as a father toward his children." Id., at 389, n.7. But the mere existence of a biological link does not merit equivalent constitutional protection. The actions of judges neither create nor sever genetic bonds. "[T]he importance of the familial relationship, to the individuals involved and to the society, stems from the emotional attachments that derive from the intimacy of daily association, and from the role it plays in 'promot[ing] a way of life' through the instruction of children as well as from the fact of blood relationship." Smith v. Organization of Foster Families for Equality and Reform, 431 U.S. 816, 844 (1977) (quoting Wisconsin v. Yoder, 406 U.S. 205, 231-233 (1972)).

The significance of the biological connection is that it offers the natural father an opportunity that no other male possesses to develop a relationship with his offspring. If he grasps that opportunity and accepts some measure of responsibility for the child's future, he may enjoy the blessings of the parent-child relationship and make uniquely valuable contributions to the child's development. If he fails to do so, the Federal Constitution will not automatically compel a state to listen to his opinion of where the child's best interests lie.

In this case, we are not assessing the constitutional adequacy of New York's procedures for terminating a developed relationship. Appellant has never had any significant custodial, personal, or financial relationship with Jessica, and he did not seek to establish a legal tie until after she was two years old.[27] We are concerned only with whether New York has adequately protected his opportunity to form such a relationship. . . .

After this Court's decision in *Stanley*, the New York Legislature appointed a special commission to recommend legislation that would accommodate both the interests of biological fathers in their children and the children's interest in prompt and certain adoption procedures. The commission recommended, and the legislature enacted, a statutory adoption scheme that automatically provides notice to seven categories of putative fathers who are likely to have assumed some responsibility for the care of their natural children. If this scheme were likely to omit many responsible fathers, and if qualification for notice were beyond the control of an interested putative father, it might be thought procedurally inadequate. Yet, as all of the New York courts that reviewed this matter observed, the right to receive notice was completely within appellant's control. By mailing a postcard to the putative father registry, he could have guaranteed that he would receive notice

---

27. This case happens to involve an adoption by the husband of the natural mother, but we do not believe the natural father has any greater right to object to such an adoption than to an adoption by two total strangers. If anything, the balance of equities tips the opposite way in a case such as this. In denying the putative father relief in *Quilloin*, we made an observation equally applicable here: "Nor is this a case in which the proposed adoption would place the child with a new set of parents with whom the child had never before lived. Rather, the result of the adoption in this case is to give full recognition to a family unit already in existence, a result desired by all concerned, except appellant. Whatever might be required in other situations, we cannot say that the State was required in this situation to find anything more than that the adoption, and denial of legitimation, were in the 'best interests of the child.'" 434 U.S., at 255.

of any proceedings to adopt Jessica. The possibility that he may have failed to do so because of his ignorance of the law cannot be a sufficient reason for criticizing the law itself. The New York legislature concluded that a more open-ended notice requirement would merely complicate the adoption process, threaten the privacy interests of unwed mothers, create the risk of unnecessary controversy, and impair the desired finality of adoption decrees. Regardless of whether we would have done likewise if we were legislators instead of judges, we surely cannot characterize the state's conclusion as arbitrary.

Appellant argues, however, that even if the putative father's opportunity to establish a relationship with an illegitimate child is adequately protected by the New York statutory scheme in the normal case, he was nevertheless entitled to special notice because the court and the mother knew that he had filed an affiliation proceeding in another court. This argument amounts to nothing more than an indirect attack on the notice provisions of the New York statute. The legitimate state interests in facilitating the adoption of young children and having the adoption proceeding completed expeditiously that underlie the entire statutory scheme also justify a trial judge's determination to require all interested parties to adhere precisely to the procedural requirements of the statute. The Constitution does not require either a trial judge or a litigant to give special notice to nonparties who are presumptively capable of asserting and protecting their own rights. Since the New York statutes adequately protected appellant's inchoate interest in establishing a relationship with Jessica, we find no merit in the claim that his constitutional rights were offended because the family court strictly complied with the notice provisions of the statute.

THE EQUAL PROTECTION CLAIM

. . . The legislation at issue in this case . . . [is] designed to promote the best interests of the child, protect the rights of interested third parties, and ensure promptness and finality. To serve those ends, the legislation guarantees to certain people the right to veto an adoption and the right to prior notice of any adoption proceeding. The mother of an illegitimate child is always within that favored class, but only certain putative fathers are included. Appellant contends that the gender-based distinction is invidious.

As we noted above, the existence or nonexistence of a substantial relationship between parent and child is a relevant criterion in evaluating both the rights of the parent and the best interests of the child. In Quilloin v. Walcott, supra, we noted that the putative father, like appellant, "ha[d] never shouldered any significant responsibility with respect to the daily supervision, education, protection, or care of the child. Appellant does not complain of his exemption from these responsibilities. . . ." 434 U.S., at 256. We therefore found that a Georgia statute that always required a mother's consent to the adoption of a child born out of wedlock, but required the father's consent only if he had legitimated the child, did not violate the Equal Protection Clause. . . .

We have held that these statutes may not constitutionally be applied in that class of cases where the mother and father are in fact similarly situated with regard to their relationship with the child. In Caban v. Mohammed, 441 U.S. 380 (1979), the Court held that it violated the Equal Protection Clause to grant the mother a veto over the adoption of a four-year-old girl and a six-year-old boy, but not to grant a veto to their father, who had admitted paternity and had participated in the rearing of the children. . . .

Jessica's parents are not like the parents involved in *Caban*. Whereas appellee had a continuous custodial responsibility for Jessica, appellant never established any custodial, personal, or financial relationship with her. If one parent has an established custodial relationship with the child and the other parent has either abandoned or never established a relationship, the Equal Protection Clause does not prevent a state from according the two parents different legal rights.

The judgment of the New York Court of Appeals is affirmed.

WHITE, J., with whom MARSHALL, J., and BLACKMUN, J., join, dissenting. . . . It is axiomatic that "[t]he fundamental requirement of due process is the opportunity to be heard 'at a meaningful time and in a meaningful manner.'" As Jessica's biological father, Lehr either had an interest protected by the Constitution or he did not. If the entry of the adoption order in this case deprived Lehr of a constitutionally protected interest, he is entitled to notice and an opportunity to be heard before the order can be accorded finality.

According to Lehr, he and Jessica's mother met in 1971 and began living together in 1974. The couple cohabited for approximately 2 years, until Jessica's birth in 1976. Throughout the pregnancy and after the birth, Lorraine acknowledged to friends and relatives that Lehr was Jessica's father; Lorraine told Lehr that she had reported to the New York State Department of Social Services that he was the father. Lehr visited Lorraine and Jessica in the hospital every day during Lorraine's confinement. According to Lehr, from the time Lorraine was discharged from the hospital until August, 1978, she concealed her whereabouts from him. During this time Lehr never ceased his efforts to locate Lorraine and Jessica and achieved sporadic success until August, 1977, after which time he was unable to locate them at all. On those occasions when he did determine Lorraine's location, he visited with her and her children to the extent she was willing to permit it. When Lehr, with the aid of a detective agency, located Lorraine and Jessica in August, 1978, Lorraine was already married to Mr. Robertson. Lehr asserts that at this time he offered to provide financial assistance and to set up a trust fund for Jessica, but that Lorraine refused. Lorraine threatened Lehr with arrest unless he stayed away and refused to permit him to see Jessica. Thereafter Lehr retained counsel who wrote to Lorraine in early December, 1978, requesting that she permit Lehr to visit Jessica and threatening legal action on Lehr's behalf. On December 21, 1978, perhaps as a response to Lehr's threatened legal action, appellees commenced the adoption action at issue here. . . .

Lehr's version of the "facts" paints a far different picture than that portrayed by the majority. The majority's recitation, that "[a]ppellant has never had any significant custodial, personal, or financial relationship with Jessica, and he did not seek to establish a legal tie until after she was two years old," obviously does not tell the whole story. Appellant has never been afforded an opportunity to present his case. The legitimation proceeding he instituted was first stayed, and then dismissed, on appellees' motions. Nor could appellant establish his interest during the adoption proceedings, for it is the failure to provide Lehr notice and an opportunity to be heard there that is at issue here. We cannot fairly make a judgment based on the quality or substance of a relationship without a complete and developed factual record. This case requires us to assume that Lehr's allegations are true — that but for the actions of the child's mother there would have been the kind of significant relationship that the majority concedes is entitled to the full panoply of procedural due process protections.

I reject the peculiar notion that the only significance of the biological connection between father and child is that "it offers the natural father an opportunity that no other male possesses to develop a relationship with his offspring." A "mere biological relationship" is not as unimportant in determining the nature of liberty interests as the majority suggests.

"[T]he usual understanding of family' implies biological relationships, and most decisions treating the relation between parent and child have stressed this element." Smith v. Organization of Foster Families, supra, 431 U.S., at 843. The "biological connection" is itself a relationship that creates a protected interest. Thus the "nature" of the interest is the parent-child relationship; how well developed that relationship has become goes to its "weight," not its "nature." Whether Lehr's interest is entitled to constitutional protection does not entail a searching inquiry into the quality of the relationship but a simple determination of the fact that the relationship exists — a fact that even the majority agrees must be assumed to be established.

Beyond that, however, because there is no established factual basis on which to proceed, it is quite untenable to conclude that a putative father's interest in his child is lacking in substance, that the father in effect has abandoned the child, or ultimately that the father's interest is not entitled to the same minimum procedural protections as the interests of other putative fathers. Any analysis of the adequacy of the notice in this case must be conducted on the assumption that the interest involved here is as strong as that of any putative father. That is not to say that due process requires actual notice to every putative father or that adoptive parents or the State must conduct an exhaustive search of records or an intensive investigation before a final adoption order may be entered. The procedures adopted by the State, however, must at least represent a reasonable effort to determine the identity of the putative father and to give him adequate notice.

II

In this case, of course, there was no question about either the identity or the location of the putative father. The mother knew exactly who he was and both she and the court entering the order of adoption knew precisely where he was and how to give him actual notice that his parental rights were about to be terminated by an adoption order. Lehr was entitled to due process, and the right to be heard is one of the fundamentals of that right, which "has little reality or worth unless one is informed that the matter is pending and can choose for himself whether to appear or default, acquiesce or contest."

The State concedes this much but insists that Lehr has had all the process that is due to him. . . . I am unpersuaded by the State's position. In the first place, § 111-a defines six categories of unwed fathers to whom notice must be given even though they have not placed their names on file pursuant to the section. Those six categories, however, do not include fathers such as Lehr who have initiated filiation proceedings, even though their identity and interest are as clearly and easily ascertainable as those fathers in the six categories. . . .

The State asserts that any problem in this respect is overcome by the seventh category of putative fathers to whom notice must be given, namely those fathers who have identified themselves in the putative father register maintained by the State. . . . I have difficulty with this position. First, it represents a grudging and crabbed approach to due process. The State is quite willing to give notice and a hearing to putative fathers who have made themselves known by resorting to the putative fathers' register. It makes little sense to me to deny notice and hearing to a father who has not placed his name in the register but who has unmistakably identified himself by filing suit to establish his paternity and has notified the adoption court of his action and his interest. I thus need not question the statutory scheme on its face. Even assuming that Lehr would have been foreclosed if his failure to utilize the register had somehow disadvantaged the State, he effectively made himself known by other means, and it is the sheerest formalism to deny him a hearing because he informed the State in the wrong manner. . . .

The State's undoubted interest in the finality of adoption orders likewise is not well served by a procedure that will deny notice and a hearing to a father whose identity and location are known. As this case well illustrates, denying notice and a hearing to such a father may result in years of additional litigation and threaten the reopening of adoption proceedings and the vacation of the adoption.

NOTES AND QUESTIONS

1. What was Lehr trying to accomplish by attempting to participate in the adoption proceeding? Was it important that this was a stepparent adoption? Should that matter? *See* In re Baby Girl Eason, 358 S.E.2d 459 (Ga. 1987).

2. What test does *Lehr* adopt for determining when an unmarried father has constitutionally protected custodial rights? What is the basis under this test for custodial rights? What interest of the child (if any) does this test protect? What interests (if any) are disserved?

3. Under the New York statute considered in *Lehr*, when was an unmarried father entitled to notice of an adoption proceeding and an opportunity to participate in it? Is this statute adequate to identify all biological fathers who are entitled to notice under the *Lehr* criteria? Is the statute intended to discover fathers who have developed a substantial relationship with their children as well as those who have not but might want to? Could there be some fathers who have developed a relationship with their children who would not be entitled to notice under the statute?

4. Section 201 of the 2002 Uniform Parentage Act, set out above, provides that an unmarried man who is rebuttably presumed to be a child's father, who has been adjudicated to be the father, or who has signed a voluntary acknowledgment of paternity with the child's mother is entitled to full parental rights, including, of course, notice of adoption and custody proceedings regarding the child. Under the Act, the rights of other putative fathers to notice vary depending on the child's age.

Sections 402 and 404 provide that if the child is less than a year old, such a putative father is entitled to notice only if he has registered with the state putative father registry or has commenced a proceeding to adjudicate his paternity. If the child is older than one year, under § 405, notice must be given to every "alleged father," regardless of whether he has registered. Section 102(3) defines "alleged father" as "a man who alleges himself to be, or is alleged to be, the genetic father or a possible genetic father of a child, but whose paternity has not been determined. The term does not include: (A) a presumed father."

The age-based distinction facilitates adoption of babies while protecting fathers who developed relationships with older children. How would *Lehr* have been decided under the UPA?

5. Statutes of limitation in a number of states provide that an adoption decree may not be collaterally attacked for any reason, including jurisdictional defects, after the statutory period (often one year) expires. If the court applies such statutes of limitation in a case in which the father has not been notified of the adoption, is the result constitutional? *See* In re M.N.M., 605 A.2d 921 (D.C. App. 1992); In re S.L.F., 27 P.3d 583 (Utah App. 2001).

6. In *Caban* and *Lehr* the unmarried father claimed that the statute unconstitutionally discriminated between mothers and fathers. Why did this claim succeed in *Caban* but fail in *Lehr*?

7. The most recent Supreme Court case on the rights of unmarried fathers is Michael H. v. Gerald D., 491 U.S. 110 (1989), which is discussed above at page 877. Michael based his challenge to the California conclusive marital presumption statute on the *Stanley-Lehr* line of cases and claimed that he fit into the category of unmarried fathers given the greatest protection because of his established relationship with the child. Justice Scalia's plurality opinion rejected this argument:

> In Lehr v. Robertson, a case involving a natural father's attempt to block his child's adoption by the unwed mother's new husband, we observed that "[t]he significance of the biological connection is that it offers the natural father an opportunity that no other male possesses to develop a relationship with his offspring," and we assumed that the Constitution might require some protection of that opportunity. Where, however, the child is born into an extant marital family, the natural father's unique opportunity conflicts with the similarly unique opportunity of the husband of the marriage; and it is not unconstitutional for the State to give categorical preference to the latter. . . . In accord with our traditions, a limit is also imposed by the circumstance that the mother is, at the time of the child's conception and birth, married to and cohabitating with another man, both of whom wish to raise the child as the offspring of their union. . . .
>
> We do not accept Justice Brennan's criticism that this result "squashes" the liberty that consists of "the freedom not to conform." It seems to us that reflects the erroneous view that there is only one side to this controversy — that one disposition can expand a "liberty" of sorts without contracting an equivalent "liberty" on the other side. Such a happy choice is rarely available. Here, to provide protection to an adulterous natural father is to deny protection to a marital father, and vice versa. If Michael has a "freedom not to conform" (whatever that means), Gerald must equivalently have a "freedom to conform." One of them will pay a price for asserting that "freedom" — Michael by being unable to act as father of the child he has adulterously

begotten, or Gerald by being unable to preserve the integrity of the traditional family unit he and Victoria have established. Our disposition does not choose between these two "freedoms," but leaves that to the people of California. Justice Brennan's approach chooses one of them as the constitutional imperative, on no apparent basis except that the unconventional is to be preferred.

491 U.S. at 128-130. Justice Brennan dissented for himself and two others, noting that five members of the Court "refuse to foreclose 'the possibility that a natural father might ever have a constitutionally protected interest in his relationship with a child whose mother was married to and cohabiting with another man at the time of the child's conception and birth.' . . . Four Members of the Court agree that Michael H. has a liberty interest in his relationship with Victoria, and one assumes for purposes of this case that he does." *Id.* at 136. The opinion criticized the plurality for ignoring "the very premise of *Stanley* and the cases following it . . . that marriage is not decisive in answering the question whether the Constitution protects the parental relationship under consideration. These cases are, after all, important precisely because they involve the rights of unwed fathers. It is important to remember, moreover, that in *Quilloin, Caban*, and *Lehr*, the putative father's demands would have disrupted a "unitary family" as the plurality defines it; in each case, the husband of the child's mother sought to adopt the child over the objections of the natural father." *Id.* at 144. Justice White also dissented, while Justices O'Connor and Stevens concurred separately.

Would *Michael H.* support state laws that limit unmarried fathers' custodial rights through means other than a conclusive marital presumption?

8. *Lehr* dealt with the rights of the biological father of an older child who never took steps to protect his relationship with the child until adoption was proposed. It did not discuss the rights of fathers of newborns, which the next case considers.

In re Adoption of A.A.T.

196 P.3d 1180 (Kan. 2008)

The opinion of the court was delivered by LUCKERT, J.: . . . This case began in New York, where the natural mother, N.T., became sexually involved with the natural father, M.P. N.T. informed M.P. in mid-October 2003 that she was pregnant with his child. Then, just before Thanksgiving, N.T. left New York to visit her parents in Wichita. She later decided to stay in Kansas.

After leaving New York, N.T. refused to give M.P. the address where she was living, but the couple remained in telephone contact. M.P.'s cell phone records show that as early as November 25, 2003, he was making calls to Wichita.

In a phone call on January 22, 2004, N.T. falsely informed M.P. that she had undergone an abortion. She later testified that she did so because she knew M.P. would not consent to an adoption. After the conversation in which N.T. lied about the abortion, M.P. continued to question N.T. about the pregnancy, doubting her veracity. In May 2004, M.P.'s expression of skepticism led to an argument with N.T. that temporarily stopped their telephone contact.

After a period of time but before the child was born, M.P. and N.T. began talking again and continued to do so throughout the remainder of the pregnancy and following their child's birth on June 24, 2004, in Wichita. During this time, M.P. continued to express his doubts about N.T.'s truthfulness, making statements like, "Why do I have a feeling you're lying to me?" and "I know I have a child, I can feel it." M.P. told a friend that he thought he had a daughter, and he bought a pair of earrings before Christmas 2004, apparently as a gift for the child he imagined he might have.

M.P. was not the only one deceived by N.T. N.T. told her mother, other family members, and friends that the baby died at delivery. She also deceived the adoption agency regarding the identity of the father, claiming not to know his last name and to have only vague information about where he lived.

The day after the birth, N.T. directed that A.A.T. be given to the adoptive parents, who took the baby home from the hospital. The adoptive parents filed their petition for adoption and for termination of the parental rights of the father on July 1, 2004, when A.A.T. was 1 week old. As part of this proceeding, N.T. again lied. She executed an affidavit that gave a false surname for the newborn child's putative father. She also falsely stated that the father was "not willing to be of assistance to [her] during the pregnancy and with regard to these proceedings" and that she had no personal knowledge of his background information.

A guardian ad litem (GAL) was appointed to represent the putative father. After interviewing N.T., the GAL filed an affidavit with the court, passing on incorrect information supplied by N.T., including a false surname for the putative father and representations that N.T. had not contacted the father since her second month of pregnancy and that he was aware of her intent to place their child for adoption. In addition, N.T. failed to pass along information such as M.P.'s address. . . .

In the absence of correct information about M.P. and his willingness or unwillingness to relinquish his parental rights under K.S.A. 59-2124, a notice including the inaccurate name of the putative father and "To Whom It May Concern" was published in the New York Post on July 30, 2004, and August 6, 2004. The item in the New York Post, which circulates to every county in New York, also contained A.A.T.'s last name and stated that Kansas was the location of the proceeding. Nothing was done to provide actual notice of the adoption to M.P.

No father appeared before the court. The natural father's parental rights thus were terminated and the adoption decree was finalized on August 24, 2004.

In late December 2004, when A.A.T. was 6 months old, N.T. finally told M.P. the truth. Within 6 weeks, M.P. had retained Kansas counsel and had begun this action to set aside the adoption . . . . M.P., possibly with the assistance of his lawyer, had been able to obtain the names, residential address, and church affiliation of the adoptive parents.

. . . At a March 23, 2005, hearing, the district court ordered the matter to proceed and considered whether genetic testing should be performed to determine if M.P. was the father and thus had standing to challenge the adoption. . . .

. . . DNA tests were performed. The results confirmed M.P.'s paternity of A.A.T. M.P. then sought a trial on the issue of whether the adoption should be set aside . . . .

After trial, the district court refused to set aside the adoption decree. The court found, *inter alia*, that the adoption agency and adoptive parents had acted in good faith in the adoption proceeding. The court also found that M.P. had not abandoned N.T. during her pregnancy and that M.P. had not learned of A.A.T.'s birth until December 24 or 25, 2004. Still, the court further found that M.P. "should have known and did suspect [N.T.] was still pregnant with his child and she gave birth to his child." Under these circumstances, M.P. "should have taken action to determine whether [N.T.] had had an abortion or was still pregnant . . . and . . . gave birth to his child." . . .

. . . In light of these circumstances, we must determine whether M.P. had a constitutionally protected liberty interest under the Due Process Clause of the Fourteenth Amendment to the United States Constitution, the only basis M.P. asserts for his claim that he was entitled to notice of the adoption proceeding. The Due Process Clause is invoked only when the State takes action to deprive any person of life, liberty, or property. Lehr v. Robertson, 463 U.S. 248, 256 (1983).

If life, liberty, or property is at stake, procedural due process requires the State to provide notice of a potential deprivation of the interest and an opportunity to be heard regarding the deprivation. It is necessarily implied that both the notice and opportunity to be heard must be provided at a meaningful time and in a meaningful manner to comport with the constitutional guarantee.

In arguing that he has a liberty interest, M.P. relies upon the United States Supreme Court's recognition of a natural parent's right to "the companionship, care, custody, and management" of his or her child as a liberty interest far more important than any property right. Santosky v. Kramer, 455 U.S. 745, 758-59 (1982); Lassiter v. Department of Social Services, 452 U.S. 18, 27 640 (1981); see also Wisconsin v. Yoder, 406 U.S. 205 (1972) (parents have protected liberty interest in controlling their children's religious upbringing); Pierce v. Society of Sisters, 268 U.S. 510 (1925) (parents have protected liberty interest in the way they choose to educate their children); Meyer v. Nebraska, 262 U.S. 390 (1923) (parents have protected liberty interest in controlling their children's education). . . .

Obviously, the liberty interest of a natural parent has its origin in the biological connection between the parent and the child. Nevertheless, a biological relationship does not guarantee the permanency of the parental rights of an unwed natural father. Rather, "[t]he significance of the biological connection is that it offers the natural father an opportunity that no other male possesses to develop a relationship with his offspring." *Lehr*, 463 U.S. at 262. The opportunity is lost, however, if the natural father does not come forward to "demonstrate[ ] a full commitment to the responsibilities of parenthood." 463 U.S. at 261.

DECISIONS REGARDING UNWED FATHERS

Several decisions of the United States Supreme Court establish this principle and emphasize the importance of an actual relationship of parental responsibility as distinguished from a mere biological relationship. [The court reviewed *Stanley*, *Quilloin*, *Caban*, and *Lehr*.] . . .

Although *Lehr* and the other decisions of the Supreme Court provide guidance, none address a newborn adoption, leaving it to the state courts to determine how to measure whether a putative father of a newborn child has fully and completely grasped his opportunity to parent.

Two of the first newborn adoption cases to apply *Lehr*'s requirement that the putative father must have taken some measure of the responsibility for the child's future were Matter of Baby Girl S., 141 Misc. 2d 905, 535 N.Y.S.2d 676 (1988), *aff'd without op.*, 150 A.D.2d 993, 543 N.Y.S.2d 602 (1989), *aff'd sub nom.* Matter of Raquel Marie X., 76 N.Y.2d 387, 559 N.Y.S.2d 855, 559 N.E.2d 418, *cert. denied sub nom.* Robert C. v. Miguel T., 498 U.S. 984 (1990), and its companion, Matter of Raquel Marie X., 76 N.Y.2d 387, 559 N.Y.S.2d 855, 559 N.E.2d 418.

New York's highest court, considering the consolidated appeal of the two cases, first compared *Caban* with *Quilloin* and *Lehr*. From those cases, the New York court discerned that "it is apparent that the biological parental interest can be lost entirely, or greatly diminished in constitutional significance, by failure to timely exercise it or by failure to take the available legal steps to substantiate it." Based upon this concept, the New York court concluded that the father of a newborn child is entitled to constitutional protection of his rights "so long as he *promptly* avails himself of *all* the possible mechanisms for forming a legal and emotional bond with his child." (Emphasis added.) . . .

The tests formulated by other courts have been similar, although most have stopped short of the New York requirement that *all* available opportunities must have been seized. *E.g.*, Adoption of Kelsey S., 1 Cal. 4th 816, 849, 4 Cal. Rptr. 2d 615, 823 P.2d 1216 (1992) (father must "promptly come forward and demonstrate a full commitment to his parental responsibilities"); In re Adoption of B.G.S., 556 So. 2d 545, 550 (La. 1990) (father of newborn child must "demonstrate that he is fit and committed to the responsibilities of parenthood" and "show that he has taken concrete actions to grasp his opportunity to be a father"); Heidbreder v. Carton, 645 N.W.2d 355, 372-73 n.12 (Minn.), *cert. denied*, 537 U.S. 1046 (2002) (father must "affirmatively demonstrate a commitment" to parenting responsibilities; merely maintaining contact with mother by e-mail, contacting attorney, and attempting to locate mother does not indicate an "intent to rear the child"); In re Dixon, 112 N.C. App. 248, 251, 435 S.E.2d 352 (1993) (father must discover birth of child and take statutory steps to demonstrate his commitment to child); In re Baby Boy K., 546 N.W.2d 86, 97 (S.D. 1996) ("Because children require early and consistent nurturing of their emotional as well as physical needs, an unwed father must act quickly to grasp the opportunity interest in his biological child."); In re Adoption of B.V., 33 P.3d 1083, 1086 (Utah App. 2001) (unwed biological father ""must fully and strictly comply"" with statutory conditions or ""is deemed to have waived and surrendered any right in relation to child""; he must initiate proceeding to establish paternity, and if he has knowledge of the pregnancy, pay reasonable amount of expenses); In re C.L., 178 Vt. 558, 560-61, 878 A.2d 207 (2005) (father must assume responsibilities in "reasonable" time and reasonableness judged from the perspective of the child's needs).

The outcomes in these cases are not perfectly consistent, given variability in fact situations and state laws. Some states limit the time period during which an adoption can be set aside, regardless of the circumstances; some require statutory compliance with procedures such as filing with a putative father registry; and others specify criteria to be used in judging motions to set aside.

Despite these differences, as we synthesize these holdings, common factors emerge. In general, a putative father has a liberty interest affording a right to notice of proceedings to adopt his newborn child if he: (1) diligently took affirmative action that manifested a full commitment to parenting responsibilities and (2) did so during the pregnancy and within a short time after he discovered or reasonably should have discovered that the biological mother was pregnant with his child.

Regarding the first factor, to determine if a natural father of a newborn child has taken diligent, affirmative action, courts measure the putative father's efforts to make a financial commitment to the upbringing of the child, to legally substantiate his relationship with the child, and to provide emotional, financial, and other support to the mother during the pregnancy. Following the holdings in *Quilloin* and *Lehr*, often courts have required the father to use those legal mechanisms within his control that would entitle him to notice under the state's statutes, *i.e.*, acknowledge or prove paternity, agree to a support order, or file with a putative father registry, and have done so even if a statute does not specify that adherence is required.

This principle has been applied in many cases where the father was unaware of the child's existence. (Citations omitted.)

The second factor — timeliness or promptness of the father's action — has been emphasized, often being cited as the most critical factor. In a newborn adoption, the father's opportunity to make a commitment to parenting must have been grasped during the pregnancy and in a prompt and timely manner as measured by the fleeting opportunity availed to the father under the circumstances of the case, in other words, within a short time after he discovered or reasonably should have discovered that the mother was pregnant with his child.

The need for promptness reflects the reality of the newborn adoption situation, which provides the father with only a limited time in which to act. The necessity of promptness results from two primary considerations. First, in a newborn adoption case, the window of opportunity for a father to have grasped an opportunity interest is constrained by the biological reality that the mother bears the child during pregnancy. As one court noted, during a pregnancy a mother must make many important decisions including whether to have an abortion, prepare an adoption plan, or keep the child. Recognizing that the natural mother, in making these decisions, "may well need emotional, financial, medical, or other assistance," the court concluded the natural father, as one of two people responsible for the pregnancy, must have " 'promptly' demonstrated a 'full commitment' to parenthood *during pregnancy* and within a short time after he discovered or reasonably should have discovered that the biological mother was pregnant with his child." Adoption of Michael H., 10 Cal. 4th 1043, 1054, 43 Cal. Rptr. 2d 445, 898 P.2d 891 (1995), *cert. denied sub nom.* Mark K. v. John S., 516 U.S. 1176 (1996). While a father cannot assume the physical aspects of pregnancy, he may assist with the financial and emotional aspects of the pregnancy and assure the mother of his commitment to fully assume parenting responsibilities both during the pregnancy and throughout the child's lifetime, including being a sole parent if necessary.

The second reason a natural father's actions must be timely was emphasized in Lehr v. Robertson, 463 U.S. 248, 262-64 n.20 (1983): States have an interest in being able to determine as early as possible in a child's life the rights, interests, and obligations of all parties, in eliminating the risk of unnecessary controversy that might impair the finality of an adoption, in encouraging adoptions, in protecting the adoption process from unnecessary controversy and complication, and in protecting the privacy and liberty interests of the natural mother and all parties to the adoption. As the California court stated in Adoption of Michael H.:

> "[I]f an unwed father is permitted to ignore his parental role during pregnancy but claim it after birth, it will often be very difficult to know with certainty whether he will be able to successfully contest an adoption until after the child is born. This uncertainty could well dissuade prospective adoptive parents from attempting to adopt the children of unwed mothers who . . . have chosen for whatever reason not to keep their child and raise it themselves. And that result would frustrate the state's clear interest in encouraging such adoptions and providing stable homes for children. [Citations omitted.]"

In addition, the finalization of an adoption gives rise to a legal relationship between the adoptive parents and the child, creating liberty interests.

In this case, M.P. did not diligently take affirmative action that manifested a full commitment to parenting responsibilities during the pregnancy and within a short time after he discovered N.T. was pregnant with his child. In fact, M.P. does not suggest he took affirmative steps that demonstrated his commitment to parenting. His only suggestion regarding his assumption of parental duties is a statement in his brief that "N.T. knew M.P. would have done anything N.T. asked to support her during her pregnancy." However, standing ready and being willing to provide support is insufficient; parenting responsibilities must be assumed; affirmative action must be taken. Furthermore, the record does not evidence any support, financial or otherwise, being provided, with the exception of some insignificant financial payments of $200 for airfare and "$20 here, $20 there."

Tellingly, M.P. offers no explanation of his failure to act during the time between his learning of the pregnancy and N.T.'s lie about the abortion, the period when N.T. was making decisions regarding adoption. Later, there was no attempt to locate N.T., confirm the pregnancy, substantiate his legal rights, or take other action even though the district court found that M.P. "should have known and did suspect [N.T.] was still pregnant with his child and she gave birth to his child."

M.P. failed to grasp the fleeting opportunity available to him to establish a firm commitment to parenting.

Fraud

M.P. suggests, however, that these considerations do not apply when the father's ability to commit to fatherhood is thwarted by the mother's actions. He suggests the calculus changes from a biology-plus-developed-parenting-relationship formula to a biology-plus-fraud formula when the natural mother is an active agent in preventing actual notice to the natural father.

This issue has not been addressed directly by the United States Supreme Court. Clearly though, in *Lehr*, the majority did not consider the mother's efforts to thwart the father as even deserving of mention. In contrast, the mother's actions were a focus of the dissenting opinion and explain much of the difference in analysis between the two opinions. Nevertheless, the *Lehr* majority did note "[t]here is no suggestion in the record that [the mother] engaged in fraudulent practices that led [the father] not to protect his rights." Thus, the question of whether fraud would change the Supreme Court's view was left unanswered.

State courts have faced the issue, however. The cases reflect that mothers, with some frequency and for a variety of reasons (many of which are very weighty), fail to provide information regarding the putative father or provide inaccurate information. When this happens, competing interests are pitted against each other, including the mother's constitutionally protected privacy interest.

Although there are variances, in general, the cases have not focused upon the natural mother's intent, the reason she was not forthcoming, whether the fraud was concealment by silence (simply failing to inform the father or the court of information) or active (knowingly misstating information), or whether the fraud was intrinsic or extrinsic. Rather, the analysis has focused upon whether the State is justified in ending the putative father's opportunity to develop a relationship and in recognizing the finality of the adoption even though the father's opportunity was burdened and truncated by the birth mother's fraud.

In general, the cases conclude that as long as the state's statutes provide a process whereby most responsible putative fathers can qualify for notice in an adoption proceeding, the interests of the State in the finality of adoption decrees, as discussed in *Lehr* — providing a child stability and security early in life, encouraging adoptions, protecting the adoption process from unnecessary controversy and complication, and protecting other parties' privacy and liberty interests — justify a rule that a putative father's opportunity to develop a parenting relationship ends with the finalization of a newborn child's adoption even if the reason the father did not grasp his opportunity was because of the mother's fraud.

This conclusion is supported by the decision in Matter of Robert O. v. Russell K., 80 N.Y.2d 254, 590 N.Y.S.2d 37, 604 N.E.2d 99 (1992). In that case, New York's highest court concluded a putative father who had assumed no responsibility during a pregnancy did not have a due process interest even though the father was unaware of the child's birth until after the adoption had been finalized. The natural parents were living together at the time of conception but, soon thereafter, the father moved out and terminated contact with the mother. The mother did not inform the father of the pregnancy, apparently because she did not want him to believe she was trying to coerce him into reconciliation. The mother placed the child for adoption. Later, the natural parents reconciled and married. Then, 18 months after the birth and 10 months after the adoption was finalized, the mother ended her fraud by silence and told the father of his child. As in this case, once learning of his child's birth, the father immediately and diligently took action to assert his legal connection with the child.

The New York court concluded, however, that this was too late and rejected the father's suggestion that "the Constitution also protects the custodial opportunity of the 'unknowing' unwed father who does nothing to manifest his parental willingness before placement because he is unaware of the child's existence." The court emphasized that "the opportunity, of limited duration, to manifest a willingness to be a parent . . . becomes protected only if grasped." The court concluded:

"[T]he timing of the father's actions is the 'most significant' element in determining whether an unwed father has created a liberty interest. [Citation omitted.] States have a legitimate concern for prompt and certain adoption procedures and their determination of the rights of unwed fathers need not be blind to the 'vital importance' of creating adoption procedures possessed of 'promptness and finality,' promoting the best interests of the child, and protecting the rights of interested third parties like adoptive parents (Lehr v. Robertson, [463 U.S.] at 263-66 n.25). Recognizing those competing interests — all of which are jeopardized when an unwed father is allowed to belatedly assert his rights . . . the period in which the biological father must manifest his parental interest is limited in duration: if the father's actions are untimely, the State can deny a right of consent. . . .

"To conclude that petitioner acted promptly once he became aware of the child is to fundamentally misconstrue whose timetable is relevant. Promptness is measured in terms of the baby's life not by the onset of the father's awareness. The demand for prompt action by the father at the child's birth is neither arbitrary nor punitive, but instead a logical and necessary outgrowth of the State's legitimate interest in the child's need for early permanence and stability."

In Matter of Robert O., the majority and concurring opinion debated whether the opportunity was a constitutionally protected interest subject to a balancing of interests under a traditional due process test or was merely an opportunity that became extinguished once the adoption was finalized. The majority adopted the latter view because the inchoate interest had never ripened into a liberty interest.

The South Dakota Supreme Court adopted a similar rationale in In re Baby Boy K., 546 N.W.2d 86 (S.D. 1996), a case where the natural mother misrepresented the natural father's identity to the court. . . .

Yet another example of a case using a similar analysis is Petition of Steve B.D., 112 Idaho 22, 730 P.2d 942, a case relied upon by the adoptive parents in this case. . . .

Almost 20 years later, in Doe v. Roe, 142 Idaho 202, 127 P.3d 105 (2005), the Idaho Supreme Court again rejected an unwed natural father's assertion of his interest in his child because of his failure to establish his rights, either pursuant to statute or by timely establishment of a relationship. . . .

Under similar rationales, several other courts have rejected fraud or deception as a substitute for showing that a parenting relationship had been established by an unwed father. (Citations omitted.)

Summarizing the rationale expressed in these cases, one commentator noted: "Blood gives the father the absolute first chance to perform the constitutional duties [of parenting]. If he fails, regardless of his blamelessness, the critical requirement of stability for the child precludes a second chance." Buchanan, *The Constitutional Rights of Unwed Fathers Before and After Lehr v. Robertson*, 45 Ohio St. L.J. 313, 368 (1984).

On the other hand, there are cases in which courts have ruled in putative fathers' favor. Generally, however, there was some circumstance that caused the interests to balance differently. For example, in some cases the adoption was not finalized or the adoptive parents were aware there were questions about the father's identity when they assumed custody or shortly thereafter. Similarly, if the father made efforts to provide financial or emotional support or to protect his legal interests but the attempts were futile because of factors outside his control, the balance may shift. Rarely, however, have the mother's actions alone been sufficient to shift the balance of interests to the point the court determined the State was not justified in ending the father's opportunity to assert his right to parent.

KANSAS ADOPTION STATUTES

With this discussion of cases in mind, we turn to the Kansas Adoption and Relinquishment Act, K.S.A. 59-2111 through K.S.A. 59-2144, and the specifics of this case.

The general rule of the Kansas Adoption and Relinquishment Act is that the consent or relinquishment of both known natural parents is required for an adoption. Departure from this general rule is permitted only if specific statutory requirements are met.

Here, N.T. relinquished custody to the adoption agency, but M.P. neither consented to the adoption nor relinquished custody. In such a case, K.S.A. 59-2136(e) requires a petition to terminate the father's parental rights.

Addressing the right to notice of the proceedings, the statute provides that "[i]n an effort to identify the father, the court shall determine by deposition, affidavit or hearing" if any man (1) is a presumed father under K.S.A. 38-1114, (2) has been determined the father by a court, (3) would be considered a father as to whom the child is a legitimate child under any state's laws, (4) has provided or has promised to provide support to the mother during the pregnancy or to the child after birth, (5) cohabitated with the mother at the time of conception or at birth, or (6) has formally or informally acknowledged or declared possible paternity.

These provisions, like the New York statutes considered in *Lehr*, place several mechanisms within a man's control which, if exercised, entitle him to notice of adoption proceedings. In addition, these categories, like those in New York, are likely to cover responsible fathers who have stepped forward to assume parenting responsibilities.

There is no showing that any of these mechanisms was utilized by M.P., explaining why he bases his arguments on a constitutional, rather than statutory, right to notice.

NEW YORK PROCEDURES

In addition to the Kansas procedures that were available to M.P., Kansas law grants full faith and credit to any proceedings or actions taken under the laws of another state. Hence, under the unique facts of this case, M.P. could have availed himself of legal protections available in New York — the state of his domicile, the location of the child's conception, N.T.'s location when M.P. first learned of the pregnancy, and the location to which N.T. promised to return. This means M.P. could have utilized the putative father registry as discussed in *Lehr*. In addition, New York allows paternity proceedings to be "instituted during the pregnancy of the mother."

M.P.'s use of these procedures might not have guaranteed he would receive notice in Kansas. Yet, cases from other jurisdictions illustrate that a putative father may develop a liberty interest or at least strengthen his argument that he has a liberty interest by attempting to utilize the procedure of his home state even though the mother moved to another state. . . .

Undoubtedly, the human and emotional tensions of this case are enormous, creating sympathy for M.P.'s position and little doubt about the sincerity of his present desire for custody. Nevertheless, the critical fact remains that the opportunity to assert his interest in parenting slipped away without any involvement of the State. The interests of the State and the adoptive family justify a conclusion that M.P.'s opportunity to demonstrate his commitment to parenting passed without developing into a liberty interest.

We hold that M.P. did not have a liberty interest in a relationship with A.A.T. and that the State did not deny him the opportunity to establish such a relationship. Consequently, we affirm the district court's conclusion that the adoption is not void. . . .

Nuss, J., dissenting: . . . In summary, the analysis should begin by viewing mother's year's worth of abortion lies through the *Danforth* lens: an acknowledgment that not even a married woman has an obligation to notify her husband of the fact of her abortion; much less does an unmarried woman have an obligation to obtain the consent of the father before aborting. As reflected in this unwed mother's own testimony, while father disagreed with her, he nevertheless fully respected and essentially felt bound by mother's *Danforth*-based rights and her resultant decision to abort.

The analysis should proceed with a consideration of whether father reasonably should have known of the continued pregnancy based upon all relevant surrounding circumstances, including not only mother's abortion lies to him but also her other efforts to conceal or otherwise obstruct and interfere. A similar standard of reasonable efforts under all the relevant circumstances should apply to father's efforts once he learned of the birth.

The adoptive parents' failure to challenge at the trial court level, much less appeal, that court's fraud findings and conclusions conclusively establishes that father reasonably and justifiably relied upon mother's lies about her abortion; that in reliance upon mother's lies, father reasonably and justifiably failed to act, *i.e.*, to attempt to verify whether she aborted; and that because of father's reliance, mother's lies caused him damage, *i.e.*, his ability to establish more than a biological link with his son. . . .

Assuming that reasonable reliance and resultant damage is not conclusively established by the failure to challenge or appeal, then as Justice Beier discusses, the evidence of record demonstrates the father made considerable efforts that were reasonable when considering all the circumstances. . . .

In my view, none of the separate opinions sufficiently consider the delicate situation created between a man and a woman when the woman, especially one who is unwed, becomes pregnant, nor do they sufficiently consider the resultant sensitivity required. . . .

In my view, the sensitivity required by the father is not only an important factor, but also one that must be kept at the forefront. One must consider whether legitimate efforts of the father, designed to ascertain the unwed pregnant woman's veracity, are nevertheless construed by her as serious assaults on her integrity. When a mother becomes aware of a father's efforts to ascertain her veracity — whether calling the grandmother or the sister, as the majority suggests, or hiring a detective or coming to Kansas himself — those efforts can backfire. They can tip what already may be a precarious balance into the mother's unappealable decision to now obtain an abortion because she considers the father's efforts to be inter- fering with her unilateral right to abort. A mother might also realistically view the father's actions as stalking and a danger to her physically. . . .

And even assuming no word of the father's veracity checks gets back to the mother, or if it does and she nevertheless elects to remain pregnant, will the father be required to monitor mother's activities for the remainder of the pregnancy "just in case" she changes her mind? And even assuming the mother has not been driven away by father's actions, how may his actions affect the chances for eventually establishing a good relationship with her for the benefit of the couple and also the child? . . .

In any event, I readily conclude as a matter of law that the father in the instant case already took enough reasonable steps to establish his constitutionally pro- tected parental relationship with his child. There was no notice given before the State took his liberty interest. Accordingly, relief from the judgment should be granted under K.S.A. 60-260(b)(4); the judgment is void because it was granted in a manner inconsistent with due process. . . .

BEIER, J., dissenting: . . . First, I do not view my differences from the majority as arising out of a disagreement over facts or, more specifically, over factual find- ings of the district court judge. Although it is a fact that M.P. was suspicious, it is not a fact that he should have known N.T. was still pregnant and gave birth to his child. N.T. did everything in her power short of muzzling her mother to prevent M.P. from knowing the true state of affairs until A.A.T. was 6 months old. M.P. may have been less than perfect, but a ruling on whether he ever had parental rights worthy of protection cannot turn on his lack of clairvoyance.

Second, I cannot help but observe that the majority's decision builds a bias into the law that will favor the wealthy or well-financed. The majority says it agrees with the district court that M.P. took "no action" to protect his parental rights, that acting on his suspicions "would have required little effort," and that he could have determined where N.T. was and learned of her continued pregnancy. The undisputed facts, however, demonstrate that M.P. sent N.T. a small amount of money, that he persisted in questioning her, and that he promptly and doggedly pursued access to and a relationship with his child as soon as he learned of N.T.'s multiple lies. I do not accept that the United States Constitution or the adoption law of Kansas require him to hire a private investigator, as was suggested at oral argument, or to incur the expense to come to Kansas personally to challenge N.T.'s story. Although the record indicates that this particular natural father may have had the resources to undertake such efforts, surely that will not be true of all men in his position. . . .

I simply cannot agree with the district judge or with the majority, who appar- ently would force M.P. to meet what I consider a nearly impossible standard, depriving him of his right to parent A.A.T. because he failed to uncover the nature, extent, and effect of N.T.'s lies at some earlier date. I see such a rule as inconsistent with the historical parental preference rule of Kansas common law and our legislature's carefully designed codification of its modern incarnation. I would hold, consistent with United States Supreme Court precedent on unwed fathers and the statutes and cases of this jurisdiction, that M.P.'s "inchoate interest" ripened into a constitutionally protected, substantive due process right not to be deprived of the companionship, care, custody, and management of his child. In the absence of his consent or relinquishment with appropriate notice he would have appeared and objected to A.A.T.'s adoption, and the process due him was that outlined by our legislature in K.S.A. 59-2136(h)(1)–(7). . . .

The possibility that a child of A.A.T.'s age will be removed from the only home A.A.T. has ever known is extremely distressing. It is hard for me to imagine a set of facts that would bring the human and legal tensions between the arguments advanced by the parties and among the interests and issues analyzed by courts into sharper relief than that set before the court here. A natural father was deliberately deceived about the continuation of a pregnancy to term, denying him the practical possibility of choosing to support the mother up to delivery or the child after birth. A mother engaged in an elaborate scheme to prevent the father from discovering that she did not have an abortion and that she placed the child for adoption without his knowledge, consent, or choice to relinquish his rights, again denying him the practical possibility of choosing to support the child. Significant time passed before the father's discovery of the mother's lies; and far more significant time, particularly when measured in child time, passed before the case came before us for decision. In that later period, according to the record before us, the father and his counsel have diligently pursued development and protection of father's legal rights. The adoptive parents and their counsel, understandably, have exercised similar diligence to guard the finality of the adoption and the family to which it gave rise. I am fully aware of the psychological and legal merits of such finality. At this late date, however, it is clear that neither M.P. nor the adoptive parents are likely to volunteer to surrender their claim to exclusive companionship, care, custody, and management of A.A.T. so that the parameters of A.A.T.'s family can be adjusted and maximized to give all of the adults who want to be parents cooperative roles. Thus, in my view, this court is bound to deliver on the promise of the federal Constitution's guarantee of due process to M.P., as that concept has been defined by our legislature. So too is the district judge. Neither this court nor the district court is permitted to default to a merely comfortable result. . . .

ROSEN, J., dissenting: I join with Justice Beier's dissent and rationale to remand to the district court for further factual findings and legal conclusions under K.S.A. 59-2136(h). I write separately, however, to express my disagreement with and concern over the apparent lack of consideration of the best interests of the child, A.A.T. While the majority and the other dissents are concerned with protecting the rights and interests of the adoptive parents and natural father, they do not provide for meaningful consideration of the best interests of the child, which I consider the principal issue in this matter. Promoting the best interests of children permeates both statutory and case law. The best interests of a child are the implicit goal of any custody determination and should be considered here, even though K.S.A. 59-2136 did not expressly require the district court to do so.

When this court makes the statutory rights of the adoptive parents and the due process rights of the natural father dispositive, it dehumanizes A.A.T., treating him as if he were a piece of chattel property with no rights and interests of his own. This court has long held, however, that "a child is not in any sense like a horse or any other chattel." Chapsky v. Wood, 26 Kan. 650, 652 (1881). "[A] parent's right to the custody of a child is not like the right of property, an absolute and uncontrollable right." 26 Kan. at 652-53. . . .

. . . I concur with Justice Beier's dissent in remanding this case for further factual findings and conclusions of law. I part from her dissent in that I believe the best interests of the child should be considered and given weight by the district court when determining whether to set aside the adoption even though such consideration is not explicitly set forth in the statute in effect at the time of the adoption proceeding.

NOTES AND QUESTIONS

1. The judges in *A.A.T.* disagree about whether the biological father took enough initiative to express his interest in the child during the pregnancy. How would you describe that difference? After this case, if you practiced in Kansas, how would you advise an unmarried man who had just learned that his girlfriend was pregnant and who was unsure of what he wanted?

If you represented would-be adoptive parents in Kansas, under what circumstances would you advise them to proceed with an adoption without first obtaining the consent of an unmarried father?

2. The judges in *A.A.T.* also disagree about whether the opportunity to establish a relationship with one's child is itself constitutionally protected. Why does this matter?

3. Would the father in *A.A.T.* have been entitled to notice of his baby's adoption under the Uniform Parentage Act, note 4, page 888, above?

States vary greatly in the extent to which they give unmarried fathers the right to prevent adoption of their children by withholding consent. A number of states have adopted a test similar to Kansas's. *See, e.g.*, Ex parte J.W.B. and K.E.M.B., 933 So. 2d 1081 (Ala. 2005); Escobedo v. Nickita, 231 S.W.3d 601 (Ark. 2006); Adoption of Michael H., 898 P.2d 891 (Cal. 1995) (en banc); Appeal of H.R., 581 A.2d 1141 (D.C. 1990), *on remand*, 630 A.2d 670 (D.C.); Matter of Adoption of Doe, 543 So. 2d 741 (Fla. 1989).

In contrast, in some states, once the fact of the father's paternity is established, his rights are the same as those of the mother. State law in two well-known cases from the mid-1990s took this form, with the result that children who had been placed by their mothers with adoptive parents at birth were eventually returned to their biological fathers after years of litigation. *See* In the Interest of B.G.C., 496 N.W.2d 239 (Iowa 1992) (Baby Jessica case); In re Petition of Kirchner, 496 N.W.2d 239 (Ill. 1995) (Baby Richard case). For a similar result on alterative grounds, *see* In re Adoption of N.L.B., 212 S.W.3d 123 (Mo. 2007) (en banc). If you practiced in a state with this rule, how would you advise the unmarried father? The would-be adoptive parents?

David D. Meyer, Family Ties: Solving the Constitutional Dilemma of the Faultless Father, 41 Ariz. L. Rev. 753 (1999), reports that after the Baby Richard and Baby Jessica cases, a number of states amended their laws to head off similar results. Some states made complete elimination of fathers' claims easier, either by expanding the definitions of abandonment and unfitness as grounds for involuntary termination of parental rights or providing that a father who did not take prescribed steps within a certain time lost his right to custody. Other states gave greater protection to the child's existing placement by providing for long-term custody with the would-be adoptive parents and visitation rights for fathers. *See also* Laura Oren, Unmarried Fathers and Adoption: "Perfecting" or "Abandoning" an Opportunity Interest, 36 Cap. U. L. Rev. 253, (2007); Jeffrey A. Parness, Adoption Notices to Genetic Fathers: No to Scarlet Letters, Yes to Good-Faith Cooperation, 36 Cumb. L. Rev. 63 (2006).

4. On unwed fathers' rights generally, *see* June Carbone, The Missing Piece of the Custody Puzzle: Creating a New Model of Parental Partnership, 39 Santa Clara L. Rev. 1091 (1999); Janet L. Dolgin, The Constitution as Family Arbiter: A Moral in the Mess?, 102 Colum. L. Rev. 337 (2002); Nancy E. Dowd, Fathers and the Supreme Court: Founding Fathers and Nurturing Fathers, 54 Emory L.J. 1271 (2005); James G. Dwyer, A Constitutional Birthright: The State, Parentage, and the Rights of Newborn Persons, 56 UCLA L. Rev. 755 (2009); Leslie J. Harris, A New Paternity Law for the Twenty-first Century: Of Biology, Social Function, Children's Interests, and Betrayal, 44 Willamette L. Rev. 297 (2007); Mark Strasser, The Often Illusory Protections of "Biology Plus": On the Supreme Court's Parental Rights Jurisprudence, 13 Tex. J. C.L. & C.R. 31 (2007); Sharon S. Townsend, Fatherhood: A Judicial Perspective: Unmarried Fathers and the Changing Role of the Family Court, 41 Fam. Ct. Rev. 354 (2003); Barbara B. Woodhouse, Hatching the Egg: A Child-Centered Perspective on Parents' Rights, 14 Cardozo L. Rev. 1747 (1993). For a discussion of these issues in child maltreatment cases, *see* Leslie Joan Harris, Involving Nonresident Fathers in Dependency Cases: New Efforts, New Problems, New Solutions, 9 J.L. Fam. Stud. 281 (2007).

5. Sahin v. Germany, Sommerfeld v. Germany, Hoffman v. Germany, decided by the European Court of Human Rights, October 11, 2001, holds that aspects of German law concerning the rights of unmarried fathers violated the European Convention for the Protection of Human Rights and Fundamental Freedoms. At the time the cases were brought, German law provided that the mother had the right to custody of a child born outside marriage and to determine whether the father could visit, subject to a court's authority to make a contrary decision in the child's best interests. Fathers could not appeal from the court decision. The Court held that the law violated Articles 14 and 8 of the Convention by unjustifiably failing to protect the relationship of the father and child and by denying the father a right to appeal. The judgments are available from the Court's website at http://www.echr.coe.int/Eng/Judgments.htm. Effective July 1, 1998, German law has been amended to provide that the father and mother share parental rights and that they have joint custody with regard to children born outside marriage.

The European Court of Human Rights has subsequently ruled that under Article 8, children have a right to identity that includes a right to determine, though DNA testing, the identity of their deceased fathers even if the "child" is

60 years old (Jaggi v. Switzerland, July 13, 2006). Alleged fathers also have a right of access to DNA testing to disprove paternity established through the marital presumption (Tavli v. Turkey, Nov. 9, 2006; Mizzi v. Malta, Dec. 1, 2006), and the statute of limitations cannot bar an action where the alleged father did not have reason to suspect he might not be a biological father until after the time period had elapsed (Shofman v. Russia, Nov. 24, 2005). Alleged fathers further have a corresponding right to establish paternity that cannot be limited to cases in which the mothers agree or state authorities choose to pursue a paternity action (Rozanski v. Poland, May 18, 2006).

PROBLEMS

1. Anita and Martin lived together for six years, though they never married. Two children were born to them during this time. Martin supported the children, cared for them, and attended school conferences concerning them. Anita and Martin separated eight months ago, when the children were six months and four years old. Six months ago Anita placed the children for adoption with Tim and Karen. She signed a valid document relinquishing her parental rights and falsely told Tim and Karen that she did not know where the children's father was. Martin learned one week later that Anita had placed the children for adoption. He searched for them unsuccessfully by calling all the adoption agencies in the community. Shortly after a court had entered the order granting Tim and Karen's adoption petition, Martin finally discovered that Anita had placed the children privately. Martin was not personally served, but a notice was published in the local newspaper. Martin has moved to set aside the adoption on the grounds of lack of notice. Under the Uniform Parentage Act, was he entitled to notice? Under *Lehr*, would it be constitutional to terminate his rights to the children without notice? If he were given notice and objected to the adoption, would it be constitutional under *A.A.T.* to grant the adoption without his consent?

2. Madelyn and Frank were dating. Madelyn told Frank that she was pregnant, but he seemed indifferent. She told him that she intended to place the baby for adoption, and he was silent. After the baby was born, Frank visited Madelyn and the baby in the hospital once, but he did not provide any financial support to Madelyn or the baby during the pregnancy or after the birth. Madelyn placed the child with an adoption agency, relinquishing her parental rights, when the baby was three days old. Madelyn told the agency that Frank was the father, and a representative of the agency contacted him. He refused to sign a form consenting to the baby's adoption but said that he would not interfere. The agency placed the baby for adoption with the Patrick family. When the baby was seven months old, Frank filed a petition seeking custody or visitation of the baby. The Patricks and the adoption agency responded by filing an adoption petition, alleging that Frank's consent was not required. Under *A.A.T.* is his consent required?

3. While Dawn was separated from her husband, Frank, she began living with Jerry and became pregnant by him. Three months later she moved back in with Frank and in due course gave birth to a son. During this time Jerry took parenting classes, purchased items for the baby for his house, and did other things to prepare himself for fatherhood. He tried unsuccessfully to see Dawn after she returned to

Frank and to persuade Dawn and Frank to let him visit the baby. Jerry has now filed a paternity suit under the Uniform Parentage Act seeking a declaration of paternity and visitation rights. What arguments should Dawn and Frank, who want to keep Jerry out of their lives, make? How should Jerry respond?

3. Biological Paternity and Child Support

Legal parenthood is not always a voluntary status. A major impetus in the evolving law of parentage over the last quarter-century, particularly as the number and needs of nonmarital children have increased, has been the effort to establish support rights. While today we consider such rights to be the most important claim of a child against parents, the common law did not recognize a generally applicable, legally enforceable support duty for any parents. The modern efforts to enhance the effectiveness of child support enforcement coincided with the expansion of welfare benefits and the desire to protect the public fisc. *See generally* Leslie J. Harris, Dennis Waldrop & Lori R. Waldrop, Making and Breaking Connections Between Parents' Duty to Support and Right to Control Their Children, 60 Or. L. Rev. 691, 692-696 (1990). As recently as 1971 some states still imposed no generally applicable support duty on unmarried fathers. Harry Krause, Illegitimacy: Law and Social Policy 22 (1971). In Gomez v. Perez, 409 U.S. 535 (1973), however, the Supreme Court held that denying a nonmarital child the right to support from the father when marital children had such a right violates the equal protection clause.

Current policy trends contrast sharply with the common law reluctance to enforce parental support duties, including the duties of unmarried fathers. The general rule is that proof of biological parenthood is sufficient for imposing a support duty, and courts and legislatures are extremely reluctant to excuse this duty. The principle of holding biological fathers responsible for supporting their children has resulted in some extreme judicial holdings, perhaps the most well-known of which are the "statutory rape" rule and the "lie about contraception" rule. Applying the statutory rape rule, a number of courts have held that teenage and even pre-teen boys, all too young to be able to consent to sexual intercourse, were liable for child support for their children born to older girls and adult women. One court reached this conclusion even though it expressly acknowledged that there was very little chance that any money would ever be collected. San Luis Obispo County v. Nathaniel J, 57 Cal. Rptr. 2d 843 (Cal. App. 1996) (15-year-old boy who had sex with a 34-year-old woman); *see also* Dep't of Revenue v. Miller, 688 So. 2d 1024 (Fla. Dist. Ct. App. 1997) (15-year-old boy and 20-year-old woman); Kansas ex rel. Hermesmann v. Seyer, 847 P.2d 1273, 1279 (Kan. 1993) (12-year-old boy held liable for support of child born to 16-year-old girl, even though the state welfare office conceded that there was very little chance any money would be collected; collecting cases from other jurisdictions).

In a number of cases from around the country, biological fathers have argued that they should not be required to pay child support because the mother intentionally lied about using birth control. Courts simply do not find this to be fraud or say that even if it is, excusing the man from the child support obligation is not the remedy. *See, e.g.*, Erwin L.D. v. Myla Jean L., 847 S.W.2d 45, 46 (Ark. Ct. App. 1993); Stephen K. v. Roni L., 164 Cal. Rptr. 618, 619-621 (Cal. App. 1980); Wallis v. Smith, 22 P.3d 682 (N.M. 2001); Douglas R. v. Suzanne M., 487 N.Y.S.2d 244, 246 (Sup. Ct. 1985); Hughes v. Hutt, 455 A.2d 623 (Pa. 1983); Linda D. v. Fritz C., 687 P.2d 223, 227 (Wash. Ct. App. 1984).

In a more sophisticated attempt to avoid liability, the biological father in L. Pamela P. v. Frank S., 449 N.E.2d 713 (N.Y. 1983), argued that he had a constitutionally protected right to choose whether to be a parent and that finding him to be the child's legal father for purposes of the support duty unconstitutionally infringed upon that right. The New York Court of Appeals rejected the argument, saying that a man has a right to decide whether to be a *biological* parent, but that the Constitution only protects against governmental interference with private choice. The court said that in this case Pamela, a private individual, interfered with his choice, and that the Constitution provides no redress for that. In contrast, the Sixth Circuit in Dubay v. Wells, 506 F.3d 422 (6th Cir. 2007), agreed with the father that the critical question in such a case is whether the man is the child's legal father, an issue determined by state law, not by the mother. However, the court also rejected the man's equal protection argument, finding that the statutory provision making him the child's legal father was rationally related to the state's interest in "ensur[ing] that the minor children born outside marriage are provided with support and education."

These and related issues are discussed in Pinhas Shifman, Involuntary Parenthood: Misrepresentation as to the Use of Contraceptives, 4 Int'l J.L. & Fam. 279 (1990); Linda L. Berger, Lies Between Mommy and Daddy: The Case for Recognizing Spousal Emotional Distress Claims Based on Domestic Deceit That Interferes with Parent-Child Relationships, 33 Loy. L.A. L. Rev. 449, 501-508 (2000); Donald C. Hubin, Daddy Dilemmas: Untangling the Puzzles of Paternity, 13 Cornell J.L. & Pub. Pol'y 29 (2003); Niccol D. Kording, Little White Lies That Destroy Children's Lives: Recreating Paternity Fraud Laws to Protect Children's Interests, 6 J.L. Fam. Stud. 237 (2004); Adrienne D. Gross, Note: A Man's Right to Choose: Searching for Remedies in the Face of Unplanned Fatherhood, 55 Drake L. Rev. 1015 (2007).

In child support cases, as in custody and visitation cases, mothers have sometimes argued that a man should be estopped to deny paternity because he represented that he would act as the child's father and the mother or child detrimentally relied on the representation. In other cases mothers have argued that the man stands *in loco parentis* to the child and so has a support duty. While some courts have held that these allegations state a claim for relief, they typically require a very strong showing of detrimental reliance on the man's representations that he would act as the father. *See, e.g.*, M.H.B. v. H.T.B., 498 A.2d 775 (N.J. 1985); A.S. v. B.S., 354 A.2d 100 (N.J. Super. 1976), *aff'd*, 374 A.2d 1259 (N.J. Super. 1977); Niesen v. Niesen, 157 N.W.2d 660 (Wis. 1968); *see also* Margaret Mahoney, Support and Custody Aspects of the Stepparent-Child Relationship, 70 Cornell L. Rev. 38 (1984). For example, in Miller v. Miller, 478 A.2d 351 (N.J. 1984), the court held that a stepfather would be liable only if he encouraged the child to rely on him for support and the child would suffer financial harm if the stepfather were allowed to repudiate the financial obligation.

Finally, mothers typically do not even bother to argue that the best interests of the child should preclude a man from disclaiming the role of father (even though, of course, it might well be in the child's best interests if the man paid child support). Best interests is just not an issue when it comes to determining parentage for purposes of child support.

The legal issue linking legal paternity and child support duties that is most frequently litigated today is under what circumstances paternity can be disestablished. We have already examined an aspect of this issue above, considering challenges to presumptions of paternity, particularly the presumption based on marriage. Paternity determinations that are theoretically more conclusive, those based on judgments or voluntary acknowledgments, are also common. The first issue in such challenges is often whether a court will order genetic testing.

State, Dep't of Revenue ex rel. Chambers v. Travis

971 So. 2d 157 (Fla. Dist. Ct. App. 2007)

BENTON, J. By petition for writ of certiorari, the Department of Revenue (DOR) seeks review of a non-final circuit court order denying DOR's motion to vacate an order requiring paternity testing. In the absence of any showing of good cause, the circuit court departed from the essential requirements of law in requiring the mother (along with respondent and the child) to submit to DNA testing. Because this departure may result in harm that cannot be remedied on plenary appeal,[28] we grant the petition. . . .

On January 20, 2003, Donneshia Chambers and Terrell D. Travis executed a "paternity affidavit by natural parents" acknowledging Mr. Travis as the biological father of a child born two days earlier. This duly notarized affidavit established a "rebuttable presumption . . . of paternity" pursuant to section 742.10(1), Florida Statutes (2003), which provides, in relevant part, as follows:

> [W]hen an affidavit or notarized voluntary acknowledgment of paternity as provided for in § 382.013 or § 382.016 is executed by both parties, it shall constitute the establishment of paternity for purposes of this chapter. If no adjudicatory proceeding was held, a notarized voluntary acknowledgment of paternity shall create a rebuttable presumption . . . of paternity and is subject to the right of any signatory to rescind the acknowledgment within 60 days of the date the acknowledgment was signed or

---

28. *See* Dep't of Revenue ex rel. Gardner v. Long, 937 So. 2d 1235, 1237 (Fla. 1st DCA 2006) ("We find that subjecting Mother and Child to a potentially intrusive [paternity] test . . . is enough to constitute irreparable harm."); Dep't of Revenue ex rel. T.E.P. v. Price, 958 So. 2d 1045, 1046 (Fla. 2d DCA 2007) ("Because this error cannot be corrected through a direct appeal, for the improper genetic testing requiring a blood draw would have already been completed, the error must be corrected through certiorari proceedings."); Reiss v. Dep't of Revenue ex rel. Sava, 753 So. 2d 764, 765 (Fla. 4th DCA 2000) (granting DOR's petition for writ of certiorari where trial court improperly ordered paternity test); Dep't of Revenue ex rel. Freckleton v. Goulbourne, 648 So. 2d 856, 858 (Fla. 4th DCA 1995) (same); Marshek v. Marshek, 599 So. 2d 175, 176 (Fla. 1st DCA 1992) (same).

the date of an administrative or judicial proceeding relating to the child, including a proceeding to establish a support order, in which the signatory is a party, whichever is earlier.

Pursuant to section 742.10(4), Florida Statutes (2007), such a signed voluntary acknowledgment of paternity, because it was not rescinded within the 60-day period following the date the acknowledgment was signed, "shall constitute an establishment of paternity and may be challenged in court only on the basis of fraud, duress, or material mistake of fact, with the burden of proof upon the challenger."

On October 17, 2005, some two years and nine months after Mr. Travis formally acknowledged paternity, the DOR filed (on behalf of Ms. Chambers) a petition for support and other relief seeking to establish that respondent had a child support obligation. . . . Although acknowledging that he signed the paternity affidavit and alleging that he had in fact acted as the child's custodial parent for most of the child's life, Mr. Travis, out of a "desire[ ] to be sure that he is the biological father of the child" in light of what he alleged to have been the mother's "past promiscuous behavior," requested DNA testing prior to the establishment of any support obligation.

Over DOR's objections that signing a paternity affidavit had made him the legal father of the child pursuant to section 742.10, Florida Statutes (2003), the hearing officer recommended to the trial court entry of an order requiring the mother, the child, and Mr. Travis to submit to DNA testing at his expense. The trial court entered an order approving and ratifying the hearing officer's recommended order. . . .

Where the putative father is not the child's biological father, the Legislature has provided that paternity established by his voluntary acknowledgment of paternity may be "disestablished" in accordance either with section 742.10(4) or with section 742.18, Florida Statutes (2007). . . .

A signed voluntary acknowledgment of paternity that establishes paternity pursuant to section 742.10(4), Florida Statutes (2007), may be challenged "on the basis of fraud, duress, or material mistake of fact, with the burden of proof upon the challenger." § 742.10(4), Fla. Stat. (2007). A challenge may be brought on these grounds under section 742.10(4), whether or not all the requirements set out in section 742.18 are met.

In addition, "a male may disestablish paternity or terminate a child support obligation when the male is not the biological father of the child," § 742.18(1), Fla. Stat. (2007), although neither fraud nor duress induced the signing of the acknowledgment of paternity, except in certain circumstances.[29] If he proceeds pursuant to section 742.18, Florida Statutes (2007), he must file a petition in circuit court that includes (1) an affidavit averring "that newly discovered evidence relating to the paternity of the child has come to the petitioner's knowledge since the initial

---

29. The statute provides that a court shall not set aside a paternity determination if the putative father engages in certain conduct *after* learning he is not the child's biological father, such as voluntarily acknowledging paternity pursuant to section 742.10(4) or consenting to be named on the child's birth certificate as the child's biological father.

paternity determination or establishment of a child support obligation"; (2) the results of a paternity test generally accepted within the scientific community demonstrating a probability that the petitioner cannot be the biological father of the child or an affidavit alleging that the petitioner lacked access to the child that scientific testing requires; and (3) an affidavit in which the petitioner avers that he has substantially complied with any child support obligation for the child and that any delinquency resulted from his "inability for just cause to pay the delinquent child support" when it became due. The circuit court must grant relief if it finds each of seven requirements is met, including a requirement that the petitioner has become aware of newly discovered evidence since paternity was initially determined or a child support obligation was initially established.

But Mr. Travis has instituted no proceedings, either under section 742.10(4) or under section 742.18, to disestablish the paternity which his notarized, voluntary acknowledgment of paternity established under section 742.10(1). In the child support proceedings pending before the support enforcement hearing officer, he made no allegation of fraud, duress, material mistake of fact, or newly discovered evidence that might have placed his paternity in controversy in circuit court. Absent any such allegation, and absent proof in support, he failed to show good cause for a court order for paternity testing.

The support hearing officer, when considering Mr. Travis's request for DNA testing in the child support proceedings DOR instituted against him on behalf of Ms. Chambers, was faced with what can be viewed as a discovery request. . . . But no party to any family law proceeding is entitled to an order requiring another party to submit to genetic testing unless (1) the proceedings place paternity "in controversy" and (2) "good cause" exists for the testing.

Here the child's legal father requested genetic testing in connection with child support proceedings instituted by DOR merely in order "to be sure" that he was the child's biological father before being required to pay child support. Absent any allegation or proof of fraud, duress, material mistake of fact, or newly discovered evidence, no good cause was shown to justify the hearing officer's recommendation to require the mother and child to submit to DNA testing. The trial court's order adopting the recommendation should have been vacated. Denial of the motion to vacate departed from the essential requirements of law.

Accordingly, we grant the petition, issue the writ, quash the order on review, and remand for further proceedings.

NOTES AND QUESTIONS

1. In many paternity disestablishment cases, the legal father alleges that the mother committed fraud by representing that he was the biological father when she knew he was not. In some cases, the evidence supports this claim of deceit, but more often the facts show that the mother just failed to disclose that another man could be the biological father. Does this amount to fraud? Does this show material mistake?

In cases involving challenges to VAPs based on genetic testing that shows that the man who signed the VAP is not the biological father, courts are remarkably consistent in ruling that a VAP will not be set aside if the man knew or suspected that he was not the biological father, regardless of whether the challenge is brought by the man who signed the VAP or the mother. *See, e.g.,* Madison v. Osburn, 396 S.W.3d 264 (Ark. App. 2013), *overruled on other grounds by* Furr v. James, 2013 Ark. App. 181; Allison v. Medlock, 983 So. 2d 789 (Fla. Dist. Ct. App. 2008); Van Weelde v. Van Weelde, 110 So. 3d 918 (Fla. Dist. Ct. App. 2013); In re Paternity of H.H. v. Hughes, 879 N.E.2d 1175 (Ind. App. 2008); In re Paternity of Cheryl, 746 N.E.2d 488 (Mass. 2001); Demetrius H. v. Mikhaila C.M., 827 N.Y.S.2d 810 (App. Div. 2006).

2. The first statute that the *Chambers* court discusses is the kind of statute enacted in all states to comply with federal law, allowing a VAP to be set aside if a party shows that it was based on fraud, duress, or material mistake of fact. The second statute is newer and representative of those that have been enacted in more than half the states that allow a legal determination of the paternity of a nonmarital child to be set aside based on evidence that the legal father is not the biological father without additional evidence of fraud, duress, mistake, or something equivalent. Of these states, 18 allow courts to refuse to set aside a judgment or a VAP based on estoppel or the child's best interests, or both, but the remainder do not. Thirteen states have statutes of limitations on motions to disestablish paternity in some or all cases; in the other states a legal determination of paternity is vulnerable to challenge at least throughout the child's minority. And almost half of these statutes are not gender neutral but instead empower only the legal father to challenge paternity, at least in some situations. Leslie Joan Harris, Reforming Paternity Law to Eliminate Gender, Status and Class Inequality, 2013 Mich. St. L. Rev. 1295, 1320-1327.

Even in states with such statutes, if the mother brings the challenge and she and the man knew or suspected that he was not the father, she loses. For the most part, courts explain this outcome by saying that the facts do not establish fraud or mistake or that they do establish that the challenger is estopped from denying the man's paternity without further comment. On the other hand, if the man petitions to set aside the VAP when he did not know or have reason to suspect that he was not the biological father, courts usually grant his petition, even though he could have sought genetic testing before signing the VAP. *See, e.g.,* Dep't of Human Servs. v. Chisum, 85 P.3d 860, 861-862 (Okla. App. 2004); Glover v. Severino, 946 A.2d 710, 716 (Pa. Super. Ct. 2008).

3. Studies show that almost always the man identified as a child's legal father is the biological father. The most comprehensive data analysis concluded that in the United States, 98 percent of the men raising children they believe to be their biological children are correct and that only 30 percent of the men who seek blood tests to confirm paternity are not the biological fathers. Kermyt G. Anderson, How Well Does Paternity Confidence Match Actual Paternity? Results from Worldwide Nonpaternity Rates, 47 Current Anthropology 513, 516 (2006).

4. For further discussion of voluntary acknowledgments and the legal status of unmarried parents, *see* Paula Roberts, Truth and Consequences: Part I. Disestablishing the Paternity of Non-Marital Children, 37 Fam. L.Q. 35 (2003); Paula Roberts, Truth and Consequences: Part II. Questioning the Paternity of Marital Children, 37 Fam. L.Q. 55 (2003); Paula Roberts, Truth and Consequences: Part III. Who Pays When Paternity Is Disestablished? 37 Fam. L.Q. 69 (2003); Jane C. Murphy, Legal Images of Fatherhood: Welfare Reform, Child

Support Enforcement and Fatherless Children, 81 Notre Dame L. Rev. 325, 346 (2005); Melanie B. Jacobs, When Daddy Doesn't Want to Be Daddy Anymore: An Argument Against Paternity Fraud Claims, 16 Yale J.L. & Feminism 193 (2004).

PROBLEM

J. was born in July 1997. Sheldon, the baby's biological father, refused to acknowledge that the child might be his and provided the mother with no support or assistance during the period leading up to the child's birth. The mother and Leon, a friend of the mother, signed and filed a voluntary declaration of paternity so that the child would have someone to look after her should something happen to her mother. After the birth, blood tests confirmed Sheldon's paternity. Sheldon then moved in with J. and her mother, and he contributed support to the household until September 2000, when he and J.'s mother separated. In an action against Sheldon for child support, what will be the result?

C. LEGAL RECOGNITION OF FUNCTIONAL PARENTS

Traditionally, the marital presumption served not just as a convenient presumption of biological paternity, but as a bright-line rule that locked functional fathers into a parental role. Pregnant women felt the pressure to marry someone, whether or not the biological father, to "give the child a name," and the courts often used estoppel principles to confirm the parental status of a man who held out the child as his own in the face of certain knowledge that he could not have fathered the child. *See, e.g.*, Clevenger v. Clevenger, 189 Cal. App. 2d 658 (1961). Conversely, however, the same courts would almost certainly refuse to recognize the parental status of a man playing the same functional role who neither married the mother nor adopted the child. If the mother married a man who was not the biological father, the law did not recognize rights and duties between him and the child. *See* Cynthia Grant Bowman, The Legal Relationship Between Cohabitants and Their Partners' Children, 13 Theoretical Inquiries L. 127 (2012); Mary Ann Mason & Nicole Zayac, Rethinking Stepparent Rights: Has the ALI Found a Better Definition?, 36 Fam. L.Q. 227, 227-228 (2002); Margaret M. Mahoney, Stepparents as Third Parties in Relation to Their Stepchildren, 40 Fam. L.Q. 81 (2006).

Today, many children live in families that include a legal parent's new partner who comes to play a parental role in the child's life. The following excerpt examines the varying nature of these relationships and suggests the difficulties that this variety creates for developing laws that afford great recognition to relationships between children and these "functional" parents.

DAVID CHAMBERS, STEPPARENTS, BIOLOGIC PARENTS, AND THE LAW'S PERCEPTIONS OF "FAMILY" AFTER DIVORCE

Divorce Reform at the Crossroads 102, 104-108, 118-119 (Stephen D. Sugarman & Herma Hill Kay eds., 1990)

The stepparent relationship, by contrast [to the biologic parent relationship] lacks — and I would argue, cannot possibly obtain — a single paradigm or model of appropriate responsibilities. As a starting point, children acquire two dramatically different and irretrievably "normal" forms of steprelations — the stepparent who is married to a custodial parent and with whom the child lives (a "residential stepparent," if you will) and the stepparent who is married to the noncustodial parent and whom the child sees, if at all, on visits. . . .

Even if we consider residential stepparents only, we still lack a single paradigm for the normal relationship of stepchild and stepparent. . . . The child who begins to live with a stepparent while still an infant is likely to develop a different relationship and bond with the stepparent than the child who begins the relationship as an adolescent.

In cases in which the biologic parents have been divorced (in contrast to cases in which one of the biologic parents has died), the course of the stepparent-child relationship is especially difficult to predict because of the very existence of the nonresidential parent and the variations in the frequency and quality of the visits between the child and the nonresidential parent. Indeed, the range of family compositions in the lives of children one or both of whose parents remarry is vast. . . .

It is thus unsurprising that . . . researchers have confirmed that stepparents and stepchildren come into these relationships uncertain what to expect and what is expected of them. As they begin a stepparent relationship, neither stepparents nor stepchildren have available to them a set of clear norms to guide their behaviors. . . .

To the extent that we do have an image of the stepparent relationship provided to us from our culture, it is a bleak one. . . . As a metaphor, "stepchild" describes a neglected issue or subject. . . . Cinderella's stepmother was wicked. Hamlet's stepfather was evil. . . . How many tales do you know of stepparents who were loving or kind? Some researchers believe that our cultural images of the stepparent increase the awkwardness of the relationship for those who are entering them. . . .

. . . [T]he relationship between many stepparents and stepchildren remains unclear and uncomfortable well beyond the initial stages. In his study of children with a residential stepparent, Furstenberg found that children were much less likely to say they felt "quite close" to their stepparent than to say they felt "quite close" to their custodial parent and much less likely to say that they wanted to grow up to be like their stepparent than to say they wanted to be like their custodial parent. In fact, about a third of children living with a stepparent did not mention that person when asked to name the members of their family. Nearly all named their noncustodial parent, even when they saw him or her erratically.

By much the same token, about half the stepfathers in the Furstenberg study said that their stepchildren did not think of them as a "real" parent, about half said that the children were harder to love than their own children, and about half said that it was easier to think of themselves as a friend than as a parent to the step-children. Stepparents had difficulty figuring out their appropriate role in disciplining the child and determining how to show affection for the child. Many stepparents and children remain uninvolved or uncomfortable with each other throughout the years they live together. . . .

Part of the difficulty for stepparents, as Furstenberg's questions themselves may suggest, is that many may believe that they are expected to be seen as a true "parent," an equal at caretaking and counseling, even when they recognize that that role is unlikely to be attainable. To be sure, not all stepparents have difficult relations with their stepchildren. Some — many of those in the other half of Furstenberg's respondents — come to see themselves as a parent and are viewed by children as such. Many others attain a comfortable relationship with the child but not in the role of a parent, establishing themselves over time not as an adult authority figure but as an adult companion and adviser. Those stepparents who prove least comfortable in the stepparent role are often those who find themselves stuck in the role of "other mother" or "other father," seen by themselves and the child as being in a parent role, but competing with and compared unfavorably with the noncustodial parent. . . .

Ultimately, the difficulty for stepparents in our society may be due in part to a want of social imagination, to an incapacity to recognize that, especially in the context of divorce, it will commonly be very hard for a stepparent either to hold a role identical to the biologic parent or, as the partner of the child's biologic parent, to become just a friend. . . . We conceive the stepparent role to be analogous to roles we already know. We expect the stepparent to be "like" someone — and he or she usually falls short.

. . . Perhaps it is impossible to forge coherent or flexible middle views. Perhaps it is psychologically inevitable that children will see a stepparent with whom they live as a person assigned to take the place of the absent parent. The least that can be said is that we as a society do not regard the advent of stepparenthood as we do the arrival of a new baby — as a treat that offers the opportunity for rich relationships.

The awkwardness of the stepparent relationship might be thought to suggest that children would in general be better off if their custodial parents did not remarry and that the law ought in general to discourage the formation of stepfamilies. That is not what the current state of research suggests. Most children living with a custodial mother become much better off economically upon their mother's remarriage. Whether they are typically better or worse off in other respects is uncertain. Research that attempts to measure the developmental effects on children of any life event — a parent's remarriage, parents' divorce, whatever — is fraught with difficulties, and thus research on the developmental effects of a parent's remarriage on children is predictably inconclusive. Clinical studies often find that children living with stepparents have adjustment problems and other difficulties, but so do children living with a single parent; empirical research typically finds few systematic differences between children raised in stepfamilies and children raised in other family configurations. . . .

Almost no information is available about actual patterns of stepparent adoption in this country or about the impact of adoption on the relationships between stepparents and children. . . . What we are able to calculate is that only a small percentage of stepparents actually adopt their stepchildren, despite the fact that the high proportion of children of divorce who never see or receive support from their noncustodial parent suggests that the number of stepparents eligible to adopt, even over the absent biologic parent's objection, must be very large. We know nothing about what distinguishes the families in which adoption occurs from the families in which it does not. . . .

While all states continue to use biology, marriage, and adoption as the principal bases for legal parenthood, all allow legal recognition of functional parents, at least in some circumstances. However, the legal doctrines, including the criteria for invoking and the consequences of these doctrines, vary substantially from state to state. One of the most common situations in which claims are raised is when a parent and stepparent divorce and the stepfather wants to maintain a relationship with the child or the mother wants the stepfather to continue contributing to the child's support. The other scenario that has been litigated in many states involves the attempt of a biological parent to exclude a former same-sex partner from the life of a child who was born during the relationship and whom both adults had been raising. In In re Parentage of L.B., 122 P.3d 161 (Wash. 2005) (en banc), the Washington Supreme Court held in the latter kind of case that a same-sex partner might attain full legal parent status through the "de facto parent" doctrine. In two succeeding cases, the court was asked to extend this ruling to stepparents when a marriage of an opposite-sex couple ended in divorce, with mixed results. The second of these cases is set out below, and the notes and materials after it examine other states' approaches to these problems.

In re Custody of B.M.H.

315 P.3d 470 (Wash. 2013) (en banc)

González, J. . . . Ms. Holt and Mr. Holt began a romantic relationship in 1993 and had a son, C.H., in 1995. The couple separated in 1998, without having married, and Ms. Holt soon became engaged to another man. Unfortunately, her fiance died in an industrial accident in 1999 while she was three months pregnant with his biological child, B.M.H.

Mr. Holt provided significant emotional support to Ms. Holt during the pregnancy, was present at B.M.H.'s birth, and even cut B.M.H.'s umbilical cord. Mr. Holt and Ms. Holt married shortly after B.M.H.'s birth but divorced in 2001. The resulting parenting plan designated Ms. Holt as C.H.'s primary residential parent and gave Mr. Holt residential time every other weekend. The parenting plan did not include provisions for B.M.H., but the parties do not dispute that B.M.H. essentially followed the same visitation schedule as C.H.

Mr. Holt was actively involved in B.M.H.'s life. In 2002, Ms. Holt changed B.M.H.'s last name from the biological father's last name to Mr. Holt's last name. Ms. Holt and Mr. Holt discussed Mr. Holt's adopting B.M.H. in 2007, but according to the guardian ad litem (GAL), adoption was not pursued because of the effect it might have on the survivor benefits that B.M.H. receives by virtue of his biological father's death.

Ms. Holt married another man in 2007 but divorced in 2008. During that relationship, Mr. Holt claims that Ms. Holt started to separate B.M.H. from Mr. Holt's visitations with C.H. In the summer of 2009, C.H. moved in with Mr. Holt. The parties dispute the reason for the move.

In late 2009 or early 2010, Mr. Holt learned that Ms. Holt planned to move with B.M.H. from Vancouver, Washington, to her new boyfriend's home in Castle Rock, about 50 miles away. On February 23, 2010, Mr. Holt filed a nonparental custody petition, alleging that Ms. Holt was not a suitable custodian for B.M.H. He explained that Ms. Holt "is threatening to move [B.M.H.] out of the area and thus disrupt the close relationship that [he] and [B.M.H.] have together." Mr. Holt also asked the court to find that he was B.M.H.'s de facto parent. Mr. Holt alleged that "[Ms. Holt] held [him] out as the child's father in all respects"; that he and B.M.H. are "extremely bonded"; and that "[B.M.H.] refers to [him] as his father." . . .

The court ordered a GAL at Mr. Holt's request and ordered Ms. Holt to keep B.M.H. in his Vancouver school pending the GAL's report and to continue to allow Mr. Holt regular residential visitation with B.M.H.

On March 24, after a hearing, the court found that Mr. Holt had established a prima facie case for de facto parentage. Ms. Holt moved for revision, and before the revision hearing this court issued *M.F.*, 168 Wash. 2d 528, 228 P.3d 1270. The parties debated *M.F.*'s effect on Mr. Holt's de facto parentage action, and after two hearings, the trial court granted Ms. Holt's revision motion and dismissed Mr. Holt's de facto parentage action, finding that "*M.F.* . . . excludes [Mr. Holt from asserting a de facto parentage cause of action] based on his former marriage to [Ms. Holt] and on the filing of a nonparental custody action." . . .

On August 20, the trial court found that adequate cause existed to proceed to a show cause hearing. The adequate cause finding reads:

> The Guardian Ad Litem has testified that it is in the child's best interest to have a continued relationship with the petitioner, [Mr. Holt]. Based upon all the affidavits, declarations and guardian ad litem report, the Court believes there is enough documentation set forth to proceed to trial on the non parental custody petition. The Court finds that if the Respondent/mother denies contact between Petitioner and minor child it would cause actual detriment to the minor child's growth and development if the relationship between the minor child and the Petitioner is not protected, and the Court has concerns that the mother may withhold visitation contact in the future.

. . . The Court of Appeals reinstated the de facto parentage petition and affirmed the order for a show cause hearing on the nonparental custody petition. . . .

1. *Adequate Cause on Third Party Custody Petition*

Under chapter 26.10 RCW, a third party can petition for child custody, but the State cannot interfere with the liberty interest of parents in the custody of their children unless a parent is unfit or custody with a parent would result in "actual detriment to the child's growth and development." The law's concept of the family rests in part on a presumption that "natural bonds of affection lead parents to act in the best interests of their children," and only under "'extraordinary circumstances'" does there exist a compelling state interest that justifies interference with the integrity of the family and with parental rights. To limit disruptions in family life, chapter 26.10 RCW places a high threshold burden on a petitioner seeking nonparental custody to allege specific facts that, if proved true, would meet this standard. If the court finds adequate cause for hearing on the petition, the burden shifts to the respondent to show cause why the requested order should not be granted.

A parent is unfit if he or she cannot meet a child's basic needs, and in such cases, the State is justified in removing the child from the home and in certain cases, permanently terminating parental rights.

Whether placement with a parent will result in actual detriment to a child's growth and development is a highly fact-specific inquiry, and "'[p]recisely what might [constitute actual detriment to] outweigh parental rights must be determined on a case-by-case basis.'" In *Shields*, we noted that when this heightened standard is properly applied, the requisite showing required by the nonparent is substantial and a nonparent will be able to meet this substantial standard in only "'extraordinary circumstances.'" The actual detriment standard has been met, for example, when a deaf child needed a caregiver who could effectively communicate with the child and the father was unable to do so, when a suicidal child required extensive therapy and stability at a level the parents could not provide, and when a child who had been physically and sexually abused required extensive therapy and stability at a level the parent could not provide.

Facts that merely support a finding that nonparental custody is in the "best interests of the child" are insufficient to establish adequate cause.

Mr. Holt does not allege that Ms. Holt is unfit. Rather, he alleges that . . . the "[mother] intends to immediately relocate the child to a situation that is unstable." Mr. Holt's petitions and declarations stated that since Ms. Holt's 2008 divorce she has "started relationships and moved several different men in and out of her home in Vancouver" and that "[t]hese relationships have been confusing and disruptive to [B.M.H.]." Mr. Holt stated that he believes "that [B.M.H.] is at risk if this pattern continues." According to Mr. Holt's declaration, "[B.M.H.] has expressed to [Mr. Holt] that he does not want to move to Castle Rock and he is missing his brother and it's all just happening too quickly for him." Mr. Holt's former wife stated in her declaration:

> "I have observed over the years how Laurie jumps right into relationships head-on leaving very little time for the boys to adjust to the new man in her life. The constant shuffling of boyfriends in and out of the household I believe has taken its toll on both boys but especially on [B.M.H.] who sees Michael as his one and only father."

Ms. Holt's biological father stated in his declaration that "having watched the choices [Laurie] has made and the men come in and out of her life over the years, I feel strongly that the choices she is making now are detrimental to the boys."

Mr. Holt's petition and declarations also stated that B.M.H. viewed Mr. Holt as his father and the two had a close relationship; Ms. Holt was threatening to move B.M.H. out of the area and thus disrupt this close relationship; Ms. Holt had occasionally tried to limit Mr. Holt's contact with B.M.H., when she was involved in relationships with other men, including during her 2007-08 marriage; and Ms. Holt had once told Mr. Holt that he could not see B.M.H. The GAL emphasized that B.M.H. viewed Mr. Holt as a father and that it would be detrimental to B.M.H. if Ms. Holt terminated his contact with Mr. Holt. The trial court found in its order that "it would cause actual detriment to the minor child's growth and development if the relationship between the minor child and the Petitioner is not protected" and that the trial court had "concerns that the mother may withhold visitation contact in the future." . . .

. . . [H]ere without more extraordinary facts bearing on B.M.H.'s welfare, the prerequisites for a nonparental custody action have not been met. The concern that Ms. Holt might interfere with Mr. Holt and B.M.H.'s relationship is insufficient to show actual detriment under *Shields* and to meet the burden of production for adequate cause under *E.A.T.W.* Although the importance of preserving fundamental psychological relationships and family units was part of the court's analysis in *Allen* and *Stell*, there were more extreme and unusual circumstances that contributed to the finding of actual detriment. In each case, the child had significant special needs that would not be met if the child were in the custody of the parent. Continuity of psychological relationships and family units was particularly important where a child had these special needs. Here, additional circumstances have not been alleged. This court has consistently held that the interests of parents yield to state interests only where "parental actions or decisions seriously conflict with the physical or mental health of the child. Other facts in the affidavits point to Ms. Holt's dating patterns and her decision to move to Castle Rock. These are not the kind of substantial and extraordinary circumstances that justify state intervention with parental rights. We reverse the Court of Appeals and dismiss the nonparental custody petition without prejudice.

2. DE FACTO PARENTAGE

. . . De facto parentage is a flexible equitable remedy that complements legislative enactments where parent-child relationships arise in ways that are not contemplated in the statutory scheme. In *L.B.*, we identified a "statutory silence regarding the interests of children begotten by artificial insemination" and we granted equitable relief. Two women who had lived together in a long-term relationship decided to have a child. One of the women conceived using donor sperm. For six years, the women coparented the child. Some time after they separated, the biological mother terminated contact between her former partner and the child, and the former partner petitioned for recognition as the child's de facto parent. Because there was no statutory means by which the former partner could establish her parental status, we adopted the de facto parentage doctrine established by the Wisconsin courts.

Establishing de facto parentage requires a showing that (1) the natural or legal parent consented to and fostered the parent-like relationship; (2) the petitioner and child lived together in the same household; (3) the petitioner assumed obligations of parenthood without expectation of financial compensation; and (4) the petitioner has been in a parental role for a length of time sufficient to have established with the child a bonded, dependent relationship, parental in nature. De facto parent status is "'limited to those adults who have fully and completely undertaken a permanent, unequivocal, committed, and responsible parental role in the child's life.'" The de facto parentage doctrine incorporates constitutionally required deference to parents by requiring that the biological or legal parent consent to and foster the parentlike relationship. Once a petitioner has made the threshold showing that the natural or legal parent consented to and fostered the parent-like relationship, the State is no longer "interfering on behalf of a third party in an insular family unit but is enforcing the rights and obligations of parenthood that attach to de facto parents." Under the test, attaining de facto parent status is "no easy task."

De facto parentage remains a viable equitable doctrine under Washington law. We respectfully disagree with the dissent's suggestion to the contrary. Since *L.B.*, legislative amendments have "clarif[ied] and expand[ed] the rights and obligations of state registered domestic partners and other couples related to parentage" but have not abrogated the common law doctrine of de facto parentage. "It is a well-established principle of statutory construction that '[t]he common law . . . ought not to be deemed repealed, unless the language of a statute be clear and explicit for this purpose.'" No such intent appears here. To the contrary, where the act formerly "govern[ed] every determination of parentage in this state," it now simply "applies to determinations of parentage" and "does not create, enlarge, or diminish parental rights or duties under other law of this state." In *L.B.*, we chronicled the long standing history of Washington courts exercising equity powers "in spite of legislative enactments that may have spoken to [an] area of law, but did so incompletely," and we determined that our state's relevant statutes do not provide the exclusive means of obtaining parental rights and responsibilities. That pronouncement stands as true today as it was then. Notwithstanding the 2011 amendments to the Uniform Parentage Act of 2002 (UPA), chapter 26.26 RCW, it is "inevitabl[e] [that] in the field of familial relations, factual scenarios arise, which even after a strict statutory analysis remain unresolved, leaving deserving parties without any appropriate remedy, often where demonstrated public policy is in favor of redress." Where the legislature remains silent with respect to determinations of parentage because it cannot anticipate every way that a parent-child relationship forms, we will continue to invoke our common law responsibility to "respond to the needs of children and families in the face of changing realities." We cannot say that legislative pronouncements on this subject preclude any redress to Mr. Holt or B.M.H., and it is our duty to apply the common law in a manner "consistent with our laws and stated legislative policy."[30]

---

30. The UPA was amended in 2011 to specifically reference state-registered domestic partnerships in various provisions and to specify that the UPA applies to persons of the same sex who have children together to the same extent it applies to opposite sex couples who have children together. Gender-specific terms in the act were replaced with gender-neutral terms. Additionally, a new provision for the presumption of parentage was adopted. Now, a party is "presumed to be the parent of a child if, for the first two years of the child's life, the person resided in the same household with the child and openly held out the child as his or her own."

Ms. Holt also argues that if de facto parentage remains a viable doctrine, our case law precludes a stepparent from becoming a de facto parent. In *M.F.*, we held that a former stepfather could not be his stepdaughter's de facto parent, but we did not preclude all stepparents as a class from being de facto parents. To do so would be contrary to legislative directive that children not be treated differently based on the marital status of their parents. Side by side, this case and *M.F.* illustrate that there is no single formula for all stepparents. *M.F.*'s biological parents separated shortly after her birth and shared parenting rights and responsibilities under a parenting plan. We found that the specific factual scenario in that case was contemplated by the legislature and addressed in chapter 26.10 RCW and that applying the equitable remedy would "infringe[ ] upon the rights and duties of *M.F.*'s existing parents." But arbitrary categorical distinctions based on a petitioner's status as a stepparent or former stepparent would preclude many legitimate parent-child relationships from being recognized. Here, where it is alleged that an individual entered a child's life at birth following the death of that child's second biological parent, and undertook an unequivocal and permanent parental role with the consent of all existing parents but does not have a statutorily protected relationship, justice prompts us to apply the de facto parent test. This adequately balances the rights of biological parents, children, and other parties.

Ms. Holt contends that as a former stepparent, Mr. Holt has a sufficient statutory remedy because he can file a nonparental custody petition under chapter 26.10 RCW. But that remedy was available in *L.B.* as well. Precluding *any* individual from petitioning for de facto parentage because he or she can file for nonparental custody would obliterate the de facto parentage doctrine because *any* person not recognized as a parent may seek nonparental custody. . . . Like the former partner in *L.B.*, Mr. Holt has no meaningful statutory means by which he can seek a determination of parentage, and nonparental custody is an inadequate remedy to protect his weighty interests relative to the child and its biological parent. By requiring proof that Ms. Holt fostered the parent-child relationship, the de facto parentage doctrine will properly balance Mr. Holt's interests in an adjudication of parentage against the deference we give natural parents. We affirm the Court of Appeals and remand to the trial court for further proceedings on Mr. Holt's de facto parent petition . . . .

MADSEN, C.J. (concurring/dissenting). . . . The majority's approach is impermissible because it allows a stepparent to seek custody in violation of a parent's fundamental constitutional rights in her child.

The majority believes, though, that the consent prong of the de facto parent test protects the parent's constitutional rights. As we pointed out in *M.F.*, the de facto parent test would be too-easily applied in the stepparent context, is ill-suited to the custody issue, and makes no meaningful distinctions in this context. We said about the consent prong: "in the vast majority of cases a parent will encourage his or her spouse, the stepparent, to act like a parent in relationship to the child." Our concern is echoed by one noted author, who says in connection with the American Law Institute's treatment of de facto parents and its test that similarly includes consent:

> Because agreement may be implied, this [part of the test] is satisfied when a mother acquiesces to the partner's behavior — behavior that virtually any mother would

welcome in her partner, such as taking the child to the doctor, reading to the child, helping the child get ready for bed, and making dinner for the family.

Robin Fretwell Wilson, *Trusting Mothers: A Critique of The American Law Institute's Treatment of De Facto Parents*, 38 Hofstra L. Rev. 1103, 1112 (2010).

Accordingly, satisfying the consent prong is meaningless in the stepparent context. Consent to coparent within the marriage and family unit is not the same as consent to a life-long, parent-child relationship on the part of the stepparent to continue no matter what happens to the marriage. Yet consent is precisely the hook upon which the majority hangs its catch.

The other prongs are not particularly probative in the stepparent context, either. We said in *M.F.*:

> [T]he second factor will nearly always be met—that "the petitioner and the child lived together in the same household." The third element is that the petitioner assumed obligations of parenthood without expectation of compensation, and one only has to envision the stepparent attending school functions, helping the child get dressed in the morning, or engaging in the other numerous events that together make up family life with a child to see how easily this factor might be satisfied. The only variable in most cases, it would appear, is the length of time the stepparent has been in a parental role, and generally this would be merely a matter of how long the relationship with the parent endures—hardly a basis for deciding parental status.

. . . Finally, I note that in *M.F.* there were two fit parents. This, of course, cannot be a viable distinction because our statutory and constitutional law plainly contemplates and protects the single parent just as it does two parents. A single parent's constitutional rights in her child must be safeguarded every bit as vigorously as the constitutional rights of two parents together.

The majority also believes that the present case is analogous to *L.B.*, and that just as the third party custody statutes were available to the same-sex nonbiological parent in *L.B.*, the de facto parent theory is applicable here.

L.B. is not like the present case. In *L.B.*, the same-sex partners could not marry, nor were rights equal to those of heterosexual parents recognized under state statutes at the time. The two parties had been in a long-term committed relationship and did everything they could do to create a child together. They could not marry and could not together conceive their child, unlike heterosexual partners, but they deliberately set out to and did initiate the pregnancy together and both before and after the child's birth acted in every way as the child's parents.

In *L.B.*, the de facto test was a necessary legal channel for attributing to the two partners the parenthood that they already shared. Because of the nature of the parties' relationship—as a same-sex couple—the parent who was not a biological parent could otherwise be cut off from parental rights under the heightened showing that applies when a nonparent seeks custody. The de facto status gave legal effect to a person who was and always had been the child's parent. No acquired parenthood was ever at issue. Recognizing this, this court applied the de facto parent theory that enabled the nonbiological parent to seek custody under the "best interests of the child" standard applicable between parents.

The circumstances in a stepparent context are not the same. Parentage exists in the two biological parents who created the child and brought into existence the parent-child relationship. Here, Laurie's child was created by her and her fiance, who passed away before the child was born.

Without doubt, a stepparent may enter the picture and assume a role as a loving, caring parental figure. Our laws permit a stepparent to seek custody of a child under the third party custody statutes. Adoption is also a possibility. But a parent's constitutional rights must be given precedence over the stepparent and it takes a very strong showing to overcome a fit parent's rights. As we held in In re Custody of Smith, 137 Wash. 2d 1, 20, 969 P.2d 21 (1998), *aff'd sub nom.* Troxel v. Granville, 530 U.S. 57 (2000) (plurality opinion), a fit parent is presumed to act in the child's best interest and there must be a showing of harm to the child to overcome this presumption.

The majority's decision that de facto parent status is available to a stepparent means that the stepparent is a parent in every respect. This means that the stepparent will be able to proceed under the "best interests of the child" standard that applies under chapter 26.09 RCW when two parents dispute custody of their child, an easier showing that places the parent's and the stepparent's interests on a par.

This result is in tension with the common law view of stepparents and their obligations to their spouses' children. One author points out how the concept of parenthood traditionally related to the duties a stepparent has toward such children, saying that stepparents generally have had a recognized relationship with the child of his or her spouse but no continuing duties if the marriage ends. June Carbone, *The Legal Definition of Parenthood: Uncertainty at the Core of Family Identity*, 65 La. L. Rev. 1295, 1311-12 (2005). "The stepparents' responsibilities . . . are not permanent" but rather "may be relinquished at will." Absent adoption, stepparents have not been viewed as having a permanent bond with the child, both because any obligation to the child is derivative of the obligation to the legal parent and because, if marriage to a legal parent triggered permanent support obligations to the child, it would discourage remarriage.

Under our state law "[t]he obligation to support stepchildren shall cease upon the entry of a decree of dissolution, decree of legal separation, or death." Thus, once the marriage ended without Michael having adopted the child, Laurie was unable to compel Michael to pay support. The statute supports the view that Michael is only in a parent-like relationship because of his marriage to Laurie and any rights and responsibilities vis-à-vis Laurie's child are derivative of that relationship. Once the relationship ends, so do these rights and responsibilities. He becomes a third party to the children when the marriage ends. Laurie cannot compel him to provide child support, a conclusion consistent with the derivative nature of his obligations.

However, if he were to obtain de facto parent status, he would have the rights and obligations of a parent, as we said in *L.B.* His relationship to the child would become primary and permanent, and he could seek custody under a "best interests of the child" standard. If he did not seek de facto parent status, however, Laurie herself cannot compel him to or make the argument herself, nor can she seek support for the child. This one-sided paradigm is fundamentally at odds with the constitutional rights she has in her child. Why should a stepparent be entitled to seek de facto parent status and then custody under the lower "best interests of the child" standard when, once the marriage ends, the parent has no ability to seek either a permanent relationship for her children with the stepparent or support for the children[?]

The majority poses a threat to parents' constitutional rights that may be far-reaching because of the sheer number of stepparents and stepchildren potentially affected, the fact that the majority's analysis applies equally well to cohabitating partners of parents, and because the majority appears inclined to find statutory "gaps" that must be filled based solely on different factual circumstances, notwithstanding recent legislation.

An estimated 25 percent of children today will become part of a family including a stepparent. Sarah H. Ramsey, *Constructing Parenthood For Stepparents: Parents By Estoppel and De Facto Parents Under the American Law Institute's Principles of the Law of Family Dissolution*, 8 Duke J. Gender & Pol'y 285, 287 (2001) (quoting Frank F. Furstenberg, Jr., *History and Current Status of Divorce in the United States*, 4 Future of Children, Spring 1994, at 29, 35). Moreover, a large number of children live with one parent, and predictably in a number of these cases there will be a stepparent who is no longer married to the parent. Some "21 million children . . . lived with one parent in 2012." Jonathan Vespa, Jamie M. Lewis, and Rose M. Kreider, U.S. Census Bureau, Population Characteristics Report No. P20-570, America's Families And Living Arrangements: 2012, at 23 (2013). "[A]pproximately 1 in 5 White, non-Hispanic children (21 percent); 1 in 3 Hispanic children (31 percent); and 1 in 2 Black children (55 percent) lived with one parent" in 2012. *Id.* at 23-26. The vast majority of family groups with one parent are mother-only groups. *Id.* at 13. . . .

Census information also shows that cohabitation continues as a growing trend. In 2012, "more cohabiting adults lived with children who were not biologically related to them than did married spouses." Vespa, Lewis & Kreider, *supra*, at 21. When such couples separate, the nonparent can readily argue that the majority's decision and analysis in this case support a de facto parent theory in the cohabitation context.

One author has described such potential for broad application of the de facto parent theory as "a thinned-out conception of parenthood" that is "primarily a function of co-residence" and that "would give former live-in partners access to a child" even when opposed by the legal parent, "nearly always a child's mother." Wilson, *supra*, at 1109. "Mothers are disproportionately affected by the extension of new parental rights to live-in partners because most non-marital children and children of divorce live with their mothers." *Id.* at 1109-10.

In short, the parents who are most likely to be affected by the majority's decision are mothers who will often be members of a minority race or group. Many women faced with custody disputes will have resources so limited that they are highly unlikely to be able to afford to hire legal assistance in private custody disputes.

In Washington, as these national statistics suggest, a significant number of parents may be subject to the majority's flawed analysis that can transform an ex-husband or ex-wife who acquires a stepparent relationship with the parent's child, or a former cohabitant, into a parent with all of the rights of a parent, including the right to seek child custody under a "best interests of the child" standard without regard to the parent's fundamental constitutional rights. . . .

We have heretofore adhered to an strict scrutiny analysis when a fit parent's right to autonomy in child-rearing decisions is at issue. We have done so to protect the fundamental liberty interest that parents have in the care and welfare of their minor children. The right to raise one's children is deemed essential. . . .

The majority excuses its constitutional violations by an analysis that can turn Michael into a parent, allowing him to proceed under the "best interests of the child" standard. Although he is not the child's natural, biological, or adoptive parent, as a de facto parent he can proceed without regard to Laurie's fitness as a parent and without having to show detriment to the child because Laurie's rights are no longer superior to his.

I do not ascribe to the majority's loosely reframed de facto parent standard for stepparents. Our cases are to the contrary, and the fundamental rights a parent has in the care, custody, and control of her child are too precious to cast aside as no longer of any moment. There is no "gap" in our statutory scheme that demands recognition of this common law theory in the stepparent context, and the de facto parent test itself is a low hurdle over a parent's constitutional rights. . . .

WIGGINS, J. (dissenting in part[31]). . . . This court adopted the de facto parentage doctrine to address a very specific statutory deficiency: the respondent in *L.B.* acted as a parent in every way but could not be L.B.'s legal parent because she was in a same-sex relationship with L.B.'s biological mother. . . . However, we also acknowledged that "the legislature may eventually choose to enact differing standards than those recognized here today, and to do so would be within its province." . . .

In 2009, the legislature did just that, filling the legislative void we addressed in *L.B.* by granting state registered domestic partners all of the privileges and rights of married spouses. . . .

The question before us today is this: given that the reason for the de facto parentage doctrine no longer exists, should we defer to the legislature and follow the statutory scheme, or should we expand the de facto parentage doctrine to include other relationships that were never omitted from the statutory scheme? By needlessly enlarging the reach of the de facto parentage doctrine in this case, the majority places its judgments above the legislature's. . . .

This case involves the UPA as it was written prior to several 2011 legislative amendments. However, the majority insists that regardless of evolving statutory law, this court should continue to provide a separate common law remedy for any factual scenario that the legislature might not have contemplated. This overlooks the fact that the common law is the rule of decision for the courts only "so far as it is not inconsistent with the . . . laws . . . of the state of Washington." . . .

Two years ago, the legislature amended the UPA significantly in a manner that further obviates the need for the de facto parentage doctrine. As part of the 2011 amendments, the legislature declared:

> The provisions [of the UPA] apply to persons in a domestic partnership to the same extent they apply to persons in a marriage, and apply to persons of the same sex

---

31. I concur with the majority's resolution of Michael Holt's third party custody claim under chapter 26.10 RCW, and do not address it further.

who have children together to the same extent they apply to persons of the opposite sex who have children together.

More importantly, the legislature has codified the de facto parentage doctrine by creating a presumption of parentage for any person "if, for the first two years of the child's life, the person resided in the same household with the child and openly held out the child as his or her own."

Furthermore, last year, the legislature passed legislation permitting same-sex couples to marry. This reflects additional legislative intent since the *L.B.* decision to treat households containing same-sex and opposite-sex couples equally.

In light of these amendments equalizing same-sex and opposite-sex couples in all respects and codifying the de facto parentage doctrine, the legislature has expressed its intent that chapter 26.26 RCW apply to all determinations of parentage. . . .

Given the legislature's provision of the very specific, enumerated ways that the parent-child relationship is formed in our state, we must rely solely on chapter 26.26 RCW when determining whether a nonparent adult may state a parentage claim. The majority's assertion that the legislature has not "anticipate[d] every way that a parent-child relationship forms," is incorrect and completely unworkable in light of the comprehensive scheme enacted by the legislature. Going forward, we cannot have parallel parentage schemes, one legislative and one judicial. Rather, we must follow the law as written by the legislature. . . .

NOTES AND QUESTIONS

1. Recall that Troxel v. Granville, above at page 855, concerned the constitutionality of the Washington state third-party visitation statute. After *Troxel*, the state amended its statute to the version discussed in *B.M.H.* What requirements does the new version of the statute impose on third parties who seek visitation? Are they required by *Troxel*? How do these requirements differ from the requirements for becoming a de facto parent? Since the version of the de facto parent doctrine adopted by Washington gives the successful claimant full legal parent status, it seems to be a greater intrusion on the parental rights of the original legal parent than a third-party visitation order. How then, does the court in *B.M.H.* reach the conclusion that the stepfather could not satisfy the requirements of the visitation statute but could become a de facto parent?

Justice Madsen's concurring and dissenting opinion in *B.M.H.* objects to the recognition of de facto parentage in part because it imposes a second parent on the first. The opinion observes that "the parents who are most likely to be affected by the majority's decision are mothers who will often be members of a minority race or group" and that the majority opinion "can turn Michael into a parent" and allow him to "proceed without regard to Laurie's fitness as a parent and without having to show detriment to the child because Laurie's rights are no longer superior to his." How does the majority respond to his argument? For a discussion of what makes someone a parent and the role of consent in extending parentage to others, *see* E. Gary Spitko, The Constitutional Function of Biological Paternity: Evidence of the Biological Mother's Consent to the Biological Father's Co-Parenting of Her Child, 48 Ariz. L. Rev. 97 (2006).

How do the majority and the two dissents differ in their definitions of what makes someone a legal parent under the U.S. Constitution and in accordance with Washington law?

2. In the earlier Washington stepparent case, *M.F.*, which is discussed in *B.M.H.*, the Washington Supreme Court held that the stepfather could not invoke the de facto parent doctrine and had to use the third-party visitation statute to assert his claim. Why? How does *B.M.H.* distinguish *M.F.*?

3. The Maine Supreme Court in Pitts v. Moore, __ A.3d __ (2014), upheld earlier decisions recognizing the de facto parent doctrine, but articulated a different test. It held that a would-be de facto parent must prove by clear and convincing evidence that "1) he or she has undertaken a 'permanent, unequivocal, committed, and responsible parental role in the child's life,' and 2) that there are exceptional circumstances sufficient to allow the court to interfere with the legal or adoptive parent's rights." *Id.* at __. The court further explained that the test requires proof that the claimant lived with the child, engaged in caretaking functions "which involve 'the direct delivery of day-to-day care and supervision of the child, including grooming, feeding, medical care, and physical supervision,'" that the legal parent and co-parent intended the co-parent to act as a parent, and "that the relationship was not undertaken for the purposes of financial compensation or with other institutional approval, as with a nanny, foster parent, or daycare provider." *Id.* at __. In addition, the claimant must prove that "the child's life would be substantially and negatively affected if the person" no longer is able to exercise these functions. *Id.* at __. How does this test differ from the *B.M.H.* test? Would the claimant in *B.M.H.* be recognized as a de facto parent under *Pitts*?

4. Some states have refused to recognize de facto parentage. For example, in Moreau v. Sylvester, __ A.3d __ (Vt. 2014), the Vermont Supreme court affirmed an earlier decision rejecting the doctrine. The unmarried mother of two children and her partner had been in an on-again, off-again relationship for eight to ten years. The partner, who was not the biological father of the children, had played a "significant, father-like role" while they lived together, and had shared responsibility for the children after the couple separated. When their relationship deteriorated, he began to harass the mother and eventually sought recognition as a de facto parent. The Vermont Supreme Court rejected the man's de facto parent claim, explaining:

> . . . [T]here are public-policy considerations that favor allowing third parties claiming a parent-like relationship to seek court-compelled parent-child contact. These considerations, however, are still not so persuasive as to compel recognition of a new cause of action, and matching equitable jurisdiction to entertain it, so that acquaintances and partners with less than adoptive or even stepparent status can seek court-compelled visitation with children of persons not legally related to them and against the wishes of their natural parents. . . . "[G]iven the complex social and practical ramifications of expanding the classes of persons entitled to assert parental rights by seeking custody or visitation, the Legislature is better equipped" to address this issue. Deference to the Legislature continues to be prudent "because the laws pertaining to parental rights and responsibilities and parent-child contact have been

developed over time solely through legislative enactment or judicial construction of legislative enactments."

Id. at A.3d ___. The *Moreau* court explained in a footnote that the ramifications of de facto parentage "could be far-reaching." It queried:

> Does recognition of a common law or equitable claim for parental contact by unrelated domestic partners include a corresponding right to claim child support from an unrelated but putative de facto parent? Can an unrelated but putative de facto parent then interfere with the biological parent's decision to move away with his or her children? Will every relief-from-abuse proceeding present an avenue for defendant partners to counterattack with de facto parentage complaints?

Id. at A.3d ___. How would the majority in *B.M.H.* have responded to such questions? Would the dissent agree with the issues raised in *Moreau*? How would the court in *B.M.H.* have dealt with the assertion of de facto parentage if Mr. Holt had been harassing and threatening Ms. Holt? If Mr. Holt had sought recognition as a de facto parent only after Ms. Holt had decided to move to another state?

5. The ALI Principles of the Law of Family Dissolution propose recognition of de facto parenthood, which gives some legal rights to a person "who, for a significant period of time not less than two years, lived with the child and, for reasons primarily other than financial compensation, and with the agreement of a legal parent to form a parent-child relationship, or as a result of a complete failure or inability of any legal parent to perform caretaking functions, (A) regularly performed a majority of the caretaking functions for the child, or (B) regularly performed a share of caretaking functions at least as great as that of the parent with whom the child primarily lived." ALI Principles of the Law of Family Dissolution §§ 203(1)(c). The rights of a de facto parent are subordinate to those of a "parent by estoppel," who has full legal parental rights and responsibilities in most situations. A parent by estoppel (1) has lived with the child for at least two years and had a reasonable good faith belief that he was the child's biological father, and continued to make reasonable, good faith efforts to accept parental responsibilities even if the belief no longer existed; or (2) lived with the child since the child's birth or for at least two years and holds out and accepts full and permanent responsibility as a parent as the result of a co-parenting arrangement with the child's legal parent if recognition of the relationship is in the child's best interests; or (3) is liable for child support. ALI Principles § 2.03(1)(b). How do the ALI elements necesssary to establish parenthood by estoppel differ from the elements necessary to establish de facto parenthood in *B.M.H.*?

For a critique of the ALI approach and discussion of the different parental statuses in the ALI, *see* Sarah H. Ramsey, Constructing Parenthood for Stepparents: Parents by Estoppel and De Facto Parents Under the American Law Institute's Principles of the Law of Family Dissolution, 8 Duke J. Gender L. & Pol'y 285 (2001). *See also* David D. Meyer, Partners, Care Givers, and the Constitutional Substance of Parenthood, Robin Fretwell Wilson, Undeserved Trust: Reflections on the ALI's Treatment of De Facto Parents, and Katharine K. Baker, Asymmetric Parenthood, all in Reconceiving the Family: Critical Reflections on the American

Law Institute's Principles of the Law of Family Dissolution (Robin Fretwell Wilson ed., 2006).

ELISA B. v. SUPERIOR COURT

117 P.3d 660 (Cal. 2005)

MORENO, J. . . . On June 7, 2001, the El Dorado County District Attorney filed a complaint in superior court to establish that Elisa B. is a parent of two-year-old twins Kaia B. and Ry B., who were born to Emily B., and to order Elisa to pay child support. Elisa filed an answer in which she denied being the children's parent.

A hearing was held at which Elisa testified that she entered into a lesbian relationship with Emily in 1993. They began living together six months later. Elisa obtained a tattoo that read "Emily, por vida," which in Spanish means Emily, for life. They introduced each other to friends as their "partner," exchanged rings, opened a joint bank account, and believed they were in a committed relationship.

Elisa and Emily discussed having children and decided that they both wished to give birth. Because Elisa earned more than twice as much money as Emily, they decided that Emily "would be the stay-at-home mother" and Elisa "would be the primary breadwinner for the family." At a sperm bank, they chose a donor they both would use so the children would "be biological brothers and sisters."

After several unsuccessful attempts, Elisa became pregnant in February, 1997. Emily was present when Elisa was inseminated. Emily began the insemination process in June of 1997 and became pregnant in August, 1997. Elisa was present when Emily was inseminated and, the next day, Elisa picked up additional sperm at the sperm bank and again inseminated Emily at their home to "make sure she got pregnant." They went to each other's medical appointments during pregnancy and attended childbirth classes together so that each could act as a "coach" for the other during birth, including cutting the children's umbilical cords.

Elisa gave birth to Chance in November, 1997, and Emily gave birth to Ry and Kaia prematurely in March, 1998. Ry had medical problems; he suffered from Down's Syndrome, and required heart surgery.

They jointly selected the children's names, joining their surnames with a hyphen to form the children's surname. They each breast-fed all of the children. Elisa claimed all three children as her dependents on her tax returns and obtained a life insurance policy on herself naming Emily as the beneficiary so that if "anything happened" to her, all three children would be "cared for." Elisa believed the children would be considered both of their children.

Elisa's parents referred to the twins as their grandchildren, and her sister referred to the twins as part of their family and referred to Elisa as the twins' mother. Elisa treated all of the children as hers and told a prospective employer that she had triplets. Elisa and Emily identified themselves as co-parents of Ry at an organization arranging care for his Down's Syndrome.

Elisa supported the household financially. Emily was not working. Emily testified that she would not have become pregnant if Elisa had not promised to support her financially, but Elisa denied that any financial arrangements were discussed before the birth of the children. Elisa later acknowledged in her testimony, however, that Emily "was going to be an at-home mom for maybe a couple of years and then the kids were going to go into day care and she was going to return to work."

They consulted an attorney regarding adopting "each other's child," but never did so. Nor did they register as domestic partners or execute a written agreement concerning the children. Elisa stated she later reconsidered adoption because she had misgivings about Emily adopting Chance.

Elisa and Emily separated in November, 1999. Elisa promised to support Emily and the twins "as much as I possibly could" and initially paid the mortgage payments of approximately $1,500 per month on the house in which Emily and the twins continued to live, as well as other expenses. Emily applied for aid. When they sold the house and Emily and the twins moved into an apartment in November, 2000, Elisa paid Emily $1,000 a month. In early 2001, Elisa stated she lost her position as a full-time employee and told Emily she no longer could support her and the twins. At the time of trial, Elisa was earning $95,000 a year.

The superior court rendered a written decision on July 11, 2002, finding that Elisa and Emily had rejected the option of using a private sperm donor because "[t]hey wanted the child to be raised *exclusively* by them as a couple." The court further found that they intended to create a child and "acted in all respects as a family," adding "that a person who uses reproductive technology is accountable as a de facto legal parent for the support of that child. Legal parentage is not determined exclusively by biology."

The court further found that Elisa was obligated to support the twins under the doctrine of equitable estoppel. . . .

Elisa petitioned the Court of Appeal for a writ of mandate, and the court directed the superior court to vacate its order and dismiss the action, concluding that Elisa had no obligation to pay child support because she was not a parent of the twins within the meaning of the Uniform Parentage Act (Fam. Code, § 7600 et seq.). We granted review. . . .

. . . The UPA defines the "'[p]arent and child relationship'" as "the legal relationship existing between a child and the child's natural or adoptive parents. . . . The term includes the mother and child relationship and the father and child relationship." (§ 7601.) One purpose of the UPA was to eliminate distinctions based upon whether a child was born into a marriage, and thus was "legitimate," or was born to unmarried parents, and thus was "illegitimate." Thus, the UPA provides that the parentage of a child does not depend upon "'the marital status of the parents'" stating: "The parent and child relationship extends equally to every child and to every parent, regardless of the marital status of the parents." (§ 7602.)

The UPA contains separate provisions defining who is a "mother" and who is a "father." Section 7610 provides that "[t]he parent and child relationship may be established . . . : [¶] (a) Between a child and the natural mother . . . by proof of her having given birth to the child, or under this part." Subdivision (b) of section 7610 states that the parental relationship "[b]etween a child and the natural father . . . may be established under this part."

Section 7611 provides several circumstances in which "[a] man is presumed to be the natural father of a child," including: if he is the husband of the child's mother, is not impotent or sterile, and was cohabiting with her (§ 7540); if he signs a voluntary declaration of paternity stating he is the "biological father of the child" (§ 7574, subd. (a)(6)); and if "[h]e receives the child into his home and openly holds out the child as his natural child."

Although, as noted above, the UPA contains separate provisions defining who is a mother and who is a father, it expressly provides that in determining the existence of a mother and child relationship, "[i]nsofar as practicable, the provisions of this part applicable to the father and child relationship apply."

The Court of Appeal correctly recognized that, under the UPA, Emily has a parent and child relationship with each of the twins because she gave birth to them. Thus, the Court of Appeal concluded, Emily is the twins' natural mother. Relying upon our statement in Johnson v. Calvert, *supra*, 5 Cal. 4th 84, 92, 19 Cal. Rptr. 2d 494, 851 P.2d 776, that "for any child California law recognizes only one natural mother," the Court of Appeal reasoned that Elisa, therefore, could not also be the natural mother of the twins and thus "has no legal maternal relationship with the children under the UPA." . . .

The issue before us in *Johnson* was whether a wife whose ovum was fertilized in vitro by her husband's sperm and implanted in a surrogate mother was the mother of the child so produced, rather than the surrogate. . . .

In *Johnson*, therefore, we addressed the situation in which three people claimed to be the child's parents: the husband, who undoubtedly was the child's father, and two women, who presented conflicting claims to being the child's mother. We rejected the suggestion of amicus curiae that both the wife and the surrogate could be the child's mother, stating that a child can have only one mother, but what we considered and rejected in *Johnson* was the argument that a child could have three parents: a father and two mothers. We did not address the question presented in this case of whether a child could have two parents, both of whom are women. The Court of Appeal in the present case erred, therefore, in concluding that our statement in *Johnson* that a child can have only one mother under California law resolved the issue presented in this case. " Language used in any opinion is of course to be understood in the light of the facts and the issue then before the court, and an opinion is not authority for a proposition not therein considered." . . .

We perceive no reason why both parents of a child cannot be women. That result now is possible under the current version of the domestic partnership statutes, which took effect this year. . . .

Prior to the effective date of the current domestic partnership statutes, we recognized in an adoption case that a child can have two parents, both of whom are women. . . . If both parents of an adopted child can be women, we see no reason why the twins in the present case cannot have two parents, both of whom are women.

. . . [W]e proceed to examine the UPA to determine whether Elisa is a parent to the twins in addition to Emily. As noted above, section 7650 provides that provisions applicable to determining a father and child relationship shall be used to determine a mother and child relationship "insofar as practicable."

Subdivision (d) of section 7611 states that a man is presumed to be the natural father of a child if "[h]e receives the child into his home and openly holds out the child as his natural child." . . .

Applying section 7611, subdivision (d), we must determine whether Elisa received the twins into her home and openly held them out as her natural children. There is no doubt that Elisa satisfied the first part of this test; it is undisputed that Elisa received the twins into her home. Our inquiry focuses, therefore, on whether she openly held out the twins as her natural children.

The circumstance that Elisa has no genetic connection to the twins does not necessarily mean that she did not hold out the twins as her "natural" children under section 7611. We held in In re Nicholas H. (2002) 28 Cal. 4th 56, 120 Cal. Rptr. 2d 146, 46 P.3d 932 that the presumption under section 7611, subdivision (d), that a man who receives a child into his home and openly holds the child out as his natural child is not necessarily rebutted when he admits he is not the child's biological father.

The presumed father in *Nicholas H.*, Thomas, met the child's mother, Kimberly, when she was pregnant with Nicholas. Nevertheless, Thomas was named as the child's father on his birth certificate and provided a home for the child and his mother for several years. Thomas did not marry Kimberly. When Nicholas was removed by the court from Kimberly's care, Thomas sought custody as the child's presumed father, although he admitted he was not Nicholas's biological father.

We held in *Nicholas H.* that Thomas was presumed to be Nicholas's father despite his admission that he was not Nicholas's biological father. The Court of Appeal had reached the opposite conclusion, observing that "the Legislature has used the term 'natural' to mean 'biological'" and concluding that the presumption under section 7611, subdivision (d) is rebutted under section 7612, subdivision (a) by clear and convincing evidence "that the man is not the child's natural, biological father." We noted, however, that the UPA does not state that the presumption under section 7611, subdivision (d), *is* rebutted by evidence that the presumed father is not the child's biological father, but rather that it *may* be rebutted *in an appropriate action* by such evidence. We held that *Nicholas H.* was not an appropriate action in which to rebut the presumption because no one had raised a conflicting claim to being the child's father. Applying the presumption, therefore, would produce the "harsh result" of leaving the child fatherless. . . .

We conclude that the present case . . . is not "an appropriate action" in which to rebut the presumption of presumed parenthood with proof that Elisa is not the twins' biological parent. This is generally a matter within the discretion of the superior court, because it would be an abuse of discretion to conclude that the presumption may be rebutted in the present case. It is undisputed that Elisa actively consented to, and participated in, the artificial insemination of her partner with the understanding that the resulting child or children would be raised by Emily and her as coparents, and they did act as coparents for a substantial period of time. Elisa received the twins into her home and held them out to the world as her natural children. She gave the twins and the child to whom she had given birth the same surname, which was formed by joining her surname to her partner's. The twins were half siblings to the child to whom Elisa had given birth. She breast-fed all three children, claimed all three children as her dependents on her tax returns, and told a prospective employer that she had triplets. Even at the hearing before the superior court, Elisa candidly testified that she considered herself to be the twins' mother.

Declaring that Elisa cannot be the twins' parent and, thus, has no obligation to support them because she is not biologically related to them would produce a result similar to the situation we sought to avoid in *Nicholas H.* of leaving the child fatherless. The twins in the present case have no father because they were conceived by means of artificial insemination using an anonymous semen donor. Rebutting the presumption that Elisa is the twin's parent would leave them with only one parent and would deprive them of the support of their second parent. Because Emily is financially unable to support the twins, the financial burden of supporting the twins would be borne by the county, rather than Elisa. . . .

We observed in dicta in *Nicholas H.* that it would be appropriate to rebut the section 7611 presumption of parentage if "a court decides that the legal rights and obligations of parenthood should devolve upon an unwilling candidate." But we decline to apply our dicta in *Nicholas H.* here, because we did not consider in *Nicholas H.* a situation like that in the present case.

Although Elisa presently is unwilling to accept the obligations of parenthood, this was not always so. She actively assisted Emily in becoming pregnant with the expressed intention of enjoying the rights and accepting the responsibilities of parenting the resulting children. She accepted those obligations and enjoyed those rights for years. Elisa's present unwillingness to accept her parental obligations does not affect her status as the children's mother based upon her conduct during the first years of their lives . . . .

We were careful in *Nicholas H.*, therefore, not to suggest that every man who begins living with a woman when she is pregnant and continues to do so after the child is born necessarily becomes a presumed father of the child, even against his wishes. The Legislature surely did not intend to punish a man like the one in *Nicholas H.* who voluntarily provides support for a child who was conceived before he met the mother, by transforming that act of kindness into a legal obligation.

But our observation in *Nicholas H.* loses its force in a case like the one at bar in which the presumed mother under section 7611, subdivision (d), acted together with the birth mother to cause the child to be conceived . . . .

The judgment of the Court of Appeal is reversed.

[The concurring opinion of Justice Kennard is omitted.]

NOTES AND QUESTIONS

1. The key precedents for *Elisa B.* are cases in which the California Supreme Court held that proof that a "holding out father" is not the biological father does not necessarily rebut the presumption that he is the legal father. What test does the court adopt for deciding when such evidence would rebut the presumption? How does this test differ from the test discussed above for resolving which of two conflicting presumptions of paternity should prevail?

2. Two earlier California cases that *Elisa B.* relies on, In re Nicholas H., 46 P.3d 932 (Cal. 2002), and In re Jesusa V., 85 P.3d 2 (Cal. 2004), were juvenile court child neglect cases in which the children were taken from their mothers; their fathers were unidentified and in prison, respectively. Both children had been living

with their mothers and their mothers' partners to whom they were not married. In both cases, these men had assumed a parental role and were willing and suitable to care for the children. However, under California juvenile court law, the court could not have simply placed the children in the custody of the men if they were unrelated third parties. Characterizing them as legal fathers via the holding out presumption allowed the children to remain in the men's care. *Elisa B.* and its companion cases, K.M. v. E.G., 117 P.3d 673 (Cal. 2005), and Kristine H. v. Lisa R., 117 P.3d 690 (Cal. 2005), all concerned children conceived by artificial insemination and born to lesbian co-parents who had raised the children. If the court had not recognized the biological mothers' partners as parents, the children would have had only one legal parent. How important are these facts in determining whether the presumption can be rebutted? For a discussion of these and related cases, *see* June Carbone, From Partners to Parents Revisited: How Will Ideas of Partnership Influence the Emerging Definition of California Parenthood?, 7 Whittier J. Child & Fam. Advoc. 3 (2007).

3. How do the criteria for invoking the presumption of parenthood in *Elisa B.* differ from those of the de facto parent theory used in *B.M.H.*? How do the legal consequences of the doctrines differ? How is the *Elisa B.* theory different from the ALI de facto parenthood doctrine? From the ALI parent by estoppel theory?

4. Courts in Colorado have held that proof that a man is not a child's biological father does not necessarily rebut a presumption that he is the child's father based on holding out or on having signed and filed a VAP. In re the Parental Responsibilities of A.D., 240 P.3d 488, 490-492 (Colo. App. 2010); People in Interest of J.C.G., 318 P.3d 576 (Colo. App. 2013). In In re S.N.V., 284 P.3d 147 (Colo. App. 2011), the court extended this principle to hold that the wife of a biological father could rely on the holding out presumption to seek a declaration of parentage of a child born to another woman, where the birth mother claimed that the child was the product of an affair, and the husband and wife claimed that they had a surrogacy arrangement with her.

Courts in New Mexico and Colorado have held that the same-sex partner of a child's mother may be a legal parent, based on holding out. Chatterjee v. King, 280 P.3d 283 (N.M. 2012); In re Parental Responsibilities of A.R.L., 318 P.3d 581 (Colo. App. 2013). *See also* Shineovich v. Kemp, 229 Or. App. 670, 214 P.3d 29, 39-40 (2009) (applying statutory presumption that a husband is the legal father of a child born to his wife through artificial insemination to same-sex couple where one conceives by artificial insemination while living with and with the consent of the other). On the other hand, the court in In re T.J.S., 16 A.3d 386 (N.J. Super. 2011), interpreted the state parentage act as allowing a declaration of legal maternity only for a woman biologically or gestationally related to a child.

NOTE: SECOND PARENT ADOPTION

De facto parenthood, parenthood by estoppel, and other judicial doctrines for recognizing functional parents can be expensive because of the need to go to court, and they are available only if, in hindsight, a court determines that the adult has become a functional parent. The latter feature alone means that unrelated adults who develop relationships with children cannot rely on these devices to protect those relationships. The fact that the doctrines are indeterminate and discretionary exacerbates this problem.

If the legal parent's partner adopts the child, at least some of these problems are solved. Adoption statutes, which will we will discuss at greater length in Chapter 14, were originally intended to permit an unrelated couple to become parents of a child who had been orphaned or born to a parent (often a single mother) unable to care for the child. The statutes accordingly provided for the birth mother and father (if known) to surrender their parental rights so that the new parents could adopt the child. Parents who remarried after the death or desertion of a spouse sometimes wanted their new spouse to adopt the child, providing legal recognition for the new family unit. The question arose as to whether the adoption statutes that had been written with stranger adoption in mind permitted adoption by a second parent where the first parent had never surrendered his or her parental rights. In Marshall v. Marshall, 196 Cal. 761, 767 (1925), for example, the California Supreme Court, addressed the issue and "effectively read second parent adoption into the statutory scheme, by approving a type of second parent adoption, stepparent adoption, which at that time the adoption statutes did not expressly authorize. In so doing, we necessarily determined that relinquishment of the birth parent's rights was not essential to adoption." Sharon S. v. Superior Court, 73 P.3d 554 (Cal. 2003).

When same-sex couples could not receive recognition for their unions, but nevertheless sought to affirm their status as co-parents, they, too, turned to adoption and, in some cases, relied on the precedent set by the stepparent cases to persuade state courts to permit an adoption by a second parent of the same sex. Thus, the term "second-parent adoption" has been used to refer to "an independent adoption whereby a child born to [or legally adopted by] one partner is adopted by his or her non-biological or non-legal second parent, with the consent of the legal parent, and without changing the latter's rights and responsibilities." Emily Doskow, The Second Parent Trap, 20 J. Juv. L. 1, 5 (1999). The result is that "the child has two legal parents who have equal legal status in terms of their relationship with the child." Sharon S. v. Superior Court, above. Human Rights Watch reported in February 2014 that 22 states and the District of Columbia now expressly authorize second-parent adoption either by statute or court rulings, eight states present obstacles to such adoptions, and the rest neither authorize nor prohibit it. Parenting Laws: Second Parent or Stepparent Adoption, available at http://hrc-assets.s3-website-us-east-1.amazonaws.com//files/assets/resources/parenting_second-parent-adoption_2-2014.pdf (last visited May 13, 2014). In a number of the latter states, trial courts have granted such adoptions without specific statutory or appellate authorization. See Ann K. Wooster, Adoption of Child by Same-Sex Partners, 61 A.L.R.6th 1 (originally published in 2011); National Center for Lesbian Rights, Adoption by LGBT Parents (Dec. 2013), http://www.nclrights.org/wp-content/uploads/2013/07/2PA_state_list.pdf (last visited May 14, 2014).

Adoption offers advantages even to couples who might otherwise receive recognition through the marital presumption in states that allow same-sex couples to marry or states that recognize de facto parentage. Adoption produces a judicial decree that is entitled to full faith and credit in all 50 states. States that refuse to recognize a same-sex marriage performed in another state or that do not recognize de facto parentage must, under the U.S. Constitution, give effect to an adoption decree. *See, e.g.*, Russell v. Bridgens, 647 N.W.2d 56 (Neb. 2002) (recognizing a Pennsylvania second-parent adoption and holding that it established Nebraska resident's parental standing to seek custody and support). This offers greater protection to parents who might some day move or travel to a jurisdiction that would otherwise not recognize their parental status. For this reason, many attorneys advise all same-sex co-parents to adopt if they are able to do so.

Some states have adoption statutes that expressly limit adoption to married couples or that refer to adoption by a "husband and wife jointly" or to an "unmarried person," suggesting that the act does not authorize adoption by unmarried couples. A number of these states have nonetheless interpreted these statutes to permit gay and lesbian couples who cannot marry to adopt a child jointly. *See, e.g.*, Adoption of M.A., 930 A.2d 1088 (Me. 2007).

An unresolved issue is whether states that permit same-sex marriage will then distinguish between married and unmarried couples in the adoption process. In April 2014, a judge in Brooklyn refused to grant a second-parent adoption to the spouse of a lesbian because, since the couple was married, New York law already recognized the two women as co-parents and the adoption was unnecessary. James C. McKinsley, Jr., N.Y. Judge Alarms Gay Parents by Finding Marriage Law Negates Need for Adoption, New York Times, Jan. 28, 2014, available at http://www.nytimes.com/2014/01/29/nyregion/ny-judge-alarms-gay-parents-by-finding-marriage-law-negates-need-for-adoption.html?_r=1 (last visited, June 26, 2014). In other states, where the trial courts had been willing to grant second parent adoption to unmarried partners who could not marry, it remains to be seen whether the practice will continue or whether the courts will require prospective adoptive parents who can marry to do so. *See* Marriage Equality and Adoption in Minnesota, http://www.bblawmn.com/1/post/2013/07/marriage-equality-and-adoption-in-minnesota.html (last visited May 14, 2014) (observing that "it is likely that the courts will no longer grant second-parent adoptions to unmarried couples in Minnesota").

See generally Courtney G. Joslin, Travel Insurance: Protecting Lesbian and Gay Parent Families Across State Lines, 4 Harv. L. & Pol'y Rev. 31 (2010); Courtney G. Joslin, Interstate Recognition of Parentage in a Time of Disharmony: Same-Sex Parent Families and Beyond, 70 Ohio St. L.J. 563 (2009); Nancy D. Polikoff, A Mother Should Not Have to Adopt Her Own Child: Parentage Laws for Children of Lesbian Couples in the Twenty-First Century, 5 Stan. J. C.R. & C.L. 201 (2009); Mark Strasser, Interstate Recognition of Adoptions: On Jurisdiction, Full Faith and Credit, and the Kinds of Challenges the Future May Bring, 2008 BYU L. Rev. 1809; Rhonda Wasserman, Are You Still My Mother? Interstate Recognition of Adoptions by Gays and Lesbians, 58 Am. U. L. Rev. 1 (2008).

PROBLEMS

1. When Hank and Wanda were divorced, Hank agreed to pay child support for Bobby, their son born during the marriage, and for Ellie, Wanda's child from a former relationship who had lived with Hank and Wanda throughout their six-year marriage. The agreement was incorporated into Hank and Wanda's divorce

decree. During the marriage Hank had signed an affidavit of paternity for Ellie and filed it with the Bureau of Vital Statistics, even though he was not in fact her biological father. He never formally adopted her, though. It is now two years since the divorce. Hank has remarried, and his new wife has just had twins. He has moved to terminate his duty to support Ellie on the basis that she is not his biological child. Ellie's biological father lives in an adjoining state. Wanda has had no contact with him since before Ellie's birth. What arguments should Wanda make? How should Hank respond?

2. Ross and Kathy were married when Kathy's child from her former marriage, Danny, was 6 months old. Ross knew that he was not Danny's biological father, but he treated him as his son in every way. Kathy died when Danny was 7 years old. Until Kathy's death Danny had no contact with his biological father, Greg, who refused to visit. After Kathy's death Greg came forward, claiming the right to Danny's custody. Ross also seeks custody. As between Ross and Greg, to whom should the court award custody and why? As between Kathy's mother and Ross, to whom should the court award custody?

D. MORE THAN TWO PARENTS?

Traditional parentage law, particularly the strong marital presumption, protected the relationships that children form with their caretakers. Today, however, large numbers of children are raised by a changing cast of adults. It is no longer clear that an insistence on two — and only two — parents continues to makes sense. In *Michael H.*, the case in which the United States Supreme Court addressed the constitutionality of the marital presumption, a guardian ad litem was appointed to represent the interests of the child, Victoria. The guardian argued that Victoria's interests would best be served by allowing her to maintain a personal relationship with both men, her mother's husband who was raising her and the biological father she called "Daddy." Justice Scalia's plurality opinion rejected this argument out of hand, saying, "California law, like nature itself, makes no provision for dual fatherhood." The case might have been decided quite differently if the lower court had had the option of recognizing both Michael and Gerald as Victoria's fathers, and then deciding what role each would play on the basis of a best-interest determination. The Louisiana courts have held that this solution is sometimes an option under state law.

T.D. v. M.M.M.

730 So. 2d 873 (La. 1999)

TRAYLOR, Justice. This avowal action arose when P.W., the biological father of the minor child, C.M., intervened in the legal parents' custody proceeding to have his parental rights acknowledged. The trial court recognized P.W. as the biological father and ordered that a hearing be conducted to resolve visitation and child support issues in the best interest of the child. On appeal, the court of appeal barred the action under the doctrine of laches. . . . We granted certioirari. . . .

The child's mother, T.D., and legal father, M.M.M., were married in October of 1984. In October of 1985, T.D. met P.W., who was also married at the time. T.D. and P.W. began having adulterous sexual relations in March or April of 1986. The affair spanned a period of approximately seven and one-half years. In March of 1988, T.D. conceived a child, C.M. T.D. informed P.W. that she suspected he was the father because she had not been intimate with her husband at the time of conception. T.D. also informed her husband that he was the father of the child.

T.D. and P.W. discontinued their sexual relations during the pregnancy, but continued with the affair shortly after the child's birth in December of 1988. P.W. testified that he regularly visited the mother and child throughout the affair and always suspected that he was the child's father. In November of 1992, T.D. and M.M.M. separated. At T.D.'s request, P.W. curbed his visits during most of the separation, but resumed them in March of 1993. In April of 1993, the child and P.W. underwent DNA paternity testing. In June of 1993, the DNA test results confirmed to a 99.5% probability that P.W. was the child's biological father. That same month, T.D. and M.M.M. were granted a divorce. In August of 1993, the trial court named T.D. as the domiciliary parent and granted M.M.M. visitation. T.D. ended the affair with P.W. in November 1993 and, thereafter, would not allow P.W. access to the child.

In December 1994, P.W. intervened in the legal parents' domestic proceedings seeking recognition of his biological paternity, joint custody, and visitation. The legal parents objected to this intervention. The court held that P.W.'s suit was not untimely because "his suspicions of parenthood were not confirmed until he received the results of the [DNA test]" and that visitation rights of any parent must be considered in light of the best interests of the child. The court recognized P.W. as the child's biological father, ordered a mental health evaluation of the child to assess possible effects of parentage information and visitation with the biological father, and, finding itself without sufficient evidence to determine the best interest of the child, the court ordered an evidentiary hearing to determine visitation rights and to assess income for potential child support issues.

The legal parents appealed from this ruling, arguing the biological father's action was untimely. The court of appeal found for the legal parents. . . . P.W. sought writs with this court, contending the court of appeal misinterpreted and misapplied the doctrine of laches and, therefore, erred in dismissing his avowal action. . . .

In order for this court to decide the timeliness of the instant action, we must first set out the jurisprudential background of avowal. Louisiana courts have traditionally recognized a biological father's right to his illegitimate child[32] by means of an avowal action. This action is available despite the La. Civ. Code art. 184 presumption that the husband of the mother is the father of all children born or conceived during the marriage.[33]

---

32. In this context, we use the term "illegitimate" to connote a child who is not born in the marriage of his biological father to his mother and/or is assumed to be the child of another man. A child who enjoys legitimacy as to his legal father may also be the illegitimate child of his biological parent. Our jurisprudence allowing dual paternity provides that such a child may filiate to his biological father or the biological father may avow the child.

33. Contrast this to the holding of the U.S. Supreme Court in Michael H. v. Gerald D., 491 U.S. 110 (1989). We find the instant case distinguishable from the former case because,

In our view, several policy factors favor allowing a biological father to avow his child where such action will result in dual paternity. First, a biological father is susceptible to suit for child support until his child reaches nineteen years of age. La. Civ. Code art. 209. Second, a child who enjoys legitimacy as to his legal father may seek to filiate to his biological father in order to receive wrongful death benefits or inheritance rights. It seems only fair, in light of the obligations to which a biological father is susceptible and the multitude of benefits available to the biological child due to the biological link, that the biological father should be afforded at least an opportunity to prove his worthiness to participate in the child's life. Alternatively, a biological father who cannot meet the best-interest-of-the-child standard retains his obligation of support but cannot claim the privilege of parental rights. Finding that a biological father clearly has the right to avow his illegitimate child under the law of this state, we now turn to the issue of whether P.W. asserted his action in a timely manner . . . .

The legal parents based their appeal on the argument that laches bars a biological father's avowal action where it is not promptly asserted. As a matter of law, the purpose of the doctrine is to prevent an injustice which might result from the enforcement of long neglected rights and to recognize the difficulty of ascertaining the truth as a result of that delay. However, this court has clearly established that the common law doctrine of laches does not prevail in Louisiana. Nevertheless, we have applied the doctrine in rare and extraordinary circumstances

We will consider the elements of the doctrine as they apply to the instant case to determine if rare and extraordinary circumstances exist in the instant case which merit application of the doctrine of laches. Regarding the first element of prejudice, we find no proof of prejudice to the child nor to the defendants in intervention, the legal parents. To the contrary, the trial judge expressly limited his ruling to a finding of fact that P.W. is the child's father. The trial court passed on the issue of the best interest of the child because it was without sufficient evidence to make a knowledgeable finding. If evidence of the best interest of the child was lacking, certainly there is insufficient proof institution of this action has caused prejudice to the child. Thus, we find no injustice or prejudice may result from this avowal action. The legal parents failed to prove the first element of laches . . . .

Regarding the second element of delay, we surmise that the delay in this case is not entirely the fault of the biological father. It is apparent that the actions of the mother have caused much of the delay. *See* Finnerty v. Boyett, 469 So. 2d at 292 (Where the mother of the child effectively causes the delay in the biological father's filing of an avowal action, the delay is not considered unreasonable so as to pre-clude avowal). P.W. regularly visited his child when he was on good terms with the mother. This appears to be the reason why he did not file suit until after the affair ended and his attempts to visit his child were thwarted. P.W. filed his suit less than one year after it became apparent that he was not free to visit his child, and approximately six years from the child's birth. We find P.W. did not seek

---

unlike Louisiana law, a California statute specifically prohibits dual paternity and mandates that the husband of the mother of the child born during marriage is **conclusively** presumed to be the father. Such a finding is not tenable in Louisiana because the law of this State allows recognition of dual paternity and the Article 184 presumption of paternity is rebuttable.

enforcement of long neglected rights because his filing was not unreasonable in light of circumstances which impute much of the delay to the mother. Thus, the legal parents failed to prove the second element of laches.

It is the province of the trial court to determine the nature and extent of a biological father's rights to his illegitimate child. For this reason, we remand this matter to the trial court for such a determination. Assuming arguendo that P.W. can convince the trial court that his involvement in C.M.'s life is in the best interest of C.M., he should not be precluded from participating in the child's life. . . .

KNOLL, J., concurring. I write separately to concur in the result only. In my view, since Louisiana law (our Civil Code and statutory law) fails to provide for an avowal action for an unwed biological father, the real focus of the majority opinion should be directed toward a consideration of the unwed biological father's constitutional rights, placed in balance with competing interests. . . .

If an unwed biological father's claim is supported by constitutionally based rights, a procedural bar cannot deny consideration of those claims based on state law or absence thereof, because state law is subordinate to the Constitution according to the supremacy clause. . . . Specifically, the majority should have addressed the unwed biological father's liberty interest in the relationship with his child and whether he may be deprived of his rights without due process of law. . . .

In the case *sub judice*, the biological father did develop a relationship with his natural child, particularly as the natural mother's marriage was drawing to a close. He should not be faulted for not coming forward during the time in which his child's mother was married to another man, because Louisiana's public policy favors protecting the marital unit. Given the presumption of paternity in La. Code Civ. P. art. 184 and the strong State interests in preserving the marital family unit that gave rise to the presumption, any efforts made during that marriage would have been properly thwarted.

The fact that a biological father is thwarted from exercising parental rights when the mother is married to another man is not constitutionally offensive, because the balance tips in favor of preserving the marital family over the biological father's individual rights. *See* Michael H. v. Gerald D., 491 U.S. 110 (1989). However, once the bonds of matrimony are dissolved *a vinculo matrimonii*, the State's interest in preserving the marital family disappears. This does not ignore the fact that some rights spring from the dissolution of a lawful marriage, but recognizes instead the policy behind the codal provision and the perspective of our times. Today's realities are that illegitimacy and "broken homes" have neither the rarity nor the stigma as in the past. When parenthood can be objectively determined by scientific evidence, and where illegitimacy is no longer stigmatized, presumptions regarding paternity are "out of place." . . . In this case, where we have conclusive scientific evidence of true paternity based on DNA testing, it is inappropriate not to address the biological father's substantive rights. . . .

For the reasons above, I respectfully concur in the results.

CALOGERO, C.J., dissenting. . . . I would hold that this biological father lacks standing to bring an avowal action, as no statutory or codal authority exists granting him standing to rebut the article 184 presumption of paternity. Rather, the

Civil Code only permits the child to seek dual paternity. La. Civ. Code art. 209. Moreover, public policy dictates that the relationships among a legal father, child, and his or her mother remain protected, even though the marital relationship has dissolved. Accordingly, I respectfully dissent.

KIMBALL, Justice, dissenting. I dissent because the majority proceeds to a discussion of laches without first determining both the validity of the avowal action and the categories of persons who are allowed to bring this action, which are issues that this court has never squarely addressed. I consider such a discussion wholly appropriate to the instant case, as there is no codal or statutory authority for the avowal action. Rather, this action is a creation of the lower courts. I also conclude that, even assuming *arguendo* that such an action exists, a careful examination of the law and the history of the law in this area shows that the intervenor in this suit lacks standing to bring this action. . . .

NOTES AND QUESTIONS

1. If Louisiana law did not allow "dual paternity," what arguments for being recognized as C.M.'s legal father might P.W. raise under the Uniform Parentage Act? What counterarguments could the mother, T.D., make? Could P.W. successfully argue that he was a de facto parent under *B.M.H.*?

2. The other Louisiana cases on dual paternity hold that an unmarried biological father whose paternity is established in Louisiana can be liable for child support, and his child may claim wrongful death benefits or inheritance rights at the father's death, but he is unlikely to prevail in an action for custody or visitation over the objection of the mother and her husband. Smith v. Cole, 553 So. 2d 847 (La. 1989); Smith v. Jones, 566 So. 2d 408 (La. App. 1990); Finnerty v. Boyett, 469 So. 2d 287 (La. 1985); Durr v. Blue, 454 So. 2d 315 (La. App. 1984).

What are the advantages of the Louisiana dual paternity approach, which allows more than two legal parents, over the other doctrines we have examined in this chapter? What problems does it create?

3. After *T.D.* was decided, the Louisiana legislature amended various statutes so that now a husband who wishes to disavow his paternity must do so within one year of a child's birth, and a man claiming to be the biological father of a child presumed to be the child of another man must bring a filiation action within a year of birth unless the mother in bad faith deceived the biological father about his paternity. In the latter situation, the suit must be brought within one year from the day the father knew or should have known of his paternity, or within ten years from the the birth of the child, whichever occurs first. La. Civ. Code art. 189, 198 (2014). For more information, *see* Katharine Shaw Spaht, Who's Your Momma, Who Are Your Daddies? Louisiana's New Law of Filiation, 67 La. L. Rev. 307 (2007).

4. In 2013, California became the first state to enact a statute explicitly authorizing recognition of three parents. Cal. Fam. Code § 7612 provides:

(c) In an appropriate action, a court may find that more than two persons with a claim to parentage under this division are parents if the court finds that recognizing only two parents would be detrimental to the child. In determining detriment to the child, the court shall consider all relevant factors, including, but not limited to, the harm of removing the child from a stable placement with a parent who has fulfilled the child's physical needs and the child's psychological needs for care and affection, and who has assumed that role for a substantial period of time. A finding of detriment to the child does not require a finding of unfitness of any of the parents or persons with a claim to parentage.

In enacting the statute, the California legislature found that "[m]ost children have two parents, but in rare cases, children have more than two people who are that child's parent in every way. Separating a child from a parent has a devastating psychological and emotional impact on the child, and courts must have the power to protect children from this harm." Senate Bill No. 274, Section 1(a) (effective Jan. 1, 2014).

The statute's requirement of a showing of "detriment to the child" is the same standard California uses to justify an award of visitation over the objections of a parent to a third party such as a grandparent or stepparent. *See* In re Marriage of W., 7 Cal. Rptr. 3d 461 (Cal. App. 2003). Does designation of a person as a "parent" or, indeed, as a third parent, rather than as a stepparent or grandparent have constitutional implications? For a summary of the constitutional debate, *see* David D. Meyer, Partners, Care Givers, and the Constitutional Substance of Parenthood, *in* Reconceiving the Family: Critical Reflections on the American Law Institute's Principles of the Law of Family Dissolution (Robin Fretwell Wilson ed., 2006).

5. Other states have occasionally recognized three parents, particularly where all three parents were in agreement on the inclusion of the third person, though most of the decisions are unreported. A Pennsylvania case is one of the first reported decisions to recognize more than two legal parents. In Jacob v. Shultz-Jacob, 923 A.2d 473 (Pa. Super. 2007), a lesbian couple, who had entered into a civil union in Vermont, were jointly raising four children. The biological father of two of the children, who had acted as a sperm donor but never sought to sever his parental standing, provided support and saw the children on a regular basis. The trial court awarded partial custody to each of the two women, and partial custody of two of the children to their biological father, but rejected the possibility of holding three parents liable for support. The appellate court, in the first reported case of its kind, vacated the support order and remanded, instructing the trial court to consider fractional support awards among the three parties. The Canadian courts have also recognized three parents, including two lesbian partners and a sperm donor in a case involving an ongoing family arrangement. *See* A.A. v. B.B., [2007] 278 D.L.R. (4th) 519, 522, 533-534 (Can.), *leave to appeal denied sub nom.* Alliance for Marriage & Family v. A.A., [2007] 3 S.C.R. 124. *See also* LaChappelle v. Mitten, 607 N.W.2d 151 (Minn. App. 2000) (lesbian couple and sperm donor agreed that sperm donor would have contact with the child but not full custodial rights); Steve Rothaus, Miami-Dade Circuit Judge OK's Plan for Gay Man, Lesbian Couple to Be on Daughter's Birth Certificate, Miami Herald, Feb. 7, 2013.

6. Thirty years ago Katharine Bartlett, the principal author of the ALI de facto parent and parent by estoppel provisions, first fully set out the

argument for legal recognition of the roles multiple adults play in some children's lives. Katharine Bartlett, Rethinking Parenthood as an Exclusive Status: The Need for Legal Alternatives When the Premise of the Nuclear Family Has Failed, 70 Va. L. Rev. 879 (1984). More recent discussions include Susan Frelich Appleton, Parents by the Numbers, 37 Hofstra L. Rev. 11 (2008); Katharine K. Baker, Bionormativity and the Construction of Parenthood, 42 Ga. L. Rev. 649, 655 (2008); Cynthia Grant Bowman, The Legal Relationship Between Cohabitants and Their Partners' Children, 13 Theoretical Inquiries L. 127 (2012); Nancy E. Dowd, Multiple Parents/Multiple Fathers, 9 J.L. & Fam. Stud. 231 (2007); Leslie Joan Harris, The Basis for Legal Parentage and the Clash Between Custody and Child Support, 42 Ind. L. Rev. 611 (2009); Melanie B. Jacobs, Why Just Two? Disaggregating Traditional Parental Rights and Responsibilities to Recognize Multiple Parents, 9 J.L. & Fam. Stud. 209 (2007); Laura T. Kessler, Community Parenting, 24 Wash. U. J.L. & Pol'y 47, 49 (2007); Melissa Murray, The Networked Family: Reframing the Legal Understanding of Caregiving and Caregivers, 94 Va. L. Rev. 385 (2008); Alison Harvison Young, Reconceiving the Family: Challenging the Paradigm of the Exclusive Family, 6 Am. U. J. Gender Soc. Pol'y & L. 505, 517-518 (1998); Comm'n on Parenthood's Future, Institute for American Values, The Revolution in Parenthood: The Emerging Global Clash Between Adult Rights and Children's Needs 10-15 (2006) (a survey of relevant developments in the United States and abroad, led by principal investigator Elizabeth Marquardt).

See also Shelly Ann Kamei, Comment, Partitioning Paternity: The German Approach to a Disjuncture Between Genetic and Legal Paternity with Implications for American Courts, 11 San Diego Int'l L.J. 509 (2010).

PROBLEMS

1. Donna and Emily were married in California. Emily supported Donna when Donna became pregnant and gave birth to a baby girl, Ingrid, named after Emily's mother. George and Harry also married in California, and they contributed sperm to Donna with the understanding that they would play an "uncle" role in the child's upbringing. George and Harry mixed their sperm before the insemination, and no one knew whether George or Harry was Ingrid's biological father. George and Harry saw Ingrid at least once every two weeks after she was born, and they often contributed financially.

Donna and Emily divorced when Ingrid was a year old, and Emily moved to the East Coast. Her relationship with Donna remained amicable, and Emily saw Ingrid two to three times a year. A few months after the split with Emily, Donna entered into a new informal relationship with Francine. When Ingrid was four, Francine and Donna separated. The separation was not amicable, and Donna refuses to let Francine continue to see Ingrid. Ingrid regards Donna and Francine as her two "mommies." Who should be regarded as Ingrid's parents and with what rights and obligations?

2. Melissa and Irene, who registered as domestic partners in their state, had a tumultuous relationship. After a particularly intense conflict, Melissa moved out and obtained a restraining order against Irene, alleging physical and emotional abuse. Melissa entered into a relationship with Jesus and became pregnant. During

the first few months of the pregnancy, she lived with Jesus and his family, and he supported her financially. Before the baby was born, however, Melissa reconciled with Irene. Melissa did not notify Jesus of her address or of the child's birth. Jesus, who had moved to Oklahoma, did not make any effort to contact Melissa through her family. Melissa listed only her name on the child's birth certificate, but she and Irene jointly cared for the child for about a month after the child's birth. Then Melissa moved out, and when the child was two months old, Irene filed for shared custody or visitation. Melissa contacted Jesus, who sent money on several occasions. At his request, Melissa regularly took the baby to visit his family.

Melissa then entered into a relationship with Jose. When the child was about 6 months old, Jose attacked Irene with a knife, stabbing her in the neck and causing severe injuries. Melissa admitted that she and Jose were using drugs at the time and that the attack was intended to scare Irene away from the baby. Melissa was arrested and charged with being an accessory to attempted murder.

Irene was badly injured in the attack. She has no means of support and has been living with friends. Melissa suffers from bipolar disorder and severe depression. Jesus has a stable job in Oklahoma and support from his fiance and grandmother in caring for the child.

Who should receive recognition as the child's parents and how should custody be allotted?

Adoption and Alternative Reproductive Technologies

14

In the last chapter we examined basic principles used to determine who the legal parents of a child are—biology, marriage, and functioning in a parental role. We also looked at traditional premises regarding parenthood, such as the proposition that each child have one mother and one father, and challenges to these premises.

The topics of this chapter—adoption and parenthood by means of alternative reproductive technologies—continue our study of these issues and add new ones. The adoption materials, for example, raise fundamental questions about the role of intention in defining parenthood, how society determines when parents can lose their legal status, and what role, if any, larger groups should play in determining how a child will be raised. Alternative reproductive technologies— artificial insemination, embryo transplantation, and others—also raise these issues and even challenge our understanding of what it means to be a biological parent.

Thus, although the issues covered in this chapter do not arise in practice nearly as often as do those in Chapter 13, they are very important for what they reveal about our understanding of legal parent-child relationships.

A. ADOPTION

Burton Z. Sokoloff, *Antecedents of American Adoption*

3(1) The Future of Children 17, 18, 21-22 (Spring 1993)[1]

Reference to adoption may be found in the Bible and in the ancient codes, laws, and writings of Babylonians, Chinese, Egyptians, Hebrews, and Hindus. It is

---

1. This journal, from which much material in this section is taken, is a publication of the Center for the Future of Children, The David and Lucille Packard Foundation.

believed that this practice was usually employed to provide male heirs to childless couples, to maintain family lines and estates, or to fulfill the requirements of specific religious practices such as ancestor worship. It is commonly stated that adoption law in the United States is based upon early Roman laws; however, as Presser points out: "In contrast with current adoption law, which has as its purpose the 'best interests of the child,' it appears that ancient adoption law . . . was clearly designed to benefit the *adopter*, and any benefits to the adoptee were secondary."[2] . . . Hollinger adds that the adoptees were all male and usually adults, not children, and concludes that the relationship between adoption as known by the Romans and adoption as practiced by Americans "is tenuous at best."[3]

Likewise, English common law cannot be cited as the precedent for American adoption law because the former makes no reference to adoption and because the first general adoption statute was not enacted in England until 1926, some 75 years after passage of the first adoption statute in the United States. Thus, as Hollinger states, American adoption is "purely a creature of the statutes which have been enacted in this country since the mid-nineteenth century."[4] . . .

During the nineteenth century, adoption laws developed in response to the desire both to give legal status to children whose care had been transferred and to encourage more available and better care for dependent children. . . .

The first comprehensive adoption statute was passed in Massachusetts in 1851.

. . . The Massachusetts statute is particularly notable in that, for the first time, the interests of the child were expressly emphasized and the adoption had to be approved by a judge.

. . . [B]y 1929 all states had enacted some form of adoption legislation. Virtually all statutes emphasized the "best interests of the child" as the basis for adoption. . . .

During the first half of the twentieth century, *secrecy, anonymity*, and the *sealing of records* became statutorily required and standard adoption practice. The Minnesota Act of 1917 is commonly credited with having initiated the secrecy and sealed records aspects of adoption. Actually, as Hollinger points out, these practices "were not designed to preserve anonymity between biological parents and adopters, but to shield the adoption proceedings from public scrutiny. These statutes barred all persons from inspecting the files and records on adoption except for the parties to the adoption and their attorneys."[5] Nevertheless, beginning in the 1920s and extending well into the 1940s, states progressively amended their statutes "to provide not only for the sealing of adoption records, but also for denial to everyone of access to these records except upon a judicial finding of 'good cause.'" In these statutes, the identities of the birthparents and the adoptive parents were to remain secret, even from each other. . . .

---

2. Presser, S. B. The historical background of the American law of adoption, Journal of Family Law (1972) 11:446.

3. Hollinger, J. H. Introduction to adoption law and practice. In Adoption Law and Practice. J. H. Hollinger, ed. New York: Matthew Bender & Co., Inc. 1991, p.1-19.

4. *See* [*id.*], p.1-18.

5. [*Id.*], p.13-5.

The movement toward secrecy is said to have been urged by social workers in child-placing agencies with the goal of removing the stigma of illegitimacy from children born out of wedlock. These workers believed that assuring the anonymity of the birth mothers and the privacy of the adoptive family would make the integration of the child into the adoptive family more secure. . . .

In addition to the passage of adoption legislation, the first half of the twentieth century is characterized by a dramatic increase in interest in adoption on the part of childless couples and in the steady trend toward adoption of infants. Prior to the 1920s very few legal adoptions of children actually took place when compared with the numbers of children in institutions, in foster care, or in situations created by informal transfers. . . .

World War I and the influenza epidemic that followed resulted in a sharp drop in the birth rate and an increased interest in infant adoption. . . . Major factors encouraging infant adoption were the development of successful formula feeding and the perception that environment, not heredity, was the major determinant of child development.

Hollinger describes the end of the first half of the twentieth century as follows:

> By the 1950s, a complete transition had occurred from the earlier interest in adopting older children to the present desire for adoptable babies. . . . A 1951 survey of 25 states indicated that nearly 70% of children being placed for adoption were under the age of one. . . . Well over half of the children were born out of wedlock, two-fifths of the mothers being under 18. The remaining children came primarily from "broken homes." . . . Fewer than 10% of the children were placed because both of their parents were dead.

For more on the history of American adoption law, in addition to the sources cited in this excerpt, *see* Jamil S. Zainaldin, The Emergence of a Modern American Family Law: Child Custody, Adoption, and the Courts, 1796-1851, 73 Nw. U. L. Rev. 1038 (1979); Yasuhide Kawashima, Adoption in Early America, 20 J. Fam. L. 677 (1981-1982); Michael Grossberg, Governing the Hearth 268-280 (1985); Naomi Cahn, Birthing Relationships, 17 Wis. Women's L.J. 162 (2002); Naomi Cahn, Perfect Substitutes or the Real Thing?, 52 Duke L.J. 1077 (2003). *See also* The Adoption History Project, available at http://darkwing.uoregon.edu/~adoption (last visited Nov. 25, 2013).

Most adoptions today are "related adoptions," that is, adoptions by stepparents and relatives. One-fifth are adoptions of foster children, and only 20 to 30 percent are adoptions of infants by adults who are strangers to them. Uniform Adoption Act, Prefatory Note (1994). In 2010, householders reported that 1.5 million adopted children under the age of 18 lived with them, a drop from 1.6 million in 2000. Adopted children made up 2.4 percent of all children under 18 living with the householders who responded to the census. Bureau of the Census, Adopted Children and Stepchildren: 2010, at 4, 6 (April 2014), available at http://www.census.gov/prod/2014pubs/p20-572.pdf (last visited June 23, 2014). Adopted children were more likely to live with two married parents (73 percent) than were biological children (69 percent). *Id.* at 16.

State law governs adoption, and specific statutory requirements vary significantly from state to state. The relative lack of success of the most recent version of the Uniform Adoption Act, promulgated in 1994, suggests the lack of consensus on how the law should treat specific issues. Only Vermont has changed its law based on the 1994 version, and it did not adopt the Uniform Act verbatim. *See* Vt. Stat. Ann. ch. 15A §§ 1-101 through 7-105. Nevertheless, it is possible generally to describe adoption as a two-stage process. The first stage is the termination of the parent-child relationship between the child and the parent who is going to be "replaced." The second stage is creation of the new parent-child relationship between the adoptive parent and the child, which under most circumstances requires a judicial proceeding.[6] The next two sections consider the adoption process; the third explores the role that a child's membership in a social group plays in determining whether a child will be adopted and, if so, by whom.

1. *Terminating the First Parent-Child Relationship*

Before a child with a living mother, married or unmarried, may be adopted by another woman, the first mother's relationship to the child must be terminated. A father's rights must be terminated before his child can be adopted if he is married to the mother or if, as an unmarried father, he is entitled to substantive custodial rights under state law (see Section B of Chapter 13). A parent may voluntarily give up parental rights by consenting to the child's adoption, and all states also have enacted statutes that allow courts to terminate parents' rights without their consent.

Generally, the legal principles for determining when a parent's rights can be terminated are the same for adoptions by both a relative and a stranger, but the most bitterly contested adoptions are probably stepparent and other in-family adoptions. Often such cases are prosecuted on the grounds that the noncustodial biological parent abandoned the child, but the next case considers the validity of a parent's consent to the adoption of a child by a stepparent.

---

6. While some of the older statutes speak of unmarried fathers "adopting" their children by acknowledging them, treating them openly as their children, or receiving them into their homes, these are really devices for legitimating the child and so are not within the process explained here. *See* Chapter 13, page 880.

In addition, the doctrine of "equitable adoption," which is based on estoppel principles, is recognized in some states. Under this doctrine, the would-be adoptive parents have agreed to adopt a child, but for some reason the adoption is never completed. Upon a showing of detrimental reliance on this agreement to adopt, the adoptive parents (and their successors) are estopped to deny that the child was adopted, and the child has the same rights that he or she would have if the adoption had been completed. Most of the equitable adoption cases arise in the context of probate of the "adoptive" parents' estates, and the effect of finding that a child was equitably adopted is to give the child inheritance rights. For purposes of Social Security survivors' benefits, equitably adopted children are considered a decedent's children. 20 C.F.R. § 404.354(a). *See also* Cynthia Grant Bowman, The New Illegitimacy: Children of Cohabiting Couples and Stepchildren, 20 Am. U. J. Gender Soc. Pol'y & L. 437 (2012).

In re Petition of S. O.

795 P.2d 254 (Colo. 1990) (en banc)

Mullarkey, J. . . . . Appellant D. J. T. began living with T. O. in 1980 and lived with her for about five years. The two were unmarried during their entire relationship. On June 13, 1983, T. O. gave birth to a son, E. E. F., who is the subject of this dispute. T. O. conceded in an affidavit filed in the subsequent adoption action that D. J. T. was E. E. F.'s natural father. Following E. E. F.'s birth, D. J. T. and T. O. continued to live together with their son for about two and one-half years. During that period, D. J. T. exercised at least some of the duties and responsibilities of a father, although the exact extent to which he did so was disputed by the parties. In the Fall of 1985, T. O. ended her relationship with D. J. T. and, together with E. E. F., ceased to live with him. On October 18, 1985, T. O. married S. O., the appellee stepfather. Following T. O.'s marriage to S. O., D. J. T. continued to maintain a relationship with E. E. F., visiting him periodically in T. O. and S. O.'s home. D. J. T. did not contribute significantly to the costs of E. E. F.'s support, and was not asked to do so by T. O.

In the Fall of 1986, T. O. approached D. J. T. to discuss the possibility that her husband S. O. adopt E. E. F. Among other reasons, according to D. J. T., T. O. and S. O. believed it would be better for the child to have S. O.'s last name and be eligible for his medical coverage. The evidence presented at the juvenile court hearing on the appellant's motion to set aside the adoption indicated that the parties understood that D. J. T. would continue to visit E. E. F. after the adoption. The parties dispute, however, whether such visitation was to be as a matter of right for D. J. T. or only so long as T. O. and S. O. consented to such visits. It is undisputed that when T. O. and S. O. obtained a consent form from the juvenile court, they and D. J. T. brought the form to the office of the clerk of the court and asked a clerk whether they could modify the consent form to include a provision recognizing D. J. T.'s right to visit E. E. F. The clerk indicated "there wasn't any way to change the wording." D. J. T. signed the unaltered form.

On October 23, 1986, T. O. and S. O. filed a Petition for Adoption of a Child in Denver Juvenile Court. Included with the petition were D. J. T.'s and T. O.'s separate consents to the adoption. D. J. T.'s consent included a provision under which D. J. T. waived his right to notice of the adoption hearing. D. J. T. received no formal notice of the hearing and D. J. T. testified without contradiction that he was not otherwise informed of the date and time of the hearing. On November 24, 1986, the juvenile court commissioner conducted a hearing on the stepfather's petition to adopt E. E. F., which D. J. T. did not attend. T. O. and S. O. appeared at the hearing without counsel and were questioned by the commissioner on whether they obtained the consent of the child's natural father. They assured the court that the father understood that the adoption decree would terminate his relationship with E. E. F. The commissioner determined that E. E. F. was available for adoption and that it "would serve the best interests of all of the parties" to enter an immediate final decree of adoption.

Following the adoption, D. J. T. continued to visit E. E. F. although over time T. O. became increasingly reluctant to permit the visits. Finally, in May of 1987, the appellees ceased permitting D. J. T. to visit the child and in August of

1987, they obtained a permanent injunction forbidding D. J. T. from contacting E. E. F. About one month after the appellees ceased permitting D. J. T. to visit E. E. F., D. J. T. contacted an attorney and petitioned the juvenile court for a good cause hearing to obtain access to the adoption file. On January 28, 1988, D. J. T. filed in juvenile court what was designated a "Verified Motion to Set Aside Adoption Decree." On October 20, 1988, the court held a hearing on D. J. T.'s motion, receiving testimony from D. J. T., S. O. and T. O., and reviewed the file in the prior adoption action. The court denied the motion to set aside the adoption decree, finding that the father's consent to the adoption was "knowingly and intelligently and voluntarily executed." D. J. T. appealed that decision to the court of appeals, and this case was transferred to this court. . . .

Before specifically addressing D. J. T.'s arguments, it is useful to review the statutory scheme governing stepparent adoptions. . . . The adoption of a child by a stepparent necessarily terminates the parental rights of the noncustodial parent. To commence a proceeding for a stepparent adoption, the stepparent files an adoption petition pursuant to section 19-5-208, 8B C.R.S. (1989 Supp.). The court must decide whether the child is "available for adoption" pursuant to section 19-5-203, 8B C.R.S. (1989 Supp.). Subsection (1) of that section provides in relevant part:

(1) A child may be available for adoption only upon:

(a) Order of the court terminating the parent-child legal relationship in a proceeding brought under article 3 or 5 of this title;

(b) Order of the court decreeing the voluntary relinquishment of the parent-child legal relationship under section 19-5-103 or 19-5-105;

(c) Written and verified consent of the guardian of the person, appointed by the court, of a child whose parents are deceased;

(d) (I) Written and verified consent of the parent in a stepparent adoption where the other parent is deceased or his parent-child legal relationship has been terminated under paragraph (a) or (b) of this subsection (1);

(II) Written and verified consent of the parent in a stepparent adoption where the other parent has abandoned the child for a period of one year or more or where he has failed without cause to provide reasonable support for such child for a period of one year or more. Upon filing of the petition in adoption, the court shall issue a notice directed to the other parent, which notice shall state the nature of the relief sought, the names of the petitioner and the child, and the time and place set for hearing on the petition. If the address of the other parent is known, service of such notice shall be in the manner provided by the Colorado rules of civil procedure for service of process. Upon affidavit by the petitioner that, after diligent search, the address of the other parent remains unknown, the court shall order service upon the other parent by one publication of the notice in a newspaper of general circulation in the county in which the hearing is to be held. The hearing shall not be held sooner than thirty days after service of the notice is complete, and, at such time, the court may enter a final decree of adoption notwithstanding the time limitation in section 19-5-210(2).

(e) Written and verified consent of the parent having only residual parental rights and responsibilities when custody has been awarded to the other parent in a dissolution of marriage proceeding where the spouse of the parent having custody wishes to adopt the child;

(f) Written and verified consent of the parent or parents as defined in section 19-1-103(21) in a stepparent adoption where the child is conceived and born out of wedlock[.]

Here, there was no independent proceeding terminating D. J. T.'s parental rights. Further, . . . the adoption proceeding did not go forward on the basis that D. J. T. had abandoned E. E. F. but rather on the basis that D. J. T. had consented to E. E. F.'s adoption. Thus, the propriety of E. E. F.'s adoption must be considered under section 19-5-203(1)(f), the only subsection by its terms applying to the circumstances of the present case. . . .

. . . D. J. T. claims that although he consented to the adoption of E. E. F., his consent was conditioned upon his retaining the right to visit E. E. F. Because such right is unenforceable, D. J. T. argues, his consent must be invalidated. . . . We disagree. . . .

The juvenile court found that D. J. T.'s consent to the adoption of E. E. F. was "knowingly and intelligently and voluntarily" executed. . . . There is sufficient evidence in the record to support the juvenile court's finding that the consent to the adoption . . . was valid. First, we note that the consent/waiver form was written in plain language, clear and unambiguous on its face. D. J. T. consented to the relinquishment of "all my rights and claim to said child," and agreed that the child would "to all legal intents and purposes, be the child of the person or persons so adopting said child." Further, D. J. T. in his testimony conceded that he was told by a court official that the consent form could not be changed to make the adoption conditional so as to grant him visitation rights. Also, T. O. testified that D. J. T. understood completely that his visitation rights would terminate under the agreement and that he would only be permitted to visit E. E. F. with S. O.'s and T. O.'s permission and that such permission would be granted only so long as D. J. T. did not use illegal drugs. Although there was conflicting evidence on this point, the juvenile court was free to reject D. J. T.'s claim that he signed the consent/waiver form only because he did not realize it would terminate his parental rights vis-à-vis E. E. F.

Because D. J. T. validly consented to the adoption of E. E. F. by S. O., there was no basis upon which to grant his motion to set aside the adoption. A parent's change of heart or subsequent regret at having consented to the adoption of his child is not by itself a sufficient reason for setting aside the adoption. Thus, because the juvenile court properly denied D. J. T.'s motion to set aside the adoption, the judgment of that court is affirmed.

QUINN, J., dissents, and ROVIRA, C.J., and ERICKSON, J., join in the dissent. . . . Because a natural parent has a constitutionally protected liberty interest in the parent-child relationship, Stanley v. Illinois, 405 U.S. 645 (1972), a natural parent's consent to an adoption must be knowingly, intelligently, and voluntarily made. A consent is knowing and intelligent when the natural parent is aware of the import and consequences of an adoption decree to which the consent is directed—that is, that the effect of the adoption decree will be to divest the natural parent "of all legal rights and obligations with respect to the child." § 19-5-211(2), 8B C.R.S. (1989 Supp.). A consent is voluntary when it is the product of a free and unconstrained choice of the maker. A consent induced by a promise or representation that the natural parent will retain the legal right of visitation after the entry of the adoption decree, when in fact the natural parent will be divested of such right, obviously does not qualify as a voluntary consent. . . .

I would resolve this case by adopting the reasoning of the Pennsylvania Supreme Court in In re Adoption of Singer, 457 Pa. 518, 326 A.2d 275 (1974), a case factually similar to the instant controversy. In *Singer*, the natural father and natural mother, Frederick and Shirley Singer, were divorced in New Jersey, and custody of their minor daughter was awarded to the mother. Upon the mother's remarriage to Thomas Forbes, the natural father executed an agreement modifying the earlier separation agreement to provide that he would consent to the adoption of his daughter by Forbes and that his visitation rights would continue. The Forbes thereafter filed a petition for adoption in Pennsylvania, and the trial court denied the petition because the natural father's consent was not unconditional. The Forbes then obtained the natural father's signature to an unconditional form of consent and, relying upon that document, again petitioned the Pennsylvania court for a decree of adoption, and the trial court entered an adoption decree. Approximately six months later the natural father filed a petition to open the decree on the basis that he had received no notice of the adoption hearing and that his signature had been obtained by deception. At the hearing to open the adoption decree, the natural father testified that Thomas Forbes told him that the judge had been informed of all the conditions that were involved in the adoption and that the new consent form had the same meaning as the one previously executed by the natural father. The trial court concluded that there was a mutual mistake of fact and law between the parties as to the legal effect and consequences of the adoption decree and ordered that the decree be opened. The Pennsylvania Supreme Court affirmed, reasoning as follows:

> A decree of adoption here would terminate forever all relations between [the daughter] and her natural father. For all purposes, legal and practical, she would be dead to [the natural father] and he would lose his right ever to see her again or ever to know of her whereabouts. . . . The [natural] father simply did not consent to such an adoption. The record clearly indicates that from the time that he first agreed to an adoption in the amendment of the New Jersey divorce decree, [the natural father] never intended to give up his parental rights. Although his signature did appear on the unconditional consent form, it was nevertheless conditioned upon the retention of these rights. . . .
>
> The problem is that the preservation of these rights, even through an informal agreement, or on a goodwill basis, conflicts with the incident of complete control and custody of an adopted child by an adopting parent as contemplated by law. We cannot say that a consent conditioned upon the preservation of certain rights with respect to the child is sufficient to effectively establish the statutorily required consent. The severance of natural ties occasioned by adoption is of such obvious finality as to demand clear and unequivocal consent by a natural parent and we believe that [the natural father's] consent here was insufficient.

457 Pa. at 524, 326 A.2d at 278; *see also* McCormick v. State, 218 Neb. 338, 354 N.W.2d 160 (1984) (relinquishment for adoption not voluntary and hence invalid where natural parents were told that they had a chance to see their son through an "open adoption"—an adoption in which the natural parents continue to have contact with the child—if they signed a relinquishment, and natural parents executed their relinquishment on that representation); McLaughlin v. Strickland,

279 S.C. 513, 309 S.E.2d 787 (S.C. App. 1983) (natural father's execution of a consent to adoption was not valid where the consent was qualified by father's intent to retain parental visitation with child).

NOTES AND QUESTIONS

1. What was the stepfather seeking to accomplish by adoption? Absent an adoption, what was his relationship to his stepchildren socially? Legally? How would adoption change these relationships?

2. Some states have special statutes that make it easier for a stepparent than a stranger to adopt without the consent of the biological parent. *See, e.g.,* Fla. Stat. Ann. § 63.112(2)(b) (2013) (eliminating the need for a home study in a stepparent adoption); Joan H. Hollinger, Adoption Law and Practice 3-10 (2006). What, if anything, justifies this different treatment of stepparent adoptions?

3. Was the biological father's consent involuntary? Uninformed? Conditional? What should be the test for determining when a parent's consent to the adoption of a child is legally sufficient? Why?

Where a parent agrees to an adoption with the understanding that he or she will have continued visitation, and the visitation agreement is unenforceable as a matter of state law, the courts vary in whether they treat the consent as valid. *Compare* Queen v. Goeddertz, 48 S.W.3d 928 (Tex. App.-Beaumont 2001, no pet.) (finding no valid consent), *with* Black v. Howard County Dep't of Child Servs. (In re M.B.), 896 N.E.2d 192 (Ind. App. 2008) (upholding consent despite unenforceability of visitation agreement).

If you represented the adoptive parents in a case in which the birth parent wished to condition agreement to the adoption on a visitation contract, and state law did not provide for the enforceability of such agreements, what measures would you recommend to ensure that the courts would not later invalidate the adoption on the ground that the consent was invalid?

4. Section (1)(d)(II) of the adoption statute quoted in *S. O.* allows a court to permit a child to be adopted without parental consent if the parent has "abandoned the child for a period of one year or more or where he has failed without cause to provide reasonable support for such child for a period of one year or more." If the stepfather in *S. O.* had petitioned to adopt on this ground, would the evidence have been sufficient to support the necessary finding of abandonment or failure to support? Under what circumstances should it be possible for a child to be adopted over the objections of a parent?

5. If the biological father in *S. O.* had sought to enforce the agreement allowing him to visit after the adoption, instead of moving to set the adoption aside, should the court have ruled in his favor? Why or why not? Are there circumstances in which a court should order postadoption visitation by a parent even when that parent and the adoptive parents have not made an agreement?

6. To what extent do and should the answers to these questions depend on the rights of the biological and adoptive parents? To what extent on the interests of the child? Just what are the interests of the child in cases like this?

7. Traditionally parents facing involuntary termination of their parental status through an adoption proceeding had no right to publicly provided legal assistance if they were indigent, but courts in several states have held that due process requires

provision of counsel in such cases. *See* Patricia C. Kussmann, Right of Indigent Parent to Appointed Counsel in Proceeding for Involuntary Termination of Parental Rights, 92 A.L.R.5th 379 (2009) (with weekly updates); Rebecca Aviel, Why Civil *Gideon* Won't Fix Family Law, 122 Yale L.J. 2106 (2013) (arguing that extending the right to counsel is unlikely to improve family law decision making).

8. To what extent can a court take a parent's undocumented status into account in a termination of parental rights proceeding? Does it matter whether the parent has been arrested or faces deportation? Does it matter whether the child is an American citizen or has legal status? *See* Anita Ortiz Maddali, The Immigrant "Other": Racialized Identity and the Devaluation of Immigrant Family Relations, 89 Ind. L.J. 643 (2014).

NOTE: PARENTAL CONSENT TO ADOPTION

All states permit a parent to consent to the adoption of a child, and all require that consent be voluntary. In addition, some statutes provide that a parent may not give legally effective consent to adopt before a child is born, and some say that effective consent cannot be given until several days (typically three to five) after the birth.

If a parent who gave apparent consent changes his or her mind and can show that consent was obtained by duress or fraud or that procedural requirements were not satisfied, the adoption may be invalidated. However, some cases refuse this remedy on theories of estoppel or laches if the parent raises this claim long after the adoptive parents have assumed physical custody.

Even consent validly given may be revocable. In some states consent is revocable for a set period; in others, it is revocable until an adoption decree is entered. In some states consent is revocable until the entry of the final decree for private adoptions; however, if consent is given to an agency, it is irrevocable. Uniform Adoption Act Section 2-404(a) provides that consent may be revoked within 192 hours (eight days) after the child's birth. If the consent is executed more than eight days after the child's birth, it is generally not revocable. The Act also requires that the biological parent have been informed about the meaning and consequences of adoption, the availability of personal and legal counseling, and procedures for release of identifying and nonidentifying information. *Id.* The document of consent must be executed in the presence of a judicial official or attorney. For further information on the revocability of parents' consent to adoption, including a survey of statutes and cases, *see* Karen D. Laverdiere, Content over Form: The Shifting of Adoption Consent Laws, 25 Whittier L. Rev. 599 (2004).

Elizabeth Samuels observes that in many European countries, consents for adoption do not become final for approximately six weeks. In contrast, in about half the U.S. states, irrevocable consent can be established in four days after birth or less. The European Convention on the Adoption of Children, which has been ratified by 18 nations, specifies that there should be a six-week period before a legal consent can be accepted. Elizabeth J. Samuels, Time to Decide? The Laws Governing Mothers' Consents to the Adoption of Their Newborn Infants, 72 Tenn. L. Rev. 509 (2005).

Physical placement of the child with a prospective adoptive family alone does not amount to consent to adoption. In most states, consent must be given to the court. In some states the biological parents must personally appear in court to give their consent, while in other states a written document expressing consent is sufficient. If the adoption is being arranged by an agency, the biological parents relinquish physical custody of the child to the agency and give written consent to termination of their rights to the agency. After the agency has placed the child with the prospective adoptive parents, it gives the necessary consent during the judicial proceedings.

In many states, adoption of an older child requires that the child consent as well. If the adoptee is an adult, only his or her consent may be required; consent of the biological parents is often dispensed with.

NOTE: GROUNDS FOR DISPENSING WITH PARENTAL CONSENT

All states permit adoption without parental consent on proof of statutory grounds, most often some variation of desertion or abandonment and serious neglect. In addition, some states dispense with the requirement for consent where the pregnancy was a result of rape. The states vary, however, in whether or not they require a criminal conviction for the rape before they dispense with the consent requirement. *Compare* Wash. Rev. Code § 26.33.170(2) (2013) ("An alleged father's, birth parent's, or parent's consent to adoption [may] be dispensed with if the court finds that . . . the alleged father, birth parent, or parent has been found guilty of rape"), *with* Wis. Stat. § 48.415(9) (2013) (allowing the termination of parental rights upon a showing "indicating that the person who may be the father of the child committed, during a possible time of conception, a sexual assault . . . against the mother of the child"). *See* Kara N. Bitar, The Parental Rights of Rapists, 19 Duke J. Gender L. & Pol'y 275, 279-280 (2012).

To establish "abandonment," courts traditionally have required proof that the parent subjectively intended to abandon the relationship; proof of behavior that objectively suggests a fixed loss of interest in the child was not sufficient. In an effort to facilitate adoption when a parent had effectively abandoned a child, even though the parent expressed a wish to maintain a parent-child relationship, some legislatures have adopted alternative grounds. For example, borrowing from modern juvenile court termination-of-parental-rights statutes, many adoption statutes make a parent's failure to provide support or to communicate with the child for some period, often six months or a year, a ground for permitting adoption without that parent's consent. *E.g.,* Uniform Adoption Act § 6(a)(2). *Compare* Roe v. Doe, 141 P.3d 1057 (Idaho 2006) (reversing termination of parental rights for abandonment where mother had moved 1,400 miles away and father, who had not seen the child nor paid support for over a year, had been unemployed and in debt), *with* In re B.E.M., 961 So. 2d 498 (La. App. 2007) (affirming stepmother adoption without the consent of the birth mother where the birth mother had not paid support or seen the child for more than six months, despite the fact that the mother's home and all her belongings had been destroyed by Hurricane Katrina).

NOTE: OPEN ADOPTION AND OPEN RECORDS

Open adoption and open adoption records are significant challenges to the traditions of closed, confidential adoption and to the "substitution" theory of adoption, which treats the adoptive relationship as wholly replacing the biological one.

"Open adoption" means different things to different people. Sometimes it means only that the birth mother or parents choose the adoptive family from a pool generated by an adoption agency. Sometimes it connotes contact between the biological and adoptive parents, before the adoption or after it on an ongoing basis. Birth parents' desire for more control over the placement of their children and for information about what happens to them, and the negative experiences of some adults adopted as children in closed (anonymous and confidential) adoptions during the 1940s and 1950s have provided the impetus for opening adoptions from the outset. In a four- to six-year period during the late 1980s and early 1990s, one study found that the number of adoption agencies offering adoption with contact increased from 35 percent to 77 percent. The primary reason for the change was client demand. Susan M. Henney et al., Changing Agency Practices Toward Openness in Adoption, 1 Adoption Q. 45, 53 (1998), cited in Naomi Cahn, Birthing Relationships, 17 Wis. Women's L.J. 162, 187-188 (2002). In addition, today adoption is more common for older children, often children who have been in foster care for extended periods, and they often remember and may benefit from ongoing contact with their biological parents. Professor Solangel Maldonado argues that ongoing contact may offer special benefits for children adopted into families of a different race; relationships with the birth families may allow greater contact not only with relatives, but with the customs and traditions of the birth community. Solangel Maldonado, Permanency v. Biology: Making the Case for Post-Adoption Contact, 37 Cap. U. L. Rev. 321 (2008). Professor Annette Appell argues that court-ordered contact may be similarly appropriate to protect the adopted child's relationships with third parties such as siblings, grandparents, or extended family members. Annette Ruth Appell, Reflections on the Movement Toward a More Child-Centered Adoption, 32 W. New Eng. L. Rev. 1 (2010).

The law regarding open adoptions has evolved significantly in the last 20 years. The Evan B. Donaldson Adoption Institute reports that almost all prospective birth mothers (approximately 90 percent) choose and meet the adoptive parents of their children, and even the majority of those who do not meet them are able to choose the new parents from profiles. Moreover, by 2004 at least 21 states had enacted statutes that expressly permit adoptive parents to enter into an enforceable postadoption contact agreement with their adopted child's biological parent, and the basic validity and finality of an adoption is not affected by the existence of an open agreement or by any dispute over its terms. The report explains:

> If a parent refuses to comply with a court order, the parent faces the usual penalties associated with refusal to obey an order — i.e., the court can hold the parent in contempt and impose a fine and/or jail time. But for most infant adoptions, there is no legal basis for enforcing verbal or written contracts made between prospective adoptive parents and birthparents regarding their agreement for ongoing information exchange or contact.

Evan B. Donaldson Adoption Institute, Safeguarding the Rights and Well-Being of Birthparents in the Adoption Process (November 2006), available at http://www.adoptioninstitute.org/publications/2006_11_Birthparent_Study_All.pdf

(last visited Sept. 21, 2013). *See also* Danny R. Veilleux, Postadoption Visitation by Natural Parent, 78 A.L.R.4th 218 (2011) (updated weekly); In re Adoption of S.K.L.H., 204 P.3d 320 (Ala. 2009) (postadoption visitation agreement is permissible only because of express statutory authorization). Some statutes, however, expressly state that postadoption visitation agreements are not enforceable. *See, e.g.,* Tenn. Code Ann. § 36-1-121(f) (2014). *See also* Postadoption Contact Agreements Between Birth and Adoptive Families, Child Welfare Information Gateway, available at http://www.childwelfare.gov/systemwide/laws_policies/statutes/cooperative.cfm (last visited Sept. 6, 2009).

Researchers in Minnesota and Texas have conducted the most extensive studies of open adoption. These researchers have followed 190 adoptive families and 169 birth mothers since the mid-1980s. The adoptions ranged from fully closed through fully disclosed. Among the most significant findings are (1) high percentages of the adoptive parents and adopted children who had ongoing contact with birth mothers were satisfied or very satisfied with the level of openness, (2) over time the level of openness generally remained the same, (3) relationships were dynamic and had to be renegotiated over time, (4) the extent to which adolescents did not have ongoing contact with their birth mothers varied but was not related to how satisfactory their relationships with their parents were, and (5) there was no relationship between the degree of openness and the children's socioemotional adjustment. Harold D. Grotevant & Ruth G. McRoy, Openness in Adoption: Outcomes for Adolescents Within Their Adoptive Kinships Networks (Nov. 2003), chapter also in Psychological Issues in Adoption: Theory, Research, and Application (D. Brodzinsky & J. Palacios eds., 2005). The lead researchers also conclude that no one type of adoption arrangement is best for all families and that the needs and desires of family members may well shift over time.

A second challenge to traditional adoption practice is the trend toward open records. While constitutional challenges to closed record laws by adopted children have generally not been successful, most states allow adult adoptees to have access to nonidentifying information about themselves from their adoption records, and all but 14 allow birth parents to access nonidentifying information about adoptive families. In most states, identifying information is available through mutual consent registries, and a few states have statutes allowing adult adoptees to gain access to their adoption records even in the absence of consent by the birth parents. Indeed, Kansas has never sealed its adoption records, and Alaska has allowed access since 1950. In the absence of such a statute, identifying information is available only by court order upon a showing of good cause. State-by-state information on access laws is available at Child Welfare Information Gateway, http://www.childwelfare.gov/systemwide/laws_policies/statutes/infoaccessap.cfm (last visited Sept. 6, 2009). *See generally* Elizabeth J. Samuels, Surrender and Subordination: Birth Mothers and Adoption Law Reform, 20 Mich. J. Gender & L. 33 (2013); Naomi Cahn & Jana Singer, Adoption, Identity, and the Constitution: The Case for Opening Closed Records, 2 U. Pa. J. Const. L. 113 (1999); Evan B. Donaldson Adoption Institute, For the Records: Restoring a Legal Right for Adult Adoptees (2007), available at http://www.adoptioninstitute.org/publications/2007_11_For_Records.pdf (last visited Apr. 25, 2014). Article 7 of the United Nations Convention on the Rights of the Child provides for registration of a child at birth and for the protection of the child's rights to name, nationality, and "as far as possible, the right to know and be cared for by his parents." Some commentators argue that this creates a right to know the identities of one's genetic parents and perhaps to have contact with them. Katherine O'Donovan, "Real" Mothers for Abandoned Children, 36 Law & Soc'y Rev. 347, 351 (2002) (citing Jane Fortin, Children's Rights: The Developing Law (1998); Michael Freeman, The New Birth Right?, 1 Int'l J. Child. Rts. 1 (1996)). In 2007 the courts in Ontario, Canada, invalidated an open records act that did not allow birth parents the option to prevent disclosure. Rather than appeal, Ontario repassed the law with such a disclosure veto. Cheskes v. Ontario (Attorney General), 2007 CanLII 38387 (ON S.C.).

As a practical matter, the Internet has been changing the nature of adoption practice. The Internet has made it easier to facilitate private placements with or without agency involvement. In addition, the information on the Internet makes it easier to track birth families. The Evan B. Donaldson Adoption Institute found:

- A growing "commodification" of adoption and a shift away from the perspective that its primary purpose is to find families for children. This is particularly the case in domestic infant adoption, where a scarcity of babies available to be adopted heightens competition. Unregulated websites compete with traditional practitioners, sometimes by making claims and utilizing practices that raise serious ethical and legal concerns.
- Finding birth relatives is becoming increasingly easy and commonplace, with significant institutional and personal implications, including the likely end of the era of "closed" adoption and a growth in relationships between adoptive families and families of origin.
- An indeterminable but growing number of minor adopted children are contacting and forming relationships with biological siblings, parents and other relatives, sometimes without their adoptive parents' knowledge and usually without guidance or preparation about the complex emotional and interpersonal repercussions for everyone involved.
- A rising number of useful, positive sites, such as ones that expedite the adoption of children and youth who need families, notably including those with special needs; and more places to get information and education, networking opportunities, support services and other resources that are a clear contribution to professionals, policymakers, researchers, journalists and the millions of personally affected individuals.

Jeanne A. Howard, Untangling the Web: The Internet's Transformative Impact on Adoption (2012), available at http://www.adoptioninstitute.org/research/2012_12_UntanglingtheWeb.php (last visited Sept. 21, 2013). See also Michelle M. Hughes, Internet Promises, Scares, and Surprises: New Realities of Adoption, 41 Cap. U. L. Rev. 279 (2013); Mary Kate Kearney & Arrielle Millstein, Meeting the Challenges of Adoption in an Internet Age, 41 Cap. U. L. Rev. 237 (2013).

PROBLEMS

1. Mary was 17 years old, unmarried, and unemployed when her baby was born. She gave the baby to her 26-year-old stepbrother and his wife shortly after

birth. Mary visited the child about twice a year and gave her stepbrother small amounts of money irregularly. She is now 23, married, and settled down. She has asked her stepbrother to return custody of her child, but he has refused, and he and his wife have filed an adoption petition alleging that Mary's consent is unnecessary because she has abandoned the child. Mary insists that she wants and has always wanted to raise her child. What arguments should each side make?

2. Father and Mother divorce and share custody. Father remarries. Father accuses Mother of abusing the child repeatedly, and subjects the child to numerous examinations in an effort to prove the abuse charges. The examinations do not substantiate the allegations. Father also threatens Mother and makes it difficult for her to see the child. Mother believes that the allegations have traumatized the child and that the judge in charge of the case has done little to protect Mother or the child. Mother moves to a different state, leaving Father with custody. She calls and attempts to maintain contact with the child, but Father obstructs these efforts. Father would like his wife to adopt the child, alleging that Mother, who has not seen the child since her move, has abandoned the child. Mother refuses to consent to the adoption. If Mother has not seen the child for two years, does Father have a good case for abandonment? If you represent Mother and agree with her sense that the judge overseeing the case has been hostile toward her and that the conflict between Father and Mother have been harmful to the child, what would you advise her to do to create the strongest possible case to prevent the adoption? *See* In re Adoption of L.J.B., 18 A.3d 1098 (Pa. 2011).

3. The mother's parental rights to L.C.S. were terminated and the biological father agreed to the child's adoption on the condition that his parents, Fletcher and Sara, be allowed to continue visitation with the child. The father agreed that he would have no contact with the child. The adoption decree did not mention the grandparents or the condition. The adoptive parents, Christopher and Brandy, initially allowed visitation but later refused to permit the grandparents to see the child, ostensibly because the grandparents had allowed the child to see the biological father during the visits. The grandparents sued to secure a visitation order. The state grandparent visitation statute specifies that the courts shall not order grandparent visitation over the objections of two fit parents in an intact family. What arguments should each side make?

4. Anne placed her month-old child with friends of her family, signing a written relinquishment of her parental rights. She told the would-be adoptive parents that she believed the child's father, George, would consent. However, he did not, and under the law in this jurisdiction there are no grounds for allowing the adoption without his consent. Moreover, unless he can be proven unfit, he is entitled to custody as against the would-be adoptive parents. Anne's lawyer has told her that under this state's law it is very unlikely that George will be found unfit. Anne believes that George will be a very bad father and that the child will actually be raised by George's mother and sister, whom Anne dislikes. Anne has therefore moved to withdraw her relinquishment of parental rights on the grounds that it was conditional on her child being adopted. How should the court rule?

5. Timmy was born to Margaret and Dave, a married couple. Dave and Margaret were divorced when Timmy was one year old. Margaret was awarded custody, and Dave was granted visitation and ordered to pay child support. For the last two years Dave has irregularly and reluctantly paid child support, and he has

rarely visited Timmy. Recently, though, he told Margaret that if he had to pay, he wanted to see Timmy more often and that he might even seek custody. Margaret, who is 23, and her father, who is 50, suggested instead that Dave relinquish his parental rights and consent to Timmy's adoption by Margaret's father. Margaret and Timmy often see Margaret's parents, who live in the same town, although they do not live with them.

Statutes in this jurisdiction provide that ordinarily when a child is adopted, the parental rights of the child's biological parents must be terminated, but provide this exception: "Whenever a parent consents to the adoption of his child by his spouse, the parent-child relationship between him and his child shall remain whether or not he is one of the petitioners in the adoption proceeding." If Margaret and her father file the adoption petition, along with Dave's written consent, is a court likely to grant the adoption? Why or why not?

6. As we saw in Chapter 13, numerous states have permitted adoption by a second parent of the same-sex without requiring termination of the parental rights of the first parent. What if D.J.T. and T.O., relying on Colorado's recognition of second-parent adoption, agree that S.O. can adopt the child without terminating D.J.T.'s parental status? What arguments would you make on their behalf? What arguments would be made in opposition to their petition? If Colorado permitted a lesbian partner to adopt without terminating the sperm donor's parental status, would that strengthen your argument? What arguments would be made to distinguish that case?

2. Establishing the New Parent-Child Relationship — Independent versus Agency Adoption and Adoption of Special-Needs Children

Four states — Delaware, Indiana, Ohio, and West Virginia — require that all adoptive placements be made by a state child welfare agency or a private child placement agency licensed by the state. Six more states — Florida, Kentucky, Massachusetts, Minnesota, New Mexico, and Rhode Island — require parents to obtain permission from the state child welfare agency or a court before they make a private placement. Child Welfare Information Gateway, Who May Adopt, Be Adopted, or Place a Child for Adoption? (2012), available at http://www.child welfare.gov/systemwide/laws_policies/statutes/parties.cfm (last visited Sept. 21, 2013). In such states an exception is usually made for stepparent adoptions. Why?

In the other states private adoptions — that is, ones not arranged by an agency — are also permitted. Private adoptions may be arranged directly between the biological parents and adoptive parents or through an intermediary such as a doctor or lawyer. Most states make it a crime for anyone but licensed adoption agencies to accept money to arrange adoptions. In such states private intermediaries such as doctors and lawyers still arrange adoptions, but they are formally paid only for their medical or legal services. Some states also require adoptive parents to disclose fully to the court all their expenses incident to the adoption. Child Welfare Information Gateway, State Regulation of Adoption Expenses (2013), available at http://www.childwelfare.gov/systemwide/laws_policies/statutes/expenses.cfm (last visited Sept. 21, 2013).

In most states it is a crime to offer or receive money or any valuable consideration for relinquishing or accepting a baby for adoption. However, it is not illegal to pay expenses to the biological parents, including pre-birth and birth medical expenses and professional fees of adoption agencies, lawyers, and doctors. Where offering or receiving money for an adoption is not illegal, payment to a mother may render her consent involuntary. Some states recognize an exception where the agreement promotes the child's welfare and the parent is not in a position to furnish proper care for the child.

Because adoptive parents ordinarily must pay an adoption agency or intermediary and often pay expenses of the biological mother, adoption can be expensive. Agency adoptions cost from $5000 to more than $40,000, and independent adoptions cost from $8000 to $40,000. Adoptions of children from foster care cost up to $25,000, and international adoptions are comparable in price to agency and independent adoptions. National Adoption Information Clearinghouse, Costs of Adopting: A Fact Sheet for Families (June 2004), available at http://njarch.org/images/NAIC_article_costs_of%20_adoption.pdf (last visited Sept. 21, 2013).

The functions of adoption agencies include counseling birth parents thinking of adoption, receiving children to be placed for adoption, screening and counseling prospective adoptive parents, placing children with prospective adoptive parents, supervising the adoptive family for an initial probationary period, approving the adoption, giving legal consent in court, and making a report to the court about the desirability of the adoption. In most states the state child welfare agency functions as an adoption agency, and private religiously affiliated and non-sectarian agencies also exist.

In many states, agencies still have a role to play in private adoptions, for statutes require that a licensed agency evaluate the adoptive parents' home and make a report to the court recommending for or against adoption. These "home studies" are typically waived in stepparent and relative adoptions. *See, e.g.,* Uniform Adoption Act part 2.

The Child Welfare Information Gateway, examining the changing nature of adoption, reported:

- The source of adoptions is no longer dominated by kinship adoptions and private agency adoptions. In 2001, public agency and intercountry adoptions accounted for more than half of all adoptions.
- These trends changed little between 2001 and 2008. In 2008, approximately two-fifths of adoptions occurred through public child welfare agencies, the same percentage reported in 2000, though up from18 percent in 1992.
- Intercountry adoptions increased from 5 percent to 15 percent of adoptions in the United States between 1992 and 2001. Intercountry adoption declined slightly to 14 percent in 2007 and 13 percent in 2008.
- The other two-fifths of adoptions are primarily private agency, kinship, or tribal adoptions. In 1992, for example, stepparent adoptions (a form of kinship adoption) alone accounted for two-fifths (42 percent) of all adoptions.

How Many Children Were Adopted in 2000 and 2001? (2004), available at http://www.childwelfare.gov/pubs/s_adopted/s_adopted.pdf (last visited Sept. 6, 2009); How Many Children Were Adopted in 2007 and 2008 (2011), available at https://www.childwelfare.gov/pubs/adopted0708.pdf (last visited Sept. 23, 2013).

As the number of newborn adoptions has declined, stranger adoptions involving agency placement of older and special-needs children have increased. The movement to find adoptive homes for special-needs children — which include older children; children with physical, mental, or emotional disabilities; children of color; and sibling groups — began in the 1970s. Judith K. McKenzie, Adoption of Children with Special Needs, 3(1) The Future of Children 62 (1993). In practice, placing special-needs children largely means finding adoptive placements in foster care for children whose parents' rights have been terminated. In addition to increased agency emphasis on placing these children, a number of programs facilitate such adoptions. Some state child welfare agencies encourage people to become foster parents with the promise that they will be able to adopt their foster child if she or he becomes free for adoption. With the support of federal funds, parents who adopt children who have been in the child welfare system may receive subsidies for medical and educational expenses up to the amount of foster care payments until the child is 18, under some circumstances. Almost all the people who adopt older foster children — 80 to 90 percent — have been the child's foster parents first. McKenzie, above, at 71. Adoption disruption has increased along with the adoption of special-needs children. The greatest risk factors are the child's age at the time of adoption, the number of prior foster care placements, and the child's behavioral and emotional needs. Some studies show disruption rates for at-risk older children as high as 25 percent. Child Welfare Information Gateway, Adoption Disruption and Dissolution: Numbers and Trends (2012), available at http://www.childwelfare.gov/pubs/s_disrup.cfm (last visited Sept. 28, 2013). For a review of the many causes of adoption disruption, including the death, illness, or incapacity of the adoptive parents, *see* Dawn J. Post & Brian Zimmerman, The Revolving Doors of Family Court: The Need to Confront Broken Adoptions, 40 Cap. U. L. Rev. 437 (2012).

Given the increase in high-risk placements, more adoptive parents have sought to abrogate adoptions. Some discover that the child has a significant physical, mental, or emotional problem, while others involve a stepparent who is divorcing the child's biological parent.

Some courts recognize an alternative remedy — a tort action against an adoption agency where the agency fraudulently induced the adoption. Recently some courts have extended this doctrine to allow adoptive parents to recover for an agency's negligent failure to disclose information they are statutorily required to disclose. The U.S. District Court in Dresser v. Cradle of Hope Adoption Ctr., Inc., 358 F. Supp. 2d 620, 639-641 (E.D. Mich. 2005), summarized the developments:

> . . . Ohio was the first state to recognize a common law fraud claim brought by adopting parents. *See* Burr v. Board of County Comm'rs, 23 Ohio St. 3d 69, 23 Ohio B. 200, 491 N.E.2d 1101 (Ohio 1986). In that case, adoption agency personnel made blatant misrepresentations about a child's current health and medical history upon which the parents relied in deciding to adopt him. The child turned out to be quite ill and suffered from a variety of physical and mental ailments. The parents eventually obtained the child's records, discovered that they had been deceived, and were allowed to bring a fraud claim against the agency. Three years later, Wisconsin held that an adoption agency could be found liable for negligence by misinforming

prospective parents about the risk of an adopted child contracting Huntington's Disease. Meracle v. Children's Serv. Soc'y, 149 Wis. 2d 19, 437 N.W.2d 532 (Wis. 1989). Since then, a majority of jurisdictions that have considered the question have extended traditional fraud and negligence theories to provide relief to parents who sought to bring claims against adoption agencies for failure to disclose accurate histories of their adopted children. . . .

The nature of the relief sought in those cases has ranged from voiding the adoption order to money damages for extraordinary expenses incurred in meeting the special needs of the child. In a few cases, damages were sought because the failure to provide an accurate medical history caused a delayed or erroneous diagnosis or improper medical treatment. In all the cases, however, the damages were awarded to the parents.

The Court has found no case in which an adopted child has recovered damages for the adoption agency's failure to convey accurate medical information to the new parents. . . .

Nonetheless, the Court believes recognition of a duty of an adoption agency to the adopted child to furnish to the new parents the medical records available to it is both a logical and incremental extension of well-recognized and firmly-rooted tort principles, and consistent with established state policy.

Some parents who find that they have adopted children they cannot handle have taken matters into their own hands. They advertise on the Internet that they would like to "rehome" the child; that is, transfer custody to new adoptive parents. These private placements often take place with little investigation of the new parents and little formality in the transfer. In some cases, the adoptive parents arrange things over the Internet, draft "power of attorney" papers (a notarized document declaring the child to be under the care of another adult), meet the new adoptive parents for the first time at the time they deliver the child, and never see either again. Reuters investigated these practices and analyzed 5029 posts from a 5-year period on one Internet message board. It discovered that:

> On average, a child was advertised for re-homing there once a week. Most of the children ranged in age from 6 to 14 and had been adopted from abroad — from countries such as Russia and China, Ethiopia and Ukraine. The youngest was 10 months old.
>
> . . . [S]ome children who were adopted and later re-homed have endured severe abuse. Speaking publicly about her experience for the first time, one girl adopted from China and later sent to a second home said she was made to dig her own grave. Another re-homed child, a Russian girl, recounted how a boy in one house urinated on her after the two had sex; she was 13 at the time and was re-homed three times in six months.

The Report found that international adoptees were particularly at risk and that between 50 and 70 percent of the children advertised on rehoming sites were from abroad. Megan Twohey, Americans Use the Internet to Abandon Children Adopted from Overseas (Sept. 9, 2013) Reuters Investigates: The Child Exchange, available at http://www.reuters.com/investigates/adoption/#article/part1 (last visited Nov. 25, 2013).

3. Child Placement, Race, and Religion

Racial and religious matching of adoptive parents and children was customary and even legally required through the first two-thirds of the twentieth century. Historically, most of the agencies that arranged foster and adoptive placements were religiously affiliated, and they strongly tended to serve only or primarily adults and children who belonged to their sect. In addition, as we have seen, the dominant approach to adoption has until fairly recently been the "complete substitution" theory, in which adoptions are made to mimic biological parent-child relationships as much as possible. Consistent with this approach, a 1954 survey of more than 250 adoption agencies about their placement practices found that the following factors were ranked as the most important matching factors for adoption: intelligence and intellectual potential, religious background, racial background, temperament needs, educational background, and the adoptive parents' physical resemblance to the child. Laura J. Schwartz, Religious Matching for Adoption: Unraveling the Interests Behind the "Best Interests" Standard, 25 Fam. L.Q. 171, 173 (1991).

During the late 1950s and into the 1960s, adoption practice moved away from this approach and toward greater acceptance of transracial adoption, in part because of the general social changes wrought by the civil rights movement. The emergence of international adoption following the Korean War accelerated the practice, since most international adoptions are transracial. Arnold R. Silverman, Outcomes of Transracial Adoption, 3(1) The Future of Children 104, 107 (1993). However, transracial adoption became the subject of strong criticism in the 1970s. Objections were particularly vehement to the high incidence of foster care and adoptive placement with white parents of Native American and African-American children. In 1978 Congress enacted the Indian Child Welfare Act (ICWA), 25 U.S.C. §§ 1901-1963, which explicitly requires racial matching in child placement for Native American children. Following enactment of ICWA, adoption of Native American children by white parents dropped dramatically. Silverman, above, at 107.

MISSISSIPPI BAND OF CHOCTAW INDIANS V. HOLYFIELD

---

490 U.S. 30 (1989)

BRENNAN, J. . . . The Indian Child Welfare Act of 1978 (ICWA), 92 Stat. 3069, 25 U.S.C. §§ 1901-1963, was the product of rising concern in the mid-1970's over the consequences to Indian children, Indian families, and Indian tribes of abusive child welfare practices that resulted in the separation of large numbers of Indian children from their families and tribes through adoption or foster care placement, usually in non-Indian homes. Senate oversight hearings in 1974 yielded numerous examples, statistical data, and expert testimony documenting what one witness called "the wholesale removal of Indian children from their homes, . . . the most tragic aspect of Indian life today." Studies undertaken by the Association on American Indian Affairs in 1969 and 1974, and presented in the Senate hearings, showed that 25 to 35 percent of all Indian children had been separated from their families and placed in adoptive families, foster care, or institutions. Adoptive placements counted significantly in this total: in the State of Minnesota, for example, one in eight Indian children under the age of 18 was in an adoptive home, and during the year 1971-1972 nearly one in every four infants under one year of age was placed for adoption. The adoption rate of Indian children was eight times that of non-Indian children. Approximately 90% of the Indian placements were in non-Indian homes. A number of witnesses also testified to the serious adjustment problems encountered by such children during adolescence, as well as the impact of the adoptions on Indian parents and the tribes themselves.

Further hearings, covering much the same ground, were held during 1977 and 1978 on the bill that became the ICWA. While much of the testimony again focused on the harm to Indian parents and their children who were involuntarily separated by decisions of local welfare authorities, there was also considerable emphasis on the impact on the tribes themselves of the massive removal of their children. For example, Mr. Calvin Isaac, Tribal Chief of the Mississippi Band of Choctaw Indians and representative of the National Tribal Chairmen's Association, testified as follows:

> Culturally, the chances of Indian survival are significantly reduced if our children, the only real means for the transmission of the tribal heritage, are to be raised in non-Indian homes and denied exposure to the ways of their People. Furthermore, these practices seriously undercut the tribes' ability to continue as self-governing communities. Probably in no area is it more important that tribal sovereignty be respected than in an area as socially and culturally determinative as family relationships.

1978 Hearings, at 193. *See also* id., at 62. Chief Isaac also summarized succinctly what numerous witnesses saw as the principal reason for the high rates of removal of Indian children:

> One of the most serious failings of the present system is that Indian children are removed from the custody of their natural parents by nontribal government authorities who have no basis for intelligently evaluating the cultural and social premises underlying Indian home life and childrearing. Many of the individuals who decide the fate of our children are at best ignorant of our cultural values, and at worst contemptful of the Indian way and convinced that removal, usually to a non-Indian household or institution, can only benefit an Indian child.

Id., at 191-192.[7]

---

7. One of the particular points of concern was the failure of non-Indian child welfare workers to understand the role of the extended family in Indian society. The House Report on the ICWA noted: "An Indian child may have scores of, perhaps more than a hundred, relatives who are counted as close, responsible members of the family. Many social workers, untutored in the ways of Indian family life or assuming them to be socially irresponsible, consider leaving the child with persons outside the nuclear family as neglect and thus as grounds for terminating parental rights." House Report, at 10, U.S. Code Cong. & Admin. News 1978, at 7532. At the conclusion of the 1974 Senate hearings, Senator Abourezk noted the role that such extended families played in the care of children: "We've had testimony here that in Indian communities throughout the Nation there is no such

The congressional findings that were incorporated into the ICWA reflect these sentiments. The Congress found:

> (3) that there is no resource that is more vital to the continued existence and integrity of Indian tribes than their children . . . ;
>
> (4) that an alarmingly high percentage of Indian families are broken up by the removal, often unwarranted, of their children from them by nontribal public and private agencies and that an alarmingly high percentage of such children are placed in non-Indian foster and adoptive homes and institutions; and
>
> (5) that the States, exercising their recognized jurisdiction over Indian child custody proceedings through administrative and judicial bodies, have often failed to recognize the essential tribal relations of Indian people and the cultural and social standards prevailing in Indian communities and families.

25 U.S.C. §1901.

At the heart of ICWA are its provisions concerning jurisdiction over Indian child custody proceedings. Section 1911 lays out a dual jurisdictional scheme. Section 1911(a) establishes exclusive jurisdiction in the tribal courts for proceedings concerning an Indian child "who resides or is domiciled within the reservation of such tribe," as well as for wards of tribal courts regardless of domicile. Section 1911(b), on the other hand, creates concurrent but presumptively tribal jurisdiction in the case of children not domiciled on the reservation: on petition of either parent or the tribe, state-court proceedings for foster care placement or termination of parental rights are to be transferred to the tribal court, except in cases of "good cause," objection by either parent, or declination of jurisdiction by the tribal court. . . .

This case involves the status of twin babies, known for our purposes as B. B. and G. B., who were born out of wedlock on December 29, 1985. Their mother, J. B., and father, W. J., were both enrolled members of appellant Mississippi Band of Choctaw Indians (Tribe), and were residents and domiciliaries of the Choctaw Reservation in Neshoba County, Mississippi. J. B. gave birth to the twins in Gulfport, Harrison County, Mississippi, some 200 miles from the reservation. On January 10, 1986, J. B. executed a consent-to-adoption form before the Chancery Court of Harrison County. Record 8-10. W. J. signed a similar form. On January 16, appellees Orrey and Vivian Holyfield filed a petition for adoption in the same court, id., at 1-5, and the chancellor issued a Final Decree of Adoption on January 28. Id., at 13-14. Despite the court's apparent awareness of the ICWA, the adoption decree contained no reference to it, nor to the infants' Indian background.

Two months later the Tribe moved in the Chancery Court to vacate the adoption decree on the ground that under the ICWA exclusive jurisdiction was vested in the tribal court. Id., at 15-18. On July 14, 1986, the court overruled the motion, holding that the Tribe "never obtained exclusive jurisdiction over the children involved herein. . . ." The court's one-page opinion relied on two facts in reaching that conclusion. The court noted first that the twins' mother "went to

---

thing as an abandoned child because when a child does have a need for parents for one reason or another, a relative or a friend will take that child in. It's the extended family concept." 1974 Hearings 473.

some efforts to see that they were born outside the confines of the Choctaw Indian Reservation" and that the parents had promptly arranged for the adoption by the Holyfields. Second, the court stated: "At no time from the birth of these children to the present date have either of them resided on or physically been on the Choctaw Indian Reservation." Id., at 78.

[The Mississippi Supreme Court affirmed on the basis that, under state law, the children's parents had abandoned them when they relinquished them for adoption and that the domicile of abandoned children is that of adults who stand in loco parentis to them.] . . .

The meaning of "domicile" in the ICWA is, of course, a matter of Congress's intent. The ICWA itself does not define it. The initial question we must confront is whether there is any reason to believe that Congress intended the ICWA definition of "domicile" to be a matter of state law. . . .

First, and most fundamentally, the purpose of the ICWA gives no reason to believe that Congress intended to rely on state law for the definition of a critical term; quite the contrary. It is clear from the very text of the ICWA, not to mention its legislative history and the hearings that led to its enactment, that Congress was concerned with the rights of Indian families and Indian communities vis-à-vis state authorities. More specifically, its purpose was, in part, to make clear that in certain situations the state courts did not have jurisdiction over child custody proceedings. . . .

Second, Congress could hardly have intended the lack of nationwide uniformity that would result from state-law definitions of domicile. . . .

That we are dealing with a uniform federal rather than a state definition does not, of course, prevent us from drawing on general state-law principles to determine "the ordinary meaning of the words used." Well-settled state law can inform our understanding of what Congress had in mind when it employed a term it did not define. . . .

"Domicile" is, of course, a concept widely used in both federal and state courts for jurisdiction and conflict-of-laws purposes. . . . "Domicile" is not necessarily synonymous with "residence," and one can reside in one place but be domiciled in another. For adults, domicile is established by physical presence in a place in connection with a certain state of mind concerning one's intent to remain there. . . . Since most minors are legally incapable of forming the requisite intent to establish a domicile, their domicile is determined by that of their parents. In the case of an illegitimate child, that has traditionally meant the domicile of its mother. . . .

It is undisputed in this case that the domicile of the mother (as well as the father) has been, at all relevant times, on the Choctaw Reservation. Thus, it is clear that at their birth the twin babies were also domiciled on the reservation, even though they themselves had never been there. . . .

Nor can the result be any different simply because the twins were "voluntarily surrendered" by their mother. Tribal jurisdiction under § 1911 (a) was not meant to be defeated by the actions of individual members of the tribe, for Congress was concerned not solely about the interests of Indian children and families, but also about the impact on the tribes themselves of the large numbers of Indian children adopted by non-Indians. . . .

In addition, it is clear that Congress's concern over the placement of Indian children in non-Indian homes was based in part on evidence of the detrimental impact on the children themselves of such placements outside their culture. Congress determined to subject such placements to the ICWA's jurisdictional and other provisions, even in cases where the parents consented to an adoption, because of concerns going beyond the wishes of individual parents. . . .

These congressional objectives make clear that a rule of domicile that would permit individual Indian parents to defeat the ICWA's jurisdictional scheme is inconsistent with what Congress intended. The appellees in this case argue strenuously that the twins' mother went to great lengths to give birth off the reservation so that her children could be adopted by the Holyfields. But that was precisely part of Congress's concern. Permitting individual members of the tribe to avoid tribal exclusive jurisdiction by the simple expedient of giving birth off the reservation would, to a large extent, nullify the purpose the ICWA was intended to accomplish.

. . . Since, for purposes of the ICWA, the twin babies in this case were domiciled on the reservation when adoption proceedings were begun, the Choctaw tribal court possessed exclusive jurisdiction pursuant to 25 U.S.C. § 1911(a). The Chancery Court of Harrison County was, accordingly, without jurisdiction to enter a decree of adoption; under ICWA § 104, 25 U.S.C. § 1914 its decree of January 28, 1986, must be vacated.

III

We are not unaware that over three years have passed since the twin babies were born and placed in the Holyfield home, and that a court deciding their fate today is not writing on a blank slate in the same way it would have in January 1986. Three years' development of family ties cannot be undone, and a separation at this point would doubtless cause considerable pain.

Whatever feelings we might have as to where the twins should live, however, it is not for us to decide that question. We have been asked to decide the legal question of who should make the custody determination concerning these children — not what the outcome of that determination should be. The law places that decision in the hands of the Choctaw tribal court. Had the mandate of the ICWA been followed in 1986, of course, much potential anguish might have been avoided, and in any case the law cannot be applied so as automatically to "reward those who obtain custody, whether lawfully or otherwise, and maintain it during any ensuing (and protracted) litigation." *Halloway*, supra, at p. 972. It is not ours to say whether the trauma that might result from removing these children from their adoptive family should outweigh the interest of the Tribe — and perhaps the children themselves — in having them raised as part of the Choctaw community. Rather, "we must defer to the experience, wisdom, and compassion of the [Choctaw] tribal courts to fashion an appropriate remedy." Ibid.

The judgment of the Supreme Court of Mississippi is reversed and the case remanded for further proceedings not inconsistent with this opinion. It is so ordered.

STEVENS, J., with whom THE CHIEF JUSTICE and KENNEDY, J., join, dissenting. . . . The [ICWA] gives Indian tribes certain rights, not to restrict the rights of parents of Indian children, but to complement and help effect them.

The Indian tribe may petition to transfer an action in state court to the tribal court, but the Indian parent may veto the transfer. § 1911(b). The Act provides for a tribal right of notice and intervention in involuntary proceedings but not in voluntary ones. §§ 1911(c), 1912(a). Finally, the tribe may petition the court to set aside a parental termination action upon a showing that the provisions of the ICWA that are designed to protect parents and Indian children have been violated. § 1914.

While the Act's substantive and procedural provisions effect a major change in state child custody proceedings, its jurisdictional provision is designed primarily to preserve tribal sovereignty over the domestic relations of tribe members and to confirm a developing line of cases which held that the tribe's exclusive jurisdiction could not be defeated by the temporary presence of an Indian child off the reservation. . . .

Although parents of Indian children are shielded from the exercise of state jurisdiction when they are temporarily off the reservation, the Act also reflects a recognition that allowing the tribe to defeat the parents' deliberate choice of jurisdiction would be conducive neither to the best interests of the child nor to the stability and security of Indian tribes and families. Section 1911(b), providing for the exercise of concurrent jurisdiction by state and tribal courts when the Indian child is not domiciled on the reservation, gives the Indian parents a veto to prevent the transfer of a state court action to tribal court. "By allowing the Indian parents to 'choose' the forum that will decide whether to sever the parent-child relationship, Congress promotes the security of Indian families by allowing the Indian parents to defend in the court system that most reflects the parents' familial standards." Jones, 21 Ariz. L. Rev., at 1141. As Mr. Calvin Isaac, Tribal Chief of the Mississippi Band of Choctaw Indians, stated in testimony to the House Subcommittee on Indian Affairs and Public Lands with respect to a different provision:

> The ultimate responsibility for child welfare rests with the parents and we would not support legislation which interfered with that basic relationship. Hearings on S. 1214 before the Subcommittee on Indian Affairs and Public Lands of the House Committee on Interior and Insular Affairs, 95th Cong., 2d Sess., 62 (1978).[8]

If J. B. and W. J. had established a domicile off the reservation, the state courts would have been required to give effect to their choice of jurisdiction; there should not be a different result when the parents have not changed their own domicile, but have expressed an unequivocal intent to establish a domicile for their children off the reservation. The law of abandonment, as enunciated by the Mississippi Supreme Court in this case, does not defeat, but serves the purposes of the Act. An abandonment occurs when a parent deserts a child and places the

---

8. Chief Isaac elsewhere expressed a similar concern for the rights of parents with reference to another provision. *See* Hearing, at 158 (Statement of Calvin Isaac on behalf of National Tribal Chairmen's Association) ("We believe the tribe should receive notice in all such cases but where the child is neither a resident nor domiciliary of the reservation intervention should require the consent of the natural parents or the blood relative in whose custody the child has been left by the natural parents. It seems there is a great potential in the provisions of section 101(c) for infringing parental wishes and rights.").

child with another with an intent to relinquish all parental rights and obligations. . . . If the child is abandoned by both parents, he takes on the domicile of a person other than the parents who stand in *loco parentis* to him. . . .

The interpretation of domicile adopted by the Court requires the custodian of an Indian child who is off the reservation to haul the child to a potentially distant tribal court unfamiliar with the child's present living conditions and best interests. Moreover, it renders any custody decision made by a state court forever suspect, susceptible to challenge at any time as void for having been entered in the absence of jurisdiction.[9] Finally, it forces parents of Indian children who desire to invoke state court jurisdiction to establish a domicile off the reservation. Only if the custodial parent has the wealth and ability to establish a domicile off the reservation will the parent be able to use the processes of state court. I fail to see how such a requirement serves the paramount congressional purpose of "promot[ing] the stability and security of Indian tribes and families." 25 U.S.C. § 1902.

NOTES AND QUESTIONS

1. The Supreme Court revisited ICWA in 2013. In Adoptive Couple v. Baby Girl, 570 U.S. ___ (2013), Justice Alito delivered the opinion of the Court.

This case is about a little girl (Baby Girl) who is classified as an Indian because she is 1.2% (3/256) Cherokee. Because Baby Girl is classified in this way, the South Carolina Supreme Court held that certain provisions of the federal Indian Child Welfare Act of 1978 required her to be taken, at the age of 27 months, from the only parents she had ever known and handed over to her biological father, who had attempted to relinquish his parental rights and who had no prior contact with the child. The provisions of the federal statute at issue here do not demand this result.

Contrary to the State Supreme Court's ruling, we hold that 25 U.S.C. § 1912(f) — which bars involuntary termination of a parent's rights in the absence of a heightened showing that serious harm to the Indian child is likely to result from the parent's "continued custody" of the child — does not apply when, as here, the

---

9. The facts of In re Adoption of Halloway, 732 P.2d 962 (Utah 1986), which the Court cites approvingly, . . . , vividly illustrate the problem. In that case, the mother, a member of an Indian Tribe in New Mexico, voluntarily abandoned an Indian child to the custody of the child's maternal aunt off the reservation with the knowledge that the child would be placed for adoption in Utah. The mother learned of the adoption two weeks after the child left the reservation and did not object and, two months later, she executed a consent to adoption. Nevertheless, some two years after the petition for adoption was filed, the Indian Tribe intervened in the proceeding and set aside the adoption. The Tribe argued successfully that regardless of whether the Indian parent consented to it, the adoption was void because she resided on the reservation and thus the tribal court had exclusive jurisdiction. Although the decision in *Halloway*, and the Court's approving reference to it, may be colored somewhat by the fact that the mother in that case withdrew her consent (a fact which would entitle her to relief even if there were only concurrent jurisdiction, *see* 25 U.S.C. § 1913(c)), the rule set forth by the majority contains no such limitation. As the Tribe acknowledged at oral argument, any adoption of an Indian child effected through a state court will be susceptible of challenge by the Indian tribe no matter how old the child and how long it has lived with its adoptive parents.

relevant parent never had custody of the child. We further hold that § 1912(d) — which conditions involuntary termination of parental rights with respect to an Indian child on a showing that remedial efforts have been made to prevent the "breakup of the Indian family" — is inapplicable when, as here, the parent abandoned the Indian child before birth and never had custody of the child. Finally, we clarify that § 1915(a), which provides placement preferences for the adoption of Indian children, does not bar a non-Indian family like Adoptive Couple from adopting an Indian child when no other eligible candidates have sought to adopt the child. We accordingly reverse the South Carolina Supreme Court's judgment and remand for further proceedings.

Justice Sotomayor, with Justices Ginsburg and Kagan, and Justice Scalia in part, dissented:

A casual reader of the Court's opinion could be forgiven for thinking this an easy case, one in which the text of the applicable statute clearly points the way to the only sensible result. In truth, however, the path from the text of the Indian Child Welfare Act of 1978 (ICWA) to the result the Court reaches is anything but clear, and its result anything but right.

The reader's first clue that the majority's supposedly straightforward reasoning is flawed is that not all Members who adopt its interpretation believe it is compelled by the text of the statute; nor are they all willing to accept the consequences it will necessarily have beyond the specific factual scenario confronted here. [Justices Thomas and Breyer filed separate concurrences.] The second clue is that the majority begins its analysis by plucking out of context a single phrase from the last clause of the last subsection of the relevant provision ["continued custody"], and then builds its entire argument upon it. That is not how we ordinarily read statutes. The third clue is that the majority openly professes its aversion to Congress' explicitly stated purpose in enacting the statute. The majority expresses concern that reading the Act to mean what it says will make it more difficult to place Indian children in adoptive homes, but the Congress that enacted the statute announced its intent to stop "an alarmingly high percentage of Indian families [from being] broken up" by, among other things, a trend of "plac[ing] [Indian children] in non-Indian . . . adoptive homes." 25 U.S.C. § 1901(4). Policy disagreement with Congress' judgment is not a valid reason for this Court to distort the provisions of the Act. Unlike the majority, I cannot adopt a reading of ICWA that is contrary to both its text and its stated purpose. I respectfully dissent.

2. *Holyfield* and *Adoptive Couple* agree on one of the purposes of ICWA. In *Adoptive Couple*, the Supreme Court quoted verbatim from *Holyfield*'s description of the legislative history condemning the involuntary removal of Indian children from their families. The two majority opinions, however, differ in their descriptions of the other purposes of the Act. The *Holyfield* majority, for example, emphasized that "Congress was concerned not solely about the interests of Indian children and families, but also about the impact on the tribes themselves of the large numbers of Indian children adopted by non-Indians. . . ." Addie Rolnick observes that *Adoptive Couple*, in contrast, gave little weight to tribal interests, explaining that:

The blow struck by [*Adoptive Couple*] . . . is significant. As the Court recognized in *Holyfield*, ICWA is about preserving the relationship between an Indian child and her tribe. The tribe has an interest in its children that may be separate from the interests of the Indian parents. The child's interests are likewise served by maintaining a connection to her tribe and her extended family, even if she no longer has a relationship with her parents. In this case, the Cherokee Nation supported Dusten Brown's effort to regain custody, but tribal intervention does not always (or even usually) mean returning the child to her Indian parent. By focusing so much on the father's actions in the case, the Court has allowed tribal rights to be subsumed by an individual parent's lack of responsibility. This is precisely the opposite of its holding in *Holyfield*, and it significantly undermines the spirit of the law.

Adoptive Couple v. Baby Girl (1 of 4): Why the Court's ICWA Ruling Matters (June 29, 2013) available at http://prawfsblawg.blogs.com/prawfsblawg/2013/06/ adoptive-couple-v-baby-girl-1-of-4-why-the-courts-icwa-ruling-matters-.html (last visited Nov. 25, 2013). Consider in both *Holyfield* and *Adoptive Couple* what the tribes' interests are and the procedures that might be adopted to protect them.

3. Does ICWA subordinate the child's interests to those of the tribe? What theory of the best interests of the child supports the ICWA approach to custody? Does vindication of tribal interests require removal of the child from the non-Indian adoptive parents in each of these cases?

4. In *Holyfield* and *Halloway*, discussed in the text and footnotes, and *Adoptive Couple*, an appellate court concluded that the court that had granted the adoption had wrongfully asserted jurisdiction years after the child had been placed with the would-be adoptive parents. In the meantime, of course, the child and the adoptive parents had been living as a family. When an error of this kind is made, what should be the remedy? Does it make sense to ignore all the expectations and relationships that have developed over time? On the other hand, is any other remedy effective? In *Holyfield* the Court held that the case had to be returned to tribal court. What discretion did the tribal court have in the final resolution?

5. Professor Solangel Maldonado reports that:

> On February 9, 1990, four years after the Holyfields first brought the twins home from the hospital, Choctaw Tribal Court Judge Roy Jim granted Joan Holyfield's petition to adopt them. Given the Tribe's interest in raising Choctaw children, not to mention the Tribe's significant legal efforts in asserting jurisdiction, one might have expected the Tribal Court to return the twins to the Tribe. However, the Tribal Court balanced the Tribes' interest in keeping tribal children in tribal communities against the children's interests in continuity and stability. . . . Even though she was an "older parent," a number of factors favored Joan. First, the twins had lived with her all their lives and "it would have been cruel to take them from the only mother they knew." Second, by all accounts, she was a loving parent who provided a stable home environment. Third, the twins had not been raised in a Choctaw home and did not speak or understand the Choctaw language, which, according to a 1974 survey, was the predominant language spoken in eighty percent of Choctaw homes. . . . Still, Judge Jim was not willing to sever the children's ties to the Tribe completely; he ordered that they maintain contact with their extended family and other tribal members.

Solangel Maldonado, Race, Culture, and Adoption: Lessons from Mississippi Band of Choctaw Indians v. Holyfield, 17 Colum. J. Gender & L. 1, 17-18

(2008). Maldonado further observes that Mr. Holyfield, the adoptive father, was one-quarter Choctaw, but that the tribe only granted tribal membership to those who were at least one-half Mississippi Choctaw. *Id.* at 23-24.

6. When the South Carolina Supreme Court, in contrast, concluded that ICWA applied in *Adoptive Couple*, it also concluded that custody had to be transferred from the adoptive parents to the father, Dusten Brown, who had never met Baby Veronica. The Court read ICWA to require recognition of the biological parent's parental standing absent a showing of "active [and ultimately futile] efforts have been made to provide remedial services and rehabilitative programs designed to prevent the breakup of the Indian family," 25 U.S.C. §1912(d), and proof beyond a reasonable doubt "that the continued custody of the child by the parent or Indian custodian is likely to result in serious emotional or physical damage to the child." 25 U.S.C. §1912(f). Adoptive Couple v. Baby Girl, 731 S.E.2d 550, 563-565 (S. Car. 2012). In applying ICWA, the state court did consider the child's best interest. In doing so, the court cited *Holyfield* to the effect that "the child's relationship with his or her tribe is an important consideration, as the ICWA is 'based on the fundamental assumption that it is in the Indian child's best interest that its relationship to the tribe be protected.'" *Id.* at 565.

After the U.S. Supreme Court decision in *Adoptive Couple*, the South Carolina Supreme Court ordered the prompt transfer of Baby Veronica back to the adoptive parents. It held that the father's consent was not required for an adoption under South Carolina law and that once a final adoption decree had been entered, "the relationship of parent and child and all the rights, duties, and other legal consequences of the natural relationship of parent and child" existed between the adoptive couple and the child. The court emphasized the need for an expeditious resolution of the case and concluded that "Adoptive Couple is the only party who has a petition pending for the adoption of Baby Girl, and thus, theirs is the only application that should be considered at this stage." It rejected consideration of a best-interest standard on the basis of the ties that had developed during the father's custody of the child for the preceding year and a half. Adoptive Couple v. Baby Girl (S.C. July 17, 2013), available at http://www.judicial.state.sc.us/court Orders/displayOrder.cfm?orderNo=2013-07-17-01 (last visited Nov. 25, 2013).

7. A number of courts have employed a general "best interests of the child" exception to the placement preferences. *See, e.g.,* In Interest of A.E., 572 N.W.2d 579 (Iowa 1997); In re Adoption of Bernard A., 77 P.3d 4, 10 (Alaska 2003). Other courts reject the best-interests exception as inconsistent with the fundamental principles of ICWA. Matter of Custody of S.E.G., 521 N.W.2d 357 (Minn. 1994); In re Adoption of Riffle, 922 P.2d 510 (Mont. 1996). *See also* In re C.H., 997 P.2d 776, 784 (Mont. 2000) ("To allow emotional bonding—a normal and desirable outcome when, as here, a child lives with a foster family for several years—to constitute an 'extraordinary' emotional need would essentially negate the ICWA presumption."). How would you characterize the South Carolina approach?

8. One of the differences between ICWA and South Carolina law is the protection accorded to the biological father. Under South Carolina law, the birth mother could place the child for adoption without the father's consent because the father had not lived with the mother for a continuous period of six months before the child's birth, nor contributed to her pregnancy-related expenses. S.C. Code Ann. §63-9-310(A)(5) (2010). ICWA in contrast treats

biological parents as parents for purposes of the statute, but excludes "the unwed father where paternity has not been acknowledged or established." 25 U.S.C. § 1903(9). Since the biological father, Dusten Brown, acknowledged paternity as soon as he learned of the proposed adoption (and ultimately had a paternity test establishing his biological connection to Baby Veronica), the South Carolina courts treated him as a father for purposes of ICWA. The U.S. Supreme Court decided that ICWA did not apply without reaching the issue of his parental status under the Act. 133 S.Ct. at 1260, n.4. What arguments could be made that Brown was not a "father" under the ICWA? Are these arguments consistent with the purposes of the statute articulated in the different Supreme Court opinions?

9. Baby Veronica's mother, Christy Maldonado, made the decision to place the child for adoption after the biological father indicated in a text that he did not want to be involved with the child, and she chose the adoptive couple without the father's involvement. She arranged for an open adoption. Shortly after the Supreme Court decision, she wrote:

> For 27 months, I watched Veronica grow and thrive with Matt and Melanie [the adoptive couple]. I got regular updates, talked to her on the phone and watched her open presents at Christmas. They are wonderful parents, and I felt proud of the decision I had made for my child. But after more than two years in her happy home, a court ruled that my choice meant nothing.

Christy Maldonado, Baby Veronica Belongs with Her Adoptive Parents, Wash. Post (July 12, 2013) available at http://articles.washingtonpost.com/2013-07-12/opinions/40529306_1_matt-and-melanie-adoptive-parents-melanie-capobianco (last visited Nov. 25, 2013). Under South Carolina law, Maldonado could make the decision to place the child for adoption and choose the adoptive couple on her own. ICWA, in contrast, places greater emphasis on contact with the biological father in spite of his lack of involvement before the child's birth and on adoptive placements that continue contact with tribal culture irrespective of the wishes of the mother, a Latina who is not a tribe member. To what extent should the mother's views be taken into account? Should either the tribe or the South Carolina courts be compelled to consider a non-Indian parent's cultural heritage in an adoptive placement?

10. A critical question for purposes of determining the applicability of the ICWA is whether the child whose custody is at stake is an "Indian child." The statute defines this term to include any unmarried person less than 18 years old who is an enrolled member of an Indian tribe, the biological child of a member of an Indian tribe, or the biological child of a member of an Indian tribe who is also eligible for membership. 25 U.S.C. § 1903(4).

Tribes vary in how they determine tribal membership. The "non-Indian" adoptive father in *Holyfield*, for example, had more Choctaw ancestry (one-quarter) than Dusten Brown had Cherokee blood, but the Choctaws require one-half Choctaw ancestry to be a tribal member while the Cherokee simply require the ability to trace a member's lineage to a particular person in the historical tribal rolls. Addie Rolnick comments:

> The definition of Indian [under ICWA] . . . is clear, and it is clearly tied to tribal enrollment. Of all the possible indicia of Indianness, formal enrollment in a

tribe is the most clearly "political" because it refers to national citizenship. . . . As Justice Sotomayor points out in her dissent, the majority's frequent references to the tribe's reliance on descent and its "second-guess[ing]" of the tribe's membership requirements are ironic in light of the fact that federal regulations require that all members demonstrate "descent from a historical Indian tribe" as a condition for tribal acknowledgement.

Adoptive Couple v. Baby Girl (2 of 4): Why the Court's ICWA Ruling Matters (June 30, 2013) available at http://prawfsblawg.blogs.com/prawfsblawg/2013/06/adoptive-couple-v-baby-girl-2-of-4-3256th-cherokee.html (last visited Nov. 25, 2013).

The first sentence in Justice Alito's majority opinion in *Adoptive Couple* reads, "This case is about a little girl (Baby Girl) who is classified as an Indian because she is 1.2% (3/256) Cherokee." Does it matter to Alito's view of the case that the tribe does not require a greater "blood quantum" of Native American ancestry as a condition for tribal membership? How does a "political" definition of tribal membership that emphasizes citizenship rather than descent affect the purposes of ICWA?

11. ICWA also contains substantive placement preferences that bind state courts. A child removed from home must be placed in the least restrictive setting (one that most approximates a family home) in which the child's special needs can be met. If the child is placed in foster care, a state court must give preference to the child's extended family or to an Indian home. If the child is being placed for adoption, a state court, in the absence of good cause to the contrary, must give preference to a member of the child's extended family, to other members of the Indian child's tribe, or to other Indian families. 25 U.S.C. § 1915. The Bureau of Indian Affairs guidelines on good cause to deviate from the placement preferences can be found at 44 Fed. Reg. 67,584-67,595 (1979). Justice Alito observed that no extended family or tribal members had applied as part of the original adoption proceeding in *Adoptive Couple*, but since the child had not been classified as an "Indian child" at that point, no effort had been made to encourage such participation. Should that have mattered to the outcome of the case? Would Dusten Brown have had a stronger case if he had applied to adopt the child rather than sought to establish paternity?

12. ICWA applies to foster care and preadoptive placements, adoption, and termination of parental rights of Indian children, but not to custody disputes following divorce. 25 U.S.C. § 1903(1). The courts are divided about its applicability to other intrafamilial custody disputes. For a summary of the case law, *see* Kurtis A. Kemper, Validity, Construction, and Application of Placement Preferences of State and Federal Indian Child Welfare Acts, 63 A.L.R.6th 429 (2011).

Professor Leslie Harris observes that:

> Adoptive Couple v. Baby Girl . . . did not change the test for whether ICWA applies to a case. If the proceeding is a "child custody proceeding" involving an "Indian child" as those terms are defined in ICWA, ICWA applies. The Court in *Adoptive Couple* took this as a given. The case also did not change ICWA's jurisdictional rules, including the provision granting exclusive jurisdiction to a tribal court if the child resides or is domiciled on the reservation. The case did not change the rights of the child's tribe to notice of foster care or termination of parental rights proceedings involving the child or the right of the tribe to intervene in such proceedings. Instead, the case limited the application of ICWA provisions that protect the parental

rights of Indian children in "child custody proceedings." Specifically, it held that a parent who does not have legal or physical custody is not protected by the requirement that active efforts to preserve the family be made before the parent's rights are terminated or by the requirement that evidence, including qualified expert testimony, support a finding beyond a reasonable doubt "that the continued custody of the child by the parent of Indian custodian is likely to result in serious emotional or physical damage to the child" before parental rights are terminated.

Leslie J. Harris, Impact of the New Supreme Court ICWA Case on Child Welfare Cases, 10(3) Juvenile Law Reader 1 (Autumn 2013), available at http://www.youthrightsjustice.org/media/2654/YRJreaderV10i3.pdf.

13. Justice Thomas, in an opinion no other member of the Court joined, concurred. He concluded that although the statute is susceptible of more than one plausible reading, the majority's reading avoids "significant constitutional problems" about whether ICWA exceeds Congress's authority under the Indian commerce clause. Justice Sotomayor commented, "No party advanced this argument, and it is inconsistent with this Court's precedents holding that Congress has 'broad general powers to legislate in respect to Indian tribes, powers that we have consistently described as plenary and exclusive,' founded not only on the Indian Commerce Clause but also the Treaty Clause."

NOTE: TRANSRACIAL PLACEMENT

In 1972 the National Association of Black Social Workers (NABSW) adopted a resolution, to which it still adheres, that provides in part:

[W]e have taken the position that Black children should be placed only with Black families whether in foster care or adoption. Black children belong physically, psychologically and culturally in Black families in order that they receive the total sense of themselves and develop a sound projection of their future. Human beings are products of their environments and develop their sense of values, attitudes and self-concept within their family structures. Black children in White homes are cut off from the healthy development of themselves as Black people.

Our position is based on:

1. the necessity of self-determination from birth to death of all Black people.
2. the need of our young ones to begin at birth to identify with all Black people in a Black community.
3. the philosophy that we need our own to build a strong nation.

The socialization process for every child begins at birth. Included in the socialization process is the child's cultural heritage, which is an important segment of the total process. This must begin at the earliest moment; otherwise our children will not have the background and knowledge which is necessary to survive in a racist society. This is impossible if the child is placed with White parents in a White environment. . . .

We the participants of the workshop have committed ourselves to go back to our communities and work to end this particular form of genocide.

Quoted in Rita J. Simon & Howard Altstein, Transracial Adoption 50, 52 (1977). After the NABSW issued its statement, transracial adoption declined sharply.

From a peak of 2574 transracial adoptions in 1971, the number fell to 831 in 1975. Elizabeth Bartholet, Where Do Black Children Belong? The Politics of Race Matching in Adoption, 139 U. Pa. L. Rev. 1163, 1180 (1991).

Interest in transracial and international adoption has resurfaced, and racial matching practices are again being challenged. Two trends underlie the increased interest in transracial adoption. The first is emphasis on placing foster children. Substantially more than half of all children waiting in foster care to be adopted are children of color. In 2011, 23 percent of the children entering foster care, and 28 percent of those waiting to be adopted—but only 23 percent of those actually adopted—were African-American; 21 percent of those entering foster care, 22 percent of those waiting to be adopted, and 21 percent of those actually adopted were Hispanic (of any race); and 40 percent of those waiting to be adopted, and 45 percent of those actually adopted were non-Hispanic white children. Children's Bureau, The AFCARS Report—Preliminary FY 2011 Estimates as of July 2012 (19), available at http://www.acf.hhs.gov/programs/cb/stats_ research/afcars/tar/report19.pdf (last visited Sept. 28, 2013). Moreover, African-Americans and Native Americans are disproportionately represented in the foster care system and less likely to be adopted, despite the fact that a higher percentage of African-Americans entering the foster care system become available for adoption. Evan B. Donaldson Adoption Institute, Finding Families for African American Children: The Role of Race and Law in Adoption from Foster Care 5, 33 (2008), available at http://www.adoptioninstitute.org/publications/MEPApaper20080527.pdf (last visited Sept. 7, 2009) (black and Native American children consistently have adoption rates around 30 percent, while all other groups' rates range from 40 to over 50 percent). A new movement seeks to address the reasons African-American children are more likely to be placed in foster care and less likely to adopted. For an assessment, *see* Elizabeth Bartholet, The Racial Disproportionality Movement in Child Welfare: False Facts and Dangerous Directions, 51 Ariz. L. Rev. 871 (2009).

The second trend is continued interest in international adoption as a way of finding available infants. International adoptions in the United States increased dramatically in the last two decades but have started to decline because of allegations of abuse and greater restrictions in the countries of origin. The number of children adopted from abroad increased from 7000 in 1990 to a peak of 22,664 in 2004, and then declined over the next four years to 8668 in 2012 and declined further in 2013. In 2012 and 2013 the largest number of children came from China and Ethiopia. Intercountry Adoptions, Office of Children's Issues, Total Adoptions to the United States: Fiscal Year 2012 Adoption Statistics, available at http://adoption.state.gov/news/total_chart.html (last visited Sept. 28, 2013).

Taken together, these factors have increased the rate of transracial adoptions. The Supreme Court has twice considered the constitutionality of laws that determined family relationships based on race, and both times it applied strict scrutiny and held that the laws violate the equal protection clause. In Loving v. Virginia, 388 U.S. 1 (1967), the Court struck down a statute that forbade interracial marriage, and in Palmore v. Sidoti, 466 U.S. 429 (1984) (see Chapter 9), it held unconstitutional the use of race to determine custody between parents.

The 1994 Multiethnic Placement Act, as amended in 1996, prohibits discrimination in a child's placement on the basis of the race, national origin, or ethnicity of the child or the prospective foster or adoptive parents. The 1996 amendments deleted language that permitted an agency to "consider" the child's cultural, ethnic, or racial background as a factor in assessing the parents' ability to meet the needs of the child. The Act imposes obligations on agencies to seek out potential adoptive families of the races and ethnicities of the children needing placement. Pub. L. No. 103-382, § 553 (1994), as amended by Pub. L. No. 104-188, § 1808 (1996), codified at 42 U.S.C. § 5115a.

Twila L. Perry, Transracial and International Adoption: Mothers, Hierarchy, Race and Feminist Legal Theory

10 Yale J.L. & Feminism 102, 115-116, 121-122 (1998)

One troubling aspect of both transracial and international adoption is that each often results in the transfer of children from the least advantaged women to the most advantaged. At the same time, such adoptions, per se, do nothing to alleviate the conditions in the societies or communities from which the children come and thus do nothing to change the conditions that place some women in the position of being unable to care for their children themselves. Perhaps for these reasons, at least in part, recent scholarship by women of color on transracial adoption suggests that many of them are less than enthusiastic about the practice. . . .

There are probably many reasons why Black women often appear to be ambivalent or even hostile toward transracial adoption. Some of the reasons certainly involve perceptions about the needs of individual Black children — there is skepticism about whether white women can provide Black children with the skills they need to survive in a racist society. Some Black women may also feel that white women often raise white children with a sense of superiority over Blacks and that they will naturally raise Black transracially adopted children to feel the same way. Some Black women may simply believe that white people cannot love a Black child the same way they would love a white one. They understand that however precious Black children may be to Black people, for many whites seeking to adopt, a Black child is a second, third or last choice, behind children that are white, Asian or Hispanic. Some Black women are quite critical of the mothering skills displayed by white mothers with respect to their own children, and thus view arguments of some advocates of transracial adoption that white families may be able to parent Black children better than Black families with amused contempt. Others may be concerned that white women are interested in adopting Black children to fulfill their own desires to parent, but have no interest in the condition of Black children in general or in conditions that threaten the stability of so many Black families.

I offer two additional explanations for the feelings some Black women may have toward transracial adoption — feelings unrelated to concerns about the competence of white women to raise Black children. I argue that many Black women feel that arguments in favor of transracial adoption that minimize the role of race in parenting devalue an important part of what motherhood means to them — a historical and contemporary struggle to raise Black children successfully in a racist world. In addition, many Black women may also resent transracial adoption because they see it as part of a larger system of racial hierarchy and privilege that advantages white women while it devalues and subordinates women of color. . . .

Because women play a dominant role in caring for children, a subtext in the debate over transracial adoption involves the issue of mothering. Thus, a question underlying the debate about giving Black children "survival skills" is: who is qualified to mother children in a society that even the advocates of transracial adoption admit is racist? It is interesting that there are ways in which this issue is discussed, and ways in which it is not discussed. I argue that society's perception of the competence of women to mother children is intricately tied to the racial hierarchies among women in this society and that these perceptions are reflected in the controversy concerning transracial adoption. All too often, Black women are seen as inadequate to the task of mothering Black children, while white women are seen as competent to raise children of any race.

I view this racial hierarchy among mothers as having a number of troubling ramifications. First, if society values the mothering of some women more than it values of the mothering of others, the separation of the devalued mother from her children is less likely to be a cause of concern. Indeed, children transferred from devalued women to valued women are deemed to have received a lucky break. Second, women who know that they are devalued as mothers are likely to resent a pattern of adoption in which children from their group are always transferred to the women of higher status. Finally, the perception of the more valued group of women as competent to mother all children may deflect other important inquiries. In the context of the controversy over transracial adoption, assumptions about the ability of white women to mother Black children avoids a different inquiry about mothering, race, and racism that deserves attention. . . . I argue for a shift of the debate from the question of who is qualified to raise Black children in a racist society to the question of what it means to raise white children in a racist society. . . .

There are important links to be drawn between the transracial adoption of Black children in the United States and the adoption of children of color from Asia and Latin America. The factors of racism and economic discrimination that result in large numbers of Black children being separated from their biological parents in this country have counterparts in the international context, where a history of colonialism, neocolonialism, cultural imperialism, and economic exploitation often results in mothers being unable to keep the children to whom they have given birth. Thus, both domestically and internationally, transracial and international adoption often result in a pattern in which there is the transfer of children from the least advantaged women to the most advantaged women. Despite the differences between the specific circumstances of Black women in America and some other third world women, there is a connection in terms of a struggle by both to function as mothers under political and economic conditions which severely challenge their ability to adequately parent their own children. Moreover, many transracial adoptions, international adoptions, and adoptions in which racial and ethnic differences are not a factor, also share another connection — a link to the institution of patriarchy.

ELIZABETH BARTHOLET, *INTERNATIONAL ADOPTION:*
THE CHILD'S STORY

24 Ga. St. U. L. Rev. 333, 338-348 (2007)

The issues at the heart of international adoption have to do with children too young to make decisions by themselves, and often too young even to voice feelings, desires, and views. Millions upon millions of infants and young children are growing up in orphanages or on the streets having been orphaned, abandoned, or placed in institutions by parents unable to care for them, or removed from such parents. . . .

International adoption is heavily regulated by the state, with applicable law typically describing itself as guided by the best interest of the child. Such law includes the domestic law of what are called "sending" and "receiving" countries, and international law like the Convention on the Rights of the Child, and the Hague Convention on Intercountry Adoption. All this law has tended to function generally to restrict rather than to facilitate international adoption. The law focuses on the bad things that might happen when a child is transferred from a birth parent to an international adoptive parent and then purports to try to protect against those things happening. . . . There are very typically so many restrictions that even when international adoption is officially allowed, it is in effect not allowed, except for a tiny percentage of children in need, leaving the rest to grow up in institutions or on the streets.

. . . [C]ritics of international adoption have been both active and significantly successful. For example, Romania was forced to eliminate international adoption in 2004 as a condition of being admitted to the European Union by those in control of the European Parliament's process at the time, who relied on the U.N. Convention on the Rights of the Child and the European Convention for the Protection of Human Rights and Fundamental Freedoms to argue that international adoption was inherently a violation of children's rights. . . . New governmental restrictions on private intermediaries involved in international adoption has resulted in significantly closing down such adoption in many countries in South and Central America, including Paraguay, Chile, Bolivia, Peru, Ecuador, Honduras, and El Salvador. The result has generally been to limit the numbers of children released so that only a relative few get out, and these only after having spent two or three years or more in the kind of institutional care that puts children at high risk for permanent disabilities.

II. CONFLICTING VERSIONS OF THE CHILD'S STORY

. . . [L]et's imagine one child whose situation is typical of many others. Let's imagine the infant in a large institution. . . .

If we could have a rational conversation with this infant about her needs and wants, and about the choices she would make among the real-world options she has, how would this conversation go? First the infant would presumably want on an immediate basis to be held, fed, comforted, and played with, and kept clean, dry and warm. She would want attention when awake, and someone to respond when she cries. As months of infancy went by, she would want to see a familiar face, to connect with someone emotionally. If we could explain to her about childhood development, about the social life that normal non-institutionalized adolescents and adults live, about education and the world of work, she would want to make sure that she got the nurturing and education as a child that would enable her to grow up as the kind of emotionally and physically healthy person who could have good relationships with friends and family, and who could survive and thrive in the world of work.

... To help the infant make a rational choice among possible future options we should give her some more information. She knows from her daily experience that the orphanage is a horrible place. Her bottle is propped, with a large hole gouged in the nipple so that the milk pours out — the idea is to give her a better chance to take in some milk since she is too young and weak to suck strongly — but she often chokes on the milk flooding into her mouth and throat, and spits the bottle out. When she screams for attention because she is hungry or cold or wet or just alone, nobody comes — attendants arrive only every four or six hours and then leave immediately after hurried diaper-changing and bottle-propping events. She would notice if she were capable of understanding that infants around her stop screaming after a while; they learn that screaming does not produce any result. We could tell her that those who study child institutions often remark with horror on the silence that characterizes them — horror in part because those experts know that for an infant to learn the lesson that it's not worth screaming is terribly damaging to their prospects for normal development. We could also tell her what the research shows about the range of institutions that exist for homeless children like her, and the problems inherent in even the best institutions. Her current orphanage is fairly typical. Some are better, providing a little more care, but still little if any opportunity to develop the kind of relationship with a nurturing parent figure that is essential for normal human development. Some are far worse, with infants dying at a high rate, and children whose biological age is in the teens lying in cribs looking as if they were toddlers, unable to talk or walk because they have been so deprived of the attention it takes for a human being to actually develop. Photographs of some of the still-living children in certain of these institutions look like photographs that could have been taken in the Nazi death camps, except here the subjects are all children, bone-thin, expressionless, staring back emptily at the camera eye.

We should also give the infant other information. We should tell her that many adults in the world place significant value on birth and national heritage. We should tell her that if she were to grow up adopted abroad, many people would ask about her "real parents," referring to her birth parents.... We should [also] tell her that the research shows adopted children do very well on all measures that social scientists use to assess human happiness, and that it reveals no evidence that children are in any way harmed by being placed internationally. Finally, we should tell her that the research shows that children raised for significant periods of time in institutions do terribly badly on all of those social science measures....

NOTES AND QUESTIONS

1. Both proponents of domestic racial matching and critics of international adoption suggest that children's interests lie with connection with home countries, families of origin, and the culture associated with them. What are the interests of children in these cases?

Does some form of open adoption, with ongoing contact between an adopted child and his or her family of origin, resolve the problem by allowing the child to form an identity that includes both families and cultures? *See* Solangel Maldonado, Permanency v. Biology: Making the Case for Post-Adoption Contact, 37 Cap. U. L. Rev. 321 (2008).

Historically, the idea of "whiteness" and "blackness" was seen through the lens of what some have called a "black-white" binary in which children were seen as having one race or the other. Today, there has been a greater willingness to see children as "biracial" and to embrace a biracial identity. How should that affect adoption practices? For discussion of this issue, *see* Twila L. Perry, Race, Color, and the Adoption of Biracial Children, 17 J. Gender Race & Just. 73 (2014).

2. How should a public adoption agency proceed in the following case, which occurred in Cincinnati, Ohio, the seat of Hamilton County?

> Leah, who is two, is African American and had been born with Fetal Alcohol Syndrome and a form of dwarfism. After she had been in the permanent custody of the county for about six months, a married couple, the Atkinsons, inquired about the possibility of adopting her. The Atkinsons had three biological children, each of whom had significant special health needs, and they were longtime foster parents to a fourth child, an Alaskan Native who, like Leah, had a form of dwarfism as well as other special needs. The Atkinsons learned about Leah from Little People of America, a national advocacy group in which the Atkinsons were active. The Atkinsons were white and lived in North Pole, Alaska, a suburb of Fairbanks.

David D. Meyer, *Palmore* Comes of Age: The Place of Race in the Placement of Children, 18 U. Fla. J.L. & Pub. Pol'y 183, 196 (2007). Is it legally permissible for the agency to inquire about the racial composition of the Atkinsons' neighborhood or church, or about the Atkinsons' attitudes or plans for raising an African-American child in Alaska? Is it permissible for the agency to delay in responding to the Atkinsons for several months while it determines whether other (perhaps racially more suitable) placements are available? Is it legally permissible for the agency to consider the presence of another child with dwarfism in the household and to make that a basis for selecting the Atkinsons over another couple?

3. Professor Barbara Fedders reports that many private adoption agencies, which are less regulated than public agencies, charge higher fees for the adoption of white infants than black infants. *See* Barbara Fedders, Race and Market Values in Domestic Infant Adoption, 88 N.C. L. Rev. 1687 (2010). Should the agencies be required to charge race-neutral fees even if that means that fewer African-American children will be adopted? Does the response to this issue replicate many of the same issues Professors Perry and Bartholet discuss?

4. What roles do race and culture play in intercountry adoptions? The Evan B. Donaldson Adoption Institute reports that:

Two international treaties established the rights of children whose families could not care for them, and the government's responsibilities for these children. The first, the Convention on the Rights of the Child, was approved by the United Nations in 1989 and ratified by more than 175 countries; only the United States and Somalia have not ratified this treaty. Among the rights of children recognized by CRC is the right to "identity." Article 20 sets forth governmental obligations in protecting a child's identity and continuity of cultural background:

1. A child temporarily or permanently deprived of his or her family environment, or in whose own best interests cannot be allowed to remain in that environment, shall be entitled to special protection and assistance provided by the State.
2. [While] such care could include . . . foster placement or adoption or, if necessary, placement in suitable institutions for the care of children, when considering solutions, due regard shall be paid to the desirability of continuity in a child's upbringing and to the child's ethnic, religious, cultural and linguistic background.

Some opponents of international adoption use the CRC to argue against children leaving their home countries for adoption; however, research and humanitarian perspectives invariably support the position that it is better for children to be raised in permanent families than to grow up in institutions or foster care.

The second treaty, the Hague Convention on Protection of Children and Cooperation in Respect of Intercountry Adoption, was adopted in 1993 in the 17th convening of the Hague Conference, with over 65 countries represented; and it has been ratified by 75 countries to date. The Hague Convention regulates international adoption practice and is designed to protect the rights of children, birthparents, and adoptive parents. Like the CRC, it recognizes the importance of a child's identity. Article 16 states that a child's country of origin must "give due consideration to the child's upbringing and to his or her ethnic, religious and cultural background" and "determine, on the basis in particular of the reports relating to the child and the prospective adoptive parents, whether the envisaged placement is in the best interests of the child."

After the U.S. signed the Hague Convention, Congress enacted the Intercountry Adoption Act of 2000, which brings this country into compliance with Hague Convention requirements. The Department of State, now the designated U.S. Central Authority for international adoption, has issued implementing regulations. These address, among a number of other issues, children's racial and ethnic needs. First, they require that prospective adoptive parents receive 10 hours of pre-adoption training which, among other topics, must address the "long-term implications for families who become multi-cultural through intercountry adoption" (Section 96.48). Second, adoption service providers are to counsel parents about the child's history, including a focus on "cultural, racial, religious, ethnic, and linguistic background" (Section 96.48). The U.S. has ratified the Hague Convention, and it took effect in this country in April 2008.

Finding Families for African American Children: The Role of Race and Law in Adoption from Foster Care 23 (2008), above, at 16-17.

A little-known development is that the United States has also become a source of children adopted abroad, often African-American children from foster care. In 2005 the United States was the third largest supplier of infants to adoptive parents in Canada, up 29 percent from the previous year. The Hague Convention provisions also apply to these children. Galit Avitan, Note, Protecting Our Children or Our Pride? Regulating the Intercountry Adoption of American Children, 40 Cornell Int'l L.J. 489, 499 (2007). *See also* Sophie Brown, Overseas Adoptions Rise — for Black American Children, CNN, Sept. 17, 2013, available at http://www.cnn.com/2013/09/16/world/international-adoption-us-children-adopted-abroad/index.html (last visited Sept. 28, 2013).

The Convention itself is available at the home page of the Hague Conference on Private International Law, http://hcch.e-vision.nl/index_en.php (last visited Sept. 29, 2013). Information about the U.S. implementation process is available at http://adoption.state.gov/hague_convention.php (last visited Sept. 29, 2013). General information on intercountry adoption from the State Department is available at http://adoption.state.gov/ (last visited Sept. 29, 2013).

5. Three separate types of laws address the role of race and identity in adoption: the Indian Child Welfare Act (ICWA), the Multi-Ethnic Placement Act and its amendments (MEPA-IEP), and international treaties on intercountry adoption. The Evan B. Donaldson Adoption Institute comments that:

> MEPA-IEP's prohibitions on addressing racial issues also run directly counter to other policies in the U.S. that recognize the role of race, ethnicity, and culture in adoption. ICWA and MEPA-IEP represent almost polar opposites in their treatment of race/ethnicity as a factor in decision-making on foster and adoptive placements — that is, ICWA puts high value on racial/ethnic heritage. Similarly, the Hague Convention and the IAA require that attention be paid to children's cultural, racial, religious, ethnic, and linguistic background needs and to the preparation of parents to meet those needs. In sharp contrast, MEPA-IEP prohibits agencies receiving federal funding from considering race and ethnicity in foster or adoptive placements except when a compelling government interest is at stake, as interpreted by DHHS. MEPA-IEP has created a different status for African American children adopted from foster care with regard to racial/ethnic/cultural identity — a status that diverges significantly from that recognized in law for American Indian/Alaskan Native children, children adopted internationally, and children who are adopted through private adoption agencies that do not receive federal funds.
>
> The very different federal approaches about race and adoption constitute a disturbing inconsistency that undermines children, families, and the agencies charged with serving them. For some children (internationally adopted and Native American), the law holds that race and culture matter, and it protects their racial and cultural interests; for African American children in foster care; however, the law minimizes the importance of race and culture, even to the point of punishing those who work to respect and protect racial and cultural interests consistent with best practice in adoption. This schism in federal policy appears to be more a function of happenstance than a considered decision to treat different children in different ways. There appears to be no principled or historic reason for giving less respect to the racial/ethnic/cultural identity needs of African American children in foster care than to those adopted internationally or from Native American communities.

Finding Families, above, at 39. For a comparison of these differences in constitutional decision making, *see* Katie Eyer, Constitutional Colorblindness and the Family, 162 U. Pa. L. Rev. 537 (2014).

Professor Solangel Maldonado notes the irony that white Americans appear reluctant to adopt African-American children while more readily adopting Asian and Latin American children from abroad. She observes that "[r]acial preferences, whether conscious or unconscious, do play a role in the decision to adopt" and that "such preferences might be, to some degree, the result of race-matching policies that effectively prohibited whites from adopting African American children. These legal barriers confirmed and contributed to social opposition and disapproval of such adoptions, even as support for international adoptions was increasing." She proposes measures to require that Americans show that they have tried to adopt domestically, irrespective of race, before they are allowed to adopt abroad. Solangel Maldonado, Discouraging Racial Preferences in Adoptions, 39 U.C. Davis L. Rev. 1415, 1467 (2006). *See also* Deleith Duke Gossett, If Charity Begins at Home, Why Do We Go Searching Abroad? Why the Federal Adoption Tax Credit Should Not Subsidize International Adoptions, 17 Lewis & Clark L. Rev. 839 (2013); David D. Meyer, *Palmore* Comes of Age: The Place of Race in the Placement of Children, 18 U. Fla. J.L. & Pub. Pol'y 183 (2007) (comparing the role of race in custody disputes with the role of race in adoption placement).

Should American law make some effort to harmonize the role of race and identity between these different forms of adoption? If so, how should it do so?

6. Professor Bartholet describes a "crisis" in international adoption in International Adoption: The Way Forward, 55 N.Y.L. Sch. L. Rev. 687, 688 (2012). The crisis includes, in addition to some of the issues described above:

- allegations of corruption, improper financial inducements, and misrepresentations or fraud. Adoptive parents have been willing to pay high fees to agencies who arrange adoptions and these fees fueled corruption, including charges that some agencies in other countries have kidnapped children or paid parents in intact families to surrender their children. *See, e.g.,* Richard Carlson, Seeking the Better Interests of Children with a New International Law of Adoption, 55 N.Y.L. Sch. L. Rev. 733 (2010-2011).

- charges from adoptive parents that they have not been fully informed of the extent of children's emotional, physical, and developmental needs, and from the sending countries that children have been harmed because of placement with unsuitable adoptive parents. Russia, for example, once a major source of adoptive children, has banned adoptions by U.S. citizens after allegations that adoptive parents have mistreated the children. *See* D. Marianne Brower Blair, Admonitions or Accountability?: U.S. Implementation of the Hague Adoption Convention Requirements for the Collection and Disclosure of Medical and Social History of Transnationally Adopted Children, 40 Cap. U. L. Rev. 325 (2012); Rachel L. Swarns & David M. Herszenhorn, World of Grief and Doubt After an Adoptee's Death, N.Y. Times, Aug. 31, 2013, available at http://www.nytimes.com/2013/09/01/us/widening-ripples-of-grief-in-adoptees-death.html?pagewanted=all (last visited Sept. 29, 2013) (describing the death of a Russian adoptive child).

- concerns that international adoptions have been romanticized by celebrities such as Madonna and Angelina Jolie, or promoted by Christian evangelicals as a religious obligation. *See* Deleith Duke Gossett, If Charity Begins at Home, Why Do We Go Searching Abroad? Why the Federal Adoption Tax Credit Should Not Subsidize International Adoptions, 17

Lewis & Clark L. Rev. 839 (2013); David M. Smolin, Of Orphans and Adoption, Parents and the Poor, Exploitation and Rescue: A Scriptural and Theological Critique of the Evangelical Christian Adoption and Orphan Care Movement, 8 Regent J. Int'l L. 267, 269 (2012).

- tension between American efforts to ensure the inclusion of gay and lesbian adoptive parents in international adoptions and the efforts of some sending countries to prohibit adoption by same-sex couples. *See* Jennifer B. Mertus, Barriers, Hurdles, and Discrimination: The Current Status of LGBT Intercountry Adoption and Why Changes Must Be Made to Effectuate the Best Interests of the Child, 39 Cap. U. L. Rev. 271 (2011).

RELIGIOUS MATCHING

Legally, religious matching in adoption and foster care, like racial matching, has been transformed from a mandatory rule to a discretionary policy. In the late 1980s one-third of the states had some form of religious matching provision regarding adoption. Note, Gregory A. Horowitz, Accommodations and Neutrality Under the Establishment Clause: The Foster Care Challenge, 98 Yale L.J. 617, 624 (1989). Practices vary significantly from state to state as well. Professor Clark has argued that religious matching rules were created to impose a truce on proselytizing and to avoid conflict among religious groups. He cites as support the New York practice during the 1950s of arbitrarily designating foundling children as one-third each Catholic, Protestant, and Jewish. Homer H. Clark, Jr., Domestic Relations in the United States § 20.7 at 917 (2d ed. 1988).

Religious matching is most deeply entrenched in New York, where the child welfare system is "completely intertwined with religion." Martin Guggenheim, State-Supported Foster Care: The Interplay Between the Prohibition of Establishing Religion and the Free Exercise Rights of Parents and Children: *Wilder v. Bernstein*, 56 Brook. L. Rev. 603, 605 (1990). New York State provides public support for children in the care of private agencies, most of which are religious. Religiously affiliated and other private agencies directly or indirectly place and supervise children in foster care. Until the Wilder v. Bernstein litigation described in Professor Guggenheim's article, sectarian agencies gave placement preferences to children from their own religious groups for homes and institutions that they ran. There were more Catholic and Jewish placements than there were children of those faiths but fewer Protestant placements than there were Protestant children, and many of the placements regarded as most desirable were Catholic and·Jewish. The result, according to the plaintiffs in *Wilder*, was that the Protestant children, who were predominantly African-American, did not have equal access to the better placements. Eventually the litigation was settled so that foster children are to be placed on a first-come, first-served basis but with religious matching permitted if it does not allow a child to jump ahead of other children who have been waiting longer.

Most of the litigation in New York and other states after *Wilder* has involved claims by parents that their own free exercise rights require that their children be placed with foster parents of the same religion. These requests are typically honored if possible, and, at least in New York, if a child is placed with foster parents of a different religion, the agency is supposed to provide support and supervision to the foster parent to ensure that the child's religious practices are protected.

See, e.g., Bruker v. City of New York, 337 F. Supp. 2d 539 (S.D.N.Y. 2004); Whalen v. Allers, 302 F. Supp. 2d 194 (S.D.N.Y. 2003).

PROBLEM

The juvenile court ordered that 14-year-old Liz be placed in foster care after finding that her mother had physically and emotionally abused her. Liz was placed in the foster home of Susan, a single mother living with two children. Liz thrived in Susan's home. Her grades improved, her depression lifted, and she described herself as happier than she had ever been in her life. After Liz had been in Susan's home for three months, Liz's mother learned that Susan is a Catholic. Liz has been raised to be an observant Jew. Statutes in this jurisdiction provide that:

> Whenever a child is committed to an agency, such commitment shall be made, when practicable, to an authorized agency under the control of persons of the same religious faith as that of the child. The placement of any child thus committed must, when practicable, be with or in the custody of a person or persons of the same religious faith or persuasion as that of the child.

Liz was not placed in a Jewish foster home originally because none was available when she was removed from her mother's home. Citing this statute, Liz's mother has asked that Liz be moved from Susan's home to the home of practicing Jewish foster parents. While Liz has resided at Susan's home, she has attended synagogue and observed Jewish holidays. However, prior case law in this jurisdiction provides that the religious matching requirement is not satisfied by placing a child with a person of another faith, even if that person tries to protect the child's faith. Liz vehemently objects to being removed from Susan's home. She believes that her mother's request has nothing to do with religion but is part of her continuing effort to control her.

Based on all the materials we have read so far and assuming that the religious-matching statute does not violate the First Amendment, how should the lawyers for Liz's mother argue that Liz must be moved to the first available Jewish foster home? Assuming that Liz is granted party status and that her guardian ad litem agrees with her position, how should Liz's lawyers argue that she should be allowed to remain at Susan's home?

B. ALTERNATIVE REPRODUCTIVE TECHNOLOGIES

1. *Artificial Insemination and In Vitro Fertilization*

The most common, most basic, and simplest "alternative reproductive tech-nology" is artificial insemination, a relatively old, relatively simple process. The first recorded application occurred in London in 1785 when Dr. John Hunter impregnated the wife of a linen merchant with her husband's sperm. The use of donor sperm was much more controversial, however, and when the first acknowledged instance occurred in 1884, the doctor did not tell the mother that the sperm came from someone other than her husband. By the end of the 1940s, married couples had quietly begun to use artificial insemination by donor (AID) in substantial numbers in cases where the husband was infertile. So long as the couple stayed together, the child's origins usually remained secret; if the couple divorced, however, questions often arose about the child's legal status and the husband's liability for child support and right to visitation. The answers to these questions in the initial cases were divided. Leading cases imposing a parent-child relationship between the husband and child on the theory that he had voluntarily taken on responsibility for the child by assenting to AID include Levin v. Levin, 626 N.E.2d 527 (Ind. 1993); People v. Sorensen, 437 P.2d 495 (Cal. 1968) (en banc); and Strnad v. Strnad, 78 N.Y.S.2d 390 (Sup. Ct. 1948). *But see* Gursky v. Gursky, 242 N.Y.S.2d 406 (Sup. Ct. 1963) (child illegitimate but husband liable for child's support because consent to the insemination implied a promise to support).

To clarify parental status, these techniques have been the subject of a number of uniform acts, most notably the Uniform Parentage Act of 1973, which was adopted by 18 states. The Uniform Parentage Act of 2002 substantially changed the 1973 Act and incorporated many of the features of the intervening uniform acts. It has been adopted by Alabama, Delaware, New Mexico, North Dakota, Oklahoma, Texas, Utah, Washington, and Wyoming, with legislation pending elsewhere.

Uniform Parentage Act (2002)

§ 702. A donor is not a parent of a child conceived by means of assisted reproduction.

§ 704. (a) Consent by a woman, and a man who intends to be a parent of a child born to the woman by assisted reproduction must be in a record signed by the woman and the man. This requirement does not apply to a donor.

(b) Failure of a man to sign a consent required by subsection (a), before or after birth of the child, does not preclude a finding of paternity if the woman and the man, during the first two years of the child's life resided together in the same household with the child and openly held out the child as their own.

§ 705. (a) Except as otherwise provided in subsection (b), the husband of a wife who gives birth to a child by means of assisted reproduction may not challenge his paternity of the child unless:

(1) within two years after learning of the birth of the child he commences a proceeding to adjudicate his paternity; and

(2) the court finds that he did not consent to the assisted reproduction, before or after birth of the child.

(b) A proceeding to adjudicate paternity may be maintained at any time if the court determines that:

(1) the husband did not provide sperm for, or before or after the birth of the child consent to, assisted reproduction by his wife;

(2) the husband and the mother of the child have not cohabited since the probable time of assisted reproduction; and

(3) the husband never openly held out the child as his own.

(c) The limitation provided in this section applies to a marriage declared invalid after assisted reproduction.

§ 706. (a) If a marriage is dissolved before placement of eggs, sperm, or embryos, the former spouse is not a parent of the resulting child unless the former spouse consented in a record that if assisted reproduction were to occur after a divorce, the former spouse would be a parent of the child.

(b) The consent of a woman or a man to assisted reproduction may be withdrawn by that individual in a record at any time before placement of eggs, sperm, or embryos. An individual who withdraws consent under this section is not a parent of the resulting child.

§ 707. If an individual who consented in a record to be a parent by assisted reproduction dies before placement of eggs, sperm, or embryos, the deceased individual is not a parent of the resulting child unless the deceased spouse consented in a record that if assisted reproduction were to occur after death, the deceased individual would be a parent of the child.

NOTES AND QUESTIONS

1. Under what circumstances does the Uniform Parentage Act of 2002 terminate the parental status of the donor? States do not ordinarily recognize the validity of parentage contracts, on the ground that the right to support belongs to the child and that the adults cannot terminate a biological parent's support duties on their own. The Uniform Parentage Act of 1973 terminated a donor's parental obligations only if the donor provided the semen to a licensed physician for insemination. Twenty-one states adopted either the UPA or other statutes referring to the execution of the procedure by a physician. The 1973 Act also limited the termination of the donor's parental status to insemination of married women. Thirteen states have codes that do not specifically mention marital status as a requirement. Sixteen states have no legislation addressing artificial insemination. These jurisdictions often employ common law principles, such as estoppel or in loco parentis, to recognize a mother's partner as a parent in case-by-case adjudications. *See* Gaia Bernstein, The Socio-Legal Acceptance of New Technologies: A Close Look at Artificial Insemination, 77 Wash. L. Rev. 1035 (2002). *See more generally* Naomi R. Cahn, Test Tube Families: Why the Fertility Market Needs Legal Regulation (2009); Naomi R. Cahn, The New Kinship: Constructing Donor-Conceived Families (2012); Glenn I. Cohen, Response: Rethinking Sperm-Donor Anonymity: Of Changed Selves, Nonidentity, and One-Night Stands, 100 Geo. L.J. 431 (2012); Susan Frelich Appleton, Adoption in the Age of Reproductive Technology, 2004 U. Chi. Legal F. 393, 428-429 (2004); Courtney I. Joslin, Protecting Children(?): Marriage, Gender, and Assisted Reproductive Technology, 83 S. Cal. L. Rev. 1177 (2010).

2. State versions of the Uniform Parentage Acts of 1973 and 2002 vary substantially both in the language the legislatures adopted and in the courts' interpretation of the statutes in various states. In Kansas, for example, the state supreme court refused to recognize the parental status of a sperm donor on the basis of that state's artificial insemination statute. The Kansas statute provides that "[t]he donor of semen provided to a licensed physician for use in artificial insemination of a

woman other than the donor's wife is treated in law as if he were not the birth father of a child thereby conceived, unless agreed to in writing by the donor and the woman." Kan. Stat. Ann. § 38-1114(f). In In Interest of K.M.H, 169 P.3d 1025 (Kan. 2007), the court held that (1) the plain language of the statute adopts an "opt out" rule in which the donor does not have parental status unless he signs a written agreement to the contrary, and (2) the statute is constitutional even in circumstances in which the donor claims to have relied on an oral agreement that he would have parental rights.

The state of Washington adopted a provision with language identical to the Kansas provisions. The Washington Supreme Court, in In re Parentage of J.M.K., 119 P.3d 840 (2005), nonetheless concluded that the former Washington artificial insemination statute and the Uniform Parentage Act did not protect the father from legal responsibility because the process of in vitro fertilization is different from the process of artificial insemination, and these laws were only designed to shield sperm donors who have no intention of becoming fathers. In this case the mother and father, who had a romantic relationship, conceived the children with the intention of raising them together, and the father signed an acknowledgment of paternity with respect to the first but not the second child.

The Uniform Parentage Act of 2002 differs from the 1973 Act in terminating a donor's parental status even if a doctor is not used for the insemination. Two of the 12 states to adopt the UPA of 2002 (Alabama and Oklahoma) have deleted that provision, and terminate the donor's parental status only if the insemination is performed by a doctor and the recipient is a married woman.

3. The use of AID has expanded from infertile heterosexual couples to single women and lesbian couples, creating more complex parentage issues. In Jacob v. Shultz-Jacob, 923 A.2d 473 (Pa. 2007), a Pennsylvania appellate court found a known sperm donor liable for child support on equitable estoppel grounds in light of the sperm donor's voluntary provision of some support, involvement in the children's lives, and award of partial custody. The court also found the child's biological mother and her partner financially liable for the children.

In Ferguson v. McKiernan, 940 A.2d 1236 (Pa. 2008), the Pennsylvania Supreme Court upheld the validity of an oral agreement in which a known donor agreed to provide sperm for in vitro fertilization (IVF) pursuant to an understanding that he would have no parental role, rights, or obligations. The court emphasized that the romantic relationship between the donor and the mother had ended before the insemination, the insemination took place in a clinical setting, the parties took steps to preserve the donor's anonymity, and he had no significant involvement with the mother or the children after their birth. The supreme court decision reversed the lower court holdings that the agreement was void as against public policy because it negated the children's right to support.

In some states, the courts have suggested, primarily in dicta, that if a state statute were interpreted to terminate the parental status of a man who contributed sperm for use in artificial insemination by a doctor even where the man and the woman had an agreement that he would retain his parental status, the statute would be unconstitutional. See, e.g., C.O. v. W.S., 639 N.E.2d 523 (Ohio 1994); In re

K.M.H., 169 P.3d 1025 (Kan. 2007). In Steven S. v. Deborah D., 127 Cal. App. 4th 319, 25 Cal. Rptr. 3d 482 (2005), however, the court terminated the parental status of the donor by operation of law, notwithstanding his allegation of an agreement to the contrary. In that case, however, the parties did not raise a constitutional challenge to the statute, and the California legislature amended the statute in 2011 to allow for an express written agreement recognizing a donor's parental status.

4. Infertile couples choose whether or not to tell their children about their use of donor gametes, but the children of single women or same-sex couples realize at a relatively young age that another adult was involved in their conception. For discussion of the child's interests in learning the identity or identifying information about the donor, *see* Wendy Kramer & Naomi Cahn, Finding Our Families: A First-of-Its-Kind Book for Donor-Conceived People and Their Families (2013); Ellen Waldman, What Do We Tell the Children?, 35 Cap. U. L. Rev. 517 (2006) (opposing mandatory disclosure as premature); Lynne Marie Kohm, What's My Place in This World? A Response to Professor Ellen Waldman's What Do We Tell the Children?, 35 Cap. U. L. Rev. 563 (2006); Annette R. Appell, The Endurance of the Biological Connection: Heteronormativity, Same-Sex Parenting and the Lessons of Adoption, 22 BYU J. Pub. L. 289 (2008); The Donor-Sibling Registry, available at https://www.donorsiblingregistry.com/ (last visited Nov. 25, 2013). Sperm banks pay extra for donors who are willing to have their identities disclosed.

5. Is egg donation the same as sperm donation? Approximately 12 states have statutes that terminate the parental status of egg donors as well as sperm donors. In K.M. v. E.G., 117 P.3d 673 (2005), the California Supreme Court addressed the question of whether a woman who donated an egg to her partner, signing the consent forms to terminate her parental status but intending to raise the child in their joint home, was a legal parent. California had adopted the Uniform Parentage Act of 1973, providing that a man is not a father if he provides semen to a physician to inseminate a woman who is not his wife, but the court held that the Act did not apply where a woman donated the egg with the intention that she would participate in raising the child in the home she maintained with her partner. The ruling generated a vigorous dissent, with protesters claiming that the decision destabilizes preconception agreements about parental status in the context of ovum donation and surrogacy. Although this was not discussed in the opinions, the ruling also has the potential to affect known sperm donors who sign preconception forms forgoing parental status with the intent, however, that the donor will play some role in the child's life. For a comparison of the egg and sperm markets, *see* Kimberly D. Krawiec, Sunny Samaritans and Egomaniacs: Price-Fixing in the Gamete Market, 72 Law & Contemp. Probs. (Summer 2009).

In D.M.T. v. T.M.H., 129 So. 3d 320 (Fla. 2013), a woman donated an egg to her same-sex partner with the intention that they would raise the child together. Florida law recognized the woman giving birth as the sole legal parent absent participation in a preconception procedure limited to heterosexual couples. The Florida Supreme Court held the statute to be unconstitutional because it deprived the genetic mother who contributed the egg with the intention of retaining her parental status of her due process rights.

PROBLEMS

1. Hank and Wendy, a married couple, went to Dr. Donaldson to discuss artificial insemination of Wendy by a donor. Hank did not consent in writing to the insemination then or at any later time, but Dr. Donaldson artificially inseminated Wendy with semen from an unknown donor three times, and Wendy became pregnant and gave birth to a healthy child. Under the Uniform Parentage Act (2002), who is the child's legal father? In a state with no legislation on the subject?

2. Helen decided to conceive a child by artificial insemination and to raise the child jointly with her partner, Victoria. Helen chose Mark as the semen donor. Helen now claims that she made clear to Mark that he was to have no role in the child's life, while Mark says that he and Helen agreed that he would see the child regularly and act as a noncustodial father. Victoria, who is a nurse, performed the artificial inseminations with Mark's semen. After several unsuccessful attempts, Helen became pregnant and gave birth to a baby girl. Mark was listed as the father on the birth certificate. Mark visited Helen in the hospital several times, purchased gifts for the baby, and visited at least monthly until last month, when Helen cut off the visits. The baby is now 18 months old. Victoria and Helen have remained close, and Victoria actively participates in raising the baby. Mark has filed a paternity suit against Helen, seeking a declaration of paternity and visitation rights.

a. How should this suit be resolved under the Uniform Parentage Act (2002)?

b. How would Mark's suit be resolved if he had impregnated Helen through intercourse? Why should artificial insemination change the result? Or should it? Should the law be structured so that there will always be a way to identify some man as a child's legal father?

c. What if Helen and Mark had signed a written agreement that provided that Mark would not petition for paternity and waived all claims to legal parenthood?

d. Would the result change if the jurisdiction allows Helen and Victoria to marry and they do so before the child's birth or shortly thereafter? If Helen and Victoria were married and they agreed that Mark would retain his status as a father, would the state recognize all three of them as parents? If not, how would the state choose between Victoria and Mark if both had a relationship with the child?

3. After having created embryos through in vitro fertilization, a married couple divorced. They could not agree about the disposition of seven frozen embryos stored in a fertility clinic. The mother, Mary Sue, asked for control of the embryos so that she could have them implanted in her uterus and perhaps bear a child. The father, Junior, objected because he was not sure he wanted to become a parent and asked that the embryos remain in cold storage. As the case progressed, both changed their minds: Mary Sue wanted the embryos donated to a childless couple, and Junior wanted them destroyed. Should the embryos be treated like children and the dispute between Mary Sue and Junior handled like a custody fight? Are the embryos property, subject to equitable division between them? If the parties have entered into an agreement with the fertility clinic about the disposition of the embryos in a situation like this, should the agreement be specifically enforced? Is either party entitled as a matter of constitutional right to control the destiny of the embryos?

4. Robert and Denise, a married couple, arranged with a fertility clinic to use in vitro fertilization to attempt a pregnancy with donated ovum and Robert's sperm. Denise successfully bore a resulting child. During the same time period, Susan, a single woman, arranged with the same clinic to attempt a pregnancy using donated ovum and sperm. She also successfully bore a resulting child, giving birth ten days after Denise. Ten months later, the fertility clinic informed the three parents that the clinic had mistakenly implanted embryos fertilized with Robert's sperm into Susan, and that Robert was the genetic father of the child to whom Susan had given birth. Robert, Denise, and Susan all seek recognition as parents and custody of the child. What is the likely result?

2. *Surrogate Motherhood and Gestational Carriers*

The idea of "surrogacy" — of one woman carrying a child to term to be raised by another — generates enormous legal and ethical disagreement. To some it is "baby selling"; to others it is an acceptable innovation that assists in the creation of families of choice. With the advent of in vitro fertilization and the possibility of separating genetic and gestational motherhood, the use of a "gestational carrier" to give birth to a child to whom she is not genetically related has become more acceptable. The law, however, continues to vary from states that outlaw the practice altogether to those that explicitly authorize and regulate it to those with no related statutory or common law provisions.

The first surrogacy case to capture national attention involved "simple" surrogate motherhood, that is, the use of AID to create a child with sperm from the intended father. William Stern and Mary Beth Whitehead entered into a contract providing that Whitehead would bear Stern's child, who would also be Mary Beth Whitehead's genetic and gestational child. The New Jersey Supreme Court ruled in that case that, absent adoption, Whitehead was Baby M's legal mother. In re Baby M, 537 A.2d 1227 (N.J. 1988). The *Baby M* decision today seems unremarkable. Most courts would continue to find that Whitehead and other traditional surrogates are the mothers of the children they bear. A notable exception, however, is a Wisconsin case where the traditional surrogate persuaded an infertile couple she knew not only to allow her to bear a child conceived with the intended father's sperm, but to do so through artificial insemination rather than use of donor eggs. The Wisconsin Supreme Court held that while the surrogacy agreement could not terminate the surrogate mother's parental status, it should be enforced absent a showing that it was contrary to the best interests of the child. In re F.T.R., 833 N.W.2d 634 (Wis. 2013).

The more complicated — and more common — cases involve gestational surrogacy. In these cases, the sperm and an egg from one woman are combined in vitro and implanted in the womb of another woman, the gestational surrogate. In the first of the cases below, the egg donor is the intended mother. In the second case, the egg donor surrenders her parental status, and the sperm donor intends that his unmarried partner will help him care for the children. The courts become involved when the relationships in these cases break down.

JOHNSON V. CALVERT

19 Cal. Rptr. 2d 494, 851 P.2d 776 (1993) (en banc)

PANELLI, J. . . . Mark and Crispina Calvert are a married couple who desired to have a child. Crispina was forced to undergo a hysterectomy in 1984. Her ovaries remained capable of producing eggs, however, and the couple eventually considered surrogacy. In 1989 Anna Johnson heard about Crispina's plight from a coworker and offered to serve as a surrogate for the Calverts.

On January 15, 1990, Mark, Crispina, and Anna signed a contract providing that an embryo created by the sperm of Mark and the egg of Crispina would be implanted in Anna and the child born would be taken into Mark and Crispina's home "as their child." Anna agreed she would relinquish "all parental rights" to the child in favor of Mark and Crispina. In return, Mark and Crispina would pay Anna $10,000 in a series of installments, the last to be paid six weeks after the child's birth. Mark and Crispina were also to pay for a $200,000 life insurance policy on Anna's life.

The zygote was implanted on January 19, 1990. Less than a month later, an ultrasound test confirmed Anna was pregnant.

Unfortunately, relations deteriorated between the two sides. . . .

The child was born on September 19, 1990, and blood samples were obtained from both Anna and the child for analysis. The blood test results excluded Anna as the genetic mother. The parties agreed to a court order providing that the child would remain with Mark and Crispina on a temporary basis with visits by Anna. . . .

Civil Code sections 7001 and 7002 replace the distinction between legitimate and illegitimate children with the concept of the "parent and child relationship." The "parent and child relationship" means "the legal relationship existing between a child and his natural or adoptive parents incident to which the law confers or imposes rights, privileges, duties, and obligations. It includes the mother and child relationship and the father and child relationship." (Civ. Code, § 7001.) "The parent and child relationship extends equally to every child and to every parent, regardless of the marital status of the parents." (Civ. Code, § 7002.) . . .

Passage of the Act clearly was not motivated by the need to resolve surrogacy disputes, which were virtually unknown in 1975. Yet it facially applies to *any* parentage determination, including the rare case in which a child's maternity is in issue. . . . Not uncommonly, courts must construe statutes in factual settings not contemplated by the enacting legislature. . . . [T]he Act offers a mechanism to resolve this dispute, albeit one not specifically tooled for it. We therefore proceed to analyze the parties' contentions within the Act's framework.

These contentions are readily summarized. Anna, of course, predicates her claim of maternity on the fact that she gave birth to the child. The Calverts contend that Crispina's genetic relationship to the child establishes that she is his mother. . . .

. . . Civil Code section 7003 provides, in relevant part, that between a child and the natural mother a parent and child relationship "*may* be established by proof of her having given birth to the child, or under [the Act]." (Civ. Code, § 7003, subd. (1), emphasis added.) Apart from Civil Code section 7003, the Act sets forth no specific means by which a natural mother can establish a parent and child relationship. . . .

Significantly for this case, Evidence Code section 892 provides that blood testing may be ordered in an action when paternity is a relevant fact. When maternity is disputed, genetic evidence derived from blood testing is likewise admissible. The Evidence Code further provides that if the court finds the conclusions of all the experts, as disclosed by the evidence based on the blood tests, are that the alleged father is not the father of the child, the question of paternity is resolved accordingly. By parity of reasoning, blood testing may also be dispositive of the question of maternity. Further, there is a rebuttable presumption of paternity (hence, maternity as well) on the finding of a certain number of genetic markers.

. . . [W]e are left with the undisputed evidence that Anna, not Crispina, gave birth to the child and that Crispina, not Anna, is genetically related to him. Both women thus have adduced evidence of a mother and child relationship as contemplated by the Act. Yet for any child California law recognizes only one natural mother, despite advances in reproductive technology rendering a different outcome biologically possible.[10]

We see no clear legislative preference in Civil Code section 7003 as between blood testing evidence and proof of having given birth. . . .

Because two women each have presented acceptable proof of maternity, we do not believe this case can be decided without enquiring into the parties' intentions as manifested in the surrogacy agreement. Mark and Crispina are a couple who desired to have a child of their own genetic stock but are physically unable to do so without the help of reproductive technology. They affirmatively intended the birth of the child, and took the steps necessary to effect in vitro fertilization. But for their acted-on intention, the child would not exist. Anna agreed to facilitate the procreation of Mark's and Crispina's child. The parties' aim was to bring Mark's and Crispina's child into the world, not for Mark and Crispina to donate a zygote to Anna. Crispina from the outset intended to be the child's mother. Although the gestative function Anna performed was necessary to bring about the child's birth, it is safe to say that Anna would not have been given the opportunity to gestate or deliver the child had she, prior to implantation of the zygote, manifested her own intent to be the child's mother. No reason appears why Anna's later change of heart should vitiate the determination that Crispina is the child's natural mother.

We conclude that although the Act recognizes both genetic consanguinity and giving birth as means of establishing a mother and child relationship, when the two means do not coincide in one woman, she who intended to procreate the

---

10. We decline to accept the contention of amicus curiae the American Civil Liberties Union (ACLU) that we should find the child has two mothers. Even though rising divorce rates have made multiple parent arrangements common in our society, we see no compelling reason to recognize such a situation here. The Calverts are the genetic and intending parents of their son and have provided him, by all accounts, with a stable, intact, and nurturing home. To recognize parental rights in a third party with whom the Calvert family has had little contact since shortly after the child's birth would diminish Crispina's role as mother.

child — that is, she who intended to bring about the birth of a child that she intended to raise as her own — is the natural mother under California law.[11]

Our conclusion finds support in the writings of several legal commentators. . . .

[One] commentator has cogently suggested, in connection with reproductive technology, that "[t]he mental concept of the child is a controlling factor of its creation, and the originators of that concept merit full credit as conceivers. The mental concept must be recognized as independently valuable; it creates expectations in the initiating parents of a child, and it creates expectations in society for adequate performance on the part of the initiators as parents of the child." (Note, Redefining Mother: A Legal Matrix for New Reproductive Technologies (1986) 96 Yale L.J. 187, at p.196.)

Moreover, as Professor Shultz recognizes, the interests of children, particularly at the outset of their lives, are "[un]likely to run contrary to those of adults who choose to bring them into being." (Shultz, Reproductive Technology and Intent-Based Parenthood: An Opportunity for Gender Neutrality (1990) Wis. L. Rev. 297 [Shultz], at p.397.) Thus, "[h]onoring the plans and expectations of adults who will be responsible for a child's welfare is likely to correlate significantly with positive outcomes for parents and children alike." (Ibid.) Under Anna's interpretation of the Act, by contrast, a woman who agreed to gestate a fetus genetically related to the intending parents would, contrary to her expectations, be held to be the child's natural mother, with all the responsibilities that ruling would entail, if the intending mother declined to accept the child after its birth. In what we must hope will be the extremely rare situation in which neither the gestator nor the woman who provided the ovum for fertilization is willing to assume custody of the child after birth, a rule recognizing the intending parents as the child's legal, natural parents should best promote certainty and stability for the child. . . .

Anna urges that surrogacy contracts violate several social policies. Relying on her contention that she is the child's legal, natural mother, she cites the public policy embodied in Penal Code section 273, prohibiting the payment for consent to adoption of a child. She argues further that the policies underlying the adoption

---

11. Thus, under our analysis, in a true "egg donation" situation, where a woman gestates and gives birth to a child formed from the egg of another woman with the intent to raise the child as her own, the birth mother is the natural mother under California law.

The dissent would decide parentage based on the best interests of the child. Such an approach raises the repugnant specter of governmental interference in matters implicating our most fundamental notions of privacy, and confuses concepts of parentage and custody. Logically, the determination of parentage must precede, and should not be dictated by, eventual custody decisions. The implicit assumption of the dissent is that a recognition of the genetic intending mother as the natural mother may sometimes harm the child. This assumption overlooks California's dependency laws, which are designed to protect all children irrespective of the manner of birth or conception. Moreover, the best interest standard poorly serves the child in the present situation: it fosters instability during litigation and, if applied to recognize the gestator as natural mother, results in a split of custody between the natural father and the gestator, an outcome not likely to benefit the child. Further, it may be argued that, by voluntarily contracting away any rights to the child, the gestator has, in effect, conceded the best interest of the child is not with her.

laws of this state are violated by the surrogacy contract because it in effect constitutes a prebirth waiver of her parental rights.

We disagree. Gestational surrogacy differs in crucial respects from adoption and so is not subject to the adoption statutes. The parties voluntarily agreed to participate in in vitro fertilization and related medical procedures before the child was conceived; at the time when Anna entered into the contract, therefore, she was not vulnerable to financial inducements to part with her own expected offspring. As discussed above, Anna was not the genetic mother of the child. The payments to Anna under the contract were meant to compensate her for her services in gestating the fetus and undergoing labor, rather than for giving up "parental" rights to the child. Payments were due both during the pregnancy and after the child's birth. We are, accordingly, unpersuaded that the contract used in this case violates the public policies embodied in Penal Code section 273 and the adoption statutes. For the same reasons, we conclude these contracts do not implicate the policies underlying the statutes governing termination of parental rights.

It has been suggested that gestational surrogacy may run afoul of prohibitions on involuntary servitude. (*See* U.S. Const., Amend. XIII; Cal. Const., art. I, § 6; Pen. Code, § 181.) Involuntary servitude has been recognized in cases of criminal punishment for refusal to work. We see no potential for that evil in the contract at issue here, and extrinsic evidence of coercion or duress is utterly lacking. We note that although at one point the contract purports to give Mark and Crispina the sole right to determine whether to abort the pregnancy, at another point it acknowledges: "All parties understand that a pregnant woman has the absolute right to abort or not abort any fetus she is carrying. Any promise to the contrary is unenforceable." We therefore need not determine the validity of a surrogacy contract purporting to deprive the gestator of her freedom to terminate the pregnancy.

Finally, Anna and some commentators have expressed concern that surrogacy contracts tend to exploit or dehumanize women, especially women of lower economic status. Anna's objections center around the psychological harm she asserts may result from the gestator's relinquishing the child to whom she has given birth. Some have also cautioned that the practice of surrogacy may encourage society to view children as commodities, subject to trade at their parents' will.

We are all too aware that the proper forum for resolution of this issue is the Legislature, where empirical data, largely lacking from this record, can be studied and rules of general applicability developed. However, in light of our responsibility to decide this case, we have considered as best we can its possible consequences.

We are unpersuaded that gestational surrogacy arrangements are so likely to cause the untoward results Anna cites as to demand their invalidation on public policy grounds. Although common sense suggests that women of lesser means serve as surrogate mothers more often than do wealthy women, there has been no proof that surrogacy contracts exploit poor women to any greater degree than economic necessity in general exploits them by inducing them to accept lower-paid or otherwise undesirable employment. We are likewise unpersuaded by the claim that surrogacy will foster the attitude that children are mere commodities; no evidence is offered to support it. The limited data available seem to reflect an absence of significant adverse effects of surrogacy on all participants.

The argument that a woman cannot knowingly and intelligently agree to gestate and deliver a baby for intending parents carries overtones of the reasoning that for centuries prevented women from attaining equal economic rights and professional status under the law. To resurrect this view is both to foreclose a personal and economic choice on the part of the surrogate mother, and to deny intending parents what may be their only means of procreating a child of their own genetic stock. Certainly in the present case it cannot seriously be argued that Anna, a licensed vocational nurse who had done well in school and who had previously borne a child, lacked the intellectual wherewithal or life experience necessary to make an informed decision to enter into the surrogacy contract. . . .

Anna relies principally on the decision of the United States Supreme Court in Michael H. v. Gerald D. (1989) 491 U.S. 110, to support her claim to a constitutionally protected liberty interest in the companionship of the child, based on her status as "birth mother." . . . The reasoning of the plurality in *Michael H.* does not assist Anna. Society has not traditionally protected the right of a woman who gestates and delivers a baby pursuant to an agreement with a couple who supply the zygote from which the baby develops and who intend to raise the child as their own; such arrangements are of too recent an origin to claim the protection of tradition. To the extent that tradition has a bearing on the present case, we believe it supports the claim of the couple who exercise their right to procreate in order to form a family of their own, albeit through novel medical procedures.

Moreover, if we were to conclude that Anna enjoys some sort of liberty interest in the companionship of the child, then the liberty interests of Mark and Crispina, the child's natural parents, in their procreative choices and their relationship with the child would perforce be infringed. Any parental rights Anna might successfully assert could come only at Crispina's expense. As we have seen, Anna has no parental rights to the child under California law, and she fails to persuade us that sufficiently strong policy reasons exist to accord her a protected liberty interest in the companionship of the child when such an interest would necessarily detract from or impair the parental bond enjoyed by Mark and Crispina. . . .

Drawing an analogy to artificial insemination, Anna argues that Mark and Crispina were mere genetic donors who are entitled to no constitutional protection. That characterization of the facts is, however, inaccurate. Mark and Crispina never intended to "donate" genetic material to anyone. Rather, they intended to procreate a child genetically related to them by the only available means. Civil Code section 7005, governing artificial insemination, has no application here. . . .

The judgment of the Court of Appeal is affirmed.

KENNARD, J., dissenting. . . . In my view, the woman who provided the fertilized ovum and the woman who gave birth to the child both have substantial claims to legal motherhood. Pregnancy entails a unique commitment, both psychological and emotional, to an unborn child. No less substantial, however, is the contribution of the woman from whose egg the child developed and without whose desire the child would not exist.

For each child, California law accords the legal rights and responsibilities of parenthood to only one "natural mother." When, as here, the female reproductive role is divided between two women, California law requires courts to make a decision as to which woman is the child's natural mother, but provides no standards by which to make that decision. The majority's resort to "intent" to break the "tie" between the genetic and gestational mothers is unsupported by statute, and in the absence of appropriate protections in the law to guard against abuse of surrogacy arrangements, it is ill-advised. To determine who is the legal mother of a child born of a gestational surrogacy arrangement, I would apply the standard most protective of child welfare — the best interests of the child. . . .

Surrogacy proponents generally contend that gestational surrogacy, like the other reproductive technologies that extend the ability to procreate to persons who might not otherwise be able to have children, enhances "individual freedom, fulfillment and responsibility." (Shultz, Reproductive Technology, *supra*, 1990 Wis. L. Rev. 297, 303.) Under this view, women capable of bearing children should be allowed to freely agree to be paid to do so by infertile couples desiring to form a family. (Shalev, Birth Power: The Case for Surrogacy, *supra*, at p.145 [arguing for a "free market in reproduction" in which the "reproducing woman" operates as an "autonomous moral and economic agent"]; *see also* Posner, Economic Analysis of Law (3d ed. 1986) p.139; Landes & Posner, The Economics of the Baby Shortage (1978) 7 J. Legal Stud. 323 [proposing a "market in babies"].) The "surrogate mother" is expected "to weigh the prospective investment in her birthing labor" before entering into the arrangement, and if her "autonomous reproductive decision" is "voluntary," she should be held responsible for it so as "to fulfill the expectations of the other parties. . . ." (Shalev, Birth Power: The Case for Surrogacy, *supra*, at p.96.) . . .

Surrogacy critics, however, maintain that the payment of money for the gestation and relinquishment of a child threatens the economic exploitation of poor women who may be induced to engage in commercial surrogacy arrangements out of financial need. (Capron & Radin, Choosing Family Law Over Contract Law as a Paradigm for Surrogate Motherhood, in Surrogate Motherhood, *supra*, p.62.) Some fear the development of a "breeder" class of poor women who will be regularly employed to bear children for the economically advantaged. (*See* Women and Children Used in Systems of Surrogacy: Position Statement of the Institute on Women and Technology, in Surrogate Motherhood, *supra*, at p.322; and Corea, Junk Liberty, testimony before Cal. Assem. Judiciary Com., April 5, 1988, in Surrogate Motherhood, *supra*, at pp.325, 335.) Others suggest that women who enter into surrogacy arrangements may underestimate the psychological impact of relinquishing a child they have nurtured in their bodies for nine months. (*See* Macklin, Artificial Means of Reproduction and Our Understanding of the Family, *supra*, 21 Hastings Center Rep. 5, 10.)

Gestational surrogacy is also said to be "dehumanizing" (Capron & Radin, Choosing Family Law Over Contract Law as a Paradigm for Surrogate Motherhood, in Surrogate Motherhood, *supra*, at p.62) and to "commodify" women and children by treating the female reproductive capacity and the children born of gestational surrogacy arrangements as products that can be bought and sold (Radin, Market-Inalienability (1987) 100 Harv. L. Rev. 1849, 1930-1932). The commodification of women and children, it is feared, will reinforce oppressive gender stereotypes and threaten the well-being of all children. (Medical Technology, *supra*, 103 Harv. L. Rev. 1519, 1550; Annas, Fairy Tales Surrogate Mothers Tell, in Surrogate Motherhood, *supra*, at p.50.) Some critics foresee promotion of an ever-expanding "business of surrogacy brokerage." (E.g., Goodwin, Determination of Legal Parentage, *supra*, 26 Fam. L.Q. at p.283.) . . .

The policy statement of the New York State Task Force on Life and the Law sums up the broad range of ethical problems that commercial surrogacy arrangements are viewed to present: "The gestation of children as a service for others in exchange for a fee is a radical departure from the way in which society understands and values pregnancy. It substitutes commercial values for the web of social, affective and moral meanings associated with human reproduction. . . . This transformation has profound implications for child-bearing, for women, and for the relationship between parents and the children they bring into the world. . . .

Surrogate parenting allows the genetic, gestational and social components of parenthood to be fragmented, creating unprecedented relationships among people bound together by contractual obligation rather than by the bonds of kinship and caring. . . .

. . . Surrogate parenting alters deep-rooted social and moral assumptions about the relationship between parents and children. . . .

. . . [It] is premised on the ability and willingness of women to abdicate [their parental] responsibility without moral compunction or regret [and] makes the obligations that accompany parenthood alienable and negotiable." (New York State Task Force on Life and the Law, Surrogate Parenting: Analysis and Recommendations for Public Policy (May 1988) in Surrogate Motherhood, *supra*, at pp.317-318.)

Proponents and critics of gestational surrogacy propose widely differing approaches for deciding who should be the legal mother of a child born of a gestational surrogacy arrangement. Surrogacy advocates propose to enforce pre-conception contracts in which gestational mothers have agreed to relinquish parental rights, and, thus, would make "bargained-for intentions determinative of legal parenthood." (Shultz, Reproductive Technology, *supra*, 1990 Wis. L. Rev. at p.323.) . . .

Surrogacy critics, on the other hand, consider the unique female role in human reproduction as the determinative factor of questions of legal parentage. They reason that although males and females both contribute genetic material for the child, the act of gestating the fetus falls only on the female. (*See* Radin, Market-Inalienability, *supra*, at p.100 Harv. L. Rev. 1849, 1932, fn.285 [pointing out the "asymmetrical" interests of males and females in human reproduction].) Accordingly, in their view, a woman who, as the result of gestational surrogacy, is not genetically related to the child she bears is like any other woman who gives birth to a child. In either situation the woman giving birth is the child's mother. (*See* Capron & Radin, Choosing Family Law Over Contract Law as a Paradigm for Surrogate Motherhood, in Surrogate Motherhood, *supra*, at pp.64-65.) Under this approach, the laws governing adoption should govern the parental rights to a child born of gestational surrogacy. Upon the birth of the child, the gestational mother can decide whether or not to relinquish her parental rights in favor of the genetic mother. (*Ibid.*) . . .

The majority offers four arguments in support of its conclusion to rely on the intent of the genetic mother as the exclusive determinant for deciding who is the natural mother of a child born of gestational surrogacy. Careful examination, however, demonstrates that none of the arguments mandates the majority's conclusion.

The first argument that the majority uses in support of its conclusion that the intent of the genetic mother to bear a child should be dispositive of the question of motherhood is "but-for" causation. . . . Neither the "but for" nor the "substantial factor" test of causation provides any basis for preferring the genetic mother's intent as the determinative factor in gestational surrogacy cases: Both the genetic and the gestational mothers are indispensable to the birth of a child in a gestational surrogacy arrangement.

. . . The majority draws its second rationale from a student note: "The mental concept of the child is a controlling factor of its creation, and the originators of that concept merit full credit as conceivers." . . .

The problem with this argument, of course, is that children are not property. Unlike songs or inventions, rights in children cannot be sold for consideration, or made freely available to the general public. Our most fundamental notions of personhood tell us it is inappropriate to treat children as property. . . .

Next, the majority offers as its third rationale the notion that bargained-for expectations support its conclusion regarding the dispositive significance of the genetic mother's intent. . . . The unsuitability of applying the notion that, because contract intentions are "voluntarily chosen, deliberate, express and bargained-for," their performance ought to be compelled by the courts is even more clear when the concept of specific performance is used to determine the course of the life of a child. Just as children are not the intellectual property of their parents, neither are they the personal property of anyone, and their delivery cannot be ordered as a contract remedy on the same terms that a court would, for example, order a breaching party to deliver a truckload of nuts and bolts.

. . . [B]efore turning to the majority's fourth rationale, I shall discuss two additional considerations, not noted by the majority, that in my view also weigh against utilizing the intent of the genetic mother as the sole determinant of the result in this case and others like it.

First, in making the intent of the genetic mother who wants to have a child the dispositive factor, the majority renders a certain result preordained and inflexible in every such case: as between an intending genetic mother and a gestational mother, the genetic mother will, under the majority's analysis, always prevail. The majority recognizes no meaningful contribution by a woman who agrees to carry a fetus to term for the genetic mother beyond that of mere employment to perform a specified biological function.

The majority's approach entirely devalues the substantial claims of motherhood by a gestational mother such as Anna. True, a woman who enters into a surrogacy arrangement intending to raise the child has by her intent manifested an assumption of parental responsibility in addition to her biological contribution of providing the genetic material. But the gestational mother's biological contribution of carrying a child for nine months and giving birth is likewise an assumption of parental responsibility. (*See* Dolgin, Just a Gene: Judicial Assumptions About Parenthood (1993) 40 UCLA L. Rev. 637, 659.) A pregnant woman's commitment to the unborn child she carries is not just physical; it is psychological and emotional as well. . . . A pregnant woman intending to bring a child into the world is more than a mere container or breeding animal; she is a conscious agent of creation no less than the genetic mother, and her humanity is implicated on a deep level. Her role should not be devalued. . . .

I find the majority's reliance on "intent" unsatisfactory for yet another reason. By making intent determinative of parental rights to a child born of a gestational surrogacy arrangement, the majority would permit enforcement of a gestational surrogacy agreement without requiring any of the protections that would be afforded by the [Uniform Status of Children of Assisted Conception Act]. . . .

In my view, protective requirements such as those set forth in the USCACA are necessary to minimize any possibility in gestational surrogacy arrangements for overreaching or abuse by a party with economic advantage. As the New Jersey Supreme Court recognized, it will be a rare instance when a low income infertile couple can employ an upper income surrogate. (Matter of Baby M., *supra*, 109 N.J. 396, 537 A.2d 1227, 1249.) The model act's carefully drafted provisions would assure that the surrogacy arrangement is a matter of medical necessity on the part of the intending parents, and not merely the product of a desire to avoid the inconveniences of pregnancy, together with the financial ability to do so. Also, by requiring both pre-conception psychological counseling for all parties and judicial approval, the model act would assure that parties enter into a surrogacy arrangement only if they are legally and psychologically capable of doing so and fully understand all the risks involved, and that the surrogacy arrangement would not be substantially detrimental to the interests of any individual. Moreover, by requiring judicial approval, the model act would significantly discourage the rapid expansion of commercial surrogacy brokerage and the resulting commodification of the products of pregnancy. In contrast, here the majority's grant of parental rights to the intending mother contains no provisions for the procedural protections suggested by the commissioners who drafted the model act. The majority opinion is a sweeping endorsement of unregulated gestational surrogacy.

The majority's final argument in support of using the intent of the genetic mother as the exclusive determinant of the outcome in gestational surrogacy cases is that preferring the intending mother serves the child's interests, which are "[u]nlikely to run contrary to those of adults who choose to bring [the child] into being." . . .

. . . In the absence of legislation that is designed to address the unique problems of gestational surrogacy, this court should look not to tort, property or contract law, but to family law, as the governing paradigm and source of a rule of decision.

The allocation of parental rights and responsibilities necessarily impacts the welfare of a minor child. And in issues of child welfare, the standard that courts frequently apply is the best interests of the child. . . . This "best interests" standard serves to assure that in the judicial resolution of disputes affecting a child's well-being, protection of the minor child is the foremost consideration. Consequently, I would apply "the best interests of the child" standard to determine who can best assume the social and legal responsibilities of motherhood for a child born of a gestational surrogacy arrangement. . . .

. . . I would remand the matter to the trial court to undertake that evaluation.

NOTES AND QUESTIONS

1. The majority concludes that the Parentage Act and provisions of the Evidence Code regarding the admissibility of blood testing are relevant to this case but that laws regarding adoption and the consequences of artificial insemination are not. Why?

2. Johnson v. Calvert was decided under the Uniform Parentage Act of 1973. Section 803 of the Uniform Parentage Act of 2002 provides:

> (a) If the requirements of subsection (b) are satisfied, a court may issue an order validating the gestational agreement and declaring that the intended parents will be the parents of a child born during the term of the of the agreement.
>
> (b) The court may issue an order under subsection (a) only on finding that:
>
> (1) the residence requirements of Section 802 have been satisfied and the parties have submitted to the jurisdiction of the court under the jurisdictional standards of this [Act];
>
> (2) unless waived by the court, the [relevant child-welfare agency] has made a home study of the intended parents and the intended parents meet the standards of suitability applicable to adoptive parents;
>
> (3) all parties have voluntarily entered into the agreement and understand its terms;
>
> (4) adequate provision has been made for all reasonable health-care expense associated with the gestational agreement until the birth of the child, including responsibility for those expenses if the agreement is terminated; and
>
> (5) the consideration, if any, paid to the prospective gestational mother is reasonable.

If the parties do not comply with these requirements, the Act recognizes the gestational mother as the mother of the child. If California were to adopt these provisions, how would they affect a subsequent case similar to Johnson v. Calvert?

3. The states continue to vary widely in their treatment of surrogacy. Twenty states still have no statutory or case law addressing surrogacy. Eleven states either ban surrogacy agreements, in some cases criminalizing commercial arrangements, or hold that they are unenforceable. Some states follow the approach of the Uniform Parentage Act and regulate surrogacy, in some cases limiting recognition of the intended parents to cases in which the intended mother is infertile, at least one of the intended parents contributed a gamete, and/or the intended parents are married. For examples of efforts to regulate surrogacy, see Fla. Stat. ch. 742.15 (2014); Va. Code Ann. § 20-160 (2014). For a summary of existing state laws, see Darra L. Hoffman, "Mama's Baby, Daddy's Maybe": A State-by-State Survey of Surrogacy Laws and Their Disparate Gender Impact, 35 Wm. Mitchell L. Rev. 449 (2009). If you were going to regulate the practice, what requirements would you impose and why? For discussion, see Jane Larkey, Redefining Motherhood: Determining Legal Maternity in Gestational Surrogacy Arrangements, 51 Drake L. Rev. 605, 622 (2003); Helene S. Shapo, Assisted Reproduction and the Law: Disharmony on a Divisive Social Issue, 100 Nw. U. L. Rev. 465, 475 (2006); Richard F. Storrow, Rescuing Children from the Marriage Movement: The Case Against Marital Status Discrimination in Adoption and Assisted Reproduction,

39 U.C. Davis L. Rev. 305 (2006); Molly J. Walker Wilson, Precommitment in Free-Market Procreation: Surrogacy, Commissioned Adoption, and Limits on Human Decision Making Capacity, 31 J. Legis. 329, 333 (2005); Jill Elaine Hasday, Intimacy and Economic Exchange, 119 Harv. L. Rev. 491 (2005).

4. One of the objections to the use of gestational surrogates involves fear of the exploitation of the women carrying the child. Agencies, however, screen for reliable surrogates and prefer older, more mature women who have given birth before. Empirical research in the United States and Britain does not support the stereotype of poor, single, young, ethnic minority women whose family, financial difficulties, or other circumstances pressure her into a surrogacy arrangement. Nor does it support the view that surrogate mothers are naively taking on a task unaware of the emotional and physical risks it might entail. Rather, the empirical research establishes that surrogate mothers are mature, experienced, stable, self-aware, and extroverted nonconformists who make the initial decision that surrogacy is something that they want to do. *See, e.g.*, Lina Peng, Surrogate Mother: An Exploration of the Empirical and the Normative, 21 Am. U. J. Gender Soc. Pol'y & L. 555 (2013).

5. Should fears of exploitation be greater where commissioning couples use foreign surrogates? Most countries do not follow the *Johnson* approach; in a contest between a genetic and a gestational mother, the gestational mother prevails as the legal mother. *See* Arlie Hochschild, Childbirth at the Global Crossroads, 20 American Prospect, Sept. 19, 2009, at 25, 27, available at http://prospect.org/article/childbirth-global-crossroads-0; Hague Conference on Private Int'l Law, Private International Law Issues Surrounding the Status of Children, Including Issues Arising from International Surrogacy Arrangements, at 3, Prel. Doc. No. 11 (Mar. 2011), available at http://www.hcch.net/upload/wop/genaff2011pd11e.pdf (last visited Nov. 25, 2013). Yet, international surrogacy appears to be a growing practice that leaves some children in limbo as they may not be recognized as the citizens of any country. Richard F. Storrow, "The Phantom Children of the Republic": International Surrogacy and the New Illegitimacy, 20 Am. U. J. Gender Soc. Pol'y & L. 561, 597 n.264 (2012). And unregulated cross-border practices raise concerns about exploitation that regulated domestic surrogacy may not. Kristiana Brugger, International Law in the Gestational Surrogacy Debate, 35 Fordham Int'l L.J. 665, 676 (2012). If couples in a state that does not permit surrogacy go abroad and bring the child back to the United States, who are the parents of the child? Should the state in that case allow an adoption for a second parent who is not biologically related to the child? For an example of two married gay men using a gestational carrier in India and then returning to New York, *see* In re Adoption of J.J., 984 N.Y.S.2d 841 (Fam. Ct. 2014).

PROBLEMS

1. Under the *Johnson* court's analysis, who would be the legal mother of the child in a case involving a surrogate who gave birth to a child genetically hers pursuant to a contract specifying that the father and his wife would have custody?

2. If Mary donated an egg to be fertilized with John's sperm and the fetus were to be gestated by John's wife Wendy, who would be the child's legal mother under Johnson v. Calvert?

3. Alison gestated a fetus conceived from the egg and sperm of anonymous donors, agreeing that the child would be adopted by Barbara and George. Shortly before the child was born, George filed for divorce, alleging that no children were born of the marriage. Barbara responded that she and George expected to adopt the soon-to-be-born child of Alison and sought custody and a child support order against George. After the baby was born, Alison made clear that she did not want custody. The trial judge ruled that the baby had no legal parents. What arguments should Barbara and George make on appeal?

J.F. v. D.B.

897 A.2d 1261 (Pa. Super. 2006)

McCaffery, J.: Appellant, J.F. ("Father"), asks us to determine whether the trial court erred in holding that D.B. ("gestational carrier") has standing to seek custody of the triplet boys she carried and delivered, after having taken them from the hospital against Father's wishes when they were eight days old. . . . Following an exhaustive review of the record, the briefs of the parties and the pertinent law, we decline to comment on the validity of surrogacy contracts, either specifically in this case or generally in this Commonwealth. That task is for the legislature. Our holding today is limited to our conclusion that gestational carrier lacked standing to seek custody or challenge Father's custody of the triplets. As a result, gestational carrier also lacked standing to seek termination of egg donor's parental rights. Accordingly, we vacate the order of the trial court and remand the matter with directions.

FACTS AND PROCEDURAL HISTORY

The unique facts and procedural history underlying these appeals are as follows. Father is a math professor and department chair at Cleveland State University in Cleveland, Ohio. He lives with E.D., who was a practicing dentist and is now retired. Father and E.D., who live together in a home they built in Ohio, are in a long-term relationship and they want to have children. E.D. is a widow,[12] with two grown children: a daughter, who is married with four children, and a son. . . . Father has no children. After enduring infertility treatments and learning that E.D. was incapable of conceiving any more children, the couple considered other options. Although willing, E.D.'s daughter was incapable of serving as a surrogate for the couple. . . .

---

12. E.D. has received a yearly pension since 1973, which she would lose should she remarry. . . . However, the couple has always been willing to give up the pension and marry, if necessary, to obtain custody of the triplets.

SMI matched the couple with gestational carrier, a married resident of Pennsylvania with three children of her own, and egg donor, a single woman residing in Texas. E.D. met gestational carrier in April 2002. In August 2002, Father, egg donor, gestational carrier and her husband executed a surrogacy contract ("the Contract" or "the Surrogacy Contract"). . . . By virtue of the Contract Father agreed, *inter alia*, to pay gestational carrier the sum of $15,000.00 for a single birth, $20,000.00 for multiple births, plus medical expenses, travel expenses, and life insurance for the duration of the pregnancy. . . . Gestational carrier agreed, *inter alia*, that she would not attempt to form a parent-child relationship with any child or children she might bear; that she would voluntarily relinquish any parental rights to any such child or children; and Father would not be responsible for any lost wages, childcare expenses for existing children, or any other expenses not expressly set forth in the Contract. . . . In the event that custody was somehow awarded to either gestational carrier or egg donor, each agreed to indemnify Father for any and all monies paid for child support, and reimburse him for any and all monies paid to either one pursuant to the Surrogacy Contract. . . . Father agreed to assume legal responsibility for any child or children of his, born pursuant to the Contract, and the Contract also provided that any such child or children should be placed in the sole custody of E.D. if Father were to die before the birth of the child or children. . . . A portion of the Surrogacy Contract contained a Release and Hold Harmless Agreement, which provided as follows:

> [Gestational carrier] and [egg donor] will undergo a procedure whereby eggs or ovum from [egg donor] will be combined with sperm from [Father], and the resulting embryo or embryos will be transferred to [gestational carrier] for the purpose of carrying [Father's] child to term. Upon the birth of the child, [gestational carrier] and/or [egg donor] will surrender any custody rights to the child to [Father]. . . .

. . . E.D. sold her dental practice in 2002 in anticipation of being a "stay at home mother."

Pursuant to the Surrogacy Contract, the parties underwent extensive medical and psychological testing. Finally, in April 2003, three of egg donor's eggs, fertilized *in vitro* with Father's sperm, were implanted in gestational carrier. Father and E.D., the intended parents, were present for this procedure as well as four weeks later for the sonogram confirming that gestational carrier was carrying triplets. . . . Intended parents also attended gestational carrier's first few doctor's appointments in Erie, Pennsylvania, but were later told by gestational carrier not to come to any more appointments. Thereafter, E.D. called to check on gestational carrier and the triplets she was carrying, apparently more often than gestational carrier liked. She asked E.D. not to call so often, and E.D. complied, as she had complied with the request to stop going to the doctor's appointments. . . . When it became necessary for gestational carrier to go on bed rest on her doctor's advice, she requested additional money for that period of time. Even though they were not required to do so by the contract, intended parents sent gestational carrier an additional $1,000 for each of the four months she was on bed rest.

As the triplets grew, the doctor became concerned that gestational carrier would go into labor prematurely. Gestational carrier scheduled a caesarean delivery ("C-section") at Hamot Medical Center ("Hamot" or "the hospital") in Erie,

Pennsylvania, for November 19, 2003, approximately thirty-five (35) weeks into the pregnancy. Although E.D. expressed her desire to be in the delivery room for the birth, gestational carrier wanted her husband there instead, and so gestational carrier did not tell intended parents about the scheduled C-section. . . . Gestational carrier knew the triplets' gender, but intended parents chose to wait to find out until the birth.

On the morning of November 19th, gestational carrier called SMI to inform the agency that she would be undergoing a C-section later that day. SMI called intended parents and informed them of this fact. The triplets were, indeed, born on that date, but their early delivery caused minor medical problems that warranted their placement in Hamot's neonatal intensive care unit ("NICU"). Intended parents, who had only learned about the birth on that same day, drove from Ohio to Erie that evening to visit the babies. . . .

Over the next few days, while the children were being monitored and cared for by Hamot doctors and nurses in the NICU, intended parents purchased a minivan, car seats, toys, and clothing, all for the care and benefit of the triplets. E.D. made repeated telephone calls to their insurance company to secure medical insurance for the infants and arrange for apnea monitors, which the babies required before they could be discharged from the hospital. E.D. spoke with gestational carrier on November 20th and the 21st.[13] E.D. also telephoned Hamot at least once a day, often more frequently, to speak with the babies' doctors, NICU nurses, and social services personnel. . . . Hamot discharged gestational carrier on Saturday, November 22nd, and she went home. Prior to and at that time, gestational carrier claimed to have had no intention of taking the triplets home with her. She also knew that E.D. was planning to adopt them. . . .

Originally, intended parents were scheduled to "nest" with the triplets on Sunday, November 23rd, to prepare to bring them home.[14] However, as intended parents were leaving their home in Ohio that day for the drive to Hamot, Dr. Jonathan Chai called them and explained that nesting had to be postponed, because two of the boys needed to go back on oxygen and all three had apnea. Dr. Chai also told E.D. that this development meant a delay in discharge until the end of the week. In addition, the couple learned that their mandatory apnea monitor training could not be accomplished on a Sunday. In light of these facts, Dr. Chai and E.D. rescheduled the nesting and monitor training for the next day.

On Monday, E.D. learned that Hamot had not yet secured apnea monitors for the triplets; therefore, nesting was postponed once again. . . . Still back in Ohio, E.D. worked to straighten out some confusion which existed between the

---

13. During these calls, gestational carrier purportedly expressed concern that the couple was not coming to the hospital frequently to visit the triplets. E.D. explained that her daughter was away for the week and E.D.'s four young grandchildren were staying with them, and it was difficult to travel from their home to Erie to visit the triplets in the NICU with four young children. Because gestational carrier had unilaterally scheduled the C-section for November 19th and had deliberately chosen not to inform intended parents, E.D. did not have any opportunity to make other plans for the care of her grandchildren.

14. "Nesting" at Hamot occurs when new parents stay at the hospital overnight with their newborn and use the apnea monitor or any other equipment as they would at home, while hospital staff is nearby to assist if necessary.

insurance company and Hamot. She was successful, and the hospital rescheduled the nesting and monitor training for Tuesday, November 25th. Hamot staff members were expecting intended parents on Tuesday evening.

In the meantime, gestational carrier was aware that E.D. had spoken with the Hamot doctors, NICU nurses and social services staff on a daily basis. Nevertheless, gestational carrier did not like what she characterized as a "lack of physical visits" to the NICU on the part of intended parents. On Tuesday morning, gestational carrier called Hamot to voice her concerns about the lack of visitation. According to gestational carrier, Huckno, Hamot's risk manager, told her that she was the legal mother and that, if she wanted to, she could take the babies home. Later that morning, gestational carrier arrived at Hamot to meet with Dr. Michele Chai, NICU nurses and social services to arrange to take the triplets home with her.[15] Gestational carrier expressed her concern about what was going to happen to the children if they were discharged to people who had not visited them frequently in the NICU. Gestational carrier also stated that she believed Father and E.D. were "not fit to be parents." At that time, gestational carrier revoked her consent for intended parents to visit the children. She also arranged to nest with the triplets that night, along with her husband, so that they could take the babies home when they were discharged.

Although gestational carrier notified Attorney Litz at SMI of her decision to take the triplets home, she did not contact intended parents, who were expecting to arrive at Hamot that evening for nesting and training. Anticipating a confrontation, Hamot staff contacted security to alert them to intended parents' impending arrival. Unaware of these events, intended parents arrived at Hamot late on Tuesday afternoon ready for training and nesting. They were met by Hamot security at the NICU nurses' station. At the direction of Huckno, Hamot staff told intended parents that the triplets had been discharged to gestational carrier, and they should seek legal advice. E.D. insisted on speaking with Huckno, who verified that the triplets had been discharged to gestational carrier with his consent. In fact, the triplets had not been discharged and gestational carrier was present at the hospital at this time, preparing for her own nesting and training with the babies that evening. Even though Hamot staff had represented to intended parents that the triplets had been discharged to gestational carrier, the triplets remained at Hamot for an additional two days, until Thursday, November 27th. . . . On that day, gestational carrier took the babies from Hamot to her home in Corry, Pennsylvania.

After being informed of the purported "discharge" of the babies, the bewildered intended parents returned to Ohio and promptly began calling gestational carrier. Each time, they left messages asking for an explanation of gestational carrier's actions. Gestational carrier did not return any of the calls.

---

15. According to Hamot witnesses, no staff member had expressed a concern to intended parents about physical visits. In fact, Dr. Jonathan Chai testified, "Not visiting in and of itself is not all that uncommon. There are a lot of reasons that parents don't come to visit their babies in the NICU. And certainly for parents that are out of town, you know, we understand that some have transportation issues, some have other children that they need to take care of. So, that in and of itself is not that unusual."

When all their calls to gestational carrier went unanswered and unreturned, intended parents began contacting attorneys. On December 4, 2003, Father signed a verification in support of a Complaint for Custody and a Motion for Emergency Special Relief naming gestational carrier as the defendant. . . .

Nearly six months after the custody trial had concluded and while the termination proceedings were ongoing, the court issued an order on January 7, 2005 ("Custody Order"), awarding primary physical custody to gestational carrier. The Custody Order also granted Father partial custody/visitation, and ordered that legal custody be shared between Father and gestational carrier. In addition, the court entered a stipulated order for child support. Father timely appealed the Custody Order. . . .

Because we find that gestational carrier has no standing to pursue custody of the children on either an *in loco parentis* basis or as the children's "legal mother," we do not reach the issue of whether the evidence presented at the custody hearings was sufficient to support the court's award of primary physical custody to gestational carrier.

STANDING BASED ON IN LOCO PARENTIS STATUS

Regarding the first part of the standing issue, Father contends that gestational carrier does not have *in loco parentis* status because she is a non-parent third party who took the children home from the hospital in defiance of his wishes. We agree. . . .

Well-settled Pennsylvania law provides that persons other than a child's biological or natural parents are "third parties" for purposes of custody disputes). . . . In addition, natural parents have a *prima facie* right to custody. McDonel v. Sohn, 2000 Pa. Super. 342, 762 A.2d 1101, 1105 (Pa. Super. 2000). "Except via dependency proceedings, third parties lack standing to seek custody as against the natural parents unless they can demonstrate a *prima facie* right to custody." *Id.* Accord Rosado v. Diaz, 425 Pa. Super. 155, 624 A.2d 193, 195 (Pa. Super. 1993). . . . Even when standing to seek custody is conferred upon a third party, the natural parent has a "*prima facie* right to custody," which will be forfeited only if clear and "convincing reasons appear that the child's best interest will be served by an award to the third party. Thus, even before the proceedings start, the evidentiary scale is tipped, and tipped hard to the [biological] parents' side." Jones v. Jones, 2005 Pa. Super. 337, 884 A.2d 915, 917 (Pa. Super. 2005) (citation omitted). . . .

> There is a stringent test for standing in third-party suits for . . . custody due to the respect for the traditionally strong right of parents to raise their children as they see fit. The courts generally find standing in third-party visitation and custody cases only where the legislature specifically authorizes the cause of action. A third party has been permitted to maintain an action for custody, however, where that party stands *in loco parentis* to the child. . . .
>
> The phrase "*in loco parentis*" refers to a person who puts oneself in the situation of a lawful parent by assuming the obligations incident to the parental relationship without going through the formality of a legal adoption. . . . The third party in this type of relationship, however, cannot place himself *in loco parentis* in defiance of the parents' wishes and the parent/child relationship.

Liebner v. Simcox, 2003 Pa. Super. 377, 834 A.2d 606, 609 (Pa. Super. 2003), *appeal denied*, Pa., 890 A.2d 1060 (2005) (quoting T.B. v. L.R.M., 567 Pa. 222, 228-29, 786 A.2d 913 at 916-17 (2001))....

In other words, a third party may not intervene and assume *in loco parentis* status where the natural parent opposes such intervention.

The facts now before us are easily distinguishable from [earlier cases involving a stepparent and an aunt acting in loco parentis with a legal parent's acquiescence].... There was no acquiescence or participation by Father in gestational carrier's unilateral decision to take *custody of the triplets*. The requirement of a natural parent's participation and acquiescence is critical to the determination of whether to accord a third party *in loco parentis* status.... The law simply cannot permit a third party to act contrary to the natural parent's wishes in obtaining custody and then benefit from that defiant conduct in a subsequent custody action. Here, the manner in which gestational carrier obtained custody of the children was fraught with impropriety, a fact completely overlooked by the trial court.

There is no dispute that intended parents came to visit the triplets the day they were born, despite gestational carrier's failure to inform them of the date which she had scheduled for the C-section. It is also undisputed that the premature infants were out of necessity under the care of trained medical professionals in the NICU for the next several days. The record is replete with chart notations and testimony concerning numerous telephone calls placed by E.D. checking on the health, status, and welfare of the triplets. Gestational carrier was discharged from Hamot on Saturday, November 22, 2003, knowing full well that intended parents were taking the necessary steps to bring the triplets home and knowing full well that E.D. was planning to adopt them. The neonatal physicians had communicated to intended parents that the triplets required medical attention and would not be ready for discharge from the NICU until Thursday or Friday, November 27th or 28th at the earliest. Nesting with the triplets had to be postponed not once, but twice, through no fault of intended parents. In fact, as intended parents were preparing to leave for Hamot on Sunday, November 23, 2003, they received a call from Dr. Jonathan Chai, who told them they could not nest that day, nor would they be able to receive mandatory monitor training that day.

Gestational carrier herself did not return to Hamot until Tuesday, November 25th. On that date, she unilaterally decided that Father and E.D. would not be "fit parents." Based on her personal judgment, gestational carrier arranged to nest with the triplets in advance of taking them home with her. Gestational carrier made these arrangements *without the consent of Father*, with full knowledge that she did not have his consent, and on the very day she knew intended parents were coming to Hamot. When intended parents arrived for their scheduled nesting and monitor training, they were *turned away* by hospital staff, who misled them by claiming that the babies had been "discharged" to gestational carrier, when in fact the triplets were still in the hospital, and gestational carrier was preparing to nest with them in intended parents' stead. Two days later, after she nested and received training, gestational carrier took the triplets to her home, again, in direct defiance of Father's wishes. E.D. left telephone messages for gestational carrier seeking to locate the triplets, and Father immediately took steps to gain custody of his children. Clearly, the facts of this case show unequivocally that Father *at no time* participated or acquiesced in gestational carrier's assuming custody of the triplets. Indeed, the very manner in which gestational carrier managed to secure custody establishes the complete lack of Father's participation and the knowledge that her actions were in defiance of Father's wishes. Hospital personnel lied to Father by telling him that the babies had been "discharged" to gestational carrier when, in fact, they were in the hospital at that moment and remained there for two more days. Our case law is very clear that there can be no finding of *in loco parentis* status where the third party obtains her status in defiance of the natural parent's wishes. . . . Accordingly, gestational carrier's standing to pursue custody of the babies cannot be sustained on the basis of *in loco parentis* status and the trial court erred in ruling otherwise. . . .

STANDING BASED ON "LEGAL MOTHER" STATUS

Father also asserts that the trial judge erred in granting gestational carrier standing on an alternate basis, namely, her status as "legal mother." Specifically, Father challenges the trial court's authority to void the Surrogacy Contract *sua sponte* and name gestational carrier as the "legal mother" of the babies without notice to the biological mother or the intended mother. We agree that these findings cannot be sustained and rely on multiple reasons why the court's actions do not withstand scrutiny.

First, it is clear from the pleadings in this case that neither Father nor gestational carrier sought invalidation of the Contract. The law of this Commonwealth provides that courts may not rule on matters not before them. . . .

In addition to assessing the validity of the Contract without a request that it do so, the trial court herein proceeded to declare the Contract void despite the absence of some of the parties to the Contract. . . . The court compounded its error by naming gestational carrier the "legal mother" without even *notifying* egg donor, the person all parties concede is the biological mother of the babies. Plainly, egg donor was an indispensable party in this action. Thus, not only was it necessary to notify egg donor because she was a party to the Contract, it was also imperative that she have notice because she is the biological mother of the triplets. In light of these facts, the court lacked jurisdiction to rule on the issue of who was the "legal mother." . . .

Even if we were to ignore the fact that the court *sua sponte* addressed the validity of the Contract without a request from the parties and without all indispensable parties present, we would conclude that the court's analysis of the issue was seriously flawed. The trial court utilized the terms of the Contract and restricted certain parties' rights based on those terms while it simultaneously deemed the Contract void. For example, in determining that gestational carrier was the "legal mother" of the triplets, the trial court treated egg donor as an anonymous biological donor who had signed her rights away by contract much like an anonymous sperm donor. . . . Of course, if the entire Surrogacy Contract is void, egg donor could not have "signed away her rights by contract." . . .

Further, the trial court simply does not offer sufficient support or a reasoned basis for its decision to void the Surrogacy Contract and name gestational carrier the "legal mother" of the babies. "Generally, a clear and unambiguous contract provision must be given its plain meaning unless to do so would be contrary to a clearly expressed public policy [and we are mindful that] public policy is more than a vague goal which may be used to circumvent the plain meaning of the contract." . . .

The trial court herein struck down the Contract primarily because the parties failed to name a legal mother. However, the designation of who is a "legal mother" is one ultimately determined by statute and/or judicial ruling. Had the parties named a legal mother in the Contract, that designation surely would not have been binding on the court. We find the trial court's basis for invalidating the Contract unsupportable. . . .

Despite the lack of applicable law, the trial court determined, *sua sponte*, that it would strike the Surrogacy Contract completely and name gestational carrier the triplets' "legal mother." The court, invoking public policy, found that gestational carrier "assumed" maternity; the court characterized her as "more a mother and a parent by her actions than by genetics." . . . The court did not cite any law in support of its finding; it merely concluded that this was the case. Our assessment of how gestational carrier came to have custody of the triplets is outlined above; we need not repeat it here. In essence, the trial court voided the Contract so that it could change the status of the parties, by naming gestational carrier "legal mother." This in turn gave gestational carrier standing to seek custody, despite the conduct in which gestational carrier had engaged. We flatly reject this reasoning and this result. . . .

This case involves a biological father seeking custody of his children from a third party gestational carrier who is not the children's biological mother, and who took the children from the hospital in direct defiance of Father's wishes after she completely changed her mind about how matters would proceed. . . . There is no law in this Commonwealth that accords standing to a surrogate with no biological connection to the child she seeks to take into her custody. Today, on these facts, we decline to grant such a party standing.

* * *

In summary, we hold that, with regard to the custody matter, Father was entitled to obtain custody of his biological children from the third party gestational carrier who has no biological connection to the children and who took custody of the children in flagrant defiance of Father's wishes. The trial court erred in finding that gestational carrier had *in loco parentis* status to challenge Father's right to custody. Gestational carrier's defiant conduct precluded such a finding. Moreover, the trial court erred in *sua sponte* voiding the Surrogacy Contract as contrary to public policy and in naming gestational carrier as the "legal mother." None of the bases upon which the trial court relied for standing can be sustained. . . .

Conclusion

We cannot conclude this matter without recognizing the profound effect its resolution will have on the three persons who matter most in this case: Father's biological children. We reach our resolution here only after lengthy, serious reflection and concern. Due in part to troubling conduct on the part of gestational carrier and Hamot personnel, and due also to the length of time it takes for matters to wend their way through our legal system, we have before us three small boys who no doubt face a challenging period of transition and change. In light of this, we urge the parties to act hereinafter with the utmost respect for the boys' right of privacy. Furthermore, we strongly recommend that the transfer of custody and the preparations therefor be conducted privately, in the presence of the parties and their immediate families only. Although it is likely unnecessary, we encourage all parties to put aside their personal positions in this case and instead place the emotional welfare of these children above all other concerns in the days ahead.

The order of the trial court awarding primary physical custody, as well as child support, to gestational carrier, with partial custody rights to Father, is hereby vacated and we direct that Father be awarded full physical and legal custody of his biological children. Further, the trial court's order terminating egg donor's parental rights is reversed. Jurisdiction is relinquished.

NOTES AND QUESTIONS

1. The appellate court noted that, in the interim between the trial court and appellate opinions,

[the] egg donor filed an action in Ohio seeking a declaration that she and the triplets had a parent/child relationship. The Ohio court, in an order dated October 29, 2004, granted egg donor relief and specifically found that it was not precluded from ruling on the matter as a direct result of the Pennsylvania court's failure to notify egg donor, the genetic parent, of the proceedings and failure to provide her with an opportunity to be heard. Despite finding that the evidence did establish a parent/child relationship between egg donor and the babies, the Ohio court refused to make further findings regarding the parenting relationships between gestational carrier and the triplets. The Ohio court held that it had no jurisdiction to make such a ruling because the issue was still before the Pennsylvania courts, which is the children's home state and which has exclusive jurisdiction over parenting determinations with respect to them. J.R. v. J.F. and D.B., 9th Dist. No. 22416, 2005-Ohio-4667.

The court observed further that "the Ohio appellate court issued an opinion in favor of Father's claims against gestational carrier, which claims had been filed by Father in that state. *See* J.F. v. D.B., et al., 9th Dist. No. 22709, 2006-Ohio-1175. The Ohio court held that the parties' surrogacy contract was enforceable under Ohio law and, further, that gestational carrier was liable to Father for reimbursement of the contract fee, as well as money paid for support." If the relationship between the intended father and the gestational carrier falls apart, what rights should the egg donor have? Should the contract be drafted to protect her interests? If it conditioned termination of her parental standing on the father's custody, would such a provision be enforceable? Should it be? For a more complete account of the different jurisdictions involved, *see* Robert E. Rains, What the Erie "Surrogate Triplets" Can Teach State Legislatures About the Need to Enact Article 8 of the Uniform Parentage Act of 2000, 56 Clev. St. L. Rev. 1 (2008).

2. The trial and appellate courts differed considerably in their description of the facts. June Carbone observes that:

> While the trial court decision clearly sympathized with the surrogate, the appellate court was dramatically more supportive of the commissioning father. The trial court treated the parties as anonymous; the appellate opinion described the father as "a math professor and department chair at Cleveland State University in Cleveland, Ohio." The trial court decision described his partner as his "paramour," and emphasized her lack of a legal relationship to the child. The appellate decision noted that she was a widowed dentist, she had retired in order to be able to take care of the children, she and the father were in a long term relationship, they had not married because of the impact of marriage on her benefits, they were willing to marry if necessary to obtain custody of the children, and they had begun preparations for adoption before the children were born. The appellate court also emphasized the intended parents' difficulties in traveling from Cleveland on short notice, particularly in light of the fact that the surrogate did not tell them of the scheduled C-section, and the misinformation they received from the hospital.

June Carbone, Assisted Reproduction in an Era of Polarization: An Institutional Examination of Why Adoption May Be the New Battleground for the Recognition of Partnership, 35 Cap. U. L. Rev. 341, 369-370 (2006). The Supreme Court of Pennsylvania denied a subsequent appeal. J.F. v. D.B., 909 A.2d 1290 (Pa. 2006). Should the different factual descriptions affect the legal determination of parentage? Under the appellate court's ruling, would the trial court's description of the facts change the outcome?

3. The appellate court concludes: "There is no law in this Commonwealth that accords standing to a surrogate with no biological connection to the child she seeks to take into her custody." What does the court mean by "biological"? Compare this outcome with the Uniform Parentage Act (2002), which treats the woman giving birth as the mother in the absence of a preconception court order under Section 803 to the contrary. (See page 1001.)

4. Could the commissioning agencies have done anything to avoid the dispute in *J.F.*? For a reconsideration of the role of commercial agencies in *Baby M*, *see* Carol Sanger, Developing Markets in Baby-Making: In the Matter of Baby M, 30 Harv. J.L. & Gender 67 (2007).

5. In In re C.K.G., 173 S.W.3d 714 (Tenn. 2005), the Tennessee Supreme Court addressed a dispute between a genetic father and his unmarried partner who gave birth to his children using donated eggs with the intention that they would jointly parent the children. In this case, the court concluded that gestation was an important factor in determining parenthood, albeit where the father had consented to his partner's conception with the intention that they jointly raise the children. What would the outcome be if the father had used a gestational carrier to give birth to a child using the father's sperm and a donor egg? Would his partner, who raised the child as her own, be recognized as a legal parent? Would it matter whether the dispute arose at birth or several years later? *See* In re T.J.S., 54 A.3d 263 (N.J. 2012).

6. The trial court in this case appeared to be concerned that the contract did not provide for anyone to be a legal mother. Should that matter? In a case of first impression, a Maryland appellate court addressed the issue of whether a gestational

carrier's name should be on the birth certificate. The biological father intended to raise the child and wished to have his name on the certificate without a mother listed. The gestational carrier, who was not genetically related to the child, agreed. The father raised equal protection arguments, maintaining that a woman could be a single parent, but not a man, if the original circuit court dismissal of the complaint stood. The court of appeal interpreted the state statute to allow the birth certificate to reflect only the father's name without reaching the constitutional issues. In re Roberto d.B., 923 A.2d 115 (Md. Ct. App. 2007). If a woman gives birth to a child, her husband is automatically presumed to be the legal father. If a man arranges for the birth of a child through the use of a gestational carrier, is his spouse presumed to be legal parent? For a discussion of the role of gender in the application of the marital presumption to same-sex couples, *see* Susan Frelich Appleton, Presuming Women: Revisiting the Presumption of Legitimacy in the Same-Sex Couples Era, 86 B.U. L. Rev. 227 (2006), Note, Peri Koll, The Use of the Intent Doctrine to Expand the Rights of Intended Homosexual Male Parents in Surrogacy Custody Disputes, 18 Cardozo J.L. & Gender 199 (2011). *See also* Raftopol v. Ramey, 12 A.3d 783 (Conn. 2011) (recognizing two gay partners as legal parents without adoption).

7. Several courts have raised questions about the constitutional validity of a statute that would sever the parental standing of a woman who provides an egg to a gestational carrier with the intention of retaining parental status. *See* J.R. v. Utah, 261 F. Supp. 2d 1268 (Utah 2002) (heterosexual couple who arrange for birth of a genetically related child through use of a gestational carrier); D.M.T. v. T.M.H., 129 So. 3d 320 (Fla. 2013) (woman who contributes an egg to her lesbian partner with the intention that they will jointly raise the child). These cases raise due process issues under the liberty clause of the Constitution. Is the constitutional issue the same with respect to the parental status of a man? Is it a matter of due process or equal protection? Consider whether the trial court opinion in *J.F.* could be attacked on constitutional grounds. Would your answer change if the trial court had recognized the gestational carrier's husband as the legal father of the child? Is there a difference under the various state approaches legally or constitutionally between the following two scenarios?

1) Married heterosexual couple arranges for the birth of a child using the wife's egg, donor sperm, and a gestational carrier.
2) Married gay couple arranges for the birth of a child using one man's sperm, a donor egg, and a gestational carrier.

8. If the court were to hold that D.B. had standing on the basis of in loco parentis without also finding that she is a legal mother on the basis of gestation, would such a ruling pose constitutional questions under *Troxel*? The trial court opinion in *J.F.* mentions the Connecticut case of Doe v. Doe, 710 A.2d 1297 (Conn. 1998), which used a best interest test to rebut the presumption in favor of parental custody in order to allow the father's wife standing to seek custody of a child she had helped raise for eight years. After *Troxel*, however, the Connecticut Supreme Court changed the doctrine on which *Doe* was based. Connecticut now requires that a "third party must allege and prove, by clear and convincing evidence, a relationship with the child that is similar in nature to a parent-child

relationship, and that denial of the visitation would cause real and significant harm to the child." In re Joshua S, 796 A.2d 1141, 1156 (2002). How would D.B. fare under the Connecticut standard? For an argument that the consent of the legal parent is constitutionally mandated for a nonparent to acquire parental rights, *see* E. Gary Spitko, The Constitutional Function of Biological Paternity: Evidence of the Biological Mother's Consent to the Biological Father's Co-Parenting of Her Child, 48 Ariz. L. Rev. 97 (2006).

9. To date, gestational surrogacy cases have involved the following combinations: egg and sperm from the intended parents (Calvert v. Johnson), sperm or egg from one of the intended parents and a gamete from a donor (*J.F.*), and donor gametes, *see* Buzzanca v. Buzzanca, 72 Cal. Rptr. 2d 280 (Cal. App. 1998) (holding that intended parents were legal parents on the basis of their role in arranging the child's birth). On the horizon, however, is the transfer of embryos from one couple to another for reproductive purposes. Would the laws governing gamete donation or surrogacy apply? If not, would the intended parents need to adopt the child in order to secure their parental standing? For discussion, *see* Elizabeth E. Swire Falker, The Disposition of Cryopreserved Embryos: Why Embryo Adoption Is an Inapposite Model for Application to Third Party Assisted Reproduction, 35 Wm. Mitchell L. Rev. 489 (2009); June Carbone & Naomi Cahn, Embryo Fundamentalism, 18 Wm. & Mary Bill Rts. L.J. 1015 (2010). For a comparison of the determination of parentage in the context of inheritance, *see* Kristine S. Knaplund, Children of Assisted Reproduction, 45 U. Mich. J.L. Reform 899 (2012).

PROBLEM

Commissioning couple live in New York, which does not recognize commercial surrogacy agreements. The couple enter into a contract with an agency in Connecticut that recruits a Connecticut woman to act as a gestational carrier. The contract specifies that Connecticut law, which treats gestational contracts as enforceable, will apply. The contract further specifies that the commissioning couple, who contribute a donor egg and the commissioning husband's sperm, shall be recognized as the child's legal parents and that they shall have the right to elect an abortion on terms of their choosing. Early in the pregnancy, the couple learn that the gestational carrier is carrying twins and that one of the twins has serious birth defects. The commissioning couple wants the carrier to have a "selective reduction," aborting the twin with the birth defects. The carrier refuses and flees to Michigan, which recognizes the woman giving birth as the legal mother. She gives birth to twins, including one with serious birth defects. The carrier places the twins for adoption in Michigan.

What are the commissioning couples' options when the carrier refuses to go through with the abortion? Do they have any recourse after the birth of the children?

Table of Cases

Index